Contemporary Authors®

NEW REVISION SERIES

ISSN 0275-7176

Contemporary Authors®

**A Bio-Bibliographical Guide to
Current Writers in Fiction, General Nonfiction,
Poetry, Journalism, Drama, Motion Pictures,
Television, and Other Fields**

NEW REVISION SERIES *volume* 120

GALE®

THOMSON
™
GALE

Detroit • New York • San Diego • San Francisco • Cleveland • New Haven, Conn. • Waterville, Maine • London • Munich

Contemporary Authors, New Revision Series, Vol. 120

Project Editor
Scot Peacock

Editorial
Katy Balcer, Shavon Burden, Sara Constantakis, Anna Marie Dahn, Alana Joli Foster, Natalie Fulkerson, Arlene M. Johnson, Michelle Kazensky, Julie Keppen, Joshua Kondek, Thomas McMahon, Jenai A. Mynatt, Judith L. Pyko, Mary Ruby, Lemma Shomali, Susan Strickland, Maikue Vang, Tracey Watson, Denay L. Wilding, Thomas Wiloch, Emiene Shija Wright

Research
Michelle Campbell, Tracie A. Richardson, Robert Whaley

Permissions
Kim Davis, Shalice Shah-Caldwell

Imaging and Multimedia
Dean Dauphinais, Robert Duncan, Leitha Etheridge-Sims, Mary K. Grimes, Lezlie Light, Dan Newell, David G. Oblender, Christine O'Bryan, Kelly A. Quin, Luke Rademacher

Composition and Electronic Capture
Carolyn A. Roney

Manufacturing
Stacy L. Melson

LIBRARY OF CONGRESS CATALOG CARD NUMBER 81-640179

ISBN 0-7876-6712-9
ISSN 0275-7176

Printed in the United States of America
10 9 8 7 6 5 4 3 2 1

Contents

Indexing note: All *Contemporary Authors* entries are indexed in the *Contemporary Authors* cumulative index, which is published separately and distributed twice a year.

As always, the most recent Contemporary Authors cumulative index continues to be the user's guide to the location of an individual author's listing.

Preface

Contemporary Authors (*CA*) provides information on approximately 115,000 writers in a wide range of media, including:

- Current writers of fiction, nonfiction, poetry, and drama whose works have been issued by commercial publishers, risk publishers, or university presses (authors whose books have been published only by known vanity or author-subsidized firms are ordinarily not included)

- Prominent print and broadcast journalists, editors, photojournalists, syndicated cartoonists, graphic novelists, screenwriters, television scriptwriters, and other media people

- Notable international authors

- Literary greats of the early twentieth century whose works are popular in today's high school and college curriculums and continue to elicit critical attention

A *CA* listing entails no charge or obligation. Authors are included on the basis of the above criteria and their interest to *CA* users. Sources of potential listees include trade periodicals, publishers' catalogs, librarians, and other users.

How to Get the Most out of *CA*: Use the Index

The key to locating an author's most recent entry is the *CA* cumulative index, which is published separately and distributed twice a year. It provides access to *all* entries in *CA* and *Contemporary Authors New Revision Series* (*CANR*). Always consult the latest index to find an author's most recent entry.

For the convenience of users, the *CA* cumulative index also includes references to all entries in these Gale literary series: *Authors and Artists for Young Adults, Authors in the News, Bestsellers, Black Literature Criticism, Black Literature Criticism Supplement, Black Writers, Children's Literature Review, Concise Dictionary of American Literary Biography, Concise Dictionary of British Literary Biography, Contemporary Authors Autobiography Series, Contemporary Authors Bibliographical Series, Contemporary Dramatists, Contemporary Literary Criticism, Contemporary Novelists, Contemporary Poets, Contemporary Popular Writers, Contemporary Southern Writers, Contemporary Women Poets, Dictionary of Literary Biography, Dictionary of Literary Biography Documentary Series, Dictionary of Literary Biography Yearbook, DISCovering Authors, DISCovering Authors: British, DISCovering Authors: Canadian, DISCovering Authors: Modules* (including modules for Dramatists, Most-Studied Authors, Multicultural Authors, Novelists, Poets, and Popular/Genre Authors), *DISCovering Authors 3.0, Drama Criticism, Drama for Students, Feminist Writers, Hispanic Literature Criticism, Hispanic Writers, Junior DISCovering Authors, Major Authors and Illustrators for Children and Young Adults, Major 20th-Century Writers, Native North American Literature, Novels for Students, Poetry Criticism, Poetry for Students, Short Stories for Students, Short Story Criticism, Something about the Author, Something about the Author Autobiography Series, St. James Guide to Children's Writers, St. James Guide to Crime & Mystery Writers, St. James Guide to Fantasy Writers, St. James Guide to Horror, Ghost & Gothic Writers, St. James Guide to Science Fiction Writers, St. James Guide to Young Adult Writers, Twentieth-Century Literary Criticism, 20th Century Romance and Historical Writers, World Literature Criticism*, and *Yesterday's Authors of Books for Children.*

A Sample Index Entry:

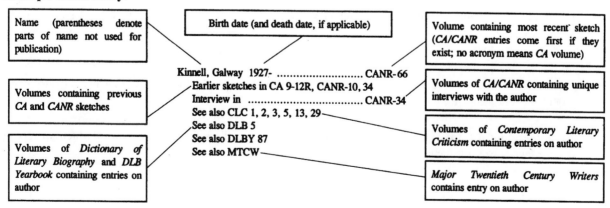

How Are Entries Compiled?

The editors make every effort to secure new information directly from the authors; listees' responses to our questionnaires and query letters provide most of the information featured in *CA*. For deceased writers, or those who fail to reply to requests for data, we consult other reliable biographical sources, such as those indexed in Gale's *Biography and Genealogy Master Index*, and bibliographical sources, including *National Union Catalog, LC MARC*, and *British National Bibliography*. Further details come from published interviews, feature stories, and book reviews, as well as information supplied by the authors' publishers and agents.

An asterisk (*) at the end of a sketch indicates that the listing has been compiled from secondary sources believed to be reliable but has not been personally verified for this edition by the author sketched.

What Kinds of Information Does An Entry Provide?

Sketches in *CA* contain the following biographical and bibliographical information:

- **Entry heading:** the most complete form of author's name, plus any pseudonyms or name variations used for writing

- **Personal information:** author's date and place of birth, family data, ethnicity, educational background, political and religious affiliations, and hobbies and leisure interests

- **Addresses:** author's home, office, or agent's addresses, plus e-mail and fax numbers, as available

- **Career summary:** name of employer, position, and dates held for each career post; resume of other vocational achievements; military service

- **Membership information:** professional, civic, and other association memberships and any official posts held

- **Awards and honors:** military and civic citations, major prizes and nominations, fellowships, grants, and honorary degrees

- **Writings:** a comprehensive, chronological list of titles, publishers, dates of original publication and revised editions, and production information for plays, television scripts, and screenplays

- **Adaptations:** a list of films, plays, and other media which have been adapted from the author's work

- **Work in progress:** current or planned projects, with dates of completion and/or publication, and expected publisher, when known

- **Sidelights:** a biographical portrait of the author's development; information about the critical reception of the author's works; revealing comments, often by the author, on personal interests, aspirations, motivations, and thoughts on writing

- **Interview:** a one-on-one discussion with authors conducted especially for *CA*, offering insight into authors' thoughts about their craft

- **Autobiographical essay:** an original essay written by noted authors for *CA*, a forum in which writers may present themselves, on their own terms, to their audience

- **Photographs:** portraits and personal photographs of notable authors

- **Biographical and critical sources:** a list of books and periodicals in which additional information on an author's life and/or writings appears

- **Obituary Notices** in *CA* provide date and place of birth as well as death information about authors whose full-length sketches appeared in the series before their deaths. The entries also summarize the authors' careers and writings and list other sources of biographical and death information.

Related Titles in the *CA* Series

Contemporary Authors Autobiography Series complements *CA* original and revised volumes with specially commissioned autobiographical essays by important current authors, illustrated with personal photographs they provide. Common topics include their motivations for writing, the people and experiences that shaped their careers, the rewards they derive from their work, and their impressions of the current literary scene.

Contemporary Authors Bibliographical Series surveys writings by and about important American authors since World War II. Each volume concentrates on a specific genre and features approximately ten writers; entries list works written by and about the author and contain a bibliographical essay discussing the merits and deficiencies of major critical and scholarly studies in detail.

Available in Electronic Formats

GaleNet. *CA* is available on a subscription basis through GaleNet, an online information resource that features an easy-to-use end-user interface, powerful search capabilities, and ease of access through the World-Wide Web. For more information, call 1-800-877-GALE.

Licensing. *CA* is available for licensing. The complete database is provided in a fielded format and is deliverable on such media as disk, CD-ROM, or tape. For more information, contact Gale's Business Development Group at 1-800-877-GALE, or visit us on our website at www.galegroup.com/bizdev.

Suggestions Are Welcome

The editors welcome comments and suggestions from users on any aspect of the *CA* series. If readers would like to recommend authors for inclusion in future volumes of the series, they are cordially invited to write the Editors at *Contemporary Authors*, Gale Group, 27500 Drake Rd., Farmington Hills, MI 48331-3535; or call at 1-248-699-4253; or fax at 1-248-699-8054.

Contemporary Authors Product Advisory Board

The editors of *Contemporary Authors* are dedicated to maintaining a high standard of excellence by publishing comprehensive, accurate, and highly readable entries on a wide array of writers. In addition to the quality of the content, the editors take pride in the graphic design of the series, which is intended to be orderly yet inviting, allowing readers to utilize the pages of *CA* easily and with efficiency. Despite the longevity of the *CA* print series, and the success of its format, we are mindful that the vitality of a literary reference product is dependent on its ability to serve its users over time. As literature, and attitudes about literature, constantly evolve, so do the reference needs of students, teachers, scholars, journalists, researchers, and book club members. To be certain that we continue to keep pace with the expectations of our customers, the editors of *CA* listen carefully to their comments regarding the value, utility, and quality of the series. Librarians, who have firsthand knowledge of the needs of library users, are a valuable resource for us. The *Contemporary Authors* Product Advisory Board, made up of school, public, and academic librarians, is a forum to promote focused feedback about *CA* on a regular basis. The seven-member advisory board includes the following individuals, whom the editors wish to thank for sharing their expertise:

- **Anne M. Christensen,** Librarian II, Phoenix Public Library, Phoenix, Arizona.

- **Barbara C. Chumard,** Reference/Adult Services Librarian, Middletown Thrall Library, Middletown, New York.

- **Eva M. Davis,** Youth Department Manager, Ann Arbor District Library, Ann Arbor, Michigan.

- **Adam Janowski, Jr.,** Library Media Specialist, Naples High School Library Media Center, Naples, Florida.

- **Robert Reginald,** Head of Technical Services and Collection Development, California State University, San Bernadino, California.

- **Katharine E. Rubin,** Head of Information and Reference Division, New Orleans Public Library, New Orleans, Louisiana.

- **Barbara A. Wencl,** Media Specialist, Como Park High School, St. Paul, Minnesota.

International Advisory Board

Well-represented among the 115,000 author entries published in *Contemporary Authors* are sketches on notable writers from many non-English-speaking countries. The primary criteria for inclusion of such authors has traditionally been the publication of at least one title in English, either as an original work or as a translation. However, the editors of *Contemporary Authors* came to observe that many important international writers were being overlooked due to a strict adherence to our inclusion criteria. In addition, writers who were publishing in languages other than English were not being covered in the traditional sources we used for identifying new listees. Intent on increasing our coverage of international authors, including those who write only in their native language and have not been translated into English, the editors enlisted the aid of a board of advisors, each of whom is an expert on the literature of a particular country or region. Among the countries we focused attention on are Mexico, Puerto Rico, Spain, Italy, France, Germany, Luxembourg, Belgium, the Netherlands, Norway, Sweden, Denmark, Finland, Taiwan, Singapore, Malaysia, Thailand, South Africa, Israel, and Japan, as well as England, Scotland, Wales, Ireland, Australia, and New Zealand. The sixteen-member advisory board includes the following individuals, whom the editors wish to thank for sharing their expertise:

- **Lowell A. Bangerter,** Professor of German, University of Wyoming, Laramie, Wyoming.

- **Nancy E. Berg,** Associate Professor of Hebrew and Comparative Literature, Washington University, St. Louis, Missouri.

- **Frances Devlin-Glass,** Associate Professor, School of Literary and Communication Studies, Deakin University, Burwood, Victoria, Australia.

- **David William Foster,** Regent's Professor of Spanish, Interdisciplinary Humanities, and Women's Studies, Arizona State University, Tempe, Arizona.

- **Hosea Hirata,** Director of the Japanese Program, Associate Professor of Japanese, Tufts University, Medford, Massachusetts.

- **Jack Kolbert,** Professor Emeritus of French Literature, Susquehanna University, Selinsgrove, Pennsylvania.

- **Mark Libin,** Professor, University of Manitoba, Winnipeg, Manitoba, Canada.

- **C. S. Lim,** Professor, University of Malaya, Kuala Lumpur, Malaysia.

- **Eloy E. Merino,** Assistant Professor of Spanish, Northern Illinois University, DeKalb, Illinois.

- **Linda M. Rodríguez Guglielmoni,** Associate Professor, University of Puerto Rico—Mayagüez, Puerto Rico.

- **Sven Hakon Rossel,** Professor and Chair of Scandinavian Studies, University of Vienna, Vienna, Austria.

- **Steven R. Serafin,** Director, Writing Center, Hunter College of the City University of New York, New York City.

- **David Smyth,** Lecturer in Thai, School of Oriental and African Studies, University of London, England.

- **Ismail S. Talib,** Senior Lecturer, Department of English Language and Literature, National University of Singapore, Singapore.

- **Dionisio Viscarri,** Assistant Professor, Ohio State University, Columbus, Ohio.

- **Mark Williams,** Associate Professor, English Department, University of Canterbury, Christchurch, New Zealand.

CA Numbering System and Volume Update Chart

Occasionally questions arise about the *CA* numbering system and which volumes, if any, can be discarded. Despite numbers like "29-32R," "97-100" and "211," the entire *CA* print series consists of only 259 physical volumes with the publication of *CA* Volume 212. The following charts note changes in the numbering system and cover design, and indicate which volumes are essential for the most complete, up-to-date coverage.

CA First Revision
- 1-4R through 41-44R (11 books)
  Cover: Brown with black and gold trim.
  There will be no further First Revision volumes because revised entries are now being handled exclusively through the more efficient *New Revision Series* mentioned below.

CA Original Volumes
- 45-48 through 97-100 (14 books)
  Cover: Brown with black and gold trim.
  101 through 212 (112 books)
  Cover: Blue and black with orange bands.
  The same as previous *CA* original volumes but with a new, simplified numbering system and new cover design.

CA Permanent Series
- *CAP*-1 and *CAP*-2 (2 books)
  Cover: Brown with red and gold trim.
  There will be no further Permanent Series volumes because revised entries are now being handled exclusively through the more efficient *New Revision Series* mentioned below.

CA New Revision Series
- CANR-1 through CANR-120 (120 books)
  Cover: Blue and black with green bands.
  Includes only sketches requiring significant changes; **sketches are taken from any previously published CA, CAP, or CANR volume.**

If You Have:	You May Discard:
CA First Revision Volumes 1-4R through 41-44R and *CA Permanent Series* Volumes 1 and 2	*CA* Original Volumes 1, 2, 3, 4 and Volumes 5-6 through 41-44
CA Original Volumes 45-48 through 97-100 and 101 through 212	**NONE:** These volumes will not be superseded by corresponding revised volumes. Individual entries from these and all other volumes appearing in the left column of this chart may be revised and included in the various volumes of the *New Revision Series*.
CA New Revision Series Volumes *CANR*-1 through *CANR*-120	**NONE:** The *New Revision Series* does not replace any single volume of *CA*. Instead, volumes of *CANR* include entries from many previous *CA* series volumes. All *New Revision Series* volumes must be retained for full coverage.

A Sampling of Authors and Media People
Featured in This Volume

Jeffrey Eugenides

Eugenides received critical acclaim for his first novel, *The Virgin Suicides,* a tale of five teenaged sisters who one by one kill themselves. Adapted to film in 2000, *The Virgin Suicides* juxtaposes the innocence and eroticism of early-1970s suburbia against the unaccountable force that drove the young women to their deaths. Eugenides published his second novel, *Middlesex,* in 2002. The tale of a multigenerational Greek-American family told through the eyes of its most unusual member, a hermaphrodite, *Middlesex* received the Pulitzer Prize for fiction.

Marshall Frady

Journalist Frady has written extensively about southern politics and culture, both as a reporter for such magazines as *Newsweek, Life,* and the *Saturday Evening Post* and in his nonfiction books. In 1979 he moved into television journalism when he became a correspondent for ABC News. Frady's writings, which include biographies of controversial politician George Wallace and of televangelist Billy Graham, draw upon his rural North Carolina background. In 1981, Frady was nominated for the Pulitzer Prize for *Southerners: A Journalist's Odyssey.*

James M. McPherson

An author of nonfiction for children and adults, McPherson generally is considered the preeminent living expert on the American Civil War through such volumes as *Battle Cry of Freedom: The Civil War Era.* A prolific writer, McPherson has written and edited numerous books about the Civil War and its aftermath, the Reconstruction, and of President Abraham Lincoln. He is also noted for his coverage of African Americans during the midnineteenth century, especially their service as soldiers and their efforts to secure their freedom from slavery, and of the abolitionists who worked to obtain equal rights for the freed slaves.

Deborah Dash Moore

Moore's book *At Home in America: Second Generation New York Jews* examines the Americanization of second-generation New York Jews during the period from 1920 to 1950. Moore turned her attention to the next era in American Jewish life in *To the Golden Cities: Pursuing the American Jewish Dream in Miami and L.A.,* a chronicle of how the post–World War II economic boom triggered the second great wave of Jewish immigration. In 2001, she co-authored *Cityscapes: A History of New York in Images.*

Blake Morrison

Though often identified as a British poet, Morrison also produces well-received nonfiction and journalism. Both his Lancashire-born father (whose life and death Blake would recount in a 1993 memoir) and Irish-born mother (commemorated in another memoir ten years later) were physicians, but the younger Morrison rejected medicine for literature, and in the process has embraced many genres. In *Things My Mother Never Told Me,* published in 2003, Morrison makes use of a collection of private letters to delve into hidden aspects of his mother's life and identity, including details about her relationship with Morrison's father.

Whitney Otto

Otto expanded a short story that used the practice of quilting as a metaphor for events in the lives of its characters into the 1991 novel *How to Make an American Quilt.* The narrative relates the stories of a group of women that regularly meets in a small California town to sew. Interspersed between each story are bits of information about the history of quilting and sets of sewing instructions. Otto is also author of the novels *Now You See Her, The Passion Dream Book,* and 2002's *A Collection of Beauties at the Height of Their Popularity.*

Laura Joh Rowland

Rowland is a historical mystery novelist whose works often take place in Japan. *Shinju,* the Japanese term for "double love suicide," is set in seventeenth-century Tokyo, where police are investigating the apparent shinju of a peasant and the daughter of a prominent citizen. *The Pillow Book of Lady Wisteria,* published in 2002, exposes the more bizarre sexual practices of old Japan in a tale of court intrigue. Rowland is also the author of 2003's *The Dragon King's Palace.*

Sara Wheeler

Travel writer Wheeler has written several books based on her visits to various parts of the world. *An Island Apart: Travels in Evia* details her journey to the Greek island of Evia. A Greek scholar, Wheeler managed to successfully explore most of the island, even the hinterlands, where civilization has yet to invade and where most tourists do not visit. She is also the author of the acclaimed biography of an Antarctic adventurer, *Cherry: A Life of Apsley Cherry-Garrard.* Published in 2001, *Cherry* received abundant praise from reviewers.

Acknowledgments

Grateful acknowledgment is made to those publishers, photographers, and artists whose work appear with these authors' essays. Following is a list of the copyright holders who have granted us permission to reproduce material in this volume of *CA*. Every effort has been made to trace copyright, but if omissions have been made, please let us know.

Photographs/Art

Nicholson Baker: Baker, photograph. AP/Wide World Photos. Reproduced by permission.

Sandra Benitez: Benitez, photograph. © 2003 Ed Bock. Reproduced by permission.

David Caute: Caute, photograph. © Jerry Bauer. Reproduced by permission.

Gillian Chan: Chan, photograph. © 2003 Gillian Chan. Reproduced by permission.

Richard J. Ellis: Ellis, photograph. © 2003 Richard Ellis. Reproduced by permission.

Jeffrey Eugenides: Eugenides, photograph by Jerry Bauer. Reproduced by permission.

Marshall Frady: Frady, photograph. Co Rentmeester/Time Life Pictures/Getty Images. Reproduced by permission.

Samuel P. Huntington: Huntington, photograph. © Reuters NewMedia Inc./Corbis. Reproduced by permission.

Peter Jennings: Jennings, photograph. AP/Wide World Photos. Reproduced by permission.

Diana Wynne Jones: Jones, photograph. Reproduced by permission of the author.

Kelly Lange: Lange, photograph. © Davis Factor/Corbis. Reproduced by permission.

David Wong Louie: Louie, photograph. Photograph courtesy of Amy Cheng. Reproduced by permission.

Deborah Dash Moore: Moore, photograph by Mik Moore. © 2003 Deborah Dash Moore. Reproduced by permission.

Edmund Morris: Morris, photograph. AP/Wide World Photos. Reproduced by permission.

Peter Nabokov: Nabokov, photograph. AP/Wide World Photos. Reproduced by permission.

Alexander Nehamas: Nehamas, photograph. © 2003 Alexander Nehamas. Reproduced by permission.

Conor Cruise O'Brien: O'Brien, photograph. AP/Wide World Photos. Reproduced by permission.

Ulick O'Connor: O'Connor, photograph. Express Newspapers/Getty Images. Reproduced by permission.

Whitney Otto: Otto, photograph. AP/Wide World Photos. Reproduced by permission.

Tamora Pierce: Pierce, photograph by Steve Dawson. Reproduced by permission of Tamora Pierce.

Dan Rottenberg: Rottenberg, photograph by Alex Lowy. Reproduced by permission.

A-B

ALEXANDER, Bevin (Ray) 1928-

PERSONAL: Born February 17, 1928, in Gastonia, NC; son of John McAuley (an executive in the textile industry) and Odessa (a homemaker; maiden name, Beaty) Alexander; married Peggy Bailey (marriage ended); children: Bevin Ray, Jr., Troy, David. *Ethnicity:* "Caucasian." *Education:* The Citadel, A.B. (history; with honors), 1949; Northwestern University, M.S. (with distinction), 1954.

ADDRESSES: Office—Arvon Grove, Bremo Bluff, VA 23022. *E-mail*—bevina@cstone.net.

CAREER: Richmond Times-Dispatch, Richmond, VA, government reporter, 1954-58; *Rural Virginia,* Richmond, editor, 1958-61; University of Virginia, Charlottesville, director of information and editor of university magazine, 1961-66; Virginia Hotel and Motel Association, Richmond, executive vice president and director of relations with government, 1966-82. *Military service:* U.S. Army, commanding officer of Fifth Historical Detachment, 1951-52; served in Korea; became first lieutenant; received Commendation Medal and three battle stars. U.S. Army Reserve, 1949-62; became captain.

MEMBER: Sigma Delta Chi, Kappa Tau Alpha, Richmond Rotary Club (president, 1985-86).

WRITINGS:

Korea: The First War We Lost, Hippocrene (New York, NY), 1986, revised edition, 2000.
The Strange Connection: U.S. Intervention in China, 1944-1972, Greenwood (Westport, CT), 1992.

Lost Victories: The Military Genius of Stonewall Jackson, Holt (New York, NY), 1992.
How Great Generals Win, Norton (New York, NY), 1993.
The Future of Warfare, Norton (New York, NY), 1995.
Robert E. Lee's Civil War, Adams Media (Holbrook, MA), 1998.
How Hitler Could Have Won World War II, Crown (New York, NY), 2000.

SIDELIGHTS: Bevin Alexander told *CA:* "I am especially interested in military strategy." Alexander operates a cattle farm in the Piedmont area of Virginia. He has traveled in the Far East, Europe, Mexico, and the Caribbean.

*   *   *

ASSMANN, Jan 1938-

PERSONAL: Born July 7, 1938, in Langelsheim, Germany; son of Hans (an architect) and Charlotte (Boening) Assmann; married Aleida Bornkamm (a professor of literature), August 10, 1968; children: Vincent, David, Marlene, Valerie, Corinna. *Education:* Attended Universities of Munich, Goettingen, Paris, and Heidelberg; earned Ph.D., 1965. *Religion:* Protestant.

ADDRESSES: Home—Im Neulich 5, 69121 Heidelberg, Germany. *Office*—Institute of Egyptology, University of Heidelberg, Marstallhof 4, 69117 Heidelberg, Germany. *E-mail*—Jan.Assmann@urz.uni-heidelberg.de.

CAREER: University of Heidelberg, Heidelberg, Germany, faculty member, 1971—, professor of Egyptology, 1976—.

MEMBER: Akademie der Wissenschaften.

AWARDS, HONORS: Max Planck Forschungs Preis, 1996; Deutscher Historiker Preis (German History Prize), 1998; honorary Dr. Theol.

WRITINGS:

Zeit und Ewigkeit im alten Aegypten: ein Beitrag zur Geschichte der Ewigkeit, (vorgelegt am 9. Nov. 1974 von Roland Hampe auf Anregung von Eberhard Otto), C. Winter, 1975.

(Compiler and author of preface) *Aegyptische Hymnen und Gebete,* Artemis-Verlag, 1975, 2nd edition, Vandenhoeck & Ruprecht, 1999.

Re und Amun: die Krise des polytheistischen Weltbilds im Aegypten der 18.-20. Dynastie, Vandenhoeck & Ruprecht, 1983.

Sonnenhymnen in thebanischen Graebern, P. von Zabern, 1983.

Aegypten: Theologie und Froemmigkeit einer fruehen Hochkultur, Kohlhammer, 1984.

(Contributor) *Das Grab des Nefersecheru (TT296),* P. von Zabern, 1985.

(Contributor) *Vom Nil zum Neckar: Kunstschaetze Aegyptens aus pharaonischer und koptischer Zeit an der Universitaet Heidelberg,* Springer-Verlag, 1986.

(Contributor) *Theologen und Theologien in Verschiedenen Kulturkreisen,* Patmos, 1986.

Ma'at: Gerechtigkeit und Unsterblichkeit im alten Aegypten, C.H. Beck, 1990.

Das Grab des Amenemope, TT 41, P. von Zabern, 1991.

(Contributor and coeditor) *Revolution und Mythos,* Fischer Taschenbuch Verlag, 1992.

Politische Theologie zwischen Aegypten und Israel, Carl Friedrich von Siemens Stiftung, 1992.

Das kulturelle Gedächtnis, Beck, 1992.

Akhanyati's Theology of Light and Time, Israel Academy of Sciences and Humanities, 1992.

Monotheismus und Kosmotheismus: Aegyptische Formen eines "Denkens des Einen" und ihre Europaeische Rezeptionsgeschichte, Winter, 1993.

Egyptian Solar Religion in the New Kingdom: Re, Amun and the Crisis of Polytheism, Kegan Paul International, 1995.

Aegypten. Eine Sinngeschichte, Hanser, 1996.

Moses the Egyptian: The Memory of Egypt in Western Monotheism, Harvard University Press (Cambridge, MA), 1997.

Das verschleierte Bild zu Sais: Schillers Ballade und ihre Griechischen und Aegyptischen Hintergruende, B.G. Teubner (Stuttgart), 1999.

Herrschaft und Heil: Politische Theologie in Altaegypten, Israel und Europa, Hanser (Munchen), 2000.

Weisheit und Mysterium: das Bild der Griechen von Aegypten, Beck (Munchen), 2000.

Der Tod als Thema der Kulturtheorie: Todesbilder und Totenriten im alten Aegypten, Suhrkamp (Frankfurt), 2000.

(Contributor) *Mose: Agypten und das Alte Testament,* Verlag Katholisches Bibelwerk (Stuttgart), 2000.

Images et Rites de la Mort dans l'Egypte Ancienne: l'Apport des Liturgies Funeraires: Quatre Seminaires a l'Ecole Pratique des Hautes Etudes, Section des Sciences Religieuses, 17-31 May 1999: Avec un Appendice sur la Theorie de la "Parole Divine" (mdw n_tr), chez Jamblique et dans les Sources Egyptiennes, Cybele (Paris), 2000.

Tod und Jenseits im Alten Agypten, Beck (Munchen), 2001.

The Search for God in Ancient Egypt, translated by David Lorton, Cornell University Press (Ithaca, NY), 2001.

The Mind of Egypt: History and Meaning in the Time of the Pharaohs, translated by Andrew Jenkins, Metropolitan Books (New York, NY), 2002.

EDITOR

(Coeditor) *Fragen an die Altaegyptische Literatur: Studien zum Gedenken an Eberhard Otto,* Reichert, 1977.

(Coeditor) *Schrift und Gedaechtnis: Beitraege zur Archaeologie der literarischen Kommunikation,* W. Fink, 1983.

(Coeditor) *Kanon und Zensur,* W. Fink, 1987.

(Coeditor) *Problems and Priorities in Egyptian Archaeology,* KPI, 1987.

(Coeditor) *Kultur und Gedaechtnis,* Suhrkamp, 1988.

(Coeditor) *Kultur und Konflikt,* Suhrkamp, 1990.

(Editor) *Das Fest und das Heilige: religioese Kontrapunkte zur Alltagswelt,* Guetersloher Verlagshaus G. Mohn, 1991.

(Editor) *Die Erfindung des inneren Menschen: Studien zur religioesen Anthropologie,* Guethersloher Verlagshaus G. Mohn, 1993.

(Coeditor) *Die politische Theologie des Paulus* (Vortraege, gehalten an der Forschungsstaette der evangelischen Studiengemeinschaft in Heidelberg, 23-27 February 1987), Wilhelm Fink, 1993.

(Coeditor) *Ocular desire = Sehnsucht des Auges,* Akademie Verlag, 1994.

(Coeditor) *Text und Kommentar,* W. Fink, 1995.

(Coeditor) *Thebanische Beamtennekropolen: neue Perspektiven archaeologischer Forschung* (Internationales Symposion Heidelberg 9-13 June 1993), Heidelberger Orientverlag, 1995.

(Coeditor) *Schuld, Gewissen, und Person: Studien zur Geschichte des inneren Menschen,* Guetersloher Verlagshaus, 1997.

(Coeditor) *Self, Soul, and Body in Religious Experience,* Brill, 1998.

(Coeditor) *Transformations of the Inner Self in Ancient Religions,* Brill (Boston, MA), 1999.

(Coeditor) *Einsamkeit,* Fink (Munchen), 2000.

(Coeditor) *Representation in Religion: Studies in Honor of Moshe Barasch,* Brill (Boston, MA), 2000.

SIDELIGHTS: Jan Assmann, a professor of Egyptology and scholar of history and literature at Heidelberg University in Germany, has, over the past three decades, published several in-depth studies of the people and culture of ancient Egypt, with a special emphasis on theology and philosophy. To date, two of Assmann's works have been translated into English. They are *The Search for God in Ancient Egypt* (2001), and *The Mind of Egypt: History and Meaning in the Time of the Pharaohs* (2002).

In *Moses the Egyptian,* Assmann traces the history of monotheism, the belief in one god, back to the Egyptian King Akhenaten, Pharaoh Amenophis IV (1360-1340 B.C.), who briefly revolutionized Egyptian religious thought when he abolished the belief in the idols of the Egyptian form of polytheism and in its place established a worship of Aton, the god of light. It is with Akhenaten that Assmann places the origin of the monotheism professed by Moses. Moses' followers later condemned the Egyptians who continued to practice polytheism, referring to them as idolaters. This, Assmann contends, began the cycle of one religion claiming to hold the truth and denouncing all others as false. It is through this historical story of Moses that

Assmann defines the study of what he calls historical memory—the ways in which fact and fiction are mixed together and then incorporated into religious belief.

"This is certainly a fascinating work," wrote David Lorton for the *Journal of Near Eastern Studies,* although he added that readers unfamiliar with this time period and the "intellectual currents of the seventeenth and eighteenth centuries will find it somewhat difficult going." Robert Louis Wilken of *First Things* suggested that the challenges of the text come from Assmann's preference for studying the past more for how "it is remembered" than for what it actually was. As an example of this, Wilken pointed out that when scholars of the Enlightenment era studied Egyptian religion they made that religion look "very much like Spinozism, Deism, pantheism, or 'natural religion,' the kinds of religious sensibilities they favored."

In 2001, Assmann's *The Search for God in Ancient Egypt* was translated and published in English. For this study, Assmann researches ancient Egyptian texts to create an educated interpretation of Egyptian thought in all its complexities. His topics include the Egyptian concept of the Cosmos, their myths, their beliefs in the New Gods, and their various rituals and cultic beliefs.

Broadening his scope, Assmann next wrote *The Mind of Egypt,* which incorporates more than just the religion of this ancient culture. According to a *Publishers Weekly* reviewer, this work is a "book about history—and how it's made and interpreted—as much as it is about Egypt." Taking notes from literature, archeology, and iconography, Assmann creates an image of Egyptian thought through approximately three thousand years of evolution.

Assmann takes his readers through careful steps in this process, wrote Edward K. Werner for *Library Journal,* "reflecting changes in attitude and world view resulting from internal and external social and historical factors." He does not do this by simply filling out his pages with the facts but rather by looking into the many cultural factors that "characterized antiquity's most technologically advanced and psychologically complex civilization," wrote Margaret Flanagan for *Booklist.* A critic for *Kirkus Reviews* called Assmann's book "an insightful look at the framework of beliefs that supported one of the world's oldest and most stable civilizations."

BIOGRAPHICAL AND CRITICAL SOURCES:

PERIODICALS

Booklist, February 15, 2002, Volume 98, number 12, Margaret Flanagan, review of *The Mind of Egypt: History and Meaning in the Time of the Pharaohs,* p. 987.

First Things: A Monthly Journal of Religion and Public Life, August 1999, Robert Louis Wilken, review of *Moses the Egyptian: The Memory of Egypt in Western Monotheism,* p. 76.

Journal of Near Eastern Studies, July 2000, Volume 59, number 3, David Lorton, review of *Moses the Egyptian: The Memory of Egypt in Western Monotheism,* p. 202.

Kirkus Reviews, February 1, 2002, Volume 70, number 3, review of *The Mind of Egypt: History and Meaning in the Time of the Pharaohs,* p. 151.

Library Journal, March 15, 2002, Volume 127, number 5, Edward K. Werner, review of *The Mind of Egypt: History and Meaning in the Time of the Pharaohs,* p. 92.

Publishers Weekly, February 18, 2002, Volume 249, number 7, review of *The Mind of Egypt: History and Meaning in the Time of the Pharaohs,* pp. 83-84.

*   *   *

ATXAGA, Bernardo
  See GARMENDIA, Joseba Irazu

*   *   *

AVI
  See WORTIS, Avi

*   *   *

BAKER, Nicholson 1957-

PERSONAL: Born January 7, 1957, in New York, NY; son of Douglas and Ann (Nicholson) Baker; married Margaret Brentano, 1985; children: Alice, Elias. *Education:* Attended Eastman School of Music, 1974-75; Haverford College, B.A., 1980.

Nicholson Baker

ADDRESSES: Agent—Melanie Jackson Agency, 250 West 57th St., Suite 1119, New York, NY 10107.

CAREER: Worked variously as an oil analyst, word processor, and technical writer, 1980-87; full-time writer, 1987—. founder of the nonprofit organization American Newspaper Repository.

AWARDS, HONORS: National Book Critics Circle Award for *Double Fold: Libraries and the Assault on Paper,* 2001.

WRITINGS:

NOVELS

The Mezzanine, Weidenfeld & Nicolson (New York, NY), 1988.

Room Temperature, Grove Weidenfeld (New York, NY), 1990.

Vox, Random House (New York, NY), 1992.

The Fermata, Random House (New York, NY), 1994.

The Everlasting Story of Nory, Random House (New York, NY), 1998.

A Box of Matches, Random House (New York, NY), 2003.

NONFICTION

U and I, Random House (New York, NY), 1991.

The Size of Thoughts: Essays and Other Lumber, Random House (New York, NY), 1996.

Double Fold: Libraries and the Assault on Paper, Random House (New York, NY). 2001.

Contributor of stories and essays to periodicals, including *Atlantic* and *New Yorker.*

SIDELIGHTS: A few years before the hit television series *Seinfeld* made comic success out of an essentially plotless "nothing," the critically acclaimed author Nicholson Baker was doing likewise in his novels. A Baker book, in fact, can consist almost entirely of digression, with virtually no plot, action, dialogue, or characterization. This offbeat approach comes naturally to Baker, although at first he tried to make his work more conventional. "I had a whole elaborate plot worked out with [my first novel]," the author told Harry Ritchie in the London *Sunday Times.* "But I'd start writing, and if the plot were, say, a foot long, I'd find I'd covered an eighth of an inch. So I got rid of the plot. I felt enormous relief that I didn't have to pretend to do something that didn't interest me."

Baker's first novel, *The Mezzanine,* celebrates the trivia of daily existence. The slim volume revolves around the largely uneventful lunch hour of the protagonist, a young office worker named Howie who uses his lunch break to buy shoelaces, eat a hot dog and a cookie, and read from second century Roman emperor Marcus Aurelius's *Meditations.* "What Howie observes of his equally worn laces—it made the variables of private life seem suddenly graspable and law-abiding—could also be said of Baker's technique," David Dowling wrote in *Contemporary Novelists.* "Whether it is a record player arm, a doorknob, a straw or a shoelace, his disquisitions make one feel the private life matters, can have logic, and even beauty. Sometimes his examinations have the aridity of a consumer magazine report, but mostly Baker surprises and charms with images which are both ingenious metaphors for the emotional subject, and exact in their own right."

Robert Taylor of the *Boston Globe* added, "The plot might in summary sound either banal or absurdist, when in fact it is a constant delight." The substance of the novel is derived not from the plot, but from the inner workings of Howie's mind. Through Baker's fascination with minutiae, Howie muses about a myriad of everyday objects and occurrences, including how paper milk cartons replaced glass milk bottles, the miracle of perforation (to which he gives a loving tribute), and the nature of plastic straws, vending machines, paper-towel dispensers, and popcorn poppers.

"What makes Howie's ruminations so mesmerizing is the razor-sharp insight and droll humor with which Mr. Baker illuminates the unseen world," said *New York Times Book Review* contributor Robert Plunket. Barbara Fisher Williamson, writing in *Washington Post Book World,* called Baker's descriptions of ordinary items "verbal ballets of incredible delicacy." Brad Leithauser, in *New York Review of Books,* cited Baker's precision by quoting a passage from *The Mezzanine:* "The upstairs doorknobs in the house I grew up in were made of faceted glass. As you extended your fingers to open a door, a cloud of flesh-color would diffuse into the glass from the opposite direction. The knobs were loosely seated in their latch mechanism, and heavy, and the combination of solidity and laxness made for a multiply staged experience as you turned the knob: a smoothness that held intermediary tumbleral fallings-into-position. Few American products recently have been able to capture that same knuckly, orthopedic quality." Though some critics considered Baker's technique a gimmick, many praised his mastery of observation. Plunket said *The Mezzanine*'s "135 pages probably contain more insight into life as we live it than anything currently on the best-seller lists." Williamson called it "the most daring and thrilling first novel since John Barth's 1955 *The Floating Opera,* which it somewhat resembles. It is innovative and original. . . . It is wonderfully readable, in fact gripping, with surprising bursts of recognition, humor, and wonder."

Baker wrote *Room Temperature* similarly. Again, the book contains little plot: Mike, the narrator, is feeding his new baby girl. The book takes place during the twenty minutes necessary for the baby, nicknamed the Bug, to finish her bottle. During this time Mike's ruminations include nose-picking, breathing, the comma, childhood, love, and eating peanut butter straight from the jar, digressions that again display what *Washington*

Post writer Michael Dirda called a "flair for noticing what we all know but don't quite remember or acknowledge." According to Dirda, *Room Temperature* is like *The Mezzanine* in "its microscopic approach to ordinary life, but is altogether more lighthearted, airier." The phrase "room temperature" describes the feel of the baby's bottle and also Mike's world, that of warm daydreams. Comparing *Room Temperature* with *The Mezzanine, Times Literary Supplement* contributor Lawrence Norfolk said the meanderings in *Room Temperature* are "brought closer to the meditations of the character, becoming credible as part of Mike's psychology rather than his author's cleverness. Not wordplay but thought-process."

Although Lesser criticized *Room Temperature* for its sentimentality and subject matter, saying "the timeless love people feel in response to their infants tells us very little about our particular moment in history," Taylor called the work "a big novel unfolding out of small devices so subtly one is scarcely aware of its magnitude until the final page." Dirda described the book as "less sheerly innovative than its more clinical, austere predecessor, . . . yet nevertheless a real charmer, a breath of fresh air, a show-stopping coloratura aria made up of the quirks of memory and the quiddities of daily life."

Critics have compared Baker's writing, noted for its warmth and power of observation, to that of novelist John Updike, but not the author himself who, when asked to name his influences, listed "*The Tailor of Gloucester,* Harold Nicolson, Richard Pryor, [Dr.] Seuss's *If I Ran the Circus,* Edmund Burke, Nabokov, Boswell, . . . Henry and William James, John Candy, *you* know, the usual crowd." Updike, however, plays a supporting role in Baker's first nonfiction book, *U and I.*

This tribute to Updike is experimental and deliberately nonacademic; early in the book, Baker surprisingly says he has read less than half of Updike's work and does not intend to read any more until he has finished writing *U and I.* Calling his method "memory criticism," Baker strives to discover how Updike truly influenced him only through what he spontaneously remembers and forgets about the author and his work. Lewis Burke Frumkes, in the *New York Times Book Review,* described *U and I* as a "fascinating if unsteady journey of literary analysis and self-discovery, shuttling back and forth between soaring, manic moments of unabashed hero-worship and sober, even critical appraisals of the man who, he says, has haunted, inspired and influenced him beyond any other." *Times Literary Supplement* contributor Galen Strawson, however, maintained that "the *I* engulfs the *U.* In the end, *U and I* is almost all about Baker." Strawson added, "[Baker] has very little of interest to say about Updike." But according to Chicago *Tribune Books* critic Joseph Coates, *U and I* contains "a host of offhand, and sometimes startling, critical observations," making it a "provocative and compelling book for any serious reader of contemporary fiction."

Baker returned to fiction with *Vox* and *The Fermata.* In *Vox,* an *Economist* reviewer wrote, Baker "turns his hand to something that should be really interesting: sex." The story centers on one phone call between a man and a woman. The two characters in this short novel both call an adult party line, then decide to converse privately, a dialogue *Time*'s Richard Stengel called "the ultimate in '90s safe sex: voices, not hands, caress each other." Readers learn very little about the characters, at least physically, as the book focuses only on what these two strangers say to one another. The conversation is sexual in nature, with some critics referring to this novel as soft porn. But Stengel said to call it just that would miss the point. Stengel preferred to call *Vox* "an anatomically correct, technology-assisted love story." He also praised Baker for his obvious love relationship with language. "*Vox* is as much about wordplay," Stengel wrote, "as it is about foreplay."

In *The Fermata,* Baker continues with a discussion of sexuality. In a *Seattle Times* review, Michael Upchurch described this novel as "an X-rated sci-fi fantasy that leaves 'Vox' seeming like mere fiber-optic foreplay." The word *fermata* refers to a so-called fold in time, which the book's socially shy protagonist, Arno Strine, uses to stop time and thus freeze the motions of other characters. Dowling found the author "freezing" spots of time "so that they, or more precisely those [spots] on the bodies of women in the vicinity, can be examined minutely. The device gives the text its typical baroque lassitude, but the hero, despite protesting: 'My curiosity has more love and tolerance in it than other men's does,' comes across as smug, and his eroticism as unpleasantly voyeuristic." Dowling further faults the narrative for taking an "adolescent male fantasy" approach, but adds that despite these flaws, *The Fermata* "contains some exquisite apercus such as . . .

the color of those older Tercels and Civics whose paint had consequently oxidized into state of frescoesque, unsaturated beauty, like M&Ms sucked for a minute and spit back out into the palm for study." However, Upchurch said the novel had an undeniable "warmth and generous spirit," and concluded that *The Fermata* confirmed Baker "as one of our most gifted and original writers."

The Size of Thoughts: Essays and Other Lumber is a collection of essays under the categories of "Thought," "Machinery," "Reading," "Mixed," "Library Science," and "Lumber." Baker examines the life's simplicities such as toenail clippers and the all-but-forgotten library index card catalog. Some critics said this collection again exemplifies Baker's passion for language. Jennie Yabroff, writing for the online publication *Hot Wired*, compared Baker to "a hip lit professor who seduces his class into reading deconstructivist criticism by referencing MTV." He "spices up his readings with outrageous metaphors," Yabroff added, to keep his readers involved. Sven Birkerts, for the *New York Times*, said Baker settles on "something commonplace yet structurally intricate [such as the nail clippers] and then, with magnified detailing and sly humor" proceeds to take his readers into "hitherto unimagined panoramas." His "incessantly effervescing prose," Birkerts wrote, "tunes" the reader's mind.

Baker returned to fiction with his novel *The Everlasting Story of Nory*, which relates the childhood story of Eleanor Winslow, a nine-year-old American girl who attends school in England. Again, Baker manipulates language to set the story apart. Baker demonstrates through his young protagonist, Eric Lorberer wrote in the *Review of Contemporary Fiction*, "how both the scientist and the surrealist inhabit a child's consciousness." Nory entices the reader with her self-defined concepts of the world, her stories, and her own peculiar language in her attempt to find meaning. Carol Herman, in *Insight on the News*, refers to Nory as a literary gem that "presents the fears, dreams and ideas of a prepubescent schoolgirl whose preoccupations are more innocent than erotic and as such all the more stunning." Though Baker has a young daughter, Herman found that the author did not write from a father's perspective. Rather, he let Nory speak for herself.

Baker stirred a lot of controversy with *Double Fold: Libraries and the Assault on Paper*, in which he rails against the commonplace destruction of index-card

files, newspapers, and other paper documents at many modern libraries across the United States. Although he admits computerized files may be more efficient, the demise of the actual paper products, especially the newspapers and old books, saddens him. According to Margaria Fichtner, writing for the *Knight-Ridder/Tribune News Service,* Baker blames the loss of "at least 925,000 books," many rare, on modernization. Baker has invested his own money in a non-profit organization, American Newspaper Repository, through which he attempts to preserve as many old newspapers as he can. In his book, he scolds many large libraries, including the Library of Congress, for their practices. Librarians, such as Francine Fialkoff in her *Library Journal* article, defended their practices; she said Baker just "doesn't get it." Though Fialkoff bemoaned Baker's negativity, other critics praised him for publicizing the loss of original publications. Baker won the National Book Critics Circle Award for this book.

Baker told *National Public Radio*'s Jeffrey Freymann-Weyr in a 2003 interview that he wrote *Box of Matches* "only by the light of a fire." Baker said he did not want "to let incandescent light intrude on my consciousness." This novel also focuses on the little things. "I want the books to be about things that you don't notice when you're noticing them," Baker told Freymann-Weyr. Protagonist Emmett, a forty-four-year-old married man, lights a fire every morning, using only one match each time, then sits down to think. He will perform this ceremony for thirty-three days, one day for every match in a box. Emmett, wrote Walter Kirn in the *New York Times*, is "something of a homebody Thoreau, camped out in the Walden Woods of his own living room." The book captures Emmett's often-funny ruminations. "There is gentle humor at work here," Michael Upchurch wrote for the *Seattle Times*. Some critics have described the humor as melancholic. Someone going through a mid-life crisis worries a lot and reminisces. "There's nothing else like" *A Box of Matches,* wrote Upchurch, except another book by Baker. *Newsweek*'s David Gates praised *A Box of Matches* as one of Baker's most "satisfying" books yet.

BIOGRAPHICAL AND CRITICAL SOURCES:

BOOKS

Contemporary Novelists, 6th edition, St. James Press (Detroit, MI), 1996.
Saltzman, Arthur M., *Understanding Nicholson Baker,* University of South Carolina Press (Columbia, SC), 1999.

PERIODICALS

America, June 4, 2001, Volume 184, number 19, Peter Heinegg, "Bureaucrat, Spare That Book!," p. 27.

Atlantic Monthly, January/February, 2003, Volume 291, number 1, Thomas Mallon, "Going to Extremes," review of *A Box of Matches*, pp. 190-93.

Booklist, March 15, 1998, Volume 94, number 14, Donna Seaman, review of *The Everlasting Story of Nory*, pp. 1178-79; February 15, 2001, Volume 97, number 12, Mark Knoblauch, review of *Double Fold: Libraries and the Assault on Paper*, p. 1087.

Boston Globe, December 14, 1988; April 18, 1990.

Columbia Journalism Review, July, 2001, Volume 40, number 2, James Boylan, review of *Double Fold: Libraries and the Assault on Paper*, p. 67.

Current Biography, August, 1994, p. 3.

Economist, April 4, 1992, Volume 323, number 7753, "Don't Call Me," review of *Vox*, p. 109.

Entertainment Weekly, March 11, 1994, p. 28; January 17, 2002, number 691, Troy Patterson, review of *A Box of Matches*, p. 85.

Esquire, February, 1994, p. 76.

Guardian (London), April 5, 1990.

Harper's Bazaar, February, 1994, p. 84.

Independent (London), September 6, 1989.

Insight on the News, August 31, 1998, Volume 14, number 32, Carol Herman, review of *The Everlasting Story of Nory*, p. 36.

Knight-Ridder/Tribune News Service, April 11, 2001, Margaria Fichtner, "Writer's Anger Is Painful, and His Book about Library Discards Is Disturbing," p. K4872.

Library Journal, January, 1994, p. 157; May 1, 1998, Volume 123, number 8, Kay Hogan, review of *The Everlasting Story of Nory*, p. 135; June 15, 2002, Volume 126, number 11, "Baker-Inspired Backlash at LC?," p. 11.

Los Angeles Times, April 19, 1990.

Los Angeles Times Book Review, April 1, 1990, p. 6.

Micrographics and Hybrid Imaging Systems Newsletter, September, 2001, Volume 33, number 9, "Fighting Back against the Double Scold," p. 7.

New Republic, May 28, 2001, Alexander Star, "The Paper Pusher," review of *Double Fold: Libraries and the Assault on Paper*, p. 38.

New Statesman, April 6, 1990, p. 38.

Newsweek, April 16, 2001, Malcolm Jones, "Paper Tiger: Taking Librarians to Task," p. 57; January 13, 2002, Volume 141, number 2, David Gates, "Monster of Exactitude," review of *A Box of Matches*, p. 60.

New York Review of Books, August 17, 1989, p. 15; April 7, 1994, p. 14; June 20, 1996, p. 65.

New York Times Book Review, February 5, 1989, p. 9; April 15, 1990, p. 17; April 14, 1991, p. 12; February 13, 1994, p. 13; April 14, 1996, Steven Birkerts, review of *The Size of Thoughts*, p. 12; February 2, 2003, Walter Kirn, "In the Beginning, There Were Paper Towels: In This Novel, Things Not Worth Noticing Eventually Become All There Is to Notice," review of *A Box of Matches*, pp. 7, 10.

Observer (London), April 1, 1990.

Philadelphia Inquirer, April 15, 1990.

Publishers Weekly, November 29, 1993, p. 52; February 7, 1994, p. 42; March 30, 1998, Volume 245, number 13, review of *The Everlasting Story of Nory*, p. 66; April 2, 2001, Volume 248, number 14, review of *Double Fold: Libraries and the Assault on Paper*, p. 53; October 14, 2002, Volume 249, number 41, Jeff Zaleski, review of *A Box of Matches*, p. 62.

Review of Contemporary Fiction, fall, 1998, Eric Lorberer, review of *The Everlasting Story of Nory*, p. 242.

San Francisco Chronicle, July 8, 1990, p. 3.

San Jose Mercury News, March 18, 1990, p. 20.

Searcher, June, 2001, Volume 9, number 6, review of *Double Fold: Libraries and the Assault on Paper*, p. 6.

Seattle Times, February 27, 1994, Michael Upchurch, "Sex Odysseys," review of *The Fermata*, p. F2; January 12, 2003, Michael Upchurch, "'Matches' Lights Up with Subtle Humor," review of *A Box of Matches*, p. L10.

Sunday Times (London), September 3, 1989; April 8, 1990, p. H8.

Time, February 3, 1992, Volume 139, number 5, Richard Stengel, "1-900-Aural Sex," review of *Vox*, p. 59; May 11, 1998, Volume 151, number 18, R. Z. Sheppard, review of *The Everlasting Story of Nory*, p. 80.

Times Literary Supplement, September 15, 1989, p. 998; April 27, 1990, p. 456; April 19, 1991, p. 20; April 5, 1996, p. 22.

Tribune Books (Chicago), April 28, 1991, p. 7.

Washington Post, May 7, 1990; September 23, 1990.

Washington Post Book World, November 13, 1988, p. 7.

Wilson Quarterly, Summer, 2001, Volume 25, number 3, James Morris, review of "*Double Fold: Libraries and the Assault on Paper*," p. 125.

ONLINE

Hot Wired Web site, http://www.hotwired.lycos.com/ (February 15, 2003), Jennie Yabroff, "Lumbering Genius."

NPR Web site, http://www.npr.org/ (January 15, 2003), Jeffrey Freymann-Weyr, "Nicholson Baker: A Life in Detail."*

* * *

BARABTARLO, Gene
  See BARABTARLO, Gennady

* * *

BARABTARLO, Gennady 1949-
  (Gene Barabtarlo)

PERSONAL: Born February 15, 1949, in Moscow, U.S.S.R (now the Russian Federation); son of Alexander (an economist) and Maria (a professor of German; maiden name, Zelvyansky) Barabtarlo; married Alla Toshchakov (a philologist), 1968; children: Maria Elizabeth. *Education:* University of Moscow, Diploma, 1972; University of Illinois at Urbana-Champaign, Ph. D., 1985. *Politics:* None. *Religion:* Russian Orthodox. *Hobbies and other interests:* Handicrafts.

ADDRESSES: Home—Columbia, MO. *Office*—451 GCB, GRAS, University of Missouri—Columbia, Columbia, MO 65211.

CAREER: Pushkin Literary Museum, Moscow, Russia, senior research fellow, 1970-78; University of Missouri—Columbia, assistant professor of Russian, 1984-90, associate professor of Russian, 1990-94, professor of Russian, 1994—.

MEMBER: International Nabokov Society (vice president, 1990-92; president, 1992-94).

WRITINGS:

(Translator) Vladimir Nabokov, *Pnin,* Ardis (Ann Arbor, MI), 1983.
Phantom of Fact, Ardis (Ann Arbor, MI), 1989.

Aerial View: Essays on Nabokov's Art and Metaphysics, Peter Lang (New York, NY), 1993.
(With Charles Nicol) *A Small Alpine Form,* Garland Publishing (New York, NY), 1993.
(Editor and writer of commentary) Alexander Solzhenitsyn, *What a Pity* (short fiction), Duckworth (London, England), 1996.
In Every Place, Stella (St. Petersburg, Russia), 1996.
(Editor and contributor) *Cold Fusion: Aspects of the German Cultural Prescience in Russia,* Berghahn Books (Oxford, England, and New York, NY), 2000.

Also writes under the name Gene Barabtarlo.

WORK IN PROGRESS: Nabokov and Pushkin: A Private Correspondence.

SIDELIGHTS: Gennady Barabtarlo told *CA:* "In all my writing, I try hard to avoid chopped sentences, split infinitives, and minced words, and to steer clear, as much as I can, of abbreviations."

* * *

BAWCUTT, Priscilla (June) 1931-

PERSONAL: Born June 3, 1931, in Malton, England; daughter of Thomas William (in local government) and Winifred Mary (Humfrey) Preston; married Nigel William Bawcutt (a university teacher), May 26, 1962; children: Nicholas David. *Education:* University of London, B.A. (first class honors), M.A., 1954.

ADDRESSES: Home—21 Dowsefield Lane, Liverpool L18 3J9, England.

CAREER: Independent scholar and writer. Honorary professor at University of Liverpool.

AWARDS, HONORS: Scottish Research Book of the Year, Saltire Society.

WRITINGS:

(Editor) *The Shorter Poems of Gavin Douglas,* Scottish Text Society (East Lothian, Scotland), 1967.
Gavin Douglas: A Critical Study, University of Edinburgh Press (Edinburgh, Scotland), 1974.

(Editor, with Felicity Riddy) *Longer Scottish Poems*, Scottish Academic Press (Edinburgh, Scotland), 1987.

Dunbar the Makar, Oxford University Press (New York, NY), 1992.

(Editor, with Riddy) *Selected Poems of Henryson and Dunbar*, Scottish Academic Press (Edinburgh, Scotland), 1992.

(Editor) *The Poems of William Dunbar* (two volumes), Association for Scottish Literary Studies (Glasgow, Scotland), 1998.

Contributor to *Discovering Scottish Writers*, Scottish Library Association, 1997. Contributor to various periodicals, including *Notes and Queries*.

SIDELIGHTS: Priscilla Bawcutt has devoted much of her career to the study of Scottish poets from the late fifteenth and early sixteenth centuries. Most notable among these are Gavin Douglas and William Dunbar, about whom she has written or edited two books each. Another volume is devoted to the work of both Dunbar and a third Scottish poet of a generation slightly earlier than his and Douglas's, Robert Henryson or Henderson.

Bawcutt's critical editions of these poets' works have been widely praised. The work was not easy; for some of the authors, particularly Dunbar, no authoritative, original manuscripts of their poems exist, so Bawcutt had to choose between competing late versions. R. James Goldstein in *Medium Aevum*, praising Bawcutt's "unrivalled knowledge of Middle Scots language and literature," maintained that with *The Poems of William Dunbar*, Bawcutt "has risen to this formidable editorial challenge, producing what will undoubtedly serve as the standard edition for years to come." Goldstein also praised Bawcutt's "copious commentary and glossary," which comprised the second volume of this two-volume work.

BIOGRAPHICAL AND CRITICAL SOURCES:

BOOKS

Mapstone, Sally, editor, *William Dunbar, "The Nobill Poyet": Essays in Honour of Priscilla Bawcutt*, Tuckwell Press (East Linton, Scotland), 2001.

Reid, Alan, and Brian D. Osborne, editors, *Discovering Scottish Writers*, Scottish Library Association (Hamilton, Scotland), 1997.

PERIODICALS

London Review of Books, May 24, 2001, Sally Mapstone, "Dunbar's Disappearance," pp. 27-29.

Medium Aevum, October, 2001, R. James Goldstein, review of *The Poems of William Dunbar*, pp. 141-2.

Modern Philology, February, 1995, review of *Dunbar the Makar*, p. 366.

Notes and Queries, December, 2000, A. S. G. Edwards, review of *The Poems of William Dunbar*, pp. 497-9.

Review of English Studies, November, 1994, review of *Dunbar the Makar*, p. 553; August, 2001, Keely Fisher, review of *The Poems of William Dunbar*, p. 435.

Speculum, July, 1994, review of *Dunbar the Makar*, p. 739.

Times Literary Supplement, May 6-12, 1988, p. 499; August 13, 1999, Patrick Crotty, "Long in Mind My Work. . .," pp. 3-4.

*   *   *

BEECHER, Jonathan French 1937-

PERSONAL: Born April 26, 1937, in Boston, MA; son of Henry K. U. (a doctor and professor) and Margaret (Swain) Beecher; married Merike Lepasaar (a translator), August 24, 1974; children: David Ilmar, Daniel Lembit. *Education:* Harvard University, A.B. (magna cum laude), 1959, Ph.D., 1968; attended Ecole Normale Superieure, 1962-64. *Politics:* Democratic socialist.

ADDRESSES: Home—401 Pine Flat Rd., Santa Cruz, CA 95060. *Office*—Department of History, University of California, Santa Cruz, CA 95064.

CAREER: Harvard University, Cambridge, MA, instructor in history, 1967-69; University of California, Santa Cruz, assistant professor, 1970-76, associate professor, 1976-86, professor of history, 1986—.

MEMBER: American Historical Association, Societe d'Histoire de la Revolution de 1848, Phi Beta Kappa.

AWARDS, HONORS: Fulbright fellow, 1959-60; fellow of American Council of Learned Societies, 1976-77; Guggenheim fellow, 1988-89; president's fellow of the University of California, 1988.

WRITINGS:

(Editor and translator, with Richard Bienvenu) *The Utopian Vision of Charles Fourier,* Beacon Press (Boston, MA), 1971, second edition, University of Missouri Press (Columbia, MO), 1983.

Charles Fourier: The Visionary and His World, University of California Press (Berkeley, CA), 1986.

Victor Considerant and the Rise and Fall of French Romantic Socialism, University of California Press (Berkeley, CA), 2001.

Contributor of articles and reviews to history journals, including *Journal of Modern History.*

SIDELIGHTS: Jonathan French Beecher once told *CA:* "In writing the biography of French social thinker Charles Fourier (1772-1837), one of my aims was to grasp the interplay between Fourier's dreams and aspirations and the world in which he lived. I tried to situate Fourier's ideas with reference to the worlds of discourse that he challenged and to understand his life by reconstructing the various social worlds that he traversed. This is not the way Fourier has normally been seen; and in taking this approach I was reacting in part against the conventional view of Fourier as an inspired lunatic who lived in a completely self-contained mental universe—a picturesque crank with a few 'modern' insights. I would describe my approach to intellectual biography as contextualist. However, my main concern in writing the book was not to prove a point about how biography should be written but rather to find a way of writing this man's biography that would not trivialize his thought and experience.

"Currently I'm at work on a second biography. Its subject, Victor Considerant (1808-1893), was a follower of Fourier who played an important role in the creation of a Fourierist movement and became one of the leaders of the French democratic socialist left in 1848. Considerant subsequently immigrated to the United States and spent much of the 1850s and 1860s attempting to establish a utopian community in Texas. What makes his long life particularly interesting to me is that through him we can trace the rise and fall of French romantic socialism and we can follow the efforts of a major figure of the generation of the 1840s to salvage his career and ideals after the debacle of 1848.

"When I'm finished with Considerant, I hope to write a volume of essays on European intellectuals and the French revolution of 1848. My central theme or question would be the relation between what such individuals did in 1848 and what they said about the revolution later."

"It is no exaggeration to say that, with [*Victor Considerant and the Rise and Fall of French Romantic Socialism*], Beecher has established himself as the world expert on French utopian socialism," K. Steven Vincent wrote in his review of that book in *French Politics, Culture and Society.* The pre-Marxist socialism of Considerant and others has been an object of scorn for modern social theorists, but as Jeremy Black observed in the *Journal of European Studies,* "Beecher seeks to rescue early socialism from condescension." Black praised Beecher's results: "This is a splendid piece of historical scholarship. . . . Beecher's study is not only destined to become the standard work on Considerant in English, it is the best study of him in any language."

BIOGRAPHICAL AND CRITICAL SOURCES:

PERIODICALS

American Historical Review, October, 1988; April, 2002, Alan B. Spitzer, review of *Victor Considerant and the Rise and Fall of French Romantic Socialism,* p. 631.

Choice, September, 2001, S. Bailey, review of *Victor Considerant and the Rise and Fall of French Romantic Socialism,* p. 194.

French Politics, Culture and Society, spring, 2002, review of *Victor Considerant and the Rise and Fall of French Romantic Socialism,* pp. 120-122.

Journal of European Studies, March, 2001, Jeremy Black, review of *Victor Considerant and the Rise and Fall of French Romantic Socialism,* pp. 125-6.

New York Times Book Review, May 17, 1987; June 21, 1987.

Political Studies, December, 2001, H. S. Jones, review of *Victor Considerant and the Rise and Fall of French Romantic Socialism,* p. 1016.

Times Literary Supplement, April 27, 2001, Bee Wilson, "Illusions Lost," pp. 4-5.

Utopian Studies, winter, 2002, George Mariz, review of *Victor Considerant and the Rise and Fall of French Socialism,* pp. 173-175.

ONLINE

University of California Press Web site, http://www. ucpress.edu/ (May 8, 2002).

*   *   *

BENDERLY, Beryl Lieff 1943-

PERSONAL: Born December 25, 1943, in Chicago, IL; daughter of Morris (a chemist) and Pearl (a sociologist; maiden name, Jacobs) Lieff; married Jordan Benderly (a government official), May 22, 1964; children: Daniel Ethan, Alicia Nadine. *Education:* Attended Universidad de los Andes, Bogota, Colombia, 1964; University of Pennsylvania, B.A., 1964, M.A., 1966; graduate study at Washington University, 1966.

ADDRESSES: Home—Washington, DC. *Agent*—Virginia Barber Literary Agency, Inc., 353 West 21st St., New York, NY 10011.

CAREER: Fisk University, Nashville, TN, instructor, 1966-67; University of Puerto Rico, Rio Piedras, Puerto Rico, instructor in sociology and anthropology, 1967-69; American University, Washington, DC, research scientist and social-cultural specialist, 1969-76; freelance writer, 1976—. Member of judging committee, MacDougal Creative Writing Prize, 1979-82.

MEMBER: National Book Critics Circle, American Society of Journalists and Authors (member of national board, 1985-87; chair of Washington, DC, chapter, 1987—), National Association of Science Writers, Authors Guild, Authors League of America, Washington Independent Writers (member of board of directors, 1978-79, 1980-81; vice-president, 1979-80), Phi Beta Kappa.

AWARDS, HONORS: Woodrow Wilson fellowship, 1964; university fellowships from Washington University and University of Pennsylvania, both 1965; national finalist in White House Fellows competition, 1974; National Media Award, American Psychological Foundation, 1981, for article "The Great Ape Debate"; honorable mention in national features category, Odyssey Institute, 1981, for article "Dialogue of the Deaf"; Exceptional Achievement Award, Council for the Advancement and Support of Education, 1984; Gallaudet Journalism Prize, 1984; American Society of Journalists and Authors Book Award, 1989.

WRITINGS:

(With Richard F. Nyrop and others) *The Area Handbook,* 18 volumes, U.S. Government Printing Office (Washington, DC), 1971-77.

(With Mary F. Gallagher and John Young) *Discovering Culture: An Introduction to Anthropology* (textbook), Van Nostrand (New York, NY), 1977.

Dancing without Music: Deafness in America, Anchor/ Doubleday (New York, NY), 1980.

Thinking about Abortion, Dial/Doubleday (New York, NY), 1984.

High Schools and the Changing Workplace, National Academy of Science (Washington, DC), 1984.

The Myth of Two Minds: What Gender Means and Doesn't Mean, Doubleday (New York, NY), 1987.

(With Renee Royak-Schaler) *Challenging the Breast Cancer Legacy: A Program of Emotional Support and Medical Care for Women at Risk,* HarperCollins (New York, NY), 1992.

In Her Own Right: The Institute of Medicine's Guide to Women's Health Issues, National Academy Press (Washington, DC), 1997.

(With Stanley I. Greenspan) *The Growth of the Mind: And the Endangered Origins of Intelligence,* Addison-Wesley (Reading, MA), 1997.

Jason's Miracle: A Hanukkah Story (juvenile fiction), Albert Whitman (Morton Grove, IL), 2000.

(With Hasia Diner) *Her Works Praise Her: A History of Jewish Women in America from Colonial Times to the Present,* Basic Books (New York, NY), 2002.

Also author of accompanying print material for Public Broadcasting Service series "The Hurt That Does Not Show," first broadcast by KOCE-TV, 1983, and of numerous news reports. Contributor of articles to magazines, including *Change, Ms., Health, Moment, Redbook, Self, Science, Smithsonian, Working Mother,* and *Woman's Day.* Contributor of book reviews to *Present Tense, The World and I, Washington Post Book World* and *Smithsonian.* Contributing editor, *Psychology Today.*

SIDELIGHTS: Beryl Lieff Benderly once told *CA:* "My writing centers on the social, or human, effects of the ideas we hold—on how what we think governs the way we act. I explore this theme mainly at the intersection of society and technology, where what is possible runs up against the way we would like the world to be." She later added that "this theme comes out particularly strongly in [*The Myth of Two Minds: What Gender Means and Doesn't Mean*], a critique of current thinking on gender differences." In a *Washington Post Book World* review, critic Susan Dooley called Benderly's work "a fascinating exploration of what science actually knows about the differences between men and women."

Similar praise was given to the author's earlier book about the deaf, *Dancing without Music: Deafness in America,* about which *Washington Post Book World* contributor Evelyn Wilde Mayerson noted: "[Benderly offers] both lay readers and interested professionals in the health sciences a comprehensive layout, as rich as an illustrated story board, of the deaf experience." Benderly described her book to *CA* as "the first general trade book on this subject to appear in almost forty years. It describes the social, educational, and psychological situation of the deaf community and outlines the historic development that produced the world that today's deaf people inhabit. Communication mode largely determines a deaf child's social future. I examine the various communications options available to deaf people in terms of their social and human outcomes."

More recently, Benderly addresses the delicate subject of abortion in *Thinking about Abortion.* Fitzhugh Mullan commented in *Washington Post Book World* that "Benderly deals straightforwardly with the subject" of abortion in her book. "Her text is thoughtful, informative and, ultimately, pro-choice," Mullan concludes. "She dutifully reviews the theological and polemical arguments against abortion as well as those made in its favor." Another controversial subject, the relationships between intelligence and environment, is tackled

in *The Growth of the Mind: And the Endangered Origins of Intelligence,* cowritten with Stanley I. Greenspan. In this book, the authors argue that a warm and nurturing environment is crucial for the full development of intelligence, and suggest radical reforms of workplace, schools, and child-care organizations to create better environments for children. A *Publishers Weekly* contributor welcomed the book as a wide-ranging and well-researched work that added significant light to a crucial social issue.

Jewish themes inform two of Benderly's most recent books. *Jason's Miracle: A Hanukkah Story* is a children's novel in which twelve-year-old Jason travels back in time to the era of the Maccabees, learning first-hand about the heroic events that came to be celebrated at Hanukkah. In *Her Works Praise Her: A History of Jewish Women in America from Colonial Times to the Present,* Benderly and coauthor Hasia Diner present the first comprehensive social history of Jewish women in America. A reviewer for *Publishers Weekly* found the book "well-researched and consistently absorbing," and noted that, though it fails to consider the role of Jewish women in the gay and lesbian movement, the book is nevertheless a "fundamental contribution" and "certain to inform and engage."

BIOGRAPHICAL AND CRITICAL SOURCES:

PERIODICALS

Booklist, February 1, 1997, William Beatty, review of *The Growth of the Mind: And the Endangered Origins of Intelligence,* p. 908.

Choice, July-August, 1997, P. Barker, review of *The Growth of the Mind,* p. 1876.

Library Journal, April 1, 1992, Janet M. Coggan, review of *Challenging the Breast Cancer Legacy: A Program of Emotional Support and Medical Care for Women at Risk,* p. 142; May 1, 1997, Barbara M. Bibel, review of *In Her Own Right: The Institute of Medicine's Guide to Women's Health Issues,* p. 133.

Psychology of Women Quarterly, June, 1994, Diane L. Gressley, review of *Challenging the Breast Cancer Legacy,* p. 316.

Publishers Weekly, January 27, 1997, review of *The Growth of the Mind,* p. 91; September 25, 2000, review of *Jason's Miracle: A Hanukkah Story,* p.

66; February 11, 2002, review of *Her Works Praise Her: A History of Jewish Women in America from Colonial Times to the Present*, p. 173.

School Library Journal, October, 2000, review of *Jason's Miracle*, p. 64.

Smithsonian, November, 1980.

Teaching English to the Deaf, fall, 1981.

Washington Post Book World, October 5, 1980, August 25, 1984; November 13, 1987.*

*   *   *

BENITEZ, Sandra (Ables) 1941-

PERSONAL: Born March 26, 1941, in Washington, DC; daughter of James Q. (a diplomat, road builder, comptroller, and writer) and Marta A. (an executive secretary and translator; maiden name, Benitez) Ables; married second husband, James F. Kondrick (a writer and game inventor), May 25, 1980; children: (first marriage) Christopher Charles Title, Jonathon James Title. *Education:* Truman State University, B.S., 1962, M.A., 1974.

ADDRESSES: Home and office—6075 Lincoln Drive, No. 210, Edina, MN 55436. *Agent*—Ellen Levine Literary Agency, Inc., 15 East 26th St., Suite 1801, New York, NY 10010-1505.

CAREER: Gaunt High School, Affton, MO, ninth-grade Spanish and English teacher, 1963-68; Northeast Missouri State University, Kirksville, teaching assistant, 1974; Wilson Learning Corporation, Eden Prairie, MN, freelance Spanish/English translator, 1975-76, marketing liaison in international division, 1977-80; fiction writer and creative writing teacher for The Loft and the University of Minnesota, Duluth, Split Rock Arts Program, 1980—. Loft Inroads Program, Hispanic mentor, 1989-92. COMPAS Writers-in-the-Schools Roster Artist, St. Paul, MN; member of the National Writers' Voice Project Reading Tour, 1994-95; University of Minnesota, Keller-Edelstein Distinguished writer-in-residence, 1997; University of San Diego, member of Knapp (chair, 2001).

MEMBER: Authors Guild, The Loft, Poets and Writers.

Sandra Benitez

AWARDS, HONORS: Loft Mentor Award for fiction, 1987; Loft-McKnight Award for fiction, 1988; Jerome Foundation Travel and Study Grant, 1989; Minnesota State Arts Board fellowship, 1991; Minnesota Hispanic Heritage Month Award, 1992; Loft-McKnight Award of Distinction for prose, 1993; Barnes and Noble Discover Great New Writers Award, 1993, and Minnesota Book Award for fiction, 1994, both for *A Place Where the Sea Remembers;* Edelstein-Keller Writer of Distinction, 1997; American Book Award, Before Columbus Foundation, 1998, for *Bitter Grounds;* Bush Artists fellowship, 1999; *Book Sense* '76 Pick, *Star Tribune* "Talking Volumes" selection, 2002, for *The Weight of All Things*; All-city book read award, 2002, for *A Place Where the Sea Remembers.*

WRITINGS:

A Place Where the Sea Remembers, Coffee House Press (Minneapolis, MN), 1993.

Mickey Pearlman, editor, "Home Views," *A Place Called Home: Twenty Writing Women Remember*, St. Martins Press (New York, NY), 1996.

Bitter Grounds, Hyperion (New York, NY), 1997.

Marilyn Kallet and Judith Ortiz Cofer, editors, *"Fire, Wax, Smoke," Sleeping with One Eye Open: Women Writers and the Art of Survival,* University of Georgia Press (Athens, GA), 1999.

The Weight of All Things, Hyperion (New York, NY), 2000.

Night of the Radishes, Hyperion (New York, NY), 2003.

Work has been published in British, Dutch, German, Spanish and French.

Work represented in several anthologies. Contributor of numerous English and Spanish articles to periodicals.

SIDELIGHTS: Sandra Benitez draws upon her experiences living in Mexico and El Salvador to craft novels that reveal how domestic life is compromised by politics in Latin America. In Benitez's novels, political discord dissolves family and friendship ties, it leaves young children orphaned and vulnerable, and it infects generation after generation. The larger social framework of Latin America becomes understandable when presented from the viewpoint of so-called "ordinary" characters with whom the reader can develop a rapport. To quote a *Publishers Weekly* writer in a review of *The Weight of All Things,* Benitez—who published her first novel at the age of fifty-two—"gives voice to the silenced."

Benitez's first novel, *A Place Where the Sea Remembers,* was published in 1993. The book reveals the aspirations and disillusionment felt by people living in the Mexican village of Santiago. Candelario Marroquin is fired from his job one afternoon and, upon returning home, discovers that his wife is pregnant. Now Candelario is unable to keep his promise to his wife's sister to take in her baby that was conceived as the result of a rape. A quarrel between the sisters ensues which triggers a series of events that touches the lives of many of the residents of Santiago. Some reviewers complimented Benitez on her ability to create a distinctive society by interweaving the stories of her characters. "Throughout *A Place Where the Sea Remembers,* Ms. Benitez's descriptions of people and places are crisp, and the staccato rhythms of her prose are just right for this dark fable of a story. She has built a little world . . . and filled it with people we care for, we root for, and whose flaws we are willing to forgive," wrote Chris Bohjalian in the *New York Times Book Review.* Cristina Garcia of the *Washington Post Book World* felt that *A Place Where the Sea Remembers* "is a quietly stunning book that leaves soft tracks in the heart." The work won Benitez the Barnes and Noble Discover Great New Writers Award in 1993, as well as a Minnesota Book Award for fiction in 1994.

In 1997 Benitez published *Bitter Grounds,* a story that follows two connected Salvadoran families through the political events of the 1930s through the 1970s. One family owns a coffee plantation; the other works in their employment. Benitez keeps her focus on the women of these families through three generations and shows despite their disparate circumstances, how they are linked by a complex mix of servitude and friendship. The author gives a careful sensory picture of their combined experiences, such as the making of sweet and salt tamales, and a ubiquitous radio soap opera called "Las Dos." The story concentrates on individual experiences, but the violence of continuous political upheaval in El Salvador is inescapable, beginning with the flight of Nahuat-descended Mercedes from the massacre in her Indian village. Political allegiances and class divisions threaten to end the generations-old relationship between the families, as each generation produces daughters who rebel against their places in the world.

Bitter Grounds received enthusiastic reviews and was admired for its cultural and social nuances, as well as for its careful treatment of a controversial political situation. Writing for *Booklist,* Grace Fill called the novel "a beautiful work of fiction that reveals the complicated roots of human drama and lays bare the truth of a troubled nation." Suzanne Ruta commended Benitez in *Entertainment Weekly,* admiring her "savory details. . . . comic touches. . . . [and] delicate, domestic look at violent history." A *Publishers Weekly* reviewer found the work "surprisingly free of propaganda" and commented that the "Spanish-sprinkled, elegant prose is mesmerizing in its simplicity and frankness." Mary Margaret Benson noted the book's "rich and fluid" prose in her review for *Library Journal* and called it a "welcome addition to the growing body of Latina literature."

The Weight of All Things offers a chilling portrait of a young boy caught up in an incomprehensible war. Nine-year-old Nicolas de la Virgen Veras accompanies his mother to the funeral of a martyred Catholic hero, Archbishop Romero. Soldiers fire on the large crowd, killing Nicolas's mother, who has tried to shield him from the flying bullets. Unaware that his mother is dead, and not just wounded, the bewildered boy makes his way home to his grandfather—only to discover that the war has arrived in his rural town as well. According to Michael Porter in the *New York Times Book Review,* through Nicolas's eyes "we see the war as a morass of fear and confusion, punctuated by acts of brutality and selfless kindness." Mimi O'Connor in *Book* magazine praised the work for its "straightforward and evocative prose" that offers "a deeply affecting and startling portrait" of a country caught in the throes of war. In *Publishers Weekly* a critic noted that the novel "seamlessly blends fact with imagination, evoking the trauma of war more vividly than any newspaper account." And Andrea Caron Kempf concluded in the *Library Journal:* "With its deceptively simple narrative, *The Weight of All Things* tells a powerful story."

Benitez once told *CA:* "I came to writing late. I was thirty-nine before I gathered enough courage to begin. When I hear other writers talk about writing, I'm amazed by those who say they always knew they had to write. When I was a girl, I never wished to do it. Being a writer was something magical I never dreamed I could attain. But while growing up, I frequently had a book in my lap, and so I was linked, even then, to writing and to the spell that stories cast.

"Over the years, I didn't know a writing life was lying in store for me. I had to live and grow before I caught the faint call at the age of thirty-nine. Since then, I've worked hard at being faithful to the call. For writing is an act of faith. We must keep faith each day with our writing if we want to be called writers.

"Since I've been writing, I've searched what's in my heart and it's from *that* core that I write and not from what seems marketable. I am a Latina American. In my heart are stored the stories of my Puerto Rican and Missourian heritage and of a childhood lived in Mexico and El Salvador. When I write, I have to suppress the knowledge that mainstream America often ignores the stories of 'la otra America.' Over the years, I've learned to write from the heart, to persevere despite the setbacks of a host of rejections.

"In the end, I've learned these things about writing: it's never too late to begin; we know all we need to know in order to do it; persistence and tenacity will take us all the way; and there are angels on our shoulders. Be still to catch their whisperings."

BIOGRAPHICAL AND CRITICAL SOURCES:

PERIODICALS

Book, January-February, 2001, Mimi O'Connor, review of *The Weight of All Things,* p. 79.
Booklist, September 15, 1997, Grace Fill, review of *Bitter Grounds,* p. 207.
Boston Globe, December 29, 1993.
Christian Science Monitor, January 21, 1998, Kathleen Kilgore, "Mayan and Modern Worlds Vie in El Salvador Tale," p. 13.
Entertainment Weekly, October 31, 1997, Suzanne Ruta, review of *Bitter Grounds,* p. 100.
Hispanic Times Magazine, May-June, 1997, Robert Kendall, review of *A Place Where the Sea Remembers,* p. 39.
Library Journal, September 1, 1997, Mary Margaret Benson, review of *Bitter Grounds,* p. 214; December, 2000, Andrea Caron Kempf, review of *The Weight of All Things,* p. 184.
Los Angeles Times, October 28, 1997, Kevin Baxter, "Rediscovering Roots through Her Writing," p. E3.
Minneapolis-St. Paul Magazine, November, 1999, Alicia Fedorczak, "The Stories of Her Life," p. 50.
New York Times Book Review, October 31, 1993; March 25, 2001, Michael Porter, review of *The Weight of All Things,* p. 22.
Publishers Weekly, August 11, 1997, review of *Bitter Grounds,* p. 384; December 11, 2000, review of *The Weight of All Things,* p. 64.
St. Louis Post-Dispatch, September 7, 1997, Susan C. Hegger, "Melodrama with Latin Accent," p. C5.
Washington Post Book World, September 5, 1993.
Women's Review of Books, June, 1998, Barbara Belejack, review of *Bitter Grounds,* p. 100.

*   *   *

BHATT, Sujata 1956-

PERSONAL: Born May 6, 1956, in Ahmedabad, India; married Michael Augustin, 1988; children: one daughter. *Education:* Goucher College, B.A., 1980; University of Iowa Writers' Workshop, M.F.A., 1986.

ADDRESSES: Home—Bremen, Germany. *Agent*—c/o Author Mail, Carcanet Press, 4th Floor, Alliance House, Cross St., Manchester M2 7AP, England.

CAREER: Freelance writer and translator. University of Victoria, British Columbia, Lansdowne visiting writer/professor, spring, 1992.

AWARDS, HONORS: Alice Hunt Bartlett Award, 1988; Dillons Commonwealth Poetry Prize, 1989; Poetry Society Book Recommendation, 1991, for *Monkey Shadows;* Cholmondeley Award, 1991.

WRITINGS:

POETRY

Brunizem, Carcanet (Manchester, England), 1988.
Monkey Shadows, Carcanet (Manchester, England), 1991.
Freak Waves (chapbook), Reference West (Victoria, British Columbia, Canada), 1992.
The Stinking Rose, Carcanet (Manchester, England), 1995.
Point No Point: Selected Poems, Carcanet (Manchester, England), 1997.
Augatora, Carcanet (Manchester, England), 2000.
My Mother's Way of Wearing a Sari, Penguin Books (New York, NY), 2000.
A Colour for Solitude, Carcanet (Manchester, England), 2002.

SIDELIGHTS: Sujata Bhatt is a poet whose work was hailed by critics from the start of her writing career. Bhatt's parents are Indian, but she grew up in the United States and later married a German citizen. Her first collection, *Brunizem,* moves through the stages and countries of her life, from India, to North America, to Europe. She is "comfortable with meditative, expansive narratives, even with shorter spells of rumination interspersed with brisk commentaries," noted K. Narayana Chandran in *World Literature Today.* Chandran found she was "not so impressive when she sketches, or when she is eager to present things in a nutshell."

Bhatt's next collection, *Monkey Shadows,* contains some work of "astonishing brilliance," according to another review by Chandran in *World Literature Today.*

Chandran praised "White Asparagus" as "a stunning onslaught of a poem, a body slipping the leash of its mind at one furious go, as it were." Bhatt covers scenes of post-World War II Germany, portrays everyday lives in India, and uses a band of Rhesus monkeys as a metaphor for the human condition in *Monkey Shadows.* Her work in this collection shows that she understands "what it means to talk about cultures, across vast and dizzying gulfs of incomprehension, to heads swollen with colonial, racial prejudices," stated Chandran.

Bhatt is "an accomplished poet using her multicultural background to its fullest effect," praised Sudeep Sen in a *World Literature Today* review of Bhatt's collection *Point No Point: Selected Poems.* This volume is "substantial," in Sen's opinion, a book that "allows us to travel, dream, and learn, but one that ultimately moves us by its quietude of stance and impeccable articulation." Summing up Bhatt's talents, Sen noted her ability to "use free verse with delicacy, poise, and effect. Her lines are tight, her metaphors unusual, and her range of themes wide." In another commentary on *Point No Point* in *World Literature Today,* Sen claimed that Bhatt's greatest strength is her ability to stretch "imagination's limits through lucid use of language, employing images that are clear and simple and locations that are surprising."

BIOGRAPHICAL AND CRITICAL SOURCES:

PERIODICALS

Antioch Review, January 1, 2001, Jane Satterfield, review of *Augatora,* p. 123.
Journal of Commonwealth Literature, spring, 2000, Cecile Sandten, "In Her Own Voice: Sujata Bhatt and the Aesthetic Articulation of the Diaspora Condition," p. 99.
Observer, October 26, 1997, review of *Point No Point: Selected Poems,* p. 15.
Times Literary Supplement, October 27, 1995, Elizabeth Lowry, review of *The Stinking Rose,* p. 27; August 8, 1997, Sudeep Sen, review of *Point No Point: Selected Poems,* p. 16; December 22, 2000, Peter Daniels Luczinski, review of *Augatora,* p. 22.
World Literature Today, September 22, 1984, K. Narayana Chandran, review of *Brunizem,* p. 884; January 1, 1995, K. Narayana Chandran, review

of *Monkey Shadows,* p. 223; September 22, 1997, Sudeep Sen, review of *Point No Point: Selected Poems,* p. 868; September 22, 2000, Sudeep Sen, review of *Recent Indian English Poetry,* p. 783.

* * *

BILL, James A(lban) 1939-

PERSONAL: Born March 2, 1939, in La Crosse, WI. *Education:* Assumption College, B.A., 1961 (class valedictorian); Pennsylvania State University, M.A., 1963; Princeton University, M.A., 1965, Ph.D., 1989.

ADDRESSES: Office—International Studies Department, College of William and Mary, P.O. Box 8795, Williamsburg, VA 23187-8795. *E-mail*—jabill@ facstaff.wm.edu.

CAREER: Political scientist, educator, and author. College of William and Mary, professor of government and director emeritus of Reves Center for International Studies. Formerly professor of government at University of Texas, Austin; visiting professor at Washington University, St. Louis, and University of Alaska, Anchorage; visiting distinguished professor at University of Delaware; lecturer on international issues at Harvard University, Yale University, Princeton University, University of Chicago, University of California, Los Angeles, and more than ninety other universities in the United States; has given lectures in Tokyo, Bonn, Toronto, London, Mexico City, Halifax, Tehran, Cairo, Jerusalem, Kuwait, Moscow, Abu Dhabi, and Dushanbe. Member of Overseers' Committee to Visit the Center for Middle Eastern Studies, Harvard University.

MEMBER: American Political Science Association, Society for Iranian Studies.

AWARDS, HONORS: Honorary doctorate, Assumption College, 1989.

WRITINGS:

The Politics of Iran: Groups, Classes, and Modernization, C. E. Merrill (Columbus, OH), 1972.
Comparative Politics: The Quest for Theory, C. E. Merrill (Columbus, OH), 1973.

Politics and Petroleum, King's Court, 1975.
(With Robert Springborg) *Politics in the Middle East,* Little, Brown (Boston, MA), 1979.
The Eagle and the Lion: The Tragedy of American-Iranian Relations, Yale University Press (New Haven, CT), 1988.
The Shah, the Ayatollah, and the United States, Foreign Policy Association (New York, NY), 1988.
(Editor, with William Roger Louis) *Musaddiq, Iranian Nationalism, and Oil,* University of Texas Press (Austin, TX), 1988.
George Ball: Behind the U.S. Foreign Policy, Yale University Press (New Haven, CT), 1997.
(With John Alden Williams) *Roman Catholics and Shi'i Muslims: Prayer, Passion, and Politics,* University of North Carolina Press (Chapel Hill, NC), 2002.

Contributor of articles to periodicals, including *Time, Newsweek, Fortune, New Yorker, Wall Street Journal,* and *Science.*

SIDELIGHTS: James A. Bill, a specialist in international studies, has traveled extensively in the Middle East and has devoted his career to the study of politics and society in that region. His focus is primarily on Iran, where he lived for two years during the 1960s and to which he returned for several visits through the 1970s. His four books on Iran have been welcomed as informative studies on a timely and important subject.

In *The Eagle and the Lion: The Tragedy of American-Iranian Relations,* Bill argues that U.S. policy toward Iran has been based on "pervasive ignorance." Seeing Iran as little more than a pawn in the Cold War, the United States failed to understand the nationalist forces building within the country and, by blindly supporting the unpopular shah, guaranteed the growth of a bitterly anti-American movement in the country. *New Republic* reviewer Alan Tonelson observed that "Bill makes a powerful case" that American policy blundered in Iran, but questioned whether a regionalist policy—one more attuned to the particularities of Iranian politics and society—would have succeeded any better. Jerrold D. Green of *New Leader,* however, found Bill's analysis well written and convincing, emphasizing his conclusion that policymakers should never maintain a narrow focus when responding to international crises.

Musaddiq, Iranian Nationalism, and Oil, a collection of scholarly essays which Bill coedited with William Roger Louis, examines the achievements of Muhammad Musaddiq, who served as premier of Iran from 1951 until his overthrow in 1953. *Middle Eastern Studies* contributor David Menashri hailed the book as a "highly valuable contribution shedding much light on one of the most controversial periods, and one of the most notable figures in twentieth-century Iran."

Bill's account of the career of diplomat George Ball, who served as presidential adviser, undersecretary of state, and ambassador to the United Nations under presidents Kennedy and Johnson, also attracted significant notice. Bill presents his subject as both pragmatic and idealistic, and shows how his handling of several international issues contributed in positive ways to American statecraft. "Bill rightly presents George Ball 'as a rare and realistic model of the prudent statesman,'" wrote Wilson D. Miscamble in *History: Review of New Books*. "This fine book should encourage policymakers of the present and the future to learn from his experience and example." Similar praise marked David C. Hendrickson's review in *Foreign Affairs*, where he commended the book as a convincing and "admirable" study, and James M. Scott's review for *American Political Science Review*, in which he hailed the book as a "first-rate piece of scholarship . . . that provides a useful biographical sketch of Ball and an often revealing glimpse of U.S. foreign policymaking." Though a writer for *Publishers Weekly* found *George Ball* almost too much in awe of its subject, the reviewer pointed out that the book "works well" in explaining the foundations of the U.S. foreign policy system.

Several of Bill's later books have tackled the subject of religion and culture. His *Roman Catholics and Shi'i Muslims: Prayer, Passion, and Politics,* cowritten with John Alden Williams, shows the significant similarities between the two faiths. Noting that the authors had chosen a difficult subject, *Library Journal* contributor Gary P. Gillum deemed the book a success, concluding that the authors "help us understand a much-maligned religion" and appreciate its common bonds with Catholicism.

BIOGRAPHICAL AND CRITICAL SOURCES:

PERIODICALS

American Historical Review, June, 1999, Jeffrey Kimball, review of *George Ball,* p. 949.

American Political Science Review, December, 1990, Shahrough Akhavi, review of *The Eagle and the Lion: The Tragedy of American-Iranian Relations,* p. 1417; September, 1999, James M. Scott, review of *George Ball,* p. 708.

Annals of the American Academy of Political and Social Science, July, 1998, Douglas Brinkley, review of *George Ball: Behind the U.S. Foreign Policy,* p. 225.

Asian Affairs, October, 1989, Desmond Harney, review of *The Eagle and the Lion,* p. 321.

Booklist, March 15, 1997, Mary Carroll, review of *George Ball,* p. 1222; February 15, 2002, Steven Schroeder, review of *Roman Catholics and Shi'i Muslims: Prayer, Passion, and Politics,* p. 973.

Diplomatic History, summer, 1990, Mark Lytle, review of *The Eagle and the Lion,* p. 461.

Foreign Affairs, summer, 1988, John C. Campbell, review of *The Eagle and the Lion,* p. 1134; May-June, 1997, David C. Hendrickson, review of *George Ball,* p. 133.

History: Review of New Books, fall, 1997, Wilson D. Miscamble, review of *George Ball,* p. 38.

History: The Journal of the Historical Association, June, 1989, Ritchie Ovendale, review of *Musaddiq, Iranian Nationalism, and Oil,* p. 266.

International Affairs, spring, 1989, Philip Robins, review of *The Eagle and the Lion,* p. 383.

International Journal of Middle East Studies, August, 1990, Said Amir Arjomand, review of *The Eagle and the Lion,* p. 335.

Journal of American Studies, April, 1999, Martin H. Folly, review of *George Ball,* p. 103.

Journal of Politics, February, 1989, Sanford R. Silverburg, review of *The Eagle and the Lion,* p. 198; May, 1998, Robert J. Bresler, review of *George Ball,* p. 583.

Library Journal, March 15, 1997, Edward Goedeken, review of *George Ball,* p. 75; March 1, 2002, Gary P. Gillum, review of *Roman Catholics and Shi'i Muslims,* p. 106.

Middle Eastern Studies, April, 1993, David Menashri, review of *Musaddiq, Iranian Nationalism, and Oil,* p. 360.

New Leader, May 2, 1988, Jerrold D. Green, review of *The Eagle and the Lion,* p. 20.

New Republic, August 1, 1988, Alan Tonelson, review of *The Eagle and the Lion,* p. 44.

New York Times Book Review, Fouad Ajami, review of *The Eagle and the Lion,* p. 3.

Publishers Weekly, January 27, 1997, review of *George Ball,* p. 89.

Times Higher Education Supplement, June 6, 1997, Susan Carruthers, review of *George Ball,* p. 25.

Wall Street Journal, April 18, 1988, Amos Perlmutter, review of *The Eagle and the Lion,* p. 20.

Washington Monthly, July-August, 1997, Robert Dallek, review of *George Ball,* p. 55.*

*   *   *

BLAINEY, Geoffrey (Norman) 1930-

PERSONAL: Born March 11, 1930, in Melbourne, Victoria, Australia; son of Samuel Clifford (a clergyman) and Hilda (maiden name, Lanyon) Blainey; married Ann Warriner Heriot (an author), February 15, 1957; children: Anna Elizabeth. *Education:* Attended Wesley College, Melbourne, and Queen's College, University of Melbourne.

ADDRESSES: Home—P.O. Box 257, E. Melbourne, Victoria 3002, Australia. *Office*—42 Hotham St., E. Melbourne, Victoria 3002, Australia.

CAREER: Freelance writer, specializing in industrial history, 1951-61; University of Melbourne, Melbourne, Victoria, Australia, senior lecturer, 1962-63, reader, 1963-68, professor of economic history, 1968-77, Ernest Scott Professor of History, 1977-88; University of Ballarat, chancellor, 1994—. Commonwealth Literary Fund, member of advisory board, 1968-71, chair, 1971-73; chair of literature board, Australia Council, 1973-74; vice-chair, Australian Government Inquiry into Museums and Galleries, 1974-75.

AWARDS, HONORS: Sir Ernest Scott Prize for Australian history, 1954, for *The Peaks of Lyell;* Harbison-Higinbotham Prize and Colonel Crouch Gold Medal of Australian Literature Society, 1963, both for *The Rush That Never Ended: A History of Australian Mining;* C. Weickhardt Award at Melbourne Festival, 1966, for *The Tyranny of Distance: How Distance Shaped Australia's History;* Captain Cook Bi-Centenary Prize for Biography, 1970, for The Steel Master: A Life of Essington Lewis. Named one of Australia's 100 "living treasures" by the National Trust, 1997.

WRITINGS:

The Peaks of Lyell, Melbourne University Press (Melbourne, Australia), 1954, 3rd edition, 1968.

(With N. H. Oliver) *The University of Melbourne: A Centenary Portrait,* Melbourne University Press (Melbourne, Australia), 1956, published as *A Centenary History of the University of Melbourne,* 1957.

Gold and Paper: A History of the National Bank of Australasia, Georgian House (Melbourne, Australia), 1958, reprinted, Macmillan (Melbourne, Australia), 1983.

Mines in the Spinifex: The Story of Mount Isa Mines, Angus & Robertson (Sydney, Australia), 1960, 3rd edition, 1970.

The Rush That Never Ended: A History of Australian Mining, Melbourne University Press (Melbourne, Australia), 1963, 4th edition, 1993.

A History of Camberwell, Jacaranda Press (Brisbane, Australia), 1964.

The Tyranny of Distance: How Distance Shaped Australia's History, Sun Books (Melbourne, Australia), 1966, St. Martin's (New York, NY), 1968, reprinted, Macmillan (Melbourne, Australia), 1982.

(Editor) *If I Remember Rightly: The Memoirs of W. S. Robinson, 1876-1963,* F. W. Cheshire (Melbourne, Australia), 1967.

Across a Red World, St. Martin's (New York, NY), 1968.

The Rise of Broken Hill, Macmillan (Melbourne, Australia), 1968.

The Steel Master: A Life of Essington Lewis, Macmillan (Melbourne, Australia), 1971, reprinted, Melbourne University Press (Melbourne, Australia), 1995.

The Causes of War, Free Press (New York, NY), 1973, reprinted, 1988.

Triumph of the Nomads: A History of Aboriginal Australia, Macmillan (Melbourne, Australia), 1975, Overlook Press (Woodstock, NY), 1976, reprinted, Macmillan (Melbourne, Australia), 1982.

(Contributor) *The Birth of Australia,* Rigby (Adelaide, Australia), 1978.

A Land Half Won, Macmillan (Melbourne, Australia), 1980.

The Blainey View, Macmillan (Melbourne, Australia), 1982.

Our Side of the Country: The Story of Victoria, Methuen Haynes (North Ryde, Australia), 1984.

All for Australia, Methuen Haynes (North Ryde, Australia), 1984.

Surrender Australia and Asian Immigration, Allen & Unwin (Boston, MA), 1985.

(Contributor) *The Birth of a Nation: Australia's Historic Heritage, from Discovery to Nationhood,* Viking O'Neil (South Yarra, Australia), 1987.

The Great Seesaw: A New View of the Western World, 1750-2000, Macmillan (Melbourne, Australia), 1988.

Australian Universities: Some Fashions and Faults, La Trobe University (Bundoora, Australia), 1989.

Blainey, Eye on Australia: Speeches and Essays of Geoffrey Blainey, Schwartz Books (Melbourne, Australia), 1991.

(With Isobel Crombie) *Sites of the Imagination: Contemporary Photographers View Melbourne and Its People,* National Gallery of Victoria (Melbourne, Australia), 1992.

The Golden Mile, Allen & Unwin (St. Leonard's, Australia), 1993.

Jumping over the Wheel, Allen & Unwin (St. Leonard's, Australia), 1993.

A Shorter History of Australia, Heinemann (Port Melbourne, Australia), 1994.

(Editor, with Ronda Jamieson) *Charles Court, the Early Years: An Autobiography,* Fremantle Arts Centre Press (South Fremantle, Australia), 1995.

White Gold: The Story of Alcoa of Australia, Allen & Unwin (St. Leonard's, Australia), 1997.

In Our Time, Information Australia (Melbourne, Australia), 1999.

A Short History of the World, Dee (Chicago, IL), 2002.

SIDELIGHTS: Geoffrey Blainey began his writing career as an industrial historian, concentrating on metal mining in his native Australia. He has since risen to prominence as a general historian of Australia, as well as a commentator on national and international issues pertaining to his country. A longtime professor at the University of Melbourne, he has written books that merge scholarship with accessible style. A *Times Literary Supplement* reviewer once commented that Blainey's work "is an example of the way a potentially ponderous subject can be turned into an interesting one by a rigorous control of material and a fluent pen."

Blainey made his academic mark with the publication of *The Peaks of Lyell* and *The Rush That Never Ended: A History of Australian Mining.* Both books look at milestones in Australian metal mining, sometimes comparing Australian events to such phenomena as the American gold rush. In an *American History Review* piece on *The Rush That Never Ended,* S. C. McCul-loch noted of Blainey that "he never fails to convey the sense of drama," and "his research is intensive. . . . Illustrations and maps are excellent."

Writing talent and an enjoyment of observation allowed Blainey to escape the boundaries of academic writing, and today he is a respected general author in Australia. A *New Yorker* correspondent described Blainey as "intelligent, observant, open-minded, gregarious, and a writer of considerable style." With books such as *Across a Red World, The Causes of War,* and *A Shorter History of Australia,* the author has attracted a wide readership both within his native land and in other English-speaking countries. To quote one *Choice* reviewer, Blainey "displays a flair for drawing historical insights while critiquing and creating explanations. . . . He looks for empirical evidence and interprets subtly and well."

The work that may well stand as the cap to Blainey's distinguished career is *A Short History of the World.* In this book, the historian provides an overview of 100,000 years of world history—a daunting task, as many critics noted. "I used to go to China frequently but I knew little of its history or Japan's," he told *Weekend Australian* writer Murray Waldron. "Or early American civilisations. I just wondered how it all fitted together. . . . And it seemed important [to write this book] at a time when clearly the world is shrinking at a dramatic pace thanks to communication and travel. That became one of the book's themes, how unshrinkable the world seemed for so long and now suddenly that doesn't hold."

Blainey's approach in the book, in the view of *Quadrant* contributor Gregory Melleuish, has "an Enlightenment feel about it" and is often Eurocentric and idealistic. "To be fair," Melleuish added, "Blainey does recognise many other civilisations apart from Europe: he deals with the Incas, China and India and he discusses the rise of Islam and Buddhism." The critic, however, faulted Blainey for a failure to appreciate, as did Deepak Lal in his book *Unintended Consequences,* that European "deviance" from older societies contributed to its development as a unique civilization. Melleuish concluded that *A Short History of the World* is "good on economics, technology, geography and environment, poor on war and the state. It doesn't really do much to improve our understanding of the Europe question, or shine any light into the engine room of human political, social and economic development.

Blainey shies away from the 'dark side of the force'—war, pestilence and human evil. In so doing he shows us only one side of the human story."

In *National Observer—Australia and World Affairs,* however, R. J. Stove offered a much more positive assessment of the book. The work, in his view, succeeds "with terrifying conviction" and is enhanced by lucid prose and enlightening insights. Praising Blainey's extraordinary erudition and narrative skill, Stove hailed *A Short History of the World* as a "triumph . . . that . . . forms in itself a liberal education."

Commenting on the controversies surrounding much of Blainey's work, Waldron pointed out that the historian "is a bona fide member of a rare club, those public intellectuals whose works are read by ordinary people." Indeed, as John Fisher observed in a *Quadrant* article, "Blainey's ability to set out his themes and insights in simple language studded with apt and colourful images and metaphors accounts for his high standing not just among his academic peers but among students and society as a whole. He can grab and hold the attention of readers in a manner than other historians cannot match."

BIOGRAPHICAL AND CRITICAL SOURCES:

BOOKS

Crawford, Raymond Maxwell, *Making History,* Penguin Books (New York, NY), 1985.

PERIODICALS

American History Review, October, 1964, p. 259; June, 1969, p. 1692.
Booklist, February 15, 2002, Gilbert Taylor, review of *A Short History of the World,* p. 987.
Choice, March, 1974, p. 160.
Kirkus Reviews, January 1, 2002, review of *A Short History of the World,* p. 26.
Library Journal, April 1, 1964, p. 1604; March 15, 2002, Clay Williams, review of *A Short History of the World,* p. 92.
National Observer—Australia and World Affairs, autumn, 2001, R. J. Stove, review of *A Short History of the World,* p. 63.

New Yorker, November 9, 1968, p. 238.
Publishers Weekly, February 4, 2002, review of *A Short History of the World,* p. 62.
Quadrant, April, 2000, John Fisher, "History Master," p. 58; December, 2000, Gregory Melleuish, "Blainey, Europe and the World," p. 28.
Times Literary Supplement, March 5, 1964, p. 194; November 21, 1968, p. 1315; March 6, 1969, p. 224; June 15, 1973, p. 659.
Weekend Australian, October 30, 2000, Murray Waldron, "The World According to Geoffrey" (interview with Blainey).*

*   *   *

BOKINA, John 1948-

PERSONAL: Born January 6, 1948, in Chicago, IL; son of Victor (an X-ray technician) and Mary (a homemaker) Bokina; married Nancy Lashaway (a professor), April 5, 1992; children: Sarah. *Education:* University of Illinois at Chicago, A.B. (political science and sociology), 1970, M.A. (political science and sociology), 1972; University of Illinois at Urbana-Champaign, Ph.D. (political theory), 1979; also attended language courses at the Goethe-Institut, Blaumeuren, Germany, 1974, Institut für Sozialforschung, 1974, Christian-Albrechts Universität, 1980, Hochschule für Ökonomie, 1988, and Europäische Akademie, 1988.

ADDRESSES: Home—303 Austin Blvd., Edinburg, TX 78539. *Office*—Department of Political Science, University of Texas-Pan American, Edinburg, TX 78539. *E-mail*—jb83e8@pamam.edu.

CAREER: University of Illinois, Chicago, IL, teaching assistant, 1971; University of Illinois at Urbana-Champaign, teaching assistant, 1972-74 and 1975-76, instructor, 1973-76; University of Detroit, Detroit, MI, visiting assistant professor, 1976-77, instructor, 1977-79, director of the honors program, 1977-80, assistant professor, 1979-81; University of Texas-Pan American, Edinburg, TX, assistant professor, 1982-85, associate professor, 1986-92, professor, 1992—. Conductor of workshops.

MEMBER: International Political Science Association, International Politics and the Arts Group, European Consortium for Political Research (institutional liaison), American Historical Association, American Political Science Association, Midwest Political Science Association, Caucus for a New Political Science, Conference Group on German Politics, Foundations of Political Theory Group, German Studies Association, Phi Kappa Phi.

AWARDS, HONORS: Fellowship, University of Illinois, 1974-75; graduate research grant, University of Illinois, 1974; German language training grants from the Council for European Studies, 1974, and the German Academic Exchange Service, 1980; Political Science Association Faculty Member of the Year, University of Detroit/Pi Sigma Alpha, 1980-81; National Endowment for the Humanities Fellowship for College Teachers, 1981-82; faculty research grants, University of Texas-Pan American, 1984-86, 1997; International Political Science Association Travel Grant, 1985; American Council of Learned Societies Travel Grant, 1986; Faculty Achievement Awards, University of Texas-Pan American, 1986, 1997.

WRITINGS:

(With Joseph P. Friedman and Joseph Miller) *Contemporary Political Theory,* University of Illinois Extension Division (Urbana, IL), 1977.
(Editor, with Timothy J. Lukes) *Marcuse: From the New Left to the Next Left,* University Press of Kansas (Lawrence, KS), 1994.
Opera and Politics: From Monteverdi to Henze, Yale University Press (New Haven, CT), 1997.

Contributor to anthologies, including *Vienna: The World of Yesterday, 1889-1914,* Westview Press (Boulder, CO), 1994, and *Wagner in Retrospect: A Centennial Reappraisal,* Rodopi (Amsterdam), 1987. Contributor to journals, including *International Political Science Review, Telos, Cultural Critique,* and *Politics and the Life Sciences.* Contributor of book reviews to journals, including *New Political Science, American Political Science Review,* and *Library Journal.* Member of editorial board, *Telos,* 1986—, and *New Political Science,* 1989-96, 1999—.

WORK IN PROGRESS: Herbert Marcuse, for Rowman & Littlefield (Lanham, MD); *The Idea of Spartacus.*

BOND, George C(lement) 1936-

PERSONAL: Born November 16, 1936; son of J. Max (in U.S. Foreign Service) and Ruth C. (a teacher) Bond; married; wife's name, Alison M. (a social worker); children: Matthew, Rebecca, Jonathan, Sarah. *Ethnicity:* "Black." *Education:* Boston University, B.A., 1959; London School of Economics and Political Science, London, M.A., 1962, Ph.D., 1968.

ADDRESSES: Home—229 Larch Ave., Teaneck, NJ 07666. *Office*—Program in Applied Anthropology, Box 10, Teachers College, Columbia University, New York, NY 10027. *E-mail*—gcb1@columbia.edu.

CAREER: University of East Anglia, Norwich, England, lecturer, 1966-68; Columbia University, New York City, assistant professor, 1968-74, associate professor at Teachers College, 1974-82, professor of anthropology, 1982—, director of the Institute of African Studies, 1989-99.

WRITINGS:

The Politics of Change in a Zambia Community, University of Chicago Press (Chicago, IL), 1976.
(Editor) *African Christianity,* Academic Press (New York, NY), 1978.
(Coeditor) *Social Construction of the Past,* Routledge & Kegan Paul (London, England), 1994.
(Editor) *AIDS in Africa and the Caribbean,* Westview (Boulder, CO), 1995.
(Coeditor) *Contested Terrain and Constructed Categories: Africa in Focus,* Westview Press (Boulder, CO), 2001.

SIDELIGHTS: George C. Bond told *CA:* "As an anthropologist, I am concerned with the manner in which societies, cultures, and bodies of knowledge are shaped. A driving theme within my writing has been to reveal the subtle, complex mechanisms that lead to the exclusion and subjugation of individuals and designated human collectivities. I wish to explore the relation of domination to resistance as a way of establishing common human properties and arriving at the meaning of unquantifiable sentiments."

BOWDEN, Charles 1945(?)-

PERSONAL: Born c. 1945.

ADDRESSES: Home—Tucson, AZ. *Agent*—c/o Harry N. Abrams, Inc., 100 Fifth Ave., New York, NY 10011.

CAREER: Writer. Reporter, *Tucson Citizen,* Tucson, AZ; editor, *City Magazine,* Tucson, AZ.

WRITINGS:

The Impact of Energy Development on Water Resources in Arid Lands: Literature Review and Annotated Bibliography, University of Arizona, Office of Arid Land Studies (Tucson, AZ), 1975.

Killing the Hidden Waters, University of Texas Press (Austin, TX), 1977.

(With Lew Kreinberg) *Street Signs Chicago: Neighborhood and Other Illusions of Big City Life,* foreword by William Appleman Williams, photographs by Richard Younker, Chicago Review Press (Chicago, IL), 1981.

Blue Desert (essays), University of Arizona Press (Tucson, AZ), 1986.

Frog Mountain Blues, photographs by Jack W. Dykinga, University of Arizona Press (Tucson, AZ), 1987.

Mezcal (autobiography), University of Arizona Press (Tucson, AZ), 1988.

Red Line, Norton (New York, NY), 1989.

Desierto: Memories of the Future, Norton (New York, NY), 1991.

The Sonoran Desert: Arizona, California, and Mexico, photographs by Jack W. Dykinga, Harry N. Abrams (New York, NY), 1992.

The Secret Forest, introduction by Paul S. Martin, photographs by Jack W. Dykinga, University of New Mexico Press (Albuquerque, NM), 1993.

(With Michael Binstein) *Trust Me: Charles Keating and the Missing Billions,* Random House (New York, NY), 1993.

Seasons of the Coyote: The Legend and Lore of an American Icon (essays), edited by Philip L. Harrison, HarperCollins (San Francisco, CA), 1994.

Blood Orchid: An Unnatural History of America, Random House (New York, NY), 1995.

Stone Canyons of the Colorado Plateau, photographs by Jack W. Dykinga, Harry N. Abrams (New York, NY), 1996.

Chihuahua: Pictures from the Edge (essays), photographs by Virgil Hancock, University of New Mexico Press (Albuquerque, NM), 1996.

Juarez: The Laboratory of Our Future, preface by Noam Chomsky, afterword by Eduardo Galeano, photographs by Javier Aguilar (and others), Aperture (New York, NY), 1998.

(Author of essay) Julian D. Hayden, *The Sierra Pinacate,* photographs by Jack Dykinga, essay by Bernard L. Fontana, University of Arizona Press (Tucson, AZ), 1998.

Paul Dickerson, 1961-1997 (essay), American Fine Art (New York, NY), 2000.

Eugene Richards, Phaidon (New York, NY), 2001.

Blues for Cannibals: The Notes from Underground, North Point Press (New York, NY), 2002.

Down by the River: Drugs, Money, Murder, and Family, Simon & Schuster (New York, NY), 2002.

Work represented in anthologies, including *The Best American Essays 1999,* selected by Edward Hoagland, Houghton Mifflin (Boston, MA), 1999. Contributor to numerous periodicals, including *Esquire, Harper's,* and *GQ.*

SIDELIGHTS: Charles Bowden is a journalist and editor who has achieved renown as both an environmental writer and a critic of modern society. *Killing the Hidden Waters* is about the use of groundwater to irrigate agricultural projects in Arizona. In this work Bowden elucidates the dire consequences of this action which, by the mid-1970s, was drawing groundwater at more than ten times the rate at which it was being replaced. Bowden contrasts this use, or misuse, of groundwater with the practices of the Papago Indians, desert inhabitants who have managed to survive in the arid region without depleting the same groundwater supply.

Blue Desert, another of Bowden's earlier books, also presents various aspects of life in the American Southwest. This volume, which was published in 1986, includes essays on the decline of a mining community, jeopardized wildlife, questionable real-estate deals conducted between capitalists and the Papago, and the illegal immigration of Mexicans into the United States. David Graber, writing in *Los Angeles Times Book Re-*

view, described *Blue Desert* as "painfully engaging" and added that Bowden "has written a series of vignettes about life in the Arizona desert which feels true the way something dark and austere feels true."

Frog Mountain Blues, a 1987 volume that Bowden produced in collaboration with photographer Jack W. Dykinga, addresses the relationship between the prospering city of Tucson and the desert and mountains that surround it. The book provides considerable background on the region's development, and discusses the environmental repercussions of that development. Bruce Brown, reviewing *Frog Mountain Blues* in *Washington Post Book World,* proclaimed Bowden's book "a personal and provocative work that entertains at almost every turn in the trail." Don Campbell, in his *Los Angeles Times Book Review* assessment, deemed *Frog Mountain Blues* "a beautifully written, handsomely illustrated love poem to a mountain range."

Mezcal is an autobiographical volume in which Bowden relates both his experiences as a drug-using radical in the 1960s and his increasing interest in the environment. Bob Sipchen reported in *Los Angeles Times Book Review* that "Bowden's self-reflexive reportage of the 1960s waxes gonzo," and he observed that "it's only when [Bowden] finally grounds his addiction to the adrenaline rush of modern life upon the tranquillity of the natural world that he finds an original voice."

In *Red Line* Bowden fuses the environmental preoccupations of *Killing the Hidden Waters* and *Blue Desert* with both the historical concerns of *Frog Mountain Blues* and the autobiographical elements of *Mezcal.* In this 1989 book he joins a narcotics officer and probes the violent death of a Mexican drug dealer and killer in Tucson. But in conducting his investigation Bowden provides autobiographical asides and comments on both the region's changes and the environmental problems that have ensued. David Rieff, writing in *Los Angeles Times Book Review,* described *Red Line* as "a hybrid of personal memoir, a historical evocation of 1849 and of the settling of the Southwest, a journalistic hunt . . . for a drug dealer . . . and a harsh and moving nature chronicle."

Bowden's *Desierto: Memories of the Future,* published in 1991, is another of the author's works on the environment. *Desierto* contains interviews conducted by Bowden with individuals who share his concerns for environmental change, but he also deals with individuals—especially notorious banker Charles Keating, Jr.—whose ethical relationship to society and the environment is more problematic. In the *New York Times Book Review,* Ron Hansen called *Desierto* "a compelling and wonderfully poetic book" and "a meditative and highly evocative narrative."

In the early 1990s Bowden teamed again with photographer Jack W. Dykinga to produce *The Sonoran Desert: Arizona, California, and Mexico* and *The Secret Forest,* two more volumes on the North American Southwest. He then collaborated with Michael Binstein on *Trust Me: Charles Keating and the Missing Billions,* an account of the Arizona bank tycoon whose fraudulent practices led to the savings-and-loan scandal in the early 1990s. In 1995 Bowden published *Blood Orchid: An Unnatural History of America,* which William Kittredge described in *Los Angeles Times Book Review* as a book that examines "the angst among . . . alienated citizens" and that provides "a passionate report on the real-world sources of their unrest." In *Blood Orchid,* Bowden writes about paranoid Americans who bear arms, suspect helicopters, and think that computer chips are being implanted in children. Kittredge declared that *Blood Orchid* is "brilliant and sometimes excessive but always compelling," and he concluded that Bowden "is becoming one of our most important voices in the so-called New West."

A frequent contributor to such publications as *Harper's, Esquire,* and *GQ,* Bowden continues to write about marginalized people and experiences. His essay "Torch Song," originally published in *Harper's,* is an autobiographical account of his years as a reporter covering sex abuse crimes, and how the experience desensitized him. The piece was chosen by Edward Hoagland for inclusion in *The Best American Essays 1999.* Bowden's *Juarez: The Laboratory of Our Future,* for which he wrote text to accompany the work of thirteen photojournalists from the city of Juarez, Mexico, began as a *Harper's* essay, originally published in December, 1996. *Los Angeles Times Book Review* contributor Saul Landau described the work as a "book-length window on the underbelly of what used to be described . . . as the new world order." The book shows that in Juarez, which lies just across the Rio Grande from El Paso, workers are oppressed by a system that, in Landau's words, "experiment[s] with how much abuse capital can heap on labor and the environment." Photographs expose the story of more than 100 young women raped and murdered on their way to and from work in foreign-owned factories; numerous victims murdered by gangs and drug cartels; children searching through garbage dumps for scraps; an uncontrollable chemical fire; and Mexicans climbing barriers or wading across the river to reach the United States and its promise of jobs. "Bowden's book," wrote Landau, "is full of embarrassing questions and is an indispensable starting point for any serious discussion of the issues of the North American Free Trade Agreement, immigration, gangs, corruption, drug trafficking and poverty."

Eugene Richards is another collection of photographs for which Bowden wrote the accompanying text. Richards, a photorealist, is known for his work documenting the lives of the poor and exploited; among his collections is *Dorchester Days,* a portrait of a working-class Boston community, and *Below the Line: Living Poor in America.* Bowden, a personal friend of Richards, provides biographical and critical commentary on the photographer's opus.

Blues for Cannibals: The Notes from Underground drew strong critical response. A work of nonnarrative nonfiction, the book, according to a *Publishers Weekly* reviewer, "explores modern American soul-sickness" and stands as a "spiritually rousing . . . punch in the gut." The book's material, some of it reworked from previously published essays, covers such subjects as Bowden's witnessing of a legal execution in Arizona, exploitation at the U.S.-Mexican border, and sex crimes. In the *New York Times Book Review,* Mark Jude Poirier observed that the book's chief strength is its author's presence, pointing out that Bowden "is observant, well read and refreshingly unpredictable" in his narration. *Atlanta Journal-Constitution* writer Frank Reiss expressed similar admiration, noting Bowden's poetically intense style and his capacity for compassion. "As a writer seeking justice in his words," wrote *Los Angeles Times Book Review* critic Susan Salter Reynolds, "he is like a man clearing brush, trying to break through, to get enough light and oxygen to see his trees and sky again before he goes back under."

Salon contributor Michelle Goldberg, however, felt that the author condescends to his readers and glorifies some aspects of violence in the book. "Bowden seems to believe that he's privy to hideous truths that most of us are too deluded to see," commented Goldberg, who disapproved of the author's "admiration for the way some of [his subjects] fuck with established order." The critic also disagreed with Bowden's contention that he is telling readers things they do not want to hear. "The fact is, almost everyone wants to hear these things," Goldberg objected, pointing out that "in Bowden's writing, the big unutterable secret about sex crimes seems to be that they're titillating." Dismissing the author's attempts to philosophize about this issue, Goldberg asked: "But don't we know all this by now? Isn't it clear to everyone that human nature harbors ghastly impulses? Does another recitation of kiddie killings do anything to illuminate the dark corners of the soul?" Other reviewers, however, appreciated Bowden's insights on such difficult topics. Poirier, for one, suggested that though *Blues for Cannibals* doesn't succeed in answering the questions it raises, the author's "frank and charged prose" helps to "point us in the direction of an answer." *San Francisco Chronicle* writer David Kipen praised Bowden's often "muscular" prose and "rapturous indignation," and deemed *Blues for Cannibals* the "best imperfect book of the year."

BIOGRAPHICAL AND CRITICAL SOURCES:

PERIODICALS

Atlanta Journal-Constitution, April 7, 2002, Frank Reiss, review of *Blues for Cannibals: The Notes from Underground,* p. H4.
Booklist, January 1, 1997, Donna Seaman, review of *Chihuahua: Pictures from the Edge,* p. 812; February 1, 2002, Donna Seaman, review of *Blues for Cannibals,* p. 918.
Business Week, August 2, 1993, p. 10.
Kirkus Reviews, January 1, 2002, review of *Blues for Cannibals,* p. 26.
Los Angeles Times Book Review, November 16, 1986, p. 6; July 5, 1987, p. 4; January 8, 1989, p. 3; December 24, 1989, pp. 3, 11; June 16, 1991, p. 6; August 20, 1995, p. 12; May 24, 1998, Saul Landau, review of *Juarez: The Laboratory of Our Future;* March 30, 2002, Susan Salter Reynolds, review of *Blues for Cannibals.*
New York Times Book Review, July 5, 1987, p. 14; September 22, 1991, p. 14; November 21, 1993, p. 33; May 19, 2002, Mark Jude Poirier, review of *Blues for Cannibals,* p. 45.

Publishers Weekly, February 4, 2002, review of *Blues for Cannibals,* p. 71.

San Francisco Chronicle, March 10, 2002, David Kipen, review of *Blues for Cannibals,* p. 1.

Washington Post Book World, August 9, 1987, Bruce Brown, review of *Frog Mountain Blues,* p. 8.

Whole Earth, fall, 1998, Dan Imhoff, review of *Juarez,* p. 95.

ONLINE

Salon, http://www.salon.com/ (March 13, 2002), Michelle Goldberg, review of *Blues for Cannibals: The Notes from Underground.**

*   *   *

BOWEN, Zack (Rhollie) 1934-

PERSONAL: Born August 10, 1934, in Philadelphia, PA; son of Zack R. (an automobile dealer) and Mary (a singer; maiden name, Upton) Bowen; married Lindsey Tucker (an English professor), February 22, 1980; children: (prior marriage) Zack, Daniel, Patricia. *Education:* University of Pennsylvania, B.A., 1956; Temple University, M.A., 1960; State University of New York at Buffalo, Ph.D., 1964.

ADDRESSES: Home—8735 Southwest 54th Ter., Miami, FL 33165. *Office*—Department of English, University of Miami, P.O. Box 248145, Coral Gables, FL 33124-4632. *E-mail*—zbowen@umiami.ir.miami.edu.

CAREER: Temple University, Philadelphia, PA, instructor, 1958-60; State University of New York College at Fredonia, assistant professor of English, 1960-64; State University of New York at Binghamton, 1964-76, began as assistant professor, became Distinguished Teaching Professor and chairman of English department; University of Delaware, Newark, professor of English and chairman of department, 1976-86; University of Miami, chairman department of English, 1986-96, professor of English, 1996—; University of Miami Caribbean Writers Summer Institute, director, 1990-92. Lecturer in poetry, drama, and English research, Philadelphia Museum College of Art, 1960; producer-director of works by James Joyce for Folkway Records, including *Lestrygonians,* 1961, *Calypso,* 1963, *Lotus Eaters,* 1963, *Hades,* 1964, and *Sirens,* 1965.

MEMBER: International James Joyce Foundation (board of trustees, 1982—; president, 1996-2000), Modern Language Association (member of Lowell Prize Committee, 1985; chairman of Lowell Prize Committee, 1986-87), James Joyce Society (president, 1977-86).

WRITINGS:

Padraic Colum: A Biographical-Critical Introduction, preface by Harry T. Moore, Southern Illinois University Press (Carbondale, IL), 1970.

Mary Lavin, Bucknell University Press (Lewisburg, PA), 1975.

Musical Allusions in the Woods of James Joyce: Early Poetry through "Ulysses," State University of New York Press (Albany, NY), 1975.

(With James Carens) *A Companion to Joyce Studies,* Greenwood Press (Westport, CT), 1984.

Ulysses as a Comic Novel, Syracuse University Press (Syracuse, NY), 1989.

A Reader's Guide to John Barth, Greenwood Press (Westport, CT), 1993.

Bloom's Old Sweet Song: A Collection of Essays on Joyce and Music, University Press of Florida (Gainesville, FL), 1995.

Also contributor of more than one hundred monographs, articles, notes, and reviews to literary journals, including *James Joyce Quarterly, Eire-Ireland, Journal of Irish Literature, Threshold, Literature and Psychology, Modern British Literature,* and the *Joyce Newsletter.* Editor, *Irish Renaissance Annual,* 1980-83; general editor, "Critical Essays in British Literature" series, G. K. Hall/Twayne/Macmillan, 1983—; editor, "The Florida James Joyce" series, University Press of Florida, 1994—; editor, *The James Joyce Literary Supplement,* 1994—; editorial board member, *Journal of Modern Literature, Joyce Studies Annual, International Review of Modernism,* and *South Atlantic Review.*

WORK IN PROGRESS: Science and Literature, a book coauthored with microbiologist David Wilson for publication by the University Press of Florida.

*   *   *

BRENNAN, Carol
See SLATE, Caroline

BRODY, Miriam 1940-

PERSONAL: Born May 12, 1940, in Philadelphia, PA; daughter of Louis (a lithographer) and Anna (a school social worker; maiden name, Rabinowitz) Brody; married Isaac Kramnick (a professor), January 20, 1963; children: Rebecca, Jonathan, Leah. *Education:* University of Pennsylvania, B.A., 1961; Boston University, M.A., 1963; Cornell University, Ph.D., 1987. *Politics:* Democrat. *Religion:* Jewish.

ADDRESSES: Home—Ithaca, NY. *Office*—Writing Program, Ithaca College, Ithaca, NY 14850. *E-mail*—miriambrody@aol.com.

CAREER: Ithaca College, Ithaca, NY, professor of writing.

WRITINGS:

(Editor) Mary Wollstonecraft, *A Vindication of the Rights of Women,* Penguin (New York, NY), 1975.
Manly Writing: Gender, Rhetoric, and the Rise of Composition, Southern Illinois University Press (Carbondale, IL), 1993.
Mary Wollstonecraft: Mother of Women's Rights, Oxford University Press, 2000.

WORK IN PROGRESS: A biography of Victoria Woodhull for Oxford University Press young adult series.

SIDELIGHTS: Miriam Brody once told *CA:* "I suppose it's axiomatic that writers cannot resist either a blank page or an invitation for self-disclosure. I cannot remember a time when I did not write. My earliest memory is inscribing my name on paper. I thought I would write fiction as an adult, and it is amusing to me that I write instead about writing. I think now that, as a child, I wanted less to write fiction and more to write simply for the sake of writing, as I am doing now. Ultimately I think we write to fill up blank pages."

She more recently added, "I have stopped writing about writing and am now writing biographies of women's lives. I think this is a delaying tactic to postpone writing my own. One day I will."

BROOKS, (Mary) Louise 1906-1985

PERSONAL: Born November 14, 1906, in Cherryvale, KS; died of a heart attack, August 8, 1985; daughter of Leonard Porter (a lawyer and assistant attorney general of Kansas) and Myra (a homemaker; maiden name, Rude) Brooks; married A. Edward Sutherland (a film director), July 12, 1926 (divorced, 1928); married Deering Davis (a dancer), October 10, 1933 (divorced, 1938). *Education:* Attended Wichita College of Music, c. 1919-21; studied under Ted Shawn and Ruth St. Denis at Denishawn School of Dance, 1922-23. *Religion:* Catholic.

CAREER: Dancer, actress, and writer. Denishawn Dancers, New York, NY, member of dance troupe, 1923-24; Café de Paris, London, England, Charleston dancer, 1924; *Ziegfeld Follies,* New York, dancer, 1925; Saks Fifth Avenue, New York, NY, sales clerk, 1946-48. Actress in motion pictures, including *The Street of Forgotten Men,* 1925, *The American Venus,* 1926, *A Social Celebrity,* 1926, *It's the Old Army Game,* 1926, *The Show-Off,* 1926, *Just Another Blonde,* 1926, *Love 'Em and Leave 'Em,* 1926, *Evening Clothes,* 1927, *Rolled Stockings,* 1927, *Now We're in the Air,* 1927, *The City Gone Wild,* 1927, *A Girl in Every Port,* 1928, *Beggars of Life,* 1928, *The Canary Murder Case,* 1929, *Pandora's Box,* 1929, *The Diary of a Lost Girl,* 1929, *Beauty Prize,* 1930, *Windy Riley Goes Hollywood,* 1931, *It Pays to Advertise,* 1931, *God's Gift to Women,* 1931, *Empty Saddles,* 1936, *King of Gamblers,* 1937, *When You're in Love,* 1937, and *Overland Stage Raiders,* 1938; actress in radio soap operas, including *Hobby Lobby* and *Ellery Queen,* 1943. Worked variously as a dance instructor, model, and publicist.

WRITINGS:

The Fundamentals of Good Ballroom Dancing, privately printed, 1940.
Lulu in Hollywood (essays), introduction by William Shawn, Knopf (New York, NY), 1982, reprinted with introduction by Kenneth Tynan, University of Minnesota Press (Minneapolis, MN), 2000.

Brooks's papers, left to the George Eastman House, are sealed until 2006. Contributor to books, including *William Wyler: An Index,* by Richard Roud, British

Film, c. 1958; *Pandora's Box,* Classic Film Scripts, Simon & Schuster (New York, NY), 1971; *Double Exposure,* by Roddy McDowall, Delacorte (New York, NY), 1976; *John Wayne,* by Allen Eyles, A. S. Barnes, 1976; and *Louise Brooks: Portrait d'une anti-star,* edited by Roland Jaccard, Phebus, 1976. Also contributor to various film magazines, including *Film Culture, Focus on Film, Image, London Magazine, Objectif, Positif,* and *Sight and Sound.*

SIDELIGHTS: Silent film beauty Louise Brooks became immortalized during the early days of Hollywood through her dazzling and carefree performances on and off the screen. World renowned for her short, bobbed haircut, delicate features, daring style of dress, and disregard for conventional mores, Brooks embodied the spirit of the flapper during the 1920s—a postwar era marked by people's pursuance of all things pleasurable. Dancing on Broadway at the age of eighteen, she became a motion picture star before her twentieth birthday and retired from the business in her early thirties, after failing to land a leading role in films for eight years. Brooks's stunted movie career as well as the politics of filmmaking during Hollywood's infancy are two of the subjects she would later describe when she pursued her writing career in earnest in her fifties. Her effect on Hollywood during the Jazz Age and the importance of her films have been discussed at length in critical studies, particularly Kenneth Tynan's profile of her in a 1979 *New Yorker* article, which is reprinted in Tynan's *Show People: Profiles in Entertainment.* Combined with the publication of her semi-autobiographical book *Lulu in Hollywood,* such tributes have renewed interest in her work and elevated her legendary films to cult classic status.

Born in 1906 in Cherryvale, Kansas, Brooks began dancing at age ten. She set her sights for the stage in her youthful years as she performed at various local events and club meetings, accompanied by her mother, a talented pianist. Brooks attended the Wichita College of Music but was expelled by the age of fifteen due to poor behavior. Within a year, she was accepted into the New York school run by professional dancers Ted Shawn and Ruth St. Denis, and soon began touring with the Denishawn Dancers. As chronicled in *Lulu in Hollywood,* Brooks was introduced to big city nightlife during her two-year stint with the troupe by a group of affluent stockbrokers who escorted her to fashionable clubs, dressed in scintillating gowns and furs. She wrote, "The most eligible bachelors in their thirties, finding debutantes a threat, turned to pretty girls in the theatre, whose mothers weren't husband-hunting. . . . The extravagant sums given to the girls for clothes were part of the fun—part of competing to see whose girl would win the best-dressed title. Sexual submission was not a condition of this arrangement, although many affairs grew out of it."

Brooks noted in *Lulu in Hollywood* that her newfound popularity propelled her to shed all traces of her rural upbringing and incorporate a new sophisticated image. She accomplished this by ridding herself of her Kansas accent with the help of an articulate soda fountain employee, discovering the essence of dress from a shop girl, and studying etiquette with cultured waiters. According to various Brooks biographers, the change in her demeanor and subsequent lack of dedication to her work reportedly led to her dismissal from the Denishawn Dancers in 1924. Immediately after, she tried Broadway and secured a part as a chorus girl in George White's *Scandals,* but her work in the musical was short-lived, as she quit within a matter of months, seeking a job as a Charleston dancer at a London nightclub. Quickly bored, she returned to New York and became a chorus girl in Florenz Ziegfeld's musical comedy *Louis the 14th.* She was again hired by the producer for his 1925 *Ziegfeld Follies* stage show, starring Will Rogers and W. C. Fields, despite her continued unpredictable behavior. During her initial dancing career, Brooks also found time to model, posing semi-nude for theatrical photographer John De Mirjian.

Brooks's Broadway chorus line days were numbered as she successfully tested for a bit part in the Paramount Pictures film *The Street of Forgotten Men.* She was soon offered contracts from both Metro-Goldwyn-Mayer and Paramount, and opted for the latter, quit dancing, and made six films at the Famous Players-Lasky studio in New York. Her work in *The American Venus* inspired the "Dixie Dugan" comic strip by John H. Striebel, which ran for more than thirty-five years. (Guido Crepax would also base his comic strip "Valentina" on her in 1965.) According to Barry Paris in his biography *Louise Brooks,* the actress continued her fast-paced, flamboyant lifestyle, which included numerous affairs with wealthy men and such Hollywood notables as comedian Charlie Chaplin. Attempting to settle down, she married A. Edward Sutherland, who directed her and Fields in *It's the Old Army Game* in 1926. When Paramount shifted its New York operations to Hollywood in 1927, Brooks soon developed a dislike for her new surroundings. According to Tynan's *New Yorker* profile, Brooks wrote that "in Hollywood . . . the studio was run by B. P. Schulberg, a coarse exploiter who propositioned every actress and policed every set. To love books was a big laugh. There was no theatre, no opera, no concerts—just those g———d movies."

Brooks's brief marriage to Sutherland ended in 1928. By that time, her meteoric rise to fame had given her sex symbol status throughout the industry, and her increasing box office appeal prompted her to demand a pay raise under the terms of her contract. Her request fell on Paramount head Schulberg's deaf ears at a time when Hollywood was converting from silent to sound pictures. Brooks later observed that studios used this transition to reduce salaries and void contracts, claiming that actors' voices had not been tested in the silent movies, and the paying public might reject the stars if their voices were deemed inappropriate to their on-screen silent image. As a result, the actress was denied an increase in income and broke her contract with Paramount.

Aware that German director Georg Wilhelm Pabst had asked Paramount repeatedly to borrow her for films, Brooks ventured abroad. In *Lulu in Hollywood* she recalled, "In Hollywood, I was a pretty flibbertigibbet whose charm for the executive department decreased with every increase in my fan mail. In Berlin, I stepped onto the station platform to meet Pabst and became an actress. I would be treated by him with a kind of decency and respect unknown to me in Hollywood. It was just as if Pabst had sat in on my whole life and career and knew exactly where I needed assurance and protection."

In fact, Pabst had first seen Brooks in the 1928 film *A Girl in Every Port*, which she had made while on loan from Paramount to Twentieth Century-Fox. In what biographer Paris equates to David O. Selznick's later search for the perfect Scarlett O'Hara for the 1939 classic film *Gone with the Wind*, Pabst scouted the world's film industry for the ultimate femme fatale for his 1929 picture *Pandora's Box*. Pabst selected the American Brooks, much to the chagrin of up-and-coming star Marlene Dietrich, hundreds of other German actresses, and the country's curious public. In *Pandora's Box*, Brooks portrays Lulu, a bewitching siren who responds with innocent calm to the destruc-

tion her beauty and amorality yield. Based on nineteenth-century German playwright Frank Wedekind's initially banned 1895 *Der Erdgeist* and its 1904 sequel *Die Buechse der Pandora*, the film follows the pleasure-seeking life of Lulu, a character who would be frequently compared to the actress herself. Tynan quoted Brooks as saying, "She's just the same kind of nitwit that I am. Like me, she'd have been an impossible wife, sitting in bed all day reading and drinking gin." Pabst and Brooks's presentation of Lulu as a victim, however, was a significant factor in the film's universally poor reception by critics and audiences alike. In fact, the film was not acknowledged as a masterpiece of the silent cinema until some twenty-five years later. Brooks made two more films abroad before returning to Hollywood despite Pabst's warning, "Your life is exactly like Lulu's, and you will end the same way."

Despite her earlier success in silent films, Brooks was unable to land a leading role in talkies upon her return to the United States in 1930. Some biographers have claimed that her failed comeback was tied to both her dispute with Paramount and the nature of the erotic films she made in Germany, while others have speculated that her reputation for being unpredictable and difficult abbreviated her movie career. Brooks contended, however, that her acting days were stunted by her innate honesty and need for independence. In *Lulu in Hollywood* she explained, "My parents' resolute pursuit of their own interests also accounted for my own early autonomy and my later inability, when I went to work in the Hollywood film factories, to submit to slavery." After a promised contract with Columbia Pictures did not materialize, she landed bit parts in movies and again tried theater. She married dancer Deering Davis in October of 1933, and left him after six months. She toured the nightclub circuit with a dance troupe in 1934 and 1935, and later returned to Hollywood for several small roles, including one in 1938's *Overland Stage Raiders* with John Wayne. She obtained an official divorce from Davis and quit the business shortly after the western was completed.

Brooks returned to Wichita and opened a dance studio in 1940. When this enterprise failed in 1943, she relocated to New York City and worked in radio soap operas for six months. "I moved on to New York," Brooks observed in *Lulu in Hollywood,* "where I found that the only well-paying career open to me, as an unsuccessful actress of thirty-six, was that of a call girl. I blacked out my past, refused to see my few remaining friends connected with the movies, and began to flirt with fancies related to little bottles filled with yellow sleeping pills."

In the mid 1940s, Brooks was employed by various publicity agencies and, for a short time, wrote a gossip column. She also signed on as an instructor for one week at an Arthur Murray dance studio. Nearly broke, she obtained a job at Saks Fifth Avenue, where she worked from 1946 to 1948 as a sales clerk. In 1948, Brooks began a memoir titled "Naked on My Goat," after a passage in Johann Wolfgang von Goethe's *Faust* that reads, "I sit here naked on my goat and show my fine young body." In *Focus on Film* magazine she recalled that she destroyed the work, as she could not write the sexual details of her life, a history she believed was necessary to make her autobiography of interest to readers. Burt A. Folkart quoted her in the *Los Angeles Times* as stating: "Nobody needs a book of mine to learn how to make a mess of life."

As documented in Tynan's *New Yorker* article, several men paid for Brooks's living expenses from the late 1940s to the early 1950s, until she ended those relationships. Destitute by 1954, she began receiving an annual annuity from former lover and friend William Paley, chairman of the Columbia Broadcasting System, to help subsidize a new writing career. After a move to Rochester, New York, in 1956, she began jotting down memories of her early life and days in Hollywood for magazines such as *Film Culture, Focus on Film,* and *Sight and Sound.* In the mid 1950s and early 1960s, Brooks's film career finally received the recognition it had been denied for almost a quarter of a century when her work was featured in a major exhibition in Paris and when French director Jean-Luc Godard modeled the heroine of his film *Vivre sa vie* after Brooks.

The actress was in her seventies, virtually reclusive, and frequently bedridden due to osteoarthritis and acute emphysema when Tynan met with her to prepare his *New Yorker* article, "The Girl in the Black Helmet." Consenting to the interview at the urging of her friend, actor Roddy McDowall, Brooks took a liking to Tynan who, according to Paris, described her as "the most seductive, sexual image of Woman ever committed to celluloid . . . the only unrepentant hedonist, the only pure pleasure-seeker, I think I've ever known." Paris noted that Brooks and Tynan's friendship ended bit-

terly, however, for she feared he was exploiting her to further his already successful career, although she had approved his manuscript prior to publication. Paris wrote that Brooks told film historian Kevin Brownlow, "Ever since old Tynan double-crossed me by converting sex gossip into the *New Yorker* profile, I have been battered with publishers' offers to print cheap sex memoirs and offers from three film outfits." She opted to compile her life's story herself and prepared *Lulu in Hollywood,* a combination of previously published manuscripts and new writings.

Although *Lulu in Hollywood* is only a partial autobiography, it features some 130 photographs from Brooks's early days of filmmaking. Its more than 100 pages include seven essays devoted to her early life in Kansas, the filming of *Beggars of Life,* her work with Pabst on *Pandora's Box,* and her observations of various Hollywood notables, including Humphrey Bogart and Fields. Generally well-received by critics, *Lulu in Hollywood* also features a discussion of Brooks's distaste for the Hollywood system, which she said destroyed many great talents, including Greta Garbo, Jeannette MacDonald, Joan Crawford, and Lillian Gish. "These essays become another kind of legacy from her," noted Charles Champlin in the *Los Angeles Times Book Review,* "and a testament to survival." James Wolcott in *Esquire* deemed *Lulu in Hollywood* "a very tart, fleet, gossipy book, a whip-flicking display of wit and spite." And Sara Laschever remarked in *New York Review of Books,* "One of the most distinctive features of Brooks's memoirs is the almost total absence of regret. Still, she is true to the persona she imagined for herself, and her self-portrait is the one undeniable success of the book."

Brooks died of a heart attack in her Rochester apartment on August 8, 1985. She summed up her career in a letter to her brother Theodore, which was published in Paris's biography: "I never read anything about myself that doesn't make me puke. That doesn't mean I don't love my latter-day fame; I simply reserve the right to find the whole thing ridiculous."

BIOGRAPHICAL AND CRITICAL SOURCES:

BOOKS

Atwell, Lee, *G. W. Pabst,* [Boston, MA], 1977.
Biographical Dictionary of Film, Morrow (New York, NY), 1976.

Brooks, Louise, *Lulu in Hollywood* (essays), introduction by William Shawn, Knopf (New York, NY), 1982, reprinted with introduction by Kenneth Tynan, University of Minnesota Press (Minneapolis, MN), 2000.

Brownlow, Kevin, *The Parade's Gone By* (essays), Knopf (New York, NY), 1968.

International Dictionary of Films and Filmmakers, Volume 3: *Actors and Actresses,* St. James Press (Detroit, MI), 1996.

Jaccard, Roland, editor, *Louise Brooks: Portrait d'une anti-star,* Phebus, 1976, translation published as *Louise Brooks: Portrait of an Anti-Star,* [London], 1987.

Liebman, Roy, *Silent Film Performers,* McFarland and Co. (Jefferson, NC), 1996.

The Oxford Companion to Film, Oxford University Press (New York, NY), 1976.

Paris, Barry, *Louis Brooks,* Knopf (New York, NY), 1989.

Tynan, Kenneth, *Show People: Profiles in Entertainment,* Simon & Schuster (New York, NY), 1980.

PERIODICALS

Esquire, May, 1982.

Focus on Film, March, 1978.

Los Angeles Times Book Review, May 30, 1982.

New Republic, December 25, 1989, David Thomson, "Saint Lulu."

Newsweek, May 24, 1982.

New York, May 31, 1982.

New Yorker, June 11, 1979, Kenneth Tynan, "The Girl in the Black Helmet"; August 16, 1982.

New York Review of Books, October 21, 1982.

New York Times, May 21, 1982.

New York Times Book Review, May 30, 1982.

Vanity Fair, October, 1989; April, 1998, Tom Dardis, "What Lulu Wanted," p. 174.

Washington Post Book World, June 13, 1982.

OBITUARIES:

PERIODICALS

Los Angeles Times, August 10, 1985.

Newsweek, August 19, 1985.

New York Times, August 10, 1985.

Time, August 19, 1985.*

BUDDE, Michael L(eo) 1958-

PERSONAL: Born July 27, 1958, in Joliet, IL; son of Richard L. and Marilyn J. (Meyers) Budde; married Terri L. Anderson. *Education:* Northwestern University, B.S.J., 1979, Ph.D., 1989; Catholic University of America, M.A., 1984.

ADDRESSES: Home—Shorewood, IL. *Office*—Department of Political Science, DePaul University, 2320 North Kenmore, Chicago, IL 60614.

CAREER: Auburn University, Auburn, AL, assistant professor of political science, 1990-93; DePaul University, Chicago, IL, associate professor of political science, 1993—; founder and coordinator, The Ekklesia Project.

WRITINGS:

The Two Churches: Catholicism and Capitalism in the World System, Duke University Press (Durham, NC), 1992.

The (Magic) Kingdom of God: Christianity and Global Culture Industries, Westview Press (Boulder, CO), 1997.

(Editor, with Robert Brimlow) *The Church As Counterculture,* State University of New York Press (Albany, NY), 2000.

(With Robert Brimlow) *Christianity Incorporated: How Big Business Is Buying the Church,* Brazos Press (Grand Rapids, MI), 2002.

Contributor to journals, including *Sociological Analysis* and *World Policy Journal.*

SIDELIGHTS: Political scientist Michael L. Budde has written extensively on the conflation of religion and socioeconomics. In *The Two Churches: Catholicism and Capitalism in the World System,* he shows that a shift from a First World to a Third World Catholic Church has begun to occur, and argues that "world Catholicism (led by the Latin American and other Third World Churches) will continue to develop in anticapitalist directions." He further argues that, in the words of *American Political Science Review* contributor Timothy R. Scully, "the future of worldwide Catholicism holds a colossal clash between the two

Churches, pitting poor against rich." Though he found Budde's analysis provocative, Scully questioned his reliance on the Latin American Church as a model of peripheral Catholicism. He also questioned Budde's conclusion that class conflict between First World and Third World Churches would be inevitable. While he also disagreed with this point, *Sociology of Religion* reviewer Joseph A. Scimecca considered *The Two Churches* a "first rate work of scholarship" that is "right on the mark" much of the time. Scimecca concluded that "It is must reading for anyone interested in understanding what the Catholic Church is doing today in relation to the political and economic changes occurring in the world."

The (Magic) Kingdom of God: Christianity and Global Culture Industries is a "wake-up call to the Christian Church" that should alert it to the ways in which its mission is being undermined by consumer culture, according to *Cross Currents* contributor William T. Cavanaugh. In this book, Budde exposes the role of entertainment media, telecommunications, and marketing firms in the subversion of Christian identity. "Budde shows how culture industries present obstacles to the construction of desire in prayer, colonize any separate Church space, and poach religious symbols and narratives for use in selling products," Cavanaugh observed, concluding that the book "is a tremendous service not just to the Church but to a world which needs people formed in Gospel ways of peace and justice."

Budde expands on this theme in *Christianity Incorporated: How Big Business Is Buying the Church*, which a reviewer for *Publishers Weekly* considered a "cogent" and readable analysis filled with "alarming anecdotes and biting humor." Among these: the use of the pope's image to market french fries in Mexico, or the idea of Jesus as a model CEO. The book doesn't break any new ground, according to *Library Journal* reviewer L. Kriz, but its argument nevertheless bears repeating at a time when Christians may be inattentive to the ways in which big business may be eroding their values.

BIOGRAPHICAL AND CRITICAL SOURCES:

PERIODICALS

American Political Science Review, June, 1993, Timothy R. Scully, review of *The Two Churches: Catholicism and Capitalism in the World System,* p. 511.

Annals of the American Academy of Political and Social Science, January, 1994, Ted G. Jelen, review of *The Two Churches,* p. 184.

Comparative Politics, July, 1995, Carol Ann Drogus, review of *The Two Churches,* p. 465.

Cross Currents, spring, 1999, William T. Cavanaugh, review of *The (Magic) Kingdom of God: Christianity and Global Culture Industries,* p. 124.

Journal for the Scientific Study of Religion, June, 1993, Hans A. Baer, review of *The Two Churches,* p. 193.

Journal of the American Academy of Religion, March, 2000, John Langan, review of *The (Magic) Kingdom of God,* p. 153.

Library Journal, February 1, 2002, L. Kriz, review of *Christianity Incorporated: How Big Business Is Buying the Church,* p. 106.

Modern Theology, October, 2001, Nicholas M. Healy, review of *The Church As Counterculture,* p. 524.

Publishers Weekly, January 28, 2002, review of *Christianity Incorporated,* p. 286.

Religion, July, 1993, Jon Davies, review of *The Two Churches,* p. 291.

Sociology of Religion, winter, 1993, Joseph A. Scimecca, review of *The Two Churches,* p. 433.

Times Literary Supplement, January 21, 1994, Peter Hebblethwaite, review of *The Two Churches,* p. 26.*

*　　*　　*

BYALICK, Marcia 1947-

PERSONAL: Born April 9, 1947, in Brooklyn, NY; daughter of Al (a dry cleaner) and Mona (Goldsmith) Finkelstein; married Robert Byalick (a psychologist), November 22, 1967; children: Jennifer, Carrie. *Education:* Brooklyn College of the City University of New York, M.A., 1969. *Politics:* "Liberal Democrat." *Religion:* Jewish. *Hobbies and other interests:* Theater, exercise, "any excuse to get together with friends and family."

ADDRESSES: Home and office—22 Lydia Ct., Albertson, NY 11507.

CAREER: Writer. Editor in chief, *Women's Record,* 1985-93. Columnist, feature writer, *Spotlight, Distinction,* 1996—. Hofstra University, C. W. Post writing teacher, 1993—. Journalist, Long Island section of the *New York Times.*

AWARDS, HONORS: Eleven awards from Long Island Press Club, 1986-2002, for work as a columnist; Books for the Teen Age, New York Public Library, 1996, for *It's a Matter of Trust; Quit It* chosen as one of Bank Street College of Education's Best Children's Books of 2003.

WRITINGS:

FOR YOUNG ADULTS

Reel Life, 1993.
You Don't Have to Be Perfect to Be Excellent, 1993.
It's a Matter of Trust, Harcourt (Orlando, FL), 1995.
Quit It, Delacorte Press (New York, NY), 2002.

OTHER

(With Linda Saslow) *The Three Career Couple: Mastering the Art of Juggling Work, Home, and Family* (humorous self-help), Peterson's Press (Princeton, NJ), 1993.
(With Linda Saslow) *How Come I Feel So Disconnected If This Is Such a User Friendly World? Reconnecting with Your Family, Your Friends—and Your Life,* Peterson's Press (Princeton, NJ), 1995.
(With Ronald A. Ruden) *The Craving Brain: The Biobalance Approach to Controlling Addictions,* HarperCollins (New York, NY), 1997, second edition published as *The Craving Brain: A Bold New Approach to Breaking Free from Drug Addiction, Overeating, Alcoholism, Gambling,* Perennial (New York, NY), 2000.

SIDELIGHTS: "Acne, clothes and friends are not all today's teens are concerned with," Marcia Byalick once told interviewer Ramin P. Jaleshgari of the *New York Times.* Byalick's young adult novels draw upon this conviction by centering on characters with serious problems, realistically depicted. In her first young adult novel to be widely reviewed, *It's a Matter of Trust,* the life of sixteen-year-old Erika Gershon is turned upside down when her father is indicted on racketeering charges. In addition to her feelings about her father, Erika must cope with the intrusion of the media upon her family, her friends' gossip, and the death of a beloved uncle. "Young readers will find a wealth of issues to discuss in this unsettling, thought-provoking novel," predicted *School Library Journal* contributor Jana R. Fine. Byalick further tests the fine-tuning on her readers' judgment when she causes her protagonist to cheat during a tennis match and then lie about it. Erika is also growing up during all this turmoil, and finds herself developing romantic feelings for her camp mate Greg. "YA girls will find much to like about Erika and her story of maturation," asserted *Voice of Youth Advocates* contributor Lucy Marx.

"My ultimate goal is to help teens become comfortable dealing with hard issues," Byalick told Jaleshgari. "Young people need to know that time always brings change. Through my writing I'd like to teach them that coping with those changes positively is always within their control." The "hard issue" young Carrie must deal with in Byalick's novel *Quit It* is Tourette's syndrome, and the involuntary twitches, tics, and throat-clearings which make her dream of disappearing into anonymity as she starts the seventh grade a mere illusion. Though Carrie has a difficult row to hoe, she has the enduring friendship of Clyde, who is bothered by obsessive compulsive disorder, but not by Carrie's twitching, and they both benefit from joining the Lunch Bunch, a support group, at school. A contributor to *Kirkus Reviews* praised Byalick's treatment of Tourette's within the framework of Carrie's story. "While [Byalick] doesn't skimp on any unpleasant details, she doesn't make it seem as if having the illness is the worst thing in the world either," this critic remarked.

Carrie's parents are in fact two people in the novel who are least able to cope with Carrie's problem honestly and in their efforts to put a brave face on their disappointment they hurt Carrie's feelings. Then, when Rebecca, a new girl at school, joins the Lunch Bunch and befriends Carrie, Byalick's protagonist is at first delighted, and then must reevaluate the relationship, for Rebecca is determined to come between Carrie and her old friend. "Carrie's voice is strong and the author tells a convincing story," asserted Linda B. Zeilstra in *School Library Journal.* Likewise, *Booklist* contributor Shelle Rosenfeld praised Byalick's protagonist and her informative, but not preachy, treatment of a neurological disorder rarely found in young adult literature: "Carrie is an engaging character, whose descriptive, first-person narrative balances a matter-of-fact tone with wry observations and lively commentary."

BIOGRAPHICAL AND CRITICAL SOURCES:

PERIODICALS

Booklist, October 1, 2002, Shelle Rosenfeld, review of *Quit It,* p. 324.

Bulletin of the Center for Children's Books, January, 1996, p.156.

Kirkus Reviews, August 1, 2002, review of *Quit It,* p. 1123.

New York Times, January 21, 1996, interview with Ramin P. Jaleshgari, p. 14.

School Library Journal, December, 1995, Jana R. Fine, review of *It's a Matter of Trust,* p. 128; November, 2002, Linda B. Zeilstra, review of *Quit It,* p. 158.

Voice of Youth Advocates, February, 1996, Lucy Marx, review of *It's a Matter of Trust,* p. 368.

C

CAIRNCROSS, Frances (Anne) 1944-

PERSONAL: Born August 30, 1944, in Otley, England; daughter of Sir Alec (an economist) and Mary (Glynn) Cairncross; married Hamish McRae (a journalist), September 10, 1971; children: Isabella, Alexandra. *Education:* St. Anne's College, Oxford, M.A. (history; first class honors), 1965; Brown University, M.A. (economics), 1966.

ADDRESSES: Home—6 Canonbury Lane, London N1, England. *Office*—*The Economist,* 25 Saint James's St., London SW1 1HG, England.

CAREER: Times, London, England, reporter, 1967-69; *Banker* (financial magazine), London, England, editorial assistant, 1969; *Observer* (weekly newspaper), London, England, economics writer, 1969-73; *Guardian* (known in United States as *Manchester Guardian;* national daily newspaper), London, England, economic correspondent, women's page editor, 1973—; *Economist* (British edition) environmental editor, media editor, public policy editor, 1984-1998, management editor, 1999—.

MEMBER: Institute for Fiscal Studies (member of council).

WRITINGS:

(With husband, Hamish McRae) *Capital City: London As a Financial Centre,* Methuen (London), 1973.
(With Hamish McRae) *The Second Great Crash,* Prentice-Hall (Englewood Cliffs, NJ), 1975.

(Editor) *Changing Perceptions of Economic Policy: Essays in Honour of the Seventieth Birthday of Sir Alec Cairncross,* Methuen (New York), 1981.
(Editor, with Phil Keeley) *The Guardian Guide to the Economy,* Methuen (New York), 1981.
Guide to the Economy, Methuen (London, England), 1987.
(Contributor) Harry G. Johnson, *Man and His Environment,* British-North America Committee (Washington, DC), 1990.
(Editor with Sir Alec Cairncross) *The Legacy of the Golden Age: The 1960s and Their Economic Consequences,* Routledge (New York), 1992.
Costing the Earth: The Challenge for Governments, the Opportunities for Business, Harvard Business School Press (Boston, MA), 1992.
Green, Inc.: A Guide to Business and the Environment, Island Press (Washington, DC), 1995.
The Death of Distance: How the Communications Revolution Will Change Our Lives, Harvard Business School Press (Boston, MA), 1997.
The Company of the Future: How the Communications Revolution Is Changing Management, Harvard Business School Press (Boston, MA), 2002.

SIDELIGHTS: Frances Cairncross spent her entire professional career as a journalist, first for the London *Observer,* later for the *Guardian,* and finally for the British headquarters of the *Economist.* Throughout her career, she also published several books, most of them dealing with her favorite topic—economics.

She wrote her first book, *Capital City: London As a Financial Centre,* with her husband, Hamish McRae, in 1973, which reviewer Alex Murray, for *Manage-*

ment Today, called a "well researched and comprehensive book," which "painted a detailed picture of the City colony as a financial centre at the start of a new decade." The book was recently revised, adding "the extraordinary activities of the '80s," giving the general reader "an easily digestible introduction" to this lively city. Cairncross also has added comments on trends that she sees developing in London.

Almost twenty years later, Cairncross published *Costing the Earth* (1992), a book in which she discusses the costs to the environment caused by big business. Cairncross looks not only into the toxic wastes that usually make the headlines but also the normal, everyday rubbish that must be dealt with. Ordinary waste, says Cairncross, as quoted in Colin Tudge's article for *Management Today,* "will preoccupy companies . . . much as other kinds of pollution" has in the past. She further points out that when making more benign products for public use, companies must not forget that the process of manufacturing these goods must also be harmless to the environment. In order to maintain a truly free enterprise in the business sector, Cairncross contends, companies must demonstrate that they can monitor their own productions without government interference that will ensure they are not guilty of further pollution of the environment. However, in the end, Cairncross believes that most companies "will only be as green as governments make them."

Tudge, after reading the book, recommended it to fellow business managers, explaining that it "is a very fine overview of issues that are infinitely complex." This book, wrote Jonathan Porritt, a fellow journalist at the *Economist,* "is rich with examples of 'best practice' from Europe and the United States." Unfortunately, Cairncross had discovered that there were very few businesses in England that she could cite as practitioners of environmentally friendly production. Not only should business managers read this book, according to John E. Karayan of the *Mid-Atlantic Journal of Business,* but it "is a must read for those merely concerned about drinking, breathing, and living in a better environment."

Cairncross uses her knowledge and experience from her position as environmental editor at the *Economist* to write *Green, Inc.: A Guide to Business and the Environment* (1995). Mick Braddick of the *British Medical Journal* summarized Cairncross's position as claiming that "continued economic growth is both de-sirable and inevitable, and that technical fixes will avert the global environmental crisis." Although Braddick did not agree with Cairncross's arguments, he did concede that she at least "provides valuable insights in the thinking of a mainstream economist." Stanley Johnson, for the *Economist,* also found some of Cairncross's statements troublesome. Johnson pointed out that Cairncross's stand on globing warming is "to wait and see" if it truly will be a problem. If it does, "adaptation will be much less costly than prevention."

Cairncross's most recent books focus on a different topic, that of communications. In *The Death of Distance: How the Communications Revolution Will Change Our Lives* (1997), she offers her predictions on how the world will change over the next half century as the speed of communication increases. Cairncross believes that this change, as stated by Joseph W. Leonard for the *Library Journal,* will be "the most important economic force shaping the upcoming century."

Although Cairncross's predictions that the international business community as well as individuals all over the globe will benefit from the fast communications of the future, some critics found her predictions a little too optimistic. "Here is the nub of the problem," wrote Eric Jones for the *National Interest,* "Although it is easy to foresee change, the definite forecasting of change is much harder." Jones pointed out that although a few countries are quickly progressing to better communications, there are still many companies that lag woefully behind. Jones also stated, "We can easily share Cairncross' hope that cheaper information will improve the world, encourage the spread of democracy, and tilt the odds toward peace," but considerations also have to be made to the "frictions" that will be "set up by different resistance to change." Not all countries will move at the same pace.

Other critics made quite favorable responses to Cairncross's book and her predictions, such as Stephen P. Banks, writing for *Public Relations Review.* Banks began his review describing *The Death of Distance* as "an ambitious, detailed, highly accessible, and fascinating examination." He commended her careful analysis and her speculative futurology. However, he did suggest that Cairncross might want to balance her reportage with "an examination of newly emergent pathologies and structural problems that attend the communications revolution." Such issues include the "loss of privacy, commodification of identities, and turning of culture into entertainment that we see every night on the evening news and in our schools and shopping malls." Overall, however, Banks recommended the book for its "lively style" and "its compilation of facts and trend information about diverse technologies."

In 2002, Cairncross published *The Company of the Future: How the Communications Revolution Is Changing Management.* In this work, she lays out ten specific rules that she believes companies should follow in order to be successful. Those rules state that a company must learn how to manage knowledge, make sound decisions, focus on key customers, manage talent, manage collaboration, build the right structure, manage communications, set standards, foster openness, and develop leadership. "At the heart of Cairncross' argument," wrote Paul B. Brown for the website *CIO Insight,* "is her call for the IT department to be more forceful in shaping its company's agenda." A reviewer from *Publishers Weekly* stated Cairncross's thesis as being: "To survive in the years ahead, companies must put technology at the very heart of everything they do." Most company managers are aware of the importance of information technology, wrote this reviewer, "but saying it should be integral to everything from marketing to managing talent may raise some eyebrows." In order to do as Cairncross suggests, most companies will have to completely restructure their businesses. The *Publishers Weekly* reviewer concluded: "It will be interesting to see which companies—if any—make those changes."

Commenting on the impetus behind her books, Cairncross writes, "I want to convey some of the excitement I felt about the changing world economic situation to people who otherwise would shy away from the subject—even though it is a subject that intimately affects everybody's life."

BIOGRAPHICAL AND CRITICAL SOURCES:

PERIODICALS

Booklist, March 15, 1992, Volume 88, number 14, Mary Carroll, review of *Costing the Earth: The Challenge for Governments, the Opportunities for Business,* p. 1324; October 15, 1997, Volume 94, number 4, Mary Whaley, review of *The Death of Distance: How the Communications Revolution Will Change Our Lives,* p. 369.

British Medical Journal, October 21, 1995, Volume 311, number 7012, Mick Braddick, review of *Green, Inc.: A Guide to Business and the Environment,* p. 1102.

Choice, September 1992, Volume 30, number 1, F. Reitman, review of *Costing the Earth,* p. 174; March 1996, Volume 33, number 7, F. Reitman, review of *Green, Inc: A Guide to Business and the Environment,* pp. 1178-79; January, 2002, Volume 389, number 5, N. J. Johnson, review of *The Death of Distance,* pp. 925-26.

Economist (UK), June 1, 1991, Volume 319, number 7709, Jonathan Porritt, review of *Costing the Earth,* pp. 86-87; July 29, 1995, Volume 336, number 7925, Stanley Johnson, review of *Green, Inc.,* p. 66; April 7, 2001, Tim Hindle, review of *The Death of Distance,* p. 119.

Foreign Affairs, November-December 1997, Volume 76, number 6, Eliot A. Cohen, review of *The Death of Distance,* p. 157.

Library Journal, October 15, 1997, Volume 122, number 17, Joseph W. Leonard, review of *The Death of Distance,* p. 72.

Management Today, August 1991, Colin Tudge, review of *Costing the Earth,* p. 75; September 1991, Alex Murray, review of *Capital City: London As a Financial Centre,* p. 129.

Mid-Atlantic Journal of Business, December 1993, Volume 29, number 3, John E. Karayan, review of *Costing the Earth,* pp. 355-56.

National Interest, fall 1998, number 53, Eric Jones, review of *The Death of Distance,* pp. 116-19.

New York Review of Books, March 26, Volume 45, number 5, Jeff Madrick, review of *The Death of Distance,* pp. 29-30.

Public Relations Review, fall 1999, Volume 25, number 3, Stephen P. Banks, review of *The Death of Distance,* p. 399.

Publishers Weekly, January 21, 2002, Volume 249, number 3, review of *The Company of the Future: How the Communications Revolution is Changing Management,* p. 80.

Wall Street Journal, June 3, 1992, Fred L. Smith, Jr., review of *Costing the Earth,* p. A12.

ONLINE

CIO Insight Web site, http://www.cioinsight.com/ (May 17, 2002), Paul B. Brown, review of *The Company of the Future.**

CAUTE, (John) David 1936-
(John Salisbury)

PERSONAL: Born December 16, 1936, in Alexandria, Egypt; son of Edward (a British military officer) and Rebecca Caute; married Catherine Shuckburgh, 1961 (divorced, 1970); married Martha Bates (an editor), 1973; children: (first marriage) Daniel, Edward; (second marriage) Rebecca, Anna. *Education:* Wadham College, Oxford, England B.A., 1959, M.A. and D.Phil., 1963. *Politics:* Labour Party.

ADDRESSES: Home—41 Westcroft Sq., London W6 0TA, England.

CAREER: All Souls College, Oxford University, Oxford, England, fellow, 1959-65; Harvard University, Cambridge, MA, Henry fellow, 1960-61; visiting professor, New York University, 1966-67, Columbia University, 1966-67, and University of Bristol, 1985; Brunel University, Uxbridge, England, reader in social and political theory, 1967-70; University of California, regents lecturer, 1974. *New Statesman,* London, England, literary editor, 1979-81. Writers Guild of Great Britain, deputy chair, 1979-80, co-chair, 1981-82. *Military service:* British Army, 1955-56, served in Africa.

MEMBER: Royal Society of Literature (fellow).

AWARDS, HONORS: London Authors' Club Award and John Llewelyn Rhys Prize, both 1960, both for *At Fever Pitch.*

WRITINGS:

At Fever Pitch (novel), Pantheon (New York, NY), 1960.
Songs for an Autumn Rifle (play), first produced at the Edinburgh Festival by the Oxford Theatre Group, 1961.
Comrade Jacob (novel), Pantheon (New York, NY), 1962.
Communism and the French Intellectuals, 1914-1960, Macmillan (New York, NY), 1964.
The Left in Europe since 1789, McGraw (New York, NY), 1966.
The Decline of the West (novel), Macmillan (New York, NY), 1966.

David Caute

(Editor) *The Essential Writings of Karl Marx,* Macmillan (New York, NY), 1967.
The Demonstration (play; first produced at Nottingham Playhouse, 1969; also see below), Deutsch (London, England), 1970.
Frantz Fanon (monograph), Viking (New York, NY), 1970, published as *Fanon,* Fontana (London, England), 1970.
The Confrontation: A Trilogy (contains *The Demonstration, The Occupation,* and *The Illusion: An Essay on Politics, Theatre and the Novel*), Deutsch (London, England), 1971.
The Occupation (novel; also see below), McGraw (New York, NY), 1972.
The Illusion: An Essay on Politics, Theatre and the Novel (also see below), Harper (New York, NY), 1972.
(With Ralph Miliband) *Nineteenth-Century European Socialism,* BFA Educational Media (Santa Monica, CA), 1972.
The Fellow-Travellers: A Postscript to the Enlightenment, Macmillan (New York, NY), 1973, revised and expanded edition published as *The Fellow-Travellers: Intellectual Friends of Communism,* Yale University Press (New Haven, CT), 1988.
Fallout (radio play), first broadcast on British Broadcasting Corp. (BBC Radio), 1973.

The Fourth World (play), first produced in London, England, at the Royal Court Theatre, 1973.

Cuba, Yes?, McGraw (New York, NY), 1974.

Collisions: Essays and Reviews, Quartet Books (London, England), 1974.

The Great Fear: The Anti-Communist Purge under Truman and Eisenhower, Simon & Schuster (New York, NY), 1978.

(Under pseudonym John Salisbury) *The Baby-Sitters* (novel), Atheneum (New York, NY), 1978, published as *The Hour before Midnight,* Dell (New York, NY), 1980.

Brecht and Company (television documentary), first produced on BBC-TV, 1979.

(Under pseudonym John Salisbury) *Moscow Gold* (novel), Futura (London, England), 1980.

Under the Skin: The Death of White Rhodesia, Northwestern University Press (Evanston, IL), 1983.

The Zimbabwe Tapes (radio play), first produced on BBC Radio, 1983.

The K-Factor (novel), M. Joseph (London, England), 1983.

The Espionage of the Saints: Two Essays on Silence and the State, Hamish Hamilton (London, England), 1986.

News from Nowhere (novel), Hamish Hamilton (London, England), 1986.

Henry and the Dogs (radio play), first produced on BBC Radio, 1986.

Sanctions (radio play), first produced on BBC Radio, 1988.

The Year of the Barricades: A Journey through 1968, Harper (New York, NY), 1988, published as *Sixty-Eight: The Year of the Barricades,* Hamish Hamilton (London, England), 1988.

Veronica; or, The Two Nations (novel), Hamish Hamilton (London, England), 1989, Arcade/Little, Brown (New York, NY), 1990.

The Women's Hour (novel), Paladin (London, England), 1991.

Dr. Orwell and Mr. Blair (novel), Weidenfeld & Nicolson (London, England), 1994.

Joseph Losey: A Revenge on Life, Oxford University Press (New York, NY), 1994.

Animal Fun Park (radio play), first produced on BBC Radio, 1995.

Fatima's Scarf (novel), Totterdown Books (London, England), 1998.

Contributor to periodicals, including *New Statesman, Partisan Review, Times Literary Supplement,* and *Spectator.*

ADAPTATIONS: Comrade Jacob was adapted as the 1975 film *Winstanley,* directed by Kevin Brownlow.

SIDELIGHTS: David Caute, an English novelist, playwright, and historian, has consistently dealt with socialism, communism, and the relationship between the West and Third World countries in his writings. His interest in these areas has led him to write several novels dealing with important political events in Africa.

But the author's forays into so many different genres—plays, novels, political theory, and history—"makes one cast about anxiously for some common thread, a unifying theme," said Alan Ryan in *Listener.* The author defines that thread in his *Collisions: Essays and Reviews* as "the inclination to walk to and fro across the bridges which join, or can be made to join, history, politics and literature." Thus, the author has striven to write fiction and nonfiction books that deal with themes pertinent to society as a whole. Caute, remarked *Dictionary of Literary Biography* contributor Gerald Steel, "is one of the most intellectually stimulating novelists of recent decades in England—a 'public' rather than a 'private' writer." In the United States, however, his work has received less attention.

Caute draws from his personal experiences in several of his books. *At Fever Pitch,* his first novel, is based on his adventures as an infantryman stationed in the Gold Coast just before it became independent Ghana. The author parallels soldier Michael Glyn's personal voyage towards sexual maturity with the confrontations between the British and Africans. Merging these two subjects, Caute attempts what Steel called an "exploration of the sexual psychology of militarism." *Spectator* writer Simon Raven described the novelist's blending of sexual and military themes as "vigorous, intelligent and keen," but some writers have said Caute tries to do too much. The "organization of the book suffers as a result," one *Times Literary Supplement* reviewer said. Still, *At Fever Pitch* received the London Authors Club Award and John Llewelyn Rhys Memorial Prize.

Caute has written several more novels set in Africa that address the alleged exploitation of Africans by white colonists. *The Decline of the West,* in particular, has drawn much attention. Set in the fictional African country of Coppernica, *The Decline of the West* describes the post-revolutionary turmoil of a newly independent nation similar to that which existed in Zaire and Algeria during their formative years. Some critics have felt that this novel about how Europeans justified their violent acts in Africa by falling back on beliefs in white superiority relies too heavily upon history. One *Times Literary Supplement* reviewer, for example, wrote that though the premise of *The Decline of the West* is "politically sound," the "characters are papier-mache versions of real public figures." In the *New York Times Book Review*, Laurence LaFore commented that *The Decline of the West* "is perhaps better as fictional history than as a work of art, but it is still an important and imposing novel." There have also been critics, such as *New Leader* contributor Raymond Rosenthal, who believe Caute overemphasizes violence in the novel. There is, Rosenthal wrote, a "hysterical wallowing in violence and torture . . . in almost every paragraph of Caute's book." Rosenthal, however, does not doubt Caute's "sincere desire to help the Africans in their struggle for independence, or at least to illuminate their struggle." And LaFore wrote that "the author's task, an enormous one, has been impressively completed. . . . He has advanced an important thesis, conceived an important tragedy and composed a fascinating story."

Zimbabwe, formerly Rhodesia, is the subject of two more Caute novels and his nonfiction work, *Under the Skin: The Death of White Rhodesia,* which concerns the author's firsthand reports and impressions of the last days of white rule in that country. *The K-Factor* is a fictional "re-working" of *Under the Skin,* dealing with racial stratification in Rhodesia, according to Roger Owen in the *Times Literary Supplement.* As with Caute's other novels, a number of reviewers felt the author gets mixed results by trying to blend complicated personal situations with political events. *London Times* critic Isabel Raphael, for one, asserted that "Caute tells a good, tense story, and writes sharp, fast-moving dialogue. But he tries to keep too many balls in the air at once." *News from Nowhere,* about an author and academician who travels to Rhodesia just as Caute had, drew similar remarks. Victoria Glendinning wrote in the *London Times* that the reporter's "adventures amid the ... fighting and betrayals of emerging Zimbabwe are frankly confusing, as is some of the writing." But she likened Caute's intricate plotting techniques to those of John le Carré as providing a "pleasurable confusion. It never did le Carré any harm."

Like Richard Stern in *News from Nowhere,* protagonist Steven Bright in Caute's trilogy, *The Confronta-*

tion, is an academician. Bright resembles his creator in several ways: he has written a book entitled *The Rise of the East,* which many critics have compared to Caute's *The Decline of the West,* has strong leanings toward leftist politics, resigned from All Souls College for political reasons, and has taught at New York University. *The Confrontation* consists of a play, *The Demonstration,* an essay ostensibly written by Bright, *The Illusion,* and a novel, *The Occupation.* "The trilogy indicates that Bright is Dr. Caute's alter ego," a *Times Literary Supplement* writer observed. "This is not a reader's deduction but an explicit suggestion by the author, repeated several times. These may not be autobiographical works but they are certainly confessional ones."

Alienation and the factors that cause it, such as the difference between art and reality, the generation gap, and the political struggles between left and right, is a major theme of all three books in *The Confrontation.* *The Illusion* addresses this subject as it relates to literature, favoring a Marxist/Brechtian approach to writing. As Bernard Bergonzi explained in *The Contemporary English Novel,* "Bright-Caute argues for an alignment of revolutionary art and radical politics; for a literature and theatre that will be dialectical in the play between art and reality—contra the structuralists, who are scathingly treated in *The Illusion,* Caute believes in distinguishing between the two—and for an exposure of the essentially illusory nature of fictional and dramatic realism, and the necessity of alienation as Brecht understood it."

The Demonstration, John Russell Taylor explained in his *The Second Wave: British Drama for the Seventies,* "illuminat[es] many of the problems the dramatist faces if he tries to use contemporary reality as the basis of art." In this play, Bright is a drama professor in England who tries to control his young, rebellious students by redirecting their energies against the establishment into a play called *Pentagon 67.* But Bright's plan backfires when illusion and reality change places and "he is brought to a realization of his own rejection and impotence." Bright's character is firmly against what he considers the decadence of capitalism, but at the same time he fears his students' extremism. He wants to "keep conscience, comforts and status equally intact," Benedict Nightingale wrote in *New Statesman,* but he becomes disillusioned when he can't.

The Occupation, which follows Bright's life as a visiting professor in New York in the same era as events in

The Demonstration, involves his personal struggle to understand his place in the world, a personal preoccupation that eventually leads to a breakdown. The plot, according to *National Review* critic John R. Coyne, Jr., is surrealistic, centering on "scenes occurring either in [Bright's] office or in his mind or both in which he argues with sitting-in New Left students." Bergonzi noticed that *The Occupation* represents Caute's "rejection of the Old Left" attitudes that are represented by character Hamilton Snout, "an ageing socialist hack writer and editor." Furthermore, Bergonzi surmised that because Snout applauds Bright's *The Rise of the East,* "Caute may here be ... disowning *The Decline of the West.*"

Caute has written numerous fiction and nonfiction works centering on leftist politics. His second novel, *Comrade Jacob,* tells of Gerard Winstanley's attempt to establish a collective settlement during Oliver Cromwell's rule. It is an allegory about contemporary communism, and as such, Bergonzi said in a *Spectator* review, that one "is constantly aware of the Marxist spectacles through which [Caute] regards his subject." Nevertheless, Bergonzi described *Comrade Jacob* as a "well-written and highly intelligent book." Similarly, a *Times Literary Supplement* reviewer called the novel "a remarkable, and moving, evocation of a stirring and significant experiment in English history."

Another fiction work, the play *Songs for an Autumn Rifle,* about the 1956 revolt in Hungary, is also directly concerned with socialism; but most of Caute's books that deal directly with socialism and communism have been nonfiction. Such works as *Communism and the French Intellectuals, 1914-1960, The Fellow-Travellers: Intellectual Friends of Communism,* and *The Great Fear: The Anti-Communist Purge under Truman and Eisenhower,* have drawn critics' praise for covering new ground about how and why communism has appealed to some and appalled others. *New Statesman* reviewer Neil McInnes praised *The Fellow-Travellers,* which is about the travels of André Gide, George Bernard Shaw, Jean-Paul Sartre, and other well-known figures to the Soviet Union and their impressions of communism, for its "rich ... fund of fascinating information." H. Stuart Hughes, writing in the *New York Review of Books,* also called Caute's study of McCarthyism in *The Great Fear,* a work "of first-rate importance." Some critics, however, said *The Great Fear* was too slanted. "The gravest deficiency in Caute's work," Sidney Hook wrote in *Encounter,*

"is its failure to state fairly and come to grips with the arguments and evidence of those whom he denounces." *New York Times Book Review* critic Arthur Schlesinger, Jr., pinpointed the problem as Caute's "accept[ance of] the fallacy that has disabled many latter-day commentators on that unhappy time: that there was no tenable middle ground; that to oppose Stalinism made McCarthyism inevitable."

Steel said the author has become aware of this tendency. In 1976, Caute wrote, "Nowadays I'm more preoccupied by questions of literary form than I used to be." His novel *Veronica; or, The Two Nations,* which appeared in 1989, "is more descriptive than prescriptive," remarked Nina King in the *Washington Post Book World,* "offering no simple solutions for the social ills it depicts." Combining a story of love and incest with social and political themes, Caute tells of the mutual love Michael Parsons and Bert Frame share for Michael's half-sister, Veronica, during their school days in England. Michael, who comes from an upper-class background, later becomes a ruthless, self-serving Tory politician and a prime candidate to succeed Margaret Thatcher, while Bert becomes a tabloid writer. Bert, who grew up in London's poor East End, resents Michael personally and opposes him politically. The novel concludes when Bert ruins Michael's career by revealing that the politician favors legalizing incest because he once committed the act with his half sister.

Sometimes referred to as a conceit of Benjamin Disraeli's *Sybil; or, The Two Nations* in which Disraeli described England as two disparate nations, one rich and one poor, *Veronica; or, The Two Nations* has drawn critical praise for its dramatic presentation of England's social ills. *New Statesman* contributor Richard Deveson, for example, called the novel a "defiantly intelligent and an instantly absorbing read [that] is partly on the state of the nation, self-consciously echoing *Sybil*: a confrontation of ruler and ruled." But unlike the author's earlier novels, *Veronica* does not clearly favor leftist politics. Caute, observed King, "seems more than a little ambivalent himself about the working-class leftists of the new era." Mark Wormald added in the *Times Literary Supplement,* "Caute invites us to question the legitimacy of any extreme assertion, any self which claims to know itself utterly." King noted that although Caute's other novels have gotten little notice in the United States this "should change with *Veronica,* which in addition to its engrossing plot and political insight, is beautifully constructed."

In *The Women's Hour,* Caute explores the implications of dogmatic feminism and postmodern ideology in a British university during the 1980s. The novel features Sydney Pyke, a lecherous professor of media studies and former leftist radical, who is accused of raping a feminist colleague in the university pool during women's swim hour. "Despite lurid moments," Nicolas Tredell wrote in the *London Review of Books,* "this novel has an elegiac, fin-de-siecle quality, evoking, even through its surface energies, the twilight of those hopes raised by the Sixties." Caute's caricatures of militant feminists and paranoid men reveal the absurdity of such stereotypes and the cynicism and divisiveness of contemporary academia. Commenting on Caute's "extravagant satire," Nicci Gerrard said in an *Observer* review, "I emerged from the experience giggling, reeling and not a little discomfited." Caute also alludes to the ambiguity of fictional truth by hinting at alternative endings and leaving Pyke's fate unresolved. According to *Times Literary Supplement* contributor Mary Beard, "This clever post-modern slipperiness, however, can turn into a glaringly misogynistic vision of the world." Yet, Beard added, "For all his irritating posing, Pyke engages our sympathies." Neil Berry added in *New Statesman,* "Caute contrives some highly satisfactory satire here."

Dr. Orwell and Mr. Blair is a fictional account of the story behind George Orwell's inspiration for his novel *Animal Farm.* Caute's version is purportedly based on Orwell's introduction to a Ukrainian edition of *Animal Farm* in which Orwell sees a young boy whipping a cart horse as the stimulus to produce his parable on the evils of tyranny and exploitation. The narrator of *Dr. Orwell and Mr. Blair* is twelve-year-old Alex Jones, who cuts school to save the family farm from foreclosure in the absence of his parents. Alex befriends a man he only knows as Eric Blair (Orwell's real name), who admits to working on a fairy tale about the farm. Though noting structural flaws in the novel's narrative perspective, Nigel Spivey commented in *Spectator,* "These problems apart, the story retains its force as an act of homage" to Orwell. According to J. K. L. Walker in the *Times Literary Supplement,* "*Dr. Orwell and Mr. Blair* is a subtle and complex novel that deserves to be read for its insight into the often murky processes of literary creativity." Colin Ward wrote in *New Statesman,* "David Caute brings an astringent intelligence to this fantasy, and protects himself from nitpickers by his disclaimer that nothing described in the book ever happened."

Caute again drew on real people and events in *Fatima's Scarf,* a sort of fictionalization of the events that occurred with the publication of Salman Rushdie's controversial novel, *The Satanic Verses.* In Caute's version, the protagonist, author Gamal Rahman, has written a book called *The Devil: An Interview* that angers Muslims, including residents of the town of Bruddersford who burn copies of the book. A "fatwa," or death sentence, is declared against Rahman, and the author, like Rushdie, becomes a marked man. Much of the rest of the book lampoons fictionalized versions of people involved in the Rushdie controversy, including Egyptian President Anwar Sadat and Muslim philosopher Shabbir Akhtar. Ziauddin Sardar, in *New Statesman,* labeled *Fatima's Scarf* "a collection of character assassinations" and a "long, unoriginal and excruciatingly boring book" that borrows heavily from Rushdie and the work of author Naguib Mahfouz. Several publishers, some wary the book's potential offensiveness, refused to publish Caute's novel. The author then published it himself. *Dictionary of Literary Biography* contributor Nicolas Tredell said, "With *Fatima's Scarf* Caute has once again demonstrated his ability to engage with large themes, employ a range of narrative techniques, and provoke controversy. He shows no sign of retiring."

Caute has also produced an extensive biography of left-wing American filmmaker Joseph Losey. Based lengthy research, *Joseph Losey: A Revenge on Life,* penetrates the personal life and critical reputation of this acclaimed cinematic artist and Marxist. Joel Siegel wrote in the *Washington Post Book World,* "David Caute takes a sledgehammer to the Losey legend. . . . Caute reveals hitherto unexposed facts of Losey's nature: misogynist, paranoid, snob, alcoholic, hypocrite, fop, tax evader, glutton and sadist. It's not a pretty picture."

Though drawing criticism for its structure, this exhaustive biography reflects Caute's skill as a historian and willingness to scrutinize a fellow leftist. Caute's "book is at times knotted and overbearing as its subject," James Saynor said in *Observer,* but "it is also a hugely impressive attempt to do the unfashionable, and make a person's art accountable to their life."

BIOGRAPHICAL AND CRITICAL SOURCES:

BOOKS

Bradbury, Malcolm, and David John Palmer, general editors, *The Contemporary English Novel,* Arnold (London, England), 1979.

Contemporary Authors Autobiography Series, Volume 4, Gale (Detroit, MI), 1986.

Contemporary Literary Criticism, Volume 29, Gale (Detroit, MI), 1984.

Dictionary of Literary Biography, Gale (Detroit, MI), Volume 14: *British Novelists since 1960,* 1982, Volume 231: *British Novelists since 1960,* Fourth Series, 2000.

Taylor, John Russell, *The Second Wave: British Drama for the Seventies,* Hill & Wang (New York, NY), 1971.

Tredell, Nicolas, *Caute's Confrontations: A Study of the Novels of David Caute,* Pauper's Press (Nottingham, England), 1994.

Tredell, *Conversations with Critics,* Carcanet (Manchester, England), 1994.

PERIODICALS

Annals of the American Academy of Political and Social Science, March, 1965.

Antioch Review, June, 1973.

Chicago Tribune Book World, July 31, 1983.

Commentary, March, 1965; June, 1973; June, 1978.

Commonweal, May 14, 1965.

Encounter, February, 1970; January, 1979, Sydney Hook, review of *The Great Fear.*

Esquire, July, 1973.

Glasgow Herald, September 13, 1986.

Harper's, January, 1967; June, 1968.

Journal of American History, March, 1989, p. 1381.

Journal of American Studies, December, 1977.

Listener, September 8, 1966; September 17, 1970; July 22, 1971; January 25, 1972; January 25, 1973; May 9, 1974; March 6, 1975; September 28, 1978; February 24, 1983; February 6, 1986.

London Magazine, September, 1966; June, 1983.

London Review of Books, July 7, 1983; May 8, 1986; November 20, 1986; November 7, 1991, p. 26.

Los Angeles Times Book Review, August 7, 1983; February 14, 1988.

Nation, June 27, 1966; January 16, 1967; April 22, 1978; May 5, 1984.

National Review, September 15, 1972; January 5, 1973; April 13, 1973; April 15, 1988, Joseph Sobran, review of *The Year of the Barricades: A Journey through 1968,* p. 46.

New Leader, November 7, 1966; December 23, 1974.

New Statesman, May 12, 1961; September 15, 1961; July 10, 1964; March 4, 1966; November 18, 1969; July 23, 1971; January 9, 1973; March 1,

1974; September 15, 1978; February 25, 1983; May 25, 1983; September 19, 1986; June 30, 1989; April 27, 1990, p. 10; October 4, 1991, p. 40; July 29, 1994, p. 40; April 3, 1998, Ziauddin Sardar, review of *Fatima's Scarf,* p. 68.

Newsweek, March 19, 1973.

New York Review of Books, April 20, 1978, H. Stuart Hughes, review of The Great Fear.

New York Times, April 27, 1962; July 28, 1970; May 9, 1978; September 5, 1978; March 4, 1988.

New York Times Book Review, October 9, 1966; May 14, 1971; April 8, 1973; March 19, 1978; May 20, 1979; April 3, 1988, p. 8.

Observer, February 1, 1959; May 14, 1961; April 10, 1966; September 11, 1966; December 18, 1966; January 11, 1970; July 25, 1971; January 21, 1973; September 21, 1973; February 10, 1974; February 27, 1977; September 10, 1978; February 27, 1983; May 22, 1983; September 7, 1986; January 10, 1988; July 2, 1989; November 3, 1991, p. 68; January 23, 1994, p. 19.

Observer Review, January 11, 1970.

Progressive, February, 1971; August, 1978.

Publishers Weekly, July 13, 1990, Sybil Steinberg, review of *Veronica; or, The Two Nations,* p. 42; August 29, 1994, review of *Joseph Losey: A Revenge on Life,* p. 59.

Saturday Review, October 8, 1966; June 6, 1970; March 18, 1978.

Society, March-April, 1989, p. 78.

Spectator, February 6, 1959; May 12, 1961; March 11, 1966; September 9, 1966; January 12, 1968; January 27, 1973; March 9, 1974; September 23, 1978; February 26, 1983; June 11, 1983; February 8, 1986; October 18, 1986; January 16, 1988; August 12, 1989; January 29, 1994, p. 41; June 18, 1994, p. 37.

Time, June 2, 1961.

Times (London), February 5, 1959; September 8, 1966; November 20, 1969; January 17, 1970; July 22, 1971; January 22, 1973; March 14, 1973; September 14, 1978; May 26, 1983; September 4, 1986; January 14, 1988; June 29, 1989.

Times Literary Supplement, February 13, 1959; May 19, 1961; October 22, 1964; September 8, 1966; November 3, 1966; January 29, 1970; December 3, 1971; July 6, 1973; May 3, 1974; November 17, 1978; March 11, 1983; June 3, 1983; November 3, 1983; April 4, 1986; September 26, 1986; January 29, 1988; April 15, 1988; August 25, 1989; September 6, 1991, p. 22; April 29, 1994; June 17, 1994.

Tribune Books (Chicago), March 27, 1988.
Village Quarterly Review, winter, 1967.
Washington Post Book World, July 22, 1979; August 7, 1983; August 26, 1990; October 9, 1994, p. 12.*

* * *

CAYLEFF, Susan E. 1954-

PERSONAL: Born March 4, 1954, in Boston, MA; daughter of Nathan (a hardware store retailer) and Frieda (a homemaker; maiden name, Kates) Cayleff. *Education:* University of Massachusetts at Amherst, B.A. (magna cum laude), 1976; Sarah Lawrence College, M.A. (women's history), 1978; Brown University, M.A. (American civilization), 1979, Ph.D., 1983. *Religion:* Jewish.

ADDRESSES: Home—San Diego, CA. *Office*—Department of Women's Studies, San Diego State University, San Diego, CA 92182.

CAREER: University of Texas Medical Branch, Galveston, assistant professor of medical humanities, 1983-87, clinical adjunct in nursing, 1986-87, humanities faculty founder of Women's History Seminar Series in the Obstetrics of Gynecology Department, 1984-87; San Diego State University, San Diego, CA, associate professor, 1987-92, professor of women's studies, 1993—, chair of department of women's studies, 1996—, member of executive committee, Lipinsky Institute for Judaic Studies, 1990—. Loma Linda University, William Frederick Norwood Lecturer, 1988; University of Texas Medical Branch, Galveston, adjunct faculty at Institute for the Medical Humanities, 1987-95; guest on radio and television programs; public speaker. Project Wildlife, member of Transport Team of Injured Animals and Birds, 1991.

MEMBER: National Women's Studies Association, American Historical Association, American Studies Association, Organization of American Historians, American Association for the History of Medicine, Society for Health and Human Values, Society for Menstrual Cycle Research, Western Association for Women Historians, Graduate Women Scholars of Southern California (faculty founder, 1990), Phi Kappa Phi.

AWARDS, HONORS: Grants from National Endowment for the Humanities, 1984, Babe Didrikson Zaharias Memorial Foundation, 1986, and American Association of Naturopathic Physicians, 1992; Pulitzer Prize nominee, 1996, for *Babe;* Outstanding Book Award, Gay and Lesbian Alliance against Defamation, 1996; Research, Scholarship and Creative Activity Award, 1997.

WRITINGS:

Wash and Be Healed: The Water-Cure Movement and Women's Health, Temple University Press (Philadelphia, PA), 1987.
(Editor, with Barbara Bair) *"Wings of Gauze": Women of Color and the Experience of Health and Illness,* Wayne State University Press (Detroit, MI), 1993.
Babe: The Life and Legend of "Babe" Didrikson Zaharias, University of Illinois Press (Urbana, IL), 1995.
Babe: The Greatest All-Sport Athlete of All-Time (young adult biography), Conari Press (Berkeley, CA), 2000.

Work represented in anthologies, including *Other Healers: Unorthodox Medicine in America,* edited by Norman Gevitz, Johns Hopkins University Press (Baltimore, MD), 1988; *Women, Health, and Medicine in America: An Encyclopedia Handbook,* Garland Publishing (New York City), 1990, *Tish Sommers, Activist,* by Patricia Huckle, University of Tennessee Press (Knoxville, TN), 1991. Contributor of more than thirty articles, poems, and reviews to academic journals. Member of editorial board, *Medical Humanities Review,* 1986-88.

WORK IN PROGRESS: "Keeping to the Path": A History of Naturopathic Healing and Professionalism in Twentieth-Century America.

* * *

CHAN, Gillian 1954-

PERSONAL: Born March 29, 1954, in Cleethorpes, England; daughter of Jimmy and Patricia Durrant; married Henry Chan (an actor), 1982; children: Theo. *Ethnicity:* "British." *Education:* Orange Hill Girls Grammar School, Edgeware, Middlesex; Rochester

Gillian Chan

Grammar School for Girls, Kent; Keswick Hall, University of East Anglia, B.Ed. *Hobbies and other interests:* Reading, traveling, cooking, calligraphy, watching baseball, playing computer games.

ADDRESSES: Home and office—41 Thornton Trail, Dundas, Ontario, Canada L9H 6Y2. *E-mail*—gillian. chan@sympatico.ca.

CAREER: English and drama teacher and librarian, 1980-90; writer, 1994—; worked variously as a mail sorter, dishwasher, bartender, bank clerk, and shop assistant.

MEMBER: Canadian Society of Children's Authors, Illustrators and Performers (CANSCAIP), Writers' Union of Canada, Canadian Children's Book Centre.

AWARDS, HONORS: Hamilton and Region Arts Council Literary Award, and Mr. Christie's Book Award finalist, Christie Brown & Co., both 1995, both for

Golden Girl and Other Stories; Governor General's Literary Award finalist, Children's Literature, Canada Council, 1996, and Mr. Christie's Book Award finalist, Christie Brown & Co., 1997, both for *Glory Days and Other Stories*; finalist for the Shining Willow Award and the Red Maple Award, both 2002, both for *The Carved Box.*

WRITINGS:

Golden Girl and Other Stories, Kids Can Press (Toronto, Ontario, Canada), 1994.
Glory Days and Other Stories, Kids Can Press (Toronto, Ontario, Canada), 1996.
The Carved Box, Kids Can Press (Toronto, Ontario, Canada), 2001.
A Foreign Field, Kids Can Press (Toronto, Ontario, Canada), 2002.

WORK IN PROGRESS: Two novels.

SIDELIGHTS: Gillian Chan was born in England into a royal air force family that moved every few years throughout that country and Germany. One of her earliest memories is of the family's Saturday morning trips to the library. Everyone in her family liked to read to young Gillian—if only to stop her from pretending to read at the top of her lungs.

When she was five, Chan announced that she was going to write a book of her own, and from then on she wrote constantly. After graduating from college, she taught English and ran a school library in Norfolk, England. Often too tired to think about writing for herself, she compromised and completed the same writing assignments she gave her students in her classes. She never told the kids this, nor did she tell them she wrote the anonymous pieces they studied when she needed a selection to fit a lesson plan.

Life changed drastically when Chan and her husband left England for Canada in 1990. Looking for something to do together, Chan and her husband had planned to open a bookstore, but the recession put that dream on hold. She then devoted her time to writing, and her husband decided to become an actor. "Canada has been a renaissance—a rebirth—for us and we've been motivated to do something completely different," Chan told Sandy Van Harten of the *Hamilton Spectator.*

Chan's first published book evolved from a writing course at McMaster University, where she was asked to write a short story in as alien a voice as possible. She chose to write as Dennis, a sixteen-year-old boy. At a blue-pencil workshop, she showed the story to Charis Wahl, editor of young adult fiction at Toronto-based Kids Can Press, who suggested she submit it to her. Chan, however, did not follow through. In fact, it wasn't until she took a second writing course at Humber College and was reassured by the instructor Paul Quarrington that Wahl's suggestion was probably sincere that she submitted the story.

Eventually, Kids Can Press published this story and four others as *Golden Girl and Other Stories,* a collection related in the first person by five different characters who attend the same high school. "I didn't set out to write a series of stories set in the same place. . . . I wrote 'The Buddy System' and when I'd finished it, I didn't want to let the two main characters, Dennis and Bob, go," Chan wrote in a promotional profile prepared by Kids Can Press. As a result, the characters in *Golden Girl* pop up in each other's stories, and some even end up telling their own stories. Elizabeth MacCallum wrote in the Toronto-based *Globe and Mail* that "Chan's descriptions of the tensions arising between adults and adolescents have the ring of truth"—and was a finalist for the Mr. Christie's Book Award in 1995.

Chan was so caught up in the lives of the Elmwood High students that she published a sequel two years later. *Glory Days and Other Stories* tells of other students there, and occasionally mentions the kids from *Golden Girl. Toronto Star* columnist Margot Griffin told a young reader, "I predict that you will find the characters in this book to be so real that you will find yourself thinking about them long after you finish the last story." Chris Sherman of *Booklist* commended the collection, commenting that the stories "are sure to touch a responsive chord" in its young readers. This book was a finalist for the Governor General's Literary Award, Children's Literature, in 1996, and for the Mr. Christie's Book Award, 1997.

Chan told the audience at Packaging Your Imagination, a workshop for children's writers, that teenagers live their lives with an intensity that frightens her. They either love something or hate it. What happens to them is all that matters at a given moment. As a result, she believes the short story is perfect for capturing the intense, episodic nature of teenage life.

A meticulous researcher, Chan reads teen magazines and makes copius notes while watching teens at high schools and hangouts. She believes that it's important to capture the voices of her narrators, using words the way she imagines they would use them and reproducing their intonation and speech patterns. This close attention to research led Chan into a new direction, with two historical novels for young adults: *The Carved Box* and *A Foreign Field.*

The starting place for most of her stories is the main character, Chan told Packaging Your Imagination. The characters come to her first, and she spends days thinking about them before worrying about a plot. She creates detailed character sketches, including things like family history, background, appearance, personality, idiosyncrasies, academic performance, friends, interests, and weaknesses, dreams, fears and ambitions. She even includes a time line of their lives and those of other family members and, in some cases, diagrams of their homes and rooms. "My feeling is that the plot has to derive from the character, she asks herself questions such as, 'What would be the worst thing that could happen to this character? The best thing?'" As she does this, she finds that the plot evolves naturally.

The Carved Box set in Upper Canada (now southern Ontario) during the late 1700s, is the story of a Scottish orphan boy, fifteen-year-old Callum Murdoch. Callum is sent to live with his uncle Rory and and his family, Canadian pioneers, after the death of both of his parents. On his arrival in the New World, Callum buys an abused black dog from a stranger, giving him the only money he has brought from Scotland. The stranger also gives Callum a mysterious carved wooden box, saying the dog will stay with him only as long as Callum keeps the box with him and it remains unopened. Callum must work hard on his uncle's farm, with only "Dog" for companionship. One day, after numerous adventures that create a deepening friendship between boy and dog, the box accidentally breaks open and leads Callum to a surprising awareness about his canine companion. Akin to old Scotch-Irish myths about the "selkies," this story has an unusual twist at the end, showing that friendship can survice even a dramatic personal change. A contributor to *Kirkus Reviews* found the book "a well-knit, outdoorsy tale." Crystal Faris of *School Library Journal,* however, wrote, "This mystical ending seems contrived . . . and adds a jarring element" to a story she otherwise enjoyed. Gail Lennon of *Resource Links* called the book a "delightful tale of life in Upper Canada" during pioneer times. Lennon highly recommended *The Carved Box* for junior or intermediate elementary students. The book was a finalist for the Shining Willow Award and the Red Maple Award, both in 2002.

In *A Foreign Field,* Ellen Logan and British pilot Stephen Dearborn develop a deep friendship during World War II. Their friendship develops into love over time, and the two continue to write after Stephen is sent to the front lines, where his plane is shot down. Carolyn Phelan in *Booklist* observed, "Chan beautifully captures the particular tensions and intensity of wartime relationships in this quiet, absorbing novel." Phelan noted that the violent subject sometimes calls for strong language, but it is "true to the [novel's] characters and events." Paula J. LaRue, writing in *School Library Journal,* commented on Chan's skillful use of "homey details, such as the teen overcooking the potatoes," and thought the book presented a story that would thoroughly engage its readers. Victoria Pennell commented in *Resource Links* that "this book presents a vivid glimpse into the way of life for many young Canadians during the years of World War II. . . . Young adults will be able to relate to Ellen and Stephen, their day-to-day experiences, their hopes and fears and the uncertainty of the times."

Chan begins her stories by writing longhand in a spiral-bound notebook, using only the right-hand side of the page. "I leave the left for notes to myself, for questions, instructions, diagrams, things that occur to me as I write and which need further work," she told the audience at Packaging Your Imagination.

Her final question is, Does the story end too neatly? Chan believes a short story is one moment in someone's life. "There has to be a sense that life continues," she once commented.

Her stories project this. Discussing one of them in the *Globe and Mail,* MacCallum wrote, "This denouement, like the others in *Golden Girl,* produces a thought-provoking, surprising ending that leaves the reader pondering the peculiarities and vagaries of human nature. Now that's a good story."

BIOGRAPHICAL AND CRITICAL SOURCES:

PERIODICALS

Booklist, September 15, 1997, review of *Golden Girl and Other Stories,* p. 220; January 1, 1998, Chris Sherman, review of *Glory Days and Other Stories,* p. 794; October 1, 2001, review of *The Carved Box,* p. 312; September 15, 2002, Carolyn Phelan, review of *A Foreign Field,* p. 226.

Books in Canada, April, 1997, review of *Glory Days,* p. 34.

Bulletin of the Center for Children's Books, January, 1998, reviews of *Golden Girl* and *Glory Days,* p. 156.

Canadian Book Review Annual, 1994, review of *Golden Girl,* p. 477; 1996, review of *Glory Days,* p. 468

Canadian Children's Literature, winter, 1996, review of *Golden Girl,* p. 106; summer, 1997, review of Glory Days, p. 83.

Children's Book News, winter, 1997, review of *Glory Days,* p. 27.

Children's Book Review Service, November, 1997, review of *Golden Girl,* p. 33.

CM: Canadian Review of Materials, November 16, 2001, review of *The Carved Box.*

Emergency Librarian, November, 1995, review of *Golden Girl,* p. 25.

Globe and Mail (Toronto), October 15, 1994, Elizabeth MacCallum, review of *Golden Girl;* October 20, 2001, review of *The Carved Box,* p. D22.

Hamilton Spectator, September 17, 1994, Sandy Van Harten.

Kirkus Reviews, August 1, 1997, review of Golden Girl, p.1219; August 15, 1997, review of *Glory Days,* p. 1303; August 15, 2001, review of *The Carved Box,* p. 1208.

Quill & Quire, September, 1994, review of *Golden Girl,* p. 73; October, 1996, review of *Glory Days,* p. 51; July, 2001, review of *The Carved Box,* p. 51.

Resource Links, February, 1997, review of *Glory Days,* p. 136; October, 2001, Gail Lennon, review of *The Carved Box,* p. 9; December, 2002, Victoria Pennell, review of *A Foreign Field,* p. 44.

School Library Journal, November, 1997, review of Golden Girl, p. 114; October, 2001, Crystal Faris, review of *The Carved Box,* p. 152; November, 2002, Paula J. LaRue, review of *A Foreign Field,* p. 159.

Toronto Star, January 12, 1997, Margot Griffin, review of *Glory Days.*

ONLINE

Gillian Chan Home Page, http://www.gillianchan.com/ (May 15, 2003).

CHAPIN, Sarah 1931-

PERSONAL: Born December 19, 1931, in Cambridge, MA; daughter of John Archibald Sessions (an accountant) and Doheny Hackett; married Charles Chapin, April 17, 1954 (divorced); children: Samuel. *Education:* Smith College, B.A., 1953; attended Boston College; Lesley College, M.Ed., 1981. *Politics:* Democrat. *Religion:* Protestant.

ADDRESSES: Home—255 Lexington Rd., Concord, MA 01742.

CAREER: Concord Free Public Library Special Collections, Concord, research scholar, 1989—.

AWARDS, HONORS: Best of Category, Forty-first Annual New England Book Show, 1997, for *A Wreath of Joy.*

WRITINGS:

The Tin Box Collection: Letters of Roger Sessions, His Family and Friends, privately printed, 1992.
(Editor) Edward Jarvis, *Traditions and Reminiscences of Concord, Massachusetts, 1779-1878,* University of Massachusetts Press (Amherst, MA), 1993.
A Wreath of Joy, The Library (Concord, MA), 1996.
Concord, Massachusetts, Aracadia (Mt. Pleasant, SC), 1997.
(With others) *Concord: Then and Now,* (Mt. Pleasant, SC), 2001.

Also editor of transcriptions from Concord Free Public Library publications, including *Journal of Alfred W. Hosmer* (1888-1903); *Thoreau—Salt's Biography* (1896), grangerized by Alfred W. Hosmer; *William Ellery Channing's Botanical Jottings* (from Channing's copy of Gray's *Manual,* 1848); and *Concord Flora 1834-1836: Observed by Edward Jarvis.* Contributor to journals, including *Psychomusicology* and *The Filson Club History Quarterly.*

*   *   *

CHOUEIRI, Youssef M. 1948-

PERSONAL: Surname is pronounced "shu-*way*-ri"; born October 15, 1948, in Douma, Lebanon; son of Michel (in business) and Milia Youssef (Habib) Choueiri; married Amal Ali Al-Ghusayn (a biochemist), October 10, 1974; children: Tarek, Hiba.

Education: American University of Beirut, B.A., 1974; University of London, M.Sc., 1978; Cambridge University, Ph.D., 1986. *Politics:* Independent. *Religion:* Humanist.

ADDRESSES: Home—19 Feltrim Ave., Exeter EX2 4RP, England. *Office*—University of Exeter, Prince of Wales Rd., Exeter EX4 4JZ, England. *E-mail*—Y.M. Choueiri@exeter.ac.uk.

CAREER: Cambridge University, Cambridge, England, lecturer in Arabic, 1983-86; University of Exeter, Exeter, England, lecturer in Middle Eastern history and Islamic studies, 1986-97, 1998—; writer. Reader in Middle Eastern History, University of Exeter, Exeter, England.

MEMBER: British Society for Middle Eastern Studies (fellow; member of council), Middle Eastern Studies Association of North America; fellow, Royal Historical Society, United Kingdom.

WRITINGS:

Margin and Text (in Arabic), Riad El-Rayyes Books, 1988.
Arab History and the Nation-State: A Study in Modern Arab Historiography, 1820-1980, Routledge & Kegan Paul (New York, NY), 1989.
Islamic Fundamentalism, Twayne (Boston, MA), 1990.
State and Society in Syria and Lebanon, St. Martin's Press (New York, NY), 1994.
Islamic Fundamentalism, Pinter (Washington, DC), 1997.
Arab Nationalism—A History: Nation and State in the Arab World, Blackwell Publishers (Malden, MA), 2000.
Modern Arab Historiography, Curzon Press, Ltd. (New York, NY), 2002.

Also author of *The Arab Nationalist Movement in the Twentieth Century,* in press. Editor in chief, *Ad-Dastour,* 1979-80.

SIDELIGHTS: In an attempt to bridge the gap between East and West, Youssef M. Choueiri has written books for more than twenty years trying to explain the

Arab world to Europeans and other non-Middle Eastern populations. In his writing, he explores the politics, the religion, the history, and the culture of the Arab nations.

His first book to be written in English, *Arab History and the Nation State* (1989) is a revised version of Choueiri's doctoral dissertation. Michael Gilsenan of the *English Historical Review* explained that, in this book, Choueiri is "highly critical of the historiographical writing of the modern period," especially of Arab historians who tend to incorporate "mostly European thought" into their writing. Exemplifying this comment, Mahmoud Haddad of the *Journal of the American Oriental Society*, quoted Choueiri as stating that "modern Arabic thought has not yet found its historian."

Also according to Haddad, Choueiri claims that many modern Arab historians share common characteristics with military officers. They both have adopted "certain Western ideas," and they have a "burning desire to reform society," as well as practice a certain "efficiency, discipline and a perceptible aloofness toward their traditional communities."

In 1994, Choueiri published his *State and Society in Syria and Lebanon,* in which, together with contributors, he examines the disintegration of the Ottoman Empire during World War I through the struggle for independence that these countries fought for until 1991. Some of the topics included in this book are the government policies and practices throughout this period and an attempt to define the concept of Arabism and nationalism as found in this area of the Middle East. Some of the subjects that Choueiri discusses in this book include the early-twentieth-century economy of Syria, the formation of a caste system in Greater Lebanon, and concepts of nation and state in Lebanon.

According to reviewer Laila Juma of the Web site *Muslimedia* (the online presence of *Crescent International,* a news magazine of Islam), in *Arab Nationalism—A History: Nation and State in the Arab World* (2000), Choueiri "traces the emergence and development of Arab nationalism rather more sympathetically than most people would." To do this, Choueiri emphasizes three distinct phases: from 1800 to 1900, what is referred to as a cultural stage; 1900 to 1945, considered an anti-imperialist phase; and 1945 to 1973, a period that saw the creation and development of a its own radical program. Choueiri believes that the Arab World is about to enter a fourth stage of development, which "he links to secular democracy and civil society."

Choueiri "provides a wealth of detail" wrote Charles Tripp for the *Times Literary Supplement,* based on the writing of several well-respected Arab writers. Choueiri "describes what they [Arab writers] had to say about the Arab nation and about the political programmes needed to realize its potential."

In Choueiri's 2002 publication, *Modern Arab Historiography,* he tightens the theme of his doctoral thesis by focusing on specific Arab historians from Egypt, Lebanon, and Morocco, and analyzing their work.

Choueiri once told *CA:* "I have been studying and teaching the modern history of the Arab world for at least two decades. As a Western-educated Arab scholar, I believe that I am in an ideal position to interpret the interaction between Western and Third World societies."

BIOGRAPHICAL AND CRITICAL SOURCES:

PERIODICALS

Choice, September 2001, Volume 39, number 1, B. Harris, Jr., review of *Arab Nationalism—A History: Nation and State in the Arab World,* p. 184.

English Historical Review, January 1993, Volume 108, number 426, Michael Bilsenan, review of *Arab History and the Nation-State: A Study in Modern Arab Historiography, 1820-1980,* p. 270.

Journal of the American Oriental Society, July-September 1992, Volume 112, number 3, Mahmoud Haddad, review of *Arab History and the Nation-State: A Study in Modern Historiography, 1820-1980,* pp. 530-31.

Times Literary Supplement, December 14, 2001, Charles Tripp, review of *Arab Nationalism—A History,* p. 29.

ONLINE

Muslimedia Web site, http://www.muslimedia.com/ (July 22, 2002), Laila Juma, "Tracing the History (and Decline) of Arab Nationalism."

CLENDINNEN, Inga 1934-

PERSONAL: Born August 17, 1934, in Geelong, Victoria, Australia; daughter of Thomas William (a cabinet maker) and Catherine (a homemaker; maiden name, Barlow) Jewell; married Frederick John Clendinnen (a philosopher), June 1, 1955; children: Stephen John, Richmond David. *Education:* University of Melbourne, B.A. (with honors), 1955, M.A., 1975; La Trobe University, D.Litt., 1991. *Politics:* "Left." *Religion:* "On the whole, against."

ADDRESSES: Home—30 Childers St., Kew, Victoria 3101, Australia. *Office*—Department of History, La Trobe University, Bundoora, Victoria 3083, Australia.

CAREER: University of Melbourne, Parkville, Australia, tutor, 1956-57, senior tutor in history, 1958-65 and 1968; La Trobe University, Bundoora, Australia, lecturer, 1969-82, senior lecturer, 1982-89, reader in history, 1989-91, emeritus scholar, 1992—. Princeton University, fellow at Shelby Cullom Davis Center for Historical Research, 1983-84; Institute for Advanced Study (Princeton, NJ), fellow at School for Historical Studies, 1987; University of Michigan, Arthur H. Aiton Memorial Lecturer, 1987. Forty-first Boyer Lecturer, Australian Broadcasting Company, 1999; and Carson Lecturer, Oregon State University, fall, 2002.

AWARDS, HONORS: Conference on Latin American History Prize, 1981, for the article "Landscape and World View: The Survival of Yucatec Maya Culture Under Spanish Conquest"; Herbert Eugene Bolton Memorial Prize, 1988, for *Ambivalent Conquests: Maya and Spaniard in Yucatan, 1517-1571;* prize from Program for Cultural Cooperation, Spanish Ministry of Culture and U.S. Universities, 1989, for *Ambivalent Conquests;* New South Wales Premier's History Prize, 1999, for *Reading the Holocaust.* Won a prize for a short story in the early 1990s; Nita Kibble Award for Women's Life Writing, 2001, and Inaugural Award for Innovative Writing, Adelaide Festival, 2002, for *Tiger's Eye: A Memoir.*

WRITINGS:

Ambivalent Conquests: Maya and Spaniard in Yucatan, 1517-1571, Cambridge University Press (New York, NY), 1987.
Aztecs: An Interpretation, Cambridge University Press (New York, NY), 1991.

Reading The Holocaust, Text Publishing (Melbourne, Australia), 1998.
True Stories, ABC Books for the Australian Broadcasting Corporation (Sydney, Australia), 1999.
Tiger's Eye: A Memoir, Text Publishing (Melbourne, Australia), 2000, Scribner (New York, NY), 2001.
Dancing with Strangers, Text Publishing (Melbourne, Australia), 2003.

Work represented in anthologies, including *Disciplines of Faith: Studies in Religion, Politics, and Patriarchy,* edited by Jim Obelkevich, Lyndal Roper, and Raphael Samuel, Routledge & Kegan Paul, 1987; *Women, Race, and Writing in the Early Modern Period,* edited by Patricia Parker and Margot Hendricks, Routledge, 1992; and *War and Society in Early America,* edited by John M. Murrin. Contributor to history and anthropology journals. *Aztecs* has been translated into Spanish and Chinese. *Reading the Holocaust* has been translated into Portuguese and Hebrew.

SIDELIGHTS: Although *Tiger's Eye: A Memoir* was Australian historian and writer Inga Clendinnen's fifth book, its deeply personal subject matter makes it a starting point for discussing her work. In 1991, she felt ill, suffering bouts of bleeding, acute fatigue, and stomach pains. Her doctors initially were at a loss as to a diagnosis. According to Jane Wheatley in the *Times,* one younger physician even told her that she had a problem "relinquishing youth gracefully." Finally a diagnosis came, and it was not pretty: active auto-immune hepatitis, a severe disease of the liver.

By that time, Clendinnen had established an international reputation as a historian with her books *Ambivalent Conquests: Maya and Spaniard in Yucatan, 1517-1571* in 1987 and *Aztecs: An Interpretation,* published the year she became sick. She ultimately recovered, but in the midst of that difficult period, when she felt certain death was approaching, she began to write stories. "Writing became a desperate enterprise as I clung to the shreds of memory I still had," she told Wheatley. "I wrote to preserve myself." Her recovery was a difficult one, and during the course of it, she underwent long hours of contemplation that led to two later nonfiction works, *Reading The Holocaust* and *True Stories.*

The latter of these is the text from a series of six half-hour broadcasts, delivered over ABC (Australian Broadcasting Corporation) Radio National in 1999. Invited to serve as the forty-first Boyer Lecturer, a great honor for Australian writers, she presented a series of historical tales illustrating the nation's past. An exemplary story was drawn from the single surviving letter by Lillie Matthews, a farmer's wife in Victoria in the 1880s who discovered that her husband was participating in attacks on Aborigines not unlike those being perpetrated against American blacks by the Ku Klux Klan at the same time. With these vignettes, wrote Leora Moldofsky in *Time International,* Clendinnen "asks her listeners and readers to join her in deciding what to make of them, what to feel about them, and finally, what to do about them."

Clendinnen took on human atrocities of a much greater scale in *Reading the Holocaust,* an unorthodox work that, in the words of Joseph Robert White in *History: Review of New Books,* "seeks to demythologize the problem of explaining" one of history's greatest crimes. Eschewing what she called the "'Gorgon effect'—the sickening of imagination and curiosity . . . which afflicts so many of us when we try to look squarely at the persons and processes implicated in the Holocaust," she sought to provide understanding of a phenomenon that is extraordinarily well documented but seldom comprehended in its immensity.

In so doing, Clendinnen took issue with the view expressed by prominent Jewish writer Elie Wiesel, that the Holocaust was a phenomenon unique to the Jews. In the words of Milton Goldin in a review on the Web site *A Teacher's Guide to the Holocaust,* it was Clendinnen's position that "the Holocaust is not beyond human comprehension, which is the exact opposite of what most writers on the subject insist. Clendinnen's common sense understanding is if these crimes involved human beings, the Holocaust is surely within human comprehension." To Daphne Merkin in the *New York Times Book Review,* the book "is not, despite its somewhat generic title, just another book about the Holocaust. It signals, instead, a radical departure point." *Reading the Holocaust,* wrote White, is "a thoughtful and sophisticated distillation of recent Holocaust scholarship accessible to general readers."

Reading the Holocaust seemed to make the point that there is no true dividing line between the political and the personal, and with *Tiger's Eye* Clendinnen approached a subject deeply personal: her own illness, from which she had by then recovered. Noting Clendinnen's observation in the book that "Illness casts you out, but it also cuts you free," Kay Hogan Smith in *Library Journal* maintained that "While this insight may be common among those who have been visited by serious illness, rarely is it delivered with the eloquence and honesty found in this work." A reviewer in *Publishers Weekly* called the memoir "a rare and original meditation on the construction of the self."

BIOGRAPHICAL AND CRITICAL SOURCES:

PERIODICALS

American Historical Review, February, 1993, review of *Aztecs: An Interpretation,* p. 278.
Americas: A Quarterly Review of Inter-American Cultural History, January, 1993, review of *Aztecs,* p. 395.
Arena Magazine, December, 1999, Ryan Scott, review of *Reading the Holocaust,* p. 55.
Australian Book Review, October, 1998, review of *Reading the Holocaust,* p. 7.
Booklist, July, 2001, Suzanne Young, review of *Tiger's Eye,* p. 1956.
German Studies Review, May, 2000, Andrew R. Carlson, review of *Reading the Holocaust,* pp. 378-79.
Guardian (Manchester, England), February 3, 2001, Julie Myerson, review of *Tiger's Eye: A Memoir.*
History: Review of New Books, winter, 2000, Joseph Robert White, review of *Reading the Holocaust,* p. 67.
History Today, April, 1999, review of *Reading the Holocaust,* p. 56.
H-Net: Humanities and Social Sciences Online, July, 1999, review of *Reading the Holocaust.*
Kirkus Reviews, February 1, 1999, review of *Reading the Holocaust,* p. 191.
Kliatt Young Adult Paperback Book Guide, November, 1993, review of *Aztecs,* p. 37.
Library Journal, July 7, 2001, Kay Hogan Smith, review of *Tiger's Eye,* p. 113.
New Leader, June 14, 1999, Alvin H. Rosenfeld, review of *Reading the Holocaust,* p. 22.
New York Times Book Review, April 11, 1999, Daphne Merkin, review of *Reading the Holocaust,* p. 17; June 6, 1999, review of *Reading the Holocaust,* p. 40; December 5, 1999, review of *Reading the Holocaust,* p. 106; August 26, 2001, Mary Gordon, "The Strangest Place to Be: In the Memoir, the Author Reports from the Expansive Continent

of the Deathly Ill," review of *Tiger's Eye,* p. 10; September 2, 2001, review of *Tiger's Eye,* p. 18; September 9, 2001, review of *Tiger's Eye,* p. 30.

Publishers Weekly, June 4, 2001, review of *Tiger's Eye,* p. 69.

Time International, November 22, 1999, Leora Moldofsky, review of *True Stories* radio broadcasts, p. 60; March 20, 2000, Michael Fitzgerald, review of *Tiger's Eye,* p. 67.

Times (London, England), January 3, 2001, Iain Finlayson, review of *Tiger's Eye,* p. 9; January 13, 2001, Jane Wheatley, "Stories from Over the Horizon," p. W-13; January 12, 2002, Fanny Blake, review of *Tiger's Eye,* p. 16.

Times Literary Supplement, June 11, 1999, review of *Reading the Holocaust,* p. 32.

William and Mary Quarterly, October, 1995, review of *Aztecs,* p. 709.

ONLINE

A Teacher's Guide to the Holocaust, http://fcit.coedu.usf.edu/ (May 17, 2002), Milton Goldin, review of *Reading the Holocaust.*

*   *   *

CONRAN, Terence Orby 1931-

PERSONAL: Born October 4, 1931, in Esher, Surrey, England; son of Rupert and Christina (Halstead) Conran; married Brenda Davison (divorced); married Shirley Ida (Pearce), 1955 (divorced, 1962); married Caroline Herbert (a writer), 1963 (divorced, 1996); children: (first marriage) Sebastian, Jasper; (second marriage) Tom, Sophie, Edmund. *Education:* Attended Central School of Art, studied textile design, 1948-50. *Hobbies and other interests:* Gardening, cooking.

ADDRESSES: Home—22 Shad Thames, London, SE1 2YU, England. *Office*—The Studio, Barton Court, Kintbury, Newbury, Berkshire, England.

CAREER: Rayon Centre, London, textile designer, 1950-51; Dennis Lennon Studio, London, interior designer, 1951-52; Conran and Company, freelance furniture designer, 1965-56; Soup Kitchen restaurants, founder-proprietor, London, 1953-56; Conran Design

Group, founder-director, 1956-71; Habitat Furnishing Stores, founder-director, 1964-71; Ryman Conran Ltd., London, joint-chairman, 1968-71; Neal Street Restaurant, London, managing director/chairman, 1968-72; Conran Stores, chairman, 1977—; Jasper Conran Fashion Company, chairman, 1977—; J. Hepworth and Son, director/chairman, 1979—; Habitat Mothercare Ltd., chairman, 1982—; Conran Roche Architectural and City Planning, director, 1982—; Conran Octopus Publishing, 1982—; Butlers Wharf Development, 1984—; Michelin House Development, director, 1985—; Bibendum Restaurant, chairman, 1986—; British Home Stores PLC and Savacentre Ltd., chairman, 1986—; Conran Foundation for Design and Industry, founder/trustee, 1982—; Design Museum, London, founder/trustee, 1989—; Conran Ink, Creative Business, and Conran Associates, Terence Conran Ltd., 1990—.

MEMBER: Royal Commission on Environmental Pollution, 1973-76; council of Royal College of Art, 1978—, and advisory council of Victoria and Albert Museum, 1979-81; Society of Industrial Artists and Designers.

AWARDS, HONORS: Presidential medals for design management from Royal Society of Arts, 1968, 1975; Society of Industrial Artists and Designers Design Medal, 1980; Royal Society of Arts Bicentenary Medal, 1982; *Daily Telegraph*/Association for Business Sponsorship Award, 1982; Queen's New Year Honours, knighthood, 1983; honorary fellow, Royal Institute of British Architects, 1984; D&AD President's Award, 1989; Commandeur des Arts et des Lettres, awarded by Jack Lang, minister of culture, France, 1992; *House Beautiful* Design Award, 2002.

WRITINGS:

Printed Textile Design, Studio Publications (New York, NY), 1957.

The House Book, Mitchell Beazley (London), 1974.

(With Maria Kroll) *The Vegetable Book,* Collins (Glasgow), 1976.

The Kitchen Book, Mitchell Beazley (London), 1977.

The Bed and Bath Book, Crown Publishers (New York), 1978.

(With Caroline Conran) *The Cook Book,* Crown Publishers (New York, NY), 1980.

Terence Conran's New House Book, Villard Books (New York, NY), 1985.

Conran Directory of Design, edited by Stephen Bayley, Villard Books (New York, NY) 1985.

(With Susan Conder) *Terence Conran's Plants at Home,* Conran Octopus (London), 1986.

The Soft Furnishings Book, edited by Judy Brittain, Conran Octopus (London), 1986.

Terence Conran's Home Furnishings, edited by Judy Brittain, Little, Brown (Boston, MA), 1986.

(With Pierrette Pompon Bailhache and Maurice Croizard) *Terence Conran's France,* Little, Brown (Boston, MA), 1987.

Original Designs for Bathrooms and Bedrooms, edited by John McGowan and Rogert DuBern, Simon & Schuster (New York, NY), 1989.

Original Designs for Kitchens and Dining Rooms, edited by John McGowan and Roger DuBern, Simon & Schuster (New York, NY), 1989.

Terence Conran's DIY by Design, edited by John McGowan and Roger DuBern, Conran Octopus (London), 1989.

Terence Conran's Garden DIY, edited by John McGowan and Roger DuBern, Conran Octopus (London), 1991.

Terence Conran's Garden Style, edited by John McGowan and Roger DuBern, Crown Publishers (New York, NY), 1991.

Children's Furniture and Toys: Stylish Projects to Make for Your Children, Macmillan: Maxwell Macmillan International (New York, NY), 1992.

Terence Conran's Kitchen Book: A Comprehensive Source Book and Guide to Planning, Fitting and Equipping Your Kitchen, edited by Elizabeth Wilhide and Deborah Smith-Morant, Overlook Press (Woodstock, NY), 1993.

The Essential House Book: Getting Back to Basics, Crown (New York, NY), 1994.

(Author of introduction) *The Cigar in Art,* Overlook Press (New York), 1996.

Terence Conran on Design, Overlook Press (Woodstock, NY), 1996.

(With Caroline Conran and Simon Hokinson) *The Essential Cook Book: The Back-to-Basics Guide to Selecting, Preparing, Cooking, and Serving the Very Best of Foods,* Stewart, Tabori & Chang (New York, NY), 1997.

(With Dan Pearson) *The Essential Garden Book,* Crown Publishers (New York, NY), 1998.

Terence Conran's Easy Living, Soma Books (San Francisco, CA), 1999.

(With Andi Clevely and Jeremy Lee) *The Chef's Garden,* Soma Books (San Francisco, CA), 1999.

Terence Conran's New House Book: The Complete Guide to Home Design, Conran Octopus (London), 1999.

Terence Conran on Restaurants, Overlook Press (Woodstock, NY), 2000.

Terence Conran Small Spaces: Inspiring Ideas and Creative Solutions, Clarkson Potter (New York, NY), 2001.

Alcazar to Zinc: The Story of Conran Restaurants, Conran Octopus (London), 2001.

Terence Conran Kitchens: The Hub of the Home, Clarkson N. Potter (New York, NY), 2002.

Q and A: A Sort of Autobiography, HarperCollins Publishers, Ltd. (London), 2002.

Terence Conran's House & Garden Design Projects: Over 45 Projects and Hundreds of Ideas for Making the Most of Your Home—Inside and Out, edited by John McGowan and Roger DuBern, Conran Octopus (London), 2002.

SIDELIGHTS: Two years after leaving the Central School of Arts and Crafts in London, where he studied textile design, Sir Terence Conran set up a freelance furniture-making business in a basement studio on Notting Hill in London. Six years later, he founded the Conran Design Group, which, over the next thirty-five years, grew to become one of the largest design consultancies in Europe, with offices in London, Paris, and Hong Kong. During this same time period, he founded Conran Roche, an award-winning architects and city planning firm, opened several restaurants, founded and managed many retail shops, and wrote a prodigious number of books.

In presenting *House Beautiful*'s 2002 award to Conran, editor-in-chief Marian McEvoy referred to him as "'the patron saint' of up-to-the-minute design," according to *Washington Post*'s by Jura Koncius. McEvoy added, "Terence Conran changed the way an entire generation looked at design."

Some of the more famous of Conran's creations include his Habitat store. The first one opened in the 1960s and has since become an international retail chain that sells stylish, practical, and affordable furniture and housewares. A by-product of Habitat was the slightly more upscale Conran Shop, which also evolved into a chain. Later, Conran opened his Mothercare shops that sold clothing for mothers and babies; while his line of Hepworth stores sold men's wear. Conran also started Benchmark Woodworking, a furniture-making company.

In the business of restaurants, The Soup Kitchen was Conran's first, followed by others such as Bibendum, Mezzo, Zinc Bar, and Bluebird. In 1983, Conran used his knowledge of the publishing industry (having already authored numerous titles) to found a publishing company called Conran Octopus. This publisher specializes in books about interior design, cookery, gardening, crafts, and the decorative arts, all of which reflect Conran's design philosophy and style.

Most of Conran's books focus on some element or theory of interior design. He has written extensively on decorating almost every room of the house, concentrating on how to make life easier, more comfortable, and more pleasing to the eye. His first successful book was simply called *The House Book* (1974). Since then, he has taken the basic concepts included in this book and revised and updated them in subsequent editions. In *The Essential House Book: Getting Back to Basics* (1994), Conran promotes his minimal design for the entire house. Some of his ideas include mixing design concepts of different cultures as well as mixing old styles with new.

With his *Terence Conran's Easy Living* (1999), he offers more than just photographs and projects about interior design. His philosophy of design and comfortable living is also included in the extensive text of this book, in which he discusses functionality and simplicity in modern life, two of his favorite topics. Partnered with *Easy Living* is his *Soft Furnishings Book* (2000), which covers household elements such as drapery, fabric screens, cushions, seat-covers, and more. For those who live in small apartments or homes, Conran offers his *Small Spaces: Inspiring Ideas and Creative Solutions* (2001). Whether decorating a houseboat or a tree-house-sized abode, Conran's ideas offer aesthetically pleasing solutions.

Another of Conran's many interests is the home garden. To this end, he has published *The Essential Garden Book* (1998), which covers the small city plot as well as the elegant country formal garden. In 2000, *Terence Conran's Garden DIY* was published, in which he makes suggestions for everything related to the gar-

den from children's playhouses, to trellises, patios, ponds, and plant containers. The same year, he also published *The Chef's Garden,* taking yet another aspect of backyard projects, this time the kitchen garden. In this book, Conran recommends that everyone, regardless of the limits or expansiveness of available space, grow herbs, fruit, and vegetables to guarantee that their diet includes chemical-free and more intensely flavored food. He offers tips on how to use herbs and edible flowers in eighteen simple but exotic recipes.

Conran has also written two books on another favorite topic of his, restaurants. His 2000 *Terence Conran on Restaurants* covers topics that anyone interested in opening a restaurant might want to read. Sharing his experience of more than forty years in the restaurant business, Conran writes about how to select the right location, plan a budget, design the space, and choose a menu and staff. Also included are profiles of some of the most successful restaurants in the world, including Big Sur's Nepenthe, Chicago's Big Bowl, and New York City's Nobu and Balthazar. Two years after the publication of this book, Conran wrote *Alcazar to Zinc: A Story of Conran Restaurants,* in which he recounts the history behind his own involvement in forty-two different restaurants, cafes, bars, clubs, and delis.

Conran offers readers a more personal look into his forty-odd-year career as author, designer, restaurateur, and founder of furniture and other retail stores with his book *Q and A: A Sort of Autobiography.* A *Publishers Weekly* reviewer commented that Conran's autobiography is "as original as his home design concept." For this book, Conran asked several friends, family members, and a few celebrities to ask him questions about his life, which he responded to in full. "Conran's chatty and forthright responses yield an engaging portrait of a man who sums himself up as a 'hard-working hedonist.'"

BIOGRAPHICAL AND CRITICAL SOURCES:

PERIODICALS

Publishers Weekly, January 14, 2002, review of *Q and A: A Sort of Autobiography,* p. 50.
Washington Post, May 30, 2002, Jura Koncius, "Terence Conran at the Peak of His Powers," p. H01.

ONLINE

Conran, http://www.conran.com/us/pressroom/ (July 21, 2002), "Conran News."*

*   *   *

CONROY, John 1951-

PERSONAL: Born March 29, 1951, in La Spezia, Italy; son of Al (in refrigerator sales) and Mary (a book-keeper; maiden name, Buckley) Conroy; married Colette Davison (a psychologist), May 31, 1986. *Education:* University of Illinois, B.A., 1973.

ADDRESSES: Home—2722 West Potomac, Chicago, IL 60622. *Agent*—Wendy Weil, 747 Third Ave., New York, NY 10017.

CAREER: Chicago Guide (now *Chicago*), Chicago, IL, senior editor, 1974-76; *Reader,* Chicago, staff writer, 1978-91; writer.

AWARDS, HONORS: Awards from Society of Professional Journalists, 1976, and Women in Communications, 1977, both for "Mill Town" series; Peter Lisagor awards, 1977 and 1991; Alicia Patterson Foundation fellow, 1979; best nonfiction book award, Friends of Literature and Society of Midland Authors, Carl Sandburg Literary Art Award, Friends of the Chicago Public Library, both 1987, and *Boston Globe* Literary Press Award finalist, 1988, all for *Belfast Diary: War As a Way of Life;* research and writing grant, John D. and Catherine T. MacArthur Foundation, 1990; John Bartlow Martin Award for public interest in magazine journalism, 1991.

WRITINGS:

Belfast Diary: War As a Way of Life, Beacon Press (Boston, MA), 1987.
Unspeakable Acts, Ordinary People: The Dynamics of Torture, Knopf (New York, NY), 2000.

Contributor to periodicals, including *Chicago.*

SIDELIGHTS: John Conroy has won significant acclaim for *Belfast Diary: War As a Way of Life,* his account of war-torn Northern Ireland in the 1980s. From the early 1920s, when an accord with Britain divided the country into Northern Ireland and the Irish Free State (later named the Republic of Ireland), violent skirmishes occurred between Northern Ireland's Protestant majority, who generally supported the political union with Great Britain, and its Catholic minority, some of whom sought a union with the Republic of Ireland, and refused to accept the division of Ireland or retention of ties with the British.

The Irish Republican Army (IRA) was formed in 1919 as a nationalist organization seeking a united, independent Ireland, yet its members claimed that terrorism—arbitrary acts of violence, often against the general population—was necessary to prompt unification. Although outlawed, the IRA continued as a clandestine organization, and when the two branches—the Officials and Provisionals—split in 1969, the Provisionals embarked on an intensified terrorist campaign. In an attempt to restore order to a province on the verge of civil war, British Army troops took to the streets in August, 1969. Thus begun what the Irish, both in Northern Ireland and the Republic of Ireland, call "the Troubles."

Although the British were initially tolerated by the Catholic community as a protective force, the tide of opinion slowly turned, and the IRA targeted both civilians and British soldiers. Since then, neither the IRA nor the British Army has been able to claim victory in the struggle, and in consequence the citizens of Northern Ireland have lived under the continual shadow of violence. During the 1990s, there were signs that the more than seventy-year-long war might be coming to an end, and peace was generally restored to Northern Ireland, but scattered outbreaks of IRA violence continued.

Conroy based *Belfast Diary* on his own observations and experiences in Belfast in 1980, when he lived in a Catholic area. There he attempted to fathom the citizenry's manner of conducting everyday affairs while exposed to violence. Conroy found himself at risk from both Catholic and Protestant factions, each of whom suspected the American freelance journalist of belonging to the opposition and questioned his political allegiance. He was held at gunpoint on three occasions by members of the Provisional IRA, and he once escaped danger from a band of intoxicated Protestants by claiming to be Jewish.

In a *Sunday Times* review, Sally Belfrage deemed the author of *Belfast Diary* as an "expert at absorbing and abstracting information" about Northern Ireland. *Boston Globe* contributor Shaun O'Connell wrote that Conroy "articulates the divided mind and sad heart of this walled-in community, illustrates its violence and dramatizes its resilience." Jamie Dettmer, reviewing the book for the London *Times,* described it as "a sensitive and perceptive chronicle," and recommended it to "anyone who is interested in understanding the problems in Northern Ireland." Likewise, Martin F. Nolan, in his assessment for the *New York Times Book Review,* lauded *Belfast Diary* as "a well-written, sympathetic and clear-eyed view" of Northern Ireland.

Ten years' worth of research all over the globe yielded *Unspeakable Acts, Ordinary People: The Dynamics of Torture,* which Tom McGrath in *U.S. Catholic* called "a compelling and disturbing new book." In writing *Unspeakable Acts,* Conroy studied torture the world over, focusing mostly on those acts of torture conducted under liberal democracies rather than on the more widely recognized instances of torture under totalitarian or authoritarian regimes. The book resulted from his work with the *Chicago Reader,* when he learned about an appalling case of police brutality, and along the way he began to collect stories of torture conducted by the British in Northern Ireland, and by Israeli soldiers against Palestinians.

Though his focus is on the acts of cruelty committed by states that generally maintain the rule of law—there is little about North Korea, Cuba, or Iraq in *Unspeakable Acts*—Conroy's purpose is not to excoriate the West. His aim, rather, is to show that torture is endemic to the human condition. Wrote David Bosco in the *New York Times Book Review,* "Conroy wants to do more than bear witness. He punctuates his reportorial chapters with essays on the history and psychology of torture. . . . The famous Stanley Milgram experiments—in which a disturbing number of test subjects willingly administered what they thought were painful electric shocks to others—are a key exhibit. Perhaps because so many people can be brutal, Conroy has trouble mustering repugnance for the actual torturers he meets. Almost ruefully, he admits that 'I never met the monster I anticipated.' Instead, he sees the monster in all of us."

Unspeakable Acts, according to Ann Collette in *Book,* is a "clear, concise and, at times (due to stomach-turning details) appalling-to-read work." In the book, Anne-Marie Cusac wrote in the *Progressive,* Conroy "manages to comprehend a phenomenon many of us find incomprehensible." She lauded him for his "intellectual honesty and unflinching humanity," revealed in observations such as this one, from the book: "When most people imagine torture, they imagine themselves the victim. The perpetrator appears as a monster—someone inhuman, uncivilized, a sadist, most likely male, foreign in accent, diabolical in manner. Yet there is more than ample evidence that most torturers are normal people, that most of us could be the barbarian of our dreams as easily as we could be the victim, and that for many perpetrators, torture is a job and nothing more."

BIOGRAPHICAL AND CRITICAL SOURCES:

PERIODICALS

Book, July-August, 2000, Ann Collette, review of *Unspeakable Acts, Ordinary People: The Dynamics of Torture,* pp. 80-81.

Booklist, March 15, 2000, Joe Collins, review of *Unspeakable Acts, Ordinary People,* p. 1297.

Boston Globe, November 1, 1987, Shaun O'Connell, review of *Belfast Diary: War As a Way of Life,* p. A16.

Chicago Tribune, March 22, 1988, review of *Belfast Diary.*

Human Rights Review, April-June, 2001, Adam Jones, review of *Unspeakable Acts, Ordinary People,* pp. 165-69.

Library Journal, March 15, 2000, Tim Delaney, review of *Unspeakable Acts, Ordinary People,* p. 108.

Los Angeles Times Book Review, January 3, 1988, review of *Belfast Diary,* p. 12.

New York Times Book Review, December 20, 1987, review of *Belfast Diary,* p. 14; October 8, 1995, review of *Belfast Diary,* p. 40; March 19, 2000, David Bosco, review of *Unspeakable Acts, Ordinary People.*

Progressive, July, 2000, Jodi Vander Molen, review of *Unspeakable Acts, Ordinary People,* p. 44; January, 2001, Anne-Marie Cusac, review of *Unspeakable Acts, Ordinary People,* p. 37.

Publishers Weekly, February 14, 2000, review of *Unspeakable Acts, Ordinary People,* p. 184.

Sunday Times (London), February 14, 1988, Sally Belfrage, review of *Belfast Diary,* p. 12.

Times (London), April 22, 1989, review of *Belfast Diary.*

Tribune Books (Chicago), October 11, 1987, review of *Belfast Diary,* p. 7.

U.S. Catholic, November, 2000, Tom McGrath, review of *Unspeakable Acts, Ordinary People,* p. 54.*

*   *   *

CONSTANTINE, David (John) 1944-

PERSONAL: Born March 4, 1944, in Salford, Lancashire, England; son of Bernard Constantine (a civil servant) and Bertha (Gleave) Constantine; married Helen Frances Best (a teacher), July 9, 1966; children: Mary-Ann, Simon. *Education:* Wadham College, B.A. (modern languages), 1966, D.Phil, 1971. *Politics:* Left.

ADDRESSES: Home—1 Hill Top Rd., Oxford OX4 1PB, England. *Office*—Queen's College, Oxford University, Oxford OX1 4AW, England.

CAREER: Writer, cultural historian, translator, and literary critic. University of Durham, Durham, England, 1969-81, began as lecturer, became senior lecturer in German; Queen's College, Oxford, tutorial fellow in German and university lecturer, 1981-2000.

AWARDS, HONORS: Alice Hunt Bartlett Award, Poetry Society (London, England), 1984, for *Watching for Dolphins;* received Anglo-Hellenic League's Runciman Prize from Book Trust (England) for *Early Greek Travellers and the Hellenic Ideal;* Southern Arts Literature Prize from Southern Arts Association for *Davies;* Robertson Prize and European Poetry Translation Prize for *Hoelderlin; Something for the Ghosts* was shortlisted for the Whitbread Prize.

WRITINGS:

(Editor) *German Short Stories 2,* Penguin (New York, NY), 1976.

The Significance of Locality in the Poetry of Friedrich Hoelderlin, Modern Humanities Research Association (London, England), 1979.

Early Greek Travellers and the Hellenic Ideal, Cambridge University Press (Cambridge, MA), 1984.

Davies (novel), Bloodaxe Books (Newcastle upon Tyne, England), 1985.

Back at the Spike (short stories), Ryburn Publishing (Keele, Staffordshire), 1994.

(Editor, with Hermione Lee and Bernard O'Donoghue) *Oxford Poets 2000: An Anthology,* Carcanet (Manchester, England), 2000.

POETRY

A Brightness to Cast Shadows (includes "In Memoriam 8571 Private J. W. Gleave"), Bloodaxe Books (Newcastle upon Tyne , England), 1980.

Watching for Dolphins (includes title poem, "Hymns," and "Islands"), Bloodaxe Books (Newcastle upon Tyne, England), 1983.

(With Noel Connor, Barry Hirst, and Rodney Pybus) *Talitha Cumi,* Bloodaxe Books (Newcastle upon Tyne, England), 1983.

Mappa Mundi, Five Seasons Press (Hereford), 1984.

Madder, Bloodaxe Books (Newcastle upon Tyne, England), 1987.

Selected Poems, Bloodaxe (Newcastle upon Tyne, England), 1991.

Caspar Hauser: A Poem in Nine Cantos, Bloodaxe Books (Newcastle upon Tyne, England), 1994.

The Pelt of Wasps, Bloodaxe (Newcastle upon Tyne, England), 1998.

Something for the Ghosts, Bloodaxe Books (Tarset, Northumberland), 2002.

Also contributor to *Ten North-East Poets,* edited by Neil Astley, Bloodaxe Books, 1980.

BIOGRAPHY

Hoelderlin, Oxford University Press (New York, NY), 1988.

Friedrich Hoelderlin, Beck Publishing (Munich, Germany), 1992.

Fields of Fire: A Life of Sir William Hamilton, Weidenfeld & Nicolson (London, England), 2001.

TRANSLATOR

(With wife, Helen Frances Constantine, from French) Henry Michaux, *Spaced, Displaced: Deplacements Degagements,* Bloodaxe (Newcastle upon Tyne, England), 1992.

(With Mark Treharne, from French) Philippe Jaccottet, *Under Clouded Skies,* Bloodaxe Books (Newcastle upon Tyne, England), 1994.

(From German) Johann Wolfgang von Goethe, *Elective Affinities,* Oxford University Press (Oxford, England), 1994.

(From German) *Selected Writings: Heinrich von Kleist,* Everyman Classic Library, 1999.

Selected Poems of Friedrich Hoelderlin, Bloodaxe (Newcastle upon Tyne, England), 1996.

(From German) *Holderlin's Sophocles: Oedipus & Antigone,* Bloodaxe (Tarset, Northumberland), 2001.

Also translator of Hans Magnus Enzenberger's *Lighter than Air,* 2002.

Former coeditor of *Argo* (literary magazine); literary editor of *Oxford.* Contributor of short stories to periodicals, including *Stand, Critical Quarterly, Iron* and *London.*

WORK IN PROGRESS: Working on a translation of Goethe's *Faust,* for Penguin Classics.

SIDELIGHTS: David Constantine is an acclaimed British poet and author, whose collections of verse include *A Brightness to Cast Shadows* and the award-winning *Watching for Dolphins.* He is a scholar of seventeenth- and eighteenth-century Greece, as reflected by his *Early Greek Travellers and the Hellenic Ideal.* Constantine has also been recognized as an authority on the early nineteenth-century German poet Friedrich Hoelderlin.

The Significance of Locality in the Poetry of Friedrich Hoelderlin was Constantine's graduate thesis and his first published work. It garnered the young scholar praise from critic Ronald Grey in the *Times Literary Supplement,* who found that, despite the restrictions imposed by the nature of the thesis, "David Constantine's modest study . . . reveals a latent talent for criticism and appreciation."

In his next critical work, Constantine shifts his emphasis from German literature to a more classical subject. *Early Greek Travellers and the Hellenic Ideal* was published in 1984 and examined what William St. Clair referred to in the *Times Literary Supplement* as "the course of Europe's discovery of Greece in the seventeenth and eighteenth centuries." Prior to that time, European travelers desirous of exploring classical antiquities confined their explorations to Rome and the other major cities of Italy. As the title implies, the book discusses accounts of early European tourists in Greece, including those who felt they had discovered customs among the Greek people that dated back to ancient times, many of whom were so steeped in classical tradition that they found the reality of Greece a disappointment. St. Clair concluded that in *Early Greek Travellers and the Hellenic Ideal,* Constantine penned an "excellent study."

Aside from *Early Greek Travellers and the Hellenic Ideal,* Constantine concentrated on his poetry during the early 1980s. His poems often combine the use of classical subjects and models with more modern topics. Mary Kinzie explained in the *American Poetry Review* that "what is remarkable about the poetry of David Constantine is that he seems to have the words for any situation, although he has as yet used very few of them. His poems keep enough in reserve that they need not always incline at the same angle, nor come down with the same flourish at the same speed in the same spot every time."

A Brightness to Cast Shadows is Constantine's first book-length collection of poems. "In Memoriam 8571 Private J. W. Gleave," one of the more noted works in the collection, is a sequence of nine poems concerned with Constantine's maternal grandfather who perished without a trace during World War I. It centers on how his grandmother over the years came to terms with the loss of her husband. Commenting on this sequence of poems in the *Times Literary Supplement,* Roger Garfitt found the work to be "not so much a raid on the inarticulate as a persistent stalking of the incomprehensible." While less impressed with the book's last group of poems, calling them "a series of portraits of the socially deprived," Garfitt lauded Constantine's first two love poems and his overall sense of classicism, finding that the poet "adheres to that severe canon of style which teaches that poetry, to be of enduring excellence, must be unostentatious in its effects."

Constantine's second volume of poetry, *Watching for Dolphins,* earned him the Alice Hunt Bartlett Prize. With the work, Constantine continued to gain attention for his classicality. As Michael Hofmann stated in a *Times Literary Supplement* review, "the 'classical mastery' achieved by Constantine . . . entails not only a classical manner and choice of subjects, but also an original creative impulse whose nature is genuinely un-modern, if not anti-modern." In addition to the segment "Hymns" (a translation from Ancient Greek), which is made up of individual poems on figures from classical mythology such as Aphrodite and Demeter, *Watching for Dolphins* includes the title poem—another Ancient Greek translation—which juxtaposes the classical conceit of waiting for dolphins to accompany one's ship, but where, as Kinzie relayed, "the dolphins alas never do come and the sacred charm of their images fades against a horizon of tankers and pollution and guilt—the skyline of unworthiness." The volume also contains a segment titled "Islands," which tells of a couple at sea in search of their daughter, who sight her on a small island as she is about to be drawn into the water by the tide. Commenting on *Watching for Dolphins,* Kinzie concluded that "Constantine's poems continue to repay close scrutiny, becoming richer with each reading, more effortlessly layered."

Madder, Constantine's 1987 collection of poems, takes its name from the root of the Eurasian madder, used to produce a moderate to deep red dye. *Times Literary Supplement* contributor Mark Ford declared that "the poems in *Madder* are written with an intensity his earlier, remoter work only obliquely aspires to." While Constantine in *Madder* draws upon classical subjects and motifs, Ford noted that "poems here evoke the Nazi death-camps, Russian political imprisonments, Vietnam, [the events surrounding the atomic bombing of] Nagasaki and Hiroshima, the El Salvador death squads."

In 1988, Constantine returned to the subject of Friedrich Hoelderlin, publishing a biography and critical introduction to the work of the German poet. As with Constantine's poems, his academic work continues to be well received. Theodore Ziolkowski of the *Times Literary Supplement,* praised Constantine's even-handed treatment of Hoelderlin, when considering that extreme left- and right-wing political camps, and existentialist and deconstructionist philosophical schools, have each co-opted his writings to suit their respective ideologies. Hoelderlin's work was, for example, adapted by the Nazi government in Germany in which, as Ziolkowski observed, "theorists of National Socialism co-opted him as a forerunner of the *voelkisch* [nationalistic] mentality." But, Ziolkowski continued, "Constantine picks his way through the

ideological extremes with knowledge and good sense, equally wary of silly theories regarding Hoelderlin's madness or politics and of the 'acquisitive reading' that characterizes the various partisan schools of interpretation." The critic completed his assessment by declaring that "Constantine . . . has now given us a readable and reliable 'critical introduction' to the works [of Hoelderlin] based on an understanding of the life." Four years after producing 1988's *Hoelderlin,* Constantine published another volume under the same title. This publication, written in German, introduces Hoelderlin's life and works.

An award-winning translator, Constantine has produced several acclaimed books. His translation of Johann Wolfgang von Goethe's *Die Wahlverwandtschaften,* which Constantine translated as *Elective Affinities* (1994), is considered to be one of Goethe's most unapproachable novels. Reviewer Nicholas Boyle of the *Journal of European Studies* explained that the story is filled with "such Romantic baggage as animal magnetism, landscape symbolism . . . medieval revivalism, Fate, coincidence, and miracle-stories." The characters speak through stilted conversation, and Boyle described the narrator as "knowing" but "aloof." Constantine warns readers in his introductory comments that Goethe's voice here is racked with "oppressive rigidity and unnaturalness," Still, Boyle commended Constantine for making the reader's effort to get through the novel well worth the time. Boyle referred to Constantine's translation as an "outstandingly accurate and beautiful version."

Constantine is also a noted biographer. Prior to *Fields of Fire: A Life of Sir William Hamilton,* Hamilton had, unfortunately, been best remembered for the indiscretions of his wife, Emma. She was a beautiful but poverty-stricken young woman, who became a mistress of the great British naval hero Vice Admiral Lord Nelson. Due to the scandalous nature of the affair, Hamilton's own scholarly achievements went largely ignored. Constantine's biography is an attempt to rectify this. During the excavation of Pompeii and Herculaneum, Hamilton collected a number of ancient vases and compiled an illustrated book of engravings depicting them. As a result, British manufacturers began producing replicas of the beautiful vases, and the British Museum ultimately purchased Hamilton's entire collection.

Fields of Fire: A Life of Sir William Hamilton, according to Aileen Reid of the London *Sunday Telegraph,* is

CONTEMPORARY AUTHORS • New Revision Series, Volume 120

an excellent book that demonstrates that the more popular view of Sir William (as a "dumb cuckold") has been a misrepresentation. Another reviewer, Miranda Seymour for the London *Sunday Times,* called the book an "excellent and sometimes scintillating biography."

BIOGRAPHICAL AND CRITICAL SOURCES:

BOOKS

Dictionary of Literary Biography, Volume 40: *Poets of Great Britain and Ireland since 1960,* Gale (Detroit, MI), 1985.

PERIODICALS

American Poetry Review, September, 1984, pp. 45-47.

Economist (UK), March 24, 2001, Kate Grimond, review of *Field of Fire: A Life of Sir William Hamilton,* pp. 122-23.

Journal of European Studies, December 1994, Volume 24, number 4, Nicholas Boyle, review of *Elective Affinities: A Novel,* pp. 411-13.

Library Journal, March 1, 2000, Volume 125, number 4, Ali Houissa, review of *Selected Writings: Heinrich von Kleist,* p. 90.

Sunday Telegraph (London, England), March 25, 2001, Aileen Reid, "The Other Man: Aileen Reid Enjoys a Life of William Hamilton, the Husband of Nelson's Mistress," p. NA.

Sunday Times (London, England), March 11, 2001, Miranda Seymour, "The Man Who Was Cuckolded by Nelson," p. 34.

Times Literary Supplement, January 11, 1980, p. 45; March 13, 1981, p. 286; November 18, 1983, p. 1272; October 12, 1984, p. 1148; May 27, 1988, p. 596; October 7, 1988, pp. 1106-07; January 27, 1995, Malcolm Bowie, review of *Spaced, Displaced: Deplacements, Degagements,* pp. 11-12, Malcolm Bowie, review of *Under Clouded Skies,* pp. 11-12; March 3, 1995, No. 4796, Lachlan MacKinnon, review of *Caspar Hauser: A Poem in Nine Cantos,* p. 24; April 6, 2001, No. 5114, L. G. Mitchell, review of *Fields of Fire: A Life of Sir William Hamilton,* p. 27.

COPE, Wendy (Mary) 1945-

PERSONAL: Born July 21, 1945, in Erith, Kent, England; daughter of Fred Stanley (a company director) and Alice Mary (a company director; maiden name, Hand) Cope; partner of Lachlan Mackinnon (a poet and writer) since 1993. *Education:* St. Hilda's College, Oxford, B.A., 1966; Westminster College of Education, Oxford, Dip.Ed. (diploma in education), 1967. *Hobbies and other interests:* Music, playing piano and guitar.

ADDRESSES: Home—London, England. *Office*—c/o Faber & Faber, 3 Queen Sq., London WC1N 3AU, England. *Agent*—Pat Kavanagh, Peters, Fraser and Dunlop, Drury House, 34-43 Russell Street, London WC2B 5HA, England.

CAREER: Portway Junior School, London, England, teacher, 1967-69; Keyworth Junior School, London, teacher, 1969-73; Cobourg Junior School, London, teacher, 1973-81, deputy headmaster, 1980-81; *Contact* (a newspaper), arts and reviews editor, 1982-84; Brindishe Primary School, London, music teacher, 1984-86; freelance writer, 1986—; *Spectator,* London, television columnist, 1986-90. Conducted readings in Amman, Jordan, at the invitation of the British Council, 2000.

AWARDS, HONORS: Cholmondeley Award for poetry, 1987; fellow of the Royal Society of Literature, 1992; Michael Braude Award, American Academy of Arts and Letters, 1995; shortlisted for Whitbread Poetry Award, 2002, for *If I Don't Know.*

WRITINGS:

Across the City, Priapus Press (Berkhamsted, England), 1980.

Shall I Call Thee Bard? A Portrait of Jason Strugnell (radio drama), British Broadcasting Corporation (BBC) Radio 3 (London, England), 1982.

Hope and the Forty-two, Other Branch Readings (Leamington Spa, England), 1984.

Making Cocoa for Kingsley Amis (poems), Faber & Faber (Boston, MA), 1986.

Poem from a Colour Chart of House Paints, Priapus Press (Berkhamsted, England), 1987.

Does She Like Word-Games? (poems), Anvil Press Poetry (London, England), 1988.

Men and Their Boring Arguments (poems), Wykeham Press (Winchester, England), 1988.

Twiddling Your Thumbs: Hand Rhymes (for children), illustrated by Sally Kindberg, Faber & Faber (Boston, MA), 1988.

The River Girl (poem), illustrations by Nicholas Garland, Faber & Faber (Boston, MA), 1991.

Serious Concerns (poems), Faber & Faber (Boston, MA), 1992.

The Squirrel and the Crow, illustrated by John Vernon Lord, Clarion Publishing (Alton, England), 1994.

Being Boring, Aralia Press (West Chester, PA), 1998.

If I Don't Know, Faber (Boston, MA), 2001.

EDITOR

Is That the New Moon?: Poems by Women Poets, illustrations by Christine Roche, Lions (London, England), 1989.

The Orchard Book of Funny Poems (anthology for children), illustrated by Amanda Vesey, Orchard Books (London, England), 1993.

The Funny Side: 101 Humorous Poems, Faber & Faber (London, England), 1998.

The Faber Book of Bedtime Stories, Faber & Faber (London, England), 1999.

Heaven on Earth: 101 Happy Poems, Faber & Faber (London, England), 2001.

MUSICAL COLLABORATIONS

(With Colin Matthews) *Strugnell's Haiku: For Voice and Piano,* Faber Music (London, England), 1990.

(With Roderik de Man) *5 Songs on Poems by Wendy Cope: For Mezzo-Soprano and Piano,* Donemus (Amsterdam, Holland), 1990.

(With Martin Read) *The Christmas Life,* Banks Music (York, England), 1999, reprinted with coauthor Roxanne Panufnik, Universal Edition (Vienna), 2002.

Has recorded several audiocassette versions of her work, including *Two Cures for Love: A Collection of Poems Introduced and Read by the Poet,* Faber & Faber Audio Poetry (London, England), 1994; (with

Samantha Bond and Tim Pigott-Smith) *The Funny Side: 101 Humorous Poems,* Penguin Audiobooks (London, England), 1998.

Contributor to anthologies, including *Spring Offensive,* Star Wheel Press (Hitchin, England), 1981; *Poetry Introduction 5,* Faber & Faber (Boston, MA), 1982; *Making for the Open,* Chatto & Windus (London, England); *The Faber Book of Twentieth Century Women's Poetry,* edited by Fleur Adcock, Faber & Faber (Boston, MA); *Faber Book of Parodies* (Boston, MA), and *The Penguin Book of Limericks,* Penguin (New York, NY). Contributor of poems and book reviews to periodicals, including *Times Literary Supplement, Observer, New Statesman,* and *London Review of Books;* contributor of poems to radio programs, including *Poetry Now,* BBC Radio 3, *Rollercoaster,* BBC Radio 4, and *Pick of the Week,* BBC Radio 4.

SIDELIGHTS: British poet Wendy Cope is the author of *Making Cocoa for Kingsley Amis,* a collection of poems that includes several parodies and other literary jokes. The title is explained in the first poem, which reads: "It was a dream I had last week / And some kind of record seemed vital. I knew it wouldn't be much of a poem, / But I loved the title." In other pieces, Cope parodies such poets as T.S. Eliot, Philip Larkin, and Ted Hughes. Cope's imitations reveal an irreverent attitude toward modernist poetry, lightly veiled beneath the guise of good clean fun. The parodies are attributed to Jason Strugnell, a character created by Cope and introduced in a British Broadcasting Corporation (BBC) radio program in 1982. An ambitious but inferior poet, Strugnell continually finds himself imitating major contemporary voices, and the results are always entertaining. Other selections in the volume use traditional poetic forms, such as the sonnet and the villanelle, to express a view of love that is both sincere and satirical.

Critical response to *Making Cocoa for Kingsley Amis* was generally favorable. Robert Nye, writing in the London *Times,* referred to Cope as "a writer of very stylish and clever light verse which is a great pleasure to read." Although *Times Literary Supplement* contributor Bernard O'Donoghue found the quality of the writing somewhat lacking, he referred to the work as an "amusing book, which you can read from cover to cover, tum-ti-tum, in a very pleasant hour."

In 1991 Cope published *The River Girl,* a single long narrative poem that had been commissioned by a marionette company, which eventually performed it on a theater barge. The tale explores a love affair between a mortal and an immortal being. John Didde, a young poet who spends his time gazing out at the river, encounters Isis, the daughter of the river king, Father Thames. Isis serves as John's muse; he immediately begins to spout glorious poetry, and he and Isis fall in love at first sight. Father Thames is distressed that his daughter has fallen in love with a poet, but he does not forbid her to associate with John. John and Isis marry, and John's book is accepted by a major publisher, Tite and Snobbo. He begins to attract a following, and his fans shower him with praise, which goes straight to his head. His egotism causes him to neglect his wife, who changes first into a bird and then into a fish as she leaves him to return to her father. George Szirtes, writing in the *Times Literary Supplement,* lauded the poem's "delicate balance between the affairs of this world and the world of under the river," and called *The River Girl* "a well-written, entertaining story with a great deal of charm."

Cope's 1992 work, *Serious Concerns,* is a volume of poetry similar to *Making Cocoa for Kingsley Amis,* prompting *Times Saturday Review* contributor Robert Nye to predict that it is "likely to please the same audience all over again." The book includes parodies by Jason Strugnell as well as poems that play directly on the lives of literary figures. Cope also includes a number of romantic pieces that mingle humor with the sadness of loss and rejection. Although the subject of *Serious Concerns* is men, Nye noted that the poet herself is usually the butt of the jokes.

Cope told *CA:* "I dislike the term 'light verse' because it is used as a way of dismissing poets who allow humor into their work. I believe that a humorous poem can also be 'serious'—i.e., deeply felt and saying something that matters.

"Although it includes a few happy poems, I think my second full-length collection, *Serious Concerns,* is a bleak book. A key poem is 'Some More Light Verse.' I see this as a poem about feeling suicidal, but managing to see the funny side, and therefore being able to carry on. I would like this poem, and the whole book, to be seen in the context of the high suicide rate of an earlier generation of poets. If we don't want to go down that road, poets of my generation have to find a different approach."

"Cope's life has not been easy," wrote Emma Brockes in the *Guardian,* "running on loneliness and depression and an anxiety which, although she is more con-

tent these days, reveals itself in a certain over-scrupulous primness of manner." Yet Cope was unquestionably happier, as revealed in *If I Didn't Know,* her first collection in nine years. The book showed a different side of her, reflective of changes in her personal life: having found fulfillment in a relationship with poet and writer Lachlan Mackinnon, she experienced what Siân Hughes in the *Times Literary Supplement* characterized as "a shift of subject matter from the vicissitudes of the pursuit of love, to the vulnerability of happiness."

Adam Newey in the *New Statesman* called *If I Didn't Know* "a patchy book," but Diana Hendry in the *Spectator* wrote that "I'm happy that Wendy's found happiness and gardens and possibly the man of her dreams; that the exceedingly witty despair that fueled the poems of *Serious Concerns* has gone and that, as she writes in 'Being Boring,' 'A happier cabbage you never did see.'" Hendry cited as her favorite poem from the collection "Present," in which Cope remembers the inscription "Psalm 98" on a confirmation present given to her by her grandmother or "Nanna" when she was a little girl. Thirty-five years later, she hears the psalm, and apostrophizes her grandmother: "At last I pay attention. // to the words she chose. / O sing unto the Lord / a new song. Nanna, / it is just what I wanted." Concluded Hendry, "Lots of new songs here. And for Cope fans, still plenty of funny poems—some of them even about men."

Hughes referred to "the central question of the collection—where to find a poetic language with which to chart slow growth." Her celebration of joy "is a territory not so thoroughly mapped in verse as that of heartbreak and confusion," Hughes noted. Cope herself has expressed the opinion that there is something deeply meaningful, and far from frivolous, at the heart of humor: "It annoys me that funny poems are not expected to be serious," she told the *Star,* a Jordanian paper, while in that country for a series of readings. "I believe that a humorous poem can also be serious, deeply felt, and [say] something that matters."

BIOGRAPHICAL AND CRITICAL SOURCES:

PERIODICALS

Books for Keeps, March, 1996, review of *The Orchard Book of Funny Poems,* p. 28; January, 1997, review of *The Orchard Book of Funny Poems,* p. 20.

Guardian (Manchester), May 26, 2001, Emma Brockes, "Laughter in the Dark" (profile of Cope), pp. R6-R7.

Independent, June 7, 2001, Thomas Sutcliffe, "The Unromantic Poet of Love," p. S-7.

Junior Bookshelf, December, 1993, review of *The Orchard Book of Funny Poems,* p. 230.

London Review of Books, April 17, 1986, pp. 20-22.

New Statesman, May 2, 1986, pp. 24-25; June 25, 2001, Adam Newey, review of *If I Don't Know,* p. 53; December 17, 2001, Adam Newey, "Lesbians Are Us: 101 Reasons to Read Poetry," pp. 113-14.

New Yorker, May 24, 1993, review of *Serious Concerns,* p. 105.

Observer (London), February 16, 1997, review of *Making Cocoa for Kingsley Amis,* p. 18.

Spectator, August 23, 1997, review of *Serious Concerns,* p. 37; June 16, 2001, Diana Hendry, review of *If I Don't Know,* p. 39.

Times (London), March 13, 1986, Robert Nye, review of *Making Cocoa for Kingsley Amis.*

Times Educational Supplement, November 12, 1993, review of *The Orchard Book of Funny Poems,* p. R-4; October 2, 1998, review of *The Funny Side: 101 Humorous Poems,* p. 11.

Times Literary Supplement, June 6, 1986, p. 616; July 12, 1991, p. 21; September 7, 2001, Siân Hughes, review of *If I Don't Know,* p. 22.

Times Saturday Review, March 14, 1992, Robert Nye, review of *Serious Concerns,* p. 37.

ONLINE

Guardian Unlimited Observer, http://www.observer.co.uk/ (May 18, 2002), Rachel Redford, review of *If I Don't Know.*

The Star: Jordan's Political, Economic, and Cultural Weekly, http://archives.star.arabia.com/ (May 18, 2002), Paula Weik, "British Humor Poet Wendy Cope: I Don't Mean to Be Funny" (June 8, 2000, issue).

*   *   *

CORNWELL, Smith
See SMITH, David (Jeddie)

CRAIG, Gordon A(lexander) 1913-

PERSONAL: Born November 26, 1913, in Glasgow, Scotland; came to the United States in 1925; U.S. citizen by derivation; son of Frank Mansfield (a composer) and Jane (Bissell) Craig; married Phyllis Halcomb (director of a school), June 16, 1939; children: Susan, Deborah Gordon, Martha Jane, Charles Grant. *Education:* Princeton University, B.A., 1936, M.A., 1939, Ph.D., 1941; Balliol College, Oxford, B.Litt., 1938. *Politics:* Democrat. *Religion:* Presbyterian.

ADDRESSES: Home—451 Oak Grove Ave., Menlo Park, CA 94025. *Office*—Department of History, Stanford University, Stanford, CA 94305. *E-mail*—GCRA@Stanford.edu

CAREER: Yale University, New Haven, CT, instructor in history, 1939-41; Princeton University, Princeton, NJ, instructor, 1941-43, assistant professor, 1943-46, associate professor, 1946-50, professor of history, 1950-61; Stanford University, Stanford, CA, professor of history, 1961-69, J. E. Wallace Sterling Professor of Humanities, beginning 1969, currently professor emeritus. Visiting professor, Columbia University, 1947-48, 1949-50; professor of modern history, Free University of Berlin, beginning 1962; fellow, Center for Advanced Study in the Behavioral Sciences, 1956-57; research associate, Office of Strategic Services, 1942; special assistant, U.S. Department of State, 1943; member of social science advisory board, U.S. Arms Control and Disarmament Agency, 1964-70; member of U.S. Air Force Academy advisory council, 1968-71. *Military service:* U.S. Marine Corps Reserve, beginning 1944; now captain (retired).

MEMBER: International Committee of Historical Sciences (vice-president, 1975-85), USAF Academy (advisory board member, 1968-73), American Historical Association (president, 1981), American Academy of Arts and Sciences, American Philosophical Society, American Academy of Political Science, Berlin Historical Commission (honorary member), Phi Beta Kappa (visiting scholar, 1965, 1972; senator, 1980-85).

AWARDS, HONORS: Rhodes scholar, 1936-38; Henry Baxter Adams Prize of American Historical Association, 1956, for *The Politics of the Prussian Army,*

1640-1945; Guggenheim fellow, 1969-70 and 1982-83; D. Litt, Princeton University, 1970; Gold Medal for Nonfiction, Commonwealth Club of California, 1979, and Historikerpreis of Muenster, West Germany, 1980, both for *Germany, 1866-1945; Los Angeles Times* history prize nomination, 1982, and American Book Award nomination in history, 1983, both for *The Germans;* D. Phil, Free University of Berlin, 1983; D. Hum., Ball State University, 1984; Commander's Cross of the Legion of Merit of the Federal Republic of Germany, 1984; Goethe medal, Goethe Inst., Fed. Republic Germany, 1987; Polit. Book prize Ebert Stiftung, 1988; Max Gerlinger prize, Max Gerlinger Foundation, Zurich, 1991; Fellow Ctr. for Advanced Study in the Behavioral Sciences, Bayerische Academy Schonen Kunste, Brit. Academy; honorable fellow, Balliol College, Oxford University, 1989.

WRITINGS:

(Editor, with Edward Meade Earle and Felix Gilbert) *Makers of Modern Strategy: Military Thought from Machiavelli to Hitler,* Princeton University Press (Princeton, NJ), 1943, reprinted, 1971, 1986.

(Editor, with Gilbert) *The Diplomats, 1919-1939,* Princeton University Press (Princeton, NJ), 1953, reprinted, Atheneum, 1971.

The Politics of the Prussian Army, 1640-1945, Clarendon Press (Oxford), 1955.

From Bismarck to Adenauer: Aspects of German Statecraft, Johns Hopkins University Press (Baltimore, MD), 1958, revised edition, Harper (New York), 1965.

Europe since 1815, Holt (New York), 1961, 2nd edition published as *Europe, 1815-1914,* 1968, 3rd edition published as *Europe since 1815,* 1971, alternate edition, 1974.

The Battle of Koeniggraetz: Prussia's Victory over Austria, 1866, Lippincott (Philadelphia, PA), 1964.

War, Politics and Diplomacy: Selected Essays, Praeger (New York), 1966.

(Editor and author of introduction) Herbert Rosinski, *The German Army,* Praeger (New York), 1966.

Military Policy and National Security, Kennikat, 1972.

(Editor and author of introduction) Heinrich Gotthard von Treitschke, *History of Germany in the Nineteenth Century: Selections from the Translations of Eden and Cedar Paul,* University of Chicago Press (Chicago, IL), 1975.

(Editor and author of introduction) *Economic Interest, Militarism and Foreign Policy: Essays by Eckart Kahr,* University of California Press, 1977.

Germany, 1866-1945, Oxford University Press (Oxford), 1978.

The Germans, Putnam (New York), 1982, New American Library (New York), 1983, Meridian (New York), 1991.

(With Alexander L. George) *Force and Statecraft: Diplomatic Problems of Our Times,* Oxford University Press (Oxford), 1983.

The End of Prussia: The Corti Lectures, 1982, University of Wisconsin Press (Madison, WI), 1984.

(Editor, with Felix Gilbert) *The Makers of Modern Strategy: From Machiavelli to the Nuclear Age,* edited by Peter Paret, Princeton University Press (Princeton, NJ), 1986.

The Triumph of Liberalism: Zurich in the Golden Age, 1830-1869, Scribner (New York, NY), 1988.

(With Nicolas Bouvier, Lionel Gossman) *Geneva, Zurich, Basel: History, Culture and National Identity,* Princeton University Press (Princeton, NJ), 1994.

(With Felix Gilbert) *The Diplomats, 1939-1979,* Princeton University Press (Princeton, NJ), 1994.

The Politics of the Unpolitical: German Writers and the Problem of Power, 1770-1871, Oxford University Press (New York, NY), 1995.

Theodor Fontane: Literature and History in the Bismarck Reich, Oxford University Press (New York, NY), 1999.

Politics and Culture in Modern Germany: Essays from The New York Review of Books, Society for the Promotion of Science and Scholarship (Palo Alto, CA), 1999.

Also contributor to *The Second Chance: America and the Peace,* edited by John B. Whitton, 1944, reprinted, Books for Libraries Press, 1971, and *The Quest for a Principle of Authority in Europe, 1715-Present,* 1948; and *Forty Years of the Grundgessetz (Basic Law),* edited by Hartmut Lehmann and Kenneth F. Ledford, in conjunction with the Research Fellows of the German Historical Institute, The Institute (Washington, DC), 1990.

SIDELIGHTS: Few American historians are as well versed in the history, politics, and modern culture of Germany as Gordon A. Craig. As Fritz Stern related in a *New York Times Book Review* article, Craig "first visited Germany as a student in 1935, attracted by the country's cultural richness, appalled by 'the many examples that I encountered of abuse of culture and, indeed, of inhumanity and barbarism.'" In the ensuing decades he became an authoritative interpreter of German political history, known especially for his study of the Prussian army and for *Germany, 1866-1945.*

In *Germany, 1866-1945,* Craig examines a most important period of that country's history: the establishment, rise, and fall of the *Reich,* beginning with the Bismarckian empire and ending with Germany's surrender in World War II. The period was characterized by a devotion to the militia and authority in general; it was also during that time that some of Germany's most distinguished literature was published. While *New York Times Book Review* contributor H. R. Trevor-Roper described Craig's book as "somewhat austere," he also cited "excellent chapters on the Weimar experiment; [the author] is particularly good on Gustav Stresemann, whose patient and successful foreign policy was frustrated by the economic and political weakness of the Republic; and he recognizes and illustrates the real political genius that enabled Hitler to re-create, out of that weakness, a new structure of authoritarian power even more formidable, because it was less conservative than the old."

New Republic reviewer Charles Maier found "individual judgments sensible and sound" in *Germany, 1866-1945,* adding, "Without being strident or anti-German as such, [the author] is as critical in his views of the 19th-century governing system as even the most acerbic German historians of the Empire. Craig's Germany enforced conformity, suppressed socialist dissent, had an egregious record on women's rights even in an epoch where no society had a good one; it encouraged lickspittle subordination to military display and bureaucratic authority. . . . Finally, Craig does not spare the German resistance to Hitler: honoring its bravery, he is frank about its often romantic and conservative objectives. He also reminds us how little of it there was."

In a companion book, *The Germans,* Craig presents a more contemporary view of Germany against a historical backdrop. "His method is to take a subject— religion, say—and go as far back as necessary to explain recent developments and the position of the German churches today," according to a *New Yorker* critic. Craig deals not only with religion, but with soldiers, women, "and other modern German themes," said Amos Perlmutter in a *New Republic* piece. "The section on 'Berlin: Athens on the Spree and City of Crisis' is nostalgic and evocative, a past-and-present

tour from an expert guide. *The Germans* is freewheeling, surprisingly entertaining for a scholarly book, and extremely eloquent." Stern, in his *New York Times Book Review* article, was likewise impressed: "It is impossible to convey fully the richness of the book. It is a splendid introduction to some of the characteristics of German life, past and present."

More than forty years ago, Craig collaborated with Felix Gilbert on a collection of essays called *The Diplomats, 1919-1939.* In 1994, Craig worked with co-editor Francis Loewenheim to produce a sequel to the original collection. In the first collection, Craig focused on the diplomats of Europe. In the second, *The Diplomats, 1939-1979,* the essays include information on the diplomatic corps from Asia and the Middle East, an element that was missing in the first. In the more recent volume, there is more attention to the political leaders, which signals, according to Arthur M. Schlesinger, Jr., writing for *Foreign Affairs,* "the decline of diplomacy as an autonomous profession." Schlesinger commented that during previous centuries, international relations were overseen primarily by ambassadors "skilled in manipulating balances of power." Schlesinger added that these nineteenth-century and early twentieth-century diplomats were "self-contained. Public opinion was irrelevant. . . ."

That all changed with the rise in democracy. "Ordinary people now felt entitled to a larger share in decisions that might send them out to die," Schlesinger explained. International concerns became a matter of what was right and what was wrong, not what the diplomats themselves decided. The essays in this collection reflect those changes, some of them splendidly so, according to Schlesinger. Mentioning particularly "illuminating" essays, William I. Hitchcock of *The Historian* pointed out five written about non-Western nations, which he found to "constitute the most innovative component of the collection."

In 1999, Craig saw publication of *Theodor Fontane: Literature and History in the Bismarck Reich* and *Politics and Culture in Modern Germany: Essays from the New York Review of Books.* In *Theodor Fontane,* Craig covers much of the life and most of the works of this very famous and very versatile German author. Fontane, born in 1819, wrote poems, ballads, travel pieces, military history, theatre criticism, novels, short stories, and worked as a journalist. Although best known for his novels, two other areas of his writing appear to have gained Craig's interest—that of his travel writing, in which Fontane also included historical accounts for each place he visited, and that of his theatre writing. Fontane's works have not enjoyed a large following in non-German-speaking countries, and his books have been slow to be translated into English. Reflecting on this, Dennis Drabelle of the *Atlantic Monthly* commented, "If Gordon Craig's useful introduction to Fontane's life and works leads to an expansion of this list [of translated works], he will have performed a distinct service for lovers of sophisticated European fiction." A similar sentiment was expressed by Stern, writing for the *New Republic:* "Gordon Craig's book should inspire the same resolve: we should read and reread Fontane—in the few translations that are available—for aesthetic pleasure and historical instruction, and as an indispensable commentary on a still-peaceful Germany with its moral and political dilemmas only partially concealed." Then Stern added, "And for further instruction we should read Craig's historical works as well. They belong together, the affinity holds."

Craig's *Politics and Culture in Modern Germany* covers the period from 1800 to the present. Here, Craig uses specific books written about Germany as a "starting point" for his "own reflections," Stuart Parkes of the *Journal of European Studies* explained. The books that have inspired Craig's thought cover such cultural figures as the authors Heinrich and Thomas Mann, themes about the Third Reich and the German Jewish population, and a discussion about the future of Germany. Parkes concluded, "Most specialists in the fields of German and European Studies will find something new" in this collection; while every reader "will surely admire the style of the writing, not least the elegance of the indirect approach to the topic that is such a characteristic feature of many of the fascinating essays in this collection."

BIOGRAPHICAL AND CRITICAL SOURCES:

PERIODICALS

Atlantic Monthly, October, 2000, Volume 286, number 4, Dennis Drabelle, "The Dickens of Berlin," review of *Theodor Fontane: Literature and History in the Bismarck Reich,* p. 134.

Foreign Affairs, July-August, 1994, Volume 73, number 4, Arthur M. Schlesinger, Jr., review of *The Diplomats, 1939-1979,* pp. 146-51.

Historian, winter 1996, Volume 58, number 2, William I. Hitchcock, review of *The Diplomats, 1939-1979,* pp. 427-28.

Journal of American History, December, 1995, Volume 82, number 3, Douglas Brinkley, review of *The Diplomats, 1939-1979,* p. 1273.

Journal of European Studies, September, 2000, Volume 30, number 3, Stuart Parkes, review of *Politics and Culture in Modern Germany: Essays from The New York Review of Books,* p. 349.

Journal of Modern History, December, 2001, Volume 73, number 4, Henry H. H. Remak, review of *Theodor Fontane: Literature and History in the Bismarck Reich,* pp. 980-83.

London Review of Books, December 13, 2001, Ruth Franklin, "Halfway to Siberia," review of *Theodor Fontane: Literature and History in the Bismarck Reich,* pp. 31-32.

Los Angeles Times Book Review, July 3, 1983.

New Republic, October 7, 1978, February 24, 1982, March 7, 1983; September 8, Volume 195, Scott D. Sagan, review of *The Makers of Modern Strategy: From Machiavelli to the Nuclear Age,* pp. 34-38; March 5, 2001, Fritz Stern, review of *Theodor Fontane: Literature and History in the Bismarck Reich,* p. 37.

New Yorker, September 11, 1978, February 8, 1982.

New York Review of Books, January 25, 1979, May 31, 1984.

New York Times Book Review, January 21, 1979, March 14, 1982; April 13, 1986, John Gooch, review of *The Makers of Modern Strategy: From Machiavelli to the Nuclear Age,* p. 34; June 18, 1989, Raymond Grew, review of *The Triumph of Liberalism: Zurich in the Golden Age, 1830-1869,* p. 15.

Pacific Affairs, fall, 1995, Volume 68, number 3, Donald W. Klein, review of *The Diplomats: 1939-1979,* pp. 412-13.

Publishers Weekly, March 24, 1989, Volume 235, number 12, Genevieve Stuttaford, review of *The Triumph of Liberalism: Zurich in the Golden Age, 1830-1869,* p. 56.

Times Literary Supplement, October 6, 1978; October 5, 1984; April 26, 1996, number 4856, D. J. Enright, review of *The Politics of the Unpolitical: German Writers and the Problem of Power, 1770-1871,* p. 29.

Washington Post Book World, March 20, 1983; May 8, 1983.*

CREWDSON, John (Mark) 1945-

PERSONAL: Born December 15, 1945, in San Francisco, CA; son of Mark Guy (a civil engineer) and Eva Rebecca (Doane) Crewdson; married Prudence Gray Tillotson, September 11, 1969; children: Anders Gray, Oliver McDuff. *Education:* University of California, Berkeley, B.A. (with great distinction; economics), 1970; Queen's College, post-graduate studies in politics, 1971-72.

ADDRESSES: Office—Chicago Tribune, 1325 G St. N.W., Washington, DC 20005. *Agent*—Kathy Robbins, The Robbins Office Inc., 2 Dag Hammarskjold Plaza, 866 Second Ave., 12th Floor, New York, NY 10017.

CAREER: New York Times, reporter in Washington, DC, 1973-77, national correspondent in Houston, TX, 1977-82; *Chicago Tribune,* Chicago, IL, national news editor, 1982-83, metropolitan news editor, 1983-84, West Coast correspondent, 1984-90, senior national correspondent, 1990-96, senior writer, 1996—.

AWARDS, HONORS: Undergraduate Prize in Economics, University of California at Berkeley, 1970; Bronze medallion from Sigma Delta Chi, 1974; James Wright Brown Award, New York Deadline Club, 1976; special achievement award, New York Press Club, 1977; George Polk Memorial Award, Long Island University, NY, for medical reporting, 1977, 1990; Page One award from the New York Newspaper Guild, 1977; Pulitzer Prize for national reporting, 1981, for *New York Times* articles on immigration to the United States; William H. Jones Award, 1990, 1995, 1997; Peter Lisagor Award, Sigma Delta Chi, Chicago Chapter, IL, 1997; Goldberg Award from the New York Deadline Club.

WRITINGS:

NONFICTION

The Tarnished Door: The New Immigrants and the Transformation of America, Times Books (New York), 1983.
By Silence Betrayed: Sexual Abuse of Children in America, Times Books (New York), 1988.

Science Fictions: A Scientific Mystery, a Massive Coverup, and the Dark Legacy of Robert Gallo, Little, Brown (Boston, MA), 2002.

Also author of *Slavery in Texas, Illegal Aliens, Seafood and Coyotes,* 1980. Contributor of articles to periodicals.

SIDELIGHTS: Journalist John Crewdson won a Pulitzer Prize as a *New York Times* reporter for his series of investigative articles on illegal immigration to the United States. Crewdson walked through the Southwestern desert with Mexican border crossers and rode the Gulf Stream to Florida with Cuban immigrants in a rickety boat; he visited dank Chicago sweatshops and lush California produce fields to see how the new arrivals labor; he interviewed U.S. immigration officials and Border Patrol officers to gauge the government's response to the vast army of undocumented workers entering the country each year. Crewdson's reporting exposed the hardship and exploitation many illegal migrants endure and uncovered extensive corruption and mismanagement in the U.S. immigration bureaucracy, prompting the Justice Department to launch its own investigation of immigration procedures.

Crewdson's *Times* reporting forms the empirical core for *The Tarnished Door: The New Immigrants and the Transformation of America* (1983), his controversial and critically praised account of the crisis in current U.S. immigration policy. The author's central conclusion is that the crisis is one of policy, not of immigration per se. While acknowledging that data on illegal immigration is necessarily sketchy, Crewdson cites evidence suggesting that undocumented workers do not take away jobs from Americans; rather, they contribute more to the American economy than they take out. The author writes that most of the undocumented arrivals are unskilled laborers from Mexico, the Caribbean, and Asia who take low-paying, arduous jobs that American workers scorn. According to Crewdson, these immigrants have helped sustain the American produce and garment industries, keeping these and many other goods and services low-priced and competitive. At the same time, undocumented workers tend to contribute proportionately more in taxes while taking less in government benefits than American citizens do. Yet, Crewdson notes, it is these immigrant laborers—rather than the thousands of educated foreign professionals who overstay their visas and *do* compete with American workers—who bear the brunt of popular anti-immigrant sentiment and are rounded up for deportation by the Immigration and Naturalization Service (I.N.S.). Many economists and immigration experts share Crewdson's conclusions, but some critics believe that the author understates immigrants' competition with Americans for menial jobs and their depressive effect on the wage scale.

Low wages are only part of the web of exploitation that ensnares many undocumented workers, according to *The Tarnished Door.* Crewdson writes that the immigrants' "unrelenting fear of attracting the attention of the authorities makes them easy prey for endless numbers of predators—dishonest landlords, gouging merchants, employers who charge them 'hiring fees,' immigration lawyers who take their money and then do nothing." The author also details some shocking crimes committed against immigrants—including extortion, rape, and torture—by Border Patrol officers operating along the Mexican border. These abuses occur in the context of increasing anti-immigrant sentiment among the American people, Crewdson notes, a phenomenon he feels is perhaps attributable to the slowdown in U.S. economic growth and the sheer number of new foreign arrivals in recent years.

Crewdson provides no easy answers to questions of what can, or should, be done about the perceived problem of illegal immigration. He writes that Third World immigrants will continue to be pushed by poverty in their home countries and pulled by the lure of opportunity to the United States, and that it would take a police state to fully control the country's porous borders and rout out aliens. The author quotes former I.N.S. commissioner Leonel Castillo's conclusion that "the only long-range answer is world economic development." But Crewdson argues that U.S. immigration policy might still be administered more efficiently and equitably if realistic targets were to be substituted for chaotic and reactive attempts to stanch the steady flow of people into the United States. Accomplishing this will require thoroughly reforming the I.N.S., which the author excoriates as "the most Kafkaesque labyrinth thus far devised by government" and as "shot through with nepotism, incompetence, corruption, and brutality." At the same time, Crewdson warns, the American people will have to adapt to the cultural and linguistic diversity that the new immigrants bring or risk increasing social conflict.

Critical response to *The Tarnished Door* was highly favorable. Joanne Omang's *Washington Post Book World* assessment, for example, praised the book as "an alarming, engrossing and levelheaded portrait of a critical national issue and of a population undergoing fundamental change." And reviewing *The Tarnished Door* in the *Los Angeles Times Book Review,* Malcolm Boyd wrote, "The sweep of the book is awesome; its fusion of complex themes is undergirded by first rate research and reporting. 'The Tarnished Door' is a splendid example of responsible journalism visiting a subject of massive significance."

Crewdson turned his investigative sights to the pervasive but usually hidden problem of child sexual abuse in his 1988 book, *By Silence Betrayed: Sexual Abuse of Children in America.* The product of two years of research and reporting, Crewdson's work describes some recent sexual abuse cases and discusses current research on the causes and extent of the problem. The author cites a *Los Angeles Times* study suggesting that almost forty million adult Americans were victims of sexual abuse as children and that thirteen million of today's children will be abused. Crewdson notes that abuse rates appear to be roughly the same for all cultural and ethnic groups and that most abusers know the child and do not use force, circumstances that conspire to keep the great majority of cases unreported.

Crewdson believes that the silence surrounding the problem of sexual abuse stems from a societal refusal to listen to children, to read the signs of abuse, or to confront a problem that often strikes at the heart of the family and other close relations of trust. The author speculates that the growing disintegration of the nuclear family and rising social inequality may be some of the factors behind this alarming trend. He also points to the eroticization of children in advertising and popular culture and notes finally that adult sexual attraction to children may have deep psychic roots. In addition, Crewdson offers a detailed analysis of two controversial, widely publicized, and unsuccessful sexual abuse prosecutions to argue that justice often miscarries even for the tiny proportion of cases that end up in court. The author shows how children's testimony is easily undermined by defense lawyers and often disbelieved when contradicted by an adult, factors that Crewdson suspects helped defeat the cases he examines.

Critics noted that although *By Silence Betrayed* offers no simple means of combating this behavior so destructive to youthful emotional health, the book is important "because it should alert parents and legislators to the seriousness of this many-faceted problem," remarked *Washington Post Book World* reviewer Marguerite Kelly. Crewdson has "researched and pulled together what has appeared piecemeal in newspapers and magazines in different parts of the country and enlivened his studies with interviews and first-person accounts by children, parents, lawyers, therapists, judges, police and molesters themselves," summarized Lois Timnick in the *Los Angeles Times Book Review. By Silence Betrayed,* the critic added, "is an excellent overview and introduction to the subject."

Crewdson released the results of another major research project on November 19, 1989, in the *Chicago Tribune.* The lengthy story was an exposé of Robert Gallo, a prominent scientist who was the chief of the tumor-cell biology laboratory at the National Cancer Institute. Gallo had claimed that he was the first to discover a test that could successfully detect the AIDS virus.

However, Crewdson's detailed article demonstrated that Gallo had taken credit for a discovery that had actually been made at the Pasteur Institute in Paris. After the article's publication, a federal investigation of Gallo ensued, and his reputation was tarnished, yet he escaped punishment. In apparent response, an indignant Crewdson wrote *Science Fictions: A Scientific Mystery, a Massive Coverup, and the Dark Legacy of Robert Gallo* (2002). John Horgan of the *New York Times Book Review* remarked, "Crewdson returns with a vengeance to the Gallo affair in more than 600 excruciatingly detailed pages."

Nathaniel C. Comfort of the *American Scientist,* summarized Crewdson's research, explaining that he "conducted interviews, pored over laboratory notes and correspondence, combed government documents, read published accounts and pieced together a scathing portrait of the Gallo affair, one of the most high-profile scandals in the history of recent science." For his efforts, Crewdson has been highly praised. Critics praise his objectivity, thorough research, and accessible writing style as the book's strengths. Despite Crewdson's original *Tribune* article and the more detailed accusations in his subsequent book, Gallo, who is now a professor at the University of Maryland and has since left the National Cancer Institute, continues to receive patent royalties from the AIDS test that he claimed as his own.

Investigating the complexities of the Gallo incident was both time-consuming and confusing. Presenting the material in a meaningful way was a challenge Crewdson was determined to meet. *Library Journal* reviewer Gregg Sapp regarded the book successful in providing a thorough and easy-to-follow account of the events. Although *Washington Monthly* reviewer Phillip J. Longman dreaded making his way through the six hundred-plus pages of technical details, footnotes, and scientific content, he admitted that "about one-third of the way through my forced march across these pages, I started to become captivated. By the end, I could hardly put the book down out of a mounting realization that this was more than a story about human vanity and political corruption. It was a compelling account of how the scientific fictions fostered by Gallo and those who believed his claims led to the deaths of innocents." A *Publishers Weekly* reviewer stated that although the details of this story had been covered previously in Crewdson's news story, "the level of detail and drama here [in the book] is unprecedented." The reviewer, like Longman, ultimately found the book hard to put down. Most critics agreed that Crewdson's narrative skill helped overcome the dry, extended scientific explanations.

BIOGRAPHICAL AND CRITICAL SOURCES:

PERIODICALS

American Scientist, May, 2002, Volume 90, number 3, Nathaniel C. Comfort, "Call Him Ishmael," review of *Science Fictions: A Scientific Mystery, a Massive Coverup, and the Dark Legacy of Robert Gallo,* pp. 268-70.

Booklist, January 1, 2002, Gilbert Taylor, review of *Science Fictions: A Scientific Mystery, a Massive Coverup, and the Dark Legacy of Robert Gallo,* p. 787.

Chicago Tribune, February 1, 1988.

Chicago Tribune Book World, September 25, 1983.

Kirkus Reviews, December 15, 2001, Volume 69, number 24, review of *Science Fictions: A Scientific Mystery, a Massive Coverup, and the Dark Legacy of Robert Gallo,* p. 1732.

Library Journal, March 15, 2002, Volume 127, number 5, Gregg Sapp, review of *Science Fictions: A Scientific Mystery, a Massive Coverup, and the Dark Legacy of Robert Gallo,* p. 104.

Los Angeles Times Book Review, October 2, 1983; January 31, 1988.

New Republic, November 7, 1983.

New York Times, January 5, 1984;

New York Times Book Review, February 7, 1988; March 3, 2002, John Horgan, "Autopsy of a Medical Breakthrough," review of *Science Fictions: A Scientific Mystery, a Massive Coverup, and the Dark Legacy of Robert Gallo, p. 9.*

Publishers Weekly, January 14, 2002, Volume 249, number 2, review of *Science Fictions: A Scientific Mystery, a Massive Coverup, and the Dark Legacy of Robert Gallo,* p. 52.

Washington Monthly, March, 2002, Volume 34, number 3, Phillip J. Longman, review of *Science Fictions: A Scientific Mystery, a Massive Coverup, and the Dark Legacy of Robert Gallo,* pp. 56-57.

Washington Post Book World, November 11, 1983; April 10, 1988.*

*   *   *

CURLEE, Lynn 1947-

PERSONAL: Born October 9, 1947, in NC. *Education:* Attended College of William and Mary, 1965-67; University of North Carolina, B.A., 1969, M.A., 1971.

ADDRESSES: Home and office—P.O. Box 699, Jamesport, NY 11947.

CAREER: Exhibiting gallery artist, 1973—; freelance writer, 1991—.

WRITINGS:

SELF-ILLUSTRATED; FOR CHILDREN

Ships of the Air, Houghton Mifflin (Boston, MA), 1996.

Into the Ice: The Story of Arctic Explorations, Houghton Mifflin (Boston, MA), 1998.

Rushmore, Scholastic (New York, NY), 1999.

Liberty, Scholastic (New York, NY), 2000.

The Brooklyn Bridge, Atheneum (New York, NY), 2001.

Seven Wonders of the Ancient World, Atheneum (New York, NY), 2002.

Capital, Atheneum (New York, NY), 2003.

The Parthenon, Atheneum (New York, NY), 2004.

OTHER

(Illustrator) Dennis Haseley, *Horses with Wings,* HarperCollins (New York, NY), 1993.

SIDELIGHTS: Lynn Curlee is best known for writing and illustrating stunning picture books starring famous landmarks of the American landscape. His first two books, however, celebrated the wonders of early human flight. *Horses with Wings,* an account of a balloon escape from Paris during the Franco-Prussian War written by Dennis Haseley, was illustrated by Curlee with acrylic paintings hailed by *Booklist* contributor Kay Weisman as "stunning." *Ships of the Air,* Curlee's second book but the first that he both wrote and illustrated, continues with the flight motif. It is a brief history of balloon and dirigible crafts. A *Kirkus Reviews* critic found that the book "delights as well as . . . informs." Susan P. Bloom, writing in the *Horn Book* magazine, noted that *Ships of the Air* provides an account of the role hot-air balloons played in Arctic explorations of the 1920s, and perhaps whetted the author's appetite for tales of Arctic explorers. His next book, *Into the Ice: The Story of Arctic Exploration,* supplies "a readable and quite beautiful treatment of Arctic exploration," according to Carolyn Phelan in *Booklist.* Here, Curlee tells the story of human explorers who were compelled to travel to the frozen lands of the far North, and of the people who called that land home. "Curlee's stark acrylic paintings seem particularly sympathetic to his subject matter," remarked Bloom. Relying on a restricted palette of blues, grays, and white, the artist "creates the forbidding and formidable landscape of the North."

Rushmore, a tribute to the making of this famous memorial to United States presidents in South Dakota, is Curlee's first book on significant American architectural sites. John Gutzon de la Mothe Borglum, a sculptor of monumental ego and ambition, undertook the project in the 1920s to transform the Black Hills of South Dakota into a tourist attraction and homage to American presidents Washington, Lincoln, Jefferson, and Theodore Roosevelt. During the nearly two decades of production, workers on the site had to climb the equivalent of a forty-story building in order to get to work each day and the artist's gray and blue acrylic paintings ably provide readers with a sense of the project's scale, reviewers noted. "Curlee conveys the sensitivity in the faces of the giant chiseled sculpture while simultaneously demonstrating a sense of scale," remarked a contributor to *Publishers Weekly.* The text of the book covers the engineering as well as the artistic feat involved in creating the monument, and describes controversies over who ought to be depicted. *Booklist* reviewer Stephanie Zvirin complained that Curlee's paintings of Rushmore sacrifice feeling for accuracy, in their predominantly blue and gray overtones, however: "they make the monument seem cold and remote, rather than a warm, forceful testament to vision, hard work, and national pride." On the other hand, Mary M. Burns, writing in *Horn Book,* found Curlee's renderings of the monument to be more than realistic, "rather, they are an exultant view into the nature of art and, yes, patriotism."

Like *Rushmore, Liberty,* Curlee's next book, showcases a famous American monument through a scientific explanation of the mechanics of bringing the original vision to reality, anecdotes of its creation, and affecting illustrations, which one critic, Alicia Eames, writing in *School Library Journal,* described as "richly hued, stylized acrylic paintings, which are both compellingly dramatic and strikingly static." The Statue of Liberty was the brainchild of French intellectuals and artists, and was brought to fruition with the timely aid of American newspaper magnate Pulitzer, in Curlee's historical overview. Here again, as in the earlier book, an unabashed patriotism infuses the artist's renderings of his subject. "Stunning, stylized portraits of the lady heighten Curlee's lucid, appreciative text," remarked a contributor to the *Horn Book* magazine. Likewise, a contributor to *Publishers Weekly* dubbed *Liberty,* "a reverent, absorbing homage to the world-renowned symbol of American freedom."

Curlee's next American landmark was the Brooklyn Bridge, which upon its completion in 1883 was by far the tallest human-made structure in its surroundings, and was the longest bridge in the world at the time. In his *Brooklyn Bridge,* Curlee details the engineering feats that went into the bridge's construction, but wraps it in the human drama of the Roebling family: John A., who conceived the vast structure but died just as it was begun, his son Washington, who took over the project until ill health forced him into seclusion, and Washington's wife, Emily, who oversaw the day-to-day operation of construction after her husband fell ill. As in his earlier tributes to the Statue of Liberty and Mount Rushmore, *Brooklyn Bridge* features stunning illustrations that work on the emotions of the viewer.

"The sweeping cityscape oil paintings of the bridge during sunset fireworks and glowing in the moonlight illustrate its majesty and pageantry," a contributor to *Publishers Weekly* attested.

The Brooklyn Bridge was once considered by some to be the eighth wonder of the world, and so it is only fitting that Curlee's next book was *Seven Wonders of the World.* The book provides a brief look at what the seven wonders of the ancient world, as deemed by the Greek poet Antipater of Sidon, would probably look like, as all but the Great Pyramid at Giza have long since disappeared. "The expanse of his ambitious subject does not allow the author to delve into the kinds of details allowed by his single-subject volumes, but he certainly whets readers' appetites," concluded a contributor to *Publishers Weekly.* Drawing upon contemporary accounts and modern archeology, Curlee creates a vision of what each might have looked like in its day, as well as an account of its destruction. Although *Booklist* contributor Ilene Cooper noted some flaws in the historical account, "there's no denying that this book is both fascinating and strongly executed," she concluded.

BIOGRAPHICAL AND CRITICAL SOURCES:

PERIODICALS

Booklist, November 15, 1993, Kay Weisman, review of *Horses with Wings,* p. 630-631; September 1, 1996; April, 1998, Carolyn Phelan, review of *Into the Ice,* p. 1316; March 1, 1999, Stephanie Zvirin, review of *Rushmore,* p. 1204; April 15, 2001, Randy Meyer, review of *Brooklyn Bridge,* p. 1548; December 1, 2001, Stephanie Zvirin, review of *Brooklyn Bridge,* p. 658; January 1, 2002, Ilene Cooper, review of *Seven Wonders of the Ancient World,* p. 850; January 1, 2003, Carolyn Phelan, review of *Capital,* p. 880.

Bulletin of the Center for Children's Books, October, 1996, pp. 53-55.

Childhood Education, Jeanie Burnett, review of *Brooklyn Bridge,* p. 171.

Horn Book, November-December, 1996, p. 757; May-June, 1998, Susan P. Bloom, review of *Into the Ice,* p. 357; March, 1999, Mary M. Burns, review of *Rushmore,* p. 221; May, 2000, review of *Liberty,* p. 330; July, 2001, review of *Brooklyn Bridge,* p. 470.

Kirkus Reviews, June 1, 1996, review of *Ships of the Air,* p. 821; January 1, 2002, review of *Seven Wonders of the Ancient World,* p. 43; December 1, 2002, review of *Capital,* p. 1766.

New York Times, December 7, 1998, Christopher Lehmann-Haupt, "Adventuring from a Child's Imagination to the Arctic," review of *Into the Ice.*

New York Times Book Review, May 20, 2001, Sam Swope, "Oz on the Hudson," review of *Brooklyn Bridge,* p. 30.

Publishers Weekly, September 13, 1993, pp. 132-137; February 15, 1999, review of *Rushmore,* p. 107; May 29, 2000, review of *Liberty,* p. 83; May 14, 2001, review of *Brooklyn Bridge,* p. 82; December 24, 2001, review of *Seven Wonders of the Ancient World,* p. 64; November 25, 2002, review of *Capital,* p. 65.

School Library Journal, December, 1993, pp. 88-89; May, 1998, Patricia Manning, review of *Into the Ice,* p. 152; March, 1999, Rosie Peasley, review of *Rushmore,* p. 191; May, 2000, Alicia Eames, review of *Liberty,* p. 180; May, 2001, Susan Lissim, review of *Brooklyn Bridge,* p. 162; March, 2002, Kathleen Baxter, "Castles in the Air: Inspire Readers with Personal Stories of Creative Vision," review of *Brooklyn Bridge,* p. 49; September, 2002, Mary Ann Carcish, review of *Seven Wonders of the Ancient World,* p. 242.*

*   *   *

CURTIS, Michael K. 1942-

PERSONAL: Born November 21, 1942, in Dallas, TX; son of Thomas Lisle and Kent (Adams) Curtis; married Deborah F. Maury (an attorney), September 18, 1983; children: Matthew F. Curtis-Maury. *Education:* University of the South, B.A. (summa cum laude), 1964; University of North Carolina at Chapel Hill, J.D. (with honors), 1969; University of Chicago, M.A., 1990. *Politics:* Democrat. *Religion:* Society of Friends (Quakers). *Hobbies and other interests:* Mediation, psychology, history and legal history, writing poetry.

ADDRESSES: Home—Greensboro, N.C. *Office*—School of Law, Wake Forest University, 3332 Worrell Professional Center, Winston-Salem, NC 27109. *E-mail*—curtismk@law.wfu.edu.

CAREER: Admitted to the Bar of North Carolina, 1969, and the Bar of the U.S. Supreme Court, 1974; North Carolina Supreme Court, Raleigh, law clerk to Chief Justice William H. Bobbitt, 1969-70; Smith, Patterson, Follin, Curtis, James & Harkavy (law firm), Greensboro, NC, partner, 1970-90; Wake Forest University School of Law, Winston-Salem, NC, visiting professor, 1990, associate professor, 1991-94, professor of law, 1994—. Instructor at Guilford College, 1974-77. Chairman of review board, North Carolina Occupational Safety and Health Administration, 1975-85; mediator at Dispute Settlement Center.

MEMBER: American Bar Association, Association of Trial Lawyers of America, North Carolina Bar Association, North Carolina Academy of Trial Lawyers (chairman, 1979-85), North Carolina Civil Liberties Union (cooperating attorney; past president; past representative to board of directors), Greensboro Bar Association, Phi Beta Kappa, Order of Coif.

AWARDS, HONORS: Frank Porter Graham Award, North Carolina Civil Liberties Union, 1985; Excellence in Teaching Award, Student Bar Association, 1997; Joseph Branch teaching award, 1999; Hugh M. Hefner First Amendment Award, Playboy Foundation, and Mayflower Cup Award, North Carolina Society of Mayflower Descendants, both 2001, both for *Free Speech, "The People's Darling Privilege": Crucial Struggles for Freedom of Expression in American History.*

WRITINGS:

No State Shall Abridge: The Fourteenth Amendment and the Bill of Rights, Duke University Press (Durham, NC), 1986.

(Editor, and author of introduction) *The Constitution and the Flag,* two volumes, Garland Publishing (New York, NY), 1993.

Free Speech, "The People's Darling Privilege": Crucial Struggles for Freedom of Expression in American History, Duke University Press (Durham, NC), 2000.

Contributor to books, including *Oxford Companion to the Supreme Court of the United States,* edited by James W. Ely, Jr. and others, Oxford University Press, 1992; *Slavery and the Law,* edited by Paul Finkelman, Madison House, 1996; *Religion and American Law: An Encyclopedia,* edited by Paul Finkelman, Garland

Publishing, 2000. Contributor of articles and reviews to journals and periodicals, including *North Carolina Law Review, UCLA Law Review, Boston College Law Review, Wake Forest Law Review, Northwestern University Law Review, William and Mary Bill of Rights Journal, Ohio State Law Journal, Harvard Journal of Law and Public Policy,* and *Constitutional Commentary.*

SIDELIGHTS: An attorney with twenty years of experience in private practice, Michael K. Curtis is a professor of law at Wake Forest University and a constitutional scholar with particular interest in the issue of free speech.

In his award-winning book, *Free Speech, "The People's Darling Privilege": Crucial Struggles for Freedom of Expression in American History,* Curtis examines the early history of the struggle for free speech in the United States, focusing on three crucial political battles—the controversy over the 1798 Sedition Act involving the right to criticize elected officials; the controversy over anti-slavery speech before the Civil War; and the controversy over anti-war speech during the Civil War. Curtis demonstrates that in each of these cases the free speech issues were decided not in the courts but in Congress, state legislatures, and in public discussion and debate. Curtis tells the stories of these struggles, often drawing upon first-person accounts gleaned from newspapers and records of town meetings. Paul Wenzer, writing in *Perspective on Political Science,* observed, "Curtis does an outstanding job of bringing [the stories] to life. He is to be commended for keeping editorial comments to a minimum and allowing the participants to make his points for him." Appreciating the author's "fresh perspective," Wenzer declared that Curtis "has made an extremely valuable contribution to the literature addressing the history of free speech in America." In his assessment of the book in the *Jewish World Review,* Nat Hentoff commented, "Curtis, as always, is free of legalese; with clarity and deep knowledge, he shows how our freedoms are nourished more insistently by the people than by the courts."

Curtis once told *CA:* "In 1833 the Supreme Court ruled that the protections of the Bill of Rights did not limit states and local governments. The Supreme Court has gradually applied Bill of Rights guarantees to the states and local governments under the Fourteenth Amendment (ratified in 1868). Some scholars have suggested that requiring states and local governments to obey the Bill of Rights was a historical mistake. This claim led me to look again at the history of the Fourteenth Amendment. I have always been interested in the history of liberty."

BIOGRAPHICAL AND CRITICAL SOURCES:

PERIODICALS

American Journal of Legal History, April, 1995, Marlyn Robinson, review of *The Constitution and the Flag,* pp. 233-234.

American Political Science Review, March, 1987, Gary J. Jacobsohn, review of *No State Shall Abridge: The Fourteenth Amendment and the Bill of Rights,* pp. 278-279.

Choice, September, 1993, R. J. Steamer, review of *The Constitution and the Flag,* Volume 1, p. 218; October, 1993, review of *The Constitution and the Flag,* Volume 2, p. 364; May, 2001, D. L. LeMahieu, review of *Free Speech, "The People's Darling Privilege": Crucial Struggles for Freedom of Expression in American History,* p. 1679.

Jewish World Review, December 4, 2000, Nat Hentoff, review of *Free Speech, "The People's Darling Privilege."*

Journal of American History, March, 1988, Glenn Linden, review of *No State Shall Abridge,* pp. 1354-1355.

Library Journal, September 15, 1986, Milton Cantor, review of *No State Shall Abridge,* pp. 96-97.

Perspectives on Political Science, fall, 2001, Paul Wenzer, review of *Free Speech, "The People's Darling Privilege,"* p. 237.

Reviews in American History, March, 1992, review of *No State Shall Abridge,* p. 59.

ONLINE

Wake Forest University School of Law Web site, http://www.law.wfu.edu/ (August 3, 2002).

D

DARTON, Eric 1950-

PERSONAL: Born May 30, 1950, in New York, NY. *Education:* Empire State College of the State University of New York, B.A., 1990; Hunter College of the City University of New York, M.A., 1994.

ADDRESSES: *Agent*—Watkins Loomis Agency, Inc., 133 East 35th St., New York, NY 10016.

CAREER: Writer.

AWARDS, HONORS: Fiction fellow, New York Foundation for the Arts, 1991, Bread Loaf fellowship, 1998.

WRITINGS:

Free City (novel), Norton (New York, NY), 1996.
Divided We Stand: A Biography of New York's World Trade Center (nonfiction), Basic Books (New York, NY), 1999.

Work anthologized in *After the World Trade Center: Rethinking New York City,* edited by Michael Sorkin and Sharon Zukin, Routledge (New York, NY), 2002, and *110 Stories: New York Writes after September 11,* edited by Ulrich Baer, New York University Press (New York, NY), 2002. Contributor to journals and periodicals, including *Metropolis, Culturefront, Designer/Builder, American Letters & Commentary,* and *New England Review.* Short fiction *Radio Tirane* appeared in *Conjunctions,* Volume 17, 1991.

WORK IN PROGRESS: A revised edition of *Divided We Stand.*

SIDELIGHTS: When Eric Darton first published *Divided We Stand: A Biography of New York's World Trade Center* in 1999, Basic Books printed a mere 5,000 copies. Two years later, as reported by Charlotte Abbott in *Publishers Weekly,* an additional 15,000 were in press, and copies were selling as fast as bookstores could stock them. "It became clear to me what had happened," Darton told *Book,* "when a woman who had bought the last copy of my book in the bookstore asked me to sign it. I was confronted with the cover of my own book—and I came close to losing it."

On September 11, 2001, terrorists flew airplanes filled with passengers into the twin towers of the World Trade Center, causing the collapse of the buildings and the deaths of more than three thousand innocent victims. One of the many consequences of this event was a sudden change in the significance of Darton's book.

Before September 11, as initial reviews of the book illustrate, *Divided We Stand* was merely a chronicle of what many architects and others regarded as an eyesore and a political boondoggle. Darton himself summed up this idea in the conclusion of his book, with an eerily prophetic discussion of the Trade Center towers as a living ruin. At that time, the buildings had already suffered one terrorist attack, though a far less devastating one, a 1993 bombing in which seven people were killed. But it was not in a literal sense that Darton considered the buildings as a ruin.

"A structure begins to fall into a state of ruin," he wrote, "when it is no longer supported by the productive relations that created it. . . . In this sense, the World Trade Center came prepackaged as a ruin that has slowly been moving in the direction of becoming a living building. But even in the wake of the [1993] bombing, New Yorkers have never been able to successfully fill [architect Minuro] Yamasaki's twin silos with the kind of psychological investment freely poured into the Empire State Building [or] the Chrysler Building. . . . From an economic standpoint, the trade center—subsidized since its inception—has never functioned, nor was it intended to function, unprotected in the rough-and-tumble real estate market."

Todd Gitlin in the *American Prospect,* reviewing the book in 2000, noted that "Dreams of spiritless rationality were Yamasaki's specialty," and went on to discuss another famous (or rather, infamous) Yamasaki creation, the Pruitt-Igoe public housing project, which won prizes at the time of its construction in St. Louis in 1955. "But it is not famous for that reason," Gitlin went on. "If the name is familiar, that is because it became notorious 17 years later" when it was demolished "because the people who lived there hated it so much. The towers of the World Trade Center were equally abstract sculptures . . . . This is what happened when architects took seriously [French modernist architect] Le Corbusier's cry of 1933: 'Death of the street!'"

When the towers experienced a very different kind of death on September 11, views of the buildings themselves changed dramatically in hindsight, even as Darton's book became vastly more significant than it had been at the time of its publication. Whereas the Trade Center towers had few champions by the end of twentieth century, once they were gone, memories became much more fond. Reviewing Darton's book along with *Twin Towers: The Life of New York City's World Trade Center* by Angus Kress Gillespie, Philip Herter of the *Boston Herald* wrote, "It is hard to read these histories of the World Trade Center as anything but elegies to a certain part of 20th century urban America, and as reminders of the way history can veer into myth in the briefest instant. Author Eric Darton probably never dreamed that *Divided We Stand,* begun as his master's degree thesis on contemporary culture and mass media, would resonate with readers worldwide." Yet even long before the bombing that catapulted the Towers into the status of a vanished na-tional icon, critics recognized the power in Darton's account: according to a *Publishers Weekly* reviewer in 1999, "This is a mesmerizing history of how deep-seated struggles over architectural aspirations, economics, city planning, and the exigencies of a democracy undergird the New York cityscape."

BIOGRAPHICAL AND CRITICAL SOURCES:

PERIODICALS

American Prospect, March 27, 2000, Todd Gitlin, review of *Divided We Stand: A Biography of New York's World Trade Center,* p. 75.
Book, Eric Wetzel, November-December, 2001, "9/11/01 One Writer's Moment of Clarity," p. 15.
Boston Herald, October 7, 2001, Philip Herter, "Authors Capture the Way We Were," p. 71.
Business Week, October 5, 2001, Eric Darton, "The Process of Creating a Ruin" (book excerpt).
Choice, October, 2000, review of *Divided We Stand,* p. 319.
Entertainment Weekly, October 12, 2001, Troy Patterson, "Pair Bonded: Two Authors Look at the Creation of the World Trade Center and How It Forever Changed the Manhattan Skyline," p. 80.
Kirkus Reviews, November 15, 1999, review of *Divided We Stand,* p. 48.
Library Journal, February 1, 2000, David Soltesz, review of *Divided We Stand,* p. 78.
New York Times, September 24, 2001, Richard Bernstein, review of *Divided We Stand,* p. E-6.
Publishers Weekly, November 22, 1999, review of *Divided We Stand,* p. 48; September 24, 2001, Charlotte Abbott, "News," p. 13.

ONLINE

Eric Darton/New York's World Trade Center: A Living Archive, http://ericdarton.net/ (May 18, 2002).
Fractalism, http://www.fractalism.com/ (May 18, 2002), review of *Divided We Stand.*

*   *   *

DAVIE, Michael 1924-

PERSONAL: Born January 15, 1924, in Cranleigh, Surrey, England; son of Russell (a stock broker) and Harriet (Browne) Davie; married Mollie Robin Atherton, November 8, 1954 (divorced, 1975); married Anne

Chisholm (a writer); children: (first marriage) Annabel, Simon, Emma. *Education:* Merton College, Oxford, B.A., 1949.

ADDRESSES: Home—136 Fellows Rd., London NW3, England. *Office*—Observer, 160 Queen Victoria St., London EC4, England.

CAREER: Journalist and writer. *Observer,* London, England, associate editor, beginning 1969; *The Age,* Melbourne, Australia, editor, 1979-81; *The Times of Papua New Guinea,* Papua, founder, 1980; *Military service:* Royal Navy, 1942-46.

AWARDS, HONORS: Yorkshire Post literary award, 1973; nominated for James Tait Black Prize, 1993, for *Lord Beaverbrook: A Life.*

WRITINGS:

LBJ: A Foreign Observer's Viewpoint, Duell, Sloan & Pearce (New York, NY), 1966.
California: The Vanishing Dream, Dodd (New York, NY), 1972.
(Editor) *The Diaries of Evelyn Waugh,* Weidenfeld & Nicolson (London, England), 1976.
The Titanic: The Full Story of a Tragedy, Bodley Head (London, England), 1986, published as *Titanic: The Death and Life of a Legend,* Knopf (New York, NY), 1987.
(Editor, with Simon Davie) *The Faber Book of Cricket,* Faber & Faber (Boston, MA), 1987.
(With wife, Anne Chisholm) *Lord Beaverbrook: A Life,* Knopf (New York, NY), 1993.
Anglo-Australian Attitudes, Secker & Warburg (London, England), 2000.

SIDELIGHTS: Michael Davie has been writing for most of his professional life. He has worked on newspapers in both England and Australia, becoming editor of *The Age* in Melbourne, Australia, and founder of the weekly investigative newspaper *The Times of Papua New Guinea.* Davie has also authored nonfiction books on a variety of subjects, ranging from Lyndon B. Johnson to the Titanic to cricket.

Davie's best-known book may be *Lord Beaverbrook: A Life,* which he coauthored with his wife, Anne Chisholm. Although they were not the first biographers of Lord Beaverbrook, political insider and early media mogul, critics generally agreed that theirs was the most complete and objective study of the man to date. Beaverbrook went from humble beginnings in maritime Canada to being a millionaire who by the 1950s controlled newspapers with a circulation of five million. Along the way, he acquired a multitude of friends and as many, if not more, enemies. His politics, which were freely expressed in his newspapers, were pro-Empire, pro-appeasement where Hitler was concerned, and pro-Soviet Union, yet serious journalists flocked to his papers, ignoring his politics for the chance to work for someone willing to spend a great deal of money to make the best paper he could.

Critical response to *Lord Beaverbrook* was overwhelmingly positive. A *Publishers Weekly* reviewer termed it an "exhaustively researched" book which "candidly describes Beaverbrook's dark side." "A rich, fair, and comprehensive inquiry," declared James D. Startt in *The Historian. American Spectator* contributor Richard Lamb wrote, "Full of . . . intimate anecdotes, this is a wonderful biography. It is detailed, informed, and vivid."

A native Englishman who spent much of his life working in the Australian newspaper industry, Davie has observed firsthand Australians' love-hate relationship with their former parent country. In *Anglo-Australian Attitudes,* he raises questions about the nature of the relationship between the two countries and takes on some Australians' more persistent myths about Great Britain, including the beliefs that British officers sent Australian soldiers to die needlessly at the battle of Gallipoli during the First World War and that the British abandoned Singapore, and thereby Australia, during the Second. He also addresses more benign spats like "Bodyline," a famous cricket match in the 1930s. Though perplexed that an Englishman can spend so many years in Australia and "still be surprised by how Australians feel about the United Kingdom," *Times Literary Supplement* reviewer Ben Ball called the book "insightful and entertaining."

BIOGRAPHICAL AND CRITICAL SOURCES:

PERIODICALS

American Spectator, December, 1987, review of *Titanic: The Death and Life of a Legend,* p. 45; May, 1993, Richard Lamb, review of *Lord Beaverbrook: A Life,* pp. 68-70.

Atlantic, September, 1987, review of *Titanic,* p. 102.

Booklist, June 1, 1987, review of *Titanic,* p. 1478; February 1, 1993, Margaret Flanagan, review of *Lord Beaverbrook,* p. 967.

British Book News, August, 1987, review of *Titanic,* p. 514.

Bulletin with Newsweek, July 18, 2000, Peter Pierce, review of *Anglo-Australian Attitudes,* p. 102.

Business History, April, 1994, Gregory P. Marchildon, review of *Lord Beaverbrook,* pp. 99-100.

Contemporary Review, February, 1993, A. L. Rowse, review of *Lord Beaverbrook,* pp. 106-108.

Europe, September, 1993, Peter Doyle, review of *Lord Beaverbrook,* pp. 44-46.

Guardian Weekly, October 5, 1986, review of *Titanic,* p. 21.

Historian, summer, 1995, James D. Startt, review of *Lord Beaverbrook,* pp. 581-582.

Kirkus Reviews, April 15, 1987, review of *Titanic,* p. 611.

Kliatt Young Adult Paperback Book Guide, April, 1989, review of *Titanic,* p. 59.

Library Journal, July, 1987, John Kenny, review of *Titanic,* p. 75; February 15, 1993, Mary Hemmings, review of *Lord Beaverbrook,* p. 172.

London Review of Books, December 4, 1986, review of *Titanic,* p. 16.

Los Angeles Times Book Review, June 28, 1987, review of *Titanic,* p. 8.

Maclean's, April 5, 1993, Anthony Wilson-Smith, review of *Lord Beaverbrook,* p. 58.

Neiman Reports, spring, 1993, Joe Hall, review of *Lord Beaverbrook,* p. 72.

New Republic, May 10, 1993, David Canadine, review of *Lord Beaverbrook,* pp. 46-49.

New Statesman & Society, Peter Clarke, review of *Lord Beaverbrook,* pp. 42-43.

Newsweek, January 18, 1993, David Gates, review of *Lord Beaverbrook,* pp. 56-57.

New Yorker, August 10, 1987, review of *Titanic,* p. 80; March 1, 1993, Naomi Bliven, review of *Lord Beaverbrook,* pp. 109-114.

Publishers Weekly, May 8, 1987, Genevieve Stuttaford, review of *Titanic,* p. 56; November 30, 1992, review of *Lord Beaverbrook,* p. 44.

Reference and Research Books News, fall, 1987, review of *Titanic,* p. 11.

Saturday Night, December, 1992, Conrad Black, review of *Lord Beaverbrook,* pp. 46-49.

SciTech Book News, September, 1987, review of *Titanic,* p. 2.

Spectator, July 1, 2000, Peter Porter, review of *Anglo-Australian Attitudes,* pp. 28-29.

Times Higher Education Supplement, September 14, 2001, Andrew Mueller, review of *Anglo-Australian Attitudes,* p. 26.

Times Literary Supplement, October 10, 1986, review of *Titanic,* p. 1129; January 5, 2001, Ben Ball, review of *Anglo-Australian Attitudes,* p. 11.

Washington Post Book World, July 19, 1987, review of *Titanic,* p. 5.

West Coast Review of Books, Volume 13, issue 2, 1987, review of *Titanic,* p. 37.

ONLINE

Foreign Correspondent Web site, http://www.abc.net.au/foreign/ (April 25, 2000), Jennifer Byrne, "Interview with Michael Davie."

Guardian Unlimited Books, http://books.guardian.co.uk/travel/ (July 2, 2000), Charles Saumarez Smith, "Upside-down View of Down Under," review of *Anglo-Australian Attitudes.**

*   *   *

DAVIS, Lydia 1947-

PERSONAL: Born 1947, in Northampton, MA; married Alan Cote (a painter); children: two sons. *Education:* Attended Barnard College, graduated 1970.

ADDRESSES: Home—Port Ewen, NY. *Agent*—c/o Author Mail, Picador USA, 175 5th Ave., New York, NY 10010.

CAREER: Translator and author. Currently teaches writing at Milton Avery Graduate School, Bard College.

AWARDS, HONORS: Whiting Writer's Award, Mrs. Giles Whiting Foundation, 1988; Fund for Poetry Award, 1992; French-American Foundation Translation Award, 1993; Guggenheim fellowship; Lannan Literary Award; French Insignia of the Order of Arts and Letters; Ingram Merrill-Foundation Grant for Fiction; National Endowment for the Arts Grant for Translation; finalist, PEN/Hemingway Foundation Award for Fiction for *Break It Down.*

WRITINGS:

The Thirteenth Woman and Other Stories, Living Hand (Berkeley, CA), 1976.

Sketches for a Life of Wassilly, Station Hill Press (Barrytown, NY), 1981.

Story, and Other Stories, The Figures (Berkeley, CA), 1983.

In a House Besieged, Dog Hair Press (West Branch, IA), 1984.

Break It Down (stories; includes "Break It Down," "Safe Love," "Five Signs of Disturbance," and "Therapy"), Farrar, Straus, and Giroux (New York, NY), 1986.

The End of the Story (novel), Farrar, Straus, and Giroux (New York, NY), 1995.

Almost No Memory (stories), Farrar, Straus, and Giroux (New York, NY), 1997.

Blind Date, Chax Press (Tucson, AZ), 1998.

Samuel Johnson Is Indignant: Stories, Picador USA (New York, NY), 2002.

Davis's work has appeared in *Conjunctions, Harper's, Hambone, Antaeus, McSweeney's, Paris Review, Bomb, Grand Street, Sulfur,* and *Doubletake,* and has been included in *Best American Short Stories of 1997* (edited by E. Annie Proulx) and other collections.

Audiocassetes include *Lydia Davis at UCSD, November 4, 1981,* (with Stephen Rodefer) *Poetry Reading, May 20, 1987,* and *Poetry Reading, April 15, 1998,* all released by the University of California, San Diego.

TRANSLATOR

(With Paul Auster) Saul Friedländer and Jean Lacouture, *Arabs and Israelis,* Holmes and Meier (London, England), 1975.

(With Paul Auster) Jean Chesneaux, Jean and Marie-Claire Bergère, *China from the 1911 Revolution to Liberation,* Harvester Press (Hassocks, England), 1977.

Attilio Colombo, and others, *Fantastic Photographs,* Gordon Fraser Gallery (London, England), 1979.

Maurice Blanchot, *The Gaze of Orpheus and Other Literary Essays,* edited with an afterword by P. Adams Sitney, Station Hill (Barrytown, NY), 1982.

Maurice Blanchot, *The Madness of the Day* (fiction), Station Hill (Barrytown, NY), 1982.

Maurice Blanchot, *Death Sentence* (fiction; original title, *L'Arret de Mort*), Station Hill (Barrytown, NY), 1982.

Maurice Blanchot, *When the Time Comes* (fiction), Station Hill (Barrytown, NY), 1986.

Françoise Giroud, *Marie Curie: A Life* (biography), Holmes and Meier (London, England), 1986.

Conrad Detrez, *Zone of Fire* (fiction), Harcourt Brace (New York, NY), 1986.

Michel Butor, *The Spirit of Mediterranean Places* (nonfiction), Marlboro Press/Northwestern (Evanston, IL), 1986.

Maurice Blanchot, *The Last Man* (fiction), Columbia University Press (New York, NY), 1987.

(With Robert Hemenway) Andre Jardin, *Tocqueville: A Biography,* Farrar, Straus, and Giroux (New York, NY), 1988.

Daniele Sallenave, *Phantom Life,* Pantheon (New York, NY), 1989.

Emmanuel Hocquard, *Aerea in the Forests of Manhattan,* Marlboro Press/Northwestern (Evanston, IL), 1992.

Pierre Jean Jouve, *Hélène,* Marlboro Press/Northwestern (Evanston, IL), 1995.

Pierre Jean Jouve, *The Desert World,* Marlboro Press/Northwestern (Evanston, IL), 1996.

Michel Leiris, *Scratches,* Johns Hopkins University Press (Baltimore, MD), 1997.

Michel Leiris, *Scraps,* Johns Hopkins University Press (Baltimore, MD), 1997.

Justine Lévy, *The Rendezvous: A Novel,* Scribner (New York, NY), 1997.

Pierre Jean Jouve, *Hecate,* Marlboro Press/Northwestern (Evanston, IL), 1997.

Pierre Jean Jouve, *Vagadu,* Marlboro Press/Northwestern (Evanston, IL), 1997.

Marquis de Sade, *Florviller and Courveal,* Libertine Reader (New York, NY), 1997.

Vivant Denon, *No Tomorrow,* Libertine Reader (New York, NY), 1997.

Abbé Prévost, *The Story of a Modern Greek Woman,* Libertine Reader (New York, NY), 1997.

Choderlos de Laclos, *On the Education of Women,* Libertine Reader (New York, NY), 1997.

Maurice Blanchot, *The Station Hill Blanchot Reader: Fiction and Literary Essays,* Station Hill/Barrytown, Ltd. (Barrytown, NY), 1999.

Maurice Blanchot, *The One Who Was Standing Apart from Me,* Station Hill/Barrytown, Ltd. (Barrytown, NY), 1999.

Also translated *Swann's Way* by Marcel Proust. Davis's stories have been translated into French, German, Polish, and Spanish.

WORK IN PROGRESS: Novel based on French grammar.

SIDELIGHTS: Lydia Davis's 1986 collection of short stories, *Break It Down,* helped win her the Whiting Writer's Award in 1988. She has also had previous collections of short fiction published, including *Sketches for a Life of Wassilly* and *Story, and Other Stories.*

In addition to her work as an author, Davis has translated novels, biographies, and other scholarly works from French to English. Notable among her translation efforts are works by French author Maurice Blanchot. According to Walter Kendrick in the *Village Voice Literary Supplement,* Blanchot is a precursor of "all the pointmen in the continuing French invasion of American thought," including Michel Foucault and Jacques Derrida. And while critic Kendrick noted in his review that Blanchot's proto-deconstructionist texts are "opaque philosophical-literary discourse," he observed that Blanchot told Davis her English translation of his *L'Arret de Mort* is "really *her* [Davis's] book."

Other critics have praised Davis's translations as well. Edouard Roditi, examining the English version of Michel Butor's *The Spirit of Mediterranean Places* in the *New York Times Book Review,* declared that Davis "deserves to be congratulated on her success in reducing this affectation of French avant-gardism to relatively readable English." Davis has also translated French biographies of Alexis de Tocqueville—author of the famed nineteenth-century analysis of the United States, *Democracy in America*—and scientist Marie Curie, discoverer of radium. Other works she has rendered into English include Conrad Detrez's novel about the Nicaraguan revolution, *Zone of Fire,* and Daniele Sallenave's fictional account of the difficulties of adultery, *Phantom Life.*

Davis's *Break It Down* was the first of her own works to be published by a major firm. (Her previous short story collections had been printed by small presses.) The title piece concerns a man totaling up the monetary cost of a failed love affair in an effort to determine whether the experience was worth having. Some of the other stories in *Break It Down,* such as "Safe Love," "are no more than a page or a paragraph long," reported critic Michiko Kakutani in the *New York Times.* In another article, Kakutani lamented that the shorter pieces "feel like little more than creative-writing-class exercises," but she hailed longer tales such as "Five Signs of Disturbance" and "Therapy" as "grounded in sufficient detail to offer a peephole into a distinct fictional world; and in doing so, they attest to the author's gifts as an observer and archivist of emotion."

Commenting on Davis's novel *The End of the Story* in the *Review of Contemporary Fiction,* Irving Malin wrote that Davis "deserves close reading (and readings)." A critic in *Publishers Weekly* called the tale, in which a nameless protagonist looks back upon a love affair with a man thirteen years younger than she, an "absorbing and lucid first novel."

Almost No Memory, a collection of stories, received widespread attention from critics. Stacey Richter in *Weekly Wire* online maintained that "Davis is by no means an easy writer. Her work is stubbornly intellectual, and many of the stories in this collection avoid the hallmarks of contemporary fiction: There are often no characters, no setting, and no events." Yet "it's impossible to read [Davis's] stories without being reminded of women's magazines like *Cosmopolitan.* She writes about the confusion of romantic longing, the boredom of raising children, the difficulty of getting along with one's husband." Wrote Liam Callanan in the *New York Times Book Review,* "Lydia Davis's latest collection of short stories fascinates in the same way that miniature portraits do. The closer one looks, the more details emerge—and the more impressed one becomes with the skill it takes to fit so much into such a tiny space."

These reviewers were not alone in noting Davis's unusual style. "Lydia Davis's new book is hardly the usual yawn-inducing traditional fiction fare," wrote Deborah Olin Unferth in *Hypertext* online. "The stories are a mixed bag, a series of short experiments with form that variously resemble fables, Sappho-like epigrams, meta-writings, counting games, recipes or word problems, all interconnected and circling around themes of distance, identity, and relationship."

The same tone of bemused admiration could be found in reviews of *Samuel Johnson Is Indignant,* another collection, of which Albert Mobilio wrote in the *New*

York Times Book Review, "Remember minimalism—those terse, tidy dramas that aimed to say so much in so little? How's this for minimal? It's the short story 'A Double Negative,' in its entirety . . .: 'At a certain point in her life, she realizes it is not so much that she wants to have a child as that she does not want not to have a child, or not to have had a child.'" Yet Mobilio went on to assert that Davis "is no minimalist . . . . Not only has she never partaken of the commercial cachet that label bestowed, but her wry voice and elliptical technique have always been particularly hers—that is, instantly recognizable and emulated at the imitator's risk."

In a similar vein, the title story of *Samuel Johnson Is Indignant*—which a commentator in *Kirkus Reviews* called "another fine collection of 54 wry, haunting pieces"—consists simply of the words "Scotland has so few trees." Discussing the story with Dave Eggers in *Interview,* Davis said, "Oh, it was from a report by [Johnson biographer James] Boswell about a trip Johnson took to Scotland. I liked it and wrote it down, and then over the years I began to see that it could make a whole piece." Quipped Eggers to Davis, "I could see a breezy reviewer calling you a humorist. Or a post-modern humorist, or a meta-post-humor-modern-meta-person. You should know that that's how we're marketing the book. You were traveling in France, so we didn't have time to tell you."

Davis has continued to turn out a wide array of translated works by French authors that include the Marquis de Sade. Her two careers necessarily impinge on one another, as she revealed in an interview with Kate Moses for *Salon* online: "I have plans for a very long book which will be a novel in the form of a French Grammar, I think. And it's going to be long and have many parts to it like a grammar book that's used to translate things. It's something I have to work on. I tend to work on it while I'm translating. I take little notes—again, of things that occur to me. I usually let things come to me instead of me going to them." Summing up the dual nature of Davis's work, Regan McMahon observed in the *San Francisco Chronicle,* "Here's the long and the short of it: Lydia Davis can translate Marcel Proust's convoluted tapestry of clauses and asides in sentences that run more than a page. Or, in her own fiction, she can capture a scene, a relationship, an existential dilemma or a philosophical conundrum in a story the size of a paragraph. It depends on the day."

BIOGRAPHICAL AND CRITICAL SOURCES:

PERIODICALS

American Poetry Review, May/June, 1984, p. 15.

Booklist, January 1, 1995, Alice Joyce, review of *The End of the Story,* p. 799; May 1, 1997, Donna Seaman, review of *Almost No Memory,* p. 1479.

Contemporary Literature, winter, 1999, Christopher J. Knight, "An Interview with Lydia Davis," p. 524.

Interview, September, 2001, Dave Eggers, "Lydia Davis" (interview), p. 136.

Kenyon Review, spring, 1999, Patricia Vigderman, reviews of *Almost No Memory, Break It Down,* and *The End of the Story,* pp. 152-59.

Kirkus Reviews, December 1, 1994, review of *The End of the Story,* p. 1559; April 1, 1997, review of *Almost No Memory,* p. 482; October 15, 2001, review of *Samuel Johnson Is Indignant,* p. 1453.

Library Journal, September 1, 1993, Ann Irvine, review of *Hélène,* pp. 221-222; January, 1995, Kimberly G. Allen, review of *The End of the Story,* p. 136; October 1, 1995, review of *The End of the Story,* p. 144; October 1, 1996, Paul Hutchison, review of *The Desert World,* p. 127; April 1, 1997, Ann Irvine, review of *Almost No Memory,* p. 132.

London Review of Books, October 31, 1996, reviews of *Break It Down* and *The End of the Story,* p. 6.

Los Angeles Times Book Review, November 16, 1986, p. 1; January 1, 1989, p. 1; July 27, 1997, review of *Almost No Memory,* p. 7; December 14, 1997, Benjamin Weissman, review of *Almost No Memory,* p. 4.

New Yorker, June 12, 1995, review of *The End of the Story,* p. 104.

New York Times Book Review, May 25, 1986, p. 23; August 31, 1986, p. 10; September 28, 1986, p. 16; November 16, 1986, p. 24; December 28, 1986, p. 19; October 11, 1987, p. 56; February 19, 1989, p. 12; December 24, 1989, p. 17; March 19, 1995, Charlotte Innes, review of *The End of the Story,* p. 22; May 12, 1996, reviews of *The End of the Story* and *Break It Down,* p. 28; January 12, 1997, David Guy, review of *The Desert World,* p. 21; September 14, 1997, Liam Callanan, review of *Almost No Memory,* p. 26; September 28, 1997, Barbara Fisher, review of *The Rendezvous,* p. 22; November 8, 1998, review of *Almost No Memory,* p. 36; December 16, 2001, Albert Mobilio, review of *Samuel Johnson Is Indignant;* December 23, 2001, review of *Samuel Johnson Is Indignant,* p. 14.

Publishers Weekly, August 2, 1993, review of *Hélène,* p. 64; December 5, 1994, review of *The End of the Story,* pp. 64-65; April 8, 1996, review of *The End of the Story,* p. 66; September 2, 1996, review of *The Desert World,* p. 114; April 14, 1997, review of *Almost No Memory,* p. 52; June 16, 1997, review of *The Rendezvous,* p. 45; September 15, 1997, reviews of *Hecate* and *Vagadu,* p. 53; October 1, 2001, review of *Samuel Johnson Is Indignant,* p. 36.

Review of Contemporary Fiction, spring, 1993, Jeff Sorensen, review of *Aerea in the Forests of Manhattan,* pp. 262-263; fall, 1994, Steve Dickinson, review of *The One Who Was Standing Apart from Me,* p. 214; January 1, 1995, Irving Malin, review of *The End of the Story,* p. 152; spring, 1996, review of *The End of the Story,* p. 152.

San Francisco Chronicle, December 9, 2001, Regan McMahon, "Q&A: Lydia Davis; Precision with Words; The Author and Translator Talks about Fiction, Teaching, and Proust," p. 2.

Time, November 19, 2001, Ben Marcus, review of *Samuel Johnson Is Indignant,* p. 143.

Times Literary Supplement, November 8, 1996, reviews of *Break It Down* and *The End of the Story,* p. 28.

Village Voice Literary Supplement, May, 1982, Walter Kendrick, review of *Death Sentence,* p. 8; summer 1997, review of *Almost No Memory,* p. 22.

Washington Post Book World, June 4, 1995, review of *The End of the Story,* p. 10; September 14, 1997, review of *Almost No Memory,* p. 8.

Women's Review of Books, July, 1997, Lisa Shea, review of *Almost No Memory,* pp. 38-39.

ONLINE

Bomb Web site, http://www.bombsite.com/ (May 18, 2002), Francine Prose, interview with Davis.

Hypertext Web site, http://www.hypertext.com/ (May 18, 2002), Deborah Olin Unferth, review of *Almost No Memory.*

Salon, http://www.salon.com/ (May 18, 2002), Kate Moses, "Not Tired of Thinking Yet: An Interview with Lydia Davis."

Timothy McSweeney's Internet Tendency, http://www.mcsweeneys.net/ (May 18, 2002), Timothy McSweeney, "Lydia Davis Week."

Weekly Wire/Tucson Weekly Web site, http://www.weeklywire.com/ (May 18, 2002), Stacey Richter, review of *Almost No Memory.**

DAVIS, Stephen 1947-

PERSONAL: Born September 8, 1947, in New York, NY; son of Howard (a television director) and Hana Charlotte (Fischer) Davis; married Judith Arons (a psychotherapist), June 12, 1976; children: Lily, India. *Education:* Boston University, A.B., 1969.

ADDRESSES: Office—Blue Hills Productions, P.O. Box 123, Milton Village, MA 02187. *Agent*—David Vigliano, Suite 809, 584 Broadway, New York, NY 10012.

CAREER: Boston Phoenix, Boston, MA, associate editor, 1970-71; *Rolling Stone,* New York, NY, associate editor, 1972-73; *New Age* (now *New Age Journal*), Brighton, MA, associate editor, 1977-85; freelance writer.

MEMBER: Boston Athenaeum (life member).

AWARDS, HONORS: ASCAP Deems Taylor Award, 1988, for excellence in music journalism.

WRITINGS:

Reggae Bloodlines: In Search of the Music and Culture of Jamaica, photographs by Peter Simon, Doubleday (New York, NY), 1977.

(Editor, with Simon, and contributor) *Reggae International,* Knopf (New York, NY), 1982.

Bob Marley, Doubleday (New York, NY), 1985.

Hammer of the Gods: The Led Zeppelin Saga, Morrow (New York, NY), 1985.

Say Kids! What Time Is It?, Little, Brown (Boston, MA), 1987.

(With Mick Fleetwood) *Fleetwood: My Life and Adventures in Fleetwood Mac,* Morrow (New York, NY), 1990, published with a sound disc as *My Twenty-Five Years in Fleetwood Mac,* discography by Frank Harding, Hyperion (New York, NY), 1992.

(With Levon Helm) *This Wheel's on Fire: Levon Helm and the Story of the Band,* Morrow (New York, NY), 1993.

Jajouka Rolling Stone: A Fable of Gods and Heroes (fiction), Random House (New York, NY), 1993.

(With the members of Aerosmith) *Walk This Way: The Autobiography of Aerosmith,* Avon Books (New York, NY), 1997.

Old Gods Almost Dead: The Forty-year Odyssey of the Rolling Stones, Broadway Books (New York, NY), 2001.

Contributor to *New Grove Dictionary of Music,* Oxford University Press (New York, NY). Contributor to periodicals, including *New York Times, Boston Globe, Rolling Stone, Newsday, Omni, CoEvolution Quarterly, Oui, The Beat, Mojo* (UK), and *Libération* (Paris).

SIDELIGHTS: Stephen Davis told *CA:* "What a writer needs most (besides a helpful spouse, an audience, an agent, and a check) is inspiration on a daily basis. I get my inspiration mostly from music (Marley, Charles Mingus, Claude Debussy) and other writers, especially Paul Bowles and Brion Gysin, and my journalistic competition. My greatest pleasure from my work, aside from being able to provide for my family, comes from seeing my books in translation and British editions. Almost all of my books are in print in Japan and are available in French and Italian editions as well."

A writer who focuses on popular culture and entertainment, Davis has devoted a number of volumes to the exploration of reggae music and to its most famous artist, Bob Marley. A worldwide pop phenomenon rooted in Jamaican culture and the millenarian visions of the Rastafarian faith, reggae is "this century's premier music of social redress," wrote Greg Tate in the *Village Voice;* it calls for the unification of Africans everywhere and for deliverance of the world's dispossessed. *Reggae International,* edited by Davis and Peter Simon, is an anthology of essays that look at Jamaica's history and culture, Rasta's tenets, reggae's international parallels and influence, and its messianic messenger Marley. Deeming the book "graphically gorgeous," Tate commended much in the volume: "The first section, 'Tracin De Riddim,' is thoughtfully long on historical homework," while he considered Rory Sanders's chapter, "The Rastafarians," "an overdue reexamination, if not reversal, of the primitivist view of Rasta which persists in the U.S." Tate also reported that Timothy White "works up a vivid mural of Jamaican folk culture that is mesmerizing."

Davis's *Bob Marley* recounts the life of the third-world superstar from his country boyhood to his death from cancer at the age of thirty-six in 1981. The son of a black Jamaican woman and a white English army captain, Marley spent his early years steeped in the mysticism of Jamaica's backwoods and later years on the tough streets of Kingston's ghettos. Interested in African-American music, the young performer showed the influence of rhythm and blues in his earliest songs. After forming the Wailers singing group, Marley adopted the Rastafarian faith, bringing its call for black unity to an international audience. His riveting musical gifts and magnetic personality granted him an almost religious following, and the singer's romantic entanglements and idealistic political involvements did little to shake his messianic appeal. "Few other popular musicians have touched people from so many different cultures," observed Randall F. Grass in the *New York Times Book Review.* "In his recordings and performances, he celebrated the struggle of dispossessed people everywhere, and he preached a natural way of life with such charismatic force that fans proclaimed him a prophet." While noting "some errors of detail [and] questions unanswered" in the biography, the critic observed, "Davis has written a straightforward journalistic narrative [that] does not ignore any facet of Marley's life." Reviewing *Bob Marley* for the Toronto *Globe and Mail,* Norman (Otis) Richmond concurred: "Davis's work captures Bob Marley as the bridge-builder he was."

Hammer of the Gods, a subsequent Davis publication, follows heavy metal British rock group Led Zeppelin while on a 1970s American tour. Scoring enormous popular success, *Hammer of the Gods* spent ten weeks on the *New York Times* best-seller list. For *Say Kids! What Time Is It?,* a behind-the-scenes look at the 1950s children's television program *Howdy Doody,* Davis draws from personal experience: his father, Howard Davis, was a writer and director for the hit show featuring the freckle-faced puppet and friends, and Stephen was a frequent visitor to *Howdy Doody*'s Peanut Gallery. The author reveals that things were not as they appeared in Doodyville: performers were made to hawk Howdy Doody merchandise relentlessly (bringing in $15 million a year), life backstage was dominated by infighting and manipulation, and "rehearsals . . . were ribald affairs," wrote Lynn Van Matre in the *Chicago Tribune Book World,* "in which the cast and crew regularly put the puppets through pornographic paces." The critic concluded, "Drawing upon interviews with former cast members as well as old Howdy kinescopes and archival material, Davis has written a richly detailed, even-handed account of the *Howdy Doody* phenomenon—and the all-too-human folks who made it all happen."

Davis returned to the subject of rock history with *Fleetwood: My Life and Adventures in Fleetwood Mac,* cowritten with Mick Fleetwood. Genevieve Stuttaford in *Publishers Weekly* promised that the book "will please avid readers and fans alike." Another rock biography, *This Wheel's on Fire: Levon Helm and the Story of the Band,* followed. According to a critic in *Publishers Weekly,* the book contrasted well with Barney Hoskyns's *Across the Great Divide: The Band and America,* also published in 1990, which focused largely on the recollections of the Band's other most prominent figure, guitarist Robbie Robertson.

Jajouka Rolling Stone: A Fable of Gods and Heroes marked a departure into the world of fiction. Based partly on Davis's own experiences, it is the story of an American journalist working for *National Geographic* in Morocco, where he has gone to study with the legendary musicians in the town of Jajouka. Despite its far-away setting, the book is still closely tied to pop cultural history: a number of western icons, most notably the late Rolling Stones guitarist Brian Jones, also traveled to Jajouka to learn from the "Master Musicians" there.

Returning to the subject of rock history, Davis worked with singer Steven Tyler, guitarist Joe Perry, and the other three members of Aerosmith on *Walk This Way: The Autobiography of Aerosmith.* Whereas the former members of Led Zeppelin had been incensed by the portrayal they received in *Hammer of the Gods,* according to Larry Katz in the *Boston Herald,* "that notorious book only convinced the members of Aerosmith that Davis was the right man to tell about the number they did on themselves." (That is, about the excesses of their personal lives prior to the late 1980s, when the group members gave up cocaine and other drugs.) Describing *Walk This Way* as "really more of an oral history than an autobiography," Katz noted that "it makes for compelling reading—especially throughout the first half, which covers Aerosmith's rise to rock stardom in the mid-1970s. Then came the years of debauchery, when Aerosmith lost its direction and career in a hellish blizzard of white powders. 'We call them "the wonder years,"' Tyler says in the book, 'because we wonder what happened to them.'"

With *Old Gods Almost Dead: The Forty-year Odyssey of the Rolling Stones,* Davis took on another group of great stature in music history. In a review for the Atlanta *Journal-Constitution* Steve Dollar noted, "as be-

fits a professional music biographer, *Old Gods* is a professional music biography, useful for its archiving of countless stray bits of information, but only as compelling as the story it has to tell." The problem, suggested some critics, was not with Davis, but with his subject. Not only had the Stones' saga already been chronicled many times, but by the time of the book's publication in 2001, their best work lay thirty years in the past. Still, wrote Steve Wilson in *Book,* "Davis's engaging history of the Rolling Stones reminds us why we still love the band."

BIOGRAPHICAL AND CRITICAL SOURCES:

PERIODICALS

Book, November-December, 2001, Steve Wilson, review of *Old Gods Almost Dead: The Forty-year Odyssey of the Rolling Stones,* p. 68.

Booklist, August, 1993, Joe Collins, review of *Jajouka Rolling Stone: A Fable of Gods and Heroes,* p. 2035; November 1, 2001, Mike Tribby, review of *Old Gods Almost Dead,* p. 454.

Boston Herald, September 8, 1997, Larry Katz, review of *Walk This Way: The Autobiography of Aerosmith,* p. 28; November 20, 2001, Larry Katz, review of *Old Gods Almost Dead,* p. 44.

Christian Science Monitor, December 28, 1993, Whitney Dodds Woodruff, review of *This Wheel's on Fire: Levon Helm and the Story of the Band,* p. 13.

Entertainment Weekly, November 16, 2001, Brian M. Raftery, review of *Old Gods Almost Dead,* p. 164.

Esquire, March, 2001, review of *Old Gods Almost Dead,* p. 110.

Globe and Mail (Toronto), August 3, 1985, Norman (Otis) Richmond, review of *Bob Marley.*

Journal-Constitution (Atlanta, GA), November 25, 2001, Steve Dollar, review of *Old Gods Almost Dead,* p. C-6.

Kirkus Reviews, April 15, 1993, review of *Jajouka Rolling Stone,* p. 475; September 15, 2001, review of *Old Gods Almost Dead,* p. 1334.

Los Angeles Times Book Review, September 12, 1993, review of *Jajouka Rolling Stone,* p. 13.

New York Times Book Review, March 31, 1985; November 18, 1990, Robert Waddell, review of *Fleetwood: My Life and Adventures in Fleetwood Mac,* p. 29; December 29, 1993, Margo Jefferson, review of *This Wheel's on Fire,* p. B4.

Notes, December, 1991, Shelley L. Rogers, review of *Fleetwood,* pp. 531-33.

Observer (London), April 10, 1994, review of *Bob Marley,* p. 21.

Publishers Weekly, August 10, 1990, Genevieve Stuttaford, review of *Fleetwood,* p. 428; May 10, 1993, review of *Jajouka Rolling Stone,* p. 50; October 4, 1993, review of *This Wheel's on Fire,* p. 62; October 8, 2001, review of *Old Gods Almost Dead,* p. 53.

Rolling Stone, October 16, 1997, Mark Coleman, review of *Walk This Way,* p. 32.

Tribune Books (Chicago, IL), March 4, 1979; January 19, 1986; October 15, 1987.

Variety, October 1, 1990, review of *Fleetwood,* p. 104.

Village Voice, September 20, 1983, Greg Tate, review of *Reggae International.*

Washington Post, December 21, 2001, David Segal, review of *Old Gods Almost Dead,* p. C2.

*   *   *

DAVIS, William C(harles) 1946-

PERSONAL: Born September 28, 1946, in Kansas City, MO; son of Eual Edward (a salesman) and Martha (an accountant; maiden name, Joan) Davis; married Pamela S. McIntyre, July 22, 1969 (divorced); children: M. Jefferson, Rebecca M. *Education:* Sonoma State College (now University), A.B., 1968, M.A., 1969. *Politics:* Democrat.

ADDRESSES: Office—History Department, Virginia Polytechnic Institute and State University, Major Williams Hall, Blacksburg, VA, 24061-0117. *E-mail*—widavis6@vt.edu.

CAREER: Historian, writer, and educator. Historical Times, Inc., Harrisburg, PA, editorial assistant, 1969-72; National Historical Society, Gettysburg, PA, editor of *American History Illustrated* and *Civil War Times Illustrated,* 1972-76, president, 1976-82; Historical Times, Inc., Harrisburg, executive director, 1982-84, corporate editorial director, 1984-85, president of Museum Editions, Ltd., 1986-1990; Virginia Polytechnic Institute and State University, began as instructor, became professor of history and Director of Programs for Virginia Center for Civil War Studies. Consultant for numerous Civil War television movie and docu-

mentary productions, including "Civil War Journal" series for Arts & Entertainment/History Channel, "The Blue and the Gray" mini-series for Columbia Pictures, "George Washington," "The Perfect Tribute," and a Florentine Production documentary for the Public Broadcasting Service (PBS). Consultant for History Book Club, Easton Press Library of Military History, U.S. Intelligence Historical Society, and Eastern National Park and Monument Association for the National Park Service.

MEMBER: Southern Historical Association.

AWARDS, HONORS: Jefferson Davis Award for the best book on Confederate history, Museum of the Confederacy and the Confederate Memorial Literary Society, 1974, for *Breckinridge: Statesman, Soldier, Symbol,* 1991, for *Jefferson Davis: The Man and His Hour,* and 1994, for *"A Government of Our Own": The Making of the Confederacy;* Jules F. Landry Award for the best book on Southern history, literature, and biography, Louisiana State University Press, 1974, and Phi Alpha Theta Award for best first work in history, 1975, both for *Breckinridge;* Pulitzer Prize nominations, 1975, for *Breckinridge,* and 1978, for *Battle at Bull Run;* fellow, U.S. Army Military History Institute, 1975, for contributions to the study of American military history; honorary doctor of humane letters, Lincoln Memorial University, 1976; Fletcher Pratt Award, 1977; fellow, Royal Photographic Society, 1985, for "The Image of War" series; Reuben M. Potter Award, 1998, for *Three Roads to the Alamo: The Lives and Fortunes of David Crockett, James Bowie, and William Barret Travis.* Several of Davis's books have been selections of the Military Book Club, History Book Club, and Literary Guild.

WRITINGS:

Breckinridge: Statesman, Soldier, Symbol, Louisiana State University Press (Baton Rouge, LA), 1974.

The Battle of New Market, Doubleday (New York, NY), 1975.

Duel between the First Ironclads, Doubleday (New York, NY), 1975.

Battle at Bull Run: A History of the First Major Campaign of the Civil War, Doubleday (New York, NY), 1977, 2nd edition, Stackpole Books (Harrisburg, PA), 1995.

The Orphan Brigade: The Kentucky Confederates Who Couldn't Go Home, Doubleday (New York, NY), 1980.

The Imperiled Union, Doubleday (New York, NY), Volume 1: *The Deep Waters of the Proud,* 1982, Volume 2: *Stand in the Day of Battle,* 1983.

Brother against Brother, Time-Life Books (Alexandria, VA), 1983.

First Blood, Time-Life Books (Alexandria, VA), 1983.

Gettysburg: The Story behind the Scenery, KC Publications (Las Vegas, NV), 1983.

Civil War Parks: The Story behind the Scenery, KC Publications (Las Vegas, NV), 1984.

Death in the Trenches, Time-Life Books (Alexandria, VA), 1986.

Fighting Men of the Civil War, W. H. Smith (New York, NY), 1989.

Commanders of the Civil War, W. H. Smith (New York, NY), 1990.

The Battlefields of the Civil War, Smithmark Publishers (New York, NY), 1991, also published as *The Battlefields of the Civil War: The Bloody Conflict of North against South Told through the Stories of Its Great Battles, Illustrated with Collections of Some of the Rarest Civil War Historical Artifacts,* University of Oklahoma Press (Norman, OK), 1996.

Jefferson Davis: The Man and His Hour, HarperCollins (New York, NY), 1991.

Generals of the Civil War, Mallard Press (New York, NY), 1991.

Battles of the Civil War, Mallard Press (New York, NY), 1991.

Memorabilia of the Civil War, Mallard Press (New York, NY), 1991.

Weapons of the Civil War, Mallard Press (New York, NY), 1991.

The American Frontier: Pioneers, Settlers and Cowboys, 1800-1899, Smithmark Publishers (New York, NY), 1992.

Trivia of the Civil War, Mallard Press (New York, NY), 1993.

Soldiers of the Civil War, Mallard Press (New York, NY), 1993.

The Civil War Cookbook, Courage Books (Philadelphia, PA), 1993.

"A Government of Our Own": The Making of the Confederacy, Free Press (New York, NY), 1994.

(With William Marvel) *A Concise History of the Civil War,* Eastern National Park and Monument Association (Conshohocken, PA), 1994.

The First Battle of Manassas, Eastern National Park and Monument Association (Conshohocken, PA), 1995.

A Way through the Wilderness: The Natchez Trace and the Civilization of the Southern Frontier, HarperCollins (New York, NY), 1995.

Brothers in Arms, Salamander Books (London, England), 1995.

The Cause Lost: Myths and Realities of the Confederacy, University Press of Kansas (Lawrence, KS), 1996.

Three Roads to the Alamo: The Lives and Fortunes of David Crockett, James Bowie, and William Barret Travis, HarperCollins (New York, NY), 1998.

Lincoln's Men: How President Lincoln Became Father to an Army and a Nation, Free Press (New York, NY), 1999.

Portraits of the Civil War: The Men and Women in Blue and Gray, Smithmark Publishers (New York, NY), 1999.

An Honorable Defeat: The Last Days of the Confederate Government, Harcourt (San Diego, CA), 2001.

The Union That Shaped the Confederacy: Robert Toombs and Alexander H. Stephens, University Press of Kansas (Lawrence, KS), 2001.

Rhett: The Turbulent Life and Times of a Fire-eater, University of South Carolina Press (Columbia, SC), 2001.

Portraits of the Riverboats, Thunder Bay Press (San Diego, CA), 2001.

Look Away!: A History of the Confederate States of America, Free Press (New York, NY), 2002.

EDITOR

The Embattled Confederacy, Doubleday (New York, NY), 1982.

Fighting for Time, Doubleday (New York, NY), 1983.

(With Bell I. Wiley) *The Image of War, 1861-1865,* Doubleday (New York, NY), Volume 1: *Shadows of the Storm,* 1981, Volume 2: *The Guns of '62,* 1982, Volume 3: *The Embattled Confederacy,* 1982, Volume 4: *Fighting for Time,* 1983, Volume 5: *The South Besieged,* 1983, Volume 6: *The End of an Era,* 1984, also published as *The Civil War Times Illustrated Photographic History of the Civil War,* Black Dog & Leventhal Publishers (New York, NY), 1994, Volume 1: *Vicksburg to Appomattox,* Volume 2: *Fort Sumter to Gettysburg,* also published in one volume as *Civil War Album:*

Complete Photographic History of the Civil War: Fort Sumter to Appomattox, Tess Press (New York, NY), 2000.

Touched by Fire: A Photographic Portrait of the Civil War, Little, Brown (Boston, MA), 1985-1986.

Diary of a Confederate Soldier: John S. Jackman of the Orphan Brigade, University of South Carolina Press (Columbia, SC), 1990.

The Confederate General, six volumes, National Historical Society (Harrisburg, PA), 1990-1991.

(With Brian C. Pohanka and Don Troiani) *Civil War Journal* (edited scripts from the television program of the same name), Rutledge Hill Press (Nashville, TN), Volume 1: *The Leaders,* 1997, Volume 2: *The Battles,* 1997, Volume 3: *The Legacies,* 1999.

(With Meredith L. Swentor) *Bluegrass Confederate: The Headquarters Diary of Edward O. Guerrant,* Louisiana State University Press (Baton Rouge, LA), 1999.

A Fire-eater Remembers: The Confederate Memoir of Robert Barnwell Rhett, University of South Carolina Press (Columbia, SC), 2000.

Author without by-line of *Spies, Scouts, and Raiders,* Time-Life Books (Alexandria, VA), 1986. Also author of introduction, Ed Porter Thompson, *History of the Orphan Brigade,* Morningside Press (Dayton, OH), 1974, and Paul M. Angle, *A Pictorial History of the Civil War Years,* Doubleday (Garden City, NY), 1980.

Contributor to books, including *Encyclopedia of Southern History,* Louisiana State University Press, 1979; *Dictionary of American Military Biography,* Greenwood Press, 1984; *Rebels Resurgent,* Time-Life Books, 1985; *Above and Beyond: The Congressional Medal of Honor,* Boston Publishing, 1985; *Historical Times Illustrated Encyclopedia of the Civil War,* Harper, 1986; *The Cavalry* (part of "The Wars of America" series), Boston Publishing, 1987; *Civil War Battlefield Guide,* edited by Francis H. Kennedy, Houghton Mifflin, 1990; *Leadership during the Civil War,* edited by Roman J. Heleniak and Lawrence L. Hewitt, White Mane, 1992; *The Way of the Warrior,* Time-Life Books, 1993; *Encyclopedia of the Confederacy,* edited by Richard N. Current, Simon & Schuster, 1993; *Encyclopedia of the American Presidency,* edited by Leonard W. Levy and Louis Fisher, Simon & Schuster, 1993; *Lee the General,* edited by Gary Gallagher, University of Nebraska Press, 1966; *Abraham Lincoln, Gettysburg, and the Civil War,* Savas, 1999.

Contributor to journals and periodicals, including *American Heritage, American History Illustrated, British Heritage, Civil War Times,* and *Smithsonian.* Consulting editor for *Great Battles of the Civil War,* Publications International, 1989; *The West: From Lewis and Clark to Wounded Knee: The Turbulent Story of the Settling of Frontier America,* Smithmark Publishers, 1994; Martin F. Graham, Richard A. Sauers, and George Skoch, *The Blue and the Gray: The Conflict between North and South,* Publications International, 1996.

SIDELIGHTS: William C. Davis has devoted his career to the history of the American Civil War and is recognized as one of the foremost historians of the period. He is the author of over thirty books on the Civil War and editor of, or contributor to, many more. In recent years, Davis has also branched out into other areas of American history, writing a joint biography of three famous men who died at the Alamo and two histories of the settlement of the American West. "I have gotten sufficiently jaded on the Civil War that now every other book I do is on some other era," he said in an interview with Dr. Stephen L. Hardin on the *Alamo de Parras* Web site.

Davis's early book, *The Orphan Brigade: The Kentucky Confederates Who Couldn't Go Home,* chronicles the Civil War activities of the those Kentucky soldiers who, unlike most of their fellow Kentuckians, elected to side with the Confederacy. Robert Kirsch of the *Los Angeles Times* noted that "Davis's intimate account captures the pride and loyalty of the regiments, brings individuals alive, draws heavily on the records and narratives left by the brigade under encouragement by Capt. Ed Porter Thompson, an amateur historian." Rory Quirk wrote in the *Washington Post* that "the battles are rich with detail," yet noted the book's lack of maps: "This absence of detailed maps is a regrettable omission in an otherwise informative, comprehensive and colorful account."

Davis's biography of Confederate leader Jefferson Davis (no relation) was described by David Herbert Donald in the *New York Times Book Review* as "the fullest and best biography yet written [of Davis], a work that will remain a standard, authoritative account of the life of the Confederate president." Jefferson Davis appears again in *"A Government of Our Own": The Making of the Confederacy,* a blow-by-blow recounting of the four-month-long discussion about the shape of the Southern constitution. The author's previous familiarity with Davis was no doubt an advantage; *Booklist* reviewer Brad Hooper noted how successfully the author "brings back to life and breath the personalities involved, particularly Jefferson Davis." The author also wrote about Jefferson Davis in "his finely drawn and highly readable" study of the sparring between Davis and Confederate Secretary of War John Breckinridge during the final days of the war, as *An Honorable Defeat: The Last Days of the Confederate Government* was described in *Library Journal* by John C. Edwards.

Davis has also written about the Union leader, Abraham Lincoln, in books such as *Lincoln's Men: How President Lincoln Became Father to an Army and a Nation.* According to Davis, Lincoln earned the respect of the rank-and-file soldiers by his obvious attention to them: Lincoln was known to personally commute the sentences of deserters, to put his own life in danger by visiting forward positions on the Union line, and to walk among the men telling jokes and stories after he had reviewed the troops. Davis also writes about Lincoln's personal thoughts about command, the roots of his sympathy for the soldiers in his own experiences during the 1832 Black Hawk War and in his historical memory of Washington as father figure during the Revolution. "Davis has cut directly to Lincoln's soul and discovered his genius," Randall M. Miller declared in *Library Journal.*

Davis's most famous non-Civil War book may be *Three Roads to the Alamo: The Lives and Fortunes of David Crockett, James Bowie, and William Barret Travis.* All three men fled failure in the East to try to reinvent themselves in the West, and all became legends, for good reasons, as Davis reveals. As Gilbert Taylor noted in *Booklist,* Davis's "integrated research . . . impress[es] the reader with a strange-but-true tone as he describes" Bowie's financial successes in smuggling slaves and conducting fraudulent land deals, for example. This "is a readable, stimulating and exceptionally well-researched narrative history," said *Library Journal* contributor Charles Cowling, who also noted that Davis was the first historian to draw substantially on the Mexican Military Archives.

In his most recent book, *Look Away!: A History of the Confederate States of America,* Davis examines the character of the Confederate nation beyond the battlefield. Jay Winik, writing in the *National Review,* identified Davis's thesis in the book: "Born out of conflict, the confederate nation was riven from Day One by endless bitter disputes and savage factional fighting." Calling the book "an important resource for students of the Civil War South," Winik pointed out that Davis "makes a convincing case that the Confederacy at home, much like its northern counterpart, was often dangerously divided, if not at war with itself." John Carver Edwards in *Library Journal* found the book a "penetrating analysis of the values and differences among the various factions of the Confederacy." "Davis eschews both present-mindedness and lost-cause romanticism in this rigorous but accessible history," wrote a *Publishers Weekly* reviewer, "and does an excellent job depicting this early failed state from a variety of angles."

Davis described his writing habits in an interview with Stephen L. Hardin: "I adhere to a very strict writing schedule. . . . I take a brisk six-mile walk in the morning, which helps clear my head and arrange thoughts for the day's work. Then I start writing at precisely ten a.m. and stay at it until at least 6:30 usually with ninety minutes off at lunch. I do that seven days a week until the book is finished, and every day I produce fourteen pages of finished copy on the word processor, or two pages an hour. Most importantly, I do not answer the telephone or knocks at the door. A ten-second phone call from some boob telemarketing burial plots or insurance can cost half an hour or more if a train of thought is interrupted and has to be recreated. . . . Once I'm done writing, I usually sort the note cards for the following day's work, and then sit down in front of the fireplace and read a book or watch a British comedy on television."

BIOGRAPHICAL AND CRITICAL SOURCES:

PERIODICALS

A. B. Bookmans's Weekly, October 5, 1992, review of *The American Frontier: Pioneers, Settlers and Cowboys, 1800-1899,* p. 1141.

American Historical Review, December, 1992, Steven E. Woodworth, review of *Jefferson Davis: The Man and His Hour,* pp. 1597-1598; February, 1997, Ronald L. F. Davis, review of *A Way through the Wilderness: The Natchez Trace and the Civilization of the Southern Frontier,* p. 177;

April, 1998, Richard E. Beringer, review of *The Cause Lost: Myths and Realities of the Confederacy,* pp. 602-603; June, 2000, Joseph Allen Frank, review of *Lincoln's Men: How President Lincoln Became Father to an Army and a Nation,* pp. 928-929; February, 2002, Gregg Cantrell, review of *The Union That Shaped the Confederacy,* p. 198.

American History, February, 1999, Joseph Gustaitis, review of *Three Roads to the Alamo: The Lives and Fortunes of David Crockett, James Bowie, and William Barret Travis,* p. 14; December, 2001, Stephen Currie, review of *An Honorable Defeat: The Last Days of the Confederate Government,* p. 66.

American Spectator, July, 1992, Paul Johnson, review of *Jefferson Davis,* pp. 54-57.

Atlantic Monthly, March, 1995, Phoebe-Lou Adams, review of *A Way through the Wilderness,* pp. 128-129.

Booklist, September 15, 1992, Ray Olson, review of *The American Frontier,* pp. 118; November 1, 1993, Barbara Jacobs, review of *A Civil War Cookbook,* pp. 494-495; October 1, 1994, Brad Hooper, review of *"A Government of Our Own": The Making of the Confederacy,* p. 233; February 15, 1995, Dorothy Lilly, review of *A Way through the Wilderness,* p. 1056; June 1, 1998, Gilbert Taylor, review of *Three Roads to the Alamo,* p. 1712; November 15, 1998, Gilbert Taylor, review of *Lincoln's Men,* p. 563; March 1, 2001, Gilbert Taylor, review of *An Honorable Defeat,* p. 1220; March 15, 2001, Gilbert Taylor, review of *The Union That Shaped the Confederacy: Robert Toombs and Alexander H. Stephens,* p. 1350.

Bookwatch, November, 1992, review of *The American Frontier,* p. 131; January, 1993, review of *Fighting Men of the Civil War, Commanders of the Civil War,* and *Battlefields of the Civil War,* p. 11; April, 1998, review of *Civil War Journal,* Volume 2: *The Battles,* p. 7.

Book World, October 25, 1992, review of *Jefferson Davis,* p. 1597; March 5, 1995, review of *A Way through the Wilderness,* p. 3.

Choice, April, 1997, review of *The Cause Lost,* p. 1403; November, 2001, J. D. Smith, review of *The Union That Shaped the Confederacy,* p. 576; January, 2002, R. A. Fischler, review of *An Honorable Defeat,* p. 945.

Christian Science Monitor, April 1, 1999, review of *Lincoln's Men,* p. 17.

Civil War History, September, 1992, Lynda Lasswell Crist, review of *The Confederate General,* Volume 1, pp. 246-247; June, 1993, Ludwell H. Johnson III, review of *Jefferson Davis,* pp. 156-158; June, 1997, Mary Munsell Monroe, review of *The Battlefields of the Civil War,* pp. 182-183; September, 1997, Gaines M. Foster, review of *The Cause Lost,* pp. 247-248; December, 1998, Glenna R. Schroeder-Lein, review of *Civil War Journal,* Volume 2: *The Battles,* p. 318; September, 1999, Michael Burlingame, review of *Lincoln's Men,* p. 275.

Civil War Times, May, 2002, Peter S. Carmichael, review of *Look Away!: A History of the Confederate States of America,* pp. 10-11.

Guardian Weekly, December 27, 1992, review of *Jefferson Davis,* p. 16.

Historian, autumn, 1995, John F. Marszalek, review of *"A Government of Our Own,"* pp. 133-134.

History: Reviews of New Books, summer, 1997, review of *The Cause Lost,* p. 153.

Journal of American History, September, 1995, John David Smith, review of *"A Government of Our Own,"* pp. 744-746; April, 1996, John McCardell, review of *"A Government of Our Own,"* pp. 569-570; September, 1997, Ludwell H. Johnson III, review of *The Cause Lost,* pp. 668-669; December, 1997, W. Stitt Robinson, review of *A Way through the Wilderness,* p. 1041; March, 2000, J. Matthew Gallman, review of *Lincoln's Men,* pp. 1740-1743.

Journal of Military History, April, 1995, review of *"A Government of Our Own,"* p. 336.

Journal of Southern History, August, 1992, Steven E. Woodworth, review of *Diary of a Confederate Soldier: John S. Jackman of the Orphan Brigade,* pp. 547-548; August, 1993, John M. McCardell, Jr., review of *Jefferson Davis,* pp. 554-555; February, 1996, George C. Rable, review of *"A Government of Our Own,"* pp. 133-134; May, 1996, John D. W. Guice, review of *A Way through the Wilderness,* pp. 361-362; February, 1998, Daniel E. Sutherland, review of *The Cause Lost,* pp. 156-157; May, 2000, Roger A. Fischer, review of *Lincoln's Men,* pp. 420-421; November, 2001, Kenneth H. Williams, review of *Bluegrass Confederate: The Headquarters Diary of Edward O. Guerrant,* p. 862.

Kirkus Reviews, October 1, 1991, review of *Jefferson Davis,* p. 1256; August 15, 1994, review of *"A Government of Our Own,"* p. 1097; December 15, 1994, review of *A Way through the Wilderness,* p. 1535; September 1, 1996, review of *The Cause Lost,* p. 1290; May 1, 1998, review of *Three Roads to the Alamo,* p. 628; November 15, 1998, review of *Lincoln's Men,* p. 1642.

Kliatt Young Adult Paperback Book Guide, September, 1997, review of *"A Government of Our Own,"* p. 37; September, 1999, review of *The American Frontier,* p. 39; February 1, 2002, review of *Look Away!,* p. 156.

Library Journal, September 15, 1990, Jason H. Silverman, review of *Diary of a Confederate Soldier,* p. 88; November 15, 1991, Randall M. Miller, review of *Jefferson Davis,* p. 90; September 15, 1994, Robert A. Curtis, review of *"A Government of Our Own,"* pp. 78-79; February 1, 1995, Dorothy Lilly, review of *A Way through the Wilderness,* p. 87; June 15, 1997, William D. Bushnell, review of *Civil War Journal,* Volume 1: *The Leaders,* p. 82; May 15, 1998, Charles Cowling, review of *Three Roads to the Alamo,* p. 95; November 1, 1998, Randall M. Miller, review of *Lincoln's Men,* p. 109; February 15, 2001, John C. Edwards, review of *An Honorable Defeat,* p. 181; April 1, 2001, David M. Alperstein, review of *The Union That Shaped the Confederacy,* p. 113; February 1, 2002, Theresa McDevitt, review of *Rhett: The Turbulent Life and Times of a Fire-eater,* p. 114; March 1, 2002, John Carver Edwards, review of *Look Away!,* pp. 117-118.

Los Angeles Times, April 18, 1980.

National Review, May 6, 2002, Jay Winik, review of *Look Away!,* p. 46.

New York Review of Books, June 13, 2002, James M. McPherson, "Could the South Have Won?," review of *Look Away!,* pp. 23-25.

New York Times, January 12, 1992, David Herbert Donald, review of *Jefferson Davis;* August 16, 1998, Paula Mitchell Marks, review of *Three Roads to the Alamo;* July 8, 2001, Daniel Sutherland, "A Civil Ending?," p. 26.

Parameters: U.S. Army War College Quarterly, autumn, 1992, review of *Jefferson Davis,* p. 123.

Publishers Weekly, November 1, 1991, review of *Jefferson Davis,* p. 68; January 9, 1995, review of *A Way through the Wilderness,* p. 53; April 6, 1998, review of *Three Roads to the Alamo,* p. 64; November 23, 1998, review of *Lincoln's Men,* p. 52; March 12, 2001, review of *The Union That Shaped the Confederacy,* p. 75; February 4, 2002, review of *Look Away!,* p. 65.

Reference & Research Book News, November, 1993, review of *The Battle of New Market,* p. 11; May, 1999, review of *The American Frontier,* p. 55.

Reviews in American History, September, 1995, review of *"A Government of Our Own,"* p. 444; September, 1999, review of *Lincoln's Men,* p. 414;

School Library Journal, March, 1993, review of *The American Frontier,* p. 240.

Times Literary Supplement, February 1, 2002, James M. McPherson, "Destroyed Utterly," review of *An Honorable Defeat,* p. 7.

Virginia Quarterly Review, autumn, 1996, review of *Jefferson Davis,* p. 141.

Wall Street Journal, November 8, 1994, review of *"A Government of Our Own,"* p. A20; February 26, 1997, review of *The Cause Lost,* p. A16.

Washington Post, May 30, 1980; May 27, 2001, Ernest B. Furguson, "On the Run," p. T04.

ONLINE

Alamo de Parras, http://alamo-de-parras.welkin.org/ (May 30, 2001), Stephen L. Hardin, interview with Davis.

Virginia Center for Civil War Studies, http://www.civilwar.vt.edu/staff/ (August 18, 2002), profile of Davis.

*   *   *

DiRENZO, Anthony 1960-

PERSONAL: Born January 22, 1960, in Brooklyn, NY; son of Philip (a fashion executive) and Maria Bilo DiRenzo (a storyteller and homemaker); married Sharon Elizabeth Ahlers (a teacher and academic counselor), May 12, 1990. *Education:* S. I. Newhouse School of Public Communications, Syracuse University, B.S., 1982; Villanova University, M.A., 1986; Syracuse University, Ph.D., 1990. *Politics:* "Conservative by Temperament, Radical by Default." *Religion:* Roman Catholic. *Hobbies and other interests:* Opera, theater.

ADDRESSES: Home—507 Hector St., Ithaca, NY. *Office*—Department of Writing, Ithaca College, Park 223, Ithaca, NY 14850.

CAREER: Syracuse University, Syracuse, NY, adjunct professor of English, 1990-93; Ithaca College, Ithaca, NY, associate professor in Department of Writing,

1990—. Also worked variously as copywriter, public relations agent, broadcaster, lector, cantor, and Eucharistic minister.

MEMBER: National Council of Teachers of English, College Composition and Communication, Modern Language Association, International Humor Society, Pirandello Society of America, Association of Business Communicators, Association of Teachers of Technical Writing, Italian American Writers Association, Onondaga historical Association.

AWARDS, HONORS: Pushcart Prize nomination, 1998, for "Exiles from Cockaigne: Pimping Sausages and Other Italian-American Tragedies"; Pushcart Prize and Best American Essays nomination, 1999, for "Coffeehouse Philosophy."

WRITINGS:

American Gargoyles: Flannery O'Connor and the Medieval Grotesque, Southern Illinois University Press (Carbondale, IL), 1993.
If I Were Boss: The Early Business Stories of Sinclair Lewis, Southern Illinois University Press (Carbondale, IL), 1997.

Also author of "Exiles from Cockaigne: Pimping Sausages and Other Italian-American Tragedies," 1997, "Coffeehouse Philosophy," 1998, "Eddie, Kiss Me Goodnight," 1998; "The Apotheosis of Brumidi," 1999, and "Tears and Onions," 2000, all appearing in *River Styx*. Stories published in literary journals, including *Il Caffé, Syracuse Scholar, Studia Mistica, Kansas Review, Coydog Review, Pangloss Papers, Quixote,* and *Saw Hill Journal*.

WORK IN PROGRESS: Novels, including *After the Fair Is Over, The Altar and the City,* and *His Master's Voice;* essay collection *Bitter Greens;* critical study *The Great American Dream Machine: John Dos Passos' USA;* opera libretto, *Canallers,* a retelling of Giacomo Puccini's *Il Tabarrro* set on the Syracuse Erie Canal circa 1910.

SIDELIGHTS: Anthony DiRenzo told *CA:* "Like those professional letter writers, who plied their trade in Little Italies all over America at the turn of the century, I find myself a messenger between two worlds, struggling with the problems of audience and language. Having been raised in a largely oral minority culture, how do I do it justice by writing about it in the words of the literate culture that has marginalized it, that has, in fact, done everything in its power to eradicate it? To be an Italian-American writer is to embrace contradiction and to court betrayal. What kind of double agent am I, and to whom do I owe my allegiance? Like the old proverb says, *Traduttore traditore.* The very hyphen between the two words, Italian and American, symbolizes this dilemma. It is both a bridge and a plank, a checkpoint and a toll gate. An American education has made me an unwilling participant in the destruction of Italian immigrant culture, but without that education I could not preserve the culture of my childhood from complete annihilation. Basically, I'm a chronicler of a fading world, a notary public recording the depositions of ghosts. My fiction and most of my scholarship can be likened to an open coroner's inquest in which an entire community agonizes over the overwhelming evidence of its own demise and asks if it was murder, suicide, or accidental death. Naturally, such business is ghastly, relieved only by the sardonic humor of its participants. But culturecide does that, turns ordinary people into self-mocking skeletons. Each time I press my fingers to my keyboard, I hear the rattling of bones.

"Put another way, my writing documents the necrophilic commodification of Italian culture in the Great Shopping Mall of America. I am appalled by how bits and pieces of my world become transubstantiated into stickers, t-shirts, and fast food. Such relentless commercialism is a Satanic parody of the Eucharist, a form of cannibalism in which my people are both consumers and the consumed."

*   *   *

DOBRIN, Arthur 1943-

PERSONAL: Born August 22, 1943, in Brooklyn, NY; son of Moe (a truck driver) and Anne (Slavin) Dobrin; married Lyn Beth Fradkin (a writer of children's books, artist, and model), August 30, 1960; children: Eric Simba, Kikora Anana. *Education:* City College of the City University of New York, B.A., 1965; New York University, M.A., 1971; additional graduate study at Nathan Ackerman Family Institute, 1973-75. *Religion:* Ethical Humanist.

ADDRESSES: Home—613 Dartmouth St., Westbury, NY 11590. *Office*—Ethical Humanist Society, 38 Old Country Rd., Garden City, NY 11530.

CAREER: Poet. U.S. Peace Corps, volunteer in Kenya, 1965-67; Ethical Humanist Society of Long Island, Garden City, NY, leader, 1968-2001, leader emeritus, 2001—. Initiator of The Learning Tree (experimental school); summer director of Encampment for Citizenship, Great Falls, MT, and Tucson, AZ, 1968, 1969, 1970, 1972; director of Institute for Leadership Development, 1971-72; teacher at Westbury Experimental High School, 1973-74; Hofstra University's New School, associate professor of social science. Board member of Westbury League of Women Voters, 1974-75.

MEMBER: World Poetry Society, Amnesty International, American Association of Marriage and Family Therapists (clinical member), Poetry Society of America, Human Subjects Review Committee of Long Island Jewish Hospital, Long Island Progressive Coalition (board member), Ethics Committee of Winthrop-University Hospital.

WRITINGS:

The Role of Cooperatives in the Development of Rural Kenya (monograph), Rutgers University Press, 1970.

(With Kenneth Briggs) *Getting Married the Way You Want,* Prentice-Hall (Englewood Cliffs, NJ), 1974.

Little Heroes, Cross-Cultural Communications (Merrick, NJ), 1977.

Lace: Poetry from the Poor, Homeless, Aged, Physically and Emotionally Handicapped, Cross-Cultural Communications (Merrick, NJ), 1979.

(Editor, with wife, Lyn Dobrin, and Thomas Liotti) *Convictions: Political Prisoners—Their Stories,* Orbis (Maryknoll, NY), 1981.

(Editor) *Being Good and Doing Right: Readings in Moral Development,* University Press of America (Lanham, MD), 1993.

Spelling God with Two O's: Thoughts, Stories and Questions on Making a Moral Life, Columbia (Bethpage, NY), 1993.

Ethical People: And How they Get to Be That Way, University Press of America (Lanham, MD), 1993.

Malaika (novel), Jomo Kenyatta Foundation (Nairobi, Kenya), 1998.

Love Your Neighbor: Stories of Values and Virtues, Scholastic (New York, NY), 1999.

Teaching Right from Wrong: 40 Things You Can Do to Raise a Moral Child, Berkley Books (New York, NY), 2001.

Ethics for Everyone: How to Increase Your Moral Intelligence, J. Wiley & Sons (New York, NY), 2002.

POETRY

Sunbird: Poems of East Africa, Cross-Cultural Communications (Merrick, NJ), 1976.

Saying My Name Out Loud, Xanadu Press, 1978.

Gentle Spears, Cross-Cultural Communications (Merrick, NJ), 1979.

Out of Place, Backstreet Press, 1982.

Angels and Chambers, Cross-Cultural Communications (Merrick, NJ), 2001.

Contributor of poems to *Bitterroot, Chelsea, Dark Waters, Street Cries, Compass, Poet, Ocarina, Xanadu,* and *East Africa Journal.*

SIDELIGHTS: Arthur Dobrin is the author of numerous nonfiction books, poetry collections, and essays. Many of his nonfiction works reflect his leadership role with the Ethical Humanist Society of Long Island, a position from which he has recently stepped down to emeritus status. Together with his wife, Lyn, he has worked in Kisii, Kenya, as a Peace Corp volunteer; he has conducted annual people-to-people tours and photo safaris to Kenya; and he is the co-founder and co-leader of Amnesty International Group #74 and the Long Island Interracial Alliance for a Common Future. He also teaches classes in religious ethics and the psychology of morality at Hofstra University.

Among Dobrin's nonfiction publications are three books focused on ethics: *Love Your Neighbor: Stories of Values and Virtues* (1999); *Teaching Right from Wrong: 40 Thing You Can Do to Raise a Moral Child* (2001); and *Ethics for Everyone: How to Increase Your Moral Intelligence* (2002). The first book in this trio is a collection of morality tales for children to help them overcome prejudice and learn cooperation, character, and kindness. Using animals to portray specific challenges in day-to-day living, Dobrin tells thirteen short stories, each ending in a question, which he urges the reader to try to answer. Megan Rutherford, writing a review for *Time,* found these tales to be "thought-provoking" and predicted that although the book is targeted toward children, parents and older students will also find something to enjoy in this book.

Teaching Right from Wrong helps guide parents in ways to teach their children to be kind, trustworthy, considerate, and fair. The concepts that Dobrin offers in this book come from current research in psychology. Dobrin demonstrates how ethical intelligence is teachable, how certain aspects of today's society shapes a child's character in either positive or negative ways, and how to avoid common pitfalls that parents often run into in educating their children.

Ethics for Everyone contains several examples of morally difficult situations that people commonly face. After defining a specific moral conflict, Dobrin considers both sides of the issue, encouraging his readers to extend their own thoughts to the broadest possible boundaries. Although Dobrin states that there are no easy answers to the dilemmas that he includes in this book, he believes that by discussing them, readers can gain better insight and make better decisions when faced with moral questions of their own. In the beginning of the book, Dobrin provides a set of questions for his readers that test their moral intelligence. After reading the book, readers are encouraged to answer the questions again and to make note of any changes in their thinking. A *Publishers Weekly* reviewer predicted that most readers will more than likely see a change in the results of the two separate sets of answers. They might find, it was suggested, that "their own ethical perspectives [have become] more nuanced and satisfying."

BIOGRAPHICAL AND CRITICAL SOURCES:

PERIODICALS

Family Circle, June, 1974.
Publishers Weekly, April 26, 1999, Volume 246, number 17, review of *Love Your Neighbor: Stories of Values and Virtues,* p. 82; February 18, 2002, Vol. 249, No. 7, review of *Ethics for Everyone: How to Increase Your Moral Intelligence,* p. 84.
School Library Journal, March 1999, Volume 45, number 3, Marianne Saccardi, review of *Love Your Neighbor: Stores of Values and Virtues,* p. 173.

Time, June 21, 1999, Volume 153, number 24, Megan Rutherford, review of *Love Your Neighbor: Stories of Values and Virtues,* p. 82K.*

*   *   *

DOWNING, Michael (Bernard) 1958-

PERSONAL: Born May 8, 1958, in Pittsfield, MA; son of John Frederick and Gertrude Nora (Martin) Downing. *Education:* Harvard University, B.A. (magna cum laude), 1980. *Politics:* Democrat. *Religion:* Roman Catholic.

ADDRESSES: Home—50 Follen St., No. 505, Cambridge, MA 02138. *Office*—Wheelock College, 200 Riverway, Boston, MA 02215-4176. *E-mail*—downing58@aol.com.

CAREER: Novelist, editor, and educator. *Oceanus* (periodical), Woods Hole, MA, senior editor, 1983-84; *FMR* (periodical), Milan, Italy, senior editor, 1984-86; Bentley College, Waltham, MA, instructor in English, 1987-88; Wheelock College, Boston, MA, instructor, 1988-91, assistant professor of humanities and director of writing program, 1992—.

MEMBER: PEN, Authors Guild, Authors League of America, Share Our Strength (Washington, DC; writers' committee).

AWARDS, HONORS: Harvard-Shrewsbury fellow in Shropshire, England, 1980-81; *Perfect Agreement* named a best book of 1997 by *Newsday.*

WRITINGS:

NOVELS

A Narrow Time, Vintage (New York, NY), 1987.
Mother of God, Simon & Schuster (New York, NY), 1990.
Perfect Agreement, Counterpoint (Washington, DC), 1997.
Breakfast with Scot: A Novel, Counterpoint (Washington, DC), 1999.

OTHER

The Last Shaker (play), produced at Triangle Theater, in Boston, MA, 1995.
Shoes Outside the Door: Desire, Devotion, and Excess at the San Francisco Zen Center, Counterpoint (Washington, DC), 2001.

Work represented in anthologies, including *Louder than Words,* Vintage (New York, NY), 1989. Contributor of stories, poems, essays, and reviews to periodicals, including *America, Commonweal, Harvard,* and *Salopian.*

SIDELIGHTS: Michael Downing's debut novel, 1987's *A Narrow Time,* is the first-person narrative of Anne Fossicker, a working Connecticut wife and mother of three children. Anne's daughter Sarah disappears from parochial school, and Anne's feelings of guilt about having a career are brought to the fore as she anxiously leads the search effort. It turns out that Sarah has been kidnapped by a novice nun who has a history of abuse. After the nun commits suicide, the daughter is found with her grandmother, who has kept the child's whereabouts a secret from the parents.

The book was hailed by Tom Nolan in the *New York Times Book Review* as a "remarkable novel" and by a *Publishers Weekly* reviewer as "impressive." The latter critic described the work as "told in an extraordinary voice" and as a "superior portrait of human suffering and pain." Reviewer Nolan commented that the author "renders his narrator's feelings and actions so skillfully that each sentence seems at once surprising and completely true." He concluded that the novel "has the emotional precision of the best fiction and the satisfying resolution of a detective story."

Downing's second novel, *Mother of God,* centers on the emotional troubles of Stephen Adamski and of his family, particularly his controlling mother, Sylvia. A young man, Stephen is arrested for vandalizing a synagogue after learning that his father is not his biological parent. A *Publishers Weekly* critic found the characters "neither likable nor inspiring," and the author's analysis of their motivations uninteresting.

In his third novel, *Perfect Agreement,* Downing again deals with religious concerns. The novel examines the life-crisis of thirty-six-year-old Mark Sternum, who has just been fired from his job as head of writing programs at a small college. His long-lost father shows up after a stint in a Shaker community and tells a complicated story about an old Shaker, Sister Celia. In the opinion of a *Publishers Weekly* reviewer, Sister Celia's story is "seamlessly woven in and out of the main plot," although perhaps too complexly resolved. The reviewer pointed out that chapters of the novel are marked with short lessons on the rules of English. Calling the book "graceful," the reviewer concluded that *Perfect Agreement* is "a novel of . . . compassion and wit" that "combines one man's tale of loss and acceptance, the lost rhythms of the Shaker world and the delights of the English language."

In 1999, Downing published his fourth novel, *Breakfast with Scot,* a critically-acclaimed tale about a sexually-confused 11-year-old, who is sent to live with two gay men after his mother dies. The story is narrated by Ed, who, along with his partner, Sam, agrees to care for Scot. But Scot is not a normal boy. He dresses like a girl and wears makeup, and many of his mannerisms are feminine. The story follows as Sam and Ed adjust to parenthood, with all its travails and pitfalls. "Having a child, I soon learned, is like having an open wound," Ed says in the story. "People ask you about it. They give you advice and secret remedies. Friends tell you to ignore it for a while and see if it doesn't heal itself. Everyone assures you that it won't kill you. And then they show you their scars." While Sam and Ed fret about Scot's safety at school and from neighborhood bullies, the two learn much about themselves. The book was hailed by several critics, including Nancy Pearl of *Library Journal,* who called it a "refreshingly off-beat take on gay parenting." J. E. Robinson, who reviewed the book for the *Lambda Book Report,* felt it was a "well-written, realistic novel." A contributor for *Publishers Weekly* called Downing's prose "melodious and lucid."

Downing got away from fiction with his next project, the nonfiction book *Shoes Outside the Door: Desire, Devotion, and Excess at the San Francisco Zen Center.* The book recalls the rise and fall of the San Francisco Zen Center and its former leader, Richard Baker. Downing discusses how Baker turned the center into a money-making empire in the 1970s and early 1980s. However, in 1983, a scandal known in Zen circles as "the Apocalypse" brought Baker down, when he used his influence and authority to have a sexual relationship with the wife of one of the center's biggest benefactors. In the years after the event took place, there was much speculation about what exactly happened. Downing wrote the book to find out. He spent three years interviewing some eighty people who were familiar with the events. One person who declined an interview, however, was Baker himself. Still, Downing achieved his goal of uncovering the details. Downing also lets readers know how the center has fared since the scandal.

Donna Seaman, who reviewed the book for *Booklist,* called the work "a fascinating, multifaceted chronicle," and "an invaluable portrait of the . . . American Buddhist movement." Several critics also lauded Downing's prose style. "Downing tells the story with a novelist's attention to character and detail," wrote a contributor for *Publishers Weekly.* Similarly, Kay Meredith of *Library Journal* felt the book had "a narrative style that flows quickly."

BIOGRAPHICAL AND CRITICAL SOURCES:

PERIODICALS

Booklist, October 1, 2001, p. 282.
Boston Review, December, 1987, p. 28.
Kirkus Reviews, September 15, 1987, p. 1338; March 15, 1990, p. 361.
Lambda Book Report, January, 2000, p. 23.
Library Journal, December, 2001, p. 212; October 1, 2001, p. 120.
New York Times Book Review, January 3, 1988, p. 18.
Publishers Weekly, October 23, 1987, p. 50; March 23, 1990, p. 64; October 13, 1997, p. 57; September 13, 1999, p. 57; October 15, 2001, p. 68.
San Francisco Chronicle, November 11, 2001, p. 3.

ONLINE

Counterpoint Press Web site, http://www.counterpointpress.com/ (May 29, 2002), "Interview with Michael Downing."
Salon.com, http://www.salon.com/ (May 29, 2002), Greg Bottoms's review of *Breakfast with Scot.**

*   *   *

DREZ, Ronald J(oseph) 1940-

PERSONAL: Born March 2, 1940, in New Orleans, LA; son of J. Roger Drez and Aline Raynaud Drez; married Judith LaCour (an interior designer), June 13, 1964; children: Ronald, Jr., Kevin, Diane Barnett, Craig. *Education:* Tulane University, B.B.A., 1962; University of New Orleans, M.A., 1985. *Religion:* Catholic.

ADDRESSES: Home and office—8516 Fordham Ct., New Orleans, LA 70127.

CAREER: Bonded Carbon and Ribbon Co., Inc., New Orleans, LA, salesperson, 1969-72; Dockside Elevators, New Orleans, operations manager, 1973-82; Delta Transload, New Orleans, general manager, 1982-86; self-employed, 1987—. University of New Orleans Metro College Eisenhower Center, assistant director, 1987—. *Military service:* U.S. Marine Corps, 1962-69; served in Vietnam; became captain; received two Bronze Stars and the Vietnamese Cross of Gallantry.

AWARDS, HONORS: Outstanding Young Men of America, 1968; George Wendell Award for outstanding thesis, University of New Orleans, 1985.

WRITINGS:

Voices of D-Day: The Story of the Allied Invasion, Told by Those Who Were There, Louisiana State University Press (Baton Rouge, LA), 1994.
Twenty-five Yards of War: The Extraordinary Courage of Ordinary Men in World War II, Hyperion Books (New York, NY), 2001.

WORK IN PROGRESS: Midnight in a Flaming Town, a novel about boat people, intrigue, and lost treasures; research about military action at Khe Sanh and in the Persian Gulf War.

SIDELIGHTS: Ronald J. Drez once told *CA:* "As the assistant director of the Eisenhower Center at the University of New Orleans, I began research into the invasion of Normandy with the idea to preserve the oral histories and thoughts of the veterans who had fought in that climactic battle of World War II. Over the next eight years I interviewed hundreds of veterans, encouraging hundreds of others to make their own oral histories to submit to the Eisenhower Center so that by the end of 1992, we possessed some 1,400 memoirs or oral histories.

"After much editing, *Voices of D-Day* emerged as a work in which the men who fought at Normandy told the story of the invasion of June 6, 1944. The guiding person who influenced the creation of *Voices* was Dr. Stephen Ambrose, the noted historian and biographer of General Dwight Eisenhower."

Another ten years of research and over 1,400 interviews resulted in *Twenty-five Yards of War: The Extraordinary Courage of Ordinary Men in World War II,* released in time for the sixtieth anniversary of the bombing of Pearl Harbor. More broadly focused than *Voices of D-Day, Twenty-five Yards of War* presents a panoramic view of the front lines from battles across the globe, representing all branches of the military. From the Battle of Midway in the Pacific to the Battle of the Bulge in Belgium, the stories of a total of ten battles are included in the book, told in the voices of those who were there. Included are the invasion of Normandy, told by Private Kenneth Russell and First Sergeant Leonard Lomell; Iwo Jima, by Private First Class Jay Rebstock of the United States Marine Corps; the sinking of the *U.S.S. Indianapolis,* by Seaman Second Class Harold Eck; and the battle at China's Namkwan Harbor, by Dr. Eugene B. Fluckey, United States Navy. First Lieutenant Lyle Bouck of the 99th Infantry Division recalls looking through his binoculars at the Battle of the Bulge and watching as German paratroopers approach the men under his command. Critic Douglas Brinkley wrote for Hyperion Books, "These tales of survival against incredible odds speak to the extraordinary combination of bravery and miracle that served to bring the men back alive." The stories, he wrote, are "riveting . . . timeless paeans to duty, honor, and country." The title of the book, *Twenty-five Yards of War,* refers to the "a soldier's 25 yards—the length and breadth of the war for him at any given moment," as noted by a *Publishers Weekly* critic. Praising Drez for his research and storytelling, the *Publishers Weekly* critic wrote, "Drez, a Vietnam veteran, is in sync with his interviewees, and his facile pen brings their stories to life." Gilbert Taylor of *Booklist* wrote, "In a palpable, unfeigned way, Drez extols their heroism and valor through his focus on the individual combat experience. Resonant reading."

BIOGRAPHICAL AND CRITICAL SOURCES:

PERIODICALS

Booklist, November 15, 2001, Gilbert Taylor, review of *Twenty-five Yards of War: The Extraordinary Courage of Ordinary Men in World War II,* p. 544.

History: The Journal of the Historical Association, April 1998, Michael Partridge, review of *Voices of D-Day: The Story of the Allied Invasion, Told by Those Who Were There,* p. 383.
Journal of American History, June, 1995, review of *Voices of D-Day,* p.338.
Kliatt Young Adult Paperback Book Guide, September, 1996, review of *Voices of D-Day,* p.32.
Virginia Quarterly Review, autumn, 1996, review of *Voices of D-Day,* p. 142.
World War II Magazine, March, 2002, Steven Martinovich, review of *Twenty-five Yards of War.*

ONLINE

Hyperion Books, www.hyperionbooks.com/ (fall, 2001), Douglas Brinkley, review of *Twenty-five Yards of War,**

*   *   *

DUFFY, Carol Ann 1955-

PERSONAL: Born December 23, 1955, in Glasgow, Scotland; daughter of Francis (an engineer) and Mary (Black) Duffy; partner of Jackie Kay (a poet), since early 1990s; children: Ella. *Education:* University of Liverpool, B.A. (with honors), 1977. *Politics:* Socialist.

ADDRESSES: Home—4 Camp View, London SW19 4UL, England. *Agent*—Penny Tackaberry, Tessa Sayle Agency, 11 Jubilee Pl., London SW3 3TE, England.

CAREER: Worked for Granada Television, c. 1977-81; *Ambit* magazine, London, England, poetry editor, 1983—; full-time freelance writer, 1985—. Writer in residence in East End schools, London, England, 1982-84; North Riding College, Scarborough, England, visiting fellow, 1985; Southern Arts, Thamesdown, England, writer in residence, 1987-88; part-time creative writing instructor, Manchester Metropolitan University, 1996—; visiting professor, Wake Forest University.

MEMBER: Royal Society of Letters (fellow).

AWARDS, HONORS: C. Day Lewis fellow of poetry, Greater London Arts Association, 1982-84; first prize, National Poetry Competition, British Broadcasting Corp., 1983, for "Whoever She Was"; Eric Gregory Award, British Society of Authors, 1984; Book Award, Scottish Arts Council, 1986, for *Standing Female Nude;* first prize, "Poems about Painting" competition, Peterloo Poets, 1986, for "The Virgin Punishing the Infant"; Somerset Maugham Award, Society of Authors, 1987, for *Selling Manhattan;* Dylan Thomas Award, 1989, for *The Other Country;* Book Award, Scottish Arts Council, 1989; Cholmondeley Award, 1992; Book Award, Scottish Arts Council, 1993, for *Mean Time;* Whitbread Award and Forward Poetry Prize, both 1993, both for *Mean Time;* Lannan Award, 1995; Order of the British Empire, 1995; Signal Poetry Award, 1997, for *Stopping for Death: Poems of Death and Loss,* 2001, for *The Oldest Girl in the World;* shortlist, Forward Poetry Prize, 1999, for *The World's Wife;* National Lottery grant, 2000.

WRITINGS:

POETRY

Fleshweathercock, and Other Poems, Outposts (Walton-on-Thames, Surrey, England), 1973.
Fifth Last Song, Headland (Wirral, Merseyside, England), 1982.
Standing Female Nude, Anvil Press (London, England), 1985.
Thrown Voices, Turret Books (London, England), 1986.
Selling Manhattan, Anvil Press (London, England), 1987.
The Other Country, Anvil Press (London, England), 1990.
Mean Time, Anvil Press (London, England), 1993.
Selected Poems, Penguin (London, England)/Anvil Press (London, England), 1994.
The Pamphlet, Anvil Press (London, England), 1999.
The World's Wife, Picador (New York, NY), Faber & Faber (London, England), 2000.

PLAYS

Take My Husband (two-act), first produced in Liverpool, England, at Liverpool Playhouse, December 4, 1982.
Cavern of Dreams (two-act), first produced in Liverpool at Liverpool Playhouse, August 3, 1984.

Loss (one-act), first broadcast by BBC-Radio, July 22, 1986.
Little Women, Big Boys (one-act), first produced in London, England, at Almeida Theatre, August 8, 1986.

FOR CHILDREN

(Adaptor) *Grimm Tales,* Faber & Faber (London, England), 1996.
Meeting Midnight (poems), Faber & Faber (London, England), 1999.
(With Jackie Kay, Roger McGough, Gareth Owen, Brian Patten) *Five Finger-Piglets* (poems), Macmillan (London, England), 1999.
The Oldest Girl in the World, Faber & Faber (London, England), 2000.

OTHER

(Editor) *Home and Away,* Southern Arts (Thamesdown, England), 1988.
(Editor and contributor) *I Wouldn't Thank You for a Valentine: Anthology of Women's Poetry,* illustrated by Trisha Rafferty, Viking (New York, NY), 1992, published as *I Wouldn't Thank You for a Valentine: Poems for Young Feminists,* Holt (New York, NY), 1993.
(Editor) *Stopping for Death: Poems of Death and Loss,* illustrated by Trisha Rafferty, Holt (New York, NY), 1996.
(Editor) *Time's Tidings: Greeting the Twenty-first Century,* Anvil Press (London, England), 1999.

Duffy's manuscripts are housed at the Robert W. Woodruff Library, Emory University.

ADAPTATIONS: Duffy's version of Grimms' fairy tales has been adapted for the stage.

SIDELIGHTS: Carol Ann Duffy is an award-winning English poet who, according to Danette DiMarco in *Mosaic,* is the poet of "post-post war England: Thatcher's England." Duffy is best known for writing love poems that often take the form of monologues. Her verses, as an *Economist* reviewer described them, are typically "spoken in the voices of the urban disaffected, people on the margins of society who harbour resentments and grudges against the world." Although she knew she was a lesbian since her days at St. Joseph's convent school, her early love poems give no indication of her homosexuality; the object of love in her verses is someone whose gender is not specified. Not until her 1993 collection, *Mean Time,* and 1994's *Selected Poems,* does she begin to write about homosexual love.

Duffy's poetry has always had a strong feminist edge, however. This position is especially well captured in her *Standing Female Nude,* in which the collection's title poem consists of an interior monologue comprising a female model's response to the male artist who is painting her image in a Cubist style. Although at first the conversation seems to indicate the model's acceptance of conventional attitudes about beauty in art—and, by extension, what an ideal woman should be—as the poem progresses Duffy deconstructs these traditional beliefs. Ultimately, the poet expresses that "the model cannot be contained by the visual art that would regulate her," explained DiMarco. "And here the way the poem ends with the model's final comment on the painting 'It does not look like me'—is especially instructive. On the one hand, her response suggests that she is naive and does not understand the nature of Cubist art. On the other hand, however, the comment suggests her own variableness, and challenges traditionalist notions that the naked model can, indeed, be transmogrified into the male artist's representation of her in the nude form. To the model, the painting does not represent either what she understands herself to be or her lifestyle."

Duffy was seriously considered for the position of poet laureate in Britain in 1999. Prime Minister Tony Blair's administration had wanted a poet laureate who exemplified the new "Cool Britannia," not an establishment figure, and Duffy was certainly anything but establishment. She is the Scottish-born lesbian daughter of two Glasgow working-class radicals. Her partner is another poet, a black woman, and the two of them are raising a child together. Duffy has a strong following among young Britons, partially as a result of her poetry collection *Mean Time* being included in Britain's A-level curriculum, but Blair was worried about how "middle England" would react to a lesbian poet laureate. There were also concerns in the administration about what Britain's notorious tabloids would write about her sexuality, and about comments that Duffy had made urging an updated role for the poet

laureate. In the end, Blair opted for the safe choice and named Andrew Motion to the post.

After Duffy had been passed over, Katherine Viner wrote in the *Guardian Weekend* that her "poems are accessible and entertaining, yet her form is classical, her technique razor-sharp. She is read by people who don't really read poetry, yet she maintains the respect of her peers. Reviewers praise her touching, sensitive, witty evocations of love, loss, dislocation, nostalgia; fans talk of greeting her at readings 'with claps and cheers that would not sound out of place at a rock concert.'" Viner lamented that Duffy only came to the attention of many people when she was caricatured and rejected as poet laureate. However, the poet got some satisfaction when she earned the National Lottery award of 75,000 pounds, a sum that far exceeded the stipend that poet laureates receive.

After the laureate debacle, Duffy was further vindicated when her next original collection of poems, *The World's Wife,* received high acclaim from critics. In what *Antioch Review* contributor Jane Satterfield called "masterful subversions of myth and history," the poems in this collection are all told from the points of view of the women behind famous male figures, both real and fictional, including the wives and lovers of Aesop, Pontius Pilate, Faust, Tiresius, Herod, Quasimodo, Lazarus, Sisyphus, Freud, Darwin, and even King Kong. Not all the women are wives, however. For example, one poem is told from Medusa's point of view as she expresses her feelings before being slain by Perseus; "Little Red-Cap" takes the story of Little Red Riding Hood to a new level as a teenage girl is seduced by a "wolf-poet." These fresh perspectives allow Duffy to indulge in a great deal of humor and wit as, for example, Mrs. Aesop grows tired of her husband's constant moralizing, Mrs. Freud complains about the great psychologist's obsession with penises, Sisyphus's bride is stuck with a workaholic, and Mrs. Lazarus, after finding a new husband, has her life ruined by the return of her formerly dead husband. There are conflicting emotions as well in such poems as "Mrs. Midas," in which the narrator is disgusted by her husband's greed, but, at the same time, longs for something she can never have: his physical touch. "*The World's Wife* appeals and astonishes," said Satterfield. "Duffy's mastery of personae allows for seamless movement through the centuries; in this complementary chorus, there's voice and vision for the coming ones." An *Economist* reviewer felt that the collection "is savage, trenchant, humorous and wonderfully inventive at its best." And Ray Olson, writing in *Booklist,* concluded that "Duffy's takes on the stuff of legends are . . . richly rewarding."

Duffy has also written verses for children, many of which are published in *Meeting Midnight* and *Five Finger-Piglets.* The poems in *Meeting Midnight,* as the title indicates, help children confront their fears by addressing them openly. "They explore the hinterland in a child's imagination where life seems built on quicksand and nameless worries move in and will not leave," explained Kate Kellaway in an *Observer* review. Kellaway also asserted that "these are real poems by one of the best English poets writing at the moment."

In addition to her original poetry, Duffy has edited two anthologies, *I Wouldn't Thank You for a Valentine: Poems for Young Feminists* and *Stopping for Death: Poems of Death and Loss,* and has adapted eight classic Brothers Grimm fairy tales in *Grimm Tales.* Not intended for young children but for older children and young adults in drama and English classes, *Grimm Tales* includes adaptations of such stories as "Hansel and Gretel" and "The Golden Goose," which are rewritten "with a poet's vigor and economy, combining traditions of style with direct, colloquial dialogue," according to Vida Conway in *School Librarian.*

BIOGRAPHICAL AND CRITICAL SOURCES:

PERIODICALS

Antioch Review, winter, 2001, Jane Satterfield, review of *The World's Wife,* p. 123.

Booklist, March 1, 1994, p. 1260; April 1, 2000, Ray Olson, review of *The World's Wife,* p. 1426.

Book Report, September, 1994, p. 49

Bulletin of the Center for Children's Books, February, 1994, Betsy Hearne, review of *I Wouldn't Thank You for a Valentine: Poems for Young Feminists,* pp. 184-185; September, 1996, Betsy Hearne, review of *Stopping for Death: Poems of Death and Loss,* pp. 9-10.

Economist, March 18, 2000, "Whose Voice Is It Anyway?," p. 14.

Guardian Weekend, September 25, 1999, Katherine Viner, "Metre Maid," pp. 20-26.

Horn Book, May, 1994, Nancy Vasilakis, review of *I Wouldn't Thank You for a Valentine: Poems for Young Feminists,* p. 329.

Independent (London, England) October 2, 1999, Christina Patterson, "Street-wise Heroines at Home," p. WR9.

Kirkus Reviews, January 1, 1994, Review of *I Wouldn't Thank You for a Valentine: Poems for Young Feminists,* p. 66; June 15, 1996, review of *Stopping for Death: Poems of Death and Loss,* p. 897.

Mosaic (Winnipeg, Canada), September, 1998, Danette DiMarco, "Exposing Nude Art: Carol Ann Duffy's Response to Robert Browning," pp. 25-39.

New Statesman, November 29, 1999, review of *Time's Tidings: Greeting the Twenty-first Century,* p. 83.

Observer (London, England), August 15, 1999, review of *The World's Wife* (audio version), p. 14; October 24, 1999, Kate Kellaway, review of *Meeting Midnight,* p. 13.

School Librarian, November, 1992, Doris Telford, review of *I Wouldn't Thank You for a Valentine: Poems for Young Feminists,* p. 154; May, 1996, Vida Conway, review of *Grimm Tales,* p. 70; summer, 1999, review of *Five Finger-Piglets,* p. 96.

School Library Journal, January, 1994, p. 66; August, 1996, Sharon Korbeck, review of *Stopping for Death: Poems of Death and Loss,* p. 168.

Sunday Times, March 28, 1999, Richard Brooks, "Laureate Favourite Tells of Lesbian Love," p. N5.

Theology, May-June, 1997, James Woodward, review of *Stopping for Death,* pp. 234-235.

Times Educational Supplement, January 22, 1999, review of *The Pamphlet,* p. 13; April 23, 1999, review of *Five Finger-Piglets,* p. 27; December 17, 1999, review of *The World's Wife,* p. 22; January 19, 2001, John Mole, review of *The Oldest Girl in the World,* p. F20.

Times Literary Supplement, March 3, 1995, p. 24; July 7, 1995, p. 32; December 3, 1999, Alan Brownjohn, review of *The World's Wife,* p. 24.

Voice of Youth Advocates, April, 1994, p. 48; October, 1996, p. 238.

ONLINE

The Knitting Circle Web site, http://www.sbu.ac.uk/~stafflag/ (July 26, 2001), "Carol Ann Duffy."*

E

ELLIS, Richard J. 1960-

PERSONAL: Born November 27, 1960, in Leicester, England; immigrated to the United States; son of John M. (a professor) and Carol Robertson (a high school teacher; maiden name, Hails) Ellis; married Juli Hakenaka (an elementary school teacher), July 18, 1987; children: Eleanor, Nicholas. *Education:* University of California, Santa Cruz, B.A., 1982; University of California, Berkeley, M.A., 1984, Ph.D., 1989.

ADDRESSES: Home—1645 Madrona Ave. S., Salem, OR 97302. *Office*—Department of Political Science, Willamette University, 900 State St., Salem, OR 97301. *E-mail*—rellis@willamette.edu

CAREER: Willamette University, Salem, OR, assistant professor, 1990-1995, associate professor of political science, 1995-99, Mark O. Hatfield professor of politics, 1999—; writer. University of California, Santa Cruz, visiting lecturer in political science, 1989.

AWARDS, HONORS: Grant from National Endowment for the Humanities, 1991; Earhart Foundation fellow, 1993, 1998; George and Eliza Gardner Howard fellow, 1993; research grant, Oregon Council for the Humanities, 1994; Donner Foundation grant, 1995; Graves Foundation grant, 1998.

WRITINGS:

(With Aaron Wildavsky) *Dilemmas of Presidential Leadership from Washington through Lincoln,* Transaction Publishers (New Brunswick, NJ), 1989.

(With Michael Thompson and Wildavsky) *Cultural Theory,* Westview Press (Boulder, CO), 1990.

Richard J. Ellis

American Political Cultures, Oxford University Press (New York, NY), 1993.

(Editor, with Dennis J. Coyle) *Politics, Policy, and Culture,* Westview Press (Boulder, CO), 1994.

Presidential Lightning Rods: The Politics of Blame Avoidance, University Press of Kansas (Lawrence, KS), 1994.

(Editor, with Thomson) *Culture Matters: Essays in Honor of Aaron Wildavsky,* Westview Press (Boulder, CO), 1997.

(Editor) *Speaking to the People: The Rhetorical Presidency in Historical Perspective,* University of Massachusetts Press (Amherst, MA), 1998.

The Dark Side of the Left: Illiberal Egalitarianism in America, University Press of Kansas (Lawrence, KS), 1998.

(Editor) *Founding the American Presidency,* Rowman & Littlefield (Lanham, MD), 1999.

Democratic Delusions: The Initiative Process in America, University Press of Kansas (Lawrence, KS), 2002.

Contributor to *Political Parties and Elections in the United States: An Encyclopedia,* edited by L. Sandy Maisel, Garland (New York, NY), 1991, and *Routledge Encyclopedia of Government and Politics,* edited by Mary Hawkesworth and Maurice Kogan, Routledge (New York, NY), 1992. Also contributor to political science, history, and economic journals.

SIDELIGHTS: Richard J. Ellis, a native of England, has built his career assessing politics in the United States. A professor of political science at Willamette University in Salem, Oregon, Ellis has written such books as *American Political Cultures* and *Presidential Lightning Rods: The Politics of Blame Avoidance.* The latter book examines how a president may use members of his inner circle—including the vice president, senior staff members, advisers, and even a spouse—to deflect criticism. For such a "lightning rod" to be effective, Ellis writes in the book, the deflector must be widely recognized. "Unknowns," he points out, "cannot function as lightning rods."

Times have changed since Harry Truman placed a sign, "The Buck Stops Here," on his desk in the Oval Office. In today's media-intrusive political environment, a chief executive may delegate blame.

Ellis cites as one example in *Presidential Lightning Rods,* Richard M. Nixon, who turned to many subordinates during the Watergate scandal. The author shows, said John Hart of *American Political Science Review,* "that the scope for lightning-rod strategies is severely constrained by numerous factors, not the least that any president 'who is serious about blame avoidance must be prepared to cede not only responsibility but power.'" Ellis concludes that deflecting blame has become a "prerequisite for effective presidential leadership," wrote Hart, who called *Presidential Lightning*

Rods "a stimulating and challenging analysis of an important aspect of presidential leadership. Not all will agree with his conclusion, but few can deny that his work opens up an area of empirical and normative significance."

In the opening of *The Dark Side of the Left: Illiberal Egalitarianism in America,* Ellis describes himself as a longtime Democrat, a "card-carrying member" of the American Civil Liberties Union, and a federalist. Still, his work looks critically at left-wing movements from the nineteenth-century utopians and abolitionists to modern-day feminists and environmental activists. In many cases, the author asserts, "ideologues abandoned their egalitarian principles in favor of rigid political correctness," as a *Publishers Weekly* contributor noted. The author finds a "common thread" among the left-wingers of yesterday and today, *Society* critic Robert Schaeffer said. "Intrinsic to all these forms of egalitarianism is the rejection of the classical liberal understanding of equality before the law." Instead, Schaeffer added, egalitarians "seek de facto equality of wealth, of status, of gender, among species, etc. These goals come into conflict with the existing rule of law in the United States. . . and the preferences of the vast majority of ordinary people." Don Herzog of *American Political Science Review* put it more simply: "The American Left has been so passionate about equality that it has run roughshod over liberty."

History critic David De Leon thought the author inadequately defined "the Left," in *The Dark Side of the Left,* omitting analysis of the New Deal initiative during the Depression in favor of a view of the 1960s New Left, "wherein the New Frontier and the Great Society [movements] are nearly invisible." To Schaeffer, Ellis "lays intellectual traps for his subjects. Either they 'idealize the oppressed,' a serious error, or they 'disdain the masses,' an equally serious fault. Under these circumstances, of course, the Left can do no right, only different wrongs." Still, Schaeffer said that "although Ellis's negative assessment of Left movements is unwarranted, his general aversion to intolerance and self-righteousness, in its many forms, is sound."

Joseph Bertolini, in *Perspectives on Political Science,* found more to recommend in *The Dark Side of the Left.* He cited the book's "excellent concluding chapter" in which Ellis "puts together all these movements and explains that they all exhibit similar qualities that make them a threat to liberalism." Alan Charles Kors, in *Reason,* criticized the author, writing about the utopian communities, for instance, that Ellis "ignores the essential point that these were wholly voluntary associations" and not designed to influence the lives of others. But Kors also felt that "there is lots of grand stuff in Ellis's work. He is at his best, displaying a fine ear for detail, when examining the dissonance between the love of radical intellectuals for the masses in the abstract and their contempt for ordinary lives in the particular." Herzog called it "elegantly written, provocative, and sometimes just plain provoking."

Democratic Delusions: The Initiative Process in America, questions the ability of the ballot initiative to affect change. In Ellis's view, "only rarely and accidentally," a *Publishers Weekly* contributor wrote, "is the public interest served by the initiative process." The same reviewer concluded that this book is one to "crystallize simmering discontent."

BIOGRAPHICAL AND CRITICAL SOURCES:

BOOKS

Ellis, Richard J., *Presidential Lightning Rods: The Politics of Blame Avoidance,* University Press of Kansas (Lawrence, KS), 1994.

Ellis, Richard J., *The Dark Side of the Left: Illiberal Egalitarianism in America,* University Press of Kansas (Lawrence, KS), 1998.

PERIODICALS

American Historical Review, February, 1995, John Patrick Diggins, review of *American Political Cultures,* p. 222; February, 1996, Robert A. Divine, review of *Presidential Lightning Rods,* p. 257; December, 1999, Michael Kazin, review of *The Dark Side of the Left,* p. 1713.

American Political Cultures, December, 1995, John Hart, review of *Presidential Lightning Rods,* p. 1021; June, 2000, Don Herzog, review of *The Dark Side of the Left,* p. 445.

American Political Science Review, September, 1994; JUne 3, 2002, Michael Nelson, "The Voter As a Legislator," p. 37.

Annals of the American Academy of Political and Social Science, March, 1996, Rhonda Kinney, review of *Presidential Lightning Rods,* p. 219.

Choice, February, 1994, H. G. Reid, review of *American Political Cultures,* p. 995; March, 1995, review of *Presidential Lightning Rods,* p. 1212; July-August, 1998, N. B. Rosenthal, review of *The Dark Side of the Left,* p. 1934; July-August, 1999, S. L. Harrison, review of *Speaking to the People: The Rhetorical Presidency in Historical Perspective,* p. 2019; July-August, 2002, H. R. Ernst, review of *Democratic Delusions: The Initiative Process in America,* p. 2040.

Chronicle of Higher Education, February 22, 2002, Nina C. Ayouh, "Nota Bene," p. 6.

Congress & the Presidency, spring, 1995, Kathryn Dunn Tenpas, review of *Presidential Lightning Rods,* p. 103.

Contemporary Sociology, November, 1994, Russell L. Hanson, review of *American Political Cultures,* p. 886.

Critical Review, winter, 1993, review of *Cultural Theory,* p. 81.

Government and Opposition, summer, 1997, Marco Verweij, review of *Politics, Policy, and Culture,* p. 421.

Historian, winter, 1994, Harry W. Fritz, review of *American Political Cultures,* p. 381; winter, 2000, W. J. Rorabaugh, review of *The Dark Side of the Left,* p. 407.

History, summer, 1995, review of *Presidential Lightning Rods,* p. 147; fall, 1998, David De Leon, review of *The Dark Side of the Left,* p. 6.

Human Events, December 4, 1998, review of *The Dark Side of the Left,* p. 18.

Independent Review, winter, 2000, Joseph R. Stromberg, review of *The Dark Side of the Left,* p. 439.

Journal of American History, March, 1995, James T. Kloppenberg, review of *American Political Cultures,* p. 1669; March, 1999, Wini Breines, review of *The Dark Side of the Left,* p. 1680.

Journal of Interdisciplinary History, autumn, 1995, John Higham, review of *American Political Cultures,* p. 326.

Journal of Politics, February, 1995, review of *American Political Cultures,* p. 270; February, 1996, Joseph A. Pika, review of *Presidential Lightning Rods,* p. 251; November, 1999, J. Donald Moon, review of *The Dark Side of the Left,* p. 1177.

Library Journal, July, 1994, review of *Presidential Lightning Rods,* p. 112.

Perspectives on Political Science, fall, 1995, review of *Presidential Lightning Rods,* p. 225; spring, 1999, Joseph C. Bertolini, review of *The Dark Side of the Left,* p. 97; summer, 1999, David C. Saffell, review of *Speaking to the People,* p. 153.

Political Science Quarterly, spring, 1995, Michael A. Genovese, review of *Presidential Lightning Rods,* p. 136.

Political Studies, June, 1994, Martin Durham, review of *American Political Cultures,* p. 354.

Presidential Studies Quarterly, September, 1999, Anthony J. Mohr, review of *Speaking to the People,* p. 728.

Publishers Weekly, February 2, 1998, review of *The Dark Side of the Left,* p. 77; January 21, 2002, review of *Democratic Delusions,* p. 79.

Reason, December, 1998, Alan Charles Kors, review of *The Dark Side of the Left.*

Reference & Research Book News, February, 1995, review of *Presidential Lightning Rods,* p. 11; February, 1998, review of *Culture Matters,* p. 93; May, 1998, review of *The Dark Side of the Left,* p. 94.

Review of Politics, winter, 1995, H. Mark Roelofs, review of *American Political Cultures,* p. 179.

Society, July-August, 1999, Robert K. Schaeffer, review of *The Dark Side of the Left,* p. 94.

Times Literary Supplement, May 22, 1998, review of *The Dark Side of the Left,* p. 11.

Washington Post Book World, March 8, 1998, review of *The Dark Side of the Left,* p. 6.

William and Mary Quarterly, July, 1994, Joshua Miller, review of *American Political Cultures,* p. 590.*

*   *   *

ETZKOWITZ, Henry 1940-

PERSONAL: Born July 9, 1940, in New York, NY; son of Benjamin and Mary (Lipschitz) Etzkowitz. *Education:* University of Chicago, B.A., 1962; New School for Social Research, Ph.D., 1969.

ADDRESSES: Office—Division of Social Science, State University of New York, Purchase, NY 10577.

CAREER: Washington University, St. Louis, MO, 1969-72, began as instructor, became assistant professor of sociology; Purchase College, State University of New York, Purchase, NY, associate professor of sociology, director, Science Policy Institute. Chair, Inter-University Seminar for Knowledge-based Economic Development in New York City; co-convenor, bi-yearly international Conference on University-Industry-Government Relations: "The Triple Helix." Contributing editor, *Technology Access Report.* Founder, World Innovation Network. Served in Peace Corps in Nigeria, 1962-64.

MEMBER: American Sociological Association, Society for the Study of Social Problems.

WRITINGS:

(With Gerald Schaflander) *Ghetto Crisis,* Little, Brown (Boston, MA), 1969.

Is America Possible?, West Publishing (St. Paul, MN), 1974.

(With Peter Schwab) *Is America Necessary?,* West Publishing (St. Paul, MN), 1976.

(Editor, with Ronald M. Glassman) *The Renascence of Sociological Theory: Classical and Contemporary,* F. E. Peacock Publishers (Itasca, IL), 1991.

(Editor, with Loet Leydesdorff) *Universities and the Global Knowledge Economy: A Triple Helix of University-Industry-Government Relations,* Pinter (New York, NY), 1997.

(Editor, with Andrew Webster and Peter Healey) *Capitalizing Knowledge: New Intersections of Industry and Academia,* State University of New York Press (Albany, NY), 1998.

(With Carol Kemelgor, Brian Uzzi, and others) *Athena Unbound: The Advancement of Women in Science and Technology,* Cambridge University Press (New York, NY), 2000.

(With Magnus Gulbrandsen and Janet Levitt) *Public Venture Capital: Government Funding Sources for Technology Entrepreneurs,* Harcourt (San Diego, CA), 2000.

WORK IN PROGRESS: The Second Academic Revolution: MIT and the Rise of Entrepreneurial Science, to be published by Gordon and Breach (London, England).

SIDELIGHTS: Sociologist Henry Etzkowitz has written and edited works on the interrelationships of government, education, and industry in contemporary society. His *Public Venture Capital: Government*

Funding Sources for Technology Entrepreneurs, a book he wrote with Magnus Gulbrandsen and Janet Levitt, was welcomed as a very useful and readable work by Steven J. Mayover in *Library Journal,* and was hailed as an "outstanding accomplishment" by *Technology Access Report* contributor Ashley J. Stevens.

Athena Unbound: The Advancement of Women in Science and Technology received significant critical attention. In this book, cowritten with Carol Kemelgor and Brian Uzzi, Etzkowitz and his colleagues examine the reasons why relatively few women enjoy successful careers in science, concluding that systemic barriers exist for women not just at the entry point but throughout all stages of a scientific career. *BioScience* contributor Jane L. Lehr agreed with the book's recommendations, but felt that the study offered nothing new to a debate that has raged for many years. Alison Winter in *American Scientist,* however, considered the book "one of the best studies I have read on contemporary issues relating to women's participation in science."

BIOGRAPHICAL AND CRITICAL SOURCES:

PERIODICALS

American Scientist, September, 2001, Alison Winter, "Separate and Unequal," p. 460.

BioScience, June, 2001, Jane L. Lehr, review of *Athena Unbound: The Advancement of Women in Science and Technology,* p. 504.

Booklist, December 1, 2000, Donna Seaman, review of *Athena Unbound,* p. 683.

Choice, May, 2001, M. H. Chaplin, review of *Athena Unbound,* p. 1646.

Economic Journal, June, 1999, review of *Universities and the Global Knowledge Economy: A Triple Helix of University-Industry-Government Relations,* p. 464.

Journal of College Science Teaching, December, 2001, Holly Priestley, review of *Athena Unbound,* p. 279.

Library Journal, February 1, 2002, Steven J. Mayover, review of *Public Venture Capital: Sources of Government Funding for Technology Enterpreneurs,* p. 111.

Nature, April 12, 2001, review of *Athena Unbound,* p. 747.

Technology Access Report, February, 2001, Ashley J. Stevens, review of *Public Venture Capital,* p. 7.

Times Higher Education Supplement, September 7, 2001, Joan Mason, review of *Athena Unbound,* p. 35.*

*   *   *

EUGENIDES, Jeffrey 1960(?)-

PERSONAL: Born c. 1960, in Grosse Pointe Park, MI; son of Constantine (a mortgage banker) and Wanda Eugenides; married, wife's name Karen (an artist); children: a daughter. *Education:* Brown University, B.A. (magna cum laude), 1983; Stanford University, M.A. (creative writing), 1986. *Religion:* Greek Orthodox.

ADDRESSES: Agent—Lynn Nesbit, Janklow & Nesbit Associates, 445 Park Ave., New York, NY 10022.

CAREER: Writer. *Yachtsman* magazine, photographer and staff writer; American Academy of Poets, New York, NY; various positions including newsletter editor, beginning in 1988. Has worked as a cab driver, busboy, and a volunteer with Mother Teresa in India.

AWARDS, HONORS: Aga Khan Prize for fiction, *Paris Review,* 1991, for an excerpt from the *The Virgin Suicides;* Writers Award, Whiting Foundation, 1993; Henry D. Vursell Memorial Award, American Academy of Arts and Letters; Pulitzer Prize in fiction, 2003, for *Middlesex;* recipient of fellowships from Guggenheim Foundation, National Endowment for the Arts, and Academy of Motion Picture Arts and Sciences; Berlin Prize fellowship, American Academy in Berlin, 2000-2001; fellow of the Berliner Kuenstlerprogramm of the DAAD.

WRITINGS:

The Virgin Suicides, Farrar, Straus & Giroux (New York, NY), 1993.

Middlesex, Farrar, Straus & Giroux (New York, NY), 2002.

Jeffrey Eugenides

Contributor to periodicals, including *Paris Review.*

ADAPTATIONS: The Virgin Suicides, a film adaptation written and directed by Sofia Coppola, was released by Paramount Pictures, 2000.

SIDELIGHTS: Novelist Jeffrey Eugenides received critical acclaim for his first novel, *The Virgin Suicides,* a tale of five teenaged sisters who one by one kill themselves. His next novel, *Middlesex,* published nine years later, won a Pulitzer Prize for fiction.

The Michigan-born writer had worked in various fields before graduating from Brown University, including driving a cab in downtown Detroit and working alongside Mother Teresa in Calcutta, India. He later wrote for the American Academy of Poets in New York, and pushed to complete his opus when he learned the organization would soon terminate his position. Eugenides also wrote part of his first novel, *The Virgin Suicides,* while traveling down the Nile through Egypt. An excerpt from the book was published in the *Paris Review* in 1991 and won the literary journal's Aga Khan Prize for fiction that year.

The author got the idea for *The Virgin Suicides* while visiting his brother's house in Michigan and chatting with the baby sitter. The young woman said that she and her sisters had all attempted suicide at one point. When Eugenides asked why, she replied simply, "pressure." The theme of inexplicable adolescent trauma amid a placid suburban landscape gave birth to the plot of the novel. *The Virgin Suicides* is set in an unnamed affluent suburb remarkably similar to Eugenides's hometown of Grosse Pointe Park, Michigan, and is told in the collective narrative voice of a group of men who were obsessed with the girls as teenagers. Now nearing middle age, they are still trying to fathom the mysterious suicides of twenty years before, haunted by their memories of the sisters.

The Virgin Suicides juxtaposes the innocence and eroticism of early-1970s suburbia against the unaccountable force that drove the young women to their deaths. The Lisbon family consists of the five lovely daughters, an overprotective and devoutly Catholic mother, and a rather invisible father. The girls are garbed in shapeless, oversized clothes and forbidden to date. The neighborhood boys, entranced by their remoteness, spy on them and rummage through the family's garbage for such collectibles as discarded cosmetics and homework papers. The reader learns how the suicides began as the voice recounts when one of them sneaked into the Lisbon house through a sewer tunnel and peeped in on the youngest, thirteen-year-old Cecilia, as she bathed. To his horror she had also slit her wrists, and her intruder turns out to be a temporary rescuer when he notifies the police. Yet a short time later, during an unlikely party at the somber Lisbon house, Cecilia jumps to her death from a window, impaling herself on a fencepost. The death of a peer fascinates the neighborhood boys: "We had stood in line with her for smallpox vaccinations," the narrator recalls of Cecilia, "had held polio sugar cubes under our tongues with her, had taught her to jump rope, to light snakes, had stopped her from picking her scabs on numerous occasions, and had cautioned her against touching her mouth to the drinking fountain at Three Mile Park."

Soon the girls are grounded permanently and disappear even from the normalcy of a school routine, further piquing the boys' obsession. They watch as one of the sisters, the sexually precocious Lux, fornicates on the roof of the house with mysterious men at night, while neighbors begin to complain about the family's unkempt lawn and the strange odors emanating from the Lisbon house. The boys maintain a distant relationship with the girls, calling them on the phone and signaling to them from neighboring houses. Finally they hatch a plan to rescue the girls in which they will all escape to Florida in a stolen car. In the end, however, the remaining girls commit suicide, leaving the boys to their lifelong preoccupation with the unexplained deaths.

Many reviewers praised the author's use of the wry, anonymous narrative. Tom Prince, in *New York* magazine, described the work as "a highly polished novel about the coarseness of adolescence, relentlessly mournful but also gruesomely funny." *New York Review of Books* critic Alice Truax remarked that "if anything is offensive about *The Virgin Suicides,* perhaps it's that reading it is such a pleasurable, melancholy experience—in spite of its ostensible subject matter." Commenting on Eugenides's style, Truax said "On his first page, he makes it clear that his title means what it says, and that he plans to spin a dreamy, elegiac tale from its terrible promise."

"Eugenides never loses his sense of humor," Kristin McCloy wrote in the *Los Angeles Times Book Review.* "Mordant to be sure, and always understated, Eugenides's sense of the absurd is relentless." Michiko Kakutani of the *New York Times* warned that unexplained elements in the novel might "grate on the reader's nerves, momentarily breaking the spell of [Eugenides's] tale." Kakutani, however, described the book's end result as "by turns lyrical and portentous, ferocious and elegiac," and noted that "*The Virgin Suicides* insinuates itself into our minds as a small but powerful opera in the unexpected form of a novel." And *People*'s Joseph Olshan added that "the novel manages to maintain a high level of suspense in what is clearly an impressive debut."

Nine years passed between *The Virgin Suicides* and the publication of *Middlesex.* The author returned to Grosse Pointe to tell about a multigenerational Greek-American family through the eyes of its most unusual member: the hermaphroditic Cal (Calliope) Stephanides. Using a male/female narrator posed a challenge: "I wanted the book to be first-person," Eugenides told Dave Welch of *Powells.* "In many ways, the point of the book is that we're all an *I* before

we're a he or a she, so I needed that *I*." For practical reasons, the author added, "I wanted the *I* because I didn't want that terrible situation where the character is she, then you turn the page and she becomes he—or even the more dreaded s/he."

In *Middlesex,* Cal's gender is the product of speculation even before conception. Parents Milton and Tessie long for a girl, and heed an uncle's advice to engage in sex twenty-four hours before ovulation; that way "the swift male sperm would rush in and die off. The female sperm, sluggish but more reliable, would arrive just as the egg dropped." After Tessie becomes pregnant, rancor builds among the relatives when grandma Desdemona, dangling a silver spoon over Tessie's abdomen, declares the child inside a boy. However, the baby born shortly after is deemed female. Calliope spends her childhood and early adolescence as what Laura Miller of the *New York Times* called a "relatively unremarkable daughter." All that changes at puberty when "she" begins sprouting facial hair and speaking in a deepening voice. It is discovered during a doctor's examination that Calliope is a hermaphrodite, possessing equally the physical and sexual characteristics of male and female. "To the extent that fetal hormones affect brain chemistry and histology," the narrator declares, "I've got a male brain."

The girl's horrified parents take her to sexologist Dr. Luce, who proposes a radical "final solution" to Cal's predicament: surgery to remove all outward traces of maleness, and hormonal therapy to reinforce the female characteristics. But for Calliope, that is not the answer. Instead, the character embraces his male identity, and grows to adulthood as an academic in Berlin (where the author lives). Meanwhile, he recounts a twentieth-century family saga that illustrates how Calliope/Cal came to be. He reveals, for example, that grandparents Desdemona and Lefty were brother and sister; and that Cal's own parents married as first cousins.

"Though its premise makes the novel sound as if it's either sensational or clinical—or both," Charles Matthews in a *Knight Ridder/Tribune News Service* review, "it isn't. That's because [*Middlesex*] is as much about the Stephanides family as it is about Cal/Calliope." Matthews added that "even with the element of incest, the story of the Stephanides family doesn't become weirdly titillating or turn into a sentimental problem drama about what's now known as intersexuality. Instead, it's a story based on the familiar dynamics of belonging and displacement." Lisa Schwarzbaum, in *Entertainment Weekly,* said the writing itself "is also about mixing things up, grafting flights of descriptive fancy with hunks of conventional dialogue, pausing briefly to sketch passing characters or explain a bit of a bygone world."

"Because it's long and wide and full of stuff," wrote Miller, the novel "will be associated by some readers with books by David Foster Wallace and Jonathan Frazen, brilliant members of Eugenides's cohort." But unlike those hard-line satirists, the critic added, Eugenides "is sunnier; the book's length feels like its author's arms stretching farther and farther to encompass more people, more life."

But Keith Gessen of *Nation* acknowledged that this "politically effective" novel displays "too much energy . . . expended" on "the assurance of the author's good intentions. The result is often a measured, highly adequate bloodlessness." Yet to *New Republic* contributor James Wood, the author showcases just the right intentions. "Eugenides's charm, his life-jammed comedy, rescues the novel from its occasional didacticism," he wrote. "One can put it this way: a novel narrated by a hermaphrodite comes to seem largely routine, as if Calliope were simply fat or tall. A fact that might scream its oddity, and that might have been used again and again heavily to explore fashionable questions of identity and gender, is here blissfully domesticated."

Comparing the two Eugenides novels, Mark Lawson of *Europe Intelligence Wire* found that while *The Virgin Suicides* "reflected on connections between sex and death, its successor considers the links between sex, life and inheritance." Lawson also found it strange that "in a novel with such a long gestation, occasional phrases seem hasty." In ten years the novelist had produced only two books, though both well-received; Rachel Collins, in *Library Journal,* said "it is Eugenides's dedication to his stories, his characters, and, yes, even his readers, that compels him to spend years on a manuscript." As for his 2003 Pulitzer Prize-winner, Eugenides told Collins that *Middlesex* "really is Cal's" book, "and I think there is nothing ugly about his life. In fact, it's as close to a triumphant story as I'm ever likely to write."

BIOGRAPHICAL AND CRITICAL SOURCES:

BOOKS

Eugenides, Jeffrey, *The Virgin Suicides,* Farrar, Straus & Giroux (New York, NY), 1993.

PERIODICALS

Atlantic Monthly, September, 2002, Stewart O'Nan, review of *Middlesex,* p. 157.

Book, September-October, 2002, Penelope Mesic, "Identity Crisis," p. 70.

Booklist, June 1, 2002, Joanne Wilkinson, review of *Middlesex,* p. 1644.

Bookseller, July 5, 2002, "A Family Story with a Difference," p. 35.

British Medical Journal, October 26, 2002, John Quin, review of *Middlesex,* p. 975.

Detroit News, April 3, 1993, review of *The Virgin Suicides,* pp. 1C, 3C.

Economist, October 5, 2002, review of *Middlesex.*

Entertainment Weekly, September 13, 2002, Lisa Schwarzbaum, "Work of Genes," p. 146.

Europe Intelligence Wire, October 5, 2002, Mark Lawson, "Gender Blender"; October 6, 2002, Geraldine Bedell, "He's Not Like Other Girls."

Kirkus Reviews, July 15, 2002, review of *Middlesex,* p. 977.

Knight Ridder/Tribune News Service, September 11, 2002, Margaria Fichtner, review of *Middlesex,* p. K7215; September 18, 2002, Charles Matthews, review of *Middlesex,* p. K2795; October 2, 2002, Carlin Romano, review of *Middlesex,* p. K4158; October 30, 2002, Marta Salij, "Pointe of View," p. K4969.

Library Journal, July, 2002, Rachel Collins, review of *Middlesex,* p. 116, author interview, p. 121.

Los Angeles Times Book Review, June 20, 1993, Kristin McCloy, review of *The Virgin Suicides,* pp. 2, 5.

Nation, October 14, 2002, Keith Gessen, "Sense and Sexibility," p. 25.

New Republic, October 7, 2002, James Wood, "Unions," p. 31.

Newsweek, September 23, 2002, David Gates, "The Gender Blender," p. 71.

New York, April 26, 1993, Tom Prince, review of *The Virgin Suicides,* pp. 54-58; September 9, 2002, John Homans, "Helen of Boy," p. 131.

New York Review of Books, June 10, 1993, Alice Truax, review of *The Virgin Suicides,* pp. 45-46; November 7, 2002, Daniel Mendelsohn, "Mighty Hermaphrodite," p. 17.

New York Times, March 19, 1993, Michiko Kakutani, review of *The Virgin Suicides,* p. C23; September 15, 2002, Laura Miller, "My Big Fat Greek Gender Identity Crisis."

People, April 19, 1993, Joseph Olshan, review of *The Virgin Suicides,* p. 27.

Spectator, October 5, 2002, Sebastian Stone, "Putting It All In," p. 43.

Time, September 23, 2002, Richard Lacayo, review of *Middlesex,* p. 78.

Times Literary Supplement, October 4, 2002, Paul Quinn, "In the Centre of the Labyrinth," p. 24.

ONLINE

Bomb, http://www.bombsite.com/ (April 9, 2003), Jonathan Safran Foer, author interview.

Powells, http://www.powells.com/ (April 9, 2003), Dave Welch, "Jeffrey Eugenides Has It Both Ways."

Read, http://www.randomhouse.ca/ (April 9, 2003), author interview.

Salon, http://www.salon.com/ (October 15, 2002), Laura Miller, "Interview with Jeffrey Eugenides."*

F

FAIRCLOUGH, Adam 1952-

PERSONAL: Born November 14, 1952, in London, England; son of Alan (a journalist) and Marian (Skea, now Wills) Fairclough; married Patricia Benard (an artist), 1976 (marriage ended); married Mary Ellen Curtin (a historian); children: (first marriage) Jennifer Lee. *Ethnicity:* "English." *Education:* Balliol College, Oxford, B.A. (with first class honors), 1975; graduate study at University of Georgia, 1975-76; University of Keele, Ph.D., 1978; postdoctoral study at Institute of Education, London, 1982-83. *Politics:* Labour Party.

ADDRESSES: Office—School of English and American Studies, University of East Anglia, Norwich NR4 7TJ, England; fax: 1603-507728. *E-mail*—adam. fairclough@uea.ac.uk.

CAREER: New University of Ulster (now University of Ulster), Coleraine, Northern Ireland, member of history department, 1978-79; University of Liverpool, Liverpool, England, member of modern history department, 1980-81; University of Wales, St. David's University College, Lampeter, member of history department, 1983-94; University of Leeds, Leeds, England, professor of modern American history, 1994-97; University of East Anglia, School of English and American Studies, Norwich, England, professor of American history, 1997—. Tulane University, visiting scholar, 1987; Carter C. Woodson Center, University of Virginia, fellow, 1990-91; National Humanities Center, fellow, 1994-95.

MEMBER: Association of University Teachers, British Association for American Studies, Southern Historical Association, Organization of American Historians, American Historical Association.

AWARDS, HONORS: American Council of Learned Societies fellowship, 1987; Lillian Smith Award, 1995, Louisiana Literary Award, 1996, and General L. Kemper Williams Prize, 1996, all for *Race and Democracy: The Civil Rights Struggle in Louisiana, 1915-1972.*

WRITINGS:

To Redeem the Soul of America: The Southern Christian Leadership Conference and Martin Luther King, Jr., University of Georgia Press (Athens, GA), 1987.

Martin Luther King, Jr., University of Georgia Press (Athens, GA), 1990.

Race and Democracy: The Civil Rights Struggle in Louisiana, 1915-1972, University of Georgia Press (Athens, GA), 1995.

Forty Acres and a Mule: Horace Mann Bond and the Lynching of Jerome Wilson, University of Georgia Press (Athens, GA), 1997.

(Editor) Horace Mann Bond and Julia W. Bond, *The Star Creek Papers: Washington Parish and the Lynching of Jerome Wilson,* foreword by Julian Bond, University of Georgia Press (Athens, GA), 1997.

Teaching Equality: Black Schools in the Age of Jim Crow, University of Georgia Press (Athens, GA), 2001.

Better Day Coming: Blacks and Equality, 1890-2000, Viking (New York, NY), 2001.

Contributor to history journals.

WORK IN PROGRESS: Constant Struggle: Blacks and Equality, 1895-1995.

SIDELIGHTS: Adam Fairclough, a historian and professor, has authored numerous articles and several books discussing the history of the South and American race relations. His writings include *To Redeem the Soul of America: The Southern Christian Leadership Conference and Martin Luther King, Jr., Martin Luther King, Jr.,* and the Lillian Smith award-winning *Race and Democracy: The Civil Rights Struggle in Louisiana, 1915-1972,* all titles influenced by the Civil Rights Movement and the leadership of Martin Luther King, Jr. Fairclough has also edited Horace Mann Bond's *The Star Creek Papers: Washington Parish and the Lynching of Jerome Wilson,* with the help of Bond's wife, Julia Bond. This book documents the early twentieth-century black family. Fairclough's most recent books are *Teaching Equality: Black Schools in the Age of Jim Crow* and *Better Day Coming: Blacks and Equality, 1890-2000.*

In *The Star Creek Papers,* Horace Mann Bond recorded his extensive research of the daily life of blacks in the South. Bond was curious to learn more about black ancestry and related history, and was interested in finding out why numerous local black farmers were land owners. A reviewer for *Publishers Weekly* noted, "If this collection is fragmentary, it once again proves Horace Bond, who died in 1972, was a shrewd observer of race relations and black family life."

Better Day Coming catalogues the historical events of the Civil Rights movement in the United States from the nineteenth century to the present. Fairclough provides details about the characters, places, and events that were woven together to create the fabric of the Civil Rights movement and includes descriptions of relationships between key figures like Ida B. Wells, Booker T. Washington, W. E. B. Du Bois, Marcus Garvey, and Martin Luther King, Jr. Diane McWhorter of the *New York Times* wrote that the book "is a novelty, a single volume that succinctly encompasses the history of black emancipation from 1890 to the present . . . and is a smart, tidy survey of a lot of ground." McWhorter concluded by calling *Better Day Coming* "a fixture of the Civil Rights bibliography."

Better Day Coming describes the different groups, pivotal court cases, and historically significant events—such as the Montgomery bus boycott of 1955-56, the demonstrations in Birmingham, Alabama, in 1963, the march from Selma to Montgomery for voting privileges in 1965, and the Los Angeles Watts Riots of 1966—that led to present day Civil Rights. A *Publishers Weekly* reviewer noted that the work "will probably suit . . . the general reader . . . who may have little or no knowledge about the history of race relations since the American Civil War." *New York Times* critic McWhorter concluded, "Fairclough has produced a reliable map of a challenging field and a sobering measure of how few have been the better days and how long the years in between."

Fairclough once told *CA:* "My work is sustained by the creative tension between political engagement and the ideal of objectivity implicit in the historian's craft. I absorbed a concern for social justice and an interest in Labour politics from my father, chief leader-writer for the London *Daily Mirror* until his death in 1973. It took exposure to the poverty of Liverpool, however, to transmute vague sympathies into concrete political activity. Whether political commitment helps or hinders my work as a historian of the American Civil Rights movement is not for me to say; but it has, I believe, deepened my understanding of the mechanics of power and of the political wisdom of Martin Luther King's leadership.

"My work on the Civil Rights movement in Louisiana, and my current research into the history of black education, have taken me much more deeply into the complexities of the Civil Rights movement, compelling me to question many of the assumptions that characterize recent interpretations—including my own."

BIOGRAPHICAL AND CRITICAL SOURCES:

PERIODICALS

American Historical Review, February, 1997, Kenneth W. Goings, review of *Race and Democracy: The Civil Rights Struggle in Louisiana, 1915-1972,* p. 219.

American Studies, spring, 1997, Hugh Davis Graham, review of *Race and Democracy,* pp. 186-187.

Booklist, July, 2001, Vernon Ford, review of *Better Day Coming: Blacks and Equality, 1890-2000,* p. 1956.

Choice, July-August, 2001, J. Watras, review of *Teaching Equality: Black Schools in the Age of Jim Crow,* p. 2009.

Journal of American Studies, December, 1997, Mark Newman, review of *Race and Democracy,* p. 455.

Journal of Southern History, November, 1998, Pamela Tyler, review of *Race and Democracy,* pp. 788-790; August, 2002, Robert G. Sherer, review of *Teaching Equality,* p. 722.

Library Journal, August, 2001, A. O. Edmonds, review of *Better Day Coming,* p. 131.

Los Angeles Times, July 30, 1987.

New York Times Book Review, July 29, 2001, Diane McWhorter, "Overcoming Repeatedly," p. 15; July 21, 2002, Scott Veale, review of *Better Day Coming,* p. 20.

Publishers Weekly, June 2, 1997, review of *The Star Creek Papers: Washington Parish and the Lynching of Jerome Wilson,* p. 60; June 4, 2001, review of *Better Day Coming,* p. 68.

Times Literary Supplement, July 17, 1987.

Western Journal of Black Studies, Paul T. Miller, review of *Better Day Coming,* p. 123.

ONLINE

University of East Anglia Web site, http://www.uea.ac.uk/ (January 19, 2002).*

*   *   *

FARRELL, Warren (Thomas) 1943-

PERSONAL: Born June 26, 1943, in New York, NY; son of Thomas Edward (an accountant) and Muriel Lee (a librarian; maiden name, Levy) Farrell; married Ursie Otte Fairbairn (senior vice president, Union Pacific), June 19, 1966 (divorced, 1977). *Education:* Montclair State College, B.A., 1965; University of California at Los Angeles, M.A., 1966; New York University, Ph.D., 1974. *Politics:* Independent. *Religion:* "Spiritual—no affiliation." *Hobbies and other interests:* Tennis, running, reading, films—"I love discussing and reviewing films."

ADDRESSES: Home—103 North Highway 101, Box 220, Encinitas, CA 92024. *Agent*—Ellen Levine, Ellen Levine Literary Agency, 15 East 26th St., No. 1801, New York, NY 10010. *E-mail*—wfarrel@home.com and warrenfarrell@adelphia.net.

CAREER: Author, lecturer, and consultant on gender, male-female relationships and men's issues. Television appearances include *Oprah, Donahue, The Today Show, Larry King Live, ABC World News with Peter Jennings, 20/20,* and *Crossfire;* consulting clients include U.S. Department of Education, Bonneville Power, National Aeronautics and Space Administration, IBM, Revlon, Toyota, AT&T, and Bell Atlantic. Lecturer, Fordham University, 1970; instructor, New Jersey State College, 1970, Rutgers University, 1971-73, American University, 1973-74, and Georgetown University, 1973-75; professor, California School of Professional Psychology, 1978-79, and San Diego State University, 1979-80; adjunct assistant professor, University of California, San Diego, 1986-88, and City University of New York (CUNY).

MEMBER: National Congress for Men and Children (board of directors, 1992—), National Coalition of Free Men (advisory board, 1996—), National Organization for Women (board of directors, New York City chapter, 1970-73), American Board of Sexology, American Coalition of Fathers and Children (board of directors, 1996-98), Children's Rights Council (advisory board, 1985—); Coastal Community Foundation, Fathers' Rights & Equality Exchange.

AWARDS, HONORS: Best Book Award, National Coalition of Free Men, 1986, for *Why Men Are the Way They Are;* Men's Rights award, 1986, for *Why Men Are the Way They Are,* and 1993, for *The Myth of Male Power;* Outstanding Contribution award, California Association of Marriage and Family Therapists, 1988; Best Book Award, National Congress for Men and Children, 1993, for *The Myth of Male Power;* Family Hero Award, Pennsylvania Family Rights Coalition, 1994. Honorary doctorate of humane letters, Professional School of Psychology, 1985.

WRITINGS:

The Liberated Man, Random House (New York, NY), 1975.

Why Men Are the Way They Are, McGraw-Hill (New York, NY), 1986.

The Myth of Male Power: Why Men Are the Disposable Sex—Fated for War, Programmed for Work, Divorced from Emotion, Simon & Schuster (New York, NY), 1993, new edition, with an updated introduction by the author, Berkley Books (New York, NY), 2001.

(Contributor, with Alan Garner) Marnie Winston-Macauley, *The Ultimate Answering Machine Message Book,* Andrews & McMeel (Kansas City, MO), 1997.

Women Can't Hear What Men Don't Say: Destroying Myths, Creating Love, Jeremy Tarcher (New York, NY), 1999.

Father and Child Reunion: How to Bring the Dads We Need to the Children We Love, Jeremy Tarcher (New York, NY), 2001.

Contributor of articles to professional journals.

ADAPTATIONS: An abridged version of *The Myth of Male Power* was adapted for audiocassette and read by the author, Simon & Schuster Audio, 1993; selections from *Why Men Are the Way They Are* were updated, adapted for audiocassette, and read by the author, Audio Partners Publishing, 1993; an abridged version of *Women Can't Hear What Men Don't Say* was adapted for audiocassette and read by the author, Audio Renaissance, 1999.

SIDELIGHTS: Working as consultant, speaker, college instructor, and author, Warren Farrell has focused on male-female relationships and men's issues in his career. Once counting himself among active feminists—during the early 1970s he was a leader in the National Organization of Women (NOW), his advocacy for the rights of women generated media attention and numerous invitations to speaking engagements and university posts. However, in the mid-1970s his thinking shifted and he began to see the movement he once championed as hurtfully flawed, advancing women's rights at the expense of men's rights. Farrell then set out to advance equality for both sexes, primarily taking the role as an outspoken advocate for the rights of men and often highlighting how society, the media, and traditional feminist thinking unfairly characterize and restrict men.

Farrell was called the "Gloria Steinem of Men's Liberation" by *Washington Post* reviewer Don Oldenburg. Generally, critics agree that Farrell's writings deal with "gender liberation." A founding member of the National Organization for Changing Men and the National Congress for Men and Children, Farrell has served on numerous boards, including the National Coalition of Free Men and the American Coalition of Fathers and Children. Oldenburg noted that Farrell's

writing reframes "'the balance of sexual power and politics in the contemporary world' in his [1986] book *Why Men Are the Way They Are.*" Farrell told the *Washington Post:* "I'm asking women and men, before they blame the other sex, to listen to the other sex's experience of the world—both their power experiences and powerless experiences. Too often people are arguing from their own self-interests."

Perhaps Farrell's most controversial observations in the gender discussion are captured in *The Myth of Male Power: Why Men Are the Disposable Sex—Fated for War, Programmed for Work, Divorced from Emotion,* a 1993 release. *Washington Post Book World* contributor Camille Paglia (herself a prominent figure in gender studies) called *The Myth of Male Power* "a bombshell. . . . It attacks the unexamined assumptions of feminist discourse with shocking candor and forces us to see our everyday world from a fresh perspective. . . . *The Myth of Male Power* is the kind of original, abrasive, heretical text that is desperately needed to restore fairness and balance the present ideology-sodden curriculum of women's studies courses."

All men have a common bond in their "wound of disposability," according to Farrell. *Business Week* reviewer Bruce Nussbaum noted that Farrell examines the paradox of male aggression: "Farrell demonstrates male powerlessness by pointing to the violence done to males in school sports (which he terms male child abuse), the selling of men's time and bodies to support wife and family (prostitution of males), and the draft (enslaving men in the military). Farrell concludes that 'the wound that unifies all men is the wound of their disposability . . . as soldiers, workers, dads.'" While Farrell's discourse on rights of men and the inequalities they face initially earned him less support, attention, and invitation than he enjoyed as an avowed feminist, his more male-focused thoughts have not gone unnoticed. *The Myth of Male Power* became "a men's movement bible," observed Cathy Young, in a *Reason* review of its successor, *Women Can't Hear What Men Don't Say: Destroying Myths, Creating Love.*

Published in 1999, *Women Can't Hear What Men Don't Say* discusses issues of miscommunication between genders and presents ideas on how to improve the situation, while giving great weight to fleshing out instances of male-bashing spurred on by the women's movement. As Peter Kocan observed in *Quadrant,* "Farrell constantly exposes the Heads-I-Win-Tails-You-Lose mode of argument which is the hallmark of radical feminism." One assertion in *Women Can't Hear What Men Don't Say* is that men have been continually forced into the role of a "human doing" especially prized for bread-winning capabilities, rather than a "human being" praised for attending to their emotional side. Though an advocate for men, Farrell believes the best goal is help further a "a gender transition movement" in which blaming the opposite gender gives way to a more collaborative, win-win thought process.

While several reviewers found his statements intriguing and his theories convincingly supported, other critics noted that Farrell sometimes exhibited the same traits he criticized in extreme activists. Young, for example, unfavorably noted some platitudes and exaggerations in Farrell's writing, and stated, "*Women Can't Hear What Men Don't Say* makes a persuasive case [documenting various] male disadvantages. . . . Unfortunately, like many feminists, Farrell can't resist overstating his case. . . . Farrell's description of anti-male biases in the media and culture while mostly on-target, also includes some dubious assertions." Flaws aside, concluded Young, in his book Farrell offers "a fairly specified (and mostly positive) agenda" to further "a gender transition movement."

One of Farrell's propositions in furthering the "gender transition movement" is to give more recognition to fathers' rights. This is his focus in his 2001 book, *Father and Child Reunion: How to Bring the Dads We Need to the Children We Love.* Farrell reports in this book that research findings indicate that children raised primarily by only one parent are better off if they are in the custody of their father and not their mother. He explores the research, examines the differing behaviors of mothers and fathers, and impacts of stepparents and the separation from the natural parent. In addition, *Father and Child Reunion* examines social actions that can foster greater equality and opportunity for men in their role as fathers. *Library Journal* contributor Douglas C. Lord felt that Farrell wrote in an "overly dramatic" manner and his "intensely pro-male tone" fostered a win-lose relationship which detracted from his "though-provoking comments."

Farrell once told *CA:* "Perhaps my writing career unconsciously began at about age twelve—during the McCarthy era—with being labeled 'Pinko' for refus-

ing to divide the world into Americans good/Communists bad. Fortunately, when I was fourteen and fifteen, my family moved to Europe, and I discovered that the questions that generated ostracism in the U.S. generated respect in Europe. It was an impressionable age at which to have my questioning process rewarded.

"When the civil rights, gay movements, and women's movements surfaced, I was again astonished at the inability of people to hear the best intent of the aggrieved groups. I got deeply enough involved in the women's movement to become the only man in the United States ever elected three times to the Board of Directors of the National Organization for Women (NOW) in New York City. This led to my writing my first book, *The Liberated Man,* in which I tried to articulate to men the value of independent women.

"Slowly, though, I began seeing the feminist leadership dividing the world into 'women good/men bad.' This led to *Why Men Are the Way They Are,* which was an attempt to take the most common questions women asked about men (e.g., 'Why are men such jerks?') and answer these from men's perspective. Men had become, in essence, the latest misunderstood group.

"As it became a definition of 'liberal' to care more about saving whales than saving males, I began to see the legal system becoming a substitute husband—doing more, for example, to protect women in the work place from dirty jokes than to protect men in the work place from faulty rafters. This led to my asking myself whether men really had the power if they felt the *obligation* to earn more money that someone else spent while they died earlier. Questions like these led to six years of research, fifty pages of footnotes, and *The Myth of Male Power: Why Men Are the Disposable Sex—Fated for War, Programmed for Work, Divorced from Emotion.*"

BIOGRAPHICAL AND CRITICAL SOURCES:

PERIODICALS

Booklist, April 1, 2000, Nancy Spillman, review of *Women Can't Hear What Men Don't Say: Destroying Myths, Creating Love* (audiobook), p. 1483.

Business Week, September 13, 1993, Bruce Nussbaum, review of *The Myth of Male Power: Why Men Are the Disposable Sex—Fated for War, Programmed for Work, Divorced from Emotion,* pp. 14-15.

Independent, Jojo Moyes, March 4, 1996, "Give a Guy a Break," p. S23.

Library Journal, November 1, 1999, Elizabeth Goeters, review of *Women Can't Hear What Men Don't Say,* p. 111; March 1, 2001, Douglas C. Lord, review of *Father and Child Reunion: How to Bring the Dads We Need to the Children We Love,* p. 118.

Maclean's, February 1, 1988, p. 58.

New Statesman and Society, March 4, 1994, p. 38.

People, June 15, 1987, p. 49.

Publishers Weekly, October 4, 1999, review of *Women Can't Hear What Men Don't Say,* p. 55.

Quadrant, June, 2000, Peter Kocan, review of *Women Can't Hear What Men Don't Say,* p. 83.

Reason, March, 2000, Cathy Young, "The Man Question," p. 64.

Time, March 7, 1994, p. 6.

Washington Post, October 17, 1986, Don Oldenburg, review of *Why Men Are the Way They Are.*

Washington Post Book World, July 25, 1993, Camille Paglia, review of *The Myth of Male Power,* p. 1.

ONLINE

Salon, http://www.salon.com/ (February 6, 2001), Amy Benfer, "Save the Males!."

Warren Farrell Home Page, http://www.warrenfarrell. com/ (April 13, 2001).*

*   *   *

FENICHELL, Stephen 1956-

PERSONAL: Born April 22, 1956, in New York, NY; son of Stephen S. (a writer and editor) and Lois (a historian; maiden name, Forde) Fenichell; married Carol Goodstein, March 4, 1995; children: Loisa Anna, Aaron Forde. *Education:* Harvard University, A.B., 1977; Trinity College, diploma in Anglo-Irish literature, 1978.

ADDRESSES: Home—523 Hudson St., New York, NY 10014. *Agent*—Julian Bach, 747 Third Ave., New York, NY 10017.

CAREER: Writer, 1977—.

MEMBER: Authors Guild, Harvard Club.

WRITINGS:

Daughters at Risk: A Personal DES History, Doubleday (New York, NY), 1981.

Other People's Money: The Rise and Fall of OPM Leasing Services, Anchor/Doubleday (New York, NY), 1985.

Plastic: The Making of a Synthetic Century, HarperBusiness (New York, NY), 1996.

(With Mark Mobius) *Passport to Profits: Why the Next Investment Windfalls Will Be Found Abroad,* Warner Books (New York, NY), 1999.

(With Scott Bedbury) *A New Brand World: Eight Principles for Achieving Brand Leadership in the Twenty-first Century,* Viking (New York, NY), 2002.

Contributor to magazines and newspapers, including *Channels, Penthouse, Diversion, Mademoiselle, New York,* and *Connoisseur.*

SIDELIGHTS: Journalist Stephen Fenichell has written on a variety of subjects relating to contemporary business practices. His first book, *Daughters at Risk: A Personal DES History,* recounts the story of women exposed to the drug diethylstilbestrol (DES), a synthetic estrogen prescribed to millions of pregnant women from about 1938 to 1971. DES was thought to protect against miscarriage, but this proved not to be the case; it was later found that children exposed to DES in utero carried a high risk of many diseases, including vaginal cancer, infertility, and changes in the structure of reproductive organs. Huge numbers of individuals affected by DES have sued the companies that manufactured the drug, and have been awarded financial compensation.

In *Other People's Money: The Rise and Fall of OPM Leasing Services,* Fenichell reports the rise and fall of Other People's Money (OPM), a company that became one of the biggest leasers of mainframe equipment but never turned a profit; in fact, the company accumulated losses of approximately 190 million dollars. OPM was founded and run by Mordecai

(Mordy) Weissman and Myron Goodman, whose business plan was to offer the lowest rates to potential customers; this brought them a huge volume of business, yet they continued to lose money. Despite these losses, as *Nation* reviewer Sol Yurick pointed out, Mordy and Myron "lived very well. Their enterprise expanded internationally, their offices were sumptuous, they held many celebrations attended by people from all over the country . . . they contributed heavily to charities, they were constantly on planes, first class . . . they bought mansions on Long Island, and also, they schmeared heavily in order to get contracts." They also, apparently, employed questionable accounting practices and tax dodges, the details of which Yurick felt Fenichell should have explained more fully. Noting that the author "writes in a breathless style: short, punchy paragraphs and sentence fragments," Yurick found the book "entertaining reading."

A New Brand World: Eight Principles for Achieving Brand Leadership in the Twenty-first Century, which Fenichell co-wrote with business coach Scott Bedbury, is another look at savvy business techniques. Reviewers found the book an informative guide to the subject. Investment strategies are shared in *Passport to Profits: Why the Next Investment Windfalls Will Be Found Abroad,* a book outlining coauthor Mark Mobius's insights on emerging markets.

Fenichell's *Plastic: The Making of a Synthetic Century* received significant critical attention. "Plastic," Fenichell told *Los Angeles Times* interviewer Connie Koenenn, "is an American phenomenon. It defines the way the twentieth century has evolved into an artificial landscape with Disney World and shopping malls and theme parks—things that are all about surface." The book covers the invention and development of plastics, but its focus is primarily social, as Fenichell draws parallels between the new medium and social change. For him, Tupperware represents the 1950s fear of outside contamination, and Formica offered "protection against internal and external attack, eternally vigilant in its struggle to wipe clean the past." Silly Putty, in his view, is a symbol of existentialism, and Velcro signifies the tenuousness of postmodern commitments. *New Republic* writer Jackson Lears considered such insights "glib and unsatisfying," and noted that this perspective ignores the economics that drove the development of plastics and shows only a "one-dimensional market model." Other reviewers,

however, praised *Plastic*. Mark Bautz in *People Weekly* described it as "quirky and informative," and a contributor to *Publishers Weekly* wrote that "This compelling, often surprising saga . . . will rivet your attention, challenge your preconceptions and open up new vistas of science, history, and popular culture."

Fenichell once told *CA:* "My journalistic interests have been in architectural and social history—including the history of New York City, high technology and its effects on social development, and biomedical issues such as DES (diethylstilbestrol). I am hoping to work more on East-West issues. I am also interested in nonfiction as dramatic art.

"I have been a freelance writer for four out of the five years since I graduated from college. (One year was spent in graduate school in Ireland.) Therefore I have been unemployed consistently during that time. The first nonfiction book on DES developed after I was contacted by a representative from a products liability firm based in Detroit (L.S. Charfoos), whose work in advancing the many hundreds of plaintiffs' suits arising from the DES debacle was, he felt, a viable basis for a book on the subject. He had the material; I was the writer; he was the active participant; I became, in effect, the observer. I felt this evolved into a worthwhile collaboration, particularly as the book developed (largely under the influence of my editor at Doubleday) into a very personal work based on the life of one woman who had been unlucky enough to be deeply affected, physically and emotionally, from exposure to this toxic drug."

He also noted, "As far as my view of nonfiction as dramatic art is concerned, I've found that the current publishing climate seems to actively encourage an artistic trend of rather massive proportions, namely the treatment of 'real life' stories in modes formerly suited only to fiction. Many critics have decried this trend, but, as in many other such developments, writers have insisted on their right to merge these once discrete categories. And the possibilities of such a merger have to date only been touched by the groundbreakers: Mailer, Capote, etc. This so-called 'New Journalism' has in fact grown into a new area of imaginative fiction. The recent award of the Booker prize in fiction for a nonfiction work by Keneally, *Schindler's List,* is a case in point."

BIOGRAPHICAL AND CRITICAL SOURCES:

PERIODICALS

ABA Journal, August, 1985, Joseph E. Kalet, review of *Other People's Money: The Rise and Fall of OPM Leasing Services,* p. 76.

Barron's, January 3, 2000, Jim Coxon, review of *Passport to Profits: Why the Next Investment Windfalls Will Be Found Abroad,* p. 52.

Booklist, July, 1996, Mary Whaley, review of *Plastic: The Making of a Synthetic Century,* p. 1786; July, 1999, David Rouse, review of *Passport to Profits,* p. 1911.

Business Week, March 25, 2002, review of *A New Brand World: Eight Principles for Achieving Brand Leadership in the Twenty-first Century,* p. 20.

Economist, October 19, 1996, review of *Plastic,* p. S13.

Entertainment Weekly, August 23, 1996, Alexandra Jacobs, review of *Plastic,* p. 116.

Library Journal, September 1, 1985, review of *Other People's Money,* p. 193; March 1, 1986, review of *Other People's Money,* p. 55; July, 1999, A. J. Sobczak, review of *Passport to Profits,* p. 108; May 15, 2000, Mark Guyer, review of *Passport to Profits,* p. 141.

Los Angeles Times, July 7, 1985, S. C. Gwynne, review of *Other People's Money,* p. B2; August 20, 1996, Connie Koenenn, review of *Plastic,* p. 5.

Military Law Review, summer, 1986, Jayson L. Spiegel, review of *Other People's Money,* pp. 265-266.

Nation, July 20, 1985, Sol Yurick, review of *Other People's Money,* p. 56.

New Republic, December 2, 1996, Jackson Lears, review of *Plastic,* p. 50.

New Yorker, October 7, 1996, review of *Plastic,* p. 96.

People Weekly, July 29, 1996, Mark Bautz, review of *Plastic,* p. 27.

Publishers Weekly, June 3, 1996, review of *Plastic,* p. 69; July 5, 1999, review of *Passport to Profits,* p. 50; February 11, 2002, review of *A New Brand World,* p. 177.

Scientific American, February, 1997, Jeffrey L. Meikle, review of *Plastic,* p. 102.

Wall Street Journal, March 7, 2002, David A. Price, review of *A New Brand World,* p. A22.

Washington Monthly, June, 1985, Eric Lewis, review of *Other People's Money,* p. 59.

Washington Post Book World, July 21, 1996, review of *Plastic,* p. 13.*

FINE, Gary Alan 1950-

PERSONAL: Born May 11, 1950, in New York, NY; son of Bernard David (a psychoanalyst) and Bernice Estelle (Tanz) Fine; married Susan Baker Hirsig (a manager), June 9, 1972; children: Todd David, Peter Gregory. *Education:* University of Pennsylvania, B.A., 1972; Harvard University, Ph.D., 1976.

ADDRESSES: Home—761 Linwood Ave., St. Paul, MN 55105. *Office*—Department of Sociology, Northwestern University, 1810 Chicago Avenue, Evanston, IL 60208.

CAREER: Boston College, Boston, MA, lecturer, 1974-75; University of Minnesota, Minneapolis, assistant professor, 1976-80, associate professor, 1980-85, became professor of sociology; faculty member, Northwestern University, Evanston, IL. Consultant to Yankelovich, Skelly, and White, New York, NY, 1979-80.

MEMBER: International Sociological Association, American Sociological Association, American Folklore Society, Association for the Study of Play (member of executive committee, 1983-85; president, 1985-86), Society for the Study of Symbolic Interaction (vice president, 1982-83), Society for the Study of Social Problems.

WRITINGS:

(With Ralph Rosnow) *Rumor and Gossip: The Social Psychology of Hearsay,* Elsevier-North Holland (New York, NY), 1976.

Shared Fantasy: Role Playing Games As Social Worlds, University of Chicago Press (Chicago, IL), 1983.

Talking Sociology, Allyn and Bacon (Boston, MA), 1985.

With the Boys: Little League Baseball and Preadolescent Culture, University of Chicago Press (Chicago, IL), 1987.

(Editor) *Meaningful Play, Playful Meaning,* Human Kinetics Publishers (Champaign, IL), 1987.

(With Kent L. Sandstrom) *Knowing Children: Participant Observation with Minors,* Sage (Newberry Park, CA), 1988.

(Editor, with John Johnson and Harvey A. Farberman) *Sociological Slices: Introductory Readings from the Interactionist Perspective,* JAI Press (Greenwich, CT), 1992.

Manufacturing Tales: Sex and Money in Contemporary Legends, University of Tennessee Press (Knoxville, TN), 1992.

(Editor, with Karen Cook and James S. House) *Sociological Perspectives on Social Psychology,* Allyn and Bacon (Boston, MA), 1994.

(Editor, with Karen S. Cook and James S. House) *Sociological Perspectives on Social Psychology,* Allyn and Bacon (Boston, MA), 1995.

(Editor) *A Second Chicago School?: The Development of a Postwar American Sociology,* University of Chicago (Chicago, IL), 1995.

Kitchens: The Culture of Restaurant Work, University of California (Berkeley, CA), 1996.

Morel Tales: The Culture of Mushrooming, Harvard University Press (Cambridge, MA), 1998.

(Editor, with Gregory W. H. Smith) *Erving Goffman,* Sage (Thousand Oaks, CA), 2000.

Difficult Reputations: Collective Memories of the Evil, Inept, and Controversial, University of Chicago Press (Chicago, IL), 2001.

Gifted Tongues: High School Debate and Adolescent Culture, Princeton University Press (Princeton, NJ), 2001.

(With Patricia A. Turner) *Whispers on the Color Line: Rumor and Race in America,* University of California (Berkeley, CA), 2001.

(With Daniel D. Martin and Kent L. Sandstrom) *Symbols, Selves, and Social Life: A Symbolic Interactionist Approach,* Roxbury (Los Angeles, CA), 2002.

Contributor to sociology journals. Editor, *Symbolic Interaction,* Society for the Study of Symbolic Interaction, 1986-89.

SIDELIGHTS: American sociologist and scholar Gary Alan Fine has authored or edited more than a dozen books since publishing his debut work, *Rumor and Gossip: The Social Psychology of Hearsay,* in 1976. Many of Fine's books have been based on his academic research conducted at the University of Minnesota, where he began teaching sociology in 1976. One such book is his 1996 effort, *Kitchens: The Culture of Restaurant Work.* The book was the result of a four-month period that Fine spent studying the work and behavior of cooks in four different restaurants during

the mid-1980s. Written from a cook's point of view, the book examines the difficulties that food preparers confront in the workplace, including having to labor in hot, confining conditions. "Consider the life of the cook, who faces enormous challenges, toiling in an environment less pastoral than infernal," Fine wrote in the book. Fine also discussed the age-old conflicts cooks often have with picky patrons, as well as with the waitstaff. Despite the troubles of the job, Fine believes that bonds of communality and friendship develop among well-run kitchen staffs.

Several literary critics lauded *Kitchens,* including Bonalyn J. Nelson, who reviewed it for *Administrative Science Quarterly.* Calling the work "well written and carefully documented," Nelson was impressed with the lengths Fine went to immerse himself in the life of a cook. "The careful presentation of both mundane and more profound aspects of this work leaves little doubt that Fine is intimately acquainted with the hectic, heated, and often humorous world of professional cooks," Nelson wrote. "This researcher has done his homework." David Farkas of the periodical *Restaurant Hospitality* also recommended the book, especially to people in the restaurant industry. "Anyone who owns or manages restaurants will be doing themselves a favor by reading this book," Farkas wrote.

A more recent work by Fine is his 2001 effort, *Whispers on the Color Line: Rumor and Race in America,* which he co-authored with Patricia A. Turner, a scholar of African-American studies. The book, which critic Donna Bell-Russel of *Library Journal* called "fascinating," examines the effect urban legends have on race relations in the United States. According to the authors, urban legend myths can have a profound effect on these relations, which in turn affect the way the legends themselves change over time among different ethnic groups. Fine and Turner describe the origins of these harmful urban legends and how they shape opinions. Bell-Russel went on to call *Whispers on the Color Line* "an important and useful book."

Fine once told *CA:* "My central research and writing focus is on the relationship between culture and social culture. This interest informs all of my writing from my study of Little League baseball to that of rumor to that of fantasy games. The question I ask is how is expressive culture shaped by the social system in which we all live and how does this social system affect the culture that we create and that we participate in. I examine the way in which small groups affect and give meaning to our shared experiences."

BIOGRAPHICAL AND CRITICAL SOURCES:

BOOKS

Fine, Gary Alan, *Kitchens: The Culture of Restaurant Work,* University of California (Berkeley), 1996.

PERIODICALS

Administrative Science Quarterly, March, 1999, pp. 197-199.
Library Journal, October 1, 2001, p. 131.
Restaurant Hospitality, April, 1996, p. 50.*

*   *   *

FRADY, Marshall (Bolton) 1940-

PERSONAL: Born January 11, 1940, in Augusta, GA; son of Joseph Yates (a Baptist minister) and Jean Marshall (Bolton) Frady; married Susanne Barker, January 20, 1961 (divorced, October, 1966); married Gloria Mochel, November 10, 1966 (divorced, 1975); married Gudrun Barbara Schunk, May 14, 1975; children: (second marriage) Katrina, Carson, Shannon. *Education:* Furman University, B.A., 1963; received degree from University of Iowa, 1966.

ADDRESSES: Office—ABC News, 7 West 66th St., New York, NY 10023.

CAREER: Newsweek, Atlanta, GA, and Los Angeles, CA, bureaus, correspondent, 1966-67; *Saturday Evening Post,* Atlanta bureau, staff writer, 1968-69; *Harper's,* Atlanta bureau, contributing editor, 1969-71; *Life,* Atlanta bureau, writer, 1971-73; American Broadcasting Corporation (ABC-TV) News, New York, NY, chief correspondent for "ABC News Closeup," 1979-86, "Nightline" correspondent, 1986—; nonfiction author.

AWARDS, HONORS: Woodrow Wilson fellow, 1963; Golden Eagle Award, Council of International Non-Theatrical Events, 1980 and 1983; Pulitzer Prize nomi-

Marshall Frady

nation for general nonfiction, Columbia University Graduate School of Journalism, 1981, for *Southerners: A Journalist's Odyssey;* Emmy Award, National Academy of Television Arts and Sciences, 1982; named distinguished alumnus, Furman University, 1982.

WRITINGS:

Wallace, World Publishing (Chicago, IL), 1968, revised edition published by New American Library (New York, NY), 1976, Random House (New York, NY), 1996.
Across a Darkling Plain: An American's Passage through the Middle East, Harper's Magazine Press (New York, NY), 1971.
Billy Graham: A Parable of American Righteousness, Little, Brown (Boston, MA), 1979.
Southerners: A Journalist's Odyssey, New American Library (New York, NY), 1980.
(With others) *To Save Our Schools, To Save Our Children: The Approaching Crisis in America's Public Schools,* introduction by Robert Coles, foreword by Peter Jennings, New Horizon Press (Far Hill, NJ), 1985.

Jesse: The Life and Pilgrimage of Jesse Jackson, Random House (New York, NY), 1996.

Martin Luther King, Jr., Viking (New York, NY), 2001.

Contributor to numerous periodicals.

ADAPTATIONS: Wallace was adapted for the miniseries, *George Wallace,* 1997, TNT television.

SIDELIGHTS: Journalist Marshall Frady has written extensively about southern politics and culture, both as a reporter for such magazines as *Newsweek, Life,* and the *Saturday Evening Post* and in his nonfiction books. In 1979 Frady moved into television journalism when he became a correspondent for ABC News. Frady's writings, which include biographies of controversial politician George Wallace and of televangelist Billy Graham, draw upon his rural North Carolina background. Reviewers often cite his skill in evoking ambiance through adjectives; some have compared Frady's descriptive talent to that of acclaimed twentieth-century southern novelist William Faulkner (author of *Light in August* and *The Sound and the Fury*). In a 1980 article, *Los Angeles Times* contributor David Shaw remarked that Frady "has always had a touch of the poet about him, an ability to use language far better than most journalists to evoke feeling, to invoke a sense of place and time and character."

Wallace, Frady's first book, attracted widespread attention for several reasons. The first was its well-timed publication in 1968, when its subject, former Alabama governor George Wallace, was a third-party presidential candidate finishing ahead of opponents Hubert Humphrey and incumbent Richard Nixon in some polls. The Vietnam conflict had divided the country, as had growing racial tensions in both impoverished northern cities and a South ravaged by the civil rights struggle, and Wallace's stance on these issues appealed to some voters. Others felt that Wallace's "populist" campaign—championing the cause of the working poor for better economic conditions and streets free from crime—was racist and divisive. As Frady's biography details, Wallace's most notorious brush with fame stemmed from his opposition to racial integration in the South. In one instance, Wallace himself, with the help of the National Guard, physically blocked the doorway of the University of Alabama after federal courts had ordered admission of the school's

first black student. Frady first came to know Wallace when he was a *Newsweek* reporter covering the 1966 Alabama gubernatorial campaign, and came to believe Wallace would be the perfect subject for a work of fiction about an ambitious southern politician.

Frady spent eight months researching the book inside the Wallace camp, interviewing his subject, friends, and advisors, and the work evolved from a novel into a direct biography. When *Wallace* was published in 1968 in the midst of the presidential campaign, the candidate was dismayed at Frady's portrayal of him and threatened to sue for libel. Another of its more controversial aspects was its cover—a caricature of Wallace with a chin cleft that resembled a swastika (a symbol of the Nazi party). Frady chronicles Wallace's impoverished background and entry into politics, revealing that when Wallace and his first wife, Lurleen, moved into the governor's mansion in 1962, they owned only the clothes on their backs. *Wallace* also recounts the near-total control of Alabama that the governor obtained, including successfully running Lurleen for governor in 1966 because the state constitution limited the office to a single term.

Frady culled his portrait of Wallace from tape-recorded conversations that are transcribed in the biography. According to reviewers, Wallace thought that Frady was a sympathetic southerner and candidly gave his views (often inflammatory) on race, bigotry, and the violent nature of American society—in the process, offering insight into the ruthless political campaigns he was infamous for waging. A considerable focus of the biography is Wallace's early career in Alabama state politics. As a young legislator he had been a protégé of Governor "Big Jim" Folsom, who was known for supporting integration and held liberal views regarding African American rights; Wallace later married Folsom's niece in 1970. Wallace's initially moderate stance on race mirrored Folsom's, as Frady demonstrates, until he lost a 1958 election to a bigoted opponent.

Because of Wallace's status as a presidential candidate, the book's publication received intense media scrutiny. Some critics felt that Frady's treatment of his subject was too superficial and faulted his portrayal of Wallace as a populist hero without delving into the charges of corruption that plagued his political career. Other reviewers, however, praised Frady's biography as rich with insight. *New York Review of Books* contributor Elizabeth Hardwick, noting Frady's original intent to write a novel, remarked that the end result is a biography with "an unusually imaginative quality." In a *New Republic* article, Robert D. Novak asserted that Frady "has established new standards in political biography by ignoring stylistic traditions and instead seeking the essence and the spirit of this unique and terrifying political figure through novelistic techniques." Ben A. Franklin of the *New York Times Book Review* described *Wallace* as "one of the finest pieces of political reporting published in years—a sensitive, informed and funny feat of high journalism that is a classic of the kind." *Saturday Review* writer Ronnie Dugger suggested that "Frady's work should convince his readers that Wallace has discovered and is hollowing out a great darkness within the American possibility." Wallace entered the presidential political foray again in 1972, but was shot and wounded in Maryland while campaigning. Partially paralyzed and confined to a wheelchair, he ran again in 1976, and a revised edition of Frady's biography was published the same year. The author added a 9,000-word addendum that incorporated the altered political climate of the 1970s as well as Wallace's triumph over adversity.

Frady continued in his career as a journalist, writing for such periodicals as *Harper's* and *Life* until 1973. *Across a Darkling Plain: An American's Passage through the Middle East* is a 1971 chronicle of the author's journey through Egypt, Jordan, and Israel. The author formed his impressions of the area through interviews with intellectuals, military personnel, and the rank-and-file; he presents them in the third person, referring to himself as "the American." Frady brings a southern perspective to his observations of life in the war-torn region, comparing Egypt to the American South in its adherence to a simpler way of life and its refusal to yield to the speed of the modern world. Despite his premise of objectivity, the author was dismayed by what he perceived as the nationalist outpost of modern technocratic civilization embodied in Israel. Alan Pryce-Jones of *Book World* noted that readers "may find the wrought prose and the third-person detachment a trifle daunting," but commended Frady's end result as "a sympathetic and evocative book."

Frady tackled a different icon of American fervor in his book on the popular and influential Reverend Billy Graham. For the 1979 biography, *Billy Graham: A Parable of American Righteousness,* Frady draws upon his background as the son of a Baptist minister to por-

tray Graham as the epitome of a peculiarly American postwar spiritual movement; Frady also speculates on what it is that drove Graham to achieve a global following. The volume chronicles Graham's rise from obscurity as a door-to-door salesperson to the leader of worldwide religious crusades that tempered a fire-and-brimstone ethic with a contemporary agenda of political conservatism. Frady writes that Graham's career as an evangelist began in the late 1940s and was assisted when tradition-bound media moguls such as William Randolph Hearst championed his mission, garnering it extensive and favorable press coverage. Effectively utilizing the medium of television to bring supporters into his fold, Graham was a household name by the 1960s and was consistently cited in polls as one of the country's most-admired men.

Frady's biography of Graham was culled from four years of research and several extended interview sessions with the minister. The biography discusses the evangelist's particular message of salvation, which incorporates a Gospel-based ideology of love and temperance with a pro-American, anti-Communist sentiment. In discussing the minister's popularity, Frady asserts that "Graham has become the only familiar American paragon left; the last hero of the old American righteousness." Frady also chronicles the more controversial aspects of Graham's career as a friend and erstwhile golfing companion to the likes of Dwight Eisenhower, Lyndon Johnson, and Richard Nixon. Graham vociferously supported American involvement in Vietnam, and remained on Nixon's side even after the president resigned from office in 1974.

In reviewing *Billy Graham, New York Times Book Review* critic Garry Wills faulted Frady's use of "over-ripe Southern rhetoric," remarking that the author's "style, clinging and sweltering, will not refrain from five adjectives where one would do." Yet Wills granted that "Graham is our nation's least-studied national institution. Marshall Frady has finally given him the kind of attention he deserves, close and critical, not condescending." Lance Morrow of *Time* also commented on Frady's prose, describing it as "a hot-wired Southern lushness of phrase and fluorescence of effect that would be insufferable were it not so accurate, so funny and, sometimes, so moving."

Southerners: A Journalist's Odyssey is a 1980 collection of eighteen of Frady's previously published magazine articles. The pieces, written for *Newsweek, Life,* and *Harper's* in the late 1960s and early 1970s, primarily focus on southern politics and personalities. Frady penned a profile of himself as an introduction, and each of the essays is premised by his commentary on the subject matter and followed by an update. One subject in the collection is a piece on former President Jimmy Carter, who, prior to 1976, had been governor of Georgia. Frady describes him at the time of his bid for national office as a "neat soft-spoken martinet of conscientiousness. . . . It was as if he were pursuing the Presidency through a kind of politics of niceness—a gentle, bread-pudding didacticism." Frady chronicles Carter's stint as governor, in addition to that of the more controversial Lester Maddox, and profiles other such luminaries as Georgia legislator and civil rights activist Julian Bond. *Southerners* also reflects upon past and present relations between blacks and whites as well as the legacy of slavery in the South. Frady once again draws upon his background as a North Carolina minister's son to provide insight into a peculiarly southern blend of fundamentalist religion and shady politics. *Los Angeles Times* critic Shaw faulted some aspects of the collection for "intrusive self-consciousness," but asserted that Frady "writes movingly of his feelings and of the feelings of his subjects." Robert Sherrill of the *New York Times Book Review* deemed *Southerners* full of "scenes you won't likely forget." The critic further praised Frady's evocation of the old South through extravagant prose, asserting that often the author's "results are excruciatingly sentimental or even incoherent. But when he brings it off, ah, the hair on your neck will stand up."

Frady tackled another controversial subject in his 1996 biography, *Jesse: The Life and Pilgrimage of Jesse Jackson.* Frady first met the black leader and heir presumptive to Martin Luther King, Jr., in 1960, then later followed Jackson in his 1988 campaigning for the failed presidential bid of Michael Dukakis, as well as during his own bids for the country's highest office. Frady's biography covers the high points of Jackson's career, from his blood-stained presence on television the day of King's assassination, through his successes and travails with the Southern Christian Leadership Conference. Reviewing the biography in *Washington Monthly,* Clarence Page felt that Frady "has written a hagiography worthy of Jackson's important place in history," though he also suspected that Jackson's "final chapters have yet to be written." According to Jack E. White, reviewing the title in *Time,* "Frady provides such a full-bodied portrait of this awesomely gifted but equally flawed man that it should provoke a repo-

sitioning of Jackson's place in history." Wayne Kayln, writing in *People Weekly,* also had praise for the book, noting that Frady's years of following Jackson for the biography resulted in the story of a "man of many parts," while the *Nation's* Debra Dickerson felt that Frady "seamlessly synthesizes" his decade of research and years of interviews with Jackson and his associates. "Frady is to be commended for putting Jackson's accomplishments in their proper perspective," Dickerson further commented. And *Entertainment Weekly's* Megan Harlan called *Jesse* a "galvanic, richly variegated, novelistic biography."

In 2001 Frady contributed a short biography of Martin Luther King, Jr. to the "Penguin Lives" series. K. Anthony Appiah, reviewing *Martin Luther King, Jr.* in the *New York Review of Books,* commented that the abbreviated text aims "to provide a lively narrative unencumbered by the scholarly apparatus of footnotes." Appiah further called Frady's work "engaging," a book that covers "elegantly and persuasively" the central facts of King's turbulent life. "Frady captures King in heroic moments and occasional failures alike," wrote a contributor for *Kirkus Reviews,* "delivering a nuanced portrait of a complex man." More praise for the King biography came from Thomas J. Davis in *Library Journal,* who observed that Frady's work "is an engrossing read for its literary prose, as well as for its tableau of the times and freshened perception of King as a personality." As with his Jackson biography, Frady was able to use his personal experience with King to add depth to his biography. *Booklist's* Vernon Ford felt that such experiences "add texture to this reflective look." And a reviewer for *Publishers Weekly,* while noting that the author covered King's negative sides—his philandering, for instance—as well as his positive aspects, concluded that "Frady's sensitive, succinct presentation never lets King's foibles obscure his tremendous contributions to American life."

BIOGRAPHICAL AND CRITICAL SOURCES:

BOOKS

Frady, Marshall, *Billy Graham: A Parable of American Righteousness,* Little, Brown (Boston, MA), 1979.

Frady, Marshall, *Southerners: A Journalist's Odyssey,* New American Library (New York, NY), 1980.

PERIODICALS

Book, January-February, 2002, Nathan Ward, "The Man Who Would Be King," pp. 18-19.

Booklist, December 15, 2001, Vernon Ford, review of *Martin Luther King, Jr.,* pp. 686-687.

Book World, May 2, 1971, Alan Pryce-Jones, review of *Across a Darkling Plain,* p. 8.

Chicago Tribune, June 25, 1979, Section 1, pp. 8, 10, Section C, pp. 8, 10.

Christian Science Monitor, February 14, 2002, Gerald Early, "A Short Biography of the Man with a Long-Term Dream," p. 15.

Entertainment Weekly, July 26, 1996, Megan Harlan, review of *Jesse,* p. 50.

Kirkus Reviews, review of *Martin Luther King, Jr.,* p. 1594.

Library Journal, December, 2001, Thomas J. Davis, review of *Martin Luther King, Jr.,* p. 138.

Los Angeles Times, December 18, 1980, David Shaw, review of *Southerners: A Journalist's Odyssey;* July 2, 1996, Michael Kennedy, "Chronicling a Man Out of Time," p. E1; January 20, 2002, David J. Garrow, "How the Dream Unfolded," p. R9.

Nation, April 10, 1976, pp. 442-44; July 8, 1996, Debra Dickerson, review of *Jesse,* pp. 25-28.

New Leader, November 4, 1968, p. 20.

New Republic, October 12, 1968, Robert D. Novak, review of *Wallace,* pp. 33-35; July 15, 1996, Eugene D. Genovese, review of *Jesse,* pp. 29-34.

Newsweek, August 12, 1968, p. 82.

New Yorker, December 16, 1996, review of *Jesse,* p. 109.

New York Review of Books, November 7, 1968, Elizabeth Hardwick, review of *Wallace,* pp. 3-4; September 19, 1996, Gary Wills, review of *Jesse,* pp. 61-72; April 11, 2002, K. Anthony Appiah, "The House of the Prophet," pp. 79-83.

New York Times, May 22, 1979, p. C9; July 29, 1996, Christopher Lehmann-Haupt, review of *Jesse,* p. B2.

New York Times Book Review, October 6, 1968, Ben A. Franklin, review of *Wallace,* p. 3; April 11, 1976, pp. 4-5; May 20, 1979, Gary Wills, review of *Billy Graham,* pp. 1, 52-53; September 28, 1980, Robert Sherrill, review of *Southerners: A Journalist's Odyssey,* pp. 3, 47; June 9, 1996, Alan Brinkley, review of *Jesse,* p. 12; January 27, 2002, Scott Malcomson, "King for Beginners," p. 10.

People Weekly, July 8, 1996, Wayne Kayln, review of *Jesse,* p. 31.

Publishers Weekly, July 1, 1996, Norman Oder, "Marshall Frady: Into Jesse's World," pp. 38-39; November 5, 2001, review of *Martin Luther King, Jr.,* pp. 49-50.

Saturday Review, October 5, 1968, Ronnie Dugger, review of *Wallace,* p. 26.

Social Science Quarterly, June, 1998, John Rouse, review of *Jesse,* pp. 478-479.

Time, May 28, 1979, Lance Morrow, review of *Billy Graham,* pp. 85-86; July 8, 1996, Jack E. White, review of *Jesse,* p. 69.

Washington Monthly, July-August, 1996, Clarence Page, review of *Jesse,* pp. 46-49.*

*　　*　　*

FREEMAN, Judith 1946-

PERSONAL: Born October 1, 1946, in Ogden, UT; daughter of LeRoy and Alice (Paul) Freeman; married Anthony Hernandez, 1986; children: Todd.

ADDRESSES: Agent—Joy Harris Literary Agency, 156 Fifth Avenue, Suite 617, New York, NY 10010.

CAREER: Writer. Contributing critic of *Los Angeles Times Book Review.*

MEMBER: PEN West.

AWARDS, HONORS: Western Heritage Award for best western novel, 1991, for *Set for Life;* John Simon Guggenheim fellowship in fiction, 1997; Utah Center for the Book Award for *Red Water,* 2003.

WRITINGS:

Family Attractions (stories), Viking (New York, NY), 1988.

NOVELS

The Chinchilla Farm, Norton (New York, NY), 1989.
Set for Life, Norton (New York, NY), 1991.
A Desert of Pure Feeling, Pantheon (New York, NY), 1996.
Red Water, Pantheon (New York, NY), 2002.

SIDELIGHTS: Judith Freeman's body of work has garnered critical praise for the author's technical skill and insight into the human condition. In an interview for *Contemporary Literary Criticism,* Freeman described what she hopes to achieve with her writing: "All writers must want to know more about themselves, but I hope my investigation extends beyond that. I look at the world partly like a photographer does. In other words, I'm recording things, and reporting on more than the state of my own life."

"*Family Attractions* marks the debut of a talented writer," wrote Michiko Kakutani, reviewer for the *New York Times.* The stories in this collection treat characters who attempt to reassemble their lives after a period of upheaval. For example, "The Death of a Mormon Elder" portrays a Mexican couple who must adapt to life in the United States, particularly in a Mormon community, and in "It Sure Is Cold Here at Night" a woman feels alienated from her boyfriend, a Vietnam War veteran. "The Botanic Gardens" is the story of a middle-aged woman vacationing in Australia after the death of her fiancé. "Freeman has a clear, unpretentious prose style and an ability to weave the small comic and tragic occurrences of domestic life into pleasingly organic narratives," asserted Kakutani. "Her voice—low-key, unsentimental and accented with the sounds of California and the West—is distinctively her own, and it allows her instinctive storytelling powers to shine through." "Freeman's writing is warmly intuitive, and many of her stories are braced with sardonic humor," commented Diane Manuel in the *Christian Science Monitor.* Writing in the *New York Times Book Review,* Beverly Lyon Clark found fault with one aspect of the style of *Family Attractions:* "Although Ms. Freeman tends to overstate her points by telling what she has already shown—sometimes making her metaphors and endings strain too obviously for significance—she is superb at capturing dialogue, especially the dialogue of cross-purposes." "Judith Freeman tells her tales in passionate voices strong with the authority of deeply felt experience, folk wisdom, and close observation of life," wrote Merrill Joan Gerber in a review in the *Los Angeles Times Book Review.* "In the best moments of these stories, we lose our awareness of reading a story and move through Freeman's fictional transparency directly into the world she wishes to reveal to us."

Freeman's debut novel, *The Chinchilla Farm,* follows the physical, mental, and spiritual voyages of Verna Fields. Unlike chinchillas, who remain with their mates for life, Fields, a thirty-four-year-old Mormon, is abandoned by her husband. Fields quits her job at a bowling alley, packs her belongings in a livestock trailer, and travels to Los Angeles, where she finds adventure. Novelist Barbara Kingsolver, writing for the *Los Angeles Times Book Review,* called *The Chinchilla Farm* "a beautiful, enigmatic novel that explores the nature of human connections and reveals itself in its own time." "*The Chinchilla Farm* is an on-the-road novel, a touching picaresque journey through the deserts of the West and the landscape of memory," noted Fern Kupfer in the *Washington Post.*

Set for Life is the story of two intertwined lives, that of an older man who is a retired Idaho carpenter and heart transplant survivor, and a sixteen-year-old pregnant girl who is a runaway trying to escape a family of neo-Nazis. The two meet accidentally and develop a father-daughter type of relationship. Jay Parini in the *Los Angeles Times Book Review* commented on Freeman's "remarkable clarity in portraying characters and her luminous often lyrical prose" in *Set for Life.* According to Parini, the novel is "starkly beautiful and focused with an almost laser-like intensity on her two protagonists." "*Set for Life* is about the heroism of ordinary people, and the strength of the characters in the novel lies in Ms. Freeman's ability to describe men and women with acumen and humor, and then go inside them," remarked novelist Katherine Paterson, in the *New York Times Book Review.* "Freeman rarely lingers in a narrative cul-de-sac; indeed, the story drives ahead like an old-fashioned steam engine stuffed with coal," added Parini. Several commentators praised Freeman's handling of the setting in *Set for Life.* "It's the kind of writing, so vivid and concrete and sonorous, that makes *Set for Life* stand apart from so much that is now being written," asserted Parini. "Freeman is at her best painting the breath-taking natural landscape of lake and mountain," observed Paterson. "Writers with Judith Freeman's heart and mind are rare; their work should be cherished and carefully tended."

Freeman delves into the microcosm of relationships in her book *A Desert of Pure Feeling.* The book is set, in part, on an ocean liner "with a cast of characters worthy of Agatha Christie," according to Susannah Hunnewell of the *New York Times.* Hunnewell added, however, that the novel suffers from "too many plot lines" and "too many ambitious subjects." A reviewer at *Publishers Weekly* remarked that *A Desert of Pure Feeling* is strong on portraying the inner workings of the characters, but it is weak "when Freeman throws in Nazis, Mormons and Guatemalan terrorism, elements that provide a false, often melodramatic sense of scope to what is, in the end, a very intimate novel."

Freeman grew up in a large Mormon family in Utah. Although she eventually left the church and moved to California, Freeman revisited her roots when she wrote her historical novel *Red Water.* In 1847 a group of Mormons and Paiutes (a Native American tribe) murdered a group of more than 100 settlers who were traveling through Utah on their way to California. The only man to be tried, convicted, and executed for the crime, known as the Mountain Meadows Massacre, was a Mormon leader named John Doyle Lee. In *O, The Oprah Magazine,* Louisa Kamps noted that the horrific story is told from the perspectives of three different women, and "in the process she creates a vivid, believable picture of the high religious fervor and red-dust-covered hardships of the Utah frontier." A *Kirkus Reviews* contributor described the book as "a sobering tale of women abused by a man and a faith that demanded total obedience. Still, lacking Lee's own testimony, the ghastly event is only partially explained." David Kipen of the *San Francisco Chronicle* commented on Freeman's writing style: "In keeping with her religious material, Freeman forsakes stylistic embellishments in her writing here, deferring almost all hints of humor, suspense or decoration." He added that "the result is a historical novel that's tough to warm up to, easier to admire than enjoy." John Freeman of the *St. Louis Post-Dispatch* described the three women who serve as narrators of the story. He felt the narrative structure worked, remarking, "Writing from each of their perspectives, Freeman gives her story the intimate feel of a diary, one that captures the nuances of a lost way of life."

In an interview with Ariel Swartley of *Los Angeles* magazine, Freeman said, "I was fascinated in my research to find this wacky, wild religion and to see how it transformed itself. Nineteenth-century Mormonism

was so kinky. They're drinking and they're really out there. Polygamy was a divine principle they were obliged to practice. It was a millennial sect: They believed the end was coming and they were preparing for it. And I think partly because of the Mountain Meadows—it brought such shame and disgrace—that when they entered the 20th century, Mormons wanted to become much more mainstream. And by God they have."

BIOGRAPHICAL AND CRITICAL SOURCES:

BOOKS

Contemporary Literary Criticism, Volume 55, Gale, 1988, pp. 55-58.

PERIODICALS

Booklist, January 15, 1988, pp. 827-28.
Christian Science Monitor, March 16, 1988, p. 20.
Kirkus Reviews, November 15, 2001, review of *Red Water,* p. 1568.
Los Angeles, January, 2002, Ariel Swartley, review of *Red Water,* p. 86.
Los Angeles Times Book Review, February 14, 1988, p. 13; November 19, 1989, p. 13; October 27, 1991, p. 3.
New York Times, February 17, 1988, p. C21; January 19, 1992, p. 21; May 26, 1996, Susannah Hunnewell, review of *A Desert of Pure Feeling,* p. 15
New York Times Book Review, March 6, 1988, p. 20; January 19, 1992.
O, The Oprah Magazine, January, 2002, Louisa Kamps, review of *Red Water,* p. 102.
Publishers Weekly, April 25, 1989, p. 51; April 8, 1996, review of *A Desert of Pure Feeling,* p. 57.
San Francisco Chronicle, January 27, 2002, David Kipen, review of *Red Water,* p. 1.
St. Louis Post-Dispatch, February 17, 2002, John Freeman, review of *Red Water,* p. F9.
Washington Post Book World, November 20, 1989, p. B4.*

G

GARMENDIA, Joseba Irazu 1951-
(Bernardo Atxaga)

PERSONAL: Born July 27, 1951, in Guipuzcoa, Spain. *Education:* Attended University of Barcelona.

ADDRESSES: Agent—c/o Harvill, 77-85 Fulham Palace Rd., Hammersmith, London W6 8JB, England.

CAREER: Writer and translator.

AWARDS, HONORS: National Prize for Literature (Spain), 1989, for *Obabakoak.*

WRITINGS:

NOVELS; UNDER PSEUDONYM BERNARDO ATXAGA

Ziutateaz, Kriselu (Donostia, Spain), 1976.
Bi anai, Erein (Donostia, Spain), 1984.
Obabakoak, Erein (Donostia, Spain), 1988, translated from the Spanish by Margaret Jull Costa, Hutchinson (London, England), 1992, Pantheon (New York, NY), 1993.
The Lone Man, translated from the Spanish by M. Costa, Harvill (London, England), 1997.
Lista de locos y otros alfabetos, Ediciones Siruela (Madrid, Spain), 1998.
(With Mikel Valverde) *Recuerdo de mis abuelos,* Ediciones Alfaguara (Madrid, Spain), 1999.

The Lone Woman, translated from the Spanish by Margaret Jull Costa, Harvill Press (London, England), 1999.
Poemas & hibridos: selección y versiones del propio autor, 1974-1989, Visor (Madrid, Spain), 1999.
Un espia llamado Sara, Ediciones SM (Madrid, Spain), 2000.
Two Brothers, translated from the Spanish by Margaret Jull Costa, Harvill Press (London, England), 2002.

OTHER

(As Bernardo Atxaga) *Sugeak txoria'ri begiratzen dionean,* Erein (Donostia, Spain), 1983, second edition, 1985.

Also author, as Bernardo Atxaga, of children's books and poetry. Contributor to *Toros,* a catalog in Basque and Spanish, 1999.

SIDELIGHTS: Bernardo Atxaga, the Basque novelist who was born Joseba Irazu Garmendia, became an internationally known author after the 1988 publication of his novel-in-stories, *Obabakoak.* Previously, he had written poetry, children's books, and two early novels. His practice is to write in Basque, then translate his own work into Spanish for publication. Even so, there is no doubt of Atxaga's allegiance to his Basque heritage, for much of his work is set in that culture, and his novel *The Lone Man,* published in the United States in 1997, sympathetically portrays Basque separatism.

Obabakoak, his best-known work, is made up of three sections, each of which contains a number of stories, some of which, in turn, are themselves made up of stories. "Its very structure, and the extraordinary method of its narrative, mark it as radically different," wrote Spanish novelist Eugenio Suarez-Galban in the *New York Times Book Review,* noting Atxaga's use of the infinite variety of storytelling forms as one of his themes. Crime stories, fairy tales, magical realism— "but not simply another docile imitation of Latin American magical realism," Suarez-Galban declared— diaries, poems, scientific papers, essays on the art of narrative, and more furnish the forms of *Obabakoak.*

The work is nominally set in a small village named Obaba; the word *Obabakoak,* according to the *Times Literary Supplement*'s Abigail Lee Six, means "the people and things of Obaba." It soon becomes apparent that for Atxaga, this tiny Basque village is the nucleus of a vast universe which extends into other lands and other times. As Suarez-Galban pointed out, the stories' long geographical and historical reach set them apart from such unified collections as Sherwood Anderson's *Winesburg, Ohio:* "The range of the author's imagination and his apparently inexhaustible fund of narrative voices alone would distinguish this book from other collections of stories. . . . What *Obabakoak* does share with all these works is a certain ironic delight in observing provincial narrowness; but this social criticism, so central to the others, is merely one element in a much deeper vision in Mr. Atxaga's book."

That vision is structured, within the book, into three sections. The first, "Childhoods," includes five tales set in Obaba. In Six's view, it is the most conventional of the sections and it "shows the author to be a skilful handler of the short-story genre, deftly mixing nostalgia with pathos and finding a good twist for his endings." The second, and shortest, section, is "Nine Words in Honour of the Villamediana," a set of anecdotes about the life of an apparently ordinary, but also magical, village. The third section, "In Search of the Last Word," was assessed by Six to be the most original in its narrative strategies. Unified by a single narrator, it contains numerous smaller stories within that frame, and its characters recur from story to story. Central to this scheme is the narrator's belief that one of his friends caused another friend to become an idiot by inserting a lizard into his ear: a hypothesis, Six added, that "appears to be borne out in the extremely effective surprise ending." In this third section, Six explained, Atxaga blends traditional storytelling with postmodern comments on that art form; Six acclaimed the "embedded" stories as "small masterpieces."

Concluded Six, "Above all, it is the tone of the novel which is one of its most attractive features, for it maintains a lightness of touch without ever becoming flippant; there is humour shot through with pathos and irony that is wry rather than biting, a novel that is entertaining without ever becoming lightweight." Suarez-Galban, who viewed *Obabakoak* as a collection of short stories rather than a novel, termed it "a delicious literary paella, very baroque and very Spanish." He found Atxaga's literary charm to be so complete that the book's brief essays on the art of narrative did not seem like digressions: "The book, you see, turns out to be a practical and theoretical manual on storytelling." In short, wrote Suarez-Galban, "Its pages make the word and the world new and fresh again, with an originality not very common in contemporary Spanish literature." *Los Angeles Times Book Review* writer Karen Stabiner, calling *Obabakoak* a "sprawling, sweet, and eccentric novel," characterized Atxaga as "clever without ever being superficial; there is poignancy in his nimble prose." His prose, in the English version, was translated by Margaret Jull Costa from Atxaga's Spanish translation of his own Basque original; Suarez-Galban said of this once-removed translation that it "beautifully retains Mr. Atxaga's magically flowing and seemingly simple style"—a style, the critic explained, which displays the talents of an inventive virtuoso.

Two related novels explore the thoughts and motives of terrorists. The title character of 1997's *The Lone Man* is Carlos, a former Basque separatist fighter who now is part owner of a Barcelona hotel. The story unfolds during World Cup action in 1982. The Polish national soccer team is staying at Carlos's hotel, as are a pair of terrorists, Jon and Jone, whom Carlos has agreed to hide on the premises. "The hotel is crawling with cops, ostensibly there to protect the Polish team, but Carlos knows it is only a matter of time before they discover his clandestine guests," reported *New York Times Book Review* critic Jenny McPhee. As Carlos bides his time, he reflects on his own violent past and finds he is emotionally unable to accept his former or future existence.

In *The Lone Woman,* central figure Irene has served four years of prison time, accused of terrorist conspiracy along with her lover, who was killed. Her incarceration, according to Amada Craig of the London *Times,* has become "the central experience of her life"; now, on a bus from Barcelona to Bilbao, Irene is shad-owed by two policemen, who suspect her of smuggling a bomb on board. As the bus trip progresses, the woman increasingly feels that prison was a more real experience than the outside world; she copes by reminiscing about her confinement and education at the hands of Margarita, an elderly Argentine murderess who was her cellmate. "Irene is hardly a sympathetic character, but she is vividly alive and uncomfortably convincing," commented Margaret Walters in a *Sunday Times* article. Walters found *The Lone Woman* "as taut and tense as a thrill, as well as an often moving meditation on the meanings of freedom."

Obaba is again the setting for *Two Brothers,* a 2001 release that is "a short novel with a long history," according to the *Guardian*'s Michael Eaude. Garmendia wrote the text in the 1970s; it was published in Basque in 1985; the author provided his own English translation for a 1995 release. The story is about two adolescent orphaned brothers in the small village. The younger brother, sixteen-year-old Paulo, inherits the family sawmill and much of the responsibility since his brother, Daniel, age twenty, has the mental age of a toddler. The emerging sexuality of both brothers adds to the pressure of making ends meet for Paulo. "Like all Atxaga's characters, they have little room for [maneuver]," said Eaude. As the author told Eaude, he deliberately set up the conflicts in Obaba because "village life is tough. People are often disagreeable and ignorant." *Daily Telegraph* contributor Lucia Graves found a "refreshing directness" in *Two Brothers.* Graves also remarked, "From the first page, Atxaga propels the reader into a compelling narrative in which fantasy and symbolism are used to tell a dramatic tale of real life." Death stalks the novel, as Ray Olsen noted in *Booklist,* and the action culminates in a tragedy in a story that is delivered "with the lightness of a Mozart aria."

In his interview with Eaude, the author said he considered *Two Brothers* his most important book, "because it showed me that my idea of how to write about village life could work." As for his writing on Basque issues, Atxaga acknowledged that he has learned to see the Basque/Spanish conflict from both sides, and has seen people from both factions killed. He realizes that in creating such books as *The Lone Man* and *The Lone Woman* he has become known as *the* Basque novelist; Garmendia also "knows he will always be a standard-bearer," wrote Eaude. The books of Atxaga, the reporter added, "have put Basque culture on the map,

but [the author's] success is also specific and literary. His simple style has not come simply."

BIOGRAPHICAL AND CRITICAL SOURCES:

PERIODICALS

Book, July, 1999, review of *The Lone Woman,* p. 84.

Booklist, June 1, 1999, Michelle Kaske, review of *The Lone Woman,* p. 1788; March 1, 2002, Ray Olson, review of *Two Brothers,* p. 1089.

Daily Telegraph (London, England), January 5, 2002, Lucia Graves, "Cast Out to the Wild," p. 06.

Guardian (London, England), October 20, 2001, Michael Eaude, "A Life in Writing: Michael Eaude Talks to Bernardo Atxaga, Basque's Strongest Literary Voice," p. 11.

Kirkus Reviews, June 15, 1999, review of *The Lone Woman,* p. 911.

Los Angeles Times Book Review, June 6, 1993, Karen Stabiner, review of *Obabakoak,* p. 6.

New Statesman, June 28, 1999, Lisa Jardine, review of *The Lone Woman,* p. 49.

New York Times Book Review, June 20, 1993, Eugenio Suarez-Galban, review of *Obabakoak,* p. 20; April 20, 1997, Jenny McPhee, review of *The Lone Man.*

Publishers Weekly, December 30, 1996, p. 55; June 28, 1999, review of *The Lone Woman,* p. 54; January 21, 2002, review of *Two Brothers,* p. 63.

Sunday Times (London, England), April 11, 1999, Margaret Walters, "Simply No Way Out," p. 12.

Times (London, England), March 27, 1999, Amanda Craig, review of *The Lone Woman,* p. 19.

Times Literary Supplement, August 21, 1992, Abigail Lee Six, review of *Obabakoak,* p. 18.

Translation Review Supplement, December, 1999, review of *The Lone Woman,* p. 31.*

*   *   *

GRANDINETTI, Fred M. 1961-

PERSONAL: Born May 1, 1961, in Watertown, MA; son of Dominic B. (a shoe repairer) and Dolores A. (in purchasing; maiden name, DeMeo) Grandinetti. *Ethnicity:* "Italian." *Education:* Northeastern University, B.S., 1984.

ADDRESSES: Home—96 Edenfield Ave., Watertown, MA 02172.

CAREER: Writer, cartoonist.

MEMBER: International Popeye Fan Club (co-founder, established 1989).

AWARDS, HONORS: Three Conti awards for *Drawing with Fred;* one Conti award for "Danny the Lifeguard," a public service announcement on water safety.

WRITINGS:

Popeye the Collectible, Krause Publications (Iola, WI), 1990.
Popeye: An Illustrated History, McFarland and Co. (Jefferson, NC), 1994.
Popeye: Le Marin, Dreamland (France), 1996.

Writer and program host for *Drawing with Fred,* a local children's television series which has aired for ten years. Contributor to magazines and newspapers. Cowriter on "Popeye" trading card series, Card Creations (New York), 1994, 1996.

WORK IN PROGRESS: A manuscript on the work of Jack Mercer who was the voice of Popeye for over forty years and writer of hundreds of animated cartoons for many studios.

SIDELIGHTS: Fred M. Grandinetti told *CA:* "The animated film career of Popeye the Sailor had never been fully covered prior to my publication. Since the sailor has had the longest run in the history of animated cartoons, someone had to tell his story. I have been a Popeye fan since the age of three and, since 1983, I have published a number of articles on the sailor."

*   *   *

GREENFELD, Liah 1954-

PERSONAL: Born August 22, 1954, in Vladivostock, U.S.S.R. (now Russia); daughter of Vladimir (a medical doctor) and Victoria (a medical doctor; maiden name, Kirschenblat) Greenfeld; married Gil Press (a marketing consultant); children: Natan. *Education:* Hebrew University of Jerusalem, B.A., 1976, M.A., 1978, Ph.D., 1982.

ADDRESSES: Home—64 Spring Ave., Arlington, MA 02174. *Office*—Department of Sociology, 558 William James Hall, Harvard University, Cambridge, MA 02138.

CAREER: Educator and author. Harvard University, Cambridge, MA, assistant professor, 1985-89, associate professor of sociology and social studies, 1989—, John L. Loeb Associate Professor of Social Sciences, 1989-92. Institute for Advanced Study, Princeton, NJ, 1989-90. Massachusetts Institute of Technology, visiting associate professor, 1992-93. Writer.

AWARDS, HONORS: Mellon fellow, 1985-86; Olin fellow, 1987-88; fellow of German Marshall Fund of the United States, 1989-90.

WRITINGS:

(Editor, with Michel Martin) *Center: Ideas and Institutions,* University of Chicago Press (Chicago, IL), 1988.
Different Worlds: A Study of Taste, Choice, and Success in Art, Cambridge University Press (New York, NY), 1989.
Nationalism: Five Roads to Modernity, Harvard University Press (Cambridge, MA), 1992.
The Spirit of Capitalism: Nationalism and Economic Growth, Harvard University Press (Cambridge, MA), 2001.

Also contributor to numerous professional journals.

WORK IN PROGRESS: Research for *The End of the Russian Revolution* which considers Russian national consciousness since perestroika.

SIDELIGHTS: As a sociologist, Liah Greenfeld broadens the scope of her research by examining the historical development of sociological issues. This methodology also allows her to expand the analysis of nationalism, which is a subject that is the focus of two of her books.

In *Nationalism: Five Roads to Modernity,* Greenfeld examines the historical and sociological development of nationalism in five countries: France, England, Russia, Germany, and the United States. Within this book, she seeks to determine what makes one nation inherently different from another nation—both culturally and politically—and why its citizens gravitate toward a nationalistic identity. Greenfeld maintains that, of these five countries, nationalism developed first in England and grew out of the specific needs of the emerging aristocracy and middle class. The French nobility used this concept of national identity to gain political power. The Russian aristocracy used nationalism as a means of promoting their identities as separate from the classes of people they considered to be beneath them. Nationalism in Germany was not based on aristocracy but, rather, on ethnic identity. American nationalism developed in a completely different manner from its European counterparts because it did not require its citizens to embrace a single, unified identity.

Describing the book as "a series of intellectual histories," *Society* reviewer Alex Inkeles quoted Greenfeld's summary of the questions the book examines as "why and how nationalism emerged, why and how it was transformed in the process of transfer from one society to another, and why and how different forms of national identity and consciousness became translated into institutional practices and patterns of culture."

In a review for *World Politics,* Yael Tamir commended Greenfeld's "significant contribution" to the body of sociological research because "she rightly argues that national identity is fundamentally 'a matter of dignity. It gives people reason to be proud.'"

Though Michele Micheletti, writing for *International Journal of Comparative Sociology,* was distracted by the book's "very detailed and long chapters," she agreed with Greenfeld that "these types of (nationalistic) struggles for recognition have historic roots." A reviewer for *Economist* also appreciated Greenfeld's historical examination of the subject and called the book "a great contribution to understanding nationalism's place in the world." In a review for *Atlantic,* Stanley Hoffman said "Greenfeld's enormous effort is serious and impressive," to describe her achievement in writing this book. He then agreed with (and quoted) Greenfeld's own statement from the book that it ". . .is an attempt to understand the world in which we live. Its fundamental premise is that nationalism lies at the basis of this world."

In *The Spirit of Capitalism: Nationalism and Economic Growth,* Greenfeld again combines historical research with sociological analysis as she examines the role of nationalism in the development of capitalistic economies. She reviews the economic and sociological histories of a number of European nations as well as Japan and the United States. A reviewer for *Choice* stated that Greenfeld ". . . weaves a rich tapestry, which reads well, and her survey of nonmainstream economic thought is encompassing and well done." In fact, because of Greenfeld's ability to describe the core concepts of this topic in a fundamentally understandable way, a *Publishers Weekly* commentator called this an ideal book ". . .for a freshman sociology course on the origins of the modern economy."

BIOGRAPHICAL AND CRITICAL SOURCES:

PERIODICALS

Atlantic, August, 1993, Stanley Hoffman, review of *Nationalism: Five Roads to Modernity,* p. 101-108.

Choice, May 1, 2002, review of *The Spirit of Capitalism: Nationalism and Economic Growth.*

Economist, March 27, 1993, review of *Nationalism,* p. 94-95.

International Journal of Comparative Sociology, January-April, 1994, Michele Micheletti, review of *Nationalism,* p. 152-154.

Publishers Weekly, October 8, 2001, review of *The Spirit of Capitalism,* p. 56.

Society, September-October, 1993, Alex Inkeles, review of *Nationalism,* p. 77-83.

World Politics, April, 1995, Yael Tamir, review of *Nationalism,* p. 418-440.*

*   *   *

GROBEL, Lawrence 1947-

PERSONAL: Surname is pronounced "*Grow*-bell"; born February 10, 1947, in New York, NY; son of Seymour and Estelle (a singer) Grobel; married Hiromi Oda (an artist), June 1, 1978; children: Maya, Hana. *Education:* University of California, Los Angeles, B.A., 1968.

ADDRESSES: Agent—Peter Matson, Literistic Ltd., 264 Fifth Ave., New York, NY 10001.

CAREER: Writer. United States Peace Corps, Washington, DC, volunteer teacher at Ghana Institute of Journalism, Accra, Ghana, 1968-71; Antioch College (now University) West Los Angeles, Venice, CA, assistant director, 1974-77, director of graduate writing program, 1977-80; writer.

AWARDS, HONORS: Winner of *Newsday* essay contest, 1963; interviewing award from *Playboy,* 1980; grant from National Endowment for the Arts, 1981; special achievement award in nonfiction from International PEN, 1986, for *Conversations with Capote.*

WRITINGS:

Conversations with Capote, New American Library (New York, NY), 1985.
The Hustons (biography), Scribner (New York, NY), 1989, updated edition, Cooper Square Press (New York, NY), 2000.
Conversations with Brando, Hyperion (New York, NY), 1991.
Talking with Michener, University Press of Mississippi (Jackson, MS), 1999.
Above the Line: Conversations about the Movies, Da Capo Press (Cambridge, MA), 2000.
Endangered Species: Writers Talk about Their Craft, Their Visions, Their Lives, Da Capo Press (Cambridge, MA), 2001.

Also author, with Sam Merrill, of screenplay "Helix." Contributing editor, *Playboy;* contributor to periodicals.

SIDELIGHTS: Lawrence Grobel, a longtime writer for such publications as *Playboy, Movieline,* and *Rolling Stone,* has specialized in chronicling the elusive, whether it's movie star Marlon Brando or the late novelist James Michener. In *Talking with Michener,* Grobel updates his interview with the *South Pacific* author twenty years earlier. Michener shared many of his strong views on race, sexual politics and education with his biographer in what *Booklist*'s Dale Edwyna Smith called a "wide-ranging romp."

In *Conversations with Brando* (titled *Conversations with Marlon Brando* in its U.K. release), Grobel portrays the enigmatic actor as a "celebrated zipped-lip merchant who turns out to be lucidly witty about his job," as Jonathan Romney wrote in *New Statesman & Society.* Adapted from a series of interviews first published in *Playboy* in 1978, *Conversations* has Brando "doing a tremendous PR job on his own supposed depth of character and political insight," Romney said. Casey Harrison, in the *London Review of Books,* said Grobel's interviews with Brando's family and associates "give glimpses of a less temperate Brando, and restore to us some of the screen personal, the murmuring hulk promising childish storms of violence and tenderness. Which is the real Brando? Both, no doubt."

Grobel's biography, *The Hustons,* follows the acting family (Walter, John, Angelica), focusing on John, a "womanizer, a heavy drinker, a man who enjoyed playing practical jokes," according to a *Kliatt* reviewer. Grobel, the critic added, "leaves nothing out."

Anthony Pucci, also in *Kliatt,* reviewed *Endangered Species: Writers Talk about Their Craft, Their Visions, Their Lives.* The work, a compilation of interviews over thirty years, presents background on the subjects and the circumstances of their conversations together. "There seems to be less emphasis on the craft," Pucci said, "and more focus on the visions and the lives" of such subjects as Saul Bellow, James Ellroy, Joseph Heller, and Joyce Carol Oates.

Another compilation of interviews, *Above the Line: Conversations about the Movies,* explores the lives and careers of those before the camera and behind the scenes, including actors Anthony Hopkins and Jodie Foster, director Oliver Stone, and producer Robert Evans. In this book, Grobel "produces entertaining, informative chapters on people who have made a difference to the way we understand movies," a critic wrote in the *Virginia Quarterly Review.*

BIOGRAPHICAL AND CRITICAL SOURCES:

PERIODICALS

Booklist, September 1, 1991, Martin Brady, review of *Conversations with Brando,* p. 20; September 1, 1999, Dale Edwyna Smith, review of *Talking with Michener,* p. 57.
Chicago Tribune, March 3, 1985.
Chicago Tribune Book World, March 9, 1986.

Films in Review, March, 1992, review of *Conversations with Brando,* p. 131.

Kliatt Young Adult Paperback Book Guide, April, 1991, review of *The Hustons,* p. 30; July, 2002, Anthony J. Pucci, review of *Endangered Species: Writers Talk about Their Craft, Their Visions, Their Lives,* p. 33.

Library Journal, January, 2000, Michael Rogers, review of *Conversations with Brando,* p. 173.

London Review of Books, November, 1991, Carey Harrison, "Harrison Rex," p. 30.

New Statesman & Society, March 27, 1992, Jonathan Romney, review of *Conversations with Brando,* p. 38.

New York Times, October 27, 1989.

New York Times Book Review, November 19, 1989; August 9, 1992, review of *The Hustons,* p. 3.

Publishers Weekly, November 23, 1984; August 23, 1999, review of *Talking with Michener,* p. 40.

Tribune Books (Chicago, IL), January 20, 1991, review of *The Hustons,* p. 12.

Variety, September 9, 1991, Stephen Schafer, review of *Conversations with Brando,* p. 104.

Washington Post Book World, April 14, 1985, December 31, 1989.*

*   *   *

GUTMANN, Amy 1949-

PERSONAL: Born November 19, 1949, in Brooklyn, NY; daughter of Kurt and Beatrice (Brenner) Gutmann; married Michael W. Doyle (a professor), May 30, 1976; children: Abigail Gutmann Doyle. *Education:* Harvard University, B.A. (magna cum laude), 1971, Ph.D., 1976; London School of Economics and Political Science, London, M.S., 1972.

ADDRESSES: Home—979 Stuart Rd., Princeton, NJ 08540. *Office*—3 Nassau Hall, Princeton University, Princeton, NJ 08544. *E-mail*—agutmann@wws. princeton.edu.

CAREER: Princeton University, Princeton, NJ, assistant professor, 1976-81, associate professor, 1981-86, professor of politics, 1987—, Andrew W. Mellon Professorship, 1987-90, Laurance S. Rockefeller University Professor of Politics and the University Center for Human Values, 1990—, director of graduate studies in politics, 1986-88, director of Program in Political Philosophy, 1987-90, director of Program in Ethics and Public Affairs, 1990-95, 1997—, director of University Center for Human Values, 1990-95, 1998—, dean of faculty, 1995-97, academic advisor to the president, 1997-98, provost, 2001—. Visitor at Institute for Advanced Study, Princeton University, 1981-82; visiting Rockefeller Faculty Fellow at Center for Philosophy and Public Policy, University of Maryland, 1984-85; visiting professor at Kennedy School of Government, Harvard University, 1988-89, participant in Saguaro Seminar, 1996-2000, member of advisory council, 1996—. Hastings Center, Institute of Society, Ethics, and the Life Sciences, fellow, 1982—, vice-president, 1986. Burkhardt Lecturer, Ball State University, 1991; Tanner Lecturer, Stanford University, 1994-95; Patten Lecturer, Indiana University—Bloomington, 1995. Member of board and executive committee, Center for Advanced Study in the Behavioral Sciences, Stanford, CA, 1998—. Lecturer at colleges and universities, including Arizona State University, Rice University, Santa Clara University, Rutgers University, and Brown University. Project on the Federal Social Role, director of Democracy and the Welfare State, 1985-86. Member of Twentieth-Century Fund Task Force on the Presidential Appointment Process, 1996; member of Penn National Commission on Society, Culture, and Community, 1996-2000; member of senior advisory panel, National Commission on Civic Renewal, 1996-2000. Member of board of trustees, Rockefeller College, 1982—, and Princeton University Press, 1996—; member of board of directors, Center for Policy Research in Education, 1985-88, and Salzburg Seminar, 1987-90. Consultant to President's Commission on Ethical Issues in Health Care, 1979-80, National Conference on Social Welfare, 1984-85, Schumann Foundation, 1996, Spencer Foundation, and Mellon Foundation Sawyer Seminar Selection Committee, 1996—.

MEMBER: American Academy of Arts and Sciences, American Academy of Political and Social Science, American Political Science Association (chairperson, Leo Strauss Award Committee, 1984-85), American Society for Political and Legal Philosophy (vice president, 1989-92; president, 2001-04), Association of Practical and Professional Ethics (founding member; member of executive committee, 1990—), American Council of Education, Whig-Cliosophic Society (chair of board of trustees, 1985-88), Paris Group for Philosophy and Social Science.

AWARDS, HONORS: Fellow, Danforth Foundation, 1973-76, National Endowment for the Humanities,

1977, and American Council of Learned Societies, 1978-79; LL.D., Kalamazoo College, 1992; McCosh Faculty Fellowship, Princeton University, 1993-94; Spencer Foundation Senior Scholar and Mentor grants, 1995-2004; Ralph J. Bunche Award, American Political Science Association, and Book Award, North American Society for Social Philosophy, both 1997, for *Color Conscious: The Political Morality of Race;* Kenneth Robinson Fellowship, University of Hong Kong, 1998-99; Gustavus Myers Center for the Study of Human Rights in North America Award, 1997; Bertram Mott Award "in recognition of outstanding achievement towards advancing the goals of higher education" from American Association of University Professors, 1998; President's Distinguished Teaching Award, Princeton University, 2000.

WRITINGS:

Liberal Equality, Cambridge University Press (New York, NY), 1980.

Democratic Education, Princeton University Press (Princeton, NJ), 1987, new expanded edition, 1999.

(With Anthony Appiah) *Color Conscious: The Political Morality of Race,* Princeton University Press (Princeton, NJ), 1996.

(With Dennis Thompson) *Democracy and Disagreement,* Belknap Press (Cambridge, MA), 1996.

Identity in Democracy: A Humanist View, Princeton University Press (Princeton, NJ), 2003.

EDITOR

(With Dennis Thompson) *Ethics and Politics: Cases and Comments,* Nelson-Hall (Chicago, IL), 1984, third edition, 1997.

Democracy and the Welfare State, Princeton University Press (Princeton, NJ), 1988.

(And author of introduction) *Multiculturalism and "The Politics of Recognition,"* Princeton University Press (Princeton, NJ), 1992, expanded edition published as *Multiculturalism: Examining the Politics of Recognition,* 1994.

(And author of introduction) *A Matter of Interpretation: Federal Courts and the Law,* Princeton University Press (Princeton, NJ), 1997.

(And author of introduction) *Freedom of Association,* Princeton University Press (Princeton, NJ), 1998.

Robert M. Solow, *Work and Welfare,* Princeton University Press (Princeton, NJ), 1998.

(And author of introduction) J. M. Coetzee and others, *The Lives of Animals,* Princeton University Press (Princeton, NJ), 1999.

Judith Jarvis Thomson, *Goodness and Advice,* Princeton University Press (Princeton, NJ), 2001.

(And author of introduction) Michael Ignatieff, *Human Rights As Politics and Idolatry,* Princeton University Press (Princeton, NJ), 2001.

(And author of introduction) Judith Jarvis Thomson, *Goodness and Advice,* Princeton University Press (Princeton, NJ), 2001.

Contributor to numerous books, including *Utilitarianism and Beyond,* edited by Amartya Sen and Bernard Williams, Cambridge University Press (Cambridge, England), 1982; *Liberal Democracy,* edited by J. Roland Pennock and John W. Chapman, New York University Press (New York, NY), 1983; *Liberalism Reconsidered,* edited by Douglas MacLean and Claudia Mills, Rowman & Allanheld (Totowa, NJ), 1983; *Moral Problems in Medicine,* edited with introductions by Samuel Gorovitz and others, second edition, Prentice-Hall (Englewood Cliffs, NJ), 1983; *Representation and Responsibility: Exploring Legislative Ethics,* edited by Bruce Jennings and Daniel Callahan, Plenum (New York, NY), 1985; *Justification,* edited by Roland Pennock and John W. Chapman, New York University Press (New York, NY), 1986; *Pluralism, Justice, and Equality,* edited by David Miller and Michael Walzer, Oxford University Press (Oxford, England), 1995; *Public Education in a Multicultural Society: Policy, Theory, Critique,* edited by Robert Fullinwider, Cambridge University Press (Cambridge, England), 1996; *Liberal Modernism and Democratic Individuality: George Kateb and the Practice of Politics,* edited by Austin Sarat and Dana R. Villa, Princeton University Press (Princeton, NJ), 1996; *Universities and Their Leadership,* edited by William G. Bowen and Harold T. Shapiro, Princeton University Press (Princeton, NJ), 1998; *Deliberative Politics: Essays on Democracy and Disagreement,* edited by Stephen Macedo, Oxford University Press (Oxford, England), 1999; *The Social Worlds of Higher Education: Handbook for Teaching in a New Century,* edited by B. A. Pescosolido and R. Aminzade, Pine Forge Press (Thousand Islands, CA), 1999; *Race and Ethnicity in the United States: Issues and Debates,* edited by Stephen Steinberg, Blackwell (Malden, MA), 1999; *Obligations of Citizenship and Demands of Faith, Religious Accommodation in Pluralist Democracies,* edited by Nancy L. Rosenblum, Princeton University Press (Princeton, NJ), 2000; *Truth vs. Justice,* edited by Robert Rotberg and Dennis Thompson, Princeton University Press (Princeton, NJ), 2001; *The Democratic Purposes of Education,* edited by L. M. McDonnell and M. Timpane, University of Press of Kansas (Lawrence, KS), 2001; *Taking Responsibility: Comparative Perspectives,* edited by Winston Davis, University of Virginia Press (Charlottesville, VA), 2001; *School Choice: The Moral Debate,* edited by Alan Wolfe, Princeton University Press (Princeton, NJ), 2002; *NOMOS: Moral and Political Education,* edited by Stephen Macedo and Y. Tamir, New York University Press (New York, NY), 2002; *Ethical Dimensions of Health Policy,* edited by M. Danis, C. Clancy, and L. Churchill, Oxford University Press (Oxford, England), 2002.

Contributor of articles to encyclopedias, including *International Encyclopedia of Social and Behavioral Sciences, Encyclopedia of Democratic Thought, Twentieth-Century Political Thinkers,* and *Encyclopaedia of Political Thought.* Editor, "University Center for Human Values Series in Ethics and Public Affairs," Princeton University Press, 1992—. Contributor of articles and reviews to numerous professional journals, including *American Political Science Review, Dissent, Milbank Memorial Fund Quarterly, Philosophy and Public Affairs, Washington Post, Studies in Philosophy and Education, Stanford Law Review, Ethics, Values and Public Policy,* and *Political Theory.* Member of editorial board, *Teachers' College Record,* 1990—, *Cambridge Studies in Philosophy and Public Policy,* 1991—, *Raritan,* 1995—, *Journal of Political Philosophy,* 1995—, and *Handbook of Political Theory,* 1999—.

Gutmann's books have been translated into Dutch, French, German, Italian, Japanese, Spanish, Swedish, Hebrew, Slovene, and Turkish.

SIDELIGHTS: Amy Gutmann's work centers on the political and philosophical implications of current issues in terms of her commitment to liberalism and democracy. In her 1987 book, *Democratic Education,* Gutmann observes that liberalism, the belief in timeless principles of equality and individual rights, and democracy, the belief in government by and for the people, are not always compatible since the will of the majority can jeopardize an individual's rights. Al-

though Benjamin R. Barber's review of the book in the *New Republic* criticized Gutmann for not sufficiently resolving this liberal/democratic conflict, he nonetheless lauded her "unimpeachable sense of fairness." In addition, Jean Floud of the *Times Literary Supplement* said Gutmann's political theory of education is "rigorously deployed and its practical implications are conscientiously demonstrated in close, well-documented and instructive discussion of controversial issues in the politics of American education."

Liberalism and democracy are also central themes in *Liberal Equality,* which examines the liberal tradition by tracing its history through such thinkers as Thomas Hobbes, John Locke, and Immanuel Kant. *Democracy and the Welfare State,* a collection of papers given at a seminar on social values and welfare in America, was sponsored by the Project on the Federal Social Role. *Color Conscious: The Political Morality of Race* examines the philosophies of language and politics as they affect race issues in the United States. In the *Annals of the American Academy of Political and Social Science,* Lewis R. Gordon wrote: "*Color Conscious* is a fine volume. Its strengths emerge . . . primarily from Gutmann's truly excellent, thought-provoking contribution, which is by far among the best scholarly treatments in U.S. liberal political thought on the struggle against racism."

Gutmann is also the editor of a series of books that collect the annual Tanner Lectures at Princeton University, as well as scholarly responses to those lectures. She is editor, as well, of *Freedom of Association,* a work that explores constitutional principles that apply to issues of "expressive association" and "public accommodation"—for instance, in the Boy Scouts of America rules that ban homosexuals from participation. William A. Galston in the *American Political Science Review* found *Freedom of Association* to be "written at a high level of clarity, rigor, and relevance to problems that matter."

Gutmann once told *CA:* "My work in moral and political philosophy and practical ethics has focused most recently on the moral challenges of democracy. *Color Conscious* won the 1997 Ralph J. Bunche Award for 'the best scholarly work in political science which explores the phenomenon of ethnic and cultural pluralism' and the North American Society for Social Philosophy award for the book that 'makes the most significant contribution to social philosophy.' *Democ-*

racy and Disagreement confronts the challenge of moral disagreement in democracy and shows how a democracy can develop mutual respect among citizens even in the face of irresolvable moral disagreements. The concept that Dennis Thompson and I develop in the book is called deliberative democracy, which is an antidote to soundbite democracy. My teaching and research interests extend to moral and political philosophy, practical ethics, education, and public policy."

In 2001 Gutmann took on a new and unique challenge as provost of Princeton University. Her appointment by university president Shirley Tilghman marked only the second time in Ivy League history that women have served as a president-provost team. Gutmann was quoted in the *Radcliffe Quarterly:* "We can't live a human life without educating others and ourselves. Education is an essential part of what it means to be a human being."

BIOGRAPHICAL AND CRITICAL SOURCES:

PERIODICALS

American Political Science Review, December, 2000, William A. Galston, review of *Freedom of Association,* p. 929.

Annals of the American Academy of Political and Social Science, March, 1998, Lewis R. Gordon, review of *Color Conscious: The Political Morality of Race,* p. 209.

Canadian Journal of Philosophy, June, 1999, Christine Sypnowich, review of *Color Conscious,* p. 275.

Choice, May, 2002, D. P. Forsythe, review of *Human Rights As Politics and Idolatry,* p. 1660.

Commonweal, February 12, 1999, Charles R. Morris, review of *Work and Welfare,* p. 24.

Current History, William W. Finan, Jr., "On Human Rights," review of *Human Rights As Politics and Idolatry,* pp. 229-231.

Ethics, April, 1998, William A. Galston, review of *Democracy and Disagreement,* p. 607.

Journal of Communication, spring, 1999, Joohan Kim, review of *Democracy and Disagreement,* p. 137.

Journal of Politics, November, 1999, Austin Sarat, review of *Freedom of Association,* p. 1212.

New Republic, October 26, 1987.

New York Review of Books, June 11, 1998, Robert Post, review of *A Matter of Interpretation: Federal Courts and the Law,* p. 57.

New York Times, Kate Zernike, "New President at Princeton Names Provost," p. A12.

Political Theory, April, 2002, Margaret Kohn, "Panacea or Privilege? New Approaches to Democracy and Association," pp. 289-298.

Publishers Weekly, August 27, 2001, review of *Human Rights As Politics and Idolatry,* p. 64.

Quarterly Review of Biology, June, 2001, David Fraser, review of *The Lives of Animals,* p. 215.

Radcliffe Quarterly, fall, 2001, Anne-Marie R. Seltzer, "Spotlight: Amy Gutmann."

Southern Economic Journal, October, 1999, Jeanne S. Ringel, review of *Work and Welfare,* p. 481.

Spectator, December 8, 2001, Caroline Moorehead, review of *Human Rights As Politics and Idolatry,* p. 52.

Times Literary Supplement, February 6, 1981; August 28, 1987; January 22, 1999, John Gray, review of *Freedom of Association,* p. 11; March 1, 2002, Saul Smilansky, review of *Goodness and Advice,* p. 28; May 10, 2002, Oliver Letwin, "But Who Are the Innocent?," p. 28.

Yale Journal of International Law, winter, 2002, Sanjukta Mitra Paul, review of *Human Rights As Politics and Idolatry,* pp. 230-233.

ONLINE

Amy Gutmann Homepage, http://www.princeton.edu/~agutmann/ (April 3, 2002).*

H

HABERS, Walther A(drianus) 1926-

PERSONAL: Born March 12, 1926, in Zwolle, Netherlands; son of Anton (a police officer) and Adriana Habers; married Helena Folmer (a social worker), January 30, 1985; children: Frederik, Esther.

ADDRESSES: Home—Reviusrondeel 197, 2902 EE Capelle a/d Ijssel, Netherlands.

CAREER: Writer. Has worked as a police officer, bookkeeper, coffee dealer, and broker of cocoa, spices, tea, and peanuts. Dutch Ground Nut Association, chair.

WRITINGS:

Involved (novel), Soho Press (New York, NY), 1994, printed in Holland as *De Winnaar,* reprinted as *The Way Back,* Gopher Publishers (online).
In Heaven It's Not All Roses Either, Gopher Publishers (online).
The Penthouse People, Gopher Publishers (online).

SIDELIGHTS: Dutch author Walther A. Habers enjoyed a number of professions, including law enforcement and coffee trading, before taking up writing after retirement. Habers's first novel, *Involved,* was published in 1994. Set in the Netherlands, *Involved* focuses on Bram Aardsen, an affluent, cavalier sports car dealer in Haarlem, and his marriage, which becomes troubled after he accidentally cripples a young boy. Twelve-year-old Dick Verwal has both feet amputated after being hit by Aardsen's Alfa Romeo, and Aardsen is racked with guilt. He visits the boy in the hospital during the recuperation, and a friendship develops between them despite the circumstances when Aardsen discovers that Dick also is an automobile aficionado. Aardsen's obsession with making amends rouses the jealous and suspicious nature of his wife, Francien, whose increasingly tempestuous rages—she thinks Aardsen and Dick's attractive mother are having an affair—eventually cripples the relationship. Francien's friend Marjet sees the Aardsen marriage is in trouble and tries to bring Bram and Francien back together.

In *Involved,* a chain of events begins that shares parallels with earlier incidents—a junkie trying to vandalize Aardsen's car gets both his legs broken, and, in Milan, Francien fractures a carjacker's skull and kills him. This incident leads to Francien's appearance on an Italian television show and being hailed as a feminist hero. Dick's mother, Pauline, also emerges as an integral character in her own right. In the end, Francien befriends the boy, Aardsen emerges as a little less self-centered, and, as *Washington Post Book World* writer Sandra Scofield explained, "everyone behaves admirably." Scofield also praised Habers's characterization of the women of *Involved,* noting that they seem to begin as mere peripheral adjuncts but emerge as "bright and tough." Scofield further asserted: "What might have been a mere comedy of marital manners shudders with reminders of fate, then trembles with tenderness." Andy Solomon in the *Detroit News* noted: "The value of marriage is not that adults produce children but that children produce adults. That might be an ideal epigraph for this quirky, heartwarming first novel." Calling Habers's writing "clinical," Chris Goodrich told *Los Angeles Times* readers that "you could almost guess [Habers is] a former policeman." The critic added that Habers's writing style "keeps the story moving along solidly, if not inventively."

Habers told *CA:* "In the early sixties I tried my hand at a novel. It was a wonderful experience, although I got no further than one chapter. I then decided I would try again after I retired. At the end of 1988 I wrote the first line of *Involved* and a year later it was finished. At least that's what I thought. I learned later that I'm one of those writers with an idea and no plot. Every page I wrote was new to me. I was the first to read my own book. Very fascinating. Before Soho Press accepted it three years later I had already revised it eight times. I am still ashamed I dared to submit the first version.

"*Involved* is about the unwritten small print on the marriage contract; whether to divorce or not to divorce? If a beautiful thing as the sparkle of love short-circuits, it shouldn't lead to hate and contempt."

BIOGRAPHICAL AND CRITICAL SOURCES:

PERIODICALS

Detroit News, December 21, 1994.
Los Angeles Times, November 27, 1994.
Publishers Weekly, August 22, 1994, pp. 39-40.
Washington Post Book World, October 30, 1994.

* * *

HAILEY, Johanna
See JARVIS, Sharon

* * *

HARRIS, Marie 1943-

PERSONAL: Born November 7, 1943, in New York, NY; daughter of Basil (a physician) and Marie (Murray) Harris; married Charter Weeks (a photographer), November 4, 1977; children: (first marriage) William, Sebastian Matthews, Manny. *Edu-*cation: Attended Georgetown University, 1961-63, and University of North Carolina, 1967-68; Goddard College, B.A., 1971.

ADDRESSES: Home—Barrington, NH. *Office*—Isinglass Marketing, P.O. Box 203, Barrington, NH 03825.

CAREER: Alice James Books, Cambridge, MA, publisher, 1974—; Maximus Advertising, Exeter, NH, copywriter, 1977—; Isinglass Marketing (business-to-business communications firm), Barrington, NH, partner, 1979—. New Hampshire Commission on the Arts Poet-in-the-Schools Program, administrator, 1972-76; Theatre-by-the-Sea, Portsmouth, NH, administrative assistant, 1976-77; gives readings at college and universities and on radio programs.

MEMBER: National Writers Union, Poetry Society of America, Academy of American Poets.

AWARDS, HONORS: National Endowment for the Arts fellow, 1976-77; New Hampshire State Council on the Arts grant; poet laureate, New Hampshire, 1999-2004.

WRITINGS:

Raw Honey (poems), Alice James Books (Cambridge, MA), 1975.
Interstate (poems), Slow Loris Press (Pittsburgh, PA), 1980.
(Editor) *Dear Winter: Poems for the Solstice,* Northwoods (Stafford, VA), 1984.
(Editor) *A Gift of Tongues: Critical Challenges in Contemporary American Poetry,* University of Georgia Press (Athens, GA), 1987.
(Coeditor) *An Ear to the Ground: An Anthology of Contemporary American Poetry,* University of Georgia Press (Athens, GA), 1989.
Weasel in the Turkey Pen, Hanging Loose Press (Brooklyn, NY), 1993.
Your Sun, Manny: A Prose Poem Narrative, New Rivers Press (Minneapolis, MN), 1999.
G Is for Granite: A New Hampshire Alphabet, Sleeping Bear Press (Chelsea, MI), 2002.

Contributor to anthologies, including *Ardis Anthology of New American Poetry,* Ardis (Ann Arbor, MI), 1977; *Blacksmith Anthology,* Volumes I-II, Blacksmith Press;

Mountain Moving Day, Crossing Press (Trumansburg, NY); *The Book of Eulogies,* Scribner, 1997; *The Party Train,* North American Prose Poetry, New Rivers, 1996; *Always the Beautiful Answer,* Kings Estate Press, 1999; and *The Unmade Bed,* Harper Collins, 1992. Contributor of articles and poems to magazines, including *Parnassus: Poetry in Review, Longhouse, Hanging Loose, Rivendell, Paragraph, New Formalist, New York Times, Boston Globe, UnionLeader,* and *American Writer.*

WORK IN PROGRESS: Catechism for a Lunar Eclipse, a book of poems.

SIDELIGHTS: Marie Harris is a New Hampshire-based poet who lives in a rural area in a home she and her husband built themselves. While not prolific, she has produced a steady stream of work for books and periodicals, in addition to running several advertising firms. Her written work includes advertising copy, travel articles, and creative nonfiction, along with poetry. She succeeded Donald Hall as poet laureate of New Hampshire.

A *Publishers Weekly* reviewer noted of *Weasel in the Turkey Pen* that the prose poems "move easily and unexpectedly between the real and the surreal." The same critic praised the "sense of doomed journey throughout."

Harris and her husband adopted a disadvantaged fourteen-year-old named Manny, a Puerto Rican young man who had long been a ward of the state. The prose poems in *Your Sun, Manny: A Prose Poem Memoir,* "place Manny at center stage," to quote Jacqueline White in *Ruminator Review.* The pieces in the book are forthright and candid about Manny's struggles to assimilate into his new life and to become a self-supporting, functioning adult. White wrote: "The mixed emotions these new parents grapple with speak to a larger cultural uncertainty. The nuclear family is imploding, children are the casualties, and yet, as a society, we hardly seem able to talk, much less act, on their behalf. [This] brave [book addresses] that silence, offering up alternative configurations of family that attempt to heal the resulting distress."

Harris is involved with arts in education, and has served as a writer-in-residence in elementary and secondary schools in New Hampshire. The New Hampshire Council on the Arts Web site says Harris's plans as poet laureate "include working with town libraries and exploring the uses of the internet to accomplish her goals." Harris told the Brewster Academy during a reading for *Your Sun, Manny* that she views herself as an advocate for poets. "[Poets] used to be visible in society," she said, "then we somehow became locked away in ivory towers, marginalized."

BIOGRAPHICAL AND CRITICAL SOURCES:

PERIODICALS

Booklist, February 15, 1993, Patricia Monaghan, review of *Weasel in the Turkey Pen,* p. 1028.
Georgia Review, fall, 1990, Anne C. Bromley, review of *An Ear to the Ground: An Anthology of Contemporary American Poetry,* p. 511.
Publishers Weekly, May 26, 1989, review of *An Ear to the Ground,* p. 60; February 1, 1993, review of *Weasel in the Turkey Pen,* p. 87.
Ruminator Review, fall, 2001, Jacqueline White, review of *Your Sun, Manny: A Prose Poem Memoir,* p. 31.

ONLINE

Brewster Academy Web site, http://www.brewsteracademy.org/ (January 7, 2002), "Marie Harris, New Hampshire's Poet Laureate."
New Hampshire Council on the Arts Web site, http://www.state.nh.us/nharts/ (June 25, 2002), "Marie Harris: New Hampshire's Poet Laureate, 1999-2004."

*   *   *

HERMAN, Walter
   See WAGER, Walter H(erman)

*   *   *

HERSEY, George Leonard 1927-

PERSONAL: Born August 30, 1927, in Cambridge, MA; son of Milton Leonard (an economist) and Katharine (Page) Hersey; married Jane Maddox Lancefield, September 2, 1953; children: Donald, James. *Education:* Harvard University, A.B., 1951; Yale University, M.F.A., 1954, M.A., 1960, Ph.D., 1964. *Politics:* Democrat.

ADDRESSES: Home—167 Linden St., New Haven, CT 06511. *Office*—Department of the History of Art, Yale University, New Haven, CT 06520. *E-mail*—george.hersey@yale.edu.

CAREER: Bucknell University, Lewisburg, PA, instructor, 1954-55, assistant professor of art, 1956-59, acting chairman of art history department, 1958-59; Yale University, New Haven, CT, assistant professor, 1965-68, associate professor, 1968-74, director of graduate studies, 1968-71, professor, 1974-92, currently professor emeritus of the history of art. Director of restoration research, Lockwood-Mathews Mansion Museum, Norwalk, CT, beginning 1970; member, Governor's Commission on the Restoration of the Connecticut State Capitol, beginning 1977. *Military service:* U.S. Army, 1946-47.

MEMBER: Society of Architectural Historians (member of board of directors, 1970-73), Victorian Society (United States), Victorian Society (Great Britain).

AWARDS, HONORS: Fulbright scholar in Italy, 1962; American Philosophical Society award, 1962; Schepp Foundation fellow of the Harvard Center for Renaissance Studies, 1971.

WRITINGS:

Alfonso II and the Artistic Renewal of Naples, 1485-95, Yale University Press (New Haven, CT), 1969.

High Victorian Gothic: A Study in Associationism, Johns Hopkins University Press (Baltimore, MD), 1972.

The Aragonese Arch at Naples, 1443-1477, Yale University Press (New Haven, CT), 1973.

Pythagorean Palaces: Architecture and Magic in the Italian Renaissance, Cornell University Press (Ithaca, NY), 1976.

Architecture, Poetry, and Number in the Royal Palace at Caserta, MIT Press (Cambridge, MA), 1983.

The Lost Meaning of Classical Architecture: Speculations on Ornament from Vitruvius to Venturi, MIT Press (Cambridge, MA), 1988.

(With Richard Freedman) *Possible Palladian Villas (Plus a Few Instructively Impossible Ones),* MIT Press (Cambridge, MA), 1992.

High Renaissance Art in St. Peter's and the Vatican: An Interpretive Guide, University of Chicago Press (Chicago, IL), 1993.

The Evolution of Allure: Sexual Selection from the Medici Venus to the Incredible Hulk, MIT Press (Cambridge, MA), 1996.

The Monumental Impulse: Architecture's Biological Roots, MIT Press (Cambridge, MA), 1999.

Architecture and Geometry in the Age of the Baroque, University of Chicago Press (Chicago, IL), 2000.

Contributor to *Mediterranean,* Aperture (New York, NY), 1995. Co-editor of *Architectura: Internationale Zeitschrift für Architektur-Geschichte,* 1971—; editor, Yale Publications on the History of Art, 1971-92.

SIDELIGHTS: For many years George Leonard Hersey was a professor of art history at Yale University. Retired in the early 1990s, Hersey has channeled his expertise on Italian Renaissance and nineteenth-century architecture into several books, including *Architecture and Geometry in the Age of the Baroque, The Monumental Impulse: Architecture's Biological Roots,* and *The Evolution of Allure: Sexual Selection from the Medici Venus to the Incredible Hulk.* Hersey has three degrees from Yale University, including an M.A. and Ph.D. in the history of art. Before becoming an instructor at Yale, he taught at Bucknell University, and became a full professor at Yale in 1974.

In *Architecture, Poetry, and Number in the Royal Palace at Caserta,* Hersey offers the first English book about Luigi Vanvitelli and his greatest work, the palace at Caserta. Work on the palace began in 1752 for Carlo di Borbone, the Bourbon king of the Two Sicilies. Hersey provides insight into the relationship literature had on Vanvitelli's work, particular the works of Giambattista Vico. Alison Armstrong Jensen noted in *Progressive Architecture* that "Hersey's book is valuable for its explanation not only of Caserta's physical history but also of Vico's influence on his contemporaries."

In *The Lost Meaning of Classical Architecture: Speculations on Ornament from Vitruvius to Venturi,* Hersey poses the question "why do we continue to use the classical orders in architecture?" Centuries after the decline of Greek's golden age, architects have continued to build columns in the form used on Greek temples. The Greeks have influenced the most celebrated monuments of modern culture, from the Capitol in Washington, D.C., to the Imperial Palace in Tokyo. Hersey's explanation for this is that ancient belief systems have a way of seeping into our language because their original meaning is somehow sacred. Mark Alden Branch commented in *Progressive Architecture* that Hersey's "exploration of the subtleties of the written and spoken language yields a greater understanding of the origins of the architectural language."

Hersey links nineteenth-century evolution proponent Charles Darwin to art history in *The Evolution of Allure: Sexual Selection from the Medici Venus to the Incredible Hulk*. According to the author, art has significantly shaped the fabric of evolution and human history. From the ancient Greeks to Hollywood and comic books, art has influenced our ideals about physical beauty, even down to the mates we choose. According to Barbara Dickson in *Criticism*, Hersey "offers rich suggestions and creative analysis which lends itself well to cultural studies of conceptualizations of the body." The book includes 146 illustrations.

Hersey continues to make connections between Darwinian science and architecture in *The Monumental Impulse: Architecture's Biological Roots*. He expands his theory by drawing comparisons between species of animal and building types. By examining the worlds of biology and architecture, Hersey hopes to demonstrate the relationship between microscopic life and buildings. In the final paragraph of the book he restates his mission by writing that "the discussion has illuminated a long and, I hope, fascinating drama of encounters, enactments, fusions, and correspondences between biology and architecture." Hersey's candid writing and the book's numerous illustrations offer a fascinating insight into his theories.

BIOGRAPHICAL AND CRITICAL SOURCES:

PERIODICALS

American Craft, February-March, 1985, review of *The Lost Meaning of Classical Architecture: Speculations on Ornament from Vitruvius to Venturi*, p. 94.

Apollo, February, 1990, review of *The Lost Meaning of Classical Architecture*, p. 35.

Architectural Record, March, 1993, review of *Possible Palladian Villas (Plus a Few Instructively Impossible Ones)*, p. 31.

Architecture, May, 1999, review of *The Monumental Impulse: Architecture's Biological Roots*, p. 55.

Burlington Magazine, November, 1984, review of *Architecture, Poetry, and Number in the Royal Palace at Caserta*, p. 714; fall, 1989, review of *The Lost Meaning of Classical Architecture*, p. 158; March, 1994, review of *High Renaissance Art in St. Peter's and the Vatican: An Interpretive Guide*, p. 186.

Choice, October, 1983, review of *Architecture, Poetry, and Number in the Royal Palace at Caserta*, p. 263; April, 1993, review of *Possible Palladian Villas (Plus a Few Instructively Impossible Ones)*, p. 1305; December, 1993, review of *High Renaissance Art in St. Peter's and the Vatican*, p. 594; March, 1997, review of *The Evolution of Allure*, p. 1152.

Classical and Modern Literature, spring, 1991, review of *The Lost Meaning of Classical Architecture*, p. 262.

Classical Review, 1990, review of *The Lost Meaning of Classical Architecture*, p. 186.

Criticism, spring, 1998, review of *The Evolution of Allure*, p. 322.

Design Book Review, summer, 1989, review of *The Lost Meaning of Classical Architecture*, p. 35.

House & Garden, January, 1984, review of *Architecture, Poetry, and Number in the Royal Palace at Caserta*, p. 30.

Hudson Review, summer, 1997, review of *The Evolution of Allure*, p. 347.

Journal of Aesthetics and Art Criticism, summer, 1992, review of *The Lost Meaning of Classical Architecture*, p. 73; spring, 1994, review of *Possible Palladian Villas*, p. 262.

Library Journal, April 1, 1983, review of *Architecture, Poetry, and Number in the Royal Palace at Caserta*, p. 735; May 1, 1988, review of *The Lost Meaning of Classical Architecture*, p. 73.

Progressive Architecture, November, 1985, review of *Architecture, Poetry, and Number in the Royal Palace at Caserta*, p. 135; May, 1988, review of *The Lost Meaning of Classical Architecture*, p. 107; March, 1993, review of *Possible Palladian Villas*, p. 111.

Renaissance Quarterly, summer, 1984, review of *Architecture, Poetry, and Number in the Royal Palace at Caserta*, p. 264.

Times Literary Supplement, February 28, 1997, review of *The Evolution of Allure*, p. 32; February 25, 2000, review of *The Lost Meaning of Classical Architecture*, p. 20.*

HIRSCH, Foster (Lance) 1943-

PERSONAL: Born December 20, 1943, in New York, NY; son of Harry (a real estate investor) and Etta (Goldberg) Hirsch. *Education:* Stanford University, B.A., 1965; Columbia University, M.F.A., 1966, M.A., 1967, Ph.D., 1971. *Religion:* Jewish.

ADDRESSES: Home—49 West Twelfth St., New York, NY 10011. *Office*—Department of Film, Brooklyn College of the City University of New York, Brooklyn, NY 11210. *Agent*—Ruth Nathan, 80 Fifth Ave., New York, NY 10011.

CAREER: Brooklyn College of the City University of New York, instructor, 1967-73, assistant professor, 1974-77, associate professor of English, 1978-85, professor of film, 1985—. New School for Social Research (now New School University), lecturer, 1970-72.

MEMBER: Authors Guild, Authors League of America, National Book Critics Circle, Phi Beta Kappa.

AWARDS, HONORS: Stanford Journalism Award, 1965.

WRITINGS:

Elizabeth Taylor, Pyramid Publications, 1973.
Edward G. Robinson, Pyramid Publications, 1975.
George Kelly, Twayne (New York, NY), 1975.
The Hollywood Epic, A. S. Barnes (San Diego, CA), 1978.
Who's Afraid of Edward Albee?, Creative Arts, 1978.
Laurence Olivier, G. K. Hall (New York, NY), 1979.
A Portrait of the Artist: The Plays of Tennessee Williams, Kennikat Press (Port Washington, NY), 1979.
Joseph Losey, Twayne (New York, NY), 1980.
Film Noir: The Dark Side of the Screen, A. S. Barnes (San Diego, CA), 1981.
Love, Sex, Death, and the Meaning of Life: Woody Allen's Comedy, McGraw (New York, NY), 1981, revised edition, 1990.
Laurence Olivier on Screen, Da Capo Press (New York, NY), 1984.

A Method to Their Madness: The History of the Actors Studio, Norton (New York, NY), 1984.
Eugene O'Neill, York Press, 1986.
Harold Prince and the American Musical Theatre, Cambridge University Press (New York, NY), 1989.
Acting Hollywood Style, Harry Abrams (New York, NY), 1991.
The Boys from Syracuse: The Shuberts' Theatrical Empire, Southern Illinois University Press (Carbondale, IL), 1998.
Detours and Lost Highways: A Map of Neo-Noir, Limelight Editions (New York, NY), 1999.
Kurt Weill on Stage: From Berlin to Broadway, Alfred A. Knopf (New York, NY), 2002.

Contributor to books, including *Contemporary Dramatists,* St. Martin's Press, 1973, and *Sexuality in Film,* edited by Thomas Atkins, Indiana University Press, 1975. Author of afterword, *Crime Movies,* Da Capo Press, 1997. Contributor of reviews to periodicals, including *Nation, America, New York Times, Commonweal,* and *Village Voice.*

SIDELIGHTS: Foster Hirsch's *A Method to Their Madness: The History of the Actors Studio* describes the evolution of Lee Strasberg's Actors Studio, which trained such notables as Marlon Brando, Paul Newman, Shelley Winters, and Marilyn Monroe. Strasberg's method-acting techniques were derived from a system formulated by Konstantin Stanislavsky in Europe but differed in significant ways, eventually causing a great rift in the American theater between those who favored Stanislavsky's original theories and those who followed Strasberg's more dogmatic beliefs. Hirsch's study not only examines Strasberg's professional influence but explores his controversial personality as well.

The first half of *A Method to Their Madness* gives a thorough analysis of the development of Stanislavsky's system. "Hirsch's imagination endows this history with new life, enriched with interviews of people who participated in the events," noted *New York Times Book Review* contributor Marshal W. Mason. The second part of Hirsch's book follows Strasberg's development of Stanislavsky's philosophies and the problems encountered therein. "His history of [the Studio] . . . is far from conventionally deferential, and his assessment of its accomplishments is properly sceptical," noted *Times Literary Supplement* critic Benedict Nightingale in appraising Hirsch's analysis.

Much of Hirsch's scepticism regarding Strasberg and his techniques arises from his concern that method acting produces actors able to portray only those aspects of a character with which they can literally identify. Hirsch's first-hand accounts of Strasberg's unusual training methods are included in his book. "The tone degenerates from historical to anecdotal as he switches from researched opinion to on-site observation," wrote Mason, who noted that Hirsch's highly critical view of Strasberg colors his subject as "a man with a monstrous ego and destructive eccentricities." Hirsch's negative assessment of Strasberg's personality is based on numerous interviews where the biographer alternately heard the famed acting teacher compared to figures as disparate as Jesus and German Chancellor Adolph Hitler. In any case, Nightingale noted, "Strasberg was rude, cowardly in a crisis, and abjectly impressed by the stars and celebrities whose glitter the Studio was in the business to resist." Nightingale maintained that Hirsch's conclusions regarding Strasberg and the Actor's Studio are more moderate and "more just" than other studies of Strasberg have been.

In *The Boys from Syracuse: The Shuberts' Theatrical Empire*, Hirsch writes about the Shubert brothers who moved south from Syracuse, New York, early in the twentieth century to find success in the theater in New York City. Although brothers Sam, Lee, and J. J. earned their share of enemies for what were perceived as tough and ruthless business tactics, they dominated New York theater in the early part of the century. The list of stars the brothers worked with includes the biggest names in the theater of their time: Al Jolson, Eddie Cantor, Fanny Brice, and Fred Astaire are but a few notables. Rachel Shteir, reviewing *The Boys from Syracuse* in *Nation*, called Hirsch's book "elegantly written."

With the publication of *Detours and Lost Highways: A Map of Neo-Noir*, Hirsch builds on the success of his earlier study of film noir by refuting the belief that the genre died with Orson Welles's classic film *Touch of Evil*. In his study of noir theory, Hirsch writes that many connections can be made linking classic noir to many modern films, including those in the horror and blaxploitation genres. *Film Criticism* reviewer William B. Covey acknowledged that "Hirsch is to be congratulated for being the first film critic to publish a book-length examination of neo-noir." *Detours and Lost Highways* includes a filmography, bibliography, and index.

The history of the Broadway musical stage is studded with giant names like Irving Berlin, Richard Rodgers, and Cole Porter, yet many have forgotten the name of another great, Kurt Weill. Hirsch hoped to renew interest in the composer with the publication of his *Kurt Weill on Stage: From Berlin to Broadway*. In his biography Hirsch incorporates an impressive amount of interviews and letters with Weill and others. He also includes a thorough list of Weill's productions, including his collaborators and the conditions he worked under to create his music. Although the musician died young at the age of fifty he left behind a catalogue of exceptional work, most notably the score to *The Threepenny Opera*. "This absorbing and well-researched work should be especially appealing to those interested in the history and evolution of musical theater," pointed out Carol J Binkowski in her review for *Library Journal*.

BIOGRAPHICAL AND CRITICAL SOURCES:

PERIODICALS

American Theatre, May, 2002, Benjamin Ivry, review of *Kurt Weill on Stage: From Berlin to Broadway*, p. 66.

Choice, March 1, 1999, Rachel Shteir, review of *Boys from Syracuse: The Shuberts' Theatrical Empire*, p. 31; April, 2000, W. P. Hogan, review of *Detours and Lost Highways: A Map of Neo-Noir*, p. 1476.

Film Comment, January-February, J. Hoberman, review of *Film Noir: The Dark Side of the Screen*, p. 69; fall, 2000, William B. Covey, review of *Detours and Lost Highways*, p. 83.

Film Quarterly, summer, 1983, Peter Hogue, review of *Film Noir*, p. 55; summer, 1985, James Naremore, review of *A Method to Their Madness: The History of the Actors Studio*, p. 43.

Kirkus Reviews, February 1, 2002, review of *Kurt Weill on Stage*, p. 159.

Library Journal, April 1, 1981, review of *Film Noir*, p. 811; September 1, 1984, Marshall W. Mason, review of *A Method to Their Madness*, p. 1683; March 15, 2002, Carol J. Binkowski, review of *Kurt Weill on Stage*, p. 83.

Los Angeles Magazine, December, 1991, Steve Root, review of *Acting Hollywood Style*, p. 93.

Nation, March 1, 1999, Ralph Shteir, review of *Boys from Syracuse*, p. 31.

New Republic, October 22, 1984, Robert Brustein, review of *A Method to Their Madness,* p. 39.

New York Times Book Review, November 4, 1984, Marshall W. Mason, review of *A Method to Their Madness,* p. 31; February 18, 1990, Andrew Harris, review of *Harold Prince and the American Musical Theatre,* p. 21.

Notes, March, 1991, David M. Kilroy, review of *Harold Prince and the American Musical Theatre,* p. 788.

Opera News, July, 2002, William V. Madison, review of *Kurt Weill on Stage,* p. 72.

Publishers Weekly, January 16, 1981, Sally A. Lodge, review of *Love, Sex, Death, and the Meaning of Life: Woody Allen's Comedy,* p. 76; July 8, 1983, Marshall W. Mason, review of *Film Noir,* p. 64; August 3, 1984, Marshall W. Mason, review of *A Method to Their Madness,* p. 57; February 11, 2002, review of *Kurt Weill on Stage,* p. 175.

San Francisco Chronicle, March 17, 2002, Steven Winn, review of *Kurt Weill on Stage,* p. 3.

Theatre History Studies, June, 1999, Joseph Kissane, review of *Boys from Syracuse,* p. 195.

Times Literary Supplement, June 27, 1986, p. 717.

Variety, June 7, 1989, review of *Harold Prince and the American Musical Theatre,* p. 81; March 2, 1992, Fred Lombardi, review of *Acting Hollywood Style,* p. 77; April 22, 2002, Joel Hirschhorn, review of *Kurt Weill on Stage: From Berlin to Broadway,* p. 32.

Washington Post Book World, December 5, 1999, review of *Detours and Lost Highways: A Map of Neo-Noir,* p. 8.*

*   *   *

HODGSON, Geoffrey M. 1946-

PERSONAL: Born July 28, 1946, in Watford, England; son of Peter Kenneth (a headmaster) and Joan Sonia (a headmistress; maiden name, Whiteman) Hodgson; married Vinny Logan (a research nurse), July 26, 1980; children: Sarah Logan, James Thomas. *Education:* Victoria University of Manchester, B.Sc., 1968, M.A., 1974. *Politics:* Labour. *Religion:* Agnostic.

ADDRESSES: Home—Malting House, West Wickham, Cambridge CB1 6SD, England. *Office*—Malting House, 1 Burton End, West Wickham, Cambridgeshire CB1 6SD, England.

CAREER: University of Northumbria, Newcastle upon Tyne, England, professor of economics, 1990-92; Cambridge University, Cambridge, England, visiting lecturer in economics, 1992—; Trinity College, Hartford, Connecticut, global visiting professor, 2001—; University of Hertfordshire, Hertford, England, research professor in business studies. Consultant to Lifespan NHS Trust and Union of Communication Workers.

MEMBER: European Association for Evolutionary Political Economy (general secretary, 1989—), Royal Economic Society.

AWARDS, HONORS: Dehn Prize, University of Manchester, 1974; Clarence E. Ayres Visiting Scholar award, Association for Evolutionary Economics Meeting, 1990.

WRITINGS:

Socialism and Parliamentary Democracy, Spokesman (Nottingham, England), 1977.

Labour at the Crossroads, Martin Robertson (Oxford, England), 1981.

Capitalism, Value, and Exploitation, Martin Robertson (Oxford, England), 1982.

The Democratic Economy, Penguin (Harmondsworth, England), 1984.

Economics and Institutions, University of Pennsylvania Press (Philadelphia, PA), 1988.

After Marx and Sraffa: Essays in Political Economy, Macmillan (London, England), 1991.

(Editor, with E. Screpanti) *Rethinking Economics,* Edward Elgar (Aldershot, England), 1991.

Economics and Evolution: Bringing Life Back into Economics, University of Michigan Press (Ann Arbor, MI), 1993.

(Editor) *The Economics of Institutions,* Edward Elgar (Aldershot, England), 1993.

(Editor, with W. Samuels and M. Tool) *The Elgar Companion to Institutional and Evolutionary Economics,* Edward Elgar (Aldershot, England), 1994.

(Editor) *Economics and Biology,* Edward Elgar (Aldershot, England), 1995.

(Editor) *The Foundations of Evolutionary Economics: 1890-1973,* Edward Elgar (Aldershot, England), 1998.

(Editor, with M. Itoh and N. Yokokawa) *Capitalism in Evolution: Global Contentions—East and West,* Edward Elgar (Aldershot, England), in press.

The Political Economy of Utopia, Routledge (London, England), in press.

Evolution and Institutions: Critical Essays on the Reconstruction of Economics, Edward Elgar (Aldershot, England), in press.

How Economics Forgot History: The Problem of Historical Specificity in Social Science, in press.

Contributor of about forty articles to economic and future studies journals.

WORK IN PROGRESS: The Political Economy of Utopia, for Routledge & Kegan Paul; research on evolutionary and institutional economics.

SIDELIGHTS: Geoffrey M. Hodgson told *CA:* "I am concerned with making economics a useful, realistic, and practical science, so that it can once again contribute to the alleviation of problems such as poverty, famine, unemployment, and environmental destruction."

*   *   *

HOLMES, Frederic L(awrence) 1932-2003

PERSONAL: Born February 6, 1932, in Cincinnati, OH; died of stomach cancer, March 27, 2003 in New Haven, CT; son of Frederic Everett (a clinical biochemist) and Florence (Jauch) Holmes; married Harriet Vann (a university teacher of English), December 29, 1959; children: Catherine, Susan, Rebecca. *Education:* Massachusetts Institute of Technology, B.S., 1954; Harvard University, M.A., 1958, Ph.D., 1962. *Politics:* Democrat. *Religion:* Protestant. *Hobbies and other interests:* Tennis, playing the clarinet.

CAREER: Massachusetts Institute of Technology, Cambridge, assistant professor of humanities and history of science, 1962-64; Yale University, New Haven, CT, assistant professor, 1964-70, associate professor, 1970-72, professor of history of medicine, 1972—, head of department, 1972-79; University of Western Ontario, London, Ontario, Canada, professor of history of medicine and science and head of department,

1972-79; Member of Hamden Human Relations Area Council, 1970-72. *Military service:* U.S. Air Force, 1955-57; became first lieutenant.

MEMBER: History of Science Society (vice president, 1978-80; president, 1981-83), American Association for the History of Medicine, Canadian Society for the History and Philosophy of Science (second vice president, 1977-79).

AWARDS, HONORS: Schumann Prize, History of Science Society, 1961; Pfizer Prize, History of Science Society, 1975, and William Welch Medal, American Association for the History of Medicine, 1978, both for *Claude Bernard and Animal Chemistry.*

WRITINGS:

Claude Bernard and Animal Chemistry, Harvard University Press (Cambridge, MA), 1974.

(Editor) *Dictionary of Scientific Biography,* Volumes 17-18, Scribner (New York, NY), 1981.

Lavoisier and the Chemistry of Life: An Exploration of Scientific Creativity, University of Wisconsin Press (Madison, WI), 1985.

(Editor, with William Coleman) *The Investigative Enterprise: Experimental Physiology in Nineteenth-Century Medicine,* University of California Press (Berkeley, CA), 1988.

Eighteenth-Century Chemistry As an Investigative Enterprise, University of California Press (Berkeley, CA), 1989.

Hans Krebs, two volumes, Oxford University Press (New York, NY), Volume 1: *The Formation of a Scientific Life, 1900-1933,* 1991, Volume 2: *Architect of Intermediary Metabolism, 1933-1937,* 1994.

Between Biology and Medicine: The Formation of Intermediary Metabolism, University of California Press (Berkeley, CA), 1992.

Antoine Lavoisier—The Next Crucial Year; or, The Sources of His Quantitative Method in Chemistry, Princeton University Press (Princeton, NJ), 1998.

(Editor, with Trevor H. Levere) *Instruments and Experimentation in the History of Chemistry,* MIT Press (Cambridge, MA), 2000.

Meselson, Stahl, and the Replication of DNA: A History of "The Most Beautiful Experiment in Biology," Yale University Press (New Haven, CT), 2001.

Contributor of articles and reviews to journals on the history of science and medicine.

SIDELIGHTS: Frederic L. Holmes once told *CA:* "For many years the normal patterns of education have continued to divide students sharply into scientists and humanists. Recently the growing sense that most public issues have at least some scientific component has renewed my hope that the history of science may still sometime play a mediating role.

"My first two teaching years gave me limited scope to develop my interest in the history of science, but by a fortunate chance I was asked to spend a year at Yale University. I stayed for eight years. There I had the opportunity to specialize in the history of the biological sciences and to benefit from a splendid library for the history of medicine.

"I left Yale in 1972 for the University of Western Ontario. I found it a rewarding experience to live in that very comfortable, attractive region of Canada, and came to recognize and appreciate the real differences between the outlook of Canadians and Americans, to feel a sense of rapport with the Canadian way of life, and at the same time to view our country from the perspective of those who live just beyond its borders.

"I had not considered myself to be a historian of medicine, since I am not medically trained, and my historical research has been principally in such areas as the history of biochemistry and physiology. The dean of medicine at Yale assured me, however, that at Yale they consider this to be a part of medicine."

Holmes's 1985 work, *Lavoisier and the Chemistry of Life: An Exploration of Scientific Creativity* is a biography of the eighteenth-century French chemist and physicist often credited as the founder of modern chemistry. Antoine Lavoisier won recognition at an early age with his introduction of quantitative methods in examining chemical reactions. The son of a wealthy Parisian lawyer, Lavoisier pursued a dual existence as scientist and leading public figure. He was actively involved in the French Revolution and is credited for developing many of its reforms, including the establishment of the metric system of weights and measures. He died tragically when he was executed at the guillotine during the Reign of Terror. *Science* magazine con-

tributor Trevor H. Levere called Holmes's book "an important and penetrating study [that] . . . will repay careful reading by scientists, historians of science, and philosophers."

In *Antoine Lavoisier—The Next Crucial Year; or, The Sources of His Quantitative Method in Chemistry,* Holmes provides an examination of the research methodology that led Lavoisier to the findings on respiration which helped him formulate his theories on the nature of perspiration. In his review of the book for the *Quarterly Review of Biology,* Arthur Donovan noted that "Holmes's contribution to the history of chemistry and biology are immense; his conclusions about how science advances deserve careful consideration."

In his two-volume biography on German physiologist *Hans Krebs,* Holmes offers the first comprehensive study of one of the twentieth century's leading scientists. Krebs, who was forced to immigrate to England in 1933, nonetheless continued to work at Cambridge and Oxford universities. In 1953 he won the Nobel Prize for Medicine for his study on the nature of metabolic processes, particularly the manner in which living organisms obtain energy from food. Krebs was knighted in 1958. In addition to discussing his scientific breakthroughs, Holmes also examines the man behind the work. According to John W. Servos of *Science,* "this magnificent biography demonstrates, as few books do, the intimate relations between personality and science."

Histories of science tend to focus on the hypothetical, technological, and human side of science, particularly those concerning the careers of scientists and their institutions. In his coediting of *Instruments and Experimentation in the History of Chemistry,* Holmes diverges from this trend by taking as his focus the development of instruments used in experiments. In these essays, edited by Holmes and Trevor Levere, the emphasis is on the tools of the trade, tools that in turn guided theories. Arthur Greenberg of *American Scientist* called the book "a must for all institutional libraries and for anyone even mildly interested in the history of chemistry."

BIOGRAPHICAL AND CRITICAL SOURCES:

PERIODICALS

American Historical Review, April, 1986, Colin A. Russell, review of *Lavoisier and the Chemistry of*

Life: An Exploration of Scientific Creativity, p. 384; December, 1995, John E. Lesch, review of *Hans Krebs,* p. 1557; June, 1999, Mary Jo Nye, review of *Antoine Lavoisier—The Next Crucial Year; or, The Sources of His Quantitative Method in Chemistry,* p. 1004.

American Scientist, January-February, 1990, W. Bruce Fye, review of *The Investigative Enterprise: Experimental Physiology in Nineteenth-Century Medicine,* p. 75; July, 2001, Arthur Greenberg, review of *Instruments and Experimentation in the History of Chemistry,* p. 1372.

Animal Biology Teacher, November-December, 1992, Maura C. Flannery, review of *Claude Bernard and Animal Chemistry,* p. 497.

British Journal for the History of Science, June, 1990, John V. Pickstone, review of *The Investigative Enterprise,* p. 207; March, 1991, Jan Golinski, review of *Eighteenth-Century Chemistry As an Investigative Enterprise,* p. 102.

Cell, November 2, 2001, Horace Freeland Judson, review of *Meselson, Stahl, and the Replication of DNA: A History of "The Most Beautiful Experiment in Biology,"* p. 264.

Choice, October, 1985, review of *Lavoisier and the Chemistry of Life,* p. 318; September, 1992, A. D. Gounaris, review of *Hans Krebs,* Volume 1, p. 144; January, 1994, A. D. Gounaris, review of *Hans Krebs,* Volume 2, p. 810; July, 1998, H. Goldwhite, review of *Antoine Lavoisier—The Next Crucial Year; or, The Sources of His Quantitative Method in Chemisty,* p. 1872; March, 2001, E. R. Webster, review of *Instruments and Experimentation in the History of Chemistry,* p. 1300.

Endeavor, June, 1998, review of *Antoine Lavoisier,* p. 85.

Isis, June, 1989, Steve Sturdy, review of *The Investigative Enterprise,* p. 289; June, 1991, John G. McEvoy, review of *Eighteenth-Century Chemistry As an Investigative Enterprise,* p. 1382; December, 1995, review of *Hans Krebs,* p. 668; March, 1999, Marco Beretta, review of *Antoine Lavoisier,* p. 123.

Journal of Interdisciplinary History, autumn, 1987, John W. Servos, review of *Lavoisier and the Chemistry of Life,* p. 346.

Journal of the American Medical Association, December 16, 1992, Nathaniel Berlin, review of *Hans Krebs,* Volume 1, p. 3379.

Library Journal, March 1, 1986, review of *Lavoisier and the Chemistry of Life,* p. 45.

Nature, February 23, 1989, W. F. Bynum, review of *The Investigative Enterprise,* p. 697; December 2, 1993, review of *Hans Krebs,* Volume 1, p. 417.

New Technology Books, November, 1986, review of *Lavoisier and the Chemistry of Life,* p. 626.

Quarterly Review of Biology, March, 1994, review of *Hans Krebs,* p. 77; September, 1999, review of *Antoine Lavoisier,* p. 331.

Science, August 23, 1985, Trevor H. Levere, review of *Lavoisier and the Chemistry of Life,* p. 751; August 7, 1992, John W. Servos, review of *Hans Krebs,* Volume 1, p. 819; December 21, 2001, Nathaniel Comfort, review of *Meselson, Stahl, and the Replication of DNA,* p. 2483.

Science Books and Films, December, 1993, review of *Hans Krebs,* p. 267.

SciTech Book News, August, 1985, review of *Lavoisier and the Chemistry of Life,* p. 13.

Technology and Culture, October, 1991, Arthur Donovan, review of *Eighteenth-Century Chemistry As an Investigative Enterprise,* p. 1106.

Times Higher Education Supplement, June 3, 1994, W. F. Bynum, review of *Hans Krebs,* p. 25.

Times Literary Supplement, October 18, 1985, review of *Lavoisier and the Chemistry of Life,* p. 1166; January 11, 2002, Thomas L. Hankins, review of *Instruments and Experimentation in the History of Chemistry,* p. 7.

Trends in Biochemical Sciences, June, 1994, review of *Hans Krebs,* p. 264.*

*   *   *

HOSKING, Geoffrey A(lan) 1942-

PERSONAL: Born April 28, 1942, in Troon, Ayrshire, Scotland; son of Stuart William Steggall (in banking) and Jean Ross (a teacher; maiden name, Smillie) Hosking; married Anne Lloyd Hirst (a teacher), December 19, 1970; children: Katya, Janet. *Education:* King's College, Cambridge, M.A., Ph.D.; attended St. Anthony's College, Oxford. *Hobbies and other interests:* Squash, chess, walking.

ADDRESSES: Home—18 Camden Mews, London NW1 9DA, England. *Office*—School of Slavonic and East European Studies, University of London, Senate House, Malet St., London WC1E 7HU, England. *Agent*—Murray Pollinger, 4 Garrick St., London WC2E 9BH, England.

CAREER: University of Essex, Colchester, England, assistant lecturer, 1966-68, lecturer in government, 1968-71, lecturer, 1972-76, senior lecturer in history,

1976-78, reader in Russian history, 1978-84; University of London, School of Slavonic and East European Studies, London, England, professor of Russian history, 1984—; currently Leverhulme Professor of History. Visiting lecturer in political science, University of Wisconsin, Madison, 1971-72; research fellow, Columbia University Russian Institute, 1976; visiting professor, University of Cologne Slaviches Institute, 1980-81. Council member, Writers and Scholars Educational Trust, 1985—; member, East-West advisory committee, 1987-89, and Council of Management, Keston College, 1989-89; BBC Reith lecturer, 1988; governor, Camden School for Girls, 1989—; trustee, J. S. Mill Institute, 1992—; jury member, Booker Prize for Russian fiction, 1993—.

MEMBER: British Universities Association of Slavists, American Association for the Advancement of Slavic Studies.

AWARDS, HONORS: Los Angeles Times Historical Book Prize, 1986, for *A History of the Soviet Union.*

WRITINGS:

The Russian Constitutional Experiment: Government and Duma, 1907-14, Cambridge University Press (Cambridge, England), 1973.

Beyond Socialist Realism: Soviet Fiction since "Ivan Denisovich," Holmes & Meier (New York, NY), 1980.

The First Socialist Society: A History of the Soviet Union from Within, Harvard University Press (Cambridge, MA), 1985, published as *History of the Soviet Union,* Collins (London, England), 1985.

The Awakening of the Soviet Union, Harvard University Press (Cambridge, MA), 1990.

Church, Nation, and State in Russia and Ukraine, St. Martin's Press (New York, NY), 1991.

(With Jonathan Aves and Peter J. S. Duncan) *The Road to Post-Communism: Independent Political Movements in the Soviet Union, 1985-1991,* St. Martin's Press (New York, NY), 1992.

Empire and Nation in Russian History, Baylor University Press (Waco, TX), 1993.

Russia: People and Empire, 1552-1917, Harvard University Press (Cambridge, MA), 1997.

Russia and the Russians: A History, Harvard University Press (Cambridge, MA), 2001.

EDITOR

(With George F. Cushing) *Perspectives on Literature and Society in Eastern and Western Europe,* St. Martin's Press (New York, NY), 1989.

(With Julian Graffy) *Culture and the Media in the USSR Today,* St. Martin's Press (New York, NY), 1989.

(With Robert Service) *Russian Nationalism, Past and Present,* St. Martin's Press (New York, NY), 1997.

(Coeditor) *Myths and Nationhood,* University of London (London, England), 1997.

(With Robert Service) *Reinterpreting Russia,* Oxford University Press (New York, NY), 1999.

Contributor to *Towards a New Community: Culture and Politics in Post-Totalitarian Europe,* edited by Peter J. S. Duncan and Martyn Rady, University of London, 1993.

SIDELIGHTS: Geoffrey A. Hosking is a wide-ranging scholar of Russian history and literature. Reviewing Hosking's career in *History Today,* Daniel Snowman observed: "The country and its people. These are what Hosking has particularly tried to know. His writings are sprinkled with references to a town here, a village there, a quotation from the letters column or local newspaper, a joke the workers or peasants would tell each other, a telling anecdote from his own experience. But Hosking is not a collage artist. On the contrary, his finely tuned mind loves nothing more than to alight upon an organising principle, perhaps a Big Hypothesis, that helps explain a mass of otherwise inchoate facts."

In *Beyond Socialist Realism,* Hosking seeks to familiarize Western readers with Soviet literature written in, and in the period following, the relaxed artistic environment of the Khrushchev years. *Beyond Socialist Realism* contains a "well-written and sensitive analysis" of the significant works of nine authors deemed by Hosking as "'representative of the renewed realism' in Soviet letters," according to *Times Literary Supplement* contributor John B. Dunlop. Hosking considers the works of Vasily Belov, Valentin Rasputin, Vladimir Tendryakov, Aleksandr Solzhenitsyn, Vladimir Maximov, Vladimir Voinovich, Georgy Vladimov, Vasily Shukshin, and Yuri Trifonov. "They have created, within the official doctrine of 'socialist realism,' a pluralistic critical literature that ranges from the 'village prose' of Belov and Rasputin to the dark urban pessimism of Trifonov," observed Stephen F. Cohen in the *New York Times Book Review*. Dunlop stated: "Hosking believes that these works, with their anti-Promethean stance, their questioning of the benefits of headlong modernization, and their existential and religious probings, may carry some lessons for us in the West."

In Dunlop's critical judgment, *Beyond Socialist Realism* has one significant weakness. "Hosking's radical refusal to acknowledge any substantive difference between 'official' and *samizdat* [underground dissident] literature leads him into the methodological error of treating such works interchangeably." Even so, the reviewer concluded, "Despite my disagreement with certain of Hosking's ideas, I would underline that *Beyond Socialist Realism* is an important study of a much-neglected field (it also contains a first-rate, detailed bibliography for which specialists will be grateful)."

In 1985 Hosking published *The First Socialist Society.* Noted Soviet affairs scholar Adam B. Ulam, writing in the *Times Literary Supplement,* praised the book's scope: "Professor Hosking's skill as a writer," Ulam commented, permitted him, "in addition to the narrative of events. . . , to squeeze in so much about the economy and cultural scene." Bohdan Nahaylo of the *Spectator* noted with approval Hosking's treatment of the Soviet Union as an empire: "Here, at last, is a book that recognises certain basic truths about the Soviet Union which other authors have tended to overlook. For one thing, Hosking treats the Soviet Union as a multinational state, [and] does not blur the distinction between the USSR's majority Russian nation and its 135 million or so non-Russians." Martin McCauley, writing in *British Book News,* observed with approval Hosking's quotations from Russian novels "as historical evidence" that give "greater color to his account." He also commended the book's approach to its subject: not from the perspective of the Soviet leadership in the Kremlin, but from that of ordinary people. In fact, the book's approach to Soviet history was sufficiently removed from "the party line" that *Choice* contributor A. K. Davis—who presented with his review an account of the USSR's history that harmonized with the official Soviet stance—expressed concern that "Hosking's tone at times may seem anti-Soviet." Most reviewers, however, described the author's standpoint as decidedly neutral.

What few critics—or few other people, for that matter—could have guessed in 1985 was that the Soviet system had little more than a half-decade of life left in it. Ulam, for instance, ended his review with the words, "I like to believe with Geoffrey Hosking that there does exist among the Soviet people a longing for freedom, a longing which one day, but, alas, not in the near future, will come to the surface." By 1990, when Hosking published *The Awakening of the Soviet Union,* the dissolution of the Communist regime was underway. The book's thesis, one that Hosking had presented in different ways for some time, is that the Russian people have long possessed the institutions for creating the civil society necessary to establish democracy. Chief among these grass-roots institutions was the communal peasant organization called the *mir,* and it was precisely this democratic tendency which ironically spawned the workers' soviets which the Bolsheviks co-opted during the 1917 revolution.

In expressing this viewpoint, Hosking often found himself at odds with the conventional wisdom that the Russian people simply lacked the capacity to govern themselves democratically, but later events seemed to corroborate his earlier thesis. Citing Hosking's 1988 Reith Lectures—which form the basis of the book— James Sherr wrote in the *Times Literary Supplement* that "the lectures will not easily date. Professor Hosking has managed to capture the spirit of the times, but unlike many today, he is not captured by it." Ulam, this time writing in the *New York Times Book Review,* commented that *The Awakening of the Soviet Union* served as an antidote to claims by members of the media and others that the end of Communism resulted primarily from the foresight of Soviet president Mikhail Gorbachev and his system of *glasnost* or "openness." Other reviewers also noted the author's evenhandedness: Leo Gruliow in *Antioch Review,* for instance, observed that Hosking "avoids the journalist's pitfall of trying to sum up a situation still fluid." In the *New York Review of Books,* Peter Reddaway wrote that Hosking's discussion "of how suppressed history was restored to people's consciousness is also highly original." Linda J. Cook, in the *Russian Review,* called the book "a remarkably informative, rich, clearly written account of the tumultuous events of 1987-1990."

Perhaps Hosking's most ambitious work is *Russia and the Russians: A History,* a comprehensive survey of Russian/Soviet history from the beginnings of the Russian state in A.D. 650 to the end of the twentieth century. Reviewing the book for *History,* Harold J. Goldberg found it an "impressive work" that aims to explore "the ambivalence of the West toward Russia . . . [and] the ambivalence that Russians often express toward themselves and their own history." In Goldberg's opinion, Hosking is "remarkably successful in achieving his goals" for the book. "This is a useful supplement to Hosking's more analytical 'Russia: People and Empire,' which appeared in 1997," noted Steven Merritt Miner in the *New York Times Book Review.* "The new book is the most up-to-date, comprehensive one-volume history of Russia in print, drawing as it does on a wealth of scholarship to provide readers with a superb, well-organized chronological narrative. The footnotes alone give the reader an excellent guide to recent scholarship." Some critics felt that *Russia and the Russians* filled a need for a readable general history of Russia. Remarking that a number of books on Russia and the Soviet Union "tackle a wide variety of narrow studies," a *Contemporary Review* correspondent commented that Hosking "is to be congratulated" for his thorough overview. Gilbert Taylor in *Booklist* suggested that the work "is especially welcome" because Hosking "links the Communist era, now that it is over, to the enduring themes of the Russian experience." Zachary T. Irwin in *Library Journal* also commended Hosking for "revealing Russia's enduring continuities," adding that *Russia and the Russians* "compares favorably with some of the best Russian histories of recent decades."

In *History Today,* Daniel Snowman concluded that Hosking has "used his intellectual versatility to help fuel his guiding light, the flame of Russian history." Snowman further commented: "Hosking was neither cold warrior nor fellow traveller. But he wasn't a dry-as-dust academic either. He felt, and feels, that you can only really understand the present if you know what produced it."

Hosking once told *CA:* "My interest in Russia goes back to my school days. We didn't study Russia or Communism at all at school; perhaps that's why I found it fascinating. I had the feeling then (and still have) that the great political, artistic, philosophical and religious issues of our day were somehow being decided in Russia. No one, of course, regards the Soviet Union any longer as a socialist paradise; few people think the country has anything particularly important to tell the world. But Russia's uniquely long experience in trying to fulfill the ideals of socialism makes it a country vitally important to study (whether or not one regards socialism as desirable). This is the

viewpoint from which I . . . examined the contemporary novel in *Beyond Socialist Realism: Soviet Fiction since "Ivan Denisovich."* The novelists (official and *samizdat*) are the most truthful and the profoundest historians of their own nation under Communist rule. They are both witnesses to and interpreters of that social reality. I have followed this up with my own history of the USSR, largely based on more orthodox sources, but drawing on diary and memoir material, and stressing internal social and cultural developments more than is usual in such general histories."

BIOGRAPHICAL AND CRITICAL SOURCES:

PERIODICALS

Antioch Review, spring, 1991, pp. 288-95.
Booklist, April 15, 2001, Gilbert Taylor, review of *Russia and the Russians: A History,* p. 1530.
British Book News, June, 1985, Martin McCauley, review of *The First Socialist Society: A History of the Soviet Union from Within,* pp. 376-77.
Choice, March, 1986, A. K. Davis, review of *The First Socialist Society,* p. 1124; February, 1993, p. 1023.
Contemporary Review, September, 2001, review of *Russia and the Russians,* p. 190.
English Historical Review, April, 2000, John Kelp, review of *Reinterpreting Russia,* p. 495.
Europe-Asia Studies, July, 2000, Wendy Slater, review of *Reinterpreting Russia,* p. 958.
History, fall, 2001, Harold J. Goldberg, review of *Russia and the Russians,* pp. 3-4.
History Today, July, 2000, Daniel Snowman, "Geoffrey Hosking," p. 28.
International Affairs, January, 2002, Michael Pursglove, review of *Russia and the Russians,* pp. 193-194.
International History Review, June, 2002, David Goldfrank, review of *Russia and the Russians,* pp. 393-394.
Library Journal, April 1, 2001, Zachary T. Irwin, review of *Russia and the Russians,* p. 114.
Los Angeles Times Book Review, January 12, 1986.
New Leader, March, 2001, Ronald Grigor Suny, review of *Russia and the Russians,* p. 30.
New Statesman, August 20, 2001, John Kampfner, "Gogolian Farce," p. 42.
New York Review of Books, November 7, 1991, Peter Reddaway, review of *The Awakening of the Soviet Union,* pp. 53-59.

New York Times Book Review, May 4, 1980; April 8, 1990, p. 14; September 29, 1991, p. 34; May 25, 1997, p. 13; July 8, 2001, Steven Merritt Miner, "Where the West Begins," p. 14.

Publishers Weekly, March 12, 2001, review of *Russia and the Russians,* p. 74.

Russian Review, January, 1993, pp. 139-40; January, 1995, pp. 155-56.

Slavic Review, winter, 2000, Elise Kimerling Wirtschafter, review of *Reinterpreting Russia,* p. 902.

Spectator, March 8, 1986, Bohdan Nahaylo, review of *The First Socialist Society,* pp. 31-32.

Times Literary Supplement, October 3, 1980, John B. Dunlop, review of *Beyond Socialist Realism: Soviet Fiction since "Ivan Denisovich";* September 13, 1985, Adam B. Ulam, review of *The First Socialist Society,* p. 1010; March 16, 1990, James Sherr, review of *The Awakening of the Soviet Union,* p. 273; August 24, 2001, Richard Pipes, review of *Russia and the Russians,* p. 7.

Virginia Quarterly Review, spring, 1986, pp. 52-53.

Washington Post Book World, July 8, 2001, Robert G. Kaiser, "Blood Red," p. 1.*

*   *   *

Samuel P. Huntington

HUNTINGTON, Samuel P(hillips) 1927-

PERSONAL: Born April 18, 1927, in New York, NY; son of Richard Thomas (a publisher of hotel trade journals) and Dorothy Sanborn (a writer; maiden name, Phillips) Huntington; married Nancy Alice Arkelyan, September 8, 1957; children: Timothy Mayo, Nicholas Phillips. *Education:* Yale University, B.A., 1946; University of Chicago, M.A., 1948; Harvard University, Ph.D., 1951.

ADDRESSES: Home—52 Brimmer St., Boston, MA 02108. *Office*—Harvard University, 1737 Cambridge St., Cambridge, MA 02138-3016.

CAREER: Harvard University, Cambridge, MA, instructor, 1950-53, assistant professor, 1953-58, professor of government, 1962-67, Frank G. Thomson Professor of Government, 1967-81, Clarence Dillon Professor of International Affairs, 1981-82, Eaton Professor of Science of Government, 1982, Albert J. Weatherhead III University Professor, 1995, chair of department, 1967-69, 1970-71, and 1982-95, Center for International Affairs, research associate, 1958-63, faculty member, 1964, executive committee, 1966, associate director, 1973-78, acting director, 1975-76, director, 1978-89, Academy of International and Area Studies, chair, 1996; Columbia University, New York, NY, research associate, 1958-63, Institute of War and Peace Studies, associate assistant director, 1958-59, associate director, 1959-62, associate professor of government, 1959-62, Ford Research Professor, 1960-61, 1962. Brookings Institution, research associate in defense policy, 1952-53; Social Science Research Council, faculty research fellow, 1954-57; All Souls College, Oxford University, visiting fellow, 1973; Woodrow Wilson International Center for Scholars, fellow, 1983-84; John M. Olin Institute for Strategic Studies, director, 1989-2000; International Institute for Strategic Studies, senior research associate, 1990; visiting lecturer at University of Michigan, University of California, Dartmouth College, Ohio State University, Carnegie Institute of Technology (now Carnegie-Mellon University), Army War College, Air War College, National War College, and Industrial College of the Armed Forces. Consultant to Institute for Defense

Analysis, 1961, Hudson Institute, 1962, U.S. Air Force Academy, 1962-64, and Office of the Secretary of Defense, 1963-68. Service to the U.S. government includes: Council on Vietnamese Studies in Southeast Asia, chair of Development Advisory Group, 1966-69; Presidential Task Force on International Development, member, 1969-70; International Development Foundation, trustee, 1969-76; Commission on U.S.-Latin American Relations, member, 1974-75; National Security Council, coordinator of security planning, 1977-78; Commission on Integrated Long Term Strategy, member, 1986-88; Commission on Protecting and Reducing Government Secrecy, 1995-97. *Military service:* U.S. Army, 1946-47.

MEMBER: International Political Science Association (council, 1973-75), International Institute of Strategic Studies, American Political Science Association (member of council, 1969-71; vice president, 1984-85; president-elect, 1985-86; president, 1986-87), Council on Foreign Relations.

AWARDS, HONORS: Silver Pen Award, Journal Fund, 1960; fellow, Center for Advanced Study in Behavioral Sciences, Stanford University, 1969-70; Guggenheim fellow, 1972-73; Grawemayer World Order award, 1992; fellow, American Academy of Arts and Sciences.

WRITINGS:

The Soldier and the State: The Theory and Politics of Civil-Military Relations, Harvard University Press (Cambridge, MA), 1957.

The Common Defense: Strategic Programs in National Politics, Columbia University Press (New York, NY), 1961.

Instability at the Non-Strategic Level of Conflict, Institute for Defense Analyses, Special Studies Group (Washington, DC), 1961.

(With Zbigniew Brzezinski) *Political Power: USA/USSR,* Viking (New York, NY), 1964.

Political Order in Changing Societies, Yale University Press (New Haven, CT), 1968.

(With Michel Crozier and Joji Watanuki) *The Crisis of Democracy: Report on the Governability of Democracies to the Trilateral Commission,* New York University Press (New York, NY), 1975.

(With others) *Can Cultures Communicate?: An AEI Round Table Held on September 23, 1976, and Sponsored by the American Enterprise Institute for Public Policy Research, Washington, D.C.,* The Institute (Washington, DC), 1975.

(With J. M. Nelson) *No Easy Choice: Political Participation in Developing Countries,* Harvard University Press (Cambridge, MA), 1976.

(With Andrew J. Goodpaster) *Civil-Military Relations,* American Enterprise Institute for Public Policy Research (Washington, DC), 1977.

American Politics: The Promise of Disharmony, Belknap Press (Cambridge, MA), 1981.

The Dilemma of American Ideals and Institutions in Foreign Policy, American Enterprise Institute for Public Policy Research (Washington, DC), 1981.

(With Albert Carnesale and Paul Doty) *Living with Nuclear Weapons,* Harvard University Press (Cambridge, MA), 1983.

American Military Strategy, Institute of International Studies, University of California (Berkeley, CA), 1986.

The Third Wave: Democratization in the Late Twentieth Century, University of Oklahoma Press (Norman, OK), 1991.

The Clash of Civilizations and the Remaking of World Order, Simon & Schuster (New York, NY), 1996.

EDITOR

Changing Patterns of Military Politics, Free Press of Glencoe (New York, NY), 1962.

(With Clement H. Moore) *Authoritarian Politics in Modern Society: The Dynamics of Established One-Party Systems,* Basic Books (New York, NY), 1970.

The Strategic Imperative: New Policies for American Security, Ballinger (Cambridge, MA), 1982.

(With Robert J. Art and Vincent Davis) *Reorganizing America's Defense: Leadership in War and Peace,* Pergamon-Brassey's (Washington, DC), 1985.

(With Joseph S. Nye, Jr.) *Global Dilemmas,* University Presses of America (Lanham, MD), 1985.

(With Myron Weiner) *Understanding Political Development: An Analytic Study,* Little, Brown (Boston, MA), 1987.

(With Lawrence E. Harrison) *Culture Matters: How Values Shape Human Progress,* Basic Books (New York, NY), 2000.

(With Peter L. Berger) *Many Globalizations: Cultural Diversity in the Contemporary World,* Oxford University Press (New York, NY), 2002.

Contributor of more than fifty articles to scholarly journals and periodicals including *Foreign Policy,*

Daedalus, World Politics, Foreign Affairs, Bangkok Post, and *American Political Science Review.* Coeditor, *Foreign Policy,* 1970-77.

ADAPTATIONS: The Clash of Civilizations and the Remaking of World Order was adapted for audiocassette, read by Paul Boehmer, Books on Tape, 2002.

SIDELIGHTS: Samuel P. Huntington is a political scientist who has held distinguished university positions as well as a number of noteworthy government posts. A scholar in global politics, Huntington has chaired Harvard's government department, coordinated activities of the United State's National Security Council, and, among other roles, directed the John M. Olin Institute for Strategic Studies, a noted think-tank. "Huntington has made many important contributions to the fields of international relations and comparative politics. He has called to our attention the distinction between quantitative and qualitative arms races, advanced our understanding of modernization and institutionalization processes in the Third World, and contributed to our knowledge of 'transnationalism in world politics' and of the effect of democratization," summarized Richard Rosecrance in *American Political Science Review,* adding: "One important measure of creativity in the field is the number of new and important variables a scholar introduces. Huntington's . . . work leaps this hurdle with room to spare." Among his most novel ideas are those elaborated on in his book *The Clash of Civilizations and the Remaking of World Order,* and related to the central topic discussed in *Culture Matters: How Values Shape Human Progress,* a collection of essays he coedited.

Among the other publications Huntington has edited or authored is *The Third Wave: Democratization in the Late Twentieth Century,* released in 1991. *The Third Wave* is a post-hoc analysis of more than thirty countries who became democratic political entities during the 1970s and 1980s, the third wave—the first two waves being from 1828 to 1926 and from 1943 to 1962. Not intending to provide a predictive theory, Huntington identifies five changes which set the stage for the change to occur, the processes bringing the nondemocratic bodies into democratic systems, and also factors related to the stabilization and consolidation of democracies. In *World Politics,* Ian Shapiro wrote: "Huntington's *The Third Wave* is . . . stunningly well informed. Essential reading for anyone who is interested in the future of democracy." "Huntington is a scholar of the first rank, and this study is, like so many of his others, a significant contribution," concluded Scott London in online *Scott London* review.

Huntington became more predictive in his political analysis for a 1993 *Foreign Affairs* article, "The Clash of Civilizations." The article "was a brilliantly provocative piece," noted Bill Powell in *Newsweek,* and it generated great scholarly discussion. Riding this momentum, Huntington expanded his thoughts, addressing more implications of his thesis, and wrote *The Clash of Civilizations and the Remaking of World Order,* published in 1996. Essentially, Huntington's theory, which breaks from more traditional international relations theories, is that the world is moving away from nation-centered unity and conflicts into a set of about eight civilizations grouped primarily along cultural lines. Currently the West—North America, Europe, Western Europe—is dominant, but according to Huntington their relative power is declining, with the Chinese/Sinic/Confucian and the Islamic civilizations contenders to take the lead. The remaining civilizations classified by Huntington are Africa, Latin America, a Japanese/Buddhist civilization centered on Japan, a Hindu civilization centered on India, and an orthodox civilization centered on Russia. When perceiving emerging world politics through this lens, asserts Huntington, one of the issues that becomes important for U.S. foreign policy is to "promote the unity of the West," he told David Gergen in a *NewsHour* interview. "Which means not just in military and economic terms but . . . also in moral terms and in commitment to western values." According to Huntington, political actions in this post-Cold War, culturally-competitive world environment should be mindful that Western values are not necessary held by, nor are they desired by, other civilizations.

Although Huntington's ideas in *The Clash of Civilizations,* formulated from both political and historical analysis, are most often recognized as well-informed, intelligent, and significant, they are also cited as flawed, typically criticized for being too narrowly focused on his civilizations thesis. As such, some reviewers have stated that he has not given enough weight to certain factors, such as influence of nationalism, and not fully described other issues, such as the specific motivators for individual states. In the "bold and brilliant book," described *National Review* contributor Robin Harris, "the author's single-minded rigor in employing the widest variety of data to make his case and his forceful sweep of assertion carry the reader along almost too easily. . . . For all its virtuosity, Huntington's analysis does not . . . ultimately pass muster." While Edward W. Said's *New Statesman* analysis of the book described Huntington's central thesis as "a gimmick," Christian Stracke stated in *Journal of International Affairs:* "Huntington offers a coherent case, backed by a wealth of well-researched empirical information, for overturning the dominant, primarily American notion that the end of the Cold War means the final victory for the West's capitalism and universalist ideals." Of the arguments presented in *The Clash of Civilizations,* Robert Jervis remarked in *Political Science Quarterly:* "His critics are not likely to be persuaded, but I cannot imagine a reader coming away without rethinking many accepted ideas."

Huntington's belief in the determining effect that culture has in shaping society is also found in *Culture Matters.* Huntington worked with Lawrence E. Harrison to edit the 2000 publication, which contains twenty-two essays originating from a 1999 symposium sponsored by the Harvard Academy for International and Area Studies, an organization Huntington once chaired. As the title suggests, the volume centers its discussions around the belief that different cultural attributes have varying effects on the economic development of a region. Within the volume's seven sections are essays that discuss culture and economic development in general, as well as more specific writing that addresses culture and gender, American minorities, anthropological debates, the recent Asian economic crisis, and change within a culture. Critics such as Thomas R. DeGregori, reviewing for *Journal of Economic Issues,* and *Quadrant* contributor Eric Jones felt the contents of *Culture Matters* did not quantify exactly how certain cultural variables affect economics. DeGregori generally agreed with the books statements, but was left wanting for "an operational understanding of how culture mattered." Jones, who found many faults with the collection, maintained "culture matters less and in different ways from many of the claims advanced in this volume." In contrast, Peter L. Berger's *Society* review praised *Culture Matters* as "an important book" filled with papers "of excellent quality." Though Berger believed the volume omitted important discussion of the role of religion and whether all or just an influential subset of a population need to hold a certain value for it to be economically significant,

the critic concluded: "Harrison and Huntington have brought out a book that should be required reading for anyone concerned with economic and political developments in the contemporary world. And the reading will not only be instructive but pleasurable."

In a recent article in the *Atlantic,* Robert D. Kaplan surveyed Huntington's career and writings. "*The Soldier and the State,*" Kaplan observed, "initiated what has become a familiar pattern in Huntington's long career: his work has not immediately earned brilliant reviews and academic awards but, rather, has garnered mixed reviews and harsh denunciations that ultimately yield to widespread if grudging acceptance. Even Huntington's enemies unwittingly define and worry about the world in ways and in phrases that originated with Huntington." Noting that Huntington's opinions have "proved to be as prescient as they have been controversial," Kaplan concluded his extended critique of the man and his work with this assertion: "If American political science leaves any lasting intellectual monument, the work of Samuel Huntington will be one of its pillars. A passage in the conclusion of *American Politics* has always seemed to me to capture the essence of Huntington's enduring judgment and political sensibility: 'Critics say that America is a lie because its reality falls so far short of its ideals. They are wrong. America is not a lie; it is a disappointment. But it can be a disappointment only because it is also a hope.'"

BIOGRAPHICAL AND CRITICAL SOURCES:

PERIODICALS

American Historical Review, October, 1982, review of *American Politics: The Promise of Disharmony,* p. 1148.

American Journal of Sociology, May, 1983, review of *American Politics,* p. 1296; September, 1997, Edward A. Tiryakian, review of *The Clash of Civilizations and the Remaking of World Order,* p. 475.

American Political Science Review, September, 1988, Ronald H. Chilcote, review of *Understanding Political Development: An Analytic Study,* p. 1025; December, 1992, Herbert Kitschelt, review of *The Third Wave: Democratization in the Late Twentieth Century,* p. 1028; December, 1998, Richard

Rosecrance, review of *The Clash of Civilizations and the Remaking of World Order,* p. 978.

American Spectator, December, 1981, review of *American Politics,* p. 14; July, 1982, review of *American Politics,* p. 12.

Annals of the American Academy of Political and Social Science, November, 1983, George H. Quester, review of *The Strategic Imperative: New Policies for American Security,* p. 196; March, 1998, William E. Naff, review of *The Clash of Civilizations and the Remaking of World Order,* p. 198.

Arab Studies Quarterly, winter, 1998, Zerougui Adbel Kader, review of *The Clash of Civilizations and the Remaking of World Order,* p. 89.

Atlantic, December, 2001, Robert D. Kaplan, "Looking the World in the Eye," extended review of Huntington's career and writings.

Booklist, October 1, 1996, Gilbert Taylor, review of *The Clash of Civilizations and the Remaking of World Order,* p. 318.

Book World, December 1, 1996, review of *The Clash of Civilizations and the Remaking of World Order,* p. 4; December 8, 1996, review of *The Clash of Civilizations and the Remaking of World Order,* p. 7.

Business Week, November 25, 1996, review of *The Clash of Civilizations and the Remaking of World Order,* p. 16.

Choice, January, 1982, review of *American Politics,* p. 685; June, 1988, review of *The Common Defense: Strategic Programs in National Politics,* p. 1519; March, 1992, R. J. Terchek, review of *The Third Wave,* p. 1154.

Christian Century, March 24, 1982, review of *American Politics,* p. 347.

Commentary, March, 1997, Richard Pipes, review of *The Clash of Civilizations and the Remaking of World Order,* p. 62.

Commonweal, March 12, 1982, William B. Hixson, Jr., review of *American Politics,* pp. 150-51.

Contemporary Sociology, November, 1997, review of *The Clash of Civilizations and the Remaking of World Order,* p. 691.

Daedalus, winter, 1981, review of *American Politics,* p. 40.

Far Eastern Economic Review, February 6, 1997, review of *The Clash of Civilizations and the Remaking of World Order,* p. 39; May 1, 1997, review of *The Clash of Civilizations and the Remaking of World Order,* p. 36.

Foreign Affairs, winter, 1982, review of *The Strategic Imperative,* p. 462; February, 1992, review of *The Third Wave,* p. 190; September, 1997, reviews of *Political Order in Changing Societies* and *The Soldier and the State: The Theory and Politics of Civil-Military Relations,* pp. 215, 220; January-February, 2001, Robert J. Samuelson, review of *Culture Matters: How Values Shape Human Progress,* p. 205.

Foreign Policy, fall, 1994, Richard E. Rubenstein and Jarle Crocker, "Challenging Huntington," p. 113; spring, 1997, Stephen M. Walt, review of *The Clash of Civilizations and the Remaking of World Order,* p. 176.

Guardian (London, England), November 23, 1996, "Professor Samuel Huntington," p. 23.

Harvard Law Review, May, 1982, Rogers M. Smith, review of *American Politics,* pp. 1691-1702.

International Affairs, July, 1997, Felipe Fernandez, review of *The Clash of Civilizations and the Remaking of World Order,* p. 547.

Journal of American History, September, 1982, review of *American Politics,* p. 417.

Journal of American Studies, August, 1983, review of *American Politics,* p. 280.

Journal of Economic Issues, December, 2001, Thomas R. DeGregori, review of *Culture Matters,* p. 1009.

Journal of International Affairs, summer, 1997, Christian Stracke, review of *The Clash of Civilizations and the Remaking of World Order,* p. 302.

Journal of Modern History, June, 1998, Walter A. McDougall, review of *The Clash of Civilizations and the Remaking of World Order,* p. 436.

Journal of Peace Research, February, 1994, Nils Petter Gleditsch, review of *The Third Wave,* p. 119; January, 1998, review of *The Clash of Civilizations and the Remaking of World Order,* p. 127.

Journal of Politics, November, 1982, review of *American Politics,* p. 1135; February, 1998, review of *The Clash of Civilizations and the Remaking of World Order,* p. 304.

Journal of Social, Political and Economic Studies, summer, 1998, review of *The Clash of Civilizations and the Remaking of World Order,* p. 215.

Journal of World History, spring, 200, Robert Marks, review of *The Clash of Civilizations and the Remaking of World Order,* p. 101.

Kirkus Reviews, August 15, 1981, review of *American Politics,* p. 1057; September 1, 1996, review of *The Clash of Civilizations and the Remaking of World Order,* p. 1295.

Library Journal, November 1, 1981, review of *American Politics,* p. 2143; October 1, 1996, David Ettinger, review of *The Clash of Civilizations and the Remaking of World Order,* p. 106; August, 1999, review of *The Clash of Civilizations and the Remaking of World Order,* p. 56; April 15, 2000, Danna Bell-Rusell, review of *Culture Matters,* p. 113.

London Review of Books, April 24, 1997, review of *The Clash of Civilizations and the Remaking of World Order,* p. 3; November 1, 2001, Bruce Robbins, review of *Culture Matters,* pp. 34-35.

Military Review, September, 1994, review of *The Third Wave,* p. 82.

Nation, November 28, 1981, Alan Wolfe, review of *American Politics,* p. 583.

National Review, November 13, 1981, Joseph Sobran, review of *American Politics,* p. 1352; October 28, 1996, Robin Harris, review of *The Clash of Civilizations and the Remaking of World Order,* p. 69.

New Perspectives Quarterly, summer, 1993, "The Islamic-Confucian Connection," p. 19; winter, 2002, "Osama bin Laden Has Given Common Identity Back to the West," interview with Huntington, pp. 5-8.

New Republic, November 11, 1981, Samuel H. Beer, review of *American Politics,* p. 30.

New Statesman, April 4, 1997, review of *The Clash of Civilizations and the Remaking of World Order,* p. 42; October 15, 2001, Edward W. Said, analysis of *The Clash of Civilizations and the Remaking of World Order,* p. 20.

Newsweek, December 9, 1996, Bill Powell, review of *The Clash of Civilizations and the Remaking of World Order,* p. 63.

New York Review of Books, January 9, 1997, review of *The Clash of Civilizations and the Remaking of World Order,* p. 18.

New York Times, November 6, 1996, Richard Bernstein, review of *The Clash of Civilizations and the Remaking of World Order,* p. B2(N); October 20, 2001, Michael Steinberger, "A Head-on Collision of Alien Cultures?," p. A11(N).

New York Times Book Review, November 15, 1981, Andrew Hacker, review of American Politics, p. 3; June 26, 1983, review of *Living with Nuclear Weapons,* p. 3; September 11, 1983, Andrew Hacker, review of *American Politics,* p. 55; December 1, 1996, Michael Ignatieff, review of *The Clash of Civilizations and the Remaking of World Order,* p. 13.

New York University Journal of International Law and Politics, winter, 1987, review of *Reorganizing America's Defense: Leadership in War and Peace,* pp. 523-24.

New Zealand International Review, May-June, 1997, John McKinnon, review of *The Clash of Civilizations and the Remaking of World Order,* p. 22A.

Observer (London), February 23, 1997, review of *The Clash of Civilizations and the Remaking of World Order,* p. 16.

Perspective, June, 1982, review of *American Politics,* p. 98.

Perspectives on Political Science, spring, 1992, review of *The Third Wave,* p. 100.

Policy Review, June-July, 2002, Stanley Kurtz, "The Future of 'History': Francis Fukuyama vs. Samuel P. Huntington," pp. 43-58.

Political Science Quarterly, fall, 1982, review of *American Politics,* p. 505; summer, 1997, Robert Jervis, review of *The Clash of Civilizations and the Remaking of World Order,* p. 307.

Political Science Review, fall, 1983, review of *American Politics,* p. 69.

Political Studies, March, 1994, Graeme Duncan, review of *The Third Wave,* p. 174.

Publishers Weekly, September 9, 1996, review of *The Clash of Civilizations and the Remaking of World Order,* p. 69.

Quadrant, May, 1997, review of *The Clash of Civilizations and the Remaking of World Order,* p. 75; September, 2000, Eric Jones, review of *Culture Matters,* p. 78.

Religious Studies Review, July, 1983, review of *American Politics,* p. 253.

Review of Politics, January, 1983, review of *American Politics,* p. 149; spring, 1993, Philippe C. Schmitter, review of *The Third Wave,* p. 348.

San Francisco Chronicle, April 6, 1997, Abbas Milani, "Western Civilization Takes on the World," p. 10.

School Library Media Quarterly, summer, 1993, review of *The Third Wave,* p. 267.

Social Science Quarterly, March, 1998, review of *The Clash of Civilizations and the Remaking of World Order,* p. 250.

Society, November, 2000, Peter L. Berger, review of *Culture Matters,* p. 103.

Spectator, April 12, 1997, review of *The Clash of Civilizations and the Remaking of World Order,* p. 35.

Time, May 22, 2000, Lance Morrow, review of *Culture Matters,* p. 26.

Times Literary Supplement, April 11, 1997, Patrick Glynn, review of *The Clash of Civilizations and the Remaking of World Order,* p. 10.

Village Voice, November 11, 1981, review of *American Politics,* p. 38.

Virginia Quarterly Review, winter, 1982, review of *American Politics,* p. 10.

Wall Street Journal, November 7, 1996, Francis Fukuyama, review of *The Clash of Civilizations and the Remaking of World Order,* p. A20(E).

Whole Earth Review, summer, 1997, review of *The Clash of Civilizations and the Remaking of World Order,* p. 39.

Wilson Quarterly, spring, 1982, review of *American Politics,* p. 155.

World Politics, October, 1993, Ian Shapiro, review of *The Third Wave,* p. 121.

ONLINE

NewsHour, http://www.pbs.org/newshour/ (January 9, 1997), David Gergen discussion with Huntington, transcript "Many World Orders."

Scott London, http://www.scottlondon.com/ (April 19, 2002), review of *The Third Wave.**

I-J

ILLIANO, Antonio 1934-

PERSONAL: Born April 21, 1934, in Italy; son of Fausto and Luigina (Scotto) Illiano; married Elfriede R. Worsthorn, June 11, 1962; children: Vincent. *Education:* University of Naples, Laurea de Dottore in Lettere, 1958; University of California, Berkeley, Ph. D., 1966.

ADDRESSES: Home—400 Ridgecrest Dr., Chapel Hill, NC 27514. *Office*—Department of Romance Languages and Literatures, University of North Carolina, Chapel Hill, NC 27514.

CAREER: University of California, Santa Barbara, instructor, 1963-66; University of Texas at Austin, assistant professor of Italian language and literature, 1966-68; University of Oregon, Eugene, assistant professor of Italian language and literature, 1968-69; University of North Carolina at Chapel Hill, assistant professor, 1969-71, associate professor of Romance languages and literatures, 1971-81, professor of romance language and literature, 1982—.

MEMBER: Modern Language Association of America, Dante Society of America.

AWARDS, HONORS: Postdoctoral fellowship from University of Texas Academic Excellence Program, 1966; Pogue Leave, University of North Carolina, 1978.

WRITINGS:

Introduzione alla critica pirandelliana, Fiorini (Verona, Italy), 1976.
Metapsichica e letteratura in Perandello, Firenze (Vallecchi, Italy), 1982.

Per l'esegesi del 'Corbaccio,' Federica & Ardia (Napoli, Italy), 1991.
Morfologia della narrazione manzoniana: dal 'Fermo e Lucia' ai 'Promessi Sposi,' Fiesole (Cadmo, Italy), 1993.
Sulle sponde del prepurgatoria: poesia e arte narrativa del preludio all' ascese, Fiesole (Cadmo, Italy), 1997.
Da Boccaccio a Pirendello: scritti e ricerche con un saggio su letteratura e cristianesimo, Federico e Ardia (Napoli, Italy), 1997.
Dalla Vita Nuova a Palomar, L'Orientale Editrice (Napoli, Italy), 1999.

Contributor to *Dante Encyclopedia,* and *Columbia Dictionary of Modern European Literature.* Contributor to *Italica, PMLA, New York Public Library Bulletin, Forum Italicum, Italianistica, Mark Twain Journal, Perspectives on Contemporary Literature,* and other journals. Editor of *Forum Italicum, Symposium;* series editor for Italian *Dictionary of Literary Biography,* Gale.

*　　*　　*

ISAACS, Anne 1949-

PERSONAL: Born March 2, 1949, in Buffalo, NY; daughter of Samuel (a materials handling engineer) and Hope (an anthropologist; maiden name, Levy) Isaacs; children: Jordan, Amy, Sarah. *Education:* University of Michigan, B.A., 1971, M.S., 1975; attended State University of New York, Buffalo, 1971-72. *Religion:* Jewish.

ADDRESSES: Home—8521 Buckingham Drive, El Cerrito, CA 94530. *Agent*—Gail Hochman, Brandt & Brandt Literary Agents, 1501 Broadway, New York, NY 10036. *E-mail*—Anne@anneisaacs.com

CAREER: Held numerous positions in environmental education from 1975 to 1990; writer of children's books and poetry, 1983—.

AWARDS, HONORS: Swamp Angel, illustrated by Paul O. Zelinsky, was a Caldecott honor book and a Notable Books selection of the American Library Association (ALA), both 1994; other awards for *Swamp Angel* include: Best Illustrated Books citation, *New York Times,* and Best Books from *School Library Journal* and *Publishers Weekly,* all 1994, and Honor Book, *Boston Globe-Horn Book,* Children's Book of the Year list, Child Study Children's Book Committee, and Notable Trade Book in Language Arts, National Council of Teachers of English, all 1995; National Jewish Book Award finalist, ALA Notable Book and Best Book for Young Adults designations, Sydney Taylor Notable Book for Young Readers designation, *Smithsonian* Notable Book for Children selection, *Booklist* Best of the Year/Holocaust Literature for Youth selection, International Reading Association Outstanding International Book and Notable Books for a Global Society selections, New York Public Library 100 Titles for Reading and Sharing selection, and Children's Literature Choice, Children's Book Council Notable Book in Social Studies, all 2000, all for *Torn Thread.*

WRITINGS:

Swamp Angel, illustrated by Paul O. Zelinsky, Dutton Children's Books (New York, NY), 1994.
Treehouse Tales, illustrated by Lloyd Bloom, Dutton Children's Books (New York, NY), 1997.
Cat up a Tree: A Story in Poems, illustrated by Stephen Mackey, Dutton Children's Books (New York, NY), 1998.
Torn Thread, Scholastic (New York, NY), 2000.
A Bowl of Soup, illustrated by Jerry Pinkney, Scholastic, in press.

ADAPTATIONS: Swamp Angel was adapted as a segment of *Storytime,* Public Broadcasting System (PBS), 1995.

WORK IN PROGRESS: The Song of Miriam (Scholastic), a historical novel, and two picture books, *Toby Littlewood* (Scholastic) and *Dust Devil* (Dutton Children's Books).

SIDELIGHTS: Anne Isaacs is best known for *Swamp Angel,* an imaginative historical tale spotlighting a young female heroine who appears larger than life. She is also the author of the fictional work *Torn Thread,* which is based on the true story of a young girl imprisoned in a Nazi labor camp during World War II.

Written in a tongue-in-cheek style, *Swamp Angel* features Angelica Longrider, who, as an infant, is a bit taller than her mother and who later accomplishes some amazing feats. In addition to building her first log cabin by the time she is two, Angelica rescues a wagon from Dejection Swamp and then defeats a bear, Thundering Tarnation, by throwing him up to the sky and creating a prairie from the bear's pelt. Commentators have compared Angelica to the legendary American folk hero Paul Bunyan. A Caldecott honor book with illustrations by Paul O. Zelinsky, *Swamp Angel* was declared "visually exciting, wonderful to read aloud . . . a picture book to remember" by a *Horn Book* contributor. A reviewer in *Kirkus Reviews* exclaimed, "It is impossible to convey the sheer pleasure, the exaggerated loopiness, of newcomer Isaacs's wonderful story."

A more serious work is Isaacs's *A Bowl of Soup,* which, as Isaacs explained, "is a fictional account of the experiences of my mother-in-law, Eva Buchbinder Koplowicz, as a young woman in a Nazi labor camp in Czechoslovakia from 1943 to 1945. All of the incidents are either true or possible." To write this emotionally painful story, Isaacs researched a number of holocaust topics; read the testimony of other holocaust survivors; visited concentration camps, death camps, and former ghettos in Europe; and visited the labor camp and factory where Eva worked. About writing the story, Isaacs revealed: "It has been hard going. I have had to invent the most wonderful father I have ever known, then hand him over to the Nazis again and again during subsequent drafts of the book. I have had to experience repeatedly many unbearable realities. But at the end of each writing day, I have been fortunate to be able to return to the safe and loving world of my family." While the holocaust is often difficult for children to understand, Isaac provides a spirited story sensitive to young readers. "Given its precise detail and sensitivity to unimaginable suffering," a *Publishers Weekly* reviewer noted, "this gripping novel reads like the strongest of Holocaust memoirs."

About her own life, Isaacs once commented: "I was born in 1949 in Buffalo, New York, and lived there until I left to attend the University of Michigan in 1967. As a child I did a limited amount of creative writing on my own. I had two poems published at the age of ten in a city-wide magazine of writing by school children. I read constantly, selecting books haphazardly from my parents' and the public library shelves. In fifth grade, for example, along with *The Wind in the Willows,* I read Shakespeare's *Romeo and Juliet* and *The Tempest,* plus *Lorna Doone* and *The Caine Mutiny.* As now, poetry affected me more profoundly than any other genre. At age ten I memorized Coleridge's 'Kubla Khan' while reading it for the first time.

"Probably the greatest childhood influence on my writing was reading and re-reading, over a period of years, Louisa May Alcott's *Little Women.* I would finish the last page and immediately start over at the first. The story became a kind of life plan for me, although I didn't realize that until a few years ago. Like Alcott's semi-autobiographical heroine, Jo, I grew up to marry a kindly, professorial man with an unpronounceable name, to raise a passel of kids in the country, and to combine careers in educational program development and children's book writing. This experience has taught me to respect the long-term influence a children's book may have on its readers.

"I studied English literature in my undergraduate years at the University of Michigan, and in a year of graduate study at the State University of New York, Buffalo. I also studied French, Russian, Latin, and American literature during these years. I have always been especially interested in nineteenth-century novels and poetry. Only as an adult have I begun to read extensively in children's literature, often experiencing a book for the first time while reading it to my children.

"As a result of reading children's and adult literature interchangeably throughout my life, I have never recognized a clear distinction between them, nor do I apply different standards."

In *Treehouse Tales,* a collection of her short stories, Isaacs links the lives of three farm children with their tree house. The stories take place in Pennsylvania during the 1880s. Whether pretending to be U.S. Civil War generals or in the midst of a dragon's lair, each of these stories is imaginatively told, combining fantasy with lessons about family harmony and affection. According to Kay Weisman of *Booklist,* "Isaac's light-hearted tales sparkle with warmth and humor."

Cat up a Tree communicates a series of mystical poems about a cat's adventures climbing a tree. Stephen Mackey's expansive, rich illustrations add a sense of enchantment to the poems, each one told from a different point of view. The poems and paintings combine to transport the reader from an ordinary event into a hidden, secretive world of mystery and imagination. "Cat Lovers will go wild for this work, as will poets and dreamers," proclaimed a contributor to *Publishers Weekly* in a review of the book.

BIOGRAPHICAL AND CRITICAL SOURCES:

PERIODICALS

Booklist, October 15, 1994, Hazel Rochman, review of *Swamp Thing,* p. 424; January 15, 1995, pp. 862, 907; April 15, 1995, p. 1412; September 15, 1997, Kay Weisman, review of *Treehouse Tales,* p. 235; March 1, 2000, Hazel Rochman, review of *Torn Thread,* p. 1236; March 15, 2001, review of *Torn Thread,* p. 1366.

Bulletin of the Center for Children's Books, October, 1997, review of *Treehouse Tales,* p. 54; November, 1998, review of *Cat up a Tree,* p. 101.

Childhood Education, fall, 2000, Jeanie Burnett, review of *Torn Thread,* p. 45.

Children's Book Review Service, August, 1997, review of *Treehouse Tales,* p. 164.

Children's Bookwatch, December, 1998, review of *Cat up a Tree,* p. 4.

Entertainment Weekly, October 21, 1994, Leonard S. Marcus, review of *Swamp Angel,* p. 83.

Horn Book, March/April, 1995, Mary M. Burns, review of *Swamp Angel,* p. 184; September-October, 1997, Ann A. Flowers, review of *Treehouse Tales,* p. 572.

Horn Book Guide, spring, 1999, review of *Cat up a Tree,* p. 132.

Kirkus Reviews, October 15, 1994, p. 1408; June 1, 1997, review of *Treehouse Tales,* p. 874; September 1, 1998, review of *Cat up a Tree,* p. 1286.

New York Times Book Review, November 13, 1994, p. 30; June 22, 1997, review of *Treehouse Tales,* p. 22; November 15, 1998, Jen Nessel, review of *Cat up a Tree,* p. 48.

Publishers Weekly, October 3, 1994, review of *Swamp Angel,* p. 69; November 7, 1994, p. 43; May 26, 1997, review of *Treehouse Tales,* p. 86; August 24, 1998, review of *Cat up a Tree,* p. 57; May 22, 2000, review of *Torn Thread,* p. 57.

San Francisco Chronicle, November 22, 1998, review of *Cat up a Tree,* p. 9.

School Library Journal, December, 1994, pp. 24, 76; July, 1997, Julie Cummins, review of *Treehouse Tales,* p. 69; November, 1997, review of *Swamp Angel,* p. 41; November 1, 1998, Miriam Lang Budin, review of *Cat up a Tree,* p. 136; April, 2000, Virginia Golodetz, review of *Torn Thread,* p. 136.

U.S. News & World Report, December 5, 1994, Marc Silver, review of *Swamp Angel,* p. 95.

*   *   *

JAKSIĆ, Iván (Andrades) 1954-

PERSONAL: Born March 14, 1954; immigrated to the United States, 1976; son of Fabian and Nidia (Andrade) Jaksić; married Carolina Arroyo, August 20, 1982; children: Ilse. *Education:* Attended Universidad de Chile, 1971-75; State University of New York at Buffalo, M.A. (American and Puerto Rican studies), 1978, M.A. (history) and Ph.D., both 1981. *Hobbies and other interests:* Reading, soccer, theater and film.

ADDRESSES: Office—Center for Latin America, University of Wisconsin, Cutin Hall, Room 902, Milwaukee, WI 53201.

CAREER: Philosophy teacher in Santiago, Chile, 1975-76; University of California, Berkeley, postdoctoral research associate at Center for Latin American Studies, 1982-83, vice chairperson of the center, 1984-89; University of Wisconsin, Milwaukee, associate professor of history, 1989—, became director of Center for Latin America, 1989; currently professor of history, University of Notre Dame, Notre Dame, IN. State University

of New York at Buffalo, assistant professor, summer, 1983; University of California, Berkeley, visiting lecturer, autumn, 1986, 1987; Stanford University, consulting assistant professor, winter, 1988.

MEMBER: Conference on Latin American History (life member), Society for Iberian and Latin American Thought (vice president, 1989-91; president, 1991-92), Latin-American Studies Association, American Historical Association, New England Council of Latin-American Studies, Cervantes Society of America, Commonwealth Club of California (chairman, Western Hemisphere section, 1985-89).

AWARDS, HONORS: State University of New York at Buffalo, travel grants, 1982-83; American Council of Learned Societies grant, 1985; Tinker Foundation and Andrew Mellon Foundation travel grants, Berkeley Center for Latin American Studies, 1985, 1988, and 1989.

WRITINGS:

(Editor, with Jorgé J. E. Gracia) *Filosofía e identidad cultural en America Latina,* Monte-Avila (Caracas, Venezuela), 1988.

Academic Rebels in Chile: The Role of Philosophy in Higher Education and Politics, State University of New York Press (Buffalo, NY), 1989.

(Editor, with Paul W. Drake, and contributor) *The Struggle for Democracy in Chile, 1982-1990,* University of Nebraska Press, 1991.

(Editor, with others) *Sarmiento: Author of a Nation,* University of California Press (Berkeley, CA), 1994.

(Editor and author of introduction) *Selected Writings of Andrés Bello,* translated by Frances M. Lopez-Morillas, Oxford University Press (New York, NY), 1997.

Andrés Bello and the Problem of Order in Post-Independence Spanish America, David Rockefeller Center for Latin American Studies (Cambridge, MA), 1997.

(Editor, with Paul W. Drake) *El modelo chileno: democracia y desarrollo en los noventa,* LOM Ediciones (Santiago, Chile), 1999.

Andrés Bello: Scholarship and Nation-building in Nineteenth-Century Latin America, Cambridge University Press (New York, NY), 2001.

Work represented in anthologies, including *Latin American Education: A Quest for Identity,* edited by Nancy J. Nystrom, Roger Thayer Stone Center for Latin American Studies, Tulane University, 1985; *Student Political Activism: An International Reference Handbook,* edited by Philip G. Altbach, Greenwood Press, 1989; and *International Yearbook of Oral History and Life Stories,* edited by Rina Benmayor and Andor Skotnes, Oxford University Press, 1993. Contributor of articles, translations, and reviews to scholarly journals. Editor, "Stanford-Berkeley Occasional Papers in Latin American Studies," 1984-89; member of editorial board, *Explicacion de textos literarios,* 1983—.

WORK IN PROGRESS: Research on modern Latin-American history, Latin-American philosophy, Latin-American higher education, and Chile.

SIDELIGHTS: Iván Jaksić once told *CA:* "I lived through the turmoil of Chile and Argentina in the 1970s. This prompted my immigration to the United States in 1976. Much of my writing is academic, but deals with subjects very close to my experience in Chile. I continue to write on non-academic subjects and hope, at some point, to produce some autobiographical reflections on immigration and personal identity, especially as it is impacted by the acquisition of a new language. I find writing to be indispensable for providing structure to one's life, but also for sharing experiences that might be of value to others."

Jaksić helped edit the twenty-two essays by leading Latin-American scholars in *Sarmiento: Author of a Nation.* The book helped shed light on the life of one of that region's most important nineteenth-century politicians. As president of Argentina from 1868 to 1874, Domingo Faustino Sarmiento helped shape politics in the region for decades with his liberal stance on export and trade. In addition to being a crafty diplomat, Sarmiento is also considered one of Argentina's finest writers. His greatest work, *Facundo,* is considered to be a brave and impassioned outcry against political oppression in the years following Argentina's independence from Spanish rule. As David Rock pointed out in a review for *Historian,* Jaksić's book "is the first collected work of its kind published in English."

Although every major city in Latin America has a statue or road named after Venezuelan Andrés Bello, very little has been written about him in the United States. Publication of the *Selected Writings of Andrés Bello* helps fill this void on the hugely influential politician, orator, teacher, and philosopher. As editor, Jaksić includes essays on subjects ranging from education, political reform, and grammar to international relations. Bello, who played a major role in establishing Venezuela as an independent nation, is often compared to Thomas Jefferson. *Booklist* contributor Mary Carroll noted that Jaksić's book "should bring him overdue attention farther north."

Jaksić's *Andrés Bello: Scholarship and Nation-building in Nineteenth-Century Latin America* is the first biography of Bello to be published in the English language. Bello was a towering intellectual figure in nineteenth-century Latin-American politics and is regarded by many as its greatest thinker. "This intellectual biography is impressively researched," according to Leo Zaibert of the *Times Literary Supplement.* In addition to examining Bello's contributions to Latin-American history, Jaksić's portrait is also a personal, poignant examination of Bello's life.

BIOGRAPHICAL AND CRITICAL SOURCES:

PERIODICALS

American Historical Review, April, 1991, p. 646.
American Political Science Review, December, 1992, p. 1082.
Americas, April, 1990, p. 547; January, 1996, Georgette Magassy Dorn, review of *Sarmiento: Author of a Nation,* p. 418.
Comparative Education Review, February, 1991, p. 196.
Foreign Affairs, summer, 1992, p. 176.
Hispania, Volume 72, number 3, 1989, p. 558; March, 1991, p. 81.
Hispanic American Historical Review, May, 1990; November, 1992, p. 637.
Historian, winter, 1994, David Rock, review of *Sarmiento,* p. 379.
Journal of Developing Areas, October, 1990, p. 137.
Journal of Latin American Studies, October, 1992, p. 702.
Latin American Literary Review, July-December, 1994, Susana Rotker, review of *Sarmiento,* p. 98.
Times Literary Supplement, January 4, 2002, Leo Zaibert, review of *Andrés Bello: Scholarship and Nation-building in Nineteenth-Century Latin America,* p. 29.*

JARVIS, Sharon 1943-
(Johanna Hailey, H. M. Major, joint pseudonyms)

PERSONAL: Born October 1, 1943, in Brooklyn, NY; daughter of Joseph and Ethel (Karger) Jarvis. *Education:* Hunter College of the City University of New York, B.F.A., 1964.

ADDRESSES: Home and office—Sharon Jarvis & Co., Toad Hall, Inc., Rural Route 2, Box 2090, Laceyville, PA 18623. *E-mail*—toadhall@aol.com.

CAREER: Ace Books, New York, NY, copy editor and copywriter, 1969-70; assistant managing editor for Popular Library, 1970-71; Ballantine Books, Inc., New York, NY, editor, 1971-74; Doubleday & Co., New York, NY, editor, 1974-77; Playboy Books, New York, NY, senior editor, 1977-82; Jarvis, Braff Ltd. (literary agency), Staten Island, NY, vice president, 1978-82; Sharon Jarvis & Co. (literary agency), Laceyville, PA, president, 1983—.

MEMBER: International Fortean Organization, Association of Author's Representatives, Science Fiction Writers of America, Holistic Consortium.

WRITINGS:

WITH KATHLEEN BUCKLEY; UNDER JOINT PSEUDONYM H. M. MAJOR

The Alien Trace, New American Library (New York, NY), 1984.
Time Twister, New American Library (New York, NY), 1984.

WITH MARCIA HOWL; UNDER JOINT PSEUDONYM JOHANNA HAILEY

Enchanted Paradise, Zebra Books (New York, NY), 1985.
Crystal Paradise, Zebra Books (New York, NY), 1986.
Beloved Paradise, Zebra Books (New York, NY), 1987.

EDITOR

True Tales of the Unknown, Bantam (New York, NY), Volume 1, 1985, Volume 2, 1989, Volume 3, 1991.

Inside Outer Space: Science Fiction Professionals Look at Their Craft, Frederick Ungar (New York, NY), 1985.
The Uninvited, Bantam (New York, NY), 1989.
Beyond Reality, Bantam (New York, NY), 1991.
Dark Zones, Warner Books (New York, NY), 1992.
Dead Zones, Warner Books (New York, NY), 1992.

Author of columns for *Mystery Scene Magazine.*

WORK IN PROGRESS: The Cosmic Countdown.

SIDELIGHTS: Sharon Jarvis told *CA:* "We do a lot of New Age and nonfiction occult, in addition to genre fiction."

*   *   *

JENNINGS, Peter (Charles Archibald Ewart) 1938-

PERSONAL: Born July 29, 1938, in Toronto, Ontario, Canada; immigrated to United States, 1964; son of Charles (a broadcast journalist and television programming executive) and Elizabeth Ewart (Osborne) Jennings; married Valerie Godsoe (a journalist; divorced, 1972); married Annie Malouf (a photographer; divorced); married Kati Ilona Marton (a writer and former journalist), 1979 (divorced, 1993); children: (third marriage) Elizabeth, Christopher. *Education:* Attended Trinity College School, Port Hope, Ontario, Canada; Carleton University, Ottawa, Ontario, Canada; Rider College, Lawrenceville, NJ. *Hobbies and other interests:* Skiing, sailing, reading thrillers and adventure novels.

ADDRESSES: Office—c/o ABC Media Relations, 47 West 66th St., New York, NY 10023-6201.

CAREER: Canadian Broadcasting Corporation (CBC), Montreal, Quebec, Canada, host of *Peter's People* (radio program of news and music for children), c. 1948; Royal Bank of Canada, Toronto, Ontario, Canada, teller, c. 1954-56; host of *Club Thirteen* (television dance party), c. 1957; CFJR-Radio, Brockville, Ontario, Canada, reporter and interviewer, 1959-61; CBC, interviewer for several radio and television programs, including *Close-Up,* and host of *Let's Face It* (public affairs program) and *Time Out* (afternoon

Peter Jennings

talk show), 1960s; CJOH-TV, Ottawa, Ontario, Canada, special events commentator and host and co-producer of *Vue* (late-night interview program), 1960s; Canadian Television Network (CTV), Ottawa, reporter for and co-anchor of *CTV National News,* 1962-64; American Broadcasting Companies Inc. (ABC-TV), New York, NY, 1964—, news correspondent, 1964, anchor of *Peter Jennings with the News,* 1965-67, roving news correspondent, 1968-73, head of Middle East bureau, 1969-74, Washington, DC, correspondent and news reader for *A.M. America,* 1975, chief foreign correspondent, 1975-78, foreign-desk anchor of *World News Tonight,* 1978-83, anchor and senior editor of ABC's *World News Tonight with Peter Jennings,* 1983—; anchor of ABC's *Peter Jennings Reporting,* 1990—. Involved in the production of numerous documentaries and series for ABC-TV, including *Sadat: Action Biography,* 1974; *Personal Note: Beirut,* 1982; *We the People,* 1987; *Ethics in America,* 1989; *The AIDS Quarterly*; *Southern Accents: Northern Ghettos*; *The Century,* 1999; and *In Search of America,* 2002. Lecturer.

MEMBER: International Radio & Television Society Foundation Inc., American Federation of Television & Radio Artists, Overseas Press Club of America.

AWARDS, HONORS: National Headliner Award, c. 1972, for behind-the-lines coverage of civil war in Bangladesh; George Foster Peabody Broadcasting Award, Henry W. Grady School of Journalism and Mass Communication at the University of Georgia, 1974, for *Sadat: Action Biography*; recipient of at least nine Emmy awards from Academy of Television Arts & Sciences, including 1982, for outstanding coverage of a single breaking news story for *Personal Note: Beirut,* and for ten-part series on ABC's *World News Tonight with Peter Jennings* titled "U.S.-U.S.S.R.—A Balance of Powers"; Alfred I. duPont-Columbia University Award in Broadcast Journalism, Columbia University Graduate School of Journalism, c. 1982, for "U.S.-U.S.S.R.—A Balance of Powers"; Bob Considine Award, St. Bonaventure University, 1984, for excellence in news reporting; named best anchor by the *Washington Journalism Review,* 1988, 1989, and 1990; Overseas Press Club of America awards for coverage of the Falkland Islands War, for coverage of the assassination of Anwar Sadat, and for coverage of life in the Soviet Union; Goldsmith Career Award, Harvard University; Radio and Television News Directors Paul White Award; LL.D. from Rider College; honorary degrees from Loyola University, University of Rhode Island, and Carleton University.

WRITINGS:

(Editor) *Face to Face with the Turin Shroud,* Mayhew-Macrimmon (Great Wakering, England), 1978.
(With Eamonn McCabe) *The Pope in Britain: Pope John Paul II British Visit, 1982,* Bodley Head (London, England), 1982.
(With Todd Brewster) *The Century,* Double Day (New York, NY), 1998 adapted by Jennifer Amrstrong as *The Century for Young People,* Random House (New York, NY), 1999.
(With Brewster) *In Search of America,* Hyperion (New York, NY), 2002.

Also author of introduction to *The '84 Vote;* co-interviewer, *Children of the Troubles: Growing Up in Northern Ireland,* 1986. Contributor to periodicals, including *Christian Science Monitor* and *Maclean's.*

SIDELIGHTS: Peter Jennings, the Canadian-born anchor of the American Broadcasting Company's (ABC) *World News Tonight,* is one of America's most visible, and sometimes controversial, television journalists.

He is actually in his second tenure as an ABC anchor. In 1965, a handsome but inexperienced Jennings anchored the ABC evening newscast, *Peter Jennings with the News,* amid uproar among media counterparts who questioned his credentials. He left the anchor desk three years later, continuing to work for ABC as a foreign correspondent. Over the next twenty-five years, Jennings proved himself as an exemplary reporter, receiving prestigious journalistic awards—George Foster Peabody, National Headliner, Emmys—and earning a reputation as an expert on the Middle East. More importantly, he won the respect of his colleagues, stilled his critics, and resumed the role of ABC evening news anchor.

Jennings was born in Toronto, the son of Charles Jennings, a pioneering journalist for the Canadian Broadcasting Corporation (CBC). Jennings was introduced to broadcasting at age nine, when his father picked him to host a weekly half-hour radio program of music and news for children, *Peter's People.* After dropping out of high school in the tenth grade—"bored," Jennings freely admitted—he spent three years as a teller in a Toronto bank before returning to the media.

Jennings then worked three years as a radio interviewer at CFIR, in Brockville, Ontario, a small city in the Thousand Islands region. In the early 1960s he joined CBC as host of *Let's Face It,* a public-affairs program, and *Time Out,* an afternoon talk show. After just a few months, he signed on with CJOH-TV in Ottawa. There, he served as special events commentator, and host and co-producer of the late-night interview program, *Vue.* The CBC then lured him back by offering him the chance to host several radio and television shows, including the prestigious documentary series, *Close-Up.*

In 1962, the CTV Television Network Limited debuted the *CTV National News,* Canada's first nationwide newscast. For the *National News* Jennings covered the North Atlantic Treaty Organization meetings in France and Ontario; he was the first Canadian journalist to arrive at U.S. President John F. Kennedy's assassination scene in Dallas, Texas, in November, 1963; and he reported on the 1964 Democratic National Convention in Atlantic City, New Jersey. While broadcasting at the convention, Jennings caught the eye of Elmer Lower, then ABC News president. Lower offered Jennings a job with his young, fledgling news organization, which the Canadian refused, terrified at the prospect of covering the news in the United States. "America was enormous," he told Norman Atkins many years later in a *Rolling Stone* interview. "I'd only been here once before, to go to a Broadway show. I'd never seen buildings so tall." Three months later, realizing he missed the opportunity of a lifetime, Jennings wrote the ABC News president back, asking if he would reconsider.

In September, 1964, Jennings was assigned to ABC headquarters in New York. One of Jennings's first reporting assignments was on the burgeoning civil rights movement in the American South. He followed civil rights activists from one small town to another, often finding himself in harrowing situations—members of the white supremacist group Ku Klux Klan chased Jennings and his camera crew out of Natchez, Mississippi. After Jennings had been with ABC for only a few months, network executives, desperate to attract viewers faithful to Columbia Broadcasting System (CBS) news icon Walter Cronkite and the well-liked National Broadcasting Company (NBC) team of Chet Huntley and David Brinkley, offered Jennings anchor position of the nightly newscast.

Ryan Murphy wrote in the *Saturday Evening Post* that upon receiving the promotion, Jennings cried "tears of sorrow and extreme bitterness." It was the last thing he wanted to do, fearing a lack of freedom to travel and cover world events. Jennings finally heeded the advice of veteran newsman Howard Smith, who told him: "It's like being nominated for president. You can't turn it down." Furthermore, the network assured him he would still be a working newsman. When Jennings took the anchor desk on February 1, 1965, at age twenty-six, he became the youngest person ever to anchor a national network newscast in the United States.

"It was a little ridiculous when you think about it," Barbara Matusow quoted Jennings in *The Evening Stars: The Making of the Network News Anchor.* "A twenty-six-year-old trying to compete with Cronkite, Huntley, and Brinkley. I was simply unqualified." Derided as a "glamorcaster" by television critics and "anchorboy" by his more seasoned colleagues, Jennings antagonized those in the media who complained that his looks got him hired. Furthermore, many resented his aristocratic air and Canadian dialect—he said "leftenant" for lieutenant and "shedule" for schedule. Viewers, at first favorable, resented his Anglicized diction and his ignorance of American history and culture. On the air he had mispronounced the site of the famed Civil War battleground, Appomattox, and misidentified the U.S. Marine Corps's official anthem, "The Marine Hymn," as "Anchors Aweigh." Animosity forced some affiliate stations not to air his newscasts or bury them in traditionally low-viewing time slots.

Nonetheless, Jennings anchored *The ABC Evening News* for three years, and earned modest ratings gains for the organization. He excelled at on-location reporting from world trouble spots such as Santo Domingo and Vietnam, and was commended for *Southern Accents: Northern Ghettos,* his television documentary exposing the plight of poor Southern blacks living in squalor in Northern urban areas. Late in 1967 when ABC was to expand its newscast from fifteen to thirty minutes, Jennings requested reassignment. His superiors agreed, and he returned to the field.

Jennings resumed his duties as a roving reporter again in January, 1968. He spent much of the following decade abroad, reporting from such places as Cuba (because it was closed to Americans—Jennings entered as a Canadian) and Bangladesh, winning a National Headliner Award for his coverage of that nation's civil war. In 1969 he helped establish and was named head of the ABC News Middle East bureau in Beirut, Lebanon, the first television news desk in the Arab world. Jennings had developed a great interest in the Middle East two years earlier, when he was a correspondent following the Arab-Israeli territorial conflicts in the Six-Day War. Soon Jennings's expertise in Middle Eastern affairs was unmatched among broadcast journalists; he was noted for filing insightful, comprehensive, and accurate reports with a fresh perspective. "I felt very strongly—and I still do—that there is much more than the Israeli side to the Middle East story," Jennings told Atkins. "There are nineteen countries in the Arab world, and I worked in them all." Jennings conducted the first televised interview with Palestine Liberation Organization leader Yassir Arafat. His 1974 profile of Egyptian President Anwar Sadat, *Sadat: Action Biography,* won a George Foster Peabody Award, one of journalism's highest accolades.

Jennings was providing routine coverage for the Summer Olympic Games in Munich, Germany in 1972, when members of the Arab terrorist group Black September seized the Israeli compound and took athletes hostage. Well-versed in the history and goals of the terrorists, Jennings filed a series of exceptional commentaries. "He also displayed considerable moxie as a reporter," Matusow recalled, "hiding himself and a camera crew inside the grounds, close enough to the scene to obtain clear pictures of the guerrillas in their floppy hats and stockinged faces, darting in and out of the balcony of the Israeli building. It was among the most gripping episodes ever shown on live television." Jennings's reports helped ABC win an Emmy Award that year for outstanding achievement in special events coverage.

In early 1975 Jennings returned to the United States as Washington correspondent and news reader for *A.M. America,* ABC's answer to NBC's popular morning news and feature program, *Today.* After ten months with *A.M. America*—it was canceled in October—Jennings was reassigned overseas as chief foreign correspondent. In July, 1978, in an innovative move to make ABC's news division more competitive with CBS and NBC, ABC executives created a three-part anchor system for the retitled evening broadcast, *World News Tonight.* Frank Reynolds would be based in Washington, D.C., Max Robinson would report from Chicago, and the now-seasoned Jennings, still chief foreign correspondent, would anchor from London.

Jennings enhanced ABC News's global coverage with his exposure to the European perspective, and, being based in London, could scoop rival networks on world stories. His curiosity in Middle Eastern affairs led him to interview the Ayatollah Ruhollah Khomeini when he was only an obscure Iranian cleric living in exile in France. In 1979, when the Ayatollah and his followers overthrew the Shah of Iran, and later when his followers seized the U.S. Embassy in Tehran, Iran, and took fifty-two hostages, Jennings provided extensive background information and in-depth commentary. In 1981, when Sadat was assassinated, Jennings noted the subdued response by the Egyptian people, who usually mourn more demonstrably. He realized that although Sadat was a hero to the West, the Egyptian president had fallen out of favor with his countrymen after signing a peace treaty with Israel. In addition, Jennings's notable coverage of the Iran hostage crisis, his Emmy Award-winning documentary, *Personal Note: Beirut,* and his penetrating insight into tumultuous world events made him the new model of the foreign correspondent.

In 1979 Jennings married Kati Marton, a reporter from ABC's Philadelphia affiliate, sent to London to replace a foreign correspondent. The two became engaged on their second date. They had two children within the next three years before divorcing in 1993.

In summer, 1983, after Reynolds died of cancer, ABC adopted the single-anchor format, to which CBS and NBC had returned. Jennings, not surprisingly, was asked to be sole anchor of the newly titled ABC *World News Tonight with Peter Jennings.* He still chafed at being tied to the anchor desk, but he accepted the job, in part to give his family greater stability and the "continuity of a home," as *Good Housekeeping* quoted him.

"He seems finally to have overcome first impressions," Joshua Hammer wrote in *People* magazine, recalling Jennings's abysmal treatment in the 1960s. Still, in the 1980s, some predicted Jennings's sophisticated manner would not appeal to American audiences. "Jennings has a great big liability," Matusow said. "He doesn't look, sound or act like Middle America, and the news is aimed at Middle America." But Harry F. Waters and Trey Ellis, in *Newsweek,* wrote that "viewers weary of studied folksiness in their newscasters might embrace Jennings's cerebral, no-nonsense demeanor as a refreshing alternative." Jennings, who reassured critics that his verbal gaffes were in the past, was convinced his decade overseas would give him an edge over his fellow anchors. "For much of the major news of the last five years," he said in *Newsweek,* "I was there."

When Jennings became solo anchor on September 5, 1983, it signaled an intensified battle among the three networks for the early-evening audience and the millions of dollars in advertising revenues the viewers represent. ABC, in last place in the ratings for decades, had been slowly gaining on the second place *NBC Nightly News with Tom Brokaw. CBS Evening News with Dan Rather* had been well in the lead for a year. By summer, 1986, however, the competition among the three newscasts was so intense a television critic likened the ratings race to a presidential campaign. During the second week in July, all three newscasts were tied; the next week, Jennings took the lead. Three years later Jennings was consistently on top in the ratings. He is reportedly the most popular anchor among big-city audiences and the preferred choice among viewers with university degrees. "Peter is urban, projecting an image with which a more youthful market can identify," Edwin Diamond wrote in *Rolling Stone.*

Jennings can improvise in intelligent, complete sentences when broadcasting live. When TWA Flight 847 was hijacked near Athens, Greece, in June, 1985, Jennings was on the air throughout the day for seventeen straight days. After the space shuttle *Challenger* exploded in 1986, ABC received 10,000 letters commending Jennings for his stabilizing presence. In September, 1988, when he moderated the first debate between presidential hopefuls George Bush and Michael Dukakis, some television critics declared Jennings the winner. In the aftermath of the terrorist attacks on America on September 11, 2001, Jennings contributed a marathon anchoring job as ABC and the other news services scrambled to provide updates.

Because his statements can steer the political thought of tens of millions of people, Jennings claims neutrality in his news coverage. He learned as a reporter in the Middle East that most issues have many angles, and, he noted in *Rolling Stone,* he inherited a sense of fairness from his father. Some political writers, however, maintain that his Middle East stories displayed a pro-Palestinian slant.

Andrea Levin, in the *Jerusalem Post,* pointed out Jennings's broadcast on the lynching of two Israeli reservists who had inadvertently entered Arab-occupied Ramallah in October, 2000. The anchor, she wrote, "introduced his report with characteristic reticence to blame the Palestinians directly. He meandered around the point, saying, 'It has been another terrible day of fighting between Israelis and Palestinians.'" The rest of the segment, reported by Gillian Findlay, "focused on Israeli retaliation [for the lynching] and Arab anger," Levin continued. While Findlay described the damage done to Palestinian police stations and broadcast transmitters, the report "failed to mention that the Israelis gave a three-hour warning of the attacks to enable evacuation and that, as a result, there were no Arab fatalities." Former New York mayor Ed Koch, in a 2002 radio address reprinted on the Web site *ZCPortal,* said Jennings has "specialized in vicious and unfair portrayals of Israel intended to injure the Jewish state and lionize Palestinians."

But others see more objectivity in Jennings. The *Washington Journalism Review* named him anchor of the year three consecutive years. In 1995, the *Boston Globe* declared that Jennings had inherited the mantle of perhaps the greatest news broadcaster of all time, Edward R. Murrow. Nor is his influence lost on television audiences—Jennings finished second only to the retired Walter Cronkite in a 1986 Gallup Poll survey of what is most important in an anchor—believability in the media.

Jennings and co-author Todd Brewster have written broadcast-related books. *The Century* also appeared as a millennium-themed series on ABC and cable television's History Channel, narrated by Jennings. *USA Today* contributor Robert Rothenberg called the show a "sweeping panorama of the 20th century" that focuses on defining moments.

The Century became a bestseller that appealed to all ages. "I was in a bookstore one day and I saw an older man buying [the book] for his grandchild, and some younger people buying it for their parents," Jennings told Shannon Maugham of *Publishers Weekly.* "That led to some wonderful conversations about how kids were enjoying the book." Jennifer Armstrong adapted the work as *The Century for Young People.* The adaptation was smooth, according to a *Publishers Weekly* reviewer who said the volume "combines the authors' affecting storytelling style with an exceedingly appealing design."

Another Jennings-Brewster collaboration, *In Search of America,* was published, and broadcast in six parts, in autumn, 2002, nearly a year after the terrorist attacks. Though some work on the book was completed before September 11, after the attacks "I was gone," as Jennings told Ron Hogan in a *Publishers Weekly* interview. "I didn't get up out of that [anchor's] chair for weeks on end. We decided we needed to go back and see how 9/11 had changed the lives of the people in our stories." "In many ways, September 11 presented people with the realization the 'American experiment,' as the founders themselves called it, is a fragile thing and that it is important for Americans, as a people, to understand their country and its ideals in order to preserve them," Brewster commented in an *ABCNews.com* interview. "So that's the premise we began with."

Each of the volume's six chapters explores what the authors call an "arena" of American life: race, government, business, immigration, religion, and culture. Jennings and Brewster use case histories, such as a South Carolina school board's interpretation of the separation between church and state "as the community campaigns to build a more 'moral' society," as

Booklist's George Cohen remarked. Though the book had some favorable reviews and a tie-in to the television presentation, *In Search of America* was lost amid a spate of September 11 anniversary books.

For all his special moments and accomplishments, Jennings recalled one encounter on his fiftieth birthday with particular fondness. During a toast, he told Murphy in the *Saturday Evening Post* interview, "A colleague . . . said of me, 'He has got this far and there are no bodies.' That's it for me. I just dissolved. What else would you want anybody to say of you?"

BIOGRAPHICAL AND CRITICAL SOURCES:

BOOKS

Goldberg, Robert, and Gerald Jay Goldberg, *Anchors: Brokaw, Jennings, Rather and the Evening News,* Carol (Secaucus, NJ), 1990.
Matusow, Barbara, *The Evening Stars: The Making of the Network News Anchor,* Houghton Mifflin (Boston, MA), 1983.
Newsmakers 1997, Issue 4, Gale (Detroit, MI), 1997.
St. James Encyclopedia of Popular Culture, St. James Press (Detroit, MI), 2000.

PERIODICALS

Booklist, November 15, 1999, Carolyn Phelan, review of *The Century for Young People,* p. 611; November 22, 1999, Shannon Maugham, "'The Century' Adapted for Kids," p. 23; August, 2002, George Cohen, review of *In Search of America,* p. 1883.
Christian Science Monitor, September 18, 1985.
Detroit Free Press, April 26, 1990.
Economist, December 4, 1999, review of *The Century: America's Time,* p. S5.
Esquire, September, 1989.
Good Housekeeping, April, 1991, p. 46.
Jerusalem Post, November 1, 2000, Andrea Levin, "Eye on the Media."
Jewish World Review, January 6, 2000, Evan Gahr, "Looking Backwards: An Anchorman's Version of the 20th Century."
Knight Ridder/Tribune News Service, October 9, 2002, Paul D. Colford, "Jennings Book Seems to Be First Stumble of Fall Publishing Season," p. K7418.

Maclean's, July 21, 1986.

Newsweek, September 12, 1983.

New York, November 30, 1987.

New York Review of Books, July 15, 1999, Garry Wills, review of *The Century,* p. 24.

New York Times, August 10, 1983; September 9, 1985; September 3, 2002, Neil Genzlinger, "Founding Fathers, How Are You Faring?," p. B5.

New York Times Magazine, July 27, 1986.

Parade, October 15, 1989.

People, August 15, 1983; February 13, 1984; August 30, 1993, p. 48.

Publishers Weekly, November 8, 1999, review of *The Century for Young People,* p. 69; December 13, 1999, Daisy Maryles, "Sequels Rule," p. 19; August 5, 2002, review of *In Search of America,* p. 64, Ron Hogan, "PW Talks with Peter Jennings and Todd Brewster," p. 65.

Rolling Stone, October 9, 1986; May 4, 1989, p. 60.

Saturday Evening Post, November, 1988, p. 42.

TV Guide, November 22, 1997, p. 67.

USA Today (magazine), July, 1999, Robert Rothenberg, review of *The Century,* p. 81.

ONLINE

CNSNews.com, http://www.cnsnews.com/, (May 1, 2003), "Pro-Marxist Slant Pushed at ABC, Retired Correspondent Claims".

ZCPortal, http://www.zcportal.com/, (December 20, 2002), "Ed Koch Commentary: Support of Israel."*

*   *   *

JOHNSTON, Robert Kent 1945-

PERSONAL: Born June 9, 1945, in Pasadena, CA; son of Roy G. (a structural engineer) and Naomi (Harmon) Johnston; married Catherine M. Barsotti; children: Elizabeth, Margaret. *Education:* Stanford University, A.B., 1967; Fuller Theological Seminary, B.D., 1970; attended North Park Theological Seminary, 1970-71; Duke University, Ph.D., 1974. *Politics:* Democrat.

ADDRESSES: Home—730 South Oak Knoll Ave., Pasadena, CA 91106. *Office*—Fuller Theological Seminary, Pasadena, CA 91182. *E-mail*—johnston@fuller.edu.

CAREER: Ordained minister of Evangelical Covenant Church, 1975; youth minister at Evangelical Covenant Church in Pasadena, CA, 1967-69; assistant minister at Evangelical Covenant Church, Chicago, IL, 1970-71; Western Kentucky University, Bowling Green, assistant professor, 1974-78, associate professor of religion, 1978-82. North Park Theological Seminary, Chicago, professor of theology and culture, 1982-93, dean, 1982-88, provost dean, 1988-93; Fuller Theological Seminary, Pasadena, CA, provost, senior vice president of theology and culture, 1993-95, professor of theology and culture, 1993—. Regular Visiting professor at the St. Petersburg Theological Academy, has also served as a visiting professor at New College Berkely and the Stockholm School of Theology.

MEMBER: American Academy of Religion, American Theological Society, Dietrich Bonhoeffer Society, Conference on Christianity and Literature, Phi Beta Kappa.

WRITINGS:

Evangelicals at an Impasse: Biblical Authority in Practice, John Knox Press (Louisville, KY), 1979.

Psalms, Regal Books (Glendale, CA), 1982.

The Christian at Play, Eerdmans (Grand Rapids, MI), 1983.

(Editor) *The Use of the Bible in Theology: Evangelical Options,* John Knox Press (Louisville, KY), 1985.

(Coeditor) *The Variety of American Evangelicalism,* The University of Tennessee Press (Knoxville, TN), 1991.

(Coeditor) *Studies in Old Testament Theology: Historical and Contemporary Images of God and God's People,* World Publishing (Cleveland, OH), 1992.

(Coeditor) *Servant Leadership,* Volumes 1-2, Covenant Publications (Chicago, IL), 1993.

(Coeditor) *Grace upon Grace,* Abingdon (New York, NY), 1999.

Reel Spirituality: Theology and Film in Dialogue, Baker Book House (Grand Rapids, MI), 2000.

Contributor of more than one hundred and fifty chapters, articles and reviews to theology and church journals. General editor of *New Testament Biblical Commentary Series, Old Testament,* Hendrickson, 1995—.

WORK IN PROGRESS: With J. Walker Smith *Life Is Not Work,*, for Wildcat Canyon Press, 2001.

SIDELIGHTS: Robert Kent Johnston worked in Japan for the Evangelical Covenant Church in 1965 and in Geneva, Switzerland, as a financial analyst trainee in 1969. He has studied in Belgium and participated in an archaeological expedition in Meiron, Israel. Johnston told *CA:* "[My] vocational interests include the relationship of Christian theology and culture. This includes particular interests in the movies and theology, the relationship of literature to religion, and the relevance of Old Testament wisdom literature for the contemporary individual."

*   *   *

JONES, Diana Wynne 1934-

PERSONAL: Born August 16, 1934, in London, England; daughter of Richard Aneurin (an educator) and Marjorie (an educator; maiden name, Jackson) Jones; married John A. Burrow (a university professor), December 23, 1956; children: Richard, Michael, Colin. Education: St. Anne's College, Oxford, B.A., 1956.

ADDRESSES: Home—9, The Polygon, Clifton, Bristol B58 4PW, England. *Agent*—Laura Cecil, 17 Alwyne Villas, London N1 2HG, England.

CAREER: Writer, 1965—.

AWARDS, HONORS: Guardian Award, 1977, for *Charmed Life; Boston Globe-Horn Book* Honor Book Award, 1984, for *Archer's Goon; Horn Book* Honor List, 1984, for *Fire and Hemlock; Horn Book* Fanfare List, 1987, for *Howl's Moving Castle;* Mythopoeic Children's Fantasy Award, 1996, for *The Crown of Dalemark.*

WRITINGS:

ADULT FICTION

Changeover, Macmillan (London, England), 1970.
A Sudden Wild Magic, Morrow (New York, NY), 1993.

Diana Wynne Jones

JUVENILE FICTION

Wilkins' Tooth, Macmillan (London, England), 1973, published as *Witch's Business,* Dutton (New York, NY), 1974.
The Ogre Downstairs, Macmillan (London, England), 1974.
Eight Days of Luke, Macmillan (London, England), 1974.
Dogsbody, Greenwillow (New York, NY), 1977.
Power of Three, Greenwillow (New York, NY), 1978.
Who Got Rid of Angus Flint?, illustrated by John Sewell, Evans Brothers (London, England), 1978.
The Four Grannies, illustrated by Thelma Lambert, Hamish Hamilton (London, England), 1980.
The Homeward Bounders, Greenwillow (New York, NY), 1981.
The Skiver's Guide, illustrated by Chris Winn, Knight Books (London, England), 1984.
Warlock at the Wheel and Other Stories, Greenwillow (New York, NY), 1984.
Archer's Goon, (also see below), Greenwillow (New York, NY), 1984.
Fire and Hemlock, Greenwillow (New York, NY), 1985.

Howl's Moving Castle, Greenwillow (New York, NY), 1986.

A Tale of Time City, Greenwillow (New York, NY), 1987.

Castle in the Air, Greenwillow (New York, NY), 1990.

Chair Person, illustrated by Glenys Ambrus, Puffin Books (New York, NY), 1991.

Black Maria, Methuen (London, England), 1991, published as *Aunt Maria,* Greenwillow (New York, NY), 1991.

A Sudden Wild Magic, Morrow (New York, NY), 1992.

Yes, Dear, illustrated by Graham Philpot, Greenwillow (New York, NY), 1992.

Hexwood, Greenwillow (New York, NY), 1993.

The Last Piece of Sky, Douglas & McIntyre (Toronto, Ontario, Canada), 1993.

Mouse in the Manger, Viking (New York, NY), 1993.

The Book of Changes, Douglas & McIntyre (Toronto, Ontario, Canada), 1994, Orchard Books (New York, NY), 1995.

The Time of the Ghost, Greenwillow (New York, NY), 1996.

Stopping for a Spell, Puffin Books (New York, NY), 1996.

The Maestro (novel), Orchard Books (New York, NY), 1996.

The Time of the Ghost, Greenwillow (New York, NY), 1996.

Minor Arcana, Gollancz (London, England), 1996.

The Tough Guide to Fantasyland, Vista (London, England), 1996.

Dark Lord of Derkholm, Greenwillow (New York, NY), 1998.

Deep Secret, Tor (New York, NY), 1999.

Believing Is Seeing: Seven Stories, illustrated by Nenad Jakesevic, Greenwillow (New York, NY), 1999.

Year of the Griffin, Greenwillow (New York, NY), 2000.

Witch's Business, Greenwillow (New York, NY), 2002.

The Merlin Conspiracy, Greenwillow (New York, NY), 2003.

"CHRESTOMANCI" CYCLE; JUVENILES

Charmed Life, Macmillan (London, England), 1977, Greenwillow (New York, NY), 1979.

The Magicians of Caprona (also see below), Greenwillow (New York, NY), 1980.

Witch Week (also see below), Greenwillow (New York, NY), 1982.

The Lives of Christopher Chant (also see below), Greenwillow (New York, NY), 1988.

Chronicles of Chrestomanci (contains *Charmed Life, The Magicians of Caprona, Witch Week,* and *The Lives of Christopher Chant,* HarperCollins (New York, NY), 2001.

Mixed Magics: Four Tales of Chrestomanci, Greenwillow (New York, NY), 2001.

"DALEMARK" CYCLE; JUVENILES

Cart and Cwidder, Macmillan (London, England), 1975, Atheneum (New York, NY), 1977, reprinted, HarperTrophy (New York, NY), 2001.

Drowned Ammet, Macmillan (London, England), 1977, Atheneum (New York, NY), 1978, reprinted, HarperTrophy (New York, NY), 2001.

The Spellcoats, Atheneum (New York, NY), 1979, reprinted, HarperTrophy (New York, NY), 2001.

The Crown of Dalemark, Greenwillow (New York, NY), 1995, reprinted, HarperTrophy (New York, NY), 2001.

JUVENILE PLAYS

The Batterpool Business, first produced in London at Arts Theatre, October, 1968.

The King's Things, first produced in London at Arts Theatre, February, 1970.

The Terrible Fisk Machine, first produced in London at Arts Theatre, January, 1971.

Archer's Goon (adapted from Jones's juvenile book of the same title), first produced on BBC, 1992.

Contributor to books, including *The Cat-Flap and the Apple Pie,* W. H. Allen (London, England), 1979; *Hecate's Cauldron,* DAW Books (New York, NY), 1981; *Hundreds and Hundreds,* Puffin Books (New York, NY), 1984; *Dragons and Dreams,* Harper (New York, NY), 1986; *Guardian Angels,* Viking Kestrel (London, England), 1987; (and editor) *Fantasy Stories,* NESFA, 1995; *Everard's Ride* (miscellany), NESFA, 1995; (and editor) *Hidden Turnings,* Greenwillow (New York, NY).

SIDELIGHTS: Diana Wynne Jones, best known for her "Chrestomanci" cycle of novels, creates works that straddle the line between fantasy and science fiction. Her fans on both sides of the Atlantic include many adults who may have read her earlier works as teens. Jones, influenced by Norse, Greek, and Welsh myth, and by an earlier generation of fantasy writers, has created both stand-alone and series fantasies that innovatively mingle magic and realism. Jane Yolen in the *Washington Post Book World* called Jones "one of those English wonders who can combine wit with wisdom. Her sense of humor weaves in and out of the most absurd plots and twists around outrageous situations with a deftness any vaudevillian would envy." *Booklist* contributor Michael Cart wrote: "To my mind, Diana Wynne Jones is one of the greatest living fantasists; that the knee of every book lover does not bow at the sound of her name has always puzzled me." Cart added that Jones is "a master of the unexpected and never fails to surprise. . . . Her powers of imagination are quite breathtaking, while her ability to create strange, quirky, offbeat, mind-tickling worlds is absolutely astonishing."

Jones as a child endured the outbreak of World War II and her parents' indifference to her. Beginning at age five, she moved frequently with her sisters and her mother, and even after the family settled in rural Essex in 1943 she was neglected and expected to care for her younger siblings. Her father doled out one book a year for the girls to share, and Jones was desperate to read more even though she suffered from dyslexia. At age eight she said she wanted to become a writer, although her family trivialized her ambitions.

After Jones married and had her own children, and the quality of the juvenile fiction she read to her sons disappointed her, she started writing her own stories and novels for children. Two of her early titles, *Wilkins' Tooth* and *The Ogre Downstairs* set the themes and tones of her later works. In both stories, intrepid youngsters must tangle with the supernatural and survive by wit and teamwork. Donna R. White wrote in *Dictionary of Literary Biography:* "An immensely funny book, *The Ogre Downstairs* also explores two of Jones's pervading themes: displacement and alienation."

Jones's neglected childhood inspired her plots, heroes and heroines. A *St. James Guide to Young Adult Writers* contributor said the typical Jones protagonist "is likely to grow up among magical folk, often in an alternative world where history ran differently, or a secondary fantasy world, but this hero/ine feels inadequate because s/he does not appear to have magic powers. Using his/her own resources to cope with the problems magic is causing, at the climax a crisis reveals that our hero/ine does truly possess magic powers, sometimes superior to the others, and certainly unique. . . . Jones's books may be classified as domestic fantasy, as magic disrupts ordinary life, sometimes combined with high fantasy, as gods and goddesses become involved." White wrote that in Jones's imagined worlds, "fathers are usually ineffective, selfish, neglectful, unloving parents. Mothers, while portrayed as negatively as fathers, often ignore their children's needs to pursue their own desires."

The Homeward Bounders, which reflects Jones's originality, is a novel in which "she postulates a fantasy war game that applies to all worlds and times," Sarah Hayes wrote in the *Times Literary Supplement.* The book, a fantasy novel with science fiction elements, "contains terror, humour, adventure, everyday problems of survival and references to mythical characters," added *Times Literary Supplement* contributor Judith Elkin. The story follows the adventures of Jamie, a teenager who accidentally witnesses how the worlds are run while randomly moving among them. Although he makes friends, including the Flying Dutchman, Ahasuerus the Wandering Jew, Prometheus chained to a rock, and several children, he cannot return home unless by accident.

The "Chrestomanci" works are set in a world where the government licenses and supervises magic. The handsome enchanter, Chrestomanci, is the recurring character in a series of loosely related stories, including *Charmed Life, The Lives of Christopher Chant, The Magicians of Caprona,* and *Witch Week.* In each of the four novels the central characters must identify their own talents and learn to make use of them—and of course, some of that talent is put to evil use, leading to conflict. A *St. James Guide to Fantasy Writers* essayist wrote: "That Jones manages to make civil servants interesting to the younger reader is a testimony to her skill; that she does this by boring her young heroes and heroines reinforces this." A *Publishers Weekly* reviewer praised the "exuberant momentum" of the Chrestomanci cycle.

The "Dalemark" series is a darker and more conventional fantasy, set in its own world. The titles *Cart and Cwidder, Drowned Ammett, The Spellcoats,* and *The Crown of Dalemark* are linked, but not chronologically.

Some critics, however, have said this series seems intended for an older audience, as it proves "full of moral uncertainties but retaining the strong sense of adventure and tension," according to the *St. James Guide to Fantasy Writers* contributor.

Jones's many stand-alone novels reflect her comfort in both fantasy and science fiction. An essayist for the *St. James Guide to Science Fiction Writers* observed: "Given the fact . . . that the author herself dislikes genre categories, it should come as no surprise that many of her books deal with themes which, depending on whose eyes they're seen through, would count as science fiction, and a good half dozen of her novels have overt science fictional ideas." Still, the reviewer noted the prevailing theme: "Many of her characters, children and teenagers, through the course of the novel, learn more about their place in their world, or find a new and more appropriate place." Popular titles such as *Sirius, Archer's Goon, A Sudden Wild Magic* and *Hexwood* present otherworldly, sometimes intergalactic, communities as a means to explore social, emotional, and political conventions in the modern world. The *St. James* essayist concluded: "I like to think that for Wynne Jones, science fiction and fantasy are merely two convenient and arbitrary points on a continuum of fiction writing and that she writes as she wishes, and leaves it to others to decide. That would certainly be in keeping with the free literary spirit which pervades these . . . novels."

White concluded: "By reworking her own childhood emotions and experiences, Diana Wynne Jones has created lively, original fantasies built on a foundation of psychological realism. Her neglected young heroes always find personal strength and are usually left in the care of at least one loving adult. Because Jones writes for her own entertainment (and for that of the literature-starved child she once was), she is able to amuse her readers as well, even while challenging them to keep up with her fast-paced, convoluted plots."

In *The Merlin Conspiracy* Arianrhod (Roddy) is a young girl who meets Nick during a magical journey. Mark McCann, on the Web site of Australia's *Sydney Morning Herald,* called the book "a generous serve of pluriversal adventure and rejigged English mythology."

Jones told *CA:* "When I write for children, my first aim is to make a story—as amusing and exciting as possible—such as I wished I could have read as a child. My second aim is equally important. It is to give children—without presuming to instruct them—the benefit of my greater experience. I like to explore the private terrors and troubles which beset children, because they can thereby be shown they are not unique in misery. Children create about a third of their misery themselves. The other two-thirds is [sic] caused by adults—inconsiderate, mysterious, and often downright frightening adults. I put adults like this in my stories, in some firmly contemporary situation beset with very real problems, and explore the implications by means of magic and old myths. What I am after is an exciting—and exacting—wisdom, in which contemporary life and potent myth are intricately involved and superimposed. I would like children to discover that potent old truths are as much part of everyone's daily life as are—say—the days of the week."

BIOGRAPHICAL AND CRITICAL SOURCES:

BOOKS

Authors and Artists for Young Adults, Gale (Detroit, MI), 1989.
Dictionary of Literary Biography, Volume 161: *British Children's Writers since 1960,* Gale (Detroit, MI), 1996, pp. 225-232.
Holtze, Sally Holmes, editor, *Fifth Book of Junior Authors,* Wilson (New York, NY), pp. 166-167.
Reading for the Love of It: Best Books for Young Readers, Prentice-Hall (Englewood Cliffs, NJ), 1987.
St. James Guide to Fantasy Writers, St. James (Detroit, MI), 1996.
St. James Guide to Science Fiction Writers, 4th edition, St. James (Detroit, MI), 1996.
St. James Guide to Young Adult Writers, 2nd edition, St. James (Detroit, MI), 1999.

PERIODICALS

Booklist, October 15, 1984, p. 300; June 1, 1986, p. 1455; April 15, 1987, p. 1274; October 1, 1988, p. 320; January 1, 1990, p. 906; March 15, 1991, p. 1503; January 15, 1992, p. 873; March 15, 1992, pp. 1364, 1372; June 1, 1994, p. 1803; April 15, 2001, Michael Cart, "Fantasy Is Flourishing," p. 1546.
Book Window, spring, 1978.

British Book News Children's Books, winter, 1987, Fiona Lafferty, "Realms of Fantasy: An Interview with Diana Wynne Jones," pp. 2-5.

Bulletin of the Center for Children's Books, July-August, 1975.

Chicago Tribune Book World, November 4, 1982.

Globe and Mail (Toronto), July 12, 1986.

Growing Point, May, 1974; April, 1975; October, 1975; December, 1975; March, 1978; May, 1981; January, 1982; November, 1982; March, 1986, p. 4580; March, 1987, p. 4772; September, 1990, p. 5395; September, 1991, p. 5584.

Horn Book, August, 1980; January, 1985, p. 58; May, 1986, p. 331; March, 1988, p. 208; March, 1991, p. 206; May, 1994, p. 345; May, 2001, review of *Mixed Magics: Four Tales of Chrestomanci,* p. 327.

Junior Bookshelf, August 1979; August, 1980; October, 1981; February, 1982; December, 1982; February, 1986, p. 42; October, 1987, p. 235; October, 1990, p. 245; April, 1994, p. 69.

Los Angeles Times, January 31, 1987; September, 1990, p. 37.

New Statesman, May 24, 1974; May 20, 1977; October 10, 1986, p. 30.

New York Times Book Review, May 5, 1974; April 19, 1992, p. 16.

Observer, November 25, 1984, p. 27; December 1, 1985, p. 20; December 13, 1987, p. 22.

Publishers Weekly, February 22, 1991, Kit Alderdice, "Diana Wynne Jones," pp. 201-202; October 19, 1998, review of *Dark Lord of Derkholm,* p. 82; October 16, 2000, review of *Year of the Griffin,* p. 77; April 23, 2001, review of *Mixed Magics,* p. 79; "For Diana Wynne Jones Fans," p. 79.

School Librarian, June, 1978; December, 1982.

School Library Journal, April, 1974; April, 1978; September, 1988, p. 184; April, 1991, p. 141; October, 1991, p. 142; March, 1994, p. 236; July, 2001, Patricia A. Dollisch, review of *Mixed Magics,* p. 110.

Spectator, June 30, 1979.

Times (London), May 1, 1986.

Times Educational Supplement, November 18, 1977; November 30, 1979; April 18, 1980; November 23, 1984, p. 38; October 24, 1986, p. 24; February 5, 1988, p. 58; November 9, 1990, p. R11; November 8, 1991, p. 38.

Times Literary Supplement, March 12, 1970; April 6, 1973; July 5, 1974; April 4, 1975; July 11, 1975; April 2, 1976; March 25, 1977; April 7, 1978; March 28, 1980; September 19, 1980; March 25,

1981; March 27, 1981; November 20, 1981; July 23, 1982; October 19, 1984; November 29, 1985; January 31, 1986; December 12, 1986; November 20-26, 1987; July 12, 1991, p. 20.

Use of English, summer, 1983, Gillian Spraggs, "True Dreams: The Fantasy Fiction of Diana Wynne Jones," pp. 17-22.

U.S. News and World Report, November 29, 1999, Holly J. Morris, "Mad about Harry? Try Diana," p. 80.

Washington Post Book World, May 13, 1984; May 12, 1985; May 11, 1986; June 14, 1987; November 8, 1987; February 11, 1990, p. 12; May 13, 1990, p. 18; May 12, 1991, p. 14; May 8, 1994, pp. 17, 19.

World of Children's Books, spring, 1978.

ONLINE

Sydney Morning Herald Web site, http://www.smh.com.au/ (May 24, 2003), Mark McCann, review of *The Merlin Conspiracy.**

*   *   *

JONES, Laurie Beth 1952-

PERSONAL: Born October 15, 1952, in El Paso, TX. *Ethnicity:* "Caucasian." *Religion:* Methodist.

ADDRESSES: Office—609 East Blacker Avenue, El Paso, TX 79902. *Agent*—Julie Castiglia, Castiglia Agency, 1155 Camino del Mar, No. 510, Del Mar, CA 92014. *E-mail*—ljones@elp.rr.com.

CAREER: U.S. Congress, Washington, DC, intern, 1970-71; Georgia State University, administrative assistant, 1974-75; YMCA, El Paso, TX, public relations director, 1975-76, women's information director, 1976-81; Jones Group (marketing, business, and leadership development firm), founder and president. Motivational speaker at businesses, educational institutions, and places of worship.

MEMBER: American Women in Radio and TV (president, El Paso chapter, 1981), Women in Communications, National Association of Female Executives.

AWARDS, HONORS: Outstanding Young Woman of America, 1981; Advertising Federation for Broadcast, Print, Copywriting, 1981-82; Notable Women of Texas, 1983.

WRITINGS:

Jesus, CEO: Using Ancient Wisdom for Visionary Leadership, Hyperion (New York, NY), 1996.

The Path: Creating Your Mission Statement for Work and for Life, Hyperion (New York, NY), 1996.

Jesus in Blue Jeans: A Practical Guide to Everyday Spirituality, Hyperion (New York, NY), 1997.

Grow Something besides Old: Seeds for a Joyful Life, Simon & Schuster (New York, NY), 1998.

The Power of Positive Prophecy: Finding the Hidden Potential in Everyday Life, Hyperion (New York, NY), 1999.

Jesus, Inc.: Doing Well by Doing Right: An Entrepreneur's Guide, Crown Business (New York, NY), 2001.

Jesus, Entrepreneur: Using Ancient Wisdom to Launch and Live Your Dreams, Crown Business (New York, NY), 2001.

Teach Your Team to Fish: Using Ancient Wisdom for Inspired Teamwork, Crown Business (New York, NY), 2002.

Also author of *The Tool Box* (poems) and *Horizons.*

SIDELIGHTS: Laurie Beth Jones is president and founder of the Jones Group, an advertising, marketing, and business development firm whose mission is "to recognize, promote, and inspire divine excellence." She has written several best-selling books, including *Jesus, CEO: Using Ancient Wisdom for Visionary Leadership, The Path: Creating Your Mission Statement for Work and for Life,* and *Jesus in Blue Jeans: A Practical Guide to Everyday Spirituality.* Jones once told *CA* that her primary motivation for writing is "to express what I know and feel." The primary influence and inspiration in her life has been the Christian Gospel.

In *Jesus, CEO* Jones delivers lessons from the New Testament that can empower business leaders to succeed. She analyzes Bible stories and discovers in them an approach to motivating and managing others. Owning and operating a business firm herself, Jones understands the problems in running a company. Tom DePoto of the Newark, New Jersey, *Star-Ledger* noted that "Her entertaining observations can motivate the mogul and the minions to find the better bottom line spiritually as well as fiscally."

Jones again finds inspiration in the Bible to illustrate how its teachings are relevant to the business world in *Jesus in Blue Jeans.* Drawing from personal reflections and offering samples from the New Testament, the author adapts the words of Jesus in ways that can be used in our day-to-day lives. Each chapter presents a daily flow of meditative action to help readers achieve their highest goals and aspirations. According to DePoto, "her style is engaging and breezy with enough personal details and humor that make it easy to be swept along."

Jones's *The Power of Positive Prophecy: Finding the Hidden Potential in Everyday Life* refers to the power in words, particularly when used positively to encourage others. To pursue our goals and fulfill out potentials, Jones urges readers to bring all their passion and creativity to the workplace. Combining management know-how and practical guidance, her book demonstrates how the language of prophecy can create more productive lives. According to a critic for *Publishers Weekly,* "with the help of sample prayers and reflective questions, she encourages readers to recognize and benefit from prophecy in all its forms."

Jones hopes to help the new breed of entrepreneur find satisfaction with the soul in *Jesus, Inc.: Doing Well by Doing Right: An Entrepreneur's Guide.* As she did in her other best-selling inspirational books, the author argues that it is possible to earn a great deal of money without compromising one's Christian beliefs.

Teach Your Team to Fish: Using Ancient Wisdom for Inspired Teamwork features several stories from the Bible in which Jones utilizes the teachings of Jesus as models for resolving management issues and building team work in the business world. Managers are responsible for setting the standards that help employees accomplish their goals. To foster improved performance, Jones advocates the use of prayer and welcomes diversity as a means of bringing people together. According to a *Publishers Weekly* contributor, "her fans will devour this book." Each chapter includes prayers and questions for self-evaluation.

BIOGRAPHICAL AND CRITICAL SOURCES:

PERIODICALS

Booklist, January 1, 1995, review of *Jesus, CEO: Using Ancient Wisdom for Visionary Leadership;* March 1, 2001, review of *Jesus, Inc.: Doing Well by Doing Right: An Entrepreneur's Guide,* p. 1214.
Fortune, July 9, 2001, review of *Jesus, CEO,* p. 136H.
Gazette (Colorado Springs, CO), April 9, 2001, review of *Jesus, Inc.,* p. B3.
Guardian (London, England), May 1, 2001, review of *Jesus, Inc.,* p. 11.
Inc., April 1, 2001, review of *Jesus, Inc.,* p. 103.
Knight-Ridder/Tribune News Services, July 5, 2001, Cecil Johnson, review of *Jesus, Inc.,* p. K5789; June 20, 2002, Dan Lee, review of *Teach Your Team to Fish: Using Ancient Wisdom for Inspired Teamwork,* p. K0152.
Publishers Weekly, August 25, 1997, review of *Jesus in Blue Jeans: A Practical Guide to Everyday Spirituality,* p. 65; August 16, 1999, review of *The Power of Positive Prophecy: Finding the Hidden Potential in Everyday Life,* p. 69; April 23, 2001, review of *Jesus, Inc.,* p. 61; March 25, 2002, review of *Teach Your Team to Fish,* p. 54.
Star-Ledger (Newark, NJ), August 31, 1997, Tom DePoto, review of *Jesus, CEO,* p. 8; August 31, 1997, Tom DePoto, review of *Jesus in Blue Jeans,* p.8.
Wall Street Journal, July 30, 2001, review of *Jesus, Inc.,* p. A17.

ONLINE

Postfun.com, http://www.postfun.com/ (June 4, 2002), Ron Hogan, review of *Jesus, CEO.*

*   *   *

JONES, P(eter) M(ichael) 1949-

PERSONAL: Born April 19, 1949, in Birmingham, England; son of Ronald Arthur and Ethel Constance (Jesper) Jones; married Carolyn Margot Ford (a school teacher), August 3, 1973; children: Nicholas, Anna, Isobel. *Education:* University of Leeds, B.A. (with honors), 1970; Oxford University, D.Phil., 1977; attended University of Toulouse le Mirail, 1971-72.

ADDRESSES: Office—Department of Modern History, University of Birmingham, Edgbaston, Birmingham B15 2TT, England.

CAREER: University of Leicester, Leicester, England, tutorial assistant, 1973-74; University of Birmingham, Birmingham, England, lecturer in history, 1974-88, reader in French history, 1988-95, professor of French history, 1995—.

WRITINGS:

Politics and Rural Society: The Southern Massif Central, ca. 1750-1880, Cambridge University Press (Cambridge, England), 1985.
The Peasantry in the French Revolution, Cambridge University Press (Cambridge, England), 1988.
Reform and Revolution in France, 1774-1791: An Essay in the Politics of Transition, Cambridge University Press (Cambridge, England), 1995.
(Editor) *The French Revolution in Social and Political Perspective,* E. Allen, 1996.

WORK IN PROGRESS: A comparative history of six French villages c. 1760-1820.

SIDELIGHTS: P. M. Jones once told *CA:* "My fascination with things French developed in the 1960s as a result of camping holidays spent on the Atlantic coast. My professional connection with France dates back to 1970, when I began doctoral research under the guidance of Richard Cobb, an Oxford-based historian of France. As the student of an endangered species (the French peasantry), I elected to trace it to one of its last known habitats—the Massif Central. The result was my first book, which explores the impact of a century of political change on the country dwellers of southern central France. This was followed by a textbook study of the peasantry during the revolution and a number of other works."

K

KELLERT, Stephen R. 1944-

PERSONAL: Born October 10, 1944, in New Haven, CT; married Priscilla W. (a teacher), October 31, 1981; children: Emily, Libby. *Education:* Received B.S. from Cornell University and Ph.D. from Yale University.

ADDRESSES: Home—57 Edgehill Rd., New Haven, CT 06511. *Office*—205 Prospect St., New Haven, CT 06511.

CAREER: Yale University, New Haven, CT, 1972—, began as assistant professor, became associate professor and later professor.

AWARDS, HONORS: Has received awards from the Society for Conservation Biology, National Wildlife Federation, and Foundation for Environmental Conservation.

WRITINGS:

Ecology, Economics, Ethics, Yale University Press (New Haven, CT), 1991.
(Coauthor) *The Biophilia Hypothesis,* Island Press (Washington, DC), 1993.
The Value of Life, Island Press (Washington, DC), 1996.
Kinship to Mastery: Biophilia in Human Evolution and Development, Island Press/Shearwater Books (Washington, DC), Fisher-Verlag (Frankfurt, Germany), 1997.

KESSLER-HARRIS, Alice 1941-

PERSONAL: Born June 2, 1941, in Leicester, England; immigrated to the United States, 1955; daughter of Zoltan and Ilona (Elefant) Kessler; married Jay Evans Harris, August 28, 1960 (divorced, 1972); married Bertram Silverman, January 22, 1982; children: (first marriage) Ilona Kay; stepchildren: Julie and Devorah. *Education:* Goucher College, B.A. (cum laude), 1961; Rutgers University, M.A., 1963, Ph.D., 1968. *Hobbies and other interests:* Cooking, tennis, theater, gardening.

ADDRESSES: Home—610 West 116th St., New York, NY 10027. *Office*—Department of History, Columbia University, New York, NY 10027. *E-mail*—ak571@ columbia.edu.

CAREER: Teacher at public schools in Baltimore, MD, 1961-62; Rutgers University, New Brunswick, NJ, assistant instructor at Douglass College, 1964-65; Hofstra University, Hempstead, NY, assistant professor, 1968-73, associate professor, 1976-81, professor of history, 1981-88, co-director of Center for the Study of Work and Leisure, 1976-88; Sarah Lawrence College, Bronxville, NY, professor of history and women's studies and director of Women's Studies Program, 1974-76; Temple University, Philadelphia, PA, professor of history, 1988-90; Rutgers University, professor of history, 1990-1999, director of Women's Studies Program, 1990-95; Columbia University, New York, NY, professor of history, 1999-2001, Gordon Hoxie Professor of American History, 2001—. University of Warwick, visiting senior lecturer, 1979-80; State University of New York at Binghamton, visiting professor,

1985; New School for Social Research, research associate at Center for Studies of Social Change, 1989-90; Swedish Collegium for Advanced Study in the Social Sciences, visiting fellow, 1991; Institute for Social Research, Oslo, Norway, research associate, 1995-96; Swedish Collegium for Advanced Study in the Social Sciences, fellow, 1997; Radcliffe Institute for Advanced Study, fellow, 2001-02. Columbia University, member of Seminar in American Civilization, 1971—, member of Seminar on Women in Society, 1975—, chair, 1983-84. Pulitzer Prize in History, member of nominating committee, 1987. Consultant to organizations.

MEMBER: American Association of University Professors, American Historical Association (chair, committee on women historians, 1984-86), Organization of American Historians, American Studies Association (member of executive council, 1973-78; chair of international committee, 1982-83; president, 1990-91), American Civil Liberties Union (member of academic freedom committee, 1971-77), American Council of Learned Societies (reader in fellowship program, 1988), Coordinating Committee of Women in the Historical Profession, Berkshire Conference of Women Historians, New York State Council for the Humanities (member of Speakers' Bureau, 1982—).

AWARDS, HONORS: Grants from Danforth Foundation Auxiliary, 1962-63, Louis M. Rabinowitz Foundation, 1973-74, and American Philosophical Society, 1973-74; fellow, National Endowment for the Humanities, 1976-77, 1985-86; Bunting Institute fellow, Radcliffe College, 1977; Philip Taft Prize for the best book in labor history, 1982, for *Out to Work: A History of Wage-Earning Women in the U.S.;* travel grant from American Council of Learned Societies, 1986; fellow, Rockefeller Foundation, 1988-89, and John Simon Guggenheim Memorial Foundation, 1989-90; John B. Commerford Award for Labor Education, 1991; LL. D., Goucher College, 1991; D.Lett., Uppsala University, 1995; Fulbright award for Australia and New Zealand, 1995; Bancroft Prize, and Herbert Hoover Book Award, both 2002, both for *In Pursuit of Equity: Women, Men, and the Quest for Economic Citizenship in Twentieth-Century America.*

WRITINGS:

(Editor, with Blanche Cook and Ronald Radosh) *Past Imperfect: Alternative Essays in American History,* Random House (New York, NY), 1972.

(Author of introduction) William Ladd, *On the Duty of Females to Promote the Cause of Peace,* Garland Publishing (New York, NY), 1972.

(Author of introduction) George Cone Beckwith, *The Peace Manual; or, War and Its Remedies,* Garland Publishing (New York, NY), 1972.

(Author of introduction) Theodore Parker, *Sermon of War,* Garland Publishing (New York, NY), 1973.

(Author of introduction) Ronald Grele, editor, *Envelopes of Sound: Six Practitioners Discuss the Theory and Method of Oral History,* Precedent Publishing (Chicago, IL), 1975, revised edition, 1985.

(Author of introduction) Anzia Yezierska, *Bread Givers,* Braziller (New York, NY), 1975.

(Editor and author of introduction) *The Open Cage: An Anzia Yezierska Collection,* Persea Books (New York, NY), 1979.

Women Have Always Worked, Feminist Press (Old Westbury, NY), 1980.

Out to Work: A History of Wage-Earning Women in the U.S., Oxford University Press (Oxford, England), 1982.

(Coauthor of introduction) Joan Kelly, *Women, History and Theory,* University of Chicago Press (Chicago, IL), 1984.

(Editor, with Judith Friedlander, Blanche Cook, and Carroll Smith-Rosenberg) *Women in Culture and Politics: A Century of Change,* Indiana University Press (Bloomington, IN), 1986.

(Editor, with William McBrien) *Faith of a Woman Writer: Essays in Twentieth-Century Literature,* Greenwood Press (Westport, CT), 1988.

(Editor, with Carroll Moody) *Perspectives on American Labor History: The Problem of Synthesis,* Northern Illinois University Press (DeKalb, IL), 1990.

A Woman's Wage: Historical Meanings and Social Consequences, University Press of Kentucky (Lexington, KY), 1990.

(Editor, with Ulla Wikander and Jane Lewis) *Protecting Women: Labor Legislation in Europe, Australia, and the United States, 1880-1920,* University of Illinois Press (Champaign, IL), 1995.

(Editor, with Linda Kerber and Kathryn Sklar) *U.S. History As Women's History,* University of North Carolina Press (Chapel Hill, NC), 1996.

In Pursuit of Equity: Women, Men, and the Quest for Economic Citizenship in Twentieth-Century America, Oxford University Press (Oxford, England), 2001.

Contributor to books, including *The Study of American History,* Volume 2, edited by Ernest Hohlnitz, Dushkin (Guilford, CT), 1974; *Cooperative History of the United States,* Dushkin (Guilford, CT), 1974; *Labor Market Segmentation,* edited by Richard Edwards and others, Lexington Books (Lexington, MA), 1975; *Liberating Women's History: Theoretical and Critical Essays,* edited by Berenice Carroll, University of Illinois Press (Champaign, IL), 1976; *Class, Sex and the Woman Worker,* edited by Milton Cantor and Bruce Laurie, Greenwood Press, 1977; *American Ethnic Groups,* edited by Thomas Sowell, Urban Institute (Washington, DC), 1978; *American Character and Culture,* edited by John Hague, revised edition, Greenwood Press (Westport, CT), 1979; *A Heritage of Her Own,* edited by Nancy Cott and Elizabeth Pleck, Simon & Schuster (New York, NY), 1979; *Notable American Women* (supplement), edited by Barbara Sicherman, Harvard University Press (Cambridge, MA), 1979; *Report from the Front Lines,* edited by Wendy Chavkin, Monthly Review Press (New York, NY), 1984; *Women, Work and Protest: A Century of Women's Labor History,* edited by Ruth Milkman, Routledge & Kegan Paul, 1985; *Woman and Work: An Annual Review,* edited by Laurie Larwood, and others, Sage Publications (Beverly Hills, CA), 1985; *Sisters and Solidarity: Workers Education for Women, 1914-1980,* edited by Joyce Kornbluh and Mary Frederickson, Temple University Press (Philadelphia, PA), 1985; *Women, Households, and the Economy,* edited by Lourdes Beneria and Catharine R. Stimpson, Rutgers University Press (New Brunswick, NJ), 1987; *Labor Leaders in America,* edited by Melvyn Dubovsky and Warren Van Tine, University of Illinois Press (Champaign, IL), 1987; *Class and the Feminist Imagination,* edited by Karen Hansen and Ilene Philipson, Temple University Press (Philadelphia, PA), 1989; and *Days of Destiny: Crossroads in American History,* edited by James McPherson and Alan Brinkley, [New York, NY], 2001.

Coeditor of the series "Working Class in American History," University of Illinois Press (Champaign, IL), 1985—. Contributor of articles and reviews to periodicals, including *Science and Society, Signs, Ms., Reviews in American History, Women's Review of Books, Nation,* and *New York Times Book Review.* Member of editorial board, *Labor History,* 1983-98, *Journal of American History,* 1985-88, *Feminist Studies, Women and History,* and *Gender and History.*

WORK IN PROGRESS: Gender and Culture: Reviewing the Historical Paradigm, for University of North Carolina Press; a political biography on Lillian Hellman.

SIDELIGHTS: Among historian Alice Kessler-Harris's most important contributions is the demonstration of the inseparability of United States labor history from women's history. Through her research and analysis, she has delineated changing attitudes toward women wage earners and the subsequent results of these attitudes as shown in legislation and social policy.

Kessler-Harris has published extensively. She is the editor and author of several books and has many articles and essays to her credit. Her teaching career has been active. She has taught at colleges and universities in the United States and abroad. She is now on the history faculty of Columbia University. In addition to her roles as teacher and writer, she participated in the development of the Labor College for District 65 of the United Auto Workers and was instrumental in building the women's studies program at Rutgers University.

Kessler-Harris's book *In Pursuit of Equity: Women, Men, and the Quest for Economic Citizenship in Twentieth-Century America,* argues that women cannot participate fully in the political process until they are economically independent. Through careful examination of the tax structure and social policies from the 1930s to the middle of the 1970s, the author shows how policies constructed to protect women actually denied them full economic citizenship by being based on deeply ingrained attitudes about women in the working world. Dale Farris, reviewing the work in *Library Journal,* felt that Kessler-Harris "succeeds in showing how gender has shaped the rules by which we live." Other than this main topic of discussion, a *Publishers Weekly* reviewer concluded that *In Pursuit of Equity* "is also a refreshingly compact and useful primer on [fifty] years of employment legislation."

BIOGRAPHICAL AND CRITICAL SOURCES:

PERIODICALS

Booklist, August, 2001, David Rouse, review of *In Pursuit of Equity: Women, Men, and the Quest for Economic Citizenship in Twentieth-Century America,* p. 2059.

Library Journal, December, 2001, Dale Farris, review of *In Pursuit of Equity,* p. 144.

Nation, July 22, 2002, Linda Gordon, review of *In Pursuit of Equity,* pp. 31-34.

Publishers Weekly, October 29, 2001, review of *In Pursuit of Equity,* p. 56.

Reference Services Review, Volume 26, review of *Out to Work: A History of Wage-Earning Women in the U.S.,* p. 33.

Women's Review of Books, January, 2002, Ruth Sidel, review of *In Pursuit of Equity,* pp. 15-17.

*   *   *

KHALVATI, Mimi 1944-

PERSONAL: Born April 28, 1944, in Tehran, Iran; daughter of Mostafa Khalvati and Malih Samii; married, c. 1963 (divorced, c. 1965); married, 1970, (divorced, 1985). children: two. *Education:* Attended a boarding school on the Isle of Wight, the University of Neuchatel (Switzerland), the Drama Centre, London, and the School of African and Oriental Studies, University of London. *Politics:* Feminist. *Religion:* None.

ADDRESSES: Home—2 North Hill Ave., London N6 4RJ, England.

CAREER: Poet, actress, and theatrical director. Theatre Workshop, Tehran, Iran, actress and director, before 1979; Theatre in Exile, London, England, co-founder; Matrix (women's experimental theater group), London, England, founder; Slade Poetry School, London, England, director; Poetry Centre, Manchester University, Manchester, England, faculty member. Visiting lecturer, Goldsmiths College; workshop facilitator, Poetry Society; poet in residence, Royal Mail, 2000; freelance tutor and poetry translator.

MEMBER: Blue Nose Poets.

AWARDS, HONORS: Poetry Business Pamphlet award, 1989; Peterloo Poets Afro-Caribbean/Asian Prize, 1990; Orbis Rhyme International award, 1992; Arts Council of England Writer's Award, 1994.

WRITINGS:

I Know a Place (for children), Dent (London, England), 1985.

Persian Miniatures/A Belfast Kiss (poems), Smith/Doorstop (Huddersfield, England), 1990.

In White Ink (poems), Carcanet (Manchester, England), 1991.

Mirrorwork (poems), Carcanet (Manchester, England), 1995.

Entries on Light (poems), Carcanet (Manchester, England), 1997.

Selected Poems, Carcanet (Manchester, England), 2000.

(Editor, with Pascale Petit) *Tying the Song: A First Anthology from the Poetry School, 1997-2000,* Enitharmon Press (London, England), 2000.

The Chine (poems), Carcanet (Manchester, England), 2001.

Work represented in anthologies, including *Anvil New Poets,* edited by Graham Fawcett, Anvil Press (London, England), 1990; *New Women Poets,* edited by Carol Rumens, Bloodaxe Books (Newcastle-upon-Tyne, England), 1990; *Sixty Women Poets,* edited by Linda France, Bloodaxe Books (Newcastle-upon-Tyne, England), 1993; *The Forward Book of Poetry,* Forward Publishing (London, England), 1993.

WORK IN PROGRESS: "Shorter poems that stand up on their own two feet rather than in a sequence or series."

SIDELIGHTS: Iranian-born British author Mimi Khalvati is probably best known for her poetry; her works include *Entries on Light,* a book-length poem about how light affects the way one sees the world, and *The Chine,* in which Khalvati explores her childhood on the Isle of Wight. Khalvati did not begin writing poems until later in her career. She worked in the theater until age forty-two, when she decided to take a class in script writing. By some mistake, she was enrolled in a poetry writing class instead. "They said, 'Oh, go and write a poem,'" she recalled in an interview with Vicki Bertram. "I'm always very obedient, so off I went and wrote a poem! And they said, 'Oh, this is all right. Well, carry on writing poems.' So I went, 'Oh, all right, I'll carry on writing. . . .' I mean, it really was like that. It was weird." Within a few years, Khalvati had decided to devote all of her energy to poetry.

Khalvati was born in Iran, but at the age of six she was sent to the Isle of Wight to attend boarding school. Her parents were separated, and it was all her single mother, a bank employee, could do to pay the school fees, so it was many years before Khalvati could return to Iran for a visit. She soon forgot how to speak Persian, and when she finally did return home for a vacation at age fourteen, "I went and met all these strange people who were family, and I couldn't speak the language," she recalled to Bertram. "It was difficult."

Khalvati returned to Iran when she was seventeen. She had wanted to go to an English university, but her mother couldn't afford it, so she moved home and became a secretary at an oil company. At nineteen, she married a much older man. He was "very Westernised," she recalled to Bertram, "until, of course, the day we were married, at which point he immediately reverted to 'Me Tarzan, you Jane'!" They divorced when Khalvati was twenty-one.

Khalvati then returned to England. She attended the Drama Centre in London and began to work as an actress. A year later, she married an English actor and moved back to Tehran. They stayed there for four years, working in the theater, and only returned to England when their daughter was born. Khalvati eventually divorced her husband, but she continued working in theater until she began her career as a poet.

Mirrorwork, Khalvati's third collection of poetry, was described as "very beautiful and highly demanding" by Christina Patterson in a review for *New Statesman & Society.* In this volume, Khalvati examines her identities—Iranian, British, female, exile—as well as debating philosophical questions about perception and truth. The work has "a depth and complexity beneath their lyrical surface that demands and rewards rereading," concluded Patterson.

In 2002 Khalvati's *Selected Poems* was published, including all of *Entries on Light* as well as selections from *In White Ink* and *Mirrorwork.* Reviewing the collection in *World Literature Today,* Bruce King observed, "A feminist ideology infuses this poetry without becoming polemics or slogans. There is a seriousness in craft as well as in tone and in what it treats." Ranking Khalvati as "one of the best" poets in England, King further remarked, "She not only has traditional poetic technique at her fingertips, but has learned to give form and structure to much of what is thought of as free verse."

Khalvati discussed the content and lyrical nature of her poetry with *Magma* contributor Mary MacRae: "I'm never actually interested much in content, either

in what I read or in my own writing, but I love the way language is used. . . . I suppose I'm tempted to say that [form] is what the poem is for me. I feel that once you've found the form—and that could be in free verse, not necessarily in metrical or fixed forms—but once a poem has found its form it's almost found itself, and then it's more like filling in. . . . I think working with forms is very creative and not just finding the right-sized box to put something in, as is sometimes thought."

BIOGRAPHICAL AND CRITICAL SOURCES:

BOOKS

Stringer, Jenny, editor, *The Oxford Companion to Twentieth-Century Literature in English,* Oxford University Press (New York, NY), 1996.

PERIODICALS

New Statesman & Society, May 19, 1995, review of *Mirrorwork,* p. 40.
Poetry Review, spring, 1992, p. 73.
Times Literary Supplement, May 10, 1991, Tim Dooley, review of *Persian Miniatures/A Belfast Kiss,* p. 23; August 14, 1992, Robert Potts, review of *In White Ink,* p. 20; March 1, 1996, review of *Mirrorwork,* p. 29; November 17, 2000, John Greening, review of *Selected Poems,* p. 24.
World Literature Today, winter, 2002, Bruce King, review of *Selected Poems,* pp. 152-153.

ONLINE

BBC Radio 3, http://www.bbc.co.uk/ (April 17, 2002), "Poetry Proms: Biographies: Mimi Khalvati."
Carcanet, http://www.carcanet.co.uk/ (February 28, 2001), Vicki Bertram, "Mimi Khalvati in Conversation."
Cyber Iran, http://www.cyberiran.com/ (April 17, 2002), Susan MacDonald, "The Price of Success Far from Home."
Magma, http://www.champignon.net/Magma/ (autumn, 2000), Mary MacRae, "A Certain Kind of Energy" (interview with Khalvati).
Poetry Class, http://www.poetryclass.net/ (August 31, 2002), Jean Sprackland, interview with Khalvati.*

KINCAID, Nanci 1950-

PERSONAL: Born September 5, 1950, in Tallahassee, FL; daughter of William Henry Pierce (an educator) and Lois (a teacher; maiden name, Swingle) Pierce Cannon; married first husband (a football coach; divorced); married Dick Tomey (a football coach), February 14, 1997; children: (first marriage) two daughters. *Education:* Athens State College, B.A., 1987; University of Alabama, M.F.A. (fiction writing), 1991. *Politics:* Democrat. *Hobbies and other interests:* Gardening, nesting, traveling.

ADDRESSES: Agent—Betsy Lerner, Genert Agency, New York, NY 10013. *E-mail*—npkincaid@aol.com.

CAREER: University of Alabama, Tuscaloosa, creative writing and literature instructor, 1987-91; University of North Carolina, Charlotte, creative writing and literature instructor, 1992-96; University of Arizona, Tucson, instructor of English, 1999—. Panelist at Southern Literacy Festival, 1992, and 1997, and Writers Today Conference, 1992; keynote speaker, Eudora Welty Writer's Conference, 1993; visiting writer, Meridian Community College, Meridian, MI, 1994; presenter, North Carolina Writer's Network, 1995.

AWARDS, HONORS: Herbert L. Hughes Fiction Award, The Rectangle, 1986-87; W. B. Yeats Writer's Award, Athens State College, 1987; Fiction Award, Southern Literacy Festival, 1987; Virginia Center for Creative Arts fellowship, 1989; Teaching Writing fellowship, University of Alabama, 1990; University of Alabama graduate council fellowship, 1990-91; National Endowment for the Arts grant, 1991; MacDowell Colony fellowship, 1993, Yaddo fellowship, 1989 and 1994; Bunting fellowship, Radcliffe College, 1994-95; Emerging Artist Award, Alabama Fine Arts Society, 1996.

WRITINGS:

NOVELS

Crossing Blood, Putnam (New York, NY), 1992.
Balls, Algonquin Books (Chapel Hill, NC), 1998.
Verbena, Algonquin Books (Chapel Hill, NC), 2002.

OTHER

Pretending the Bed Is a Raft (short stories), Algonquin Books (Chapel Hill, NC), 1997.

Contributor of short stories to anthologies, including *New Stories from the South: The Year's Best, 1991,* edited by Shannon Ravenel, Algonquin Books, 1991; *New Stories from the South: The Year's Best, 1994,* edited by Ravenel, Algonquin Books, 1994; and *Short Stories of the American South.* Contributor of short stories and poetry to periodicals, including *Carolina Quarterly, Missouri Review, Ontario Review, Oxford American, Southern Exposure,* and *Southern Humanities Review.*

SIDELIGHTS: Nanci Kincaid grew up in Tallahassee, Florida, and married at age nineteen. Her two daughters were nearly grown when she returned to school to earn a bachelor's degree from Athens State College and a master's degree in fiction writing from the University of Alabama. Her poetry and short stories have been published in periodicals and anthologies, and Kincaid has taught creative writing at the college level.

Kincaid's novel *Crossing Blood* is a coming-of-age tale set in the American South during the 1960s. "Kincaid's adept characterization, blend of humor and pathos, and ear for dialogue mark this promising debut novel," wrote *Publishers Weekly* contributor Sybil Steinberg. The novel's narrator is adolescent Lucy Conyers, whose white family lives on the edge of French Town, a region of Tallahassee consisting mostly of African-American residents. Lucy's mother advocates racial equality while her stepfather does not. Lucy has an older brother, Roy, and a younger brother, Benny, and her brothers' best friends are two African-American boys who live nearby. Benny's friends are the sons of Melvina Williams, a woman who keeps house for the Conyers family. Melvina is the mother of four other children and is married to an alcoholic and abusive husband. Lucy's mother attempts to make up for white racism by helping Melvina's children, and in doing so, jeopardizes her marriage. Reviewing *Crossing Blood* in the *New York Times Book Review,* Steven Stark concluded: "It's easy to wish that Ms. Kincaid had taken more risks with her characters, that the narrative had been more concise. Still, she offers a fresh, honest, and complex portrait of love and hate in the South of the 1960s."

"Eight exquisite examples of great short story writing" is the phrase *Library Journal* contributor Ann H. Fisher used to describe Kincaid's *Pretending the Bed Is a Raft.* In the title story, Belinda, a young mother and cancer patient, makes a list of things she wants to do before she dies. In "Won't Nobody Ever Love You Like Your Daddy Does," the same male neighbor attracts a girl and her mother. An instructor in love with his student contemplates leaving his wife in "Why Richard Can't." *Booklist* contributor Mary Ellen Quinn noted that "the narrative voice in all the stories is sure and strong," and praised the author's "fresh insights and quirky humor." A *Publishers Weekly* reviewer called Kincaid "a master at revealing personality through dialogue" and labeled *Pretending the Bed Is a Raft* a "fine debut story collection."

Balls is Kincaid's novel about the culture of southern college football as seen through the eyes of fifteen female narrators. Having been married to two football coaches, Kincaid brings an insider's view to the game as it affects coaches, their families, and the players. The story begins in 1968, and the novel's main narrator is Dixie Carraway, a former homecoming queen married to former college quarterback Mac Gibbs. Mac coaches high school teams, then becomes the coach of the (fictional) Birmingham University Black Bears. Kincaid also depicts the recruiting of players and southern fans' passion for college football. When Mac starts a black quarterback, he hears from the Ku Klux Klan. Mac also commits recruiting violations and experiences problems in both his marriage and career. A contributor to *Kirkus Reviews* wrote that "Kincaid handles this rather pulpy material more-or-less evenhandedly" and noted that her "gritty, down-to-earth dialogue dominates the novel, saving it from its worst miscalculations."

Reviewing *Balls* in *Library Journal,* Wilda Williams praised "the novel's warm humor and eccentric characters." *Booklist* contributor Dennis Dodge noted that although *Balls* "seems to center on the most macho of sports, it is all about the inner lives of women," and called the novel "unfailingly perceptive and deeply moving." While a *Publishers Weekly* reviewer noted that Kincaid "hasn't quite found the shape to show her wit and wisdom to their best advantage," she "is a fresh, promising voice in the serio-comic good ol' girl school."

Bena Eckert McKale is the exceptionally strong protagonist in Kincaid's third novel, *Verbena.* Bena's life is dramatically altered after her husband dies in an automobile accident while seated next to another woman half his age. Later, Bena learns a baby also died in the crash. Kincaid thrusts more than her fair share of heartache on Bena, but the character perseveres and manages to maintain her friendly southern virtues and raise five teenage children. William W. Starr of the *Knight-Ridder/Tribune News Service* commented that "readers likely will cheer her choices in this engaging but tough characterization, shorn of sitcom sentimentality and blessed with an ending so gently satisfying." The final chapters in the novel were inspired by the real-life drama of Kincaid's own mother, as Bena battles to find meaning in a life of continuous setbacks and painful lessons. "This is an authentic story," a *Publishers Weekly* contributor noted in reviewing Kincaid's book, "of a resilient woman's doubts, troubles, heartbreak and survival."

Kincaid once told *CA:* "How can you grow up Southern and not develop a passion for stories and the words that give them life? In the poor South of my childhood money was something only a few people had—words were the true currency of the culture. I also loved the way the truth hid inside the language, how artfully camouflaged it always was and is.

"I have over-listened all my life. All that listening built up and spills out into voices and stories. Some people speak when spoken to. I write when spoken to—whether by the inner voice or by the amazing external voices that surround me. I never have writer's block. (Even when I should!)

"I don't choose my subjects. They choose me. Race. Gender. The power of place. And lately, forgiveness."

BIOGRAPHICAL AND CRITICAL SOURCES:

BOOKS

Contemporary Southern Writers, St. James Press (Detroit, MI), 1999.

PERIODICALS

Aethlon, fall, 1999, review of *Balls,* p. 188.
Atlanta Journal-Constitution, September 27, 1998, Carolyn Nizzi Warmbold, review of *Balls,* p. L11; October 30, 1998, Don Briant, review of *Balls,* p. K10.

Booklist, March 15, 1993, p. 1342; October 1, 1997, Mary Ellen Quinn, review of *Pretending the Bed Is a Raft,* p. 308; July, 1998, Dennis Dodge, review of *Balls,* p. 1829.

Entertainment Weekly, December 12, 1997, Alexandra Jacobs, review of *Pretending the Bed Is a Raft,* p. 81; November 20, 1998, Rhonda Johnson, review of *Balls,* p. 120; November 26, 1999, review of *Balls,* p. 85.

Kirkus Reviews, April 1, 1992, p. 419; August 1, 1998; March 1, 2002, review of *Verbena,* p. 280.

Knight-Ridder/Tribune News Service, June 5, 2002, Polly Paddock, review of *Verbena,* p. K0104.

Library Journal, May 1, 1992, p. 118; September 1, 1997, Ann H. Fisher, review of *Pretending the Bed Is a Raft,* p. 222; September 1, 1998, Wilda Williams, review of *Balls,* p. 214.

New Yorker, September 7, 1992, p. 95; February 1, 1999, review of *Balls,* p. 14.

New York Times, December 13, 1998, Erica Sanders, review of *Balls,* p. 35.

New York Times Book Review, January 31, 1993, p. 21; February 13, 1994, p. 32.

Publishers Weekly, March 30, 1992, review of *Crossing Blood,* p. 87; August 18, 1997, review of *Pretending the Bed Is a Raft,* p. 66; August 3, 1998, review of *Balls,* p. 71; February 18, 2002, review of *Verbena,* p. 69.

Rapport, June, 1999, review of *Balls,* p. 25.

School Library Journal, November, 1992, p. 142.

Southern Living, December, 1992, p. 82; November, 1997, p. 126.

Winston-Salem Journal, November 22, 1998, Anne Barnhill, review of *Balls,* p. A20.

ONLINE

Algonquin Books of Chapel Hill Web site, http://www.algonquin.com/ (November 12, 1998).

*   *   *

KRAUSE, Herbert (Arthur) 1905-1976

PERSONAL: Born May 25, 1905, in Fergus Falls, MN; died September 22, 1976, in Sioux Falls, SD; son of Arthur Adolph (a farmer and blacksmith) and Bertha (Peters) Krause. *Education:* St. Olaf College, B.A., 1933; University of Iowa, M.A., 1935. *Politics:* Independent.

CAREER: University of Iowa, Iowa City, instructor in English, 1938-39; Augustana College, Sioux Falls, SD, professor of English, 1939-76, chair of department, 1939-45, writer-in-residence, 1945-76, director of Center for Western Studies, 1970-76. Fulbright lecturer at University of Witwatersrand and University of Natal, 1961; Rockefeller visiting professor at University of the Philippines, 1966-69; lecturer at American universities, and for National Audubon Society, 1963.

MEMBER: Western History Association, Western Literature Association (member of executive council, 1971-74), Champlain Society, Hudson's Bay Record Society, South Dakota History Society, Wisconsin Historical Society, Minnesota Historical Society, South Dakota Ornithologists' Union (president, 1958-59; member of board of directors, 1960-65).

AWARDS, HONORS: Bread Loaf Writers' Conference fellowship, 1937; Friends of American Writers Award, 1939, for *Wind without Rain;* American Association for the Advancement of Science grant to compile the literature of South Dakota ornithology, 1958; various commissions to write commemorative poems, including one for Minnesota Statehood Centennial, 1958; Litt.D., Augustana College, 1970.

WRITINGS:

Bondsman to the Hills (play), first produced in Cape Girardeau, MO, at the Midwestern Folk Drama Tournament, April 4, 1936.

Wind without Rain (novel), Bobbs-Merrill (Indianapolis, IN), 1939.

Neighbor Boy (poems), Midland House (Iowa City, IA), 1939.

The Thresher (novel), Bobbs-Merrill (Indianapolis, IN), 1945.

The Oxcart Trail (novel), Bobbs-Merrill (Indianapolis, IN), 1954.

Myth and Reality on the High Plains, St. Olaf College (Northfield, MN), 1962.

The Big Four (television documentary), 1962.

Ornithology of the Great Plains, Art Press, 1964.

The Canada Warbler, Laboratory of Ornithology, Cornell University (Ithaca, NY), 1965.

The Half-Horse Alligator, University of the Philippines Press (Manila, Philippines), 1968.

The McCown's Longspur: A Life History, Benipayo (Manila, Philippines), 1968.

(Editor and author of afterword) *Fiction 151-1: Short Stories,* MDB Publishing (Manila, Philippines), 1968.

(Editor, with Gary Olson) *Prelude to Glory: A Newspaper Accounting of Custer's 1874 Expedition to the Black Hills,* Brevet Press (Sioux Falls, SD), 1974.

Poems and Essays of Herbert Krause, edited by Arthur R. Huseboe, Center for Western Studies, Augustana College (Sioux Falls, SD), 1990.

Crazy Horse: A Drama of the Plains Indians and the Black Hills (play), first produced in Sioux Falls, SD, at the Center for Western Studies, June 20, 1994.

Contributor to *The Bird Watcher's America,* edited by Olin Sewall Pettingill, McGraw (New York, NY), 1965; and to *Bent's Life Histories of North American Birds.* Work represented in periodicals, including *Living Bird* and *Chicago Sun Book Week.* Regional editor, National Audubon Society *Field Notes,* 1958-60.

SIDELIGHTS: Herbert Krause established a literary reputation on the strength of his three novels and various pieces of poetry, all of which reflected life in the harsh prairie environments of the American West. His novels explored life on prairie farms in the nineteenth and early twentieth centuries, and his poetry and nonfiction celebrated the natural beauties of an otherwise demanding environment. In *Twentieth-Century Western Writers,* Kristoffer F. Paulson characterized Krause as "a poet of dark reality and 'shadow-haunted' beauty."

Krause's first novel, *Wind without Rain,* was published in 1939, the same year the author began his long association with Augustana College in Sioux Falls, South Dakota. Set on a farm along the Minnesota-South Dakota border at the turn of the century, *Wind without Rain* follows the harsh and difficult life of Franz Vildvogel, a sensitive young man whose artistic tendencies are stifled by his strict family and the demands of farming. "This first novel presents a bleak and dramatic story so vigorously and cunningly that it leaves behind a singular sense of veracity and power," wrote Iris Barry in *Books.* According to John Mair in *New Statesman & Nation,* the book "is highly impressive, and though any isolated page may seem over-written,

its culminating effect is undeniably moving. Mr. Krause presents his characters as wholly of a piece with their environment, and sees their toils and wild junketings . . . as almost animal reflexes to their conditions of life." Wallace Stegner commended the work in the *Saturday Review of Literature* as "one of the best first novels in a good many years."

Nearly a decade passed before Krause published his second novel, *The Thresher,* another grim story of frontier life. Johnny Black, an orphaned farm boy, becomes obsessed with cornering the threshing business in his community, with tragic results for himself and for his wife. "The reader of 'The Thresher' . . . is immediately impressed by the language in which the book is written," declared J. T. Frederick in the *Chicago Sun Book Week.* "Krause is a poet, and he loves and uses words as a poet does." Nancy Groberg Chaikin offered a similar view in the *Saturday Review of Literature:* "Mr. Krause's characters are vivid, strong, absorbing," the critic wrote. "We are consumed with a kind of ambivalent attitude, an attitude which understands and loves these people even as it acknowledges their injustices and hates for them. . . . The writing is as powerful as the forces with which it deals—each word obviously loved and carefully chosen, each phrase adding to a total surging, poetic effect."

The Oxcart Trail follows the fortunes of Minnesota pioneers of the 1840s as they settle along the Red River. Although Paulson declared the novel to be "structurally faulty and thematically uncertain," Walter Havighurst in the *Chicago Sunday Tribune* found the book to be "a serious and substantial historical novel in which the carefully researched background is more memorable than the characters." As James Gray noted in the *New York Herald Tribune Book Review,* Krause "has put together in his long, highly readable book, hundreds of small incidents which reveal what is probably a close approximation of the truth."

In 1974 Krause published *Prelude to Glory: A Newspaper Accounting of Custer's 1874 Expedition to the Black Hills,* a gathering of the newspaper reports filed by journalists who accompanied General George Custer into the Black Hills of South Dakota in 1874. The expedition was for scientific purposes, but the enthusiastic reports written by the newspapermen stirred a gold rush in the region, leading to trouble with the Sioux Indians and to Custer's eventual death in battle at the Little Bighorn. Carl R. Baldwin of the *St. Louis Post-Dispatch* called the book "a masterpiece of sorts, in the words of the reporters, scientists and military men who participated in the 'scientific foray' into the sacred land of the Sioux and Cheyenne."

According to Arthur R. Huseboe, writing in the *Dictionary of Literary Biography*, "Krause's work on *Prelude to Glory* was closely related to the creation of the Center for Western Studies at Augustana College, which he had founded in part to increase the publication of important books about the northern plains. Throughout his teaching career at the college . . . Krause set his mind on encouraging his students to tell the stories of the people who settled the West and of the Native Americans whom they met there. Thus, in 1970, approximately thirty-one years after Krause started teaching at the college, he established the center with the support of several colleagues and the Board of Regents at Augustana. Upon his death of a stroke on 22 September 1976, Krause—who had never married—bequeathed his modest estate and his thirty-thousand-volume library to the center. A place devoted to interpreting and preserving the history and cultures of the northern prairie plains, the Center for Western Studies signified a project that in Krause's final years was as vital to him as his career as a writer of the American West."

Krause once told *CA* that his most important motivation was the "conflict between great talent or beauty (the artistic, for instance) and destructive circumstance, whether in human life or in the intrusion of thoughtless humanity upon unspoiled environments."

BIOGRAPHICAL AND CRITICAL SOURCES:

BOOKS

Dictionary of Literary Biography, Volume 256: *Twentieth-Century Western Writers,* Third Series, Gale (Detroit, MI), 2002.

Dunmire, Raymond Veryl, compiler, *The Herbert Krause Collection Bibliography,* two volumes, Augustana College (Sioux Falls, SD), 1974.

Huseboe, Arthur R., and William Geyer, editors, *Where the West Begins: Essays on Middle Border and Siouxland Writing, in Honor of Herbert Krause,* Center for Western Studies Press (Sioux Falls, SD), 1978.

Huseboe, Arthur R., *Herbert Krause,* Boise State University (Boise, ID), 1985.

Lyon, Thomas J., editor, *A Literary History of the American West,* Texas Christian University Press (Fort Worth, TX), 1987.

Meyer, Roy W., *The Middle Western Farm Novel in the Twentieth Century,* University of Nebraska Press (Lincoln, NE), 1965.

Twentieth-Century Western Writers, 2nd edition, St. James Press (Detroit, MI), 1991.

PERIODICALS

Books, February 12, 1939, Iris Barry, review of *Wind without Rain,* p. 5.

Chicago Sun Book Week, January 19, 1947, J. T. Frederick, review of *The Thresher,* p. 4.

Chicago Sunday Tribune, April 4, 1954, Walter Havighurst, review of *The Oxcart Trail,* p. 5.

New Republic, March 8, 1939, p. 144.

New Statesman & Nation, July 15, 1939, John Mair, review of *Wind without Rain,* p. 90.

New Yorker, February 11, 1939, p. 81; January 18, 1947, p. 93.

New York Herald Tribune Book Review, January 12, 1947, Walter Havighurst, "Driving Force on the Prairie," p. 4; April 4, 1954, James Gray, "Liquor, Love and Brawling on the Long Road Westward," p. 5.

New York Times, February 12, 1939, Margaret Wallace, "*Wind without Rain* and Other Recent Works of Fiction," p. 6; April 11, 1954, p. 25.

Saturday Review of Literature, February 11, 1939, Wallace Stegner, "A Strong Novel of the Minnesota Land," p. 5; February 8, 1947, Nancy Groberg Chaikin, "A Man's Drive for Power," p. 12.

South Dakota Review, spring, 1967, Judith M. Janssen, "Black Frost in Summer: Central Themes in the Novels of Herbert Krause," pp. 55-65.

St. Louis Post-Dispatch, August 25, 1974, Carl R. Baldwin, "What Custer Was After," p. 4B.

Times Literary Supplement, July 15, 1939, p. 419.*

L

LANDAU, Elaine 1948-

PERSONAL: Born February 15, 1948, in Lakewood, NJ; daughter of James and May (a department store manager; maiden name, Tudor) Garmiza; married Edward William Landau (an electrical engineer), December 16, 1968; children: Michael Brent. *Education:* New York University, B.A., 1970; Pratt Institute, M.L.S., 1975. *Religion:* Jewish. *Hobbies and other interests:* Botany.

ADDRESSES: Home—11810 Southwest 92nd Lane, Miami, FL 33186.

CAREER: Reporter on community newspaper in New York, NY, 1970-72; Simon & Schuster, New York, NY, editor, 1972-73; Tuckahoe Public Library, Tuckahoe, NY, director, 1975-79; Sparta Public Library, Sparta, NJ, director.

MEMBER: Society of Children's Book Writers and Illustrators, American Library Association.

AWARDS, HONORS: New Jersey Institute of Technology awards, 1977, for both *Death: Everyone's Heritage* and *Hidden Heroines: Women in American History,* 1981, for both *Occult Visions: A Mystical Gaze into the Future* and *The Teen Guide to Dating,* and 1989, for both *Alzheimer's Disease* and *Surrogate Mothers;* NCSS/CBC Notable Children's Trade Book in the Field of Social Studies, 1990, for *We Have AIDS,* 1991, for *We Survived the Holocaust,* 2002, for *Columbus Day: Celebrating a Famous Explorer* and *Heroine of the Titanic: The Real Unsinkable Molly Brown,* and 2003, for *Osama bin Laden: A War against the West;* ALA Quick Picks for Reluctant Young Adult Readers, 1991, for *We Have AIDS;* Science Books and Films (SB&F) Annual Best Children's Science Book List, 1991, for *Neptune,* 1994, for *Rabies,* 1996, for *ESP* and *The Curse of Tutankhamen,* 1997, for *Ocean Mammals* and *Tropical Forest Mammals,* and 1998, for *Joined at Birth: The Lives of Conjoined Twins;* Society of School Librarians, "Best of 1993," for *The White Power Movement;* NSTA/CBC Outstanding Science Trade Books for Children, 1994, for *Rabies; Booklist* Selection of the Best Rain Forest Books of the Decade, 1997, for *Tropical Rain Forests around the World,* and *Tropical Forest Mammals;* SB&F Best Science Books for Junior High and High School Readers, 1998, for *Tourette Syndrome* and *Joined at Birth: The Lives of Conjoined Twins;* Ohio Farm Bureau Award for Children's Literature, 2000, for *Corn;* New York Public Library Books for the Teenage, 2001, for *Heroine of the Titanic: The Real Unsinkable Molly Brown; Voya* 7th Annual Nonfiction Honor List, 2001, for *Heroine of the Titanic: The Real Unsinkable Molly Brown;* Society of School Librarians International Book Award, Honor Book, 2002, for *Osama bin Laden: A War against the West; Booklist* Top 10 Biographies for Youth, 2002, for *Osama bin Laden: A War against the West;* International Reading Association Young Adult's Choice, 2003, for *Slave Narratives: The Journey to Freedom;* Texas Bluebonnet Award Master List, 2003-2004, for *Smokejumpers;*

WRITINGS:

(With Jesse Jackson) *Black in America: A Fight for Freedom,* Messner (New York, NY), 1973.

Woman, Woman! Feminism in America, Messner (New York, NY), 1974.

Hidden Heroines: Women in American History, Messner (New York, NY), 1975.

Death: Everyone's Heritage, Messner (New York, NY), 1976.

Yoga for You, Messner (New York, NY), 1977.

Occult Visions: A Mystical Gaze into the Future, illustrated by Carol Gjertsen, Messner (New York, NY), 1979.

The Teen Guide to Dating, Messner (New York, NY), 1980.

The Smart Spending Guide for Teens, Messner (New York, NY), 1982.

Why Are They Starving Themselves?: Understanding Anorexia Nervosa and Bulimia, Messner (New York, NY), 1983.

Child Abuse: An American Epidemic, Messner (New York, NY), 1984, 2nd edition, 1990.

Growing Old in America, Messner (New York, NY), 1985.

Different Drummer: Homosexuality in America, Messner (New York, NY), 1986.

Sexually Transmitted Diseases, Enslow (Berkeley Heights, NJ), 1986.

Alzheimer's Disease, Franklin Watts (New York, NY), 1987.

The Homeless, Messner (New York, NY), 1987.

On the Streets: The Lives of Adolescent Prostitutes, Messner (New York, NY), 1987.

Surrogate Mothers, Franklin Watts (New York, NY), 1988.

Teenagers Talk about School—and Open Their Hearts about Their Closest Concerns, Messner (New York, NY), 1988.

The Sioux, Franklin Watts (New York, NY), 1989.

Black Market Adoption and the Sale of Children, Franklin Watts (New York, NY), 1990.

Cowboys, Franklin Watts (New York, NY), 1990.

Teenage Violence, Messner (New York, NY), 1990.

Tropical Rain Forests around the World, Franklin Watts (New York, NY), 1990.

Nazi War Criminals, Franklin Watts (New York, NY), 1990.

Lyme Disease, Franklin Watts (New York, NY), 1990.

We Have AIDS, Franklin Watts (New York, NY), 1990.

Weight: A Teenage Concern, Lodestar (New York, NY), 1991.

Wildflowers around the World, Franklin Watts (New York, NY), 1991.

We Survived the Holocaust, Franklin Watts (New York, NY), 1991.

Armed America: The Status of Gun Control, Messner (New York, NY), 1991.

Dyslexia, Franklin Watts (New York, NY), 1991.

Mars, Franklin Watts (New York, NY), 1991.

Chemical and Biological Warfare, Lodestar (New York, NY), 1991.

Interesting Invertebrates: A Look at Some Animals without Backbones, Franklin Watts (New York, NY), 1991.

Colin Powell: Four-Star General, Franklin Watts (New York, NY), 1991.

Jupiter, Franklin Watts (New York, NY), 1991.

Robert Fulton, Franklin Watts (New York, NY), 1991.

Saturn, Franklin Watts (New York, NY), 1991.

Neptune, Franklin Watts (New York, NY), 1991.

Endangered Plants, Franklin Watts (New York, NY), 1992.

The Warsaw Ghetto Uprising, New Discovery (New York, NY), 1992.

Terrorism: America's Growing Threat, Lodestar (New York, NY), 1992.

Big Brother Is Watching: Secret Police and Intelligence Services, Walker (New York, NY), 1992.

Teens and the Death Penalty, Enslow (Berkeley Heights, NJ), 1992.

The Cherokees, Franklin Watts (New York, NY), 1992.

State Birds: Including the Commonwealth of Puerto Rico, Franklin Watts (New York, NY), 1992.

State Flowers: Including the Commonwealth of Puerto Rico, Franklin Watts (New York, NY), 1992.

Bill Clinton, Franklin Watts (New York, NY), 1993.

Sexual Harassment, Walker (New York, NY), 1993.

Yeti: Abominable Snowman of the Himalayas, Millbrook Press (Brookfield, CT), 1993.

The White Power Movement: America's Racist Hate Groups, Millbrook Press (Brookfield, CT), 1993.

Sasquatch: Wild Man of the Woods, Millbrook Press (Brookfield, CT), 1993.

The Loch Ness Monster, Millbrook Press (Brookfield, CT), 1993.

Rabies, Lodestar (New York, NY), 1993.

The Right to Die, Franklin Watts (New York, NY), 1993.

Interracial Dating and Marriage, Messner (New York, NY), 1993.

Environmental Groups: The Earth Savers, Enslow (Berkeley Heights, NJ), 1993.

Allergies, Twenty-first Century Books (Brookfield, CT), 1994.

Epilepsy, Twenty-first Century Books (Brookfield, CT), 1994.

Deafness, Twenty-first Century Books (Brookfield, CT), 1994.

Teenage Drinking, Enslow (Berkeley Heights, NJ), 1994.

The Chilulas, Franklin Watts (New York, NY), 1994.

Blindness, Twenty-first Century Books (Brookfield, CT), 1994.

The Beauty Trap, New Discovery (New York, NY), 1994.

Sibling Rivalry: Brothers and Sisters at Odds, Millbrook Press (Brookfield, CT), 1994.

Diabetes, Twenty-first Century Books (Brookfield, CT), 1994.

The Pomo, Franklin Watts (New York, NY), 1994.

Cancer, Twenty-first Century Books (Brookfield, CT), 1994.

The Hopi, Franklin Watts (New York, NY), 1994.

Breast Cancer, Franklin Watts (New York, NY), 1995.

Your Legal Rights: From Custody Battles to School Searches, the Headline-making Cases That Affect Your Life, Walker (New York, NY), 1995.

Hooked: Talking about Addiction, Millbrook Press (Brookfield, CT), 1995.

Ghosts, Millbrook Press (Brookfield, CT), 1995.

Tuberculosis, Franklin Watts (New York, NY), 1995.

The Abenaki, Franklin Watts (New York, NY), 1996.

Temperate Forest Mammals, Children's Press (New York, NY), 1996.

Tropical Forest Mammals, Children's Press (New York, NY), 1996.

ESP, Millbrook Press (Brookfield, CT), 1996.

UFO's, Millbrook Press (Brookfield, CT), 1996.

Mountain Mammals, Children's Press (New York, NY), 1996.

Stalking, Franklin Watts (New York, NY), 1996.

The Ottawas, Franklin Watts (New York, NY), 1996.

Fortune Telling, Millbrook Press (Brookfield, CT), 1996.

Foretelling the Future, Millbrook Press (Brookfield, CT), 1996.

Grassland Mammals, Children's Press (New York, NY), 1996.

Desert Mammals, Children's Press (New York, NY), 1996.

Ocean Mammals, Children's Press (New York, NY), 1996.

Near-Death Experiences, Millbrook Press (Brookfield, CT), 1996.

The Shawnee, Franklin Watts (New York, NY), 1996.

The Curse of Tutankhamen, Millbrook Press (Brookfield, CT), 1996.

Bill Clinton and His Presidency, Franklin Watts (New York, NY), 1997.

Joined at Birth: The Lives of Conjoined Twins, Franklin Watts (New York, NY), 1997.

Short Stature: From Folklore to Fact, Franklin Watts (New York, NY), 1997.

Standing Tall: Unusually Tall People, Franklin Watts (New York, NY), 1997.

Living with Albinism, Franklin Watts (New York, NY), 1997.

The Sumerians, Millbrook Press (Brookfield, CT), 1997.

Your Pet Cat, Children's Press (New York, NY), 1997.

Your Pet Dog, Children's Press (New York, NY), 1997.

Your Pet Gerbil, Children's Press (New York, NY), 1997.

Your Pet Hamster, Children's Press (New York, NY), 1997.

Your Pet Iguana, Children's Press (New York, NY), 1997.

Your Pet Tropical Fish, Children's Press (New York, NY), 1997.

Minibeasts As Pets, Children's Press (New York, NY), 1997.

Parrots and Parakeets As Pets, Children's Press (New York, NY), 1997.

Wild Children: Growing Up without Human Contact, Franklin Watts (New York, NY), 1998.

Multiple Births, Franklin Watts (New York, NY), 1998.

Tourette Syndrome, Franklin Watts (New York, NY), 1998.

Apatosaurus, Children's Press (New York, NY), 1999.

Pterodactyls, Children's Press (New York, NY), 1999.

Stegosaurus, Children's Press (New York, NY), 1999.

Triceratops, Children's Press (New York, NY), 1999.

Tyrannosaurus Rex, Children's Press (New York, NY), 1999.

Velociraptor, Children's Press (New York, NY), 1999.

Angelfish, Children's Press (New York, NY), 1999.

Electric Fish, Children's Press (New York, NY), 1999.

Jellyfish, Children's Press (New York, NY), 1999.

Piranhas, Children's Press (New York, NY), 1999.

Sea Horses, Children's Press (New York, NY), 1999.

Siamese Fighting Fish, Children's Press (New York, NY), 1999.

Apples, Children's Press (New York, NY), 1999.

Bananas, Children's Press (New York, NY), 1999.

Corn, Children's Press (New York, NY), 1999.

Sugar, Children's Press (New York, NY), 1999.

Tomatoes, Children's Press (New York, NY), 1999.

Wheat, Children's Press (New York, NY), 1999.

Australia and New Zealand, Children's Press (New York, NY), 1999.

India, Children's Press (New York, NY), 1999.

Israel, Children's Press (New York, NY), 1999.

Korea, Children's Press (New York, NY), 1999.

Norway, Children's Press (New York, NY), 1999.

Puerto Rico, Children's Press (New York, NY), 1999.

Parkinson's Disease, Franklin Watts (New York, NY), 1999.

Jupiter, Franklin Watts (New York, NY), 1999.

Mars, Franklin Watts (New York, NY), 1999.

Saturn, Franklin Watts (New York, NY), 1999.

Air Crashes, Franklin Watts (New York, NY), 1999.

Fires, Franklin Watts (New York, NY), 1999.

Space Disasters, Franklin Watts (New York, NY), 1999.

Maritime Disasters, Franklin Watts (New York, NY), 1999.

Canada, Children's Press (New York, NY), 2000.

France, Children's Press (New York, NY), 2000.

Dominican Republic, Children's Press (New York, NY), 2000.

Egypt, Children's Press (New York, NY), 2000.

Peru, Children's Press (New York, NY), 2000.

Land Mines: 100 Million Hidden Killers, Enslow Publishers (Berkeley Heights, NJ), 2000.

Pizza: The Pie That's Not a Dessert, Rourke Press (Vero Beach, FL), 2000.

John F. Kennedy, Jr., Twenty-first Century Books (Brookfield, CT), 2000.

The New Nuclear Reality, Twenty-first Century Books (Brookfield, CT), 2000.

Holocaust Memories: Speaking the Truth in Their Own Words, Franklin Watts (New York, NY), 2001.

Slave Narratives: The Journey to Freedom, Franklin Watts (New York, NY), 2001.

Autism, Franklin Watts (New York, NY), 2001.

Heroine of the Titanic: The Real Unsinkable Molly Brown, Clarion Books (New York, NY), 2001.

Ice Cream: The Cold Creamy Treat, Rourke Press (Vero Beach, FL), 2001.

Chocolate: Savor the Flavor, Rourke Press (Vero Beach, FL), 2001.

Pretzels: One of the World's Oldest Snack Foods, Rourke Press (Vero Beach, FL), 2001.

Chewing Gum: A Sticky Treat, Rourke Press (Vero Beach, FL), 2001.

Hamburgers: Bad News for Cows, Rourke Press (Vero Beach, FL), 2001.

Canals, Children's Press (New York, NY), 2001.

Bridges, Children's Press (New York, NY), 2001.

Tunnels, Children's Press (New York, NY), 2001.

Skyscrapers, Children's Press (New York, NY), 2001.

Independence Day: Birthday of the United States, Enslow Publishers (Berkeley Heights, NJ), 2001.

Columbus Day: Celebrating a Famous Explorer, Enslow Publishers (Berkeley Heights, NJ), 2001.

Thanksgiving Day: A Time to Be Thankful, Enslow Publishers (Berkeley Heights, NJ), 2001.

Spinal Cord Injuries, Enslow Publishers (Berkeley Heights, NJ), 2001.

Presidential Election 2000, Children's Press (New York, NY), 2002.

Prince William: W. O. W., William of Wales, Millbrook Press (Brookfield, CT), 2002.

Smokejumpers, photographs by Ben Klaffke, Millbrook Press (Brookfield, CT), 2002.

Head and Brain Injuries, Enslow Publishers (Berkeley Heights, NJ), 2002.

St. Patrick's Day, Enslow Publishers (Berkeley Heights, NJ), 2002.

Valentine's Day: Candy, Love, and Hearts, Enslow Publishers (Berkeley Heights, NJ), 2002.

Veterans Day: Remembering Our War Heroes, Enslow Publishers (Berkeley Heights, NJ), 2002.

Earth Day: Keeping Our Planet Clean, Enslow Publishers (Berkeley Heights, NJ), 2002.

Mardi Gras: Music, Parades, and Costumes, Enslow Publishers (Berkeley Heights, NJ), 2002.

Osama bin Laden: A War against the West, Twenty-first Century Books (Brookfield, CT), 2002.

Popcorn!, illustrated by Brian Lies, Charlesbridge (Watertown, MA), 2003.

Fearsome Alligators, Enslow Publishers (Berkeley Heights, NJ), 2003.

Scary Sharks, Enslow Publishers (Berkeley Heights, NJ), 2003.

Sinister Snakes, Enslow Publishers (Berkeley Heights, NJ), 2003.

Killer Bees, Enslow Publishers (Berkeley Heights, NJ), 2003.

Creepy Spiders, Enslow Publishers (Berkeley Heights, NJ), 2003.

Fierce Cats, Enslow Publishers (Berkeley Heights, NJ), 2003.

A Healthy Diet, Franklin Watts (New York, NY), 2003.

Alcohol, Franklin Watts (New York, NY), 2003.

Cigarettes, Franklin Watts (New York, NY), 2003.

Cocaine, Franklin Watts (New York, NY), 2003.

The Civil Rights Movement, Franklin Watts (New York, NY), 2003.

A President's Work: A Look at the Executive Branch, Lerner Books (Minneapolis, MN), 2003.

Friendly Foes: A Look at Political Parties, Lerner Books (Minneapolis, MN), 2003.

Contributor of reviews to *New York Times Book Review.*

SIDELIGHTS: A prolific author of nonfiction for younger readers, Elaine Landau has been praised by reviewers for her well-researched and well-written books. In topics ranging from the legendary Loch Ness Monster to the presidency of Bill Clinton and the terrorist Osama bin Laden, and from UFO's and ESP to up-to-the minute advances in Alzheimer's disease research, Landau presents factual information often highlighted by case studies, interviews, and other information that provides readers with added insight into the topic at hand.

Born in New Jersey in 1948, Landau had written her first book by the time she was nine years old, composing it "in the children's room of my local library," as she once recalled to *CA.* "I spent a lot of time in that room, reading and growing, while remaining safely hidden from a mother, older sister, and aunt who assured me that to dream of becoming an author was an unrealistic career aspiration." But Landau was not to be discouraged by the advice of her family. "The relative hasn't been born who can dampen the magic of a well-spun story," she declared. "Besides, I was a very determined little girl. So determined that by the time I was fifteen, I had written over two dozen books—the longest of which was a full nine pages!"

When Landau was in her mid-twenties and living in New York City, she published the first of her many books. "Although being a 'real' author is often a very lonely occupation (you can't entertain friends while completing a chapter), it is also my greatest joy," she once explained. "I've always loved the idea of reaching out to share my thoughts and feelings with others, and I still can't think of a better way to do so."

Many of Landau's books have been of particular interest to modern teens facing a far different world than that of previous generations, a fact that makes older nonfiction books irrelevant. Eating disorders are dealt with in detail in *Why Are They Starving Themselves? Understanding Anorexia Nervosa and Bulimia,* which contains interviews with several women and teens, as well as a list of resources on where to get help for both anorexics and their families. The book received a starred review from *Booklist.* Landau's related work, *Weight: A Teenage Concern,* published in 1991, examines the social pressures on young women to be thin, and the prejudice that overweight teens often face. "Readers will enjoy the testimonials of teens and appreciate the author's nonjudgmental tone," according to *Voice of Youth Advocates* reviewer Joyce Hamilton. *The Beauty Trap,* which Landau published in 1994, focuses on the root cause of eating disorders: society's obsession with physical beauty and how that obsession is internalized and acted upon by women. Providing basic information on the consequences of falling into the beauty trap in four chapters, the book also includes a list of organizations that offers readers more information on ways to break the cycle. "Landau's insightful and disturbing examination" of modern culture's obsession with the physical appearance of women and girls "should be required reading for all young girls, their parents, and their teachers," according to Jeanne Triner in *Booklist.*

Other books of interest to teen readers have concerned topics of equal seriousness. *Teenage Drinking,* published in 1994, involves readers in the personal life of teens whose lives are controlled by the out-of-control drinking of either themselves or someone close to them. Praised for her ability to "reveal the impact and danger of alcoholism much more clearly and compellingly than the typical statistics and charts" by *Voice of Youth Advocates* reviewer Joanne Eglash, Landau combines stories of young alcoholics with information and advice to family members and friends. Similarly, in *Hooked: Talking about Addiction,* the author divides her discussion into causes of addiction, its effects, and the steps that must be taken in the recovery process, using three case histories of teens as the focus of the book. Susan Dove Lempke, writing in *Booklist,* felt that Landau's book is a "good jumping-off point for students who want to learn about addictions." *Teenagers Talk about School—and Open Their Hearts about Their Concerns,* which features interviews with a wide variety of students across the United States, encompasses many of the topics covered in more detail in Landau's other books. "Teens will surely recognize themselves and their friends in Landau's bittersweet mosaic of the American teen social environment," according to Libby K. White, reviewing the 1989 work for *School Library Journal.*

Sexuality figures prominently in teen life, and Landau has written several books dealing with various aspects of human sexual relationships, from dating to marriage. *Interracial Dating and Marriage* covers everything from the history of cross-race relationships between men and women to interviews with those involved with partners of a different race. White praised the book in *School Library Journal,* calling Landau's approach "warmly supportive of those who find love outside their own group," adding that "there is no attempt to minimize potential difficulties." Concerns over the medical hazards associated with sexual intercourse are covered in 1987's *Sexually Transmitted Diseases* and *We Have AIDS,* a 1990 work that "will surely help to dispel the notion among teenagers that, 'it can't happen to me,'" according to *Appraisal* reviewer Tippin McDaniel. Landau speaks with nine young adults who have contracted the deadly disease, illustrating the fact that AIDS does strike across racial, cultural, and economic boundaries. The AIDS epidemic also serves as one of Landau's topics in her *Different Drummer: Homosexuality in America.* Examining homosexuality as it currently exists throughout the American social fabric—from same-sex parenting to homophobia—the author "aims to foster a better understanding of homosexuality rather than to offer direct support to those who are questioning their sexual orientation," in the words of Stephanie Zvirin in *Booklist.*

Landau has also examined social issues such as child abuse, sexual harassment, homelessness, and surrogate parenting. *The Homeless,* published in 1988, features several interviews that illustrate the serious plight of Americans with no permanent place to live. Landau's "writing is sober, the text carefully organized, the topic important," noted Zena Sutherland in *Bulletin of the Center for Children's Books.* In *Surrogate Mothers,* the author discusses the various causes of infertility, and the ethics involved in some of the solutions to this problem. In addition to providing an in-depth examination of the "Baby M" case, Landau also includes several other case studies involving couples who wished to have children but, for various reasons, were unable to either bear children of their own or adopt. "The clarity of the writing and the organization of the material work together to capture and hold the reader's interest," commented Leonard J. Garigliano in *Appraisal.*

Additionally, Landau has turned her attention to medical topics. Her 1996 title *Alzheimer's Disease* is constructed to aid young readers understand this devastating illness. Using real life stories as an opener, Landau goes on to describe the progressive effects of the disease, including loss of memory and physical debilitation. Landau takes a similar approach in *Parkinson's Disease* and *Living with Albinism.* In the former title, she explains the basics of this motor disorder, from its subsequent tremors to speech problems as well as the problems doctors have in diagnosing it. Landau "has crafted another well-written, well-organized overview," declared Christine A. Moesch in a *School Library Journal* review of this title.

Also writing in *School Library Journal,* Joyce Adams Burner found Landau's *Living with Albinism* a "positive book, written without sensationalism." Focusing on one eleven-year-old with the condition, Landau again personalizes medical problems and thereby makes them more understandable. *Spinal Cord Injuries* is another title with appeal for young teens, a survey that includes the personal histories of celebrities such as Gloria Estafan and Christopher Reeves. *Booklist*'s Roger Leslie called the book "informative" as well as "accessible."

Noting that "kids are fascinated by those who look different from them," *Booklist*'s Ilene Cooper found that Landau answers such queries "in a straightforward way" in two different books: *Short Stature: From Folklore to Fact,* and *Joined at Birth: The Lives of Conjoined Twins.* The author deals with height in *Short Stature,* a book that lets young readers know that people with dwarfism can lead normal and productive lives. In *Joined at Birth,* Landau takes a look at several examples of such cases, from Eng and Chang to Angela and Amy Lakesberg, who shared a heart before they were separated, and to Abigail and Brittany Hensel, twins sharing one body from below the waist. Thomas Plaut, reviewing the latter title in *Science Books and Films,* felt the "writing style is comfortable and suited to late elementary school youngsters," and Cooper also praised the text, noting that "as always, Landau's writing is clear and cogent." In *Tourette Syndrome* Landau investigates this neurological condition that gives rise to tics and overly verbal behavior. Again using case histories—from athletes to an actor and a surgeon—to explain the disorder, Landau employs an "unadorned style and easily understandable language," according to Randy Meyer in *Booklist.* Moesch, writing in *School Library Journal,* also noted that the "writing is clear and well organized," providing for young readers an "excellent overview of a misunderstood condition." Similarly, Kevin S. Beach, writing in *Voice of Youth Advocates,* found that the "attractive format and accessible reading level make this an effective guide."

Natural history is another specialty for Landau, who has written books about the planets, dinosaurs, and plants and animals. Working in the "True Book" series, she has written about a wide array of fish, including angelfish and piranhas. Writing in *School Library Journal,* Karey Wehner called the books of this series "clearly written, well-organized, and attractively formatted introductions." Carolyn Phelan, reviewing *Jellyfish* and *Siamese Fighting Fish* in *Booklist,* commented on the "distinctive look" of the books, dealing with types of fish that are of "special interest to children." Animals as pets is the subject for another series, dealing with the acquisition, care, and feeding of animals from fish to dogs. Reviewing *Your Pet Tropical Fish* in *Teacher Librarian,* Jessica Higgs remarked that it was a "good title for younger readers."

Landau also turns her attention to flora as well as fauna in *Apples* and *Corn,* "simple introductions to food staples," according to Ilene Cooper in *Booklist.* In 2000 *Corn* was awarded the Ohio Farm Bureau Award for Children's Literature. Corn is again examined in Landau's first picture book, *Popcorn!* Kay Weisman noted of the book in *Booklist,* that Landau "uses a lighthearted approach in this picture book for older children." *School Library Journal*'s Barbara L. McMullin wrote, "Children will love this enjoyable, oversized compilation of historical facts, legends, trivia, and recipes."

History and biography provide further inspiration for Landau. Her *John F. Kennedy, Jr.* is a "poignant tribute," according to William McLoughlin in a *School Library Journal* review. Landau tells of the last days and tragic airplane death of this young man who was the son of the assassinated president, John F. Kennedy. McLaughlin further noted that this biography was an "appealing choice." Peter D. Sieruta, writing in *Horn Book Guide,* found the biography "balanced and well-rounded." *Booklist*'s Cooper also had praise for the profile, noting that Landau does "an excellent job" in detailing the events in the life of this young man who "meant more to his country than just his resume." In *Heroine of the Titanic: The Real Unsinkable Molly Brown,* Landau provides a "realistic biography of an independent and strong-willed woman," according to Andrew Medlar writing in *School Library Journal.* A socialite and social activist, Margaret Brown orga-

nized relief for survivors when the ship she was sailing on, the famous Titanic, sunk in 1912. Landau traces the humble origins of Brown until her marriage with a wealthy silver miner thrust her into the socialite role. However, she remained a tireless crusader for social justice, crusading for miners' rights, and her strong character came to the fore when the Titanic went down and she took charge of her lifeboat, helping to rescue others in the water. "Landau hits just the right tone in this complete portrait," Medlar concluded. Another biography with contemporary appeal is Landau's 2002 *Osama bin Laden: A War against the West.* Cooper, writing in *Booklist,* noted the urgent need for such a book, praising the author's "absorbing" narrative. "Landau, who is known for her solid research, applies her considerable talents here," Cooper further remarked. A contributor for *Kirkus Reviews* wrote that the story of bin Laden's transformation from son of a privileged family to international terrorist is "intrinsically chilling."

History of a more general nature is presented in several volumes from Landau, including *Maritime Disasters, Space Disasters,* and *Slave Narratives.* In the first two titles, the author deals with disasters such as the Titanic, the Lusitania, and the Andrea Doria as examples of accidents at sea, and with the Challenger and several other less high-profile disasters in space. Kathy Broderick praised both *Space Disasters* and *Maritime Disasters* in *Booklist,* calling them "clearly written," and sure to "enhance a school's curriculum." In her *Slave Narratives: The Journey to Freedom,* Landau combines both a general historical outlook with four first-person voices and testimonies of one-time slaves, replaying the daily drudgery and terror of the slave life, as well as the dangers of escape and of finding a new home. Edith Ching, reviewing the title in *School Library Journal,* thought it was a "good introduction to the topic as well as a telling account about slave life in various circumstances."

Landau also deals with current affairs in titles such as *The New Nuclear Reality* and *Land Mines.* Anne G. Brouse found the former title to be a "clearly written, accessible overview" in a *School Library Journal* review, and John Peters, writing in *Booklist,* felt this "systematic look . . . will leave readers marveling that the world hasn't already been bombed into radioactive slag." Landau points out nuclear dangers which include rogue states with nuclear weapons, the selling of such weapons by the former Soviet Union, and the danger of such weapons falling into the hands of terrorists. *Land Mines* paints an equally chilling picture of the thousands of mines in the world and the awful toll they take on a civilian population. "Landau offers important and persuasive facts about this problem in an effective resource for students," wrote Lynn Evarts in a *Voice of Youth Advocates* review. Further social history, of a less urgent sort, is served up in the "Finding Out about Holidays" series, in which Landau profiles such national holidays as Thanksgiving and Columbus Day. Reviewing *Columbus Day: Celebrating a Famous Explorer,* Janie Schomberg noted in *School Library Journal* that "Landau gently challenges the myths and assumptions about Columbus" in a book that "gives readers food for thought about the man, the period, and how the holiday might be interpreted and celebrated in today's world."

Writing nonfiction remains Landau's chosen occupation. "Being a nonfiction writer is like taking an unending voyage in a sea of fascinating facts," Landau explained to *CA.* "Through extensive research and travel, I've learned about desert camels, dolphin intelligence, UFO's, the Loch Ness Monster, and some very deadly diseases. The best part of the experience is sharing the information with young people across America. Even though I may never meet all my readers, I feel as though I'm talking to them whenever they open one of my books."

BIOGRAPHICAL AND CRITICAL SOURCES:

PERIODICALS

Appraisal, winter, 1989, Leonard J. Garigliano, review of *Surrogate Mothers,* pp. 44-45; summer, 1990, Tippin McDaniel, review of *We Have AIDS,* pp. 31-32; winter, 1991, p. 35; winter, 1994, pp. 55-56; winter, 1995, pp. 118-119; summer, 1996, p. 54.

Booklist, November 1, 1979, p. 450; March 15, 1986, Stephanie Zvirin, *Different Drummer: Homosexuality in America,* p. 1074; December 15, 1987, p. 710; February 1, 1989, p. 932; May 1, 1993, p. 1586; March 15, 1994, Jeanne Triner, review of *The Beauty Trap,* p. 1340; June 1, 1995, Merri Monks, review of *Tuberculosis,* p. 1744; September 15, 1997, Ilene Cooper, review of *Joined at Birth* and *Short Stature,* p. 228, April Judge, review of *Bill Clinton and His Presidency,* p. 228;

December 1, 1997, Carolyn Phelan, "The Rain Forest Collection," pp. 628-629; January 1, 1998, Lauren Peterson, review of *The Sumerians,* p. 805; July, 1998, Randy Meyer, review of *Tourette Syndrome,* pp. 1870-1871; November 15, 1998, Karen Hutt, review of *Multiple Births* and *Living with Albinism,* p. 583; June 1, 1999, Carolyn Phelan, review of *Jellyfish* and *Siamese Fighting Fish,* p. 1818; July, 1999, Roger Leslie, review of *Parkinson's Disease,* p. 1936; October 15, 1999, Ilene Cooper, review of *Apples* and *Corn,* p. 449; February 1, 2000, Kathy Broderick, review of *Space Disasters* and *Maritime Disasters,* p. 1020; July, 2000, John Peters, review of *The New Nuclear Reality,* p. 2017; December 15, 2000, Ilene Cooper, review of *John F. Kennedy, Jr.,* p. 806; August, 2001, Hazel Rochman, review of *Slave Narratives,* p. 2105; September 1, 2001, Hazel Rochman, review of *Holocaust Memories,* p. 94; September 15, 2001, Gillian Engberg, review of *Thanksgiving Day,* p. 234; January 1, 2002, Ilene Cooper, review of *Osama bin Laden,* p. 834; February 1, 2002, Roger Leslie, review of *Spinal Cord Injuries,* p. 933; June 1, 2002, Susan Dove Lempke, review of *Smokejumpers;* February 1, 2003, Kay Weisman, review of *Popcorn!*

Bulletin of the Center for Children's Books, December, 1976, pp. 59-60; October, 1983, p. 31; June, 1986, pp. 187-188; January, 1988, Zena Sutherland, review of *The Homeless,* pp. 94-95; November, 1988, p. 76; June, 1991, p. 242; September, 1993, p. 15; February, 1994, pp. 191-192.

Horn Book Guide, fall, 1998, Gail Hedges, review of *Tourette Syndrome* and *Living with Albinism,* p. 389; fall, 1999, Gail Hedges, review of *Parkinson's Disease,* p. 353; spring, 2001, Peter D. Sieruta, review of *John F. Kennedy, Jr.,* p. 146.

Kirkus Reviews, November 15, 1975, p. 1292; December 15, 1982, p. 1339; May 1, 1986, p. 722; October 15, 1991, p. 1345; June 15, 1993, review of *Sexual Harassment,* p. 787; December 1, 1993, review of *The Right to Die,* p. 1525; February 1, 2002, review of *Osama bin Laden,* p. 183.

Publishers Weekly, May 7, 2001, review of *Heroine of the Titanic,* p. 248.

School Library Journal, February, 1976, p. 46; March, 1980, p. 134; February, 1981; September, 1983, p. 131; November, 1987, p. 110; January, 1989, Libby K. White, review of *Teenagers Talk about School—and Open Their Hearts about Their Closest Concerns,* p. 100; June, 1990, Nancy E. Curran, review of *Black Market Adoption and the Sale of Children,* p. 142; September, 1993, Libby K. White, review of *Interracial Dating and Marriage,* p. 257; January, 1994, p. 138; March, 1994, p. 243; January, 1996, p. 134; September, 1997, Rosie Peasley, review of *Bill Clinton and His Presidency,* p. 232; March, 1998, Cynthia M. Sturgis, review of *The Sumerians* et al, pp. 234-235; July, 1998, Christine A. Moesch, review of *Tourette Syndrome,* p. 107; August, 1998, Joyce Adams Burner, review of *Living with Albinism,* p. 177; June, 1999, Christine A. Moesch, review of *Parkinson's Disease,* pp. 148, 150; August, 1999, Karey Wehner, review of *Piranhas* and *Siamese Fighting Fish,* p. 147; February, 2000, John Peters, review of *Mars* and *Jupiter,* p. 135, Eldon Younce, review of *Space Disasters* and *Maritime Disasters,* p. 135; September, 2000, Anne G. Brouse, review of *The New Nuclear Reality,* p. 250; February, 2001, Joyce Adams Burner, review of *Hamburgers* and *Chewing Gum,* p. 113; March, 2001, William McLoughlin, review of *John F. Kennedy, Jr.,* p. 271; July, 2001, Andrew Medlar, review of *Heroine of the Titanic,* p. 126; August, 2001, Edith Ching, review of *Slave Narratives,* p. 200; September, 2001, Janie Schomberg, review of *Columbus Day* and *Independence Day,* p. 216; December, 2001, Linda Beck, review of *Autism,* p. 165; January, 2002, Pamela K. Bomboy, review of *Thanksgiving Day,* p. 120; July, 2002, Anne Chapman Callaghan, review of *Smokejumpers;* March, 2003, Pamela K. Bomboy, review of *The 2000 Presidential Election,* p. 220; April, 2003, Barbara L. McMullin, review of *Popcorn!*

Science Books and Films, May, 1998, Thomas Plaut, review of *Joined at Birth,* p. 114.

Teacher Librarian, March, 1999, Jessica Higgs, review of *Your Pet Tropical Fish,* p. 48.

Voice of Youth Advocates, April, 1981, p. 45; December, 1987, pp. 46-47; April, 1989, p. 60; August, 1990, p. 177; June, 1991, Joyce Hamilton, review of *Weight: A Teenage Concern,* p. 126; December, 1991, p. 337; June, 1992, Colleen Macklin, review of *Teens and the Death Penalty;* August, 1993, p. 179; February, 1994, p. 397; December, 1994, Joanne Eglash, review of *Teenage Drinking,* p. 300; February, 1995, p. 360; December, 1998, Kevin S. Beach, review of *Tourette Syndrome,* p. 382; February, 2001, Lynn Evarts, review of *Land Mines,* p. 443.

ONLINE

Elaine Landau Web Site, http://www.elainelandau.com/ (May 11, 2003).

LANGE, Kelly

PERSONAL: Born Kelly Snyder in New York, NY; daughter of Edmund V. (a pharmacist) and Alice (Reason) Scafard; divorced; children: Kelly Snyder. *Education:* Merrimack College, B.A.

ADDRESSES: Home—Beverly Hills, CA. *Office*—NBC-TV News, 3000 West Alameda Ave., Burbank, CA 91503.

CAREER: KABC radio and television, Los Angeles, CA, radio talk show host, 1967-74, television reporter, 1969-70; KNBC-TV News, Burbank, CA, newscaster, host of *Sunday Show,* and correspondent for *Women 2 Women,* 1971-98 (co-host 1999-2001). Creator and host of *The Kelly Lange Show,* as well as host of *America* and *The Great American Garage Sale.* Has hosted several programs on NBC-TV, including *Rose Parade,* 1975-76, and *Take My Advice,* 1976; has guest hosted the *Today Show* and the *Tomorrow Show;* co-hosted the *Emmy Awards,* and has made guest appearances on several television shows.

AWARDS, HONORS: Genii Award, American Women in Radio and Television, 1979, for contributions to the media and to the community; Governor's Award, Academy of Television Arts and Sciences, 1999; several Emmy Awards, including outstanding achievement as a news anchorperson; several Los Angeles Press Club Awards for best news series, best news reporting, and best writing.

WRITINGS:

Trophy Wife (novel), Simon & Schuster (New York, NY), 1995.
Gossip (novel), Simon & Schuster (New York, NY), 1998.
The Reporter, Mysterious Press (New York, NY), 2002.
Dead File, Mysterious Press (New York, NY), 2003.

SIDELIGHTS: After her divorce in the early 1960s, Kelly Lange was left with "two things . . . a steam iron and a baby." Today she is recognized as a pioneer in news broadcasting and an author of best-selling novels set in the glitzy surrounds of Hollywood. Lange

Kelly Lange

worked odd jobs as a model and as a cocktail waitress to support herself and her daughter before she landed a position as a radio station traffic reporter. Her jobs as a talk show host and newscaster soon followed, leading her to various other television appearances. Lange's success in the field was highlighted in 1979 when she received the Genii Award for successfully combining career, community, and home life. (One other candidate for the award was Barbara Walters; past recipients include Lucille Ball, Carol Burnett, Mary Tyler Moore, and Julie Andrews.)

As one who struggled to become a success in the male-dominated broadcasting industry, Lange sympathizes with women who are beginning to seek their own careers. She realizes that "everybody feels insecure, I do, you do," but insists "the doors are opening so now you [women] have to get the confidence and the skills, train yourselves and get those jobs." This sense of female empowerment has become an important component of Lange's fiction as well. In an interview with *Publishers Weekly,* Simon and Schuster editor Laurie Bernstein said, "Kelly has brought . . . women's commercial fiction into the '90s. So we've still got sex, we've still got shopping, but Kelly's backdrop in-

cludes a political and social conscience—after all, this is L.A. after the riots."

Even before retiring from daily news casting in 1998, Lange had begun to devote herself to writing novels in which women are called upon to exert their full powers against brutality, neglect, and suspicion. Her debut work, *Trophy Wife,* revolves around Devin Yorke, an unloved "trophy wife" of a wealthy clothing manufacturer. When the husband she wanted to divorce is murdered instead, Devin takes over the garment business and actually improves production and working conditions for her employees. Her husband's brother and mistress, who team to plot Devin's downfall, threaten her newfound sense of accomplishment. A *Publishers Weekly* reviewer hailed the book as a "fast-paced, glittery mix of mystery and romance" as well as a "lively, knowing tale."

Gossip and *The Reporter* follow the same formula as *Trophy Wife* in that they present wealthy women who must seek to solve murders before they themselves become prime suspects. In *Gossip,* four long-time friends seek the killer of a man who was husband to one friend and lover to another. *Library Journal* correspondent Mary Ellen Elsbernd praised the novel for its "spicy plot rife with mayhem, murder, and revenge." Harriet Klausner in *BookBrowser* deemed it a "wonderful modern work of contemporary women's fiction that will thrill fans of the genre." In *The Reporter,* it is television correspondent Maxi Poole who investigates the shooting death of her ex-husband, handsome movie star Jack Nathanson. Poole's short list of suspects includes mistresses, a grown woman who was abused by Nathanson as a child, and a plethora of other shady Hollywood characters. A *Publishers Weekly* reviewer felt that Lange's experience as a reporter helped the plot to "ring bright and true" with "original moments." A *TW Bookmark* critic wrote: "*The Reporter* takes you on a virtuoso tour de force of murder and sizzling intrigue in the company of a sexy, chic, and wickedly clever sleuth."

Lange began working on her fiction while still serving as anchorwoman for the KNBC nightly news, and she has continued writing since her broadcasting duties have eased. She told the *News-Times* that she is pleased with the number of women working in television today. "Some of my colleagues feel they laid the foundation for the women that came after us," she said, "but I owe a great deal to the women who came before me, the real pioneers in broadcasting, many whose names have never been known."

BIOGRAPHICAL AND CRITICAL SOURCES:

PERIODICALS

Booklist, June 1, 1995, Mary Carroll, review of *Trophy Wife,* p. 1734; February 1, 2002, Jenny McLarin, review of *The Reporter,* p. 926.
Kirkus Reviews, December 15, 2001, review of *The Reporter,* p. 1725.
Library Journal, October 15, 1998, Mary Ellen Elsbernd, review of *Gossip,* p. 98; February 1, 2002, Rex E. Klett, review of *The Reporter,* p.135.
Los Angeles Times, December 18, 1998, Brian Lowry, "Television: The Anchor and Former 'Weather Girl' Has Decided to Pursue Other Opportunities," p. 6.
People, August 21, 1995, Joanne Kaufman, review of *Trophy Wife,* p. 35.
Publishers Weekly, January 23, 1995, Dick Donahue, "Wordsmiths Practicing What They Preach?," p. 41; May 8, 1995, review of *Trophy Wife,* p. 288; September 7, 1998, review of *Gossip,* p. 85; February 4, 2002, review of *The Reporter,* p. 56.
Saturday Evening Post, September 1978.
Valley, May 1979.

ONLINE

BookBrowser, http://www.bookbrowser.com/ reviews/ (March 26, 2002), Harriet Klausner, review of *Gossip.*
News-Times, http://www.newstimes.com/archive95/ (March 26, 2002), "For News Anchor Kelly Lange, Writing Is Icing on Her Cake."
TW Bookmark, http://www.twbookmark.com/ (March 26, 2002), review of *The Reporter.**

*   *   *

LEESON, Ted 1954-

PERSONAL: Born April 15, 1954, in Beloit, WI; son of James and Betty (a musician) Leeson; married Elizabeth Campbell (a professor), August 4, 1984. *Education:* Marquette University, B.A., B.S., 1976; University of Virginia, Ph.D., 1984. *Politics:* "When necessary."

ADDRESSES: Home—2855 Northwest Jackson, Corvallis, OR 97330. *Office*—Moreland Hall, Oregon State University, Corvallis, OR 97331. *E-mail*—tleeson@ orst.edu.

CAREER: Oregon State University, Corvallis, senior instructor, 1984—.

WRITINGS:

The Habit of Rivers: Reflections on Trout Streams and Fly Fishing, Lyons & Burford (New York, NY), 1994.
(Editor) *The Gift of Trout,* Lyons & Burford (New York, NY), 1996.
(With Jim Schollmeyer) *The Fly-Tier's Benchside Reference to Techniques and Dressing Styles,* F. Amato (Portland, OR), 1998.
(With Jim Schollmeyer) *Trout Flies of the West: Best Contemporary Patterns from the Rockies, West,* F. Amato (Portland, OR), 1998.
(With Jim Schollmeyer) *Trout Flies of the East: Best Contemporary Patterns from East of the Rockies,* F. Amato (Portland, OR), 1999.
(With Jim Schollmeyer) *Inshore Flies: Best Contemporary Patterns from the Atlantic and Gulf Coasts,* F. Amato (Portland, OR), 2000.
Jerusalem Creek: Journeys into Driftless Country, Lyons (New York, NY), 2002.

Contributing editor, *Fly Rod and Reel,* 1988—, and *Field and Stream,* 1994—.

SIDELIGHTS: The growing popularity of sport fishing in the United States has given rise to several books by Ted Leeson, an instructor at Oregon State University. With reading audiences eager for advice and information, books on fly-tying have grown in both scope and size; indeed, commented Gerald Hoffnagle in *Rackelhanen Flyfishing,* one of Leeson's guides, *The Fly-Tier's Benchside Reference to Techniques and Dressing Styles,* looks like one of "two Stone Tablets of flytying." The volume is not inexpensive, Hoffnagle noted, but for all its size, the *Fly-Tier's Benchside Reference* "has a good argument for its price." The reviewer pointed to the work's comprehensive format, organized "not by style, pattern, fish, or even progressive skill levels, but ad hoc tying problems—sometimes more than one solution per problem—that apply across all three." Hoffnagle called the guide "all technique and no fat," while also praising Leeson for text that is "actually stylish."

Leeson and coauthor Jim Schollmeyer have followed *The Fly-Tier's Benchside Reference to Techniques and Dressing Styles* with a series of books focusing on different fishing regions in the United States. *Trout Flies of the West* and *Trout Flies of the East* contain not only information on fishing lodges and related retailers in each region, but also comments from experts in the field on flytying patterns, known as "recipes." A *Fly Fisherman* reviewer said that the combination of *The Fly-Tier's Benchside Reference to Techniques and Dressing Styles* and the two regional books is "all making sense: Hit with a killer how-to book . . . and then follow up with two recipe books."

Leeson has also produced fishing books of a different sort. Titles such as *The Habit of Rivers: Reflections on Trout Streams and Fly Fishing* and *Jerusalem Creek: Journeys into Driftless Country* are less technical manuals than books of personal reflection and philosophy. *The Habit of Rivers* tells of Leeson's passion for his sport, and his experiences as a newcomer to the Pacific Northwest, which he calls "the land of unceasing seasons." *Jerusalem Creek* is set in the author's native Wisconsin, where Leeson "enters into a discriminating rapport with the entire landscape," according to a *Kirkus Reviews* contributor. John Rowen of *Booklist* admired the way Leeson takes "arcane subjects" related to the area's geography and "brings them alive with style and insight in this remarkable memoir." Like the best fishing books, Rowan concluded, *Jerusalem Creek* "transcends its topic," adding that its appeal extends beyond the fishing audience to "those who savor the nonfiction of Annie Dillard, John McPhee, and William Least-Heat Moon."

BIOGRAPHICAL AND CRITICAL SOURCES:

PERIODICALS

Aethlon, summer, 1995, review of *The Habit of Rivers: Reflections on Trout Streams and Fly Fishing*, p. 154.

Booklist, April 1, 2002, John Rowen, review of *Jerusalem Creek: Journeys into Driftless Country*, p. 1293.

Fly Fisherman, February, 2000, review of *Trout Flies of the West*, p. 22; May, 2000, review of *Trout Flies of the East*, p. 26.

Kirkus Reviews, September 1, 1996, review of *The Gift of Trout*, p. 1298; May 1, 2002, review of *Jerusalem Creek*, p. 638.

Los Angeles Times Book Review, March 26, 1995, review of *The Habit of Rivers*, p. 15.

Publishers Weekly, January 30, 1995, review of *The Habit of Rivers*, p. 98.

ONLINE

Rackelhanen Flyfishing, http://www.algonet.se/ (June 13 2002), Gerald Hoffnagle, review of *The Fly-Tier's Benchside Reference*.*

*   *   *

LEIGH, Janet 1927-

PERSONAL: Born Jeanette Helen Morrison, July 6, 1927, in Merced, CA; married John K. Carlyle, 1942 (marriage annulled, 1942); married Stanley Reames (a bandleader), 1946 (divorced, 1948); married Tony Curtis (an actor), 1951 (divorced, 1963); married Robert Brant (a stockbroker), 1964; children: (third marriage) Kelly Lee, Jamie Lee Curtis. *Education:* Attended College (now University) of the Pacific.

ADDRESSES: Home—1625 Summit Ridge Dr., Beverly Hills, CA 90210. *Agent*—Amsel Eisenstadt & Frazier, 5757 Wilshire Blvd., Suite 510, Los Angeles, CA 90036-3628.

CAREER: Actor in motion pictures, including *The Romance of Rosey Ridge*, 1947, *Hills of Home*, 1948, *Little Women*, 1949, *Strictly Dishonorable*, 1951, *It's a Big Country*, 1952, *Fearless Fagan*, 1952, *Houdini*, 1953, *Living It Up*, 1954, *Pete Kelly's Blues*, 1955, *Safari*, 1956, *Jet Pilot*, 1957, *Touch of Evil*, 1958, *Psycho*, 1960, *The Manchurian Candidate*, 1962, *Bye, Bye Birdie*, 1963, *Three on a Couch*, 1966, *An American Dream*, 1966, *Hello Down There*, Paramount, 1968, *The Deadly Dream*, 1971, *One Is a Lonely Number*, 1972, *Boardwalk*, 1979, *The Fog*, 1980, and *Halloween: H2O*, 1998; in television films, including *The Monk*, 1969, *Honeymoon with a Stranger*, 1969, and

The House on Greenapple Road, 1970; and in television programs, including *World Series Murders* and *Death's Head.*

AWARDS, HONORS: Academy Award nomination for best supporting actress, Academy of Motion Picture Arts and Sciences, 1960, for *Psycho.*

WRITINGS:

There Really Was a Hollywood (autobiography), Doubleday (New York, NY), 1984.
House of Destiny (novel), Mira (Ontario, Canada) 1995.
(With Christopher Nickens) *Psycho: Behind the Scenes of the Classic Thriller,* Harmony Books (New York, NY), 1995.
The Dream Factory (novel), Mira (Ontario, Canada), 2001.

SIDELIGHTS: For generations of film fans, the quick-cutting chills of a naked, screaming Marion Crane meeting her fate at the hands of a shower-invading, knife-wielding maniac is a quintessential moment in movie history. For Janet Leigh, who played the doomed Marion in Alfred Hitchcock's horror classic *Psycho,* the role led to a respected career in movies, television, and publishing.

Born Jeanette Helen Morrison in Merced, California, Leigh was discovered by actor Norma Shearer in 1946; the young ingénue's marquee name was personally chosen by Metro-Goldwyn-Mayer studio head Louis B. Mayer. After getting her start in such films as *Houdini* and *Pete Kelly's Blues,* Leigh landed the role of Marion Crane. She went on to appear in such varied features as the musical *Bye, Bye Birdie* and the psychological thriller *The Manchurian Candidate.* Leigh's dramatic turn in Orson Welles's *Touch of Evil* was well received, and the movie itself enjoyed a revival 1998. A member of the celebrity elite in the 1960s, Leigh made headlines for her marriage to actor Tony Curtis. One of the couple's daughters is actor Jamie Lee Curtis, a horror-star in her own right; mother and daughter appeared together in *The Fog* and *Halloween: H2O.*

Despite her wide-ranging Hollywood career, Leigh is still most strongly associated with *Psycho.* Though the movie opened to mixed reviews in 1960, it has come to be regarded as a cult classic and director Hitchcock's grace note. In 1995, the thirty-fifth anniversary of the movie's release, Leigh collaborated with Hollywood biographer Christopher Nickens on *Psycho: Behind the Scenes of the Classic Thriller.* In this volume, Leigh offers her impressions of the complicated filming of *Psycho,* along the way providing "some fascinating glimpses of Hitchcock's on-set technique," according to Gordon Flagg of *Booklist.* Among the revelations, Leigh comments that, contrary to rumor, the *Psycho* set was a jovial one; that she wore strategically placed moleskin to film the shower scene; and that making the film led to a new personal habit for the actor: "I stopped taking showers and I take baths, only baths," Leigh remarked in a 1995 *New York Times* interview with Bernard Weinraub. When only a shower is available, "I make sure the doors and windows of the house are locked, and I leave the bathroom door open and [the] shower curtain open. I'm always facing the door, watching, no matter where the shower head is." Studying the infamous shower sequence, according to Weinraub's article, Leigh noticed "a light, almost an ethereal light, a heavenly light on Marion. It was like she was being purified. Cleansed. The water—it was like she was being baptized. She was cleaning not only her body but also the inner dirt. And this made the attack even more horrible."

Leigh is also the author of two Hollywood-insider novels, *House of Destiny* and *The Dream Factory.* Of the former, a *Publishers Weekly* contributor noted that the actor/author "will never win any prizes for style" but that Leigh "weaves fact and fiction bravely." *Booklist*'s Melanie Duncan said that the story of a young man's show-business ambitions "will appeal to devotees of Hollywood fact and fiction," adding that Leigh "manages to insert personal history in several places."

BIOGRAPHICAL AND CRITICAL SOURCES:

PERIODICALS

Booklist, June 1, 1995, Gordon Flagg, review of *Psycho: Behind the Scenes of the Classic Thriller,* p. 1715; September 1, 1995, Melanie Duncan, review of *House of Destiny,* p. 40.
Books, February, 1996, review of *House of Destiny,* p. 25.

Entertainment Weekly, June 23, 1995, review of *Psycho,* p. 49.

Films in Review, September, 1995, review of *Psycho,* p. 69.

Interview, September, 1998, Patrick Giles, "Just When You Thought It Was Safe to Go Back into the Shower," p. 66.

Journal of American Culture, spring, 1998, review of *Psycho,* p. 98.

Kirkus Reviews, April 1, 1995, review of *Psycho,* p. 445.

Library Journal, May 15, 1995, review of *Psycho,* p. 74; August, 1995, review of *House of Destiny,* p. 64.

New York Times, May 1, 1995, Bernard Weinraub, "'Psycho' Deep in Janet Leigh's Psyche"; July 6, 1995, review of *Psycho,* p. C13.

New York Times Book Review, November 4, 1984, pg. 13; June 18, 1995, review of *Psycho,* p. 20; November 26, 1995, review of *House of Destiny,* p. 19.

People, August 7, 1995, Cynthia Sanz, "Coming Clean: Janet Leigh, Still Shower-Shy, Tells All about Psycho," p. 85; November 9, 1998, Elizabeth Leonard, "Talking with Janet Leigh," p. 33.

Publishers Weekly, May 22, 1995, review of *Psycho,* p. 42; July 31, 1995, review of *House of Destiny,* p. 66; January 21, 2002, review of *The Dream Factory,* p. 66.

Rapport, February, 1996, review of *House of Destiny,* p. 33.

Sight and Sound, November, 1995, review of *Psycho,* p. 37.

Washington Post Book World, August 13, 1995, review of *Psycho,* p. 11.

ONLINE

E!Online, http://www.eonline.com/ (April 1, 2002).*

*   *   *

LESSER, Michael 1939-

PERSONAL: Born March 8, 1939, in Mitchell, SD; son of Samuel A. and Edith (Shapiro) Lesser; married Deborah Langman, April 6, 1969; children: Elijah Ben, Rebecca. *Education:* Washington University, St. Louis, MO, B.A.; Cornell University, M.D.

ADDRESSES: *Office*—2340 Parker St., Berkeley, CA 94704.

CAREER: In private practice of psychiatry and nutrition in Berkeley, CA, 1971—. Founder of Othomolecular Medical Society and Nutritional Medicine. *Military service:* U.S. Public Health Service, 1968-70; became lieutenant commander.

MEMBER: Alameda-Contra Costa Medical Society.

WRITINGS:

Nutrition and Vitamin Therapy, Grove (New York, NY), 1980.

The Brain Chemistry Diet: The Personalized Prescription for Balancing Mood, Relieving Stress, and Conquering Depression, Based on Your Personality Profile, Putnam (New York, NY), 2002.

SIDELIGHTS: Dr. Michael Lesser is one of the founders of the orthomolecular movement in psychiatry, a movement that advocates treating psychiatric and mood disorders with therapies based on nutrition and vitamin supplements. Lesser's 2002 title, *The Brain Chemistry Diet: The Personalized Prescription for Balancing Mood, Relieving Stress, and Conquering Depression, Based on Your Personality Profile,* presents six personality types—including the Stoic, the Warrior, and the Star—and tailors diets to meet the specific needs of those personality types. Lesser also includes general recommendations on better psychiatric health through nutrition. A *Publishers Weekly* reviewer praised Lesser for offering case studies from his own practice and hailed the book for its "sensible recommendations."

BIOGRAPHICAL AND CRITICAL SOURCES:

PERIODICALS

Library Journal, January, 2002, Anne C. Tomlin, review of *The Brain Chemistry Diet: The Personalized Prescription for Balancing Mood, Relieving Stress, and Conquering Depression, Based on Your Personality Profile,* p. 144.

Publishers Weekly, January 21, 2002, review of *The Brain Chemistry Diet,* p. 84.*

LEVERE, Trevor H(arvey) 1944-

PERSONAL: Born March 21, 1944, in London, England; son of Godfrey and Vicki (Mendes da Costa) Levere; married Jennifer Tiesing (a teacher), July 30, 1966; children: Kevin Christopher, Rebecca Catherine. *Education:* New College, Oxford, B.A., 1966, D.Phil., 1969. *Religion:* Jewish. *Hobbies and other interests:* Bird watching, music, reading.

ADDRESSES: Home—Toronto, Ontario, Canada. *Office*—Institute for the History and Philosophy of Science and Technology, Victoria College, University of Toronto, 91 Charles Street West, Toronto M5S 1K7, Ontario, Canada. *E-mail*—trevor.levere@utoronto.ca.

CAREER: University of Toronto, Toronto, Ontario, Canada, assistant professor, 1969-74, associate professor, 1974-81, professor of the history of science, 1981—, director, Institute for the History and Philosophy of Science and Technology, 1981-86, 1993-98, director, Museum Studies Program, 1982. Fellow, Victoria College, 1982. Visiting fellow, Clare Hall, Cambridge University, 1983; resident fellow, Dibner Institute, Massachusetts Institute of Technology, 1995. Visiting scholar, Scott Polar Research Institute, 1983-84

MEMBER: International Academy of the History of Science (corresponding member), Royal Society of Canada (fellow), Canadian Society for the History of Science, History of Science Society, Royal Geographical Society (fellow), British Society for the History of Science, Royal Dutch Society of Sciences (foreign member), Académie Internationale d'Histoire des Sciences (Paris).

AWARDS, HONORS: Killam fellow, 1975-77; Guggenheim fellow, 1983-84; D.Litt., Oxford University, 1999.

WRITINGS:

Affinity and Matter: Elements of Chemical Philosophy, 1800-1865, Clarendon Press (Oxford, England), 1971.
(With G. L'E. Turner) *Martinus Van Marum,* Volume 4, Noordhoff International, 1973.

Poetry Realized in Nature: Samuel Taylor Coleridge and Early Nineteenth-Century Science, Cambridge University Press (Cambridge, England), 1981.
Science and the Canadian Arctic: A Century of Exploration, 1818-1918, Cambridge University Press (Cambridge, England), 1993.
Chemists and Chemistry in Science and Society, 1770-1878, Variorum (Brookfield, VT), 1994.
Transforming Matter: A History of Chemistry from Alchemy to the Buckyball, John Hopkins University Press (Baltimore, MD), 2001.
(With Gerard L'E. Turner) *Discussing Chemistry and Steam: The Minutes of a Coffee House Philosophical Society, 1780-1787,* Oxford university Press (Oxford, England), 2002.

EDITOR

(With R. Jarrell) *A Curious Field-Book: Science and Society in Canadian History,* Oxford University Press (Oxford, England), 1973.
Editing Texts in the History of Science and Medicine, Garland Publishing (New York, NY), 1982.
(With W. Shea) *Nature, Experiment, and the Sciences: Essays on Galileo and the History of Science,* Kluwer (Boston, MA), 1990.
(With N. M. Swerdlow) Stillman Drake, *Essays on Galileo and the History and Philosophy of Science,* University of Toronto Press (Buffalo, NY), 1999.
(With F. L. Holmes) *Instruments and Experimentation in the History of Chemistry,* MIT Press (Cambridge, MA), 2000.

Also editor of the *Annals of Science,* 1999—.

WORK IN PROGRESS: Research on the history of chemistry from the eighteenth through the nineteenth centuries; research on late eighteenth-century scientific society in England.

SIDELIGHTS: Trevor H. Levere is a scholar pursuing research in the history of chemistry. Levere's particular interests include the history of items of chemical apparatus, and he has used archeological discoveries to dispute some of the written records of instrument use through the Middle Ages and early Renaissance. He has also written about the gradual transformation of chemical research from a matter of speculative alchemy to a science of cumulative, research-based conclusions. *Instruments and Experimentation in the History of Chemistry,* which Levere edited with Frederic L. Holmes, drew praise from *American Scientist* contributor Arthur Greenberg, who felt that the chapters "are uniformly well-written and well edited. . . . They are written both for chemical historians and for a more general readership, since unfamiliar terms are defined, and often the workings of unfamiliar apparatus are explained. Each chapter ends with an extremely useful summary." Thomas L. Hankins in the *Times Literary Supplement* found the book to contain "important additions and corrections to the history of science."

Transforming Matter: A History of Chemistry from Alchemy to the Buckyball is a survey textbook based on Levere's lectures to his students at the University of Toronto. Anthony R. Butler in *American Scientist* maintained that the topic "is explained with precision and clarity." The critic concluded: "The general reader with more than a passing interest in the development of modern science would find much of interest."

Levere once told *CA:* "My first degree was in chemistry, but I had a lively historical interest and was delighted to find that history of science enabled me to combine my interests. I have been fortunate in working at a university that encourages me to pursue research and writing. My principal current project involves looking at historical chemical apparatus, as well as manuscripts and publications from the eighteenth and nineteenth centuries, to gain some understanding of the practice of science and the interplay between ideas and instruments."

BIOGRAPHICAL AND CRITICAL SOURCES:

PERIODICALS

American Scientist, July, 2001, Arthur Greenberg, "Apparatus and Acumen," p. 372; September, 2001, Anthony R. Butler, "Chemistry's Coming of Age," p. 473.
Times Literary Supplement, January 11, 2002, Thomas L. Hankins, review of *Instruments and Experimentation in the History of Chemistry,* p. 7.

LEVINE, Stephen 1937-

PERSONAL: Born July 17, 1937, in Albany, NY; son of Clarence S. (a chemist) and Ruth (Wien) Levine; married third wife, Ondrea, 1978; children: Tara, Noah, Luke. *Education:* Attended University of Miami, Coral Gables, FL, 1955-57.

ADDRESSES: Office—Warm Rock Tapes, P.O. Box 100, Chamisal, NM 87521.

CAREER: Frederick Fell Publishing Co., New York, NY, special editor, 1961-62; *Rikers Review,* Rikers Island, NY, editor in chief, 1962; Unity Press, San Francisco, CA, owner and editor, beginning 1965; *San Francisco Oracle,* San Francisco, CA, editor, 1966-68; Hanuman Foundation Dying Project, Taos, NM, co-director, beginning 1978. Writer-in-residence, Canelo Hills Wildlife Sanctuary, 1969-70; has lectured and given poetry readings at universities across the United States. Consultant to hospitals and hospices around the world.

WRITINGS:

A Resonance of Hope, Arahat Press, 1959.
Synapse: Visions of the Retinal Circus, Unity Press (San Francisco, CA), 1965.
Lovebeast, Unity Press (San Francisco, CA), 1968, revised edition, 1972.
(Editor) *Death Row: An Affirmation of Life,* Glide Publications (San Francisco, CA), 1972.
(Editor) Mae Hickman, *Care of the Wild Feathered and Furred,* Unity Press (Santa Cruz, CA), 1973.
Planet Steward: Journal of a Wildlife Sanctuary, Unity Press (Santa Cruz, CA), 1974.
(With Ram Dass) *Grist for the Mill,* Unity Press (Santa Cruz, CA), 1977, revised edition, Celestial Arts (Berkeley, CA), 1987.
A Gradual Awakening, Anchor Press (Garden City, NY), 1979, second edition, Anchor Books (New York, NY), 1989.
Who Dies?: An Investigation of Conscious Living and Conscious Dying, Anchor Press (Garden City, NY), 1982.
Meetings at the Edge: Dialogues with the Grieving and the Dying, the Healing and the Healed, Anchor Press (Garden City, NY), 1984.

Healing into Life and Death, Anchor Press (Garden City, NY), 1987.

Healers on Healing, Anchor Press (Garden City, NY), 1989.

For the Love of God, New World Library, 1990.

Guided Meditations, Explorations, and Healings, Anchor Books (New York, NY), 1991.

(With Ondrea Levine) *Embracing the Beloved: Relationship as a Path of Awakening,* Doubleday (New York, NY), 1995.

A Year to Live: How to Live This Year As If It Were Your Last, Bell Tower (New York, NY), 1997.

Turning toward the Mystery: A Seeker's Journey, HarperSanFrancisco (San Francisco, CA), 2002.

Contributor to anthologies, including *Writers in Revolt,* 1962. Contributor to audio recording *The Heart of a Relationship,* 1994. Contributor to periodicals, including *San Francisco Review of Books.*

SIDELIGHTS: Stephen Levine brings a background of study and collaboration with spiritualist Ram Dass and psychiatrist Elisabeth Kübler-Ross to his books on pain, dying, and grief. Levine uses meditative techniques to aid the terminally ill and their loved ones in exploring their emotions. For many years Levine and his wife, Ondrea, ran a telephone counseling service for those dealing with illness in their lives. "Their advice, in general, is to be open to whatever feelings arise, to accept them as a natural part of the process of dying," *Psychology Today* writer Daniel Goleman explained. While Levine has no academic background in psychology, Goleman noted, he and his wife "are good listeners who are more familiar than most of us are with the emotional territory that surrounds death. . . . The Levines' message and service," the critic concluded, fill "an essential need in American life."

Levine used the insight gleaned from work with the terminally ill to shape his own life, and to give him the thesis for his book *A Year to Live: How to Live This Year As If It Were Your Last.* Levine had seen that those who are told they have a limited time to live usually experience a profound shift in values that makes their life seem much more precious and meaningful. Careers and relationships that seemed vital may seem irrelevant, or become more important than ever. Levine and his wife decided to pick an imaginary end date for their lives and live a year as if it were really destined to happen. "In practicing to die, Levine practices living—or tries to perfect it," reported Keith Powers in *Natural Health.* Levine suggests reviewing one's life to see why past choices have been made, and recommends carefully examining those motives. Drawing on many faiths, including Christianity, Buddhism, and Native American religions, the author "argues with integrity and practical suggestions for a more focused life," stated Powers.

The Levines collaborated on *Embracing the Beloved: Relationship As a Path of Awakening.* In an era focused on individual realization and independent action, the Levines offer "a poetic and compassionate book" about the redemptive and healing power of loving relationships, according to a *Publishers Weekly* reviewer. These relationships may be with a spouse or partner, parents, other relatives, or friends, but truly loving and unselfish interaction with people offers great rewards in many ways, according to the Levines. Made up of personal anecdotes, poetry, meditation techniques and ideas from other spiritual leaders including Ram Dass, the book is valuable to anyone looking for greater insight into "their own—and their partners'—deeper natures," claimed the reviewer.

Levine urges opening oneself up to the unknowable in *Turning toward Mystery: A Seeker's Journey.* Noting that Levine's background includes time spent for drug possession in Rikers Island Penitentiary, a *Publishers Weekly* writer pointed out: "This is a man who has known fear, craving and fire in the belly and learned bravery and transcendence of self. Also a poet, Levine is able to convey his unfolding insights in fresh language."

BIOGRAPHICAL AND CRITICAL SOURCES:

PERIODICALS

Booklist, January 15, 1994, Joseph Keppler, review of *The Heart of a Relationship,* p. 955.

Library Journal, January, 1995, review of *Embracing the Beloved: Relationship As a Path of Awakening,* p. 108; February 1, 1998, Beth Farrell, review of *A Year to Live: How to Live This year As If It Were Your Last* (audio version), p. 131.

Natural Health, September-October, 1997, Keith Powers, review of *A Year to Live: How to Live This Year As If It Were Your Last,* p. 148.

Psychology Today, September, 1982.

Publishers Weekly, November 7, 1994, review of *Embracing the Beloved: Relationship As a Path of Awakening,* p. 54; February 25, 2002, review of *Turning toward the Mystery: A Seeker's Journey,* p. 61.

Tricycle: The Buddhist Review, fall, 1997, review of *A Year to Live: How to Live This Year As If It Were Your Last,* p. 92, review of *Who Dies?: An Investigation of Conscious Living and Conscious Dying,* p. 93.

Utne Reader, May, 1997, review of *A Year to Live: How to Live This Year As If It Were Your Last,* p. 84.

ONLINE

Thinking Allowed Web site, http://www.thinking allowed.com/ (January 6, 2003), interview with Stephen Levine.*

* * *

LEVY, Robert 1945-

PERSONAL: Born July 11, 1945, in Mussoorie, IN; son of Walter and Grete (Losch) Levy; married Ilsa Karger (a teacher). *Education:* University of Tampa, B.A., 1968; City University of New York, Hunter College, M.A., 1974, Brooklyn College, advanced certificate in education, 1977.

ADDRESSES: Agent—c/o Author Mail, Houghton Mifflin, 222 Berkeley, MA 02116-3764.

CAREER: Writer and educator. New York Board of Education, New York, NY, teacher and computer coordinator, 1968—.

AWARDS, HONORS: Texas Lone Star Reading List citation, for *Escape from Exile,* 1995.

WRITINGS:

YOUNG ADULT NOVELS

Escape from Exile, Houghton Mifflin (Boston, MA), 1993.

Clan of the Shape-Changers, Houghton Mifflin (Boston, MA), 1994.

The Misfit Apprentice, Houghton Mifflin (Boston, MA), 1995.

WORK IN PROGRESS: Magic Key, a fantasy adventure novel for young children.

SIDELIGHTS: Science-fiction writer Robert Levy once told *CA* that he has been "in love with fantasy ever since reading J. R. R. Tolkien's *The Hobbit* and *The Lord of the Rings.*" Making up his own worlds and telling his own stories fostered his talent for writing: "When my nieces were little, I made up stories for them about Martha Tooth Faerie and Horace the Belly Button Monster. By imagining that I'm just telling a longer story to them or to the sixth-grade students I teach, I sit in front of my Mac and wait. If I'm lucky, a character pops into my head and tells me his or her adventure. All I do is write what I'm told."

The story in *Escape from Exile* begins as Daniel Taylor works his way home through a blizzard. When a bolt of lightning hits the thirteen year old, he is knocked unconscious and wakes to find himself in a world destroyed by civil war. He soon finds that his survival depends on the help of the feline animals—the "samkits"—that have befriended him. Mentally communicating with Daniel, the samkits manage to get him to help them as well and save Queen Lauren from Resson, the evil man who keeps her from her throne. In the end, Daniel again loses consciousness and wakes to find himself near home. Li Stark of *School Library Journal* wrote that the "story is well paced, with some nice touches of humor." A *Publishers Weekly* reviewer called *Escape from Exile* a "well-founded fantasy with abundant action."

In *Clan of the Shape-Changers* sixteen-year-old Susan has the ability to change her shape to that of an animal. When Ometerer, the ruler of Reune, begins searching for those with green eyes and the shape-changing power, Susan and her wolf, Farrun, flee her village. As she travels, Susan rescues a twelve-year-old boy who, unlike herself, can't control his power to change his shape. Together they challenge Ometerer's plans by attempting to save the people of their green-eyed clan. Noting the book's "solid premise" and "exciting action," *Voice of Youth Advocates* reviewer Wendy E. Betts commented that *Clan of the Shape-Changers* is "an improvement over Levy's first book." Susan L. Rogers wrote in *School Library Journal* that "there is much more to be explained about this interesting planet and its inhabitants." In the opinion of *Booklist* contributor Chris Sherman, the "suspense" in *Clan of the Shape-Changers* "builds steadily to a dangerous climax that will satisfy fantasy and adventure lovers."

Levy also wrote a companion book to *Clan of the Shape-Changers* titled *The Misfit Apprentice*. This third novel follows the adventures of Maria, a magician's apprentice who, because she is unable to control her magic, must seek her fortune in some other line of work. During her ensuing travels, Maria meets a mute boy named Tristan. Along with a catlike being named Jerrold, they embark on a journey to steal magical scrolls from a nearby country, defeating a malicious king in the process. "In this well-crafted fantasy-adventure, magic becomes a real and believable force," Chris Sherman commented in *Booklist*.

In all of his novels, Levy demonstrates a strong affection for fantasy and adventure stories and for the characters who inhabit his imaginative lands. As he once told *CA*, the "values I hold—people having a sense of honor, caring for the land they live on and the animals they share the land with—appear in my characters and help them come alive in my own mind."

BIOGRAPHICAL AND CRITICAL SOURCES:

PERIODICALS

Booklist, April 1, 1994, Chris Sherman, review of *Clan of the Shape-Changers*, p. 1436; August, 1995, Chris Sherman, review of *The Misfit Apprentice*, pp. 1940-1941; November 1, 1997, review of *Clan of the Shape-Changers*, p. 475.
Book Report, September-October, 1994, Susan Martin, review of *Clan of the Shape-Changers*, p. 40.
Horn Book Guide, fall, 1993, p. 301.
Kirkus Reviews, March 15, 1994, p. 398.
Publishers Weekly, April 12, 1993, p. 64.
School Library Journal, May, 1993, p. 106; May, 1994, Susan L. Rogers, review of *Clan of the Shape-Changers*, p. 128; April, 1995, Patricia A. Dollisch, review of *The Misfit Apprentice*, p. 154.
Voice of Youth Advocates, August, 1993, pp. 166-167; June, 1994, pp. 99-100.*

*   *   *

LICHTENSTEIN, Nelson 1944-

PERSONAL: Born November 15, 1944, in Frederick, MD; son of Theodore Samuel and Beryl Rose Lichtenstein; married Eileen Boris, January 26, 1979; children: Daniel. *Ethnicity:* "Jewish." *Education:* University of California—Berkeley, Ph.D. (history), 1974. *Politics:* Socialist. *Religion:* Jewish. *Hobbies and other interests:* Skiing, running, mountaineering.

ADDRESSES: Office—Department of History, University of California, Santa Barbara, Santa Barbara, CA 93106. *E-mail*—nelson@history.ucsb.edu.

CAREER: Catholic University of America, Washington, DC, assistant professor, then associate professor of history, 1981-89; University of Virginia, Charlottesville, professor of history, 1989-2001; University of California, Santa Barbara, 2001—.

MEMBER: American Historical Association, Organization of American Historians, Labor and Working Class History Association.

AWARDS, HONORS: University of Virginia, Phi Beta Kappa Book Award; National Endowment for the Humanities fellowships, 1982, 1993; William E. Dornan Prize for Teaching Excellence, 1986; John Simon Guggenheim Memorial Foundation fellowship, 1998; Rockefeller Bellagio fellowship, 1999; Oregon Center for the Humanities fellowship, 2000.

WRITINGS:

(Editor) *Political Profiles: The Johnson Years*, Facts on File (New York, NY), 1976.
(Editor) *Political Profiles: The Kennedy Years*, Facts on File, 1976.
Labor's War at Home: The CIO in World War II, Cambridge University Press (New York, NY), 1982, with a new introduction, Temple University Press (Philadelphia, PA), 2003.
(Editor, with Stephen Meyer) *On the Line: Essays in the History of Auto Work*, University of Illinois Press (Urbana, IL), 1989.
(Editor, with Eileen Boris) *Major Problems in the History of American Workers: Documents and Essays*, D.C. Heath (Lexington, MA), 1991, 2nd edition, Houghton Mifflin (Boston, MA), 2003.
(Editor, with Howell John Harris) *Industrial Democracy in America: The Ambiguous Promise*, Woodrow Wilson Center Press (New York, NY), 1993.
(With Henry Kraus) *Heroes of Unwritten Story: The UAW, 1934-39*, University of Illinois Press (Urbana, IL), 1994.

The Most Dangerous Man in Detroit: Walter Reuther and the Fate of American Labor, Basic Books (New York, NY), 1995, published as *Walter Reuther: The Most Dangerous Man in Detroit,* University of Illinois Press (Urbana, IL), 1997.

What's Next for Organized Labor?: Report of the Century Foundation Task Force on the Future of Unions, Century Foundation Press (New York, NY), 1999.

(With Joshua Freeman and Stephen Brier) *Who Built America?: Working People and the Nation's Economy, Politics, Culture, and Society,* Worth (New York, NY), 2000.

State of the Union: A Century of American Labor, Princeton University Press (Princeton, NJ), 2002.

WORK IN PROGRESS: Triumphalism and Apocalypse: Thinking about Capitalism in Twentieth-Century America.

SIDELIGHTS: Historian and educator Nelson Lichtenstein has written on a number of topics related to twentieth-century American labor history, but the first titles associated with his name were two presidential biographies published in 1976, *Political Profiles: The Johnson Years* and *Political Profiles: The Kennedy Years,* which he edited for Facts on File, Inc. Lichtenstein's first full-length book came six years later with *Labor's War at Home: The CIO in World War II,* a revision of his doctoral dissertation. He posits that during the war, the leadership of the Congress of Industrial Unions—with its five million members one of the largest organized labor forces in the United States at the time—subordinated the interests of rank-and-file workers to the Roosevelt Administration's demand for social peace and war production.

Using information from labor archives, *Labor's War at Home* charts the shift in the CIO's goals. In the 1930s it was a radical, decentralized organization whose member unions, like the powerful United Automobile Workers on whom the book concentrates, were not averse to shutting down factories in their struggle to win fair pay and safe working conditions for American workers. World War II, however, brought changes to how the CIO leadership cooperated with the federal government, as Lichtenstein demonstrates. When it became evident that uninterrupted wartime production was crucial to victory against Germany and Japan, the CIO agreed that in exchange for a no-strike policy,

companies would now deduct union dues from members' paychecks. Such a deal enriched the coffers of the CIO, but often left the rank and file dissatisfied, having essentially lost two of their most powerful tools—the right to strike and the right to withhold dues. Maurice Isserman of the *Nation* termed *Labor's War at Home* "an impressive work which offers a useful perspective on the origins of the crisis the labor movement faces today."

Lichtenstein further explored the relationship between the country's most prominent industrialized sector, the auto industry, and the development of unionism in the United States in *On the Line: Essays in the History of Auto Work,* a 1989 work he edited with Stephen Meyer. For the book he contributed "'The Man in the Middle': A Social History of Automobile Industry Foremen." Concentrating specifically on the line bosses at the Ford Motor Company, Lichtenstein "shows how wartime conditions encouraged the proletarianization of low-level supervisors and how their white-collar status was only re-established in 1947 when management crushed the Foremen's Association," noted Ronald Edsforth in the *Journal of American History.* This work was followed with two books edited by Lichtenstein: *Major Problems in the History of American Workers: Documents and Essays* and *Industrial Democracy in America: The Ambiguous Promise,* the second which was coedited with Howell John Harris.

Lichtenstein, by this time a professor at the University of Virginia, gained more attention outside of academic circles with his book on labor leader Walter Reuther. Published in 1995, *The Most Dangerous Man in Detroit: Walter Reuther and the Fate of American Labor* examines the long crusade of the autoworker-turned-CIO president that began with his engineering of a sit-down strike at General Motors in 1937. Prior to that, he had been a die-maker at Ford, the last of the automakers to unionize.

In *The Most Dangerous Man in Detroit* Lichtenstein comments that his work "demonstrates that Reuther became a 'prisoner' of the institutions he helped to build: the bureaucratic UAW, routinized collective bargaining, and the Democratic Party." Lichtenstein also chronicles the friendship Reuther enjoyed over the years with a succession of U.S. presidents, and his outspoken support of the civil rights movement. "Recounting Reuther's maneuverings during World War II, Lichtenstein's assessment of the UAW leader becomes more critical," noted Robert Bussel in *Industrial and Labor Relations Review.* In the labor leader's "quest for political influence," Bussel continued, the author argues that Reuther "embraced a 'Faustian bargain,' muting 'shop-floor syndicalism' and criticism of the New Deal state in exchange for institutional acceptance and what turned out to be a limited role in shaping wartime production and industrial policy." Later, as president of the UAW, Reuther succeeded in again leading a 1946 strike against GM that culminated in what has come to be seen as a landmark labor agreement. Reuther died in 1970 in a plane crash.

Reviewing *The Most Dangerous Man in Detroit,* Bussel praised the author's research while noting that Lichtenstein "does not consistently examine the interplay between Reuther's public and private identities that might explain his motivation." Other reviewers held fewer reservations, *Washington Post Book World* critic Jeffrey E. Garten terming the book "a meticulously researched, clearly written and quickly paced story," and concluding: "Reuther's life, as portrayed by Lichtenstein, is also a story about the rise of the middle class in America as both an economic reality and a political force, and its symbiotic relationship with the growth of labor unions." To *Labor Studies Journal* contributor Ken Fones-Wolf, the author has produced "what will surely become the standard biography of Reuther." For his part, Lichtenstein once told *CA:* "The publication of my Reuther biography coincided with the election of a reform leadership in the AFL-CIO. Thus I have had the opportunity and credibility to become active as an organizer of conferences and symposia linking the trade union leadership and academic intellectuals once again."

In Volume 2 of the textbook series *Who Built America?* subtitled *Working People and the Nation's Economy, Politics, Culture, and Society,* Lichtenstein and his co-editors examine the state of labor since 1877. "Many students are surprised by what they find in these pages," noted Lisa Phillips in a review for *Teaching History.* Noting that in the past, history writers usually focused on similar groups of people, Phillips added that the *Who Built America?* writers "structure the narrative so that these 'groups' of people are the driving force behind the major developments traditionally discussed in American history." By spotlighting the influence of farmers, immigrants, women, and African Americans in shaping labor's history, Lichtenstein's book "makes clear, in a way in which other texts do

not, the role of 'ordinary' people in influence the events we deem central in American history," Phillips continued.

Lichtenstein marked one hundred years of trade unionism with his 2001 release *State of the Union: A Century of American Labor.* The author traces organized labor from its days as a male-oriented bastion of heavy industry to the more modern view of unions as heavily slanted toward government workers, service workers, and teachers. In the view of *Library Journal* critic Duncan Stewart, the author "examines both the positive and the negative sides of American labor—unions have been champions of civil rights . . . and economically self-interested clubs." Contemporary union leaders such as John Sweeney, whom Lichtenstein identifies as an advocate of a "social wage" and a nationalized health system, "embody the author's vision," added *Booklist* contributor Gilbert Taylor, "of the labor movement's agenda."

BIOGRAPHICAL AND CRITICAL SOURCES:

PERIODICALS

American Historical Review, April, 1979, p. 591; June, 1984, p. 866; February, 1991, p. 312; October, 1997, review of *The Most Dangerous Man in Detroit: Walter Reuther and the Fate of American Labor,* p. 1250.

Booklist, March 15, 2002, Gilbert Taylor, review of *State of the Union: A Century of American Labor.*

Business History Review, winter, 1993, p. 656.

Choice, July/August, 1977, p. 654; September, 1983, p. 154.

Contemporary Psychology, November, 1978, p. 197.

Contemporary Sociology, March, 1997, review of *The Most Dangerous Man in Detroit,* p. 165.

Industrial and Labor Relations Review, January, 1997, Robert Bussel, review of *The Most Dangerous Man in Detroit,* p. 363.

Journal of American History, December, 1983, p. 719; December, 1991, Ronald Edsforth, review of *On the Line: Essays in the History of Auto Work,* p. 114.

Journal of Economic History, March, 1984, p. 220; March, 1992, p. 251.

Labor Studies Journal, fall, 1997, Ken Fones-Wolf, review of *The Most Dangerous Man in Detroit,* p. 103.

Library Journal, February 1, 1977, p. 370; April 1, 2002, Duncan Stewart, review of *State of the Union,* p. 124.

Monthly Labor Review, May, 1994, p. 64.

Nation, April 30, 1983, p. 544.

Publishers Weekly, October 9, 1995, p. 71.

RQ, fall, 1977, p. 80.

Teaching History, spring, 2002, Lisa Phillips, review of *Who Built America?: Working People and the Nation's Economy, Politics, Culture, and Society,* p. 44.

Washington Post Book World, November 26, 1995, Jeffrey E. Garten, review of *The Most Dangerous Man in Detroit,* p. 1.

Wilson Library Bulletin, June, 1977, p. 815.

*   *   *

LOEWER, (Henry) Peter 1934-

PERSONAL: Born February 13, 1934, in Buffalo, NY; son of Henry Christian (a design engineer) and Ruth Isabelle (a fashion designer; maiden name, Duerstein) Loewer; married Jean Jenkins (an illustrator), February 13, 1959. *Education:* University of Buffalo, B.F. A., 1958. *Politics:* Republican. *Religion:* Episcopalian.

ADDRESSES: Office—Graphos Studio, P.O. Box 5039, Biltmore Station, Asheville, NC 28813. *Agent*—Dominick Abel, 146 West 82nd St., New York, NY 10024. *E-mail*—thewildgardener@earthlink.net.

CAREER: Gardener, artist, journalist, and writer. Graphos Studio, Asheville, NC, owner and art director, 1963—. *Upper Delaware,* art director, 1979-80; *Sullivan County Democrat,* editor, 1979-81; *Warwick Photo Advertiser,* production manager, 1983-86. Host of television series *The Wild Gardener,* WCQS, Asheville, NC. Botanical Gardens at Asheville, member of board of directors. *Military service:* U.S. Army, 1959-61.

MEMBER: American Society of Journalists and Authors, American Conifer Society, American Rock Garden Society, Alpine Garden Society, Himalayan Plant Society, Royal Horticultural Society, Men's Garden Club of Asheville (member of board of directors).

AWARDS, HONORS: Philadelphia Book Clinic Award, 1987, for *Gardens by Design;* National Agricultural Library, one of the fifty great garden books citation, 1988, for *The Annual Garden;* three awards from Garden Writers Association of America.

WRITINGS:

(And illustrator) *The Indoor Water Gardener's How-to Handbook,* Walker (New York, NY), 1973.

(And illustrator) *Bringing the Outdoors In,* Walker (New York, NY), 1974, 2nd edition, Contemporary Books, 1988.

(And illustrator) *Seeds and Cuttings,* Walker (New York, NY), 1975.

(And illustrator) *Growing and Decorating with Grasses,* Walker (New York, NY), 1977.

(And illustrator) *Growing Plants in Water,* Penguin (New York, NY), 1980.

(And illustrator) *Evergreens: A Guide for Landscape, Lawn, and Garden,* Walker (New York, NY), 1981.

(And illustrator) *The Month-by-Month Garden Almanac,* Putnam (New York, NY), 1983.

(And illustrator) *Gardens by Design,* Rodale Press (Emmaus, PA), 1986.

(Editor and photographer) *Taylor's Guide to Annuals,* Houghton (Boston, MA), 1986.

(Editor) *Garden Ornaments,* Brooklyn Botanic Garden (New York, NY), 1987.

(And illustrator) *The Annual Garden,* Rodale Press (Emmaus, PA), 1988.

(And illustrator) *American Gardens,* Simon & Schuster (New York, NY), 1988.

(Editor) *Ornamental Grasses,* Brooklyn Botanic Garden (New York, NY), 1988.

(And illustrator) *A Year of Flowers,* Rodale Press (Emmaus, PA), 1989.

A World of Plants: The Missouri Botanical Garden, Abrams (New York, NY), 1989.

Letters to Sarah (juvenile), Fort Delaware Museum, 1989.

(And illustrator) *The Indoor Window Garden,* Contemporary Books (Lincolnwood, IL), 1990.

The Inside-out Stomach (juvenile), Atheneum (New York, NY), 1990.

(And illustrator) *The Wild Gardener: On Flowers and Foliage for the Natural Border,* Stackpole (Mechanicsburg, PA), 1991.

(And illustrator) *Tough Plants for Tough Places: How to Grow 101 Easy-Care Plants for Every Part of Your Yard,* Rodale Press (Emmaus, PA), 1991.

(With Anne Halpin) *Secrets of the Great Gardeners: How to Make Your Garden As Beautiful As Theirs,* Summit Books, 1991.

(And illustrator) *The Evening Garden: Flowers and Fragrance from Dusk till Dawn,* Macmillan (New York, NY), 1992.

Step-by-Step Annuals, Better Homes & Gardens Books (Des Moines, IA), 1994.

Wildflowers and Native Plants, Better Homes & Gardens Books (Des Moines, IA), 1995.

(With Craig Tufts) *The National Wildlife Federation's Guide to Gardening for Wildlife: How to Create a Beautiful Backyard Habitat for Birds, Butterflies, and Other Wildlife,* Rodale Press (Emmaus, PA), 1995.

Thoreau's Garden: Native Plants for the American Landscape, Stackpole (Mechanicsburg, PA), 1996.

Pond Water Zoo: An Introduction to Microscopic Life, Atheneum (New York, NY), 1996.

(With Larry Mellichamp) *The Winter Garden: Planning and Planting for the Southeast,* Stackpole (Mechanicsburg, PA), 1997.

Fragrant Gardens: How to Select and Make the Most of Scented Flowers and Leaves, Houghton Mifflin (Boston, MA), 1999.

Outwitting Weeds, Lyons Press (Guilford, CT), 2001.

Solving Deer Problems: How to Keep Them out of the Garden, Avoid Them on the Road, and Deal with Them Anywhere!, Lyons Press (Guilford, CT), 2003.

Small-Space Gardening: How to Successfully Grow Flowers and Vegetables in Containers and Pots, Lyons Press (Guilford, CT), 2003.

Also author of *The New Small Garden,* 1994; and *Seeds: The Definitive Guide to Growing, History, and Lore,* 1996. Illustrator of ten natural science books, primarily for Macmillan. Author of the column "Back to the Garden," *Sullivan County Democrat,* 1977—. Contributor of articles and illustrations to magazines, including *Woman's Day, Green Scene, American Horticulturist, Organic Gardening, Garden Design,* and *Gardens and Landscapes.* Editor, *Quill and Trowel,* 1988-91, and *American Conifer Society Bulletin,* 1991—; contributing editor, *Carolina Gardener.*

ILLUSTRATOR

Alan E. Simmons, *Growing Unusual Fruit,* Walker (New York, NY), 1972.

Bebe Miles, *Wildflower Perennials for Your Garden,* Hawthorn (New York, NY), 1976.

Jean Loewer, *The Moonflower* (juvenile), Peachtree (Atlanta, GA), 1998.

SIDELIGHTS: Peter Loewer once told *CA:* "I have been both a writer and artist since I was a teenager. An overwhelming love of nature, nurtured by both family and friends, has led to a critically successful career." As both an author and as the host of *The Wild Gardener* on an Asheville, North Carolina, television station, Loewer dispenses advice on how to nurture plants both domestic and wild. His *Secrets of the Great Gardeners: How to Make Your Garden As Beautiful As Theirs* contains a guided tour through the famed Brooklyn Botanical Gardens, including tips from the staff who tends to the foliage. For "gardeners hankering to crate a robust, unaffectedly lovely natural border," a *Publishers Weekly* reviewer recommended Loewer's *The Wild Gardener,* which the reviewer characterized as a set of "charmingly eclectic essays."

Not every garden is well-suited to its task, which is why Loewer wrote *Tough Plants for Tough Places: How to Grow 101 Easy-Care Plants for Every Part of Your Yard.* In this book the author shows how to transform problem spots into "spaces flourishing with green," as a contributor to *Publishers Weekly* put it, adding that Loewer "stubbornly—and charmingly—refuses to give up on areas that seem forbidding to plants." The reviewer also praised Loewer for offering, "as usual," a practical and comprehensive menu of gardening options. By the time *The Evening Garden: Flowers and Fragrance from Dusk till Dawn* was released in 1992, Loewer was recognized as "one of the very best gardening enthusiasts now writing today," in the view of a *Publishers Weekly* reviewer. *The Evening Garden* shows how day-lilies, cactuses, wildflowers, and orchids thrive during the evening hours; the book also covers the care and feeding of both indoor and outdoor plants. The author, said *Horticulture* contributor Christopher Reed, "celebrates in a most readably evocative style" the fauna that releases its fragrance at night, and "reflects on the beauty of 'the night and the light of the moon and the stars.'"

The Winter Garden: Planning and Planting for the Southeast addresses the needs of that portion of the United States that sees a relatively mild winter but is not entirely free of the occasional ice storm or heavy snow. Loewer and coauthor Larry Mellichamp list the suggested plants to withstand such conditions, and explain that even in winter some flowers will release their perfume during the winter months. The authors include "delightful tidbits," according to a *Publishers Weekly* critic, including the origin of the roast-beef iris, named because its crushed leaves smell like cooked meat. In *Thoreau's Garden: Native Plants for the American Landscape,* Loewer weaves excerpts from Henry David Thoreau's famous journals with his own notes on the named plants. "Yet another admirable book" was Reed's opinion of this release; his praise was echoed by Alice Joyce of *Booklist,* who said that for gardeners, "a new book by Loewer is cause for celebration."

For younger readers, Loewer has produced such books as *Pond Water Zoo: An Introduction to Microscopic Life.* An acclaimed horticultural illustrator, Loewer also provides the artwork for a book written by his wife, Jean Loewer. *The Moonflower* is a picture book that provides child-oriented scientific information along with the story of how the moonflower blooms and the many night creatures who share its world. A *School Library Journal* reviewer applauded the "beautiful illustrations" accompanying the "lyrical text" of *The Moonflower.*

BIOGRAPHICAL AND CRITICAL SOURCES:

PERIODICALS

Booklist, August, 1996, Alice Joyce, review of *Thoreau's Garden: Native Plants for the American Landscape,* p. 1870; September 15, 1996, Susan DeRonne, review of *Pond Water Zoo: An Introduction to Microscopic Life,* p. 235; September 1, 1997, George Cohen, review of *The Winter Garden: Planning and Planting for the Southeast,* p. 47.

Bulletin of the Center for Children's Books, December, 1996, review of *Pond Water Zoo,* p. 141.

Fine Gardening, May, 1994, review of *The Evening Garden: Flowers and Fragrance from Dusk till Dawn,* p. 30.

Horn Book Guide, spring, 1997, review of *Pond Water Zoo,* p. 118; fall, 1998, review of *The Moonflower,* p. 379.

Horticulture, October, 1993, Christopher Reed, review of *The Evening Garden,* p. 72; November, 1997, Reed, review of *Thoreau's Garden,* p. 69.

Library Journal, January, 1993, review of *The Evening Garden,* p. 154; August, 1996, review of *Thoreau's Garden,* p. 99; July, 1997, Beth Clewis Crim, review of *The Winter Garden,* p. 113.

New York Times Book Review, June 6, 1993, review of *The Evening Garden,* p. 44.

People, June 4, 1990, Kristin McMurran, review of *A World of Plants: The Missouri Botanical Garden,* p. 33.

Publishers Weekly, March 23, 1990, Molly McQuade, review of *A World of Plants,* p. 76; March 29, 1991, McQuade, review of *Secrets of the Great Gardeners: How to Make Your Garden As Beautiful As Theirs,* p. 91; September 27, 1991, review of *The Wild Gardener: On Flowers and Foliage for the Natural Border,* p. 62; November 22, 1991, review of *Tough Plants for Tough Places: How to Grow 101 Easy-Care Plants for Every Part of Your Yard,* p. 53; December 28, 1992, review of *The Evening Garden,* p. 68; April 4, 1994, review of *The New Small Garden,* p. 76; April 1, 1996, review of *Seeds: The Definitive Guide to Growing, History, and Lore,* p. 73; August 4, 1997, review of *The Winter Garden,* p. 71.

School Library Journal, February, 1997, review of *Pond Water Zoo,* p. 120; August, 1998, review of *The Moonflower,* p. 153.

Southern Living, February, 1994, review of *The Evening Garden,* p. 70.

Washington Post Book World, December 5, 1993, review of *The Evening Garden,* p. 8.*

* * *

LOUIE, David Wong 1954-

PERSONAL: Born 1954, in Rockville Centre, NY; son of laundry workers; married, 1982 (divorced); married, 1995; children: (first marriage) Julian. *Ethnicity:* "Chinese-American." *Education:* Vassar College, B.A., 1977; University of Iowa, M.F.A., 1981.

ADDRESSES: Office—Department of English, University of California, Los Angeles, 405 Hilgard Ave., Los Angeles, CA 90024.

CAREER: Writer and teacher. Worked in advertising in New York; teacher of creative writing and literature at University of California at Berkeley, 1988, Vassar College, 1988-92, and University of California at Los Angeles, 1992—.

AWARDS, HONORS: Art Seidenbaum Award, first fiction, *Los Angeles Times,* and John C. Zacharis First Book Award, *Ploughshares*/Emerson College, both 1991, both for *Pangs of Love, and Other Stories;* Lannan Foundation Literary fellowship, 2002.

David Wong Louie

WRITINGS:

Pangs of Love, and Other Stories, Knopf (New York, NY), 1991.
The Barbarians Are Coming, Putnam (New York, NY), 2000.

Work represented in anthologies, including *The Best American Short Stories of 1989,* Houghton, (Boston, MA), 1989; *The Big Aiiieeeee! An Anthology of Chinese American and Japanese American Literature,* edited by Jeffery P. Chan, Dutton (New York, NY), 1991; *Other Sides of Silence: A Ploughshares Anthology,* Faber (New York, NY), 1993; and *Charlie Chan Is Dead: An Anthology of Contemporary Asian American Fiction,* Viking (New York, NY), 1993.

Contributor to periodicals, including *Chicago Review, Fiction International, Iowa Review, New York Times Book Review,* and *Ploughshares.*

SIDELIGHTS: David Wong Louie has won acclaim with his first book, *Pangs of Love, and Other Stories,* in which he concentrates on the world of Asian Americans. Among the notable tales in this offbeat collection are the title entry, in which a woman's son belittles her because she cannot speak English; "Disturbing the Universe," which recasts baseball as Chinese in origin; "The Movers," in which a young man finds himself alone in an empty house and gradually assumes the identity of its previous occupant; and "Bottle of Beaujolais," in which a sushi-bar worker, who keeps an otter in his storefront window, falls under the romantic spell of a mysterious woman.

Pangs of Love also includes "Displacement," in which an immigrant cleaning woman feigns ignorance of English and silently suffers the verbal harangues of her elderly employer. This story won inclusion in the anthology *The Best American Short Stories of 1989.* According to Dewitt Henry of *Ploughshares,* the prestigious literary journal of Emerson College in Boston, "the complexity of the story" arises from "the complexity of Mrs. Chow's character," an aristocratic, displaced Chinese female artist. DeWitt wrote, "The story as I read it resolves not with assimilation, but with her resigned and forward-looking ironic accommodation."

Upon publication in 1991 *Pangs of Love* gained recognition as an impressive literary debut for Louie. Janice C. Simpson, writing in *Time,* proclaimed Louie's volume "a sharp and quirky collection," and Gary Krist, in his assessment for the *New York Times Book Review,* affirmed that *Pangs of Love* is an "inventive first collection." Krist added that Louie's "affectionate and mildly surrealistic vision is embodied in imaginative narratives that . . . at least succeed in persuading us of their own manic integrity." *Pangs of Love,* Krist concluded, "refuses to be pigeonholed—and that in itself is a valiant achievement." Chief among the themes of the collection's eleven stories are "alienation, human suffering, compassion, healing, and forgiveness," as Betty Wang noted in *Jade Dragon.*

Louie's first novel, *The Barbarians Are Coming,* is the story of an immigrant Chinese family on Long Island in the late 1970s. Sterling Lung, son of Chinese laundry owners and a first-generation American, narrates the tale. Paul Gray of *Time* called it "a sprightly novel of assimilation." Resisting his parents' wishes to become a doctor, Sterling instead studies cooking at the Culinary Institute of America and intends to become a chef. He breaks the news to his parents, as Richard Eder described it in the *New York Times Book Review,* "outfitted with a chef's knife, a napkin and white coat.

Doctor's coat, his mother surmises. Knife for surgery. Napkin for wiping up blood. It is one of many misunderstandings that apply a comical distress to the surface of a more painful tale." Sterling lands a job cooking at an upscale Connecticut ladies' club, only to receive requests for Chinese food, which he never learned to cook. Although the Lungs have arranged for a young woman from Hong Kong to come to the United States to marry their son, he makes plans to marry Bliss Sass, his pregnant Jewish-American girlfriend. The younger Lung succeeds in disappointing his parents on all fronts, with major and minor episodes creating even greater distances between father and son.

The tenor of the novel bounces between pathos and humor, as Louie explores the discord that confronts Chinese-American families. Don Lee of *Ploughshares* noted that "the heart and power of Louie's novel lies more in the tragedy, not the comedy, of the Lung men." Wanting their son to assimilate, the Lungs also want him to remain Chinese, creating an impossible dilemma for him. Sterling, meanwhile, wishes to become the All-American male. Shirley N. Quan of *Library Journal* observed, "Louie writes with wit, intelligence, sensitivity, and insight, presenting an incredible yet believable assortment of characters who are all tied together in one emotionally moving and satisfying story." *Publishers Weekly* called the book "brilliant in its scathing insights. . . . Louie dazzlingly captures the bitter ironies of Asian-American life, but it is the scenes between father and son and, eventually, the scenes between Sterling and his sons, that expose the most complex realities of Chinese-American identity. . . . Louie's coruscating novel is full of astonishing writing, but the real delight is his wit and humor as he keeps plucking away the prickly petals of his characters' desires until he finds their hearts."

BIOGRAPHICAL AND CRITICAL SOURCES:

PERIODICALS

Amerasia Journal, spring, 1996, Lisa Lowe, review of *Pangs of Love,* p. 253.
Biography, winter, 2001, Lisa Marie Cacho, "Asian Americans," p. 363.

Boston Sunday Globe, March 5, 2000, review of *The Barbarians Are Coming.*
Elle Magazine, March, 2000, review of *The Barbarians Are Coming.*
Fiction Readers' Advisory, October 10, 2000, Charlotte Thompson, review of *The Barbarians Are Coming.*
Library Journal, June 1, 1991, Glenn Masuchika, review of *Pangs of Love,* p. 194; February 15, 2000, Shirley N. Quan, review of *The Barbarians Are Coming,* p. 197.
Newsday, March 6, 2000, review of *The Barbarians Are Coming.*
New York Times Book Review, July 14, 1991, Gary Krist, review of *Pangs of Love,* p. 13; July 14, 1991, Laurel Graeb, "It's Hard to Explain Mother," p. 13; Richard Eder, "Now We're Cooking" (review of *The Barbarians Are Coming*), p. 8.
Ploughshares, fall, 2000, Don Lee, review of *The Barbarians Are Coming,* p. 225.
Poets & Writers Magazine, July-August, 2000, Cheryl Pearl, "David Wong Louie: Traveling the Distance between Fathers and Sons," p. 48.
Publishers Weekly, February 8, 1991, Gayle Feldman, "Spring's Five Fictional Encounters of the Chinese American Kind," p. 25; May 10, 1991, review of *Pangs of Love,* p. 270; November 22, 1991, Lisa See, "Kesey Wins Kirsch Award at 12th *L.A. Times*' Prizegiving" (prizewinners include David Wong Louie), p. 15; January 10, 2000, review of *The Barbarians Are Coming,* p. 43.
San Francisco Chronicle, March 5-11, 2000, review of *The Barbarians Are Coming.*
Seattle Weekly, March 2, 2000, review of *The Barbarians Are Coming.*
Time, June 3, 1991, Janice C. Simpson and Iyer Pico, "Fresh Voices above the Noisy Din; New Works by Four Chinese Americans Splendidly Illustrate the Frustrations, Humor and Eternal Wonder of the Immigrant's Life," pp. 66-67; March 27, 2000, Paul Gray, review of *The Barbarians Are Coming,* p. 97.

ONLINE

BookBrowser, http://www.bookbrowser.com/ (March 28, 2002), Harriet Klausner, review of *The Barbarians Are Coming.*
Ploughshares Web site, http://www.pshares.org/ (fall, 1988), DeWitt Henry, "On David Wong Louie."

M

MAJOR, H. M.
 See JARVIS, Sharon

*   *   *

McCABE, Eugene 1930-

PERSONAL: Born July 7, 1930, in Glasgow, Scotland; son of Owen (a publican) and Helen (a teacher and musician; maiden name, MacMahon) McCabe; married Margot Bowen (an air hostess with Aer Lingus), 1955; children: Ruth, Marcus, Patrick, Stephen. *Education:* Attended Castleknock College, Dublin; University College, Cork, B.A., 1953. *Politics:* "Disenchanted left of center." *Religion:* "Not Christ's cup of tea, *luke*warm, God has a lot to answer for." *Hobbies and other interests:* "Pastoral, historical."

ADDRESSES: Home—Drumard, Clones, County Monaghan, Ireland. *Agent*—A. P. Watt Michelin House, 81 Fulham Rd., London SW3 6RB, England.

CAREER: Farmer, 1955-96; writer, 1955—.

AWARDS, HONORS: Irish Life Award, 1964, for *The King of the Castle;* Prague Festival Award, for television play, 1974; Irish Critics Award, for television play, 1976; Royal Society of Literature Winifred Holtby prize for fiction, 1977; Reading Association of Ireland Award, for *Cyril: The Quest of an Orphaned Squirrel,* 1987.

WRITINGS:

PLAYS

The King of the Castle (produced in Dublin, Ireland, 1964, produced in New York, 1978), Gallery Press (Dublin, Ireland), 1978, Dufour Editions (Chester Springs, PA), 1997.
Breakdown (produced in Dublin, Ireland, 1966).
Pull Down a Horseman (produced in Dublin, Ireland, 1966), published with *Gale Day* (also see below), Gallery Press (Dublin, Ireland), 1979.
Swift (produced in Dublin, Ireland, 1969).
Victims (includes *Cancer, Heritage,* and *Victims*), adapted from his own fiction (televised, 1976; produced in Belfast, Ireland, 1981), Mercier Press (County Cork, Ireland), 1976; *Cancer,* published by Proscenium Press (Newark, DE), 1980.
Roma (adaptation of his own story; televised, 1979), Turoe Press (Dublin, Ireland), 1979.
Gale Day (televised, 1979; produced in Dublin, Ireland, 1979), published with *Pull Down a Horseman,* Gallery Press (Dublin, Ireland), 1979.

FICTION

Victims: A Tale from Fermanagh (novel; also see below), Gollancz (London, England), 1976.
Heritage and Other Stories, Gollancz (London, England), 1978; reprinted, 1985.
Cyril: The Quest of an Orphaned Squirrel (juvenile), illustrated by Al O'Donnell, O'Brien Books (Dublin, Ireland), 1987.

Death and Nightingales (novel), Secker and Warburg (London, England), 1992, Bloomsbury (New York, NY), 2002.

Christ in the Fields: A Fermanagh Trilogy (stories), Minerva (London, England), 1993.

Tales from the Poorhouse, Gallery Press (Oldcastle, County Meath, Ireland), 1999.

Contributor of screenplays to television, including *A Matter of Conscience,* 1962; *Some Women on the Island,* 1966; *The Funeral,* 1969; *Victims* (trilogy; includes *Heritage* and *Cancer*), 1976; *Roma,* 1979; *Gale Day,* 1979; *Music at Annahullion* (based on his own short story), 1982; (with Pierre Lary) *The Year of the French,* adapted from the novel by Thomas Flanagan, 1983. Author of essay on County Monaghan for *32 Counties: Photographs by Donovan Wylie,* by Donovan Wylie, Secker and Warburg (London, England), 1989; introduction to *Shadows from the Pale,* by John Minihan, Secker and Warburg (London, England), 1996; short story "Heaven Lies about Us," in *Irish Short Stories,* edited by David Morcu, Phoenix, 1997.

SIDELIGHTS: From his border farm in County Monaghan, Ireland, Eugene McCabe has published a stream of plays, screenplays, short stories, and novels that treat life in Ireland, present and past. A common thread of his works has been the theme of the emotional or physical breakdown under the stress of life in a violent land. McCabe has yet to earn the worldwide audience that other Irish writers of his generation have enjoyed, but he is highly respected by critics, who feel that his best work offers an unflinching portrait of Ireland's ills. In the *Dictionary of Irish Literature,* Christopher Murray wrote, "McCabe's voice is distinctive: penetrating, clear, and forthright. His honest style and . . . confrontation of the violence inherent in the Irish character provide a refreshing antidote to the marketable charm of much Irish writing."

For his first play, *The King of the Castle,* in which he dared treat the then taboo subject of fertility and surrogate fatherhood, McCabe earned the coveted *Irish Life* award. While *The King of the Castle* was a success when mounted in 1964, McCabe's other works for the stage were not well received, and the author turned to writing for television, where he earned greater acclaim.

McCabe's three-part drama cycle about the situation in Northern Ireland, *Cancer, Heritage,* and *Victims,* has been praised for a realistic and objective quality that made it fresh and powerful to television viewers. The trilogy of dramas was based on earlier or simultaneously written works. For example, the screenplay for *Heritage* was adapted from *Heritage and Other Stories,* which includes the novella *Heritage* and five short stories. In the short story collection, McCabe focused on bigotry, and the novella revolves around the activities of a young Protestant man who must decide whether to become involved in the sectarian violence around him or flee to England. "A brilliant piece of writing, but the final effect is frustrating," Frank Tuohy wrote about *Heritage* in the *Times Literary Supplement.* "Bigotry as portrayed here forces the reader to keep his distance. This is a pity since Eugene McCabe is a writer of undoubted gifts."

Likewise, the screenplay for *Victims* was written in tandem with McCabe's first novel, *Victims: A Tale from Fermanagh,* which tells the story of a kidnapping of dinner party guests by terrorists of the Irish Republican Army (IRA) and the ensuing siege by authorities. In *Victims,* McCabe portrays the different kinds of people who are drawn to the IRA, including an alienated student, a psychopath, and several devout farm workers. "McCabe has constructed a microcosm of the Ulster stalemate so neat that only the polish of the writing prevents one calling it glib," remarked Frank Pike in the *Times Literary Supplement.* "The author is well known as a stage and television playwright in Ireland, and the professional assurance shows." *Film West* contributor Vincent Brown stated that the "Victims Trilogy" in its Irish television incarnation, gave viewers "some of the best television drama ever produced."

In an interview published on the *Clones Home Page,* McCabe is quoted as saying that he was compelled to write the "Victims Trilogy" out of a sense that he could not turn his back on the Troubles, especially since he lives in a border territory. He said that the writing of the three works eased his conscience. He added: "It will, of course change nothing, but if it has truth it must in time be of consequence. The overall theme is, of course, the futility of violence. It does also show that there is an underlying cause for violence but it proffers no solution and there is no message."

McCabe's more recent works include *Christ in the Fields,* a collection of short stories, and the historical novel *Death and Nightingales,* which takes place in

Ireland of the 1880s. The novel deals with a Protestant landowner and Beth, the illegitimate daughter of his late wife, whom he had abused. Beth, unable to withstand the stress of life, finally takes action after government officials begin an investigation of the man with whom she had hoped to run away. The work is "a shattering story, breathtaking in scope," declared an *Observer* critic. A *Publishers Weekly* reviewer found the book's climax "riveting," concluding that McCabe has written "a fine book that rarely blinks at the bitter truths of life, loss and war." A *Kirkus Reviews* correspondent likewise deemed *Death and Nightingales* "a haunting novel of love and deception. . . . Brilliant, richly conceived, and perfectly narrated with the suspense of a good thriller."

Tales from the Poorhouse presents a series of four interwoven monologues that reveal the wretched poverty and casual abuse that ran rampant in nineteenth-century Ireland. As the title implies, the stories are set in a poorhouse, the last resort for those men and women who were starving and penniless in a time of famine. In a *World of Hibernia* review of the book, Des Traynor observed: "If McCabe continues producing work of this high a standard to put alongside his novel *Death and Nightingales* and his stories . . . it is surely only a matter of time before his work reaches the wider audience it deserves."

McCabe once told *CA:* "I always felt that farming was 'real' work, and writing a much lesser trade. Somewhere in an interview I described myself as a tenth rate farmer (I got by) and a third rate writer. Even to describe myself as third rate may be presumptuous. It implies that some of my work will be viable a hundred years from now. This is far from certain. I decided to be a writer after reading a boys adventure novel called *Boys Trapped in the Rockies!* When I was seven to write such a story, I thought, must be wonderful. No one has even read or heard of this book, but it does (did!) exist. I'd love to read it again sixty years later!"

BIOGRAPHICAL AND CRITICAL SOURCES:

BOOKS

Berney, K. A., editor, *Contemporary British Dramatists,* 5th edition, St. James Press (Detroit, MI), 1993.

Riggs, Thomas, editor, *Contemporary Dramatists,* 6th edition, St. James Press (Detroit, MI), 1996.

PERIODICALS

Kirkus Reviews, January 1, 2002, review of *Death and Nightingales,* p. 13.

Listener, January 4, 1979, p. 30.

Los Angeles Times, April 28, 2002, Susan Salter Reynolds, review of *Death and Nightingales,* p. R-15.

New Statesman, August 13, 1976, p. 216.

Observer (London), August 15, 1976, p. 20; July 25, 1993, p. 55.

O, The Oprah Magazine, March, 2002, Francine Prose, review of *Death and Nightingales,* p. 128.

Publishers Weekly, February 18, 2002, review of *Death and Nightingales,* p. 75; January 17, 2002, review of *Tales from the Poor House,* p.45.

Spectator, August 14, 1976, p. 16.

Times Literary Supplement, August 13, 1976, p. 1005; September 1, 1978, p. 965.

World of Hibernia, fall, 1999, Des Traynor, review of *Tales from the Poorhouse,* p. 169.

ONLINE

Clones Home Page, http://www.clones.ie/ (April 1, 2002), "Eugene McCabe."

Film West, http://www.iol.ie/~galfilm/filmwest/29eugene.htm/ (April 1, 2002), Vincent Browne, "Interview with Eugene McCabe."

Irish Writers, http://www.irishwriters-online.com/ (April 1, 2002).*

*　　*　　*

McCURDY, Howard E(arl) 1941-

PERSONAL: Born December 18, 1941, in Atascadero, CA; son of Howard E. (a chemist) and Jo (an office manager; maiden name, Test) McCurdy; married Margaret M. Hurley (a teacher), June 27, 1970 (divorced, 1999). *Education:* Attended Oregon State University, 1959-61; University of Washington, Seattle, B.A., 1962, M.A., 1965; Cornell University, Ph.D., 1969.

ADDRESSES: Office—School of Government and Public Affairs, American University, Washington, DC 20016. *E-mail*—mccurdy@american.edu.

CAREER: American University, Washington, DC, assistant professor, 1968-72, associate professor, 1972-78, professor of public administration, 1978, director of public administration, 1976-80, director of key executive program, 1978-81, chair of the department of public administration, 2002—. Conductor of study on administration of national park system in Kenya, 1975; Fulbright-Hays lecturer in management and public administration at University of Zambia, 1978. Media consultant on public policy; has appeared on television shows *MacNeil-Lehrer Report, Firing Line,* and *Newsmaker Saturday.*

MEMBER: American Society for Public Administration.

AWARDS, HONORS: Henry Adams prize, Society for History in the Federal Government, 1994, for *Inside NASA: High Technology and Organizational Change in the U. S. Space Program;* Eugene M. Emme Astronautical Literature Award, American Astronautical Association, 1999, for *Space and the American Imagination;* Distinguished Research Award, National Association of Schools of Public Affairs and Administrations/American Society of Public Administration, 2001.

WRITINGS:

Public Administration: A Bibliography, College of Public Affairs, American University (Washington, DC), 1972.

An Insider's Guide to the Capitol, College of Public Affairs, American University (Washington, DC), 1977.

Public Administration: A Synthesis, Cummings (Menlo Park, CA), 1977.

Public Administration: A Bibliographic Guide to the Literature, Dekker (New York, NY), 1986.

The Space Station Decision: Incremental Politics and Technological Choice, John Hopkins University Press (Baltimore, MD), 1990.

Inside NASA: High Technology and Organizational Change in the U.S. Space Program, Johns Hopkins University Press (Baltimore, MD), 1993.

Space and the American Imagination, Smithsonian Institution Press (Washington, DC), 1997.

(Editor, with Roger D. Launius) *Spaceflight and the Myth of Presidential Leadership,* University of Illinois Press (Urbana, IL), 1997.

Faster, Better, Cheaper: Low-Cost Innovation in the U.S. Space Program, Johns Hopkins University Press (Baltimore, MD), 2001.

(With Roger D. Launius) *Imagining Space: Achievements, Predictions,· Possibilities: 1950-2050,* Chronicle Books (San Francisco, CA), 2001.

Contributor to business and public administration journals.

SIDELIGHTS: Several of public affairs expert Howard E. McCurdy's public-policy volumes are aimed at the U.S. space program. In the award-winning *Inside NASA: High Technology and Organizational Change in the U.S. Space Program,* the author tracks the National Aeronautics and Space Administration from its early triumphs, including the first moon landing in 1969, through the years of criticism and scrutiny following the explosion of space-shuttle *Challenger* in 1986. Using archival evidence and interviews, McCurdy investigates how the performance of the space program compares to NASA's organizational culture. What he found was an agency that was founded on research-and-development principles. "The combination of youthful talent, a supportive political environment, and the historical opportunity to invent exciting technology fostered an agency that valued inquiry, open communication, attention to detail, honesty, idealism, and romance," as Erwin C. Hargrove wrote in an *American Political Science Review* article.

But after the initial excitement of the moon landings, public interest in space exploration waned. Political support declined, and NASA became what Hargrove called "an operating agency, offering less challenge to its engineers and more opportunities to outside contractors." According to *Texas Monthly*'s Gregory Curtis, "even the simplest components, those NASA might once have designed and built itself, are now wastefully contracted to outside suppliers, because . . . supervising outside contracts is really all today's NASA employees know how to do." Using NASA as his example, McCurdy "concludes that high-performance bureaucratic cultures are inherently unstable," noted Hargrove, who called the author's efforts "extraordinarily comprehensive."

McCurdy's 1997 book *Space and the American Imagination,* "is guaranteed to disturb technophiles and policy wonks," commented a *Publishers Weekly* contributor. This book examines how the space program is perceived by the public; in NASA's case, as the author writes, "Advocates took fantastic ideas and laid upon them images already rooted in the American culture, such as the myth of the frontier." The early space program thrived, McCurdy continues, "not because of its technical superiority but because it aroused the imaginations of people who viewed it." Public attitudes were further influenced by the 1957 launch of Sputnik; Russia's technological excellence was often promoted as a threat to U.S. security. The author "criticizes the manipulation of public opinion though outrageous cultural images suggesting that America faced nuclear annihilation if it let the former Soviet Union maintain the upper-hand in space exploration," wrote Norman Weinstein. In his article assessing *Space and the American Imagination* for *MIT's Technology Review,* Weinstein suggested that from the Sputnik chapters to the its conclusion, the book "sheds the trappings of an academic study and becomes a sermon attacking the unsavory aspects of romantic imagination pertaining to space." *Library Journal* contributor Thomas Frieling called *Space and the American Imagination* a "masterly study" of the subject.

In 2002 McCurdy and coauthor Roger Launius—chief historian for NASA—produced *Imagining Space: Achievements, Predictions, Possibilities: 1950-2050,* a work for general readers that uses "engaging text sprinkled with over 150 archival photos and illustrations" to tell its story, according to *Astronomy* reviewer Andrew Fazekas. The authors, Fazekas continued, "give an all-embracing view of space flight, covering not only space exploration, but also its commercialization and role in warfare."

McCurdy told *CA:* "I would like to see my professional colleagues break away from their conventional views of public administration as policy-making, staffing, and budgeting and acquire a broader view of the types of management problems encountered in government agencies and the fields of study that contribute solutions to these problems. The generalist approach to public administration is going to be outstripped by the contributions made by more technical and sophisticated fields of study and we had better be prepared to absorb these contributions into our profession or face the prospect of losing our relevance in the eyes of students and public managers."

BIOGRAPHICAL AND CRITICAL SOURCES:

BOOKS

McCurdy, Howard, *Space and the American Imagination,* Smithsonian Institution Press (Washington, DC), 1997.

PERIODICALS

American Historical Review, June, 1994, review of *Inside NASA: High Technology and Organizational Change in the U.S. Space Program,* p. 996; October, 1998, review of *Space and the American Imagination,* p. 1351.
American Political Science Review, June, 1994, Erwin C. Hargrove, review of *Inside NASA,* p. 473.
American Scientist, July, 1992, review of *The Space Station Decision: Incremental Politics and Technological Choice,* p. 403.
Astronomy, February, 2002, Andrew Fazekas, review of *Imagining Space: Achievements, Predictions, Possibilities: 1950-2050,* p. 94.
Choice, May, 1991, review of *The Space Station Decision,* p. 1511; September, 1993, review of *Inside NASA,* p. 150.
Chronicle of Higher Education, December 19, 1990, review of *The Space Station Decision,* p. A10.
Historical Journal of Film, Radio and Television, June, 1998, James Schwoch, review of *Spaceflight and the Myth of Presidential Leadership,* p. 295.
Isis, September, 1999, review of *Space and the American Imagination,* p. 635.
Journal of Politics, February, 1995, review of *Inside NASA,* p. 249.
Library Journal, November 15, 1997, review of *Space and the American Imagination,* p. 74.
London Review of Books, March 5, 1998, review of *Space and the American Imagination,* p. 13.
Magazine of Fantasy and Science Fiction, January, 1999, review of *Space and the American Imagination,* p. 46.
MIT's Technology Review, March-April, 1998, Norman Weinstein, review of *Space and the American Imagination,* p. 65.
Natural History, February, 1998, review of *Space and the American Imagination,* p. 17.
Nature, June 3, 1993, review of *Inside NASA,* p. 407; March 12, 1998, review of *Space and the American Imagination,* p. 143.

New England Quarterly, December, 1998, review of *Space and the American Imagination,* p. 655.

New Scientist, April 11, 1998, review of *Space and the American Imagination,* p. 48.

New Technical Books, July, 1993, review of *Inside NASA,* p. 655.

Publishers Weekly, October 27, 1997, review of *Space and the American Imagination,* p. 60.

SciTech Book News, January, 1991, review of *The Space Station Decision,* p. 32; May, 1993, review of *Inside NASA,* p. 37.

Sky & Telescope, May, 1991, review of *The Space Station Decision,* p. 502; August, 1993, review of *Inside NASA,* p. 56.

Technology and Culture, April, 1992, review of *The Space Station Decision,* p. 385.

Texas Monthly, September, 1994, Gregory Curtis, review of *Inside NASA,* p. 5.

Wall Street Journal, November 12, 1990, review of *The Space Station Decision,* p. A12.

*   *   *

McDOWELL, Robert 1953-

PERSONAL: Born April 8, 1953, in Alhambra, CA; son of Gordon R. and Rita Terese (Grum) McDowell; married first wife, Patricia Lynn, October 30, 1976 (divorced, April, 1979); married Lysa Howard (a painter, designer, and editor), July 6, 1985; children: Dylan Randall. *Education:* University of California, Santa Cruz, B.A., 1974; Columbia University, M.F.A., 1976.

ADDRESSES: Home and office—403 Continental St., Santa Cruz, CA 95060.

CAREER: University of Southern Indiana, Evansville, assistant professor of creative writing and English, 1978-84; University of California, Santa Cruz, visiting lecturer, 1984, coordinator of Reading Series, 1987-88; Story Line Press, Santa Cruz, CA, publisher and editor, 1985-88; CTB/McGraw-Hill, associate editor, 1986-87; writer. Chairman of The Reaper, Inc., 1980—; chairman of Ohio River Writers Conference, 1980; member of board of directors, Poets' Prize Committee, Inc.

MEMBER: Academy of American Poets, Associated Writing Programs, Poets and Writers.

WRITINGS:

At the House of the Tin Man (poetry), Chowder Press, 1980.

Quiet Money (poetry), Holt (New York, NY), 1987.

(With Kevin Brennan) *Kingmaker* (screenplay), New Line Cinema, 1989.

(Editor) *Poetry after Modernism,* Story Line Press (Brownsville, OR), 1991.

The Diviners (poetry), Story Line Press (Brownsville, OR), 1995.

(With Mark Jarman) *The Reaper Essays,* Story Line Press (Brownsville, OR), 1996.

(With Harvey Gross) *Sound and Form in Modern Poetry,* second edition, University of Michigan Press (Ann Arbor, MI), 1996.

(Editor and author of introduction) *Cowboy Poetry Matters: From Abilene to the Mainstream,* Story Line Press (Ashland, OR), 2000.

On Foot, in Flames (poetry), University of Pittsburgh Press (Pittsburgh, PA), 2002.

Contributor of poems, fiction, essays, and reviews to periodicals, including *Hudson Review, American Scholar, London Magazine,* and *Poetry.* Editor, with Mark Jarman, of *The Reaper,* 1980-90.

SIDELIGHTS: Robert McDowell once told *CA:* "My fiction, rooted in realism, also focuses more on the lives of others and the creation of character than on the weather in my head. My criticism and reviews, mostly of poetry, often contain a polemical edge consistent with my striving for literature that turns away from the solipsism and self-indulgence of so much late-modern work and toward the rich subjects of the world outside the writer."

Among McDowell's works he compiled and edited *Cowboy Poetry Matters: From Abilene to the Mainstream.* The poets in this volume write knowledgeably of cattle, horses, and ranch life, even if, as *Booklist* contributor Ray Olson pointed out, they don't actually make their living ranching or farming. Olson recognizes that the themes of the poetry that predominate are "hard, painful work" endured by the cowhands and their horses, as well as the "otherness of the natural world in which it is done." The critic also noted the Old West-appeal of the anthology, adding that some of the best entries are written by women.

In addition to his editorial work, McDowell has published his own books of original verse. From 1980 to 1990 he served as editor of *The Reaper,* a magazine "devoted to the resurgence of narrative in contemporary poetry," as McDowell told *CA.* "Not surprisingly, my own poetry features a commitment to the story line, to lyrical, hard-boiled speech that evokes the lives of women and men in America. The long title poem of my book *Quiet Money,* for example, tells the story of a bootlegging pilot who flies the Atlantic solo before Charles Lindbergh, but he cannot go public because he was engaged in an illegal activity."

McDowell's *The Diviners,* published in 1995, is a long narrative poem covering five decades in the life of a family. The poems track a couple, Al and Eleanor, as they raise their son and face old age. Olson, in another *Booklist* article, compared *The Diviners* to a novel-in-stories, but maintained that the narrative suffers somewhat from "colorless material description." The critic felt, however, that the talent McDowell displays in the book is enough to make readers "wish for more—more detail, more color, more authorial daring."

On Foot, in Flames is a poetry collection "filled with loneliness," according to *American Poetry Review* contributor Kim Addonizio—but the selections are also "prayerful," the critic added. Also in *American Poetry Review,* critic Chase Twichell likewise found religious reference in the collection. To Twichell, the surface images of hymns and reveries to family, farm, and God serve to reveal "an ambitious scrutiny of those subjects." Olson's *Booklist* assessment found *On Foot, in Flames* rife with "more vivid, meatier poems" than those found in *The Diviners.* Olson added that the book's longest poem, "The Pact," a story of rural adultery, shows McDowell "venturing artfully on the terrain of the dour twentieth-century narrative master" Robinson Jeffers.

BIOGRAPHICAL AND CRITICAL SOURCES:

PERIODICALS

American Poetry Review, May, 2002, Chase Twichell and Kim Addonizio, review of *On Foot, in Flames,* p. 44.

Booklist, August, 1995, Ray Olson, review of *The Diviners,* p. 1924; May 1, 2000, Olson, review of *Cowboy Poetry Matters: From Abilene to the Mainstream,* p. 1646; March 15, 2002, Olson, review of *On Foot, in Flames.*

Choice, June, 1996, review of *The Diviners,* p. 1645.

Hudson Review, summer, 1996, review of *The Diviners,* p. 331.

Kenyon Review, summer, 1992, review of *Poetry after Modernism,* p. 188.

Library Journal, January, 1991, review of *Poetry after Modernism,* p. 105.

Los Angeles Times Book Review, March 15, 1987.

New York Times Book Review, November 8, 1987.

Publishers Weekly, December 14, 1990, review of *Poetry after Modernism,* p. 61.

Reference and Research Book News, November, 1998, review of *Poetry after Modernism,* p. 212.

School Librarian, April, 1992, review of *Poetry after Modernism,* p. 311; August, 1996, review of *The Diviners,* p. 116.

Sewanee Review, January, 1989, review of *Quiet Money,* p. R21.

Washington Post Book World, May 3, 1987.*

*   *   *

McGRATH, Campbell 1962-

PERSONAL: Born January 26, 1962, in Chicago, IL; married; wife's name, Elizabeth; children: two sons. *Education:* University of Chicago, B.A., 1984; Columbia University, M.F.A., 1988.

ADDRESSES: Home—Miami Beach, FL. *Office*—Florida International University Creative Writing Program, 3000 N.E. 151st St., North Miami, FL 33181.

CAREER: Professor and poet. University of Chicago, assistant professor; Northwestern University, assistant professor; Florida International University, assistant professor and director of poetry program, 1993—.

AWARDS, HONORS: Pushcart Prize; Academy of American Poets Prizes, 1984, 1985, and 1987; Illinois Arts Council Literary Achievement Grant, 1991; Kingsley Tufts Poetry Award from Claremont Graduate School, 1997; Cohen Prize from Emerson College, 1997; Presidential Award for Excellence in Teaching from Florida International University, 1997; Guggenheim fellowship, 1998; Witter Bynner fellowship from Library of Congress, 1998-99; John D. and Catherine T. MacArthur Foundation grant, 1999.

WRITINGS:

Capitalism, Wesleyan University Press (Hanover, NH), 1990.

American Noise, Ecco Press (Hopewell, NJ), 1993.

Spring Comes to Chicago, Ecco Press (Hopewell, NJ), 1996.

Road Atlas: Prose & Other Poems, Ecco Press (Hopewell, NJ), 1999.

(Co-translator) Aristophanes, *The Wasps,* Penn Greek Drama Series (Philadelphia, PA), 2001.

Florida Poems, Ecco Press (New York, NY), 2002.

Contributor of poems to periodicals, including *Ploughshares, New Yorker, Harper's, New York Times, Antaeus, Paris Review, TriQuarterly,* and *Kenyon Review.*

SOUND RECORDINGS

Sharing the Gifts, Library of Congress, 1999.

The Poet and the Poem from the Library of Congress, Library of Congress, 2001.

SIDELIGHTS: The prolific and energetic poet Campbell McGrath has received numerous prestigious awards for work that seeks to capture the cultural and natural landscapes of modern America. McGrath, winner of a MacArthur "genius grant," has established a reputation as a contemporary successor, both thematically and stylistically, to Walt Whitman and Allen Ginsberg. Adopting these poets' approach of cataloging many disparate items and using extremely long poetic lines, McGrath looks at the vast complexity of America and seeks to penetrate its paradoxes and attractions. His poetry collections include *Capitalism, Spring Comes to Chicago, Road Atlas: Prose & Other Poems,* and *Florida Poems.* To quote Tim Gavin in *Library Journal,* McGrath's poetic works "encompass the breadth and range of America."

Though his first collection, 1990's *Capitalism,* received little mainstream notice, it drew the attention of critics, who subsequently bestowed a Kingsley Tufts Poetry Award on the author for showing outstanding promise early in his career. McGrath's second book, 1993's *American Noise,* enjoyed more widespread readership. Critics recognized the strong influence of

Whitman in the poems in *American Noise,* while Mary Kinzie, writing in *Tribune Books,* observed that McGrath could also be compared favorably to T. S. Eliot, Ranier Maria Rilke, James Schuyler, and Robert Pinsky. Kinzie admired McGrath's "gentle and tenaciously intelligent verses" and "fierce insights in language and cadences of casual transparency" but characterized the poet's many references to popular culture "both adolescent and essentially male." *Washington Post Book World* reviewer Eric Murphy Selinger found McGrath's work "witty [and] stimulated" and praised its search for America's soul, but noted that the poet sometimes slipped into clichéd images such as "Nighthawks of the twenty-four-hour donut shops" and "dance music from the Union Hall."

McGrath's third collection, 1996's *Spring Comes to Chicago,* continues his thematic quest for what *Hungry Mind Review* critic David Biespiel called, "the simultaneous fellowship and enmity in America between intuition and reason, humanism and vulgarity, pop and high art, virtue and corruption." The collection focuses on one central work, "The Bob Hope Poem," which comprises seventy of the volume's eighty-seven pages. Biespiel assessed the poem as "a scathing examination of both the commercialism and exportation of the American myth and the American myth of exportation and commercialism" and likened the work to William Carlos Williams's *Paterson* in its ambition to "expose America to itself." Biespiel praised McGrath's blending of the serious and comic in this poem, which is, he concluded, "both a self-portrait and a raillery of the American story." McGrath, Biespiel found, is "the most Swiftian poet of his generation" and a sensitive observer of late twentieth-century American angst.

McGrath's subsequent books, *Road Atlas* and *Florida Poems,* continue to address consumerism's ills through evocative prose poems based on the author's travels through North America, Latin America, and Florida. "All the places the poet sees seem to stand for the human spirit," observed a *Publishers Weekly* reviewer of *Road Atlas.* Another *Publishers Weekly* reviewer noted that, in *Florida Poems,* "McGrath's gregarious phraseologies and expandable forms . . . suit his odd blend of comedy and jeremiad."

The MacArthur fellowship and a Guggenheim fellowship have allowed McGrath to lighten his teaching duties in favor of more writing time. He told the *University of Chicago Alumni Magazine:* "I have books coming, books backed up in the creative pipeline."

BIOGRAPHICAL AND CRITICAL SOURCES:

PERIODICALS

Library Journal, June 15, 1999, Tim Gavin, review of *Road Atlas: Prose & Other Poems,* p. 81.

Nation, April 15, 2002, "Song of the Sunshine State," p. 30.

New York Times Book Review, April 28, 2002, Andy Brumer, review of *Florida Poems,* p. 21.

Publishers Weekly, January 3, 1994, p. 72; May 31, 1999, review of *Road Atlas,* p. 87; January 21, 2002, review of *Florida Poems,* p. 86.

Tribune Books (Chicago, IL), October 2, 1994, p. 8.

Washington Post Book World, May 22, 1994, p. 11.

ONLINE

Bookwire, http://bookwire.com/ (April 1, 1997).

Columbia University News, http://www.columbia.edu/ (April 16, 1997).

Lafayette College, http://www.Lafayette.edu/ (April 4, 2002).

Ploughshares, http://www.pshares.org/issues/ (April 2, 2002), "Cohen Awards."

University of Chicago Magazine Web site, http://www.alumni.uchicago.edu/ (April 2, 2002), "Poet Campbell McGrath Has Plenty of Material and a Voice All His Own."*

*   *   *

McMILLAN, John 1951-

PERSONAL: Born January 22, 1951, in Christchurch, New Zealand; son of John Alexander (a plumber) and Alice Isobella (a homemaker) McMillan; married Patrice Ann Lord (an editor), November 2, 2002. *Education:* University of Canterbury, B.Sc. (with first class honors), 1971, M.Com (with first-class honors), 1974; University of New South Wales, Ph.D., 1978.

ADDRESSES: Office—Graduate School of Business, Stanford University, 518 Memorial Way, Stanford, CA 94305-5015. *E-mail*—mcmillan_john@gsb.stanford.edu.

CAREER: University of Canterbury, Canterbury, New Zealand, assistant lecturer in economics, 1974; University of Western Ontario, London, Ontario, Canada, assistant professor, 1978-82, associate professor of economics, 1982-87; University of California, San Diego, La Jolla, professor of international relations and Pacific studies and adjunct professor of economics, 1987-99; Stanford University, Stanford, CA, professor of international management and economics, 1999—, Jonathan B. Lovelace chair, 2001—, senior fellow, Center for Research and Economic Development, Stanford Institute for Economic Policy Research. Visiting professor, University of Mannheim, 1980-81, and Netherlands Network of Economics, 1998; writer.

MEMBER: American Economic Association, New Zealand Association of Economists, Econometric Society.

AWARDS, HONORS: Harry Johnson Prize, Canadian Economics Association, 1988; Econometric Society fellowship; grants from National Science Council of Taiwan, National Science Foundation, Social Sciences and Humanities Research Council of Canada, and Ontario Economic Council.

WRITINGS:

Game Theory in International Economics, Harwood (New York, NY), 1986.

(With R. Preston McAfee) *Incentives in Government Contracting,* University of Toronto Press (Toronto, Ontario, Canada), 1988.

Commonwealth Constitutional Power over Health, Consumers' Health Forum of Australia, 1992.

Games, Strategies, and Managers, Oxford University Press (New York, NY), 1992.

(Editor, with Barry Naughton) *Reforming Asian Socialism: The Growth of Market Institutions,* University of Michigan Press (Ann Arbor, MI), 1996.

Reinventing the Bazaar: A Natural History of Markets, Norton (New York, NY), 2002.

Contributor to anthologies, including *Recent Developments in Game Theory,* edited by J. Borland, J. Creedy, and J. Eichberger, Edward Elgar, 1992; *Trade, Welfare, and Economic Policies: Essays in Honor of Murray C. Kemp,* edited by Horst Herberg and Ngo Van Long, University of Michigan Press, 1992; and *Hand-*

book of Game Theory with Economic Applications, edited by Robert J. Aumann and Sergiu Hart, North-Holland, in press. Editor of monograph series "Micro-economic Studies," Springer-Verlag, 1985—. Contributor of articles to management, economic, and international studies journals. Editor, *Journal of Economic Literature,* 1999—; co-editor, *Journal of Economics and Management Strategy,* 1996-97; associate editor, *Economics and Politics* and *Journal of the Japanese and International Economies,* both 1990—; member of board of editors, *Canadian Journal of Economics,* 1982-84, *American Economic Review,* 1991-95, *Risk, Decision, and Policy,* 1995—, *Economics and Politics,* 1990-99, and *Contemporary Economic Policy,* 2000—.

WORK IN PROGRESS: Research on game theory and on the reform of planned economies.

SIDELIGHTS: John McMillan's expertise in international economics has led to several volumes aimed at both the specialist and generalist reader. In 1997 he coedited *Reforming Asian Socialism: The Growth of Market Institutions,* a study of economic evolution in China, Vietnam, North Korea, and other Asian nations which underwent significant political and cultural changes in the latter part of the twentieth century. "China is by far the most important transition country in Asia and also one with the longest track record," noted *Economic Record* critic J. Malcolm Dowling. *Reforming Asian Socialism* compares the changing economic climate from the reign of communist Chairman Mao Tse-tung to the nation's transition into a market economy. Several sections in the work focus on post-Mao China, as the country adopted a more decentralized economy. "A prominent feature of the reform period is that local governments have been given responsibilities for regional development and welfare," commented Russell Smyth in *Journal of Contemporary Asia.* With municipalities setting the standard for economic growth, what developed were "strong incentives to set up enterprises for revenue-raising purposes," creating a "horizontal relationship between regions which fosters regional competition and imitation," explained the critic.

According to Dowling, "The basic thrust of the book is to analyze the economic transition within the spirit and framework of the new institutional economics. It goes beyond the big-bang versus gradualism policy debates to examine the development of [Asia's] market institutions." To Smyth, "The main strength of this book lies in its careful attention to detail." The *Journal of Contemporary Asia* critic pointed to discussions regarding which direction China's development should take. *Reforming Asian Socialism* also "makes excellent use of Chinese language sources," added Smyth.

In *Reinventing the Bazaar: A Natural History of Markets,* McMillan takes a wide-ranging look at how economic markets work, showing how "sophisticated computerized markets are just the high-tech version of the bazaar," as *Booklist* contributor Mary Whaley put it. It is the author's contention that not much has changed since the days of the street peddler; the best markets are always those that are well structured. Appraising *Reinventing the Bazaar* in the midst of the scandal-ridden breakdown of U.S. mega-corporations such as Enron and WorldCom during 2001-2002, Barry Gwen suggested in the *New York Times Book Review* that McMillan's work "is the perfect book for the Age of Enron" because it provides what Gwen called "a long-term perspective, an intellectual framework, for understanding what went wrong, how we should be thinking about correctives and what a properly functioning market economy should look like."

Markets are set up in any conceivable condition where people gather. As McMillan relates in *Reinventing the Bazaar,* even under dire conditions, such as prison camps and refugee centers, food exchanges and general stores spring up. "So far, so familiar," said Gwen. "But McMillan has another shoe to drop. Markets may arise spontaneously as 'the most potent antipoverty engine there is,' yet as they develop, becoming more complex; they need rules and structures to perform properly." Interaction by government must also be considered; "Why, for instance, did Silicon Valley become the center of the computer industry and not Route 128 in Massachusetts?" asked Gwen. The answer, according to McMillan: Massachusetts has an intellectual-property law that forbids employees from taking knowledge gained at one company and bringing it to another. California has no such prohibition, and during high-tech's boom days when "job-hopping was rampant," although individual companies suffered when their secrets were shared with competitors, "the industry as a whole prospered" due to the anti-restrictive climate offered in Silicon Valley.

A *Publishers Weekly* contributor found some fault with *Reinventing the Bazaar,* citing a tone that is "by turns condescending and frustratingly abstruse." However, a *Kirkus Reviews* writer had fewer reservations, maintaining that "McMillan's prose resembles single malt, going down easy as it stimulates." According to Richard Drezen of *Library Journal,* "Readers looking for a basic primer" on market economy "will find no better treatment" than in *Reinventing the Bazaar.*

BIOGRAPHICAL AND CRITICAL SOURCES:

PERIODICALS

Booklist, April 15, 2002, Mary Whaley, review of *Reinventing the Bazaar: A Natural History of Markets,* p. 1368.

Economic Journal, January, 1994, review of *Games, Strategies, and Managers,* p. 203; January, 1998, review of *Reforming Asian Socialism: The Growth of Market Institutions,* p. 276.

Economic Record, September, 1997, J. Malcolm Dowling, review of *Reforming Asian Socialism,* p. 296.

Institutional Investor International, April, 2002, Deepak Gopinath, "They Can't Go It Alone," p. 92.

Journal of Contemporary Asia, August, 1998, Russell Smyth, review of *Reforming Asian Socialism,* p. 402.

Journal of Economic Literature, June, 1993, review of *Games, Strategies, and Managers,* p. 890; March, 1997, review of *Reforming Asian Socialism,* p. 291.

Kirkus Reviews, March 15, 2002, review of *Reinventing the Bazaar,* p. 387.

Library Journal, April 15, 2002, Richard Drezen, review of *Reinventing the Bazaar,* p. 102.

Publishers Weekly, April 8, 2002, review of *Reinventing the Bazaar,* p. 218.

*   *   *

McPHERSON, James M(unro) 1936-

PERSONAL: Born October 11, 1936, in Valley City, ND; son of James Munro (a high school teacher and administrator) and Miriam (an elementary school teacher; maiden name, Osborn) McPherson; married Patricia A. Rasche (an editor), December 28, 1957; children: Joanna. *Education:* Gustavus Adolphus College, B.A. (magna cum laude), 1958; Johns Hopkins University, Ph.D. (with highest distinction), 1963. *Politics:* Democratic. *Religion:* Presbyterian. *Hobbies and other interests:* Tennis, bicycling, sailing, reading mystery and adventure novels, playing with his granddaughter.

ADDRESSES: Home—15 Randall Rd., Princeton, NJ 08540-3609. *Office*—Department of History, Dickinson Hall, Princeton University, Princeton, NJ 08544.

CAREER: Author, editor, educator, preservationist, and consultant. Princeton University, Princeton, NJ, instructor, 1962-65, assistant professor, 1965-68, associate professor, 1968-72, professor of history, 1972-82, Edwards Professor of American History, 1982-91, George Henry Davis '86 Professor of American History, 1991—. Commonwealth Fund Lecturer, University College, London, England, 1982. Fellow, Behavioral Sciences Center, Stanford University, 1982-83. Consultant on the film *Gettysburg,* Turner Pictures, 1993; on the television documentary *The Civil War* by Ken Burns, Public Broadcasting System, 1999; and on the television documentary *Abraham and Mary Lincoln: A House Divided,* Public Broadcasting System, 2001; also consultant, Social Science program, Educational Research Council, Cleveland, OH. President, Protect Historic America, 1993-94; Society of American Historians, 2000-01; and American Historical Association, 2003—. Member of board of directors, Civil War Trust and Association for the Preservation of Civil War Sites (now the Civil War Preservation Trust), 1991-93; member of Civil War Sites Advisory Committee, a committee created by the U.S. Congress, 1991-93. Member of advisory board, George Tyler Moore College of the Study of the Civil War, Shepherdstown, WV. Member of board of advisors, Lincoln Forum. Member of editorial board of magazine *Civil War History.*

McPherson provided the narration for the video *Abraham Lincoln,* Atlas Video, 1990; is interviewed in the documentary *Smithsonian's Great Battles of the Civil War,* Volume One, Mastervision Studio, 1992, on the videos *The Civil War Legends: Robert E. Lee* and *The Civil War Legends: Abraham Lincoln* (both from Acorn Video), and on the audio cassette *American Heritage's Great Minds of History,* Simon & Schuster, 1999. He also provided the audio commentary on the DVD of the film *Gettysburg,* Turner Home Entertainment, 2000.

MEMBER: Organization of American Historians, Society of American Historians, American Philosophical Society, American Historical Association (president 2003-04), Southern Historical Association, Phi Beta Kappa.

AWARDS, HONORS: Woodrow Wilson National Fellowship, 1958; Danforth fellow, 1958-62; Proctor & Gamble faculty fellowship; Anisfield Wolff Award in Race Relations, Cleveland Foundation, 1965, for _The Struggle for Equality: Abolitionists and the Negro in the Civil War and Reconstruction;_ Guggenheim fellow, 1967-58; Huntington fellowship, National Endowment for the Humanities, 1977-78; Huntington Seaver fellow, 1987-88; National Book Award nomination, 1988, National Book Critics Circle nomination, 1988, Pulitzer Prize in history, 1989, Distinguished Book Award, U.S. Military Academy, West Point, 1989, and citation, 100 Best English-Language Books of the 20th Century, Board of the Modern Library, 1999, all for _Battle Cry of Freedom: The Civil War Era;_ Lincoln Prize, 1998, for _For Cause and Comrades: Why Men Fought the Civil War;_ Michael Award, New Jersey Literary Hall of Fame, 1989; Gustavus Adolphus College Alumni Award, Gustavus Alumni Association, 1990; R. Stanton Avery fellow, Huntington Library, 1995-96; Theodore and Franklin D. Roosevelt Prize in Naval History, 1998, with wife, Patricia McPherson, for _Lamson of the Gettysburg: The Civil War Letters of Lieutenant Roswell H. Lamson, U.S. Navy;_ Jefferson Lecturer in the Humanities, National Endowment for the Humanities, 2000; Richard Nelson Current Award of Achievement, 2002; recipient of honorary degrees from Gustavus Adolphus College, Gettysburg College, Muhlenberg College, Lehigh University, Bowdoin College, and Monmouth University.

WRITINGS:

FOR CHILDREN; NONFICTION

Marching toward Freedom: The Negro in the Civil War, 1861-1865, Knopf (New York, NY), 1968, published as _Marching toward Freedom: Blacks in the Civil War,_ Facts on File (New York, NY), 1991.

(With Joyce Oldham Appleby and Alan Brinkley) _The American Journey_ (textbook; student edition), National Geographic Society/Glencoe/McGraw-Hill (New York, NY), 1998, also published as _The American Journey: Building a Nation,_ teacher's wraparound edition, National Geographic Society/Glencoe/McGraw-Hill (New York, NY), 2000.

Fields of Fury: The American Civil War, Atheneum (New York, NY), 2002.

(With Appleby, Brinkley, Albert S. Broussard, and Donald A. Ritchie) _The American Vision_ (textbook), National Geographic Society/Glencoe/McGraw-Hill (New York, NY), 2003.

FOR ADULTS; NONFICTION

The Struggle for Equality: Abolitionists and the Negro in the Civil War and Reconstruction, Princeton University Press (Princeton, NJ), 1964, 2nd edition with new preface by the author, 1995.

The Negro's Civil War: How American Negroes Felt and Acted in the War for the Union, Pantheon (New York, NY), 1965, University of Illinois Press (Urbana, IL), 1982, published as _The Negro's Civil War: How American Blacks Felt and Acted during the War for the Union,_ Ballantine Books (New York, NY), 1991.

The Abolitionist Legacy: From Reconstruction to the NAACP, Princeton University Press (Princeton, NJ), 1975, 2nd edition, with a new preface by the author, 1995.

Ordeal by Fire: The Civil War and Reconstruction, Knopf (New York, NY), 1982, McGraw-Hill (New York, NY), 2001, published as _The Civil War_ (reprint of the second part of _Ordeal by Fire_), Knopf (New York, NY), 1982, McGraw-Hill (New York, NY), 1982, published as two separate volumes, _Ordeal by Fire: The Coming of War_ and _Ordeal by Fire: The Civil War,_ McGraw-Hill (New York, NY), 1993, 3rd edition, McGraw-Hill (New York, NY), 2001.

Images of the Civil War, paintings by Mort Künstler, Gramercy Books (New York, NY), 1982.

Battle Cry of Freedom: The Civil War Era, Oxford University Press (New York, NY), 1988, published as collector's edition, Easton Press (Norwalk, CT), 2002.

Gettysburg (companion volume to film of the same name), paintings by Mort Künstler, Turner Publishing (Atlanta, GA), 1993, Rutledge Hill Press (Nashville, TN), 1998.

What They Fought For, 1861-1865, Louisiana State University Press (Baton Rouge, LA), 1994.

Drawn with the Sword: Reflections on the American Civil War, Oxford University Press (New York, NY), 1996.

For Cause and Comrades: Why Men Fought in the Civil War, Oxford University Press (New York, NY), 1997.

Crossroads of Freedom: Antietam, Oxford University Press (New York, NY), 2002.

Hallowed Ground: A Walk in Gettysburg, Crown (New York, NY), 2003

ESSAYS AND LECTURES

Lincoln and the Strategy of Unconditional Surrender, Gettysburg College (Gettysburg, PA), 1984.

How Lincoln Won the War with Metaphor, Louis A. Warren Lincoln Library and Museum (Fort Wayne, IN), 1985.

Abraham Lincoln and the Second American Revolution, Oxford University Press (New York, NY), 1990, published as collector's edition, Easton Press (Norwalk, CT), 1991.

Why the Confederacy Lost, edited by Gabor S. Boritt, Oxford University Press (New York, NY), 1992.

Is Blood Thicker Than Water? Crises of Nationalism in the Modern World, Vintage Canada (Toronto, Ontario, Canada), 1998, Vintage Books (New York, NY), 1999.

(With Douglas J. Wilson) *Accepting the Prize: Two Historians Speak,* Lincoln and Soldiers Institute (Gettysburg, PA), 2000.

"For a Vast Future Also": Lincoln and the Millennium, National Endowment for the Humanities (Washington, DC), 2000.

EDITOR

(With others) *Blacks in America: Bibliographical Essays,* Doubleday (Garden City, NY), 1971.

(With Corner Vann Woodward and J. Morgan Kousser) *Region, Race, and Reconstruction: Essays in Honor of C. Vann Woodward,* Oxford University Press (New York, NY), 1982.

Battle Chronicles of the Civil War, six volumes, Grey Castle Press (Lakeville, CT), Macmillan (New York, NY), 1989.

(Consulting editor) Steve O'Brien and others, editors, *American Political Leaders: From Colonial Times to the Present,* ABC-CLIO (Santa Barbara, CA), 1991.

The Atlas of the Civil War, Macmillan (New York, NY), 1994.

"We Cannot Escape History": Lincoln and the Last Best Hope on Earth, University of Illinois Press (Urbana, IL), 1995.

(With Bruce Catton) *The American Heritage New History of the Civil War,* Viking (New York, NY), 1996, revised edition, with contributing editor Noah Andre Trudeau, MetroBooks (New York, NY), 2001.

(With wife, Patricia R. McPherson) *Lamson of the Gettysburg: The Civil War Letters of Lieutenant Roswell H. Lamson, U.S. Navy,* Oxford University Press (New York, NY), 1997.

(With William J. Cooper) *Writing the Civil War: The Quest to Understand,* University of South Carolina Press (Columbia, SC), 1998.

To the Best of My Ability: The American Presidents, Dorling Kindersley (New York, NY), 2000, revised edition, 2001.

Encyclopedia of Civil War Biographies, Sharpe Reference (Armonk, NY), 2000.

(Editor and contributor, with Alan Brinkley and David Rubel) *Days of Destiny: Crossroads in American History: America's Greatest Historians Examine Thirty-one Uncelebrated Days That Changed the Course of History,* DK Publishing (New York, NY), 2001.

The Civil War Reader, 1862, Simon & Schuster (New York, NY), 2002.

Also author of *How Abolitionists Fought On after the Civil War,* Princeton University (Princeton, NJ), a reprint in book form of an article from the quarterly magazine *University,* 1968-69; *White Liberals and Black Power in Negro Education, 1865-1915,* 1969; *First Black Power Bid in U.S. Education,* Princeton University (Princeton, NJ), from *University,* 1970; and *Who Freed the Slaves?: Lincoln and Emancipation,* Lincoln Memorial Association (Redlands, CA), 1993. McPherson's works have been translated into other languages, including French, German, and Spanish. Contributor to books, including *The Anti-Slavery Vanguard: New Essays on Abolitionism,* edited by Martin M. Duberman, Princeton University Press (Princeton, NJ), 1965; *Towards a New Past: Dissenting Essays in American History,* edited by Barton J. Bernstein, Pantheon (New York, NY), 1968; and *How I Met Lincoln: Some Distinguished Enthusiasts Reveal Just How They Fell under His Spell,* compiled by Harold Holzer, American Heritage (New York, NY), 1999. Contributor of forewords and afterwords to books, including *Brother against Brother,* edited by Diane Stine Thomas, Silver Burdett Press (Englewood Cliffs, NJ), 1990; *Personal Memoirs of Ulysses S. Grant,* by Ulysses S. Grant, Penguin Books (New York, NY), 1999; and *The Birth of the Grand Old Republican Party: The Republicans' First Generation,* edited by Robert F. Engs and Randall M. Miller, University of Pennsylvania Press (Philadelphia, PA), 2002. Contributor to periodicals, including *American Historical Review, Caribbean Studies, Journal of American History, Journal of Negro History, Mid-America, Phylon,* and others.

ADAPTATIONS: Battle Cry of Freedom: The Civil War Era was released on audio tape by Books on Tape, 1989; *Abraham Lincoln and the Second American Revolution* was released on audio tape by Books on Tape, 1992; *Crossroads of Freedom: Antietam* was released as an audio CD by Oxford University Press, 2002.

SIDELIGHTS: An American author of nonfiction for children and adults, James M. McPherson generally is considered the preeminent living expert on the American Civil War. The war, which took place from 1861 to 1865, pitted the Union Army from the northern United States against the Confederate Army from the southern United States. More than six hundred thousand soldiers died in the Civil War—more than in any other war involving Americans. A prolific writer, McPherson has written and edited numerous books about the Civil War and its aftermath, the Reconstruction, and of President Abraham Lincoln. McPherson is noted for his coverage of African Americans during the mid-nineteenth century, especially their service as soldiers and their efforts to secure their freedom from slavery, and of the abolitionists who worked to obtain equal rights for the freed slaves. He is also a preservationist, working to protect Civil War battlefields and other important sites as well as resource materials in libraries and other places. Finally, McPherson is credited with helping to initiate a resurgence of interest in the Civil War among the American public. Several of his books have been bestsellers and are considered to have paved the way for the success of the films *Glory* and *Gettysburg* and the television documentary *The Civil War* by Ken Burns. McPherson wrote the text for a book of paintings by Mort Künstler that was issued as a companion to the motion picture *Gettsyburg* and also provided narration on the DVD of the film; in ad-

dition, McPherson served as a consultant in the making of the Ken Burns documentary.

McPherson perhaps is best known for *Battle Cry of Freedom: The Civil War Era,* an informational book for adults that was published in 1988 and won the Pulitzer Prize for history the next year. Often acknowledged as the best single-volume study of the Civil War, *Battle Cry of Freedom* offers readers a reassessment of the war and its outcome. McPherson theorizes that the victory of the Union Army was not inevitable; in addition, he calls the Civil War a turning point in American history, a revolutionary event that brought sweeping changes to society, such as the end of slavery and a new emphasis on industrialization. A professor of history at Princeton University for more than forty years, McPherson directs most of his works to readers at the college level and above; however, several of his books, especially *Battle Cry of Freedom,* have appeal for young people and are used as supplemental reading in high schools. As an author for children, McPherson has written informational books about the Civil War and its soldiers, both black and white; he also is the coauthor of textbooks on the history of America for students in middle school.

Thematically, McPherson emphasizes the moral and ideological aspects of war. He is noted for being empathic in his treatment of the soldiers who fought on both sides of the Civil War and for writing works that stress the human dimension of this event. In several of his books, McPherson draws upon letters and diaries, many of which are unpublished, and he also includes little-known facts about his subjects. As a literary stylist, McPherson characteristically uses a narrative approach rather than the topical or thematic approaches that historians often favor. He is credited for the thoroughness of his research and for writing with authority, balance, eloquence, and clarity. In addition, McPherson has been commended for his ability to satisfy both scholars and general readers with his works, which are praised for providing accurate facts and insightful opinions in an accessible, engaging manner. McPherson occasionally is accused of not offering many new revelations about the Civil War and for not making clear whose side he is on in the controversies surrounding it. However, he usually is viewed as an exceptional historian as well as a writer of integrity and literary skill whose works demonstrate his respect for both his subject and his audience. Writing in *Salon,* Kathleen Whittamore stated, "As anyone who reads James McPherson knows, the broadest topics deliver the gold. This Princeton historian is an expert silversmith with detail, but a true artist when he solders the big questions. . . . Other writers in the Civil War may be better at emotive drama (Shelby Foote) or crackling narrative (Bruce Catton), but if you want the most astute synthesis possible, McPherson's the man." Calling McPherson "a remarkable and admirable figure," David Walsh of the *World Socialist Web site* projected, "When, in the future, historians consider the ideological landscape of our time, in all its general dreariness and moral and political renegacy, it seems certain that some consideration will be given to James McPherson as a contradictory figure of the period itself. And it will be noted—with approval and appreciation, one trusts—that he contributed to an intellectual ferment with far-reaching consequences." In his assessment of McPherson in *America,* Tom O'Brien concluded that his "whole corpus displays patriotism, not as the last refuge of a scoundrel, but as the civic-mindedness of a first-class mind and first-class person. Would American history suffer if there were even more of him?"

Born in Valley City, North Dakota, McPherson grew up in a small town in Minnesota. He is the son of James Munro McPherson, a high school teacher and administrator, and Miriam Osborn McPherson, an elementary school teacher who went back to get her degree after her children were grown. The author told Joseph Deitch of *Publishers Weekly* that having two teachers as parents "clearly had an influence on me. I see them as role models." Some of McPherson's siblings also became educators: both of his sisters have taught in elementary schools and one of his brothers was a teacher at the university level. McPherson's interest in the Civil War perhaps also has roots in his family background: his great-grandfather and great-great-grandfather both fought in the Union Army, a fact of which McPherson was unaware until he became a historian. McPherson was first inspired to study the past by a history teacher at his high school, a man who had fought in World War II. The author told Joseph Deitch of *Publishers Weekly* that he and his classmates "got a lot of personal reminiscences about the war that aroused my interest in the historical dimensions and in the war itself." After high school, McPherson went to Gustavus Adophus College in Saint Peter, Minnesota. McPherson once told *CA,* "I became fascinated with American history while in college, and it was natural that I should combine my interest in teaching and history to become a teacher of history and a writer of books about American history that I hope have been useful in teaching and learning."

While attending Gustavus Adolphus College, McPherson married Patricia A. Rasche; the couple have a daughter, Joanna. With her husband, Patricia McPherson served as the coeditor of a collection of letters by Lieutenant Roswell H. Lamson, one of the most talented naval officers of the Civil War. After graduating from college, James McPherson decided to attend graduate school to acquire his doctorate in history. At the time, the Civil Rights Movement was beginning to take place in the South. McPherson told David Walsh of the *World Socialist Web Site,* "This was in the late '50s, at the time of the Little Rock school desegregation crisis and the Montgomery bus boycott. I was just becoming conscious of what was going on in the world at this time, so I thought, 'This is a strange place, this South.' So I decided that maybe I'd like to find out more about it, study Southern history." McPherson decided to attend graduate school at Johns Hopkins University in Baltimore, Maryland. He told Walsh, "I really went to Hopkins because C. Vann Woodward [a specialist on Southern history and on segregation] was there. And when I got there, . . . I was suddenly struck by the parallels between the times in which I was living and what had happened exactly, I mean exactly in some cases, 100 years earlier." In 1982, McPherson coedited *Race, Region, and Reconstruction,* a volume of essays in honor of his mentor C. Vann Woodward. As he noted in a statement that he made to the U.S. House of Representatives regarding the preservation of historical documents, a statement that was reprinted in *National Humanities Alliance (NHA) Testimony,* McPherson also chose to attend John Hopkins for another reason: "its proximity to Washington and to one of the great research libraries of the world, the Library of Congress. Nor was I disappointed in the wealth of sources in that marvelous institution just up the street. I remember with fondness my many trips from Baltimore on the old Pennsylvania Railroad or the B & O or by car-pooling with other graduate students in an ancient Volkswagen Beetle or Chevrolet gas-guzzler. I spent many hundreds of happy hours going over books, pamphlets, and newspapers as well as manuscript collections for my doctoral dissertation. . . ."

As a northerner, McPherson became fascinated by the role that the North had played in trying to change race relations in the South. He studied eighteenth-century abolitionists and wrote about their role during and after the Civil War in trying to obtain equal rights, equal justice, and education for the freed slaves. In an interview with William R. Ferris in *Humanities,* McPherson recalled, "I did my Ph.D. dissertation on people that I called—perhaps with a little bit of exaggeration—the civil rights activists of the 1860s, the abolitionists, both black and white." He told Amy Lifson on the *Meet James McPherson* Web site, "I was struck by all of these parallels between what was a freedom crusade of the 1860s and a freedom crusade of the 1960s. My first entrée into Civil War scholarship focused on that very theme." While attending Johns Hopkins, McPherson participated in civil rights activities in the Baltimore area. In 1962, he moved to Princeton, New Jersey, to work as an instructor of history at Princeton University. The next year, McPherson received his doctorate from Johns Hopkins. His doctoral dissertation became his first book, *The Struggle for Equality: Abolitionists and the Negro in the Civil War and Reconstruction,* a volume published in 1964. In *NHA Testimony,* McPherson called this work "a study of the continuing activities of abolitionists on behalf of civil rights and education for freed slaves after the abolition of slavery." He added, "The challenges and excitement of discovery in this research really launched my career as a historian."

Three years after the publication of *The Struggle for Equality,* McPherson produced *The Negro's Civil War: How American Negroes Felt and Acted in the War for the Union* (later published as *The Negro's Civil War: How American Blacks Felt and Acted during the War for the Union*). With *Marching toward Freedom: The Negro in the Civil War* (later published as *Marching toward Freedom: Blacks in the Civil War*), McPherson adapted material from *The Negro's Civil War* for a young audience. In this work, which was published in 1968, McPherson presents children with a history of how African Americans served in the Civil War, first in supporting roles and then, after they were allowed to enlist, as effective soldiers. The author supplements his story with passages from diaries, letters, speeches, newspapers, and songs as well as prints and photographs from the period. Writing in the *New York Times Book Review* about McPherson's accomplishment in *Marching toward Freedom,* Mel Watkins commented, "Using numerous quotes from politicians, slaves, and freedmen, he shows that military and political expediency, not idealism, dictated the Union's altered stance." A writer in *Commonweal* dubbed *Marching toward Freedom* a "well-documented account" and "an impressive study" before noting, "Its brevity is an addi-

tional asset." Writing in *Book World,* Paul M. Angle said, "Mr. McPherson brings a fresh approach. Half of the text, perhaps more, consists of quotations from what the historians call first-hand sources. . . . Skillfully used by the author, these sources give the book an unusual degree of directness (read 'punch') and realism. The story—and the facts—give more credit to the black man than to the white." A critic in *Booklist* concluded, "Numerous excerpts . . . add authenticity and conviction to McPherson's telling portrayal of Negro attitudes and experiences, including impressive performances on the battlefield." McPherson told *CA,* "I enjoyed the experience of writing *Marching toward Freedom.* My two youngest brothers were then in junior high and high school, and I tried out the book on them as I was writing it in order to see whether it would appeal to a high-school age audience. They liked it, and I hope that other students who have read it have also liked it."

In 1972, McPherson became a full professor of history at Princeton; in 1982, he became the Edwards Professor of American History at the school. In addition to his academic career, McPherson continued to write and edit books on the Civil War and its key players. Asked by C. Vann Woodward and Richard Hofstadter to contribute a volume to the Oxford History of the United States, a multi-volume collection of individual books by historians that was published by Oxford University Press, he began to write about the period 1848 to 1865. In 1988, McPherson produced *Battle Cry of Freedom: The Civil War Era,* the book that established him as perhaps the best historian ever to have written about the War between the States. In this work, which takes its title from a song adopted by both the North and the South, the author outlines the history of the period by incorporating its most relevant political, social, economic, and military aspects. In addition, he combines scholarship on the subject with his own research and interpretations and tells the story of the Civil War as if he were writing fiction, with plot, conflict, character development, and other literary characteristics.

Battle Cry of Freedom was a best-seller in both hardcover and paperback. In addition, critical commentary on the volume was almost unanimously laudatory. McPherson was praised for his ability to synthesize a wealth of information—material that previous writers had taken from three to eight volumes to decipher—and place it into a single, cohesive, well-written volume. Writing in the *New York Times Book Review,* Hugh Brogan noted, "This is the best one-volume treatment of a subject I have ever come across. It may actually be the best ever published. It is comprehensive and succinct, scholarly without being pedantic, eloquent but unrhetorical. It is compellingly readable. I was swept away, feeling as if I had never heard the saga before. It is most welcome. . . . A deeply satisfying book." Huston Horn of the *Los Angeles Times Book Review* commented, "Deftly coordinated, gracefully composed, charitably argued, and suspensefully laid out, McPherson's book is just the compass of the tumultuous middle years of the 18th century it was intended to be, and as narrative history, it is surpassing. Bright with details and fresh quotations, sold with carefully-arrived-at conclusions, it must surely be, of the 50,000 books written on the Civil War, the finest compression of that national paroxysm ever fitted between two covers." Martin Flagg of the *Times Educational Supplement* called McPherson's book "a miracle of lucidity, proportion, and ripe judgment. It is also, for a one-volume chronicle, marvelously inclusive, and one cannot imagine a more telling or compelling account of this, the most tragic episode (and enduring trauma) of American history." Writing in *School Library Journal,* Audrey B. Eaglon dubbed *Battle Cry of Freedom* "probably the best one-volume history of the Civil War ever written; it reads like a suspense novel, pulling readers into the story of a nation riven by conflict."

In 1991, McPherson became the George Henry Davis '86 Professor American History at Princeton. In the same year, the United States Senate appointed McPherson to the Civil War Sites Advisory Commission, which was responsible for determining the major battle sites of the war, evaluating their condition, and recommending proposals for their preservation. As a teacher, he has taken his students on regular tours of Civil War battlefields; for example, they go to Pennsylvania every spring to visit Gettysburg. At the battlefields, McPherson often is asked by his students why the soldiers were willing to fight—and to stay in the war—when they knew that they may not be coming home. These questions prompted *For Cause and Comrades: Why Men Fought in the Civil War,* a title published in 1997. In order to create this work, McPherson studied the diaries and letters of over a thousand enlistees from both the Union and Confederate armies. He concluded that the soldiers were motivated by courage, self-respect, and group cohesion and were sustained by duty, faith, personal honor, patriotism, and ideol-

ogy, especially the preservation of liberty. Writing about *For Cause and Comrades* in *Kliatt Young Adult Paperback Book Guide,* Raymond L. Puffer commented, "A good scholar can always be depended upon to come up with an interesting new approach to a worked-over subject. In this title, Princeton historian McPherson shows again why he deserves to be called the dean of Civil War scholars." Puffer concluded by calling *For Cause and Comrades* a "legitimate and readable antidote to the romanticized motives so often cited in other works. This book also packs a visceral punch; it is full of fascinating quotations and first-person recollections, making it an often vivid experience for the reader. This is 'living history' indeed." Calling *For Cause and Comrades* "one of the most comprehensive and valuable analyses of the Civil War ever written," Daniel Baracskay of *Presidential Studies Quarterly* commended the author's "painstaking detail and incredible insight" before concluding that McPherson "has provided a tremendous contribution to the study of the Civil War, and the disciplines of history and political science. . . . McPherson has set a new standard for research for times to come." Roland Green of *Booklist* observed that, in *For Cause and Comrades,* McPherson "has written more eloquently than almost any Civil War historian since Bruce Catton. The result is an invaluable book, though a saddening one." *For Cause and Comrades* was awarded the Lincoln Prize in 1998.

In 2002, McPherson produced *Fields of Fury: the American Civil War,* a history of the war for children that spans events from the initial Confederate attack at Fort Sumter to the triumph of the Union at Appomattox. McPherson defines major battles; provides eyewitness accounts, many by children; profiles historical luminaries; gives personal anecdotes from the soldiers; and addresses such issues as slavery, the roles of women and African Americans, health care on the battlefield, treatment of prisoners of war, and the effects of Reconstruction. McPherson also includes sidebars of information; a timeline; and many photographs, drawings, and maps. With this volume, the author is credited for doing for a young audience what he did for adults with *Battle Cry of Freedom.* Writing in *School Library Journal,* Starr E. Smith commented, "A distinguished historian has used his formidable talents to produce a concise, accessible, and appealing history in an attractive format. . . . McPherson summarizes the major facts of the war and relates anecdotes that bring to life the conflict's participants. . . . A good pick for researchers and browsers alike." Noting that there is always a need for another good overview on the Civil War, a critic in *Kirkus Reviews* declared that *Fields of Fury* "fills that need." The reviewer called the work a "thoughtfully and clearly constructed offering that will appeal to history buffs, young and old, and a must for any Civil War history collection." Carolyn Phelan of *Booklist* stated, "This large-format book provides an attractive and readable introduction to the Civil War. . . . McPherson writes with authority, offering a broad overview as well as many details and anecdotes that give his account a human dimension." Phelan concluded by calling *Fields of Fury* a "good balance of information and illustration on a topic of perennial interest."

McPherson continues to write and edit books on his specialties, to teach at Princeton, to serve as a consultant and on committees, and to act as a crusader for the preservation of the major battle sites of the Civil War. He has argued publicly against the exploitation of these sites by commercial vendors; in addition, he guides both new students and the general public through battlefields and other locations that are relevant to the war. In his interview with William R. Ferris of *Humanities,* McPherson suggested why he thinks that the Civil War has an enduring fascination: "One reason is the continuing salience of many of the issues over which the war was fought. Even though the War resolved the issues of Union and slavery, it didn't entirely resolve the issues that underlay those two questions. The relationships between the national government and regions, race relations, the role of government in trying to bring about change in race relations—these issues are still important in American society today. . . . The continuing relevance of these issues, I think, is one reason for the continuing fascination with the Civil War." When asked why writers in academia do not create more books for general readers, McPherson said, "Look at the large membership in the history book club, the interest in the History Channel on television, and the interest in documentaries by Ken Burns and by other historical filmmakers. There is a real hunger out there which is not always reached by academic historians. I think they ought to reach out more than they do, and that is what I try to do." He concluded, "I think it's possible to break new ground or offer new interpretations or to write a narrative work of history in such a way as it can appeal to a general audience, but also have something for a more academic and specialized audience. It has something to do with being convinced that history is a story of change over time, with a beginning, a development, a climax of consequences, and writing that story in such a way as it will retain the interest of a broad audience, but also have something new and interesting in the way of insight or interpretation for the specialist as well. It is not easy to explain. I just try to do it, and sometimes I think I've succeeded."

BIOGRAPHICAL AND CRITICAL SOURCES:

PERIODICALS

America, September 16, 2002, Tom O'Brien, "A Qualified Victory," p. 23.
Booklist, October 1, 1968, review of *Marching toward Freedom: The Negro in the Civil War, 1861-1865,* pp. 189-190; February 1, 1997, Roland Green, review of *For Cause and Comrades: Why Men Fought in the Civil War,* p. 924; November 15, 2002, Carolyn Phelan, review of *Fields of Fury: The American Civil War,* p. 586.
Book World, May 5, 1968, Paul M. Angle, "The Battle against Prejudice," p. 30.
Commonweal, May 24, 1968, review of *Marching toward Freedom: The Negro in the Civil War, 1861-1865,* p. 302.
Humanities, May-June, 2000, William R. Ferris, "'The War That Never Goes Away': A Conversation with Civil War Historian James M. McPherson."
Kirkus Reviews, September 1, 2002, review of *Fields of Fury: The American Civil War,* p. 1315.
Kliatt Young Adult Paperback Book Guide, January, 1999, Raymond L. Puffer, review of *For Cause and Comrades: Why Men Fought in the Civil War,* p. 31.
Los Angeles Times Book Review, March 20, 1988, Huston Horn, "The Finest One-Volume Civil War Ever Written," p. 10.
New York Times Book Review, May 5, 1968, Mel Watkins, review of *Marching toward Freedom: The Negro in the Civil War, 1861-1865,* p. 49; February 14, 1988, Hugh Brogan, review of *Battle Cry of Freedom: The Civil War Era,* p. 1.
Presidential Studies Quarterly, summer, 1997, Daniel Baracskay, review of *For Cause and Comrades: Whey Men Fought in the Civil War,* p. 612.
Publishers Weekly, January 18, 1991, Joseph Deitch, "James M. McPherson: The Civil War Historian Continues to Find New Material about That Profoundly Influential Conflict," p. 40.

School Library Journal, March, 1989, Audrey B. Eaglon, "Beautiful Losers," p. 131; October, 2002, Starr E. Smith, review of *Fields of Fury: The American Civil War,* p. 188.

Times Educational Supplement, March 13, 1992, Martin Flagg, review of *Battle Cry of Freedom: The Civil War Era,* p. 28.

ONLINE

National Endowment for the Humanities, http://www.neh.fed.us/ (March 22, 2003), Amy Lifson, "Meet James McPherson."

National Humanities Alliance (NEH) Testimony, http://www.nhalliance.org/ (April 18, 1991), "James M. McPherson, 18 April 1991."

Salon, http://www.salon.com/ (March 22, 2003), Katherine Whittamore, review of *Drawn with the Sword.*

World Socialist Web site, http://www.wsws.org/ (May 19, 1999), David Walsh, "Historian James M. McPherson and the Cause of Intellectual Integrity."

Deborah Dash Moore

*   *   *

MOORE, Deborah Dash 1946-

PERSONAL: Born August 6, 1946, in New York, NY; daughter of Martin (in business) and Irene (a professor; maiden name, Golden) Dash; married MacDonald Moore (in music business), June 15, 1967; children: Mordecai, Mikhael. *Education:* Brandeis University, B.A., 1967; Columbia University, M.A., 1968, Ph.D., 1975. *Politics:* Liberal. *Religion:* Jewish. *Hobbies and other interests:* "My major avocational concerns revolve around the problem of integrating a family and other womanly responsibilities with a professional career."

ADDRESSES: Home—620 Ft. Washington Ave., New York, NY 10041. *Office*—Department of Religion, Vassar College, Poughkeepsie, NY 12601. *E-mail*—moored@vassar.edu.

CAREER: Vassar College, Poughkeepsie, NY, assistant professor, 1976-84, associate professor, 1984-88, chairman of department of religion, 1983-87, professor of religion, 1988—; director of program in American culture, 1992-95. Director of research, YIVO Institute for Jewish Research, 1976—; Fulbright-Hays senior lecturer, department of American studies, Hebrew University, 1984-85; Skirball Visiting fellow, Oxford Centre for Hebrew and Jewish Studies, 1996; visiting fellow, Center for Judaic Studies, University of Pennsylvania, 1996; Pew Visiting fellow, Institute for the Advanced Study of Religion, Yale University, 2001-02.

MEMBER: Association for Jewish Studies (member of board of governors, 1982-85; vice president for membership, 2000-03), American Jewish Historical Society (member of academic council, 1978—; member of executive committee, 1998-2001), American Academy of Jewish Research, American Historical Association, American Studies Association, Organization of American Historians, Urban History Association, Immigration History Society.

AWARDS, HONORS: National Endowment for the Humanities fellowship for college teachers, 1978-79; National Jewish Book Award Honor Book, 1994; Saul Viener Prize, 1994 and 1995, for best book in American Jewish History; Dartmouth Medal of American Library Association for best reference work, 1997; Outstanding Academic Book, *Choice,* 1998; D.H.L., Reconstructionist Rabbinical College, 2001.

WRITINGS:

At Home in America: Second Generation New York Jews, Columbia University Press (New York, NY), 1981.

B'nai B'rith and the Challenge of Ethnic Leadership, State University of New York Press (Albany, NY), 1981.

(Editor) *East European Jews in Two Worlds: Studies from the YIVO Annual,* YIVO Institute for Jewish Research (New York, NY), 1990.

(Editor, with Ronald Dotterer and Steven M. Cohen) *Jewish Settlement and Community in the Modern Western World,* Susquehanna University Press (Selinsgrove, PA), 1991.

To the Golden Cities: Pursuing the American Jewish Dream in Miami and L.A., Free Press (New York, NY), 1994.

When Jews Were GIs: How World War II Changed a Generation and Remade American Jewry (pamphlet), University of Michigan Press (Ann Arbor, MI), 1994.

(Editor, with Paula Hyman) *Jewish Women in America: An Historical Encyclopedia,* Routledge (New York, NY), 1997.

(Editor, with S. Ilan Troen) *Divergent Jewish Cultures: Israel and America,* Yale University Press (New Haven, CT), 2001.

(With Howard B. Rock) *Cityscapes: A History of New York in Images,* Columbia University Press (New York, NY), 2001.

General editor, with Paula Hyman, "The Modern Jewish Experience" series, Indiana University Press (Bloomington, IN), 1982—. Also author of pamphlet, *Worshipping Together in Uniform: Christians and World War II,* Swig Judaic Studies Program at the University of University of San Francisco (San Francisco, CA), 2001. Contributor of articles to scholarly journals, including *Jewish Journal of Sociology* and *American Jewish History.*

SIDELIGHTS: Deborah Dash Moore's book *At Home in America: Second Generation New York Jews* examines the Americanization of second-generation New York Jews during the period from 1920 to 1950. According to Moore, the children of the Eastern European Jewish immigrants who came to the country between 1880 and 1920 established the American Jewish prototype for an "ethnicity consonant with middle-class values." Focusing on housing patterns and key institutions, such as public schools and synagogue centers, the author explains how members of the second generation succeeded in creating an ethnic lifestyle that insured a continuance of Jewish identity.

Moore turned her attention to the next era in American Jewish life in *To the Golden Cities: Pursuing the American Jewish Dream in Miami and L. A.* In this book, she chronicled how the post-World War II economic boom triggered the second great wave of Jewish immigration—from the cold, well-established cities in the Northeast and the Midwest to the warm, expansive communities in the sunny climates of California and Florida. Following individual life stories, Moore identifies Miami as a suburb of New York City and illustrates how certain neighborhoods from the old cities recreated themselves in the sunbelt. Jews leaving behind their old haunts in Brooklyn, New York, even had the satisfaction of seeing the Brooklyn Dodgers relocate to Los Angeles. In both California and Florida, the new Jewish residents did face opposition, sometimes in as blatant a form as Ku Klux Klan bombings, at other times in more subtle forms of discrimination and exclusivity from the ruling WASP elite. Moore's research is painstaking; a writer for *Kirkus Reviews* pointed out that she "is careful to delineate the demographic, sociological, and religious factors that made Jewish Miami and L.A. distinct." *To the Golden Cities* is a "lively" and "lucid account," concluded the reviewer.

In *Cityscapes: A History of New York in Images,* Moore teamed with Howard B. Rock to present a pictorial history of Manhattan from its beginning in the seventeenth century, as a tiny settlement on the southern tip of the island, to the period just before the destruction of the World Trade Center, when towers covered virtually the entire island. Pictures and text work together like "a classy stop-motion film," wrote Donna Seaman in *Booklist,* providing a "fascinating, artistic, and, most importantly, humanistic chronicle."

Moore told *CA:* "I am concerned in my work to bring my competence as a historian to an understanding of contemporary situations affecting American Jews.

While I rarely study the present, I must confess to a certain present-mindedness in my choice of subjects to study. I make an effort, also, to bridge the gap between the world of scholarship and the world of community without destroying the integrity of the former or the vitality of the latter."

BIOGRAPHICAL AND CRITICAL SOURCES:

PERIODICALS

American Historical Review, December, 1981; February, 1983, review of *B'nai B'rith and the Challenge of Ethnic Leadership,* p. 197.
Booklist, December 1, 2001, Donna Seaman, review of *Cityscapes: A History New York in Images,* p. 626.
Choice, September, 1994, review of *To the Golden Cities: Pursuing the American Jewish Dream in Miami and L.A.,* p. 196.
Commentary, July, 1981.
Journal of Church and State, winter, 1992, review of *East European Jews in Two Worlds,* p. 154.
Journal of Urban History, February, 1986, review of *At Home in America: Second Generation New York Jews,* p. 191; November, 1999, review of *To the Golden Cities: Pursuing the American Jewish Dream in Miami and L.A.,* p. 98.
Kirkus Reviews, February 15, 1994, review of *To the Golden Cities: Pursuing the American Jewish Dream in Miami and L.A.,* p. 206.
Library Journal, March 15, 1994, review of *To the Golden Cities: Pursuing the American Jewish Dream in Miami and L.A.,* p. 89.
Publishers Weekly, February 16, 1990, review of *East European Jews in Two Worlds: Studies from the YIVO Annual,* p. 72; March 14, 1994, review of *To the Golden Cities: Pursuing the American Jewish Dream in Miami and L.A.,* p. 57.
Religious Studies Review, April, 1995, review of *To the Golden Cities: Pursuing the American Jewish Dream in Miami and L.A.,* p. 159.
Reviews in American History, December, 1995, review of *To the Golden Cities: Pursuing the American Jewish Dream in Miami and L.A.,* p. 739.
Slavic Review, winter, 1994, review of *East European Jews in Two Worlds: Studies from the YIVO Annual,* p. 1124.
Times Literary Supplement, December 18, 1981; November 23, 1990, review of *East European Jews in Two Worlds: Studies from the YIVO Annual,* p. 1261.

University Press Book News, June, 1990, review of *East European Jews in Two Worlds: Studies from the YIVO Annual,* p. 7.

* * *

MORRIS, Edmund 1940-

PERSONAL: Born May 27, 1940, in Nairobi, Kenya; immigrated to the United States, 1968, naturalized citizen, 1979; son of Eric Edmund (an airline pilot) and May (Dowling) Morris; married Sylvia Jukes (a writer), May 28, 1966. *Education:* Attended Rhodes University, 1959-60.

ADDRESSES: Home and office—240 Central Park S., New York, NY 10019-1413; and Washington, D.C. *Agent*—Georges Borchardt, Inc., 136 East 57th St., New York, N.Y. 10022.

CAREER: Historian and writer. Worked as advertising copywriter in London, England, 1964-68, and in New York, NY, 1968-71; writer and biographer, 1971—. Contributing editor to *New York Times,* 1975-76.

MEMBER: Society of American Historians.

AWARDS, HONORS: Pulitzer Prize for Biography and the National Book Award, 1980, for *The Rise of Theodore Roosevelt.*

WRITINGS:

The Rise of Theodore Roosevelt, Coward, McMann, and Geoghegan, (New York, NY), 1979, reprinted, Modern Library (New York, NY), 2001.
Dutch: A Memoir of Ronald Reagan, Random House (New York, NY), 1999.
(Author of introduction) *The Education of Henry Adams,* Random House (New York, NY), 1999.
(Author of introduction) *America's Library: The Story of the Library of Congress, 1800-2000,* Yale University Press (New Haven, CT), 2000.
Theodore Rex, Random House (New York, NY), 2001.

Contributor to publications, including the *New Yorker,* the *New York Times,* and *Harper's Magazine.*

Edmund Morris

ADAPTATIONS: *The Rise of Theodore Roosevelt* was adapted for audio cassette by Books on Tape, 1991. *Dutch* was adapted for audio cassette by Random Audio, 1999.

SIDELIGHTS: Edmund Morris told CA: "I care very much for form and technique, and find that my imagination works best when shaped by the one and disciplined by the other. For example, *The Rise of Theodore Roosevelt* follows the symmetrical form of Bach's *Goldberg Variations,* and the prologue is technically written in the second person, while seeming to be cast in the third. Of course readers should not be aware of such private contrivances; if they are, then one's art has not sufficiently concealed the art. I believe that literary talent, however slight, is a gift inscrutably bestowed, and that the recipient should pay for it by working very hard at the mechanics, which are, after all, ninety-nine per cent of any perfect manuscript."

Morris was born in Nairobi, Kenya, to British parents and there attended the Prince of Wales School. He de-

scribed this experience as typical of a British public school in the years before World War I, with students wearing flannel trousers, collars and ties, blazers—and all this in the searing Kenyan heat. He first became interested in literature through one of his teachers, W. W. Atkinson, and began writing novels, hiding them in his atlas while seating himself at the back of the classroom. Alexander the Great, Chuck Yeager, and Winston Churchill were his early childhood heroes, joined by Theodore Roosevelt after he saw a textbook photograph that sparked in him a passion for America. "I saw the 'friendly, peering snarl' of his face," said Morris during an interview with Martin Miller of the *Los Angeles Times,* and quickly added he was quoting H. G. Wells. "And I thought, 'He looks like a grown-up that would be fun to be with.'"

It would be twenty-five years before his passion for America and Roosevelt was rekindled. After graduating from high school, he studied music and history at Rhodes University in South Africa for one year. Four years later, he moved to London to become an advertising copywriter and, four years after that, he immigrated to New York where he felt he could not only explore his talents, but get paid to do so. In New York City, he wrote on a freelance basis, exploring a diverse range of subject matter—from advertising copy and mail-order catalogues, to poetry and radio scripts. He became a contributing editor to the *New York Times* in 1975, and—between writing assignments—independently researched and wrote a biographical study of Russian-born piano virtuoso Josef Lhévinne for WNCN radio in New York City. The three-and-one-half-hour broadcast was met with tremendous listener response.

Morris's idea for a biography on Roosevelt was actually inspired by Richard M. Nixon's words in his 1974 televised resignation speech. Nixon said of his mother, "She was beautiful in face and form . . . as a flower she lived, and as a fair young flower she died." Nixon then attributed the original words to Roosevelt. This quote sparked Morris's curiosity, and he began researching the life of Roosevelt. He soon set off for the Bad Lands of the Dakotas to research and write a screenplay, titled "Dude from New York." Although optioned by a Hollywood producer, the screenplay remained unstaged; however, Morris's agent suggested turning it into a short biography. The "short biography" grew to the 886-page *The Rise of Theodore Roosevelt,* which covers Roosevelt's life from his birth in 1895 to President William McKinley's assassination in 1901. The book became a best seller, made the Book-of-the-Month Club, and ultimately won the Pulitzer Prize and the American Book Award.

This would become the first book in a planned trilogy by Morris on Roosevelt. However, the second book of the trio was postponed when President Ronald W. Reagan granted Morris authority to become his authorized biographer. Morris received an unprecedented level of access to Reagan and his political affairs, and, in return, was asked that the biography not be published until two years after the termination of Reagan's presidency.

Morris, however, did not want to become a historian-in-residence at the White House. In an interview with Fred Barnes for the *New Republic,* Morris commented "The danger is you immediately become one of the team. You become partisan. You lose your independence." However, in 1985, Morris contacted Nancy Reagan and the deal was closed. Because of his success with his first book, the remarkable access he had to Reagan and his political affairs, and public perception of the importance of Reagan's presidency, the publisher provided Morris with a $3 million advance. The Reagans left the White House and they—and the reading public—awaited Morris's book with great expectation.

The much-anticipated release of *Dutch: A Memoir of Ronald Reagan* immediately created a controversy. The reason is well summarized by Fred Greenstein in *Political Science Quarterly.* He wrote: "Morris casts his book as the memoir of a fictional contemporary of Reagan's, who has observed him in Illinois as a young man and in California as a movie actor, conservative political activist, and governor of the state. That memoir writer is an altered version of Morris himself . . . the invented Morris was born in Chicago in 1912, the year after Reagan's birth. In addition to his fictionally-aged self, Morris populates his book with no fewer than nine made-up members of the Morris family, including a 1960's University of California student radical, who provides a highly selective account of Reagan's governorship."

"Morris's book is an intellectual embarrassment," Greenstein continued. "It blurs fact with fiction, substitutes effusion for rigorous analysis, and is riddled with errors. It also is seriously incomplete, especially in its treatment of the aspect of Reagan's experience to which Morris might have been expected to have the most to add—his White House years."

While Harvey Sicherman commented in *Orbis* that "*Dutch* soon became a byword for the way a biography should not be done," Rich Karlgaard, writing for *Forbes,* viewed the unusual style from a different perspective. He observed, "The same critics who complain about this unconventional technique whine that Morris tags Reagan as a middlebrow rube, an airhead and as intellectually incurious. Morris did this intentionally. . . . The Morris character can't fathom how *Dutch,* son of an alcoholic skip-town father, is able to transcend his poverty and limitations time and time again. But isn't that precisely how snobs and intellectuals always saw Reagan? . . . Thus, the Morris technique, odd though it may be, is a brilliant way to convey snob cynicism toward Reagan."

Morris returned from his fourteen-year hiatus of Reagan research to his favorite historical figure—Roosevelt. "It's a mysterious attraction," he explained to Miller. "I find him endlessly interesting in the mysterious way all biographers find their subjects interesting. . . . I do not think I'm in love with him, which is very dangerous for a biographer," Morris commented. "To be in love with your subject is to be protective. But even worse is to be in hate with your subject." Miller noted that, whatever Morris's emotional relationship to Roosevelt, "the reading public and critics are again in love with Morris and *Theodore Rex.* The book immediately appeared on the major bestseller lists, and reviewers are heaping on the praise."

Theodore Rex (a title taken from a quip by Henry James) begins as the youngest president in America's history rides from Mount Marcy, New York, to Buffalo, to take the oath of office. The prologue follows Roosevelt's journey to Washington and follows Roosevelt through his seven-and-a-half-year presidency. A reviewer for *Publishers Weekly* commented that "Morris succeeds brilliantly at capturing all of TR's many energized sides, producing a book that is every bit as complex, engaging and invigorating as the vibrant president it depicts."

The final volume in the trilogy will depict Roosevelt's post-presidential career, including his aborted effort to regain office as head of the Bull Moose ticket in 1912.

BIOGRAPHICAL AND CRITICAL SOURCES:

PERIODICALS

American Historical Review, April 2001, review of *Dutch: A Memoir of Ronald Reagan,* p. 535.

Book, January-February 2002, Terry Teachout, review, "*Theodore Rex,* (Review and Opinion: Moderately Mad, Madly Moderate)," p. 62.

Book-of-the-Month Club News, April, 1979, Jack Newcombe, interview of Edmund Morris, p. 5.

Book World, December 7, 1980, review of *The Rise of Theodore Roosevelt,* p. 6; October 3, 1999, review of *Dutch,* p. 1.

Columbia Journalism Review, November 199, review of *Dutch,* p. 70.

Economist, January 5, 2002, "King Ted; Theodore Roosevelt," review of *Theodore Rex.*

Entertainment Weekly, October 22, 1999, Clarissa Cruz, "Grate Communicator: *Dutch* Scores Low Approval Ratings," p. 81.

Forbes, December 13, 1999, Rich Karlgaard, "Reagan's Century," review of *Theodore Rex,* p. 51.

Los Angeles Times, December 26, 2001, interview by Martin Miller, "On the Trail of a Rough Rider, with Stories Yet to Tell; Biographer Edmund Morris' *Theodore Rex* Is Only the Second Part of the Trilogy," p. E-1.

New Republic, February 3, 1986, interview with Fred Barnes, p. 10; December 6, 1999, review of *Dutch,* p. 42.

New Statesman, November 8, 1999, review of *Dutch,* p. 56.

New York, October 18, 1999, Michael Wolff, "Dutch Treat," review of *Dutch,* p. 24.

New York Times, May 21, 1979, Christopher Lehmann-Haupt, review of *The Rise of Theodore Roosevelt;* September, 1999, Doreen Carvajal, "Writer As Character in Reagan Biography," review of *Dutch,* p. 1450-1451.

New York Times Book Review, March 25, 1979; March 30, 1980, review of *The Rise of Theodore Roosevelt,* p. 33.

Observer, (London, England), October 31, 1999, review of *Dutch,* p. 13.

Orbis, summer, 2000, Harvey Sicherman, review of *Dutch,* p. 477.

Political Science Quarterly, winter, 1980, review of *The Rise of Theodore Roosevelt,* p. 718; spring, 2000, Fred I. Greenstein, "Reckoning with Reagan: A Review Essay on Edmund Morris's *Dutch,*" p. 115.

Presidential Studies Quarterly, June 200, Peter Hannaford and Robert D. Schulzinger, review of *Dutch,* p. 338.

Publishers Weekly, February 15, 1980, review of *The Rise of Theodore Roosevelt,* p. 109; October 15, 2001, review of *Theodore Rex,* p. 55.

Wall Street Journal, June 15, 1989, review of *The Rise of Theodore Roosevelt,* p. A11; October 1, 1999, review of *Dutch,* p. W1.

Wilson Quarterly, summer, 1983, article by Edmund Morris, p. 165; April, 1991, review of *The Rise of Theodore Roosevelt,* p. 56.*

* * *

MORRISON, Jeanette Helen
See LEIGH, Janet

* * *

MORRISON, (Philip) Blake 1950-

PERSONAL: Born October 8, 1950, in Burnley, Lancashire, England; son of Arthur Blakemore (a physician) and Agnes (a physician; maiden name, O'Shea) Morrison; married Katherine Ann Drake (a social worker), July 15, 1976; children: Seth, Aphra, Gabriel. *Education:* Nottingham University, B.A. (with honors), 1972; McMaster University, M.A.; University College, London, Ph.D. *Politics:* "Left-of-centre." *Religion:* Atheist.

ADDRESSES: Home—54 Blackheath Pk., London SE3 9SQ, England. *Agent*—Pat Kavanagh, Peters, Fraser, & Dunlop, Drury House, 34-43 Russell St., London WC2B 5HA, England.

CAREER: Writer and poet. *Times Literary Supplement,* London, England, assistant editor, 1978-81; *Observer,* London, deputy literary editor, 1981-86, literary editor, 1986-89; *Independent on Sunday,* London, literary editor, 1990—. Poetry Book Society, chair, 1984-87.

MEMBER: Royal Society of Literature fellow, Poetry Book Society (board member, 1981—), Poetry Society (executive and general council member, 1980—), Arts Council (literature panel member, 1988—), English PEN (vice president, 1999—).

AWARDS, HONORS: Eric Gregory Award, Society of Authors, 1980; Somerset Maugham Award, Society of Authors, 1985, for *Dark Glasses;* Dylan Thomas Award, Poetry Society, 1986; E. M. Forster Award, American Academy and Institute of Arts and Letters, 1988; Esquire/Volvo/Waterstone's Nonfiction Award, 1993, for *And When Did You Last See Your Father?;* J. R. Ackerley Award, 1994.

WRITINGS:

The Movement: English Poetry and Fiction of the 1950s, Oxford University Press (New York, NY), 1980.

Seamus Heaney, Methuen (New York, NY), 1982.

(Editor, with Andrew Motion) *Penguin Book of Contemporary British Poetry,* Penguin (New York, NY), 1982.

Dark Glasses (poetry), Chatto and Windus (London, England), 1984, revised and expanded edition, 1989.

The Ballad of the Yorkshire Ripper and Other Poems, Chatto and Windus (London, England), 1987.

The Yellow House (children's novel), illustrated by Helen Craig, Harcourt Brace (San Diego, CA), 1987, Candlewick Press (Cambridge, MA) 1994.

And When Did You Last See Your Father?: A Son's Memoir of Love and Loss (memoir), Picador (New York, NY), 1993.

(Adapter and translator) Heinrich von Kleist, *The Cracked Pot: A Play,* Samuel French (New York, NY), 1996.

Pendle Witches (poetry), etchings by Paula Rego, Enitharmon Press (Chester Springs, PA), 1996.

As If: A Crime, a Trial, a Question of Childhood (nonfiction), Picador (New York, NY), 1997.

Too True, Granta Books (London, England), 1998.

Selected Poems, Granta Books (London, England), 1999.

The Justification of Johann Gutenberg, Chatto and Windus (London, England), 2000, William Morrow (New York, NY), 2002.

Things My Mother Never Told Me (memoir), Chatto and Windus (London, England), 2003, Granta Books (New York, NY), 2003.

Contributor to *Poetry Introduction 5,* Faber, 1982. Regular literary reviewer, critic, and contributor to *The Guardian* and *The Independent* (London, England).

SIDELIGHTS: Though often identified as a poet, Blake Morrison also produces well-received nonfiction and journalism. Both his Lancashire-born father (whose life and death Blake would recount in a 1993 memoir) and Irish-born mother (commemorated in *Things My Mother Never Told Me* ten years later) were physicians, but the younger Morrison rejected medicine for literature, and in the process has embraced many genres. Indeed, noted *Contemporary Poets* essayist Wes Magee, Morrison's "activities as editor, anthropologist, and competition adjudicator in London's literary whirlpools have tended to deflect attention from his two excellent collections of verse."

In 1984 Morrison published his first poetry collection, *Dark Glasses,* a work the author described in *Contemporary Poets* as "much preoccupied with secrecy, lies, privacy, the difficulty of openness in both private and public life." This volume, said Magee, represents "a notable debut for its clarity of expression . . . , the carefully achieved polish and finish, and the emergence of a voice, albeit with [poet] Philip Larkin looming hugely in the background."

Three years later came the publication of *The Ballad of the Yorkshire Ripper and Other Poems,* a collection "dominated by the title poem, a fourteen-page monologue [from] an unnamed Yorkshireman speaking in dialect," according to Magee. In giving an artistic spin to the true tale of a killer, Morrison "manages a compassionate and thoughtful tone."

When Magee wrote that Morrison "deals with such contemporary matters as criminality and domesticity in an unassuming, quiet manner," he could have been referring to Morrison's non-poetic work as well. In the early 1990s, Morrison covered a famous murder trial for *New Yorker* magazine. The experience of attending the trial was developed into his 1997 book, *As If: A Crime, a Trial, a Question of Childhood.* Recounting the events that began in 1993—when two British ten-year-olds lured a toddler from a shopping mall, then battered him to death near some train tracks—Morrison examines the lives of the accused boys and the resulting public furor that accompanied the trial and conviction.

Recognized as an effort that goes beyond simple crime reporting, *As If* earned kudos from a number of publications. An *Economist* critic praised Morrison for providing a balanced tone: "Rather than write the two boys off as evil incarnate, he searches for a more thoughtful explanation." *Library Journal* critic Christine Moesch found the writing "excellent," citing Morrison's "own dark thoughts as a parent who worries for his child's safety and of his concern about the larger problem of crimes committed worldwide by children."

Themes of domesticity imbued Morrison's 1993 memoir, *And When Did You Last See Your Father?* In this work the author examines the life of his father, physician Arthur Morrison, a man who, despite his education and standing in his community, reveled in committing minor offenses: sneaking past traffic lines, getting into events without paying, speeding his sports car through country roads at night. "His conversation was studded with clichés and banalities," noted Irvine Loudon in the British medical journal *Lancet*. "He had a prolonged affair with a married woman whom he called 'Aunt Beaty.'"

Though hardly a role model for his frequently embarrassed son, Arthur Morrison is also remembered as a blunt, earthy character, popular with his patients. In 1991, at age seventy-five, he was diagnosed with inoperable bowel cancer. *And When* offers Morrison's detailed report of his father's quick and painful decline, while at the same time he "ruminates on the contradictions in his father's character and tries to see him as a person separate from the parent-child relationship," a *Publishers Weekly* reviewer stated. In Loudon's view, such a book may have been accused of poor taste "if it had been badly done and motivated by hatred." On the contrary, he added, *And When* "is quite superbly written. Much of it is extremely funny, but it is humour of wry affection, tinged with exasperation and sadness. Nowhere have I read an account of death from cancer that rang so true from the initial deception about the true diagnosis, through the moments of frustrated hopes, into the relentless deterioration . . . and for the family, the long weary nights of physical and emotional exhaustion, and the fervent longing for a 'happy release.'"

Not all reviewers of Morrison's works have sung his praises, however. Thomas Jones of *London Review of Books* reviewed *The Justification of Johann Gutenberg* by beginning with an assessment of *As If* and *And When*. In both books, Morrison is extremely introspective. In confessing his experiences and emotions, however, he sometimes oversteps the bounds of decency, according to Jones, who wrote that in *As If,* Morrison's "self-absorption has some unfortunate consequences. There's the all too famous passage in the book in which Morrison describes in unashamedly erotic terms undressing his daughter. . . . Elsewhere, he informs us in detail of the 'ritual' of taking his sleeping son from his bed 'to pre-empt his bedwetting'. . . . What is objectionable about these passages is the fact of their publication. He . . . never pauses to consider the effect of writing about it. One of the many responsibilities of parents should be to respect their children's privacy."

"By the time he wrote *As If,*" Jones continued, "Morrison had already exposed his father in a similar way. He refers so often to the dying man's genitals that at times it seems a more appropriate title would have been *And When Did You Last See Your Father's Penis?* Morrison senior didn't want friends to visit him in hospital; when he got home he boarded up the window in the front door. . . . And when Morrison reproduces not only his father's medical records but a letter from his father's lover which she makes perfectly clear is for his eyes only, it's hard not to see [the book] less as a memorial than an act of Oedipal revenge."

The Justification of Johann Gutenberg is a fictional account of a man who—as the twentieth century drew to a close—was hailed by many surveys as being the most influential man of the last millennium. His name—Johann Gutenberg; his influence—movable type. Little is known of Gutenberg, and Morrison notes at the end of the book that "for much of this novel, I have had to make things up." Critics such as Jones remarked that this fictionalizing is, of course, what makes the book a novel rather than a biography. Ian Sansom, reviewing the book for *The Guardian,* commented, "Like all Morrison's work, and for all its range, *The Justification of Johann Gutenberg* ultimately focuses on that irreducible spot of unhappiness—that little inky stain—at the heart of the human condition. Morrison gives us Gutenberg as an old man, bitter, half-blind, ruined, living in exile in Eltville, dictating his memoirs to a young scribe, dreaming of 'print pilgrims' coming to visit him. . . . Morrison is, however, much less interested in Gutenberg's invention than in its human cost. The book's justification lies not in its description of Gutenberg's famous success but in its account of his many private failings."

Morrison's second memoir, *Things My Mother Never Told Me,* is an epistolary tribute to his mother, written after her death. With the aid of a collection of private letters, the author delves into hidden aspects of his mother's life and identity, including details about her relationship with Morrison's father. The couple's correspondence during World War II, when their courtship began, revealed to Morrison a romance that was passionate but tempestuous, troubled by personality conflicts, religious differences, and personal sacrifice. Morrison narrates as one who knows the outcome—the emotional pain his mother faced later in life as a result of his father—without knowing the backstory. As a result, Morrison noted in the memoir, reading the letters his then twenty-something parents wrote to one another made him feel "protective, avuncular, parental. Unlike them, I knew what the future looked like." *New York Times* reviewer Rob Nixon said the author "deploys this Tristram Shandy-like vantage point to witty, poignant effect." In this way, Morrison supplements the history with personal, introspective details. Nixon called the memoir, "enthralling," and praised Morrison for his "historical empathy and storytelling prowess."

BIOGRAPHICAL AND CRITICAL SOURCES:

BOOKS

Contemporary Poets, 6th edition, St. James Press (Detroit, MI), 1996.

PERIODICALS

Economist, February 15, 1997, review of *As If: A Crime, a Trial, a Question of Childhood,* p. 8004.
Entertainment Weekly, August 18, 1995, Joseph Olshan, review of *And When Did You Last See Your Father?,* p. 50.
Guardian (London, England), August 19, 2000, Ian Sansom, "Blood and Ink: Ian Sansom Weighs the Cost of Genius," review of *The Justification of Johann Gutenberg,* p. 10.
Lancet, December 18, 1993, Irvine Loudon, review of *And When Did You Last See Your Father?,* p. 1539.
Library Journal, August, 1997, p. 107.
London Review of Books, December 6, 1984, pp. 19-20; July 23, 1987, pp. 16-18; September 7, 2000, Thomas Jones, "Taking Flight," *The Justification of Johann Gutenberg,* p. 14.
New Statesman & Society, February 8, 1985, p. 32; May 28, 1993, Tony Gould, review of *And When Did You Last See Your Father?: A Son's Memoir of Love and Loss,* p. 41; April 24, 2000, p. 10.
New York Times Book Review, April 11, 2003, Rob Nixon, "Mother of Invention."
Observer (London, England), Tim Adams, "Medium Fine. Pity about the Message," review of *Justification of Johann Gutenberg,* p. 11.
People, October 9, 1995, p. 37; October 20, 1997, p. 42; October 20, 1997, David Lehman, review of *As If,* p. 42.
Publishers Weekly, April 24, 1995, review of *And When Did You Last See Your Father?,* p. 52; August 11, 1997, review of *As If,* p. 395.
Spectator, May 24, 1980, pp. 17-18.
Times Literary Supplement, April 4, 1980, pp. 333-35; June 20, 1980, p. 699; August 13, 1982, p. 876; p. 941; January 28, 1983, p. 78; May 29, 1987, p. 574; November 20, 1987.

N

NABOKOV, Peter (Francis) 1940-
(Peter Towne)

PERSONAL: Born October 11, 1940, in Auburn, NY; son of Nicolas (a writer and composer) and Constance (Holladay) Nabokov. *Education:* Attended St. Johns College; Columbia University, B.A. (English), 1965; Goddard College, M.A. (ethnic studies and language arts), 1972; University of California, Berkeley, Ph.D. (anthropology), 1988.

ADDRESSES: Office—World Arts and Cultures, 200Q Kinross Bldg., 267-2037, 11000 Kinross Ave., Box 951608, Los Angeles, CA 90095-1608.

CAREER: Worked on Navaho, Sioux, and Crow reservations in Montana, 1962, and later sailed with the Merchant Marine; *New Mexican,* Santa Fe, NM, staff reporter, 1967-68; Monterey Peninsula College, Monterey, CA, coordinator of college preparatory program for veterans, 1970, instructor in American Indian studies, 1970-73, 1977-78; Human Resources Research Organization, Carmel, CA, research associate, 1972-75; University of California, Berkeley, instructor, 1979-82, 1984-85, 1989; Native American Educational Services College, Chicago, IL, co-instructor, 1987; University of California, Santa Cruz, CA, lecturer, 1987-89; California State University, Hayward, lecturer, 1989; University of Wisconsin, Madison, assistant professor of anthropology, 1991-96; University of California, Los Angeles, professor of world arts and cultures, 1997—, department chair, 2002-03. Research associate, Museum of the American Indian, Heye Foundation, 1962-85, and Santa Barbara Museum of

Peter Nabokov

Natural History, 1978-82. Visiting lecturer at Center for the Study of Indian History, Haskell Indian Junior College, University of California, Santa Barbara, College of the Virgin Islands, Colorado College, University of North Dakota, University of Montana, and University of Colorado, Boulder. Recorded "Land As a Symbol" (sound recording), National Public Radio, 1979.

MEMBER: Society for the Prevention of Cruelty to Children.

AWARDS, HONORS: Albuquerque Press Club awards, two first prizes, and New Mexico Press Association, first prize in editorial writing, all 1967; American Library Association Best Book for Young Adults citation, *Library School Journal* Best Book citation, and Carter G. Woodson Book Award from National Council for the Social Studies, all 1978, all for *Native American Testimony: An Anthology of Indian and White Relations,* Volume I: *First Encounter to Dispossession;* Newberry Library predoctoral fellowship, D'Arcy McNickle Center for the History of the American Indian, 1986-87; Bay Area Book Reviewers Association Award for Nonfiction: Arts and Letters, 1990, and American Institute of Architects Institute Honor Award, 1991, both with coauthor Robert Easton, both for *Native American Architecture;* Indo-U.S. Subcommission on Education and Culture research fellowship in India, 1990-91; Ford Foundation Ethnic Studies Course Development Award, University of Wisconson, 1995; American Institute of Indian Studies senior research fellowship, 1997; UCLA Council on Research Award, 1997, 1999.

WRITINGS:

(Editor) *Two Leggings: The Making of a Crow Warrior,* Crowell (New York, NY), 1967.

Tijerina and the Courthouse Raid, University of New Mexico Press (Albuquerque, NM), 1969, revised edition, Ramparts (Berkeley, CA), 1971.

(Under pseudonym Peter Towne) *George Washington Carver,* Crowell (New York, NY), 1975.

(Editor) *Native American Testimony: An Anthology of Indian and White Relations,* Crowell (New York, NY), Volume I: *First Encounter to Dispossession,* 1978, Volume II: *Reservation to Resurgence,* 1988, new expanded edition published as *Native American Testimony: A Chronicle of Indian-White Relations from Prophecy to the Present, 1492-1992,* Viking (New York, NY), 1991.

Adobe, Pueblo and Hispanic Folk Traditions of the Southwest, Smithsonian Institute (Washington, DC), 1981.

Indian Running, Capra Press (Santa Barbara, CA), 1981, published as *Indian Running: Native American History and Tradition,* Ancient City Press, 1987.

Architecture of Acoma Pueblo: The 1934 Historic American Buildings Survey Project, Ancient City Press (Santa Fe, NM), 1986.

(With Wayne Olts) *Peoples of the Earthlodge* (film), North Dakota Council for the Humanities and Public Issues, 1987.

(With Robert Easton) *Dwellings at the Source: Architecture of the American Indian,* Oxford University Press (New York, NY), 1989.

Sacred Geography: Reflections and Sources on Environment/Religion, Harper (New York, NY), 1989.

Bibliography of the Crow, Scarecrow Press (Lanham, MD), 1989.

(With Robert Easton) *Native American Architecture,* Oxford University Press (New York, NY), 1989.

(With Lawrence Loendorf) *American Indians and Yellowstone National Park: A Documentary Overview,* National Park Service (Yellowstone National Park, WY), 2002.

A Forest of Time: American Indian Ways of History, Cambridge University Press (New York, NY), 2002.

CONTRIBUTOR

Solving "The Indian Problem": The White Man's Burdensome Business, edited by Murray L. Wax and Robert Buchanan, New York Times (New York, NY), 1975.

Methods and Materials of Continuing Education, edited by Chester Klevens, Klevens Publishing, 1976.

Shelter II, Shelter Publications, 1978.

The American Indian and the Problem of History, edited by Calvin Martin, Oxford University Press (New York, NY), 1987.

Roots: America's Vernacular Heritage, edited by Dell Upton, American Heritage Press, 1987.

(Author of introduction) *A Study of Pueblo Architecture in Tusayan and Cibola,* Smithsonian Institute (Washington, DC), 1989.

Contributor to *Our Indian Heritage,* and Reader's Digest. Contributor to numerous periodicals, including *Nation, Co-Evolution Quarterly, New Scholar, East West Journal, Camera Arts, American West, Parabola, Progressive, Washington Post,* and *New York Times Book Review.*

SIDELIGHTS: In his books about Native Americans, Peter Nabokov presents a sympathetic and compelling view of their history and traditions. His *Two Leggings:*

The Making of a Crow Warrior is "a crisp, unexaggerated re-creation of the life of a nineteenth-century Plains Indian warrior," as Meredith Brown of *Saturday Review* stated. A detailed biography that also examines Indian society of the time, it is "a unique record of a vanished culture," wrote Hardin E. Smith in *Library Journal*. Similarly, Brown assessed it "a handbook to the values and patterns of leadership in a culture that flourished less than 100 years ago."

Calling Nabokov's *Tijerina and the Courthouse Raid* "centrally the history of a social movement," Edgar Z. Friedenberg explained in the *New York Review of Books* that it chronicles "the formation and development, under [Reies Lopes] Tijerina's leadership, of the Alianzo Federal de los Pueblos Libres—the Federation of Free City States—and of the remarkable events in which the Alianzo has been involved in its organizing of so called 'Mexican-Americans' in the state of New Mexico." Friedenberg said that the book is "even more valuable as sociology than as history, because it shows so clearly how things work, and on the basis of such carefully and quite literally painfully gathered evidence, both by observation and documentation." Similarly, the value of the two-volume *Native American Testimony: An Anthology of Indian and White Relations,* according to N. Scott Momaday of the *New York Times Book Review,* is through its "keen insight into the mind and spirit of the American Indian. In these many utterances, there emerges one voice, and it is one of great poignancy and power, often one of great beauty."

A new and revised edition of the *Native American Testimony* volumes was released to coincide with the five-hundredth anniversary of Christopher Columbus's voyage to the New World. Now titled *Native American Testimony: A Chronicle of Indian-White Relations from Prophecy to the Present, 1492-1992,* the volumes feature contemporary Native American leaders speaking to Nabokov on the "continued resistance of our major institutions—the media, academia, government—to offering Indian voice and opinions," stated *Nation* reviewer Jerry Mander. At the same time, the author uses traditional narratives, oral histories, letters, and news clips, to reach back into history, presenting the testimonies of figures such as Sitting Bull and Tecumseh. In doing so the author achieves, said Mander, "what no one has before: the retelling of a half-millennium of history from an Indian viewpoint." There are accounts of battles between Indian nations and European settlers, "internal disputes and debates

among the Indians themselves, intellectual discourses about the virtues and failings of the non-Indian ways, [and] painful accounts of deliberately misleading agreements," according to the critic.

In a review for *American Indian Quarterly,* Francis Jennings took exception to one aspect of Nabokov's study; specifically, how the book "stresses the relations of Indians with other people in terms of race. Peoples of European descent are whites, a term that has bad tradition behind it and is simply not literally true." For example, the critic continued, Nabokov writes of Indians as "bronze-skinned men and women" facing the coming of the "white man." But many Spanish settlers, noted Jennings, "were pigmented . . . and the earliest Indians on record varied widely in skin color from region to region." *Sierra* writer Kathleen Courrier, however, had more to recommend about *Native American Traditions,* calling it a "monumental" work that "deflates the romantic but patronizing notion that Native Americans somehow speak as one."

In *Indian Running,* Nabokov studies ceremonial running through an account of the six-day trek from Taos, New Mexico, to Second Mesa, Hopi, Arizona, to commemorate the three-hundredth anniversary of the Pueblo Indian revolt. "Nabokov has assembled an amazing array of written knowledge on Native Americans running," noted Kenneth Funston in the *Los Angeles Times Book Review.* And although Funston faulted its "bookishness" and Nabokov's reluctance in "poking around the present world, the living people," he also thought that "ironically, in the dust of his retiring journalism, Nabokov opens a whole system of Native American etiquette, a way of being—and a way of letting others be."

Native American Architecture, a widely reviewed 1989 book, is a work that "serves many reading audiences equally well," noted William Swagerty in *American Indian Quarterly.* Nabokov, with architect coauthor Robert Easton, surveys the settlement landscapes of Native nations north of Mexico and the Caribbean, offering a review of traditional dwellings, community housing, and religious structures. "Additional interpretative value is found in Nabokov's correlation of village and camp designs and layouts with social structure," Swagerty said, adding that the book "has no age boundaries. It is suitable for junior readers as well as senior scholars."

"Totem poles were our history books," says a Tlingit man in Nabokov's 2002 publication, *A Forest of Time: American Indian Ways of History.* This work compares the Native American oral traditions with the European-based dependence on print as a way of recording history. For the Indians, "storytelling was everything," as *Los Angeles Times* critic Anthony Day noted. The book relates how white scholars have attempted over the years to understand Indian ways of thought, leading Day to say that the author "is an excellent guide to the diverse and changing trends in the various fields of anthropology as applied to American Indians. Unfortunately, for the general reader [Nabokov's] approach is heavily academic and his format does not afford room for many of the haunting and moving Indian tales and ways of seeing the world that his book refers to." To *Library Journal*'s John Burch, however, the problem of cross-cultural communication is "brilliantly demonstrated" by Nabokov in this volume.

BIOGRAPHICAL AND CRITICAL SOURCES:

PERIODICALS

American Anthropologist, September, 1990, review of *Native American Architecture,* p. 765.

American Ethnologist, May, 1994, review of *Native American Architecture,* p. 429.

American Indian Culture and Research Journal, Volume 4, 1997, review of *Native American Testimony: A Chronicle of Indian-White Relations from Prophecy to the Present, 1492-1992,* p. 217.

American Indian Quarterly, summer, 1993, Francis Jennings, review of *Native American Testimony: A Chronicle of Indian-White Relations from Prophecy to the Present, 1492-1992,* p. 403; spring, 1994, William Swagerty, review of *Native American Testimony: A Chronicle of Indian-White Relations from Prophecy to the Present, 1492-1992,*

American Quarterly, September, 1991, review of *Native American Architecture,* p. 502.

American Reference Books Annual, Volume 21, 1990, review of *Native American Architecture,* p. 412.

Bloomsbury Review, July, 1993, review of *Native American Testimony: A Chronicle of Indian-White Relations from Prophecy to the Present, 1492-1992,* p. 17.

Booklist, October 15, 1991, review of *Native American Testimony: A Chronicle of Indian-White Relations from Prophecy to the Present, 1492-1992,* p. 372; December 1, 1991, review of *Native American Testimony: A Chronicle of Indian-White Relations from Prophecy to the Present, 1492-1992,* p. 675.

Bookwatch, February, 1992, review of *Native American Testimony: A Chronicle of Indian-White Relations from Prophecy to the Present, 1492-1992,* p. 2.

Christian Science Monitor, November 21, 1991, review of *Native American Testimony: A Chronicle of Indian-White Relations from Prophecy to the Present, 1492-1992,* p. 10.

Commonweal, November 10, 1978.

Design Book Review, winter, 1989, review of *Native American Architecture,* p. 78.

Guardian Weekly, June 21, 1992, review of *Native American Testimony: A Chronicle of Indian-White Relations from Prophecy to the Present, 1492-1992,* p. 18.

Journal of American Folklore, April, 1990, review of *Native American Architecture,* p. 241.

Kirkus Reviews, November 15, 1991, review of *Native American Testimony: A Chronicle of Indian-White Relations from Prophecy to the Present, 1492-1992,* p. 1462.

Kliatt Young Adult Paperback Book Guide, January, 1991, review of *Native American Architecture,* p. 51; January, 1993, review of *Native American Testimony: A Chronicle of Indian-White Relations from Prophecy to the Present, 1492-1992,* p. 34.

Library Journal, June 15, 1967, Hardin E. Smith, review of *Two Leggings: The Making of a Crow Warrior;* November 15, 1991, review of *Native American Testimony: A Chronicle of Indian-White Relations from Prophecy to the Present, 1492-1992,* p. 94; March 15, 2002, John Burch, review of *A Forest of Time: American Indian Ways of History,* p. 94.

Los Angeles Times, March 15, 2002, Anthony Day, review of *A Forest of Time,* p. E3.

Los Angeles Times Book Review, November 29, 1981, Kenneth Funston, review of *Indian Running.*

Nation, June 1, 1970; April 6, 1992, Jerry Mander, review of *Native American Testimony: A Chronicle of Indian-White Relations from Prophecy to the Present, 1492-1992,* p. 461.

Natural History, July, 1989, review of *Native American Architecture,* p. 56.

New Leader, February 16, 1970.

New Yorker, June 1, 1992, review of *Native American Testimony: A Chronicle of Indian-White Relations from Prophecy to the Present, 1492-1992,* p. 84.

New York Review of Books, December 18, 1969, Edgar Z. Friedenberg, review of *Tijerina and the Courthouse Raid.*

New York Times, February 19, 1992, review of *Native American Testimony: A Chronicle of Indian-White*

Relations from Prophecy to the Present, 1492-1992, p. C20.

New York Times Book Review, January 11, 1970, April 30, 1978, N. Scott Momaday, review of *Native American Testimony: An Anthology of Indian and White Relations; First Encounter to Dispossession.*

Parabola, May, 1989, review of *Native American Architecture,* p. 116.

Publishers Weekly, November 1, 1991, review of *Native American Testimony: A Chronicle of Indian-White Relations from Prophecy to the Present, 1492-1992,* p. 66.

Religious Studies Review, April, 1991, review of *Native American Architecture,* p. 182.

San Francisco Review of Books, number 1, 1989, review of *Native American Architecture,* p. 27; number 1, 1992, review of *Native American Testimony: A Chronicle of Indian-White Relations from Prophecy to the Present, 1492-1992,* p. 40.

Saturday Review, September 9, 1967, Meredith Brown, review of *Two Leggings: The Making of a Crow Warrior.*

School Library Journal, August, 1992, review of *Native American Testimony: A Chronicle of Indian-White Relations from Prophecy to the Present, 1492-1992,* p. 195.

Sierra, November-December, 1992, Kathleen Courrier, review of *Native American Testimony: A Chronicle of Indian-White Relations from Prophecy to the Present, 1492-1992,* p. 116.

Technology and Culture, April, 1990, review of *Native American Architecture,* p. 305.

Village Voice Literary Supplement, November, 1991, review of *Native American Testimony: A Chronicle of Indian-White Relations from Prophecy to the Present, 1492-1992,* p. 10.

Washington Post Book World, March 29, 1992, review of *Native American Testimony: A Chronicle of Indian-White Relations from Prophecy to the Present, 1492-1992,* p. 13.

Western Historical Quarterly, November, 1990, review of *Native American Architecture,* p. 501.

Yale Review, June, 1970.

*   *   *

NAGRIN, Daniel 1917-

PERSONAL: Born May 22, 1917, in New York, NY; son of Harry Samuel (a cutter of women's coats) and Clara (a homemaker; maiden name, Wexler) Nagrin; married Helen Tamiris (a dancer), 1946 (died, 1966);

married Phyllis Steele (a painter), January 24, 1992. *Education:* City College (now of the City University of New York), B.S., 1940.

ADDRESSES: Home—Daniel Nagrin Theatre, Film, and Dance Foundation, Inc., 208 East 14th St., Tempe, AZ 85281.

CAREER: Dancer, choreographer, teacher, and writer. Arizona State University, Tempe, professor of dance, 1982-92, professor emeritus, 1992—. Tamiris-Nagrin Dance Company, codirector; Workgroup (improvisational dance company), director; American Dance Festival, held Balasaraswati/Joy Ann Dewey Beineke Chair for Distinguished Teaching, 1992. *Military service:* U.S. Army Air Forces, 1942-43.

MEMBER: Actors' Equity Association, Phi Kappa Phi, American Dance Guild.

AWARDS, HONORS: D.F.A., State University of New York College at Brockport, 1991; grant from National Endowment for the Arts, 1991-92; D.H.L., Arizona State University, 1992; named Master Teacher/Mentor by National Education Association, 1993; *The Nagrin Videotape Library of Dances* was presented in New York City, at Joyce Theatre, as a fifteen-hour retrospective of his work; grant from New York State Council for the Arts.

WRITINGS:

How to Dance Forever: Surviving As a Dancer, Morrow (New York, NY), 1988.

Dance and the Specific Image: Improvisation, University of Pittsburgh Press (Pittsburgh, PA), 1993.

The Six Questions: Acting Technique for Dance Performance, University of Pittsburgh Press (Pittsburgh, PA), 1997.

Choreography and the Specific Image: Nineteen Essays and a Workbook, University of Pittsburgh Press (Pittsburgh, PA), 2001.

Contributor to dance journals.

*   *   *

NAUGHTON, John P. 1933-

PERSONAL: Born May 20, 1933, in West Nanticoke, PA; son of John Patrick (a restaurant owner) and Anne Frances (McCormik) Naughton; married Margaret Louise Fox; children: Bruce, Marcia, Lisa, George,

Michael, Thomas. *Education:* Cameron State College, A.A., 1952; St. Louis University, B.S., 1954; University of Oklahoma, M.D., 1958, postgraduate cardiovascular traineeship, 1961-64. *Politics:* Independent Democrat. *Religion:* Episcopalian.

ADDRESSES: Home—85 Hillipine Rd., Cheektowaga, NY 14227. *Office*—School of Medicine, Room 128 Farber Hall, State University of New York at Buffalo, Buffalo, NY 14214. *E-mail*—jpn@Buffalo.Edu.

CAREER: George Washington University Medical Center, Washington, DC, intern, 1958-59; University of Oklahoma Health Sciences Center, Oklahoma City, Medical Center, resident, 1959-61, chief resident, 1962-63, School of Medicine, instructor, 1964-66, assistant professor of medicine and physiology, 1966-68; University of Illinois at the Medical Center, Chicago, associate professor of medicine and director of Rehabilitation Center, 1968-70; George Washington University Medical Center, professor of medicine, 1970-75, director of division of rehabilitation medicine, 1970-75, director of regional Rehabilitation and Training Center, 1970-75, director of coordinating Center for National Study in Exercise and Heart Disease, beginning 1972, acting associate dean for academic affairs, 1972-73, dean for academic affairs, 1973-75; State University of New York at Buffalo, professor of physiology, biophysics, social and preventive medicine, 1975—, dean of School of Medicine, 1975. Member, Governing Board of D.C. General Hospital, beginning 1972, National Heart and Lung Institute Task Force on Cardiac Rehabilitation, beginning 1973, and Mayor's Task Force on Out-Patient Care in District of Columbia, beginning 1973. Professor of rehabilitation medicine, Erie County Medical Center. Member, Uniform Data Systems for Rehabilitation Research.

MEMBER: American Medical Association, American College of Cardiology (fellow), American College of Physicians (fellow), American Heart Association, American Congress of Physical Medicine and Rehabilitation, American Physiologic Society, American Psychosomatic Society, American Society of Internal Medicine, American College of Sports Physicians (vice-president, 1967-69; president, 1970-71; fellow), American Association of University Professors, New York Academy of Sciences, District of Columbia Medical Society, Washington Heart Association, American Cancer Society of DC (member of board of trustees, beginning 1973).

AWARDS, HONORS: Career Development Award, National Heart Institute, 1966; International Health Research Act fellowships, 1971-74.

WRITINGS:

(Editor with H. Hellerstein and I. Mohler) *Exercise Testing and Exercise Training in Coronary Heart Disease,* Academic Press (New York, NY), 1973.
(Contributor) E. Levine and J. Garrett, *Rehabilitation Practices with the Physically Disabled,* Columbia University Press (New York, NY), 1973.
Exercise Testing: Physiological, Biomechanical, and Clinical Principles, Futura (Mount Kisco, NY), 1988.

Contributor to periodicals, including *American Journal of Cardiology, Comprehensive Therapy, Teaching and Learning in Medicine,* and *American Journal of Public Health.*

SIDELIGHTS: John P. Naughton is a physician and research scientist whose work is dedicated to improving the prognosis of patients with coronary heart disease and congestive heart failure. Naughton's books and papers address the use of exercise as a diagnostic tool in heart disease. Longer term experiments are in progress to determine the benefits of regular exercise in improving lifespan and quality of life for heart attack survivors.

BIOGRAPHICAL AND CRITICAL SOURCES:

ONLINE

John P. Naughton Home Page, http://www.smbs. buffalo.edu/ (June 4, 2002), Naughton's vita.

*   *   *

NAVASKY, Victor S(aul) 1932-

PERSONAL: Born July 5, 1932, in New York, NY; son of Macy and Esther (Goldberg) Navasky; married Anne Strongin, March 27, 1966; children: Bruno, Miri. *Education:* Swarthmore College, B.A. (magna cum laude), 1954; Yale University, LL.B., 1959. *Politics:* Democratic. *Religion:* Jewish.

ADDRESSES: Office—*The Nation,* 33 Irving Pl., New York, NY 10003. *E-mail*—vic@thenation.com.

CAREER: State of Michigan, Lansing, special assistant to the Governor, 1959-60; *Monocle* (political satire magazine), New York, NY, editor and publisher, 1961-70; *New York Times Magazine,* New York, NY, manuscript editor, 1970-72; *The Nation,* editor in chief, 1978—, publisher and editorial director, 1995—; Columbia University, New York, NY, Delacorte Professor of Journalism and director of George Delacorte Center for Magazine Journalism, 1999—. Adjunct associate professor, New York University, 1972-73; visiting professor, Wesleyan University, 1975; visiting scholar, Russell-Sage Foundation, 1975-76; Ferris Visiting Professor of Journalism, Princeton University, 1976-77. Consultant, U.S. Civil Rights Commission, 1961. *Military service:* U.S. Army, 1954-56.

MEMBER: Phi Beta Kappa.

AWARDS, HONORS: Guggenheim memorial fellowship, 1974-75; American Book Award in paperback nonfiction category, 1982, for *Naming Names;* Carey McWilliams Award from American Political Science Association, 2001.

WRITINGS:

(Editor, with Richard R. Lingeman) *The Monocle Peep Show,* Bantam (New York, NY), 1965.

Kennedy Justice, Atheneum (New York, NY), 1971, reprinted, toExcel (San Jose, CA), 1999.

Naming Names, Viking (New York, NY), 1980.

The Blacklist, Who Really Lost? (sound recording), CBS News Audio Resource Library (New York, NY), 1980.

(Compiler, with Christopher Cerf) *The Experts Speak: The Definitive Compendium of Authoritative Misinformation,* Pantheon (New York, NY), 1984.

(Editor, with Katrina vanden Heuvel) *The Best of "The Nation": Selections from the Independent Magazine of Politics and Culture,* Thunder's Mouth Press (New York, NY), 2000.

Author of monthly column, "In Cold Print," *New York Times Book Review,* 1972-76. Has contributed articles and reviews to professional journals. Contributing editor, *Antioch Review.*

SIDELIGHTS: As a student at Yale Law School, Victor S. Navasky learned how to explain complicated political issues in accessible terms. This ability has served him well in his career as a political journalist, for he wrestles with complicated legal questions in almost all his writing, whether for books or magazines. While his duties as editor-in-chief of the *Nation* sharply limit his time for outside projects, Navasky has written several books, including *Kennedy Justice, Naming Names,* and *The Experts Speak: The Definitive Compendium of Authoritative Misinformation.* These works on politically-charged subjects reflect the tenor Navasky brings to all his work. "He bores in relentlessly, works hard, and scores by sheer perseverance and sharpness of mind," according to *Washington Post Book World* reviewer David Caute.

Navasky's first book, *Kennedy Justice,* is a detailed study of the justice department under Robert Kennedy. The book took more than five years to research and write, but when it was published, critics deemed the time well spent. "This is probably the best book ever written on a Kennedy brother, and it may be the best book ever written on an executive department of the Federal Government," wrote George F. Will in the *National Review.* In his *New York Times Book Review* critique, Joseph Kraft explained why the book warrants such lavish praise: "It comes as close as seems humanly possible to an understanding of the relation between Robert Kennedy and J. Edgar Hoover. There is an abundance of new information on such portentous business as civil rights, crime, legislative reapportionment, the bugging of Martin Luther King, and the getting of Jimmy Hoffa. The narrative, which is strong, and the judgment, which is fine, express Mr. Navasky's dual career as a journalist . . . and a lawyer (trained at Yale)."

Central to Navasky's account is the dynamic personality of Robert Kennedy who, as Attorney General and brother to the President, wielded enormous governmental power. Aware that "the law may be used as a political weapon—especially where the Attorney General enjoys a 'relationship to the President,'" Navasky questions whether Kennedy compromised justice for political ends, especially in his relationship with Hoover and in his use of wiretapping.

Despite the opportunity for bias inherent in such a subject, most critics felt that *Kennedy Justice* presents a balanced view. "This is no anti-Kennedy diatribe.

Far from it," declared John J. Fried in the *New Republic*. Fried added, "It is an intricate and thorough study of Robert Kennedy's tenure as Attorney General, a scholarly work. Navasky gives Kennedy high marks for bringing intelligent and humane law to the justice department, for using the best and most imaginative ideas available to him, for inspiring those who surrounded him, for committing himself to social reform and equal justice." As Laurence I. Barrett put it in *Time* magazine, "Kennedy's power sources were also disguised traps. The brother in the White House had to be protected; that meant trying to salvage some support for white Southerners and avoiding a showdown with Hoover," who became "more firmly entrenched than ever."

"The final moral is melancholy," reported Robert Lekachman in the *New Leader*. "In many ways [Kennedy] was a man of exemplary virtue, faithful to friends, loyal to his associates, and compassionate to those who touched his emotions. . . . Yet most of the marks of his term as Attorney General were easily erased by the agents of a new Administration. Nothing permanent was changed." Barrett counted it a measure of Navasky's skill that Kennedy's image remains intact at the book's close. "The remarkable thing about Navasky's critical treatment is that Kennedy does not emerge as a shattered icon; the zest and the victories he brought to his department are not merely noted for the record, but given equal time." George F. Will concluded, "Navasky's book is a good biography and more. And it is a good biography precisely because it is more."

In Navasky's second book, *Naming Names,* he turns his reporting skills to an investigation of the blacklist period in Hollywood. As he explained to *Publishers Weekly* interviewer John F. Baker, the project was prompted as much by personal interest as public concern: "I grew up in a very liberal milieu. And I became aware, as I was going to school in Greenwich Village, that the parents of some of my classmates were out of a job because of their politics." As a college student, Navasky worked at the lodge where actor and ex-communist J. Edward Bromberg was staying and witnessed his harassment by the FBI. Despite a medical certificate advising against it, Bromberg was summoned to testify before the House Un-American Activities Committee (HUAC) and, shortly thereafter, died of heart failure.

It was not until years later, when Navasky was writing *Kennedy Justice,* that he found a focus for his concern.

"I became interested in the role of the informer," Navasky told Baker, "because Kennedy got Jimmy Hoffa jailed on the basis of information from a man under criminal indictment. Yet this informer was regarded as some kind of hero for helping put Hoffa away."

In his extensive search for information, Navasky interviewed more than 150 actors, writers, directors, and producers questioned by HUAC between 1947 and 1953. The process took eight years, but Navasky's diligence was rewarded with another critical success. "One can only applaud the adroitness with which he has put together a lucid and persuasive narrative from such a mare's nest of fact and supposition," Daniel Aaron wrote in the *New York Review of Books* when *Naming Names* was finally published in 1980.

Toward the informers, his approach, according to Caute, "is that of a compassionate but unflinching moralist: Like Sartre before him, he wishes to discover why a person under stress may be said to have acted honorably—or not." Or, as *Time*'s Melvin Maddocks put it, Navasky questions "at what price—not only to their victims and themselves, but to the country as a whole—did these singers sing?"

Navasky told *CA* that his thesis is essentially that "those who resisted the committee and refused to name names were acting in the spirit of the Constitution and defending the First Amendment. Those who named names ended up contributing to the worst aspects of the domestic cold war."

While Richard Sennett maintained in the *New York Times Book Review* that Navasky's treatment of his subjects in *Naming Names* is "striking in its fairness," a few reviewers disagreed. Kenneth S. Lynn commented in the *National Review,* "In addition to asking loaded questions, Navasky is also given to loaded characterizations." Lynn added, "Thus Elia Kazan, who adamantly refused to be interrogated, is described with withering sarcasm. . . . About those witnesses, however, who cooperated with Navasky by telling him they were sorry they had cooperated with the Committee, *Naming Names* is all sweetness and light. . . . Yet even though we are meant to admire their sensitivity, the real heroes of *Naming Names* are not the repentant weepers . . . but the tough guys who resisted the Committee first and last, the so-called Hollywood Ten." Lynn reached the ultimate conclusion that "the actual business of the author of *Naming Names* is the perpetuation of leftist myths."

Maddocks, on the other hand, reached a very different conclusion: "Navasky's findings are the material of continuing debate, but his achievement is unarguable. With *Naming Names,* the author of *Kennedy Justice* establishes himself as that rare historian who can, like a novelist, illuminate the boundaries where power and conscience meet."

The same kind of controversy that surrounds Navasky's books also marks his editorship of America's oldest continuous weekly—the *Nation.* On April 7, 1979, the journal published excerpts from a leaked copy of Gerald Ford's then unpublished memoir, *A Time to Heal.* Because the manuscript included new material on Ford's unprecedented pardon of former President Richard M. Nixon, Navasky regarded it as "news." To Harper & Row, Ford's publishers, however, it was "slavish copying and wholesale usurpation" and they sued for violation of copyright law. The $12,500 settlement sought by the plaintiff represents the amount they lost when *Time* magazine canceled its plans to publish selections of the book because they had already appeared in Navasky's magazine.

The publishers say they brought the suit to keep "the law of the jungle from supplanting the rule of law in the publishing business," and to prevent what they call "an open season on copyrighted materials of public officials," according to David Margolick in the *New York Times.* But Navasky viewed the matter differently. "We consider this case involves two issues—the right to publish under the First Amendment and the public's right to access to Presidential papers," he told Margolick. "Former public officials should be able to copyright their memoirs, but they have no right to withhold the news for private profit," he added in a telephone conversation with *CA.*

In February, 1983, U.S. District Judge Richard Owen ruled in favor of the publishers. "The *Nation* took what was essentially the heart of the book," Owen commented, according to *Time* magazine. But Navasky still maintains the excerpts were newsworthy. Furthermore, he told *CA,* "It is improper for judges to make decisions about what is and what is not news."

In 1995 Navasky assembled a group of investors (which included the actor Paul Newman and the author E. L. Doctorow) and together purchased the *Nation* from Arthur L. Carter. Navasky has since served as the liberal magazine's publisher and editorial director. Mary Carroll noted in *Booklist* that despite the modest circulation of the magazine, its "contributors are first-rate." The magazine presents topical issues from America and abroad and has been praised for its even-handed assessments of liberal viewpoints. When Navasky earned the Carey McWilliams Award from the American Political Science Association in 2001, the association praised the *Nation*'s "willingness to alienate" its own readership.

Navasky and coeditor Katrina Vanden Heuvel put together *The Best of "The Nation": Selections from the Independent Magazine of Politics and Culture,* a compendium of the magazine's best articles from the 1990s. *Library Journal* contributor Stephen L. Hupp praised the book as "thoughtful, lively political and social discussion from a leftist perspective." Carroll too deemed the volume "lively, opinionated commentary on issues that matter."

Between his duties at the *Nation* and his appointment as Delacorte Professor of Journalism at Columbia University, Navasky has little time to produce books. He and Christopher Cerf collaborated on *The Experts Speak: The Definitive Compendium of Authoritative Misinformation,* a collection of absurd forecasts and patently false remarks by experts who truly believed what they were saying at the time. These statements range from medical advice to prognostications on inventions and their usefulness, and even to predictions of the future that turned out completely wrong. Notable among these is the 1930 statement by the U.S. Labor Department that it would be a *splendid employment year,* and the 1975 statement by the new owner of the New York Yankees, George Steinbrenner, who said, "We plan absentee ownership. I'll stick to building ships." A reviewer for *Forbes* magazine declared that *The Experts Speak* is "a total delight for dipping into or swimming right on through." Donald Morrison in *Time* likewise observed: "This book is irreverent, unfair and subversive. What more could anyone ask for? . . . After digesting a few dozen . . . nuggets of certified knowledge, one may feel a tendency to distrust experts of all sorts."

BIOGRAPHICAL AND CRITICAL SOURCES:

PERIODICALS

Booklist, August, 2000, Mary Carroll, review of *The Best of "The Nation": Selections from the Independent Magazine of Politics and Culture,* p. 2103.

Chicago Tribune, October 22, 1980.

Esquire, December, 1980.

Forbes, April 29, 1985, review of *The Experts Speak: The Definitive Compendium of Authoritative Misinformation,* p. 39.

Library Journal, September 1, 2000, Stephen L. Hupp, review of *The Best of "The Nation,"* p. 231.

Los Angeles Times Book Review, November 16, 1980.

Mediaweek, January 23, 1995, "Navasky wins 'The Nation,'" p. 41.

National Review, November 19, 1971, George F. Will, review of *Kennedy Justice;* March 6, 1981, Kenneth S. Lynn, review of *Naming Names.*

New Leader, December 13, 1971, Robert Lekachman, review of *Kennedy Justice.*

New Republic, October 9, 1971, John J. Fried, review of *Kennedy Justice;* April 18, 1981.

New Statesman, May 21, 1982, David Caute, review of *Naming Names,* p. 18.

New York Review of Books, June 29, 1972; December 4, 1980, Daniel Aaron, review of *Naming Names.*

New York Times, October 8, 1971; October, 16, 1980; February 25, 1980; January 25, 1982; January 28, 1982, Richard Sennett, review of *Naming Names.*

New York Times Book Review, October 10, 1971, Joseph Kratt, review of *Kennedy Justice;* October 19, 1980.

Partisan Review, Volume 49, number 3, 1982.

Publishers Weekly, October 10, 1980; March 4, 1983.

Saturday Review, October, 1980.

Time, November 15, 1971; February 28, 1983, Melvin Maddock, review of *Naming Names;* August 13, 1984, Donald Morrison, review of *The Experts Speak,* p. 92.

Washington Post, January 3, 1981.

Washington Post Book World, October 12, 1980.

ONLINE

Victor S. Navasky, http://www.jrn.columbia.edu/ (June 5, 2002), web page on Navasky, includes photographs.*

*   *   *

NEELY, Barbara 1941-

PERSONAL: Born in 1941, in Lebanon, PA; daughter of Bernard and Ann Neely. *Ethnicity:* African American. *Education:* University of Pittsburgh, M.A.

ADDRESSES: Home—Jamaica Plain, MA. *Agent*—c/o author correspondence, Viking Press, 40 W. 23rd St., New York, NY 10010.

CAREER: Mystery novelist and short story writer. Former designer and director of community-based corrections facility for women; former branch director, YWCA; former head of consulting firm for nonprofit organizations. Visiting researcher, Institute for Social Research. Executive director, Women for Economic Justice. Radio producer, Africa News Service, and host of radio interview program, *Commonwealth Justice,* Massachusetts.

AWARDS, HONORS: Agatha Award, Anthony Award, Macavity Award, and Go On, Girl! Award from Black Women's Reading Club, all for best first mystery novel, all 1993, all for *Blanche on the Lam.*

WRITINGS:

NOVELS

Blanche on the Lam, St. Martin's Press (New York, NY), 1992.

Blanche among the Talented Tenth, St. Martin's Press (New York, NY), 1994.

Blanche Cleans Up, Viking (New York, NY), 1998.

Blanche Passes Go, Viking (New York, NY), 2000.

Also author of short stories in various anthologies and periodicals, including *Things That Divide Us, Speaking for Ourselves, Constellations, Literature: Reading and Writing the Human Experience, Breaking Ice, Essence,* and *Obsidian II.*

SIDELIGHTS: With her first novel, the 1992 mystery *Blanche on the Lam,* Barbara Neely infused new vigor into the whodunit genre. As Charles Champlin put it in the *Los Angeles Times Book Review,* Neely "entertainingly corrected" the absence of female African-American writers and characters in that genre. Her series sleuth, Blanche White, is a middle-aged domestic worker with a sharp tongue and a sharper mind, an independent working woman who must juggle her job, her child-rearing duties, and her penchant for solving crimes. "Neely took a giant step into unknown territory for a crime novel and succeeded brilliantly," observed a contributor to the *St. James Guide to Crime & Mystery Writers*. The contributor added, "Although racism is not new to fiction, the viewpoint of a domestic worker is. Although Blanche is not the first African-American protagonist—not even the first black woman detective—she is the first of her type. And she is a formidable character." *Library Journal* reviewer Alice Di Nizo called Blanche "one of the best fictional 'detectives' conjured up in years."

Readers are introduced to Blanche in Neely's award-winning *Blanche on the Lam*. As the novel opens, Neely's heroine is a domestic working in North Carolina. Her name means "White White," but her personality is anything but that: Blanche is feisty, independent, strong-willed, and proudly scornful of her white employers. Blanche is jailed for writing $42.50 in bad checks, a misfortune she fell into because four of her employers left town without paying her. She manages to escape and ends up working for the Carters, a "Faulknerian cast of oddballs," according to a *Kirkus Reviews* contributor.

Blanche discovers that the Carters may be involved in some arcane plots against one another in quest of an inheritance. Aunt Emmeline, the rich recluse whose inheritance is sought, may be an alcoholic; Cousin Mumsfield, a mildly retarded young man, may be more clever than he seems; and Miz Grace and Everett, Blanche's employers, are affluent neurotics. This family constitutes, Champlin suggests, a "Eugene O'Neill plot seen from the pantry door." Blanche, given the society in which she must operate, can only observe them rather than openly investigate, a limitation which, in Champlin's admiring view, Neely overcomes with "special ingenuity."

After the local sheriff is murdered, Blanche stirs things up enough for suspicion to be thrown not only upon her, but also upon an innocent African American gardener. Forced to solve the crime in order to avoid being accused of it, Blanche successfully takes charge in what a *Publishers Weekly* critic called a "deftly written debut." The *Publishers Weekly* critic appreciated *Blanche on the Lam*, too, for paying "heartfelt tribute to the community and culture of a working-class African American woman." A contributor to *Kirkus Reviews* approved of the "prickly view of class-clashes, race relations, and family foibles" but described the author's "folk-talk" style as somewhat "forced" in this "quirky" novel. For Champlin, a ma-

jor attraction of the book was Blanche's hard-nosed social commentary. Champlin was not alone in looking forward to Neely's follow-up novel, and *Blanche on the Lam* received three major awards as best first mystery novel of 1993.

The hoped-for sequel, and presumably the second in a projected longer series, was *Blanche among the Talented Tenth*. The scene has shifted from North Carolina to Boston, without a reduction in the racism of the surrounding community, but with an added spotlight on a different form of class snobbery, that of light-skinned middle-class blacks toward their darker-skinned, less affluent brothers and sisters. Blanche, a working-class, dark-skinned woman whose obvious talents make the phrase "talented tenth" sound ironic, pays a summer visit to a niece and nephew on Amber Cove, a Maine resort frequented by middle-class African Americans. Having ensconced herself in the local community against the grain of some of its members, Blanche learns that the local gossip, Faith Brown, has been electrocuted in her bathtub, and that an MIT professor named Hank has apparently drowned himself in the ocean, after leaving a note confessing to Faith's murder. That seems cut-and-dried, but Blanche suspects that something more is involved, and as she probes into local history and current relationships, she finds ample material for suspense and scandal.

Some reviewers found this novel less gripping than the first. A *Kirkus Reviews* correspondent felt that the whodunit element was less effective than Neely's "acerbic portrait of class infighting at its most corrosive." A *Publishers Weekly* critic wrote, "Blanche continues to appeal in her so-what-if-I've-got-an-attitude way, but while . . . *Blanche on the Lam* was a mystery with a bit of message, this one is a message with a bit of mystery." Blanche herself, however, and the varied environments into which she might conceivably be set, remained so captivating that thousands of readers eagerly anticipated a third installment.

Blanche Cleans Up finds the feisty detective serving as a temporary cook for the Allister Brindle family in Boston. Allister Brindle is running for governor of Massachusetts, but Blanche soon discovers a plethora of dirty secrets leading to a string of murders that ultimately threaten her and her teenaged children in their Roxbury neighborhood. Once again Blanche must step in to solve the crimes as a matter of self-preservation—but she proves adept at piercing the veneer of civility in her employers' home. A *Publishers Weekly* reviewer noted that in this installment Blanche proves to be "direct, endlessly entertaining and nobody's fool." The reviewer added that Blanche's "streetwise attitude and lusty approach to life . . . add sparks to an already sizzling mystery." Di Nizo also styled Neely "a skilled and pleasing writer . . . whose plot lines flow pleasantly."

Many novel plots revolve around characters coming to terms with their pasts, and *Blanche Passes Go* is in line with this tradition. Returning to North Carolina from Boston to help in a friend's catering business, Blanche must face the wealthy white man, David Palmer, who raped her with impunity years before. After a young woman is murdered, Blanche finds herself investigating Palmer's sister—and by default, Palmer as well—in an effort to solve a number of unsolved violent crimes against women. "Blanche's quest, both for vengeance and to reclaim her life, drives a compelling plot," stated a *Publishers Weekly* reviewer. Rex Klett in *Library Journal* praised *Blanche Passes Go* for its "unique, ancestor-worshiping protagonist" and "wonderful plotting." In *Black Issues Book Review,* Sharita Hunt characterized the novel as "an emotionally charged, multilayered exploration of violence and abuse" that also sheds light on fostering relationships with those we love—parents, friends, children, and lovers.

"Barbara Neely's talent makes music of what linguistic scholars have called 'neighborhood language,'" observed the *St. James Guide to Crime & Mystery Writers* essayist. "This is not the street slang made familiar by novels based on police procedure and the cop shows. It's a language white people seldom hear unless you go hunting for it—the language African Americans speak at home where no whites sit in judgment—and the changes Neely rings give it an added dimension of color and vividness."

BIOGRAPHICAL AND CRITICAL SOURCES:

BOOKS

Heising, Willetta L., *Detecting Women 2,* Purple Moon Press (Dearborn, MI), 1996.
St. James Guide to Crime & Mystery Writers, 4th edition, St. James Press (Detroit, MI), 1996.

PERIODICALS

Black Issues Book Review, November, 2000, Sharita Hunt, review of *Blanche Passes Go,* p. 22.
Booklist, March 15, 1998, GraceAnne A. DeCandido, review of *Blanche Cleans Up,* p. 1206; April 15, 1999, GraceAnne A. DeCandido, review of *Blanche Cleans Up,* p. 1461.
Kirkus Reviews, December 15, 1991, pp. 1560-1561; July 1, 1994, p. 889.
Library Journal, March 15, 1998, Alice DiNizo, review of *Blanche Cleans Up,* p. 95; June 15, 1999, Suzan Connell, review of *Blanche Cleans Up,* p. 132; July, 2000, Rex Klett, review of *Blanche Passes Go,* p. 145.
Los Angeles Times Book Review, March 8, 1992, p. 8, Charles Champlin, review of *Blanche on the Lam.*
Publishers Weekly, January 20, 1992, p. 50; July 18, 1994, p. 238; March 30, 1998, review of *Blanche Cleans Up,* p. 73; May 29, 2000, review of *Blanche Passes Go,* p. 55.

OTHER

Barbara Neely, http://www.blanchewhite.com/ (June 4, 2002), author's home page.
Voices from the Gaps: Women Writers of Color, http://voices.cla.umn.edu/authors/NEELYbarbara.html/ (March 20, 2003).*

*   *   *

NEHAMAS, Alexander 1946-

PERSONAL: Born March 22, 1946, in Athens, Greece; son of Albert (a banker) and Christine (Yannuli) Nehamas; married Susan D. Glimcher (an attorney), June 22, 1983; children: Nicholas Albert. *Ethnicity:* "Greek." *Education:* Swarthmore College, B.A., 1967; Princeton University, Ph.D., 1971. *Hobbies and other interests:* Arts, literature, travel, opera, film.

ADDRESSES: Home—692 Pretty Brook Road, Princeton, NJ 08540. *Office*—Princeton University, Program in Hellenic Studies, Henry House, Princeton, NJ 08540. *E-mail*—nehamas@princeton.edu.

CAREER: Educator and author. University of Pittsburgh, Pittsburgh, PA, assistant professor, 1971-76, associate professor, 1976-81, professor of philosophy,

Alexander Nehamas

1981-86; University of Pennsylvania, professor of philosophy, 1986-90; Princeton University, Princeton, NJ, professor of philosophy, comparative literature, and humanities, 1990—, chairman of Hellenic studies program, 1994-2003, head of Council of the Humanities, 1994-2003, head of society of fellows in the liberal arts, 1999-2003. Visiting professor at University of California at Berkeley, 1983, 1993, and at Princeton University, 1988.

MEMBER: American Philosophical Association (program chairman, 1982-83; president, eastern division, 2003-04), American Society for Aesthetics, Modern Language Association, Society for Ancient Greek Philosophy, Modern Greek Studies Association, North America Nietzsche Society, Phi Beta Kappa.

AWARDS, HONORS: Grant from National Endowment for the Humanities 1978-79; Guggenheim fellowship, 1983-84; Lindback Foundation Teaching Award, University of Pennsylvania, 1989; Behrman Award in humanities, Princeton University, 1999; International Nietzsche Prize (co-recipient), 2001; Mellon Distinguished Achievement Award in the Humanities, 2002.

WRITINGS:

Nietzsche: Life As Literature, Harvard University Press (Cambridge, MA), 1986.
(Translator, with Paul Woodruff, and author of introduction and notes) Plato, *Symposium,* Hackett (Indianapolis, IN), 1989.
(Coeditor, with David J. Furley) *Aristotle's Rhetoric: Philosophical Essays,* Princeton University Press (Princeton, NJ), 1994.
(Translator and author of introduction, with Paul Woodruff) Plato, *Phaedrus,* Hackett (Indianapolis, IN), 1995.
The Art of Living: Socratic Reflections from Plato to Foucault, University of California Press (Berkeley, CA), 1998.
Virtues of Authenticity: Essays on Plato and Socrates, Princeton University Press (Princeton, NJ), 1998.

WORK IN PROGRESS: A Promise of Happiness: The Place of Beauty in a World of Art.

SIDELIGHTS: Educator Alexander Nehamas was born in Greece into a banking family. He came to the United States for his education and in 1967, after completing his bachelor's degree at Swarthmore College, decided not to return home, yet. There had been a coup d'etat in Greece that spring, so Nehamas chose to apply for graduate school at Princeton University. At Princeton he majored in philosophy, a study he enjoyed, although his father, a banker, considered it to be a mistake. "From my family's point of view, I'm a failure," Nehamas joked with David Carrier in an interview posted at the *Sanford Presidential Lectures* Web site. "Greece was not and is not a country where an intellectual and academic career is considered proper." Nehamas added: "It's all right to be cultured and educated, but you are not really supposed to live off your education. You work; it's a mercantile society."

By the time he finished his doctorate at Princeton University, Nehamas realized it was too late in his life for him to get a degree in business, so he stuck with philosophy, despite the fact that his "official plan was to go into business and retire at a relatively young age in order to discuss intellectual issues" on his yacht. In his interview, he added: "I never got a yacht, I got tenure instead."

The first book that Nehamas published, 1986's *Nietzsche: Life As Literature,* focuses on the nineteenth-century German philosopher Nehamas refers to as one of his intellectual heroes. One reason Nehamas is attracted to Friedrich Nietzsche's thought is that Nietzsche believed that "many things happen for no particular reason. But once they happen you can use them for your purposes." If you successfully use such arbitrary occurrences, by your action "you have given them a reason," Nehamas explained during his interview.

Times Literary Supplement reviewer Michael Tanner proclaimed *Nietzsche: Life As Literature* to be "the best and most important book on Nietzsche in English." In this scholarly critical work, Nehamas offers a post-structuralist analysis of Nietzsche's philosophy. Writing in the *New York Times Book Review,* Karsten Harries deemed the volume an "elegant and challenging interpretation" unified by the related themes of Nietzsche's perspectivism—"we know no fact independent of interpretation; there is no vision of reality untainted by prejudice and perspective," noted Harries—and his aestheticism—that one can view the world as one would a literary text, wherein "persons and things," according to Harries, are "characters or entities in some work of fiction, [and] our relationship to the world . . . [is] textual interpretation."

The Art of Living: Socratic Reflections from Plato to Foucault is Nehamas's second published book. In this work, the author focuses on three philosophers, Michel Montaigne, Nietzsche, and Michel Foucault, all of whom, according to Kenneth Baker in the *San Francisco Chronicle,* "translated into modern terms the question [of] what it is to live a good life." These philosophers were all inspired by Socrates, emulating the ancient thinker's emphasis on the examined life. They were attracted to Socrates for the freedom of interpretation his philosophy allows. As *New Republic* contributor Martha C. Nussbaum put it, Nehamas wrote this book to demonstrate his own belief that "philosophy is an art of individual self-cultivation through which one may eventually succeed in forging a unique and unified personality, as unforgettable as that of a major literary character."

It is through *The Art of Living,* Nussbaum wrote, that Nehamas traces the "origins of this aesthetic model of philosophy," which the author believes should be "a practical discipline, capable of shaping the conduct of life." Unfortunately, modern society has lost sight of this fact, forgetting that an understanding of philoso-

phy can change lives. Baker commented that "to appreciate Nehamas's book one need not have read all the thinkers he discusses. Nehamas is a fine explainer and tells his readers what they need to know to feel the force of his arguments." Writing for the *Philosophical Review,* C. C. W. Taylor stated: "Nehamas is at home in a wide range of disciplines, including classics, philosophy, and literary studies, and has much to say to the specialist in each of those areas, as well as to the general reader. His is a rich and complex work, which invites and rewards repeated study."

Nehamas's third book, 1998's *Virtues of Authenticity: Essays on Plato and Socrates,* collects sixteen essays Nehamas wrote on various themes concerning Socrates and Plato. The topics include goodness, metaphysics, and aesthetics as well as discussions of Plato's *Republic, Phaedrus,* and the *Symposium. Library Journal* contributor Terry C. Skeats commented that *Virtues of Authenticity* offers "an excellent introduction" to Nehamas's work.

Nehamas once told *CA:* "It is extremely difficult to write philosophical works that meet the high standards of rigor and detailed discussion necessary to deal with abstract problems and also focus on issues that a broad public will find engaging and important. To be able to do so has been an important concern of mine in recent years. Plato and Nietzsche, the two philosophers I most admire, and the most different thinkers one can imagine, were masters of this. I continue studying them in the hope that I can learn from them a little about their art."

In addition to writing his own books and continuing his teaching duties at Princeton University, Nehamas also has translated several works and has coedited a collection of essays by other writers.

BIOGRAPHICAL AND CRITICAL SOURCES:

PERIODICALS

Choice, March, 1999, J. Bussanich, review of *The Art of Living: Socratic Reflections from Plato to Foucault,* p. 1280.

Library Journal, November 1, 1998, Terry C. Skeats, review of *The Art of Living* and *Virtues of Authenticity: Essays on Plato and Socrates,* pp. 86-87,

New Republic, January 4, 1999, Martha C. Nussbaum, "The Cult of the Personality," p. 32.

New York Times Book Review, January 19, 1986, Karsten Harries, review of *Nietzsche: Life As Literature,* p. 14; October 25, 2998, Jonathan Lear, review of *The Art of Living,* p. 26.

Philosophical Review, July, 2000, C. C. W. Taylor, review of *The Art of Living,* p. 423.

Philosophy Today, summer, 2000, James S. Hans, "Alexander Nehamas and 'The Art of Living,'" pp. 190-205.

San Francisco Chronicle, October 4, 1998, Kenneth Baker, "Modern Philosophers Still Look to Socrates for Guidance," p. 8.

Times Literary Supplement, May 16, 1986.

ONLINE

Stanford Presidential Lectures Web site, http://prelectur.stanford.edu/ (June 12, 2002), David Carrier, "Alexander Nehamas."

*   *   *

NEUHAUS, Richard John 1936-

PERSONAL: Born May 14, 1936, in Pembroke, Ontario, Canada; son of Clemens H. (a clergyman) and Ella (Prange) Neuhaus. *Education:* Lutheran Concordia College (now Concordia Lutheran College), B.A., 1957, M.Div., 1960; graduate study at Concordia Seminary, Wayne State University, and Washington University.

ADDRESSES: Office—Institute on Religion in Public Life, 156 Fifth Ave., Suite 400, New York, NY 10010-7002.

CAREER: Ordained Lutheran pastor, 1960; ordained Roman Catholic priest, 1991. Church of St. John the Evangelist, Brooklyn, NY, pastor, 1961-78; Rockford Institute Center on Religion and Society, New York, NY, director, 1984-89; Institute on Religion and Public Life, New York, NY, director, 1989—. Clergy and Laymen Concerned about Vietnam, founder, 1966, affiliate, 1966-75.

AWARDS, HONORS: Catholic Press Association Award, 1968; honorary degrees from Benedictine College, 1985, Gonzaga University, 1985, Valparaiso University, 1986, Nichols College, 1986, and Boston University, 1988.

WRITINGS:

(With Peter Berger) *Movement and Revolution,* Doubleday (Garden City, NY), 1970.

In Defense of People: Ecology and the Seduction of Radicalism, Macmillan (New York, NY), 1971.

Time toward Home: The American Experiment as Revelation, Seabury (New York, NY), 1975.

(With Berger) *Against the World for the World: The Hartford Appeal and the Future of American Religion,* Seabury (New York, NY), 1976.

Christian Faith and Public Policy: Thinking and Acting in the Courage of Uncertainty, Augsburg (Minneapolis, MN), 1977.

(With Berger) *To Empower People: The Role of Mediating Structures in Public Policy,* American Enterprise Institute (Washington, DC), 1977.

Freedom for Ministry, Harper (San Francisco, CA), 1979, revised edition, Eerdmans (Grand Rapids, MI), 1992.

(With others) *Christianity and Politics: Catholic and Protestant Perspectives,* Ethics and Public Policy Center (Washington, DC), 1981.

The Naked Public Square: Religion and Democracy in America, Eerdmans (Grand Rapids, MI), 1984.

Pluralism and Paralysis in American Society, National Conference of Christians and Jews (New York, NY), 1984.

Dispensations: The Future of South Africa as South Africans See It, Eerdmans (Grand Rapids, MI), 1986.

The Catholic Moment: The Paradox of the Church in the Postmodern World, Harper (San Francisco, CA), 1987.

(With Leon Klenicki) *Believing Today: Jew and Christian in Conversation,* Eerdmans (Grand Rapids, MI), 1989.

(With George Weigel) *Being Christian Today: An American Conversation,* Ethics and Public Policy Center (Washington, DC), 1992.

Doing Well and Doing Good: The Challenge to the Christian Capitalist, Doubleday (New York, NY), 1992.

America against Itself: Moral Vision and the Public Order, University of Notre Dame Press (Notre Dame, IN), 1992.

(With others) *Welfare Reformed: A Compassionate Approach,* P & R Publishers (Phillipsburg, NJ), 1994.

(With Berger) *To Empower People: From State to Civil Society,* American Enterprise Institute (Washington, DC), 1996.

The End of Democracy?: The Celebrated First Things Debate, with Arguments Pro and Con; and, The Anatomy of a Controversy, Spence Publishing (Dallas, TX), 1997.

The Best of "The Public Square": Selections from Richard John Neuhaus's Celebrated Column in "First Things,", Institute on Religion and Public Life (New York, NY), 1997.

Appointment in Rome: The Church in America Awakening, Crossroad (New York, NY), 1999.

Death on a Friday Afternoon: Meditations on the Words of Jesus from the Cross, Basic Books (New York, NY), 2000.

The Best of 'The Public Square,' Book Two, Eerdmans (Grand Rapids, MI), 2001.

As I Lay Dying: Meditations upon Returning, Basic Books (New York, NY), 2002.

EDITOR

Theology and the Kingdom of God, Westminster (Philadelphia, PA), 1969.

(And author of introduction) *Confession, Conflict, and Community,* Eerdmans (Grand Rapids, MI), 1986.

(And author of introduction) *Virtue, Public and Private,* Eerdmans (Grand Rapids, MI), 1986.

(And author of introduction) *Unsecular America,* Eerdmans (Grand Rapids, MI), 1986.

(And author of introduction) *Democracy and the Renewal of Public Education: Essays,* Eerdmans (Grand Rapids, MI), 1987.

(And author of introduction) *The Bible, Politics, and Democracy: Essays,* Eerdmans (Grand Rapids, MI), 1987.

(And co-author of introduction) *Jews in Unsecular America: Essays,* Eerdmans (Grand Rapids, MI), 1987.

(With Richard Cromartie) *Piety and Politics: Evangelicals and Fundamentalists Confront the World,* Ethics and Public Policy Center (Washington, DC), 1987.

(And author of introduction) *The Believable Futures of American Protestantism,* Eerdmans (Grand Rapids, MI), 1988.

(And author of introduction) *The Preferential Option for the Poor: Essays,* Eerdmans (Grand Rapids, MI), 1988.

(And author of introduction) *American Apostasy: The Triumph of the "Other" Gospels,* Eerdmans (Grand Rapids, MI), 1989.

(And author of introduction) *Reinhold Niebuhr Today: Essays,* Eerdmans (Grand Rapids, MI), 1989.

(And author of introduction) *Law and the Ordering of Our Life Together: Essays,* Eerdmans (Grand Rapids, MI), 1989.

(And author of introduction) *Biblical Interpretation in Crisis: The Ratzinger Conference on Bible and Church,* Eerdmans (Grand Rapids, MI), 1989.

(And author of introduction) *Guaranteeing the Good Life: Medicine and the Return of Eugenics,* Eerdmans (Grand Rapids, MI), 1990.

(And author of introduction) *The Structure of Freedom: Correlations, Causes, and Cautions,* Eerdmans (Grand Rapids, MI), 1991.

(And author of introduction) *Theological Education and Moral Formation,* Eerdmans (Grand Rapids, MI), 1992.

(And author of introduction) *Augustine Today,* Eerdmans (Grand Rapids, MI), 1993.

(With Charles Colson) *Evangelicals and Catholics Together: Toward a Common Mission,* Word Publishing (Dallas, TX), 1995.

The Eternal Pity: Reflections on Dying, University of Notre Dame Press (Notre Dame, IN), 2000.

The Second 1,000 Years: Ten People Who Defined a Millennium, Eerdmans (Grand Rapids, MI), 2001.

The Chosen People in an Almost Chosen Land: Jews and Judaism in America, Eerdmans (Grand Rapids, MI), 2002.

(With Charles Colson) *Your World Is Truth: A Project of Evangelicals and Catholics Together,* Eerdmans (Grand Rapids, MI), 2002.

Editor, *Una Sancta,* 1963-68; senior editor, *Worldview,* 1972-82; editor-in-chief, *First Things,* 1989—; religion editor, *National Review.* Regular contributor to *Commonweal, National Catholic Reporter, Harper's, New York Review of Books,* and *Christian Century.*

SIDELIGHTS: Richard John Neuhaus became a public figure in the 1960s when, as a Lutheran pastor of an inner city church, he spoke out for civil rights and against the Vietnam War. His subsequent spiritual journey has included ordination as a Catholic priest and the authorship and editorship of numerous books on the role of Christianity in public life. As the director of the Manhattan-based Institute on Religion and Public Life, he has served as an advisor to presidents from Carter to George Bush, Sr., and he is a respected voice in the conservative Christian movement, where he has sought to bridge gaps between Roman Catholics and fundamentalist Protestants. "Pastor Richard John Neuhaus is a very cool cat," observed William F. Buckley in the *National Review.* "He is a brilliant and learned writer and theologian, but he isn't going to let those awful weights keep him out of the public discussion." *Christian Century* correspondent Dennis P. McCann called Neuhaus "a significant voice among Christians engaged in public-policy debate."

The son of a Lutheran pastor, Neuhaus was born and raised in Ontario, Canada. He moved south to the United States when he was fourteen and eventually obtained ownership of a gas station and a grocery store in Cisco, Texas. He felt called to the ministry, however, and worked his way through high school and a Lutheran seminary in Austin, Texas. He also did graduate work at Concordia Theological Seminary in St. Louis, Missouri. Although of a scholarly bent, he served an internship at an urban church in Chicago, and this ignited his desire to serve the poor. In 1961 he became pastor of St. John the Evangelist Church in the Bedford-Stuyvesant section of Brooklyn, New York. There his congregation of African-American and Puerto Rican parishioners welcomed his involvement not only in their spiritual growth but also in their political empowerment.

Neuhaus was prominent among the activist clerics who demonstrated for civil rights. He became associated with Dr. Martin Luther King, Jr. not only on civil rights issues but also on the cessation of the Vietnam War. By the time he was arrested for protesting at the 1968 Democratic National Convention, he was already well known as an author and orator on theology and public ethics. His early books, such as *Theology and the Kingdom of God* and *Movement and Revolution,* the latter which he co-authored with Peter L. Berger, address the issues of racism and international affairs, taking strong exception to then-prevailing social trends.

The early 1970s brought a transformation in Neuhaus's mission. He began to question the amount of attention clergymen were paying to social issues as opposed to spiritual ones. Once perceived as a committed leftist, Neuhaus moved into a new phase of his career, a phase that would link him with the conservative Christian right and lead him to become one of the earliest advocates of faith-based charities. His writings of this period reflect a movement away from addressing trendy issues and more toward a fundamental understanding of the individual's relationship with God—a relationship that inevitably includes the desire to help the poor. In books such as *Christian Faith and Public Policy* and *To Empower People,* he argues for a reduction in the government's formation of social policy in favor of grassroots Christian involvement in the amelioration of social ills.

In 1984 Neuhaus published one of his most influential books, *The Naked Public Square: Religion and Democracy in America.* This work offers a reasoned explanation of the aims of Christian conservatives such as the Moral Majority and calls for a dialogue between right-wing Christians and more mainstream Christian believers. It also illustrates the fact that religion continues to inform politics and makes plain the fact that debate on moral, social, and religious issues must continue in a productive fashion—in the so-called "public square" of the title. Buckley noted that *The Naked Public Square* "has had a considerable impact." To quote Harvey Cox in the *New York Times Book Review,* "The urgency of this book's message is that it underlines the fragility of the democratic experiment in this country and the awful threat posed by the ruthless banning from the public square of the very moral language most of its citizens need to make real political choices." *National Review* correspondent Joseph Sobran concluded: "*The Naked Public Square* is a model of taking-everything-into-account. . . . [Neuhaus] is fair to everyone even as he is decisive. And his decisions are, as far as I can see, right. If this book is read as widely as it deserves to be, secular humanists (or whatever they're calling themselves these days) will henceforth have a hard time imposing their values while pretending they're morally neutral."

Neuhaus had long considered Lutheranism not a denomination in its own right but rather a circle of believers advocating reform within the Roman Catholic Church. In 1991 he became an ordained Roman Catholic priest while continuing his tenure at the Institute on Religion and Public Life. In an interview posted on the *AD2000 Web site,* Neuhaus noted that "Cardinal Newman wrote that when he was received into the Catholic Church it was like coming into safe harbour after years on the stormy sea. My experience is the opposite. I was in safe harbour in the Lutheran Church and, in entering the Catholic Church, have embarked on a very stormy sea."

Neuhaus's writings through the 1990s reflect his many concerns as a theologian. Throughout the period he sought to kindle understanding and dialogue between the Catholic Church and Protestant denominations and continues to maintain that capitalism within a Christian framework is the best economic plan in terms of provision for the poor. *Doing Well and Doing Good: The Challenge to the Christian Capitalist* sets out Neuhaus's views on *Centesimus Annus,* a papal encyclical on economic development and a market economy. To quote Dennis McCann, "The ultimate burden of *Doing Well and Doing Good,* however, does not lie at the level of public debate over economic policy. One is tempted to summarize: 'It's the ecclesiology, stupid!' The book is a lucid and impressive argument not just on behalf of Catholic social teaching, but also in support of the relevance of religious faith generally to questions of political economy." McCann concluded that *Doing Well and Doing Good* "is to be welcomed, especially for continuing a theological conversation about the premises for social activism within the framework of Christian tradition." In his *National Review* piece on *Doing Well and Doing Good,* William E. Simon stated: "Many will disagree with the moral and economic teachings of *Centesimus Annus.* Those who still cling to outworn ideas of socialism and collectivism will object to the idea that, as Neuhaus puts it, 'the answer to abuses of the free market is not always to be found in the economic system . . . but is finally moral and spiritual.' The great contribution of John Paul's historic encyclical, and of Father Neuhaus's compelling interpretation, is in the understanding that the moral guidance of the kind provided by *Centesimus Annus* will always be needed and will never be made obsolete by secular reforms."

In the wake of life-threatening health problems encountered during the late 1990s, Neuhaus has also published several works of meditation on suffering and death. *Death on a Friday Afternoon: Meditations on the Last Words of Jesus from the Cross* examines the "seven last words" Christ uttered on the cross, a longtime subject of reflection in Catholic theology. In his *National Review* essay on the book, Michael Potemra wrote: "Very few religious works succeed in appealing acros inter-confessional boundaries without sacrificing a great deal in terms of both literary quality and intellectual heft. This book is a rare exception to the rule. It's well written and intellectually challenging for all readers, not just those who profess Neuhaus's faith, or indeed any faith at all. To understand this book, all a reader needs is an interest in the basics of the human condition." *As I Lay Dying: Meditations upon Returning* examines Neuhaus's own brush with

death for insight into death and dying. A *Publishers Weekly* reviewer maintained that those readers interested in "pondering the complexities of mortality and the Christian promise of eternal life will emerge all the richer from his sojourn into mystery."

In addition to writing and editing numerous volumes, Neuhaus has served as editor of the monthly journal *First Things,* for which he writes a column titled "The Public Square." He is also religion editor for the *National Review.* Considering the author's body of work, McCann commented: "If Neuhaus challenges liberals to become just as alert and articulate about their differences with neoconservatives as they tend to be with the prophets of countercultural radicalism, he will have helped all Christian activists acquire a more insightful understanding of their responsibilities in public life."

BIOGRAPHICAL AND CRITICAL SOURCES:

BOOKS

Finn, James, *Protest, Politics and Pacifism,* Random House (New York, NY), 1968.
Gray, Francine, *Divine Disobedience,* Christian Classics (Westminster, MD), 1970.

PERIODICALS

America, April 3, 1993, James B. Nickloff, review of *America against Itself: Moral Vision and the Public Order,* p. 21.
Catholic Insight, April, 2000, Leonard Kennedy, review of *Appointment in Rome: The Church in America Awakening,* p. 36.
Christian Century, October 6, 1993, Dennis P. McCann, review of *Doing Well and Doing Good: The Challenge to the Christian Capitalist,* p. 941; November 7, 2001, David A. Hoekema, review of *The Second 1,000 Years: Ten People Who Defined a Millennium,* p. 31.
Christianity Today, March 8, 1993, Doug Bandow, review of *Doing Well and Doing Good: The Challenge to the Christian Capitalist,* p. 43.
First Things, May, 2001, Alan Jacobs, review of *The Eternal Pity: Reflections on Dying,* p. 37.

Library Journal, March 1, 2002, Mary Prokop, review of *As I Lay Dying: Meditations upon Returning,* p. 107.

Lutheran Forum, spring, 1972.

National Review, April 7, 1970; July 27, 1984, Joseph Sobran, review of *The Naked Public Square: Religion and Democracy in America,* p. 42; July 12, 1985, William F. Buckley, Jr., "On Fearing the Religious Right," p. 62; December 25, 1995, Janet Marsden, review of *Evangelicals and Catholics Together: Toward a Common Mission,* p. 58; October 19, 1992, William E. Simon, review of *Doing Well and Doing Good,* p. 56; March 20, 2000, Michael Potemra, "A World Renewed," p. 52.

New York Times Book Review, August 26, 1984, Harvey Cox, review of *The Naked Public Square.*

Publishers Weekly, January 14, 2002, review of *As I Lay Dying,* p. 55.

ONLINE

AD2000 Web site, http://www.ad2000.com.au/ (June, 1991), Mary Arnold, interview with Richard John Neuhaus.

Plough Web site, http://www.plough.com/uk/ (April 2, 2002), review of *Death on a Friday Afternoon: Meditations on the Last Words of Jesus from the Cross.*

*   *   *

NICKERSON, Sheila B(unker) 1942-

PERSONAL: Born April 14, 1942, in New York, NY; daughter of Charles Cantine (an investment analyst) and Mavis (McGuire) Bunker; married Martinus Hoffman Nickerson (a traffic engineer), September 5, 1964; children: Helen, Thomas Merriman, Samuel Bunker. *Education:* Bryn Mawr College, B.A. (English, with honors; magna cum laude), 1964; Union Institute, Ph.D. (creative writing), 1985.

ADDRESSES: Home—242 Bayside Road, Bellingham, WA 98225.

CAREER: University Within Walls (statewide prison education system), Alaska, editor of prison literary magazine, 1979-82, associate director, instructor, and director of arts program, 1981-82; State of Alaska, Department of Administration, Word Processing Center, proofreader and assistant supervisor, 1983-85, acting supervisor, 1985; editor of *Alaska Fish and Game* (magazine), 1985-92; writer. Alaska State Council on the Arts, Artists-in-the-Schools Program, writer-in-residence at schools in Juneau, Petersburg, Skagway, Cordova, Ketchikan, and Tenakee Springs, 1974-81; Writer-in-residence and designer of writing program for the Alaska State Library system, 1979; University Within Walls, Alaska, part-time instructor in English and creative writing, 1979-81; University of Alaska, part-time instructor in creative and technical writing, 1979-83, became assistant professor; State of Alaska, part-time instructor in technical writing for employees, 1979-83; Sitka Summer Writers Symposium in Sitka, Alaska, faculty member, 1984 and 1993. Member of the grants panel for the National Endowment for the Arts literature program, 1980. Has given readings at libraries, bookstores, colleges, and conferences throughout Alaska.

MEMBER: PEN West.

AWARDS, HONORS: Top Hand awards for best book of poetry, 1975, 1980, and 1982; Pushcart Prizes from Pushcart Press, 1976 and 1985-86; publication assistance grant, Alaska State Council on the Arts, 1977; Alaska poet laureate, 1977-81; merit and purchase awards for poetry, Alaska State Council on the Arts, 1980; literacy award, Delta Kappa Gamma, 1980.

WRITINGS:

Letter from Alaska and Other Poems, Thorp Springs Press (Berkeley, CA), 1972.

To the Waters and the Wild: Poems of Alaska, Thorp Springs Press (Berkeley, CA), 1975.

In Rooms of Falling Rain (novel), Thorp Springs Press (Berkeley, CA), 1976.

Songs of the Pine-Wife (poetry), Copper Canyon Press (Port Townsend, WA), 1980.

(Author of text) *The Enchanted Halibut* (full-length musical play), music by Jack Cannon, first produced in Douglas, AK, at Perseverance Theatre, April, 1981.

Waiting for the News of Death (poetry chapbook), Bits Press (Cleveland, OH), 1982.

Writers in the Public Library (nonfiction), Shoe String (Hamden, CT), 1984.

On Why the Quilt-Maker Became a Dragon (poetry), Vanessa Press (Fairbanks, AK), 1985.

Feast of the Animals: An Alaska Bestiary, Volume 1 (poetry), Old Harbor Press (Sitka, AK), 1987.

In the Compass of Unrest (poetry chapbook), Trout Creek Press (Parkdale, OR), 1988.

Feast of the Animals: An Alaska Bestiary, Volume 2 (poetry), Old Harbor Press (Sitka, AK), 1991.

Disappearance, a Map: A Meditation on Death and Loss in the High Latitudes, Doubleday (New York, NY), 1996.

In an August Garden (poetry), Black Spruce Press (Sandpoint, ID), 1997.

Midnight to the North: The Untold Story of the Inuit Woman Who Saved the Polaris Expedition, J. P. Tarcher/Putnam (New York, NY), 2002.

Also contributor to *Grrrr,* a book of bear poems. Author of text for *Songs from the Dragon Quilt* (orchestral and choral composition), music by Alice Parker, performed December, 1984, and author of half-hour videotape documentary for educational television, released 1982. Work represented in anthologies, including *The Pushcart Prize: Best of the Small Presses,* Pushcart (Wainscott, NY), 1976, 1985-86; *Windflower Almanac,* Windflower Press (Lincoln, NE), 1980; *Hunger and Dreams,* edited by Pat Monoghan, Fireweed Press (Falls Church, VA), 1983; *In the Dreamlight: Twenty-one Alaskan Writers,* Copper Canyon Press (Port Townsend, WA), 1984; *Only Morning in Her Shoes,* Utah State University Press (Logan, UT), 1990; *Heart of the Flower,* Chicory Blue Press, 1991; and *From the Island's Edge: A Sitka Reader,* Graywolf Press (St. Paul, MN), 1995. Contributor of poems to magazines, including *Bits, Crab Creek Review, Croton Review, Hyperion, Ms., New Laurel Review, Permafrost,* and *Tar River Poetry Review.* Coeditor of *Lemon Creek Gold: A Journal of Prison Literature,* 1979-85; coeditor of *Juneau 2000 Proceedings,* November, 1982; member of editorial board of *On People and Things Alaskan,* edited by Bridget Smith, Firsthand Press (Douglas, AK), 1982.

WORK IN PROGRESS: Poetry collection and nonfiction.

SIDELIGHTS: Sheila B. Nickerson, a former poet laureate of Alaska, is known for her lyrical explorations of wilderness both external and internal. Nickerson became interested in writing while a child and found her voice after settling in Alaska in the 1970s. She is widely represented in anthologies, as well as in books of poetry she has published with small presses in Alaska and on the mainland.

Disappearance, a Map: Meditations on Death and Loss in the High Latitudes was inspired by the loss of one of the poet's colleagues in a plane crash in rural Alaska. The book recounts the deaths of Arctic explorers as well as the disappearance of the unique cultures of native Alaskans. A *Publishers Weekly* reviewer commended *Disappearance, a Map* as "beautifully written," adding that the book "gives us a sense of place not found in ordinary maps." Donna Seaman in *Booklist* likewise praised the work as "an unusual, magnetically beautiful, and lyrically thoughtful meditation."

Nickerson's *Midnight to the North: The Untold Story of the Inuit Woman Who Saved the Polaris Expedition* tells the tale of a native woman, Tookoolito, who offered aid to the stranded crew of the ship Polaris after it was lost in ice. Though forgotten by history, Tookoolito and her husband have been credited with saving the lives of half of the Polaris crew, when logic dictated that the knowledgeable Inuit should have just abandoned the crew. "Few Arctic exploration books offer a more compelling subject," noted a *Publishers Weekly* reviewer of *Midnight to the North.* The reviewer added that Nickerson "is outstanding in illustrating Inuit customs, culture and legends." In *Booklist,* Gavin Quinn praised Nickerson for being "the first to shed light on this little-mentioned historical figure." A *Kirkus Reviews* critic found the book "a probing literary and historical contribution of consequence and beauty . . . making a significant addition to the truncated record of women's achievements there."

Nickerson once told *CA:* "Although I live in an area of compelling landscape, I am more concerned with inner landscape than outer. On the ferry trip to Juneau, Alaska, in 1971 when I moved there, people asked me, 'Do you think you will like it?' In retrospect I find that a stranger question now than I did at the time. I have written a great deal on Alaska—the land and what the connection with the land has meant to me—but I have come to realize through the years that the place of power is inside, not outside, and that we determine our view of a place by the level of awareness we bring to it. As a writer I work to observe. By observing, I learn to connect with what is there. As I connect, I break through the distractions of the everyday world and find union with the harmony of the universe. The 'tao of Writing' is my goal—finding in writing the path with a heart, the process that leads us to greater awareness, no matter what the product."

BIOGRAPHICAL AND CRITICAL SOURCES:

PERIODICALS

Booklist, December 15, 1995, Donna Seaman, review of *Disappearance, a Map: Meditation on Death and Loss in the High Latitudes,* p. 684; February 1, 2002, Gavin Quinn, review of *Midnight to the North: The Untold Story of the Inuit Woman Who Saved the Polaris Expedition,* p. 918.

Kirkus Reviews, January 1, 2002, review of *Midnight to the North,* p. 34.

Library Journal, February 1, 2002, Alison Hopkins, review of *Midnight to the North,* p. 120.

Publishers Weekly, January 1, 1996, review of *Disappearance, a Map,* p. 65; February 18, 2002, review of *Midnight to the North,* p. 89.

*   *   *

NILES, Douglas

PERSONAL: Male.

ADDRESSES: Office—c/o Author's Mail, TSR Inc., 201 Sheridan Springs Rd., P.O. Box 756, Lake Geneva, WI 53147.

CAREER: Fantasy novelist, game designer, and author of interactive fiction. Taught high school until 1982.

MEMBER: Alliterates.

AWARDS, HONORS: H.G. Wells and Origins awards for game designs.

WRITINGS:

"FORGOTTEN REALMS" FANTASY ADVENTURE SERIES: MOONSHAE TRILOGY

Darkwalker on Moonshae, TSR (Lake Geneva, WI), 1987.
Black Wizards, TSR (Lake Geneva, WI), 1988.
Darkwell, TSR (Lake Geneva, WI), 1989.

"FORGOTTEN REALMS" FANTASY ADVENTURE SERIES: MAZTICA TRILOGY

Ironhelm, TSR (Lake Geneva, WI), 1990.
Viperhand, TSR (Lake Geneva, WI), 1990.
Feathered Dragon, TSR (Lake Geneva, WI), 1991.

"FORGOTTEN REALMS" FANTASY ADVENTURE SERIES: DRUIDHOME TRILOGY

Prophet of Moonshae, TSR (Lake Geneva, WI), 1992.
The Coral Kingdom, TSR (Lake Geneva, WI), 1992.
The Druid Queen, TSR (Lake Geneva, WI), 1993.

OTHER

Tarzan and the Well of Slaves ("Tarzan" Series: Endless Quest #26), TSR (Lake Geneva, WI), 1985.
Escape from Castle Quarras ("Super Endless Quest" Adventure Gamebook #3), TSR (Lake Geneva, WI), 1985.
Lords of Doom: A Dragonlance Adventure ("Advanced Dungeons and Dragons" Adventure Gamebook #10), TSR (Lake Geneva, WI), 1986.
Dungeoneer's Survival Guide: A Sourcebook for Advanced Dungeons and Dragons Game Adventures in the Unknown Depths of Underdark! (nonfiction), TSR (Lake Geneva, WI), 1986.
Flint, the King ("Dragonlance Preludes II" Series), Penguin (New York, NY), 1990.
The Dragonlance Saga: The Kinslayer Wars ("Dragonlance Elven Nations" Trilogy #2), TSR (Lake Geneva, WI), 1991.
Emperor of Ansalon ("Dragonlance Saga Villains," Volume Three), TSR (Lake Geneva, WI), 1993.
A Breach in the Watershed ("The Watershed" Trilogy, Book One), Ace (New York, NY), 1995.
The Kagonesti ("Dragonlance: The Lost Histories," Volume One), TSR (Lake Geneva, WI), 1995.
Immortal Game ("Quest Triad," Book Three), TSR (Lake Geneva, WI), 1996.
The Rod of Seven Parts, TSR (Lake Geneva, WI), 1996.
Darkenheight, Ace Books (New York, NY), 1996.
Firstandantilus Reborn, TSR (Renton, WA), 1998.
The Last Thane, TSR (Renton, WA), 1998.
(With Steve Miller) *Dragonlance Reader's Companion: The Odyssey of Gilthanas,* TSR, Inc. (Renton, WA), 1999.

The Puppet King, Random House (New York, NY), 1999.

(With Michael Dobson) *Fox on the Rhine,* Forge (New York, NY.), 2000.

Circle at Center, Ace Books (New York, NY), 2000.

World Fall, Ace Books (New York, NY), 2001.

The Golden Orb, Wizards of the Coast (Renton, WA), 2002.

Also the author of the fantasy novels *The Lord of Lowhill, The First Moonwell,* and *Firstborn.*

SIDELIGHTS: Game designer Douglas Niles became a published author in the mid-1980s when he turned his attention to the writing of gamebooks for the "Advanced Dungeons and Dragons" and "Super Endless Quest" series. Niles was a high school teacher until 1982, when he turned his full attention to designing role-playing and military simulation games. His designs for such firms as the Wisconsin-based TSR, Inc., have earned Niles several accolades, including the H.G. Wells and Origins awards. While at TSR, he penned a 1985 volume in the "Tarzan" series, *Tarzan and the Well of Slaves.* An early work that established Niles as an authority in the field of fantasy games was *Dungeoneer's Survival Guide: A Sourcebook for Advanced Dungeons and Dragons Game Adventures in the Unknown Depths of Underdark!,* a 1986 hardback supplement to the rules of the popular role-playing game. Reviewer Alaric Fox, in *Voice of Youth Advocates,* cautioned that a knowledge of previous volumes of rules for the game was essential to an understanding of this one. He called Niles's work "very well written" and deemed the information conveyed by the book "very useful."

After that nonfiction volume, Niles began writing fantasy novels, and now has more than two dozen to his credit. These generally came in the form of trilogies, many appearing under the umbrella title *Forgotten Realms Fantasy Adventure.* The *Forgotten Realms* novels, which began emerging in 1986, take place in a fantasy game world. Niles's first set of books, the *Moonshae Trilogy,* consisted of the novels *Darkwalker on Moonshae, Black Wizards,* and *Darkwell.* Reviewing *Black Wizards* for *Voice of Youth Advocates,* Mary Ann Gilpatrick commented on the novel's slow start, which she ascribed to the introduction of many characters, but she added that the action picked up and that "many different scenes of action are well woven

together." The novel, like the rest of the series, is set in a land called "The Isles" and features such creatures as wizards, unicorns, orcs, and ogres, involved in battles between good and evil.

After the *Moonshae Trilogy,* which sold more than 600,000 copies, came a second *Forgotten Realms* fantasy series, the *Maztica Trilogy,* consisting of *Ironhelm, Viperhand,* and *Feathered Dragon.* The third trilogy in Niles's sequence, the *Druidhome* novels, began with *Prophet of Moonshae* in 1992. The plot of *Prophet of Moonshae* involves a conflict between the Northmen and the Folk, who have coexisted peacefully for twenty-five years in their fantasy game world before the god of chaos, Talos, attempts to usurp the Moonshae domain. A beautiful evil princess and a beautiful good princess enliven the action. Stacey Conrad, writing in *Kliatt,* declared, "I would recommend this book to lovers of fantasy series." She also noted that readers of this novel would probably be drawn into reading future volumes in the series as well.

In 1995, Niles issued the first volume in a popular new series, the *Watershed Trilogy.* The first book in the series, titled *A Breach in the Watershed,* is a fantasy that takes place among three imaginary lands which are protected by a supposedly invulnerable Watershed. The central conflict involves a breach made in the Watershed by a being named Sleepstealer. The task of saving the world is left to a small group of humans and magical folk, including a mountain climber named Rudy the Iceman and a woman marked by three prophecies. A burning tower, enchanted swamps, magic ice, and disappearing cliffs play roles in the action of the story. A *Library Journal* critic praised the book, saying it "bears the trademarks of classic fantasy." *Voice of Youth Advocates* placed the novel on its list of "Best Science Fiction, Fantasy and Horror" for the year 1995.

One of Niles's later series, titled the *Seven Circles Trilogy,* began with *Circle at Center* and followed by *World Fall.* Both books are set in the realm of the Seven Circles, which is populated by typical fantasy beings such as elves, griffons, centaurs, trolls, and dragons. Both books also feature a Druid priestess named Mirandel. In *Circle at Center,* the peace of the Seven Circles is threatened when an evil dwarf named Delver leads a rebellion. Mirandel uses her power as an enchantress to teleport a number of human warriors from Earth's past, hoping they can train her people to fend off Delver's evil forces. A contributor for *Publishers Weekly* appreciated the author's ability to create intriguing settings in the first book. "Niles has again conceived a fantasy setting of great richness and scope," the reviewer wrote.

World Fall picks up after Mirandel's actions save the Seven Circles, though she is exiled to live for a time among the barbaric humans for breaking her order's sacred laws. When Mirandel finally returns to her home city, she is forced to take even more drastic measures to protect the entire realm from the evil Karlath-Fayd, who attempts to conquer the Seven Circles with his army of dead soldiers from Earth's past. Several reviewers recommended the work to fantasy readers. Jackie Cassada, who reviewed the book for *Library Journal,* called it "a fast-paced tale of epic adventure." A contributor for *Kirkus Reviews* believed "unjaded fans" would find the book "awesomely cool."

With his 2000 effort called *Fox on the Rhine,* Niles utilized his experience designing military games. Co-written by fellow game designer Michael Dobson, the book offers a theoretical and fictional account of what would have happened during World War II had a 1944 assassination attempt on Adolf Hitler's life succeeded. In Hitler's absence, figures such as Heinrich Himmler and Erwin Rommel rise to prominence, help make peace with Russia, and plan an offensive against the other Allies near the city of Antwerp. A reviewer for *Publishers Weekly* felt the book had "several notable problems," while still believing the authors had "crafted a vividly realistic study of a memorable time."

BIOGRAPHICAL AND CRITICAL SOURCES:

BOOKS

Reginald, Robert, *Science Fiction and Fantasy Literature, 1975-1991,* Gale (Detroit, MI), 1992.

PERIODICALS

Booklist, June 1, 2000, p. 1860.
Kirkus Reviews, August 1, 2001, p. 1076.
Kliatt, September, 1992, p. 22; July, 1995, p. 16.
Library Journal, August, 1995, p. 122; September 15, 2001, p. 116.

Publishers Weekly, February 10, 1992, p. 78; May 15, 2000, pp. 89, 94; August 13, 2001, p. 292.
Voice of Youth Advocates, February, 1987, p. 301; February, 1989, p. 295; April, 1996, p. 17.

ONLINE

Alliterates Web site, http://www.alliterates.com/ (April 8, 2002), profile of Douglas Niles.*

*   *   *

NOOTEBOOM, Cees 1933-

PERSONAL: Surname is pronounced "*Noh*-te-bohm"; born July 31, 1933, in The Hague, Netherlands; son of Hubertus and Johanna (Pessers) Nooteboom. *Education:* Educated at an Augustinian monastery school in Eindhoven, Netherlands.

ADDRESSES: Agent—Aitken & Stone, 29 Fernshaw Rd., London SW10 0TG, England.

CAREER: Writer and lecturer.

MEMBER: Arti et Amicitiae (Amsterdam).

AWARDS, HONORS: Pegasus Prize from Mobil Oil Company, 1980, for *Rituelen;* Regents' lecturer at University of California, Berkeley, 1986-87; Anne Frank Prize; Poetry Prize of the City of Amsterdam; European Literary Prize, 1993, for *The Following Story;* International Prize Composetela-Xunta de Galicia, IVth edition, 2002.

WRITINGS:

De doden zoeben een huis (poetry), Querido (Amsterdam, The Netherlands), 1956.
Philip en de anderen (novel), Querido (Amsterdam, The Netherlands), 1956, translation by Adrienne Dixon published as *Philip and the Others,* Louisiana State University Press (Baton Rouge, LA), 1988.
De verliefde gevangene (fiction), Querido (Amsterdam, The Netherlands), 1958.

Koude gedichten (poetry), Querido (Amsterdam, The Netherlands), 1959.

De Zwanen van de Theems: Toneelstuk in drie bedrijven, Querido (Amsterdam, The Netherlands), 1959.

Het zwarte gedicht (poetry), Querido (Amsterdam, The Netherlands), 1960.

De koning is dood, De Roos (Utrecht, The Netherlands), 1961.

Een middag in Bruay (essays), De Bezige Bij (Amsterdam, The Netherlands), 1963.

De ridder is gestorven (fiction), Querido (Amsterdam, The Netherlands), 1963.

Gesloten gedichten (poetry), De Bezige Bij (Amsterdam, The Netherlands), 1964.

Een nacht in Tunesie, De Bezige Bij (Amsterdam, The Netherlands), 1965.

Een ochtend in Bahia (travel writings), De Bezige Bij (Amsterdam, The Netherlands), 1968.

De Parijse beroerte, De Bezige Bij (Amsterdam, The Netherlands), 1968.

Gemaakte gedichten (poetry), De Bezige Bij (Amsterdam, The Netherlands), 1970.

Bitter Bolivia, Maanland Mali (travel writings; first published in *Avenue*), De Bezige Bij (Amsterdam, The Netherlands), 1971.

Een avond in Isfahan: Reisverhalen uit Perzie, Gambia, Duitsland, Japan, Engeland, Madeira, en Maleisie (travel writings and biography), Arbeiderspers (Amsterdam, The Netherlands), 1978.

Open als een schelp, dicht als een steen: Gedichten (poetry), Arbeiderspers (Amsterdam, The Netherlands), 1978.

Rituelen (novel), Arbeiderspers (Amsterdam, The Netherlands), 1980, translation by Adrienne Dixon published as *Rituals,* Louisiana State University Press (Baton Rouge, LA), 1983.

Een lied van schijn en wezen (novel), Arbeiderspers (Amsterdam, The Netherlands), 1981, translation by Adrienne Dixon published as *A Song of Truth and Semblance,* Louisiana State University Press (Baton Rouge, LA), 1984.

Voorbije passages, Arbeiderspers (Amsterdam, The Netherlands), 1981.

Aas: Gedichten (poetry), Arbeiderspers (Amsterdam, The Netherlands), 1982.

Gyges en Kandaules: Een koningsdrama, Arbeiderspers (Amsterdam, The Netherlands), 1982.

Mokusei! Een liefdesverhaal, Arbeiderspers (Amsterdam, The Netherlands), 1982.

Nooit gebouwd Nederland (nonfiction), edited by Cees de Jong, Frank den Oudsten, and Willem Schilder, Unieboek/Moussault (Weesp, The Netherlands), 1983, translation published as *Unbuilt Netherlands: Visionary Projects by Berlage, Ond, Duiker, Van den Broek, Van Eyck, Herzberg, and Others,* Rizzoli (New York, NY), 1985.

Waar je gevallen bent, blijf je (essays), Arbeiderspers (Amsterdam, The Netherlands), 1983.

Fantasma, color illustrations by Sjoerd Bakker, Bonnefant (Banholt, The Netherlands), 1983.

In Nederland (novel), Arbeiderspers (Amsterdam, The Netherlands), 1984, translation by Adrienne Dixon published as *In the Dutch Mountains,* Louisiana State University Press, 1987.

Vuurtijd, ijstijd: Gedichten, 1955-1983 (poetry), Arbeiderspers (Amsterdam, The Netherlands), 1984.

De zucht naar het Westen (title means "The Yearning for the West"; travel writings and biography), Arbeiderspers (Amsterdam, The Netherlands), 1985.

De Boeddha achter de schutting: Aan de oever van de Chaophraya; een verhaal, Kwadraat (Utrecht, The Netherlands), 1986.

De brief, Arbeiderspers (Amsterdam, The Netherlands), 1988.

Het gezicht van het oog, Arbeiderspers (Amsterdam, The Netherlands), 1989.

De wereld een reiziger, Arbeiderspers (Amsterdam, The Netherlands), 1989.

Vreemd water, Arbeiderspers (Amsterdam, The Netherlands), 1991.

Berliner Notizen, Suhrhamp (Frankfurt, Germany), 1991.

Het volgende verhaal, Arbeiderspers (Amsterdam, The Netherlands), 1991; translation by Ina Rilke published as *The Following Story,* Harcourt Brace (New York, NY), 1994.

Rollende stenen, Stichting Plint (Eindhoven, The Netherlands), 1991.

Zurbaran & Cees Nooteboom, Atlas (Amsterdam, The Netherlands), 1992.

De omweg naar Santiago, Atlas (Amsterdam, The Netherlands), 1992; translation by Ina Rilke published as *Roads to Santiago,* Harcourt Brace (New York, NY), 1997.

De ontvoering van Europa, Atlas (Amsterdam, The Netherlands), 1993.

De koning van Suriname, M. Muntinga (Amsterdam, The Netherlands), 1993.

Van de lente de dauw: Oosterse reizen, Arbeiderspers (Amsterdam, The Netherlands), 1995.

The Captain of the Butterflies (poetry), translation from the Dutch by Leonard Nathan and Herlinde Spahr, Sun & Moon Press, 1997.

De filosoof zonder ogen: Europese reizen, Arbeiders-
spers (Amsterdam, The Netherlands), 1997.

Terugkeer naar Berlijn, Atlas (Amsterdam, The
Netherlands), 1998.

Allerzielen, Atlas (Amsterdam, The Netherlands),
1998.

Zo kon het zijn: gedichten, Atlas (Amsterdam, The
Netherlands), 1999.

*Bitterzoet: Honderd gedechten van vroeger en zeven-
tien nieuwe,* De Arbeiderspers (Amsterdam, The
Netherlands), 2000.

All Souls' Day, translated by Susan Massotty, Harcourt
(New York, NY), 2001.

Also author of two plays. Travel columnist for the
Dutch periodicals *Avenue* and *Elsevier's.* Producer of
an hour-long film on the pilgrimage to the Spanish
shrine at Santiago de Compostela.

SIDELIGHTS: Cees Nooteboom is a Dutch poet, travel
writer, playwright, and novelist who is best known in
the United States for his award-winning fiction. His
novel *Rituelen* received the Pegasus Prize in 1980, and
three years later, under the title *Rituals,* it became
Nooteboom's first work to be published in English
translation. Two more novels quickly followed; *Een
lied van schijn en wezen* (*A Song of Truth and
Semblance*) and *In Nederland* (*In the Dutch
Mountains*) were both written during the early 1980s
and translated soon after. The author's first novel,
Philip en de anderen (*Philip and the Others*), was
written in 1956 but not translated until 1988. Nooteboom has also had one nonfiction book published in
English, *Nooit gebouwd Nederland* (*Unbuilt
Netherlands*), which describes several unrealized
projects conceived by Dutch architects.

Nooteboom's fiction is considered remarkable for its
exploration of life's incongruities. In the author's most
highly praised novel, *Rituals,* this exploration takes
the form of a comparison between chaos and order.
The first of the book's three sections introduces Inni, a
wayward, emotionless man whose wife has just left
him. The second section describes Inni's encounter ten
years earlier with Arnold Taads, a man so obsessed by
order that he tries to spend every day exactly alike;
and the third section jumps ahead twenty years to
show Inni's meeting with Taads's estranged son, who
has adopted the ritualistic life of a Japanese tea master.
Both father and son live and die—in carefully orches-
trated suicides—according to their self-imposed
regimens. Throughout the book, Inni encounters im-
pulsive women whose free-spirited lives contrast
sharply with those of the disciplined father and son.
"The novel itself seems to embody something of both
these qualities, randomness and order," observed Linda
Barrett Osborne in her *Washington Post Book World*
review. "Told from Inni's point of view," she explained, "it moves, as he does, freely from idea to
idea. . . . At the same time, there are numerous connections among the images and symbols used throughout the book."

New Statesman reviewer Sheila MacLeod, who lauded
especially the descriptions of the obsessive father and
son, called *Rituals* "an enigmatic and somewhat mer-
ciless parable which never fails to compel." Jonathan
Keates in the London *Observer* likewise deemed *Rituals* an "insidious, elegantly-wrought work," and Osborne praised the book's "passages of clarity, beauty,
and vividness" and Nooteboom's "painter's eye." Noting the diversity of the book's characters and the variety of philosophies they illustrate, Osborne concluded,
"Reading *Rituals* is like walking through a very modern, well-proportioned art gallery full of light and air
and visually striking paintings, offering a wealth of
subjects and perspectives for contemplation. . . . One
could spend days in such a place, or book, pondering
the nature of the world, or an hour simply enjoying
the skillful craftsmanship."

Nooteboom's next two novels, *A Song of Truth and
Semblance* and *In the Dutch Mountains,* compare myth
and reality by juxtaposing the lives of the books' narrators—who are both authors—with the fictional lives
of the characters they create. *A Song of Truth and
Semblance,* in addition, compares the contemplative,
insecure narrator, known only as "the writer," with his
superficial, confident colleague, called "the other
writer." Despite his friend's advice against infusing
too much meaning into his work, the writer attempts
to answer eternal questions about truth and falsehood
through the development of his story's plot. He fails,
however, both in answering the questions and in de-
vising a satisfactory conclusion to his story. In a fit of
despair he tears up his manuscript and thus nullifies
the existence of his imagined world. While calling
Nooteboom's handling of the two levels of reality
"somehow unsubtle," *Times Literary Supplement* contributor Toby Fitton praised the "fugal interaction" of
the two plot lines and likened their resolutions to those
of "mixed doubles tournaments."

Unlike the writer in *A Song of Truth and Semblance,* the narrator in Nooteboom's next novel, *In the Dutch Mountains,* knows how his tale will end. The story he writes is a recasting of the fairy tale "The Snow Queen"; it concerns two circus performers, Kai and Lucia, who become separated when Kai is kidnapped by the coldhearted Snow Queen. Lucia and a circus clown journey north to the Snow Queen's castle and, after a series of adventures, succeed in rescuing Kai. "Engaging as this tale is," according to *Times Literary Supplement* reviewer Savkar Altinel, "[the storyteller's] running commentary on it is even more so." The narrator, Alfonso Tiburon de Mendoza, is a road surveyor by vocation and a writer by avocation. As Alfonso recounts his fairy tale he frequently digresses into musings about etymology, literary genres, the physical construction of roads, and the abstract construction of literary plots. Unlike the writer in *A Song of Truth and Semblance,* Alfonso feels no compulsion to resolve the mysteries of existence or truth through his characters; instead, he uses the simple, precise genre of the fairy tale to avoid having to explore those issues. When he finishes his story, Alfonso wanders outdoors, plays a game, sits down, "and," he writes, "I sat there happily ever after."

In the Dutch Mountains was praised almost unconditionally as a "charming and compact fable," as *Voice Literary Supplement* contributor Sven Birkerts called it, and for its lively interplay of the fanciful and the ordinary. Michael Malone, writing for *New York Times Book Review,* admired the "symbolic, digressive and self-consciously playful" novel and commended the way "a writer as fine as Mr. Nooteboom" manages to hold the reader's interest in both the fairy tale and the narrator's ruminations. Nooteboom's "strange, metaphysical novel . . . is an astonishing achievement," concurred Bernard Levin in his London *Sunday Times* review. "In fewer than 40,000 words he juggles with reality and meaning, fate and symbol, [and] cold north and hot south." Levin concluded, "[*In the Dutch Mountains*] is the brilliant and original fruit of a deep (and well-read) imagination."

Several of Nooteboom's other works have also been published in English, including a collection of poetry, titled *The Captain of the Butterflies,* which critic Frank Allen of *Library Journal* called "a window on a surreal landscape." The book's poems include many of those Nooteboom penned between 1955 and 1996. According to a contributor for *Publishers Weekly,* the poems show Nooteboom to be "much concerned with time and the pain of the inexpressible."

The Following Story, Ina Rilke's translation of Nooteboom's 1991 novel, *Het volgende verhaal,* appeared in English in 1993. The winner of the 1993 European Literary Prize, the novel revolves around the relationship between a middle-aged Latin professor and an unusual student, which ends in tragedy when the student is killed in an automobile accident. Narrated by the professor some twenty years after the accident, the book tackles a number of philosophical questions, including coming to grips with mortality and the vanity of human endeavor. In fact, a contributor for *Publishers Weekly* called the work a "baffling postmodernist fable." According to the narrator, the book is "about how an immeasurable space of memories can be stored in the most minute timespan." Several literary critics lauded the effort. "Nooteboom presents the reader with a wonderfully ironic and highly allusive tale. Its complexities are carefully interwoven," wrote Arie Staal of *World Literature Today.* According to Guy Mannes-Abbot of *New Statesman & Society,* the book "has a compelling energy and rare elegance to equal its extraordinary ambitions."

Rilke also translated *Roads to Santiago,* a book of essays that Nooteboom wrote about Spain and its people. Calling Spain his "adopted country," Nooteboom takes the reader from Barcelona to Santiago, on a pilgrimage to see the tomb of St. James, just as Christian pilgrims did in the twelfth century. Along the route, Nooteboom takes many detours, visiting the people and institutions of the Spanish countryside. For example, in one essay he provides anecdotes and personal observations about the Prado museum in Madrid. In other essays, Nooteboom simply reflects on Spanish culture and his appreciation for it. A number of critics enjoyed the effort, including Brad Santiago of *Booklist,* who felt Nooteboom refracted "all his observations through keen senses of history and human nature." Richard L. Kagan, who reviewed the book for the *New York Times,* called the author "a solitary traveler caught in an extended reverie, a dreamer for whom every monument, every work of art transforms itself into a memory palace that unlocks Spain's history."

A more recent work of Nooteboom's to appear in English is *All Souls' Day.* Translated by Susan Massotty, the book is a contemplative story about the growing relationship between two lovers, who are both haunted by earlier traumatic events. In typical Nooteboom fashion, the novel is filled with philosophical and reflective ramblings about history, art, and the meaning of life, which are as important to the work as the love affair of its protagonists. Critic Patrick Sullivan, who reviewed *All Souls' Day* for *Library Journal,* commented on this duality, calling the work "part love story, part novel of ideas." Sullivan went on to refer to the work as "an imposing and richly nuanced novel." Other critics, however, including a contributor for *Publishers Weekly,* felt the work was too convoluted. "More enervating than invigorating, the book fails to communicate the vitality of a life of thought," the contributor wrote.

BIOGRAPHICAL AND CRITICAL SOURCES:

BOOKS

Encyclopedia of World Literature in the Twentieth Century, Volume 3, St. James (Detroit, MI), 1999.

PERIODICALS

Booklist, March 15, 1997, p. 1221.
Kirkus Reviews, October 1, 2001, p. 1387.
Library Journal, April 15, 1997, p. 105; July, 1997, p. 72; August, 2001, p. 163.
New Statesman, December 21, 1984.
New York Times Book Review, October 11, 1987; April 6, 1997.
Observer (London), February 17, 1985.
Publishers Weekly, June 30, 1997, p. 72; October 8, 2001, p. 41.
San Francisco Chronicle, August 12, 1983; April 25, 1997, p. D8.
Sunday Times (London), May 22, 1987; January 13, 2002, p. 45.
The Times, January 5, 2002, p. 15.
Times Literary Supplement, December 28, 1984; January 8, 1988.
Voice Literary Supplement, December, 1987.
Washington Post Book World, June 26, 1983.
World Literature Today, fall, 1996, p. 974.*

*　　*　　*

NOZICK, Robert 1938-2002

PERSONAL: Born November 16, 1938, in Brooklyn, NY; died of stomach cancer, January 23, 2002, in Cambridge, MA; son of Max (a manufacturer) and Sophie (Cohen) Nozick; married Barbara Claire Fierer

(a teacher), August 15, 1959; children: Emily Sarah, David Joshua. *Education:* Columbia University, A.B., 1959; Princeton University, A.M., 1961, Ph.D., 1963. *Politics:* Libertarian. *Religion:* Jewish.

CAREER: Princeton University, Princeton, NJ, assistant professor of philosophy, 1962-63, 1964-65; Harvard University, Cambridge, MA, assistant professor of philosophy, 1965-67; Rockefeller University, New York, NY, associate professor of philosophy, 1967-69; Harvard University, professor of philosophy, beginning 1969, named University Professor, 1998. Fellow, Center for Advanced Study in the Behavioral Sciences, 1971-72.

MEMBER: American Association of University Professors, American Civil Liberties Union, American Philosophical Association, Society for Ethical and Legal Philosophy, Jewish Vegetarian Society, Phi Beta Kappa.

AWARDS, HONORS: National Book Award, 1975, for *Anarchy, State, and Utopia;* Ralph Waldo Emerson Award, Phi Beta Kappa, 1982, for *Philosophical Explanations.*

WRITINGS:

Anarchy, State, and Utopia, Basic Books (New York, NY), 1974.
Philosophical Explanations, Harvard University Press (Cambridge, MA), 1981.
The Examined Life: Philosophical Meditations, Simon & Schuster (New York, NY), 1989.
The Normative History of Individual Choice, Garland (New York, NY), 1990.
The Nature of Rationality, Princeton University Press (Princeton, NJ), 1993.
Socratic Puzzles, Harvard University Press (Cambridge, MA), 1997.
Invariances: The Structure of the Objective World, Belknap Press (Cambridge, MA), 2001.
The 2001 Annotated Competition Act, Carswell (Scarborough, Ontario, Canada), 2001.

Contributor to professional journals. Member of editorial board, *Philosophy and Public Affairs,* beginning 1971.

SIDELIGHTS: Robert Nozick established his reputation as an advocate of radical libertarianism—the political tenet that argues for maximum individual rights and minimal government involvement. Nozick's death in early 2002 silenced the voice of "one of the great philosophers of our day," in the words of *New Statesman* contributor Nicholas Fearn.

Born in Brooklyn, New York, Nozick was the son of Jewish immigrants, and he often described himself as just one generation from the *shtetl* (the Jewish ghettos of Eastern Europe). Nozick's penchant for philosophy emerged at an early age. "When I was 15 years old, or 16, I carried around on the streets of Brooklyn a paperback copy of Plato's *Republic,* front cover facing outward," he was once quoted in the *Harvard Gazette.* "I had read only some of it and understood less, but I was excited by it and knew it was something wonderful." As a Princeton graduate student in the 1960s, Nozick had already formed his personality and his philosophy; he was "known as the visiting professor's ordeal," noted an *Economist* writer. "However deeply the eminent guest had thought through the counterarguments and rejoinders, young Mr. Nozick could be relied on to spot a hole in the [defenses] and work away at it until the structure of argument lay in ruins."

After serving an instructor's post at Princeton University, Nozick began his Harvard University career, beginning as an assistant professor and eventually being named University Professor, an honorary post awarded to faculty members whose work crosses the boundaries of different disciplines. As the author of several philosophical books, Nozick is best remembered for *Anarchy, State, and Utopia,* which won the National Book Award in 1975. This work, said Alasdair Palmer of *Spectator,* was "a revelation. Here was a work that uses all the latest gadgetry of analytical philosophy, yet, unlike all the other books of analytical philosophy, is not just intelligible, but is actually readable, even enjoyable." This is not to say that the book wasn't controversial. *Anarchy, State, and Utopia* argued for a kind of absolute right of the individual, the right "to use whatever powers he has for whatever purposes he chooses," as Palmer described it. "The subtext is overwhelming: morals are only for suckers, for those too stupid to have 'seen through' them."

Critics would point to the contradictions of such complete freedom. "Do employers' rights to hire and fire nullify totally workers' rights to jobs?" asked a contributor to *Encyclopedia of World Biography.* "Are rights to food, housing, health care, and protection from poverty in old age as important as the right to amass a fortune?" Noting that Nozick was a vegetarian, the essayist also wondered, "what human rights should be restricted for the sake of animal rights?" Nozick, the essayist added, admitted that his thesis was "unfinished," but "he was clear on the main point: it is no more the business of the state to distribute wealth than to distribute mates for marriage."

The books following *Anarchy, State, and Utopia* leaned more toward pure philosophy than politics; the author would joke "that he did not want to write 'Anarchy, State and Utopia II,'" said the *Economist* writer. In 1981 Nozick produced *Philosophical Explanations,* "best remembered for an ingenious argument against scepticism, and for a dispositional account of knowledge as true belief that would reliably stick with the truth (or self-correct) as relevant circumstances changed." Nozick's last major book before his death, 2001's *Invariances: The Structure of the Objective World,* is "an ambitious, stimulating effort to revitalize the notions of truth and objectivity in a way that takes account of contemporary physics and biology," according to a *Publishers Weekly* critic. Robert Hoffman of *Library Journal* had a more reserved view, saying that *Invariances*'s reliance on "unanswered questions, numerous parenthetical hints, and frequent indefinite suggestions" made the author's conclusions a challenge to uncover.

"Philosophy," Nozick wrote in *Invariances,* "begins in wonder"; to the *Economist* writer, the author "had a Romantic streak, both in his Utopian vision of society and in his conduct of philosophy. But this Byronic restlessness was the fault of his virtues: rare fluency and audacity—a fearless readiness to follow an idea where it led. Like any endeavor, philosophy needs explorers as well as mapmakers. As [Nozick] liked to say, there is room for words that are not last words."

BIOGRAPHICAL AND CRITICAL SOURCES:

BOOKS

Encyclopedia of World Biography, second edition, Gale (Detroit, MI), 1998.

PERIODICALS

American Journal of Sociology, September, 1976, review of *Anarchy, State, and Utopia,* p. 428.

American Political Science Review, December, 1976, review of *Anarchy, State, and Utopia,* p. 1289; September, 1994, review of *The Nature of Rationality,* p. 745.

American Scholar, winter, 1976, review of *Anarchy, State, and Utopia,* p. 816; summer, 1982, review of *Philosophical Explanations,* p. 426; summer, 1990, review of *The Examined Life: Philosophical Meditations,* p. 458.

American Spectator, January, 1982, review of *Philosophical Explanations,* p. 11; December, 1989, review of *The Examined Life,* p. 30.

Antioch Review, summer, 1976, review of *Anarchy, State, and Utopia,* p. 377.

Booklist, December 1, 1989, review of *The Examined Life,* p. 708.

Canadian Philosophical Reviews, February, 1993, review of *The Examined Life,* p. 47; June, 1994, review of *The Nature of Rationality,* p. 195.

Choice, January, 1982, review of *Philosophical Explanations,* p. 638; January, 1994, review of *The Nature of Rationality,* p. 803.

Christian Century, June 13, 1990, review of *The Examined Life,* p. 608.

Commentary, September, 1982, review of *Philosophical Explanations,* p. 55; April, 1990, review of *The Examined Life,* p. 68.

Commonweal, January 15, 1982, review of *Philosophical Explanations,* p. 24; November 30, 1984, review of *Anarchy, State, and Utopia,* p. 663.

Dialogue, fall, 1999, John Skorupski, "In a Socratic Way," p. 871.

Economist, April 26, 1986, review of *Philosophical Explanations,* p. 98.

Esquire, May, 1994, review of *The Examined Life,* p. 138.

Ethics, April, 1995, review of *The Nature of Rationality,* p. 659.

Harvard Educational Review, February, 1983, review of *Philosophical Explanations,* p. 82.

International Philosophical Quarterly, December, 1995, review of *The Nature of Rationality,* p. 491; September, 1998, review of *Socratic Puzzles,* p. 340.

Journal of Economic Literature, March, 1994, review of *The Nature of Rationality,* p. 195.

Journal of Philosophy, December, 1983, review of *Philosophical Explanations,* p. 819.

Journal of Political Economy, June, 1976, review of *Anarchy, State, and Utopia,* p. 574.

Journal of Politics, August, 1985, review of *Anarchy, State, and Utopia,* p. 996.

Journal of Religion, January, 1985, review of *Philosophical Explanations,* p. 133.

Kirkus Reviews, July 1, 1981, review of *Philosophical Explanations,* p. 857; October 1, 1989, review of *The Examined Life,* p. 1454.

Library Journal, November 1, 1981, review of *Philosophical Explanations,* p. 142; December, 1989, review of *The Examined Life,* p. 127; May 15, 1993, review of *The Nature of Rationality,* p. 71; September 1, 2001, Robert Hoffman, review of *Invariances: The Structure of the Objective World,* p. 183.

London Review of Books, May 20, 1982, review of *Philosophical Explanations,* p. 4; January 27, 1994, review of *The Nature of Rationality,* p. 17.

Mind, July, 2001, Hallvard Lillehammer, review of *Socratic Puzzles,* p. 802.

National Review, December 31, 1989, review of *The Examined Life,* p. 38.

New Boston Review, February, 1982, review of *Philosophical Explanations,* p. 9.

New Republic, October 7, 1981, review of *Philosophical Explanations,* p. 32; November 6, 1989, review of *The Examined Life,* p. 122.

New Yorker, January 29, 1990, review of *The Examined Life,* p. 96.

New York Review of Books, February 18, 1982, review of *Philosophical Explanations,* p. 32.

New York Times Book Review, September 20, 1981, review of *Philosophical Explanations,* p. 7; April 24, 1983, review of *Philosophical Explanations,* p. 31; October 29, 1989, review of *The Examined Life,* p. 15; December 9, 1990, review of *The Examined Life,* p. 38; August 22, 1993, review of *The Nature of Rationality,* p. 11; October 22, 1995, review of *The Nature of Rationality,* p. 44.

Observer (London, England), April 18, 1982, review of *Philosophical Explanations,* p. 31.

Partisan Review, fall, 1982, review of *Philosophical Explanations,* p. 609.

Philosophical Review, January, 1983, review of *Philosophical Explanations,* p. 81; April, 1995, review of *The Nature of Rationality,* p. 324.

Publishers Weekly, July 31, 1981, review of *Philosophical Explanations,* p. 53; October 13, 1989, review of *The Examined Life,* p. 34; November 2, 1990, review of *The Examined Life,* p. 71; May 31, 1993, review of *The Nature of Rationality,* p. 34; August 6, 2001, review of *Invariances,* p. 72.

Reason, June, 1994, review of *The Nature of Rationality,* p. 61.

Reference and Research Book News, November, 1997, review of *Socratic Puzzles,* p. 4.

Review of Metaphysics, September, 1976, review of *Anarchy, State, and Utopia,* p. 134; June, 1999, review of *Socratic Puzzles,* p. 966.

Sewanee Review, spring, 1983, review of *Philosophical Explanations,* p. 309.

Social Research, spring, 1976, review of *Anarchy, State, and Utopia,* p. 169.

Theology Today, October, 1982, review of *Philosophical Explanations,* p. 327.

Times Literary Supplement, October 15, 1982, review of *Philosophical Explanations,* p. 1136; June 18, 1993, review of *The Nature of Rationality,* p. 7.

Tribune Books (Chicago, IL), December 10, 1989, review of *The Examined Life,* p. 3.

Village Voice Literary Supplement, October, 1981, review of *Philosophical Explanations,* p. 13, and *Anarchy, State, and Utopia,* p. 22; June, 1988, review of *Anarchy, State, and Utopia,* p. 20.

Washington Post Book World, October 18, 1981, review of *Philosophical Explanations,* p. 10; June 26, 1983, review of *Philosophical Explanations,* p. 12; November 19, 1989, review of *The Examined Life,* p. 4.

Wilson Quarterly, February, 1990, review of *The Examined Life,* p. 92.

Yale Review, spring, 1982, review of *Philosophical Explanations,* p. 404.

ONLINE

Harvard Gazette Web Site, http://www.news.harvard.edu/gazette/1998/ (October 1, 1998), Alvin Powell, "Robert Nozick Named University Professor."

OBITUARIES:

PERIODICALS

Economist, February 2, 2002, p. 86.
Independent, January 30, 2002, p. S6.
New Statesman, February 11, 2002, p. 53.
New York Times, January 24, 2002, p. A29.
Spectator (London, England), February 9, 2002, p. 18.
Times (London, England), January 26, 2002, p. 25.
Washington Post, January 27, 2002, p. C08.*

O

OBERMAN, Sheldon 1949-

PERSONAL: Born May 20, 1949, in Winnipeg, Manitoba, Canada; son of Allan Oberman (a champion weightlifter and cafe owner) and Dorothy Stein (known as Dot Dobie, a psychic counselor); married Lee Anne Block (a teacher/director), August 9, 1973 (divorced, March, 1990); married Lisa Dveris (a therapist/social worker), September 2, 1990; children: Adam and Mira (first marriage), Jesse (second marriage). *Education:* University of Winnipeg, B.A. (with honors), 1972; University of Jerusalem, graduate study, 1973; University of Manitoba, B.Ed. *Religion:* Jewish. *Hobbies and other interests:* Creating collage art, camping, canoeing.

ADDRESSES: Home—822 Dorchester Ave., Winnipeg, Manitoba R3M 0R7, Canada. *E-mail*—soberman@ mts.net.

CAREER: High school teacher at Joseph Wolinsky Collegiate, Winnipeg, Manitoba, Canada, 1976—; writer. Has worked variously as a journalist, editor, scriptwriter, playwright, songwriter, actor, and director of short films. Performs regularly as a storyteller and guest speaker; gives readings at libraries, schools and conferences; conducts storytelling workshops; and is a writers' mentor.

MEMBER: Society of Children's Book Writers and Illustrators, Canadian Society of Children's Authors, Illustrators, and Performers, Society of Composers, Authors, and Music Publishers of Canada, Manitoba Writer's Guild, Manitoba Association of Playwrights, Winnipeg Film Group.

AWARDS, HONORS: Canadian Authors Association Short Story Award, 1987; International Silver Medal, Leipzig Book Fair, 1990, for *The Lion in the Lake/Le Lion dans le Lac;* $10,000 Journey Prize nomination, 1991, for best Canadian short story of the year; McNally Robinson Book of the Year nomination, 1994, for *This Business with Elijah;* National Jewish Book Award; Sydney Taylor American Librarians Award; American Bookseller Pick of the List Award; *A Child's Magazine* Best Book of the Year citation, and International Reading Association Choice citation, for *The Always Prayer Shawl;* five Juno nominations for children's albums which include his songs; Norma Fleck Award for Canadian children's nonfiction (shared with Simon Tookoome), 2000, for *The Shaman's Nephew: A Life in the Far North.*

WRITINGS:

(With Steve Johnson) *The Folk Festival Book: The Stories of the Winnipeg Folk Festival,* photographs by David Landy, Turnstone Press (Winnipeg, Manitoba, Canada), 1983.

(Editor, with Elaine Newton) *Mirror of a People: Canadian Jewish Experience in Poetry and Prose,* Coteau Press (Regina, Saskatchewan, Canada), 1985.

Julie Gerond and the Polka Dot Pony, Hyperion Press (Winnipeg, Manitoba, Canada), 1988.

The Lion in the Lake/Le Lion dans le Lac (alphabet book), Peguis Publishers (Winnipeg, Manitoba, Canada), 1988.

TV Sal and the Game Show from Outer Space, illustrated by Craig Terlson, Red Deer Press (Red Deer, Alberta, Canada), 1993.

This Business with Elijah (interrelated short stories), Turnstone Press (Winnipeg, Manitoba, Canada), 1993.

The Always Prayer Shawl, illustrated by Ted Lewin, Boyds Mills Press (Honesdale, PA), 1994.

The White Stone in the Castle Wall, illustrated by Les Tait, Tundra Books of Northern New York (Plattsburgh, NY), 1995.

By the Hanukkah Light, illustrated by Neil Waldman, Boyds Mills Press (Honesdale, PA), 1997.

(With Simon Tookoome) *The Shaman's Nephew: A Life in the Far North,* Stoddart Kids (New York, NY), 1999.

The Wisdom Bird: A Tale of Solomon and Sheba, illustrated by Neil Waldman, Boyds Mills Press (Honesdale, PA) 2000.

Also author of the family play *The Always Prayer Shawl,* 1995, based on the book of the same name. Numerous articles have been published in the *Winnipeg Free Press.*

WORK IN PROGRESS: Greek myths of Crete; researching Jewish folklore.

SIDELIGHTS: Sheldon Oberman grew up an only child in the North End area of Winnipeg, Manitoba, Canada. Though this environment had much to offer in terms of cultural diversity, it had little physical space, and Oberman spent his childhood sharing a room with a boarder over his parents' store. Both of his parents had colorful histories: Oberman's father's family of weightlifters ran the local steam bath and pool hall, while his mother possessed remarkable psychic powers. They both worked long hours in the family cafe, leaving Oberman to spend his time on the streets but making sure they got him to the library frequently, and he thus became an avid reader.

As a young teen, Oberman was solitary, self-conscious, and lacking in basic social skills. In an effort to help him overcome his introversion, his mother took him to—of all people—the local butcher, the person Oberman believes to be one of his greatest teachers. Mr. Freedman had a shop down the street from the Oberman store. This short, stocky, homely man had a lisp and thick glasses yet, with confidence and poise, could hold a room full of people captive as he spoke. Mr. Freedman had the young Oberman write and memorize a short speech and present it to him in his living room. Over the months, he taught the boy how to interject appropriate pauses, hand gestures, and other techniques. Oberman's first speech at Toastmasters was rather a flop, but Mr. Freeman remained undaunted. The boy practiced and spoke in front of the Toastmaster audience until they grudgingly applauded. It was Mr. Freedman who gave Oberman his voice.

Adolescence—and working his way through university—brought Oberman an assortment of jobs, including that of a train porter, a door-to-door salesman, a cook, and a factory worker. With the jobs came a period of traveling, first across Canada, and then overseas. The end of these travels saw Oberman back in Winnipeg, though, where he eventually began teaching English at a Jewish high school in the neighborhood of his childhood. In addition to teaching, Oberman wrote, and he still devotes the majority of his time to these two activities.

The White Stone in the Castle Wall has a personal story behind it. Just outside of Toronto stands the Casa Loma, built by Sir Henry Pellat, the rich and powerful magnate of Toronto's electric streetcar and telephone companies. In the philanthropic mindset of the early 1900s, Pellat's gift to the townspeople was to pay one dollar for every stone brought to his castle and chosen by him for construction of a surrounding wall. One dollar then equaled the wages of a ten-hour day. Of the 250,000 rocks in the wall, only one is white. While visiting friends in Toronto and jogging daily around the castle, Oberman began wondering why only one white stone. So he conjured up a story about a Scottish boy's determination to bring the stone to America. The story actually became a legend in Toronto. Of the book, Susan Perren wrote in *Globe and Mail,* "This is a very satisfying work of historical fiction for the young."

In *By the Hanukkah Light,* young Rachel and her grandfather faithfully polish the family's old silver menorah each year as Grandpa retells to his gathered family a story of the Festival of Lights and the Old Testament battle between the Jews and the Syrians. This time, however, he adds his own story—of fighting the Nazis only to return home to find his town destroyed. As if by a miracle, in the devastation, he sees the family's menorah gleaming in the ashes of what was once his home. Rachel vows to tell the story to her own children, passing on tradition and strengthening family ties. Ellen Mandel, reviewing the book for *Holiday Books Roundup,* commented, "Oberman weaves a memorable story around a religious artifact that has survived brutalities and hazards to be lovingly handed down through generations."

The Shaman's Nephew: A Life in the Far North, a story in picture form, was ten years in the making. This is a memoir of Inuit nomad, artist, and traditional hunter Simon Tookoome, coauthor and illustrator of the book. When Oberman was touring the Northwest Territories in 1989 promoting his works, he asked to be housed with a traditional Inuit family and was welcomed into the Tookoome household. Simon Tookoome is one of the last Inuit to hold firmly to his ancestral heritage of living off the land, providing food and clothing for his large family by hunting caribou and seal. Tookoome, a shaman's nephew who speaks no English, asked Oberman to write down the stories of a lifestyle and tradition that has almost disappeared. Michele Landsberg, reviewing the book for the *Toronto Star,* wrote, "Many translators, as well as Tookoome's daughter, worked with the pair as they pierced through layers and layers of difference to get at the heart of Tookoome's amazing narrative and make it accessible to us 'kabloona,' or non-Inuit." Landsberg called Tookoome's illustrations "eerie and captivating," adding what a shame it would have been for her to miss this book. It was only through her membership on the jury for the Fleck Award that she became aware of its importance in the telling of Aboriginal tales.

BIOGRAPHICAL AND CRITICAL SOURCES:

BOOKS

Children's Literature Review, Volume 54, Gale (Detroit, MI), 1999.

PERIODICALS

Booklist, December 15, 1993, p. 750; October 1, 2000, Hazel Rochman, review of *The Wisdom Bird: A Tale of Solomon and Sheba,* p. 362.
Books for Young People, February, 1989, p. 8.
Books in Canada, October, 1985, pp. 21-22; November, 1993, pp. 57-58.

Canadian Book Review Annual, 1999, review of *The Shaman's Nephew: A Life in the Far North,* p. 468.
Children's Book News, spring, 1999, review of *The Always Prayer Shawl,* p. 17.
Globe and Mail, October 28, 1995, Susan Perren, review of *The White Stone in the Castle Wall.*
Holiday Books Roundup, September 1, 1997, Ellen Mandel, review of *By the Hanukkah Light,* p. 32.
Horn Book Guide, spring, 1998, review of *By the Hanukkah Light,* p. 42; spring, 2001, review of *The Wisdom Bird: A Tale of Solomon and Sheba,* p. 46.
Maclean's, November 22, 1999, review of *The Shaman's Nephew.*
Multicultural Review, March, 1998, review of *By the Hanukkah Light.*
New York Times Book Review, December 21, 1997, review of *By the Hanukkah Light,* p. 18.
Quill & Quire, October, 1993, p. 40; January, 1994, p. 36.
Reading Teacher, April, 2001, review of *The Wisdom Bird: A Tale of Solomon and Sheba,* p. 727.
Toronto Star, December 17, 2000, Michele Landsberg, "Finally, a Fresh Look at the Inuit Experience," review of *The Shaman's Nephew.*
Winnipeg Free Press, September, 1993, "Author's Life Is Fodder for Fiction," review of *This Business with Elijah;* November, 1993, Chris Kent, "Family Portraits Are Lovingly Drawn," review of *This Business with Elijah.*

ONLINE

Sheldon Oberman Home Page, http://www.sheldonoberman.com/ (March 20, 2003).

*   *   *

O'BRIEN, Conor Cruise 1917-
(Donat O'Donnell)

PERSONAL: Surname listed in some sources as Cruise O'Brien; born November 3, 1917, in Dublin, Ireland; son of Francis Cruise (a journalist and literary critic) and Katherine (Sheehy) O'Brien; married Christine Foster, 1939 (divorced, 1962); married Maire MacEntee, January 9, 1962; children: Donal, Fedelma, Kathleen, Sean Patrick, Margaret. *Education:* Trinity College, B.A., 1941, Ph.D., 1953. *Hobbies and other interests:* Travel.

Conor Cruise O'Brien

ADDRESSES: Home—Whitewater, Howth Summit, Dublin, Ireland.

CAREER: Entered Irish Civil Service, 1942; Department of Finance, member of staff, 1942-44; Department of External Affairs, member of staff, 1944-61; Irish News Agency, information and cultural section, department head and managing director, 1948-55; Irish Embassy, Paris, France, counselor, 1955-56; United Nations Irish delegate and head, 1955-61, Department of External Affairs, assistant secretary, 1960, secretariat executive staff member, 1961, Secretary-General's representative in Katanga (now Shaba, Zaire), 1961; Dail Eireann, Labour Party member representing Dublin North-East, 1969-77; minister for posts and telegraphs, 1973-77; Republic of Ireland, member of Senate, 1977-79. University of Ghana, vice-chancellor, 1962-65; New York University, Albert Schweitzer chair in the humanities, 1965-69; Nuffield College, Oxford, visiting fellow, 1973-75; University of Dublin, pro-chancellor, 1973—; Dartmouth College, visiting professor of history and Montgomery fellow, 1984-85. Editor-in-chief, *Observer* (London) 1979-81, consultant editor, 1981—; *The Atlantic,* contributing editor, 1986—.

MEMBER: Royal Irish Academy, Royal Society of Literature, Athenaeum Club.

AWARDS, HONORS: D.Litt. from University of Bradford, 1971, University of Ghana, 1974, University of Edinburgh, 1976, University of Nice, 1978, University of Coleraine, 1981, and Queen's University, Belfast, 1984; Valiant for Truth Media Award, 1979.

WRITINGS:

(Under pseudonym Donat O'Donnell) *Maria Cross: Imaginative Patterns in a Group of Modern Catholic Writers,* Oxford University Press (New York, NY), 1952.

Parnell and His Party: 1880-90, Oxford University Press (New York, NY), 1957.

To Katanga and Back: A U.N. Case, Hutchinson (London, England), 1962, Simon and Schuster (New York, NY), 1963.

Conflicting Concepts of the United Nations, Leeds University Press (Leeds, England), 1964.

Writers and Politics (essays), Pantheon (New York, NY), 1965.

(With Northrop Frye and Stuart Hampshire) *The Morality of Scholarship,* edited by Max Black, Cornell University Press (New York, NY), 1967.

The United Nations: Sacred Drama, illustrated by Feliks Topolski, Simon and Schuster (New York, NY), 1968.

Conor Cruise O'Brien Introduces Ireland, edited by Owen Dudley Edwards, Deutsch (London, England), 1969, McGraw-Hill (New York, NY), 1970.

Albert Camus of Europe and Africa, Viking (New York, NY), 1970, published as *Camus,* Fontana (London, England), 1970.

(With wife, Maire MacEntee O'Brien) *The Story of Ireland,* Viking (New York, NY), 1972, published as *A Concise History of Ireland,* Thames and Hudson (London, England), 1972.

The Suspecting Glance, Faber and Faber (London, England), 1972.

States of Ireland, Pantheon (New York, NY), 1972.

Herod: Reflections on Political Violence, Hutchinson (London, England), 1978.

(With Cark Bonham Carter) *Resolving Racial Conflict in South Africa: Some Outside Views,* edited by David Thomas, South African Institute of Race Relations (Johannesburg, South Africa), 1979.

Neighbours: Four Lectures, edited by Thomas Pakenham, Faber and Faber (Boston, MA), 1980.

The Press and the World, Birkbeck College (London, England), 1980.

Edmund Burke: Master of English, English Association, University of Leicester (Leicester, England), 1981.

Religion and Politics, New University of Ulster (Ireland), 1984.

The Siege: The Saga of Israel and Zionism, Simon and Schuster (New York, NY), 1986.

Passion and Cunning: Essays on Nationalism, Terrorism and Revolution, Simon and Schuster (New York, NY), 1988.

God Land: Reflections on Religion and Nationalism, Harvard University Press (Cambridge, MA), 1988.

The Great Melody: A Thematic Biography of Edmund Burke, University of Chicago Press (Chicago, IL), 1993.

Conor Cruise O'Brien: An Anthology, selections by Donald H. Akenson, Cornell University Press (Ithaca, NY), 1994.

Ancestral Voices: Religion and Nationalism in Ireland, Poolbeg (Dublin, Ireland), 1994, University Press of Chicago (Chicago, IL), 1995.

On the Eve of the Millennium: The Future of Democracy through an Age of Unreason, Free Press (New York, NY), 1995.

The Long Affair: Thomas Jefferson and the French Revolution, 1785-1800, University of Chicago Press (Chicago, IL), 1996.

Ideas Matter: Essays in Honour of Conor Cruise O'Brien, (selected works), edited by Richard English and Joseph Morrison, Poolbeg (Dublin, Ireland), 1998, University Press of America (Lanham, MD), 2000.

Memoir: My Life and Themes, Poolbeg (Dublin, Ireland), 1998, Cooper Square (New York, NY), 2000.

EDITOR

The Shaping of Modern Ireland, University of Toronto Press (Toronto, Canada), 1960.

Edmund Burke, *Reflections on the Revolution in France,* Penguin (New York, NY), 1969.

(With William Dean Vanech) *Power and Consciousness,* New York University Press (New York, NY), 1969.

CONTRIBUTOR

Irving Howe, editor, *The Idea of the Modern in Literature and the Arts,* Horizon Press (New York, NY), 1968.

Arthur I. Blaustein and R. R. Woock, editors, *Man against Poverty: World War III,* introduction by John W. Gardner, Random House (New York, NY), 1968.

George A. White and C. H. Newman, editors, *Literature in Revolution,* Henry Holt (New York, NY), 1972.

Teilhard de Chardin: In Quest of the Perfection of Man, Fairleigh Dickinson University Press (Madison, NJ), 1973.

Speeches Delivered at the 35th Annual Dinner of the Anglo-Israel Association, Anglo-Israel Association (London, England), 1983.

(Author of foreword) Andrew Malraux, *The Walnut Trees of Altenburg,* University of Chicago Press (Chicago, IL), 1992.

PLAYS

King Herod Explains, produced in Dublin, Ireland, 1969.

Murderous Angels: A Political Tragedy and Comedy in Black and White (produced in Los Angeles and New York City, 1970), Little, Brown (Boston MA), 1968.

OTHER

Contributor of articles to periodicals, including *Atlantic, Nation, New Statesman,* and *Saturday Review.*

SIDELIGHTS: Conor Cruise O'Brien is a distinguished and controversial literary critic, diplomat, dramatist, biographer, historian, and politician. He rose to world prominence as Irish delegate to the United Nations (U.N.) and as special representative of U.N. Secretary-General Dag Hammarskjold. A *New Statesman* writer stated that "In so far as a civil servant can, [O'Brien] became a minor national hero; the Irish independent, asserting his country's independence along with his own." The article went on to describe O'Brien as "a modern version of that nineteenth-century radical phenomenon, the Only White Man the Natives Trust."

It has been suggested that Hammarskjold's knowledge of and admiration for *Maria Cross,* a volume of critical essays that O'Brien published in 1952 under the pseudonym of Donat O'Donnell, was influential in his decision to ask O'Brien to serve on his executive staff.

Under Hammarskjold, O'Brien was assigned to oversee U.N. operations at Katanga in the Congo in 1961, a time of violent political upheavals. Later that year he was relieved of these duties at his own request and resigned from the foreign service altogether. Following his resignation, O'Brien made public his intention to publish a book about the difficulties he had encountered in the service of the U.N. in the Congo. Shortly thereafter, he received a letter from then acting Secretary-General U Thant advising him that unauthorized disclosure of U.N. affairs was prohibited by regulation. Thant's letter serves as the preface of *To Katanga and Back,* an autobiographical narrative of the crisis in the Congo, which O'Brien published in 1963 despite U.N. censure.

Although his ties with the U.N. were officially broken, O'Brien remained concerned with the intricate workings of the organization. In *The United Nations: Sacred Drama,* O'Brien portrays the U.N. as both temple and stage, with the U.N. Secretary-General serving as a kind of high priest with a spiritual authority. As John Osborne explained in the *New Republic,* "A profanation occurs . . . when [the Secretary-General] 'steps down from the religious level of politics, to the level of applied politics.'" Critic Albert Bremel commented favorably on O'Brien's conception of the dramatic aspects of the U.N. "Theater is an art. If it is to be good theater, it requires the exercise of imagination," he noted in the *New York Times Book Review.* "That is what Mr. O'Brien is really concerned with. Imaginative participants will recognize (some have already recognized) the U.N. as a superb arena for dramatizing the threats to survival."

As an extension of his conception of the U.N. as drama, O'Brien drew on his experiences in Katanga to write the play *Murderous Angels: A Political Tragedy and Comedy in Black and White.* The play provoked controversy even before it was staged due to O'Brien's reworking of historical events in the Congo. The author did not intend *Murderous Angels* to be viewed as a documentary drama or as 'theatre of fact,' but rather as a tragedy, as its subtitle implies. "While the historian must hesitate, lacking absolute proof, the dramatist may present the hypothesis which he finds most convincing," O'Brien writes as an introduction to his work, justifying his dramatic license.

In *States of Ireland,* O'Brien again courts controversy through his views on the Irish conflict in which he was actively involved as a left-wing Irish Labour Party

deputy. Wrote Vivian Mercier in the *Nation,* "The most unpopular statement in the whole book is probably this: 'While two communities are as bitterly antagonistic as are Catholics and Protestants [in Northern Ireland] now, it is not merely futile but actually mischievous to talk about uniting Ireland.' What he means is that in a united Ireland Catholics would outnumber Protestants by at least three to one." In *States of Ireland,* O'Brien argues that the two distinct Catholic and Protestant communities are a reality, the existence of which makes any goal of Irish unification impractical, if not impossible. O'Brien, whose maternal ancestors were Catholic and whose first wife, Christine Foster, was a Protestant, examines the situation from both a historical and an autobiographical perspective. "To Conor," Mercier observed, "Irish history came first of all as the history of his family."

A reviewer for the *Times Literary Supplement* described the contents of *States of Ireland* as sometimes confusing because of the breadth of O'Brien's undertaking: "some general history, fragments of literary criticism, spasms of autobiography, an extract from Dr. Cruise O'Brien's political diary for the ominous summer of 1970, an extended account of the developing situation in Northern Ireland and, by way of appendix, a splendid diatribe against Sinn Fein which was intended to flatten the President of that organization . . . in public debate and by all accounts did just that." In the *New York Review of Books,* John Horgan summed up a widely held view of what *States of Ireland* achieved: "Dr. O'Brien's great contribution to the Irish situation can be easily and quickly stated: he has forced people to face up to the fact that the tradition of the majority of people living in Ireland is a sectarian and a nationalist one, and that the link between its sectarian and its nationalist aspects will not be dissolved simply by wishful thinking."

Several reviewers of *The Siege: The Saga of Israel and Zionism* have echoed the same question: Why would an Irish historian choose to write the history of Zionism, from its pre-Herzl days to the state of Israel in the post-Begin era? "The answer," noted Walter Reich in the *Washington Post Book World,* "lies in [O'Brien's] past—in his identity as a member of a nationality, Irish Catholic, that has experienced stigmatization, and in his identity as the son of a lapsed Catholic growing up in a southern Irish sea of disapproving believers. These identities, he says, helped him form a bond with the story of a people whose stigmatization has been profound and whose experience with disapproval has been catastrophic."

At least one reviewer was less convinced about O'Brien's qualifications for the task. Milton Viorst, writing in the *Chicago Tribune Book World,* complained that "O'Brien is an Irishman, which scarcely disqualifies him from writing about Jews, but he comes to the subject as a researcher, with no discernible 'feel.'" On the other hand, in the *New Republic* Walter Laqueur argued that O'Brien's critical distance proves an advantage. He noted, "But his vantage point—he is the detached but friendly outsider—gives his work a freshness lacking in most of the committed literature on the subject." Although Patrick Seale in the *Spectator* disagreed with O'Brien's position, he praised O'Brien's ability as a writer: "He is almost incapable of writing a dull sentence. He is also an immensely persuasive advocate, clear, master of his sources, able to marshall his arguments, skilled at demolishing his adversaries with slur and innuendo." And Abba Eban, who reviewed *The Siege* in the *Los Angeles Times Book Review,* noted that the strengths of the work reflect well on its author. The book, Eban observed, "bears the mark of a restless, original idiosyncratic mind and—more surprisingly—a talent for the patient toil required by meticulous research."

On the Eve of the Millennium: The Future of Democracy through an Age of Unreason, is a collection of twenty-two lectures given at the University of Toronto's Massey College and broadcast by Canadian radio in 1994. These lectures address religion, spirituality, diversity, nationalism, and cultural and political concerns from influential individuals such as Aleksandr Solzhenitzyn, Ivan Illich, Pierre Trudeau, Daniel Boorstin, David Rockefeller, Nelson Mandella, Francois Mitterrand, and Shimon Peres.

Conor Cruise O'Brien: An Anthology begins with an in-depth account from Donald Harman Akenson of O'Brien's ancestral heritage, "searching for reasons why his subject is the most unusual yet most appropriate critic of Irish life," explained Gerard J. Russello in *Commonweal.* "O'Brien's roots lie deep in Irish history," continued Russello. "An eighteenth-century ancestor, Father Nicholas Sheehy, was martyred for the cause of an independent Ireland, and later O'Brien's maternal grandfather broke with a disgraced Parnell in the 'Committee Room 15.'" On a literary note—as James Carroll noted in his *New York Times* review of

Memoir: My Life and Themes—James Joyce often frequented the Sheehy household, memorializing O'Brien's mother, Kathleen Sheehy, in *The Dead,* and giving O'Brien's grandmother a mention in *Ulysses.* Also, O'Brien's father knew Yeats. In all, his familial background gave him a firm foundation for his political and literary careers. Carroll commented, "In *Memoir: My Life and Themes,* Conor Cruise O'Brien retraces what must rank as one of the most remarkable lives of the twentieth century. A man of eccentric brilliance . . . And each manifestation [of his career] was marked by a contentiousness that seems to have resulted partly from his commitment to principle and partly from a personality rooted in the contradictions of Irish history."

From an interview with Harry Kreisler that appears on the University of California at Berkeley Web site, one gets a brief glimpse at those contradictions and its effect on O'Brien's career. His mother was a strong Irish Catholic; his father (whom O'Brien—at the age of ten—watched die) was an agnostic who disapproved of Catholic education. Thus, O'Brien (himself an agnostic) attended a Protestant school. "One third of the pupils were people of Catholic origin like myself, but somewhat detached from that background," O'Brien commented to Kreisler. "One third were Protestants, somewhat disoriented in the new Catholic-dominated state and feeling nervous. And one third were Jews who had their own sensitivities there. So we were all a bit disoriented, a bit hypertensive, which I think is good in some ways, because it stimulates thought. When we are educated in an entirely homogeneous background, we simply inhale a comprehensive but possibly deceptive body of thought, but in the kind of [school] I was brought up in you have to start thinking for yourself, and we all did in different ways."

During the interview, Kreisler asked if, as a politician and a writer, O'Brien were ever torn between rationality and emotions about specific issues. O'Brien replied, "I would take that as a constant in people who write at all about social and political issues. You have to think about the issues, but the feelings precede the thoughts as it were, and then, of course, are qualified by the thoughts. There's a dialectic process going on the whole time. I'm very conscious about that. I'm not someone who could claim that I've been consistent in all things in my life, but I think I've been consistent in trying to think things through and then qualify the thinking in light of experience and moving along from there."

When asked by Kreisler about his thoughts on the appropriate role of intellectuals in the political arena, O'Brien commented, "I think the intellectual [to function honestly] either will have to be on the margin of actual practical politics or, having been in practical politics, as is my case, will have to move to the margin or beyond it. Because if you're immersed in politics you can't, as I found, tell the truth without hesitation. . . . [The function of the intellectual should be] to think as best they can and say what they think they find, and modify that when they find the need to do it, not because of pressure but because of their own view of developing events. I think the intellectual in relation to politics is something like the Greek chorus, outside the action but telling you quite a lot about the action."

BIOGRAPHICAL AND CRITICAL SOURCES:

BOOKS

Hughes, Catherine, *Plays, Politics, and Polemics,* Drama Book Specialist Publications (New York, NY), 1973.

O'Brien, Conor Cruise, *Murderous Angels: A Political Tragedy and Comedy in Black and White,* Little, Brown (Boston, MA), 1968.

Weightman, John, *The Concept of the Avant-Garde: Explorations in Modernism,* Library Press (La Salle, IL), 1973.

PERIODICALS

Booklist, December 1, 1995, Mary Carroll, review of *On the Eve of the Millennium: The Future of Democracy through an Age of Unreason,* p. 606.

Chicago Tribune Book World, March 9, 1986, p. 39.

Christianity Today, April 29, 1996, Bruce Barron, review of *On the Eve of the Millennium,* p. 34.

Commentary, September, 1965.

Commonweal, December 2, 1988; March 24, 1995, Gerard J. Russello, review of *Conor Cruise O'Brien: An Anthology,* p. 23.

Economist, December 6, 1997, "A War of Myth and Memory," review of *The Long Affair: Thomas Jefferson and the French Revolution, 1785-1800,* p. 95.

Guardian Weekly, April 27, 1986; March 27, 1988, p. 28; December 4, 1988.

History Today, May, 1997, Stuart Andrews, review of *The Long Affair,* p. 53.

Listener, May 30, 1968.

Los Angeles Times Book Review, March 16, 1986.

Nation, December 20, 1965, p. 502; February 23, 1970; March 27, 1972; March 12, 1973; May 26, 1997, Benjamin Schwartz, review of *The Long Affair,* p. 29.

National Review, April 8, 1996, John Gray, review of *On the Eve of the Millennium,* p. 53.

New Republic, September 11, 1965; September 7, 1968; March 3, 1986; September 12, 1988; March 10, 1997, Sean Wilentz, review of *The Long Affair,* p. 32.

New Statesman, December 6, 1968.

Newsweek, October 17, 1966; March 24, 1986.

New York Review of Books, September 8, 1966; July 31, 1969; May 3, 1973.

New York Times, September 15, 1961; February 25, 1986; May 13, 1986; February 22, 1991; November 12, 1995, Gertrude Himmelfarb, "Slouching toward the Apocalypse," review of *On the Eve of the Millennium;* December 31, 1995, Colm Toibin, "The Blood of Martyrs," review of *Ancestral Voices: Religion and Nationalism in Ireland;* September 10, 2000, James Carroll, "Against the Tide," review of *Memoir: My Life and Themes,* p. 45.

New York Times Book Review, October 31, 1965; August 4, 1968; February 11, 1973; March 2, 1986; February 15, 1987, p. 38; July 24, 1988.

Observer (London), January 26, 1969; June 1, 1986; July 20, 1986; November 30, 1986; February 28, 1988, p. 26; March 13, 1988, p. 42; February 2, 1990.

Partisan Review, number 2, 1988.

Spectator, June 17, 1978; January 3, 1981; June 14, 1986; December 6, 1986, p. 32; March 12, 1988; May 7, 1988.

Time, April 21, 1986.

Times Educational Supplement, June 10, 1988.

Times Literary Supplement, December 23, 1965; June 27, 1968; July 17, 1969; January 29, 1970; July 7, 1972; November 10, 1972; August 11, 1978; November 14, 1980; October 10, 1986; March 18, 1988, p. 298; August 5, 1988; April 13, 1990.

Washington Post Book World, February 16, 1986, p. 1; October 23, 1988, p. 13; February 25, 1990.

ONLINE

University of California at Berkeley Web site, http://globetrotter.berkeley.edu/ (April 4, 2000), Harry

Kreisler, "The Power of Ideas: Conversation with Conor Cruise O'Brien, Irish Statesman and Writer." *

*   *   *

O'CONNOR, Ulick 1928-

PERSONAL: Born October 12, 1928, in Dublin, Ireland; son of Matthew P. (a dean of Royal College of Surgeons) and Eileen (Murphy) Harris-O'Connor. *Education:* National University of Ireland, B.A.; King's Inns, Dublin, Barrister-at-Law; Loyola University, New Orleans, LA, Diploma in Dramatic Literature. *Religion:* Roman Catholic.

ADDRESSES: Home and office—15 Fairfield Park, Rathgar, Dublin, Ireland. *Agent*—(books) Howard Buck Agency, 145 East 52nd St., New York, NY 10022; (lectures) Keedick Lecture Bureau, Inc., 475 Fifth Ave., New York, NY 10017.

CAREER: Has written for *Sunday Independent,* Dublin, Ireland, *Observer,* London, England, and *Times,* London. Lecturer on Irish literary renaissance in Stockholm, Paris, and Rome. Lecturer and reader at poetry recitals at women's clubs and colleges in United States, 1965—.

MEMBER: Wanderer's Club, Pipers Club (both Dublin).

WRITINGS:

Poems, Sceptre Press (Bedfordshire, England), 1957.

The Gresham Hotel, 1865-1965, Guy & Co. (Cork, Ireland), 1964.

James Joyce and Oliver St. John Gogarty: A Famous Friendship, Texas Quarterly, University of Texas Press (Austin, TX), 1960.

The Times I've Seen: Oliver St. John Gogarty—A Biography, Obolensky (New York, NY), 1964, published as *Oliver St. John Gogarty: A Poet and His Times,* J. Cape (London, England), 1964.

Sputnik and Other Poems, Devin (New York, NY), 1967.

Ulick O'Connor

Travels with Ulick, Mercier Press (Dublin, Ireland), 1967.

(Editor) *The Joyce We Knew: Memoirs by Eugene Sheehy and Others,* Mercier Press (Dublin, Ireland), 1967.

The Dark Lovers (play), first produced in Dublin, Ireland, 1968.

Brendan Behan (biography), Hamish Hamilton (London, England), 1970, published as *Brendan,* Prentice-Hall (Paramus, NJ), 1971.

(Editor) *The Yeats We Knew,* British Book Center (New York, NY), 1971.

Life Styles (poetry), Humanities (Boston, MA), 1973.

The Troubles: Ireland, 1912-1922, Bobbs-Merrill (Indianapolis, IN), 1975, published as *A Terrible Beauty Is Born: Irish Troubles, 1912-1922,* Hamish Hamilton (London, England), 1975.

The Fitzwilliam Story, 1877-1977, Fitzwilliam Tennis Club, 1977.

Three Noh Plays (contains *The Grand Inquisitor, Submarine,* and *Deirdre*), Wolfhound Press (Dublin, Ireland), 1980.

Celtic Dawn: A Portrait of the Irish Literary Renaissance, Hamish Hamilton (London, England), 1984.

Sport Is My Lifeline: Essays from the Sunday Times, Pelham Books (London, England), 1984.

All the Olympians: A Biographical Portrait of the Irish Literary Renaissance, Atheneum (New York, NY), 1984.

All Things Counter, Dedalus (Dublin, Ireland), 1986.

Brian Friel: Crisis and Commitment: The Writer and Northern Ireland, Elo Publications (Dublin, Ireland), 1989.

The Yeats Companion, Pavilion (London, England), 1990.

Biographers and the Art of Biography, Wolfhound Press (Dublin, Ireland), 1991.

One Is Animate, Beaver Row Press (Dublin, Ireland), 1992.

Executions, Brandon (Dingle, Ireland), 1992.

Irish Tales and Sagas, Town House (Dublin, Ireland), 1993.

(Editor) *The Campbell Companion: The Best of Patrick Campbell,* Pavilion (London, England), 1994.

(Translator) *Poems of the Damned: Charles Baudelaire's Les Fleurs du Mal—The Flowers of Evil,* Wolfhound Press (Dublin, Ireland), 1995.

Michael Collins and the Troubles: The Struggle for Irish Freedom, 1912-1922, Norton (New York, NY), 1996.

The Ulick O'Connor Diaries, 1970-1981: A Cavalier Irishman, John Murray (London, England), 2001.

Also author of *Irish Liberation* and of two recordings, "An Evening with Oliver Gogarty" and "Poems of the Insurrection," both Mercier Press. Contributor to *Spectator, Listener, Theatre Arts,* and other periodicals.

SIDELIGHTS: With more than two dozen works to his credit, Irish author Ulick O'Connor has spent much of his career chronicling the tumultuous history of his Irish homeland. Born October 12, 1928, in Dublin, O'Connor has gained recognition in the literary world for his biographies of Brendan Behan, Oliver St. John Gogarty, and Michael Collins, all leading figures in Ireland's struggle for independence from British rule.

For example, in *Michael Collins and the Troubles: The Struggle for Irish Freedom, 1912-1922,* O'Connor examined the life of Collins, who played an instrumental role in Ireland's bloody resistance against the British during the early years of the twentieth century.

Culling information from a variety of sources, including historical archives and personal interviews with some of Collins's contemporaries, O'Connor presented readers with an array of previously unknown information about the man many people feel was integral to Irish independence. O'Connor is also well known for his book *Celtic Dawn,* in which he examined the Irish literary renaissance that took place at the end of the nineteenth century. Some critics feel the work is among his most important contributions.

An impressive athlete in his younger days, O'Connor was the British universities boxing champion in 1950 and held the Irish native record in pole vault, 1951-55. In 2001, O'Connor published an autobiographical work, titled *The Ulick O'Connor Diaries, 1970-1981: A Cavalier Irishman.* The book chronicles probably the most important period of O'Connor's career. Known to be brash, both as a person and a writer, O'Connor discusses many aspects of his life in the book, both professional and personal.

Between 1970 and 1981 O'Connor completed his acclaimed biographies of Behan and Gogarty and he began writing *Celtic Dawn.* Also during this time O'Connor became a household name in Ireland, largely because of his regular appearances on a popular television program called the *Late Late Show.* He discusses these experiences, as well as his forays to such places as New York City, Oslo, and Stockholm. However, some literary critics felt the book's importance was due to O'Connor's personal accounts of the political battles between Unionists and Nationalists in Northern Ireland. According to Toby Barnard, who reviewed the book for the *Times Literary Supplement,* the work has "permanent historical value." Liam Fay of the *Sunday Times* commented on O'Connor's brash writing style that reminded him of an earlier era. "The irascible and indignant writer is a throwback to the days before political correctness and sexual equality," Fay wrote. While he enjoyed certain aspects of the book, Fay felt it showed O'Connor to be overly conceited and self-centered. "What strikes one about O'Connor's diaries . . . is not so much his fearless truth telling as his self-absorption," Fay wrote. "There's barely a trace of even the mildest self-mockery anywhere in the book and little or no self-doubt. Virtually every anecdote seems to have been selected to bathe the author in a positive and often positively heroic light."

BIOGRAPHICAL AND CRITICAL SOURCES:

PERIODICALS

Economist, August 16, 1975.
New Republic, March 27, 1976.
New York Times Book Review, April 25, 1971; June 6, 1971.
Observer Review, July 26, 1970.
Plays and Players, October, 1970.
Saturday Review, August 7, 1976.
Sunday Times, July 1, 2001, p. 6; November 18, 2001, p. 40.
Times Literary Supplement, July 31, 1970; February 28, 1976; September 19, 1980; August 17, 2001, p. 26.
Variety, June 9, 1971.*

* * *

ODERMAN, Stuart (Douglas) 1940-

PERSONAL: Born February 7, 1940, in Elizabeth, NJ; son of Abraham D. (in sales) and Helen (Greenwald) Oderman; married Janet Sovey (an actor), July 18, 1983. *Education:* Attended Kean College of New Jersey, 1961; Columbia University, B.A., 1963; State University of New York College at New Paltz, M.A., 1967.

ADDRESSES: Home—243 South Harrison St., Apt. 9H, East Orange, NJ 07018.

CAREER: Silent film pianist, 1959—, including work at Museum of Modern Art, Public Theater, and New School for Social Research, all in New York, NY; Royal British Columbia Museum, Vancouver; Athens Concert Hall, Athens, Greece; and for Public Broadcasting Service television series.

WRITINGS:

Roscoe "Fatty" Arbuckle, McFarland (Jefferson, NC), 1994.
Lillian Gish, McFarland (Jefferson, NC), 2000.

Author of five plays produced off-Broadway. Composer for the television series *Laurel and Hardy Laughtunes,* 1976; composer for a documentary film about Charlie Chaplin, 1965. Contributor of articles, stories, and reviews to periodicals, including *Entertaining Yesteryear, Films in Review,* and *Films of the Golden Age.*

WORK IN PROGRESS: Anthology of silent film actor's interviews.

SIDELIGHTS: Stuart Oderman told *CA:* "I became interested in playing the piano for silent films in 1954, as a fourteen-year-old student cutting high school classes in Newark to attend Wednesday matinees at the theater. When I couldn't get the affordable second balcony seat, I would go to the Museum of Modern Art, where they would show silent films. On one of these occasions, I met Lillian Gish, and she introduced me to the museum's pianist, Arthur Kleiner. He became my teacher, while Miss Gish remained a constant source of encouragement for the next thirty-nine years, until her passing in 1993.

"I have worked with other silent film stars, including Gloria Swanson, Aileen Pringle, and Ann Pennington. I began recording my reminiscences of them when a television director said I would be the last person to hear them 'talk about the old days,' that I would be recording a history of an era that would otherwise be forgotten.

"For nearly forty-two years I have performed all over the United States and in England and Greece. As an active silent film pianist, I am the last of a dying breed."

* * *

O'DONNELL, Donat
    See O'BRIEN, Conor Cruise

* * *

O'DWYER, Tess 1966-

PERSONAL: Born June 2, 1966, in Red Bank, NJ; daughter of J. F. (a contractor) and Chung Soon (an artist; maiden name, Fwhang) O'Dwyer. *Education:* Rutgers University, M.A., 1990. *Religion:* Roman Catholic. *Hobbies and other interests:* Painting, fiction.

ADDRESSES: Home—187 Heyers Mill Rd., Colts Neck, New Jersey 07722.

CAREER: Freelance translator (Spanish literature), 1990—.

MEMBER: Modern Language Association, Poetry Society of America, Phi Beta Kappa, Phi Sigma Iota, Salmagundi Club.

AWARDS, HONORS: Awards from Columbia University's Translation Center and from Salmagundi Club.

WRITINGS:

(Translator) Giannina Braschi, *Empire of Dreams* (poems and fiction), Yale University Press (New Haven, CT), 1994.
(Translator) Alberto Blest Gana, *Martin Rivas* (novel), Oxford University Press, 2000.

Contributor of translations to periodicals.

WORK IN PROGRESS: Translating *Yo-Yo Boing,* a bilingual novel by Giannina Braschi for Latin American Literary Press.

SIDELIGHTS: Tess O'Dwyer told *CA:* "The only way to know precisely what an author means is to become the author. The translator becomes the author in the same way that an actor becomes the character. Memorizing the lines in Spanish and reciting the words as if they were my own, I traded my voice for the dramatic voices of the lyric 'I,' whose adventures and emotional states vary from book to book in *Empire of Dreams.* Swapping names, ages, nationalities, and genders, Giannina Braschi's characters are a cast of actors playing the roles of other characters. As a translator, I tried out for every part.

"I played the writer Giannina Braschi, who played the writer Mariquita Samper, who played the writer Berta Singerman and an array of other characters. With red-dyed hair, surgically implanted freckles, and a gold tooth, I especially enjoyed the role of Drag Queen. But the most gratifying moment was when I shot the narrator of the Latin American Boom, who kept rewriting my diary. Once he was out of the way, my thoughts flowed freely onto the pages. By the end of *Empire of Dreams,* I had lived so many lives that I no longer felt I was a character. I was all of them and, therefore, the author herself. I fancied myself annoyed that Giannina had translated the work into Spanish before I had the chance to write it in English! I thought of all my transformations. Had they been in vain? I became the actor who became the character who became the author. Now what would I become? The translator. And how was I to do it? With the respect that great literature deserves."

* * *

OFFNER, Arnold A. 1937-

PERSONAL: Born September 6, 1937, in Brooklyn, NY; son of Samuel (a salesman) and Helen (Wolowitz) Offner; married Ellen Siegel (a freelance editor), April 22, 1962; children: two. *Education:* Columbia University, B.A., 1959; Indiana University, M.A., 1960, Ph.D., 1964. *Religion:* Jewish. *Hobbies and other interests:* History of U.S. foreign policy, twentieth-century international relations, and American political history.

ADDRESSES: Office—Department of History, Lafayette College, Easton, PA 18042. *E-mail*—offnera@lafvax.lafayette.edu.

CAREER: Syracuse University, Syracuse, NY, instructor, 1963-65, assistant professor of history, 1965-68; Boston University, Boston, MA, associate professor, 1968-73, professor of history, 1973-1991; Lafayette College, professor of history, history department head, 1991—.

MEMBER: American Historical Association, Organization of American Historians, Society for Historians of American Foreign Relations.

AWARDS, HONORS: George P. Hammond Essay Award, Phi Alpha Theta and *Historian* (journal), 1961, for essay on William E. Dodd; American Council of Learned Societies grants-in-aid, 1967, 1969; Phi Alpha Theta National Book Award, 1969, for *American Appeasement: United States Foreign Policy and Ger-*

many, 1933-38; National Endowment for the Humanities summer stipend, 1969; American Philosophical Society research grant, 1977.

WRITINGS:

(Contributor) W. B. Hamilton and others, *A Decade of the Commonwealth, 1955-64,* Duke University Press (Durham, NC), 1966.

American Appeasement: United States Foreign Policy and Germany, 1933-1938, Belknap Press of Harvard University (Cambridge, MA), 1969.

(Editor and compiler) *America and the Origins of World War II, 1933-1941,* Houghton Mifflin (Boston, MA), 1971.

The Origins of the Second World War: American Foreign Policy and World Politics, 1917-1941, Praeger (New York, NY), 1975.

(Editor, with Theodore A. Wilson) *Victory in Europe, 1945: From World War to Cold War,* University Press of Kansas (Lawrence, KS), 2000.

"Another Such Victory": President Truman and the Cold War, 1945-1953, Stanford University Press (Stanford, CA), 2002.

Contributor of essays to numerous anthologies such as *Franklin D. Roosevelt: His Life and Times, The Fascist Challenge and the Policy of Appeasement,* and *America and the Germans: An Assessment of a 300 Year History.* Contributor of articles to many journals, including *Boston University Journal, Boston University Literary Currents, The Philadelphia Inquirer, Diplomatic History,* and *Journal of American History.*

SIDELIGHTS: History professor and scholar Arnold Offner has lectured at colleges, universities, symposiums, and conferences around the nation and in other countries. He was a featured commentator for WBZ-T, Boston's "For Kids Only" on the Vietnam War in 1974, and on a British Broadcasting Corporation documentary film "The Road to War, 1917-1941" in 1987. Offner combines his two professions—teaching and writing—in a unique manner: In the preface of *"Another Such Victory": President Truman and the Cold War, 1945- 1953,* Offner explains how when he compliments two former students for their "great help in searching out and assessing materials and serving as highly interactive sounding boards for my ideas." In a press release for a lecture at the Woodrow Wilson Center for International Studies and aired on C-Span2's "Book TV," David J. Reynolds quotes Offner as saying, "My research has an enormous impact in the classroom. I am unequivocal in my belief that a good research program feeds dramatically into teaching. They're not conflicting, but complementary, interactive, and rewarding in both directions."

"Another Such Victory" is a revisionist account of Harry Truman's presidential policies, particularly regarding relations with the Soviet Union and China. Reynolds commented that Offner's book "sharply challenges the prevailing view of historians who have uncritically praised Truman for repulsing the Soviet Union." Reynolds noted the book is based on extensive research, complemented by information that has become available since the end of the Cold War. "The book demonstrates," said Reynolds, "how Truman's simplistic analogies, exaggerated beliefs in U.S. supremacy and limited grasp of world affairs exacerbated conflicts with the Soviet Union and the People's Republic of China." Reynolds quoted Offner as commenting: "It's the duty of the historian to look behind the Fourth of July speeches and rhetoric. That doesn't negate the constructive things that have been accomplished, but it looks at the prices paid. The question is whether there were better ways of accomplishing the same objectives that would have resulted in less cost and conflict."

While a critic for *Publishers Weekly* called the book a "cramped assessment of foreign policy during Truman's watch," Karl Helicher, reviewing the book for *Library Journal,* wrote, "This excellent revisionist account . . . is enthusiastically recommended for academic diplomatic history collections."

As coeditors of *Victory in Europe, 1945: From World War to Cold War,* Offner and Theodore Wilson compiled an impressive collection of essays from a conference held in 1995 at the University of Kansas. There, a distinguished gathering of experts (including the editors) on international affairs, historians, and eye witnesses reassessed questions surrounding the end of World War II—a war that left Europe devastated, with 35 million dead, and the remaining population facing extreme economic difficulties. *Victory in Europe* offers a case study in war termination that examines choices made and opportunities lost as it considers the transition from coalition to cooperation to mutual suspicion in the face of new political realities.

BIOGRAPHICAL AND CRITICAL SOURCES:

PERIODICALS

History: Review of New Books, spring, 2001, review of *Victory in Europe, 1945: From World War to Cold War,* p. 117.
Library Journal, March 1, 2002, Karl Helicher, review of *"Another Such Victory": President Truman and the Cold War, 1945-1953,* p. 118.
Publishers Weekly, February 18, 2002, review of *"Another Such Victory,"* p. 86.

ONLINE

Lafayette College Web site, http://www.lafayette.edu/ (July 1, 2002), David J. Reynolds, "Lafayette History Professor Arnold Offner Authors Major New Book Reassessing Foreign Policy of President Harry Truman."*

Whitney Otto

*   *   *

OTTO, Whitney 1955-

PERSONAL: Born March 5, 1955, in Burbank, CA; daughter of William B., Sr. (an electrical engineer) and Constance D. Vambert (a professional public speaker; maiden name, di Silvestro) Otto; married John A. Riley, December 8, 1991; children: Samuel Morganfield Riley. *Education:* Attended Raymond College, University of the Pacific, 1973-74, and San Diego State University, 1974-75; University of California, Irvine, B.A., 1987, M.F.A., 1990. *Politics:* "Yes. Predictably liberal." *Hobbies and other interests:* Making boxes and screens.

ADDRESSES: Agent—Joy Harris, Robert Lantz-Joy Harris Literary Agency, 156 Fifth Ave., New York, NY 10010.

CAREER: Novelist and educator. University of California, Irvine, member of staff, 1975-78, instructor in creative writing and composition, 1987-89; bookkeeper in San Francisco, CA, 1980-86; Irvine Valley College, instructor in composition, 1990.

MEMBER: PEN.

AWARDS, HONORS: Art Siedenbaum Award nomination for first novel, *Los Angeles Times,* 1990, for *How to Make an American Quilt.*

WRITINGS:

How to Make an American Quilt (novel), Villard Books (New York, NY), 1991.
Now You See Her (novel), Villard Books (New York, NY), 1994.
The Passion Dream Book (novel), Harper (New York, NY), 1997.
(Contributor of photographs, drawings, and essays) Margret Aldrich, editor, *This Old Quilt: A Heartwarming Celebration of Quilts and Quilting Memories,* Voyageur Press (Stillwater, MN), 2001.
A Collection of Beauties at the Height of Their Popularity (novel), Random House (New York, NY), 2002.

ADAPTATIONS: How to Make an American Quilt was adapted as an audiobook read by Judith Ivey, Random Audio, 1992, and was adapted as a film starring Winona Ryder; *Now You See Her* was adapted as an audiobook, 1995.

SIDELIGHTS: While working toward her Master of Fine Arts degree at the University of California at Irvine, Whitney Otto wrote a short story that used the practice of quilting as a metaphor for events in the lives of its characters. On the advice of Donald Heiney, a university faculty member and writer, she eventually expanded the work into a novel, *How to Make an American Quilt.* The narrative relates the stories of a group of women that regularly meets in the small California town of Grasse—just outside Bakersfield—to sew. Their current project involves making a quilt that they intend to give as a wedding present to Finn Bennett-Dodd, the twenty-six-year-old woman who narrates the story. Finn's grandmother, Hy Dodd, and great aunt, Glady Joe Cleary, are among members of the quilting circle who tell about their marriages, their relationships with family and friends, and their connections to one another in separate chapters of the novel. Interspersed between each story are bits of information about the history of quilting and sets of sewing instructions.

David McLellan, in an article printed in the *Los Angeles Times,* referred to an interview in which Otto spoke about the use of the quilt in her novel: "It fascinated me—the idea that each patch, for example, has its own life or wholeness to it and when you join them together you get another sense of wholeness. Quilting also interested me as an urge, or impulse; people have to be joined in marriage, or friendship, or love, or to join clubs. . . . When I wrote the short story, I just sort of wrote it and didn't think about all these things. When I finished it, I thought it's like this metaphor of coming together and looking at each woman and talking about friendship, marriage, children, and lives that pull apart." Otto once told *CA* that "the impulse to join is countered by the equally strong impulse to be singular or solitary. And I feel that the lives of my characters are driven by these contradictory desires. A quilt, metaphorically, can be an illustration of fusion and separation." Barbara Fisher in the *Washington Post* praised the author for her use of the practice of quilting in her novel, stating that "Otto has made this metaphor personal and vivid. The quilting analogy seems so right, one wonders why it has never been made before."

Upon its release, *How to Make an American Quilt* elicited praise from several reviewers. Judith Freeman in the *Los Angeles Times Book Review* commended Otto for the economy and efficiency used in depicting the characters, noting that "one of the truly remarkable things about this novel is how powerfully, and succinctly, an entire life can be portrayed in just a few pages." A reviewer for *Publishers Weekly* also lauded Otto, acknowledging that *How to Make an American Quilt* is a "remarkable first novel" that is "imaginative in concept and execution." In the *Los Angeles Times Book Review,* Freeman also complimented Otto on her literary debut, pointing out that the novel includes "beautiful individual stories, stitched into a profoundly moving whole. There is a sense of history here, a feeling for quilting that elevates this somewhat arcane, feminine activity to a level of Zen-like wonder."

In *The Passion Dream Book,* Otto tells the story of Romy March, a young woman who drops out of college in 1918 to take a menial job at a movie studio. There she meets Augustine Marks, a black gardener with whom she falls in love. When Romy's family disowns her over the relationship, the couple head to New York where Augustine pursues a career as a photographer. Romy, too, pursues an artistic career and eventually the two separate as their careers become too consuming for each of them. Harriet Klausner in *BookBrowser* found that *The Passion Dream Book* "symbolizes the struggle of women to find a niche in a man's world" and praised its "story of an open bi-racial couple" for encouraging "readers to rise above the stereotypes expected of them by society and family."

Otto's 2002 novel *A Collection of Beauties at the Height of Their Popularity* follows a group of twenty-something San Franciscans who are "floating" through their lives. Drawing the novel's title from a series of famous Japanese woodblock prints of courtesans and much of its structure from the ancient Japanese *Pillow Book,* Otto presents "changeable, unmoored young characters 'who are adrift in pleasure,'" as Janet Maslin explained in the *New York Times*. Otto claimed in an online interview with Ellen Kanner of *BookPage* that she has lived that life herself: "You're hanging out with your friends, in a job not a career. You know this isn't what you should be doing, but it's so pleasant to be doing nothing." Maslin found that the novel featured "thin, wafting characters who have little seriousness or ballast. . . . It all adds up to less than meets the eye." But Kanner believed that the book's "characters are awash in the joy and madness and terror that's all part of love."

Otto once told *CA:* "In terms of my writing style, I think I am a maker of collages, in a way. I tend to fashion things by juxtaposition, overlapping, working through the larger structure piece by piece. I love being a writer and agree with James Baldwin, who said, 'I consider that I have many responsibilities, but none greater than this: to last, as Hemingway says, and get my work done. I want to be an honest man and a good writer.'"

BIOGRAPHICAL AND CRITICAL SOURCES:

BOOKS

Contemporary Literary Criticism, Volume 70, Gale (Detroit, MI), 1991.

PERIODICALS

Atlantic Monthly, May, 1994, review of *Now You See Her,* p. 145.

Biography, fall, 1998, review of *The Passion Dream Book,* p. 488.

Booklist, March 15, 1997, review of *The Passion Dream Book,* p. 1204.

Bookwatch, August, 1994, review of *Now You See Her,* p. 12.

Christian Science Monitor, June 14, 1994, review of *Now You See Her,* p. 13.

Detroit Free Press, March 17, 1991.

Entertainment Weekly, April 14, 1995, review of *Now You See Her,* p. 61; May 22, 1998, review of *The Passion Dream Book,* p. 63.

Globe and Mail (Toronto, Ontario, Canada), April 6, 1991, p. C7.

Kirkus Reviews, February 15, 1994, review of *Now You See Her,* p. 171; March 1, 1997, review of *The Passion Dream Book,* p. 330.

Library Journal, January, 1995, review of *Now You See Her,* p. 176; April 1, 1997, review of *The Passion Dream Book,* p. 130.

Los Angeles Times, March 28, 1991, Dennis McLellan, "A Thread of Brilliance in Novelist's Debut," p. E7.

Los Angeles Times Book Review, March 24, 1991, Judith Freeman, "Filling in the Blankets," p. 3.

New York Times, March 30, 1994, review of *Now You See Her,* p. C23; March 6, 2002, Janet Maslin, "The Pleasurable Life Afloat in San Francisco," p. E8.

New York Times Book Review, March 24, 1991, Jill McCorkle, "Cover Stories," p. 10; April 23, 1995, review of *Now You See Her,* p. 32; July 27, 1997, review of *The Passion Dream Book,* p. 17.

Publishers Weekly, February 8, 1991, review of *How to Make an American Quilt,* p. 46; January 24, 1994, review of *Now You See Her,* p. 38; March 17, 1997, review of *The Passion Dream Book,* p. 74.

School Library Journal, November, 1997, review of *The Passion Dream Book,* p. 148.

Times (London, England), July 18, 1991, p. 14.

Times Literary Supplement, July 26, 1991, p. 19.

Tribune Books (Chicago, IL), April 28, 1991, Roberta Rubenstein, "Discovery among Differences," pp. 6-7; May 1, 1994, review of *Now You See Her,* p. 6; July 13, 1997, review of *The Passion Dream Book,* p. 10.

Virginia Quarterly Review, autumn, 1997, review of *The Passion Dream Book,* p. 131.

Washington Post, May 27, 1991, Barbara Fisher, "Stories Stitched from Women's Lives," p. C3.

Women's Review of Books, July, 1994, review of *Now You See Her,* p. 46.

ONLINE

BookBrowser, http://www.bookbrowser.com/ (May 12, 1998), Harriet Klausner, review of *The Passion Dream Book.*

BookPage, http://www.bookpage.com/ (March, 2002), Ellen Kanner, "A Modern Floating World: Whitney Otto's Beauties Set Adrift."*

*　　　*　　　*

OUSBY, Ian (Vaughan Kenneth) 1947-2001

PERSONAL: Surname is pronounced *Ooz*-bee; born June 26, 1947, in Marlborough, Wiltshire, England; came to the United States, 1968; died from lung and liver cancer, August 6, 2001; son of Arthur Valentine (a soldier) and Betty Lettice Grace (Green) Ousby; married Heather Dubrow, June 23, 1969 (divorced, 1979); married Mary Dustan Turner (divorced, 1993); married Anna Saunders. *Education:* Magdalene College, Cambridge, B.A., 1968, M.A., 1972; Harvard University, Ph.D., 1973. *Hobbies and other interests:* Looking at pictures and buildings; listening to music.

CAREER: University of Durham, Durham, England, temporary lecturer and tutor in English, 1974-75; University of Maryland, College Park, assistant professor, 1975-78, associate professor of English, 1978-2001. Participant in scholarly meetings. Guest on Canadian radio program, "Ideas."

AWARDS, HONORS: Fulbright travel grant, 1968-73; faculty research awards, University of Maryland, 1977 and 1978; Guggenheim fellowship, 1980-81; Edith McLeod Literary Prize, Stern Silver PEN Award, 1998, for *Occupation: The Ordeal of France, 1940-1944.*

WRITINGS:

Bloodhounds of Heaven: The Detective in English Fiction from Godwin to Doyle, Harvard University Press (Cambridge, MA), 1976.

An Introduction to Fifty American Novels, Barnes & Noble (New York, NY), 1979.

(Editor, with John Lewis Bradley) *Guide to Literature in English,* Cambridge University Press (New York, NY), 1987.

(Editor) *Correspondence of John Ruskin and Charles Eliot Norton,* Cambridge University Press (New York, NY), 1987.

The Cambridge Guide to Literature in English, Cambridge University Press (New York, NY), 1988, new edition, 1993.

The Englishman's England: Taste, Travel, and the Rise of Tourism, Cambridge University Press (New York, NY), 1990.

England, 10th edition (Ousby not associated with earlier editions), Norton (New York, NY), 1989.

Literary Britain and Ireland, 2nd edition, Norton (New York, NY), 1990.

(Editor) *James Plumptre's Britain: The Journals of a Tourist in the 1790s,* Hutchinson (London, England), 1992.

The Blue Guide to Burgundy, 1992.

Cambridge Paperback Guide to Literature in English, Cambridge University Press (New York, NY), 1996.

Guilty Parties: A Mystery Lover's Companion, Thames & Hudson (New York, NY), 1997.

The Crime and Mystery Book, 1997.

Cambridge Guide to Fiction in English, Cambridge University Press (New York, NY), 1998.

Occupation: The Ordeal of France, 1940-1944, Cooper Square Press (New York, NY), 1998.

The Road to Verdun: World War I's Most Momentous Battle and the Folly of Nationalism, Doubleday (New York, NY), 2002, published as *The Road to Verdun: France, Nationalism and the First World War,* J. Cape (London, England), 2002.

Also editor, with John L. Bradley, of *The Letters of John Ruskin to His Father, 1862.* Contributing editor, *Bleak House* (critical edition), Norton (New York, NY), 1977. Contributor of column, *Lone Star Book Review.* Contributor to *Mystery Encyclopedia, The Yearbook of English Studies,* and *Mystery and Detection Annual.* Contributor of about thirty articles and reviews to literature journals, including *University of Toronto Quarterly, Modern Language Review, Nineteenth-Century Fiction, Poe Studies, Victorian Poetry,* and *James Joyce Quarterly.*

SIDELIGHTS: Ian Ousby examined two critical subjects in French history with his books *The Road to Verdun: Nationalism and the Folly of World War I's Most Momentous Battle* and *Occupation: The Ordeal of France, 1940-1944.* The battle of Verdun was a grisly bloodbath that lasted for months. The city of Verdun, France, was surrounded by nineteen forts, and the countryside around it filled with hundreds of thousands of French and German soldiers. The fighting began on February 21, 1916, and continued until December of that year. The French forces were known for their heroism in the face of overwhelming odds. The source of their courage is usually held to be their strong sense that France must be protected at all costs. Drawing on published and unpublished accounts, letters, and diaries from combatants in the battle, as well as scholars and artists who interpreted it later, Ousby gives the military details of the critical battle of Verdun and a historical analysis of French nationalism and its power. In doing so, he creates "a unique view of a specific battle and of warfare in general," remarked a writer for *Kirkus Reviews.* "To understand modern political thinking in France and the enthusiasm that France has for greater integration in Europe, one must understand Verdun—and the French people's determination that it can never be allowed to happen again," commented Michael Rose in *Spectator.* Ousby's account is a "consistently intelligent and readable" analysis of *The Road to Verdun,* stated a *New Statesman* reviewer.

Some of those fighting at Verdun went on to play major roles in World War II as well, including Charles de Gaulle and Marshal Petain; the former was the leader of the French resistance movement following German occupation, while the latter was the head of the Vichy government that cooperated with the Nazis. Ousby examined the painful years when the Nazis occupied France in *Occupation: The Ordeal of France, 1940-1944.* While a popular myth exists that most French people were resistant to the Vichy regime and its Nazi sponsors, Ousby shows that collaboration was unfortunately common. On the other hand, he does not discredit even the most seemingly trivial acts of resistance, stating that they did much to demoralize the Germans. *Occupation* is "comprehensive, incisive, compassionate, remarkably free of prejudice and condescension, and eminently readable," claimed Stanley Hoffmann in *Foreign Affairs*. Hoffmann noted that although the book does not delve deeply into all aspects of its subject, "it succeeds in showing how complex, painful, and often atrocious these years were for the French. . . . [Ousby] has captured the atmosphere of the occupation splendidly."

Ousby once told *CA:* "My book on detectives in nineteenth-century fiction grew out of a double love affair I'd been conducting for many years with detective fiction and with Victorian literature and culture. Since then, as teacher and scholar, I've pursued my interest in Victorian literature, working on Dickens, Hardy and, most recently, Ruskin. In my spare time, I continue to read detective fiction and have just started writing a regular monthly column about it, for the *Lone Star Book Review,* in a belated attempt to turn an apparently profitless vice into a profitable virtue."

BIOGRAPHICAL AND CRITICAL SOURCES:

PERIODICALS

American Literature, September, 1994, review of *Cambridge Guide to Literature in English,* p. 635.
American Reference Books Annual, 1995, review of *The Cambridge Guide to Literature in English,* p. 480; 1997, review of *Cambridge Paperback Guide to Literature in English,* p. 412.
Booklist, April 1, 1994, review of *The Cambridge Guide to Literature in English,* p. 1473; August, 1996, review of *The Cambridge Paperback Guide*

to Literature in English, p. 1922; April 1, 1998, Gilbert Taylor, review of *Occupation: The Ordeal of France, 1940-1944,* p. 1302.
Book Report, March, 1992, review of *Cambridge Guide to Literature in English,* p. 51.
Books, spring, 1999, review of *Occupation: The Ordeal of France, 1940-1944,* p. 21.
Bookwatch, October, 1997, review of *Guilty Parties: A Mystery Lover's Companion,* p. 3; March, 1999, review of *Cambridge Guide to Fiction in English,* p. 1.
Book World, February 15, 1998, review of *Guilty Parties: A Mystery Lover's Companion,* p. 6.
Catholic Library World, December, 1996, review of *Cambridge Paperback Guide to Literature in English,* p. 51.
Choice, July, 1994, review of *Cambridge Guide to Literature in English,* p. 1698; October, 1996, review of *The Cambridge Paperback Guide to Literature in English,* p. 256.
College & Research Libraries, September, 1994, review of *Cambridge Guide to Literature in English,* p. 424.
Contemporary Review, April, 1998, Geoffrey Heptonstall, review of *Occupation: The Ordeal of France, 1940-1944,* p. 216; February, 1999, review of *Cambridge Guide to Fiction in English,* p. 110.
Foreign Affairs, July-August, 1998, Stanley Hoffmann, review of *Occupation: The Ordeal of France, 1940-1944,* p. 129.
Globe and Mail (Toronto), January 21, 1989.
Guardian, April 30, 2002, Malcolm Brown, review of *The Road to Verdun: France, Nationalism and the First World War.*
History Today, October, 1997, review of *Occupation: The Ordeal of France, 1940-1944,* p. 59.
Journal of Military History, January, 1999, review of *Occupation: The Ordeal of France, 1940-1944,* p. 209.
Kirkus Reviews, March 15, 1998, review of *Occupation: The Ordeal of France, 1940-1944,* p. 388; March 15, 2002, review of *The Road to Verdun,* p. 390.
Kliatt Young Adult Paperback Book Guide, May, 1999, review of *Cambridge Guide to Fiction in English,* p. 30.
Library Association Record, April, 1996, review of *Cambridge Paperback Guide to Literature in English,* p. 215; May, 1999, review of *Cambridge Guide to Fiction in English,* p. 301.

Library Journal, May 1, 1992, review of *Cambridge Guide to Literature in English,* p. 123; November 15, 1997, Kelli N. Perkins, review of *Guilty Parties: A Mystery Lover's Companion,* p. 58.

New Statesman, January 21, 2002, Ben Shephard, review of *The Road to Verdun: Nationalism and the Folly of World War I's Most Momentous Battle,* p. 50.

New York Times Book Review, August 9, 1998, review of *Occupation: The Ordeal of France, 1940-1944,* p. 18.

Nineteenth-Century Literature, December, 1994, review of *Cambridge Guide to Literature in English,* p. 412.

Publishers Weekly, March 16, 1998, review of *Occupation: The Ordeal of France, 1940-1944,* p. 48.

Review of English Studies, May, 1992, review of *The Englishman's England: Taste, Travel, and the Rise of Tourism,* p. 302.

School Librarian, February, 1993, review of *Cambridge Guide to Literature in English,* p. 38; August, 1996, review of *Cambridge Paperback Guide to Literature in English,* p. 128; spring, 1999, review of *Cambridge Guide to Fiction in English,* p. 54.

School Library Journal, November, 1994, review of *Cambridge Guide to Literature in English,* p. 138.

School Library Media Quarterly, fall, 1996, review of *Cambridge Paperback Guide to Literature in English,* p. 65.

Sewanee Review, July, 1994, review of *Cambridge Guide to Literature in English,* p. 90.

Spectator, January 29, 2002, Michael Rose, review of *The Road to Verdun: France, Nationalism and the First World War,* p. 30.

Times (London, England), April 12, 1990.

Times Literary Supplement, April 21, 1989; May 1, 1998, review of *Occupation: The Ordeal of France, 1940-1944,* p. 11.

Voice of Youth Advocates, December, 1998, review of *Guilty Parties: A Mystery Lover's Companion,* p. 331.

World & I, April, 1998, review of *Occupation: The Ordeal of France, 1940-1944,* p. 258.

ONLINE

Strand, http://www.strandmag.com/ (April 30, 2002), Martin Friedenthal, review of *Guilty Parties: A Mystery Lover's Companion.**

OVERY, R(ichard) J(ames) 1947-

PERSONAL: Born December 23, 1947, in London, England; son of James Herbert (a design engineer) and Margaret Grace (Sutherland) Overy; married Tessa Coles, 1969 (divorced, 1976); married Jane Giddens, 1979 (divorced, 1992); married Kim Turner, 1992; children: Emma, Rebecca, Jonathan. *Education:* Gonville and Caius College, Cambridge University, Cambridge, England, B.A., 1969, M.A., 1972, Ph.D., 1977. *Politics:* Labour. *Religion:* None.

ADDRESSES: Home—120 Chesterton Rd., Cambridge, Cambridgeshire CB4 1BZ, England. *Office*—Department of History, King's College, University of London, Strand, London WC2R 2LS, England. *E-mail*—rjovery@ukonline.co.uk.

CAREER: Cambridge University, Cambridge, England, research fellow at Churchill College, 1972-73, fellow and lecturer at Queen's College, 1973-79, assistant lecturer in history, 1976-79; University of London, King's College, London, England, lecturer in history, 1980-88, reader in history, 1988-92, professor of modern European history, 1992—.

AWARDS, HONORS: T. S. Ashton Memorial Prize from Economic History Society, 1983, for article "Hitler, War, and the German Economy"; Cass Prize for Business History, 1987.

WRITINGS:

William Morris, Viscount Nuffield, Europa (London, England), 1976.

The Air War, 1939-1945, Europa (London, England), 1980, Stein and Day (New York, NY), 1980, 1st paperback edition, Scarborough House (Chelsea, MI), 1991.

The Nazi Economic Recovery, 1932-1938, prepared for Economic History Society, Macmillan (London, England), 1982, 2nd edition, Cambridge University Press (Cambridge, England, and New York, NY), 1996.

(With Peter Pagnamenta) *All Our Working Lives,* British Broadcasting Corporation Publications (London, England), 1984.

Goering: The "Iron Man," Routledge & Kegan Paul (London, England, and Boston, MA), 1984, published as *Goering,* Phoenix Press (London, England), 2000.

The Origins of the Second World War, Longman (London, England, and New York, NY), 1987, 2nd edition, 1998.

The Nazi Economy, Routledge & Kegan Paul (London, England, and Boston, MA), 1987.

Nazism, Routledge & Kegan Paul (London, England, and Boston, MA), 1987.

(With Andrew Wheatcroft) *The Road to War,* Random House (New York, NY), 1990, 2nd edition, revised and updated, Penguin (London, England, and New York, NY), 1999.

War and Economy in the Third Reich, Clarendon Press (Oxford, England), Oxford University Press (New York, NY), 1994.

The Inter-war Crisis, 1919-1939, Longman (London, England, and New York, NY), 1994.

Why the Allies Won, Norton (New York, NY), 1995, Hebrew edition, translated by Amos Karmel, Devir (Tel-Aviv, Israel), 1999.

The Penguin Historical Atlas of the Third Reich, Penguin (London, England, and New York, NY), 1996.

Bomber Command, 1939-1945, HarperCollins (London, England), 1997.

Russia's War: Blood upon the Snow, TV Books, distributed by Penguin Putnam (New York, NY), 1997, Allen Lane (London, England), 1998, Hebrew edition, translated by Ofer Shor, Devir (Lod, Israel), 2001.

The Battle, Penguin (London, England), 2000, 1st American edition published as *The Battle of Britain: The Myth and the Reality,* Norton (New York, NY), 2001.

(Author of introduction) Mark Arnold-Forster, *The World at War,* new edition, Pimlico (London, England), 2001.

Interrogations: The Nazi Elite in Allied Hands, 1945, Viking (New York, NY), 2001.

EDITOR

Times Atlas of the Twentieth Century, Times Books (London, England), 1996.

(With Gerhard Otto and Johannes Houwink ten Cate) *Die "Neuordnung" Europas: NS-Wirtschaftspolitik in besetzten Gebieten,* Series: National Socialist Occupation Policy in Europe, 1939-1945, number 3, Metropol (Berlin, Germany), 1997.

The Hammond Atlas of the 20th Century, Hammond (Maplewood, NJ), 1996, 2nd edition, Times Books (London, England), 1999.

The Times History of the World, 5th edition, Times Books (London, England), 1999.

The Times History of the 20th Century, new edition, Times Books (London, England), 1999.

Contributor to history journals and *Journal of Strategic Studies.*

SIDELIGHTS: A respected historian, author, and professor of modern European history at King's College, University of London, R. J. Overy has written several important and acclaimed books about the Second World War and the Nazi regime of Adolf Hitler. Overy specializes in German history from 1900 to 1945, the Second World War, and the history of air battles. He has also compiled and edited a number of atlases and has edited historical volumes for Times Books (London). His most widely praised books include *The Road to War, War and Economy in the Third Reich, The Battle of Britain: The Myth and the Reality, Why the Allies Won, Russia's War: Blood upon the Snow,* and *Interrogations: The Nazi Elite in Allied Hands, 1945.*

Overy collaborated with British historian Andrew Wheatcroft for *The Road to War,* a companion to a British Broadcasting Corporation television series that critics regard as a valuable work in itself. It traces the development of World War II from the end of World War I to the beginning of the second world war in seven nations: Germany, Britain, France, the Soviet Union, Italy, Japan, and the United States. Lenny Glynn and John Bemrose, in a review for *Maclean's,* said the book shows "how each pursued its own national interests to the detriment of the international situation." Glynn and Bemrose praised the book for its "strikingly original" treatment of the relationship between Adolf Hitler and the British prime minister Neville Chamberlain. Genevieve Stuttaford of *Publishers Weekly* found the book's emphasis to be on "the national prejudices and illusions" that allowed each of the seven countries to be "sucked into the maelstrom" of World War II, including the United States' isolation and ignorance of other nations and peoples.

In his highly acclaimed and widely reviewed book *Why the Allies Won,* Overy explores the Allied victory in World War II on three levels: government, military, and popular effort and support. In the first half of the book, he defines the areas in which the Allied military forces gained the upper hand—on the Eastern front, on the oceans, in the air, in bombing campaigns, and finally through the invasion of Normandy in 1944. The second half of the book explains how the people of the Allied nations helped this to happen. Mobilization of national economies, making the most of existing technology, the ability to form a strong alliance, and the belief that they were in the right, says Overy, were deciding factors in the Allied victory. Yet, as Thomas A. Britten of *The Historian* acknowledged, an Allied victory was by no means certain in the early years of the war. "Overy's goal," he wrote, "is to explain and assess how the Allies' wartime sacrifices, both on the battlefield and on the homefront, changed the fortunes of war between 1942-1944. . . . the war's outcome depended as much on the successful mobilization of the economic, scientific, and moral resources of the nations involved as it did on the fighting itself."

Clifford R. Krieger of *Armed Forces & Society: An Interdisciplinary Journal* observed, "Perhaps most important, [Overy] gives the reader an opportunity to see how slender was the thread of Allied victory. The realization that failure was possible helps us understand that each of the elements of the Allied effort was important." Overy discusses weaponry, leadership among the different nations, and the impact of morale on industrial production. Krieger praised Overy's review of military operations but said that the meat of the book remains in the second half. Krieger asked a question that is a compelling historical query: "Had the war lasted another year, would the Allies have been able to sustain their air superiority over Germany in the face of a jet-powered interceptor force and surface-to-air missiles?" Krieger concluded that Overy "warns us that in war there are no sure winners. That should be a humbling insight and a spur to reflect continuously on our received wisdom and assumptions."

Overy's well regarded *Russia's War: Blood upon the Snow* reveals new information, coming to light some fifty years after the end of World War II. This information demonstrates the crucial and decisive role that Russian soldiers and civilians played in the Allied victory. Written as a companion to IBP Films' television documentary and using previously unavailable Russian archives, the book educates the Western reader about the magnitude of the war on the Eastern Front. It probes the reasons for the Soviets' willingness to

make great sacrifices and answers questions about Stalin's ability as a military leader and the Russian preparedness for war.

In *The Battle of Britain: The Myth and the Reality,* originally published as simply *The Battle,* Overy considers many of the so-called myths about the great 1940 battle between the Royal Air Force and the German Luftwaffe over southern England. Instead of recounting the battle itself in detail, however, Overy explores the German and British strategies behind the battle and gets at the truth behind information that some revisionist historians have discounted. Richard Mullen of *Contemporary Review* praised Overy's book as "a masterful account" that "provides a perfect introduction to a complicated story." He makes a special effort to note that Britain had equipment and organizational advantages in the battle and that the Luftwaffe's "dazzling tactics . . . which made them so formidable in their victory against the French proved a handicap . . . [in] a different type of war against the RAF." Gilbert Taylor of *Booklist* commended *The Battle of Britain* as an "expert recounting of an epic drama." Edwin B. Burgess, writing a review for *Library Journal,* said the reader who is unfamiliar with World War II history will need companion sources in reading Overy's book, but he praised the author's "insightful analyses" on the successes of the Battle of Britain.

Interrogations: The Nazi Elite in Allied Hands, 1945 covers a little-known period after the Second World War, when Allied leaders decided the immediate fate of top Nazi officials who had been captured in May and June 1945. The book chronicles the lengthy interviews—conducted during the months before the Nuremburg War Crimes Tribunal began in late November—with such infamous commanders as Goering, von Ribbentrop, Hess, Ley, Speer, and more than two dozen others, as they reflect on Hitler's leadership and recall their own part in Nazi war crimes. The interrogations of these high officials are published for the first time in full in the book, with an introduction and analyses by Overy.

Anne Applebaum, in a review of the book for *Spectator,* wrote: "It makes for mesmerising reading. Overy's interests are broad, and his background knowledge extensive, enabling him to explore a number of issues at length: the different interrogation strategies deployed by different internees, their reflections on life at the top of the Nazi power structure, their memories of Hitler, their explanation of the Nazi defeat. . . . Overy's analysis of who knew what about the Holocaust is particularly fascinating." Jay Freeman of *Booklist* praised the book, concluding, "This is a riveting but deeply disturbing book, which will make an essential contribution to our understanding of the Nazi era." A contributor to *Contemporary Review* called it "a valuable contribution to our understanding of the Second World War and of man's capacity for evil and self-delusion."

Overy once told *CA:* "Communicating to a wider public than academic colleagues is of great importance to me. Historians must share their history, not make it into a specialized, inaccessible discipline. I feel this is particularly important for those historians who work on the Third Reich. Confronting the moral dilemmas posed by Nazism is as important today as it was at the time. The present generation of students needs to be reminded of what happened, but also to have it explained as honestly and scrupulously as possible. There is much myth and casual explanation in the history of Nazism, and of the war, which must be constantly challenged."

BIOGRAPHICAL AND CRITICAL SOURCES:

PERIODICALS

Air Power History, spring, 1997, review of *Why the Allies Won,* p. 58.

American Historical Review, October, 1981.

Armed Forces & Society: An Interdisciplinary Journal, fall, 1998, Clifford R. Krieger, review of *Why the Allies Won,* p. 180.

Booklist, May 1, 1990, review of *The Road to War,* p. 1683; March 15, 1996, review of *Why the Allies Won,* pp. 1237 and 1247; December 15, 1996, review of *The Hammond Atlas of the 20th Century,* p. 748; March 1, 2001, Gilbert Taylor, review of *The Battle of Britain: The Myth and the Reality,* p. 1223; September 15, 2001, Jay Freeman, review of *Interrogations: The Nazi Elite in Allied Hands, 1945,* p. 169.

Books (formerly *Books and Bookmen*), July, 1987, review of *Goering: The "Iron Man,"* p. 29; August, 1989, review of *The Road to War,* p. 21.

Books Magazine, autumn, 1998, review of *Russia's War: Blood upon the Snow,* p. 22.

British Book News, April, 1987, reviews of *Goering: The "Iron Man,"* and *The Air War, 1939-1945,* p. 219.

Business History Review, winter, 1994, review of *War and Economy in the Third Reich,* p. 614.

Choice, December, 1990, review of *The Road to War,* p. 685; September, 1996, review of *Why the Allies Won,* p. 182; February, 1998, review of *Blood upon the Snow,* p. 1048.

Contemporary Review, December, 1989, review of *The Road to War,* p. 335; August, 1999, review of *The Times History of the World,* p. 111; October, 1999, review of *Blood upon the Snow,* p. 219; September, 2000, Richard Mullen, "The Battle of Britain Remembered," p. 182; January, 2002, review of *Interrogations,* p. 61.

Economist, September 2, 1989, review of *The Road to War,* p. 83.

English Historical Review, September, 1995, review of *War and Economy in the Third Reich,* p. 958.

Foreign Affairs, September, 1994, review of *War and Economy in the Third Reich,* p. 156; May, 1996, review of *Why the Allies Won,* p. 139.

Guardian Weekly, September 10, 1989, review of *The Road to War,* p. 29; August 5, 1990, review of *The Road to War,* p. 20.

Historian, autumn, 1995, review of *War and Economy in the Third Reich,* p. 183; winter, 1998, Thomas A. Britten, review of *Why the Allies Won,* p. 450.

History: Reviews of New Books, summer, 1995, review of *War and Economy in the Third Reich,* p. 178; fall, 1996, review of *Why the Allies Won,* p. 44; summer, 1998, review of *Blood upon the Snow,* p. 191.

History Today, April, 1994, review of *War and Economy in the Third Reich,* p. 54; May, 1996, review of *Why the Allies Won,* p. 56; July, 1996, review of *War and Economy in the Third Reich,* p. 52.

Journal of Economic Literature, March, 1995, review of *War and Economy in the Third Reich,* p. 357; March, 1997, review of *The Nazi Economic Recovery, 1932-1938,* 2nd edition, p. 259.

Journal of Interdisciplinary History, spring, 1996, review of *War and Economy in the Third Reich,* p. 709.

Journal of Military History, October, 1995, review of *War and Economy in the Third Reich,* p. 735; October, 1996, review of *Why the Allies Won,* p. 797.

Journal of Modern History, June, 1996, review of *War and Economy in the Third Reich,* p. 502.

Kirkus Reviews, March 1, 1996, review of *Why the Allies Won,* p. 357; February 15, 2001, review of *The Battle of Britain,* p. 242.

Kliatt Young Adult Paperback Book Guide, September, 1997, review of *The Penguin Historical Atlas of the Third Reich,* p. 38.

Library Journal, May 1, 1990, review of *The Road to War,* p. 98; March 15, 1996, review of *Why the Allies Won,* p. 83; March 1, 2001, Edwin B. Burgess, review of *The Battle of Britain,* p. 114.

Listener, September 7, 1989, review of *The Road to War,* p. 25.

London Review of Books, July 15, 1999, review of *Blood upon the Snow,* p. 18.

Maclean's, November 13, 1989, Lenny Glynn and John Bemrose, review of *The Road to War,* p. 68.

National Review, September 16, 1996, review of *Why the Allies Won,* p. 70.

New Statesman and Society, September 1, 1989, review of *The Road to War,* p. 35; March 29, 1996, review of *Why the Allies Won,* p. 35.

New York Times, August 4, 1995, review of *Why the Allies Won,* p. 39; April 19, 1996, late edition, review of *Why the Allies Won,* p. C 27.

New York Times Book Review, June 2, 1996, review of *Why the Allies Won,* p. 20; June 22, 1997, review of *Why the Allies Won,* p. 32; January 11, 1998, review of *Blood upon the Snow,* p. 15; September 27, 1998, review of *Blood upon the Snow,* p. 32.

Observer (London), June 7, 1987, review of *Goering: The "Iron Man,"* p. 25; August 20, 1989, review of *The Road to War,* p. 38; August 4, 1991, review of *The Road to War,* p. 51; August 6, 1995, review of *Why the Allies Won,* p. 19; September 12, 1999, review of *Blood upon the Snow,* p. 14.

Presidential Studies Quarterly, fall, 1996, review of *Why the Allies Won,* p. 1172.

Publishers Weekly, March 9, 1990, Genevieve Stuttaford, review of *The Road to War,* p. 55; February 26, 1996, review of *Why the Allies Won,* p. 93; April 14, 1997, review of *Why the Allies Won,* p. 72.

Rapport: The Modern Guide to Books, Music & More, May, 1996, review of *Why the Allies Won,* p. 44.

Reference and Research Book News, February, 1998, review of *Blood upon the Snow,* p. 15.

Sewanee Review, January, 1992, review of *The Road to War,* p. 141.

Spectator, September 26, 1998, review of *Blood upon the Snow,* p. 41; November 3, 2001, Anne Applebaum, review of *Interrogations,* p. 55.

Times Educational Supplement, December 11, 1987, review of *The Origins of the Second World War,* p. 24; April 21, 1995, review of *The Inter-war Crisis, 1919-1939,* p. 17; April 30, 1999, review of *The Times History of the World,* p. 19.

Times Literary Supplement (London), December 26, 1980; September 1, 1989, review of *The Road to War,* p. 935; June 3, 1994, review of *War and Economy in the Third Reich,* p. 28; August 18, 1995, review of *Why the Allies Won,* p. 7; November 1, 1996, review of *Times Atlas of the Twentieth Century,* p. 7; August 28, 1998, review of *Blood upon the Snow,* p. 11.

Washington Post Book World, July 1, 1990, review of *The Road to War,* p. 13.

Wilson Quarterly, spring, 1996, review of *Why the Allies Won,* p. 75.

ONLINE

King's College London, History Department, http://www.kcl.ac.uk/humanities/history/ (April 19, 2002), "Professor Richard Overy."

Penguin Putnam Books, http://www.penguinputnam.com/ (April 30, 2002), synopsis of *Interrogations.**

P

PELL, Arthur R. 1920-

PERSONAL: Born January 22, 1920, in New York, NY; son of Harry and Rae (Meyers) Pell; married Erica Frost (a music teacher), May 19, 1946; children: Douglas, Hilary. *Education:* New York University, B.A., 1939, M.A., 1944; Cornell University, Professional Diploma, 1943; California Coast University, Ph.D., 1977.

ADDRESSES: Home and office—111 Dietz St., Hempstead, NY 11550.

CAREER: Eagle Electric Manufacturing Co., Long Island, NY, personnel manager, 1946-50; North Atlantic Construction Co., New York, NY, personnel manager, 1950-53; Harper Associates (personnel consultants), New York, NY, vice-president, 1953-73; consultant in human resources management in Long Island, 1975—. Professor of management in evening classes at City College of the City University of New York, 1947-67. Adjunct professor of management at New York University, 1960-81, and St. John's University, 1971-77. *Military service:* U.S. Army, 1942-46; became warrant officer.

AWARDS, HONORS: Embracing Excellence named one of the Top 30 Business Books of 2002, by *Soundview Executive Book Summaries.*

WRITINGS:

Placing Salesmen, Impact Publishers (San Ramon, CA), 1963.
(With Walter Patterson) *Fire Officers Guide to Leadership,* privately printed, 1963.
Placing Executives, Impact Publishers (San Ramon, CA), 1964.
Police Leadership, C. C. Thomas (Springfield, IL), 1967.
(With Maxwell Harper) *How to Get the Job You Want after Forty,* Pilot Books (Babylon, NY), 1967.
Recruiting and Selecting Personnel, Simon & Schuster (New York, NY), 1969.
(With Harper) *Starting and Managing an Employment Agency,* U.S. Small Business Administration (Washington, DC), 1971.
Advancing Your Career (home study program), Management Games Institute, 1971.
College Graduate Guide to Job Finding, Simon & Schuster (New York, NY), 1973.
Recruiting, Training and Motivating Volunteer Workers, Pilot Books (Babylon, NY), 1973.
Interviewing and Selecting Sales, Advertising and Marketing Personnel, Personnel Publications, 1974, revised edition, 1981.
Be a Better Employment Interviewer, Personnel Publications, 1974, second revised edition, 1994.
(With Wilma Rogalin) *Women's Guide to Management Positions,* Simon & Schuster (New York, NY), 1975.
(With Albert Furbay) *The College Student Guide to Career Planning,* Simon & Schuster (New York, NY), 1975.
Managing through People, Simon & Schuster (New York, NY), 1975, revised edition, 1987.
Choosing a College Major: Business, McKay (New York, NY), 1978.
Enrich Your Life the Dale Carnegie Way, Dale Carnegie & Associates (Garden City, NY), 1979.
Interviewing and Selecting Engineering and Computer Personnel, Personnel Publications, 1980.

(Editor) Dale Carnegie, *How to Win Friends and Influence People,* revised edition (Pell was not associated with previous edition), Simon & Schuster (New York, NY), 1981.

(With George Sadek) *Resumes for Engineers,* Simon & Schuster (New York, NY), 1982.

Interviewing and Selecting Financial and Data Processing Personnel, Personnel Publications, 1982.

How to Sell Yourself on an Interview, Simon & Schuster (New York, NY), 1982.

(With Sadek) *Resumes for Computer Professionals,* Simon & Schuster (New York, NY), 1984.

The Part-Time Job Book, Simon & Schuster (New York, NY), 1984.

Making the Most of Medicare, Prentice-Hall (Englewood Cliffs, NJ), 1987, revised edition, Chronimed, 1990.

How to Be a Successful Supervisor, Dun & Bradstreet (New York, NY), 1988.

Diagnosing Your Doctor, Chronimed, 1991.

The Supervisor's Infobank: 1000 Quick Answers to Your Toughest Problems, McGraw-Hill (New York, NY), 1994.

The Complete Idiot's Guide to Managing People, Macmillan (New York, NY), 1995.

The Pocket Idiot's Guide to One Minute Managing, Macmillan (New York, NY), 1999.

The Complete Idiot's Guide to Team Building, Macmillan (New York, NY), 1999.

The Complete Idiot's Guide to Recruiting the Right Stuff, Macmillan (New York, NY), 2000.

(With Franklin C. Ashby) *Embracing Excellence: Become an Employer of Choice to Attract and Keep the Best Talent,* Prentice-Hall (Englewood Cliffs, NJ), 2001.

Author of audiocassettes, including *The Job Finders Program,* Prentice Hall, 1989; *Getting the Most from Your People* (published in Japanese), Prentice Hall, 1990; and *The 21 Keys to Success Achievement,* ICCT, 1998. Also author of "Career Aid Pamphlets" series for Personnel Publications, syndicated monthly feature "The Human Side," published in eighty periodicals, Dale Carnegie Associates, Inc., 1987-94. Contributor of more than one hundred articles to trade and professional magazines, including syndicated newspaper series, "When Your Husband Loses His Job," 1971.

SIDELIGHTS: Arthur R. Pell has authored or edited dozens of books about business management, including several in the "Complete Idiot's Guide" series.

Pell, who is the senior vice president of the New York-based Leadership Capital Group, specializes in the human resources field, and many of his works concentrate on this area of business management. He has also given many lectures on the subject. Born in 1920 in New York City, Pell began publishing books in 1963 with his debut work, *Placing Salesmen,* and the privately published *Fire Officers Guide to Leadership.*

An example of Pell's later work is his 2001 book, *Embracing Excellence: Become an Employer of Choice to Attract and Keep the Best Talent,* which he coauthored with Franklin C. Ashby. The critically lauded book offers advice to employers on how to recruit and retain exemplary employees, which the authors feel is a major challenge facing the corporate world. The book describes how companies can use a system Pell and Ashby developed called the Organizational MRI, which is designed to analyze corporate culture and show its relationship to employee retention. They also offer advice on how to find talented workers, as well as use effective screening procedures during the interviewing process. The book includes helpful lists of publications and Web sites that employers can use to find information about human resources, jobs, careers, and management.

Several critics lauded *Embracing Excellence.* Lucy Heckman of *Library Journal* called it "a practical and informative guide to strategies employers can use." Similarly, a contributor for *Publishers Weekly* referred to the book as "a solid reference for managers and HR professionals."

Pell once told *CA:* "The mission of my writing is to utilize my God-given talents to help others identify, develop, and make the most of their capabilities in their work and in their lives."

BIOGRAPHICAL AND CRITICAL SOURCES:

PERIODICALS

Library Journal, October 1, 2001, p. 116.
Publishers Weekly, August 27, 2001, p. 72.

*   *   *

PENN, James R. 1949-

PERSONAL: Born May 26, 1949, in Madison, WI; married Laura de Andrade, November 27, 1985; children: April Marie, Eric Raymond. *Ethnicity:* "Caucasian." *Education:* University of Wisconsin—

Madison, B.S., 1974, M.D., 1977, Ph.D., 1983. *Hobbies and other interests:* Collecting books, coins, and stamps.

ADDRESSES: Home—106 Sherry Dr., Hammond, LA 70401. *Office*—Department of Sociology, SLU 10572, Southeastern Louisiana University, Hammond, LA 70402. *E-mail*—jpenn2@selu.edu.

CAREER: Southeastern Louisiana University, Hammond, assistant professor of geography and anthropology, 1989—. Columbia Players, member.

MEMBER: Association of American Geographers, American Numismatic Association.

WRITINGS:

(With Peter M. Ross) *The Economic Geography of the Northern Lakes Region,* Lake Superior Project, University of Wisconsin—Madison (Madison, WI), 1978.
Encyclopedia of Geographical Features in World History: Europe and the Americas, American Bibliographical Center-Clio Press (Santa Barbara, CA), 1997.
Rivers of the World: A Social, Geographical, and Environmental Sourcebook, American Bibliographical Center-Clio Press (Santa Barbara, CA), 2001.

SIDELIGHTS: Professor of geography James R. Penn is the author of *Encyclopedia of Geographical Features in World History: Europe and the Americas,* a study called "fascinating" by a *Booklist* reviewer. The volume covers the geography of North, South, and Central America, and all of Europe, including parts of Russia. The alphabetical entries include locations both mythological, such as the imaginary island Hy-Brazil; and manmade, including Hadrian's Wall and the Mason-Dixon Line. The author concentrates on the general geological characteristics of each region and so does not list towns, cities, principalities, or states; but does note battlefields where "water or terrain was significant to the outcome of the battle," according to the *Booklist* contributor.

Penn turned his attention to a specific kind of geographical feature in his 2001 book *Rivers of the World: A Social, Geographical, and Environmental Source-*

book. The Amazon, Nile, Mississippi, Yangtze, and Wei are just a few of the two hundred rivers examined in detail. The author lists the characteristics of the rivers with their lengths, major tributaries, and outlets. To another *Booklist* critic, the entries "feature geographical information but, much like a river, often gently meander into historical and environmental discussions." Comparing *Rivers of the World* with similar reference works, *Library Journal* reviewer Eva Lautemann found Penn's book "more in-depth" than the better known *Rand McNally Encyclopedia of World Rivers.*

BIOGRAPHICAL AND CRITICAL SOURCES:

PERIODICALS

Booklist, May 15, 1998, review of *Encyclopedia of Geographical Features in World History: Europe and the Americas,* p. 1658; May 15, 2002, review of *Rivers of the World: A Social, Geographical, and Environmental Sourcebook,* p. 1636.
Library Journal, March 15, 2002, Eva Lautemann, review of *Rivers of the World,* p. 74.*

*   *   *

PERENYI, Eleanor (Spencer Stone) 1918-

PERSONAL: Born January 4, 1918, in WA; daughter of Ellis S. and Grace (Zaring) Stone; married F. Sigmond Perenyi, September 23, 1937 (divorced); children: Peter. *Education:* Attended Phillips Gallery of Art School, 1936.

ADDRESSES: Home—53 Main St., Stonington, CT 06378.

CAREER: Harper's Bazaar, New York, NY, decoration editor, 1947-50, copy editor, 1955-57, feature and travel editor, 1956-58; *Living for Young Homemakers,* New York, NY, copy editor, 1951; *Charm,* New York, NY, feature editor, 1958-59, managing editor, 1959; *Mademoiselle,* New York, NY, managing editor, 1959-62; writer.

AWARDS, HONORS: National Book Award nomination, 1974, for *Liszt: The Artist As Romantic Hero;* American Academy and Institute of Arts and Letters award for literature, 1982.

WRITINGS:

More Was Lost (memoir), Little, Brown (Boston, MA), 1946, reprinted, Helen Marx Books, 2001.

The Bright Sword (novel), Rinehart (New York, NY), 1955.

Liszt: The Artist As Romantic Hero, Little, Brown (Boston, MA), 1974, Weidenfeld and Nicolson (London, England), 1975.

Green Thoughts: A Writer in the Garden (essays), Random House (New York, NY), 1981, new edition, with an introduction by Allen Lacy, Modern Library (New York, NY), 2002.

Contributor of articles to popular magazines, including *Atlantic Monthly, Harper's,* and *Esquire.*

SIDELIGHTS: Editor and writer Eleanor Perenyi first attracted critical attention in 1974 with *Liszt: The Artist As Romantic Hero.* In this biography of the innovative Hungarian composer and piano virtuoso Franz Liszt, Perenyi traces the musician's life from his birth in 1811 until 1861, when he entered the Franciscan Order in Rome, Italy. Throughout the work, the author presents Liszt as a prototypical romantic hero by revealing his abiding spirituality—he is considered by many to be the nineteenth century's greatest religious composer—and his generosity. Liszt's efforts to aid his contemporaries, in fact, were often offered at the expense of his own musical reputation; he popularized the operatic and symphonic works of Richard Wagner, for instance, through his own piano transcriptions. Augmenting his reputation as a great romantic, Perenyi maintains that women were quite attracted to Liszt and often pursued him relentlessly. Yet the author discredits many of the scandalous rumors surrounding the Hungarian composer's life, in particular his alleged mistreatment of his first mistress, Marie d'Agoult, the mother of his three children. Although critical reaction to *Liszt* was mixed, many reviewers agreed that Perenyi possesses a thorough understanding of the romantic period. "Her intelligence is most obvious in her penetrating treatment of Liszt's relationship to the Romantic movement," declared Christopher Lehmann-Haupt in the *New York Times. National Review* contributor Aram Bakshian, Jr., similarly praised the biography as "a real tour de force as both a character study and an overview of the Romantic movement." Perenyi has written, lauded Richard Howard in the *New York Times Book Review,* "surely one of the most searching, sophisticated and sensible books about . . . the romantic hero."

Perenyi wrote a memoir of her marriage to the young liberal Hungarian baron Zsiga (F. Sigmond) Perenyi, followed by a novel about the American Civil War battle of Chickamauga, *The Bright Sword,* published in 1955. Her memoir, *More Was Lost,* first published in 1946, was republished in paperback in 2001 and released to a new audience, for whom it is still fascinating. Perenyi married the young baron in 1937, and the couple lived in a castle in Hungary (or Czechoslovakia, as Nazi German ruler Adolf Hitler changed the boundaries of his possessions). With 700 acres of farmland, a vineyard, a forest, and a way of life that was still quite similar to that of the 1400s, young Eleanor and her husband stayed busy gardening, preserving food, and making their own repairs. Eleanor learned Hungarian from her mother-in-law, and became friends with the local people, including the old steward Gyorffy, the massive hunter Bottka, and the patriotic and proud Cousin Laci. Perenyi writes about her perception that Hungarians vaguely "looked down on" the Jews, as quoted by Gore Vidal in an article for the *New York Review of Books,* because they took on work in business and the professions that no one else wanted to do. As World War II broke out, Zsiga Perenyi persuaded the pregnant Eleanor to return to the United States to have their child. She first went to join her parents in Paris, where her father was a military attaché to the American embassy, telling Zsiga she would come back "war or no war," as quoted by Vidal. On September 2, 1939, Eleanor and her mother watched from their window in Paris as war was declared on Germany. Although Eleanor rejoined her husband for a short time that fall, he was soon called to fight in the Hungarian army, and, home on leave, insisted that she return to the United States. "I left as if I expected to be back the following week," Vidal quoted, "[with] a hasty glance around the garden over which I had worked so hard. . . . I didn't pay any farewell calls. I didn't go to take a last look at my trees in the orchard. I walked out with only one bag, got into the carriage to be driven to the station . . . and never looked back." As Eleanor and Zsiga parted in Budapest, Perenyi writes, "We had only a few bad moments . . . and I don't remember how we got through them." She returned to New York and made a new life in publishing. Zsiga stayed in Hungary, where he lived under a Russian Communist government. Their castle became a museum. In 1947, he visited Eleanor in New York, and they arranged for a divorce before he returned home. Eleanor stayed in New York with her parents and raised her son. She sums up her marriage in *More Was Lost* by recalling her husband's liberalism and "hatred of bigotry and cruelty and prejudice," while also remembering his cynicism and pessimism. A contributor to *Turtle Point* commented on Perenyi's "lucid, crisp, and unpretentious" style in the book, which "yields much that history and dispatches omit."

In 1981 Perenyi capitalized on her more than thirty years of amateur gardening experience with *Green Thoughts: A Writer in the Garden.* In this collection of seventy-two meditations and witty essays inspired by her own garden, Perenyi offers practical wisdom on such horticultural topics as compost, gardening failures, weeds, and weather conditions. Yet Perenyi's ruminations extend further than her garden. Greek legend, European history and politics, world literature, and religion and spirituality number among the sundry topics addressed in these essays, arranged alphabetically from "Annuals" to "Woman's Place." Literary figures, including Cato, John Milton, Edith Wharton, and Robert Frost, are quoted and deliberated over, as is the subject of mazes: "Should you ever find yourself lost in one," Perenyi writes, as quoted by Mary McCarthy in the *New York Review of Books,* "choose either the right or the left wall and follow its every turning. You can't fail to emerge." *Green Thoughts* met with an enthusiastic critical response. "As I read, I was constantly delighted by the nuggets of knowledge and [Perenyi's] enchanting turns of mind and phrase," claimed Brooke Astor in the *New York Times Book Review.* This volume "is quite unlike any other gardening book I know," the critic continued, "with its Old World charm, its down-to-earth practicality, its whimsy and sophistication." *Washington Post Book World* reviewer Bertha Benkard Rose simply proclaimed *Green Thoughts* "a delight," while *New Republic* reviewer John Hollander concluded: "This perennial book springs from the ground of intelligence, candor, and good humor which has not yet, artificial fertilizers to the contrary, been worn out." Jane Barker Wright, in a review for *Horticulture: The Magazine of American Gardening,* compared Perenyi's book to "a soft cheese, a hunk of good bread, and a glass of strong red wine," something to chew on and savor. "Perenyi is unapologetic in her opinions, robust in her arguments, and disarmingly graceful in her prose style," Wright concluded. "This combination," she said, "would ensure success in almost any genre; it is without doubt the key to the timelessness of *Green Thoughts.*"

BIOGRAPHICAL AND CRITICAL SOURCES:

PERIODICALS

Globe and Mail (Toronto), May 19, 1984.

Horticulture: The Magazine of American Gardening, October, 1995, Jane Barker Wright, review of *Green Thoughts: A Writer in the Garden,* p. 71.

Library Journal, December, 2001, Michael Rogers, review of *Green Thoughts,* p. 182.

Los Angeles Times Book Review, April 3, 1994, review of *Green Thoughts,* p. 1.

National Review, March 28, 1975, Aram Bakshian, Jr., review of *Liszt: The Artist As Romantic Hero.*

New Republic, January 25, 1975; October 7, 1981, John Hollander, review of *Green Thoughts.*

Newsweek, October 12, 1981.

New Yorker, October 5, 1981.

New York Review of Books, February 6, 1975; November 5, 1981, Mary McCarthy, review of *Green Thoughts;* February 28, 2002, Gore Vidal, "Everything Is Yesterday," review of *More Was Lost,* pp. 22-23.

New York Times, December 10, 1974, Christopher Lehmann-Haupt, review of *Liszt.*

New York Times Book Review, November 24, 1974, Richard Howard, review of *Liszt;* October 11, 1981, Brooke Astor, review of *Green Thoughts;* May 31, 1998, "Dear Mr. Jefferson," p. 7.

Observer (London), February 27, 1994, review of *Green Thoughts,* p. 22; November 26, 1995, review of *Green Thoughts,* p. 8.

Spectator, October 23, 1982.

Times Literary Supplement, November 7, 1975; November 26, 1982; August 4, 1995, review of *Green Thoughts,* p. 12.

Washington Post Book World, October 11, 1981, Bertha Benkard Rose, review of *Green Thoughts.*

ONLINE

Turtle Point, http://www.turtlepoint.com/ (April 30, 2002), review of *More Was Lost.**

*   *   *

PERETTI, Frank E. 1951-

PERSONAL: Born January 13, 1951, in Lethbridge, Alberta, Canada; son of Gene E. (a minister) and Joyce E. (a homemaker; maiden name, Schneider) Peretti; married Barbara Jean Ammon (a homemaker), June 24, 1972. *Education:* Attended University of California—Los Angeles, 1976-78. *Politics:* Conservative. *Religion:* Christian. *Hobbies and other interests:* Carpentry, sculpturing, bicycling, hiking, music, aviation.

ADDRESSES: Home—ID. *Agent*—c/o Blanton/Harrell, Inc., 2910 Poston Ave., Nashville, TN 37203.

CAREER: Licensed minister; associate pastor of community church in Washington state, 1978-84; K-2 Ski Factory, Washington state, production worker (ski maker), 1985-88; writer and public speaker, 1986—. Has worked as a musician and storyteller.

AWARDS, HONORS: Gold Medallion Award, Evangelical Christian Publishers Association, and Readers' and Editors' Choice awards, *Christianity Today,* all for *Piercing the Darkness.*

WRITINGS:

"COOPER KIDS ADVENTURES" SERIES

The Door in the Dragon's Throat, Crossway (Westchester, IL), 1986.
Escape from the Island of Aquarius, Crossway (Westchester, IL), 1986.
The Tombs of Anak, Crossway (Westchester, IL), 1987.
Trapped at the Bottom of the Sea, Crossway (Westchester, IL), 1988.
The Secret of the Desert Stone, Word Publications (Nashville, TN), 1996.
The Legend of Annie Murphy, Word Publications (Nashville, TN), 1997.
The Deadly Curse of Toco-Rey, Word Publications (Nashville, TN), 1996.
Flying Blind, Tommy Nelson (Nashville, TN), 1997.

THE VERITAS PROJECT

Hangman's Curse, Tommy Nelson (Nashville, TN), 2001.
Nightmare Academy, Tommy Nelson (Nashville, TN), 2002.

OTHER

This Present Darkness (novel), Crossway (Westchester, IL), 1986.
Tilly (novel; based on his radio play), Crossway (Westchester, IL), 1988.

Piercing the Darkness (also see below), Crossway Books (Westchester, IL), 1989.
All Is Well, illustrated by Robert Sauber, Word (Dallas, TX), 1991.
Prophet, Crossway Books (Westchester, IL), 1992.
The Oath, Word Publications (Nashville, TN), 1995.
The Visitation, Word Publications (Nashville, TN), 1999.
This Present Darkness and *Piercing the Darkness,* Crossway Books (Westchester, IL), 2000.
The Wounded Spirit (memoir), Word Publications (Nashville, TN), 2000.
No More Victims, Word Publications (Nashville, TN), 2001.
(Reteller, with Sharon Lamson, Cheryl McKay, and Bill Ross) *Wild & Wacky Totally True Bible Stories: All About Obedience,* Tommy Nelson (Nashville, TN), 2002.
(Reteller, with Bill Ross) *Wild & Wacky Totally True Bible Stories: All About Faith,* Tommy Nelson (Nashville, TN), 2002.
(Reteller, with Bill Ross) *Wild & Wacky Totally True Bible Stories: All About Courage,* Tommy Nelson (Nashville, TN), 2002.
(Reteller, with Bill Ross) *Wild & Wacky Totally True Bible Stories: All About Helping Others,* Tommy Nelson (Nashville, TN), 2002.
No More Bullies: For Those Who Wound or Are Wounded, Word Publications (Nashville, TN), 2003.

Author of the radio drama *Tilly.* The *Wild & Wacky Totally True Bible Stories* series has been produced on videocassette and DVD. Contributor to Christian periodicals.

SIDELIGHTS: Frank E. Peretti is a bestselling author of Christian fiction, with over nine million copies of his books sold. "Mr. Peretti's publisher acclaims him the successor to C. S. Lewis; the *Darkness* novels have sold millions. Yet the author's name is virtually unknown outside the Christian community," wrote Jared Lobdell in the *National Review.* Writing in *Christianity Today,* Michael G. Maudlin called Peretti the "great fundamentalist novelist, the father of the block-buster Christian fiction."

Hailed in *Time* and *Newsweek* as the creator of the crossover Christian thriller, Peretti is the son of a minister and an ordained minister himself, and writes evangelical stories that celebrate the divine power of God and prayer. In his writing, inspired by conservative Christian theology, angels vanquish demons and good always prevails over evil. "The battle against the demonic has always been Peretti's principal theme," wrote Etta Wilson in *BookPage.*With novels such as *This Present Darkness, Piercing the Darkness, Prophet, The Oath,* and *The Visitation,* Peretti almost single-handedly created the genre of Christian thrillers for adult readers. His books for young readers, including the titles in the "Cooper Kids Adventure" series and the "Veritas Project" series have done the same for middle-grade and young adult readers.

Born in 1951, in Canada, Peretti had, as Jeremy Lott noted in *Christianity Today,* "a hellish childhood." A glandular birth defect known as cystic hygroma led to infected and swollen lymph nodes in his neck as a baby, a condition that caused a baseball-sized lump on his throat. When his father's Pentecostal ministry led the family from Canada to Seattle, Washington, the infant Peretti had the first of seven operations. However, once the cyst was removed, his tongue became affected, swelling and elongating, turning black, and oozing blood. "I was having trouble eating—imagine trying to swallow, even to chew, without the help of your tongue," Peretti told Lott. More operations followed, but the child's tongue—affected by toxins sent by the lymph glands—continued to protrude from his mouth, making speaking another trying event in his life. Even the faith healer Oral Roberts could do nothing for the symptoms the child showed.

When Peretti was at home, people did not stare or torment him for his differences. At school, however, he was embarrassed not only by his long, black tongue, but also by his diminutive size. As he told Jana Riess in *Publishers Weekly,* he looked like a "small, frail freak" as a kid. He began to retreat from public life of any sort, feeling safe only at home with his loving parents and siblings, and tucked away in his room with comic books, trading cards, and an active imagination that created stories starring various movie monsters. As Peretti noted in his memoir, *The Wounded Spirit,* "I think part of me wanted to be one, at least a monster who wins. I wouldn't have minded being Frankenstein. At least monsters could do something about their pain." He began to write monster stories, and he and his brother even built their own monsters, one of them called Xenarthex.

Peretti's condition slowly improved, aided in part by a speech therapist who trained Peretti at age twelve to be able to talk with his tongue inside his mouth. His Christian background also helped him through these difficult years, as he has commented. By the time he was in high school in Seattle, his storytelling skills had attracted a group of neighborhood kids. After graduating, he began playing banjo with a local bluegrass group. Married in 1972, he left the band and started a Christian music ministry, then studied English and film at UCLA for a time before he assisted in pastoring a small Assembly of God church on Vashon Island, Washington, with his father.

Peretti gave up the ministry in 1983, however, working in a ski factory, and began writing short stories and his first adult novel, *This Present Darkness.* Once the novel was finished, Peretti tried unsuccessfully to get his manuscript published with mainstream publishers. Finally Crossway Books, a Christian publishing house in Illinois, bought the book. *This Present Darkness* features protagonist Pastor Hank Busche and his heroic efforts to save a small college town from the Legions of Hell. The demons, in the guise of the Universal Consciousness Society, conspire to purchase the college and then subjugate humankind with the help of a Satanist professor, a New Age minister, a corrupt multinational corporation, and a police chief. Pastor Busche is aided in his efforts by a skeptical reporter who begins to see that this nefarious plot means to subjugate not only the townspeople, but the entire human race. The conspiracy is dramatically defeated when Pastor Busche summons an army of angels to repel the demons.

Published in 1986, this debut novel sold poorly for a year, suffering from poor distribution and a lack of promotion. Then the Christian singer Amy Grant began to praise the book to her audience, and word of mouth picked up. By 1988, the novel was selling 40,000 copies a month and Peretti was deep into a sequel, *The Piercing Darkness.* Peretti had a succession of blockbuster novels thereafter, including *Prophet, The Oath,* and *The Visitation.*

Peretti's first nonfiction book, *The Wounded Spirit,* was inspired by the 1999 shootings at Columbine High School that left thirteen people dead. Peretti explores the causes of youth violence and suggests some possible solutions by relating experiences from his own childhood and young adult years. In the book he details his painful youth and the cystic hygroma which caused him to be branded as an outsider, suffering the jibes and taunts of fellow students. Peretti compares this to the condition of Eric Harris and Dylan Klebold, the perpetrators of the Columbine tragedy, who had been teased and ostracized for their differences. It was a high school gym teacher who finally came to Peretti's aid, merely by being someone with whom a troubled young man could speak about his problems. Peretti urges those who hurt others to be kinder and more aware of the effects of their actions. He also encourages those who are injured by the pettiness and insensitivity of others to speak out about their pain, rather than letting resentments build. Reviewing *The Wounded Spirit* in *Publishers Weekly,* a critic stated: "This book is full of painful stories, but also memorable moments of hope, as Peretti recounts instances when a peer or a teacher stood up for him. This remarkable memoir will inspire readers to undertake similar acts of courageous compassion."

Peretti has also written a number of books specifically for young readers. In 1990, he created the first in a series of exotic adventure stories featuring Christian archaeologist Dr. Jake Cooper and his children, Jay and Lila. The first, *The Door in the Dragon's Throat,* involves a treasure hunt in the Middle East, while the second, *Escape from the Island of Aquarius,* tells of a manhunt for a missionary missing amongst a satanic cult in the South Pacific. In eight books, Peretti takes readers into cave tombs with a mysterious religion, and even into a battle between Soviet and CIA agents. In *The Secret of the Desert Stone,* the children and their father investigate a bizarre two-mile-high stone that appears overnight in Togwana. *The Deadly Curse of Toco-Rey* finds the trio in the jungles of Central America fighting the eponymous curse. *The Legend of Annie Murphy* has them dealing with a hundred-year-old ghost. And in *Flying Blind,* the importance of faith is emphasized when Jay must try to land his uncle's Cessna after suffering a head injury that has left him temporarily blind.

In "The Veritas Project" series, inaugurated in 2000 with *Hangman's Curse,* Peretti has developed books targeted at both teens and "tweens." Again using a family as the center of action, the author posits a secret government project, the Veritas Project, which is meant to aid the FBI in breaking drug rings and solving other crimes. *School Library Journal*'s Elaine Fort Weischedel called the series an "evangelical Christian X-Files." Featured in each title are Nate and Sarah Springfield, and their twin children, Elijah and Elisha.

In the debut title in the series, *Hangman's Curse,* the family goes undercover in a small town high school to try and solve a baffling crime. A mysterious curse has struck several of the football players, leaving them raving and crazed, tied to their hospital beds. In their delirium, they all mutter the name Abel Frye. Elijah and Elisha befriend many of the kids at school in an attempt to get the bottom of this Abel Frye mystery. Soon it becomes clear that the deadly madness is connected to a spider breeding in the walls of the school, and Elisha is put into mortal danger.

Weischedel felt that Peretti "develops the plot nicely," and that the religiosity of the Springfield family "does not interrupt the flow of the story, nor does anyone get preachy." Weischedel concluded, "Young teens should enjoy this fast-paced and atmospheric novel." A contributor for *Publishers Weekly* similarly praised *Hangman's Curse,* noting that Peretti's "comfortably paced, compelling performance consistently draws readers along." The same reviewer concluded, "Peretti has an obvious knack . . . for emphasizing his beliefs without preaching."

Peretti returns to the "Veritas Project" with the 2002 title, *Nightmare Academy,* in which the project team has a new assignment—to find out what really happened to two runaways. The Springfield twins go undercover again, posing as runaways themselves, ending up in an academy where there is no such thing as absolute truth.

Peretti has also coauthored, with Bill Ross, a series of books about the Bible, "Wild & Wacky Bible Stories," humorous retellings of stories that deal with themes including courage, helping others, obedience, and faith. A character named Mr. Henry relates the experiences of various biblical figures as they pertain to the topic at hand and how they connect to today's world. The books have also been adapted for videocassette and DVD, with Peretti himself playing the "absent-minded professor-type host," according to Kirsten Martindale in *School Library Journal.* Martindale further noted that the series "embraces biblical philosophy and religious values" and will have viewers "smiling their way through some traditionally serious subjects."

Commenting on the appeal of Peretti's novels, Lobdell wrote, "Whatever their genre may be, it is not 'fantasy.' . . . Still, Mr. Peretti deserves his sales, and many readers will get exactly what they want from his books."

BIOGRAPHICAL AND CRITICAL SOURCES:

BOOKS

Peretti, Frank E., *The Wounded Spirit* (memoir), Word Publications (Nashville, TN), 2000.

PERIODICALS

Booklist, September 1, 1995, John Mort, review of *The Oath,* p. 6; June, 1999, John Mort, review of *The Visitation,* p. 1743.
Bookstore Journal, January, 1988, p. 163.
Christianity Today, April 29, 1996, Michael G. Maudlin, review of *The Oath,* p. 24; August 9, 1999, Susan Wise Bauer, review of *The Visitation,* p. 70; March 4, 2001, Jeremy Lott, review of *The Wounded Spirit,* p. 99.
Dallas Morning News, December 2, 2000, Berta Delgado, "Author Tells All to Help Heal Others," p. 1G.
Harper's, September, 1996, Vince Passaro, review of *The Oath,* pp. 64-70.
Journal of Popular Culture, winter, 1994, Jay R. Howard, "Vilifying the Enemy: The Christian Right and the Novels of Frank Peretti," pp. 193-206.
Library Journal, August, 1989, p. 165; October 15, 1989, p. 50; November 1, 1991, p. 68; September 1, 1995, p. 158.
Nation, February 19, 1996, Donna Minkowitz, review of *The Oath,* pp. 25-28.
National Review, August 20, 1990, Jared Lobdell, review of *This Present Darkness,* pp. 45-47.
People, June 18, 1990, Andrew Abrahams, "Moved by the Spirit of the Lord, Frank Peretti Writes Theological Thrillers That Sell to Heaven," pp. 62-63.
Publishers Weekly, May 15, 1995, p. 15; August 17, 1998, Carol Chapman Stertzer, "Frank Peretti," p. S28; July 31, 2000, Marcia Nelson, "Post-Columbine Reflections," p. 44; October 30, 2000, review of *The Wounded Spirit,* p. 68, Jana Riess, "PW Talks with Frank Peretti," p. 69; May 14, 2001, review of *Hangman's Curse,* p. 40.
School Library Journal, February, 1986, p. 89; May, 1986, p. 96; July, 2001, Elaine Fort Weischedel, review of *Hangman's Curse,* p. 112; Kirsten Martindale, review of *Mr. Henry's Wild & Wacky World* (videocassettes), p. 64.
Seattle Times, September 1, 1999, Sally Macdonald, "'Christian Thrillers' Convert Readers," p. B1; June, 2002.
Time, November 13, 1995, Martha Duffy, review of *The Oath,* p. 105.
Voice Literary Supplement, July, 1990, p. 15.

OTHER

BookPage, http://www.bookpage.com/ (January 6, 2001), Etta Wilson, "Maturity Marks Frank Peretti's *The Visitation.*"
Frank Peretti Home Page, http://thewoundedspirit.com/ (June 11, 2002).
Steeling the Mind of America, http://www.steelingthemind.com/ (January 6, 2001), "Steeling Speaker, Frank Peretti Page."*

* * *

PÉREZ-REVERTE, Arturo 1951-

PERSONAL: Born November 24, 1951, in Cartagena, Spain. *Hobbies and other interests:* Sailing.

ADDRESSES: Agent—Harcourt Brace, 15 E. 26th St., New York, NY 10003; Alfaguara, Juan Bravo 38, 28006 Madrid, Spain.

CAREER: Journalist and author. War correspondent in African countries for the *Pueblo;* war correspondent for Spanish national television.

WRITINGS:

El húsar, Akal (Madrid, Spain), 1986.
El maestro de esgrima, Mondadori (Madrid, Spain), 1988, translation by Margaret Jull Costa published as *The Fencing Master,* Harcourt Brace (New York, NY), 1999.
La tabla de Flandes, Alfaguara (Madrid, Spain), 1990, translation by Margaret Jull Costa published as *The Flanders Panel,* Harcourt Brace (New York, NY), 1994, 1st paperback edition, Bantam Books (New York, NY), 1996.

El club Dumas, Santillana (Madrid, Spain), 1993, translation by Sonia Soto published as *The Club Dumas,* Harcourt Brace (New York, NY), 1996, 1st paperback edition, Vintage International (New York, NY), 1998.

La sombra del águila, Alfaguara (Madrid, Spain), 1993, new edition, Editorial Castalia (Madrid, Spain), 1999.

Territorio comanche: un relato, Ollero & Ramos (Madrid, Spain), 1994.

La piel del tambor (title means "The Skin of the Drum"), Santillana (Madrid, Spain), 1995, translation by Sonia Soto published as *The Seville Communion,* Harcourt Brace (New York, NY), 1998.

Los héroes cansados (collection), introduction by Santos Sanz Villanueva, Espasa Calpe (Madrid, Spain), 1995.

Obra breve (title means "Short Works"), Santillana (Madrid, Spain), 1995.

Patente de corso: 1993-1998, introduction and selection by José Luis Martín Nogales, Alfaguara (Madrid, Spain), 1998.

La carta esférica, Alfaguara (Madrid, Spain), 2000, translation by Margaret Sayers Peden published as *The Nautical Chart,* Harcourt (New York, NY), 2001.

"ADVENTURES OF CAPITÁN ALATRISTE" SERIES

El capitán Alatriste, Alfaguara (Madrid, Spain), 1996.
Limpieza de sangre, Alfaguara (Madrid, Spain), 1997.
El sol de Breda, Alfaguara (Madrid, Spain), 1998.
El oro del rey, Alfaguara (Madrid, Spain), 2000.

ADAPTATIONS: The Club Dumas was adapted for film as *The Ninth Door,* directed by Roman Polanski, 1999.

SIDELIGHTS: The Spanish novelist Arturo Pérez-Reverte may have been aided in his writing career by his popularity as a war correspondent and television personality, but it is his intelligence and literary acumen that have allowed him to remain a best-selling author in his native country and around the world. His novels have been translated into some nineteen languages and have sold more than three million copies. Five of his literary thrillers have been translated into English.

El maestro de esgrima, first released in 1988, was translated by Margaret Jull Costa as *The Fencing Master,* published in 1999. The tale is set in 1868 Madrid, where the fencing master Don Jaime Astarloa teaches his skill to young noblemen. He is approached by the beautiful Adela de Otero and offered a large sum of money to teach her his difficult secret sword thrust. He initially declines but her persistence outlasts his resolve. She soon improves on her already excellent swordmanship, and when a wealthy client who has taken Adela for his own is killed by Don Jaime's famous technique, she becomes a suspect. Barbara Hoffert of *Library Journal* called the novel "a fine tale of political intrigue with a lot of fencing lore deftly mixed in." A *Publishers Weekly* contributor commended Pérez-Reverte for his "lushly atmospheric suspense" and "spellbinding" prose that combines fencing, Spanish politics, and "the eternal lure of the femme fatale." Brad Hooper of *Booklist* explained that Don Jaime finally learns "what purpose his involuntary participation served—and this leads to a walloping ending."

The Flanders Panel, published in 1994, is a translation of Pérez-Reverte's 1990 novel *La tabla de Flandes.* It belongs to the genre of postmodern mysteries made popular by Italian author Umberto Eco, but in the opinion of the *Times Literary Supplement*'s Michael Eaude, "Pérez-Reverte's plotting is much tighter and his narrative is more exciting." The novel's heroine, Julia, is an art restorer who discovers a murder mystery hidden in a medieval painting of a chess game. The game's moves are continued in the form of messages and events in Julia's life amid the Madrid art world; gradually, she realizes that she has become a target in the centuries-old mystery.

Discussing the book with reservations about its "undistinguished" prose style and stereotyped characters, Eaude maintained that *The Flanders Panel* is never boring." The critic commended the way Pérez-Reverte worked background material, including chess moves, into the plot, and noted "a number of shocking twists." "Above all," Eaude concluded, "Pérez-Reverte makes use of a vivid imagination." Plaudits also came from a reviewer for the London *Observer,* who called the novel a "delightfully absorbing confection" and "ingenious hocus-pocus from start to finish." A *Publishers Weekly* contributor characterized the novel as "uneven but intriguing." That reviewer, like Eaude, faulted the characters as underdeveloped and also felt that the mystery was solved unconvincingly and conventionally. The reviewer responded most favorably to Pérez-Reverte's use of chess metaphors for human actions and to Julia's analyses of the painting, termed "clever and quite suspenseful."

Pérez-Reverte's most acclaimed novel is *El club Dumas* (1993), translated into English in 1997 as *The Club Dumas*. In this book, the author's proclivity for multi-layered wit is given full play. The novel revolves around a rare-book scout, Lucas Corso, who is asked to find the last two of the three existing copies of the Renaissance work *The Book of the Nine Doors to the Kingdom of Shadows,* in which each door is represented by an illustration that is crucial to Pérez-Reverte's plot. The murder of the owner of one copy in Portugal, and the theft of that volume's illustrations lead Corso and Irene Adler, an intriguing young woman who has been following him, to Paris in search of the third copy. As a favor to a bookseller friend, Corso has also taken on the job of verifying the authenticity of a manuscript, supposed to be Chapter 42 of Alexandre Dumas's *The Three Musketeers.* After many adventures, Corso finds himself caught up in the activities of a clandestine society known as the Club Dumas.

Margot Livesey of the *New York Times Book Review* wrote, "Mr. Pérez-Reverte . . . is extremely good on the business of book collecting. Among the pleasures of *The Club Dumas* is the intimate sense it conveys of this highly specialized type of commerce. . . . [He] does an admirable job of describing these bibliophiles, as well as of creating works like *The Nine Doors,* whose illustrations are reproduced and described in fascinating detail." A *Times Literary Supplement* reviewer reported, "Readers get, together with a mass of tables, diagrams, clues, decoys, and nudgings about intertextuality . . . all twenty-seven illustrations so that they can play spot-the-differences, and draw their own conclusions." The reviewer called *The Club Dumas* a "wayward and moderately enjoyable" mystery novel. *Booklist* contributor Brian Kenney labeled the novel "witty, suspenseful, and intellectually provocative." Although Livesey said she found herself "growing impatient" with some of the plot twists and narrative techniques, she called the book an "intelligent and delightful novel." *The Club Dumas* was adapted as the 1999 film *The Ninth Door,* starring the American actor Johnny Depp.

Pérez-Reverte's 1995 novel *La piel del tambor,* translated by Sonia Soto as *The Seville Communion* (1998), was noted by reviewers for its enjoyably skillful plotting, rich use of background information (including in this case a map of Seville, Spain), and intellectual gamesmanship. The premise of the narrative is that the secret files of the Vatican have been broken into by a computer hacker whose message implores the Pope to help save a seventeenth-century Seville church destined to be demolished. The church, it is said, "kills to defend itself." Father Lorenzo Quart, a tall, good-looking priest-sleuth, is called in to investigate. Meanwhile, the parish priest, aided by an American nun, is fighting the corrupt real-estate developer who wants to build on the church site. Quart's self-discipline is challenged by the presence of a beautiful duchess whose estranged husband is a banker involved in the real-estate deal.

A reviewer for the *Economist* called Pérez-Reverte "a master of intelligent suspense and reader-friendly action" and pointed out that this novel was "a hymn to Seville" and a work in which "postmodernistic tics do not interfere with a smoothly written, realist novel." Paul Baumann, in a review for the *New York Times Book Review,* called Quart "a St. James Bond, an agent in a Roman collar and handmade leather shoes who wields a Mont Blanc pen instead of a snub-nosed Beretta." Baumann found the novel "good fun," "entertaining," and sometimes "silly." A *Publishers Weekly* contributor commented, "Despite some unconvincing plotting and a few heavy-handed moments, Pérez-Reverte's characters capture the imagination." John Elson of *Time* called the book "one of those infrequent whodunits that transcend the genre." Baumann wrote, "Pérez-Reverte writes with wit, narrative economy, a sharp eye for the telling detail and a feel for history. . . . you'd have to be a remarkably faithless reader not to want to visit Seville after finishing this flavorful confection." Elson concluded that the novel "may well inspire readers to order round-trip tickets to an ancient city redolent of jasmine and orange blossoms."

La carta esférica comes from the author's lifelong love for the sea and sailing. Translated by Margaret Sayers Peden as *The Nautical Chart,* it involves an undersea treasure hunt for a fortune in emeralds amid the wreckage of a Jesuit ship sunk in the Mediterranean during the mid-eighteenth century. The protagonist, an exiled sailor named Manuel Coy, meets the beautiful Tanger Soto of Madrid's Naval Museum after she wins the bid for an old nautical map at an auction in Barcelona. Coy joins Soto in her search for the sunken treasure off the coast of Spain in the wreckage of the *Dei Gloria.* However, they encounter a group of sinister treasure seekers who want to stand in their way. As Coy falls in love with Soto, the reader begins to wonder whether she will betray him.

A *Publishers Weekly* contributor commented on the fact that the book was half over before the plot reached the sea but thought "the underwater sequences that climax the story are masterfully done." Bill Ott of *Booklist* wrote, "There is no universal meridian . . . when the course being charted attempts to penetrate the human heart." Ott wrote of Pérez-Reverte that he has "established himself as a master of the literary thriller" and "unfailingly melds a multifaceted tale of intrigue with characters of depth and dimension."

BIOGRAPHICAL AND CRITICAL SOURCES:

PERIODICALS

Atlantic, September, 1994, p. 114.

Booklist, May 15, 1994, p. 1667; October 1, 1996, Brian Kenney, review of *The Club Dumas,* p. 292; February 1, 1999, Brad Hooper, review of *The Fencing Master,* p. 941; July, 2001, Bill Ott, review of *The Nautical Chart,* p. 1951; January 1 and 15, 2002, Editors' Choice 2001, review of *The Nautical Chart,* p. 762.

Books, September, 1994, p. 26; September, 1995, p. 25.

Book World, July 18, 1999, review of *The Fencing Master,* p. 15.

Economist, July 20, 1996, pp. 14-15.

Globe and Mail, June 19, 1999, review of *The Fencing Master,* p. D 12.

Kirkus Reviews, February 15, 1998, review of *The Seville Communion,* p. 218; April 1, 1999, review of *The Fencing Master,* p. 478; July 15, 2001, review of *The Nautical Chart.*

Library Journal, June 15, 1994, p. 96; September 1, 1996, p. 211; March 15, 1998, review of *The Seville Communion,* p. 95; March 15, 1999, Barbara Hoffert, review of *The Fencing Master,* p. 110.

Los Angeles Times Book Review, June 28, 1998, review of *The Seville Communion,* p. 7; September 5, 1999, reviews of *The Seville Communion, The Flanders Panel, The Club Dumas,* and *The Fencing Master,* p. 9.

Maclean's, June 21, 1999, review of *The Fencing Master,* p. 52.

New Yorker, April 27, 1998, review of *The Seville Communion,* p. 161.

New York Times Book Review, June 12, 1994, p. 42; December 4, 1994, p. 69; September 22, 1996, p. 40; March 23, 1997, Margot Livesey, "The Book Case," review of *The Club Dumas,* Late Edition, Final, Section 7, p. 10; May 3, 1998, Paul Baumann, "Holy Orders," review of *The Seville Communion,* Late Edition, Final, Section 7, p. 33; June 7, 1998, review of *The Club Dumas,* p. 36; May 23, 1999, review of *The Seville Communion,* p. 36; June 6, 1999, review of *The Fencing Master,* p. 26.

Observer (London), July 31, 1994, review of *The Flanders Panel,* p. 5B; March 7, 1999, review of *The Fencing Master,* p. 11.

People Weekly, May 12, 1997, p. 30.

Publishers Weekly, May 2, 1994, review of *The Flanders Panel,* p. 284; July 15, 1996, p. 23; November 18, 1996, p. 61; February 23, 1998, review of *The Seville Communion,* p. 49; March 1, 1999, review of *The Fencing Master,* p. 57; August 13, 2001, review of *The Nautical Chart,* p. 281.

Time, June 1, 1998, John Elson, review of *The Seville Communion,* p. 87; July 12, 1999, review of *The Fencing Master,* p. 77.

Times Educational Supplement, December 29, 1995, p. 12.

Times Literary Supplement, August 12, 1994, Michael Eaude, review of *The Flanders Panel,* p. 23; September 6, 1996, review of *The Club Dumas,* p. 23; July 24, 1998, review of *The Seville Communion,* p. 21; December 4, 1998, review of *Patente de corso: 1993-1998,* p. 8; April 9, 1999, review of *The Fencing Master,* p. 27.

Translation Review Supplement, December, 1999, review of *The Fencing Master,* p. 33.

ONLINE

Freelance Spain, http://www.spainview.com/ (April 30, 2002), "Arturo Perez-Reverte."

Mostly Fiction, http://mostlyfiction.com/ (April 30, 2002), "Arturo Pérez-Reverte," review of *The Seville Communion.**

PETERSON, Audrey

PERSONAL: Born in Los Angeles, CA; daughter of Alvin (an engineer) and Alice (a homemaker; maiden name, Corwin) Nelson; married Roscoe Buckland (a university professor); children: three daughters. *Education:* University of California, Los Angeles, A.B.; Long Beach State College (now California State University, Long Beach, M.A.); University of Southern California, Ph.D.

ADDRESSES: Home—931 High St., Bellingham, WA 98225. *Agent*—Mitchell J. Hamilburg, Mitchell J. Hamilburg Agency, 292 South La Cienega Blvd., Suite 212, Beverly Hills, CA 90211.

CAREER: California State University, Long Beach, CA, professor of English literature, 1966-86; writer, 1974—.

MEMBER: Mystery Writers of America, Sisters in Crime, Crime Writers Association of Great Britain.

WRITINGS:

Victorian Masters of Mystery: From Wilkie Collins to Conan Doyle (nonfiction), Ungar (New York, NY), 1984.
An Unmourned Death (novel), Five Star (Waterville, ME), 2002.

"CLAIRE CAMDEN" MYSTERIES

The Nocturne Murder, Arbor House (New York, NY), 1987.
Death in Wessex, Pocket Books (New York, NY), 1989.
Murder in Burgundy, Pocket Books (New York, NY), 1989.
Deadly Rehearsal, Pocket Books (New York, NY), 1990.
Elegy in a Country Graveyard, Pocket Books (New York, NY), 1990.
Lament for Christabel, Pocket Books (New York, NY), 1991.

"ANDREW QUENTIN AND JANE WINFIELD" MYSTERIES

Dartmoor Burial, Pocket Books (New York, NY), 1992.
Death Too Soon, Pocket Books (New York, NY), 1994.
Shroud for a Scholar, Pocket Books (New York, NY), 1995.

Contributor to journals, including *Victorian Newsletter, Victorian Studies,* and *Western American Literature.*

SIDELIGHTS: Audrey Peterson once told *CA* that her mystery series sleuths "spend a lot of time in England and on the continent, places which I enjoy and visit often . . . . [They] inhabit the academic world with which I am familiar, and I make use of my lifelong pleasure in opera and concert-going to provide a musical background to my books." Peterson has written two series of mystery books. The first, which includes titles such as *Dartmoor Burial, Death Too Soon,* and *Shroud for a Scholar,* features lead character Claire Camden, a California English professor living in London. The second series is about music professor Andrew Quentin and his former student, Jane Winfield, a British-born journalist and music writer. The pair stars in Peterson's *Nocturne Murder, Death in Wessex, Murder in Burgundy, Deadly Rehearsal, Elegy in a Country Graveyard,* and *Lament for Christabel.*

In the historical mystery *An Unmourned Death,* Peterson reaches back to 1885 England to relate the tale of a female private eye. Jasmine Malloy, widowed at thirty and employed by a London firm, travels to upper-class Devon to investigate the disappearance of the Baron Renstone's teenage daughter. The plot thickens when the unpleasant Renstone himself is discovered murdered, with the Baron's son evidently framed for the crime. Pregnant maidservants, incest, and a new theory of evolution also enter into the puzzle. Meanwhile, Jasmine's sleuthing may result in a love interest for her in the form of James Keeler, a co-worker. A *Kirkus Reviews* contributor praised *An Unmourned Death* as "an adroit novel in the 'Upstairs, Downstairs' tradition." GraceAnne A. DeCandido of *Booklist,* while finding the novel "slight and overstuffed at the same time," nonetheless decided that Peterson's book "still manages to be a page-turner." Peterson is also the author of a nonfiction guide, *Victorian Masters of Mystery: From Wilkie Collins to Conan Doyle.*

BIOGRAPHICAL AND CRITICAL SOURCES:

PERIODICALS

Armchair Detective, summer, 1993, review of *Dartmoor Burial,* p. 102; spring, 1996, review of *Shroud for a Scholar,* p. 232.

Booklist, April 1, 2002, GraceAnne A. DeCandido, review of *An Unmourned Death,* p. 1310.

Kirkus Reviews, February 15, 2002, review of *An Unmourned Death,* p. 225.

Kliatt Young Adult Paperback Book Guide, January, 1993, review of *Dartmoor Burial,* p. 11; September, 1994, review of *Death Too Soon,* p. 10.

Los Angeles Times, September 27, 1987.*

*   *   *

PETERSON, Michael L. 1950-

PERSONAL: Born January 7, 1950; married Rebecca Shannon (a Christian education director); children: Aaron, Adam. *Education:* Asbury College, B.A. (cum laude), 1972; University of Kentucky, M.A. (summa cum laude), 1974; State University of New York at Buffalo, Ph.D. (with distinction), 1976. *Hobbies and other interests:* Basketball, chess.

ADDRESSES: Home—113 Lowry Ln., Wilmore, KY 40390. *Office*—Department of Philosophy, Asbury College, Wilmore, KY 40390.

CAREER: Roberts Wesleyan College, Rochester, NY, professor of philosophy, 1974-78; Asbury College, Wilmore, KY, professor of philosophy, 1978—. *Faith and Philosophy,* managing editor.

MEMBER: American Philosophical Association, Society of Christian Philosophers, Wesleyan Theological Society.

AWARDS, HONORS: Fellow of Institute of Advanced Christian Studies, 1979-80, and Pew Evangelical Scholarship Initiative.

WRITINGS:

Evil and the Christian God, Baker Book House (Grand Rapids, MI), 1982.

(Editor) *A Spectrum of Thought: Essays in Honor of Dennis F. Kinlaw,* Francis Asbury (Grand Rapids, MI), 1982.

Philosophy of Education: Issues and Options, Inter-Varsity Press (Downers Grove, IL), 1986.

(With William Hasker, B. Reichenbach, and D. Basinger) *Reason and Religious Belief: An Introduction to the Philosophy of Religion,* Oxford University Press, 1990.

(Editor) *The Problem of Evil: Selected Readings,* University of Notre Dame Press (Notre Dame, IN), 1992, second edition, 1998.

(With William Hasker, B. Reichenbach, and D. Basinger) *Philosophy of Religion: Selected Readings,* Oxford University Press, 1995, second edition, 2001.

God and Evil: An Introduction to the Issues, Westview Press (Boulder, CO), 1998.

Contributor to philosophy journals.

WORK IN PROGRESS: Christian Theism and the Problem of Evil; The Case of Job: A Theological and Philosophical Study; Against a Silent Sky, a documentary film based on the book *The Problem of Evil,* to be broadcast by Public Broadcasting Service in 2003.

SIDELIGHTS: Michael L. Peterson told *CA:* "Born in a mining town in southwestern Indiana, I always enjoyed thinking hard about things. During my high school years, I began to read the classics. During my college years, I declared a philosophy major and married my high school sweetheart, two events that have shaped my life. Throughout my career, the enjoyment of teaching and research has been surpassed only by the benefits and wonders of married family life.

"Although my doctoral dissertation was in the philosophy of science, quite a lot of my professional writing has been in the philosophy of religion. My career is characterized by a couple of basic themes: the mutual compatibility and fruitful relation between intellectual pursuit and Christian faith, and the necessity (and nobility) of rational dialogue among people of all points of view."

*   *   *

PETRY, Alice Hall 1951-

PERSONAL: Born July 8, 1951, in Hartford, CT; daughter of James B. and Elizabeth K. Hall; married John E. Farley, 1997. *Education:* University of Connecticut, B.S. (with highest honors), 1973; Connecticut College, M.A., 1976; Brown University, Ph.D. (with distinction), 1979. *Politics:* Independent. *Religion:* Episcopalian.

ADDRESSES: Office—Department of English, Southern Illinois University at Edwardsville, Edwardsville, IL 62026-1431.

CAREER: Rhode Island School of Design, Providence, instructor, 1979-80, assistant professor, 1980-86, associate professor of English, 1986-95; Southern Illinois University at Edwardsville, professor and chair of English department, 1995-2001. Visiting professor at University of Colorado, Boulder, spring, 1987. Consultant to Center for Contemporary Media, Los Angeles, CA, USIA lecturer in Japan, 1991.

AWARDS, HONORS: Grant from National Endowment for the Humanities, 1982; Fulbright scholar at Universidade Federal do Parana (Brazil), 1985; senior postdoctoral fellow of American Council of Learned Societies, 1987-88.

WRITINGS:

A Genius in His Way: The Art of Cable's "Old Creole Days," Fairleigh Dickinson University Press (Teaneck, NJ), 1988.

Fitzgerald's Craft of Short Fiction: The Collected Stories, 1920-1935, UMI Research Press (Ann Arbor, MI), 1989.

Understanding Anne Tyler, University of South Carolina Press (Columbia, SC), 1990.

Critical Essays on Anne Tyler, Macmillan (New York, NY)/G. K. Hall (Boston, MA), 1992.

Critical Essays on Kate Chopin, Macmillan (New York, NY)/G. K. Hall (Boston, MA), 1996.

Contributor of more than forty-nine articles and more than one hundred reviews to literature, humanities, and southern studies journals.

SIDELIGHTS: Alice Hall Petry told *CA:* "My interest in southern literature came about due to one of those serendipitous situations that make scholarly activity so endlessly intriguing. In graduate school I was preparing a term paper on the New England local colorists when it occurred to me that it might be interesting to investigate other aspects of regional writing as well. So for the sake of a balanced paper I decided to look at a handful of southern writers—and discovered, to my Yankee horror, that this body of literature was far more powerful, technically innovative, and poignant than anything I had encountered from New England. From that moment, my career was effectively redirected, with the bulk of my research thereafter focusing on southern literature."

*   *   *

PIERCE, Tamora 1954-

PERSONAL: Born December 13, 1954, in South Connellsville, PA; daughter of Wayne Franklin and Jacqueline S. Pierce. *Education:* University of Pennsylvania, B.A., 1976. *Hobbies and other interests:* "I am interested in medieval customs, life, and chivalry. I study Japanese, Central Asian, and Arabic history and culture; wildlife and nature; crime; the American Civil War; and the conflicts between Islam and Christianity in the Middle Ages and the Renaissance. Occasionally I rescue hurt or homeless animals in a local park . . . visit schools as often as I can, and read, read, read."

ADDRESSES: Agent—Craig R. Tenney, Harold Ober Associates, 425 Madison Ave., New York, NY 10017.

CAREER: City of Kingston, NY, tax data collector, 1977-78; towns of Hardenburgh and Denning, NY, tax clerk, 1978; McAuley Home for Girls, Buhl, ID, social worker and housemother, 1978-79; Harold Ober Associates, New York, NY, assistant to literary agent, 1979-82; ZPPR Productions, Inc. (radio producers), creative director, 1982-86; Chase Investment Bank, New York, NY, secretary, 1985-89; freelance writer, 1990—. Former instructor, Free Woman's University, University of Pennsylvania.

MEMBER: Authors Guild, Science Fiction, and Fantasy Writers of America.

AWARDS, HONORS: Author's Citation, Alumni Association of the New Jersey Institute of Technology, 1984, for *Alanna: The First Adventure;* Schüler-Express ZDF Preis (Germany), 1985, and South Carolina Children's Book Award nomination, 1985-86, both

Tamora Pierce

for *In the Hand of the Goddess;* Children's Paperbacks Bestseller, *Australian Bookseller and Publisher,* 1995, for *Wolf-Speaker;* Best Books for Young Adults list, Hawaii State Library, Best Science Fiction, Fantasy and Horror list,*Voice of Youth Advocates,* both 1995, and Best Books for Young Adults list, American Library Association, 1996, all for *The Emperor Mage;* Best Science Fiction, Fantasy and Horror list, *Voice of Youth Advocates,* 1996, and Best Books for the Teen Age list, New York Public Library, 1997, both for *The Realms of the Gods.*

WRITINGS:

"SONG OF THE LIONESS" SERIES; FANTASY NOVELS; FOR YOUNG PEOPLE

Alanna: The First Adventure, Atheneum (New York, NY), 1983.
In the Hand of the Goddess, Atheneum (New York, NY), 1984.
The Woman Who Rides Like a Man, Atheneum (New York, NY), 1986.
Lioness Rampant, Atheneum (New York, NY), 1988.

"THE IMMORTALS" SERIES; FANTASY NOVELS; FOR YOUNG PEOPLE

Wild Magic, Atheneum (New York, NY), 1992.
Wolf-Speaker, Atheneum (New York, NY), 1994.
The Emperor Mage, Atheneum (New York, NY), 1995.
The Realms of the Gods, Atheneum (New York, NY), 1996.

"CIRCLE OF MAGIC" SERIES; FANTASY NOVELS; FOR YOUNG PEOPLE

Sandry's Book, Scholastic (New York, NY), 1996.
Tris's Book, Scholastic (New York, NY), 1998.
Daja's Book, Scholastic (New York, NY), 1998.
Briar's Book, Scholastic (New York, NY), in press.

OTHER

(Contributor) Steve Ditlea, editor, *Digital Deli,* Workman (New York, NY), 1984.
(Contributor) Douglas Hill, editor, *Planetfall,* Oxford University Press (New York , NY), 1985.
First Test, Random House (New York, NY), 1999.
Magic Steps, Scholastic Press (New York, NY), 2000.
Page, Random House (New York, NY), 2000.
Street Images, Scholastic Press (New York, NY), 2001.

Author of radio scripts aired on National Public Radio, 1987-89. Contributor to periodicals, including *Christian Century* and *School Library Journal.* Pierce's works have been translated into German, Danish, and Spanish.

SIDELIGHTS: Tamora Pierce's fantasy novels for young readers are noted for their strong female protagonists and imaginative, well-drawn plots. In her "Song of the Lioness" quartet, Pierce features Alanna, a young woman who disguises herself as a man in order to train as a knight, and then uses her physical strength and healing capabilities to serve Prince Jonathan and engage in numerous medieval adventures. "I enjoy writing for teenagers," Pierce once told *CA,* "because I feel I help to make life easier for kids who are like I was.

"I owe my career as a writer and my approach to writing to people like my writing mentor, David Bradley, who taught me that writing is not an arcane and mystical process, administered by the initiate and fraught with obstacles, but an enjoyable pastime that gives other people as much pleasure as it does me. I enjoy telling stories, and, although some of my topics are grim, people get caught up in them."

Alanna: The First Adventure, the first novel in the "Song of the Lioness" series, focuses on the title character's determination to avoid the traditional fate of young women her age—life in a secluded convent. Instead, she changes identities with her brother and begins training to become a knight in the service of her country's king. In Pierce's second novel, *In the Hand of the Goddess,* Alanna, now a squire, struggles to master skills necessary to survive her test for knighthood. After successfully protecting Prince Jonathan in battle, she eventually decides to leave royal service in search of further adventures. Proving her worth in physical combat, Alanna is accepted by a tribe of desert warriors, and ultimately becomes their shaman, in *The Woman Who Rides Like a Man.* Alanna broadens the outlook of these desert people, raising a few women of the tribe to an equal level with the men before moving on to other adventures. And in *Lioness Rampant,* the final volume of the quartet, the stubborn heroine, now legendary for her magical powers and skills in battle, goes on a quest for the King of Tortall. She also encounters love in the warrior Liam; his dislike of her magical powers, however, makes their relationship fragile. Calling Pierce "a great storyteller," a *Junior Bookshelf* reviewer praised the series' inventive characters in particular, saying the heroine's "sword, her companion and her cat will always be ready to rise to any emergency." In a *School Library Journal* review of *In the Hand of the Goddess,* Isabel Soffer praised Pierce's books about Alanna as "sprightly, filled with adventure and marvelously satisfying."

Pierce followed her "Song of the Lioness" novels with a second series, "The Immortals," which began with *Wild Magic.* Although Alanna appears in the novel, the new protagonist is thirteen-year-old Daine, an orphaned teen who has an unexplained empathy with wild creatures and a sixth sense that allows her to foresee danger. In fact, she is in danger of reverting to a wild creature herself until the wizard Numair teaches her to channel her "wild magic." Daine then uses her powers to stop evil humans from coercing the newly arrived Immortals—dragons, griffins, spidrens, and Stormwings—to help them accomplish destructive purposes. Sally Estes in *Booklist* called *Wild Magic* "a

dynamic story sure to engross fantasy fans," and Anne A. Flowers, in *Horn Book,* said readers will "find in Daine a strong heroine whose humble beginning makes her well-deserved rewards even more gratifying."

Reviewing *Wolf-Speaker,* the sequel to *Wild Magic,* Mary L. Adams wrote in *Voice of Youth Advocates*: "Daine is a super new heroine who makes this action-packed fantasy a joy to read." Bonnie Kunzel commented in *School Library Journal* that *Wolf-Speaker* "is a compulsively readable novel that [young adults] won't be able to put down until the final battle is over and good triumphs. Pierce's faithful readers as well as any action-adventure or animal fantasy fans will be delighted with this new series." Daine's adventures continue in other "Immortals" novels, which include *The Emperor Mage* and *The Realms of the Gods,* the concluding novel of the series in which Pierce's young female protagonist convinces dragons and other Immortal creatures to fight on her side against evil.

Magic again is central to Pierce's fantasy series, "Circle of Magic." In *Sandry's Book,* "a rich and satisfying read," according to a *Kirkus Reviews* critic, Sandry, Daja, Briar, and Trisana—four young people from various walks of life—meet and become friends while living in a temple community. As the four protagonists overcome the negative aspects of their lives, they learn a variety of crafts as well as the use of their unique powers, including magic.

BIOGRAPHICAL AND CRITICAL SOURCES:

BOOKS

Twentieth-Century Young Adult Writers, St. James Press (Detroit, MI), 1994.

PERIODICALS

Booklist, October 15, 1992, p. 419; March 15, 1994, p. 1344; June 1-15, 1995, p. 1757; October 15, 1996, p. 414.
Bulletin of the Center for Children's Books, November, 1984, p. 53; April, 1986, p. 156; November, 1997, pp. 97-98.
Horn Book, May-June, 1986, pp. 333-34; March-April, 1989, p. 234; January-February, 1993, p. 93; September-October, 1994, p. 613; July-August, 1995, p. 485.

Junior Bookshelf, October, 1989, p. 243.

Kirkus Reviews, August 1, 1988, pp. 1154-55; October 15, 1992, p. 1314; July 15, 1997.

School Library Journal, December, 1984, p. 94; July, 1995, p. 80; August, 1995, pp. 37-38; November, 1996, p. 124.

Voice of Youth Advocates, April, 1985, p. 56; December, 1988, p. 248; August, 1994, p. 159; April, 1995, p. 14.*

*   *   *

PINEIRO, R. J. 1961-

PERSONAL: Born April 17, 1961, in Havana, Cuba; U.S. citizen; son of Rogelio A. (an electrical engineer) and Dora R. (a homemaker) Pineiro; married Lory M., October 15, 1983; children: Cameron R. *Ethnicity:* "Hispanic." *Education:* Louisiana State University, B.S., 1983. *Religion:* Roman Catholic. *Hobbies and other interests:* Tae kwon do (second-degree black belt), flying (private pilot's license), playing classical guitar.

ADDRESSES: Home—Austin, TX. *Agent*—Trident Media Group, 152 West 57th Street, New York, NY, 10019. *E-mail*—author@rjpineiro.com.

CAREER: Engineering manager and writer. Advanced Micro Devices, Austin, TX, engineering manager, 1983—.

WRITINGS:

Siege of Lightning, Berkley Publishing (New York, NY), 1993.

Ultimatum, Tor Books (New York, NY), 1994.

Retribution, Tor Books (New York, NY), 1995.

Exposure, Tor Books (New York, NY), 1996.

Breakthrough, Forge (New York, NY), 1997.

01-01-00: A Novel of the Millennium, Forge (New York, NY), 1999.

Y2K, Tor Books (New York, NY), 1999.

Shutdown, Forge (New York, NY), 2000.

Conspiracy.com, Forge (New York, NY), 2001.

Firewall, Tom Doherty Associates (New York, NY), 2002.

Cyberterror, Tom Doherty Associates (New York, NY), 2003.

Also author of novellas and short stories titled *Combat—Fight of Endeavour, A Spook in Paradise, From Havana to Silicon Hills, Green Zeroes,* and *Air Infantry.*

ADAPTATIONS: Several works are available on audiocassette.

SIDELIGHTS: R. J. Pineiro was born in Cuba and grew up in Central America. A longtime worker in the computer industry, accomplished pilot, expert in martial arts, and gun buff, Pineiro combines his enthusiasm in these arenas to make his internationally acclaimed techno-thrillers not only exciting but intricately detailed and technically correct. He travels extensively throughout Asia, the Americas, and Europe, gathering research for his novels as well as his computer career.

The plot of *01-01-00: A Novel of the Millennium* centers around cybercop Susan Garnett and her arch enemy Bloodaxe, an expert computer hacker who sabotaged the Washington, DC, computer-based transportation code after he was fired by government officials. Bloodaxe's actions resulted in the death of Susan's husband and daughter and put Susan in a coma. Two years later, Susan tracks down Bloodaxe and he lands in prison. Her goal achieved and her family gone, a depressed Susan is considering suicide when the head of the FBI's high-tech crime department solicits her expertise and aid in averting a worldwide catastrophe. Twenty days before the millennium and at exactly the same time, every computer in the world froze for twenty seconds; with nineteen days to go, they froze for nineteen seconds. The millennium countdown is on, and Susan's life takes on new meaning. Her dilemma, however, is that the one person with the skill to help her prevent disaster is Bloodaxe. Together they determine that the computer virus originated in an ancient Mayan city. Susan heads for the jungles of Guatemala, where, with the aid of a Mayan anthropologist, she attempts to find and exterminate the deadly virus.

Harriet Klausner, reviewing the book for *BookBrowser Review* online, commented: "*01-01-00* is a well-designed millennium high tech thriller. The story is unique, fast-paced, and never buries the reader in scientific jargon. One of the charms of R.J. Pineiro's novel is those understandable explanations that always completely flow within the plot. Thus, asides to the audience or simply ignoring the reader never occurs. The complex sub-plots merge into an interesting climax where the modern world converges with the ancient world in a wondrous novel that deserves much acclaim."

Shutdown, called "fast paced and cutting edge" by Carol DeAngelo in *School Library Journal,* hooks the reader quickly and presents a believable and terrifying scenario in which a covert group within the Japanese Defense Agency coerces discontented engineers to sabotage semiconductors manufactured in the United States. These faulty components cause plane and train crashes that kill hundreds of people in various places and leave Detroit totally without electric power. Erika Conklin—a young woman caught hacking the computer system at the University of Berkeley and now employed by the FBI in lieu of a prison sentence—becomes an invaluable member of the team attempting to uncover the deadly operation. DeAngelo wrote: "The appeal to young adults stems from the personalities of Erika and the government forces with which she works. . . . Readers are taken along on a mission by a crack Navy SEAL team whose exploits, abilities, and bravery are compelling and illuminating."

Conspiracy.com, Lynn Nutwell wrote in *School Library Journal,* is "a techno-thriller in which virtual-reality scenarios woven smoothly into the plot inject sufficient energy and intrigue to compensate for short-comings in character development and dialogue." An IRS money-laundering scheme involves a major bank, a giant software company, and a wealthy business owner connected with Cuba and Castro. Big Brother-type invasions into individuals' private lives, assassinations of people and careers, and a kidnapping are among the ingredients that make this technically complex and intricately detailed novel an action-packed suspense thriller.

Action and suspense again combine with technical intricacy in *Firewall,* in which international intrigue leads the characters on a dangerous and deadly path through North Korea and to the isle of Capri. When a former East German agent is hired by North Korea to steal the access codes to a U.S. spy satellite capable of causing mass destruction, Bruce Tucker and Monica Fox—who have each been given respective halves of the password to the codes—become entangled in a web of terrorism, counterterrorism, and spies. "Pineiro

has a knack of spinning cliffhanging twists into impossible situations resolved by explosively clever means," commented a reviewer for *Publishers Weekly.*

BIOGRAPHICAL AND CRITICAL SOURCES:

PERIODICALS

Armchair Detective, winter, 1997, review of *Exposure,* p. 116.
Booklist, June 1, 1999, David Pitt, review of *01-01-00: A Novel of the Millennium,* p. 1800; March 1, 2001, David Pitt, review of *Conspiracy.com,* p. 1231.
Kirkus Reviews, July 15, 1997, review of *Breakthrough,* p. 1057.
Publishers Weekly, February 18, 2002, review of *Firewall,* p. 77.
School Library Journal, September, 2000, Carol DeAngelo, review of *Shutdown,* p. 259; September, 2001, Lynn Nutwell, review of *Conspiracy.com,* p. 259.

ONLINE

BookBrowser Review, http://www.bookbrowser.com/Reviews/ (April 2, 2002), Harriet Klausner, review of *01-01-00: A Novel of the Millennium.*
R.J. Pineiro Web page, http://www.rjpineiro.com/ (April 2, 2002).

*   *   *

PLUCKROSE, Henry (Arthur) 1931-

PERSONAL: Born October 23, 1931, in London, England; son of Henry and Ethel Pluckrose; married Helen Fox, May 31, 1955; children: Patrick, Elspeth, Hilary. *Education:* Attended St. Mark and St. John College, 1952-54, and Institute of Education, London, part-time, 1958-60; College of Preceptors, F.C.P., 1976.

ADDRESSES: Home—3 Butts Lane, Danbury, Essex, England. *Office*—Evans Brothers Ltd., Montague House, Russell Sq., London WC1B 5BX, England.

CAREER: Teacher of elementary school-aged children in inner London, England, 1954-68; Prior Weston School, London, headteacher, beginning 1968; Evans Brothers Ltd., London, editor for art and craft in education, 1968—. *Military service:* British Army, Royal Army Education Corps, 1950-52.

WRITINGS:

Let's Make Pictures, Mills & Boon (London, England), 1965, 2nd edition, 1972, Taplinger (New York, NY), 1967.

Creative Arts and Crafts: A Handbook for Teachers in Primary Schools, Macdonald (London, England), 1966, 2nd edition, 1969, Roy (New York, NY), 1967.

Introducing Crayon Techniques, Watson-Guptill (New York, NY), 1967.

Let's Work Large: A Handbook of Art Techniques for Teachers in Primary Schools, Taplinger (New York, NY), 1967.

Introducing Acrylic Painting, Watson-Guptill (New York, NY), 1968.

(Compiler) *The Art and Craft Book,* Evans Brothers (London, England), 1969.

(Editor, with Frank Peacock) *A Dickens Anthology,* Mills & Boon (London, England), 1970.

Creative Themes, Evans Brothers (London, England), 1969, International Publications Service (Levittown, PA), 1970.

(Editor) *A Book of Crafts,* Regnery (Chicago, IL), 1971.

Art & Craft Today, Evans Brothers (London, England), 1971.

Art, Citation Press (New York, NY), 1972.

(Compiler) *A Craft Collection,* Evans Brothers (London, England), 1973.

Open School, Open Society, Evans Brothers (London, England), 1975.

Seen in Britain, Mills & Boon (London, England), 1977.

A Sourcebook of Picture Making, Evans Brothers (London, England), 1977.

(Editor, with Peter Wilby) *The Condition of English Schools,* Penguin (London, England), 1980.

(Editor, with Peter Wilby) *Education 2000,* Temple Smith (London, England), 1980.

Print Ideas, Evans Brothers (London, England), 1980.

Talk about Growing, illustrated by Chris Fairclough, Watts (London, England), 1980.

Play and Learn Book, Watts (London, England), 1981.

"THINGS" SERIES

Things to See, F. Watts (New York, NY), 1971.

Things to Touch, F. Watts (New York, NY), 1971.

Things to Hear, F. Watts (New York, NY), 1973.

Things That Move, F. Watts (New York, NY), 1973.

Things Big and Small, F. Watts (New York, NY), 1974.

Things Have Shapes, F. Watts (New York, NY), 1974.

Things That Pull, F. Watts (New York, NY), 1974.

Things That Push, F. Watts (New York, NY), 1974.

Things Light and Heavy, F. Watts (New York, NY), 1975.

Things That Cut, F. Watts (New York, NY), 1975.

Things Left and Right, F. Watts (New York, NY), 1975.

Things That Grow, F. Watts (New York, NY), 1975.

Things That Float, F. Watts (New York, NY), 1975.

Things That Hold, F. Watts (New York, NY), 1975.

Things Hard and Soft, F. Watts (New York, NY), 1976.

Things Up and Down, F. Watts (New York, NY), 1976.

Things to Smell, F. Watts (New York, NY), 1977.

Things Hot and Cold, F. Watts (New York, NY), 1977.

"STARTING POINT" SERIES; EDITOR

Let's Use the Locality, Mills & Boon (London, England), 1971.

Let's Paint, Mills & Boon (London, England), 1971.

Let's Print, Mills & Boon (London, England), 1971.

Let's Make a Picture, Mills & Boon (London, England), 1971.

Let's Make a Puppet, Mills & Boon (London, England), 1971.

"ON LOCATION" SERIES

Castles, Mills & Boon (London, England), 1973.

Churches, Mills & Boon (London, England), 1973.

Houses, Mills & Boon (London, England), 1974.

Farms, Mills & Boon (London, England), 1974.

Monasteries, Mills & Boon (London, England), 1975.

"SMALL WORLD" SERIES; EDITOR

Apes, F. Watts (New York, NY), 1979.

Dinosaurs, F. Watts (New York, NY), 1979.

Birds, F. Watts (New York, NY), 1979.

Lions and Tigers, F. Watts (New York, NY), 1979.

Ants, F. Watts (New York, NY), 1980.
Bees and Wasps, F. Watts (New York, NY), 1980.
Reptiles, F. Watts (New York, NY), 1980.
Bears, F. Watts (New York, NY), 1980.
Elephants, F. Watts (New York, NY), 1980.
Horses, F. Watts (New York, NY), 1980.
Birds, F. Watts (New York, NY), 1981.
Whales, F. Watts (New York, NY), 1981.
Eskimos, F. Watts (New York, NY), 1981.
Plains Indians, F. Watts (New York, NY), 1981.
Butterflies and Moths, F. Watts (New York, NY), 1981.
Ancient Greeks, F. Watts (New York, NY), 1981.
Romans, F. Watts (New York, NY), 1982.
Jungles, F. Watts (New York, NY), 1982.
Aborigines, F. Watts (New York, NY), 1982.
Arctic Lands, F. Watts (New York, NY), 1982.
Vikings, F. Watts (New York, NY), 1982.

"THINKABOUT" SERIES

Big and Little, illustrated by Chris Fairclough, F. Watts (New York, NY), 1986.
Floating and Sinking, illustrated by Chris Fairclough, F. Watts (New York, NY), 1986.
Hearing, illustrated by Chris Fairclough, F. Watts (New York, NY), 1986.
Hot and Cold, illustrated by Chris Fairclough, F. Watts (New York, NY), 1986.
Seeing, illustrated by Chris Fairclough, F. Watts (New York, NY), 1986.
Shape, illustrated by Chris Fairclough, F. Watts (New York, NY), 1986.
Smelling, illustrated by Chris Fairclough, F. Watts (New York, NY), 1986.
Tasting, illustrated by Chris Fairclough, F. Watts (New York, NY), 1986.
Touching, illustrated by Chris Fairclough, F. Watts (New York, NY), 1986.

"FRESH START" SERIES

Crayons, illustrated by Chris Fairclough, F. Watts (New Yeeks, NY), 1987.
Paints, illustrated by Chris Fairclough, F. Watts (New York, NY), 1987.
Decorated Lettering, illustrated by Chris Fairclough, F. Watts (New York, NY), 1990.
Book Craft, illustrated by Chris Fairclough, F. Watts (New York, NY), 1992.

"KNOWABOUT" SERIES

Knowabout Capacity, illustrated by Chris Fairclough, F. Watts (New York, NY), 1988.
Knowabout Counting, illustrated by Chris Fairclough, F. Watts (New York, NY), 1988.
Knowabout Lengths, illustrated by Chris Fairclough, F. Watts (New York, NY), 1988.
Knowabout Numbers, illustrated by Chris Fairclough, F. Watts (New York, NY), 1988.
Knowabout Pattern, illustrated by Chris Fairclough, F. Watts (New York, NY), 1988.
Knowabout Sorting, illustrated by Chris Fairclough, F. Watts (New York, NY), 1988.
Knowabout Time, illustrated by Chris Fairclough, F. Watts (New York, NY), 1988.
Knowabout Weight, illustrated by Chris Fairclough, F. Watts (New York, NY), 1988.

"LOOK AT" SERIES

Faces, illustrated by Mike Galletly, F. Watts (New York, NY), 1988.
Feet, illustrated by Mike Galletly, F. Watts (New York, NY), 1988.
Teeth, illustrated by Mike Galletly, F. Watts (New York, NY), 1988.
Paws and Claws, illustrated by Simon Roulstone, F. Watts (New York, NY), 1988.
Fur and Feathers, illustrated by Simon Roulstone, F. Watts (New York, NY), 1989.
Fingers and Feelers, F. Watts (New York, NY), 1990.
Homes, Holes, and Hives, F. Watts (New York, NY), 1990.
Tongues and Tasters, F. Watts (New York, NY), 1990.
Whoops, Words, and Whistles, F. Watts (New York, NY), 1990.

"WAYS TO" SERIES

Move It!, illustrated by Chris Fairclough, F. Watts (New York, NY), 1989.
Build It!, F. Watts (New York, NY), 1990.
Change It!, F. Watts (New York, NY), 1990.
Clean It!, illustrated by Chris Fairclough, F. Watts (New York, NY), 1990.
Store It!, illustrated by Chris Fairclough, F. Watts (New York, NY), 1990.
Wear It!, F. Watts (New York, NY), 1990.

Cut It!, F. Watts (New York, NY), 1990.

Join It!, illustrated by Chris Fairclough, F. Watts (New York, NY), 1990.

"READABOUT" SERIES

Tools, illustrated by Chris Fairclough, F. Watts (New York, NY), 1992.

Machines, illustrated by Chris Fairclough, F. Watts (New York, NY), 1992.

Directions, illustrated by Chris Fairclough, F. Watts (New York, NY), 1992.

Communications, illustrated by Chris Fairclough, F. Watts (New York, NY), 1992.

Energy, illustrated by Chris Fairclough, F. Watts (New York, NY), 1992.

Wheels, illustrated by Chris Fairclough, F. Watts (New York, NY), 1992.

"WALKABOUT" SERIES

Changing Seasons, Children's Press (New York, NY), 1994.

In the Air, Children's Press (New York, NY), 1994.

Minibeasts, Children's Press (New York, NY), 1994.

Seashore, Children's Press (New York, NY), 1994.

Tree, Children's Press (New York, NY), 1994.

Under the Ground, Children's Press (New York, NY), 1994.

Weather, Children's Press (New York, NY), 1994.

"FIND OUT ABOUT" SERIES

Paper, F. Watts (New York, NY), 1994.

Metal, F. Watts (New York, NY), 1994.

Rock and Stone, F. Watts (New York, NY), 1994.

Wood, F. Watts (New York, NY), 1994.

"EXPLORING OUR SENSES" SERIES

Hearing, illustrated by Chris Fairclough, Gareth Stevens (Milwaukee, WI), 1995.

Seeing, illustrated by Chris Fairclough, Gareth Stevens (Milwaukee, WI), 1995.

Smelling, illustrated by Chris Fairclough, Gareth Stevens (Milwaukee, WI), 1995.

Tasting, illustrated by Chris Fairclough, Gareth Stevens (Milwaukee, WI), 1995.

Touching, illustrated by Chris Fairclough, Gareth Stevens (Milwaukee, WI), 1995.

"MATH COUNTS" SERIES

Capacity, Children's Press (Chicago, IL), 1995.

Counting, Children's Press (Chicago, IL), 1995.

Length, Children's Press (New York, NY), 1995.

Numbers, Children's Press (New York, NY), 1995.

Pattern, Children's Press (New York, NY), 1995.

Shape, Children's Press (New York, NY), 1995.

Size, Children's Press (New York, NY), 1995.

Sorting, Children's Press (New York, NY), 1995.

Time, Children's Press (New York, NY), 1995.

Weight, Children's Press (New York, NY), 1995.

"NEW LOOK" SERIES

Inside and Outside, illustrated by Stephen Shoot, Children's Press (Chicago, IL), 1995.

Holes, illustrated by Stephen Shoot, Children's Press (Chicago, IL), 1995.

Beginnings and Endings, illustrated by Stephen Shoot, Children's Press (Chicago, IL), 1996.

Walls, illustrated by Stephen Shoot, Children's Press (Chicago, IL), 1996.

"SENSES" SERIES

Eating and Tasting, Raintree Steck-Vaughn (Austin, TX), 1998.

Listening and Hearing, Raintree Steck-Vaughn (Austin, TX), 1998.

Looking and Seeing, Raintree Steck-Vaughn (Austin, TX), 1998.

Sniffing and Smelling, Raintree Steck-Vaughn (Austin, TX), 1998.

Touching and Feeling, Raintree Steck-Vaughn (Austin, TX), 1998.

"PICTURE A COUNTRY" SERIES

France, F. Watts (New York, NY), 1998.

Egypt, F. Watts (New York, NY), 1998.

Germany, F. Watts (New York, NY), 1998.

India, F. Watts (New York, NY), 1998.

Italy, F. Watts (New York, NY), 1998.

Jamaica, F. Watts (New York, NY), 1998.

Japan, F. Watts (New York, NY), 1998.

Spain, F. Watts (New York, NY), 1998.

Australia, F. Watts (New York, NY), 1999.

China, F. Watts (New York, NY), 1999.

Czech Republic, F. Watts (New York, NY), 1999.

Russia, F. Watts (New York, NY), 1999.

"MACHINES AT WORK" SERIES

In the Supermarket, F. Watts (New York, NY), 1998.

Building a Road, illustrated by Teri Gower, F. Watts (New York, NY), 1998.

On a Building Site, F. Watts (New York, NY), 1998.

On the Farm, illustrated by Teri Gower, F. Watts (New York, NY), 1998.

On the Move, illustrated by Teri Gower, F. Watts (New York, NY), 1998.

Under the Ground, F. Watts (New York, NY), 1999.

"LET'S EXPLORE" SERIES

What Shape Is It?, F. Watts (London, England), 1999, published as *Discovering Shapes,* Gareth Stevens (Milwaukee, WI), 2001.

What Size Is It?, F. Watts (London, England), 1999, published as *Measuring Size,* Gareth Stevens (Milwaukee, WI), 2001.

How Many Are There?, F. Watts (London, England), 1999, published as *Numbers and Counting,* Gareth Stevens (Milwaukee, WI), 2001.

Air, Gareth Stevens (Milwaukee, WI), 2001.

Day and Night, Gareth Stevens (Milwaukee, WI), 2001.

Earth, Gareth Stevens (Milwaukee, WI), 2001.

Fire, Gareth Stevens (Milwaukee, WI), 2001.

My Day, Gareth Stevens (Milwaukee, WI), 2001.

Seasons, Gareth Stevens (Milwaukee, WI), 2001.

Sorting and Sets, Gareth Stevens (Milwaukee, WI), 2001.

Time, Gareth Stevens (Milwaukee, WI), 2001.

Water, Gareth Stevens (Milwaukee, WI), 2001.

SIDELIGHTS: Author of over two hundred nonfiction titles for young and very young readers, Henry Pluckrose has "always been an exception" to the dry-as-toast approach to educational books, according to a reviewer for *Books for Keeps.* The British writer's success comes, as this same critic noted, from Pluckrose's ability "to enter into a partnership with his reader, gently tapping that reader's experience to allow more things to be learnt than his books 'teach'." Pluckrose has written for a dozen series both in his native England and in the United States. Among these are the popular "Thinkabout," "Knowabout," "Readabout," "Walkabout," and "Look At" series; his subjects range from basic concept books, to titles dealing with math, science, art, history, and geography. In the "Small World" series, which he edited, Pluckrose tackles topics from the Plains Indians of North America to ants and apes.

Born in London, England, in 1931, Pluckrose grew up in the difficult generation that experienced both the Depression and the Second World War as children. After serving in the British Army from 1950 to 1952, Pluckrose went to college and became an educator, teaching elementary school children in inner London from the early 1950s to 1968. His work in education, as well as his experiences as a father of three, convinced him there were not enough titles for young children on a wide range of basic skills and concepts.

Interest in the use of arts and crafts in education led to some of Pluckrose's earliest titles. In 1965 he published *Let's Make Pictures,* an easy-to-follow guide for budding young artists. Writing both for the student and the instructor, he assembled many titles around the art theme; one of the most popular was *The Art and Craft Book,* a collection of writings by a variety of contributors on topics from puppet-making to designing classroom space. A contributor for the *Times Literary Supplement* found the range of contributions to the guide "impressivley wide," and commended Pluckrose for producing a book "which is useful and interesting." *A Craft Collection* from 1973 similarly presents a variety of projects in media from clay to fabrics, employing a "deliberately experimental approach," according to a reviewer for the *Times Literary Supplement,* while also supplying sufficient instructions for each project. *Print Ideas* further expands on the use of arts and crafts in the classroom in a "thoroughly practical introduction to printing," according to a contributor for the *Junior Bookshelf.* Experimentation again is the key word in this art how-to. C. Lynham, writing in *School Librarian* praised the author for a book that "goes further and says more than many of its predecessors."

From such stand-alone titles, Pluckrose moved to series work, and some of the first work was again in the arts, for the "Starting Point" books. Basic concept books, however, soon became his focus. His "Things" series explores topics from sight to hearing to touch and comparison of qualities, all designed to teach very young children about the five senses. Reviewing his *Things Light and Heavy,* a reviewer for *Growing Point* noted the use of photographs with a brief text as well as simple activities, and dubbed the whole a "practical arrangement of contrasting objects." Reviewing *Things That Float* in *Growing Point,* a contributor praised the use of questions with each picture which "encourage observation, reason and memory." A reviewer for *Junior Bookshelf* praised the "excellent" use of black-and-white photography in the same title, while another reviewer for *Junior Bookshelf* lauded *Things That Push,* noting that Pluckrose demonstrates that he "understands the mind of a young child, and knows how to get the information across with the minimum strain."

More basic concepts are served up in the "Thinkabout" series, with photographic illustrations by Chris Fairclough, with whom Pluckrose often collaborates. Geared for ages two to seven, these books, similarly to the "Things" series, examine concepts such as big and little, hot and cold, the five senses, and the nature of floating versus sinking. Designed as part picture book and part springboard for discussion between young child and parent or teacher, the books focus on everyday elements of life that small children and their adults can too often take for granted. Again the author blends brief text with "handsome photography," as a reviewer noted in a *Booklist* review of *Big and Little* and several other titles in the series. Writing about several books in the series in *Appraisal: Science Books for Young People,* a reviewer noted that "preschoolers may find these [titles] appealing," but also complained of the "homogeniety of the families and communities portrayed." Denise M. Wilms, in a *Booklist* review of *Hearing* and the other four books in the series on the senses, remarked that Pluckrose puts together "striking full-color photographs with simple texts that invite readers to think about their personal environment." Wilms concluded that the titles provide "handsome, effective lessons." Reviewing *Hearing* and other titles on the senses in *British Books News,* Elizabeth J. King felt that "anyone with small children will find [the books] invaluable as a starting point for talk and exploration." Sr. Edna Demanche echoed this sentiment in a *Science Books and Films* review of *Seeing* and other titles in the series: "Any parent or primary teacher who wants a top-flight teaching aid will find it in this set of books." Demanche further praised the "vivid, full-page photographs [that] seem to leap off the page," as well as Pluckrose's "scant, direct text [that] points the direction for discussion with very young children."

With his "Knowabout" and "Math Counts" series, Pluckrose assumes a similar approach to mathematical concepts such as numbers, counting, lengths, pattern, and measurement. The "Knowabout" books again combine the photography of Fairclough with brief, succinct text from Pluckrose in works geared at children three to six. Phillis Wilson, writing in *Booklist,* found that *Counting* and other titles in the series are "no shelf-sitters." Wilson further noted that "skilful connections are evident as Pluckrose's text, in tandem with the photos, generate dialogue." Pluckrose employs simple objects from the home, nature, and shop for more abstract titles such as *Capacity* and *Weight.* Reviewing *Pattern* and other titles in the series, *Booklist*'s Wilson praised the books as "examples of quality bookmaking," and remarked that they would also be useful for English-as-a-second-language instruction. A critic for *Kirkus Reviews* in a review of *Length* and other titles called the entire series "useful" and "high-quality," while Roger Sutton, reviewing *Counting* in *Bulletin of the Center for Children's Books,* praised the use of "familiar objects," such as fingers or stairs, and the "very simple question" placed on each page. Renee Steinberg, writing in *School Library Journal,* found that *Counting* and other series titles combine "vibrantly colored photographs of familiar objects . . . with informative text and related questions to encourage active shared participation." Much the same ground is covered in "Math Counts," a series of ten books from Children's press also dealing with capacity, counting, shape, sorting, and measurement. "This series will fill a void in most school and public libraries for good books on these ten topics," wrote a reviewer for *Appraisal.* Writing in *Science Books and Films,* Viktor Mastrovincenzo and Christopher Mastrovincenzo lauded the *colorful and striking photography* in *Counting* and other titles in the "Math Counts" series, finding that such images allow very young children "to easily visualize and understand some elementary topics of mathematics." The same reviewers also noted that the books in the series "stimulate children's thinking and encourage them to experiment with and experience mathematics all around them."

Similar generalized concept books are found in series such as "Readabout" and "Find Out About," both of which adopt the same format as "Thinkabout" and "Knowabout" in presenting an introduction to topics such as materials (rock and stone, metal, wood, paper), and machines. Reviewing *Paper* and other titles in the "Find Out About" series, a contributor for *Books for Keeps* commended the books for taking a "strong, unequivocal line about the environment, stressing the need for conservation and the recycling of waste." In a *Books for Keeps* review of titles in the "Readabout" series, a critic noted that Pluckrose's brief text is "effective, making useful points that can be applied beyond the pages of the book." Fundamental concepts of physics are presented in *Energy* and *Wheels,* books designed to "stimulate interest, observation, and thought rather than to inform," wrote Kevin Steinberger in *Magpies.* Steinberger went on to conclude that these "attractive books will be very useful in the infant classroom in many ways." Stuart Hannabuss, writing in *School Librarian,* also had praise for the series. In a review of *Directions* and *Messages,* he commented that both Pluckrose and Fairclough "are well known and deservedly successful in this field," and that "discussion and independent research activities spring out on every page."

A plethora of subjects are offered in the "Small World" series, edited by Pluckrose in collaboration with variety of photographers. These picture book introductions generally are geared for a primary school audience, have more text than Pluckrose's more basic concept books, and are less focused thematically. Reviewing *Arctic Lands* and *Vikings* in *Booklist,* Ilene Cooper praised Pluckrose for bringing "rather involved subjects" to primary grade readers with his "simple yet meaningful texts." In a *Booklist* review of several animal books in the series, including *Apes,* Barbara Elleman felt that the mixture of brief text and illustrations "give young readers a satisfactory introduction to . . . different animal groups," and Peter Dance, writing in the *Times Literary Supplement,* lauded the "clear, simple texts" in *Ants* and other animal books in the series. Reviewing *Butterflies and Moths* in *School Librarian,* C. M. Ball felt that the brief information "is interesting and likely to encourage questions and further reading." *Romans* and *Ancient Greeks,* two further titles in the "Small World" series, also were commended by David N. Pauli, writing in *School Library Journal.* "Teachers and librarians," Pauli wrote, "couldn't do better than to introduce these two books" to children learning about past cultures. Barbara Hawkins also commented on the "succinctly covered" information and "well-executed color illustrations, in-cluding many cutaway diagrams," which grace series books such as *Ants.* However, some reviewers voiced dissatisfaction with similar aspects of the books. Barbara B. Murphy, writing in *School Library Journal* on *Bears* and other series titles, felt the texts "occasionally become confusing due to oversimplification." Joan C. Heidelberg, writing in *Science Books and Films,* remarked that *Dinosaurs* "offers little new information from what has been published in earlier children's books." Cooper, writing in *Booklist,* pointed to "a few confusing statements" in *Romans* and *Ancient Greeks,* and Donna J. Neylon forgave what she considered "only . . . fair quality" writing in *Vikings* because there are so few books dealing with the topic for primary grade students. Harsher criticism came from Marion Glastonbury, reviewing *Aborigines* in the *Times Educational Supplement.* Glastonbury thought that Pluckrose's title "does much to perpetuate" such "educationally unhelpful" concepts as a belief that people from other countries or races are necessarily more superstitious or aggressive or, as the same reviewer put it, "freaks."

Pluckrose returns to more focused thematic approaches in several other series, each dealing with scientific and practical topics. His "Look At" series examines parts of the human body and parts of other animals' bodies, as well. Wilms, writing in *Booklist,* found that his *Fur and Feathers* would help in "sharpening children's observation skills and comprehension of analogous physiological structures." In a *Booklist* review of *Faces* and other titles in the series dealing with parts of the human body, Wilms wrote that the "beautifully photographed books encourage youngsters to look and learn about parts of their body that they no doubt take for granted." Reviewing *Faces* in *Appraisal,* Louise Ritsema commented that an effort is made to "involve the child in observation and experimentation, with the use of stimulating questions relating to the illustrations." Anne Rowe, in a *School Librarian* review of *Paws and Claws,* commended the books in the series as an "exciting new approach to the natural world." A contributor for *Books for Keeps,* in a review of *Feet* and other titles in the series, felt they provide an "excellent introduction to . . . parts of the body." And in a review of *Tongues and Tasters, School Librarian's* Lynda Jones concluded, "This is the sort of material that teachers in primary education have been wanting for years."

Pluckrose tackles the senses in two separate series, "Exploring Our Senses" for Gareth Stevens Publishing, and "Senses" for Raintree. Reviewing the latter series, a contributor for *Horn Book Guide* remarked that the books combine simple text with color photos to "encourage articulate and thoughtful observation" rather than to provide anatomical descriptions. "Exploring Our Senses" also takes the picture book approach to the subject, encouraging young readers to begin thinking about the senses. Kenneth Skau, writing in *Appraisal,* felt the books in "Exploring Our Senses" were most appropriate for pre-school children, "because they are relatively simplistic." Pluckrose's "Machines at Work" series employs the familiar blend of color photography and simple text to introduce machines at home, on the farm, at building sites, and airports. *Booklist*'s Hazel Rochman felt that *On the Farm* and *On the Move* "will appeal to those preschoolers who are fascinated by machines." P. Jenkins, writing in *Books for Your Children,* found the entire set of six books a "really jolly series." A more hands-on approach is taken with the "Ways To" series, describing basic functions such as cleaning, joining, cutting, and wearing. Targeted at preschoolers to second graders, the books combine basic information with color photographs, along with questions to stimulate involvement and suggested activities. A reviewer for *Books for Keeps* thought that the books in the series "provide an approach to their subjects which children could valuably extend to other areas." Focusing on specific action verbs, the books employ "excellent color photographs," according to Pamela K. Bomboy in *School Library Journal,* and "will be useful as tradebook supplements in science classes." Reviewing *Cut It!* and *Join It!* in *Bulletin of the Center for Children's Books,* Sutton praised the books' design as having the "eyecatching appeal of an upscale housewares catalog." Sutton also lauded the fact that concepts are "logically introduced and developed."

In addition to language arts, Pluckrose deals with actual arts in the "Fresh Start" series. In titles such as *Crayons, Paints, Puppets,* and *Book Craft,* Pluckrose offers a wealth of craft projects for eager young artists. With *Book Craft,* he presents projects from simple folded papers books to ones with sewn sections. Derek Lomas, writing in *School Librarian,* felt that "techniques are explained simply" and that there are "plenty of clear, coloured photographs to supplement the text." A contributor for *Junior Bookshelf* found *Paints* and *Crayons* to be "instructive and useful," and a critic for *Kirkus Reviews* called the same titles "two inspiring introductions to the versatility of easily obtained art materials" as well a "fine resource for teachers and

parents." Wilms in *Booklist* also felt that both those activity books "present a nice batch of ideas for working."

Pluckrose takes to the road in the "Picture a Country" series for Watts. Geared for kindergarten through third grade, each of the thirty-page books in the series devotes two pages to the basic geography of the country, along with cultural information such as schooling, home life, work, and typical food. Additionally, color photographs are accompanied by captions. A reviewer for *Horn Book Guide* felt that four books in the series "proffer overgeneralized facts," while another contributor for the same publication, in a review for *India* and *Japan,* complained that the books provide "very little in the way of concrete information." Another critic for *Horn Book Guide* called the entries on *Germany* and *Italy* a "bland, overgeneralized introduction." Elizabeth Talbot, writing in *School Library Journal,* found what she termed "egregious errors" in titles on *China, Czech Republic,* and *Russia.* However, other critics found more to like in the series. *School Librarian*'s Janet Fisher called *Australia* and *China* "useful additions to the library," and Ann W. Moore, in a *School Library Journal* review of *Egypt* and *France,* felt the books "are attractive and could spawn much discussion."

In his over two hundred titles, Pluckrose has proved himself to be not only a versatile writer, but also a tireless promoter of basic concept books for the very young. His books about art, math, and basic science concepts have introduced a generation of readers to principles and ideas they will later more fully explore in school, while works on geography and history ply readers with questions and make them more aware of the world around them.

BIOGRAPHICAL AND CRITICAL SOURCES:

PERIODICALS

Appraisal: Science Books for Young People, fall, 1986, review of "Thinkabout" series, pp. 117-118; autumn, 1989, Louise Ritsema, review of *Faces,* pp. 74-75; spring-summer, 1995, Kenneth Skau, review of "Exploring Our Senses" series, p. 65; winter-spring, 1996, review of "Math Counts" series, pp. 79-80.

Booklist, December 1, 1979, Barbara Elleman, review of *Apes,* p. 552; July 1, 1981, review of *Bees and Wasps,* p. 1393; July, 1982, Ilene Cooper, review of *Ancient Greeks* and *Romans,* p. 1439; January 15, 1983, Ilene Cooper, review of *Arctic Lands* and *Vikings,* p. 673; May 1, 1986, Denise M. Wilms, review of *Hearing,* p. 1316; November 1, 1987, review of *Big and Little,* p. 484; April 15, 1988, Denise M. Wilms, review of *Paints* and *Crayons,* p. 1437; May 1, 1988, Phillis Wilson, review of *Counting,* p. 1528; November 1, 1988, Phillis Wilson, review of *Pattern,* p. 486; October 1, 1989, Denise Wilms, review of *Paws and Claws,* p. 354; February 1, 1989, Denise M. Wilms, review of *Faces,* p. 941; December 1, 1998, Hazel Rochman, review of *On the Farm* and *On the Move,* p. 682.

Books for Keeps, March, 1988, review of "Look At" series, p. 24; September, 1990, review of "Ways To" series, p. 18; January, 1992, review of "Read-about" series, p. 14; May, 1993, review of "Walk-about" series, p. 22; September, 1994, review of *Paper,* p. 14.

Books for Your Children, autumn, 1990, P. Jenkins, review of "Machines at Work" series, p. 21.

British Book News, March, 1986, Elizabeth J. King, review of *Hearing,* p. 27.

Bulletin of the Center for Children's Books, June, 1988, Roger Sutton, review of *Counting,* p. 214; February, 1990, Roger Sutton, review of *Cut It!* and *Join It!,* p. 145.

Growing Point, April, 1975, review of *Things Light and Heavy,* p. 2594; March, 1976, review of *Things That Float* and *Things That Hold,* p. 2814.

Horn Book Guide, fall, 1998, review of "Senses" series, p. 390, review of *Italy* and *Germany,* pp. 424-425, review of *Japan* and *India,* p. 425; fall, 1999, review of "Picture a Country" series, p. 391.

Junior Bookshelf, April, 1975, review of *Things That Push,* p. 111; April, 1976, review of *Things That Float,* pp. 94-95; October, 1980, review of *Print Ideas,* pp. 255-256; February, 1988, review of *Crayons* and *Paints,* p. 35.

Kirkus Reviews, March 1, 1988, review of *Crayons* and *Paints,* p. 368; October 1, 1988, review of "Knowabout" series, pp. 1474-1475.

Magpies, November, 1992, Kevin Steinberger, review of *Energy* and *Wheels,* p. 35.

School Librarian, December, 1980, C. Lynham, review of *Print Ideas,* p. 405; June, 1981, C. M. Ball, review of *Butterflies and Moths,* p. 147; November, 1989, Anne Rowe, review of *Paws and Claws,* p. 156; February, 1991, Lynda Jones, review of *Tongues and Tasters,* p. 26; August, 1992, Stuart Hannabuss, review of *Directions* and *Messages,* p. 109, Derek Lomas, review of *Book Craft,* p. 109; winter, 1999, Janet Fisher, review of *Australia* and *China,* p. 204.

School Library Journal, February, 1980, Barbara B. Murphy, review of *Bears,* p. 49; September, 1981, Barbara Hawkins, review of *Reptiles,* pp. 112-113; October, 1982, David N. Pauli, review of *Ancient Greeks* and *Romans,* p. 144; March, 1983, Donna J. Neylon, review of *Vikings,* p. 166; November, 1983, review of *Arctic Lands,* p. 39; October, 1986, Denise L. Moll, review of "Thinkabout" series, p. 166; October, 1988, Renee Steinberg, review of *Counting,* p. 136; April, 1989, Denise L. Moll, review of *Length,* pp. 97-98; June, 1990, Pamela K. Bomboy, review of "Ways To" series, p. 115; February, 1999, Ann W. Moore, review of *Egypt* and *France,* p. 101; January, 2000, Elizabeth Talbot, review of *China, Czech Republic,* and *Russia,* pp. 125-126.

Science Books and Films, November, 1980, Joan C. Heidelberg, review of *Dinosaurs,* p. 92; November, 1986, Sr. Edna Demanche, review of *Hearing,* pp. 106-107; January, 1996, Victor Mastrovincenzo and Christopher Mastrovincenzo, review of *Counting,* p. 15.

Times Educational Supplement, November 5, 1982, Marion Glastonbury, review of *Aborigines,* p. 22.

Times Literary Supplement, April, 15, 1970, review of *The Art and Craft Book,* p. 427l; March 27, 1981, Peter Dance, review of *Ants,* p. 347.*

*   *   *

PORCEL, Baltasar 1937-

PERSONAL: Born March 14, 1937, in Andratx, Mallorca, Spain; son of Baltasar (a sailor and farmer) and Sebastiana (a homemaker; maiden name, Pujol) Porcel; married Maria-Angels Roque (an anthropologist), July, 1972; children: Baltasar, Violant. *Ethnicity:* "Catalan." *Politics:* Democrat. *Religion:* Roman Catholic.

ADDRESSES: Home—Barcelona, Spain. *Office*—Institut Català de la Mediterrània, Ave. Diagonal, 407 bis, 08008 Barcelona, Spain; fax: 34-4-218-4513. *Agent*—

Antonia Kerrigan, Agencia Literaria Kerrigan/Miro/Calonje, Travessera de Gracia, 12 5e 2a, 08021 Barcelona, Spain.

CAREER: Writer. Campus Universitari de la Mediterrània, Barcelona, Spain, president of Institut Català de la Mediterrània.

AWARDS, HONORS: Sant Jordi Prize, Joan Creixells Prize, and Generalitat de Catalunya, all 1986, all for *Primaveres i les tardors;* Best Books of 1995 citation, *Publisher's Weekly* and *Critics' Choice,* for *Horses into the Night;* Ramon Llull prize for Catalan literature, 2001, for *El emperador o l'ull del vent.*

WRITINGS:

IN ENGLISH TRANSLATION

Horses into the Night (novel), translated and with an introduction by John L. Getman, University of Arkansas Press (Fayetteville, AR), 1995, originally published in Catalan as *Cavalls cap a la fosca,* Edicions 62 (Barcelona, Spain), 1975, also published in Spanish translation as *Caballos hacia la noche,* Plaza & Janès (Barcelona, Spain), 1977.

Springs and Autumns, translation by John L. Getman, University of Arkansas Press (Fayetteville, AR), 2000, originally published in Catalan as *Primaveres i les tardors,* Edicions Proa (Barcelona, Spain), 1986, also published in Spanish translation as *Primaveras y otoños,* Anagrama (Barcelona, Spain), 1986.

UNTRANSLATED WORKS

Els condemnats; tragèdia en tres actes (play), Editorial Moll (Palma de Mallorca, Spain), 1959.

Solnegre (novel), Albertí (Barcelona, Spain), 1961.

La simbomba fosca; tragicomèdia, Editorial Moll (Palma de Mallorca, Spain), 1962.

La lluna i el "cala llamp," Albertí (Barcelona, Spain), 1963.

Majorca (travel book), translated from the Spanish by Betty Morris, Editorial Planeta (Barcelona, Spain), 1964.

Teatre (plays), Editorial Daedalus (Palma de Mallorca, Spain), 1965.

Els escorpins, Edicions Proa (Barcelona, Spain), 1965.

(Editor) *Viatge literari a Mallorca* (prose and poetry), Edicions Destino (Barcelona, Spain), 1967.

Arran de mar; viatges i fantasies (travel book), Editorial Selecta (Barcelona, Spain), 1967.

Las sombras chinescas, Editorial Taber (Barcelona, Spain), 1968.

Els argonautes, Edicions 62 (Barcelona, Spain), 1968.

Los encuentros; primara serie (interviews), Ediciones Destino (Barcelona, Spain), 1969.

Els xuetes, Edicions 62 (Barcelona, Spain), 1969, revised and expanded edition published as *Els xuetes mallorquins: quinze segles de racisme,* 2002.

Exercicis más o menys espirituals, Edicions 62 (Barcelona, Spain), 1969.

Difunts sota ametllers en flor, Edicions Destino (Barcelona, Spain), 1970.

(Editor) *Cataluña vista desde fuera,* Libres de Sinera (Barcelona, Spain), 1970.

Los encuentros: segunda serie (interviews), Ediciones Destino (Barcelona, Spain), 1971.

Los chuetas mallorquines; siete siglos de racismo, Barral (Barcelona, Spain), 1971, revised and expanded edition published as *Los chuetas mallorquines; quince siglos de racismo,* 2002.

Los catalanes de hoy (biographies), Seix Barral (Barcelona, Spain), 1971.

Crónica d'atabalades navegacions, Edicions 62 (Barcelona, Spain), 1971.

La luna y el velero (novel), Plaza & Janès (Esplugas de Llobregat, Spain), 1972.

Grans catalans d'ara (biographies), Edicions Destino (Barcelona, Spain), 1972.

Desintegraciones capitalistas, Editorial Planeta (Barcelona, Spain), 1972.

Los alacranes, Plaza & Janés (Barcelona, Spain), 1972.

Debat català; polèmica-diàleg amb la intellectualitat castellana, Editorial Selecta (Barcelona, Spain), 1973.

China, una revolución en pie, Ediciones Destino (Barcelona, Spain), 1974.

La palabra del arte (interviews), Ediciones Rayuela (Madrid, Spain), 1976.

Josep Tarradellas: "President de la Generalitat" (interview), Editorial A.C. (Barcelona, Spain), 1977.

Josep Pallach (interview), Editorial A.C. (Barcelona, Spain), 1977.

Jordi Pujol (interview), Editorial A.C. (Barcelona, Spain), 1977.

Conversaciones con el honorable Tarradellas (interview), Plaza & Janès (Esplugas de Llobregat, Spain), 1977.

Camins i ombres: del Llobregat a l'Alguer, una visión encantada de les terres catalanes (travel book), Editorial Selecta (Barcelona, Spain), 1977.

La revuelta permanente (biography), Editorial Planeta (Barcelona, Spain), 1978.

Personajes excitantes (biography), Plaza & Janès (Barcelona, Spain), 1978.

Reivindicació de la vídua Txing i altres relats, Edicions 62 (Barcelona, Spain), 1979.

Les pomes d'or, Edicions 62 (Barcelona, Spain), 1980.

Xavier Carbonell (biography), La Gran Enciclopedia Vasca (Bilbao, Spain), 1981.

Todos los espejos, Espasa-Calpe (Madrid, Spain), 1981.

El dolços murmuria del mar, Edicions 62 (Barcelona, Spain), 1981.

El misteri de l'alzinar i altres contes, Edicions 62 (Barcelona, Spain), 1982.

Tots els contes, Edicions 62 (Barcelona, Spain), 1984.

José Bascones (biography), La Gran Enciclopedia Vasca (Bilbao, Spain), 1984.

Les illes, encantades, Edicions 62 (Barcelona, Spain), 1984.

Els dies immortals, Edicions 62 (Barcelona, Spain), 1984.

Poemes i dibuixos, Taller de Picasso (Barcelona, Spain), 1985.

El divorci de Berta Barca, Edicions Proa (Barcelona, Spain), 1989.

A totes les illes, Editorial Moll (Palma de Mallorca, Spain), 1990.

Totes les Balears, Edicions Proa (Barcelona, Spain), 1991.

Reis, polítics i anarquistes, Edicions Proa (Barcelona, Spain), 1991.

Punts cardinals, Edicions Proa (Barcelona, Spain), 1991.

Obres completes, seven volumes, Edicions Proa (Barcelona, Spain), 1991-1997.

L'alba i terra, Edicions Proa (Barcelona, Spain), 1991.

Vayreda C.: els anys de París, Xavier Amir (Barcelona, Spain), 1992.

Molts paradisos perduts, Edicions Proa (Barcelona, Spain), 1993.

El mite d'Andratx, Edicions Proa (Barcelona, Spain), 1993.

Viajes expectantes: de Marrakech a Pekín (travel book), Edicións de Bitzoc (Palma de Mallorca, Spain), 1994.

Retrato de Julio Caro Baroja, Galaxia Gutenberg (Valencia, Spain), 1994.

Lola i els peixos morts, Edicions Proa (Barcelona, Spain), 1994.

Grans catalans (biography), Edicions Proa (Barcelona, Spain), 1994.

Mediterráneo: Tumultos del oleaje, Editorial Planeta (Barcelona, Spain), 1996.

El Mediterráneo: una globalidad emergente, Editorial Complutense (Madrid, Spain), 1996.

Ulisses a alta mar, Edicions 62 (Barcelona, Spain), 1997.

Les màscares, Edicions Proa (Barcelona, Spain), 1997.

El gran galiot, Edicions Proa (Barcelona, Spain), 1997.

Mallorca (travel book), photographs by Rainer Hackenberg and others, Lunwerg (Barcelona, Spain), 1999.

(Author of prologue) Carlos Garrido, *Mallorca mágica,* José J. de Olañeta (Palma de Mallorca, Spain), 2000.

El cor del senglar, Edicions 62 (Barcelona, Spain), 2000.

El emperador o l'ull del vent, Editorial Planeta (Barcelona, Spain), 2001, also published in Spanish translation as *El emperador o el ojo del ciclón,* 2001.

Domèstics i salvatges (short stories), Editorial Planeta (Barcelona, Spain), 2001.

Les maniobres de l'amor: tots els contes, 1958-2001, Ediciones Destino (Barcelona, Spain), 2002.

Also author of a daily opinion feature for the newspaper *La Vanguardia.*

SIDELIGHTS: Baltasar Porcel, a prolific Catalan writer of fiction and nonfiction, once commented on his work: "My primary motivation for writing is a desire to interpret the world through imagination, through the strength of words, and to communicate this to people. What particularly influences my work is the world that I know about, the Mediterranean, and man in its passions. My writing process is to absorb sensations, to glimpse ideas. It is a slow elaboration of mental and emotional atmosphere, a redaction as exigent as enthusiastic. Definitively, what inspires me to write on the subjects that I choose is my relation with reality.

"In 1996 I published, in Spanish, *Mediterráneo: Tumultos del oleaje,* a long book that is a historical report, through all the countries that include the Mediterranean cultures and their great creative moments from prehistory until today, with frequent lyrical incidences."

Of the dozen novels he has published in his native tongue of Catalan, two of Baltasar Porcel's novels have been translated into English, both thanks to translator John L. Getman and the University of Arkansas Press. The first, *Cavalls cap a la fosca* (sometimes cited by its Spanish title, *Caballos hacia la noche*), appeared as *Horses into the Night* in 1995, but was not widely reviewed. The second, *Primaveres i les tardors,* first published in 1986, appeared in English translation in 2000 to considerable praise. The novel itself, a melange of stories told by the members of a large Catalan family which has gathered to celebrate Christmas, sacrifices the linear certitude of plot in order to create a pastiche of Mallorcan culture in which old family feuds and allegiances, love affairs, and crimes of passion are as real today as they were in the decades that spawned them. "Through skillful interplay between the caustic and the tender, and between the poetic and the mysterious and mythical, Porcel masterfully portrays in microcosm the closed but sprightly peculiar Mediterranean spirit of the Majorcans," observed Albert M. Forcadas in *World Literature Today.* For Jack Shreve, who reviewed *Springs and Autumns* in *Library Journal,* the characters' desire to retell their stories exposes "the age-old need to impose order upon the chaos of memory" that is common to all humanity. Furthermore, a contributor to *Publishers Weekly* added, "Porcel scrupulously avoids nostalgia and idealization, the chief pitfalls of this genre."

Mallorcan history is also at the heart of *El emperador o l'ull del vent,* Porcel's 2001 novel, which was awarded several prizes in his own country. In 1808, ten thousand defeated French troops were imprisoned on a tiny Mallorcan island while they awaited the end of the Napoleonic Wars. The story of the imprisonment is told by Honoré Grapain some thirty years later, and fictional letters to Grapain written by his lover and his publisher, as well as an epilogue by Porcel each alter the reader's initial impression of Grapain's story in surprising ways. Nick Caistor, who reviewed *El emperador o el ojo del ciclón* (the Spanish translation of the novel) for the *Times Literary Supplement,* dubbed this "the work of an author who is keen to provoke and challenge his readers as well as to entertain them."

BIOGRAPHICAL AND CRITICAL SOURCES:

BOOKS

Baltasar Porcel, Edicions La Campana (Barcelona, Spain), 1987.

PERIODICALS

Library Journal, June 15, 2000, Jack Shreve, review of *Springs and Autumns,* p. 117.
Publishers Weekly, May 22, 2000, review of *Springs and Autumns,* p. 75.
Times Literary Supplement, July 13, 2001, Nick Caistor, "Incarcerated in Cadiz," review of *El emperador o el ojo del ciclón,* p. 22.
World Literature Today, spring, 2001, Albert M. Forcadas, review of *Springs and Autumns,* p. 408.*

* * *

POSNER, Richard A. 1939-

PERSONAL: Born January 11, 1939, in New York, NY; married Charlene Horn (a freelance editor), August 13, 1962; children: Kenneth, Eric. *Education:* Yale University, A.B. (summa cum laude), 1959; Harvard University, LL.B. (magna cum laude), 1962.

ADDRESSES: Office—U.S. Court of Appeals for the Seventh Circuit, 219 South Dearborn St., Chicago, IL 60604.

CAREER: Lawyer, judge, and author. Called to the Bar of New York, 1963, and of the U.S. Supreme Court, 1996; law clerk to Supreme Court Justice William J. Brennan, Jr., Washington, DC, 1962-63; assistant to Federal Trade Commissioner Philip Elman, 1963-65; assistant to U.S. Solicitor General Thurgood Marshall, Washington, DC, 1965-67; general counsel of President Lyndon B. Johnson's Task Force on Communications Policy, Washington, DC, 1967-68; Stanford University Law School, Stanford, CA, associate professor of law, 1968-69; University of Chicago Law School, Chicago, IL, professor, 1969-78, Lee and Brena Freeman Professor of Law, 1978-81, senior lecturer, 1981—; U.S. Court of Appeals, Seventh Circuit,

Chicago, circuit judge, 1981—, chief judge, 1993-2000; research associate, National Bureau of Economic Research, Cambridge, MA, 1971-81; president and co-founder, Lexecon, Inc. (economic and legal consultants), 1977-81; consultant to the Library of America. President, *Harvard Law Review;* founder, *Journal of Legal Studies.*

MEMBER: American Bar Association, American Economic Association, American Law and Economics Association (president, 1995-96), American Law Institute, Mont Pelerin Society, American Academy of Arts and Sciences (fellow), British Academy (corresponding fellow), Phi Beta Kappa.

AWARDS, HONORS: Honorary LL.D., Syracuse University, 1986, Duquesne University, 1987, Georgetown University, 1993, Yale University, 1996, University of Pennsylvania, 1997, Northwestern University, 2001; Thomas Jefferson Memorial Foundation Award in Law, University of Virginia, 1994; Dr. Honoris Causa, University of Ghent, 1995; Marshall-Whythe Medallion, College of William and Mary, 1998; honorary president, Bentham Club of University College, London, 1998; J.D., Brooklyn Law School, 2000. Honorary fellow, College of Labor and Employment Lawyers; honorary Bencher of the Inner Temple.

WRITINGS:

Cable Television: The Problem of Local Monopoly, Rand Corporation (Santa Monica, CA), 1970.
Economic Analysis of Law, Little, Brown (Boston, MA), 1972, 5th edition, Aspen Law and Business (New York, NY), 1998.
Regulation of Advertising by the FTC, American Enterprise Institute for Public Policy Research (Washington, DC), 1973.
Antitrust Cases, Economic Notes, and Other Materials, West Publishing (St. Paul, MN), 1974, 2nd edition, with Frank H. Easterbrook, West Publishing (St. Paul, MN), 1981.
(With Gerhard Casper) *A Study of the Supreme Court's Caseload,* American Bar Foundation (Chicago, IL), 1974.
The Social Costs of Monopoly and Regulation, University of Chicago Press (Chicago, IL), 1975.
Antitrust Law: An Economic Perspective, University of Chicago Press (Chicago, IL), 1976, 2nd edition, 2001.

(With Gerhard Casper) *The Workload of the Supreme Court,* American Bar Foundation (Chicago, IL), 1976.
The Robinson-Patman Act: Federal Regulation of Differences, American Enterprise Institute for Policy Research (Washington, DC), 1976.
(With John H. Langbein) *Market Funds and Trust-Investment Law, II,* American Bar Foundation (Chicago, IL), 1977.
(With Anthony T. Kronman) *The Economics of Contract Law,* Little, Brown (Boston, MA), 1979.
(Editor, with Kenneth E. Scott) *Economics of Corporation Law and Securities Regulation,* Little, Brown (Boston, MA), 1981.
Cases and Economic Notes on Antitrust, 2nd edition, West Publishing (St. Paul, MN), 1981.
The Economics of Justice, Harvard University Press (Cambridge, MA), 1981.
(With Frank H. Easterbrook) *1982-83 Supplement to Antitrust Cases, Economic Notes, and Other Materials,* West Publishing (St. Paul, MN), 1982.
Tort Law: Cases and Economic Analysis, Little, Brown (Boston, MA), 1982.
The Federal Courts: Crisis and Reform, Harvard University Press (Cambridge, MA), 1985.
(With William M. Landes) *The Economic Structure of Tort Law,* Harvard University Press (Cambridge, MA), 1987.
Law and Literature: A Misunderstood Relation, Harvard University Press (Cambridge, MA), 1988.
The Problems of Jurisprudence, Harvard University Press (Cambridge, MA), 1990.
Cardozo: A Study in Reputation, University of Chicago Press (Chicago, IL), 1990.
A Theory of Sexuality, Harvard University Press (Cambridge, MA), 1992.
(Editor and author of introduction) *The Essential Holmes: Selections from the Letters, Speeches, Judicial Opinions, and Other Writings of Oliver Wendell Holmes, Jr.,* University of Chicago Press (Chicago, IL), 1992.
Sex and Reason, Harvard University Press (Cambridge, MA), 1992.
(With Thomas J. Philipson) *Private Choices and Public Health: The AIDS Epidemic in an Economic Perspective,* Harvard University Press (Cambridge, MA), 1993.
Economics, Time, and Age, 25th Geary Lecture, Economic and Social Research Institute (Dublin, Ireland), 1994.
Aging and Old Age, University of Chicago Press (Chicago, IL), 1995.

Overcoming Law, Harvard University Press (Cambridge, MA), 1995.

Law and Legal Theory in England and America, Clarendon Press (New York, NY), 1996.

(With Katharine B. Silbaugh) *A Guide to America's Sex Laws,* University of Chicago Press (Chicago, IL), 1996.

(Editor, with Francesco Parisi) *Law and Economics,* Edward Elgar Publishing (Lyme, NH), 1997.

Natural Monopoly and Its Regulation, Cato Institute (Washington, DC), 1999.

The Problematics of Moral and Legal Theory, Belknap Press of Harvard University (Cambridge, MA), 1999.

An Affair of State: The Investigation, Impeachment, and Trial of President Clinton, Harvard University Press (Cambridge, MA), 1999.

The Economic Structure of the Law, edited by Francesco Parisi, Edward Elgar Publishing (Northampton, MA), 2000.

Frontiers of Legal Theory, Harvard University Press (Cambridge, MA), 2001.

Breaking the Deadlock: The 2000 Election, the Constitution, and the Courts, Princeton University Press (Princeton, NJ), 2001.

Public Intellectuals: A Study of Decline, Harvard University Press (Cambridge, MA), 2001.

Contributor of hundreds of articles to law journals. Academic writings have been translated into French, German, Italian, Spanish, Chinese, Japanese, Korean, and Greek.

SIDELIGHTS: "As a federal appeals court judge, Richard A. Posner has an exalted job, but one held by a few hundred others. But to a wide swath of intellectuals, he is one of the most fascinating thinkers in the nation, especially about contemporary American social issues," wrote Neil A. Lewis for *The New York Times Biographical Service.* A prolific author, he has written more than thirty books (not to mention his hundreds of articles) on subjects as diverse as literary criticism, sex and sexuality, economics and the law, and age and aging. Opinionated and fearless of heavy-hitting critics, Posner unabashedly expresses his well-informed perspectives, as evidenced in *An Affair of State: The Investigation, Impeachment, and Trial of President Clinton,* a book in which, according to Lewis, "he did not shrink from concluding that the president had committed perjury and obstruction of justice."

Posner was born in New York City and reared in its suburbs. The honor student, who graduated first in his class at Harvard Law School and was the president of the *Harvard Law Review,* began his career in Washington, DC, in several different governmental capacities. He started teaching law at Stanford and later became professor of law at the University of Chicago. During this time, Posner wrote several books on economics and the law, covering subjects such as antitrust, public utility and common carrier regulation, torts, and contracts. In fact, he is known as one of the founders of the "law-and-economics movement" of the 1970s. He introduced economic analysis of the law into areas such as family law, racial discrimination, and jurisprudence and privacy. Lewis commented that in his book *Antitrust Law: An Economic Perspective,* Posner "argues for a narrow view of antitrust law in which the best candidates for regulation are hard-core examples of price-fixing by corporate coalitions or cartels and mergers that would obviously stifle competition." Lewis also quoted professor William Kovacic of the George Washington University Law School—a leading antitrust scholar—as having commented that "Richard Posner is one of the most important antitrust scholars of the past half-century." In an indication of his standing, Posner was appointed as mediator in all settlement talks between Microsoft and the U.S. antitrust authorities during their battle at the turn of the twenty-first century.

In keeping with Posner's wide array of interests and knowledge, his *An Affair of State* moves on to a topic entirely different from antitrust laws. "He has long been interested in the relationship between sex and legal and moral theory," wrote Andrew Sullivan in the *New York Times.* "He is a grown-up and thinking conservative, so in many ways he is a perfect man for the task, and this book doesn't disappoint. Posner makes you recall all over again why 1998 and the first six weeks of 1999 were such a riveting time, and how those months dramatized our culture's deepest political and moral disagreements and, in some strange fashion, helped restore them. But his most valuable contribution is legal. In a way only good judges can do, he manages both to portray the ambiguity of constitutional law . . . and yet not shy from judgment about what actually happened and what to make of it." Sullivan noted that, while Posner has little time for the "'Clinton-haters,'" he does, however, unequivocally expose the manner in which Clinton's "casuistic evasions of the truth" were perjurious and how he obstructed justice for almost an entire year, then discusses whether or not such acts were sufficient cause for impeachment. Sullivan commented that Posner "shows that there is a final answer to the question of what perjury and obstruction of justice are, and at least some large common ground as to what might be the constitutional grounds for impeachment."

With *Public Intellectuals: A Study of Decline,* Posner turns his sights on the role of the academic media superstars, or the "public intellectuals." In his review of the book for *Washington Monthly,* Jamie Malanowski defined this group of writers as "the big-brained types who have some academic background or relationship and who discourse on matters of public interest." Malanowski noted that Posner believes modern pubic intellectuals contribute inferior commentary in comparison to the early "giants" such as George Orwell, Albert Camus, and John Stuart Mill. He believes there are several reasons for the "decline." One is academic specialization, which limits the number of disciplines studied by the intellectual community and handicaps those who step out of their area of expertise in their social and political writings targeted to the general public. He also blames a market that lacks quality control—an audience (themselves often specialists) that lacks the knowledge to evaluate what has been written, and a peer group that seldom monitors the work of its members. In other words, noted Carol Polsgrove in her review of the book for *American Prospect,* "Freed from knowledgeable scrutiny, intellectuals can pretty much say what they want and get away with it."

In an interview with Larissa MacFarquam for the *New Yorker,* Posner said: "I have exactly the same personality as my cat. I am cold, furtive, callous, snobbish, selfish, and playful, but with a streak of cruelty." Referring to this comment, Malanowski wrote: "Knowing the man to be both brilliant and mean—playful with a streak of cruelty—it seems to me quite possible that *Public Intellectuals* is merely a massive 398-page, chart-filled practical joke perpetrated upon a vain intelligentsia and credulous media, all for the perverse, cat-stroking amusement of Richard Posner." Other reviewers, too, wondered at Posner's intent with this book. Regardless, Samuel Brittan, reviewer with the *Financial Times,* commented: "The sad thing is that this book will most likely be read by people who already agree with the message . . . rather than those who would benefit most, but who are more likely to read the attempted rebuttals which have already been proliferating in the U.S."

Following her interview with Posner, MacFarquam made this comment: "It is not apparent from his mild exterior that Posner is the most mercilessly seditious legal theorist of this generation. Nor is it obvious that, as a judge on the Seventh Circuit Court of Appeals, he is one of the most powerful jurists in the country, second only to those on the Supreme Court. . . . Posner did not set out to seize power: he spotted it drifting and gleefully pocketed it, like a stray hundred-dollar bill." She remarked that Posner is "aggressively unconventional in his judging [and] ten times as much so in his books." She also commented that "He is not the type to spend years testing his arguments for leakage, sealing tiny cracks and worrying endlessly over possible ripostes: he would rather risk sending them young into the world, flawed but forceful, with the advantage of surprise. And yet the uproarious pugilism and the desire to shock evident in his pages are nowhere visible on the surface of the man."

Steve Kurtz commented after interviewing Posner for the online magazine *Reason:* "Oscar Wilde once said of George Bernard Shaw that 'he hasn't an enemy in the world, and none of his friends like him.' Posner is the opposite: Plenty of people strongly disagree with his writings, but he's such a genial, hardworking person that even his enemies can't help but admire him."

BIOGRAPHICAL AND CRITICAL SOURCES:

PERIODICALS

American Prospect, February 11, 2002, Carol Polsgrove, review of *Public Intellectuals: A Study of Decline,* p. 42.
American Quarterly, September, 1992, review of *Law and Literature,* p. 494.
Bookworld, July 5, 1992, review of *Sex and Reason,* p. 6; November 3, 1996, review of *A Guide to America's Sex Laws,* p. 13.
Columbia Law Review, October, 1995, review of *Overcoming Law,* p. 1568.
Economist, September 18, 1999, review of *The Problematics of Moral and Legal Theory,* p. 7.
Ethics, April, 1995, review of *Sex and Reason,* p. 670; April, 1998, review of *Aging and Old Age,* p. 569.
Financial Times, February 2, 2002, Samuel Brittan, "Get Thee to an Ivory Tower, and Stay Put: Richard Posner Deplores the Sloppy Thinking of Academics Who Hog the Media Spotlight," review of *Public Intellectuals,* p. 6.

Journal of Interdisciplinary History, winter, 1992, review of *Cardozo: A Study in Reputation,* p. 547.

Law Quarterly Review, July, 1998, review of *Law and Legal Theory in England and America,* p. 511.

New Republic, August 23, 1999, review of *The Problematics of Moral and Legal Theory,* p. 38.

New Yorker, December 10, 2001, Larissa MacFarquam, "The Bench Burner: An Interview with Richard Posner."

New York Times, September 26, 1999, Andrew Sullivan, "A View from the Bench," review of *An Affair of State: The Investigation, Impeachment, and Trial of President Clinton.*

New York Times Book Review, September 9, 1990, p. 15; April, 1996, review of *Aging and Old Age,* p. 26; September 26, 1999, review of *An Affair of State,* p. 13.

Perspectives on Political Science, winter, 1992, review of *Cardozo,* p. 42.

Times Literary Supplement, May 8, 1998, review of *Law and Literature: A Misunderstood Relation;* November 19, 1999, review of *An Affair of State,* p. 8.

Tribune Books, April 11, 1993, review of *The Problems of Jurisprudence,* p. 8.

Village Voice, May 25, 1993, review of *Sex and Reason,* p. 81.

Wall Street Journal, September 14, 1999, review of *An Affair of State,* p. A20.

Washington Monthly, Jamie Malanowski, review of *Public Intellectuals,* p. 57.

ONLINE

Complete Review, http://www.complete-review.com/ (July 15, 2002), "Richard Posner at the *Complete Review.*"

Reason, http://reason.com/ (April 2001), Steve Kurtz, "Sex, Economics, and Other Legal Matters" (interview with Richard A. Posner).*

*   *   *

POWER, Jonathan 1941-

PERSONAL: Born June 4, 1941, in North Mimms, England; son of Patrick and Dorothy Power; married Anne Hayward (a government housing consultant); children: Carmen, Miriam, Lucy. *Education:* Victoria University of Manchester, B.A., 1963; University of Wisconsin, M.A., 1966. *Politics:* Social Democrat. *Religion:* Roman Catholic.

ADDRESSES: Agent—Curtis Brown, Haymarket House, 28-29 Haymarket, London SW1Y 4SP, England. *E-mail*—jonatpower@aol.com.

CAREER: Freelance writer, broadcaster, columnist, and filmmaker, 1967—. Ministry of Agriculture, Tanzania, volunteer, 1963-64; member of staff of Reverend Martin Luther King, Jr., 1966. *International Herald Tribune,* foreign affairs correspondent; conducted fieldwork in Lesotho; visiting fellow of Overseas Development Council, Washington, DC, and International Institute for Strategic Studies, London; editorial adviser to International Commission on Disarmament and Security Issues; consultant to World Council of Churches, International Institute for the Environment and Development, and Aspen Institute.

MEMBER: International Institute for Strategic Studies, Royal Society for International Affairs.

AWARDS, HONORS: Silver medal from Venice Film Festival, 1972, for "It's Ours Whatever They Say."

WRITINGS:

Economic Development, Longman (London, England), 1971.

World of Hunger, Temple Smith (London, England), 1976.

(With Ann-Marie Holenstein) *Migrant Workers in Western Europe and the United States,* Pergamon (London, England), 1979.

Amnesty International, McGraw Hill (New York, NY), 1981.

A Vision of Hope: The Fiftieth Anniversary of the United Nations, National Committee of the USA for UN50 (New York, NY), 1995.

(Editor) *Like Water on a Stone: The Story of Amnesty International,* Northeastern University Press (Boston, MA), 2001.

FILMS

The Black American Dream, first broadcast by British Broadcasting Corporation (BBC-TV), 1971.

It's Ours Whatever They Say, first broadcast by BBC-TV, 1972.

The Diplomatic Style of Andrew Young, first broadcast by BBC-TV, 1979.

Also author of several other films. Columnist for *International Herald Tribune,* 1974- 1991; guest columnist, *New York Times,* 1979, syndicated columnist, 1994—. Contributor to magazines and newspapers in England, Europe, and the United States, including *International Affairs, London Times, Guardian, Observer, Washington Post, El Pais, Die Zeit, Politiken, Commonweal, Encounter,* and *Prospect.*

SIDELIGHTS: "Amnesty [International] may not yet have changed the world, but it hasn't left the world as it found it either," said Jonathan Power on the 40th anniversary of the indefatigable human rights organization. In his book, *Like Water on Stone: The Story of Amnesty International,* Power chronicles the history of the organization from its inception, through triumphs and controversies, to its position as a potent influence in the global struggle for human rights, the humane treatment of prisoners, and the elimination of oppression.

Founded by British lawyer Peter Benenson in 1961, Amnesty International began as "a group to push for the release of prisoners locked up solely for exercising their freedom of speech on political matters," wrote a reviewer in *Publishers Weekly.* In late 1960, Benenson read "a newspaper report about two Portuguese students in Lisbon during the dark days of the Salazar dictatorship," Power wrote in *Guardian* (London). "They had been arrested and sentenced to seven years' imprisonment for raising their glasses in a toast to freedom."

Benenson pondered how to persuade the Portuguese authorities to "release these victims of outrageous oppression," Power wrote. "A way must be devised to bombard the Salazar regime with written protests." As the idea developed, Benenson believed that a wider and stronger response would be "a one-year campaign to draw public attention to the plight of political and religious prisoners throughout the world," Power wrote. Joined by prominent Londoners Eric Barker and Louis Blom-Cooper, the "Appeal for Amnesty, 1961" was launched in the newspaper, *Observer,* in late May.

"At Benenson's office in London, they collected and published information on people whom Benenson was later to call 'prisoners of conscience,'" Power wrote. "The three men soon had a nucleus of supporters, principally lawyers, journalists, politicians and intellectuals."

Upon its 40th anniversary in 2001, Amnesty International's rolls boasted an international membership of more than a million, with supporters in 160 countries and territories. "Amnesty has dealt with the cases of 47,000 prisoners of conscience and other victims of human-rights violation," Power wrote. "More than 45,000 of these cases are now closed."

In *Like Water on Stone,* Power "charts the ways in which Amnesty has contributed to the march of human rights, sometimes dramatically but mostly modestly and quietly," wrote reviewer Alex de Waal in *London Review of Books.* "And it is a truly impressive story, of many small, mostly invisible and unattributable victories, in the form of prisoners released or treated better, local human rights groups founded around the world, and legal reforms, all adding up to slowly raising the bar on what it is acceptable for a government to do." A reviewer in *Publishers Weekly* called the book a "sympathetic account." Caroline Moorehaed wrote in the *Times Literary Supplement* that it is a "very readable book. . . . Never was Amnesty International more needed. And never, to judge from Jonathan Power's carefully argued book, has it been better placed to play its part."

Power "strongly supports the increased attention that groups like Amnesty have brought to human rights, and he devotes a good deal of discussion to the group's 'success stories,'" wrote the *Publishers Weekly* reviewer. But, "to his credit, Power is willing to offer some criticisms of the group where its efforts have gone awry." Power's book "is not an uncritical history," de Waal wrote. "He refers both to the scandal of Benenson's links with the Foreign Office (which brought the organization to the point of collapse) and—glancingly—to the view that Amnesty's focus on prisoners contributed to the preference of some Latin American dictatorships for having their victims 'disappear' instead." Prominent among the group's failures, de Waal observed, is "the continuing use of the death penalty in the U.S."

The pursuit of "human rights is an activity as well as a theory; it is an exercise in power," de Waal commented. With the increased prominence of Amnesty International and other private and governmental organizations, "the discourse of human rights has widened considerably and the activity now encompasses not only the old-style campaigns against manifest injustice, torture and political detention, for example, but the promotion of democracy, conflict resolution, 'good governance,' humanitarian principles and the increasingly fashionable notion of 'civil society.'"

But there is no shortage of "horror stories encountered by Amnesty" in Power's book, Tariq Ali remarked in the *Times*, "and unlike the more pliable HR scholar/ journalists, he is not shy of naming names." Although some readers "may wish that Power had more distance from his subject," a *Publishers Weekly* reviewer wrote, "this book is a valuable addition to a growing library on the recent advances in human rights."

BIOGRAPHICAL AND CRITICAL SOURCES:

PERIODICALS

British Book News, July, 1984, review of *Amnesty International,* p. 393.
Guardian (London, England), May 12, 2001, Jonathan Power, article on Amnesty International and *Like Water on Stone: The Story of Amnesty International,* p. 3.
Library Journal, October 1, 1995, Wilda Williams, review of *A Vision of Hope: The Fiftieth Anniversary of the United Nations,* p. 102; October 1, 1995, Wilda Williams, review of *A Vision of Hope,* p. 102.
London Review of Books, August 23, 2001, Alex de Waal, "The Moral Solipsism of Global Ethics Inc," review of *Like Water on Stone,* pp. 15-18.
New Statesman, April 2, 1976.
Publishers Weekly, July 30, 2001, review of *Like Water on Stone,* p. 72.
School Librarian, May, 1996, review of *A Vision of Hope,* p. 83.
Social Education, summer, 1985, review of *Amnesty International,* p. 526.
Spectator, March 27, 1976.
Times (London, England), June 6, 2001, Tariq Ali, "How Amnesty Fought the Enemy Inside and Out," p. 13.
Washington Monthly, December, 1981, Michael Hiestand, review of *Amnesty International,* p. 58.

ONLINE

Penguin UK Web site, http://www.penguin.co.uk/ (October 7, 2001), interview with Jonathan Power.

R

RACHLIN, Nahid 1944-

PERSONAL: Born June 6, 1944, in Abadan, Iran; came to the United States in 1962, naturalized citizen, 1969; daughter of Manoochehr (a lawyer) and Mohtaram Bozorgmehri; married Howard Rachlin (a professor of psychology); children: Leila. *Education:* Lindenwood College, B.A.; attended Columbia University.

ADDRESSES: Home—300 E. 93rd St., Apt. 43-D, New York, NY 10028. *Agent*—Harriet Wasserman, 230 East 48th St., New York, NY 10017.

CAREER: Writer. Children's Hospital, Boston, MA, research assistant, 1968-69; New York University, Continuing Education Division, adjunct assistant professor of creative writing, 1979-90. Barnard College, creative writing instructor, 1991—. Appointments at Marymount Manhattan College, 1986-87; Hofstra University, 1988-90; Yale University, 1989-90; Hunter College, 1990.

AWARDS, HONORS: Bennett Cerf Award from Columbia University, 1974, for short story "Ruins"; Doubleday-Columbia fellowship for creative writing, 1974-75; Wallace Stegner fellowship, Stanford, 1975-76; National Endowment for the Arts fiction grant, 1979; PEN syndicated fiction project prize, 1983.

WRITINGS:

Foreigner, Norton (New York, NY), 1978.
Married to a Stranger, Dutton (New York, NY), 1983.
Veils: Short Stories, City Lights Books (San Francisco, CA), 1992.
The Heart's Desire: A Novel, City Lights Books (San Francisco, CA), 1995.

Contributor to *Elements of Fiction,* edited by Jack Carpenter, W.M.C. Brown (Dubuque, IA), 1979; *A Writer's Workbook,* St. Martin's Press (New York, NY), 1987; *The Uncommon Touch,* Stanford University Press (Stanford, CA), 1989; *Stories from the American Mosaic,* Graywolf Press (St. Paul, MN), 1990; *The Confidence Woman,* edited by Eve Shelnutt, Longstreet Press (Marietta, GA), 1991; and *Lovers,* Crossing Press (Santa Cruz, CA), 1992. Also contributor of stories to popular magazines and literary journals, including *Crazy Horse, Literary Review, Redbook, Shenandoah, Four Quarters, Confrontation,* and *Ararat.*

Stories have been translated into the Iranian language.

SIDELIGHTS: Nahid Rachlin, the most published Iranian author in the United States, was born in Abadan, Iran, but spent the early years of her life in Tehran. At the age of nine months she was taken by her grandmother to be raised by her mother's sister, because her mother, who already had four living children, had promised her childless sister that the next child would be hers. Rachlin's childhood was one of fun, freedom, and acceptance, surrounded by the love and devotion of her mother-aunt and other members of her extended family. Rarely did she see her true parents, for whom she naturally developed little affection. However, circumstances led to her father arriving unexpectedly and taking her back at about the age of seven.

In *Contemporary Authors Autobiography Series (CAAS),* Rachlin related the shock, pain, and sadness of being yanked away from the only true mother she ever knew and having to adjust to a strange place and a rigid lifestyle in a home where her biological mother was cool and aloof. She begins her story remembering how, coming home from high school, she would search out her older sister, Pari, and read to her whatever story she had written that day while she should have been listening to a lecture. Her stories expressed real-life events or perceptions she had experienced. "Pari always responded not to the story itself but to the anguish that the story expressed," writes Rachlin. "She listened not so much to my story as to me. I remember the intensity of my desire to express my feelings and reactions to what went on around me, and equally matched eagerness to hear her reassuring voice. I was also an avid reader. I would read some of the passages to her and she would say, 'You could do that.'" To this day, Rachlin wonders whether she would have become a writer had her sister not encouraged her.

By the time she was halfway through high school, Rachlin began reading anything she could obtain, using the stories to transport her into other peoples' lives through their emotions. She was reading translations of Hemingway, Dostoyevsky, and Balzac; writing sketches and stories; and dreaming of escape from a life destined for an arranged marriage right out of high school—the type of life that eventually caused Pari to slip into manic-depression, divorce, the loss of custody of her only child, and several months each year spent in a psychiatric institution.

Rachlin began pleading with her parents to let her join her two older brothers, who were by that time living in the United States. Although hesitant, her father finally agreed because she was the only one of his daughters who read and did so well in school. Her brothers obtained a significant scholarship for her at Lindenwood College, where she studied psychology and devoted time every day to her writing. Only after marriage and the birth of a child, however, did she feel she could justify taking time out of each day to write fiction. She began taking writing courses at Columbia University, during which time she wrote three one-page sketches—all fiction based on personal experiences in her homeland during her youth—that were published in a small literary magazine.

Rachlin's first return to Iran, twelve years after she had left, inspired her first novel, *Foreigner,* written on a Stegner fellowship at Stanford. Her second novel, *Married to a Stranger,* centers around the deteriorating marriage of her second sister and her own adolescent dreams. Reviewing the book for *Belles Lettres: A Review of Books by Women,* Saideh Pakravan noted that Rachlin is the direct descendent of people living in a culture where telling stories at home in the family setting was a way of life. These storytellers, often a parent or a nanny, engaged their rapt audiences with fascinating sagas about events that shaped peoples' lives and destinies. "Reading anything Rachlin writes is like sitting at the foot of a storyteller of yore," commented Pakravan. "Except, having lost the innocent rapture with which children listen, we also observe the sleight of hand, and wonder how Rachlin manages to hold us, how her restrained writing can exercise such pull. There is no answer, unless it lies in the very lack of artifice."

And Rachlin prefers to write—in what Pakravan called the unobtrusive voice of a powerful storyteller—about her past. She commented in *CAAS,* "It has to do with a desire to bring into the present a reality which is no longer represented in my present life. The differences between the Iranian and American cultures are so vast that in order for me to have adjusted to the American way of life I have had to, without always being conscious of it, suppress much of my own childhood and upbringing. Sometimes I wake in the middle of the night with a nightmare that my past has vanished altogether and I am floating unanchored. I get out of the bed and begin to write. Then it is all with me again."

Rachlin commented: "I have always written fiction rather than nonfiction because I feel that only fiction can convey the complexity of character and situation that I see around me. I think that the purpose of fiction in society is to provide models for alternate courses of life—not so much as a guide for action but as a vehicle for understanding people. *Foreigner,* my first published novel, for instance, seems autobiographical because of many parallels in the protagonist's life and my own life (a young woman coming to the U.S., marrying an American and then returning home for a visit).

"The same with my second novel, *Married to a Stranger,* which is about a young woman in Iran, yearning to break through the rigid traditions around her."

According to Barbara Thompson in the *New York Times Book Review,* "Rachlin captures the range of forces that were brought to bear on personal relationships in the changing political and social setting of the last years of Shah Mohammed Reza Pahlavi's reign. She shows us not only the tranquil inner courtyards with sweets and gossip exchanged by the fishpond, the flower bedecked bridal chamber, but also the political, social and religious factions contending for primacy in the streets outside." Carolyn See described it as "a woman's novel in a very particular sense," in the *Los Angeles Times.* "The reader has the feeling that these are the facts, ma'am; perhaps the real facts of one ordinary relationship, matter-of-factly described against the larger background of a country ripped by war and revolution. But it's the single human beings who are important here; that is, perhaps, what makes it a woman's novel."

The Heart's Desire, the material for which again came from Rachlin's personal experiences, centers on an Iranian/American couple dealing with cultural issues in a post-revolutionary Iran. "The plot immediately reminds one of *Not without My Daughter,* the controversial novel (also made into a film starring Sally Field) about an American mother fighting to save her child from an abusive Iranian husband in a country basically described as an insect-infested black hole," wrote a reviewer for the online publication *Iranbooks.* The reviewer also commented that Rachlin's uncomplicated style is a "blessing. Instead of trying to solve literary riddles and metaphors and hallucinating in magical realism, the reader is left free with a clear head to grasp complicated human and cultural issues."

BIOGRAPHICAL AND CRITICAL SOURCES:

BOOKS

Contemporary Authors Autobiography Series, Volume 17, Gale (Detroit, MI), 1993, pp. 215-229.

PERIODICALS

Belles Lettres: A Review of Books by Women, fall, 1992, Marilyn Booth, review of *Veils: Short Stories,* p. 52; spring, 1994, Saideh Pakravan, review of *Married to a Stranger,* p. 53.
Literary Review, fall, 1996, Thomas Filbin, review of *Married to a Stranger, Veils,* and *Foreigner,* p. 172.
Los Angeles Times, September 16, 1983, Carolyn See, review of *Married to a Stranger,* p. 20.

New York Times Book Review, October 2, 1983, Barbara Thompson, review of *Married to a Stranger,* p. 14; November 29, 1992, Laurel Graeber, review of *Veils,* p. 18.
Publishers Weekly, April 20, 1992, review of *Veils,* p. 19; October 2, 1995, review of *The Heart's Desire,* p. 66.
World Literature Today, spring, 1996, Nasrin Rahimieh, review of *The Heart's Desire,* p. 463.

ONLINE

Iranbooks, http://www.iranian.com/ (April 9, 2002), "A Tale of Two Cultures," review of *The Heart's Desire.**

*   *   *

RILEY, Dick
    See RILEY, Richard Anthony

*   *   *

RILEY, Richard Anthony 1946-
    (Dick Riley)

PERSONAL: Born May 31, 1946, in Youngstown, OH; son of Richard Anthony (in newspaper work) and Eleanor (Donnelly) Riley; married Marcia Jo Clendenen (a psychotherapist), August 23, 1975; children: Richard Ian. *Education:* University of Notre Dame, B.A., 1968; Columbia University, M.A., 1969.

ADDRESSES: Agent—Gloria Safier, Inc., 667 Madison Ave., New York, NY 10021.

CAREER: Associated Press and *New York Post,* New York, NY, reporter, 1969-70 and 1971-75; freelance writer, 1975—. *Military service:* U.S. Army, 1970-71; became first lieutenant.

MEMBER: Mystery Writers of America.

WRITINGS:

AS DICK RILEY

(With T. Harris and S. Maull) *Black Sunday,* Putnam (New York, NY), 1975.
Rite of Expiation, Putnam (New York, NY), 1976.

(Editor) *Critical Encounters: Writers and Themes in Science Fiction,* Ungar (New York, NY), 1978.

(Editor, with Pam McAllister) *The Bedside, Bathtub, & Armchair Companion to Agatha Christie,* Ungar (New York, NY), 1979, 2nd edition published as *The New Bedtime, Bathtub & Armchair Companion to Agatha Christie,* additional material edited by Pam McAllister and Bruce Cassiday, with foreword by Julian Symons, Ungar (New York, NY), 1986.

(With Pam McAllister) *The Bedside, Bathtub & Armchair Companion to Sherlock Holmes,* Continuum (New York, NY), 1999.

(With Pam McAllister) *The Bedside, Bathtub & Armchair Companion to Shakespeare,* Continuum (New York, NY), 2001.

Also author of *Middleman Out* (one-act play), first broadcast by National Public Radio, 1980.

SIDELIGHTS: Journalist, playwright, and freelance writer Dick Riley, along with coauthor Pam McAllister, has written "The Bedside, Bathtub & Armchair Companion" series. The series has included books on two important writers in the mystery genre, Agatha Christie and Arthur Conan Doyle, including Doyle's well-known sleuth, Sherlock Holmes. Another book in the series covers one of the key figures in literature, William Shakespeare.

The books consist of numerous short, illustrated chapters, designed to be read in short bursts rather than extended sittings. *The Bedside, Bathtub & Armchair Companion to Sherlock Holmes* includes brief summaries of all stories in the Holmes canon, plus an essay on the traditional image of Holmes (complete with deerstalker hat), commentary on Holmes parodies and pastiches, and a short biography of Doyle. Also included is information on Victorian England, British government, illustrators of Holmes stories, actors who have played Holmes and Watson, contact information for Holmes societies throughout the world, and other browser-friendly data. Mary Carroll, writing in *Booklist,* remarked that "this new celebration of Arthur Conan Doyle's canon should have appeal," while a critic writing in *Publishers Weekly* called *The Bedside, Bathtub & Armchair Companion to Sherlock Holmes* "a thorough—and thoroughly entertaining—survey of Sherlockiana."

Similarly, *The Bedside, Bathtub & Armchair Companion to Shakespeare* provides plot summaries of thirty-six plays (*Pericles* and *The Two Noble Kinsmen* are excluded), plus information on the Bard's likely sources, assessments of each play's most notable aspects, and other concise material on Shakespeare and his works. Other chapters cover Shakespeare's sonnets, women's roles in Shakespearean times, Shakespeare's use of language, and more. "This irreverent guide invokes pop culture to unravel some of the mysteries and difficulties associated with Shakespeare," observed Sarah Hart in *American Theatre.* Jack Helbig, writing in *Booklist,* concluded, "The accessible little volume constitutes a fine introduction to Shakespeare for neophytes."

BIOGRAPHICAL AND CRITICAL SOURCES:

PERIODICALS

American Theatre, December, 2001, Sarah Hart, review of *The Bedside, Bathtub & Armchair Companion to Shakespeare,* p. 73.

Analog Science Fiction & Fact, February, 2000, Tom Easton, review of *The Bedside, Bathtub & Armchair Companion to Sherlock Holmes,* p. 132.

Armchair Detective, winter, 1987, review of *The New Bedside, Bathtub & Armchair Companion to Agatha Christie,* p. 73.

Booklist, January 1, 1999, Mary Carroll, review of *The Bedside, Bathtub & Armchair Companion to Sherlock Holmes,* p. 820; July, 2001, Jack Helbig, review of *The Bedside, Bathtub & Armchair Companion to Shakespeare,* p. 1971.

Bookwatch, January, 1999, review of *The Bedside, Bathtub & Armchair Companion to Sherlock Holmes,* p. 6.

Library Journal, July, 2001, Shana C. Fair, review of *The Bedside, Bathtub & Armchair Companion to Shakespeare,* p. 90.

New York Times Book Review, July 6, 1986, review of *The New Bedside, Bathtub & Armchair Companion to Agatha Christie,* p. 24.

Publishers Weekly, February 22, 1999, review of *The Bedside, Bathtub & Armchair Companion to Sherlock Holmes,* p. 70.

Reference & Research Book News, November, 1999, review of *The Bedside, Bathtub & Armchair Companion to Sherlock Holmes,* p. 192.

School Library Journal, July, 1999, Pam Johnson, review of *The Bedside, Bathtub & Armchair Companion to Sherlock Holmes,* p. 118.

Wilson Library Bulletin, May, 1980, Jon Breen, review of *The Bedside, Bathtub & Armchair Companion to Agatha Christie,* p. 581, Charles Bunge, review of *The Bedside, Bathtub & Armchair Companion to Agatha Christie,* p. 592.*

*   *   *

ROBERTS, Andrew 1963-

PERSONAL: Born January 13, 1963, in London, England; son of Simon (a company director) and Katie (Hilary-Collins) Roberts. *Education:* Attended Gonville and Caius College, Cambridge. *Politics:* Conservative. *Religion:* Church of England.

ADDRESSES: Home and office—19 Collingham Place, London SW5 0QF, England. *Agent*—A. Lownie, 15 Heddon St., London WC2 2LF, England.

CAREER: Robert Fleming and Co., London, England, investment banker, 1985-88; writer. Director of private companies.

WRITINGS:

The Holy Fox: A Biography of Lord Halifax, Weidenfeld & Nicolson (London, England), 1991.
Eminent Churchillians, Weidenfeld & Nicolson (London, England), 1994, Simon & Schuster (New York, NY), 1995.
The Aachen Memorandum, Weidenfeld & Nicolson (London, England), 1995.
Salisbury: Victorian Titan, Weidenfeld & Nicolson (London, England), 1999.
(With Antonia Fraser) *The House of Windsor,* University of California Press (Berkeley, CA) 2000.
Napoleon and Wellington: The Long Duel, Weidenfeld & Nicolson (London, England), 2001, published as *Napoleon and Wellington: The Battle of Waterloo—And the Great Commanders Who Fought It,* Simon & Schuster (New York, NY), 2002.

SIDELIGHTS: British author Andrew Roberts is the author of several books of history, from the 1991 *The Holy Fox: A Biography of Lord Halifax* to *Napoleon and Wellington,* published in 2001. In his first title,

Roberts provides a revisionist account of Lord Halifax, a one-time viceroy to India and the Foreign Secretary in Prime Minister Chamberlain's government. Long charged with appeasement, along with his Prime Minister, Lord Halifax in fact began to move his government away from that policy vis-à-vis Hitler's Germany, according to Roberts, and wisely made way for Winston Churchill to become prime minister instead of himself. "The scholarship is sound and the account is thoroughly readable," noted Keith Robbins in the *English Historical Review.* Robbins further commented that "Roberts perhaps overstates the extent of the Foreign Secretary's role in abandoning appeasement, but his study is generally cogent and worth careful attention." A reviewer for the *Economist* also found Roberts's account praiseworthy, noticing that his narrative "grips and convinces," though he also felt that Halifax still "emerges from these friendly pages as just the cold, compromising nobleman of legend." And reviewing the same title in *History Today,* Steven Fielding felt that "Roberts writes with some elegance and to good effect."

Roberts next published a best-selling collection of essays about friends and enemies of Winston Churchill, entitled *Eminent Churchillians.* Reviewing that book, a contributor to the *Economist* wrote that Roberts, "a young right-wing revisionist historian from Cambridge, has brought off an odd feat. He follows his first book, 'The Holy Fox,' a rightly acclaimed life of Edward Wood, Lord Halifax, with a much ruder and a much worse one . . . written in a tone calculated to infuriate the old, the staid and the loyal." A large part of the book is an attack on Lord Mountbatten and other prominent members of the ruling class. Roberts's essays managed to rub many the wrong way, in and out of the press. However, Kenneth O. Morgan, writing in *New Statesman & Society,* called the book a "sparky collection of essays," both "forceful and opinionated," which "provide an excellent read by a very promising young scholar." Reviewing the American publication of *Eminent Churchillians,* a contributor for *Publishers Weekly* was less complimentary, calling it a "slashing and unsettling reappraisal of key figures in Britain of the period 1940-55." Among these was Roberts's portrayal of Churchill as a "profound, unrepentant racist and white supremacist." And *Booklist*'s Gilbert Taylor concluded that "Roberts pushes World War II revisionism to a new—some might say snarlingly scandalous—level."

Roberts also tackled a heavyweight of the nineteenth century—Lord Salisbury; his *Salisbury: Victorian Ti-*

tan weighed in at almost one thousand pages. "This is a big book because the author has a lot to say," wrote Richard Wilkinson in *History Review,* "both about the importance of Salisbury's career and about his unusual and entertaining personality. My interest never flagged." Salisbury, who dominated Victorian politics, held high office for twenty-one years, for thirteen of which he was Prime Minister. Yet he is, according to a reviewer for the *Economist,* "unpopular or neglected among historians and biographers." In fact he is one of those leaders whom few historians bother to research—something of an unsolved puzzle. "Andrew Roberts's new biography helps answer the puzzle," commented the *Economist* reviewer. "Even if Mr. Roberts is enthusiastic about his subject for all the wrong reasons, this biography represents an achievement." Wilkinson also had praise for Roberts's research and writing: "Roberts brilliantly establishes what a character Salisbury was. Nothing could be further from the stereotype of Victorian grandee."

In *Napoleon and Wellington,* Roberts compares the two leaders who met each other in battle at Waterloo. Roberts organizes this unusual double biography chronologically, from their births in 1769, and their subsequent famous rivalry throughout the Napoleonic Wars. In his study, Roberts once again takes to task the received interpretation of this rivalry. "The chief triumph of this book is its depiction of Wellington," commented a critic for the *Economist.* "He remains a great general, but is shown to have had feet of clay inside those famous boots . . . . [The book] redefines Wellington without diminishing his achievements." Praise for Roberts's book also came from Christopher Hibbert in the London *Sunday Times,* noting that though the "field of Napoleonic studies may be a crowded one . . . Roberts, one of our brightest young historians, is by no means overshadowed in his new book." Hibbert found *Napoleon and Wellington* "well written and well organised" and as "entertaining as it is instructive . . . , original and judicious both as military and personal history." Jeremy Black, writing in *History Today,* called the book a "sparkling new work [which] offers a different approach, a study of the personal relationship between Napoleon and Wellington and of the way it changed across their careers." Black further noted that Roberts avoids "the stodgy route of joint biography," but instead "focuses on what each man thought, wrote and said about the other." Black also had praise for the narrative itself: "Beautifully written, stuffed full with a fabulous cast, and proceeding by a series of excellent anecdotes. . . ." A "brilliant work," Black concluded.

In a *Spectator* review of *Napoleon and Wellington,* Jane Ridley remarked that "Roberts has an enviable knack for hitting on neat, sexy subjects which combine history and biography and give a fresh spin to old chestnuts."

BIOGRAPHICAL AND CRITICAL SOURCES:

PERIODICALS

Booklist, July, 1995, Gilbert Taylor, review of *Eminent Churchillians,* pp. 1857-1858.
Contemporary Review, January, 1995, p. 56.
Economist, March 30, 1991, review of *The Holy Fox,* p. 86; August 6, 1994, review of *Eminent Churchillians,* pp. 71-72; November 13, 1999, "British Politicians: Just Say No," p. 7; September 29, 2001, "Fighting Words: Napoleon and Wellington."
English Historical Review, September, 1994, Keith Robbins, review *of The Holy Fox,* pp. 1031-1032.
Foreign Affairs, November-December, 1995, pp. 127-128.
History Review, March, 2001, Richard Wilkinson, review of *Salisbury: Victorian Titan,* p. 51.
History Today, March, 1994, Steven Fielding, review of *The Holy Fox,* p. 55; January, 1996, Steven Fielding, review of *Eminent Churchillians,* p. 56; December, 2001, Jeremy Black, review of *Napoleon and Wellington,* p. 54.
Library Journal, June 15, 2001, Michael Rogers, review of *The House of Windsor,* p. 108.
New Leader, October 9, 1995, pp. 16-18.
New Statesman & Society, August 12, 1994, Kenneth O. Morgan, review of *Eminent Churchillians,* p. 36.
Publishers Weekly, June 5, 1995, review of *Eminent Churchillians,* p. 47.
Spectator, September 18, 1999, Jane Ridley, review of *Salisbury: Victorian Titan,* pp. 54-55; August 25, 2001, Jane Ridley, review of *Napoleon and Wellington,* p. 30.
Sunday Times (London), September 9, 2001, Christopher Hibbert, "The Best of Enemies," p. 35.
Times Literary Supplement, October 22, 1999, p. 3.

ONLINE

Andrew Roberts Home Page, http://www.andrew-roberts.net/ (January 28, 2002).

ROBERTS, Michele (Brigitte) 1949-

PERSONAL: Born May 20, 1949, in Bushey, Hertfordshire, England; daughter of Reginald George (a businessman) and Monique Pauline Joseph (a teacher; maiden name, Caulle) Roberts; married Jim Latter (an artist). *Education:* Oxford University, B.A. (with honors), 1970; University of London Library Associate, 1972. *Politics:* "Socialist-feminist." *Religion:* "Unconventional." *Hobbies and other interests:* Cooking and eating, painting, mountain walking, dancing, swimming, traveling.

ADDRESSES: Home—London, England, and Mayenne, France. *Agent*—Caroline Dawnay, A.D. Peters, 10 Buckingham St., London WC2, England. *E-mail*—micheroberts@excite.co.uk.

CAREER: Writer. Has worked as a librarian, cook, teacher, cleaner, pregnancy counselor, researcher, book reviewer, and broadcaster; Nottingham Trent University, visiting fellow, 1995-1996, and visiting professor, 1996—. Writer-in-residence, Lambeth Borough, London, England, 1981-82; writer-in-residence, Bromley Borough, London, 1983-84; cofounder, Feminist Writers Group.

MEMBER: Writers Guild.

AWARDS, HONORS: Gay News Literary Award, 1978, for *A Piece of the Night;* Arts Council grant, 1978; Booker Prize shortlist, 1992, and W. H. Smith Literary Award, 1993, both for *Daughters of the House.*

WRITINGS:

POETRY

(Editor, with Michelene Wandor) *Cutlasses and Earrings,* Playbooks (London, England), 1977.
Licking the Bed Clean, [London], 1978.
Smile, Smile, Smile, Smile, [London], 1980.
(With Judith Karantris and Michelene Wandor) *Touch Papers,* Allison & Busby (London, England), 1982.
The Mirror of the Mother: Selected Poems, 1975-1985, Methuen (London, England), 1985.
All the Selves I Was: New and Selected Poems, Virago (London, England), 1995.

NOVELS

A Piece of the Night, Women's Press (London, England), 1978.
The Visitation, Women's Press (London, England), 1983.
The Wild Girl, Methuen (London, England), 1984.
The Book of Mrs. Noah, Methuen (London, England), 1987.
In the Red Kitchen, Methuen (London, England), 1990.
Psyche and the Hurricane, Methuen, 1991.
Daughters of the House, Morrow (New York, NY), 1992.
During Mother's Absence, Virago (London, England), 1993.
Flesh and Blood, Virago (London, England), 1994.
Impossible Saints, Little, Brown (Boston, MA), 1997.
Fair Exchange, Little, Brown (Boston, MA), 1999.
The Looking Glass, Little, Brown (Boston, MA), 2000.

SHORT STORIES

(With Alison Fell and others) *Tales I Tell My Mother,* Journeyman Press (London, England), 1978.
(With others) *More Tales I Tell My Mother,* Journeyman Press (London, England), 1987.
Playing Sardines, Virago (London, England), 2001.

NONFICTION

(Editor, with Sara Dunn and Blake Morrison) *Mind Readings: Writers' Journeys through Mental States,* Minerva (London, England), 1996.
Food, Sex and God: On Inspiration and Writing, Virago (London, England), 1998.

Contributor of nonfiction to *City Limits* and of poems to periodicals. Poetry editor, *Spare Rib,* 1975-77, and *City Limits,* 1981-83.

SIDELIGHTS: Michele Roberts has received much acclaim in some circles for her fictional evocations of feminist themes. Born in England of a French Catholic mother and a British father, Roberts grew up speaking both languages and spending time in both countries. As a child, Roberts strongly identified with her mother's faith. She attended a convent school, and throughout her teenage years she wanted to be a nun.

"She perceived the convent as a safe haven from a world in which women had no freedom of choice and had to submit to conflicting images of femininity," Genevieve Brassard explained in the *Dictionary of Literary Biography*.

However, Roberts decided to attend college before entering the convent. While at Somerville College, Oxford, Roberts discovered feminism. After graduation, she moved to London, joined a Marxist commune "in which rooms, possessions, and sexual partners were liberally shared," as Brassard described it, and abandoned her former commitment to Catholicism as petit-bourgeois spirituality. After a brief period of time working in Thailand, Roberts returned to London and became active as a feminist and as a writer.

Roberts writes of strong female characters who rebel against a male-dominated society. She sometimes employs Christian religious symbolism, as in the novels *The Wild Girl*, about the life of Mary Magdalene, and *The Book of Mrs. Noah*, in which Mrs. Noah and five other women journey in a metaphorical ark through history to examine the condition of women throughout the ages.

Roberts's first novel, *A Piece of the Night*, tells of a woman's journey to self-realization—from convent schoolgirl to wife and mother to feminist and lesbian. Writing in the *New Statesman*, Valentine Cunningham described the novel as "a runaway chaos of inchoate bits, an incoherence that slumps well short of the better novel it might with more toil have become." "Much of *A Piece of the Night*," according to Blake Morrison in the *Times Literary Supplement*, "gives the same impression of a book written under the stern eye of a women's workshop group, and not much interested in winning the hearts of those outside the charmed circle."

In *The Wild Girl*, Roberts writes of biblical figure Mary Magdalene and her life as a prostitute and as a follower of Christ. Because of its frank, fictionalized account of Mary Magdalene's life, *The Wild Girl* received harsh criticism. "A few people," according to Tracy Clark in *Feminist Writers*, "went so far as to seek formal accusation of Roberts for blasphemy." A reviewer for *Time Out* described this work as "a powerful attack on the law of the Father and a timely reminder that old myths do not just fade away." Writing

in the *Times Literary Supplement*, Emma Fisher found that "Roberts is intelligent and passionate; by her rich use of symbols and metaphor she transforms feminist cliche into something alive and moving." Kate Fullbrook in *British Book News* admitted that "the sentiments that animate this novel are fine, even noble. But the fiction itself never comes alive. Mary Magdalene remains nothing but a committed feminist of the 1980s; Jesus becomes nothing but a simple archetype for the non-sexist male."

Religious concerns also figure in *The Visitation*, the story of Helen, who contacts female archetypal figures in her dreams. Roberts, wrote Laura Marcus in the *Times Literary Supplement*, blurs "the distinctions between reality and fantasy in a prose which is full, resonant and at times over-charged." Tracy Clark found that Roberts employs "lush physical description and enchanting mental imagery. Every once in a while, she also skillfully flashes back to Helen's younger days in order to give her readers a fuller perspective on the adult Helen's attitude toward conventional religion in general, and the Catholic church of her youth, specifically."

The Book of Mrs. Noah is, according to Helen Birch in the *New Statesman*, "Roberts' most ambitious and carefully conceived novel to date." Mrs. Noah, a librarian, imagines an ark filled with disenfranchised women from all periods in history, all of them wishing to write the story of womankind. "The ark becomes," Birch wrote, "Protean, a womb, the mother's body, containing the history and dreams of all the women." Calling the ark of the novel a "rather self-condoning time-capsule" carrying a load of "bourgeois and hyper-literate" women "aloof from the problems of working-class women," Valentine Cunningham found the novel to be "familiar stuff to followers of feminist theory." "The trouble," wrote Jennifer McKay in the *Listener*, "is that as a novel of ideas Mrs. Noah's ideas are not especially novel and they form too heavy a load for the fragile narrative."

Daughters of the House concerns Therese, a woman who is returning to her family after living for many years in a convent. "As is typical in Roberts's work," Clark wrote, "the novel is full of spiritual imagery: the convent, imagined concepts of heaven, and a favorite religious statue. Also present are numerous detailed physical descriptions: Therese's feeling too naked in street clothes because she is used to her thick, brown dress, for instance. This combination of highly styled description, heavy symbolism, and riveting plot was very well-received by critics." *Daughters of the House* was nominated for England's Booker Prize.

Religious themes also appear in *Impossible Saints,* a novel about ten people who would be saints, including Josephine, a nun who tries to seduce her father, fails, enters a convent, and successfully seduces a priest, yet still becomes a saint. As Jason Cowley of *New Statesman* told it, the writing of "*Impossible Saints* was her final attempt 'to exorcise' what Catholicism had done to her as a child." As Roberts explained in an interview with *January Magazine's* Linda Richards, "Because . . . the body is very scorned in Catholicism—particularly the female body—I wanted to rescue the body and cherish it and love it and touch it and smell it and make it into language." Roberts's women, who give into the pleasures of the body yet still become saints, show us "canonization as it might have been if the church were overseen by a matriarchy that celebrated human energy, weakness and desire," as a *Publishers Weekly* reviewer described it.

In *The Looking Glass,* the story of an early twentieth-century French poet (partially inspired by Mallarme) and the four women who love him, Roberts again returns to her French and her feminist roots. The book received mixed reviews; *Library Journal* critic Rebecca Stuhr called the latter portions of the book "didactic and plodding," while *Booklist* reviewer Carol Haggas praised Roberts's "powerful prose and poetic imagery." Roberts was inspired to write a story set in France after her mother was forced to sell the cottage where they had spent summers when Roberts was a child. "My theory is that inspiration is born of loss," she explained to Richards. "I felt I proved that with this novel. It just began, 'It is the sea I miss most,' and that was my truth. And then I found that the voice talking wasn't my voice. . . . That's the interesting thing when you write in the first person. . . . You've been taken over and possessed by somebody else and you write to find out who it is."

Roberts told *CA:* "My writing generally is fueled by the fact that I am a woman. I need to write in order to break through the silence imposed on women in this culture. The love of friends is central to my life."

BIOGRAPHICAL AND CRITICAL SOURCES:

BOOKS

Contemporary Literary Criticism, Volume 48, Gale (Detroit, MI), 1988.

Contemporary Novelists, 7th edition, St. James Press (Detroit, MI), 2001.
Feminist Writers, St. James Press (Detroit, MI), 1996.
Kenyon, Olga, *Women Writers Talk,* Carroll & Graf (New York, NY), 1990.
Moseley, Merritt, editor, *Dictionary of Literary Biography,* Volume 231: *British Novelists since 1960,* fourth series, Gale (Detroit, MI), 2000.

PERIODICALS

Booklist, July, 2001, Carol Haggas, review of *The Looking Glass,* p. 1983.
Books Magazine, spring, 1999, review of *Fair Exchange,* p. 22.
British Book News, January, 1985, pp. 49-50; April, 1986, p. 246.
Christian Science Monitor, July 2, 1998, review of *Impossible Saints,* p. B8.
Globe and Mail, July 10, 1999, review of *Fair Exchange,* p. D12.
Journal of Gender Studies, March, 1999, Susan Rowland, "Michele Roberts's Virgins: Contesting Gender in Fictions, Re-Writing Jungian Theory and Christian Myth," pp. 35-42.
Kirkus Reviews, April 15, 1998, review of *Impossible Saints,* pp. 521.
Library Journal, March 1, 1998, review of *Impossible Saints,* p. 129; June 1, 2001, Rebecca Stuhr, review of *The Looking Glass,* p. 218.
Listener, September 10, 1987, p. 23.
London Review of Books, February 16, 1984; October 2, 1997, review of *Impossible Saints,* p. 34.
New Statesman, November 3, 1978, p. 590; April 22, 1983, pp. 27-28; October 5, 1984, p. 30; May 22, 1987, pp. 27-28; May 23, 1997, Jason Cowley, review of *Impossible Saints,* p. 49; July 4, 1997, Stephen Brasher, interview with Michele Roberts, p. 21; May 22, 2000, "Quite Contrary," p. 55; June 18, 2001, Patricia Duncker, "Cookery Lessons," p. 58.
New York Times Book Review, September 20, 1998, David Guy, review of *Impossible Saints,* p. 24; October 10, 1999, review of *Impossible Saints,* p. 36; July 22, 2001, Catherine Lockerbie, "A Dangerous Muse."
Observer (London), March 9, 1986, p. 27; May 24, 1987, p. 25; January 17, 1999, review of *Fair Exchange,* p. 23.
People Weekly, August 20, 2001, review of *The Looking Glass,* p. 41.

Publishers Weekly, April 20, 1998, review of *Impossible Saints,* p. 49.

Punch, November 12, 1986, pp. 78, 80.

Spectator, November 4, 1978; January 16, 1999, Andrew Barrow, review of *Fair Exchange,* p. 30.

Time Out, December, 1984.

Times Educational Supplement, August 28, 1998, review of *Food, Sex and God: On Inspiration and Writing,* p. 23.

Times Literary Supplement, December 1, 1978, p. 1404; October 26, 1984, p. 1224; September 27, 1985, p. 1070; July 10, 1987, p. 748; July 24, 1987, p. 801; April 25, 1997, review of *Impossible Saints,* p. 24; October 16, 1998, review of *Food, Sex and God,* p. 32; January 15, 1999, review of *Fair Exchange,* p. 21.

Woman's Journal, January, 1999, review of *Fair Exchange,* p. 14.

ONLINE

January Magazine, http://www.januarymagazine.com/ (December, 2000), Linda Richards, "January Talks to Michele Roberts."

Trace Online Writing Center Web site, http://www.trace.tu.ac.uk/ (September 30, 2001), "Michele Roberts, Novelist and Poet."*

*   *   *

ROBERTS, Wesley K. 1946-
(Wess Roberts)

PERSONAL: Born October 8, 1946, in Cedar City, UT; son of Lester W. and Lura V. (Russell) Roberts; married Cheryl L. Barron, March 22, 1968; children: Justin, Jaime, Jeremy. *Education:* Southern Utah State College, B.S., 1970; Utah State University, M.S., 1972, Ph.D., 1974.

ADDRESSES: Agent—c/o Richard Pine, 1780 Broadway, New York, NY 10019.

CAREER: Writer, producer, and business executive. Courseware, Inc., San Diego, CA, project director and instructional psychologist, 1976-78; Northrop Service, Inc., project engineer and training systems specialist, 1978-79; American Express, New York, NY, director of operations training, 1979-80, director of human resources in Ft. Lauderdale, FL, 1981; American Express Travel Related Services, New York, NY, vice president of human resources in Ft. Lauderdale, 1982, vice president of human resources, travelers' check products, and domestic operations training, 1982-83, vice president of human resources and domestic operations training in Salt Lake City, UT, 1983-84, vice president of human resources and administration in Salt Lake City, 1984-85; Fireman's Fund Insurance Companies, Novato, CA, vice president of management development and training, 1985-86, vice president of human resources, beginning 1987. Executive producer of instructional business films, including *Join the Leader* and *College Recruiting.* Consultant to Utah State University Development Center, 1970-75, and Naval Instructional Technology Development Center, 1975; evaluation committee director, Columbus College's Rape Crisis Counseling Workshops, 1975. Member of board of trustees of Ft. Lauderdale Discovery Center, 1981-82; member of board of directors of Nova University's Executive Council Forum, 1981-82, and Health Plan of the Redwoods, 1987; member of board of advisors of Westminster College's School of Professional Studies, 1983-84, and University of Utah's Institute for Human Resource Management, 1983-85; member of communications committee of Great Salt Lake United Way, 1984; member of dean's advisory council of Utah State University's College of Business, 1984-85. Adjunct professor, Nova University, 1981-85. *Military service:* Utah Army National Guard, 1970-73; U.S. Army, 1973-76.

MEMBER: American Educational Research Association, American Psychological Association, American Society for Personnel Administration, Kiwanis.

AWARDS, HONORS: Bronze medals, International Film and Television Festival, 1982, for *The United Way: Broward County* and *WROC: Blue Chip Leadership,* and 1983, for *The United Way: Salt Lake City;* patriotic service award, U.S. Department of the Treasury, 1984; merit award, U.S. Department of the Treasury, 1985, for *You and U.S. Savings Bonds: A Winning Team;* professional achievement award, Utah State University's College of Business and Alumni Association, 1986; silver medal, Chicago International Film Festival, 1986, for *The Insurance Story;* finalist certificate, International Film and Television Festival, 1987, for *Join the Leader;* certificate for creative excellence, U.S. Film and Video Festival, 1988, for *College Recruiting.*

WRITINGS:

AS WESS ROBERTS

Leadership Secrets of Attila the Hun, Lester Group (Sandy, UT), 1985, reprinted as *Leadership Secrets of Attila the Hun: A Metaphorical Primer,* Warner Books (New York, NY), 1989.

Straight A's Never Made Anybody Rich, HarperCollins (New York, NY), 1991.

Victory Secrets of Attila the Hun, Doubleday (New York, NY), 1993.

(With Bill Ross) *Make It So: Leadership Lessons from Star Trek, the Next Generation,* Pocket Books (New York, NY), 1995.

Protect Your Achilles Heel: Crafting Armor for the New Age at Work, Andrews McMeel (Kansas City, MO), 1997.

It Takes More Than a Carrot and a Stick: Practical Ways for Getting Along with People You Can't Avoid at Work, Andrews McMeel (Kansas City, MO), 2001.

(Editor and compiler) *The Best Advice Ever for Leaders,* Andrews McMeel (Kansas City, MO), 2002.

Contributor to periodicals, including *American Psychologist, Educational Technology,* and *Military Review.*

Leadership Secrets of Attila the Hun has been translated into Dutch, Spanish, Japanese, Norwegian, German, Portuguese, and Swedish.

SIDELIGHTS: Wesley K. Roberts, who writes as Wess Roberts, is a psychologist and human resources executive who is probably best known to the general public as the author of the book *Leadership Secrets of Attila the Hun,* which guides readers in basic management skills. "Attila is the perfect paradigm for modern executives," noted Roberts to Stephen Madden in *M: The Civilized Man.* "We don't know much about Attila, but he does have a reputation for being daring, determined and a bit ruthless, something today's leaders need to be, too." Roberts added that by writing the book from the fifth-century warlord's perspective, he was able "to impart some basic fundamentals of leadership in an interesting and offbeat way."

Although *Leadership Secrets of Attila the Hun* eventually became a *Publishers Weekly* bestseller, it was initially rejected by many publishers. In 1985 Roberts ar-

ranged for a modest publication of the volume and then distributed copies to prominent business executives. The book quickly found favor with maverick business leader H. Ross Perot, who heartily endorsed it to others. Because of enthusiasm within the business community, the book was reprinted in 1989 to more widespread success. Perot later stated in *Success* magazine that *Leadership Secrets of Attila the Hun* "illustrates that in a rapidly changing world, the principles of leadership are timeless." Another executive, Robert L. Crandall, told *Success,* "It's the rare executive who chooses to be identified with Attila. But after reading Wess Roberts's book, and appreciating its wisdom, you become a little more open-minded." Norman R. Augustine, top executive at the Martin Marietta Corporation, wrote in *Success* that *Leadership Secrets of Attila the Hun* is "fun to read and full of very sound information." A *Publishers Weekly* critic concluded, "Businesspeople and others seeking counsel could do worse than to heed their inner Hun."

Roberts turned from historical to fictional inspiration in *Make It So: Leadership Lessons from Star Trek, the Next Generation,* written with Bill Ross. The book enlists Captain Jean-Luc Picard as a guide through detailed lessons in leadership. In each chapter, a specific episode of the show is used to illustrate one of nine particular leadership traits: focus, urgency, initiative, communication, competence, politics, intellectual honesty, interdependence, and resilience. Each chapter includes a narrative of the episode from Captain Picard's point of view, plus discussion of the lessons to be learned from the episode. "You do not have to be a fan of *Star Trek* to appreciate the authors' insights into how specific *Star Trek* episodes offer lessons for us all about leadership," wrote Becky Oliphant in *Journal of Personal Selling & Sales Management.* For Oliphant, "the one criticism that may be made of the book is that it spends too much time on the narrative of each episode and too little time discussing the lessons and observations." However, Oliphant observed, this could also be seen as a means of helping readers unfamiliar with the series to grasp the importance of the ideas being covered within the context of the *Star Trek* universe. Debra Phillips, in a review for *Entrepreneur,* observed that "even sci-fi illiterate entrepreneurs will benefit from reading *Make It So.*" Phillips concluded that the captain's "handling of crew and crises alike makes for interesting case studies in leadership."

BIOGRAPHICAL AND CRITICAL SOURCES:

PERIODICALS

Booklist, September 1, 1995, David Rouse, review of *Make It So: Leadership Lessons from Star Trek, the Next Generation,* p. 22; May 15, 1998, review of *Make It So,* p. 1609.

Entrepreneur, April, 1997, Debra Phillips, review of *Make It So,* p. 146.

Fortune, July 3, 1989, p. 137.

InfoWorld, October 15, 2001, Bob Lewis, review of *It Takes More Than a Carrot and a Stick: Practical Ways for Getting Along with People You Can't Avoid at Work,* p. 54.

Journal of Personal Selling & Sales Management, summer, 2000, Becky Oliphant, review of *Make It So,* p. 190.

Library Journal, September 15, 1997, review of *Protect Your Achilles Heel: Crafting Armor for the New Age at Work,* p. 117.

M: The Civilized Man, June, 1989, Stephen Madden, review of *Leadership Secrets of Attila the Hun,* pp. 62-64.

New York Times, April 1, 1989.

Publishers Weekly, January 4, 1993, p. 66; August 7, 1995, review of *Make It So,* p. 455; June 24, 1996, review of *Make It So,* p. 56; April 28, 1997, review of *Protect Your Achilles Heel,* p. 67; July 3, 2000, "Revival of the Fittest: Leadership Wisdom from Attila the Hun for the Twenty-first Century," p. 30; August 13, 2001, review of *It Takes More Than a Carrot and a Stick,* p. 298.

Quill & Quire, January, 1996, review of *Leadership Secrets of Attila the Hun,* p. 23.

Science Fiction Chronicle, October, 1997, review of *Make It So,* p. 50.

Success, March, 1989, pp. 52-55.*

*   *   *

ROBERTS, Wess
   See ROBERTS, Wesley K.

*   *   *

ROBINSON, Jill 1936-
   (Jill Schary, Jill Schary Zimmer)

PERSONAL: Born May 30, 1936, in Los AngelesCA; daughter of Dore (a playwright, director, and film producer) and Miriam (a painter; maiden name, Svet)

Schary; married Jon Zimmer (a stockbroker), January 8, 1956 (divorced, 1966); married Jeremiah Robinson (a computer analyst), April 7, 1968 (divorced, 1977); married Stuart Shaw (a consultant and writer), June 21, 1980; children: Jeremy Zimmer, Johanna Schary Robinson. *Education:* Attended Stanford University, 1954-55. *Politics:* "Left-wing eclectic." *Religion:* Jewish.

ADDRESSES: Home—6 Willow Rd., Weston, CT 06883. *Agent*—Lynn Nesbit, Janklow & Nesbit Assoc., 445 Park Ave., New York, NY 10022.

CAREER: Writer. Foote, Cone & Belding, Los Angeles, CA, advertising copywriter, 1956-57; free-lance journalist, 1964—; freelance book reviewer, 1973—. Host of "The Jill Schary Show" on KLAC-Radio in Los Angeles, 1966-68. Writing teacher at Womanschool in New York, NY 1975-77.

WRITINGS:

(Under name Jill Schary Zimmer) *With a Cast of Thousands: A Hollywood Childhood* (autobiographical), Stein & Day, 1963.

(Under name Jill Schary) *Thanks for the Rubies, Now Please Pass the Moon,* Dial, 1972.

Bed/Time/Story (autobiographical), Random House, 1974; *Perdido* (novel), Knopf (New York, NY), 1978.

Doctor Rocksinger and the Age of Longing (novel), Knopf (New York, NY), 1981.

Star Country, Fawcett Columbine (New York), 1996.

Past Forgetting: My Memory Lost and Found, Cliff Street Books (New York, NY), 1999.

(With Stuart Shaw) *Falling in Love when You Thought You Were Through,* HarperCollins (New York, NY), 2002.

Contributor to periodicals, including *Cosmopolitan, Vogue, House and Garden, New York Times, Los Angeles Times, Soho Weekly News, Chicago Tribune,* and *Village Voice.*

WORK IN PROGRESS: A screenplay of *Falling in Love* and a book about the life of a film distributor.

SIDELIGHTS: Jill Robinson is the author of novels and personal memoirs filled with many of Hollywood's classic royalty. Although two of her memoirs focus on her marriages, her most compelling personal story may be *Past Forgetting,* in which she details her true-life experience with amnesia. Writing in *Pif* magazine, Emily Banner noted that "Robinson mounts a fascinating and thought-provoking investigation into just what role memory plays in making us who we are."

Robinson's first book, *With a Cast of Thousands,* focuses on her childhood in Hollywood as the daughter of Dore Schary, the head of production at Metro-Goldwyn-Mayer (MGM). Robinson relates anecdotes about personalities such as John F. Kennedy, Loretta Young, Adlai Stevenson, Elizabeth Taylor, Marlon Brando, and Humphrey Bogart. C. P. Collier of *Best Sellers* commented that *With a Cast of Thousands* "could easily have become over-the-backyard-fence gossip, but even the most barbed . . . observations, while sometimes hilariously perceptive, are devoid of maliciousness." *Book Week*'s Joe Hyams similarly noted that Robinson tells "with astonishing frankness stories about her schoolmates, the multi-parented children of Hollywood's famous folk." He continued, however, that "the reader is never embarrassed for the people she so hilariously dissects, analyzes and pins down on paper with needle-sharp words."

Bed/Time/Story also met with a favorable reception. The book details the story of Robinson's second marriage to Jeremiah Robinson. "It is about two people whose love for each other slowly conquered their hatred for themselves," explained Annie Gottlieb in the *New York Times Book Review.* "It is, quite literally, about the lifesaving and healing power of love." With her husband's help, Robinson quit drinking and taking speed, acquired a good job, and began to piece her life together again. Gottlieb further stated: "Robinson portrays herself, with candor and humor, as having been so anxious to please, so terrified of rejection, so padded and propped by drugs, that she had no idea what she wanted or felt. The book tells about her discovery of herself, not as is currently fashionable, through lonely search, but through the unexpected, ferocious strength of her feeling for another." *Nation*'s Nancy Lynn Schwartz contended that "*Bed/Time/Story* . . . [is] a beautifully written book which forces the reader to care about the characters and their fate."

Robinson's next book, *Perdido,* is about teenager Susanna Howard, the granddaughter of a Hollywood pioneer who founded his own film studios. Susanna narrates this 1950's Hollywood story with a backdrop that includes the Cold War, blacklisting, and the rise of television. Tinged with an "epic, rather tragic flavor," as Schwartz described it, *Perdido* tells of things lost or soon to be lost. The heroine searches for her father, who left when she was still an infant. She is unhappy with her remote mother and stepfather and longs for the love of her missing parent. Constantly comparing real life to life in the movies, Susanna speculates that her grandfather "invented the happy American family and put it into the movies to drive everyone crazy."

Robinson wrote two more novels, *Doctor Rocksinger and the Age of Longing* and *Star Country,* in which she tells the tale of the daughter of an old Hollywood family trying to buy back a studio that her family once ran. Joanne Wilkinson in *Booklist* said that in *Star Country* Robinson managed "to communicate her deep love for L.A." despite a plot that was "overwrought." Wilkinson also noted that "Robinson . . . delivers the goods for fans of flashy melodrama."

Robinson returned to her forte with the memoir *Past Forgetting: My Memory Lost and Found.* This time, Robinson had a real-life plot device right out of the movies. After suffering a massive seizure from undiagnosed epilepsy, she wakes up in a hospital with amnesia. Robinson does not even recognize her husband dutifully sitting at her bedside. In the book Robinson recounts the many episodes involved as she recovers. At first she slowly regains pieces of her memory, with her childhood life in 1944 Los Angeles coming back the clearest. She still does not remember that her parents are dead, however, or that the children she remembers have grown. Nevertheless she uses clues from these memories and from photos to start piecing her life together. In one instance she calls up an old childhood friend from grade school to see if he remembers her. The friend, actor Robert Redford, does remember her, and the two meet to reminisce about childhood. Eventually Robinson returns to writing, a task doctors never thought she would perform again. In *Booklist,* reviewer Marlene Chamberlain said that "Robinson provides a colorful, sometimes frightening roadmap of her efforts" and called the book "a particularly moving account." A contributor to *Publishers Weekly* called the tale "an unflinching account of amnesia and the terror of being a writer without memory." And Jonathen Lethem in a review for *Salon.com* called it "a gemlike, seductively readable and quietly moving memoir."

Robinson also teamed up with her husband Stuart Shaw to write a dual memoir, in which the husband and wife team tell of their meeting and finding love when they thought romance was gone forever from their lives. In the book, the authors employ the "his" and "her" points of view. Although some reviewers found the story dull, Melissa Hirschl, writing for *Wrangler News* in Tempe, Arizona, called it a "compelling" book that was "candid and insightful."

"I'm most unhappy when I'm not working," Robinson told Hirschl. "To me, doing work is like being in love. That's the way it is sometimes when you have a talent; you can't bear not to do it."

BIOGRAPHICAL AND CRITICAL SOURCES:

BOOKS

Contemporary Literary Criticism, Volume 10, Gale (Detroit, MI), 1979.

PERIODICALS

Best Sellers, November 1, 1963.
Booklist, July, 1996, Joanne Wilkinson, review of *Star Country,* p. 1805; October 15, 1999, Marlene Chamberlain, review of *Past Forgetting: My Memory Lost and Found,* p. 410.
Book Week December 22, 1963.
Harper, August, 1978.
Kirkus Reviews, May 15, 2002, review of *Falling in Love when You Thought You Were Through,* p. 721.
Nation, April 22, 1978.
Newsweek, April 24, 1978.
New York Times Book Review, October 27, 1974; April 23, 1978.
Publishers Weekly, June 10, 1996, review of *Star Country,* p. 84; July 5, 1999, review of *Past Forgetting: My Memory Lost and Found,* p. 44; June 10, 2002, review of *Falling in Love when You Thought You Were Through,* p. 49.
Times Literary Supplement, September 22, 1978.
Washington Post, May 2, 1978.

ONLINE

Pif, http://www.pifmagazine.com (October 9, 2002), Emily Banner, review of *Past Forgetting: My Memory Lost and Found.*

Salon.com, http://www.salon.com (October 9, 2002), Jonathan Lethem, review of *Past Forgetting: My Memory Lost and Found.*
Wrangler News, (Tempe, Arizona), http://www.wranglernews.com (October 8, 2002), Melissa Hirschl, "Couple's 'How-To' Primer: Keeping the Spark of Romance Alive," August 17, 2001 issue.*

*   *   *

ROCK, Howard B. 1944-

PERSONAL: Born July 11, 1944, in Cleveland, OH; son of Manuel E. (an attorney and business executive) and Lenore (Lavin) Rock; married Ellen Bernstein (a psychotherapist), August 17, 1975; children: David, Daniel. *Education:* Brandeis University, B.A., 1966; New York University, M.A., 1969, Ph.D., 1974. *Politics:* Democrat. *Religion:* Jewish.

ADDRESSES: Home—6030 Southwest Ninety-third Ave., Miami, FL 33173. *Office*—Department of History, Florida International University, Miami, FL 33199.

CAREER: Florida International University, Miami, assistant professor, 1973-79, associate professor, 1979-80, professor of history, 1990—, chair of department of history, 1982-89.

MEMBER: American Historical Association, Organization of American Historians, New York State Historical Association.

AWARDS, HONORS: National Endowment for the Humanities fellow in residence; grant from American Council of Learned Societies; New York State Historical Association Bicentennial Award, 1976; Lilly Endowment, 1992; Florida International University awards of excellence, 1990, 1992, 1995, 1998.

WRITINGS:

Artisans of the New Republic, New York University Press (New York, NY), 1979.
(Editor) *The New York City Artisan, 1789-1825: A Documentary History,* State University of New York Press (Albany, NY), 1989.

(Editor,with Paul Gilje) *Keepers of the Revolution: The Workers of NYC in the New Republic,* Cornell University Press (Ithaca, NY), 1992.

(Editor, with Gilje and Robert Asher) *American Artisans: Crafting Social Identity, 1750-1850,* Johns Hopkins University Press (Baltimore, MD), 1995.

(With Deborah Dash Moore) *Cityscapes: A History of New York in Images,* Columbia University Press (New York, NY), 2001.

Contributor to *Worktime and Industrialization: An International History,* edited by Gary Cross, Temple University Press, 1988; *New York City in the Age of the Constitution,* Farleigh Dickinson University Press, 1992; and *The Unvanquished* by Howard Fast, 1997. Contributor of articles to periodicals, including *Labor History, New York Historical Society Quarterly,* and *Journal of Urban History.*

SIDELIGHTS: Howard B. Rock once told *CA:* "I was one of the first historians to write about the role of early American artisans, particularly their social, political, and economic place. I have extended this interest to bringing out documentary evidence of their lives and, most recently, of other groups of workingmen and workingwomen."

"A critical transformation in craft production occurred between the American Revolution and the Civil War," wrote Donna Rilling in the opening of her review of *American Artisans: Crafting Social Identity, 1750-1850.* The study, coedited by Rock, outlines the political and social evolution of the American craft worker. Between the two wars, the life of the artisan was a difficult one. Economic independence was elusive; "journeymen unable to climb the craft ladder led a growing pool of permanent wage laborers," continued Rilling in her article for *Business History Review.* The essays in *American Artisans,* said the critic, inform and challenge the reader's perceptions by pointing out, for example, the diversity of experience between the pre-industrial North and the slave-labor-driven South. "Bondage barred slave artisans from a white craftsman's world the celebrated political and economic autonomy," Rilling noted, adding that in *American Artisans* "business historians unfamiliar with artisan scholarship will find . . . a rich introduction to the diversity of early America. No longer is our vision constricted to organized labor activities in the urban northeast."

To Graham Hodges, writing in *Industrial and Labor Relations Review,* Rock contributes a "beautifully written essay" on artisan iconography, in which the writer/editor "also addresses the question of why mechanics revived English antecedents immediately after the Revolution, at a time when hostility to the English was a hallmark of artisan radicalism." Rock's answer, added Hodges: "Artisan regalia were largely used by elite masters to evoke older days of craft solidarity."

In *Cityscapes: A History of New York in Images,* Rock and Deborah Dash Moore "identify and trace the strands that make up the complex, vibrant genetic code of the mighty city of New York," according to *Booklist*'s Donna Seaman. The authors provide the text to accompany archival photographs, paintings, broadsides, and maps that recount the metropolis from its beginnings as a Dutch trading settlement to its emergence as the world's most powerful center of business and culture. The book includes a study of New York City's distinctive skyline, a detailed street grid, and a look at the ethnic enclaves that give the city its flavor. *Cityscapes,* released in late 2001, closes with images of the World Trade Center, lost to terrorist attacks on September 11 of that year.

BIOGRAPHICAL AND CRITICAL SOURCES:

PERIODICALS

Booklist, December 1, 2001, Donna Seaman, review of *Cityscapes: A History of New York in Images,* p. 626.

Business History, January, 1997, Phillip Scranton, review of *American Artisans: Crafting Social Identity, 1750-1850,* p. 123.

Business History Review, spring, 1993, Graham Hodges, review of *Keepers of the Revolution: The Workers of NYC in the New Republic,* p. 144; summer, 1996, Donna Rilling, review of *American Artisans,* p. 267.

Choice, April, 1996, review of *American Artisans,* p. 1376.

Historian, spring, 1997, review of *American Artisans,* p. 666.

Industrial and Labor Relations Review, October, 1996, Graham Hodges, review of *American Artisans,* p. 182.

Journal of Economic History, March, 1998, review of *American Artisans,* p. 283.

Journal of Economic Literature, March, 1996, review of *American Artisans,* p. 259.

Journal of Southern History, February, 1997, review of *American Artisans,* p. 145.

Library Journal, February 15, 2001, Harry Frumerman, review of *Cityscapes,* p. 161.

Reference and Research Book News, March, 1996, review of *American Artisans,* p. 24.

Technology and Culture, April, 1998, review of *American Artisans,* p. 303.

William and Mary Quarterly, July, 1997, review of *American Artisans,* p. 650.*

*　　*　　*

ROSE, Joel 1948-

PERSONAL: Born March 1, 1948, in Los Angeles, CA; son of Milton (a waiter) and Edna (a homemaker; maiden name, Greenfield) Rose; married Catherine Texier (a writer); children: Celine Texier. *Education:* Hobart College, B.A., 1970; attended Western Washington State University, 1970-71; Columbia University, M.F.A., 1973.

ADDRESSES: Home and office—255 East Seventh St., New York, NY 10009. *Agent*—Michael Carlisle, William Morris Agency, 1350 Avenue of the Americas, New York, NY 10019.

CAREER: Freelance writer, 1973—. Publisher and co-editor of *Between C and D: Lower East Side Fiction,* New York, NY, 1983—. Writer of television scripts for *Kojak, Miami Vice,* and other shows.

MEMBER: Poets and Writers (Coordinating Committee of Literary Magazines).

AWARDS, HONORS: Fellowships from National Endowment for the Arts, 1986; New York State Foundation for the Arts, 1986 and 1989.

WRITINGS:

The Vegetarian Connection, Facts of Life Publications, 1985.

Kill the Poor (novel), Atlantic Monthly Press (New York, NY), 1988.

(Editor, with wife, Catherine Texier) *Between C and D: New Writing from the Lower East Side Fiction Magazine,* Penguin (New York, NY), 1988.

(Editor, with Texier) *Love Is Strange: Stories of Postmodern Romance,* Norton (New York, NY), 1993.

(With Amos Poe) *La Pacifica* (with art by Tayyar Ozkan), Paradox Press (New York, NY), 1994.

The Big Book of Thugs, Paradox Press (New York, NY), 1996.

Dead Weekend (screenplay), Showtime Network, Inc., 1996.

Kill, Kill, Faster, Faster: A Novel, Crown (New York, NY), 1997.

New York Sawed in Half: An Urban Historical, Bloomsbury (New York, NY), 2001.

SIDELIGHTS: Joel Rose, a native New Yorker, has helped to disseminate literature about Manhattan's tough Lower East Side. Through anthologies of short stories by other writers, the periodical *Between C and D,* and his own fiction, Rose has introduced readers to the shocking levels of drug abuse, sexual vice, and criminal activity that have become part of the urban landscape. A former drug addict who has helped to bring authentic vernacular and plot points to television shows, Rose might echo the sentiments of one of his fictional characters, Joey One-Way, who declared: "I have a lot of violence and anger in me, and writing delivers me from that. I think if I wasn't writing, I would be dead."

Rose's first novel, *Kill the Poor,* tells the story of one group of Manhattan residents who try to upgrade a ghetto apartment building on the Lower East Side. As Gary Dretzka remarked in *Tribune Books,* the tenants "are poor, but some have put together enough money to rehabilitate the building, turning it into a sort of condo from Hell." Dretzka added that *Kill the Poor* "has many problems, but the book's undeniable charm and gritty rhythm help it dance over the rough spots." In the *New York Times Book Review,* Wendy Smith wrote: "Sharp, savage and extremely well written, this provocative first novel examines a politically troublesome and ethically troubling issue—the gentrification of impoverished urban neighborhoods—with the stylistic flair and easy nihilism characteristic of New York's downtown scene."

In the mid-1980s Rose launched a successful small magazine, *Between C and D,* that published fiction and poetry by New York writers. He also began working as a scriptwriter and consultant for television shows, often in partnership with an ex-convict named Miquel Pinero. It was Rose's and Pinero's job to give the criminals on such shows as *Miami Vice* and *Kojak* an authenticity in dialogue and action. The partnership also inspired Rose to write his novel, *Kill, Kill, Faster, Faster.*

With a title inspired by a well-known Russ Meyer exploitation film, *Kill, Kill, Faster, Faster* tells the story of Joey One-Way, a convicted murderer who wins release from prison after writing a play about life behind bars. Hired by a television and movie producer to write scripts, Joey One-Way begins an affair with the producer's wife which ultimately ends in violence. "This quintessentially postmodern New York novel won't be everyone's cup of tea," noted *Booklist* contributor Thomas Gaughan. "Its milieu, characters and voice are down and dirty. . . . But it's also a compelling novel with flawed and fated characters worth coming to know." A *Publishers Weekly* reviewer characterized *Kill, Kill, Faster, Faster* as "a satire of contemporary America, land of opportunity even for convicted murderers." The reviewer concluded: "Staccato rhythms and street vernacular give the narrative a genuine, manic music as it tells of Joey's life on New York's streets."

Rose's 2001 effort, *New York Sawed in Half: An Urban Historical,* is a fictional account of a legendary hoax that was played on the people of New York City in 1824. The publisher Bloomsbury used the book to launch its "Urban Historicals" series. According to the legend that Rose depicts in the book, John DeVoe and a man known as Lozier convinced the people of New York City that the island of Manhattan was overdeveloped and, as a result, would sink into the surrounding harbor. To resolve the problem, the two men proposed a massive project, in which workers would cut Manhattan in half and use boats to pull one end over so it could be attached to the mainland. Although seemingly farfetched, the idea was embraced by a multitude of people in the city, largely because many of them were out of work and needed jobs. On the day that DeVoe and Lozier said the project was to begin, thousands of people came out to lend a hand. "The men began to arrive early, as they had been instructed. Some were carrying tools. Shovels, axes, picks. Some pushed wheelbarrows. Some came with their wives and children," Rose writes in the book. After waiting all day for something to happen, the people began to

realize the whole project was a hoax. "Gradually it dawned on more and more of them that they had been 'handsomely sold,'" Rose writes.

Rose explains to the reader, however, that the entire story may have been a hoax itself. In his old age, De-Voe told the story to a nephew, who happened to be an amateur historian. Rose feels there is a good chance DeVoe may have fabricated the story, although many people, including his nephew, believed it to be true. In fact, early in the book, Rose describes the work as "an entertainment, a reimagining of a piece of the past that may well have been imagined in the first place." Despite that feeling, Rose thinks the story is still important. "The hoax may never have occurred, and therefore deserved no further notice," he writes in the book. "But . . . it became evident that the hoax's authenticity no longer mattered. The story was part of the fabric of the city's history."

Several literary critics lauded *New York Sawed in Half,* including Margaret Flanagan of *Booklist,* who felt it would "appeal to popular culture buffs." Nathan Ward, who reviewed the book for *Library Journal,* called it "a charming, atmospheric portrait of old New York."

Rose once told *CA:* "I believe in the confrontational aspect of my writing, the ability of the printed word to reach out and grab the reader and not let go. I am an emotional writer, and in this sense I felt *Kill the Poor* was given to me. By happenstance, I moved to the very block in New York City where my grandmother had come when she first arrived in America from Hungary as a little girl in 1903. My mother was born here and I remember the neighborhood vividly from when I was a boy. It was important that I somehow translate and juxtapose the feelings of then and now, to sit down with my grandmother (who is ninety-six years old), to listen, and to weave a story that might reflect the conflict of the inner city.

"In the same respect the literary journal *Between C and D* gives a forum to a wide array of new voices and writing whose connection was originally the Lower East Side of Manhattan but now has grown to include the urban centers of the United States and Europe. *Between C and D* publishes writers with an edge. Their work may be gritty, shocking, ironic, moody, violent, sexual. We see them as urban archeologists, playing with form, but not at the expense of narration."

BIOGRAPHICAL AND CRITICAL SOURCES:

BOOKS

Rose, Joel, *Kill, Kill, Faster, Faster,* Crown (New York, NY), 1997.

Rose, Joel, *New York Sawed in Half: An Urban Historical,* Bloomsbury (New York City), 2001.

PERIODICALS

Baltimore Sun, December 13, 1988.

Booklist, March 1, 1997, p. 1112; April 15, 2001, p. 1528.

Denver Post, December 11, 1988.

Guardian, May 28, 1997, pp. 17-18.

Kirkus Reviews, February 1, 1988, p. 152; August 15, 1988, p. 1187; January 15, 1997, p. 91.

Library Journal, April 1, 2001, p. 112.

Los Angeles Weekly, October 23, 1987.

New Statesman & Society, February 11, 1994, p. 38.

New York Times Book Review, March 5, 1988, p. 22.

Observer, February 13, 1994, p. 21.

Philadelphia Inquirer, December 20, 1988.

Playboy, June, 1993, p. 38.

Publishers Weekly, March 3, 1997, p. 64.

Review of Contemporary Fiction, summer, 1988, p. 327.

Tribune Books (Chicago), October 16, 1988, p. 8.

Voice Literary Supplement, October, 1988, p. 3.*

*   *   *

ROSE, Richard 1933-

PERSONAL: Born April 9, 1933, in St. Louis, MO; son of Charles I. (a merchant) and Mary (Conely) Rose; married Rosemary J. Kenny, April 14, 1956; children: Clare, Charles, Lincoln. *Education:* Johns Hopkins University, B.A., 1953; London School of Economics and Political Science, graduate study, 1953-54; Oxford University, D.Phil., 1959. *Politics:* "Border-state democrat." *Religion:* "Lapsed Southern Presbyterian." *Hobbies and other interests:* Architecture, music, travel.

ADDRESSES: Home—Bennochy, 1 East Abercromby St., Helensburgh, Dunbartonshire G84 7SP, Scotland. *Office*—Centre for the Study of Public Policy, University of Strathclyde, Glasgow G1 1XH, Scotland.

CAREER: St. Louis Post-Dispatch, St. Louis, Mo., reporter, 1955-57; University of Manchester, Manchester, England, lecturer in politics, 1961-66; University of Strathclyde, Glasgow, Scotland, professor of politics, 1966-81, professor of public policy, 1982—, director of Centre for the Study of Public Policy, 1976—. Visiting scholar at Brookings Institution, 1976; visiting professor at European University Institute, Florence, Italy, 1977 and 1978; visiting fellow at American Enterprise Institute, 1980; Hinkley Distinguished Professor, John Hopkins University, 1987; lecturer at universities in Europe, North America, and Australia. Member of United States-United Kingdom Fulbright Education Commission, 1971-75. Consultant to Northern Ireland Constitutional Convention, 1975-76, and to Organization for Economic Cooperation and Development.

MEMBER: International Political Science Association (member of Council, 1976-82), International Sociological Association, European Consortium for Political Research (co-founder), American Political Science Association, Political Studies Association (United Kingdom, honorary vice president), American Civil Liberties Union, British Politics Group (co-founder), United Kingdom Politics Work Group (chairman, 1978—), Reform Club (London), Cosmos Club (Washington, DC), International Monetary Fund (member, 1984), Phi Beta Kappa.

AWARDS, HONORS: Guggenheim fellow at Woodrow Wilson Center, 1974; Japan Foundation fellow, 1984; lifetime achievement award, Political Studies Association; fellow of the British Academy, 1992.

WRITINGS:

(With D. E. Butler) *The British General Election of 1959,* St. Martin's (New York, NY), 1960.

(With Mark Abrams) *Must Labour Lose?,* Penguin (London, England), 1960.

Politics in England: An Interpretation, Little, Brown (Boston, MA), 1964, 2nd edition, 1974 (published in England as *Politics in England Today: An Interpretation,* Faber (London, England), 1974), 3rd edition published as *Politics in England: An Interpretation for the 1980s,* 4th edition published as *Politics in England: Resistance and Change,* 1985.

Influencing Voters, St. Martin's (New York, NY), 1967.

Class and Party Divisions: Britain and a Test Center, University of Strathclyde, Center for the Study of Public Policy (Glasgow, Scotland), 1968.

People in Politics: Observations across the Atlantic, Basic Books (New York, NY), 1970.

Governing without Consensus: An Irish Perspective, Beacon Press (Boston, MA), 1971.

The Problem of Party Government, Macmillan (London), 1974, Free Press (New York, NY), 1975.

(With T. Mackie) *International Almanac of Electoral History,* Macmillan (New York, NY), 1974, 2nd edition, 1982.

(With D. W. Urwin) *Regional Differentiation and Political Unity in Western Nations,* Sage (New York, NY), 1975.

The Future of Scottish Politics: A Dynamic Analysis, Scottish Academic Press (Edinburgh, Scotland), 1975.

Northern Ireland: A Time of Choice, American Enterprise Institute (Washington, DC), 1976.

Managing Presidential Objectives, Free Press (New York, NY), 1976.

Ordinary People in Extraordinary Economic Circumstances, University of Strathclyde (Glasgow, Scotland), 1977.

The Political Consequences of Economic Overload: On the Possibility of Political Bankruptcy, University of Strathclyde (Glasgow, Scotland), 1977.

The United Kingdom As an Intellectual Puzzle, University of Strathclyde (Glasgow, Scotland), 1977.

Governing and "Ungovernability": A Sceptical Inquiry, University of Strathclyde (Glasgow, Scotland), 1977.

From Steady State to Fluid State: The Unity of the Kingdom Today, University of Strathclyde (Glasgow, Scotland), 1978.

(With B. Guy Peters) *The Juggernaut of Incrementalism: A Comparative Perspective on the Growth of Public Policy,* University of Strathclyde (Glasgow, Scotland), 1978.

What Is Governing?: Purpose and Policy in Washington, Prentice-Hall (Paramus, NJ), 1978.

(With B. Guy Peters) *Can Government Go Bankrupt?,* Basic Books (New York, NY), 1978.

(With Ian McAllister and Peter Mair) *Is There a Concurring Majority about Northern Ireland?,* University of Strathclyde (Glasgow, Scotland), 1978.

Towards Normality: Public Opinion Polls in the 1979 Election, University of Strathclyde (Glasgow, Scotland), 1979.

(With Ian McAllister and Richard Parry) *United Kingdom Rankings: The Territorial Dimension in Social Indicators,* University of Strathclyde (Glasgow, Scotland), 1979.

Changes in Public Employment: A Multi-Dimensional Comparative Analysis, University of Strathclyde (Glasgow, Scotland), 1980.

(With Ian McAllister) *Can Violent Political Conflict Be Resolved by Social Change?,* University of Strathclyde (Glasgow, Scotland), 1982.

British MPs: A Bite As Well As a Bark?, University of Strathclyde (Glasgow, Scotland), 1982.

The Role of Laws in Comparative Perspective, University of Strathclyde (Glasgow, Scotland), 1982.

Policy Research and Government Policy, University of Strathclyde (Glasgow, Scotland), 1982.

The Territorial Dimension in Government: Understanding the Untied Kingdom, Chatham House, 1982.

(With Ian McAllister) *United Kingdom Facts,* Holmes & Meier (New York, NY), 1982.

(With Tom Garvin) *The Public Policy Effects of Independence: Ireland As a Test Case,* University of Strathclyde (Glasgow, Scotland), 1983.

Getting By in Three Economies: The Resources of the Official, Unofficial, and Domestic Economies, University of Strathclyde (Glasgow, Scotland), 1983.

(With Terence Karran) *Increasing Taxes, Stable Taxes, or Both? The Dynamics of United Kingdom Tax Revenues since 1948,* University of Strathclyde (Glasgow, Scotland), 1983.

Is the United Kingdom a State?: Northern Ireland As a Test Case, University of Strathclyde (Glasgow, Scotland), 1983.

Opinion Polls As Feedback Mechanism: From Cavalry Charge to Electronic Warfare, University of Strathclyde (Glasgow, Scotland), 1983.

Do Parties Make a Difference?, Chatham House, 1980, 2nd edition, 1984.

Understanding Big Government, Sage (New York, NY), 1984.

(With McAllister) *The Nationwide Competition for Votes,* Frances Pinter, 1984.

National Pride: Cross-National Surveys, University of Strathclyde (Glasgow, Scotland), 1984.

(With Ian McAllister) *European Parliament Constituencies in Britain in 1984,* University of Strathclyde (Glasgow, Scotland), 1984.

(With Thomas T. Mackie) *Do Parties Persist of Disappear?: The Big Trade Off Facing Organizations,* University of Strathclyde (Glasgow, Scotland), 1984.

Comparative Policy Analysis: The Programme Approach, University of Strathclyde (Glasgow, Scotland), 1984.

The Capacity of the President: A Comparative Analysis, University of Strathclyde (Glasgow, Scotland), 1984.

(With Terence Karran) *Inertia or Incrementalism?: A Long-Term View of the Growth of Government,* University of Strathclyde (Glasgow, Scotland), 1984.

Public Employment in Western Nations, Cambridge University Press, 1985.

The State's Contribution to the Welfare Mix, University of Strathclyde (Glasgow, Scotland), 1985.

Maximizing Revenue and Minimizing Political Costs: Taxation by Inertia, University of Strathclyde (Glasgow, Scotland), 1985.

Accountability to Electorates and the Market: The Alternatives for Public Organizations, University of Strathclyde (Glasgow, Scotland), 1985.

(With McAllister) *Voters Begin to Choose,* Sage (New York, NY), 1986.

(With D. Van Mechelen) *Patterns of Parliamentary Legislation,* Gower, 1986.

Ministers and Ministries, Oxford University Press, 1987.

(With T. Karran) *Taxation by Political Inertia,* Allen & Unwin, 1987.

The Post-Modern Presidency, Chatham House, 1988.

(With Klaus-Dieter Schmidt and Guenter Wignanek) *Who Is and Is Not Employed?: A Population Analysis of Britain and Germany,* University of Strathclyde (Glasgow, Scotland), 1988.

Loyalty, Voice or Exit?: Margaret Thatcher's Challenge to the Civil Service, University of Strathclyde (Glasgow, Scotland), 1988.

(With Ian McAllister) *Tactical versus Expressive Voting in Britain: Testing Schumpeter's Theory,* University of Strathclyde (Glasgow, Scotland), 1989.

Ordinary People in Public Policy: A Behavioural Analysis, Sage (New York, NY), 1989.

Prime Ministers in Parliamentary Democracies, University of Strathclyde (Glasgow, Scotland), 1990.

Evaluating the Presidency: A Positive-and-Normative Approach, University of Strathclyde (Glasgow, Scotland), 1990.

(With Ian McAllister) *The Loyalties of Voters: A Lifetime Learning Model,* Sage (New York, NY), 1990.

Lesson-Drawing in Public Policy: A Guide to Learning across Time and Space, Chatham House, 1993.

(With Phillip L. Davies) *Inheritance in Public Policy: Change without Choice in Britain,* Yale University Press, 1994.

What Is Europe?: A Dynamic Perspective, HarperCollins, 1996.

(With Ian McAllister and Stephen White) *How Russia Votes,* Chatham House, 1997.

(With William Mishler and Christian Haerpfer) *Democracy and Its Alternatives: Understanding Post-Communist Societies,* Johns Hopkins University Press, 1998.

The Prime Minister in a Shrinking World, Polity Press (Cambridge, UK) and Blackwell (Malden, MA), 2001.

EDITOR

The Polls and the 1970 Election, University of Strathclyde (Glasgow, Scotland),1970.

Studies in British Politics: A Reader in Political Sociology, St. Martin's, 1966, 3rd edition, 1976.

Policy-Making in Britain, Free Press, 1969.

(With M. Dugan) *European Politics,* Little, Brown, 1974.

Electoral Behavior: A Comparative Handbook, Free Press, 1974.

Lessons from America: An Exploration, Wiley, 1974.

The Management of Urban Change in Britain and Germany, Sage (New York, NY), 1974.

The Dynamics of Public Policies, Sage (New York, NY), 1976.

Comparing Public Policies, Ossolineum, 1977.

(With Dennis Kavanagh) *New Trends in British Politics,* Sage (New York, NY), 1977.

(With G. Hermet and Alain Rouquie) *Elections without Choice,* Macmillan, 1978.

(With Ezra Suleiman) *Residents and Prime Ministers,* American Enterprise Institute (Washington, DC), 1980.

Challenge to Governance, Sage (New York, NY), 1980.

(With William B. Gwyn) *Britain: Progress and Decline,* Tulane University (New Orleans, LA), 1980.

Electoral Participation: A Comparative Analysis, Sage (New York, NY), 1980.

(With P. Madgwick) *The Territorial Dimension in United Kingdom Politics,* Academic Press (New York, NY), 1982.

(With E. Page) *Fiscal Stress in Cities,* Cambridge University Press (Cambridge, England), 1982.

(With R. Shiratori) *The Welfare State East and West,* Oxford University Press (New York, NY), 1986.

(Editor-in-chief) *International Encyclopedia of Elections,* CQ Press (Washington, DC), 2000.

OTHER

Election correspondent, London *Times,* 1964, and *Daily Telegraph,* 1979—. Contributor to London *Times, New Society,* and journals in Great Britain, United States, and Europe, and to television networks, including British Broadcasting Corp.

SIDELIGHTS: Author Richard Rose has either written or served as editor for several dozen books about British and international politics, including many textbooks widely used in British academic institutions. A longtime professor of politics at the University of Strathclyde in Glasgow, Scotland, Rose began his publishing career in 1960 with *The British General Election of 1959* and has continued to be active in the new century with titles including *The Prime Minister in a Shrinking World* and *International Encyclopedia of Elections.* Rose's work has been translated into French, German, Italian, Spanish, Norwegian, Swedish, Hebrew, Chinese, and Japanese.

Rose employed his more than fifty years of knowledge of the British political world when writing *The Prime Minister in a Shrinking World,* a critically-acclaimed book detailing how the position of British prime minister has changed in the era in which Great Britain is no longer an international superpower. According to *Frontline* reviewer A. G. Noorani, the book "describes the current state of the office of the Prime Minister with stark realism." It is Rose's supposition that recent prime ministers, such as Margaret Thatcher and Tony Blair, have been media celebrities as much as politicians. The book includes in-depth examinations of each prime minister over the course of the last century and shows just how the roles they have played altered with the blossoming of the mass media. "This is a book for the student and the general reader," wrote a *Times Literary Supplement* contributor after reviewing *The Prime Minister in a Shrinking World.* "The book is both informative and a pleasure to read." According to Noorani of *Frontline,* the work "abounds in delightful quotes" and the author's own well chosen words.

BIOGRAPHICAL AND CRITICAL SOURCES:

PERIODICALS

Economist, March 3, 2001, p. 3.
Frontline, September 15-28, 2001.
Times (London, England), February 17, 1981.

ONLINE

Polity Web site, http://www.polity.co.uk/book/ (May 12, 2001), reviews of *The Prime Minister in a Shrinking World.**

* * *

ROSEN, R. D.
   See ROSEN, Richard (Dean)

* * *

ROSEN, Richard (Dean) 1949-
   (R. D. Rosen)

PERSONAL: Born February 18, 1949, in Chicago, IL; son of Sol A. and Carolyn (Baskin) Rosen; married Diane McWhorter (a journalist); children: Lucy. *Education:* Attended Brown University, 1967-68; Harvard University, B.A., 1972. *Religion:* Jewish.

ADDRESSES: Home—166 East 96th St., Apt. 10-B, New York, NY 10128. *Agent*—(literary) Robert Lescher, 155 East 71st St., New York, NY 10021; (television) Arthur Kaminsky, Athletes & Artists, 421 Seventh Ave., New York, NY 10001.

CAREER: Writer. *Boston Phoenix,* Boston, MA, staff writer and arts editor, 1972-76; Harvard University, Cambridge, MA, teacher of expository writing, 1975-76; *Boston Magazine,* Boston, staff writer and columnist, 1977-78; WGBH-TV, Boston, television news reporter and columnist, 1978-79; *The Real Paper,* Boston, editor-in-chief, 1979-80; WGBH-TV, Boston, television reporter, writer, actor-producer of national humor special, *The Generic News,* and director-producer of *Enterprise* documentary, 1982-84; National Broadcasting Company (NBC-TV), New York, NY, staff writer for *Saturday Night Live* comedy series, 1985; Home Box Office (HBO), Los Angeles, CA, cast member and writer for *Not Necessarily the News,* 1989-90. Associate, "I Have a Dream" Project, East Harlem, NY, 1986-87.

MEMBER: Writers Guild of America, Mystery Writers of America.

AWARDS, HONORS: Academy of American Poets prize, 1970; three Emmy Awards (New England region), 1984; Edgar Allan Poe Award for best first mystery novel, Mystery Writers of America, 1985, for *Strike Three, You're Dead.*

WRITINGS:

(As R. D. Rosen) *Me and My Friends, We No Longer Profess Any Graces: A Premature Memoir,* Macmillan (New York, NY), 1971.

(As R. D. Rosen) *Psychobabble: Fast Talk and Quick Cure in the Era of Feeling,* Atheneum (New York, NY), 1977.

Not Available in Any Store: The Complete Catalog of the Most Amazing Products Never Made!, Pantheon (New York, NY), 1990.

MYSTERY NOVELS

(As R. D. Rosen) *Strike Three, You're Dead,* Walker & Company (New York, NY), 1984.

Fadeaway, Harper (New York, NY), 1986.

Saturday Night Dead, Viking (New York, NY), 1988.

World of Hurt, Walker & Company (New York, NY), 1994.

(As R. D. Rosen) *Dead Ball,* Walker & Company (New York, NY), 2001.

(As R. D. Rosen) *Mean Streak: A Harvey Blissberg Mystery,* Walker & Company (New York, NY), 2001.

OTHER

(As R. D. Rosen) *The Generic News* (script), Public Broadcasting System, 1983.

(As R. D. Rosen) *Workout* (script), Public Broadcasting System, 1984.

Contributor to numerous periodicals, including *New York Times, New York, Sports Illustrated, New Republic, New Times,* and *Psychology Today.*

SIDELIGHTS: Richard Rosen, whose first novel, *Strike Three, You're Dead,* won the prestigious Edgar Allan Poe Award, is a veteran journalist, television writer, producer, and performer. Rosen's career has included

stints with WGBH-TV, Boston's public broadcasting station, and the popular *Saturday Night Live* comedy series on NBC. He has also authored several books of nonfiction (in one of which he coined a new term, "psychobabble"), and even penned some poetry. Since 1984, he has become known for his mystery novels, featuring a ballplayer-turned-detective named Harvey Blissberg.

According to Marvin Lachman in the *St. James Guide to Crime and Mystery Writers,* Rosen "has used two subjects enormously popular with millions of people, sports and television, and combined them with vivid descriptions of how people talk and what they buy. The historians and sociologists of the future may turn to his books to find, in addition to the freshness and vigor of the mysteries, graphic descriptions of life in New England and New York during the 1980s."

Strike Three, You're Dead introduces Blissberg, an aging center fielder for the fictitious Providence Jewels. When his roommate is found murdered, Blissberg undertakes his own investigation, during which he himself becomes a target for murder. Rosen drew upon his extensive knowledge of major league baseball—and his own experiences as a player—in order to add realism to the novel. Bob Wiemer, writing in *Newsday,* remarked that the resulting work is "the literary equivalent of an in-the-park home run." *New York Times Book Review* columnist Newgate Callendar called *Strike Three, You're Dead* "an entertaining and well-written book," adding, "Mr. Rosen can write. His dialogue is smart and sophisticated and his characters altogether three-dimensional. Clearly the author loves baseball, but he does not get sentimental about it. His approach is entirely professional." The Mystery Writers of America found *Strike Three, You're Dead* the best first mystery novel of the year in 1985.

In subsequent books, Blissberg has retired from baseball and is a full-time gumshoe. *Fadeaway* concerns the violent deaths of two professional basketball players, both found in Boston's Logan Airport. Called in to track the murderer, Blissberg uncovers a sordid trail of drug abuse and recruiting violations. *Washington Post Book World* contributor Jean M. White noted that in *Fadeaway* Rosen "writes with a light, sure touch. He has done his homework on the drug problem and recruiting pressures in basketball. . . . The ending is a corker." Both *Strike Three, You're Dead* and *Fadeaway* "authentically report those sensational aspects [of sports], especially the drug and alcohol addictions of young millionaire athletes," Lachman wrote. Likewise, concluded Lachman, "Rosen conveys the hypocrisy in college recruiting and the operation of lucrative professional franchises."

Saturday Night Dead follows Blissberg onto the set of a late-night television comedy show where the reigning executive is suddenly killed. The fictitious show, *Last Laughs,* is based upon *Saturday Night Live,* a long-running television comedy series that Rosen worked for briefly in 1985. A *Publisher's Weekly* reviewer wrote of the mystery: "The story's skillful contrasts of edged satire and pathos make it irresistible, the third triumph for Blissberg and his creator." While Lachman thought the solution of *Saturday Night Dead* is "overly melodramatic," he nonetheless observed that the novel "has many strengths, notably its New York atmosphere and the behind-the-scenes look at television, especially its comedy programs."

Rosen once told *CA* he conceived of Harvey Blissberg by observing the age-old rule "that you should write about what you know." He added: "When I sat down to plan my first mystery, I thought about what I knew, and I know a lot about baseball. In fact, when I think about the things I've written over the years, I realize that baseball has found its way into almost every form. I've written journalism and poetry about baseball. I've written pieces that were odes to Fenway Park. I've drawn baseball parks. Baseball was sewn into my character at an early age, so I wasn't surprised when baseball popped into my head as the setting for my first novel."

Rosen's 2001 novel *Dead Ball* finds former baseball outfielder and motivational speaker Harvey Blissberg accepting a job as bodyguard to professional ball player Moss Cooley, a black man close to breaking Joe DiMaggio's hitting record. When Cooley begins receiving hate mail and death threats (including a headless lawn jockey), Blissberg risks his own life to uncover the source of the threats. "*Dead Ball* is a chilling look at our national pastime," wrote a reviewer on the Walker & Company Web site. "It is also a troubling look at our national disgrace of racism."

Reflecting on the source of his inspirations, Rosen once told *CA:* "Having experience in other professions is very valuable for a writer. You always want to be writing about something. You don't want to be writing about different versions of yourself or different versions of what the inside of your brain looks like. The things I find most fascinating about novels sometimes are what they have to say about what other people do for a living. . . . I think what people do is very interesting, so my experience in journalism, although it's clearly related to being a writer, gave me a larger frame of reference. I'm afflicted, and blessed, by curiosity about what people *do.*"

BIOGRAPHICAL AND CRITICAL SOURCES:

BOOKS

Contemporary Literary Criticism, Volume 39, Gale (Detroit, MI), 1987.
St. James Guide to Crime and Mystery Writers, 4th edition, St. James Press (Detroit, MI), 1996.

PERIODICALS

Boston Magazine, August, 1984, Lee Grove, review of *Strike Three, You're Dead,* pp. 114-115; May, 1987, Gail Banks, review of *Fadeaway,* pp. 128-129.
Change, April, 1978.
Eagle (Providence, RI), October 21, 1984.
Kirkus Reviews, June 15, 1984, p. 554.
Library Journal, September 1, 1986, Jo Ann Vicarel, review of *Fadeaway,* p. 218.
New Republic, August 22, 1981; August 29, 1981.
Newsday, August 19, 1984.
New Yorker, November 24, 1986.
New York Times, June 24, 1988, John Gross, review of *Saturday Night Dead,* p. 17.
New York Times Book Review, October 28, 1984; October 9, 1994, Marilyn Stasio, review of *World of Hurt,* p. 34; February 15, 1987, Edna Stumpf, review of *Fadeaway,* p. 20.
Partisan Review, Winter, 1988, David Lehman, review of *Fadeaway,* p. 149.
Publishers Weekly, May 11, 1984, p. 263; July 25, 1986, Sybil Steinberg, review of *Fadeaway,* p. 174; April 22, 1988, Sybil Steinberg, review of *Saturday Night Dead,* pp. 66-67; October 3, 1994, review of *World of Hurt,* p. 55.
Sports Illustrated, April 18, 1985.
Tribune Books (Chicago, IL) July 3, 1988.

Washington Post Book World, January 20, 1985; November 16, 1986.
Wilson Library Bulletin, November, 1984.

ONLINE

Walker & Company Web site, http://www.walkerbooks. com/ (January 6, 2002), Harriet Klausner, review of *Dead Ball.**

*   *   *

ROTTENBERG, Dan(iel) 1942-

PERSONAL: Born June 10, 1942, in New York, NY; son of Herman and Lenore (Goldstein) Rottenberg; married Barbara Rubin (a music teacher), January 4, 1964; children: Lisa Yellin, Julie. *Education:* University of Pennsylvania, B.A., 1964. *Religion:* Jewish.

ADDRESSES: Home—1618 Waverly St., Philadelphia, PA 19103. *Office*—1530 Chestnut St., Room 330, Philadelphia, PA 19102. *Agent*—Ellen Levine Literary Agency, 15 East 26th St., New York, NY 10010.

CAREER: Author and journalist. *Commercial Review,* Portland, IN, sports editor, 1964-66, editor, 1966-68; *Wall Street Journal,* Chicago, IL, reporter, 1968-70; *Chicago Journalism Review,* Chicago, managing editor, 1970-72; *Philadelphia* magazine, Philadelphia, PA, executive editor, 1972-75; *Philadelphia Inquirer,* Philadelphia, PA, columnist, 1977-1996; *Welcomat,* Philadelphia, PA, editor, 1981-1996; *Seven Arts* magazine, editor, 1993-1994; *Philadelphia Forum,* editor, 1996-1998; *Family Business* magazine, editor, 2000—; freelance writer, 1975—.

AWARDS, HONORS: Penney-Missouri Newspaper Award from J. C. Penney Co. and University of Missouri, 1976, for article, "Fernanda"; Clarion Award from Women in Communications, 1977, for article, "Edison's Nuclear Gamble"; Peter Lisagor Award for financial writing from Chicago Headline Club, 1982, for article "The Bank That Couldn't Say No"; Peter Lisagor Award for magazine reporting, 1984, for article "The Last Run of the Rock Island Line"; Temple University Free Speech award, 1992; American Soci-

Dan Rottenberg

ety of Business Publication Editors, National Gold award, 2002, for article "Where Old Money Meets New," 2001, for "When Retirement Needs a Cure."

WRITINGS:

Finding Our Fathers, Random House (New York, NY), 1977.
Fight On, Pennsylvania, University of Pennsylvania Press, 1985.
Wolf, Block, Schorr, 1988.
Main Line WASP, Norton (New York, NY), 1990.
(With Marshall E. Blume and Jeremy J. Siegel) *Revolution on Wall Street,* Norton (New York, NY), 1993.
(Editor) *Middletown Jews: The Tenuous Survival of an American Jewish Community,* Indiana University Press (Bloomington, IN), 1997.
The Inheritor's Handbook: A Definitive Guide for Beneficiaries, Bloomberg Press, 1999.

The Man Who Made Wall Street: Anthony J. Drexel and the Rise of Modern Finance, University of Pennsylvania Press (Philadelphia, PA), 2001.

Author of monthly film column syndicated to city magazines, 1971-83, and weekly column in *Philadelphia Inquirer,* 1978—. Contributing editor, *Chicago,* 1971-86, and *Town and Country,* 1976—. Contributor to *Jewish Life in Philadelphia,* Institute for the Study of Human Issues, 1983.

SIDELIGHTS: American journalist and author Dan Rottenberg has authored eight books during a career that dates back to the mid-1960s when he began as a sports editor for the *Commercial Review* in Portland, Indiana. Since then, Rottenberg has worked for numerous publications, including the *Wall Street Journal, Chicago Journalism Review,* and *Philadelphia.* He has worked as a freelance journalist since 1975, contributing articles to the *New York Times Magazine, Town & Country, Forbes, Civilization, TV Guide,* and *Rolling Stone.*

Rottenberg published his first book, *Finding Our Fathers,* in 1977. Many of Rottenberg's books describe the world of finance and investment, including his later work, *The Man Who Made Wall Street: Anthony J. Drexel and the Rise of Modern Finance.* Rottenberg once described to *CA* his areas of expertise as "business, the law, news media, movies, the super-rich, and Judaica."

In *The Man Who Made Wall Street,* Rottenberg describes the life and times of Anthony J. Drexel (1826-1893), one of the men, along with J. P. Morgan, who helped build Wall Street into the world's greatest financial center. The biography is the first published about Drexel, who founded Drexel University in Philadelphia, Pennsylvania. Since Drexel was a rather private man, Rottenberg had to track down what little information exists about him, including previously unknown letters and cables in Drexel's hand. Rottenberg also interviewed a number of Drexel's surviving relatives. The work led literary critic Patrick J. Brunet to describe Rottenberg as "an especially smooth literary stylist." Calling the book "a solid, scholarly biography," Brunet went on to characterize it as "well documented, thoughtful, and analytical but not uncritical." A reviewer for *Publishers Weekly* similarly described the book as "rigorously researched and solidly presented."

BIOGRAPHICAL AND CRITICAL SOURCES:

PERIODICALS

Library Journal, September 15, 2001, p. 88.
Publishers Weekly, September 17, 2001, p. 70.

ONLINE

University of Pennsylvania Press Web site, http://www.upenn.edu/pennpress/book/ (May 22, 2002), description of *The Man Who Made Wall Street: Anthony J. Drexel and the Rise of Modern Finance.*

*   *   *

ROUDINESCO, Elisabeth 1944-

PERSONAL: Born October 9, 1944, in Paris, France; daughter of Alexandre Roudinesco (a doctor) and Jenny Weiss (a psychiatrist and psychoanalyst); married Michel Favart, 1966 (divorced, 1969). *Education:* Sorbonne, University of Paris, Licence de Lettres Modernes, 1968; Universite de Paris VIII, Doctorat de Lettres, 1975; psychoanalytic training at Ecole Freudienne de Paris; Universite de Paris VII, These d'Etat en Histoire, 1991. *Hobbies and other interests:* Cinema, television, newspapers, history of feminism, history of communism, history of Freudianism.

ADDRESSES: Home—89 ave. Denfert-Rochereau, 75014 Paris, France. *Agent*—Olivier Betourne, Artheme Fayard, 75 rue des Saints-Peres, 75006 Paris, France.

CAREER: Writer; psychoanalyst. Member of Ecole Freudienne de Paris, 1969-80; Universite de Paris VII, Paris, France, director of research of history department, 1992—; L'Ecole des Hautes Etudes en Sciences Sociales, minister of conferences, 1992—; Maison des Ecrivains, committee member.

MEMBER: Society of the History of Psychiatry and Psychoanalysis (vice president).

WRITINGS:

Un discours au réel: Théorie de l'inconscient et politique de la psychanalyse, Mame (Tours, France), 1973.

L'inconscient et ses lettres, Mame (Tours, France), 1975.

Pour une politique de la psychanalyse, F. Maspero (Paris, France), 1977.

(With Henri Deluy) *La psychanalyse mère et chienne,* Union générale d'éditions, 1979.

La bataille de cent ans: Histoire de la psychanalyse en France, two volumes, Editions du Seuil (Paris, France), 1982, translation by Jeffrey Mehlman published as *Jacques Lacan & Co.: A History of Psychoanalysis in France, 1925-1985,* University of Chicago Press (Chicago, IL), 1990.

Theroigne de Mericourt, une femme melancolique sous la revolution, Editions du Seuil (Paris, France) 1989, translation published as *Theroigne de Mericourt: A Melancholic Woman during the French Revolution,* Verso (New York, NY), 1991.

Madness and Revolution: The Lives and Legends of Theroigne de Mericourt, Verson (New York, NY), 1992.

Jacques Lacan: Esquisse d'une vie, histoire d'un systeme de pensee, Editions Artheme Fayard (Paris, France), 1993, translation published as *Jacques Lacan: His Life and Work,* Columbia University Press (New York, NY), 1997.

Généalogies, Fayard (Paris, France), 1994.

Pourquoi la psychanalyse?, Fayard (Paris, France), 1999, translation by Rachel Bowlby published as *Why Psychoanalysis?,* Columbia University Press (New York, NY), 2001.

(Editor, with Michel Plon) *Dictionnaire de la psychanalyse,* Fayard (Paris, France), 1997, new edition, 2000.

Also author of *Initiation à la linguistique générale.* Contributor to *Penser la folie: Essais sur Michel Foucault,* Galilée (Paris, France), 1992. Contributor to *Action Poetique,* 1969-79, and *Liberation,* 1986—.

WORK IN PROGRESS: Studies in the history of Freudianism.

SIDELIGHTS: Elisabeth Roudinesco has given readers several in-depth studies of psychoanalysis and its practitioners. In her biography *Jacques Lacan: His Life and Work,* she details the life and work of Jacques Marie Emile Lacan, the most famous follower of Sigmund Freud to come from France. Lacan's reputation was established in the late 1960s, when at the age of sixty-five he published a collection of papers on psy-choanalysis, describing himself as Freud's true heir. In fact, his work was also strongly influenced by Claude Levi-Strauss and many others, and it was "frequently opaque to the point of incomprehensibility," commented Richard Webster in *New Statesman.* Lacan was also known for his short, intense therapy sessions, some lasting as little as a few moments. Lacan's detractors described him as an intellectual terrorist. Roudinesco's biography reveals his powerful personality and is "a welcome aid to keeping him in perspective," advised Perry Meisel in the *New York Times Book Review. Booklist* contributor Kathleen Hughes also recommended the book, stating, "This absorbing study is both fascinating and highly readable."

In *Why Psychoanalysis?,* Roudinesco challenges the modern practice of using medication to alleviate symptoms of mental illness, rather than trying to get to the root of the problem and cure it. By trying to remove symptoms deemed undesirable, rather than probe individual psyches, the psychiatric establishment is undermining the qualities that make humanity valuable and unique, contends Roudinesco. Her book is an "eloquent defense of psychoanalysis," reported Mary Carroll in *Booklist,* one that offers "valuable insights" into the profession. Carroll contended that Roudinesco's greatest achievement in *Why Psychoanalysis?* is her "insistence that the human subjectivity at the heart of psychoanalysis is ignored and defeated by the scientific approaches dominant today."

Roudinesco once told *CA:* "After studying arts and linguistics at the Sorbonne, I attended Gilles Deleuze's seminars at the University of Paris VIII from 1969 to 1971. I was also a pupil of Michel de Certeau, who introduced me to the study of history. I also attended Michel Foucault's courses and was close to Louis Althusser. From 1969 to 1979 I collaborated on the journal *Action Poetique* and wrote numerous articles devoted to works of literature (including the works of Raymond Roussel, Antonin Artaud, and Louis Ferdinand Celine), Freudian Marxism, and psychoanalysis. I received my psychoanalytical training under the auspices of the Ecole Freudienne de Paris and since 1979 I have specialized in psychoanalysis and its history, Freudianism, and madness."

BIOGRAPHICAL AND CRITICAL SOURCES:

PERIODICALS

America, November 29, 1997, review of *Jacques Lacan: His Life and Work,* p. 35.

Booklist, March 15, 1997, Kathleen Hughes, review of *Jacques Lacan: His Life and Work,* p. 1206; December 15, 2001, Mary Carroll, review of *Why Psychoanalysis?,* p. 685.

Canadian Literature, autumn, 1995, review of *Jacques Lacan & Co.: A History of Psychoanalysis in France, 1925-1985,* p. 111.

Choice, September, 1997, review of *Jacques Lacan: His Life and Work,* p. 144.

Dissent, summer, 1998, review of *Jacques Lacan: His Life and Work,* p. 118.

Kirkus Reviews, February 15, 1997, review of *Jacques Lacan: His Life and Work,* p. 284.

Library Journal, April 15, 1997, review of *Jacques Lacan: His Life and Work,* p. 102; January, 2002, E. James Lieberman, p. 131.

New Statesman, July 11, 1997, Richard Webster, review of *Jacques Lacan: His Life and Work,* p. 44.

New York Times Book Review, April 13, 1997, Perry Meisel, review of *Jacques Lacan: His Life and Work,* p. 12.

Publishers Weekly, March 3, 1997, review of *Jacques Lacan: His Life and Work,* p. 56.

Reference & Research Book News, August, 1997, review of *Jacques Lacan: His Life and Work,* p. 5.

Society, November, 1994, review of *Jacques Lacan & Co.: A History of Psychoanalysis in France, 1925-1985,* p. 92.

Times Literary Supplement, January 28, 1994, review of *Jacques Lacan: Esquisse d'une vie, histoire d'un systeme de pensee,* p. 23; October 17, 1997, review of *Jacques Lacan: His Life and Work,* p. 15.

Translation Review Supplement, July, 1997, review of *Jacques Lacan: His Life and Work,* p. 18.

Village Voice Literary Supplement, summer, 1997, review of *Jacques Lacan: His Life and Work,* p. 8.*

*   *   *

ROWLAND, Laura Joh 1953-

PERSONAL: Born 1953, in Harper Woods, MI; married; husband's name Marty.

ADDRESSES: Home—New Orleans, LA. *Agent*—Pamela Ahearn, Ahearn Agency Inc., 2021 Pine St., New Orleans, LA 70118.

CAREER: Engineer and writer. Martin Marietta, New Orleans, LA, senior quality control engineer.

WRITINGS:

MYSTERY NOVELS

Shinju, Random House (New York, NY), 1994.
Bundori, Villard (New York, NY), 1996.
The Way of the Traitor, Villard (New York, NY), 1997.
The Concubine's Tattoo, St. Martin's Press (New York, NY), 1998.
The Samurai's Wife, St. Martin's Press (New York, NY), 2000.
Black Lotus, St. Martin's Minotaur (New York, NY), 2001.
The Pillow Book of Lady Wisteria, St. Martin's Minotaur (New York, NY), 2002.
The Dragon King's Palace, St. Martin's Minotaur (New York, NY), 2003.

SIDELIGHTS: Before becoming a published author, Laura Joh Rowland worked as a quality control engineer at an aerospace company, using her lunch hours and weekends to pursue her dream of being a novelist. Her first two novels were repeatedly rejected for publication, but the undaunted Rowland wrote a third, *Shinju,* which she presented to a Random House editor at a writers' conference. Rowland's agent, meanwhile, sent the book to several other publishers. Three publishers auctioned for the rights to *Shinju* and its sequel, with Random House winning at a cost of one hundred thousand dollars.

Shinju, the Japanese term for "double love suicide," is set in seventeenth-century Tokyo, where police are investigating the apparent shinju of a peasant and the daughter of a prominent citizen. Although the investigating officer, Sano Ichiro, is instructed to close the case because it looks like a suicide, he strongly suspects this crime to be a murder. Sano subsequently launches his own investigation, which leads him to confront corrupt and deceitful elements in the upper echelon of Japanese society. F. G. Notehelfer, director of Japanese studies at the University of California, Los Angeles, wrote in his *New York Times Book Review* assessment of *Shinju:* "An interesting and even exciting tale, Ms. Rowland's novel introduces us to a new detective who, I suspect, will appear in further adventures." While Notehelfer indicated flaws in Rowland's historical research, he nevertheless concluded: "I trust that her considerable talent for historical fiction will not be undermined by a crotchety historian's own concerns for the truth." *Shinju* was also applauded by a *Publishers Weekly* critic: "Rowland crafts a competent mystery her first time out, shows sure command of her background material and demonstrates that she is a writer of depth and potential."

Sano Ichiro returns in *Bundori*, the story of a series of particularly gruesome murders in 1690s Tokyo: the killer leaves his victims severed heads in public places. All the victims are descendants of warriors involved a century earlier in the murder of a Japanese warlord. Sano's investigation leads him to members of Tokyo's ruling elite who have revenge in mind. According to the critic for *Publishers Weekly*, "The novel reads smoothly and positively smokes with historical atmospherics."

The Way of the Traitor finds Sano trying to locate a missing Dutch trade director in the city of Nagasaki. When the missing man is found murdered, the Dutch demand a quick accounting of the facts by training their warships' heavy guns on the city. Amid the international tension caused by the death, Sano must confront powerful government officials in unraveling the case. Rex E. Klett in *Library Journal* called the novel "exciting, exotic entertainment," while David Pitt in *Booklist* labeled the mystery "well constructed, superbly written, and very entertaining" and concludes that it is "an excellent whodunit."

Sano is marrying the Lady Ueda Reiko at the opening of *The Concubine's Tattoo;* he is called away unexpectedly by the death of a concubine employed by the local shogun. The concubine has been poisoned by ink she used in a tattoo. Sano's investigation must be successful or the shogun threatens to put him to death; and his new bride insists on involving herself in the dangerous case as well. "Rowland's understanding of the society she depicts," wrote the critic for *Publishers Weekly*, "shines through, and she succeeds in presenting Sano as an intriguing combination of wiliness and decency, making this a good bet for fans of historicals as well as of mysteries past."

Sano and Reiko combine their skills to unravel the mystery surrounding the murder of an imperial minister in *The Samauri's Wife*. The dead man was a spy with many valuable secrets, and was killed by a rare martial art. Sano learns that he had uncovered a plot against the shogun. Civil war is a possibility if the assassin is not found. Rowland portrays the "class distinctions of her characters with subtlety and pulls together the strands of her multifaceted plot with enviable grace," commented a *Publishers Weekly* writer. The author's "fascinating insights" into life in seventeenth-century Japan are also praised by George Needham in *Booklist*.

Rowland's series husband-and-wife team are pitted against each other in *Black Lotus*, in which a teenaged girl is accused of arson and murder. Sano feels the girl is guilty, but Reiko does not. As they take different tacks in investigating the crime, their dogged pursuit "for the truth threatens the fabric of their marriage," observed a *Publishers Weekly* writer. The critic added, "The question of religious cults and the abuse of their influence gives this story contemporary resonance."

The Pillow Book of Lady Wisteria exposes the more bizarre sexual practices of old Japan in another tale of court intrigue. When the shogun's heir apparent is found dead in an opulent brothel, everyone in Japan hopes to find the killer and thus win the favor of the shogun. But rivalries and loves among those who seek to solve the crime complicate the issue. Readers must decide for themselves if the "salacious details spice or undercut Sano's struggle to remain honorable in a dishonorable world," advised a *Kirkus Reviews* contributor. A *Publishers Weekly* writer found that "all the animosity and fear in this seamless work is put forth in demure language that perfectly suits the culture Rowland portrays."

BIOGRAPHICAL AND CRITICAL SOURCES:

PERIODICALS

AB Bookman's Weekly, September 20, 1999, review of *The Concubine's Tattoo*, p. 380.

Booklist, April 15, 1997, p. 1412; March 1, 2000, George Needham, review of *The Samurai's Wife*, p. 1199.

Book World, February 25, 2001, review of *Black Lotus*, p. 4.

Drood Review of Mystery, January, 2001, reviews of *The Samauri's Wife* and *Black Lotus*, p. 23.

Kirkus Reviews, February 15, 2002, review of *The Pillow Book of Lady Wisteria*, p. 226.

Library Journal, May 1, 1997, p. 143; March 1, 2001, Rex Klett, review of *Black Lotus*, p. 133.

New York Times, July 28, 1993, p. C15.

New York Times Book Review, October 9, 1994, p. 11.

Publishers Weekly, August 8, 1994, p. 368; January 15, 1996, p. 443; May 12, 1997, p. 62; September 21, 1998, p. 77; March 6, 2000, review of *The Samurai's Wife,* p. 86; January 29, 2001, review of *Black Lotus,* p. 68; March 11, 2002, review of *The Pillow Book of Lady Wisteria,* p. 54.

Tribune Books (Chicago, IL), April 1, 2001, review of *Black Lotus,* p. 2.

ONLINE

Bookreporter, http://www.bookreporter.com/ (May 1, 2002), Michelle Calabro Hubbard, review of *The Samurai's Wife.*

The Mystery Reader, http://www.themysteryreader. com/ (May 1, 2002), Lesley Dunlap, review of *Black Lotus.**

S

SACHAR, Howard Morley 1928-

PERSONAL: Born February 10, 1928, in St. Louis, MO; son of Abram Leon (a founder and president of Brandeis University) and Thelma (Horwitz) Sachar; married Eliana Steimatzky, July 23, 1964; children: Sharon, Michele, Daniel. *Education:* Swarthmore College, B.A., 1947; Harvard University, M.A., 1950, Ph. D., 1953. *Politics:* Democrat. *Religion:* Jewish.

ADDRESSES: Home—9807 Hillridge Dr., Kensington, MD 20895-3228. *Office*—Department of History, George Washington University, Washington, DC 20052. *E-mail*—sachar@gwls2.circ.gwu.edu.

CAREER: University of Massachusetts, Amherst, instructor, 1953-54; University of California, Los Angeles, director of Hillel Foundation, 1954-57; Stanford University, Palo Alto, CA, director of Hillel Foundation, 1959-61; Brandeis University, Jacob Hiatt Institute, Jerusalem, Israel, director, 1961-64; George Washington University, Washington, DC, associate professor, 1965-66, professor of history, 1966—.

MEMBER: American Historical Association, American Jewish History Society, Phi Beta Kappa, Delta Sigma Rho.

AWARDS, HONORS: Charles Brown fellow, 1957-58; National Endowment for the Humanities fellow, 1970-71; National Jewish Book Award, 1976, 1981; D.H.L., Hebrew Union College, Jewish Institute of Religion, 1996.

WRITINGS:

The Course of Modern Jewish History, World Publishing (Cleveland, OH), 1958, revised edition, 1990.

Aliyah: The Peoples of Israel, World Publishing (Cleveland, OH), 1961.

From the Ends of the Earth: The Peoples of Israel, World Publishing (Cleveland, OH), 1964.

The Emergence of the Middle East, 1914-1924, Knopf (New York, NY), 1969.

Europe Leaves the Middle East, 1936-1954, Knopf (New York, NY), 1972.

A History of Israel, Knopf (New York, NY), Volume 1: *From the Rise of Zionism to Our Time,* 1976, Volume 2: *The Aftermath of the Yom Kippur War,* 1987, 2nd edition, revised and updated, Knopf (New York, NY), 1996.

The Man on the Camel (novel), Times Books (New York, NY), 1980.

Egypt and Israel, R. Marek (New York, NY), 1981.

The Last Century of Jewish Hope: An Historian's Critique, Syracuse University Press (Syracuse, NY), 1983.

Diaspora: An Inquiry into the Contemporary Jewish World, Harper (New York, NY), 1985.

A History of the Jews in America, Knopf (New York, NY), 1992.

Farewell España: The World of the Sephardim Remembered, Knopf (New York, NY), 1994.

Israel and Europe: An Appraisal in History, Knopf (New York, NY), 1999.

Dreamland: Europeans and Jews in the Aftermath of the Great War, Knopf (New York, NY), 2002.

Contributor to periodicals.

SIDELIGHTS: Howard M. Sachar is the author of several highly praised historical studies of modern Israel, the Zionist movement, and the Middle East. Unlike the works of many of his fellow academics, Sachar's "encyclopedic" books have consistently been praised for their readability. *Commentary*'s Joseph Shattan, for example, called *A History of Israel* "an extraordinary work, a triumph of comprehensive scholarship which is also a delight to read," while the *New York Times Book Review*'s Meyer Levin wrote: "With masterful control of the extraordinarily complex and profuse accumulation of material, with an underlying universal compassion, and an historical objectivity that nevertheless does not disguise his personal viewpoint, Sachar has provided the overall picture of the Jewish movement to statehood, and since statehood. . . . Though written in the controlled, even tone of the historian, the work, particularly in its accounts of the wars of survival, has enormous tension."

The *Nation*'s Phebe Marr pointed to *The Emergence of the Middle East* as "the best and most comprehensive account thus far [of the events in that area from 1914 to 1924]. It is also among the most balanced and by far the most fascinating." The same book prompted Lord Kinross to comment in the *New York Times Book Review:* "Historians do not always combine scholarship with narrative style, a dramatic sense, an eye for human personality and a feeling for atmosphere. Churchill, the man of action, had these talents to perfection. They are shared to a distinct if unassuming degree by Howard M. Sachar. . . . In unfolding [his] story . . ., he clothes the bare bones of historical fact with the flesh and blood of living, warring peoples."

In a review of *The Course of Modern Jewish History,* the *Springfield Republican*'s Donald Derby summarized this skill as the ability to write "with learning and with feeling," a sentiment echoed by Ellis Rivkin in a *New York Herald Tribune Book Review* article on the same work. Concluded Rivkin: "Howard Sachar . . . has gone far towards writing the kind of Jewish history that yields understanding. . . . Although the volume is packed with facts, his presentation is anything but pedantic. He has strong opinions and he expresses them; he never shrinks from candid appraisal. He attempts to explain phenomena, and he holds the reader's interest by the pace, the enthusiasm, and sometimes even the excitement of his writing. . . . [His book] is a work of merit, full of fine insights, written with clarity, enthusiasm, and passion, brimming with data, sweeping in its ambitious scope."

Reviewing *Israel and Europe: An Appraisal in History,* a *Publishers Weekly* writer advised, "Sachar succeeds at a very difficult task, lucidly tracing the history of Israel's relations with Europe in one book." Sachar's stance is pro-Israeli, and his personal feelings do color the book, commented Serge Schmemann in *New York Times Book Review.* He tends to paint European leaders starkly, as either friends of the Jews or supporters of Arab partisans; still, maintained Schmemann, he "does not allow his love of Israel to cloud his judgement. He offsets his feelings with ample objective evidence, and is scrupulously fair in explaining the full range of factors shaping European attitudes toward Israel." The reviewer concluded, "What Sachar achieves in collating the history of European-Israeli relations and in keeping it clear, compelling and accessible is a remarkable feat. It is a critical background for any appreciation of the Jewish state."

In *Farewell España: The World of the Sephardim Remembered,* Sachar traces the history of the Spanish Jews, who flourished during the centuries of Roman rule before the time of Christ. After the conversion to Christianity of the Emperor Constantine, they suffered persecution, even subjected to massacres in Spain. Even those Jews who converted to Christianity were regarded with suspicion, and their sincerity, or lack of it, was one of the issues leading to the infamous Spanish Inquisition. Sachar's book reveals the history of the Spanish Jews and what became of them after they were expelled from Spain in 1492. It is "a feast for students of Jewish culture and history," advised a *Publishers Weekly* reviewer.

Dreamland: Europeans and Jews in the Aftermath of the Great War looks at the relationship between Jews and Gentiles following World War I. While the horrors perpetrated upon the Jews by the Nazis during World War II are notorious, the crimes committed against the Jews by earlier Europeans and Russians are less well known. During the Russian Civil War, Jews were routinely burned, buried alive, drowned, and otherwise tortured and mutilated. Still, there were positive aspects to the era between wars, and Sachar avoids depicting "Jews as merely passive victims, regarding them as active participants in the tumultuous events of the interwar years," reported a *Library Journal* reviewer. Sachar "has a keen eye for historical detail, and a fine sense of narrative," found a *Publishers Weekly* reviewer. The reviewer also remarked that Sachar "weaves a broad tapestry of social, economic and political conditions that is at times dizzying in its complexity and breadth."

BIOGRAPHICAL AND CRITICAL SOURCES:

PERIODICALS

AB Bookman's Weekly, April 25, 1988, review of *The Course of Modern Jewish History,* p. 1731.

America, March 5, 1983, review of *Egypt and Israel,* p. 171; December 28, 1985, review of *Diaspora: An Inquiry into the Contemporary Jewish World,* p. 469.

American Historical Review, June, 1993, review of *A History of the Jews in America,* p. 934.

Annals of the American Academy of Political and Social Science, July, 1973; September, 1987, review of *Diaspora: An Inquiry into the Contemporary Jewish World,* p. 212.

Booklist, April 1, 1985, review of *Diaspora: An Inquiry into the Contemporary Jewish World,* p. 1097; April 1, 1987, review of *A History of Israel,* p. 1174; March 15, 1992, review of *A History of the Jews in America,* p. 1314; February 15, 1996, review of *A History of Israel,* p. 987; December 15, 1998, Jay Freeman, review of *Israel and Europe: An Appraisal in History,* p. 711.

Bookwatch, April, 1999, review of *Israel and Europe: An Appraisal in History,* p. 6.

Book World, May 26, 1985, review of *Diaspora: An Inquiry into the Contemporary Jewish World,* p. 4; May 31, 1987, review of *A History of Israel,* p. 10; May 17, 1992, review of *A History of the Jews in America,* p. 1; December 11, 1994, review of *Farewell España: The World of the Sephardim Remembered,* p. 4.

Choice, February, 1977; September, 1985, review of *Diaspora: An Inquiry into the Contemporary Jewish World,* p. 178; November, 1987, review of *A History of Israel,* p. 534; July, 1999, review of *Israel and Europe: An Appraisal in History,* p. 1999.

Christian Century, August 14, 1985, review of *Diaspora: An Inquiry into the Contemporary Jewish World,* p. 745.

Commentary, February, 1977; December, 1985, review of *Diaspora: An Inquiry into the Contemporary Jewish World,* p. 68; August, 1993, review of *A History of the Jews in America,* p. 45.

Contemporary Jewish World, p. 68; August, 1993, review of *A History of the Jews in America,* p. 45.

Foreign Affairs, number 1, 1987, review of *A History of Israel,* p. 203; May, 1999, review of *Israel and Europe: An Appraisal in History,* p. 148.

Guardian Weekly, July 5, 1992, review of *A History of the Jews in America,* p. 20.

Historian, autumn, 1993, review of *A History of the Jews in America,* p. 178.

History: Reviews of New Books, spring, 1988, review of *A History of Israel,* p. 134; spring, 1993, review of *A History of the Jews in America,* p. 111.

Journal of American History, June, 1993, review of *A History of the Jews in America,* p. 236.

Journal of Interdisciplinary History, autumn, 1994, Robert I. Weiner, review of *A History of Jews in America,* pp. 335-336.

Kirkus Reviews, April 1, 1985, review of *Diaspora: An Inquiry into the Contemporary Jewish World,* p. 327; March 15, 1992, review of *A History of the Jews in America,* p. 379; September 1, 1994, review of *Farewell España: The World of the Sephardim Remembered,* p. 1200; November 15, 1998, review of *Israel and Europe: An Appraisal in History,* p. 1656; February 1, 2002, review of *Dreamland: Europeans and Jews in the Aftermath of the Great War,* p. 168.

Library Journal, March 15, 1985, review of *Diaspora: An Inquiry into the Contemporary Jewish World,* p. 69; May 1, 1987, review of *A History of Israel,* p. 67; July, 1992, review of *A History of the Jews in America,* p. 103; November 15, 1994, review of *Farewell España: The World of the Sephardim Remembered,* p. 77; February 15, 2002, Frederic Krome, review of *Dreamland: Europeans and Jews in the Aftermath of the Great War,* p. 162.

Los Angeles Times Book Review, November 2, 1980; June 9, 1985, review of *Diaspora: An Inquiry into the Contemporary Jewish World,* p. 1; May 31, 1992, review of *A History of the Jews in America,* p. 11.

Nation, January 26, 1970.

National Review, December 5, 1994, Ben C. Toledano, review of *Farewell España: The World of the Sephardim Remembered,* p. 75.

New Republic, April 12, 1993, review of *A History of the Jews in America,* p. 29.

New York Herald Tribune Book Review, May 25, 1958.

New York Times, April 16, 1985, review of *Diaspora: An Inquiry into the Contemporary Jewish World,* p. 25.

New York Times Book Review, November 23, 1969; January 21, 1973; August 7, 1977; April 21, 1985, review of *Diaspora: An Inquiry into the Contem-*

porary Jewish World, p. 17; July 26, 1987, review of *A History of Israel,* p. 13; February 13, 1994, review of *A History of the Jews in America,* p. 32; November 27, 1994, review of *Farewell España: The World of the Sephardim Remembered,* p. 18; May 2, 1999, Serge Schmemann, review of *Israel and Europe: An Appraisal in History,* p. 31.

Publishers Weekly, March 1, 1985, review of *Diaspora: An Inquiry into the Contemporary Jewish World,* p. 75; May 1, 1987, review of *A History of Israel,* p. 60; March 16, 1992, review of *A History of Jews in America,* p. 68; September 5, 1994, review of *Farewell España: The World of the Sephardim Remembered,* p. 103; September 11, 1995, review of *Farewell España: The World of the Sephardim Remembered,* p. 82; December 7, 1998, review of *Israel and Europe: An Appraisal in History,* p. 41; March 11, 2002, review of *Dreamland: Europeans and Jews in the Aftermath of the Great War,* p. 67.

Reference & Research Book News, May, 1999, review of *Israel and Europe: An Appraisal,* p. 35.

Reference Services Review, fall, 1984, review of *A History of Israel,* p. 28.

Reviews in American History, June, 1993, review of *A History of the Jews in America,* p. 190.

Saturday Review, August 2, 1958.

Springfield Republican, July 20, 1958.

Times Literary Supplement, June 4, 1993, review of *A History of the Jews in America,* p. 10.

Tribune Books (Chicago, IL), February 7, 1993, review of *A History of the Jews in America,* p. 7; February 13, 1994, review of *A History of the Jews in America,* p. 8.

Virginia Quarterly Review, autumn, 1992, review of *A History of the Jews in America,* p. 116; autumn, 1993, review of *A History of the Jews in America,* p. 749; spring, 1995, review of *Farewell España: The World of the Sephardim Remembered,* p. 45.

Washington Post Book World, January 9, 1977.

West Coast Review of Books, January, 1977.

Wilson Quarterly, winter, 1983, review of *A History of Israel* and *Aliyah: The Peoples of Israel,* p. 87.

*   *   *

SALISBURY, John
  See CAUTE, (John) David

SCHARY, Jill
  See ROBINSON, Jill

*   *   *

SHEHADEH, Raja 1951-

PERSONAL: Born July 6, 1951, in Ramallah, Israel; son of Aziz (an attorney) and Wedad Shehadeh; married Penny Johnson (a writer), 1988. *Education:* B.A., 1973. *Religion:* Christian.

ADDRESSES: Home and office—P.O. Box 74, Ramallah, Israel.

CAREER: Called to the Bar at Lincoln's Inn, England, 1976; attorney in private practice in Ramallah, West Bank, Israel, 1980—. Bethlehem University, part-time instructor in law, 1978-80; International Commission of Jurists, founder and codirector of the West Bank affiliate Al-Haq/Law in the Service of Man, 1979-90; World Council of Churches, member of human rights advisory group, Commission of the Churches on International Affairs; Netherlands Institute of Human Rights, member of international advisory council; legal adviser to the Palestinian delegation to peace talks with Israel. American Friends Service Committee, lecturer in the United States, 1985; Harvard Law School, visiting fellow in Human Rights Program, 1988.

AWARDS, HONORS: Issam Sartawi Award from International Center for Peace in the Middle East, 1984, for *The Third Way;* Rothko Cahpel Award for commitment to truth and freedom, 1986; award from Jewish Committee for Israeli-Palestinian Peace, 1988.

WRITINGS:

(With Jonathan Kuttab) *The West Bank and the Rule of Law,* International Commission of Jurists (Geneva, Switzerland), 1980.

The Third Way: A Journal of Life in the West Bank, Quartet Books (New York, NY), 1982, reprinted as *Samed: Journal of a West Bank Palestinian,* Adama Books (New York, NY), 1984.

(With Jonathan Kuttab) *Civilian Administration in the Occupied West Bank,* Law in the Service of Man (Ramallah, West Bank), 1982.

Occupier's Law: Israel and the West Bank, 1985, Institute for Palestine Studies (Washington, DC), 2nd edition, 1989.

The Sealed Room, Quartet Books (New York, NY), 1993.

The Law of the Land: Settlements and Land Issues under Israeli Military Occupation, Palestinian Academic Society for Study of International Affairs (Jerusalem, Israel), 1993.

The Declaration of Principles and the Legal System in the West Bank, Palestinian Academic Society for Study of International Affairs (Jerusalem, Israel), 1994.

From Occupation to Interim Accords: Israel and the Palestinian Territories, Kluwer Law International (Boston, MA), 1997.

Strangers in the House: Coming of Age in Occupied Palestine, Steerforth Press (South Royalton, VT), 2002.

Also author of government pamphlet *Israeli Proposed Road Plan for the West Bank: A Question for the International Court of Justice,* 1984. Contributor to periodicals, including *Life, Harper's, Middle East International, Journal of Palestinian Studies,* and *Journal of Peace Negotiations.*

SIDELIGHTS: Raja Shehadeh is a Palestinian who was born in Israel shortly after his family fled Jaffa to escape Israeli aggression. Although he had never lived there, he was reared with a strong sense of Jaffa as home; his family never lost their sense of exile. Shehadeh's father, Aziz, was an attorney and a strong supporter of the Palestinian cause. He was also one of the first to espouse a peaceful, two-state solution to the Israeli-Palestinian conflict. Raja followed his father into law, but their collaborative work for peace and human rights ended when Aziz was murdered in 1985. Shehadeh relates his father's story and his own in *Strangers in the House: Coming of Age in Occupied Palestine. New York Times Book Review* critic Ethan Bronner noted that the Shehadehs' story is "a heroic one, a rare tale of principle, conviction and kindness operating in harsh circumstances. But it is also an exceptionally sad one. Their efforts had minimal impact—the Israeli military walked all over them, ransacking their offices, threatening their workers and repeatedly delaying their court dates. Meanwhile, the Palestinians ignored and condemned them."

Strangers in the House is a "fascinating memoir," one that "offers a chilling a moving view of life inside the Occupied Territories," claimed a *Publishers Weekly* reviewer. Shehadeh relates the routine humiliation and harassment Palestinians suffer at the hands of the Israeli government, including random searches, constant surveillance, and detentions at checkpoint. Noting that the Palestinian perspective is frequently overlooked in the West, the reviewer concluded, "Anyone seeking a nuanced view of Palestinian experience should read this brave and lyrical book." Naomi Hafter, a contributor to *Library Journal,* also praised Shehadeh's portrait of Palestinian life, noting especially his "strong voice that is without diatribe, melodrama, or anger."

Shehadeh once told *CA:* "I have always agreed with Yeats that writing is the social act of a solitary being. In my solitary journey, I travel through the events of my day as a Palestinian living under Israeli occupation. In literary terms, the terrain I traverse is uncharted. In my writing, I try to transform it into a shared experience."

BIOGRAPHICAL AND CRITICAL SOURCES:

PERIODICALS

Booklist, November 15, 2001, John Green, review of *Strangers in the House: Coming of Age in Occupied Palestine,* p. 546.

Hartford Courant, February 17, 2002, Steve Courtney, review of *Strangers in the House: Coming of Age in Occupied Palestine.*

Journal of Palestine Studies, spring, 1998, John Quigley, review of *From Occupation to Interim Accords: Israel and the Palestinian Territories,* p. 106.

Library Journal, January, 2002, Naomi Hafter, review of *Strangers in the House: Coming of Age in Occupied Palestine,* p. 116.

Middle East Journal, spring, 1998, review of *From Occupation to Interim Accords: Israel and the Palestinian Territories,* p. 308.

New York Times Book Review, December 30, 2001, Ethan Bronner, review of *Strangers in the House: Coming of Age in Occupied Palestine,* p. 18.

Publishers Weekly, December 24, 2001, review of *Strangers in the House: Coming of Age in Occupied Palestine,* p. 55.

Times (London, England), August 22, 1992, p. 33.*

SHEPARD, Sam 1943-

PERSONAL: Given name Samuel Shepard Rogers VII; born November 5, 1943, in Fort Sheridan, IL; son of Samuel Shepard (a teacher and farmer) and Elaine (Schook) Rogers; married O-Lan Johnson Dark (an actress), November 9, 1969 (divorced); currently living with Jessica Lange (an actress and film producer); children: (first marriage) Jesse Mojo; (with Lange) Hannah Jane, Samuel Walker. *Education:* Attended Mount Antonio Junior College, California, 1960- 61. *Hobbies and other interests:* Polo, rodeo.

ADDRESSES: Office—Sam Shepard, International Creative Management, 8942 Wilshire Blvd., Beverly Hills, California, CA 90211-1934. *Agent*—Toby Cole, 234 West 44th St., New York, NY 10036.

CAREER: Writer, 1964—. Conley Arabian Horse Ranch, Chino, CA, stable hand, 1958-60; Bishop's Company Repertory Players (touring theatre group), actor, 1962-63; Village Gate, New York, NY, busboy, 1963-64. Rock musician (drums and guitar) with Holy Modal Rounders, 1968-71; playwright in residence at Magic Theatre, San Francisco, CA, 1974-84; actor in feature films, including *Days of Heaven,* 1978, *Resurrection,* 1980, *Raggedy Man,* 1981, *Frances,* 1982, *The Right Stuff,* 1983, *Country,* 1984, *Fool for Love,* 1985, and *Crimes of the Heart,* 1986, *Baby Boom,* 1987, *Steel Magnolias,* 1989, *The Hot Spot,* 1990, *Defenseless,* 1991, *Voyager,* 1991, *Thunderheart,* 1992, *The Pelican Brief,* 1993, *Silent Tongue,* 1994, *Safe Passage,* 1994, and *Black Hawk Down,* 2002; director of feature film *Far North,* 1988.

MEMBER: American Academy and Institute of Arts and Letters, 1992.

AWARDS, HONORS: Obie Awards from *Village Voice* for best plays of the Off-Broadway season, 1966, for *Chicago, Icarus's Mother,* and *Red Cross,* 1967, for *La Turista,* 1968, for *Forensic and the Navigators* and *Melodrama Play,* 1973, for *The Tooth of Crime,* 1975, for *Action,* 1977, for *Curse of the Starving Class,* 1979, for *Buried Child,* and 1984, for *Fool for Love;* grant from University of Minnesota, 1966; Rockefeller foundation grant and Yale University fellowship, 1967; Guggenheim foundation memorial fellowships, 1968 and 1971; National Institute and American Academy

Sam Shepard

award for literature, 1974; Brandeis University creative arts award, 1975-76; Pulitzer Prize for drama, 1979, for *Buried Child;* Academy Award for best supporting actor nomination from Academy of Motion Picture Arts and Sciences, 1984, for *The Right Stuff;* Golden Palm Award from Cannes Film Festival, 1984, for *Paris, Texas;* New York Drama Critics' Circle Award, 1986, for *A Lie of the Mind;* American Academy of Arts and Letters Gold Medal for Drama, 1992; Theater Hall of Fame, 1994; Antoinette Perry Award Nomination for best play, 1996, for *Buried Child;* revised version of *True West,* first produced off-Broadway in 1980, nominated for a Tony Award for best play, 2000.

WRITINGS:

PLAYS

Cowboys (one-act), first produced Off-Off-Broadway at St. Mark Church in-the-Bowery, October 16, 1964.

The Rock Garden (one-act; also see below), first produced Off-Off-Broadway at St. Mark Church in-the-Bowery, October 16, 1964.

4-H Club (one act; also see below), first produced Off-Broadway at Cherry Lane Theatre, 1965.

Up to Thursday (one-act), first produced Off-Broadway at Cherry Lane Theatre, February 10, 1965.

Dog (one-act), first produced Off-Broadway at La Mama Experimental Theatre Club, February 10, 1965.

Chicago (one-act; also see below), first produced Off-Off-Broadway at St. Mark Church in-the-Bowery, April 16, 1965.

Icarus's Mother (one-act; also see below), first produced Off-Off-Broadway at Caffe Cino, November 16, 1965.

Fourteen Hundred Thousand (one-act; also see below), first produced at Firehouse Theater, Minneapolis, MN, 1966.

Red Cross (one-act; also see below), first produced Off-Broadway at Martinique Theatre, April 12, 1966.

La Turista (two-act; first produced Off-Broadway at American Place Theatre, March 4, 1967; also see below), Bobbs-Merrill (Indianapolis, IN), 1968.

Cowboys #2 (one-act; also see below), first produced Off-Broadway at Old Reliable, August 12, 1967.

Forensic and the Navigators (one-act; also see below), first produced Off-Off-Broadway at St. Mark Church in-the-Bowery, December 29, 1967.

(Contributor) *Oh! Calcutta!,* first produced on Broadway at Eden Theatre, 1969.

The Unseen Hand (one-act; also see below), first produced Off-Broadway at La Mama Experimental Theatre Club, December 26, 1969.

Holy Ghostly (one-act; also see below), first produced in New York, NY, 1970.

Operation Sidewinder (two-act; first produced Off-Broadway at Vivian Beaumont Theatre, March 12, 1970; also see below), Bobbs-Merrill, 1970.

Shaved Splits (also see below), first produced Off-Broadway at La Mama Experimental Theatre Club, July 29, 1970.

Mad Dog Blues (one-act; also see below), first produced Off-Off-Broadway at St. Mark Church in-the-Bowery, March 4, 1971.

(With Patti Smith) *Cowboy Mouth* (also see below), first produced at Transverse Theatre, Edinburgh, Scotland, April 2, 1971, produced Off-Broadway at American Place Theatre, April 29, 1971.

Back Bog Beast Bait (one-act; also see below), first produced Off-Broadway at American Place Theatre, April 29, 1971.

The Tooth of Crime (two-act; also see below), first produced at McCarter Theatre, Princeton, NJ, 1972, produced Off-Off-Broadway at Performing Garage, March 7, 1973.

Blue Bitch (also see below), first produced Off-Off-Broadway at Theatre Genesis, February, 1973.

(With Megan Terry and Jean-Claude van Itallie) *Nightwalk* (also see below), first produced Off-Off-Broadway at St. Clement's Church, September 8, 1973.

Geography of a Horse Dreamer (two-act; also see below), first produced at Theatre Upstairs, London, England, February 2, 1974.

Little Ocean, first produced at Hampstead Theatre Club, London, England, March 25, 1974.

Action (one-act; also see below), first produced Off-Broadway at American Place Theatre, April 4, 1975.

Killer's Head (one-act; also see below), first produced Off-Broadway at American Place Theatre, April 4, 1975.

Angel City (also see below), first produced at Magic Theatre, San Francisco, CA, 1976.

Curse of the Starving Class (two-act; also see below), first produced Off-Broadway at Newman/Public Theatre, March, 1978.

Buried Child (two-act; also see below), first produced Off-Broadway at Theatre of the New City, November, 1978.

Seduced (also see below), first produced Off-Broadway at American Place Theatre, February 1, 1979.

Suicide in B-flat (also see below), first produced Off-Off-Broadway at Impossible Ragtime Theatre, March 14, 1979.

Tongues, first produced at Eureka Theatre Festival, CA, 1979, produced Off-Off-Broadway at The Other Stage, November 6, 1979.

Savage/Love, first produced at Eureka Theater Festival, CA, 1979, produced Off-Off-Broadway at The Other Stage, November 6, 1979.

True West (two-act; first produced Off-Broadway at Public Theatre, December 23, 1980), Doubleday, 1981.

(Also director of original production) *Fool for Love* (one-act; also see below), first produced at Magic Theatre, San Francisco, 1983, produced Off-Broadway by Circle Repertory Company, May 27, 1983.

The Sad Lament of Pecos Bill on the Eve of Killing His Wife (one-act; also see below), first produced Off-Broadway at La Mama Experimental Theatre Club, September 25, 1983.

Superstitions (one-act), first produced Off-Broadway at La Mama Experimental Theatre Club, September 25, 1983.

(Also director of original production) *A Lie of the Mind* (three-act; first produced Off-Broadway at Promenade Theatre, December, 1985), published with *The War in Heaven* (also see below), New American Library (New York, NY), 1987.

Hawk Moon, produced in London, England, 1989.

States of Shock, produced in New York, NY, 1991.

Simpatico, Dramatists Play Service (New York, NY), 1995.

Curse of the Starving Class, Dramatists Play Service (New York, NY), 1997.

Eyes for Consuela, from the story "The Blue Bouquet" by Octavio Paz, Dramatists Play Service (New York, NY), 1999.

The Late Henry Moss, produced at the Signature Theater in New York, NY, 2001.

PLAY COLLECTIONS

Five Plays by Sam Shepard (contains *Icarus's Mother, Chicago, Melodrama Play, Red Cross,* and *Fourteen Hundred Thousand*), Bobbs-Merrill (Indianapolis, IN), 1967.

The Unseen Hand and Other Plays (contains *The Unseen Hand, 4-H Club, Shaved Splits, Forensic and the Navigators, Holy Ghostly,* and *Back Bog Beast Bait*), Bobbs-Merrill (Indianapolis, IN), 1971.

Mad Dog Blues and Other Plays (includes *Mad Dog Blues, The Rock Garden, Cowboys #2, Cowboy Mouth, Blue Bitch,* and *Nightwalk*), Winter House (New York, NY), 1972.

The Tooth of Crime [and] *Geography of a Horse Dreamer,* Grove (New York, NY), 1974.

Angel City, Curse of the Starving Class and Other Plays (includes *Angel City, Curse of the Starving Class, Killer's Head,* and *Action*), Urizen Books (New York, NY), 1976.

Buried Child, Seduced, Suicide in B-flat, Urizen Books (New York, NY), 1979.

Four Two-Act Plays by Sam Shepard (contains *La Turista, The Tooth of Crime, Geography of a Horse Dreamer,* and *Operation Sidewinder*), Urizen Books (New York, NY), 1980.

Chicago and Other Plays, Urizen Books (New York, NY), 1981.

The Unseen Hand and Other Plays, Urizen Books (New York, NY), 1981.

Seven Plays by Sam Shepard, Bantam (New York, NY), 1981.

Fool for Love [and] *The Sad Lament of Pecos Bill on the Eve of Killing His Wife,* City Lights Books (San Francisco, CA), 1983.

Fool for Love and Other Plays, Bantam (New York, NY), 1984.

The Unseen Hand and Other Plays, Bantam (New York, NY), 1986.

States of Shock, Far North, [and] Silent Tongue, Vintage (New York, NY), 1993.

The Late Henry Moss, Eyes for Consuela, [and] When the World Was Green, Vintage (New York, NY), 2002.

SCREENPLAYS

(With Michelangelo Antonioni, Tonino Guerra, Fred Graham, and Clare Peploe) *Zabriskie Point* (produced by Metro-Goldwyn-Mayer, 1970), Cappelli (Bologna, Italy), 1970, published with Antonioni's *Red Desert,* Simon & Schuster (New York, NY), 1972.

(With L. M. Kit Carson) *Paris, Texas,* Twentieth Century-Fox, 1984.

Fool for Love (based on Shepard's play of the same title), Golan Globus, 1985.

Far North, Alive, 1988.

Silent Tongue, Trimark, 1992.

OTHER

Hawk Moon: A Book of Short Stories, Poems, and Monologues, Black Sparrow Press (Santa Barbara, CA), 1973.

Rolling Thunder Logbook, Viking (New York, NY), 1977.

Motel Chronicles, City Lights Books (San Francisco, CA), 1982.

(With Joseph Chaikin) *The War in Heaven* (radio drama; first broadcast over WBAI in January, 1985), published with *A Lie of the Mind,* New American Library (New York, NY), 1987.

Joseph Chaikin and Sam Shepard: Letters and Texts, 1972-1984, edited by Barry V. Daniels, New American Library (New York, NY), 1989.

Cruising Paradise: Tales, Knopf (New York, NY), 1996.

Great Dream of Heaven: Stories, Knopf (New York, NY), 2002.

Also author, with Robert Frank, of *Me and My Brother,* and with Murray Mednick, of *Ringaleerio.*

ADAPTATIONS: Fourteen Hundred Thousand was filmed for NET *Playhouse,* 1969; *Blue Bitch* was filmed by the British Broadcasting Corporation (BBC), 1973; *True West* was filmed for the Public Broadcasting Service (PBS) series *American Playhouse.*

SIDELIGHTS: Sam Shepard has devoted more than two decades to a highly eclectic—and critically acclaimed—career in the performing arts. He is considered the preeminent literary playwright of his generation. Shepard has also directed plays of his authorship, played drums and guitar in rock bands and jazz ensembles, and acted in major feature films. His movie appearances include leading roles in *The Right Stuff* and *Country,* but acting is a sideline for the man *Newsweek*'s Jack Kroll called "the poet laureate of America's emotional Badlands." Despite his success in Hollywood, Shepard is primarily a playwright whose dramas explore mythic images of modern America in the nation's own eccentric vernacular.

Shepard established himself by writing numerous one-act plays and vignettes for the Off-Off-Broadway experimental theatre. Although his audiences have grown and his plays have been widely produced in America and abroad, he has yet to stage a production on Broadway. *New Republic* contributor Robert Brustein, who found Shepard "one of our most celebrated writers," contends that the lack of attention from Broadway "has not limited Shepard's powers." Brustein added: "Unlike those predecessors who wilted under such conditions, Shepard has flourished in a state of marginality. . . . Shepard's work has been a model of growth and variety." From his early surreal one-acts to his more realistic two- and three-act plays, Shepard has stressed artistic integrity rather than marketability. As a result, Kroll contended, Shepard plays have "overturned theatrical conventions and created a new kind of drama filled with violence, lyricism and an intensely American compound of comic and tragic power."

Shepard has won eleven Obie Awards for best Off-Broadway plays, a Pulitzer Prize for *Buried Child,* and a New York Drama Critics' Circle Award in 1986 for *A Lie of the Mind.* Richard A. Davis wrote in *Plays and Players* magazine that Shepard has both "a tremendous ability to make words bring the imagination of an audience to life" and "a talent for creating with words alone extremely believable emotional experiences."

According to *Village Voice* correspondent Michael Feingold, Shepard "has the real playwright's gift of habitually transposing his feelings and visions into drama as a mere matter of praxis. He speaks through the theatre as naturally as most of us speak through the telephone." Shepard's plays use modern idiomatic language as well as such prevailing themes of American popular culture, particularly the American West, Hollywood and the rock-and-roll industry. "No one knows better than Sam Shepard that the true American West is gone forever," wrote Frank Rich in the *New York Times,* "but there may be no writer alive more gifted at reinventing it out of pure literary air."

Shepard's modern cowboys, drifters, farmers, and other offspring of the frontier era yearn for a purer past that may never have existed as they quarrel with family members. *Journal of Popular Culture* contributor George Stambolian maintained that, like many of his fellow playwrights, Shepard "knows that the old frontier myths of America's youth are no longer a valid expression of our modern anxieties, even though they continue to influence our thoughts." Stambolian said Shepard seeks "a new mythology that will encompass all the diverse figures of our cultural history together with the psychological and social conditions they represent. . . . Shepard's greatest contribution to a new American mythology may well be his elaboration of a new myth of the modern artist."

Sam Shepard's theater is marked by "a spirit of comedy that tosses and turns in a bed of revulsion," as Richard Eder wrote in the *New York Times.* Malicious mischief and comic mayhem intensify Shepard's tragic vision; in many of his plays, inventive dialogue supplements vigorous action. As David Richards wrote in the *Washington Post,* actors and directors "respond to the slam-bang potential in [Shepard's] scripts, which allows them to go for broke, trash the furniture, and generally shred the scenery. Whatever else you've got, you've got a wild and wooly fight on your hands." The theatrical fisticuffs, sometimes physical, sometimes verbal, is on the overriding American musical rhythms. *New York Times* theatre critic Clive Barnes said: "Mr. Shepard writes mythic plays in American jazz-poetry. . . . He is trying to express truths wrapped up in legends and with the kind of symbolism you often find nowadays in pop music. His command of language is daring and inventive—some of the words sound new, and quite a few of them actually are." Richard L. Homan makes a similar point in *Criti-*

cal Quarterly: "Shepard's vivid use of language and flair for fantasy have suggested something less like drama and more like poetry in some unfamiliar oral tradition."

While Shepard's subjects—nostalgia, power struggles, family tensions—may seem simple at first, his plays remain "extraordinarily resistant to thematic exegesis," Richard Gilman wrote in his introduction to *Seven Plays by Sam Shepard*. Gilman added that standard criticism of Shepard is inadequate because the dramatist "slips out of all the categories" and seems to have come "out of no literary or theatrical tradition at all but precisely for the breakdown or absence—on the level of art if not of commerce—of all such traditions in America." Gilman added that several of the plays "seem like fragments, chunks of various sizes thrown out from some mother lode of urgent and heterogeneous imagination in which [Shepard] has scrabbled with pick, shovel, gun-butt and hands. The reason so many of them seem incomplete is that they lack the clear boundaries as artifact, the internal order, the progress toward a denouement ... and the consistency of tone and procedure that ordinarily characterize good drama."

In *American Dreams: The Imagination of Sam Shepard*, Michael Earley said Shepard "seems to have forged a whole new kind of American play that has yet to receive adequate reckoning." Earley called the playwright "a true American primitive, a literary naif coursing the stage of American drama as if for the first time" who brings to his work "a liberating interplay of word, theme and image that has always been the hallmark of the romantic impulse. His plays don't work like plays in the traditional sense but more like romances, where the imaginary landscape (his version of America) is so remote and open that it allows for the depiction of legend, adventure, and even the supernatural."*Partisan Review* contributor Ross Wetzsteon contended that viewers respond to Shepard's plays "not by interpreting their plots or analyzing their characters or dissecting their themes, but simply by experiencing their resonance. . . . Shepard's arias seek to soar into a disembodied freedom, to create emotions beyond rational structure, to induce in both player and audience a trancelike state of grace."

Shepard, born in Fort Sheridan, Illinois, was given the name his forebears had used for six generations—Samuel Shepard Rogers. His father was a career army officer, so as a youngster Shepard moved from base to base in the United States and even spent some time in Guam. When Shepard's father retired from the service, the family settled on a ranch in Duarte, California, where they grew avocados and raised sheep. Although the livelihood was precarious, Shepard enjoyed the atmosphere on the ranch and liked working with horses and other animals. Influenced by his father's interest in Dixieland jazz, Shepard gravitated to music; he began to play the drums and started what *Dictionary of Literary Biography* contributor David W. Engel called "his lifelong involvement with rock-and-roll music and its subculture." He graduated from Duarte High School in 1960 and spent one year studying agricultural science at the local junior college, but his family situation deteriorated as his father began drinking excessively. Shepard fled by joining a touring theatrical group called the Bishop's Company Repertory Players. At age nineteen, he found himself in New York, determined to seek his fortune with only a few months' acting experience.

By chance Shepard encountered a high school friend in New York, Charles Mingus, Jr., son of the renowned jazz musician. Mingus found Shepard a job at The Village Gate, a jazz club, and the two young men became roommates. While working at The Village Gate, Shepard met Ralph Cook, founder of the Off-Off-Broadway company Theatre Genesis. Cook encouraged Shepard to write plays, and Shepard produced *Cowboys* and *The Rock Garden,* two one-acts that became part of the first Theatre Genesis show at St. Mark Church in-the-Bowery. Though Engel notes that most of the critics regarded Shepard's first two works as "bad imitations of Beckett," the *Village Voice* columnist "gave the plays a rave review." Shepard began to rapidly turn out one-act pieces, many performed Off-Off-Broadway; they attracted a cult following within that theatrical circuit. Shepard also continued his association with jazz and rock music, incorporating the rhythms into his dialogue and including musical riffs in the scripts. He reminisced about his early career in *New York* magazine: "When I arrived in New York there was this environment of *art* going on. I mean, it was really tangible. And you were right *in* the thing, especially on the Lower East Side. La Mama, Theatre Genesis, . . . all those theaters were just starting. So that was a great coincidence. I had a place to go and put something on without having to go through a producer or go through the commercial network. All of that was in response to the tightness of Broadway and Off-Broadway, where you couldn't get a play done."

Shepard told *New York* he did his early work hastily. "There wasn't much rewriting done," he said. "I had this whole attitude toward that work that it was somehow violating it to go back and rework it. . . . Why spend the time rewriting when there was another one to do?" Kroll said: "The true artist starts with his obsessions, then makes them ours as well. The very young Sam Shepard exploded his obsessions like firecrackers; in his crazy, brilliant early plays he was escaping his demons, not speaking to ours." *New York Times* correspondent Mel Gussow, who has monitored Shepard's career, calls the playwright's early works "a series of mystical epics (on both a large and small scale) mixing figures from folklore with visitors from the outer space of fantasy fiction." The Shepard one-acts, still frequently performed at theatre festivals and universities, juxtapose visual and verbal images with dramatic collage. Stambolian said the technique "forces the spectator to view the surface, so to speak, from behind, from within the imagination that conceived it."

"Shepard draws much of his material from popular culture sources such as B-grade westerns, sci-fi and horror films, popular folklore, country and rock music and murder-mysteries," *Modern Drama* critic Charles R. Bachman wrote. "In his best work he transforms the original stereotyped characters and situations into an imaginative, linguistically brilliant, quasi-surrealistic chemistry of text and stage presentation which is original and authentically his own." According to Stanley Kauffmann in the *New Republic,* the deliberate use of movie types "is part of Shepard's general method: the language and music of rock, spaceman fantasies, Wild West fantasies, gangster fantasies—pop-culture forms that he uses as building blocks, rituals of contemporary religion to heighten communion."

Some critics have dismissed Shepard's early work as undisciplined and obscure. *Massachusetts Review* essayist David Madden found the plays "mired in swampy attitudes toward Mom and Dad. Their main line of reasoning seems to be that if Mom and Dad's middle class values are false, that if they and the institutions they uphold are complacent and indifferent, the only alternative is some form of outlaw behavior or ideology." Other national drama critics have evaluated the one-act plays quite differently. In the *New York Review of Books,* Robert Mazzocco wrote: "If one is content to follow this hard-nosed, drug-induced, pop-flavored style, this perpetual retuning of old genres

and old myths, one encounters, finally, a profuse and unique panorama of where we are now and where we have been." Stambolian said that Shepard "is in fact showing to what extent the mind, and particularly the modern American mind, can become and has become entrapped by its own verbal and imaginative creations." And, according to Barnes, Shepard "is so sweetly unserious about his plays, and so desperately serious about what he is saying. . . . There is more in them than meets the mind. They are very easy to be funny about, yet they linger oddly in the imagination." In his own assessment of his first plays, Shepard told *New York* he thinks of them as "survival kits, in a way. They were explosions that were coming out of some kind of inner turmoil in me that I didn't understand at all. There are areas in some of them that are still mysterious to me."

Shepard's first major production, *Operation Sidewinder,* premiered at the Vivian Beaumont Theatre in 1970. Engel described the two-act play as "an excellent example of how [Shepard] combines the roles of poet, musician, and playwright." Set in the Hopi Indian country of the American Southwest, *Operation Sidewinder* follows the attempts to control a huge, mechanical rattlesnake originally designed to trace unidentified flying objects. Air force commandos, Hopi snake-worshippers, black power activists, and even a beautiful but foolish blonde named Honey try to use the computerized sidewinder for their own ends. Engel notes that the "playful and satiric action is amplified by Shepard's production techniques. He assaults the senses of the audience by the use of intense sound and lights, and by various chants and songs." Shepard himself performed music in the play with a rock band, the Holy Modal Rounders. Although Engel said "the psychological resonance of stylized production, and not its sociological satire, is Shepard's aim," some critics called the work overly moralistic and stylistically confusing. "The difficulty of the play is in the writing," Barnes said. "The symbolic progression, while clearly charting the progress to atomic holocaust, is altogether too symbolic." Kroll maintains that the play's energy "has congealed in a half-slick pop machine with the feel of celluloid and the clackey sound of doctrinaire contemporaneity." Martin Gottfried viewed the play differently in *Women's Wear Daily.* "Everything about Sam Shepard's *Operation Sidewinder* is important to our theatre," Gottfried wrote. "More than any recent major production, it is built upon exactly the style and the mentality energizing the youth movement in America today."

In 1971 Shepard took his wife and infant son and moved to England. Having long experimented with drugs, the playwright sought escape from the abusive patterns he saw destroying fellow artists in New York. He also hoped to become more involved with rock music, still a central obsession. He did not accomplish that goal, but as Engel noted, he did "write and produce some of his finest works" while living in London. Gussow wrote: "As the author became recognized as an artist and found himself courted by such unearthly powers as Hollywood, he went through a Faustian phase. The result was a series of plays about art and the seduction of the artist." Plays such as *Angel City, Geography of a Horse Dreamer,* and *The Tooth of Crime* explore various aspects of the artist/visionary's dilemma when faced with public tastes or corporate profit-taking. Mazzocco felt that at this stage in his career Shepard chose to examine "not so much in political or economic parallels as in those of domination and submission, the nature of power in America. Or, more precisely, the duplicitous nature of 'success' and 'failure,' where it's implied that a failure of nerve and not that of a 'life' is at the basis of both." The playwright also discovered, as Richard A. Davis wrote, that "it is only within the individual mind that one finds his 'shelter' from the world; and even this shelter is not permanent, for the mind and body are tied together. To a great extent, Shepard's dramas have all been caught in this continual exploration of the same human problem."

The Tooth of Crime further strengthened Shepard's literary reputation. A two-act study of rock-and-roll stars who fight to gain status and "turf," the play "depicts a society which worships raw power," in Engel's words. London *Times* reviewer Irving Wardle wrote: "Its central battle to the death between an aging superstar and a young pretender to his throne is as timeless as a myth . . . and . . . has proved a durably amazing reflection of the West Coast scene. If any classic has emerged from the last 20 years of the American experimental theatre, this is it."

"Moving freely from gangster movies of the 40's to punk rock of the 70's, Mr. Shepard speaks in a language that is vividly idiomatic," Gussow wrote. Mazzocco called *The Tooth of Crime* "undoubtedly the quintessential Shepard play" and "a dazzlingly corrosive work . . . one of the most original achievements in contemporary theater. It is also the play that best illustrates the various facets—at once highly eclectic and highly singular—of [Shepard's] genius."

The Tooth of Crime, represented a stylistic departure for Shepard. Bachman contended that the work "utilizes . . . the traditional dramatic values of taut, disciplined structure, vivid and consistent characterization, and crescendo of suspense." The transition, however, from modernist to traditional style has hardly been smooth. According to Richard L. Homan in *Critical Quarterly,* Shepard has learned "to express the outrage, which gave rise to the experimental theatre, in plays which work through realistic conventions to challenge our everyday sense of reality." Shepard told *New York* that he sees a growing emphasis on character in his plays since 1972. "When I started writing," he said, "I wasn't interested in character at all. In fact, I thought it was useless, old-fashioned, stuck in a certain way. . . . I preferred a character that was constantly unidentifiable, shifting through the actor, so that the actor could almost play anything, and the audience was never expected to identify with the character.... But I had broken away from the idea of character without understanding it." Shepard's more recent plays explore characters—especially idiosyncratic and eccentric ones—for dramatic effect.

Gussow believed Shepard's new phase of writing reflects the changes in his own life. The playwright increasingly seeks to expose "the erosion and the conflagration of the ill-American family," Gussow said. Mazzocco said Shepard has "turned from the game to the trap, from the trail back to the hearth, from warfare in a 'buddy culture' to warfare among kith and kin." Four of Shepard's plays, *Buried Child, Curse of the Starving Class, True West,* and *A Lie of the Mind,* document in scenes of black humor the peculiar savagery of modern American family life. *New York Times* contributor Benedict Nightingale found these plays peopled by a "legion of the lost," whose "essential tragedy . . . seems . . . to be that they are simultaneously searching for things that are incompatible and possibly not attainable anyway: excitement and security, the exhilaration of self-fulfillment and a sense of belonging, freedom and roots."

Buried Child and *A Lie of the Mind,* separated by seven years, examine disturbed families. In *Buried Child,* David Richards wrote in the *Washington Post,* Shepard "delivers a requiem for America, land of the surreal and home of the crazed. . . . Beyond the white frame farmhouse that contains the evening's action, the amber waves of grain mask a dark secret. The fruited plain is rotting and the purple mountain's majesty is like a bad bruise on the landscape." In *Buried Child,* son Vince arrives at his midwestern farm home after a long absence. A dangerous cast of relatives confronts him, harboring secrets of incest and murder. Richard Christiansen, in the *Chicago Tribune,* called the Pulitzer Prize-winning play "a Norman Rockwell portrait created for *Mad Magazine,* a scene from America's heartland that reeks with 'the stench of sin.'" Similarly, *A Lie of the Mind* presents a tale of "interior domestic violence, the damage that one does to filial, fraternal and marital bonds—and the love that lingers in the air after the havoc has run its natural course," Gussow wrote. In that work, two families are galvanized into violence when a jealous husband beats his wife, almost fatally. *A Lie of the Mind* won the New York Drama Critics' Circle Award for best new Off-Broadway play of 1985, and Shepard himself directed the original production.

Fool for Love, which Shepard also directed, is probably his best-known work. The one-act piece has been produced for the stage and has also been made into a feature film in which Shepard starred. *Fool for Love* alternates submission and rejection between two lovers who may also be half-brother and half-sister. New York *Daily News* critic Douglas Watt said the ninety-minute, non-stop drama "is Sam Shepard's purest and most beautiful play. An aching love story of classical symmetry, it is . . . like watching the division of an amoeba in reverse, ending with a perfect whole." *Fool for Love,* wrote *New York Times* reviewer Frank Rich, "is a western for our time. We watch a pair of figurative gunslingers fight to the finish—not with bullets, but with piercing words that give ballast to the weight of a nation's buried dreams. . . . As Shepard's people race verbally through the debris of the West, they search for the identities and familial roots that have disappeared with the landscape of legend." In the *New Republic,* Brustein found "nothing very thick or complicated about either the characters or the plot" and a lack of resolution to the play's ending. Still, the critic concluded that *Fool for Love* is "not so much a text as a legend, not so much a play as a scenario for stage choreography, and under the miraculous direction of the playwright, each moment is rich with balletic nuances."

Since 1978 Shepard has taken a major movie role each year, and was nominated for an Academy Award for his performance in *The Right Stuff.* He has, despite his discomfort with the image, assumed a certain matinee

idol status. "Shepard did not become famous by writing plays," Stephen Fay wrote in *Vogue.* "Like it or not, acting [has] made him a celebrity." Shepard does *not* like to be considered a screen celebrity; his attitude toward film work is ambivalent, and public scrutiny has made him a recluse. He told *New York:* "There's a definite fear about being diminished through film. It's very easy to do too much of it, to a point where you're lost. Image-making is really what film acting is about. It's image-making, as opposed to character-making, and in some cases it's not true." But *Film Comment* essayist David Thomson contended that Shepard's long-standing fascination with movies lures him into that sort of work. "His sternness wants to be tested against their decadence," Thomson wrote. "His restraint struggles to reconcile a simultaneous contempt and need for movies. The uneasiness hovers between passion and foolishness, between the lack of skill and a monolith of intractability."

Shepard has often contradicted his own persona. In *Country,* for instance, he portrays a farmer who wilts under pressure when threatened with foreclosure, and in *Fool for Love* he appears as a womanizing, luckless rodeo rider. According to Thomson, Shepard brings the same sort of integrity to his movie roles that he brings to his writing. "For five years or so," Thomson wrote, "he has been prowling around the house of cinema, coming in a little way, armored with disdain, slipping out, but coming back, as if it intrigued and tempted his large talent. And movies need him. . . . But as with all prowlers, there remains a doubt as to whether this roaming, wolfen, mongrel lurcher wants to live in the house or tear it to pieces with his jaws and then howl at the desert moon, queen of dead worlds." Shepard told *New York:* "I'm a writer. The more I act, the more resistance I have to it. Now it seems to me that being an actor in films is like being sentenced to a trailer for twelve weeks."

In 1983, German director Wim Wenders commissioned Shepard to write a screenplay based loosely on the playwright's book *Motel Chronicles.* The resulting work, *Paris, Texas,* was a unanimous winner of the Golden Palm Award at the 1984 Cannes Film Festival. The film recasts many of Shepard's central concerns—broken families, the myth of the loner, and the elegy for the old West—in a story of reunion between a father and a son. In *People* magazine, Peter Travers called *Paris, Texas* the "most disturbing film ever about the roots of family relationships. Shepard's words and Wenders' images blend in a magical poetry." *New York* reviewer David Denby found the film "a lifeless art-world hallucination—a movie composed entirely of self-conscious flourishes," but most other critics praised the work.

For all his work in other media, Shepard is still most highly regarded for his playwriting. "He is indeed an original," wrote Edith Oliver in the *New Yorker,* "but it might be pointed out that the qualities that make him so valuable are the enduring ones—good writing, wit, dramatic invention, and the ability to create characters." Stambolian added, "It is certain that in a society drifting rapidly into the escapism of a permanent, and often instant, nostalgia, Shepard's plays are a sign of artistic health and awareness, and are, therefore, worthy of our attention." John Lahr elaborated on this idea in *Plays and Players*: "Shepard, who has put himself outside the killing commercial climate of American life and theatre for the last few years, seems to be saying . . . that the only real geography is internal." And, as *New York Times* correspondent Walter Kerr concludes, "everyone's got to admire [Shepard's] steadfast insistence on pursuing the vision in his head."

Shepard himself sees room for growth in his writing. "I guess I'm always hoping for one play that will end my need to write plays," he told *Vogue*. "Sort of the definitive piece, but it never happens. There's always disappointment, something missing, some level that hasn't been touched, and the more you write the more you struggle, even if you are riding a wave of inspiration. And if the piece does touch something, you always know you haven't got to the depths of certain emotional territory. So you go out and try another one." According to *New Statesman* reviewer Benedict Nightingale, "we can rely on [Shepard] to continue bringing a distinctively American eye, ear and intelligence to the diagnosis of what are, if you think about it, universal anxieties."

The playwright told the *New York Times* that he has no plans to stop. "I want to do the work that fascinates me," he said.

BIOGRAPHICAL AND CRITICAL SOURCES:

BOOKS

Almanac of Famous People, 6th edition, Gale (Detroit, MI), 1998.

Auerbach, Doris, *Sam Shepard, Arthur Kopit, and the Off Broadway Theater,* Twayne (Boston, MA), 1982.

Banham, Martin, editor, *The Cambridge Guide to World Theatre,* Cambridge University Press (New York, NY), 1988.

Bowman, John S., editor, *Cambridge Dictionary of American Biography,* Cambridge University Press (New York, NY), 1996.

Contemporary Dramatists, 6th edition, St. James (Detroit, MI), 1999.

Contemporary Literary Criticism, Gale (Detroit, MI), Volume 4, 1975, Volume 6, 1976, Volume 17, 1981, Volume 34, 1985, Volume 41, 1987, Volume 44, 1987.

Contemporary Theatre, Film, and Television, Volume 25, Gale (Detroit, MI), 2000,

Dictionary of Literary Biography, Volume 8: *Twentieth-Century American Dramatists,* 1981, Volume 212: *Twentieth-Century American Western Writers, Second Series,* 1999, Gale (Detroit, MI).

Drabble, Margaret, editor, *The Oxford Companion to English Literature,* 6th edition, Oxford University Press (New York, NY), 2000.

Drama Criticism, Volume 5, Gale (Detroit, MI), 1995.

Drama for Students, Volume 14, Greg Barnhisel, "Critical Essay on *Curse of the Starving Class,*" Gale (Detroit, MI), 2002.

Earl Blackwell's Celebrity Register 1990, Gale (Detroit, MI), 1990.

Encyclopedia of World Biography, 2nd edition, Gale (Detroit, MI), 1998.

Encyclopedia of World Literature in the 20th Century, Volume 4, St. James (Detroit, MI), 1999.

Graham, Laura, *Sam Shepard: Theme, Image, and the Director,* Lang (New York, NY), 1995.

Greasley, Philip, editor, *Dictionary of Midwestern Literature,* Volume 1: *The Authors,* Indiana University Press (Bloomington, IN), 2001.

Harmon, Justin, et al, *American Cultural Leaders from Colonial Times to the Present,* ABC-CLIO (Santa Barbara, CA), 1993.

Hart, James D., editor, *The Oxford Companion to American Literature,* 6th edition, Oxford University Press (New York, NY), 1995.

Hart, Lynda, *Sam Shepard's Metaphorical Stages,* Greenwood Press (Westport, CT), 1987.

International Dictionary of Films and Filmmakers, Volume 3: *Actors and Actresses,* St. James (Detroit, MI), 1996.

International Dictionary of Theatre, Volume 2: *Playwrights,* St. James (Detroit, MI), 1993.

King, Kimball, *Ten Modern American Playwrights,* Garland (New York, NY), 1982.

King, Kimball, *Sam Shepard: A Case Book,* Garland (New York, NY), 1988.

Magill, Frank N., editor, *Critical Survey of Drama,* revised edition, Volume 6, Salem Press (Pasadena, CA), 1994.

Magill, Frank N., editor, *Cyclopedia of World Authors,* revised 3rd edition, Volume 5, Salem Press (Pasadena, CA), 1997.

Magill, Frank N., editor, *Magill's Survey of American Literature,* Volume 5, Marshall Cavendish (New York, NY), 1991.

Marranca, Bonnie, editor, *American Dramas: The Imagination of Sam Shepard,* Performing Arts Journal Publications (New York, NY), 1981.

Mottram, Ron, *Inner Landscapes: The Theater of Sam Shepard,* University of Missouri Press (Columbia, MO), 1984.

Newsmakers 1996, Issue 4, Gale (Detroit, MI), 1996.

New York Times Theatre Reviews, New York Times Company (New York, NY), 1971.

Oumano, Ellen, *Sam Shepard: The Life and Work of an American Dreamer,* St. Martin's Press (New York, NY), 1986.

Parker, Peter, editor, *A Reader's Guide to Twentieth-Century Writers,* Oxford University Press (New York, NY), 1996.

Patraka, Vivian M., and Siegel, Mark, *Sam Shepard,* Boise State University (Boise, ID), 1985.

Peck, David, editor, *Identities and Issues in Literature,* Volume 3, Salem Press (Pasadena, CA), 1997.

Riggs, Thomas, editor, *Reference Guide to American Literature,* 4th edition, St. James (Detroit, MI), 2000.

St. James Encyclopedia of Popular Culture, St. James (Detroit, MI), 2000.

Schlueter, Paul and June, editors, *Modern American Literature,* Volume 5, second supplement to the 4th edition, *A Library of Literary Criticism,* Continuum (New York, NY), 1985.

Serafin, Steven R., editor, *Encyclopedia of American Literature,* Continuum (New York, NY), 1999.

Shepard, Sam, *Five Plays by Sam Shepard,* Bobbs-Merrill (Indianapolis, IN), 1967.

Shepard, Sam, *Mad Dog Blues and Other Plays,* Winter House, 1972.

Shepard, Sam, *Seven Plays by Sam Shepard,* Bantam (New York, NY), 1981.

Shewey, Don, *Sam Shepard,* Dell (New York, NY), 1985.

Tucker, Martin, editor, *Modern American Literature,* Volume 6, supplement to the 4th edition, *A Library of Literary Criticism,* Continuum (New York, NY), 1985.

Tucker, Martin, editor, *Literary Exile in the Twentieth Century: An Analysis and Biographical Dictionary,* Greenwood (New York, NY), 1991.

Trussler, Simon, *File on Shepard,* Methuen (London, England), 1989.

Wallflower Critical Guide to Contemporary North American Directors, Columbia University Press (New York, NY), 2001.

Weales, Gerald, *The Jumping-Off Place: American Drama in the 1960's ,* Macmillan (New York, NY), 1969.

PERIODICALS

After Dark, June, 1975.

America, November 5, 1983.

American Film, October, 1984.

American Theatre, October, 2000, "Alma Pater," p. 40.

Back Stage, May 3, 1996, Daniel Sheward, review of *Buried Child,* p. 48; May 16, 1997, Peter Shaughnessy, review of *Curse of the Starving Class,* p. 64; March 24, 2000, Eric Grode, review of *True West,* p. 64; October 26, 2001, David Sheward, review of *The Late Henry Moss,* p. 56.

Back Stage West, September 28, 2000, Kristina Mannion, review of *Simpatico,* p. 18; January 18, 2001, Michael Green, review of *Fool for Love,* p. 14.

Booklist, April 15, 1996, Donna Seaman, review of *Cruising Paradise,* p. 1422.

Books, December, 1997, review of *Cruising Paradise,* p. 20.

Canadian Forum, March, 1985.

Chicago Tribune, December 15, 1978; December 7, 1979; July 2, 1980; April 23, 1982; December 16, 1985; December 18, 1985.

Christian Century, November 21, 1984.

Christian Science Monitor, June 9, 1983.

Commonweal, June 14, 1968; May 8, 1970; November 30, 1984; July 12, 1991.

Cosmopolitan, January, 1985.

Critical Quarterly, spring, 1982.

Cue, April 11, 1970; July 18, 1970; February 17, 1973; March 31, 1973; March 18, 1978.

Daily News (New York), May 27, 1983.

Drama, winter, 1965; spring, 1969; autumn, 1973; summer, 1976.

Educational Theatre Journal, October, 1977.

Entertainment Weekly, May 31, 1996, Margot Mifflin, review of *Cruising Paradise,* p. 54.

Esquire, February, 1980; November, 1988.

Film Comment, November-December, 1983; June, 1984.

Globe and Mail (Toronto), December 21, 1985.

Guardian, February 20, 1974.

Harper's Bazaar, September, 1985; November, 1994, p. 98.

Hollywood Reporter, August 12, 2002, Barry Garron, review of *True West,* pp. 33-34.

Hudson Review, spring, 1979; spring, 1984.

Interview, September, 1988.

Journal of Popular Culture, spring, 1974.

Kirkus Reviews, March 15, 1996, review of *Cruising Paradise,* p. 403; August 1, 2002, review of *Great Dream of Heaven,* p. 1071.

Kliatt, November, 1996, review of *Cruising Paradise* (audio recording), p. 47.

Library Journal, May 15, 1996, review of *Cruising Paradise* (audio recording), p. 100; June 15, 1996, review of *Cruising Paradise,* p. 95, reviews of *Simpatico* and *The Unseen Hand and Other Plays,* p. 97.

Listener, September 26, 1974.

London Magazine, December, 1968.

Los Angeles Magazine, March, 1988.

Los Angeles Times, May 12, 1982; February 12, 1983; October 1, 1983; December 12, 1983; March 14, 1984; November 16, 1984; September 25, 1985; December 6, 1985; January 25, 1986; April 11, 1986; August 11, 1986.

Los Angeles Times Book Review, July 28, 1996, review of *Cruising Paradise,* p. 6.

Maclean's, October 29, 1984; December 24, 1984; January 13, 1986; January 18, 1988; November 21, 1988; October 2, 2000, "Actor, Playwright, Cowboy," p. 74.

Mademoiselle, March, 1985.

Massachusetts Review, autumn, 1967.

Modern Drama, December, 1976, March, 1979; March, 1981.

Ms., November, 1984.

Nation, February 21, 1966; April 4, 1966; March 30, 1970; March 26, 1973; May 3, 1975; January 10, 1976; February 24, 1979; January 31, 1981; October 27, 1984; December 29, 1984; January 5, 1985; January 11, 1986; February 22, 1986.

New Leader, April 10, 1967.

New Republic, April 21, 1973; April 8, 1978; January 31, 1981; June 27, 1983; October 29, 1984; December 3, 1984; December 23, 1985; September 29, 1986; February 2, 1987; November 28, 1988, Stanley Kauffmann, review of *Far North,* pp. 22-23; July 15, 1995, p. 27.

New Statesman, August 24, 1984; October 12, 1984; March 1, 1985; July 4, 1986; October 30, 1987; February 9, 1990; September 6, 1991; July 23, 2001, Katherine Duncan-Jones, "A Little Legend about Love" (review of *A Lie of the Mind*), p. 45.

Newsweek, March 23, 1970; January 5, 1981; June 6, 1983; October 1, 1984; November 19, 1984; November 11, 1985; December 16, 1985.

New York, November 27, 1978; February 19, 1979; June 13, 1983; December 5, 1983; October 15, 1984; November 19, 1984; December 9, 1985; May 27, 1991; May 13, 1996, p. 64.

New Yorker, May 11, 1968; March 21, 1970; March 17, 1973; May 5, 1975; December 22, 1975; November 29, 1982; October 1, 1984; September 2, 1985; January 27, 1986; December 15, 1986; June 3, 1991; April 22, 1996, p. 84; May 27, 1996, p. 138.

New York Post, May 27, 1983.

New York Review of Books, April 6, 1967; May 9, 1985.

New York Times, February 11, 1965; April 13, 1966; May 28, 1968; April 13, 1969; March 15, 1970; April 2, 1970; March 8, 1971; June 28, 1971; March 7, 1973; September 17, 1977; March 3, 1978; April 28, 1978; November 7, 1978; December 10, 1978; February 2, 1979; March 4, 1979; March 14, 1979; April 17, 1979; June 3, 1979; February 7, 1980; March 12, 1980; December 24, 1980; November 9, 1981; January 6, 1982; October 18, 1982; March 2, 1983; May 27, 1983; June 5, 1983; September 20, 1983; September 25, 1983; May 27, 1983; January 29, 1984; September 28, 1984; September 30, 1984; November 9, 1984; November 14, 1984; November 18, 1984; November 22, 1984; November 29, 1984; November 30, 1984; August 15, 1985; October 1, 1985; October 4, 1985; November 14, 1985; December 1, 1985; December 15, 1985; January 12, 1986; January 21, 1986; April 13, 1986; May 17, 1996, review of *Cruising Paradise,* p. B12; June 16, 1996, review of *Buried Child,* p. H5.

New York Times Book Review, June 23, 1996, review of *Cruising Paradise,* p. 23; September 7, 1997, review of *Cruising Paradise,* p. 40.

Partisan Review, Volume XLI, number 2, 1974; Volume XLIX, number 2, 1982.

People, December 26, 1983; January 2, 1984; October 15, 1984; November 5, 1984; December 9, 1985;

January 6, 1986; June 10, 1996, p. 15; November 14, 1988, Peter Travers, review of *Far North,* p. 24.

Plays and Players, June, 1970; October-November, 1971; April, 1974; May, 1974; November, 1974; April, 1979.

Publishers Weekly, April 1, 1996, review of *Cruising Paradise,* p. 38; April 15, 1996, review of *Cruising Paradise,* p. 48; September 9, 2002, review of *Great Dream of Heaven,* pp. 40-41.

Quill & Quire, February, 1980.

Rolling Stone, August 11, 1977; December 18, 1986; February 24, 1994.

Saturday Review, December, 1984.

Spectator, November 16, 1996, review of *Cruising Paradise,* p. 51.

Theatre Journal, March, 1984.

Theatre Quarterly, August, 1974.

Time, November 27, 1972; June 6, 1983; October 8, 1984; August 12, 1985; December 2, 1985; December 16, 1985; November 7, 1988, Richard Corliss, review of *Far North,* pp. 108-109; May 20, 1996, Richard Zoglin, review of *Buried Child,* p. 77.

Times (London), September 24, 1983; September 26, 1983; October 6, 1984; January 7, 1986.

Times Literary Supplement, November 24, 1978; March 1, 1985; November 22, 1996, review of *Cruising Paradise,* p. 22.

Variety, September 14, 1988; May 20, 1991; February 8, 1993; September 19, 1994; May 5, 1997, Robert L. Daniels, review of *Curse of the Starving Class,* p. 213; February 16, 1998, Greg Evans, review of *Eyes for Consuela,* p. 68; July 16, 2001, Matt Wolf, review of *A Lie of the Mind,* p 25.

Village Voice, April 4, 1977; August 15, 1977; February 12, 1979.

Vogue, February, 1984; February, 1985.

Washington Post, January 14, 1979; June 2, 1979; March 5, 1983; April 22, 1983; October 23, 1983; April 12, 1985; October 15, 1985; May 1, 1986; September 12, 1986.

Western American Literature, fall, 1989, review of *True West,* p. 225.

Women's Wear Daily, March 13, 1970; May 27, 1983.

World Literature Today, winter, 1997, review of *Cruising Paradise,* p. 152.

ONLINE

Moonstruck Drama Bookstore Web site, http://www.imagi-nation.com/moonstruck/ (March 5, 2003), biography of Sam Shepard.

Pegasos Web site, http://www.kirjasto.sci.fi/ (March 5, 2003), biography of Sam Shepard.

Thespian Net Web site, http://www.thespiannet.com/ (March 5, 2003), biography of Sam Shepard.*

*   *   *

SLATE, Caroline 1934-
(Carol Brennan)

PERSONAL: Born December 23, 1934, in New York, NY; daughter of William (a dentist) and Irene (maiden name, Israel; present surnmae, Sayovitz) Gutzman; married Edward Beatty (a physician), December 19, 1954 (divorced, 1963); married Charles Leedham, 1968 (divorced, 1974); married Eamon Brennan (a public relations consultant), October 31, 1975; children: Richard Beatty and Joanna Maddock. *Education:* New York University, B.S., 1956; doctoral study at Hunter College of the City University of New York, 1965-69. *Politics:* "Democrat (usually)." *Religion:* "Jewish (culturally)." *Hobbies and other interests:* Theater, reading, walking.

ADDRESSES: Home—New York, NY. *Agent*—c/o Author Mail, Simon & Schuster, 1230 Avenue of the Americas, New York, NY 10020. *E-mail*—caroline@carolineslate.com.

CAREER: Author and Off-Broadway actress. Brennan & Brennan, New York, NY, partner, 1980, vice-president, 1985. Has worked in various positions, including as a teacher for speech-disabled children in the New York City Schools, a traveling television spokeswoman, a public relations manager for banks and corporate interests, a publicist for New York City's Planned Parenthood, a consultant to the Child Welfare League of America, the National Council of Juvenile Court Judges, and the Council of Adoptable Children.

WRITINGS:

(Under pseudonym Carol Brennan) *Headhunt,* Carroll & Graf (New York, NY), 1991.

(Under pseudonym Carol Brennan) *Full Commission,* Carroll & Graf (New York, NY), 1993.

(Under pseudonym Carol Brennan) *In the Dark,* Putnam (New York, NY), 1994.

(Under pseudonym Carol Brennan) *Chill of Summer,* Putnam (New York, NY), 1995.

The House on Sprucewood Lane, Pocket Books (New York, NY), 2002.

A Fractured Truth, Pocket Books (New York, NY), 2003.

SIDELIGHTS: Caroline Slate once told *CA* that she chose to first write mystery novels "not only as a release for hostility and because I like to read them, but because I figured the implicit need for structure would be an enormous help for a beginning writer, and it was." When her first novel, *Headhunt,* was published the author was "hooked." She told *CA:* "As though from nowhere, I wanted to write, and the 'perks' of wonderful places I could live while doing it rapidly took a back seat." The sequel to *Headhunt, Full Commission* follows the same protagonist (as the previous novel): a public relations executive in her early forties who carries battle scars from both the marriage and career wars, whose hostages to fortune include two children (each with a college tuition) and two cats, and who suffers the occasional dark night of the soul over growing old, possibly alone. All in all, the story is somewhat autobiographical.

Her novel *The House on Sprucewood Lane* is based on the real-life murder of six-year-old Jon Benet Ramsey of Boulder, Colorado. The death of the little girl captured headlines for months as police investigated possible suspects, including her parents. In Slate's novel, a fictionalized account based on the Ramsey case, the McQuade family is the focus of the investigation. The seemingly average American family is thrown into the limelight following the murder of Calista McQuade, their gifted ten-year-old gymnast daughter. As the investigation delves into the McQuade's life, the murky relationship between the various family members emerges, forming the backdrop to the mystery. Calista's father, Tom, a journalist, her mother, Melanie, the driving force behind her career, and Jared, her older brother, were all present in the house on the night of the murder and thus all of them are suspects.

The story unfolds through the eyes of Alexis Cavanaugh, Melanie's estranged sister, who has been summoned via e-mail by Jared, Calista's twelve-year-

old brother. Alexis and Melanie, although sisters, have been estranged for some time now because of Alexis's previous affair with Tom. As Alexis tries to solve the mystery of Calista's murder, she finds herself drawn to Jared, who reminds her of her own childhood. A reviewer for *Publishers Weekly* commented that Slate handles the subject of her novel "deftly, rounding her characters so that the reader can hear their ragged breathing."

BIOGRAPHICAL AND CRITICAL SOURCES:

PERIODICALS

Kirkus Reviews, February 1, 2002, review of *The House on Sprucewood Lane,* p. 137.

Publishers Weekly, February 18, 2002, review of *The House on Sprucewood Lane,* p. 76.

ONLINE

BookReporter, http://www.bookreporter.com/ (June 18, 2002), review of *The House on Sprucewood Lane.*

Caroline Slate Web site, http://www.carolineslate.com/ (May 9, 2002).*

*   *   *

SMITH, Dave
See SMITH, David (Jeddie)

*   *   *

SMITH, David (Jeddie) 1942-
(Smith Cornwell, Dave Smith)

PERSONAL: Born December 19, 1942, in Portsmouth, VA; son of Ralph Gerald (a naval engineer) and Catherine (Cornwell) Smith; married second wife, Deloras Mae Weaver, March 31, 1966; children: (second marriage) David Jeddie, Jr., Lael Cornwell, Mary Catherine. *Education:* University of Virginia, B.A. (with highest distinction), 1965; College of William and Mary, graduate study, 1966; Southern Illinois University, M.A., 1969; Ohio University, Ph.D., 1976.

ADDRESSES: Office—Department of English, Louisiana State University, 43 Allen Hall, Baton Rouge, LA 70803. *Agent*—Timothy Seldes, Russell and Volkening Inc., 50 West 29th Street, New York, NY 10001. *E-mail*—davesm@lsu.edu.

CAREER: High school teacher of French and English, and football coach, in Poquoson, VA, 1965-67; instructor at Night School Divisions, College of William and Mary, Williamsburg, VA, Christopher Newport College, Newport News, VA, and Thomas Nelson Community College, Hampton, VA, all 1969-72; Western Michigan University, Kalamazoo, instructor, 1973-74, assistant professor of English, Cottey College, Nevada, MO, 1974-75; University of Utah, Salt Lake City, associate professor of English and director of creative writing, 1976-80; State University of New York at Binghamton, visiting professor of English, 1980-81; creative writing summer program staff, Bennington College, VT, 1980-87; University of Florida, Gainesville, associate professor of English, 1981-82; Virginia Commonwealth University, Richmond, professor of American Literature 1982-89; Louisiana State University, Baton Rouge, professor of American Literature, 1990-96, Hopkins P. Breazle Foundation Professor of English, 1997-98; Boyd professor of English, 1998—. Editor, *Sou'wester,* 1967-68; editor, founder, and publisher, *Back Door* magazine, 1969-79; poetry editor, *Rocky Mountain Review,* 1978-80; poetry columnist, *American Poetry Review,* 1978-82; coeditor, *Southern Review,* 1990—. Has conducted poetry readings at colleges and universities. *Military service:* U.S. Air Force, 1969-72; became staff sergeant.

MEMBER: National Book Critics Circle, American Association of University Professors, Modern Language Association, Poetry Society of America, Poetry Society of Virginia, PEN, Associated Writing Programs (vice-president, 1982), Writers in Virginia, Academy of American Poets, Fellowship of Southern Writers, Phi Delta Theta.

AWARDS, HONORS: Fiction prize, *Miscellany,* 1972; Breadloaf Writers' Conference scholarship, summer, 1973; poetry prize, *Sou'wester,* 1973; *Kansas Quarterly Prize,* 1975; Borestone Mountain award, 1976; National Endowment for the Arts fellowship in poetry, 1976, 1981; Academy-Institute Award, American Academy and Institute of Arts and Letters, 1979;

David P. Gardner Award, 1979; *Portland Review* poetry prize, 1979; *Prairie Schooner* poetry prize, 1980; Guggenheim fellowship, 1981; Lyndhurst fellowship, 1987-89; Virginia Prize in Poetry, 1988; *Prairie Schooner* Reader's Award, 1995.

WRITINGS:

POETRY; UNDER NAME DAVE SMITH

Bull Island, Back Door Press (Poquoson, VA), 1970.

Mean Rufus Throw Down, Basilisk Press (Fredonia, NY), 1973.

The Fisherman's Whore, Ohio University Press (Athens, OH), 1974.

Drunks, Sou'wester (Edwardsville, IL), 1974.

Cumberland Station (also see below), University of Illinois Press (Urbana, IL), 1976.

In Dark, Sudden with Light, Croissant & Co. (Athens, OH), 1977.

Goshawk, Antelope (also see below), University of Illinois Press (Urbana, IL), 1979.

Homage to Edgar Allan Poe, Louisiana State University Press (Baton Rouge, LA), 1981.

Apparitions, Lord John (Northridge, CA), 1981.

Blue Spruce, Tamarack Editions (Syracuse, NY), 1981.

Dream Flights, University of Illinois Press (Urbana, IL), 1981.

In the House of the Judge, Harper & Row (New York, NY), 1983.

Gray Soldiers, Stuart Wright (Winston-Salem, NC), 1983.

The Roundhouse Voices: Selected and New Poems, Harper & Row (New York, NY), 1985.

Three Poems, Words Press, 1988.

Cuba Night, Morrow (New York, NY), 1990.

Night Pleasures: New and Selected Poems, Bloodaxe Books (Newcastle upon Tyne, UK), 1992.

Fate's Kite: Poems, 1991-1995, Louisiana State University Press (Baton Rouge, LA), 1995.

Tremble, Black Warrior Review, 1996.

Floating on Solitude: Three Volumes of Poetry (contains *Cumberland Station, Goshawk, Antelope,* and *Dream Flights*), University of Illinois Press (Urbana, IL), 1996.

The Wick of Memory: New and Selected Poems, 1970-2000, Louisiana State University Press (Baton Rouge, LA), 2000.

EDITOR; UNDER NAME DAVE SMITH

The Pure Clear Word: Essays on the Poetry of James Wright, University of Illinois Press (Urbana, IL), 1982.

(With David Bottoms) *The Morrow Anthology of Younger American Poets,* Morrow (New York, NY), 1985.

(And author of introduction) *The Essential Poe,* Ecco Press (New York, NY), 1990.

New Virginia Review, New Virginia Review, Inc., 1986.

New Virginia Review Anthology Four, New Virginia Review, Inc., 1986.

(And author of introduction) *The Essential Poe,* Ecco Press (New York, NY), 1991.

OTHER; UNDER NAME DAVE SMITH

Onliness (novel), Louisiana State University Press (Baton Rouge, LA), 1981.

Southern Delights: Poems and Stories, Croissant & Co. (Athens, OH), 1984.

Local Assays: On Contemporary American Poetry, University of Illinois Press (Urbana, IL), 1985.

Poems represented in many anthologies, including *I Love You All Day: It Is That Simple,* edited by Philip Dacey and Gerald Knoll, Abbey Press, 1970; *Heartland II,* edited by Lucien Stryk, Northern Illinois University Press (DeKalb, IL), 1975; and *American Poets in 1976,* edited by William Heyen, Bobbs-Merrill (New York, NY), 1976. *The Colors of Our Age* was released as a sound recording, Watershed, 1988. Contributor, sometimes under pseudonym Smith Cornwell, of short stories, poems, articles, and reviews to numerous popular and poetry magazines, including *American Poetry Review, Anteus, Nation, Southern Review, Shenandoah, New Yorker, Poetry, Poetry Northwest, Prairie Schooner,* and *Kenyon Review.* Poetry editor, University of Utah Press, 1977-87.

WORK IN PROGRESS: Against Oblivion: Essays on James Dickey's Poetry, for University of South Carolina Press; *The Crab's Pincer: New and Selected Essays on Poetry; Southern Poetry: An Anthology with Historical Introduction;* and *Below the Line: Essays on Southern Poetry,* all for Louisiana State University Press.

SIDELIGHTS: David Smith is "the legitimate heir to the Romantic tradition in America," according to Smith's friend and fellow poet Robert DeMott in *Dictionary of Literary Biography.* Smith told H. A. Maxon in the *Sam Houston Literary Review* that, like the great Transcendentalists Henry David Thoreau and Ralph Waldo Emerson, he sees writing poetry as a redemptive act: "In my life, poetry was very near a conversion. It was like a religious conviction had come into my life." As in the work of Robert Penn Warren, James Dickey, and other Southern poets, Smith's poems tend to explore the Southern narrative heritage, in the vein of Robert Penn Warren and James Dickey. His work includes the occasional grotesque image, and expresses a distinct regional sense of place, such as the Virginia tidewater region in which many of his early poems are set; Maryland in *Cumberland Station;* and Wyoming and Utah in *Goshawk, Antelope.* The books of poems that Smith has published range from full-length collections by major publishers to limited edition chapbooks by small presses, an indication of the kind of broad-range appeal he possesses.

Smith's first book, *Bull Island,* was a limited edition chapbook published by his own Back Door Press. It is structured around a journey back to the tidewater Virginia of his childhood, searching for a father figure. *Mean Rufus Throw Down,* his second small press book, shows the poet beginning to explore domestic subjects as well as regional ones, alternating narrative poems with short imagist poems. *The Fisherman's Whore* heralds both Smith's publication by a larger press and his notice by critics. Michael Heffernan, writing in *Commonweal,* praised its "fusion of poetry and prose," and Helen Vendler, in *Parnassus,* called Smith "a poet already capable of great control."

Cumberland Station was the book that brought Smith substantial critical notice. It is a circular quest in three movements: the first part, starting on the Virginia coast, concerns family origin and the historical past as he travels to the Cumberland, Maryland, railroad station where his grandfather was a ticket-seller; the second part has the poet in exile, encountering Midwest states, working hard to decode the parables they teach; and the final part brings the poet home to the coast, where, as Robert DeMott wrote, "the linked patterns of flowing images—boats, water, fish, rivers, music—capture the processional quality of Smith's vision." Dana Wier, in *Hollins Critic,* praised the book as "a celebration" and "a rich presentation of America's people, culture and landscape."

"It was not until his fourth collection, *Goshawk, Antelope,*" wrote Robert Phillips in *Hudson Review,* "that Dave Smith began to receive the wide critical attention his work deserves." The book, divided into four sections of about a dozen poems each, presents a number of poems that take on the starkness of the western landscape of Utah where Smith was teaching during this period. This collection, noted Michael McFee in *Parnassus,* shows "the mature Dave Smith," whose poems offer the "ambitious wordage" of "a poet of community and continuity" and "the complexity of shared experience."

In 1981, Smith published two new books. *Homage to Edgar Allan Poe* is a collection of brief poems, many less than a page, re-exploring family and sense of place, and the title sequence, in six sections, wrote Phillips, "entwines Poe's personal history with Smith's." *Dream Flights* presents seventeen poems that, as Thomas Swiss pointed out in *Sewanee Review,* "work through association, a complex linking that succeeds because of Smith's gift for creating a rich texture and backdrop for the action." *In The House of the Judge* received mixed reviews. Fred Chappell, in *Western Humanities Review,* criticized Smith's "heavy veneer of false elegance," and charged that "many of the lines are burdened with pronouns having unclear antecedents." Swiss, however, noted that "Smith is engaged with the literal and symbolic geographies of place," offering "less violence" and "less physical drama," so that this book has "a gentler touch." Following publication of *The Roundhouse Voices: Selected and New Poems,* a volume which Helen Vendler in the *New Yorker* called "a book too austerely thinned to give an adequate overview of his twenty years of poetic production," Smith published *Cuba Night.* Vendler singled out the book for its "Southern-gothic themes—family, memory, fear, fate, sex, violence," and indicated that, although Smith "walks a difficult line between the indignant and the overripe, . . . he manages a balance between the natural wrongness of life and the genuine rightness of art." Kathleen Norris, writing in *Library Journal,* called it "a deeply reflective, elegiac work full of . . . pleasurable music." *Night Pleasures: New and Selected Poems,* published in 1993, was Smith's first collection to appear in Britain.

The Wick of Memory: New and Selected Poems, 1970-2000, Smith's seventeenth collection, was published in 2001 and included more than one hundred poems. According to *New York Review of Books* critic Helen Vendler, the classic elements of Southern poetry are all present in *The Wick of Memory,* including images of rural life, a religious backdrop, echoes of the Civil War, and interracial relations. The collection is presented chronologically, and a *Publishers Weekly* reviewer noticed that the earlier work represented has "a formal elegance and a maritime musical panache akin to early [Robert] Lowell." The later work is less vital, according to that critic, especially when the poet takes on a "more confessional tone" and gives way to "prosaic speech." With other poems, "the wick catches anew," and the language takes on new energy.

Smith once told *CA:* "Whatever I write in the future will have to conform to two principles: I want poetry whose clarity is pronounced and resonant and I want poetry whose validity will be proved to the extent the poems embody the true, durable, and felt experience of emotional life." He named medievalist Robert Kellogg, jazz musician Dan Havens, novelist Jack Matthews, and singer Little Richard as artists most influential to him.

BIOGRAPHICAL AND CRITICAL SOURCES:

BOOKS

Contemporary Authors Autobiography Series, Volume 7, Gale (Detroit, MI), 1988.

Contemporary Literary Criticism, Volume 22, Gale (Detroit, MI), 1982, Volume 42, 1987.

Dictionary of Literary Biography, Volume 5: *American Poets since World War II,* Gale (Detroit, MI), 1980.

Evans, David Allan, editor, *New Voices in American Poetry,* Winthrop (Boston, MA), 1973.

Hales, Corrine, editor, *Contemporary Poets, Dramatists, Essayists, and Novelists of the South,* Greenwood Press, 1994.

Harris, Alex, editor, *A World Unsuspected,* University of North Carolina Press (Chapel Hill, NC), 1987.

Turner, Alberta, editor, *Poets Teaching,* Longman (New York, NY), 1980.

Vendler, Helen, *Part of Nature, Part of Us,* Harvard University Press (Cambridge, MA), 1980, pp. 289-302.

Weigl, Bruce, editor, *The Giver of Morning: On the Poetry of Dave Smith,* Thunder City Press (Birmingham, AL), 1982.

PERIODICALS

America, July 10, 1982, p. 36; December 15, 1990, p. 490.

American Book Review, May, 1982, p. 7.

American Literature, December, 1982, p. 632; October, 1986, p. 481.

American Poetry Review, November, 1977, p. 46; January/February, 1978, pp. 15-19; January/February, 1982, p. 32-35.

Antioch Review, spring, 1982, p. 225.

Booklist, September 15, 1979, p. 89; June 15, 1981, p. 1330; November 15, 1981, p. 427; September 15, 1981, p. 88; December 15, 1982, p. 550; January 15, 1986, p. 728.

Chicago Review, autumn, 1977, pp. 123-126.

Choice, January, 1975, p. 1635; May, 1977, p. 379; January, 1982, p. 630; November, 1982, p. 430; January, 1986, p. 745.

College Literature, spring, 1984, p. 200.

Commonweal, August 15, 1975, p. 346; January 6, 1978, p. 23; December 7, 1979, p. 701; March 11, 1983, p. 157.

Denver Quarterly, autumn, 1983, pp. 123-138.

Georgia Review, spring, 1980, pp. 202-212; fall, 1982, p. 675; winter, 1985, p. 849.

Hollins Critic, October, 1977, p. 18.

Hudson Review, winter, 1974-75, pp. 611-614; spring, 1978, p. 211; summer 1980, p. 301; autumn, 1981, p. 420; autumn, 1983, p. 589; summer, 1986, p. 345; winter, 1990, p. 598.

Journal of American Studies, August, 1983, p. 295.

Kenyon Review, spring, 1986, p. 113.

Kliatt Young Adult Paperback Book Guide, winter, 1982, p. 28.

Library Journal, February 15, 1974, p. 492; September 1, 1974, p. 2070; December 1, 1976, p. 2494; August, 1979, p. 1570; June 1, 1981, p. 1226; September 1, 1981, p. 1636; October 15, 1981, p. 2050; June 1, 1982, p. 1098; December 15, 1982, p. 2342; March 15, 1984, p. 598; August, 1985, p. 98; November 1, 1985, p. 100; February 1, 1990, p. 87; December, 1995, p. 116.

Nation, December 22, 1984, p. 687; October 5, 1985, p. 320.

New Criterion, December, 1985, p. 27-33.

New England Review, spring, 1982, p. 489; winter, 1983, p. 348; fall, 1991, p. 149.

New Leader, December 14, 1981, p. 16.

New Statesman and Society, July 30, 1993, p. 40.

New Yorker, June 30, 1980, p. 96; April 2, 1990, pp. 113-116.

New York Review of Books, November 7, 1985, p. 53; March 8, 2001, Helen Vendler, review of *The Wick of Memory: New and Selected Poems.*

New York Times Book Review, November 15, 1981, p. 14; April 18, 1982, p. 15; February 13, 1983, p. 15; January 12, 1986, p. 346.

North American Review, spring, 1977, p. 75; spring, 1980, p. 72.

Parnassus, fall-winter, 1975, pp. 195-205; spring-summer, 1977; fall-winter, 1980, p. 102; spring, 1983, p. 58; fall-winter, 1984, pp. 154-182.

Poetry, August, 1982, p. 293; February, 1984, p. 304; March, 1986, p. 346.

Poetry in Review, fall-winter, 1980, pp. 102-110.

Poetry Review, January-February, 1978, pp. 15-19.

Prairie Schooner, spring, 1974, p. 92; summer, 1984, p. 100.

Publishers Weekly, November 1, 1976, p. 73; June 25, 1979, p. 121; June 12, 1981, p. 50; August 7, 1981, p. 77; August 14, 1981, p. 50; December 17, 1982, p. 73; August 9, 1985, p. 72; January 5, 1990, p. 67; October 23, 1995, p. 64; March 27, 2000, review of *The Wick of Memory: New and Selected Poems, 1970-2000.*

Sam Houston Literary Review, November, 1977, pp. 64-74.

Saturday Review, September 16, 1978, p. 42.

Sewanee Review, summer, 1980, p. 474; fall, 1982, p. 612; summer, 1983, p. 483; fall, 1983, p. 83; winter, 1989, pp. 543-555; spring, 1992, p. 311.

Southern Humanities Review, winter, 1987, p. 94; winter, 1991, p. 99.

Southern Review, spring, 1990, p. 456.

Sou'wester, spring-summer, 1974, pp. 56-64.

Stand, summer, 1988, p. 72; winter, 1993, pp. 77-80.

Sulfur, March, 1986, p. 175.

Three Rivers Poetry Journal, spring, 1977, pp. 6-9.

Times Literary Supplement, November 27, 1981, p. 1388; May 22, 1987, p. 557; April 30, 1993, p. 23.

TriQuarterly, fall, 1985, pp. 245-258.

Village Voice, May 5, 1980, p. 36; November 25, 1981, p. 47.

Virginia Quarterly Review, spring, 1980, p. 62; spring, 1982, p. 60; autumn, 1983, p. 135; winter, 1986, p. 27; summer, 1990, p. 99.

Washington Post Book World, October 4, 1981, p. 4; April 3, 1983, p. 10; January 5, 1986, p. 6.

Western Humanities Review, autumn, 1977, p. 371; autumn, 1983, p. 251; spring, 1987, p. 87.

Wilson Quarterly, winter, 1981, p. 158.

Yale Review, March, 1977, p. 407.*

STACKPOLE, Michael A(ustin) 1957-

PERSONAL: Born November 27, 1957, in Wausau WI; son of James Ward (a physician) and Janet (an educator and community volunteer; maiden name, Kerin) Stackpole; companion of Elizabeth Turner Danforth (an artist). *Ethnicity:* "Caucasian/Irish-American." *Education:* University of Vermont, B.A., 1979. *Politics:* Democrat. *Religion:* Roman Catholic. *Hobbies and other interests:* Indoor soccer, arena football, gaming, shooting.

ADDRESSES: Agent—Ricia Mainhardt, 612 Argyle, No. 5-L, Brooklyn, NY 11230.

CAREER: Flying Buffalo, Inc., Scottsdale, AZ, game designer, 1979-87; writer, 1987—.

MEMBER: Game Manufacturers Association (chairperson of Industry Watch Committee), Science Fiction and Fantasy Writers of America, Academy of Gaming Arts and Design, Phoenix Skeptics (executive director, 1988—).

AWARDS, HONORS: H. G. Wells Awards, best role playing adventure, 1983, for *Citybook I,* and 1984, for *Stormhaven;* Best Adventure Game, Computer Gaming World, 1988, for *Wasteland,* and 1989, for *Neuromancer; Wasteland* was inducted into the Computer Gaming World's Hall of Fame, 1993; Meritorious Service Award, Game Manufacturers Association, 1993; inducted into Academy of Gaming Arts and Design Hall of Fame, 1994.

WRITINGS:

NOVELS

Natural Selection, FASA Corp. (Chicago, IL), 1992.
Assumption of Risk, FASA Corp. (Chicago, IL), 1993.
Bred for War, FASA Corp. (Chicago, IL), 1994.
Once a Hero, Bantam (New York), 1994.
Mutant Chronicles: Dementia, FASA Corp. (Chicago, IL), 1994.
Malicious Intent, FASA Corp. (Chicago, IL), 1996.

"WARRIOR" SERIES

Warrior: En Garde, FASA Corp. (Chicago, IL), 1988.
Warrior: Riposte, FASA Corp. (Chicago, IL), 1988.
Warrior: Coupe, FASA Corp. (Chicago, IL) 1989.

"BLOOD OF KERENSKY" SERIES

Lethal Heritage, FASA Corp. (Chicago, IL), 1990.
Blood Legacy, FASA Corp. (Chicago, IL), 1990.
Lost Destiny, FASA Corp. (Chicago, IL), 1991.

"DARK CONSPIRACY" SERIES

A Gathering Evil, Game Designers Workshop (Bloomington, IL), 1991.
Evil Ascending, Game Designers Workshop (Bloomington, IL), 1991.
Evil Triumphant, Game Designers Workshop (Bloomington, IL), 1992.

"STAR WARS X-WING" SERIES

The Krytos Trap, Bantam (New York, NY), 1996.
Rogue Squadron, Bantam (New York, NY), 1996.
Wedge's Gamble, Bantam (New York, NY), 1996.
The Bacta War, Bantam (New York, NY), 1998.
Battleground: Tatooine, Dark Horse Comics (Milwaukie, OR), 1998.
The Phantom Affair, Dark Horse Comics (Milwaukie, OR), 1998.
The Warrior Princess, Dark Horse Comics (Milwaukie, OR), 1998.
(With Steve Crespo, James W. Hall, and Drew Johnson) *Blood and Honor,* Dark Horse Comics (Milwaukie, OR), 1999.
In the Empire's Service, Dark Horse Comics (Milwaukie, OR), 1999.
Isard's Revenge, Bantam (New York, NY), 1999.
Requiem for a Rogue, Dark Horse Comics (Milwaukie, OR), 1999.
Masquerade, Dark Horse Comics (Milwaukie, OR), 2000.
Mandatory Retirement, Dark Horse Comics (Milwaukie, OR), 2001.

"STAR WARS: THE NEW JEDI ORDER" SERIES

Dark Tide I: Onslaught, Del Rey (New York, NY), 2000.
Dark Tide II: Ruin, Del Rey (New York), 2000.

"DRAGONCROWN WAR CYCLE" SERIES

The Dark Glory War: A Prelude to the DragonCrown War Cycle, Bantam (New York, NY), 2000.
Fortress Draconis, Bantam (New York, NY), 2001.
When Dragons Rage, Bantam Books (New York, NY), 2002.

"MECHWARRIOR DARK AGE" SERIES

Ghost War, Roc, 2002.

"BATTLETECH" SERIES

Bred for War, New American Library (New York, NY), 1995.
Malicious Intent, New American Library (New York, NY), 1996.
The Twilight of the Clans II: Grave Covenant, New American Library (New York, NY), 1997.
Prince of Havoc, Roc, 1998.
Warrior: Coupe, Roc, 1998.

"REALMS OF CHAOS" SERIES

A Hero Born, Harper Mass Market Paperbacks (New York, NY), 1997.
An Enemy Reborn, Harper Mass Market Paperbacks (New York, NY), 1998.

OTHER

(Editor, with Liz Danforth) *Mages Blood and Old Bones,* Flying Buffalo (Scottsdale, AZ), 1992.
Talion: Revenant, Spectra (New York, NY), 1997.
Eyes of Silver, Spectra (New York, NY), 1998.
I, Jedi, Bantam (New York, NY), 1998.
(Contributor) *Magic: The Gathering Distant Planes,* Harper Collins Canada (Toronto, ON), 1999.
(With Timothy Zahn and Carlos Ezquerra) *Star Wars— Mara Jade: By the Emperor's Hand,* Dark Horse Comics (Milwaukie, OR), 1999.
Star Wars: Union, Dark Horse Comics (Milwaukie, OR), 2000.

GAMES

Citybook I, Flying Buffalo (Scottsdale, AZ), 1983.
Stormhaven, Flying Buffalo (Scottsdale, AZ), 1984.
Wasteland, Interplay Productions (Los Angeles, CA), 1988.
Neuromancer, Interplay Productions (Los Angeles), 1989.
Wolf and Raven, Roc, 1998.
(Author of foreword) *Core Rulebook (Star Wars Role Playing Game),* Wizards of the Coast (Renton, WA), 2000.

Author of nonfiction books on gaming. Work represented in anthologies, including *Shrapnel,* FASA Corp., 1988; *Into the Shadows,* FASA Corp., 1990; *An Armory of Swords,* edited by Fred Saberhagen, Tor Books (New York, NY), 1995; *Warriors of Blood and Dreams,* Avon (New York, NY), 1995; *Superheroes,* Ace (New York, NY), 1995; and *Insufficient Evidence: Distant Planes,* Harper, 1996.

Contributor of short stories to magazines, including *Amazing Stories,Challenge, Star Wars Adventure Journal, Kage, Autoduel Quarterly,* and *Space Gamer.*

SIDELIGHTS: As a prolific writer and creator of computer games, Michael A. Stackpole relies heavily on the science fiction universe for inspiration and tradition. His numerous books make up various series, some of his own creation, and others drawn from existing fictional worlds, as in his "Star Wars" series. In either case, reviewers are generally impressed with Stackpole's efforts. Reviewing 1998's *I, Jedi,* a critic for *Publishers Weekly* praised the novel as "lavish" and found the hero, Corran Han, to be "a more complex protagonist than many, formidably competent but with believable limitations." Roland Green of *Booklist* commented on the secondary characters, noting that that it is "unusual and pleasurable to see Luke, Leia, and Han as comparative bit players in the SW [Star Wars] universe."

Years of writing science fiction novels apparently have not dulled Stackpole's ability to write innovative stories, if the reviews of 2001's *Fortress Draconis* are any indication. *Booklist*'s Paula Luedtke declared, "With a deliciously evil antagonist and some truly remarkable supporting characters, this is a terrific read."

Jackie Cassada of *Library Journal* regarded the books as "a solid addition to the epic fantasy genre." A reviewer for *Publishers Weekly* made special mention of the novel's exciting conclusion, commenting, "As usual, Stackpole provides a compelling and engaging escape."

Stackpole once told *CA:* "My writing process is pretty basic. I tend to work in three-hour blocks, morning and afternoon, usually turning out a chapter per session. I work very fast by comparison with many of my peers. It is often suggested that a writer who works fast cannot do good work, but I think that's utterly fallacious. People in all manner of professions work at different speeds and, in almost all of them, efficiency and speed is considered a good thing. Whether I write well when writing fast is a matter for each reader to decide.

"I believe that writers and readers are involved in an elaborate game of 'Name That Tune.' A reader's job is to say to himself, 'Okay, it's page ninety-seven, and I know how this story will end.' The writer's job is to keep laying the story out in a manner that precludes the reader from being right. When it is done correctly, the reader can look back and find all the clues laid out there. While I seldom reread novels myself, I know my readers do, so I like to toss in little details that emerge only on a second or third read.

"My motivations for writing are simple. I want to write the kind of story I like to read. I want to create stories that entertain the readers. I want to make readers feel for characters and care about what happens to them because, by involving a reader on an emotional level, a book can allow the reader to experience things that are outside the purview of a normal life. I also write for money, because bills have to be paid.

"Much of my work is set in brand-name universes, areas where other writers refuse to work because they think they will be too restricted. I don't feel restricted, because I do my research and learn very quickly what is out of bounds and what areas I am free to explore. I also make a corner of that universe my own, so I am at home there and can tell the kind of story I like to tell. Readers bring to these books a set of assumptions about the kind of story that will be told, and that allows me to thwart them, distract them, and ultimately surprise them. No one really wants to read a story in which they know what will happen, so I constantly work at exploding preconceptions while providing an entertaining story.

"A number of writers have influenced me. From Edgar Rice Burroughs I learned how to structure a plot, and I got a refresher course in that from Frederick Forsyth. Walter Gibson, Lester Dent, and Rex Stout all showed me how to make fascinating characters from individuals who are largely unknowable. J. R. R. Tolkien showed how a contemporary author can tap into the elements of myth, Dennis L. McKiernan and Stephan Donaldson showed how it could be done differently and better, and Roger Zelazny showed how the use of detail can suggest whole universes.

"Much of my work is military in nature. I find warfare fascinating and decidedly terrifying. Except for a natural disaster, war is the most catastrophic thing that can happen to a human being. Despite its horrors, war is a crucible that creates heroes, and it is their stories that I like to tell. My books don't praise war, but they praise the triumph of individuals over war.

"I also include politics in my books, because I find the games people play to obtain and preserve power are very interesting. Political maneuvering often resembles a game of chess, with gambits set up, exchanges offered, and traps set. The fun part about stories is that, every so often, a pawn can stand up and refuse to be used. Politics is not an exact science, and that makes it tricky to deal with and fun to write about (and vilifying politicians is so cathartic!)."

BIOGRAPHICAL AND CRITICAL SOURCES:

PERIODICALS

Booklist, April 15, 1998, Roland Green, review of *I, Jedi,* p. 1357; November 15, 2001, Paula Luedtke, review of *Fortress Draconis,* p. 560.

Library Journal, December, 2001, Jackie Cassada, review of *Fortress Draconis,* p. 181.

Publishers Weekly, April 27, 1998, review of *I, Jedi,* pp. 50-51; November 26, 2001, review of *Fortress Draconis,* pp. 44-45.

ONLINE

Michael A. Stackpole's Home Page, http://www.storm wolf.com/ (March 23, 2003).*

STERN, Richard (Gustave) 1928-

PERSONAL: Born February 25, 1928, in New York, NY; son of Henry George (a dentist) and Marion (Veit) Stern; married Gay Clark, March 14, 1950 (divorced, February, 1972); married Alane Rollings, August 9, 1985; children: (first marriage) Christopher, Kate, Andrew, Nicholas. *Education:* University of North Carolina, B.A., 1947; Harvard University, M.A., 1949; University of Iowa, Ph.D., 1954.

ADDRESSES: Office—Department of English, University of Chicago, 1050 East 59th St., Chicago, IL 60637.

CAREER: Jules Ferry College, Versailles, France, lecturer, 1949-50; University of Heidelberg, Heidelberg, Germany, lecturer, 1950-51; educational advisor, U.S. Army, 1951-52; Connecticut College, New London, CT, instructor, 1954-55; University of Chicago, Chicago, IL, assistant professor, 1956-61, associate professor, 1962-64, professor of English, 1965—, Helen Regenstein professor of English, 1990—. Visiting lecturer, University of Venice, 1962-63, University of California, Santa Barbara, 1964 and 1968, State University of New York at Buffalo, 1966, Harvard University, 1969, University of Nice, 1970, University of Urbino, 1977.

MEMBER: American Academy of Arts and Sciences, Philological Society (University of Chicago), Phi Beta Kappa.

AWARDS, HONORS: Longwood Award, 1960; Friends of Literature Award; Rockefeller grant, 1965; *Stitch* was selected as one of the American Library Association's books of the year, 1965; National Institute of Arts and Letters grant, 1968; Guggenheim fellowship, 1973-74; Carl Sandburg Award, Friends of the Chicago Public Library, 1979, for *Natural Shocks;* Award of Merit for the Novel, American Academy and Institute of Arts and Letters, 1986; Chicago *Sun-Times* book of the year award for *Noble Rot: Stories, 1949-1988,* 1989; Heartland Award, best work of non-fiction, 1995.

WRITINGS:

Golk (novel), Criterion (Torrance, CA), 1960.
Europe; or, Up and Down with Schreiber and Baggish (novel), McGraw-Hill (New York, NY), 1961,

Richard Stern

published as *Europe; or, Up and Down with Baggish and Schreiber,* MacGibbon & Kee (London, England), 1962.
In Any Case (novel), McGraw, 1963, published as *The Chaleur Network,* Second Chance (Sag Harbor, NY), 1981.
Teeth, Dying, and Other Matters [and] *The Gamesman's Island: A Play,* Harper (New York, NY), 1964.
Stitch (novel), Harper (New York, NY), 1965.
(Editor) *Honey and Wax: Pleasures and Powers of Narrative,* University of Chicago Press (Chicago, IL), 1966.
1968: A Short Novel, an Urban Idyll, Five Stories, and Two Trade Notes, Holt (New York, NY), 1970.
The Books in Fred Hampton's Apartment (essays), Dutton (New York, NY), 1973.
Other Men's Daughters (novel), Dutton (New York, NY), 1973.
Natural Shocks (novel), Coward, McCann and Geoghegan (New York, NY), 1978.

Packages (short-story collection), Coward, McCann and Geoghegan (New York, NY), 1980.

The Invention of the Real (collected essays and poems), University of Georgia Press (Athens, GA), 1982.

A Father's Words (novel), Arbor House (New York, NY), 1986.

The Position of the Body, Northwestern University Press (Evanston, IL), 1986.

Noble Rot: Stories, 1949-1988, Grove Press (New York, NY), 1988.

Shares and Other Fictions, Delphinium (Harrison, NY), 1992.

One Person and Another: On Writers and Writing, Baskerville (Dallas, TX), 1993.

A Sistermony, Donald I. Fine (New York, NY), 1995.

Pacific Tremors (novel), Northwestern University Press (Evanston, IL), 2001.

Contributor to numerous periodicals, including *Partisan Review* and the *New York Times.* Manuscript collection is housed at the Regenstein Library, University of Chicago.

SIDELIGHTS: "Richard Stern is American letters' unsung comic writer about serious matters," Doris Grumbach wrote in the *Chicago Tribune.* "He is, further, that oddity among novelists, a writers' writer, a critics' writer, whose name is not part of household vocabulary." Unlike Saul Bellow, with whom he shares artistic and thematic concerns, Stern has not gained wide recognition in popular circles or among the mainstream of academe. As Julian Barnes observed in *New Statesman,* "An obstinate and selfish attachment to lucidity debars his work from the attention of problem-solving academics; while his tense intelligence discourages holiday skimmers." Yet the long-time University of Chicago professor, in over fifty years of writing poetry, fiction, and nonfiction, has earned a significant amount of respect in the world of literature, as is evidenced by the Award of Merit for the Novel he received in 1986 from the American Academy and Institute of Arts and Letters.

Stern's approach to writing has often been at the heart of critical evaluation of his work. "A novelist who began by writing poetry," Peter Straub noted in *New Statesman,* "[he] was always concerned with, and fiercely delighted by, the possibilities within language and narrative technique, and shares with the best

American prose its self-awareness and daring." Typically, in his writing less means more. "Stern's short stories are short," explained *New Republic* contributor Mark Harris. "His novels and reportage have always been concise, compressed. Economy of language is his rule." As the reviewer pointed out, this characteristic, while viewed by Stern's proponents as an important strength, may be one of the reasons the author's works have not enjoyed more popular readership. "This is regrettable," Harris concluded, "since, if the task of reading him requires a greater concentration than we are accustomed to apply to mere jewels of literary art, the reward of reading him is proportionately greater as well."

Stern emerged on the literary scene in 1960, publishing his first novel in that year and two others by 1963. "What struck one from the first was Stern's command of the novelist's resources: an ample and supple language, a lively, vigorous narrative style, a sense of character and scene, of place, person and significant action," Saul Maloff asserted in *Commonweal.* "The generosity and sophistication of his mind, those characteristics which emerge first in depth of style, evident in his first novel, *Golk,* were fully present a year later in his second, *Europe; or, Up and Down with Baggish and Schreiber,*" commented Straub, "giving deep tones to that book's comedy—the bank he's been drawing on ever since." Of Stern's third novel, *In Any Case,* a story of espionage and treason during World War II, Straub added: "Every chapter is packed with know-how and knowingness, a hundred different kinds of sentence, stunning usages, metaphorically apt information, brilliant speculation and question."

In his 1973 novel, *Other Men's Daughters,* Stern addresses the theme of a middle-aged, married man's love for a young college student. Robert Merriwether, a doctor who teaches at Harvard University, is caught in an unhappy marriage to Sara when he meets Cynthia, half his age, "beautiful, witty, intelligent, understanding, well-educated and wholly in love with him," wrote *New York Times* critic Anatole Broyard. "He is decent, kindly and modest, she is eager, intelligent and sad, and without his wife or her father their relationship would have no problems," a *Times Literary Supplement* reviewer observed, "unless one perversely concludes that without these problems there would be no relationship, a view Merriwether himself seems to have some time for."

Other Men's Daughters "is a consideration, at once witty and painful, of marital malaise, extra-marital rejuvenation and the hard emotional burdens attendant to both," wrote Jonathan Yardley in *Washington Post Book World.* While the reviewer pointed out that the novel's subject is nothing new—it is, in fact, common to the time in which it was written—he admitted, "I cannot recall its being treated elsewhere in recent fiction with more fidelity to and understanding of the truths of separation, divorce and readjustment."

Here as before, Stern's technique and style drew significant critical attention. James R. Frakes commented in the *New York Times Book Review* that "though not really experimental in structure, *Other Men's Daughters* makes use of some unusual time-patterns, with convolutions and overlays, flashbacks and flash-forwards." In the reviewer's opinion, "The end result is not obscurantism but enrichment."

New York Review of Books contributor Michael Wood focused on the style conveyed in the novel. "Style," he wrote, "is what saves buried lives from extinction, style is the mark of an exceptional and delicate attention." Moreover, according to Wood, "Stern has a style in a perfectly old-fashioned sense, and *Other Men's Daughters* is an old-fashioned novel, an impressive plea for the private life as a continuing subject for serious fiction."

Natural Shocks examines another, yet more complicated, relationship between an older man and a younger woman. Frederick Wursup, a worldly, caustic journalist, accepts an assignment for an article on death. His subject becomes Cicia, a young woman losing her battle with cancer. As he becomes more involved with Cicia's case, Wursup's private feelings begin to intrude on his professional decisions, and he starts to realize, as *Newsweek*'s Peter S. Prescott observed, "how fully his life had become mired in the trivialities of his profession, how stunted his education in feeling."

Prescott found the author of *Natural Shocks* "a remarkably deft and witty writer" and characterized the novel as "wound so tight as to have a springy texture; aphorisms abound." *National Review* contributor Paul Lukacs, however, expressed reservations about Stern's emphasis on idea over character. He described *Natural Shocks*'s supporting characters as "formless; they are specimens of life . . . but they are not characters in a work of fiction." He also argued that the novel is not

so much the story of Wursup's growing self-awareness, but rather "in truth it is about Stern's one dominant *idea*—namely, a man's relationship with death and with his self."

New York Times book reviewer Christopher Lehmann-Haupt drew different conclusions. He wrote that the novel "has a superstructure that is as solid and timeless as a folktale, . . . fairly teems with vividly realized men and women, . . . and prose—energetic, muscular, intelligent, playful prose, bristling with epigrams and allusions, yet never distracting from the onward rush of the story it unfolds." Furthermore, Lehmann-Haupt remarked that "the book is about death, yes, but more than that, it is about the deaths of fathers and children and lovers and mentors. And it is about journalism—public events viewed by public men for the consumption of the public. And about the relationship between the public and the private."

In his 1986 novel *A Father's Words,* Stern offers the story of Cy Riemer, editor of a Chicago science newsletter, and his four grown children. Divorced from his children's mother, Cy is beginning a relationship with a young girlfriend and trying to set in order his relationships with his sons and daughters. "Family is the novel's subject," wrote Geoffrey Wolff in *Los Angeles Times Book Review,* "and particularly the idiom of a particular family, particularly American."

Central to this examination of the family is Cy's troubles with his son Jack. "The discord between father and son is one of the oldest stories and traditionally told from the son's point of view," commented Prescott in another *Newsweek* article. But as the reviewer pointed out, "What Stern has done here is to explore it from the father's perspective." This break from tradition can also be seen in the role given Cy in this novel. In an interview with Garry Abrams published in the *Los Angeles Times,* the author discussed his novel and the changing nature of fatherhood in our day and age. Fathers are "having relationships with their children that they didn't have in the past," Stern said. "The father is a competitor, a brother, a friend in a way that didn't exist for most of human history. . . . The old paternal-filial decorum is under a lot of pressure."

In *A Father's Words,* commented John Bowers in the *New York Times Book Review,* "Stern gives us a glimmer of fatherhood and how it goes to the marrow of one's bones." The author creates his portrait of the present-day father "by forgoing straight narrative and employing intelligent bits of business, little snippets of comment, disregarding sequence of time," Bowers added. This effort earned Stern praise from *New York Times* contributor John Gross. The reviewer wrote: "he is an unusually crisp and intelligent writer, with a sharp edge to his wit; and in *A Father's Words* he runs true to form. Many of the book's pleasures are incidental: jokes, intellectual cadenzas, agile turns of phrase." Bowers concluded, "Richard Stern may be compared to a jeweler. He worries and frets and tinkers to get the smallest matters just right—the jewellike *Father's Words* is an example."

A collection of Stern's short works of fiction are found in *Noble Rot: Stories, 1949-1988.* The title alludes to the putrid soil that is necessary to produce fine wines. Among the characters in the book's thirty-two stories are what Sven Birkerts of *New Republic* called "grumbling husbands and wives, depressed grad students, small-time operators, lovelorn spinsters, struggling retirees. . . . All have been rendered with a fascination for circumstance and setting . . . and with an eye for their psychological particularity." David R. Slavitt observed in *American Book Review* that "the stories are lively, well-crafted pieces, with a tough-guy Chicago voice that allows the narrator a certain freedom."

Stern stayed with the shorter form in his next book, *Shares and Other Fictions,* which contains two novellas and several short stories. The theme of the collection is the uncertain emotional ground between fathers and sons. "This ancient theme becomes original in Stern's hands," wrote Joseph Coates for *Chicago Tribune Book World,* "because it is handled so consistently from the father's viewpoint." In *One Person and Another,* a collection of essays also culled from a period of forty years, Stern examines the literary world with his usual forthright style. "Stern's observations are resolutely intelligent and interesting," noted August Kleinzahler of *Small Press,* who added that the author is "opinionated and proud of it." Mark Shechner of the *Chicago Tribune* wrote, "This flurry of auto-compilation is good news for the reader who has acquired a taste for that mixture of piquant detail and sharp irony that is Stern's signature." Among the subjects for Stern's analysis are twentieth-century authors Lillian Hellman, Ezra Pound, Samuel Beckett, Joyce Carol Oates, and Norman Mailer. The collection also includes a satirical play that speculates on how Dante and Shakespeare would fare in a modern litigious society.

In the memoir titled *Sistermony,* Stern chronicles his sister's battle with uterine cancer and his own insights into their ambivalent relationship. The effect, according to Scott Donaldson of the *Chicago Tribune,* is far from a romantic tribute. While Stern honestly presents what he considers his sister's shortcomings, the author is even harder on himself. But, as Donaldson noted, "as Ruth's illness runs its course, Richard begins to emerge from such obsessive self-repugnance into what his sister meant to him." This new insight also extends to other areas of the writer's life. A review in the *Los Angeles Book Review* chided Stern for the book's solipsism, but for Aaron Cohen of *Booklist,* the book's wide-ranging scope was a sign of craft. "Stern can conjure up a complex characterization in a few paragraphs," he commented.

After a long spell away from novels, Stern published *Pacific Tremors,* about which Donna Seaman commented in *Booklist,* "Happily, this vital and extraordinarily touching novel about two old friends and the romance of movies exceeds all expectations." The "old friends" are a renowned movie director, Ezra Kenert, and a film historian, Wendell Spear, an aging pair dealing with the literal and emotional implications involved in the realization that their creative days are drawing to an end. "The specters of physical disability and loss of vocation provide tension of one sort, while flashbacks and flash-forwards reveal familial problems," wrote Jack Hafer for *Library Journal.* "Mirroring the unsteady emotional condition of those living on the Pacific Rim, the title is fitting." Richard Schickel noted in his review of the book in the *Los Angeles Times* that here, Stern "flirts with the discovery of myth." While he commented that Stern gives little time to "detail and structural nicety," nor has a realistic grasp on the workings of the film industry, Schickel called the book ". . . artful, eccentric and pleasing . . . flawed in [its] way but notably—sometimes even nobly—resistant to the conventions of Hollywood fictions, the cliches of Hollywood historiography." Seaman concluded her review by commenting: "Stern covers a stupendous amount of emotional territory with verve and masterful economy, expressing great warmth and affection for humanity, fretful creatures bedazzled by illusion yet devoted to truth."

Stern's writing stands apart from much of the fiction created by his contemporaries in that, as Charles Monaghan suggested in *Commonweal,* it concentrates on "personal moral questions." David Kubal elaborated on the author's place in contemporary fiction in an essay in *Hudson Review:* "Mr. Stern's lucidity, together with his capacity for affection and the comic, are very rare qualities, shortages in contemporary literature. The informed reading public, at least, wants its fictive realities uncontaminated by an author's suggestion that human character is greater than its circumstances, or that the condition itself has its goodness, or that anyone should be forgiven or tolerated." Yet, as Kubal concluded, "That Mr. Stern continues to offer these consolations in a body of work . . . tells us of his artistic integrity."

BIOGRAPHICAL AND CRITICAL SOURCES:

PERIODICALS

American Book Review, October-November, 1994, David R. Slavitt, review of *Noble Rot: Stories, 1949-1988.*

Booklist, June 15, 1992; October 15, 1993; February 15, 1995, p. 1054; December 15, 2001, Donna Seaman, review of *Pacific Tremors,* p. 705.

Chicago Tribune, April 6, 1986; December 11, 1986; January 22, 1989; October 31, 1993, p. 6; March 19, 1995, p. 3.

Chicago Tribune Book World, April 6, 1986; September 6, 1992, pp. 4-5.

Commonweal, May 13, 1960, Charles Monaghan, "New Traditions," review of *Golk,* pp. 188-190; December 14, 1962, Saul Maloff, "A Personal Quest," review of *In Any Case,* pp. 319-320.

Hudson Review, autumn, 1981, David Kubal, review of *Packages,* pp. 458-459.

Library Journal, January, 2002, Jack Hafer, review of *Pacific Tremors,* p. 155.

Los Angeles Times, June 15, 1986; February 17, 1989; October 11, 1992; April 2, 1995; February 10, 2002, Richard Schickel, review of *Pacific Tremors,* p. R-2.

Los Angeles Times Book Review, May 9, 1986, Geoffrey Wolff, review of *A Father's Words,* p. 1; April 2, 1995, p.6.

National Review, May 26, 1978.

New Republic, November 15, 1980, Mark Harris, review of *Packages;* February 20, 1989.

New Statesman, May 10, 1974, Peter Straub, pp. 668-669; September 22, 1978, Julian Barnes, review of *Natural Shocks,* pp. 377-378.

Newsweek, January 2, 1978; November 3, 1980, Peter S. Prescott, review of *Packages,* p. 88; March 24, 1986.

New York Review of Books, August 13, 1970; December 13, 1973, Michael Wood, review of *Other Men's Daughters,* pp. 19-23; February 23, 1978, Roger Sale, review of *Natural Shocks,* pp. 42-44.

New York Times, October 16, 1973, Anatole Broyard, review of *Other Men's Daughters,* p. 41; January 9, 1978, Christopher Lehmann-Haupt, review of *Natural Shocks,* p. C29; April 11, 1986.

New York Times Book Review, May 1, 1960; October 14, 1962; December 19, 1965; March 25, 1973; November 18, 1973, James R. Frakes, review of *Other Men's Daughters,* pp. 4-5; January 1, 1978, Anatole Broyard, review of *Natural Shocks,* pp. 12, 21; January 9, 1978; September 7, 1980; June 15, 1986; September 27, 1992.

Partisan Review, spring, 1965.

Publishers Weekly, January 20, 1989; June 22, 1992; January 2, 1995, pp. 64-65.

Saturday Review, December 11, 1965; January 21, 1978.

Small Press, spring, 1994, August Kleinzahler, review of *One Person and Another,* p. 79.

Times Literary Supplement, May 10, 1974, review of *Other Men's Daughters,* p. 493; October 27, 1978; November 21, 1980, Nicholas Spoliar, review of *Packages,* p. 1342.

Virginia Quarterly Review, winter, 1983.

Washington Post, May 9, 1986.

Washington Post Book World, October 28, 1973, Jonathan Yardley, review of *Other Men's Daughters;* October 19, 1980; February 1, 1987.*

T-V

TIGER, John
    See WAGER, Walter H(erman)

*   *   *

TOWNE, Peter
    See NABOKOV, Peter (Francis)

*   *   *

TRUBO, Richard 1946-

PERSONAL: Born April 2, 1946, in Los Angeles, CA; son of William and Ida (Singer) Trubo; married Donna Grodin (a teacher), June 24, 1973; children: Melissa Suzanne. *Education:* University of California, Los Angeles, B.A., 1967, M.A., 1968.

ADDRESSES: Home—Irvine, CA. *Agent*—c/o Author Mail, 1332 North Halsted St., Chicago, IL 60622-2694.

CAREER: KOST Radio, Los Angeles, CA, producer-writer, 1968-71; free-lance writer, 1971—.

MEMBER: American Society of Journalists and Authors, Authors Guild.

WRITINGS:

An Act of Mercy, Nash Publishing (Los Angeles, CA), 1973.
(With Richard Guarino) *The Great American Insurance Hoax,* Nash Publishing (Los Angeles, CA), 1974.
(With Guarino) *Your Insurance Handbook,* Doubleday (New York, NY), 1975.
How to Get a Good Night's Sleep, Little, Brown (Boston, MA), 1978.
The Consumer's Book of Hints and Tips, Jonathan David (New York, NY), 1978.
(With David E. Bresler) *Free Yourself from Pain,* Simon & Schuster (New York, NY), 1979.
(With Barry Behrstock) *The Parents' When-Not-to-Worry Book: Straight Talk about All Those Myths You've Learned from Your Parents, Friends—and Even Doctors,* Harper (New York, NY), 1981.
(With Harold H. Benjamin) *From Victim to Victor: The Wellness Community Guide to Fighting for Recovery for Cancer Patients and Their Families,* Jeremy P. Tarcher (Los Angeles, CA), 1987.
(With Michael Yessis) *Secrets of Soviet Sports Fitness and Training,* Arbor House (New York, NY), 1987.
(With Sam Arkoff) *Flying through Hollywood by the Seat of My Pants: From the Man Who Brought You "I Was a Teenage Werewolf" and "Muscle Beach Party,"* Carol Publishing (Secaucus, NJ), 1992.
(With Richard Cole) *Stairway to Heaven: Led Zeppelin Uncensored,* HarperCollins (New York, NY), 1992.
(With D. Ariel Kerman) *The H.A.R.T. Program: Lower Your Blood Pressure without Drugs,* HarperCollins (New York, NY), 1992.
(With the editors of *Prevention* magazine) *Cholesterol Cures: From Almonds and Antioxidants to Garlic, Golf, Wine, and Yogurt—Three Hundred Twenty-five Quick and Easy Ways to Lower Cholesterol and Live Longer,* Rodale Press (Emmaus, PA), 1996.

(With Jim Walsh) *Everything You Need to Know about College Sports Recruiting: A Guide for Players and Parents,* foreword by Thomas Beckett, Andrews & McMeel (Kansas City, MO), 1997.

The Natural Way to Beat the Common Cold and Flu: A Holistic Approach for Prevention and Relief, Berkley (New York, NY), 1998.

(With Kenneth Baum) *The Mental Edge: Maximize Your Sports Potential with the Mind-Body Connection,* foreword by Karch Kiraly, Berkley (New York, NY), 1999.

(With Kenneth Baum) *Metabolize: The Personalized Program for Weight Loss,* Putnam (New York, NY), 2000.

(With Roger J. Callahan) *Tapping the Healer Within: Using Thought Field Therapy to Instantly Conquer Your Fears, Anxieties, and Emotional Distress,* foreword by Earl Mindell, Contemporary Books (Lincolnwood, IL), 2001.

Courage: The Story of the Mighty Effort to End the Devastating Effects of Multiple Sclerosis, Ivan R. Dee (Chicago, IL), 2001.

Contributor to popular magazines, including *Holiday, True, Coronet, TV Guide, Parade,* and *Family Weekly;* contributor to newspapers, including *Detroit News, San Francisco Chronicle, Chicago Sun-Times, Chicago Tribune,* and *Los Angeles Times.*

SIDELIGHTS: Richard Trubo's biography *Courage: The Story of the Mighty Effort to End the Devastating Effects of Multiple Sclerosis* tells the life story of Sylvia Lawry, the founder of the National Multiple Sclerosis Society.

Lawry first became involved in finding a cure for multiple sclerosis (MS) when her brother Bernard was diagnosed with the disease in 1937. Doctors explained to the family that MS is incurable, but Lawry tried to contact other patients who perhaps had recovered from the disease. Her efforts led to contact with a core group of some forty-five people, all of whom had MS and were not recovering from it. In 1947 Lawry established the National Multiple Sclerosis Society as a group to support research into a cure as well as to provide support for patients and their families. While there is still no cure for MS as of the early 2000s, Lawry's organization has spearheaded the development of drugs to alleviate the disease's symptoms. Whitney Scott in *Booklist* called Trubo's *Courage* "a

valuable resource for medical and social activists," and Mary J. Nickum in *Library Journal* found Trubo's book to be "a fascinating account of the power of one woman to affect the lives of millions."

BIOGRAPHICAL AND CRITICAL SOURCES:

PERIODICALS

Booklist, October 15, 2001, Whitney Scott, review of *Courage: The Story of the Mighty Effort to End the Devastating Effects of Multiple Sclerosis,* p. 366.

InsideMS, fall, 2001, review of *Courage.*

Library Journal, October 15, 2001, Mary J. Nickum, review of *Courage,* p. 101.

Publishers Weekly, March 11, 1996, review of *Cholesterol Cures: From Almonds and Antioxidants to Garlic, Golf, Wine, and Yogurt Three Hundred Twenty-five Quick and Easy Ways to Lower Cholesterol and Live Longer,* p. 61; September 24, 2001, review of *Courage,* p. 87.*

*   *   *

TUTEN, Frederic 1936-

PERSONAL: Born December 2, 1936, in New York, NY; son of Rex and Madelyn (Scelfo) Tuten; married Simona Morini (a writer), September 9, 1962 (divorced, 1972); married Elke Krajewska, November, 1996. *Education:* College of the City of New York (now City College of the City University of New York), B.A., 1959; New York University, M.A., 1964, Ph.D., 1971.

ADDRESSES: *Agent*—Watkins Loomis Agency, 133 East 35 St., Suite 1, New York, NY 10016. *E-mail*—frederictuten@earthlink.net.

CAREER: City College of the City University of New York, New York, NY, instructor, 1963-70, assistant professor, 1971-1975, associate professor, 1975-85, professor of English, 1985—, director of graduate English and creative writing program, 1974-79, 1984-95. University of Paris, Paris, France, visiting professor, 1979, 1981-83.

MEMBER: Modern Language Association, Melville Society, Popular Culture Association, P.E.N.

AWARDS, HONORS: Guggenheim fellowship in creative writing, 1973-1974; DAAD Award, 1997-1998; Distinguished Writing Award, American Academy of Arts and Letters, 2000.

WRITINGS:

(Translator, with wife, Simona Morini) G. R. Solari, *The House of Farnese,* Doubleday (New York, NY), 1968.

(Translator, with Simona Morini) *Charles Baudelaire: Letters from His Youth,* Doubleday (New York, NY), 1970.

The Adventures of Mao on the Long March (fiction), Citadel (Sacramento, CA), 1971.

Tallien: A Brief Romance, Farrar, Straus & Giroux (New York, NY), 1988.

Roy Lichtenstein Bronze Sculpture, 1976-1989: May 19-July 1, 1989, 65 Thompson Street (New York, NY), 1989.

Tintin in the New World (romance), Morrow (New York, NY), 1993.

Van Gogh's Bad Cafe: A Love Story, Morrow (New York, NY), 1997.

The Green Hour: A Novel, Norton (New York, NY), 2002.

Short fiction included in anthologies and journals, including *Tri-Quarterly, Fiction,* and *Statements: An Anthology of Recent American Fiction;* contributor to periodicals, including *Art in America, Vogue,* and *Artforum;* book editor for *Artforum,* 1983-1985.

SIDELIGHTS: Frederic Tuten's novels are well-known for being experimental, often mixing historical figures within the contexts of his own invented fictions. "I never wanted to write a first-person, autobiographical novel," Tuten once told Wendy Smith in *Publishers Weekly.* "I wanted, as a challenge, to do something totally distinct from anything I supposedly had lived or knew except in my mind."

When Tuten submitted the manuscript for his first novel, *The Adventures of Mao on the Long March,* editors were reluctant to publish the unusually nonlin-

ear and intellectually challenging work. "It was universally disdained," Tuten told Smith; "the nicest comment was, 'This is not a novel.'" However, after Tuten's friend, Roy Lichtenstein, agreed to do the cover, the book was published and slowly gained a small following. Tuten wrote in *Archipelago* that he was "taken by the idea of an impersonal fiction, one whose personality was the novel's and not apparently that of its author, an ironic work impervious to irony, its tone a matte gun-metal gray with just a flash of color here and there to warm the reader."

After the publication of *The Adventures of Mao on the Long March,* Tuten busied himself with his other work, including teaching at New York City College and writing for various art magazines. He also received a Guggenheim fellowship. After a seventeen-year break from writing fiction, Tuten published his second novel, *Tallien: A Brief Romance,* which *New York Times Book Review*'s James A. Snead called "an exceptionally erudite and often witty meditation on political and erotic betrayal." *Tallien* is framed by the story of a son dealing with his dying father; the essence of the book, however, is the fictionalized story of Jean Lambert Tallien, a real-life French revolutionary. Tuten's narrative shifts back and forth between 18th-century France and the present day.

Like *Tallien* and *Mao,* Tuten's next novel, *Tintin in the New World,* draws upon a previously existing character—in this case, the beloved comic-strip teenager created by the Belgian cartoonist Herge. Tuten told Smith, "Tintin was a ready-made boy hero I could invest lots of fantasy in. I didn't have to create an unknown youth who was innocent and valiant; he was already there for me, and I could build on that to create the kind of ennobled and mystical reacher for truth I wanted to have." Tuten throws his Tintin in with the characters from Thomas Mann's novel *The Magic Mountain,* a bunch of European expatriates living near Macchu Picchu in Peru, and watches as the eternal boy-hero struggles with the emerging adult issues of sexuality, sin, and philosophy. Although some critics found the discord to be forced, many were impressed by the sheer inventiveness of the story and the excellence of the writing. Tom De Haven, in *Artforum International,* particularly appreciated that "the entire enterprise, this invention, is so bizarre in its plunderings (why Tintin? why Mann?) and so unapologetically itself."

With the publication of his fourth novel, *Van Gogh's Bad Cafe,* critics noted that Tuten's impersonal intellectualism was beginning to expand into a more openly emotional style. "I'm giving myself permission to burn on the page," Tuten told Smith; "I'm much more inclined toward passion in fiction: obvious passion, not subdued and wrestled to the ground." The passion in *Van Gogh's Bad Cafe* is still presented with Tuten's characteristic juxtapositions of the familiar and unfamiliar: in this surrealistic novel, Tuten follows his time-traveling heroine, Ursula, through her dual life as Vincent Van Gogh's lover and as a late-20th-century New Yorker. In *Review of Contemporary Fiction*, Philip Landon commented on the "hallucinatory, anachronistic form of the novel" and noted that it "intelligently contemplates the validity of the aesthetic in an age that has threatened to strike art silent." As with his previous novels, many critics admired the provocative writing style. "A stylistic tour de force, the novel is exuberantly baroque," commented John Taylor in *Antioch Review*. "Here is an oft-hilarious satire of contemporary America and a heady spoof on the classical menage-a-trois."

Booklist's Donna Seaman called Tuten's next novel, *The Green Hour*, an "intellectual romance" that "artfully ponders the reconditeness of love." Here Tuten explores love, passion, art, and death through the eyes of his heroine Dominique, a brilliant art historian. Despite her successful career and her love for her work, Dominique is unable to disentangle herself from an old lover who reappears periodically throughout her life. *The Green Hour*, however, is "no ordinary love story," wrote a *Publishers Weekly* reviewer; "the novel, while a study of character, embraces art and culture as integral elements."

BIOGRAPHICAL AND CRITICAL SOURCES:

PERIODICALS

American Book Review, July, 1989, review of *Tallien: A Brief Romance*, p. 21.

Antioch Review, fall, 1997, John Taylor, review of *Van Gogh's Bad Cafe*, p. 498.

Artforum International, summer, 1993, Tom De Haven, review of *Tintin in the New World*, p. 103.

Booklist, May 15, 1993, review of *Tintin in the New World*, p. 1676; March 1, 1997, Donna Seaman, review of *Van Gogh's Bad Cafe*, p. 1112; September 1, 2002, Donna Seaman, review of *The Green Hour*, p. 61.

Book World, July 4, 1993, review of *Tintin in the New World*, p. 2.

Guardian Weekly, January 29, 1988, review of *Tallien: A Brief Romance*, p. 27; August 8, 1993, review of *Tintin in the New World*, p. 20.

Hungry Mind Review, fall, 1993, review of *Tintin in the New World*, p. 32.

Kirkus Reviews, February 1, 1988, review of *Tallien: A Brief Romance*, p. 156; March 15, 1993, review of *Tintin in the New World*, p. 330; December 15, 1996, review of *Van Gogh's Bad Cafe*, p. 1765; July 15, 2002, review of *The Green Hour*, pp. 991-992.

Library Journal, March 15, 1988, review of *Tallien: A Brief Romance*, p. 69; June 15, 1993, review of *Tintin in the New World*, p. 99; February 1, 1997, Starr E. Smith, review of *Van Gogh's Bad Cafe*, p. 108.

Listener, February 9, 1989, review of *Tallien: A Brief Romance*, p. 24; April 15, 1997, review of *The Adventures of Mao on the Long March*, p. 125.

Locus, July, 1993, review of *Tintin in the New World*, p. 46.

London Review of Books, December 2, 1993, review of *Tintin in the New World*, p. 28; April 6, 1995, review of *Tallien: A Brief Romance*, p. 25.

Los Angeles Times Book Review, May 15, 1988, review of *Tallien: A Brief Romance*, p. 3; June 6, 1993, review of *Tintin in the New World*, p. 3; March 23, 1997, review of *Van Gogh's Bad Cafe*, p. 2.

New Statesman, December 5, 1997, review of *Van Gogh's Bad Cafe*, p. 42.

New York Times Book Review, May 29, 1988, James A. Snead, review of *Tallien: A Brief Romance*, p. 15; December 5, 1993, review of *Tintin in the New World*, p. 65; June 6, 1993, review of *Tintin in the New World*, p. 9; February 26, 1995, review of *Tallien: A Brief Romance*, p. 28; February 25, 1996, review of *Tintin in the New World*, p. 32; March 20, 1997, review of *Van Gogh's Bad Cafe*, p. 16.

Observer (London, England), October 10, 1993, review of *Tintin in the New World*, p. 20; January 19, 1999, review of *Van Gogh's Bad Cafe*, p. 14.

Publishers Weekly, March 11, 1988, review of *Tallien: A Brief Romance*, p. 87; April 19, 1993, review of *Tintin in the New World*, p. 49; December 11, 1995, review of *Tintin in the New World*, p. 69; December 2, 1996, review of *Van Gogh's Bad Cafe*, p. 38; February 17, 1997, review of *The Adventures of Mao on the Long March*, p. 217;

March 3, 1997, Wendy Smith, "Frederic Tuten: Novels of Feeling and Fine Art," pp. 50-51; July 8, 2002, review of *The Green Hour*, p. 27.

Rapport: The Modern Guide to Books, Music & More, Volume 20, number 1, 1997, review of *Van Gogh's Bad Cafe*, p. 15.

Review of Contemporary Fiction, fall, 1988, review of *Tallien: A Brief Romance*, p. 161; fall, 1993, Eamonn Wall, review of *Tintin in the New World*, p. 211; fall, 1997, Philip Landon, review of *Van Gogh's Bad Cafe*, pp. 234-235.

Times Literary Supplement, November 12, 1993, review of *Tintin in the New World*, p. 22.

Village Voice Literary Supplement, July, 1985, review of *The Adventures of Mao on the Long March*, p. 15; May, 1993, reviews of *The Adventures of Mao on the Long March*, *Tallien: A Brief Romance*, and *Tintin in the New World*, p. 29.

ONLINE

Archipelago Web site, http://www.archipelago.org/ (March 3, 2003), Frederic Tuten, "Twenty-Five Years After: *The Adventures of Mao on the Long March*."

City College of New York Web site, http://www.ccny.cuny.edu/ (March 3, 2003), biography of Frederic Tuten.

W. W. Norton Web site, http://www.wwnorton.com/ (March 3, 2003), description of *The Green Hour*.

*   *   *

VAN ALLSBURG, Chris 1949-

PERSONAL: Born June 18, 1949, in Grand Rapids, MI; son of Richard (a dairy owner) and Chris Van Allsburg; married Lisa Morrison (a self-employed consultant), August, 1976; children: Sophie, Anna. *Education:* University of Michigan, B.F.A., 1972; Rhode Island School of Design, M.F.A., 1975. *Religion:* Jewish. *Hobbies and other interests:* "When I'm not drawing, I enjoy taking walks and going to museums. I play tennis a few times a week, like to sail—although I have fewer opportunities to do it now (I used to have more friends with boats). I read quite a lot."

ADDRESSES: Agent—Author's Mail, c/o Houghton-Mifflin, 2 Park St., Boston, MA 02107.

Chris Van Allsburg

CAREER: Artist; author and children's book illustrator. Rhode Island School of Design, Providence, RI, teacher of illustration, 1977—. Has exhibited his work at Whitney Museum of American Art, New York, NY; Museum of Modern Art, New York, NY; Allan Stone Gallery, New York, NY; Grand Rapids Art Museum, Grand Rapids, MI; and Port Washington Public Library, Port Washington, NY.

AWARDS, HONORS: New York Times Best Illustrated Children's Books citations, 1979, for *The Garden of Abdul Gasazi*, 1981, for *Jumanji*, 1982, for *Ben's Dream*, 1983, for *The Wreck of the Zephyr*, 1984, for *The Mysteries of Harris Burdick*, 1985, for *The Polar Express*, and 1986, for *The Stranger*; Caldecott Honor Book citation from the American Library Association, and *Boston Globe-Horn Book* Award for illustration, both 1980, and International Board on Books for Young People citation for illustration, 1982, all for *The Garden of Abdul Gasazi*; Irma Simonton Black Award from Bank Street College of Education, 1980, for *The Garden of Abdul Gasazi*, and 1985, for *The Mysteries of Harris Burdick*; *New York Times* Outstanding Books citations, 1981, for *Jumanji*, and 1983, for *The Wreck of the Zephyr*; Caldecott Medal, 1982, for *Jumanji*, and 1986, for *The Polar Express*; *Boston Globe-Horn Book* Award citation for illustration, 1982, for *Jumanji*, and 1986, for *The Polar Express*;

Children's Choice from the International Reading Association, and American Book Award for illustration from Association of American Publishers, both 1982, Kentucky Bluegrass Award from Northern Kentucky University, and Buckeye Children's Book Award from Ohio State Library, both 1983, Washington Children's Choice Picture Book Award from the Washington Library Media Association, 1984, and West Virginia Children's Book Award, 1985, all for *Jumanji;* Parents' Choice Award for Illustration from the Parents' Choice Foundation, 1982, for *Ben's Dream,* 1984, for *The Mysteries of Harris Burdick,* 1985, for *The Polar Express,* and 1986, for *The Stranger;* Kentucky Bluegrass Award from Northern Kentucky University, 1987, for *The Polar Express. Ben's Dream* was included in the American Institute of Graphic Arts Book Show in 1983, *The Wreck of the Zephyr* was included in 1984, and *The Mysteries of Harris Burdick* in 1985; *The Wreck of the Zephyr* was chosen one of New York Public Library's Children's Books in 1983, and *The Polar Express* was chosen in 1985; *Boston Globe-Horn Book* Award, 1985, for *The Mysteries of Harris Burdick; The Polar Express* was chosen one of *Redbook*'s Ten Best Picture Books for Kids, and one of Child Study Association's Children's Books of the Year, both 1985; Hans Christian Andersen Award nomination, 1985; *The Stranger* was chosen one of Child Study Association's Children's Books of the Year, 1987.

WRITINGS:

SELF-ILLUSTRATED CHILDREN'S BOOKS

The Garden of Abdul Gasazi, Houghton Mifflin (Boston, MA), 1979.

Jumanji, Houghton Mifflin (Boston, MA), 1981.

Ben's Dream, Houghton Mifflin (Boston, MA), 1982.

The Wreck of the Zephyr, Houghton Mifflin (Boston, MA), 1983.

The Mysteries of Harris Burdick, Houghton Mifflin (Boston, MA), 1984.

The Polar Express, Houghton Mifflin (Boston, MA), 1985, CD-ROM edition, 1995.

The Stranger, Houghton Mifflin (Boston, MA), 1986.

The Z Was Zapped: A Play in Twenty-Six Acts, Houghton Mifflin (Boston, MA), 1987.

Two Bad Ants, Houghton Mifflin (Boston, MA), 1988.

Just a Dream, Houghton Mifflin (Boston, MA), 1990.

The Wretched Stone, Houghton Mifflin (Boston, MA), 1991.

The Widow's Broom, Houghton Mifflin (Boston, MA), 1992.

The Sweetest Fig, Houghton Mifflin (Boston, MA), 1993.

Bad Day at Riverbend, Houghton Mifflin (Boston, MA), 1995.

ILLUSTRATOR

Mark Helprin, *Swan Lake,* Houghton Mifflin (Boston, MA), 1989.

Mark Helprin, *A City in Winter,* Viking (New York, NY), 1996.

Mark Helprin, *The Veil of Snows,* Viking (New York, NY), 1997.

A selection of Chris Van Allsburg's work is held in the Kerlan Collection at the University of Minnesota, Twin Cities, Minneapolis, MN.

ADAPTATIONS: A movie by Castle Rock Entertainment, based on *Polar Express* and starring Tom Hanks, is scheduled for release in 2004.

SIDELIGHTS: Chris Van Allsburg, wrote Jim Roginski in *Parents' Choice,* "is one of the most extraordinarily gifted artists working in children's book illustration. His immediately recognizable style—technical genius and startling images—has placed him in the forefront of active illustrators who are advancing the art of book illustration." Although Van Allsburg began his career as a book illustrator as recently as 1979, he has received numerous awards and honors. *The Polar Express* has become a Christmas classic since it first appeared in 1985, and publisher Houghton Mifflin bought the rights to *Swan Lake,* Van Allsburg's 1989 collaboration with author Mark Helprin, for $801,000.

"Growing up, I liked to do normal kid things like playing baseball and building model cars, trucks, and planes," Van Allsburg told Catherine Ruello in an interview for *Something about the Author.* "I also used to drive a go-cart on public streets, which was illegal. I lived in a growing suburb with half-built houses, great to spook around in, especially in those with only the stud work sticking out of the top of the foundations. We were not supposed to do this—it was taboo. Obviously parents were afraid we'd hurt ourselves."

"There were open fields, trees, wandering dirt roads," he recalled in an interview with Kim Heron of the *New York Times*. "The houses weren't big—they were nice, small houses for families of four or maybe five. There were still places nearby where I could catch tadpoles, there were places to go sledding, there were fields where you could play baseball—not someplace surrounded by a fence, just open fields. And I rode my bike to school."

"The first book I remember reading is probably the same book many people my age recall as their first," Van Allsburg recalled in his *Horn Book* acceptance speech for the Caldecott medal. "It was profusely illustrated and recounted the adventures and conflicts of its three protagonists, Dick, Jane, and Spot. Actually, the lives of this trio were not all that interesting. A young reader's reward for struggling through those syllables at the bottom of the page was to discover that Spot got a bath. Not exactly an exciting revelation. Especially since you'd already seen Spot getting his bath in the picture at the top of the page."

Van Allsburg's first work, *The Garden of Abdul Gasazi,* is about a young boy who pursues a runaway dog into a magician's eerie garden of topiary creatures. The artist's evocative, surreal black-and-white pencil illustrations attracted reviewers. "Critics," Laura Ingram wrote in the *Dictionary of Literary Biography,* "hailed *The Garden of Abdul Gasazi* as a graphic masterpiece, praising not only his technical but also his artistic vision"; but, she added, others felt the author allowed the illustrations to eclipse the written elements. Van Allsburg told Ruello that he "had no expectations at all. I remember thinking, 'Maybe a few copies will sell; I'll buy the remainder and give them to friends for Christmas.' But *The Garden of Abdul Gasazi* sold quite well." Some of Van Allsburg's original drawings from the book were included in an exhibition of his works at the Allan Stone Gallery in New York.

Jumanji is about two bored suburban children, Judy and Peter, who accidentally let loose wild animals in their home while playing a board game. "True to its claim," Ingram wrote, "the game dispels the children's listlessness when lions materialize in the living room,

monkeys appear on the kitchen table and help themselves to bananas, a volcano erupts, and a herd of rhinos rampage through the house." The game ends when Judy reaches the final destination, and all the animals and other effects of the game mysteriously vanish without a trace. Like *The Garden of Abdul Gasazi, Jumanji*'s black-and-white illustrations blur the boundary between fantasy and reality. "Van Allsburg's pictures," Ingram wrote, "which at first glance could be mistaken for photographs, are impressive not only for their realism but for the skill with which he manipulates light and shadow to create a vaguely unsettling mood and for the odd angles which present disconcerting views of common scenes."

Ben's Dream, in which a young boy falls asleep while studying geography and dreams that his house is floating around the world, and *The Wreck of the Zephyr,* about a young man who learns to sail his boat through the air, followed *Jumanji. The Wreck of the Zephyr,* Van Allsburg's first full-color book, received praise, wrote Ingram, "as 'the work of a master; stunning, luminescent and conveying a sense of the mystical and magical.'" But the artist returned to black-and-white for *The Mysteries of Harris Burdick,* perhaps his most idiosyncratic book. It consists of a series of pictures with titles and captions that only suggest the story that might accompany the illustrations. "Designed to challenge even those who claim to have no imagination," Ingram wrote, "these pictures possess a haunting quality that hints at unseen mysteries. Though this collection appears on the children's shelves in most libraries and bookstores, Van Allsburg's teasing scenes are sophisticated enough to provoke fantasies in the adult as well as prereaders and school-aged children."

Van Allsburg won his second Caldecott Medal for his second full-color project, *The Polar Express.* "Told as a first-person recollection," Heron wrote, "*The Polar Express* is the story of a Christmas Eve long ago, when a little boy boards a mysterious train to the North Pole. There, he meets Santa Claus and gets to choose the first gift of Christmas—a reindeer bell from Santa's sleigh." He loses the bell through a hole in the pocket of his bathrobe, but it is rediscovered under the Christmas tree the following morning with a cryptic note: "Found this on the seat of my sleigh. Fix that hole in your pocket. Mr. C." The boy, his young sister, and their friends can hear the sound of the bell clearly, while their parents cannot; although, as the youngsters grow older, many of them can no longer hear the sound. "But the bell still rings for me," the narrator concludes, "as it does for all who truly believe."

"Van Allsburg," Heron wrote, "has frequently observed that *The Polar Express* is about faith—the faith that children, trailing clouds of glory, bring into the world and that is slowly lifted from them during childhood, in the name of growth." "The rationality we all embrace as adults makes believing in the fantastic difficult, if not impossible," Van Allsburg explained in his Caldecott medal speech. "Lucky are the children who *know* there is a jolly fat man in a red suit who pilots a flying sleigh. We should envy them. And we should envy the people who are so certain Martians will land in their back yard that they keep a loaded Polaroid camera by the back door. The inclination to believe in the fantastic may strike some as a failure in logic, or gullibility, but it's really a gift. A world that might have Bigfoot and the Loch Ness monster is clearly superior to one that definitely does not."

Van Allsburg continues exploring the fantastic in such works as *The Stranger,* in which a mute young man becomes part of Farmer Bailey's family, but his arrival delays the beginning of autumn. *The Z Was Zapped: A Play in Twenty-Six Acts* is "a sort of crazed alphabet book," according to Heron, in which the letters suffer alliterative fates. Other recent works include *Two Bad Ants, Just a Dream,* and *The Wretched Stone.*

"A book is a four-and-a-half-month commitment," Van Allsburg told Ruello, "and the challenge is to actually finish it. My problem is maintaining self-motivation after the tenth drawing. There are fourteen to fifteen drawings in a conventionally laid-out book and by the tenth drawing I'm ready to start another project. I've got a 'sketchbook' in my head with thousands of pieces of sculpture and enough descriptions for ten books. But I let those things sit in the back of my mind whereby the weaker ideas settle out by themselves. I would like to be six people at once, so that I could get more of them out of the way."

BIOGRAPHICAL AND CRITICAL SOURCES:

BOOKS

Children's Literature Review, Gale (Detroit, MI), Volume 5, 1983, Volume 13, 1987.
Dictionary of Literary Biography, Volume 61: *American Writers for Children since 1960: Poets, Illustrators, and Nonfiction Authors,* Gale (Detroit, MI), 1987, pp. 306-13.

Kingman, Lee, editor, *Newbery and Caldecott Medal Books, 1976-1985,* Horn Book (Boston, MA), 1986.
Holtze, Sally Holmes, *Fifth Book of Junior Authors and Illustrators,* H. W. Wilson (New York, NY), 1983.
Something about the Author, Volume 53, Gale (Detroit, MI), 1988.

PERIODICALS

Chicago Tribune Book World, August 1, 1982.
Horn Book, August, 1982, pp. 384-87; July/August, 1986, pp. 420-24, 425-29; September/October, 1986, pp. 566-71.
Los Angeles Times Book Review, March 21, 1982; April 3, 1983.
Newsweek, December 17, 1979.
New Yorker, December 7, 1981.
New York Times, December 24, 1989.
New York Times Book Review, November 11, 1979; November 25, 1979; April 26, 1981; April 25, 1982; June 5, 1983; November 10, 1985; November 9, 1986; November 8, 1987; November 13, 1988.
Parents' Choice, Volume 10, number 3, 1987, pp. 21, 36, 38.
Publishers Weekly, April 8, 1983.
School Library Journal, May, 1982; May, 1988, p. 70.
Time, December 3, 1979; December 21, 1981; December 20, 1982.
Times Literary Supplement, September 18, 1981.
Washington Post Book World, November 11, 1979; July 12, 1981; May 9, 1982; October 14, 1984.
World and I, December, 1991, pp. 252-61.*

*   *   *

VANDE VELDE, Vivian 1951-

PERSONAL: Born June 18, 1951, in New York, NY; daughter of Pasquale (a linotype operator) and Marcelle (Giglio) Brucato; married Jim Vande Velde (a computer analyst), April 20, 1974; children: Elizabeth. *Education:* Attended State University of New York at Brockport, 1969-70, and Rochester Business Institute, 1970-71. *Religion:* Catholic. *Hobbies and other interests:* Reading, needlecrafts, "quiet family things."

ADDRESSES: Agent—c/o Author Mail, Harcourt Brace, 525 B Street, Suite 1900, San Diego, CA 92101.

CAREER: Writer.

MEMBER: Society of Children's Book Writers and Illustrators, Rochester Area Children's Writers and Illustrators.

AWARDS, HONORS: Child Study Association Book of the Year, 1986, Bro-Dart Foundation Elementary School Library Collection, International Reading Association (IRA) List, National Council of Teachers of English Notable Trade Books in the Language Arts, and the New York Public Library Children's Books 100 Titles for Reading and Sharing, all for *A Hidden Magic;* Author of the Month Award, *Highlights for Children,* 1988; "Pick of the Lists" citation, American Booksellers Association (ABA), "Best Book for Young Adults" and "Quick Pick for Reluctant Young Adult Readers" citations, American Library Association (ALA), "Popular Paperback for Young Adults" citation, Young Adult Library Services Association, Blue Ribbon Book award, Bulletin of the Center for Children's Books, and Nevada Young Readers award, 1998, all for *Companions of the Night;* "Quick Pick" and "Recommended Books for the Reluctant Young Adult Reader" citations, ALA, Junior Library Guild Selection, New York Public Library Books for the Teen Age, and Texas Lone Star reading list citation, Texas Library Association, all for *Dragon's Bait;* Junior Guild Selection for *A Well-Timed Enchantment;* "Best Book for Young Adults" and "Quick Pick for Reluctant Young Adult Readers" citations, ALA, "Young Adult's Choice" citation, IRA, and winner of "Tellable" stories, 1996, all for *Tales from the Brothers Grimm and the Sisters Weird;* "Quick Pick" citation, ALA, for *Curses, Inc.;* "Quick Pick for Reluctant Young Adult Readers" citation, ALA, 1999, for *Ghost of a Hanged Man;* Edgar Allan Poe Award for best young adult mystery, 2000, for *Never Trust a Dead Man;* Anne Spencer Lindbergh Prize in Children's Literature, 2001/2002, and New York Public Library Books for the Teen Age, 2003, both for *Heir Apparent;* Black-Eyed Susan Award (Maryland), 2002, for *There's a Dead Person Following My Sister Around;* and Volunteer State Book Award (Tennessee), 2002, for *Smart Dog.*

WRITINGS:

Once Upon a Test: Three Light Tales of Love, illustrated by Diane Dawson Hearn, A. Whitman (Morton Grove, IL), 1984.

A Hidden Magic, illustrated by Trina Schart Hyman, Crown (New York, NY), 1985.
A Well-Timed Enchantment, Crown (New York, NY), 1990.
User Unfriendly, Harcourt (San Diego, CA), 1991.
Dragon's Bait, Harcourt (San Diego, CA), 1992.
Tales from the Brothers Grimm and the Sisters Weird, Harcourt (San Diego, CA), 1995.
Companions of the Night, Harcourt (San Diego, CA), 1995.
Curses, Inc., Harcourt (San Diego, CA), 1997.
The Conjurer Princess, HarperPrism (New York, NY), 1997.
The Changeling Prince, HarperPrism (New York, NY), 1998.
Ghost of a Hanged Man, Marshall Cavendish (Tarrytown, NY), 1998.
A Coming Evil, Houghton Mifflin (Boston, MA), 1998.
Smart Dog, Harcourt Brace (San Diego, CA), 1998.
Spellbound, Science Fiction Book Club (New York, NY), 1998.
Never Trust a Dead Man, Harcourt Brace (San Diego, CA), 1999.
There's a Dead Person Following My Sister Around, Harcourt Brace (San Diego, CA), 1999.
Magic Can Be Murder, Harcourt Brace (San Diego, CA), 2000.
Troll Teacher, illustrated by Mary Jane Auch, Holiday House (New York, NY), 2000.
The Rumpelstiltskin Problem, Houghton Mifflin (Boston, MA), 2000.
Alison, Who Went Away, Houghton Mifflin (Boston, MA), 2001.
Being Dead: Stories, Harcourt Brace (San Diego, CA), 2001.
Heir Apparent, Harcourt Brace (San Diego, CA), 2002.
Wizard at Work, Harcourt Brace (San Diego, CA), 2003.
Witch's Wishes, Holiday House (New York, NY), 2003.

Contributor of short stories to *Cricket, Disney Adventures, Electric Company, Highlights for Children, Kid City, School, Storyworks,* and *Young American.* Contributor to anthologies, including *A Wizard's Dozen, A Nightmare's Dozen, Girls to the Rescue,* and several Bruce Coville anthologies.

SIDELIGHTS: Vivian Vande Velde is the author of two dozen books for young readers that blend fantasy with mystery elements, or that turn fairy tales on their heads with fresh new perspectives and with humorous touches. Vande Velde once commented that she has been "making up stories" since she was a child just to please herself. She recalled, "most of my stories were a mish-mash; I might take part of the Cinderella story here, part of the legend of Ivanhoe there, throw in a dash of Superman." Now that Vande Velde makes her career as a writer, and her stories are entertaining others as well, she still has fun with the characters and plots of well-known tales. Offbeat, fantastic, and even sarcastic, Vande Velde's books contain intriguing, suspenseful situations and provocative messages that eschew traditional themes and story-types. Christy Tyson of *Voice of Youth Advocates* noted that Vande Velde's early books *Dragon's Bait* and *User Unfriendly* "have been very popular." Vande Velde has gone on to write about vampires in *Companions of the Night,* to take a new look at fairy tales in *Tales from the Brothers Grimm and the Sisters Weird* and *The Rumpelstiltskin Problem,* to tell of a sixteen-year-old who turns to magic to help find her kidnapped sister in *The Conjurer Princess,* to play with the conventions of the Western in *The Ghost of the a Hanged Man,* to create magical mysteries in *Never Trust a Dead Man* and *Magic Can Be Murder,* and even to tackle a realistic novel in *Alison, Who Went Away.* But whatever genre the inventive Vande Velde is writing in, one thing remains the same: the high entertainment value of her books.

Born in New York City in 1951, Vande Velde grew up in New York state, enjoying reading and story-making. Such skills, however, did not lead to a successful time in school, where she was a self-confessed average student, even in English classes. Graduating from high school, she moved on to college for a year, but quit when she had exhausted all the literature course offerings she was interested in. Thereafter she attended a business school and trained as a secretary. Married in 1974, Vande Velde soon was a stay-at-home mom with a daughter, and this is when she began thinking of making a career in writing, enrolling in a writing course. Feedback from that class finally directed her to fantasy writing.

One of Vande Velde's early books exemplifies her talent for transforming old tales into new ones. According to Karen P. Smith of *School Library Journal, A Hidden Magic* is a "delightful parody of the classic fairy tale genre." Vande Velde's princess, instead of being beautiful, is plain. Her handsome prince is far from noble—he's spoiled and vain. Moreover, the prin-

cess in the story does not have to be saved by a prince—she saves him. At the close of the story, the princess refuses to marry the prince. Readers may be surprised by the man she prefers. "[Vande] Velde's approach remains fresh and definitely amusing," remarked Smith.

It was another five years before Vande Velde published her next book, *A Well-Timed Enchantment,* about a teenage girl sent back in time by T-shirt-wearing elves after she has accidentally messed up history by dropping her digital watch into a wishing well. Her next novel, *User Unfriendly,* in the words of Diane G. Yates of *Voice of Youth Advocates,* contains an "interesting premise . . . nicely developed with some lively fights and mildly scary situations." The story takes place in cyberspace and a teenager's basement. After Arvin's friend pirates an interactive computer game, he assures Arvin and five other high school pals that it's fine to use. But Arvin, his friends, and even his mother have no idea that playing the game without anyone monitoring their play will be truly dangerous. As they begin to play the game, they discover that there are glitches and holes in the program. They find themselves playing the roles of medieval characters and fighting for survival, with no hope of quitting the game before they finish their quest. To make matters worse, Arvin's mother begins to display terrifying symptoms of an unknown illness. Arvin has to win the game by facing orcs and wolves and rescuing a princess who has been kidnapped. According to a *Kirkus Reviews* critic, the "adventures" in this book "are vivid and diverting." A reviewer commented in *Publishers Weekly* that some readers "will not be able to put this swashbuckler down."

Alys, the protagonist in *Dragon's Bait,* feels ready to die after she has been accused and condemned for witchcraft. Her punishment is to be devoured by a dragon, and she is tied up on a hill to await her fate. There is no one who can save Alys (her father died when he heard the sentence placed upon her), and she thinks her life is over. But instead of eating her, the dragon decides to help her. Moreover, the dragon, Selendrile, is only a part-time dragon. He can assume human form, and by doing so, he helps Alys get back at those who falsely accused her. As a *Publishers Weekly* reviewer asserted, this novel with a "gently feminist slant" is also a "gripping adventure" which "probes the issues associated with revenge." If, as a *Kirkus Reviews* critic noted, the novel's subtexts include the notion that "revenge is not nearly as sweet as advertised," readers won't find easy answers in this book: "lessons—if any—are a little hard to follow."

While, according to Kim Carter of *Voice of Youth Advocates,* the dragon is the "only truly unusual element" in *Dragon's Bait,* the fantastic element in *Companions of the Night* is a handsome college-student vampire. Kerry, just sixteen and with a driver's permit instead of license, drives out alone late at night to the laundromat to recover her little brother's toy bear. Yet Kerry finds something else: Ethan, a young man thought to be a vampire, about to be killed by a mob. When Kerry saves him, she is accused of being a vampire herself; when she returns home, she finds that her father and brother have been kidnapped by the vampire hunters. Eventually, Kerry learns that Ethan really is a vampire, but she asks him to help her find her family anyway. Despite the fact that she doesn't quite know whether to fear him or trust him, Kerry finds herself attracted to Ethan. As Deborah Stevenson wrote in *Bulletin of the Center for Children's Books,* the novel is "an intellectual adventure more than a sensual one, its challenges more cerebral than hormonal. . . . It's a freshly written thriller, an offbeat love story, an engaging twist on the vampire novel, and an exciting tale of moral complexity." "*Companions of the Night* should attract a loyal following of its own," concluded Marilyn Makowski of *School Library Journal.*

Tales from the Brothers Grimm and the Sisters Weird consists of thirteen familiar folktales, revised in "both amusing and touching versions," as Ann A. Flowers of *Horn Book* explained. In one story, Rumpelstiltskin is a young, handsome elf. In another, Hansel and Gretel are murderers. The wolf in the story of Little Red Riding Hood is Granny's friend, the princess in the story of the Princess and the Pea requests more mattresses on her own, and the beauty in the Beauty and the Beast story is not pleased with the Beast's human appearance. "[Vande] Velde challenges readers' notions of good, bad, and ugly," observed Luann Toth in *School Library Journal.* A *Kirkus Reviews* critic remarked that the work is "Terrific fun." Vande Velde returned to fairy tales with her year 2000 *The Rumpelstiltskin Problem,* a book that presents six variations on that tale. Susan L. Rogers, writing in *School Library Journal,* found this offering to be an "interesting experiment." A reviewer for *Publishers Weekly* had stronger praise, writing that "Vande Velde's takes on this fairy tale are always humorous and often heartwarming."

In her later fantasy novels, Vande Velde has taken her penchant for unusual situations and combined it with in-depth examinations of moral issues. *The Conjurer Princess,* for instance, begins as a standard adventure when sixteen-year-old Lylene determines to rescue her older sister from the man who kidnapped her and murdered her fiancé on their wedding day. Lylene first turns to magic to aid her on her quest, promising to work for a wizard as payment for magical training. When magic proves less helpful than she had hoped, Lylene enlists the aid of two soldiers who turn out to be violent mercenaries. Many people have been hurt by the time Lylene finds her sister, only to realize that perhaps her rescue attempt was ill-advised in the first place. As Diane G. Yates remarked in *Voice of Youth Advocates,* "Vande Velde packs a lot into an enjoyable, short, quickly read narrative," including a portrayal of Lylene's growing maturity.

The 1998 novel *The Changeling Prince* likewise illuminates issues of fate and responsibility. Weiland has lived an uneasy existence since the sinister sorceress Daria transformed him from a wolf cub into a human child. He is only one of a group of similarly changed people who live their lives in fear of when Daria might suddenly become angry and return them to their animal forms. When Daria decides to leave her fortress and move into a town, Weiland has a new adjustment to make. He learns to live among the townspeople and eventually makes a friend, the thief Shile. As Daria's power becomes more evil, Weiland finally must make a stand. *Voice of Youth Advocates* contributor Nancy Eaton found the protagonist compelling, writing that "Weiland's detailed agonies of indecision evoke compassion in the reader: everything could go either way; there are no right choices." The result, the critic concluded, is a work that "raises thoughtful questions about individual responsibility."

In *Ghost of a Hanged Man,* the author combines an element of the supernatural with yet another genre, the Western. The infamous criminal Jake Barnette is sentenced to hang in the summer of 1877, and no one really takes it seriously when he swears in court he will revenge himself against those responsible for his punishment. The next spring, however, floods spill through the town, forcing several coffins—including Barnette's—to emerge from the inundated cemetery. When the foreman of Barnette's jury and the judge who presided at the trial suddenly die, the young son of the town sheriff knows he must take action before his family is destroyed. "This unsettling novel has many appealing elements," Carrie Schadle noted in *School Library Journal,* including the sinister ghost, Old West setting, and the scared yet brave protagonists. Janice M. Del Negro likewise found the "colorful characters" and "easy immediacy" of the dialogue appealing, and concluded in *Bulletin of the Center for Children's Books* that "Vande Velde has a knack for creepy understatement that effectively delivers unexpected chills, and the climax . . . brings the book to its shuddery, satisfying conclusion."

A murder mystery also figures in 1999's *Never Trust a Dead Man,* albeit one with a more lighthearted approach. Seventeen-year-old Selwyn has been wrongly convicted of murder by his medieval village, and has been sentenced to be entombed alive in the burial cave of his supposed victim, Farold. Selwyn has almost resigned himself to his fate when the imperious witch Elswyth enters the cave while looking for spell components. She makes Selwyn a bargain: she will release him from the cave and give him one week to find the real killers in exchange for years of his service. Elswyth complicates the deal by resurrecting the spirit of the annoying Farold as a bat and disguising Selwyn as a beautiful girl. As this unlikely duo of sleuths searches for the answer, many mishaps and humorous truths follow in their wake, making for an entertaining adventure. "Favoring the comic over the macabre," Kitty Flynn wrote in *Horn Book,* "Vande Velde offers a funny and imaginative murder mystery that intrigues as much as it entertains." A *Kirkus Reviews* critic similarly hailed the novel, writing that "the sympathetic hero, original humor, sharp dialogue, and surprising plot twists make this read universally appealing and difficult to put down."

Vande Velde's first picture book, *Troll Teacher,* had its start with a seed of truth and then with the author asking herself 'But what if?' "During the summer between second grade and third," Vande Velde once explained, "my daughter was talking with a friend who was trying to make her nervous about her upcoming teacher. 'Oooh, I've heard about her,' the friend said (though she lived in a town an hour and a half away). 'Isn't she the one who gives three hours of homework every night? And when girls have long hair, she likes to pull on their hair and make them cry.' I started thinking: What if there really was a teacher that was this bad? Or worse? Or—worst of all—what if there was a teacher who wasn't even human?" From that premise Vande Velde wrote *Troll Teacher* as a short story, and it became a picture book after her friend, writer-illustrator M. J. Auch, created her own illustrations for the story and sent it to her publisher. The result proved to be a successful collaborative effort. Reviewing the picture book in *Booklist,* Marta Segal noted, "As in her young adult novels, Vande Velde vividly captures a young person's feelings about being the only one in the world who really understands what's going on."

With *Magic Can Be Murder,* Vande Velde "throws murder, witchcraft, and romance into the brew," according to Laura Glaser in *School Library Journal.* Nola and her witch mother live in something of a medieval netherworld, traveling from town to town to work. Nola manages to use her powers to good effect, solving a murder, saving herself and her mother, and even finding true love in a book that is, according to Glaser, "most likely to cast a spell on Vande Velde's fans." *Booklist*'s Helen Rosenberg praised this "lighthearted mystery," concluding that kids "who like mystery and fantasy fans . . . will like this."

Mysteries of a more serious nature are presented in *Alison, Who Went Away.* Fourteen-year-old Susan, or Sibyl as she has taken to calling herself, "lives in the shadow of her older sister, Alison," as *Booklist*'s Frances Bradburn pointed out. Missing, Alison is something of an enigma to her sister and readers alike. While Susan thinks her rebellious sister has merely run away, the reader begins to believe otherwise, for we learn that Susan's is a "family in denial," as Betty S. Evans noted in *School Library Journal.* Things come to a climax in a student play in which Susan acts. Vande Velde's first venture into realistic fiction, *Alison, Who Went Away* is a "high-school story laced with a dose of sadness and mystery," according to Bradburn.

Being Dead is a collection of seven "deliciously creepy tales," according to Miranda Doyle in *School Library Journal.* Doyle went on to note that most of the tales "deal with everyday teens in seemingly ordinary situations." Once lulled by the commonplace, the reader will be all the more shocked when things turn decidedly "gruesome," as Doyle further mentioned. A critic for *Kirkus Reviews* concluded that Vande Velde "again chills, charms, moves and startles with her customary effectiveness." Similarly, GraceAnne A. DeCandido, writing in *Booklist,* praised Vande Velde's "sure hand," and went on to prophesy that "these spirits are destined to find their audience." And *Horn Book*'s Anita L. Burkam, noted that humor is the furthest thing from Vande Velde's mind in these stories. "Long known for stories that leaven supernatural elements with comedy," Burkam wrote, "Vande Velde here forgoes the humor to present a set of ghost stories for readers who enjoy being really scared."

In her 2002 novel, *Heir Apparent,* Vande Velde tells a "plausible, suspenseful" story, according to a contributor for *Kirkus Reviews,* of a girl in the near future who becomes trapped in a total immersion virtual reality game. Giannine becomes stranded in a game of kings and intrigue called "Heir Apparent" after some antifantasy protestors purposely damaged the equipment; now if she does not become successor to the medieval throne within three days, her brain could suffer permanent damage. The critic for *Kirkus Reviews* added that the book is "riveting reading for experienced gamers and tyros alike." A reviewer for *Publishers Weekly* also had praise for the title, noting that "hilarious characters . . . plus fantastical elements . . . will spur readers on toward the satisfying conclusion." Similarly, Linda Miles, writing in *School Library Journal,* commented that "all of the elements of a good fantasy are present in this adventure." Miles further lauded the book as a "unique combination of futuristic and medieval themes."

As fantastic as Vande Velde's stories are, readers may not be surprised to learn that her "stories aren't usually based on things that really happened." Yet facing dragons that turn into humans and vampires in a small New York town seems to do wonders for building character. Vande Velde once commented that her stories, based "on real feelings," force her characters to meet unexpected challenges. "Often the people in my stories are uncomfortable with the way they look, or they feel clumsy, or they find themselves having to take charge in a situation for which they are totally unprepared." She continued, "Most of my characters are quite surprised to find—by the story's end—that they can cope after all." A contributor for *The Oxford Companion to Fairy Tales* summed up Vande Velde's achievement in much of her fiction: "Though shocking, the tales are told in a light comic vein aimed at exposing social contradictions in such a manner that young adults can easily grasp the targets of criticism."

BIOGRAPHICAL AND CRITICAL SOURCES:

BOOKS

Oxford Companion to Fairy Tales, edited by Jack Zipes, Oxford University Press (New York, NY), 2000, p. 534.

Reginald, Robert, *Science Fiction and Fantasy Literature, 1975-1991,* Gale (Detroit, MI), 1992.

PERIODICALS

Booklist, April 1, 1995, p. 1389; September 1, 1998, p. 121; November 15, 1998, Chris Sherman, review or *Ghost of a Hanged Man,* p. 591; April 1, 1999, Holly Koelling, review of *Never Trust a Dead Man,* p. 1402; September 1, 1999, Candace Smith, review of *There's a Dead Person Following My Sister Around,* p. 124; November 15, 2000, Marta Segal, review of *Troll Teacher,* p. 650; December 15, 2000, Helen Rosenberg, review of *Magic Can Be Murder,* p. 809; April 1, 2001, Frances Bradburn, review of *Alison, Who Went Away,* p. 1459; September 1, 2001, GraceAnne A. DeCandido, review of *Being Dead,* p. 97; February 1, 2003, Gillian Engberg, review of *Heir Apparent,* p. 982; April 15, 2003, GraceAnne A. DeCandido, review of *Wizard at Work,* p. 1466.

Bulletin of the Center for Children's Books, July-August, 1995, Deborah Stevenson, review of *Companions of the Night,* pp. 373-374; October, 1998, Deborah Stevenson, review of *Ghost of a Hanged Man,* p. 75; October, 1999, Janice M. Del Negro, review of *There's a Dead Person Following My Sister Around,* p. 72; February, 2001, Janice M. Del Negro, review of *The Rumpelstiltskin Problem,* p. 239; September, 2001, Janice M. Del Negro, review of *Being Dead,* p. 29.

Horn Book, March-April, 1996, Ann A. Flowers, review of *Tales from the Brothers Grimm and the Sisters Weird,* pp. 201-202; May-June, 1998, Kitty Flynn, review of *Never Trust a Dead Man,* pp. 339-340; November-December, 1998, Kitty Flynn, review of *Ghost of a Hanged Man,* p. 742; November-December, 2001, Anita L. Burkam, review of *Being Dead,* p. 758.

Kirkus Reviews, August 1, 1991, review of *User Unfriendly,* p. 1017; August 1, 1992, review of *Dragon's Bait,* p. 994; August 1, 1995, review of

Tales from the Brothers Grimm and the Sisters Weird, p. 1118; October 15, 1998, review of *A Coming Evil,* p. 1539; March 15, 1999, review of *Never Trust a Dead Man;* August 1, 2001, review of *Being Dead,* p. 1133; March 1, 2003, review of *Wizard at Work,* p. 401.

Magazine of Fantasy and Science Fiction, June, 1996, p. 27; August, 1999, Michelle West, review of *Never Trust a Dead Man,* p. 45; March, 2002, Michelle West, review of *Being Dead,* pp. 34-39.

New York Times Book Review, March 9, 2003, review of *Heir Apparent,* p. 24.

Publishers Weekly, August 23, 1991, review of *User Unfriendly,* pp. 63-64; July 27, 1992, review of *Dragon's Bait,* p. 63; August 10, 1998, review of *Smart Dog,* p. 389; November 9, 1998, review of *Ghost of a Hanged Man,* p. 77; August 30, 1999, review of *There's a Dead Person Following My Sister Around,* p. 85; October 2, 2000, review of *Magic Can Be Murder,* p. 82, review of *The Rumpelstiltskin Problem,* p. 82; February 5, 2001, review of *Alison, Who Went Away,* p. 89; September 16, 2002, review of *Heir Apparent,* p. 69.

School Library Journal, December, 1985, Karen P. Smith, review of *A Hidden Magic,* pp. 95-96; September, 1992, p. 261; May, 1995, Marilyn Makowski, review of *Companions of the Night,* pp. 123-124; January, 1996, Luann Toth, review of *Tales from the Brothers Grimm and the Sisters Weird,* p. 126; October, 1998, Carrie Schadle, re-view of *Ghost of a Hanged Man,* p. 147; November, 1998, p. 131; May, 1999, Laura Glaser, re-view of *Never Trust a Dead Man,* p. 131; September, 1999, Timothy Capehart, review of *There's a Dead Person Following My Sister Around,* pp. 229-230; October, 2000, Gay Lynn Van Vleck, review of *Troll Teacher,* p. 140; November, 2000, Laura Glaser, review of *Magic Can Be Murder,* p. 164, Susan L. Rogers, review of *The Rumpelstiltskin Problem,* p. 177; April, 2001, Betty S. Evans, review of *Alison, Who Went Away,* p. 151; September, 2001, Miranda Doyle, review of *Being Dead,* p. 234; October, 2002, Lana Miles, review of *Heir Apparent,* p. 174.

Science Fiction Chronicle, October, 1995, p. 50.

Voice of Youth Advocates, December, 1991, Diane G. Yates, review of *User Unfriendly,* p. 327; April, 1993, Kim Carter, review of *Dragon's Bait,* p. 48; October, 1995, Christy Tyson, review of *Companions of the Night,* pp. 238-239; February, 1998, Diane G. Yates, review of *The Conjurer Princess,* pp. 396-397 June, 1998, Nancy Eaton, review of *The Changeling Prince,* pp. 134, 136; February, 1998, review of *The Conjurer Princess,* p. 396.

ONLINE

Vivian Vande Velde—All Books, http://www.non.com/ (March 14, 2003).

W

WAELTI-WALTERS, Jennifer (Rose) 1942-

PERSONAL: Born March 13, 1942, in Wolverhampton, England; daughter of Thomas Gilbert (an electrician) and Joan Ellen (a shopkeeper; maiden name, Mills) Walters; married Frank Carl Waelti, December 30, 1972 (divorced, 1991). *Education:* University College, London, B.A. (with honors), 1964, Ph. D., 1968; Université de Lille, Licence-es-Lettres, 1965. *Hobbies and other interests:* Painting, singing, photography.

ADDRESSES: Home—1934 Crescent Rd., Victoria, British Columbia, Canada V8S 2H1. *Office*—Women's Studies Department, University of Victoria, Victoria, British Columbia, Canada V8W 3P4.

CAREER: Goldsmith's College, London, lecturer, 1966-67; Sorbonne, Paris, France, lecturer in English, 1967-68; University of Victoria, Victoria, British Columbia, 1968-97, began as assistant professor of French, became associate professor, professor of French, chair of French Department, 1979-84, professor of women's studies, 1979-97, director of women's studies, 1983-95, professor emerita of French and of women's studies, 1997—; writer.

MEMBER: Canadian Federation for the Humanities, Humanities Association of Canada, Canadian Association for Women's Studies, Canadian Research Institute for the Advancement of Women, Association des professeurs de Français des universités et collèges Canadiens, Senior Women Academic Administrators of Canada.

AWARDS, HONORS: Publication award, Canadian Federation for the Humanities, 1977, for *Michel Butor;* Association des professeurs de Français des universités et collèges Canadiens (APFUCC) Prize, Best Book of Literary Criticism in French, 1989, for *Jeanne Hyvrard.*

WRITINGS:

Alchimie et litterature: Une étude de "Portrait de l'artiste en jeune singe," Dossiers des Lettres Nouvelles, Denoël (Paris, France), 1975.

J. M. G. Le Clézio, Twayne (Boston, MA), 1977.

Michel Butor: A Study of His View of the World and a Panorama of His Work, 1954-1974, Sono Nis Press (Victoria, British Columbia, Canada), 1977.

Icare, ou l'évasion impossible: Étude psycho-mythique de l'oeuvre de J. M. G. Le Clézio, Editions Naaman (Sherbrooke, Quebec, Canada), 1981.

Fairy Tales and the Female Imagination, Eden Press (Montreal, Canada, and St. Albans, VT), 1982.

(With Maïr Verthuy-Williams) *Jeanne Hyvrard,* Rodopi (Amsterdam, Holland), 1988.

Jeanne Hyvrard: La Langue d'avenir, papers presented at a workshop of the 31st Congrès of the Association des professeurs de français des universités et collèges canadiens (APFUCC) in 1987, APFUCC (Victoria, British Columbia, Canada), 1988.

Feminist Novelists of the Belle Epoque: Love As a Lifestyle, Indiana University Press (Bloomington, IN), 1990.

(Editor, with Steven C. Hause) *Feminisms of the Belle Epoque: A Historical and Literary Anthology,* texts translated by Jette Kjaer, Lydia Willis, and Jennifer Waelti-Walters, University of Nebraska Press (Lincoln, NE), 1994.

Jeanne Hyvrard: Theorist of the Modern World, Edinburgh University Press (Edinburgh, Scotland), 1996.

(Translator, with Jean-Pierre Mentha, and author of introduction) Jeanne Hyvrard, *Jeune morte en robe de dentelle* (title means "The Dead Girl in a Lace Dress"), Edinburgh University Press (Edinburgh, Scotland), 1996.

Damned Women: Lesbians in French Novels, 1796-1996, McGill-Queen's University Press (Montreal, Canada), 2000.

WORK IN PROGRESS: A second book on Michel Butor.

SIDELIGHTS: Canadian professor of French and women's studies Jennifer Waelti-Walters is perhaps best known for her writings about lesbians in literature, particularly in French novels. She has also won awards for books of literary criticism on authors Michel Butor and Jeanne Hyvrard.

Waelti-Walters's *Damned Women: Lesbians in French Novels, 1796-1996,* published in 2000, received mixed reviews. The book shows how lesbians were portrayed by male authors from Denis Diderot—whose character Suzanne in *La Religieuse* ("The Nun," 1796) was the first lesbian character in French novels—to Balzac, Gautier, and Proust. The author then covers the portrayal of lesbians by French women authors, including Adrienne Saint-Agen, Monique Wittig, Colette, Violette Leduc, Clarisse Françillon, Jocelyne François, Hélène de Monferrand, Liane de Pougy, Mireille Best, and many others.

The book's title is taken from a poem by Baudelaire in his book *Les Fleurs du mal* ("Flowers of Evil"), which raised a scandal when published in 1857. Waelti-Walters proposes in *Damned Women* that lesbians in French literature are given a lowly status throughout history. Male authors represented them as stereotypical at best and monstrous at worst, yet they remained within view because of the authors' popularity. When French women began writing about lesbians, their characters were more honestly portrayed, but the authors themselves, except for a few, had only a small following of readers. Julia Creet of *Books in Canada* wrote, "Oddly, some of the most valuable parts of the book do not fit Waelti-Walters' thesis very well." Creet used the author's comments

about Diderot's *La Religieuse* as an example: Waelti-Walters wrote that the book is "remarkably modern" in its tolerance and understanding of circumstances that could set the stage for lesbian sexuality. Another male author, Guy de Maupassant, in his short story "La Femme de Paul" (1881), also deals with the subject in a compassionate way, according to Waelti-Walters.

Creet called *Damned Women* "an important, but unfortunately heavy-handed contribution to the fields of queer studies and French literature." However, she added that the author "does offer some astute analyses of the social factors that propel and impede lesbian literary love," such as the way young girls of the late 1800s were raised to exalt love in all forms. Creet was less pleased with Waelti-Walters's treatment of contemporary French novels, whose texts, she wrote, "attempted to lesbianize language itself, rather than the life of characters." Yet Creet praised the author's "wealth of historical information" and "sheer fun" of her plot synopses of the French novels.

Martha Stone of *The Gay & Lesbian Review* thought that Waelti-Walters "wears her academic mantle lightly" in *Damned Women,* resulting in "an incisive, readable history" of lesbian characters in French novels. She was pleased with Waelti-Walters's bibliography of French lesbian novels and the many French passages translated for English readers. Stone called the book "a thoughtful glimpse into a body of literature that deserves our attention."

A contributor to the McGill-Queen's University Press Web site wrote, *Damned Women* "tells a story of alienation, persecution, and isolation within a culture. It is a cultural and literary commentary full of new information, forgotten or little known authors, poignant surprises, and unexpected interrelationships."

BIOGRAPHICAL AND CRITICAL SOURCES:

BOOKS

Canadian Who's Who, Volume 35, 2000.

Directory of American Scholars, 10th edition, Gale (Detroit, MI), 2001.

International Authors and Writers Who's Who, 13th edition, consultant editor, M. J. Shields, International Biographical Centre (Cambridge, England), 1993.

Writers Directory 2001, 16th edition, edited by Miranda H. Ferrara, St. James Press (Detroit, MI), 2001.

PERIODICALS

Books in Canada, April, 2002, Julia Creet, "Charmeuses des femmes," review of *Damned Women: Lesbians in French Novels, 1796-1996,* p. 19.

Canadian Literature, spring, 1995, review of *Feminist Novelists of the Belle Epoque: Love As a Lifestyle,* p. 171.

Christian Science Monitor, April 8, 1994, review of *Feminisms of the Belle Epoque,* p. 13.

French Review, February, 1998, review of *Jeanne Hyvrard: Theorist of the Modern World,* p. 479.

Gay & Lesbian Review and *Gay & Lesbian Review Worldwide,* March, 2001, Martha Stone, review of *Damned Women,* p. 38.

Library Journal, April 1, 1994, review of *Feminisms of the Belle Epoque: A Historical and Literary Anthology,* p. 97.

Modern Language Review, January, 1996, review of *Feminisms of the Belle Epoque,* p. 226.

World Literature Today, autumn, 1997, review of *Jeanne Hyvrard: Theorist of the Modern World,* p. 758.

OTHER

McGill-Queen's University Press, http://www.mqup. mcgill.ca/ (June 17, 2002), review of *Damned Women.* *

*   *   *

WAGER, Walter H(erman) 1924-
(Walter Herman, John Tiger)

PERSONAL: Born September 4, 1924, in New York, NY; son of Max Louis (a doctor) and Jessie (Smith) Wager; married Sylvia Leonard (a writer), May 6, 1951 (divorced, May, 1975); married Winifred McIvor (a goldsmith and Shiatsu practitioner), June 4, 1975; children: (first marriage) Lisa Wendy. *Education:* Columbia University, B.A., 1943; Harvard University, LL.B., 1946; Northwestern University, LL.M., 1949. *Politics:* Democrat. *Religion:* Jewish. *Hobbies and other interests:* Travel (has been to thirty-four countries in North, Central, and South America, Asia, Africa, and Europe).

ADDRESSES: Home and office—200 West 79th St., New York, NY 10024. *Agent*—Curtis Brown Ltd., Ten Astor Pl., New York, NY 10022; fax: 212-769-2725. *E-mail*—WPotogold2000@aol.com.

CAREER: Admitted to the Bar of New York State, 1946; Aeroutes, Inc., New York, NY, director of editorial research, 1947; *Journal of Air Law and Commerce,* Chicago, IL, federal department editor, 1948-49; Israeli Department of Civil Aviation, Lydda Airport, Tel Aviv, Israel, international affairs and law adviser, 1951-52; freelance writer in New York, NY, 1952-54; United Nations Secretariat, New York, NY, senior editor, 1954-56; Columbia Broadcasting System, Inc. (CBS), New York, NY, writer for radio and television, 1956; National Broadcasting Co., Inc. (NBC-TV), New York, NY, writer and producer, 1957; freelance writer for magazines, radio, and television, 1958-63; *Playbill,* New York, NY, editor in chief, 1963-66; *Show* magazine, senior editor, 1965; American Society of Composers, Authors, and Publishers, New York, NY, public relations consultant and editor of *ASCAP Today,* 1966-72, director of public relations, 1972-78; National Music Publishers' Association, New York, NY, public relations counselor, 1978-84; Juilliard School, New York, NY, director of communications, 1985-86; Mann Music Center, Philadelphia, PA, public relations counselor, 1986-87; Eugene O'Neill Theater Center, New York, NY, public relations counselor, 1987-89; University of Bridgeport, Bridgeport, CT, director of public information, 1991-93. Lecturer at Northwestern University, 1949, and at Columbia University, 1955-56. Special assistant to Attorney General of the State of New York for investigation of hate literature in elections, 1962. Member of board of directors, Jazz Hall of Fame, 1975-77.

MEMBER: National Academy of Popular Music (member of governing board), Writers Guild of America, Authors League of America, Mystery Writers of America (member of board of directors, 1988-94, 1997-2000; secretary, 2001—).

AWARDS, HONORS: Fulbright fellow, Sorbonne, Paris, France, 1949-50; Northwestern University Law School fellow, 1948-49.

WRITINGS:

NOVELS

(Under pseudonym Walter Herman) *Operation Intrigue,* Avon (New York, NY), 1956.
The Girl Who Split, Dell (New York, NY), 1969.

Sledgehammer, Macmillan (New York, NY), 1970.

Viper Three, Macmillan (New York, NY), 1971.

Swap, Macmillan (New York, NY), 1972.

Telefon, Macmillan (New York, NY), 1975.

My Side, by King Kong As Told to Walter Wager (farce), Macmillan, Collier Books (New York, NY), 1976.

Time of Reckoning, Playboy Press (Chicago, IL), 1979.

Blue Leader, Arbor House (New York, NY), 1979; large print edition, J. Curley & Associates (South Yarmouth, MA), 1980.

Blue Moon, Arbor House (New York, NY), 1980.

Blue Murder, Arbor House (New York, NY), 1981.

Designated Hitter, Arbor House (New York, NY), 1982.

Otto's Boy, Macmillan (New York, NY), 1985.

Raw Deal, Warner Books (New York, NY), 1986.

58 Minutes, Macmillan (New York, NY), 1987.

The Spirit Team, Forge (New York, NY), 1996.

Tunnel, Forge (New York, NY), 2000.

Kelly's People, Tom Doherty Associates (New York, NY), 2002.

UNDER PSEUDONYM JOHN TIGER

Death Hits the Jackpot, Avon (New York, NY), 1954.

I Spy, Popular Library, 1965.

Masterstroke, Popular Library, 1966.

Wipeout, Popular Library, 1967.

Countertrap, Popular Library, 1967.

Mission Impossible, Popular Library, 1967.

Death Twist, Popular Library, 1968.

Doomdate, Popular Library, 1968.

Mission Impossible Number Four: Code Name Little Ivan, Popular Library, 1969.

OTHER

Frontier Formalities for International Airlines, [Chicago, IL], 1949.

(Editor) *Some Selected Readings on International Air Transportation,* [Chicago, IL], 1949.

Camp Century: City under the Ice (nonfiction), Chilton Books (Philadelphia, PA), 1962.

(Editor) *The Playwrights Speak* (interviews, with introduction by Harold Clurman), Delacorte (New York, NY), 1967, (with introduction by John Russell Taylor), Longman's, 1969.

(With Mel Tillis) *Stutterin' Boy: The Autobiography of Mel Tillis, America's Beloved Star of Country Music,* Rawson (New York, NY), 1984.

Also author of screenplay *Swap,* 1974, based on his novel; author of documentary films on jazz, spirituals, guerrilla warfare, organized crime in America, U.S. disarmament policy, Alliance for Progress in Colombia and Venezuela, the U.S. decision to use the atomic bomb against Japan, and the lives of a Roman legionary and an American soldier. Contributor of articles on theater and music to periodicals.

ADAPTATIONS: Telefon was adapted for film by Metro-Goldwyn-Mayer, 1977; *Viper Three* was released in 1977 by Lorimar as *Twilight's Last Gleaming; 58 Minutes* was the basis for Twentieth Century-Fox's 1990 hit film *Die Hard 2.*

SIDELIGHTS: Lawyer, editor, freelance writer, public relations specialist, and novelist Walter H. Wager once commented, "I have written for pleasure since I was ten but never thought that one could make a living at it. I had no idea how to get started in the writing world and really wandered into writing casually as a source of income while waiting for a security clearance to become a U.N. editor." Since that time during the 1950s, Wager has turned out more than twenty-five novels, several nonfiction books, numerous articles, and a screenplay and has written for documentary films on a variety of subjects. He began writing action thrillers during the mid-1950s. Most of those he completed during the 1960s were written under the pseudonym John Tiger. Three of Wager's novels, *Viper Three* (1971), *Telefon* (1975), and *58 Minutes* (1987), were adapted for film.

Wager once explained, "I joke about how I literally stumbled into hardcover fiction. In June, 1967, I was in [Washington] D.C. autographing paperbacks at an American Booksellers Association convention. There were many parties, and I was among those who imbibed conscientiously. Somewhat tipsy, I was struggling through a throng in the crowded Harper & Row suite when I stumbled and bumped into a good-natured chap. We exchanged boozy witticisms, and later my good friend and super editor, James A. Bryans, told me that the stranger was impressed. Bryans urged me to send that man a book. The fellow was Richard Oldenberg, then managing editor at Macmillan and now head of the Museum of Modern Art. I sent him a proposal for an anthology, was directed to another bright Macmillan editor, Bob Markel—later editor in chief—who urged me to do a novel. I did quite a few. I never did get to thank Oldenberg, but I certainly will if we ever meet again."

Wager's many fans who love international intrigue, medical and biological science fiction, and fast-paced action can thank Oldenberg as well. Wager's novel *The Spirit Team* involves a highly skilled, but legally dead, five-person team put together by the CIA and the Pentagon to battle a deadly blue fungus developed by a North African dictator. Government officials later betray the team, but they find a way to take what is owed them. William Beatty of *Booklist* wrote that Wager "knows just how far suspense can be drawn out." He also includes a bit of humor in the otherwise gripping thriller, Beatty observed. A *Publishers Weekly* contributor foresaw a movie or television series resulting from the novel, calling Wager's books "plot-driven story vehicles . . . maximized for narrative flow."

Another of Wager's recent novels, *Tunnel,* is set in New York City, where the brilliant but evil terrorist Gunther, leading a gang of former East German spies in order to extort $10 million from the city, plants a bomb and seals off the Lincoln Tunnel, filled with vehicles and desperate citizens. Human drama unfolds both inside and outside the tunnel as police captain Jake Malloy, a former Navy SEAL, organizes an underwater rescue team to try and save the hundreds being ransomed, knowing that his girlfriend is among them. George Needham of *Booklist* called the book "a runaway thrill" whose "breathtaking action propels [it] like jet fuel." However, a *Publishers Weekly* contributor found it less appealing than other Wager novels, saying its tone is "inappropriately jocular" considering the number of innocent people who are killed throughout the story. While it might not be so glaring on the movie screen, the contributor concluded, the "casual, cartoonish tone" is stark in print, even though the novel is a rapid read. Harriet Klausner of *BookBrowser Review* called *Tunnel* "another triumphant thriller that never eases off the throttle."

In *Kelly's People,* Wager again turns to medical science and terrorism to create a heart-pounding mix. Five top U.S. spies have received organ transplants to save their lives, and now they must stop a terrorist armed with five nuclear weapons stolen from the Rus-

sian underground in what Roland Green of *Booklist* called "a scenario that seems uncomfortably plausible." The five U.S. agents have gained extrasensory powers along with their transplants, but the Russian agents have gained ESP through chemical treatments. A kidnapping and the destruction of an African city lead one CIA agent to a discovery that requires all five to join their new-found forces to prevent nuclear devastation. A *Publishers Weekly* contributor thought too much science fiction and improbable scenarios might cause some readers to be put off by the novel but also called it "a great thrill ride for those willing to suspend disbelief and take the plunge."

Wager once talked about his success and offered words for aspiring writers: "I've been very lucky, and I've enjoyed what I do," he said. "I'm still surprised by all the people who want to be novelists and consider writing and writers exotic and superior. Fortunately, writers themselves are not as arrogant as lawyers, doctors, or movie producers—but who is? On the other hand, I'm bored with cry-baby novelists who write irate articles about their horrid experiences with 'boorish' movie or television folk. I am also dismayed by certain defensive or hostile types who resent anyone who creates personally and works at home. However, I'm generally in a cheery mood, doing my thing.

"I don't see writers as competing with each other or with anyone else. None of us writes like any other writer, thank God. I have pointed this out to my daughter, who is a caring and excellent senior editor at Putnam. I try to assist young writers by introducing them to agents and editors, and by encouraging them if/when they are temporarily uncertain. I tell them of the 'luck' factor and how a 'real' writer will go on writing—no matter what."

BIOGRAPHICAL AND CRITICAL SOURCES:

PERIODICALS

Armchair Detective, fall, 1996, review of *The Spirit Team,* p. 503.

Booklist, July, 1996, William Beatty, review of *The Spirit Team,* pp. 1806, 1815; April 1, 2000, George Needham, review of *Tunnel,* p. 1440; April 15, 2002, Roland Green, review of *Kelly's People,* p. 1384.

Kirkus Reviews, June 1, 1996, review of *The Spirit Team,* p. 779.

Library Journal, July, 1996, review of *The Spirit Team,* p. 164.

Los Angeles Times, July 28, 1990.

New York Times, January 27, 1977; August 22, 1982.

Publishers Weekly, June 3, 1996, review of *The Spirit Team,* p. 64; April 17, 2000, review of *Tunnel,* p. 53; March 18, 2002, review of *Kelly's People,* p. 78.

ONLINE

BookBrowser Review, http://www.bookbrowser.com/ (April 22, 2000), Harriet Klausner, review of *Tunnel.*

Fictionwise, http://www.fictionwise.com/ (June 17, 2002), review of *Kelly's People.**

* * *

WALLACE, Ian 1950-

PERSONAL: Born March 31, 1950, in Niagara Falls, Ontario, Canada; son of Robert Amiens and Kathleen (Watts) Wallace; married Debra Wiedman. *Education:* Graduated from Ontario College of Art, 1973; graduate studies, 1973-74. *Hobbies and other interests:* Walking, movies, travel, dining out.

ADDRESSES: Home—184 Major St., Toronto, Ontario, Canada M5S 2L3.

CAREER: Writer and illustrator of children's books. Staff writer and illustrator for Kids Can Press, 1974-76; Art Gallery of Ontario, Toronto, information officer, 1976-80. Artist. *Exhibitions:* "Chin Chiang and the Dragon's Dance," Art Gallery of Ontario, 1986; "Once upon a Time," Vancouver Art Gallery, 1988; "Canada at Bologna," Bologna Children's Book Fair, 1990.

MEMBER: Writers Union of Canada, Canadian Children's Book Centre, Canadian Society of Children's Authors, Illustrators and Performers (CANSCAIP).

AWARDS, HONORS: Runner-up for City of Toronto Book Awards, 1976; "Our Choice" Selection, Children's Book Centre, 1977-81, Canada Council grants, 1980, 1981, 1983, 1986, 1987; Imperial Order of Daughters of the Empire (IODE) Book Award, 1984, Amelia Frances Howard-Gibbon Illustrator's Award, 1984, International Board on Books for Young People Honor List citation, 1986, all for *Chin Chiang and the Dragon's Dance;* Ontario Arts Council grants, 1985, 1988; American Library Association Notable Book citation, 1987, and White Raven Award, International Youth Library, 1987, both for *Very Last First Time;* Mr. Christie Award and Elizabeth Mrazik Cleaver Award, both for *The Name of the Tree;* nominee from Canada for Hans Christian Andersen medal (illustration), 1994; Gibbon Medal short list, 1994, for *Hansel & Gretel;* IODE Book Award, 1997, for *A Winter's Tale;* and Smithsonian Notable Book, 1999, and IBBY Honour Book, 2000, both for *Boy of the Deeps.*

WRITINGS:

JUVENILE

Julie News (self-illustrated), Kids Can Press (Toronto, Ontario, Canada), 1974.

(With Angela Wood) *The Sandwich,* Kids Can Press (Toronto, Ontario, Canada), 1975, revised edition, 1985.

The Christmas Tree House (self-illustrated), Kids Can Press (Toronto, Ontario, Canada), 1976.

Chin Chiang and the Dragon's Dance (self-illustrated), Atheneum (New York, NY), 1984.

The Sparrow's Song (self-illustrated), Viking (New York, NY), 1986.

Morgan the Magnificent (self-illustrated), Macmillan (New York, NY), 1987.

Mr. Kneebone's New Digs (self-illustrated), Groundwood (Toronto, Ontario, Canada), 1991.

(Reteller) Brothers Grimm, *Hansel & Gretel,* Groundwood (Toronto, Ontario, Canada), 1994.

A Winter's Tale, (self-illustrated), Groundwood (Toronto, Ontario, Canada), 1997.

Boy of the Deeps, (self-illustrated), DK Ink (New York, NY), 1999.

Duncan's Way, (self-illustrated), DK Ink (New York, NY), 2000.

The True Story of Trapper Jack's Left Big Toe, (self-illustrated), Groundwood (Toronto, Ontario, Canada), 2002.

The Naked Lady, (self-illustrated), Roaring Brook Press (Brookfield, CT), 2002.

ILLUSTRATOR

Jan Andrews, *Very Last First Time,* Atheneum (New York, NY), 1985, Groundwood Books (Toronto, Ontario, Canada), 2003, published as *Eva's Ice Adventure,* Methuen (London, England), 1986.

Tim Wynne-Jones, *The Architect of the Moon,* Groundwood Books (Toronto, Ontario, Canada), 1988, published as *Builder of the Moon,* Macmillan (New York, NY), 1989.

Celia Barker Lottridge, *The Name of the Tree: A Bantu Folktale,* Macmillan (New York, NY), 1990.

Teddy Jam, *The Year of the Fire,* Macmillan (New York, NY), 1993.

Bud Davidge, *The Mummer's Song,* Orchard Books (New York, NY), 1994.

W.D. Valgardson, *Sarah and the People of Sand River,* Groundwood (Toronto, Ontario, Canada), 1996.

Contributor to periodicals, including *Canadian Books for Young People.*

SIDELIGHTS: Canadian author/illustrator Ian Wallace has produced a number of award-winning self-illustrated picture books, including *Chin Chiang and the Dragon's Dance, Morgan the Magnificent, A Winter's Tale, Boy of the Deeps,* and *Duncan's Way.* One of Wallace's major themes is "the initiation process by which a child moves to understanding of self and the larger world," according to a contributor for *St. James Guide to Children's Writers.* Dealing with subjects such as young boys and girls from a variety of social and ethnic backgrounds who are on the cusp of growing up, as well as with the aged poor in his own books, Wallace also is a talented illustrator of the works of other writers such as Tim Wynne-Jones. In a profile of the author/writer in *Language Arts,* Jon C. Stott noted, "As admirers of Ian Wallace's books know, they're not only beautiful and engaging, they're very carefully planned and structured. Reading one of them is a total experience."

Born on the Canadian side of Niagara Falls in 1950, Wallace spent peaceful Sunday afternoons on family road trips, seeing how many trees of a certain species or how many cows he could count. "My first exposure to the world of art came not through pictures hung on gallery and museum walls," Wallace once told *CA,* "but through the picture books my brothers and I carted out of our local library." The stories he encoun-

tered in these books transported him out of provincial Ontario to exotic and not so exotic locales around the world. One of his favorite books from those years is *Wind in the Willows* by Kenneth Grahame, and the image of Toad flying along in his orange bi-plane. "Just as important," Wallace continued to *CA,* "[these books] made us keenly aware of the fact that a painter was not merely somebody who, like our father, picked up a brush or roller and stroked or rolled it over the walls of our house whenever the rooms had grown tired around the edges. But rather, an artist was someone who made dreams real." By age thirteen, Wallace had decided that he wanted to be one such person himself. From a simple declaration, the impulse to become an artist continued to grow through Wallace's teenage years, in part nourished by his parents, and he spent hours alone with pencil and paper learning how to sketch.

After attending the Ontario College of Art, Wallace worked as a staff writer and illustrator for a Canadian children's book publisher. Ultimately such work led him to trying his hand at his own titles; *The Sandwich* and *The Christmas Tree House* are two early examples of his picture-book work. In the former title, young Vincenzo despairs about being teased for eating a mortadella and provolone sandwich, but is reassured by his father that it is okay to be different. Nick and his friend Gloria discover a tree house in *The Christmas Tree House,* and they think it is the work of Don Valley Rose, who everyone figures is an evil old witch. However, when Nick makes friends with the old eccentric, he learns that she is actually a kind person. Reviewing the artwork in that book, Stott commented that the "greypencil illustrations suggest the wintry settings and create a luminous quality which reflects the warmth of new friendship the children experience."

Chin Chiang and the Dragon's Dance, Wallace's next title, was six years in the works. "I cannot stress enough the value of time," Wallace told *CA.* "Time to allow the right words to come forth, time to allow the drawings to formulate in the head before they appear on the paper, and time to allow both to be as polished as a piece of rare jade." *Chin Chiang* is the story of a young boy who wants to participate in the Chinese New Year celebrations for the Year of the Dragon, yet his stage fright gets in the way. The boy is getting ready for his first dragon dance, but his shyness sends him fleeing the street and his grandfather for the rooftop of the local library. Here he meets an old lady named Pu Yee who assists him in learning the steps to the dance without him even knowing it. He is then able to return and take part in the dance and his place in his own cultural heritage, his fears of failure left behind.

Wallace's years of work paid off; critics were full of praise and the picture book won numerous awards. Writing in the *Globe and Mail,* Sandra Martin lauded the "astonishing panoply of 16 watercolor paintings" which are "subtle yet brilliantly colored." Martin was so impressed with the "authenticity and meticulous care" of the artwork that she remarked the illustrations "speak eloquently of centuries of Chinese heritage transplanted onto the Canadian West coast." Mingshoi Cai, writing in *Children's Literature in Education,* felt that same title "captures the spirit of young people who try to carry on the cultural tradition," while Lee Galda, writing in the *Reading Teacher,* praised the manner in which the book "explodes with a cacophony of sound and a crescendoing intensity of brilliant colours, resplendent with exquisite details of Westcoast Chinese culture."

The Sparrow's Song, Wallace's next self-illustrated title, is set in the Niagara Falls region where the artist grew up, but is transposed to the early years of the 20th century. Young Charles kills a sparrow and his sister Katie takes care of the baby sparrow left motherless by this cruel act. Together they both learn important lessons: she of forgiveness, and he of repentance, as they work together gathering food for the fledgling and teach it to fly. Carol Gerson, reviewing the book in *Canadian Children's Literature,* noted that "text and illustrations interact magically" in this picture book. The contributor for *St. James Guide to Children's Writers* also praised Wallace's "free flowing depictions of water, rocks, and trees [that] symbolize the ever-changing panorama of nature." Several reviewers also commented on the background of the gorge and Niagara falls in the illustrations which acts like a spiritual power for the young children.

The circus is the inspiration for *Morgan the Magnificent,* the tale of another little child, like Chin, frozen by stage fright. Morgan lives alone with her single father and dreams of being a circus performer, using the beams in the barn for her tightrope-walking stage. One day she sneaks off to the circus and into the tent of the star aerialist, Anastasia. There she puts on the woman's costume and climbs up to the highwire only to be pet-

rified once she realizes what she has done and where she is. Ultimately saved by Anastasia and cajoled into performing her own act, Morgan is wiser at the end of her adventure, for she understands both her strengths and limitations. Wallace employs various viewpoints in his illustrations in order to bring the viewer into the action of the story, both from the perspective of the highwire itself looking down, and from the spectator on the ground looking up. Catherine Sheldrick Ross, reviewing *Morgan the Magnificent* in *Canadian Literature,* called attention to the "spare and dramatic" text, and to the fact that Wallace's golden-hued pictures "do not so much illustrate the text as extend and enrich it." Ulrike Walker, writing in *Canadian Children's Literature,* similarly found that the title is an "excellent, meticulously designed picture book." Walker also commented on the happy ending, brought about with the help of Anastasia: "The secure 'reality' of the father's farm world is happily mingled with Morgan's own dream world," Walker wrote.

During much of the late 1980s, Wallace concentrated on illustrating the books of others, including *Architect of the Moon* by Wynne-Jones, the Bantu tale, *The Name of the Tree,* Teddy Jam's *The Year of the Fire,* and Bud Davidge's *The Mummer's Song.* Reviewing *The Name of the Tree* in *Reading Teacher,* Galda praised Wallace's artwork, which works "beautifully to convey the mood of intense heat." According to Denia Lewis Hester in a *School Library Journal* review of that same title, "Wallace masterfully utilizes muted pinks, grays, and greens that bring to life the cracked, dry land that threatens the animals' very existence."

With the 1991 *Mr. Kneebone's New Digs,* Wallace returns to a theme initially worked in *The Christmas Tree,* namely the situation of the elderly poor in an urban environment. April Moth lives in a miserable one-room flat with her dog, Mr. Kneebone. She grows so disgusted with the rat-infested place that she sets off to find better lodgings, and ends up in a cave in the park, at least safe from the big buildings of the city. She at last has found a bit of independence in the city, but it is a fragile independence. Lynn Wytenbroek, writing in *Canadian Literature,* praised Wallace's "wonderful pastel pictures . . . [which] help make the book come alive." Annette Goldsmith, writing in *Quill and Quire,* also commented on the "quite lovely" illustrations, but was less impressed with the book as a whole, calling it a "disappointment" for long-time fans. Theo Hersh, however, found more to like in the book in a *Canadian Materials* review, describing the artwork as "among Wallace's best," and further remarking that the "complex, unsettling book" was both "unusual" and "wonderful."

Adapting the work of the Brothers Grimm, Wallace provides his own take on a classic fairy tale in *Hansel and Gretel,* a work that "may well be his most ambitious book," according to Raymond E. Jones and Jon C. Stott in *Canadian Children's Books: A Critical Guide to Authors and Illustrators.* The same authors pointed out that with so many retellings of this classic tale, "the creator of a new version faces the challenge of providing pictures that both enhance the traditional meanings of the story and communicate new ones. Wallace succeeds admirably on both counts." Wallace's retelling remains true to the original tale in spirit, but does modernize and localize parts of it, making the father a poor Atlantic Coast fisherman. Jones and Stott found the illustrations for this book "the darkest of any in Wallace's books." Reviewing *Hansel and Gretel* in *Booklist,* Hazel Rochman found the retelling "sinister but not gruesome." *School Library Journal*'s Judith Constantinides called the book a "brooding, surrealistic version of the classic fairy tale" and a "distinguished book to savor." Similarly, Patty Lawlor, reviewing the same title in *Quill and Quire,* concluded that "Wallace offers readers the opportunity to experience *Hansel and Gretel* in an intriguing and provocative picture-book format."

More uplifting material is presented in *A Winter's Tale* in which nine-year-old Abigail takes her first winter camping trip with her father and in the process helps to save a trapped fawn. *Booklist*'s Linda Perkins found that "the story is a successful vehicle for Wallace's exquisite art," while Audrey Laski, writing in *School Librarian,* called it an "enchanting picture story." Deborah Stevenson, reviewing the work in *Bulletin of the Center for Children's Books,* thought the tale was "appealing," and a "rare outdoor rite-of-passage story about a girl." A young boy has his own rite of passage in *Boy of the Deeps,* in which young James goes to his first day of work in the Nova Scotian coal mines at the turn of the 20th century. This momentous day is made even more dramatic with a cave-in, which traps the boy and his father far beneath the earth. A reviewer for *Publishers Weekly* felt that Wallace's "taut yet descriptive narrative appeals to the senses," while *Booklist*'s Rochman noted that the illustrations in

shades of "black, brown, and blue are lit with the flickering glow of miners' lamps in the dark." *Quill and Quire*'s Hadley Dyer remarked that "Wallace is one of the few children's book illustrators unafraid to let sombre colours dominate," and went on to conclude that the book would appeal to anyone who appreciates that "rare combination of fine writing and illustration."

Another adolescent boy is featured in *Duncan's Way,* which recounts the way in which a boy helps his out-of-work father. Duncan's family have long been fishermen in Newfoundland, but now the cod are not plentiful and after eighteen months of unemployment, something needs to be done. Duncan suddenly hits on the idea of using the family boat as a floating delivery van for a bakery. Linda Ludke, reviewing the work in *School Library Journal,* praised both the artwork, which "capture[s] the beauty of the landscape," and the text, which "eloquently conveys Duncan's anxiety." A contributor for *Publishers Weekly* also commended this simple tale: "Wallace creates some memorable portraits within this larger picture of a vanishing way of life."

Another rite of passage is served up in *The True Story of Trapper Jack's Left Big Toe,* set in the Yukon Territory. Josh and Gabe hear that a local trapper's amputated toe resides in a tobacco tin in the town's saloon, and conspire to get a look at it. First, however, they run into the trapper himself, who explains how his toe came to be frostbitten and subsequently amputated, and then he takes the youths to the saloon himself so they can get a look at it. A contributor for *Kirkus Reviews* called this a "great" and "well-paced" story. *Horn Book*'s Betty Carter likewise praised the "fast-moving plot and ample dialogue." Linda Berezowski, writing in *Resource Links,* found that Wallace's illustrations "complement the script and provide a strong visual setting for the story," and Lauren Peterson of *Booklist* also praised the artwork, noting that Wallace "adds to the fun [of this tall tale] with nicely rendered, superrealistic illustrations." And a contributor for *Publishers Weekly* called the book a "wry and absorbing initiation story."

In the 2002 publication, *The Naked Lady,* Wallace tells the semi-autobiographical story of his own beginnings as an artist. Young Tom takes a welcoming pie to the new neighbor, Pieter, and is shocked to see a statue of a naked lady in the man's yard. When the widowed sculptor informs Tom the statue is nude rather than naked, a friendship and mentorship begin between the lonely older man and the inquisitive farm boy, reflecting Wallace's own first teacher-student relationship as an artist. Reviewers responded warmly to this tribute. A contributor for *Publishers Weekly* applauded the "clean lines and uncluttered composition" of the artwork which in turn "reflect the directness and economy of the prose." The same reviewer called the book a "heartfelt tribute to the important role of mentors in any artist's life." Carolyn Janssen, reviewing the book in *School Library Journal,* likewise found the story to be "inspiring" as well as "appealing and enriching." And a contributor for *Kirkus Reviews* dubbed the tale "haunting" and "beautifully written and illustrated."

In an article for *Five Owls,* Wallace described his illustration process, and the importance of patience. "I always wait for the moment of revelation when I can smell the characters' blood in the media I am using, when I can see the tracks their history has left on the paper's tooth, and when I can watch them climb out of the dark and into the light of my studio. When that moment comes, I can finally say, 'So *that's* what that character or that situation is all about!'"

Jones and Stott concluded that Wallace is "one of Canada's major picture-book artists," and that his books "present a significant and strong vision of life. They emphasize not only the individual's successful quest for self-worth, but also the importance of individuals understanding themselves in relation to family, friends, community, tradition, and the powerful world of nature of which they are a part." Writing in *St. James Guide to Children's Writers,* Wallace explained his mission as a children's book author and illustrator. "In my work as an author I do not sit down to write stories, nor do I consciously choose stories to illustrate because they will be distinguished as being multicultural or Canadian or whatever flag one chooses to wave over them. I write or illustrate stories because first and foremost they are stories that will intrigue, inspire, and touch young readers. The characters who inhabit these tales are people who have earned my sympathy and are ones with whom I can empathize on a personal level. They are universal characters with universal emotions and universal experiences that make us human. They are characters who struggle, who test limits, and who endure. But most importantly they are characters who through the story go through some kind of change. At the end of a good story, a reader comes away with the confidence that the protagonist will never be the same and will treasure the memory. It is my hope that the reader of my books will never be the same either."

BIOGRAPHICAL AND CRITICAL SOURCES:

BOOKS

Children's Literature Review, Volume 37, Gale (Detroit, MI), 1996.
Continuum Encyclopedia of Children's Literature, edited by Bernice E. Cullinan and Diane G. Person, Continuum International (New York, NY), 2001.
Jones, Raymond E., and Jon C. Scott, *Canadian Children's Books: A Critical Guide to Authors and Illustrators,* Oxford University Press (Toronto, Ontario, Canada), 2000, pp. 459-565.
St. James Guide to Children's Writers, edited by Sara Pendergast and Tom Pendergast, St. James Press (Detroit, MI), 1999.
Writers on Writing, Overlea House (Toronto, Ontario, Canada), 1989.

PERIODICALS

Booklist, June 1, 1996, Hazel Rochman, review of *Hansel and Gretel,* p. 1729; November 1, 1996, Carolyn Phelan, review of *Sarah and the People of Sand River,* p. 496; October 15, 1997, Linda Perkins, review of *A Winter's Tale,* p. 417; March 15, 1999, Hazel Rochman, review of *Boy of the Deeps,* p. 1336; February 15, 2000, Susan Dove Lempke, review of *Duncan's Way,* p. 1122; June 1, 2002, Lauren Peterson, review of *The True Story of Trapper Jack's Left Big Toe,* p. 1744.
Bulletin of the Center for Children's Books, January, 1998, Deborah Stevenson, review of *A Winter's Tale,* p. 180.
Canadian Children's Literature, number 57-58, 1990, Carole Gerson, review of *The Sparrow's Song,* pp. 135-136; number 60, 1990, Ulrike Walker, review of *Morgan the Magnificent,* pp. 113-114.
Canadian Literature, autumn, 1989, Catherine Sheldrick Ross, review of *Morgan the Magnificent,* pp. 246-247; autumn, 1992, Lynn Wytenbroek, review of *Mr. Kneebone's New Digs,* p. 162.
Canadian Materials, May, 1991, Joan McGrath, "Making Friends," pp. 153-156; March, 1992, Theo Hersh, review of *Mr. Kneebone's New Digs,* p. 85.

Children's Literature in Education, September, 1994, Mingshoi Cai, review of *Chin Chiang and the Dragon's Dance,* p. 169.

Emergency Librarian, September, 1990, review of *Chin Chiang and the Dragon's Dance,* p. 51.

Five Owls, May-June, 1999, Ian Wallace, "Waiting for the Raven," pp. 102-103.

Globe and Mail (Toronto, Ontario, Canada), August 4, 1984, Sandra Martin, review of *Chin Chiang and the Dragon's Dance;* November 1, 1986.

Horn Book, May-June, 2002, Betty Carter, review of *The True Story of Trapper Jack's Left Big Toe,* p. 323.

Horn Book Guide, spring, 2001, Carolyn Shute, review of *Duncan's Way,* p. 52.

Kirkus Reviews, March 15, 1999, review of *Boy of the Deeps,* pp. 458-459; April 1, 2002, review of *The True Story of Trapper Jack's Left Big Toe,* p. 501; October 1, 2002, review of *The Naked Lady,* p. 1483.

Language Arts, April, 1989, Jon C. Stott, "Profile: Ian Wallace," pp. 443-449.

Maclean's, December 9, 2002, review of *The Naked Lady,* p. 77.

Pubishers Weekly, September 23, 1996, review of *Sarah and the People of Sand River,* p. 76; April 26, 1999, review of *Boy of the Deeps,* p. 83; March 6, 2000, review of *Duncan's Way,* p. 110; March 18, 2002, review of *The True Story of Trapper Jack's Left Big Toe,* p. 104; November 11, 2002, review of *The Naked Lady,* p. 63.

Quill and Quire, November, 1991, Annette Goldsmith, review of *The Name of the Tree,* p. 26; October, 1994, Patty Lawlor, review of *Hansel and Gretel,* pp. 40-41; March, 1999, Hadley Dyer, review of *Boy of the Deeps,* p. 67.

Reading Teacher, February, 1991, Lee Galda, review of *The Name of the Tree,* p. 411; April, 1992, Lee Galda, review of *Chin Chiang and the Dragon's Dance,* p. 635.

Resource Links, April, 2001, review of *Duncan's Way,* p. 49; June, 2002, Linda Berezowski, review of *The True Story of Trapper Jack's Left Big Toe,* pp. 8-10.

School Librarian, spring, 1998, Audrey Laski, review of *A Winter's Tale,* p. 37.

School Library Journal, March, 1990, Denia Lewis Hester, review of *The Name of the Tree,* p. 209; June, 1990, p. 80; May, 1996, Judith Constantinides, review of *Hansel and Gretel,* p. 104; December, 1996, Sally R. Dow, review of *Sarah and the People of Sand River,* p. 108; December, 1997,

Patricia Manning, review of *A Winter's Tale,* p. 102; July, 1999, Kathleen Whalin, review of *Boy of the Deeps,* p. 82; March, 2000, Linda Ludke, review of *Duncan's Way,* p. 219; April, 2002, Beth Tegart, review of *The True Story of Trapper Jack's Left Big Toe,* p. 159; November, 2002, Carolyn Janssen, review of *The Naked Lady,* p. 139.

OTHER

Meet the Author/Illustrator: Ian Wallace (videotape), Meade Education Services, 1990.

*   *   *

WALTERS, Jennifer Waelti
See WAELTI-WALTERS, Jennifer

*   *   *

WATSON, Lyall 1939-

PERSONAL: Born April 12, 1939, in Johannesburg, South Africa; son of Douglas (an architect) and Mary (Morkel) Watson; married Vivienne Mawson, 1961 (divorced, 1966). *Education:* University of Witwatersrand, B.S., 1958; University of Natal, M.S., 1959; University of London, Ph.D., 1963. *Politics:* "Absolutely none." *Religion:* "Animist." *Hobbies and other interests:* Tribal art, bird-watching, archaeology, ethnobotany, conchology.

ADDRESSES: Home—Ballplehob, West Cork, Ireland; also lived on oceangoing trawler Amazon, 1982-94. *Office*—BCM-Biologic, London WC1N 3XX, England. *Agent*—David Higham Associates, 5-8 Lower John Street, Golden Square, London W1R 4HA, England.

CAREER: Zoological Garden of Johannesburg, Johannesburg, South Africa, director, 1964-65; British Broadcasting Corp., London, England, producer of documentary films, 1966-67; BCM-Biologic (life science consultancy), London, founder and director, 1968; writer, 1970—. Once apprenticed to Desmond Morris, London Zoo; worked in archaeology with American School of Oriental Research, Jordan and Saudi Arabia;

worked in anthropology in northern Nigeria; expedition leader and researcher in Antarctica, Amazon River area, the Seychelles, Galapagos, and Indonesia, etc., 1968; commissioner for Seychelles on International Whaling Commission, 1978-82; Indian Ocean Whale Sanctuary, founder.

AWARDS, HONORS: Appointed Knight of the Golden Ark by The Netherlands, 1983.

WRITINGS:

The Omnivorous Ape, Coward, McCann & Geoghegan (New York, NY), 1971.

Supernature: The Natural History of the Supernatural, Hodder and Stoughton (London, England), 1973, first U.S. edition published as *Supernature,* Anchor (Garden City, NY), 1973, also published with original title, Coronet (London, England), 1974.

The Romeo Error: A Matter of Life and Death, Hodder and Stoughton (London, England), 1974, first paperback edition, Anchor (Garden City, NY), 1975.

Gifts of Unknown Things, Hodder and Stoughton (London, England), 1976, Simon & Schuster (New York City), 1976, published as *Gifts of Unknown Things: A True Story of Nature, Healing, and Initiation from Indonesia's "Dancing Island,"* Destiny Books (Rochester, VT), 1991.

Lifetide: The Biology of the Unconscious, Hodder and Stoughton (London, England), 1979, Simon & Schuster (New York, NY), 1979.

Sea Guide to Whales of the World, illustrated by Tom Ritchie, Hutchinson (London, England), 1981, Dutton (New York, NY), 1981.

Lightning Bird: The Story of One Man's Journey into Africa's Past (biography), Dutton (New York, NY), 1982, first paperback edition, Simon & Schuster (New York, NY), 1983.

Heaven's Breath: A Natural History of the Wind, Hodder and Stoughton (London, England), 1984, first U.S. edition, Morrow (New York, NY), 1984.

Earthworks: Ideas on the Edge of Natural History, with illustrations by Fujio Watanabe, Hodder and Stoughton (London, England), 1986.

The Dreams of Dragons: Riddles of Natural History, Morrow (New York, NY), 1987, published as *The Dreams of Dragons: An Exploration and Celebration of the Mysteries of Nature,* Destiny Books (Rochester, VT), 1992.

Beyond Supernature: A New Natural History of the Supernatural (sequel to *Supernature*), Hodder and Stoughton (London, England), 1986, first paperback edition, Bantam (New York, NY), 1988.

The Water Planet: A Celebration of the Wonder of Water, with images by Jerry Derbyshire, Crown (New York, NY), 1988.

Sumo, Sidgwick & Jackson (London, England), 1988.

The Nature of Things: The Secret Life of Inanimate Objects, Hodder and Stoughton (London, England), 1990, Destiny Books (Rochester, VT), 1992.

Neophilia, Sceptre (London, England), 1993.

Dark Nature: A Natural History of Evil, HarperCollins (New York, NY), 1995.

(Author of essay) *Turtle Islands: Balinese Ritual and the Green Turtle,* photography and journals by Charles Lindsay, Takarajima Books (New York, NY), 1995.

By the River of the Elephants: An African Childhood, Kingfisher (New York, NY), 1997.

(For children) *Warriors, Warthogs, and Wisdom: Growing Up in Africa,* illustrated by Keith West, first American edition, Kingfisher (New York, NY), 1997.

Jacobson's Organ and the Remarkable Nature of Smell, Penguin (London, England), 1999, first American edition, Norton (New York, NY), 2000.

Elephantoms: Tracking the Elephant, Norton (New York, NY), 2002.

Also author of screenplays for feature films *Gifts of Unknown Things* and *Lifetide: The Biology of the Unconscious.* Contributor to Reader's Digest Services' *Living World of Animals* series, 1970. Contributor to professional journals.

WORK IN PROGRESS: Research on the building of a bridge between scientific investigation and mystic revelation.

SIDELIGHTS: Biologist, naturalist, and writer Lyall Watson grew up in South Africa, where he learned much about life from an elderly Zulu friend and the natural world around him as a child. At college he studied with Raymond Dart, who discovered the early hominid Australopithecus; later studies in Europe led to an apprenticeship with Desmond Morris at the London Zoo. Archaeological fieldwork in Jordan in the late 1960s led Watson to an offer to direct the rebuilding of a Johannesburg zoo. He later became a producer of documentary nature films for the British Broadcasting Corp. (BBC) in London. Following this career, he founded Biologic of London, a company that designs zoos, organizes safaris, and consults on various life science projects. In 1973, Watson had his first big success with a book, *Supernature: The Natural History of the Supernatural,* which sold a million copies and launched his writing career.

"Since 1967 I have traveled constantly," Watson once said, "looking and listening, collecting bits and pieces of apparently useless and unconnected information, stopping every two years to put the fragments together into some sort of meaningful pattern. Sometimes it works out. And so far, enough people have enjoyed the results to justify publishing several million copies in fourteen languages."

Gifts of Unknown Things is an account of Watson's brief visit to Nus Tarian, a small Indonesian island, and the seemingly supernatural occurrences he witnessed there. Many of the paranormal phenomena in the book center on a young girl named Tia, and several of the book's reviewers found the events incredible. John Naughton, for example, wrote in the *New Statesman* that Watson's "chronicle of [Tia's] more spectacular exploits stretches the reader's credulity to breaking point and beyond." Christopher Lehmann-Haupt of the *New York Times* remarked: "I don't believe that Tia, the young orphan girl of the island, learned to heal burns by touching them with her hand, to cure schizophrenia by drawing out bad chemicals, to raise a man from the dead, and, finally, when the Muslim natives begin to find Tia's powers too disturbing to their orthodoxy, to transform herself into a porpoise. . . . Now it may well be, as Mr. Watson argues, that my Western rationalism is woefully limited—that it fails to perceive what children and poets and Eastern mystics and with-it physicists see with the greatest of ease, which is that 'There are levels of reality far too mysterious for totally objective common sense. There are things that cannot be known by exercise only of the scientific method.' Fair enough. But just because Newton has turned out to be wrong doesn't make *all* things possible. . . . Yet this is how Mr. Watson reasons."

In *Lifetide: The Biology of the Unconscious,* Watson attempts to construct a unified model of life and the universe that accounts for phenomena currently unexplained by modern science. Using a plethora of examples from biology—his own area of expertise—as well as such disciplines as physics, anthropology, medicine, psychology, and paleontology, Watson argues that evolution and everything else in the cosmos is deliberately directed by a kind of collective unconscious of all living things (including biological components). He calls this "contingent system" the Lifetide and describes it as "the whole panoply of hidden forces that shape life in all its miraculous guises, . . . the eddies and vortices of nature that flow together to form the living stream." Reviewing the book for *Washington Post Book World,* Dan Sperling commented: "Watson builds an admirable case in favor of the existence of such a contingent system, and believes that the eventual discovery of its parameters and properties will reveal it to be the source of much that we now call the paranormal, . . . [although] even this, he feels, will not solve the underlying mysteries of the Lifetide." Sperling also pointed out that Watson's description of this system contains "language so rich and lively that at times the book seems as though it were written by a poet rather than a scientist."

Dark Nature: A Natural History of Evil examines the nature of evil from the perspective of that which upsets the natural order of a society. Evil, Watson explains in the book, is anything "that is bad for ecology." As a *Kirkus Reviews* contributor explained, "evil is anything that disrupts the integrity of the ecological moment—the sense of place and community—anything that disturbs diversity, relative abundance, and communication." Evil, as Watson defines the term, is a force of nature. For example, headhunters in Indonesia are ethically sound from this point of view because their killings are done with cultural purpose and serve as population controls in an area with limited resources. Serial killers in America are evil because there are no apparent societal or ecological benefits. As Charles C. Mann commented in the *Washington Post Book World,* Watson examines the "baffling intersection of morality and biology" and "the apparent ethical implications of genetics and evolutionary theory." In examining the nature of evil, Watson "ranges through philosophy, psychology, anthropology, history, ecology, and especially biology," a *Publishers Weekly* contributor wrote.

Watson acknowledges that genes play the major role in determining individual behavior and that aggression and violence seem genetically inherent in human beings. He confronts the idea of natural selection and finds it at great odds with morality and aesthetics. "Natural selection," Watson writes, "is extraordinarily good at maximising immediate genetic interests, but it is uncommonly bad at long-term planning." He calls natural selection "a blind man married to a beautiful woman; and we are the products of that union."

Robert Edgerton praised the work in the *National Review,* writing, with "admirable judgement and superb craftsmanship, Watson ranges widely over such topics as the nature of ecology, genetic fitness, the selfish and deceptive behavior of gorillas, the premeditated violence of chimpanzees, and the altruism of false killer whales." Mann found that "most nonfiction has small factual errors of the sort that reviewers cite to demonstrate their own superiority. But *Dark Nature* has an astonishing number of them." He also cited several "odd lapses in logic and tone," but concluded that "buried within the factual and logical muddle is an energetic, thoughtful discussion of an important issue."

Jacobson's Organ and the Remarkable Nature of Smell is a book about the traditional sense of smell and a kind of sixth sense, the vomeronasal organ in the human nose, discovered by a Danish anatomist named Jacobson in 1809. The organ is said to pick up subtle pheromonal, sexual, and chemical odors and transmit them to the hypothalamus in the brain. Watson writes about this type of sensing ability and how it is found throughout the animal and plant kingdoms as well. Donna Seaman of *Booklist* praised Watson's "intriguing and instructive examples" and "passages of sheer wonder" as he details the amazing senses of smell—how smell can rekindle memories, help us recognize others, and distinguish between good and bad encounters—and what odors mean in the natural world. A writer for W. W. Norton's Web site observed, "In this surprising and delightful book, Lyall Watson rescues our most unappreciated sense from obscurity." A *Publisher's Weekly* contributor was less convinced, however, concluding, "As with his earlier work, Watson provides tantalizing conjectures, but his uncritical acceptance of the paranormal reduces his credibility." Ann Finkbeiner, writing a review of the book for the *New York Times,* pointed out that Watson reminds his readers that some of his theory is pure speculation and disagrees with traditional science, but she concluded, "I like scientists' care with belief. But Watson's book is loving, the writing is lively. . . . Also, he's having

such a delightful time up there in his cottage on the cliff, spinning facts and foaming nonsense into this vision of the world's creatures, Jacobsonly joined."

Watson's *Elephantoms: Tracking the Elephant* is a combination of memoir, myth, and scientific facts about this intelligent, powerful, yet emotional species. A writer for W. W. Norton called the book "part meditation on an elusive animal, part evocation of the power of place." It includes what a *Kirkus Reviews* contributor called a "superbly rendered account," told with "wonderful freshness and enthusiasm," of events from Watson's boyhood, when he and friends sighted a wild white elephant and met a South African Khoi tribesman who passed on wisdom about the creatures during days on the beach. Stories of ancient myths about elephants are woven together with accounts of Watson's later experiences with the animals in his zoological work and with facts presented by elephant researchers. Reports of how elephants have shaped their land and how hunters have sought to destroy them are also included. The *Kirkus* contributor concluded that Watson, "much more evocatively than any zoologist has ever managed," treats his readers to powerful insight into the elephant's place in nature and time. "His chronicle of these majestic creatures will cast a spell on readers," a *Publishers Weekly* contributor wrote. Edell M. Schaefer, reviewing the book for *Library Journal,* observed, "The rambling narrative style does not diminish the treasures to be gleaned from Watson's personal experiences," even though she thought some readers simply looking for facts might be disappointed. Nancy Bent of *Booklist* wrote that Watson "has created a lyrical paean to an animal that is as much myth as fact."

Although Watson maintains on his new Web site that he has never been one for using computers and technology in his writing and research, preferring instead to write "with a fountain pen, in black ink, on paper with the reassuring colour and feel of old vellum," he agrees that his readers might enjoy finding him on the Web. His world travels and simple lifestyle—he lived on a converted shrimp trawler for twelve years and now lives in a restored farm cottage on Ireland's rocky coast—allow him to take what comes and report, he said on his Web site, "what I find along the way." Out to prove no premise or promote any philosophy, Watson explained, "All I do is look, listen and try to make sense of what I find, in biological terms. Which means asking, again and again, the three essential questions that put discoveries and insights into evolutionary perspective: 'Where did it come from?, Does it have survival value?, and What happens next?'" Watson said he considers it worthwhile to pursue "the soft edges of science"—those answers that have not yet reached the level of human understanding but may reconcile science with the human experience.

BIOGRAPHICAL AND CRITICAL SOURCES:

BOOKS

International Who's Who 2000, 63rd edition, Europa (London, England), 2000.
Watson, Lyall, *Lifetide: The Biology of the Unconscious,* Simon & Schuster, 1978.
Watson, Lyall, *Dark Nature: A Natural History of Evil,* HarperCollins, 1995.
Writers Directory 2001, 16th edition, edited by Miranda H. Ferrara, St. James Press (Detroit, MI), 2001.

PERIODICALS

Booklist, February 15, 1996, p. 967; April 1, 2000, Donna Seaman, review of *Jacobson's Organ and the Remarkable Nature of Smell,* p. 1423; April 1, 2002, Nancy Bent, review of *Elephantoms: Tracking the Elephant,* p. 1290.
Cruising World, September, 1982, p. 146.
Earth Science, winter, 1988, pp. 32-33.
Fate, January, 1980, p. 106; March, 1983, p. 93.
Globe and Mail (Toronto), December 8, 1984; October 4, 1986.
Horn Book Guide, spring, 1998, review of *Warriors, Warthogs, and Wisdom,* p. 182.
Kirkus Reviews, December 15, 1995, review of *Dark Nature: A Natural History of Evil,* pp. 1760-61; February 15, 2002, review of *Elephantoms,* p. 243.
Library Journal, March 15, 2002, Edell M. Schaefer, review of *Elephantoms,* p. 105.
National Review, September 2, 1996, Robert Edgerton, review of *Dark Nature,* p. 92.
Natural History, April, 2000, review of *Jacobson's Organ,* p. 90.
New Scientist, December 25, 1999, review of *Jacobson's Organ,* p. 81.
New Statesman, July 2, 1976, John Naughton, review of *Gifts of Unknown Things.*
New Yorker, July 22, 1996, p. 62.
New York Times, April 13, 1977, Christopher Lehmann-Haupt, review of *Gifts of Unknown Things;* April 9, 2000, Ann Finkbeiner, "The Sixth Sense," review of *Jacobson's Organ,* Late Edition, Section 7, p. 25.
New York Times Book Review, June 3, 1979; April 18, 1982; May 10, 1987.
Oceans, September-October, 1982, p. 60.
Parabola, February, 1986, p. 104.
Publishers Weekly, January 15, 1996, review of *Dark Nature,* p. 456; March 20, 2000, review of *Jacobson's Organ,* p. 82; April 8, 2002, review of *Elephantoms,* p. 213.
Sea Frontiers, March-April, 1982, p. 121.
Skeptical Inquirer, fall, 1993, pp. 76-79.
Social Education, April, 1998, review of *Warriors, Warthogs, and Wisdom,* p. 8.
Spectator, October 26, 1974.
Times Literary Supplement, December 20, 1974; August 20, 1982.
Washington Post Book World, April 10, 1977; July 15, 1979, Dan Sperling, review of *Lifetide: The Biology of the Unconscious;* May 23, 1982; March 31, 1996, Charles C. Mann, review of *Dark Nature,* p. 9.
Wilson Library Bulletin, February, 1982, p. 464; December, 1985, p. 70.
Yachting, May, 1982, p. 32.

ONLINE

Lyall Watson Home Page, http://www.lyallwatson.com/ (June 17, 2002), biography, bibliography.
W. W. Norton, http://wwnorton.com/ (June 17, 2002), description of *Jacobson's Organ* and *Elephantoms.**

*   *   *

WEISSMANN, Gerald 1930-

PERSONAL: Born August 7, 1930, in Vienna, Austria; immigrated to the United States, 1938, naturalized citizen, 1943; son of Adolf (a medical doctor) and Greta (Lustbader) Weissmann; married Ann Raphael, April 1, 1953; children: Andrew, Lisa Beth. *Ethnicity:* "Austrian." *Education:* Columbia University, B.A., 1950; New York University, M.D., 1954; postdoctoral research in biochemistry at New York University and in cell biology at Cambridge University. *Hobbies and other interests:* Tennis.

ADDRESSES: Office—Department of Medicine, School of Medicine, New York University Medical Center, 550 First Ave., New York, NY 10016-6402. *E-mail*—gerald.weissmann@med.nyu.edu.

CAREER: Licensed to practice medicine in New York. Mt. Sinai Hospital, New York, NY, intern, 1954-55; Bellevue Hospital, New York, NY, resident and chief resident, 1955-58; Arthritis and Rheumatism Foundation, New York, NY, research fellow in biochemistry, 1958-59; New York University Medical Center, New York, NY, research assistant, Department of Medicine, 1959-60, instructor, 1959-61, assistant professor, 1961-65, associate professor, 1965-70, professor of medicine, 1970—, director of Division of Cell Biology, 1969-73, director of Division of Rheumatology, 1974-2000, director of Biotechnology Study Center, 2000—. U.S. Public Health Service special research fellow at Strangeways Research Laboratory, Cambridge University, 1960-61; senior investigator of Arthritis and Rheumatism Foundation, 1961-65; Diplomate of American Board of Internal Medicine, 1963; visiting investigator, ARC Institute of Animal Physiology, Babraham, England, 1964-69; career investigator of Health Research Council of New York, 1966-70; investigator and instructor at Woods Hole Marine Biological Laboratory, 1970-77, trustee, 1993—; visiting investigator at Centre de Physiologie et d'Immunologie Cellulaires, Hospital St. Antoine, Paris, France, 1973-74; lecturer at Johns Hopkins University, 1976; lecturer at Medical College of Georgia, Augusta, 1980; Rockefeller Foundation resident at the Villa Serbelloni, Bellagio, Italy, 1987; visiting investigator at William Harvey Research Institute, London, England, 1987; lecturer at Medical College of Pennsylvania, 1988; centennial lecturer at the Marine Biological Laboratory, 1988, and at Johns Hopkins Medical School, 1989. Consultant to Pfizer, Searle, Riker, Upjohn, 1972—; *Clinical Immunology and Immunopathology*, member of editorial board, 1972-88; consultant to U.S. Food and Drug Administration and National Heart and Lung Institute; Ethicon Company, scientific advisory board, 1973-76; BioResponse, scientific advisory board, 1982-86; The Liposome Company, director, cofounder (with E. C. Whitehead), and chair of scientific advisory board, 1982 ; member of postdoctoral fellowships review commission, Pfizer International, New York, NY,

1983-89; member of scholarship selection committee, Pew Scholars in the Biomedical Sciences, New Haven, CT, 1984-94; Ellison Medical Foundation, national advisory board, 1997—. *Military service:* U. S. Army Medical Corps, 1955-57; became captain.

MEMBER: International Association of Poets, Playwrights, Editors, Essayists and Novelists (PEN) American Center, American Society of Cell Biology, American Society of Biological Chemistry and Molecular Biology, American Society of Experimental Pathology, American Society for Clinical Investigation, American Federation of Clinical Research, American Society of Pharmacology and Experimental Therapeutics, American Association of Immunologists, American Association of Physicians, American Rheumatism Association, American College of Rheumatology (president, 1982-83; master, 1996), American Association for the Advancement of Science (fellow, 1982), Society for Experimental Biology and Medicine, New York Academy of Medicine (fellow, 1993), Phi Beta Kappa, Alpha Omega Alpha, Harvey Society of New York (president, 1981-82), Interurban Club.

AWARDS, HONORS: Alessandro Robecchi Prize for Rheumatology, International League against Rheumatism, 1972, for research on mechanisms of inflammation; Guggenheim fellow at Center of Immunology and Physiology, Paris, France, 1973-74; Marine Biology Laboratory Prize in cell biology, 1974 and 1979, for work in cell biology of inflammation; University of Bologna medal, Bologna, Italy, 1978; Lila Gruber Cancer Research Award (coholder with Emil Frei, Jr.), 1979; Solomon A. Berson Medical Alumni Achievement Award in Clinical Sciences, New York University, 1980; National Institutes of Health MERIT Award, 1987; Marine Biological Laboratory Centennial Award for Leadership in Biomedical Sciences, 1988; Hiram Maxim Award for Scientific Communication, 1990; American College of Rheumatology Distinguished Investigator Award, 1992; Charles Plotz Award, Arthritis Foundation (NY), 1993; Paul Klemperer Award, New York Academy of Medicine, 1997; award from Accademia Nazionale dei Lincei (Rome), 2002.

WRITINGS:

(Editor) *Mediators of Inflammation,* Plenum Press (New York, NY), 1974.
(Editor, with Robert Claiborne) *Cell Membranes, Biochemistry, Cell Biology and Pathology,* Hospital Practice Press (New York, NY), 1975.

(Editor) *The Biological Revolution: Applications of Cell Biology to Public Welfare,* Plenum Press (New York, NY), 1979.

(Series editor, with Leonard Eleazar Glynn, and John C. Houck) *Handbook of Inflammation,* four volumes, Elsevier/North-Holland Biomedical Press (Amsterdam, Holland, and New York, NY), 1979-83.

(Editor) *The Cell Biology of Inflammation,* Elsevier/North-Holland Biomedical Press (Amsterdam, Holland, and New York, NY), 1980.

The Woods Hole Cantata: Essays on Science and Society, foreword by Lewis Thomas, Dodd, Mead (New York, NY), 1985, paperback edition, Houghton Mifflin (Boston, MA), 1986.

They All Laughed at Christopher Columbus: Tales of Medicine and the Art of Discovery, Times Books (New York, NY), 1987.

The Doctor with Two Heads, and Other Essays, Knopf (New York, NY), 1990, Vintage Books (New York, NY), 1991.

The Doctor Dilemma, Whittle Direct Books (Knoxville, TN), 1992.

(Editor, with Robert Barlow and John Dowling) *The Biological Century: Friday Evening Talks at the Marine Biological Laboratory,* Harvard University Press (Cambridge, MA), 1994.

Democracy and DNA: American Dreams and Medical Progress, Hill & Wang (New York, NY), 1995.

Darwin's Audubon: Science and the Liberal Imagination, Plenum Trade (New York, NY), 1998.

The Year of the Genome: A Diary of the Biological Revolution, Times Books (New York, NY), 2002.

Contributor of more than 300 articles to professional journals; contributor of book reviews and essays to periodicals, including the *New York Times Book Review,* the *London Review of Books,* and *The New Republic;* contributor of essays to books; author of "This Week" column in online magazine the *Praxis Post.*

SIDELIGHTS: Gerald Weissmann, a professor of medicine at New York University Medical Center, is the author of five volumes of essays on the art and science of medicine. The essays in his first collection, *The Woods Hole Cantata: Essays on Science and Society,* relate the science of medicine to its social context. One piece concerns a medical researcher who is a prisoner in a concentration camp. Another describes the fate of a severe schizophrenic whose physical illness is treated with new wonder drugs; the pa-

tient is then released to the community with little apparent regard for the psychological and social aspects of her illness. The author discusses a wide range of medical and social issues that reflect his own routine as a scientific researcher. Anna Fels, a reviewer for the *New York Times Book Review,* found Weissmann's insights "original and provocative." She wrote: "It is not only Dr. Weissmann's observations that enliven these essays, but also the palpable delight he derives from the occasions that gave rise to them."

Weissmann's second volume of essays, *They All Laughed at Christopher Columbus: Tales of Medicine and the Art of Discovery,* was published in 1987. In an article for the *New York Times Book Review,* Martha Weinman Lear called the book a "graceful, feisty collection" that conveys "the promise of adventure, of voyages of discovery, near-palpable each morning . . . when the laboratory doors are opened." Weissmann uses examples from his own practice to inform the general reader about the world of scientific discovery and to air his views on some of the medico-social issues of our time. An essay on one of his asthma patients allows the physician to discuss the fluctuations in the history of asthma treatment over the years and the debate between those who consider it a physical ailment and others who treat asthma as a psychosomatic disorder. A female AIDS victim prompts Weissmann to consider the fear of science that permeates our age. Lear recommended *They All Laughed at Christopher Columbus* as "a book filled with graceful and generous themes, written in a spirit of caring that defines medicine in the fullest sense."

In his third collection, *The Doctor with Two Heads, and Other Essays,* Weissmann comments on the relationship between art and medicine. Gloria Hochman, writing in the *New York Times Book Review,* stated that the "reader comes away with a tasty repertory of cultural hors d'oeuvres."

In 1996, Weissmann published his fourth book of essays, *Democracy and DNA: American Dreams and Medical Progress,* in which he presents his arguments against the use of nontraditional therapies, pointing out the ineffectiveness of unconventional medicine on pandemics and the positive effects of American meliorists. *New York Times Book Review* contributor Lance Morrow described the book as "surprising and elegantly indignant." Morrow wrote, "Although *Democracy and DNA* is a passionately cranky tract, it sparkles here and there with charm and style. Dr. Weissmann explores the moral connection between medicine and literature, following such civilized examples as those of Sir Thomas Browne, Oliver Wendell Holmes, Sr., and Lewis Thomas. . . . He writes at length about the young Holmes's medical studies in Paris in the 1930s, when clinical medicine began to be an observational science." In conclusion, Morrow found that Weissmann "clings to an American ideal of inclusive democracy fortified by a medical habit of . . . 'explaining facts by facts.'"

Lynn Phillips, in a review of *Democracy and DNA* for *The Nation,* viewed Weissmann's use of history in the book less favorably. Phillips wrote, "Gerald Weissmann's unfortunate strategy is to hang himself with an untenable string of historical connections. He claims that modern DNA research ascends in a direct line from the nineteenth-century Anglo-American tradition of meliorism, and we should therefore love it." Phillips commented that meliorism was attributed to figures who actually had their self-interest in mind when making medical discoveries and that Weissmann does not properly credit women doctors and researchers, including Elizabeth Blackwell and Rosalind Franklin. Phillips also pointed out that the book is lacking in Weissmann's own viewpoint on the issues. "It might have been interesting," said Phillips, "to learn what he thinks the great medical potential of DNA research is, or on what grounds he equates the ethical ambiguities of genetic engineering with the simple benefits of good sanitation, or why he's so convinced that democracy is alive and well in the increasingly corporatized world of medical research." William Beatty of *Booklist* praised *Democracy and DNA,* noting Weissmann's "delightful style and wide-ranging knowledge" and commending the author for admitting that medicine still has a long way to go in spite of its progress in the past.

In a fifth book of essays, *Darwin's Audubon: Science and the Liberal Imagination,* Weissmann again touches on a number of subjects related to science and the humanities. He delves into the lives and discoveries of some of history's most famous in their fields, including Marie Curie, Gertrude Stein, Oliver Wendell Holmes, Charles Darwin, and Honore Daumier, as well as lesser known scientists such as Ludwik Fleck, who did research while a prisoner in German concentration camps. Anthony Daniels, in a review for *New Criterion,* had both praise and criticism for this volume of essays, saying, "Weissmann is best when he is at his most straightforwardly historical." He called the essay on Fleck "a work of genuine piety about a man who deserves not to be forgotten, but otherwise might be." Daniels also commented that Weissmann's "interests and learning are wide ranging. . . . He writes with equal facility of Charles Darwin and Honore Daumier, of liposomes and literature, of immunology and impasto. He is also a humane and decent man." However, Daniels thought that Weissmann "has a habit of avoiding the really difficult questions that his essays raise," for example, "why, after so much technical and material progress, mankind finds itself very little happier than before." Apart from any criticism of the book, however, Daniels had a high opinion of Weissmann's work, saying, "In recent years there have been a more than usual number of elegant scientist- and doctor-essayists. . . . Gerald Weissmann . . . is of their company." A *Publishers Weekly* contributor, although expressing some reservations about choppy prose and unnatural references to history and poetry, concluded, "these essays demonstrate the working of a considerable intellect."

The Year of the Genome: A Diary of the Biological Revolution is a collection of thirty-four of Weissmann's columns from the online magazine *Praxis Post,* written between April 3, 2000, and October 2, 2001. Their subjects are the scientific history of and modern-day public reaction to major scientific issues of the year, including the release of the so-called abortion pill, RU 486; the mapping of the human genome; cloning; stem cell research; outbreaks of the Ebola virus and typhus; mad cow disease; anthrax; and new treatments for Alzheimer's disease, Parkinson's disease, and AIDS. Mary Chitty of *Library Journal* called the book "erudite, engaging, and accessible." A *Publishers Weekly* contributor also noted that Weissmann "is articulate and erudite, and he lucidly distills scientific concepts for the layman," although the contributor felt some readers might be put off by some smugness of language. A contributor to *Kirkus Reviews* noted that Weissmann "reveals an impatience with the way things are, a sense that we haven't come all that far." The contributor concluded, "There's wisdom here to be sure, but it's mingled with plenty of self-indulgence." Gilbert Taylor of *Booklist* praised the volume as packed with information and providing "cultural context [that] goes a level deeper than the daily newspaper."

Weissmann once told CA: "I have been writing all my life and am always pleased when someone actually reads my work, not in the course of duty, but in the pursuit of pleasure."

BIOGRAPHICAL AND CRITICAL SOURCES:

BOOKS

Complete Marquis Who's Who, Marquis Who's Who, 2001.

PERIODICALS

Booklist, February 1, 1996, William Beatty, review of *Democracy and DNA: American Dreams and Medical Progress,* p. 908; April 15, 2002, Gilbert Taylor, review of *The Year of the Genome: A Diary of the Biological Revolution,* p. 1370.

Choice, February, 1999, review of *Darwin's Audubon: Science and the Liberal Imagination,* p. 1080.

Kirkus Reviews, March 15, 2002, review of *The Year of the Genome,* p. 399.

Library Journal, January, 1996, review of *Democracy and DNA,* p. 133; May 1, 2002, Mary Chitty, review of *The Year of the Genome,* p. 129.

Nation, May 20, 1996, Lynn Phillips, review of *Democracy and DNA,* p. 25.

New Criterion, March, 2002, Anthony Daniels, review of *Darwin's Audubon,* p. 65.

New Scientist, December 5, 1998, review of *Darwin's Audubon,* p. 45.

New York Times Book Review, September 29, 1985, Anna Fels, review of *The Woods Hole Cantata: Essays on Science and Society;* April 5, 1987, Martha Weinman Lear, review of *They All Laughed at Christopher Columbus: Tales of Medicine and the Art of Discovery;* July 15, 1990, Gloria Hochman, review of *The Doctor with Two Heads, and Other Essays;* March 3, 1996, Lance Morrow, "Irrational Medicine," review of *Democracy and DNA,* pp. 11-12.

Publishers Weekly, October 19, 1998, review of *Darwin's Audubon,* p. 64; April 29, 2002, review of *The Year of the Genome,* p. 52.

Science Books and Films, January, 1999, review of *Darwin's Audubon,* p. 28.

SciTech Book News, December, 1998, review of *Darwin's Audubon,* p. 10.

ONLINE

Ellison Medical Foundation Web site, http//www. ellison-med-fn.org/ (June 17, 2002), "Gerald Weissmann, M.D."

Henry Holt/Times Books Web site, http://www.holtz brinckpublishers.com/henryholt/ (June 17, 2002), review of *The Year of the Genome.*

Rheumatology Web Board, http://www.rheumatology web.com/board/ (June 17, 2002) "Gerald Weissmann, M.D."

*   *   *

WELLS, Rosemary 1943-

PERSONAL: Born January 29, 1943, in New York, NY; married Thomas Moore Wells (an architect), 1963; children: Victoria, Marguerite. *Education:* Attended Boston Museum School, Boston, MA.

ADDRESSES: Home—738 Sleepy Hollow Rd., Briarcliff Manor, NY 10510. *Agent*—c/o Doubleday, 666 Fifth Avenue, New York, NY 10103.

CAREER: Freelance author and illustrator, 1968—. Worked for Allyn & Bacon, Boston, MA, and Macmillan Publishing Co., New York, NY.

AWARDS, HONORS: Honor Book citation, *Book World* Spring Children's Book Festival, 1972, for *The Fog Comes on Little Pig Feet;* Children's Book Showcase Award, Children's Book Council, 1974, for *Noisy Nora;* Citation of Merit, Society of Illustrators, 1974, for *Benjamin and Tulip;* Art Book for Children citation, Brooklyn Museum and Brooklyn Public Library, 1975, 1976, and 1977, all for *Benjamin and Tulip;* Irma Simonton Black Award, Bank Street College of Education, for *Morris's Disappearing Bag: A Christmas Story;* Edgar Allan Poe Special Award, Mystery Writers of America, 1981, for *When No One Was Looking; Hazel's Amazing Mother* was named one of the *New York Times* Best Illustrated Books, 1985; Washington Irving Children's Book Choice Award, Westchester Library Association, 1986, for *Peabody,* and 1988, for *Max's Christmas; Boston Globe-Horn Book* Award, 1989, for *Shy Charles;* Child Study Association Children's Books of the Year citations for

Rosemary Wells

Morris's Disappearing Bag and *Don't Spill It Again, James; Booklist* Children's Editor's Choice citations for *Max's Toys: A Counting Book, Timothy Goes to School,* and *Through the Hidden Door; Horn Book* Fanfare citation and West Australian Young Readers' Book Award, both for *When No One Was Looking;* International Reading Association/Children's Book Council Children's Choice citations for *Timothy Goes to School, A Lion for Lewis,* and *Peabody;* Virginia Young Readers Award, and New York Public Library Books for the Teenage citation, both for *The Man in the Woods;* Cooperative Children's Book Center citation for *Max's Bedtime;* runner-up for Edgar Allan Poe Award, Mystery Writers of America, and ALA Best Books for Young Adults citation for *Through the Hidden Door; Bulletin of the Center for Children's Books* Blue Ribbon for *The Little Lame Prince;* Parents' Choice Award, Parents' Choice Foundation, for *Shy Charles;* Golden Kite Award, Society of Children's Book Writers, and International Reading Association Teacher's Choices list, both for *Forest of Dreams;* International Reading Association Children's Choices citation for *Max's Chocolate Chicken;* many of Wells's books were named among the best books of the year by *School Library Journal* or received American Li-

brary Association (ALA) Notable Book citations or *American Bookseller* "Pick of the Lists" citations.

WRITINGS:

CHILDREN'S BOOKS; SELF-ILLUSTRATED

John and Rarey, Funk (New York, NY), 1969.
Michael and the Mitten Test, Bradbury (Scarsdale, NY), 1969.
The First Child, Hawthorn (New York, NY), 1970.
Martha's Birthday, Bradbury (Scarsdale, NY), 1970.
Miranda's Pilgrims, Bradbury (Scarsdale, NY), 1970.
Unfortunately Harriet, Dial (New York, NY), 1972.
Benjamin and Tulip, Dial (New York, NY), 1973.
Noisy Nora, Dial (New York, NY), 1973.
Abdul, Dial (New York, NY), 1975.
Morris's Disappearing Bag: A Christmas Story, Dial (New York, NY), 1975.
Don't Spill It Again, James, Dial (New York, NY), 1977.
Stanley and Rhoda, Dial (New York, NY), 1978.
Good Night, Fred, Dial (New York, NY), 1981.
Timothy Goes to School, Dial (New York, NY), 1981.
A Lion for Lewis, Dial (New York, NY), 1982.
Peabody, Dial (New York, NY), 1983.
Hazel's Amazing Mother, Dial (New York, NY), 1985.
Shy Charles, Dial (New York, NY), 1988.
The Little Lame Prince (based on a story by Dinah Mulock Craik), Dial (New York, NY), 1990.
Fritz and the Mess Fairy, Dial (New York, NY), 1991.
Edward Unready for School, Dial (New York, NY), 1995.
Edward in Deep Water, Dial (New York, NY), 1995.
Edward's Overwhelming Overnight, Dial (New York, NY), 1995.
Read to Your Bunny, Scholastic (New York, NY), 1998.
Old MacDonald, Scholastic (New York, NY), 1998.
The Bear Went over the Mountain, Scholastic (New York, NY), 1998.
The Itsy-Bitsy Spider, Scholastic (New York, NY), 1998.
Yoko, Hyperion (New York, NY), 1998.
B-I-N-G-O, Scholastic (New York, NY), 1999.
Emily's First 100 Days of School, Hyperion (New York, NY), 2000.
Timothy Goes to School, Viking (New York, NY), 2000.
Timothy's Lost and Found Day, Viking (New York, NY), 2000.

Timothy's Class Trip: Based on Timothy Goes to School and Other Stories, Viking (New York, NY), 2001.

Be My Valentine, Hyperion (New York, NY), 2001.

Doris's Dinosaur, Hyperion (New York, NY), 2001.

Felix Feels Better, Candlewick Press (Cambridge, MA), 2001.

The Halloween Parade, Hyperion (New York, NY), 2001.

Letters and Sounds, Puffin (New York, NY), 2001.

Mama, Don't Go!, Hyperion (New York, NY), 2001.

The School Play, Hyperion (New York, NY), 2001.

Yoko's Paper Cranes, Hyperion (New York, NY), 2001.

The Germ Busters, Hyperion (New York, NY), 2002.

Emily's World of Wonders, Hyperion (New York, NY), 2003.

Felix and the Worrier, Candlewick Press (Cambridge, MA), 2003.

"MAX" SERIES; SELF-ILLUSTRATED

Max's First Word, Dial (New York, NY), 1979.

Max's New Suit, Dial (New York, NY), 1979.

Max's Ride, Dial (New York, NY), 1979.

Max's Toys: A Counting Book, Dial (New York, NY), 1979.

Max's Bath, Dial (New York, NY), 1985.

Max's Bedtime, Dial (New York, NY), 1985.

Max's Breakfast, Dial (New York, NY), 1985.

Max's Birthday, Dial (New York, NY), 1985.

Max's Christmas, Dial (New York, NY), 1986.

Max's Chocolate Chicken, Dial (New York, NY), 1989.

Max's Dragon Shirt, Dial (New York, NY), 1991.

Max and Ruby's First Greek Myth: Pandora's Box, Dial (New York, NY), 1993.

Max and Ruby's Midas: Another Greek Myth, Dial (New York, NY), 1995.

Bunny Money, HarperCollins (New York, NY), 1997.

Bunny Cakes, Dial (New York, NY), 1997.

Max Cleans Up, Viking (New York, NY), 2000.

Goodnight Max, Viking (New York, NY), 2000.

Max in the Tub, Grosset & Dunlap (New York, NY), 2001.

Ruby's Beauty Shop, Viking (New York, NY), 2002.

Play with Max and Ruby, Grosset & Dunlap (New York, NY), 2002.

"VOYAGE TO THE BUNNY PLANET" SERIES; SELF-ILLUSTRATED

First Tomato: A Voyage to the Bunny Planet, Dial (New York, NY), 1992.

The Island Light: A Voyage to the Bunny Planet, Dial (New York, NY), 1992.

Moss Pillows: A Voyage to the Bunny Planet, Dial (New York, NY), 1992.

"MCDUFF" SERIES; ILLUSTRATED BY SUSAN JEFFERS

McDuff Moves In, Hyperion (New York, NY), 1997.

McDuff Shows the Way, HarperFestival (New York, NY), 1997.

McDuff Comes Home, Hyperion (New York, NY), 1997.

McDuff and the Baby, illustrated by Susan Jeffers, Hyperion (New York, NY), 1997.

McDuff's New Friend, Hyperion (New York, NY), 1998.

The McDuff Stories, Hyperion (New York, NY), 2000.

McDuff Goes to School, Hyperion (New York, NY), 2001.

OTHER CHILDREN'S BOOKS

Forest of Dreams, illustrated by Susan Jeffers, Dial (New York, NY), 1988.

Lucy's Come to Stay, illustrated by Patricia Cullen-Clark, Dial (New York, NY), 1992.

Waiting for the Evening Star, illustrated by Jeffers, Dial (New York, NY), 1993.

Night Sounds, Morning Colors, pictures by David McPhail, Dial (New York, NY), 1994.

Lucy Comes to Stay, paintings by Mark Graham, Dial (New York, NY), 1994.

Lassie Come-Home, illustrations by Susan Jeffers, Holt (New York, NY), 1995.

The Fisherman and His Wife: A Brand New Version, Dial (New York, NY), 1996.

The Language of Doves, pictures by Greg Shed, Dial (New York, NY), 1996.

Jack and the Beanstalk, illustrated by Norman Messenger, DK Publishing (New York, NY), 1997.

Mary on Horseback: Three Mountain Stories, pictures by Peter McCarthy, Dial (New York, NY), 1998.

(With Susan Jeffers) *Rachel Field's Hitty, Her First Hundred Years with New Adventures,* Simon & Schuster (New York, NY), 1999.

(With Tom Wells) *The House in the Mail,* illustrated by Dan Andreasen, DK Publishing (New York, NY), 1999.

Streets of Gold, pictures by Dan Andreasen, Dial (New York, NY), 1999.

Adding It Up: Based on Timothy Goes to School and Other Stories, illustrated by Michael Koelsch, Viking (New York, NY), 2001.

Discover and Explore: Based on Timothy goes to School and Other Stories, illustrated by Michael Koelsch, Puffin (New York, NY), 2001.

How Many? How Much?: Based on Timothy Goes to School and Other Stories, illustrated by Michael Koelsch, Puffin (New York, NY), 2001.

Letters and Sounds, illustrated by Michael Koelsch, Viking (New York, NY), 2001.

Ready to Read: Based on Timothy Goes to School and Other Stories, illustrated by Michael Koelsch, Viking (New York, NY), 2001.

The World around Us: Based on Timothy Goes to School and Other Stories, illustrated by Michael Koelsch, Viking (New York, NY), 2001.

Read Me a Story, Hyperion (New York, NY), 2001.

Make New Friends, Hyperion (New York, NY), 2002.

Practice Makes Perfect, Hyperion (New York, NY), 2002.

Timothy's Tales from Hilltop School, Viking (New York, NY), 2002.

When I Grow Up, Hyperion (New York, NY), 2002.

Wingwalker, illustrated by Brian Selznick, Hyperion (New York, NY), 2002.

YOUNG ADULT FICTION

(And illustrator) *The Fog Comes on Little Pig Feet,* Dial (New York, NY), 1972.

None of the Above, Dial (New York, NY), 1974.

Leave Well Enough Alone, Dial (New York, NY), 1977.

When No One Was Looking, Dial (New York, NY), 1980.

The Man in the Woods, Dial (New York, NY), 1984.

(And illustrator) *Through the Hidden Door,* Dial (New York, NY), 1987.

ILLUSTRATOR

William S. Gilbert and Arthur Sullivan, *A Song to Sing, O!* (from *The Yeoman of the Guard*), Macmillan (New York, NY), 1968.

Gilbert and Sullivan, *W. S. Gilbert's "The Duke of Plaza Toro"* (from *The Gondoliers*), Macmillan (New York, NY), 1969.

Paula Fox, *Hungry Fred,* Bradbury (Scarsdale, NY), 1969.

Robert W. Service, *The Shooting of Dan McGrew [and] The Cremation of Sam McGee,* Young Scott Books, 1969.

(With Susan Jeffers) Charlotte Pomerantz, *Why You Look Like You When I Tend to Look Like Me,* Young Scott Books, 1969.

Rudyard Kipling, *The Cat That Walked by Himself,* Hawthorn, 1970.

Winifred Rosen Casey, *Marvin's Manhole,* Dial (New York, NY), 1970.

Marjorie Weinman Sharmat, *A Hot Thirsty Day,* Macmillan (New York, NY), 1971.

Ellen Conford, *Impossible, Possum,* Little, Brown (Boston, MA),1971.

Beryl Williams and Dorrit Davis, *Two Sisters and Some Hornets,* Holiday House (New York, NY), 1972.

Virginia A. Tashjian, editor, *With a Deep-Sea Smile: Story Hour Stretches for Large or Small Groups,* Little, Brown (Boston, MA), 1974.

Lore G. Segal, *Tell Me a Trudy,* Farrar Straus & Giroux (New York, NY), 1977.

Jostein Gaarder, *The Christmas Mystery,* translated by Elizabeth Rokkan, Farrar, Straus & Giroux (New York, NY), 1996.

Iona Opie, editor, *My Very First Mother Goose,* Candlewick Press, (Cambridge, MA), 1996.

Here Comes Mother Goose, Candlewick Press, (Cambridge, MA), 1999.

OTHER

(With Johanna Hurley) *Cooking for Nitwits* (adult nonfiction), Dutton (New York, NY), 1989.

(Contributor) *Worlds of Childhood: The Art and Craft of Writing for Children* (adult nonfiction), edited by William Zinsser, Houghton Mifflin (Boston, MA), 1990.

(Contributor) *So I Shall Tell You a Story: The Magic World of Beatrix Potter,* Warne (New York, NY), 1993.

(With Maria Tallchief) *Tallchief: America's Prima Ballerina,* illustrations by Gary Kelley, Viking (New York, NY), 1999.

E. B. White, *Charlotte's Web,* pictures by Garth Williams, HarperCollins (New York, NY), 1999.

E. B. White, *Stuart Little,* pictures by Garth Williams, HarperCollins (New York, NY), 1999.

Garth Williams, *Benjamin's Treasure,* pictures by Garth Williams, HarperCollins (New York, NY), 2001.

ADAPTATIONS: *Max's Christmas* and *Morris's Disappearing Bag* have been adapted as short films by Weston Woods.

SIDELIGHTS: "I do not feel that I get ideas. Books come on the [word processing] screen from outer space," writes Rosemary Wells, author and illustrator of picture books for toddlers and novels for teens, in an autobiographical *Horn Book* essay.

Wells, however, admits to more conventional sources of ideas, including observing her own children, for inspiration for many of her books for her youngest readers, or consulting memories from her own youth for her work for young adults. "I put into my books," she said in her *Something about the Author Autobiography Series* (SAAS) sketch, "all of the things I remember. . . . Those remembrances are jumbled up and churned because fiction is always more palatable than truth. They become more true as they are honed and whittled into characters and stories."

Wells began her career as an art editor in the publishing industry in the early 1960s when she took what appeared to be a temporary position filling in for a vacationing art editor at textbook publisher Allyn & Bacon. She was soon hired, however, on a permanent basis. In *SAAS* Wells called this her "first lucky break and the only one I ever needed." Two years later, with her husband, Tom, studying architecture at Columbia University, Wells found a job at the children's books division of Macmillan. She set her course for a career as an art director.

One day Wells heard a song from the Gilbert and Sullivan opera, *The Yeoman of the Guard,* and quickly made some sketches using birds, not people, to illustrate the lyrics. She gave the sketches, bound to resemble a finished book, to editor in chief Susan Hirschman. In *Horn Book,* Wells recalled: "She looked at it. Then she put it down and sang the whole thing. Several other editors were invited into her office to join choruses from [two other Gilbert and Sullivan operas] *The Mikado* and *H.M.S. Pinafore.* Then, by the by, she said, 'Sit down, Rosemary, you're a Macmillan author now.'" Encouraged by the success of her first book, *A Song to Sing, O!,* Wells decided to illustrate another Gilbert and Sullivan song, this time "The Duke of Plaza Toro" from *The Gondoliers.*

Wells secured her reputation as a children's editor with the books featuring Max and his sister, Ruby. After listening to how her daughter, Victoria, bossed around her younger sister Marguerite (more commonly known as Beezoo), Wells seized upon the idea for what would become the first installment in the Max series, *Max's First Word.* Working on pieces of illustration board on her drawing table, Wells took only a few hours to produce a major innovation in children's literature. In "The Well-Tempered Children's Book," Wells's essay in *Worlds of Childhood: The Art and Craft of Writing for Children,* she recalled: "I couldn't really understand what had happened. I had created what was clearly a picture book, but it was only sixteen pages long and wasn't for the usual nursery school and kindergarten crew. Picture books were thirty-two pages long, some even forty."

Wells's editor loved the sixteen-page story and asked her for three more. *Max's Ride, Max's New Suit,* and *Max's Toys: A Counting Book* followed. Wells added: "Thus were born what came to be known in book circles as 'board books'—books that could survive a certain amount of infant vandalizing without coming apart and, even more important, could make mothers and fathers and their babies laugh at themselves and each other and the world around them."

Max and Ruby are only two of the many characters Wells has created for her picture books—each one an individual with his or her own engaging childhood drama. Often, as did Max and Ruby, these characters appear in their own series. Edward, the "unready" little bear, stars in three books about overcoming fear: *Edward Unready for School, Edward in Deep Water,* and *Edward's Overwhelming Overnight.* Yoko, Timothy, Charles, and Nora make up another set of young animals—all students in Mrs. Jenkins's class, they often share in each other's stories.

Wells worked with illustrator Susan Jeffers to create the "McDuff" stories, starring the irrepressible West Highland terrier whom a young couple adopts. Wells joined forces with Caldecott award-winning artist Brian Selznick on 2002's *Wingwalker,* a book for slightly older readers that tells of a young boy's pivotal summer. "This big-hearted, Depression-era, American fairy tale seems to come alive out of a former generation like a well-worn family yarn," a *Kirkus Reviews* contributor wrote. Wells also collaborated with her husband to create *The House in the Mail,* what *Booklist*'s Connie Fletcher called "a remarkable picture book for older children;" it takes the form of a scrapbook kept by a young girl in the 1920s as her family builds their mail-order house.

Interaction, particularly sibling rivalry, surfaces among family members in Wells's juvenile fiction, as well as in several of her young adult novels. But Wells's novels for young people differ so much from her picture books that even librarians are often startled to find the same person wrote them. Some readers might even question why such a successful illustrator would write lengthy books, mostly with no illustrations. Wells wrote in *Publishers Weekly:* "I am both an artist and a writer, but I am firmly convinced that the story comes first. . . . The child may be charmed, intrigued or even inspired by good illustration, but it is the sound of the words and the story that first holds the child's attention." Wells calls herself "a better writer than . . . an illustrator."

Wells's first young-adult novel, *The Fog Comes on Little Pig Feet,* includes about a half a dozen full-page line drawings to illustrate the story. It is the only young adult novel she illustrated throughout, although her 1987 mystery novel, *Through the Hidden Door,* does contain a few of her small drawings.

For inspiration for *The Fog Comes on Little Pig Feet,* Wells searched her own memories. The novel tells the similar story of Rachel Saseekian, who at thirteen is sent unwillingly to a boarding school. The novel is told in diary form through entries covering a two-week period. Critics praised Wells for using many autobiographical details to help the main character come alive. "The book won raves, with most reviewers impressed by the real-life feel of the chief character," *Publishers Weekly*'s Jean F. Mercier wrote. Mrs. John G. Gray said in *Best Sellers* that *The Fog Comes On Little Pig Feet* proves Wells's "writing abilities are an easy match for her already famous artistic talents." In *School Library Journal,* Alice Miller Bregman said, "Young teens will devour this fast-paced, adequately written entertainment."

With *Leave Well Enough Alone,* Wells began writing mystery novels for young adults. The teenaged protagonists of Wells's mysteries must make important ethical choices, with the wrong ones possibly leading to physical danger. Wells, predictably, again bases her narrative on her past. Wells weaves the story of Dorothy Coughlin, aged fourteen, from Newburgh, New York, who also spends one summer working as a mother's helper in Pennsylvania, as did Wells at that age. Wells sets the novel in 1956, when she began her teens.

Although Zena Sutherland in *Bulletin of the Center for Children's Books* found the plot a little "overcrowded," Katherine Paterson wrote *Book World,* "I began this book laughing with delight at Rosemary Wells's marvelous re-creation of fourteenness."

In *When No One Was Looking,* Wells features Kathy Bardy, a fourteen-year-old tennis star from Plymouth, Massachusetts, who loves tennis but harbors a secret ambition—as Wells did, according to her *SAAS* entry—to be a baseball player. Kathy looks forward to the New England Championship competition where a win would guarantee her a spot in the nationals. As Paul Heins wrote in *Horn Book,* while *When No One Was Looking* begins "as a story of athletic prowess, the novel gradually develops as a series of moral issues that take on tragic overtones." When Ruth Gumm, the one tennis player skilled enough to beat Kathy, is found dead in the swimming pool at the Plymouth Bath and Tennis Club where Kathy practices with her coach, Marty, Kathy and her supporters are immediately under suspicion. One by one the suspects are cleared, but Kathy feels compelled to continue her sleuthing even after the real detectives consider the case closed. Her moral compulsion to solve the crime leads her to an unexpected conclusion.

Realizing what consequences the truth will bring, Kathy cries bitterly to herself: "If only I hadn't bothered to go down to the police station, then at least I wouldn't know. I don't want to know. Why wasn't it enough for me to just know that I didn't do it?"

Robert Unsworth observed in *School Library Journal*: "There is a lot to this novel and most of it is excellent." Anne Tyler wrote in the *New York Times Book Review* that the book "has energy and style, and it ought to rivet the most restless young reader."

As in Wells's earlier novels, *The Man in the Woods* features a teenage heroine who must struggle with a moral dilemma. In this case, Helen Curragh, also fourteen, tries to figure out the identity of the Punk Rock Thrower after she accidentally sees him causing yet another car crash after breaking its windshield with a tossed rock. Helen and fifteen-year-old Pinky Levy meet on the second day of school at New Bedford Regional High School, discover they are both on the staff of the school paper, the *Whaler,* and soon become embroiled in a frantic search through New Bedford documents, dating to the Civil War. Together they gather clues, narrowly escape death, and uncover a secret one of New Bedford's oldest families has been covering up for more than a hundred years. As the story ends, Helen must decide whether to write a story for the *Whaler* about their search and have a chance at being the first freshman ever to win the coveted gold medal for best story of the year, or to keep what she knows to herself.

Drew Stevenson, in *School Library Journal,* finds the historical details in *The Man in the Woods* "a fascinating subplot," and in an additional comment wrote, "the book . . . boasts an array of interesting characters, deftly brought to life." In *Horn Book,* Ethel L. Heins also called attention to the novel's "wealth of vivid characters" and labeled the work "a riveting contemporary tale of emotion, mystery, and suspense."

Although Pinky figured prominently in *The Man in the Woods, Through the Hidden Door* is Wells's first young adult offering that depends almost entirely on male characters. Barney Pennimen, from Landry, Colorado, attends Winchester Boys' Academy in the East because his mother is dead and his father's antiques business requires travel. Like parents in other Wells novels, Barney's father has ambitious goals for his son. "The Plan," according to Barney, includes the following: "Go to Winchester. Graduate with honors. Go on to Hotchkiss. Graduate with honors. Get into Harvard. Magma cum laude from there and on to Yale or Oxford (as he did)." Barney is an honor student who, to fit in, befriends a group of cruel but popular boys. As the friendships go sour and even the school headmaster turns against him, Barney seeks the company of Snowy Cobb, a bookish freshman loner. The younger boy eventually leads Barney to a hidden cave where the two spend hours uncovering archaeological treasures. The cave becomes a safe haven for Snowy and Barney.

Through the Hidden Door was a runner-up for the Edgar Allan Poe Award of the Mystery Writers of America and received citations recognizing it as both one of the American Library Association's Best Books for Young Adults and one of *Booklist*'s Children's Editor's Choices for the year. In her *Bulletin of the Center for Children's Books* review, Sutherland gave the novel her highest recommendation, calling it "one of the best stories Rosemary Wells has written."

"I believe," Wells wrote in *Worlds of Childhood,* "that all stories and plays and paintings and songs and

dances come from a palpable but unseen space in the cosmos. Ballets and symphonies written during our lifetime were there before we were born. According to how gifted we are, we are all given a large or small key to this treasury of wonders. I have been blessed with a small key to the world of the young."

BIOGRAPHICAL AND CRITICAL SOURCES:

BOOKS

Children's Literature Review, Volume 69, Gale (Detroit, MI), 2001.

Sadker, Myra Pollack, and David Miller Sadker, *Now upon a Time: A Contemporary View of Children's Literature,* HarperCollins (New York, NY), 1977, pp. 66-67.

St. James Guide to Children's Writers, fifth edition, St. James Press (Detroit, MI), 1999.

Silvey, Anita, editor, *Children's Books and Their Creators,* Houghton Mifflin (Boston, MA), 1995.

Something about the Author Autobiography Series, Volume 1, 1986, Gale (Detroit, MI), pp. 279-291.

Wells, Rosemary, *The Fog Comes on Little Pig Feet,* Dial (New York, NY), 1972.

Wells, *None of the Above,* Dial (New York, NY), 1974.

Wells, *Leave Well Enough Alone,* Dial (New York, NY), 1977.

Wells, *When No One Was Looking,* Dial (New York, NY), 1980.

Wells, *Through the Hidden Door,* Dial (New York, NY), 1987.

Zinsser, William, editor, *Worlds of Childhood: The Art and Craft of Writing for Children,* Houghton Mifflin (Boston, MA), 1990, pp. 121-143.

PERIODICALS

Best Sellers, July 15, 1972, p. 200; February 15, 1975, p. 519- 520.

Bookbird, Volume 37, number 2, 1999, review of *Yoko,* p. 64.

Booklist, April 15, 1987, p. 1296; May 1, 1995, review of *Max and Ruby's Midas,* p. 1581; September 1, 1995, reviews of *Edward in Deep Water, Edward Unready for School,* and *Edward's Overwhelming Overnight,* p. 75; December 1, 1995, review of *Lassie Come Home,* p. 637; January 1, 1996, review of *Edward's Overwhelming Over-*

night, p. 744; August, 1996, review of *The Language of Doves,* p. 1909; January 1, 1997, Hazel Rochman, review of *Bunny Cakes,* p. 857; April 1, 1997, review of *McDuff Moves In,* p. 1331; June 1, 1997, review of *McDuff Comes Home,* p. 1723; August, 1997, Stephanie Zvirin, review of *Noisy Nora,* p. 1908; September 15, 1997, review of *McDuff and the Baby,* p. 243; November 1, 1997, review of *Jack and the Beanstalk,* p. 476; December 15, 1997, review of *Noisy Nora,* p. 707; January 1, 1998, review of *Bunny Cakes,* p. 736; March 1, 1998, Denia Hester, review of *Pussycat, Pussycat and Other Rhymes,* p. 1141; May 1, 1998, review of *Read to Your Bunny,* p. 1524; July, 1998, Helen Rosenberg, review of *The Fisherman and His Wife,* p. 1884; September 1, 1998, review of *Mary on Horseback,* p. 113; review of *Bunny Cakes,* p. 130; November 15, 1998, review of *Yoko,* p. 589; December 1, 1998, review of *McDuff's New Friend,* p. 673; December 15, 1998, Carolyn Phelan, review of *The Itsy-Bitsy Spider* and *The Bear Went over the Mountain,* p. 756; January 1, 1999, review of *Yoko,* p. 785; May 1, 1999, review of *Streets of Gold,* p. 1593; November 15, 1999, review of *Rachel Field's Hitty,* p. 638; January 1, 2000, Shelley Townsend-Hudson, review of *Morris's Disappearing Bag,* p. 938; March 1, 2000, Stephanie Zvirin, reviews of *Mary on Horseback* and *Streets of Gold,* p. 1249; June 1, 2000, Hazel Rochman, review of *Timothy Goes to School,* p. 1911; February 1, 2001, Kathy Broderick, review of *Max Cleans Up,* p. 1059; May 1, 2001, Hazel Rochman, review of *Felix Feels Better,* p. 1693; August, 2001, review of *Bunny Party,* p. 2133; September 15, 2001, Hazel Rochman, review of *Yoko's Paper Cranes,* p. 233; October 1, 2001, review of *McDuff Goes to School,* p. 330; November 1, 2001, review of *The Language of Doves,* p. 475; December 15, 2001, Stephanie Zvirin, review of *Felix Feels Better,* p. 728; March 1, 2002, review of *The House in the Mail,* p. 1137; July, 2002, Shelle Rosenfeld, review of *McDuff Saves the Day,* p. 1861; August, 2002, Hazel Rochman, review of *Ruby's Beauty Shop,* p. 1977.

Books, April, 1996, review of *Edward the Unready,* p. 26; April, 1997, review of *Jack and the Beanstalk,* p. 24.

Books for Keeps, March, 1998, review of *Lassie Come Home,* p. 21; May, 1998, review of *Bunny Money,* p. 3; March, 1999, review of *Noisy Nora,* p. 19.

Book World, October 1, 1995, review of *Lassie Come Home,* p. 6; May 4, 1997, review of *Bunny Cakes,*

p. 18; December 9, 2001, review of *Yoko's Paper Cranes,* p. 8.

Bulletin of the Center for Children's Books, April, 1975, p. 139; October, 1977, p. 40; July-August, 1987, p. 220; June, 1995, review of *Max and Ruby's Midas,* p. 362; November, 1995, reviews of *Edward Unready for School, Edward in Deep Water,* and *Edward's Overwhelming Overnight,* p. 108; February, 1996, review of *Lassie Come Home,* p. 208; September, 1996, review of *The Language of Doves,* p. 36; March, 1997, review of *Bunny Cakes,* p. 261; April, 1997, review of *McDuff Moves In,* p. 300; October, 1997, review of *Bunny Money,* p. 71; April, 1998, review of *Read to Your Bunny,* p. 300; January, 1999, review of *Mary on Horseback,* p. 184; July, 1999, review of *Streets of Gold,* p. 405; May, 2001, reviews of *Letters and Sounds* and *How Many? How Much?,* p. 339; June, 2001, review of *Felix Feels Better,* p. 391; December, 2001, review of *Yoko's Paper Cranes,* p. 155.

Catholic Library World, June, 1996, review of *Lassie Come Home,* p. 48; June, 1998, review of *Jack and the Beanstalk,* p. 60.

Children's Book and Play Review, March, 2001, review of *Timothy Goes to School,* p. 25; May, 2001, review of *The Man in the Woods,* p. 26; September, 2001, review of *Felix Feels Better,* p. 26; November, 2001, review of *Emily's Fist 100 Days of School,* p. 20.

Children's Book Review Service, December, 1996, review of *The Language of Doves,* p. 43; June, 1997, review of *McDuff Comes Home,* p. 125; September, 1998, review of *The Fisherman and His Wife,* p. 8; November, 1998, review of *Yoko,* p. 30; December, 1998, review of *Mary on Horseback,* p. 43; July, 1999, review of *Streets of Gold,* p. 151.

Children's Bookwatch, December, 1995, review of *Edward Unready for School,* p. 4; October, 1996, review of *The Language of Doves,* p. 5; March, 1997, review of *Bunny Cakes,* p. 7; June, 1997, review of *McDuff Moves In,* p. 6; October, 1997, review of *Bunny Money,* p. 6; January, 1998, review of *McDuff and the Baby,* p. 1; June, 1998, review of *Read to Your Bunny,* p. 6; December, 1998, reviews of *McDuff's New Friend* and *Max's Christmas,* p. 1, review of *The Fisherman and His Wife,* p. 4; July, 1999, review of *Streets of Gold,* p. 2; October, 1999, review of *Yoko,* p. 6; February, 2001, review of *Max Cleans Up,* p. 3; December, 2001, review of *Bunny Party,* p. 7.

Christian Science Monitor, March 6, 1974, p. F2; September 28, 1995, review of *Lassie Come Home,* p. B1.

Commonweal, December 1, 1995, review of *Lassie Come Home,* p. 25.

Early Childhood Education Journal, winter, 1999, review of *The Itsy-Bitsy Spider,* p. 105.

Emergency Librarian, November, 1995, reviews of *Edward in Deep Water, Edward Unready for School,* and *Edward's Overwhelming Overnight,* p. 45; January, 1996, review of *Lassie Come Home,* p. 42; March, 1996, review of *Edward Unready for School,* p. 56.

Five Owls, November, 1995, review of *Lassie Come Home,* p. 35; January, 1996, review of *Max and Ruby's Midas,* p. 50, review of *Max and Ruby's Midas,* p. 52.

Globe and Mail, January 20, 2001, review of *Max Cleans Up,* p. D13; April 28, 2001, review of *Felix Feels Better,* p. D37; November 17, 2001, review of *McDuff Goes to School,* p. D26.

Growing Point, May, 1976, pp. 2891-92.

Horn Book, October, 1980, pp. 529-30; September-October, 1984, pp. 601-02; March-April, 1987, pp. 163-170; May-June, 1987, pp. 368-71; May-June, 1993, pp. 307-310; July, 1995, review of *Max and Ruby's Midas,* p. 455; November, 1995, reviews of *Edward Unready for School, Edward in Deep Water,* and *Edward's Overwhelming Overnight,* p. 739; March, 1996, review of *Lassie Come Home,* p. 192; March, 1997, review of *Max's First Word,* p. 186; July-August,1997, Elizabeth S. Watson, reviews of *McDuff Comes Home* and *McDuff Moves In,* pp. 446-447; January-February, 1998, Roger Sutton, review of *McDuff and the Baby,* p. 65; November, 1998, review of *Mary on Horseback,* p. 744; November, 1999, Matha V. Parravano, review of *Here Comes Mother Goose,* p. 749; January, 2000, Cathryn Mercier, review of *Rachel Field's Hitty,* p. 107; September, 2001, Kitty Flynn, review of *Bunny Party,* p. 579; January-February, 2002, Kitty Flynn, review of *McDuff Goes to School,* pp. 73-74.

Horn Book Guide, spring, 1995, review of *Night Sounds, Morning Colors,* p. 60; fall, 1995, review of *Max and Ruby's Midas,* p. 286; spring, 1996, reviews of *Edward Unready for School, Edward in Deep Water,* and *Edward's Overwhelming Overnight,* p. 16, review of *Lassie Come Home,* p. 58; spring, 1997, review of *The Language of Doves,* p. 53; fall, 1997, review of *Noisy Nora,* p. 285, reviews of *Bunny Cakes, McDuff Comes Home,* and *McDuff Moves In,* p. 284; spring, 1998, review of *McDuff and the Baby,* p. 20, review of *Bunny Money,* p. 52, review of *Jack and the Beanstalk,*

p. 109, review of *Noisy Nora,* p. 118; fall, 1998, reviews of *Read to Your Bunny, Old MacDonald, Max's Toys, Max's Ride, Max's New Suit, Max's First Word, Max's Breakfast, Max's Birthday, Max's Bedtime,* and *Max's Bath,* p. 281; spring, 1999, reviews of *The Itsy-Bitsy Spider, Max's Christmas,* and *The Bear Went over the Mountain,* p. 19, review of *Yoko* and *McDuff's New Friend,* p. 48, review of *Mary on Horseback,* p. 76, review of *The Fisherman and His Wife,* p. 99; fall, 1999, review of *Max's Chocolate Chicken,* p. 242; spring, 2001, review of *Timothy Goes to School,* p. 25; fall, 2001, reviews of *Letters and Sounds* and *How Many? How Much?,* p. 233, reviews of *Max Cleans Up* and *Felix Feels Better,* p. 243, review of *The McDuff Stories,* p. 280.

Instructor, April, 1996, review of *Lassie Come Home,* p. 60; May, 1996, review of *Max and Ruby's Midas,* p. 69; January, 1998, review of *Bunny Cakes* and *Bunny Money,* p. 30; May, 1998, review of *McDuff Moves In,* p. 60, review of *Bunny Money,* p. 61; May, 1999, review of *McDuff Moves In* and *Bunny Cakes,* p. 12.

Journal of Youth Services in Libraries, fall, 1995, review of *Waiting for the Evening Star,* p. 101; January, 1998, reviews of *McDuff and the Baby, McDuff Comes Home,* and *McDuff Moves In,* p. 30.

Kirkus Reviews, May 1, 1995, review of *Max and Ruby's Midas,* p. 641; October 1, 1995, review of *Edward in Deep Water,* p. 1437; October 15, 1995, review of *Lassie Come Home,* p. 1504; August 1, 1996, review of *The Language of Doves,* p. 1159; January 1, 1997, review of *Bunny Cakes,* p. 67; March 1, 1997, review of *McDuff Moves In,* p. 389; July 15, 1997, review of *Bunny Money,* p. 1119; November 15, 1998, review of *McDuff's New Friend,* p. 1673, review of *Yoko,* p. 1674; August 15, 2001, review of *McDuff Goes to School* and *Bunny Party,* p. 1222, review of *Yoko's Paper Cranes,* p. 1223; May 15, 2002, review of *McDuff Saves the Day,* p. 743; April 15, 2002, review of *Wingwalker,* p. 581; June 15, 2002, review of *Timothy's Tales from Hilltop School,* p. 890; July 15, 2002, review of *Ruby's Beauty Shop,* p. 1047.

Kliatt Young Adult Paperback Book Guide, April, 1989, p. 20.

Learning, November, 1997, review of *Bunny Money,* p. 29.

Library Talk, September, 1995, review of *Lassie Come Home,* p. 23; June 1, 1998, review of *The Fisherman and His Wife,* p. 817.

Los Angeles Times Book Review, December 3, 1995, reviews of *Edward in Deep Water, Edward Un-*

ready for School, and *Edward's Overwhelming Overnight,* p. 30; June 14, 1998, review of *Max and Ruby's Midas* and *Max and Ruby's First Greek Myth,* p. 11.

Magpies, March, 1996, review of *Lassie Come Home,* p. 33; July, 1997, reviews of *Edward's First Swimming Party, Edward's First Night Away,* and *Edward's First Day at School,* p. 28; November, 1997, review of *Bunny Cakes,* p. 27; March, 1999, review of *The Fisherman and His Wife,* p. 31; March 15, 2001, review of *Felix Feels Better,* p. 423.

Newsweek, November 27, 1995, reviews of *Edward in Deep Water, Edward Unready for School,* and *Edward's Overwhelming Overnight,* p. 82.

New York Times Book Review, July 10, 1977, pp. 20-21; February 1, 1981, p. 28; November 19, 1995, review of *Lassie Come Home,* p. 37; January 28, 1996, reviews of *Edward in Deep Water, Edward Unready for School,* and *Edward's Overwhelming Overnight,* p. 27; April 11, 1999, review of *Yoko,* p. 32; November 21, 1999, review of *Rachel Field's Hitty,* p. 45.

Parents' Choice, September, 1995, review of *Lassie Come Home,* p. 3; November, 1995, reviews of *Edward in Deep Water, Edward Unready for School,* and *Edward's Overwhelming Overnight,* p. 3; March, 1997, review of *The Language of Doves,* p. 8; December 21, 1997, reviews of *McDuff and the Baby, McDuff Comes Home,* and *McDuff Moves In,* p. 18.

Parents Magazine, December, 1995, review of *Edward's Overwhelming Overnight,* p. 229; December, 1997, review of *Bunny Cakes* and *Bunny Money,* p. 202, reviews of *McDuff and the Baby, McDuff Comes Home,* and *McDuff Moves In,* p. 204; December, 1998, review of *Yoko,* p. 234.

Publishers Weekly, August 5, 1974, p. 58; February 29, 1980, pp. 72-73; February 27, 1987, p. 146; May 15, 1995, review of *Max and Ruby's Midas,* p. 71; September 18, 1995, review of *Lassie Come Home,* p. 130, review of *Edward in Deep Water,* p. 131; November 6, 1995, review of *Lassie Come Home,* p. 68; July, 1996, review of *The Language of Doves,* p. 60; August 5, 1996, review of *My Very First Mother Goose,* p. 442; November 25, 1996, review of *Bunny Cakes,* p. 74; January 27, 1997, review of *Max's Dragon Shirt,* p. 108; February 17, 1997, review of *McDuff Moves In,* p. 218; April 7, 1997, review of *Noisy Nora,* p. 93; May 26, 1997, review of *Bunny Money,* p. 85; August 25, 1997, review of *McDuff and the Baby,*

p. 73; November 3, 1997, review of *McDuff Comes Home, McDuff and the Baby,* and *McDuff Moves In,* p. 59; December 15, 1997, review of *Waiting for the Evening Star,* p. 78; February 16, 1998, reviews of *Max's New Suit, Max's First Word, Max's Breakfast,* and *Max's Birthday,* p. 213.

Reading Teacher, October, 1996, review of *Max and Ruby's Midas,* p. 134; December, 1997, review of *The Language of Doves,* p. 335; January 26, 1998, review of *Read to Your Bunny,* p. 90; March 23, 1998, review of *Old MacDonald,* p. 101; July 6, 1998, review of *The Fisherman and His Wife,* p. 60; September 14, 1998, review of *Mary on Horseback,* p. 70; September 28, 1998, review of *McDuff's New Friend* and *Max's Christmas,* p. 62; October 5, 1998, reviews of *The Itsy Bitsy Spider* and *The Bear Went over the Mountain,* p. 93; October 12, 1998, review of *Lassie Come Home,* p. 79; October 19, 1998, review of *Yoko,* p. 78; October, 1998, review of *Bunny Cakes,* p. 150; January 25, 1999, review of *Max's Chocolate Chicken,* p. 98; March 1, 1999, review of *B-I-N-G-O,* p. 71; April 19, 1999, review of *Streets of Gold,* p. 73; August 16, 1999, review of *Read to Your Bunny,* p. 87; September, 1999, review of *Mary on Horseback,* p. 83; October 11, 1999, review of *Rachel Field's Hitty,* p. 76; October 25, 1999, review of *Tallchief: America's Prima Ballerina,* p. 80; November, 1999, review of *Mary on Horseback,* p. 253; December, 1999, review of *Streets of Gold,* p. 351; October 16, 2000, reviews of *Mary on Horseback* and *When No One Was Looking,* p. 78; June 4, 2001, review of *Felix Feels Better,* p. 79; July 9, 2001, "Welcome Back!" (review of *Shy Charles*), p. 69; August 20, 2001, review of *Yoko's Paper Cranes,* p. 79; September 3, 2001, review of *McDuff Goes to School,* p. 89; October 8, 2001, reviews of *The School Play* and *Mama, Don't Go!,* p. 67; October 15, 2001, "Familiar Faces" (review of *Bunny Party*), p. 73; October 29, 2001, reviews of *Ready to Read* and *Adding It Up,* p. 66; November 5, 2001, review of *Max's Snowsuit,* p. 71; March 25, 2002, review of *Wingwalker,* p. 65; May 27, 2002, review of *Happy Anniversary, Charlotte & Wilbur,* p. 61.

School Librarian, February, 1996, review of *Lassie Come Home,* p. 18; November, 1997, review of *Jack and the Beanstalk,* p. 188.

School Library Journal, May, 1972, p. 89; November, 1974, p. 69; May, 1977, p. 73; October, 1980, p. 159; May, 1984, p. 104; April, 1987, p. 114; May, 1995, review of *Max and Ruby's Midas,*

p. 97; September, 1996, review of *The Language of Doves,* p. 193; January, 1997, review of *Bunny Cakes,* p. 94; May, 1997, reviews of *McDuff Moves In* and *Bunny Cakes,* p. 116; July, 1997, reviews of *Bunny Money* and *McDuff Comes Home,* p. 78; August, 1997, review of *Noisy Nora,* p. 181; November, 1997, review of *Max and Ruby's First Greek Myth,* p. 41, review of *Bunny Cakes,* p. 188 ; December, 1997, review of *Bunny Cakes* and *McDuff Moves In,* p. 29, review of *Jack and the Beanstalk,* p. 103; January, 1998, review of *Max and Ruby's First Greek Myth,* p. 43; March, 1998, review of *Read to Your Bunny,* p. 189; May, 1998, review of *McDuff Moves In,* p. 53; July, 1998, review of *Max's Ride, Max's Toys, Max's Bedtime,* and *Max's Bath,* p. 86; August, 1998, review of *The Fisherman and His Wife,* p. 157; October, 1998, reviews of *Yoko* and *Old MacDonald,* p. 118, review of *McDuff's New Friend,* p. 46, review of *Mary on Horseback,* p. 130; December, 1998, reviews of *Yoko* and *Mary on Horseback,* p. 28; February, 1999, reviews of *The Itsy-Bitsy Spider* and *The Bear Went over the Mountain,* p. 91; June, 1999, review of *Streets of Gold,* p. 124; July, 1999, review of *B-I-N-G-O,* p. 83; May, 2001, review of *Felix Feels Better,* p. 138; August, 2001, review of *Bunny Party,* p. 166; October, 2001, Linda M. Kenton, review of *Discover and Explore,* p. 147; November, 2001, Rosalyn Pierini, review of *Yoko's Paper Cranes,* p. 138; December, 2001, review of *McDuff Goes to School,* p. 114, Lisa Gangemi Krapp, review of *The World around Us,* p. 129; January, 2002, Marilyn Taniguchi, review of *Mama, Don't Go!,* p. 112; March, 2002, Grace Oliff, review of *The House in the Mail,* pp. 205-206; May, 2002, Heide Piehler, review of *Wingwalker,* p. 162; July, 2002, Shara Alpern, review of *Be My Valentine,* p. 100, Janie Schomberg, review of *The Germ Busters,* pp. 100-101; August, 2002, Maryann H. Owen, review of *McDuff Saves the Day,* p. 172.

Smithsonian, November, 1996, review of *The Language of Doves,* p. 173.

Social Education, April, 1997, review of *The Language of Doves,* p. 13; May, 1999, review of *Mary on Horseback,* p. 10.

Teacher Librarian, March, 1999, review of *Yoko,* p. 44; May 1999, Shirley Lewis, review of *Yoko,* p. 48.

Time, December 7, 1998, review of *Yoko,* p. 220.

Times Educational Supplement, September 29, 1995, review of *Max and Ruby's Midas,* p. 13; April 5, 1996, reviews of *Helping Children Cope with Di-*

vorce and *Helping Children Cope with Grief,* p. 12; September 27, 1996, reviews of *Edward's First Swimming Party, Edward's First Night Away,* and *Edward's First Day at School,* p. 12; September 21, 2001, review of *Making Friends with Your Stepchildren,* p. 21.

Times Literary Supplement, October 1, 1976, p. 1243.

Tribune Books (Chicago, IL), August 13, 1995, review of *Edward Unready for School,* p. 3; November 12, 1995, review of *Lassie Come Home,* p. 6; June 3, 2001, review of *Felix Feels Better,* p. 4.

Washington Post Book World, May 1, 1977, p. E4.

Wilson Library Bulletin, January, 1995, review of *Noisy Nora* (audio recording), p. 114.

ONLINE

Book Page, http://www.bookpage.com/ (March 4, 2003), Deborah Hopkinson, "The Magic of Rosemary Wells."

CM: Canadian Review of Materials, http://www.umanitoba.ca/cm/ (June 5, 1998), Dave Jenkinson, review of *Read to Your Bunny.*

Horn Book, http://www.hbook.com/ (March 4, 2003), "Horn Book Radio Review" (Rosemary Wells interviewed by Anita Silvey).

The World of Rosemary Wells, http://www.rosemary wells.com/ (March 4, 2003), biography of Rosemary Wells.*

*   *   *

WHEELER, Sara 1961-

PERSONAL: Born March 20, 1961, in Bristol, England. *Education:* Brasenose College, Oxford University, B.A. (honors), 1984.

ADDRESSES: Agent—Gillon Aitkin, c/o Aitkin & Stone, 29 Fernshaw Rd., London SW10 OT9, England.

CAREER: Travel writer and frequent contributor to BBC (British Broadcasting Company) Radio; writer in residence, U.S. Polar Program, 1995.

MEMBER: Fellow of the Royal Geographic Society.

AWARDS, HONORS: Shortlisted for Travel Book of the Year, 1996, and finalist for Thomas Cook Award, both for *Travels in a Thin Country; Terra Incognita: Travels in Antarctica* chosen by Beryl Bainbridge, *Daily Mail,* as one of the best books of 1998, also chosen one of *Seattle Times's* top ten travel books of the year.

WRITINGS:

An Island Apart: Travels in Evia, Little, Brown (London, England), 1992, paperback edition, Abacus (London, England), 1993.

Travels in a Thin Country: A Journey through Chile, Little, Brown (Boston, MA), 1994, Abacus (London, England), 1995, paperback edition, Modern Library (New York, NY), 1999.

Antarctica, the Falklands & South Georgia, Cadogan (London, England), 1997.

(Editor, with Dea Birkett) *Amazonian: The Penguin Book of Women's New Travel Writing,* Penguin (London, England), 1998.

Terra Incognita: Travels in Antarctica, Jonathan Cape (London, England), 1996, U.S. edition, Random House (New York, NY), 1998, paperback edition, Modern Library (New York, NY), 1999.

Greetings from Antarctica (children's book, with illustrations by the author), Peter Bedrick Books (New York, NY), 1999.

Cherry: A Life of Apsley Cherry-Garrard, Jonathan Cape (London, England), 2001, Random House (New York, NY), 2002.

Author of a BBC Radio documentary about the Antarctic titled *The Big White;* reviewer of travel books for newspapers in the United States and the United Kingdom.

SIDELIGHTS: Travel writer Sara Wheeler has written several books based on her visits to various parts of the world. *An Island Apart: Travels in Evia* details her journey to the Greek island of Evia and into its culture. A Greek scholar, Wheeler managed to successfully explore most of the island—even the hinterlands, where civilization has yet to invade and where most tourists do not visit. Her fluency in Greek gained her access to households, and she even received the honor of serving as a godmother to a newborn infant. In her book, Wheeler provides readers with insight into the Greek

persona through such disarming displays as when villagers find it humorous when a donkey is struck by lightning. According to Frederic Raphael, writing in the *Times Literary Supplement,* Wheeler is "unusually forthright on the selfishness and cruelties of the Greeks, and on their sometimes dismaying sense of humor." While Raphael admired both Wheeler's tireless pursuit to find ruins and her evident knowledge of the subject, he remarked that her writing style was "full of cliches." Overall, however, the reviewer found Wheeler's look into the island of Evia "intimidatingly seductive."

According to *New Statesman* reviewer Tony Gould, Wheeler's adaptability and refusal to take "no" for an answer yields fine results in *Travels in a Thin Country.* The book details her exploration through Chile, from the northern deserts to the very southernmost tip, a part of the country she obviously favors. Wheeler has all manner of experiences in Chile and takes full advantage of just about any opportunity for travel journalism. She manages to stay at a deluxe family hacienda, teams up for three days with three policemen at a remote forest outpost, and unknowingly is given a free air travel ticket because an official finds her "pretty." Wheeler, according to Gould, is adaptable enough to make the most of each situation and also able to bear it when she spends long periods of time alone. Politically, much is taking place in Chile during Wheeler's travels—the aftermath of the fall of a dictatorship, growing poverty and despair in the slums, and a concern with national identity—and Wheeler provides some political context in the form of history (a description of the Chilean emergence from Spanish rule in the 1800s). Gould called the work "a perceptive and entertaining account of a little-known country." However, a *Times Literary Supplement* contributor called Wheeler's observations "banal" and concluded that the reader is "none the wiser" about Chile after reading the book.

Wheeler's next travels, funded in part by the National Science Foundation and the British Antarctic Survey, produced the best-selling work *Terra Incognita: Travels in Antarctica.* Wheeler spent seven months in Antarctica, living with the male inhabitants of the region's scientific research stations. Not only does she provide overtones of her own spirituality and how it is affected by the otherworldly terrain, but she gives insight into the day-to-day life of the Antarctic researchers. According to Erik Stokstad of the *New Scientist,* Wheeler does not seem interested in the actual research being carried out at stations, which includes studies on ozone depletion as well as studies of organisms in penguin vomit that may indicate life on Mars. Instead, Wheeler describes the "seedy bars, practical jokes, and tedium that are all features of days in the frozen vastness." Wheeler also pays due respect to the many Antarctic expeditions in history. Lucretia Stewart, writing for the *Times Literary Supplement,* found Wheeler's "nostalgic affection genuine and moving." Stokstad commented that *Terra Incognita* could leave the reader "out in the cold." However, *Observer* contributor Cressida Connolly called the work "funny, informative, touching, and candid." Michiko Kakutani, writing in the *New York Times Book Review,* stated that Wheeler "zeroes in on the people who have charted and continue to chart the region's stark and unforgiving terrain." A *Publishers Weekly* reviewer concluded that "Wheeler writes elegantly and movingly about the unearthly landscape and its effects."

Wheeler once told *CA,* "Antarctica, the subject of my book *Terra Incognita,* was the culmination of many other destinations. I found it was the perfect *tabula rasa.* Through it I was able to reach further into the psychic landscape: the most foreign country of them all."

Wheeler's acclaimed biography of an Antarctic adventurer, *Cherry: A Life of Apsley Cherry-Garrard,* received abundant praise from reviewers. The young privileged Englishman known as "Cherry" was sent to meet the ill-fated Robert Scott expedition returning from the South Pole in February 1912, but Scott and his men—two of whom were Cherry's best friends—froze to death just twelve miles away, before Cherry could find them. After the Antarctic winter had passed, ten months later, Cherry and a search party found their bodies inside a tent. The discovery represented a national tragedy for England. After Cherry returned home to his estate, he began a downward decline in health, tormented by depression and guilt over what he might have done to prevent the expedition's disastrous ending. After ten years of introspection, encouraged by his friend and neighbor George Bernard Shaw, he wrote a book about the two-year expedition. It includes the story of a five-week excursion to Cape Crozier in 1911, in which he and the two friends who later died with Scott went in search of the eggs of emperor penguins for scientific study. He titled his book *The Worst Journey in the World* after the egg-hunting

journey, in which he and his friends nearly succumbed in the minus-75-degree temperatures of the frozen Antarctic. Cherry's book is considered one of the top adventure books of all time. Wheeler drew on his book, on Cherry's journals and those of other members of the expedition, and on interviews with his widow to construct her biography.

A writer for *Books@Random* wrote, "Wheeler's biography brings to life this great hero . . . and gives us a glimpse of the terrible human cost of his adventures." Jay Freeman of *Booklist* commented that *Cherry* "examines the man and his times with credibility." Caroline Alexander, writing in the *New York Times Book Review,* also praised Wheeler's biography, saying, "one turns from her biography back to Cherry's own work with renewed, not undiminished, relish," adding that "her book, beautifully written throughout, takes fire in the Antarctic chapters, where irresistible forces converge." Philip Hensher writing in *Spectator* concluded: "If there is not a great deal to say about the last 30 years of [Cherry's] life, at least Sara Wheeler tells it with evident affection and admiration; she clearly loves her subject deeply. The polar material . . . gains here from a biographer who knows the Antartic extremely well, and can tell us with feeling exactly what it is like to stand in a wind-chill factor of minus 115 degrees."

Wheeler once told CA:"I write narrative travel books. I try to lead the reader by the hand through the landscapes I observe. I try to travel inward as well as outward, back as well as forward."

BIOGRAPHICAL AND CRITICAL SOURCES:

PERIODICALS

Booklist, March 15, 2002, Jay Freeman, review of *Cherry: A Life of Apsley Cherry-Garrard,* p. 1206.
Book World, July 18, 1999, reviews of *Travels in a Thin Country: A Journey through Chile* and *Terra Incognita: Travels in Antarctica,* p. 10.
Children's Bookwatch, June, 1999, review of *Greetings from Antarctica,* p. 1.
Globe and Mail (London), April 17, 1999, review of *Travels in a Thin Country,* p. D16.
Kirkus Reviews, June 15, 1999, review of *Greetings from Antarctica,* p. 971; January 15, 2002, review of *Cherry,* p. 96.

New Scientist, September 21, 1996, Eric Stokstad, review of *Terra Incognita,* p. 54.

New Statesman, January 28, 1994, Tony Gould, review of *Travels in a Thin Country,* p. 39.

New York Times Book Review, March 17, 1998; May 9, 1999, Michiko Kakutani, review of *Terra Incognita,* p. 42; June 6, 1999, review of *Travels in a Thin Country,* p. 29; May 5, 2002, Caroline Alexander, "The Best Fellows in the World," review of *Cherry,* Late Edition, Section 7, p. 10.

Observer, October 6, 1996, Cressida Connolly, review of *Terra Incognita,* p. 18.

Publishers Weekly, February 23, 1998, review of *Terra Incognita;* June 7, 1999, review of *Greetings from Antarctica,* p. 84; March 18, 2002, review of *Cherry,* p. 90.

School Library Journal, August, 1999, review of *Greetings from Antarctica,* p. 151.

Science Books and Films, September, 1999, review of *Greetings from Antarctica,* p. 223.

Spectator, November 3, 2001, Philip Hensher, review of *Cherry,* p. 48.

Times Literary Supplement (London), July 31, 1992, Frederic Raphael, review of *An Island Apart: Travels in Evia,* p. 10; March 4, 1994, review of *Travels in a Thin Country,* p. 28; December 13, 1996, Lucretia Stewart, review of *Terra Incognita,* p. 30; February 22, 2002, Jonathan Dore, "Blaming the Weather," review of *Cherry,* p. 5.

ONLINE

Books@Random, http://www.randomhouse.com/catalog/ (June 17, 2002), reviews of *Cherry* and *Terra Incognita.**

Roger Wilkins

*   *   *

WILKINS, Roger (Wood) 1932-

PERSONAL: Born March 25, 1932, in Kansas City, MO; son of Earl Williams (a journalist) and Helen Natalie (a national board member of the Young Women's Christian Association; maiden name, Jackson) Wilkins; married Eve Estelle Tyler (a public service executive), June 16, 1956 (divorced, 1976); married May Meyers (a stained glass artist), April 4, 1977 (divorced, 1978); married Patricia King (a teacher of law), February 21, 1981; children: (first marriage) Amy T., David E.; (third marriage) Elizabeth W. C. *Education:* University of Michigan, A.B., 1953, LL.B., 1956. *Politics:* Democrat. *Religion:* Christian.

ADDRESSES: Home—Washington, DC. *Office*—c/o Institute for Policy Studies, 1901 Q St. NW, Washington, DC 20009.

CAREER: Welfare worker in Cleveland, OH, 1957; admitted to the Bar of the State of New York, 1958; Delson & Gordon (law firm), New York, NY, attorney, 1958-62; Agency for International Development (AID), Washington, DC, special assistant administrator, 1962-64; U.S. Department of Commerce, Washington, DC, director of community relations, 1964-66; U.S. Department of Justice, Washington, DC, assistant attorney general, 1966-69; Ford Foundation, New York, NY, program director and adviser to foundation president, 1969-72; *Washington Post,* Washington, DC, member of editorial page staff, 1972-74; *New York Times,* New York, NY, member of editorial board, 1974-77, urban affairs columnist, 1977-79; *Nation,* New York, NY, member of editorial board, 1979—; *Washington Star,* Washington, DC, associate editor,

1980-81; CBS-Radio, New York, NY, commentator for "Spectrum" program, 1980-83; Institute for Policy Studies, Washington, DC, senior fellow, 1982—; George Mason University, Fairfax, VA, currently Clarence J. Robinson Professor of History and American Culture. Member of board of directors of Washington, DC, Family and Child Service, Arena Stage, New York City Cultural Council, National Association for the Advancement of Colored People (NAACP), and Legal Defense and Educational Fund, Inc.; member of board of visitors of University of Michigan Law School; member of board of trustees of African-American Institute, 1979—, and Fund for Investigative Journalism, 1981—; senior adviser to Jesse Jackson's presidential campaign, 1983-84; member of steering committee of Free South Africa Movement, 1984—; member of visiting committee of Afro-American Studies Program, Harvard University, 1984—.

MEMBER: National Association for the Advancement of Colored People (NAACP), National Urban League, American Academy of Public Administration, Americans for Democratic Action.

AWARDS, HONORS: Marc Corporation senior fellow, 1971; co-recipient of Pulitzer Prize, 1972, for editorial writing on the Watergate scandal; LL.D. from Central Michigan University, 1974; named to the Pulitzer Prize board, 1979; D.H.L. from Wilberforce University, 1982; Regents' Lectureship, University of California, 1985; Otis Lecturer, Wheaton College, 1985; Commonwealth Professor, George Mason University, 1985-86; Roger Baldwin Civil Liberties Award, New York Civil Liberties Union, 1987.

WRITINGS:

A Man's Life: An Autobiography, Simon & Schuster (New York, NY), 1982.
(Editor, with Fred R. Harris) *Quiet Riots: Race and Poverty in the United States,* Pantheon (New York, NY), 1988.
Jefferson's Pillow: The Founding Fathers and the Dilemma of Black Patriotism, Beacon Press (Boston, MA), 2001.

Contributor of articles to periodicals, including *Esquire, Foreign Policy, Fortune, Mother Jones, Nation, New Yorker,* and *Village Voice,* and to newspapers, including *Los Angeles Times, New York Times, Washington Post,* and *Washington Star.*

WORK IN PROGRESS: "A book assessing the strengths and weaknesses of Great Society programs, based primarily on the experiences and insights of poor, black, inner-city residents who were the objects of those programs."

SIDELIGHTS: The only son of college-educated, middle-class black parents and nephew of former National Association for the Advancement of Colored People (NAACP) director Roy Wilkins, Roger Wilkins spent the early years of his childhood in Kansas City, Missouri, until his father died of tuberculosis when Wilkins was only eight years old. He and his mother then moved to New York City, where they lived with relatives in the Sugar Hill section of Harlem that was, according to Wilkins, "where blacks who had it made were said to have lived the sweet life." In 1943 his mother remarried and Wilkins became the stepson of a successful Grand Rapids, Michigan, doctor, living in an all-white neighborhood and attending an all-white school.

Wilkins "came from the genteel Negro middle class at a time when the popular image of blackness was raw, poverty-stricken, angry," wrote Joseph Sobran in a *National Review* assessment of Wilkins's book *A Man's Life: An Autobiography.* Painfully aware of the differences between him and his Grand Rapids schoolmates, Wilkins relates that "with my friends in the north, race was never mentioned. Ever. I carried my race around with me like an open basket of rotten eggs. I knew I could drop one at any moment and it would explode with a stench over everything." He excelled in after-school football games with the neighborhood boys only because members of the opposing team would avoid him, afraid that he might be carrying a knife.

His efforts to gain acceptance as a black adolescent in a predominantly white setting also created cultural gaps between Wilkins and other blacks his age. By trying to demonstrate to the white world—socially and academically—that he was not inferior (a term the young Wilkins associated with blackness), he grew increasingly disdainful of and uncomfortable with his black peers: "One day I was standing outside the church trying, probably at my mother's urging, to make contact," Wilkins recalls in his book. "Conversational sallies flew around me while I stood there stiff and mute, unable to participate. Because the language was so foreign to me, I understood little of what was being said, but I did know that the word used for a white was *paddy.* Then a boy named Nickerson, the one whom my mother particularly wanted me to be friends with, inclined his head slightly toward me and said, to whoops of laughter, 'technicolor paddy.' My feet felt rooted in stone, and my head was aflame, I never forgot that phrase."

Despite the obstacles he encountered and the conflicts he felt growing up in a white environment, Wilkins was elected president of his high school's student council in his senior year. "It was a breakthrough of sorts," he remarked in *A Man's Life.* After graduation he attended the University of Michigan, where he earned a degree in law in 1956. He then practiced international law in New York City for several years before joining the Agency for International Development (AID) in Washington, DC. Sensitive to the demands of being successful in a field traditionally occupied by whites, Wilkins adapted to what he called "white power." Recalling those early years of his career in his autobiography, Wilkins wrote: "I had begun to know how white people operated in the world and had begun to emulate them. I had no aspirations that would have seemed foreign to my white contemporaries. I had abdicated my birthright and had become an ersatz white man." Even during the civil rights movements of the sixties and with the emergence of what he terms "the new black thought," Wilkins still felt a "sense of exclusion" and a degree of envy toward his white counterparts who, he assumed, were secure in "the absolute knowledge that America was their country."

From AID, Wilkins went on to serve as assistant attorney general with the U.S. Department of Justice from 1966 to 1969. He then left government work to accept a position with the Ford Foundation in New York City. As director of the foundation's domestic program that provided funds for job training, drug rehabilitation, education for the poor, and other such minority-related projects, Wilkins had a "daily connection with blackness." It was, however, a connection that only seemed to underscore the ambivalence he felt as a black man operating within a predominantly white institution.

During his years with the Ford Foundation, Wilkins socialized with many of Manhattan's cultural elite, including writers Norman Mailer, Gore Vidal, and Arthur Miller, as well as conductor-composer Leonard Bernstein and his wife. His circle of eminent friends "seemed as devoid of racism as any group of whites I had ever encountered," Wilkins explained in his book. Given such acceptance, he nevertheless felt out of place: "Because my work was not individualistic, creative, or as celebrated as that of most of the people I saw around me, I didn't believe I belonged." He further reflected that he "was enjoying a kind of life that was far beyond the actual or even imaginative grasp of the poor blacks to whom the serious efforts of my life were supposed to be committed . . . . It was as if, by entering that world at night, I was betraying everything I told myself I stood for during the day."

What happened—according to *New York Times Book Review* critic Joel Dreyfuss—was that Wilkins "gradually abandoned the desperate search for white approval and took on a role as an advocate for all blacks." Realizing his mistake in joining the Ford Foundation (he viewed it as "another way station in the white establishment"), he left his post there in 1972 to serve on the editorial staff of the *Washington Post,* where his editorials, along with the contributions of other staff members, earned the paper a special Pulitzer Prize nomination for its coverage of the Watergate scandal. Wilkins also held editorial posts with the *New York Times* before joining the *Nation* in 1979 as a member of the publication's editorial board.

When *A Man's Life* was published in 1982, it attracted national critical attention. Writing in the *Washington Post Book World,* award-winning author James Baldwin praised the autobiography as "so unprecedented a performance . . . that I consider it to be indispensable reading." Baldwin added that "Wilkins has written a most beautiful book, has delivered an impeccable testimony out of that implacable private place where a man either lives or dies." Dreyfuss, who called *A Man's Life* "an important, ground-breaking work," reflected that in the book Wilkins "asks for the acceptance—if not approval—of his own people, abandons his efforts to please white America and takes an important first step toward his personal liberation as an American." Such liberation, as suggested by John Leonard in his *New York Times* critique, is the result of the author's having been "for most of his life, underground, a fabrication." In the autobiography, Leonard continued, Wilkins "emerges to scream. All those false identities gag and choke. He spits them out. There is an excess Dostoyevsky would have understood." Richard Rodriguez, who praised *A Man's Life* in the *Los Angeles Times Book Review,* wrote: "Struggling to learn what it means to be black and middle class, Wilkins compels attention."

A *Publishers Weekly* reviewer called Wilkins's 2001 work, *Jefferson's Pillow: The Founding Fathers and the Dilemma of Black Patriotism,* "a brief but tremendously incisive demythologizing of four Virginian founders [George Washington, Thomas Jefferson, James Madison, and George Mason] and their conflicted attitudes toward race, in the process humanizing them and deepening our appreciation of the internal struggles involved in achieving their greatness, however flawed or incomplete."

In *Jefferson's Pillow,* Wilkins addresses how the Founding Fathers' achievements in creating a free American society contradict their practice of slave ownership. "Casting himself as a black Everyman, Wilkins recounts his struggle to reconcile his admiration for the achievements of the Founding Fathers and his revulsion at their moral failings with regard to slaveholding," wrote Mark Goldblatt in *Reason.* "More generally, his memoir asks whether African Americans can maintain that admiration in the face of the revulsion. Given the history of slavery, is black patriotism possible?"

Jefferson's Pillow, which derives its title from Thomas Jefferson's earliest recorded memory of being carried around on a pillow by a slave, is "an elegantly written, cogent study of the contrast between principles of American egalitarianism and the sociological limits many of its 'founding brothers' placed on it—whether by belief or necessity," wrote Tom O'Brien in *America.*

Through historical accounts, excerpts from personal correspondence, fragments of speeches and formal declarations, and other primary sources, Wilkins makes clear that "the Founding Fathers recognized full well that slavery was a moral abomination," Goldblatt wrote. Their lives were made easier by material possessions and privileges derived from slavery, and they became wealthy through the labor of the slaves. Possession of slaves as property was even considered a symbol of status, which gave slave owners a justification for equality with the peerage of the English ruling class. "The paradox, and for Wilkins it's a ghastly one, is that the egalitarian sentiment among the colonial leaders seems to have been genuine," Goldblatt observed. "The portraits he constructs of the four prin-

cipals are fair-minded and surprisingly thorough for such a brief work," Goldblatt remarked. "But the portraits are also, invariably, indictments." To O'Brien, "Wilkins's book is also personal, in part a meditation on his ancestors and in part an explanation of how he can love a country that enslaved them and teach at a school named after a slaveholder."

Wilkins does not make complicated excuses for the actions of the founders, nor does he absolve them of their responsibility in their role as slaveholders. "The closest Wilkins comes to solving the 'dilemma' of black patriotism is his acknowledgement that the Founding Fathers were, in the end, bound by the moral and intellectual conventions of the age in which they lived," Goldblatt remarked. "Judged by their time, they were no worse than many and better than most." In the end, O'Brien wrote, Wilkins concludes that the principles put forth by the founders "were greater than their defects," and "their heritage is worth preserving and their names worth honoring, even if in a qualified way. America deserves his loyalty, he says, because its foundational principles proved stronger over time than the slaveholding doctrine that injured his ancestors, many of whom he brings alive in these pages." Vernon Ford, writing in *Booklist,* called *Jefferson's Pillow* "an important look at the essential and ongoing contradictions at the heart of American ideals of liberty and patriotism."

Wilkins once told *CA:* "Your request for a comment arrived on a day when I had read a fine essay by Arthur Miller and the obituary of E. B. White. Those readings reminded me of how many miles short I had fallen of achieving my youthful dream of becoming a true professional writer. Whether for lack of urgent inclination or because of other pressures, whatever natural talent I may have had has not been shaped and honed by the hard year-by-year toil required to make me an artist or even a fine craftsman. Rather, the sentences, the paragraphs, and even the book have been forged as weapons and hurled into the struggle for justice, which has been my real lifelong occupation. That way of working has made a rich life, but it has not made out."

BIOGRAPHICAL AND CRITICAL SOURCES:

BOOKS

Wilkins, Roger, *A Man's Life: An Autobiography,* Simon & Schuster (New York, NY), 1982.

PERIODICALS

America, November 26, 2001, Tom O'Brien, "To Have and to Hold," review of *Jefferson's Pillow: The Founding Fathers and the Dilemma of Black Patriotism,* p. 23.

Booklist, June 1, 2001, Vernon Ford, review of *Jefferson's Pillow,* p. 1834.

Choice: Current Reviews for Academic Libraries, January, 2002, R. Detweiler, review of *Jefferson's Pillow,* p. 950.

Ebony, July, 1982, review of *A Man's Life,* p. 24; September, 2001, review of *Jefferson's Pillow,* p. 22.

Essence, November, 1982, Carole Bovoso, review of *A Man's Life,* p. 20.

Library Journal, July, 1982, review of *A Man's Life,* p. 1320.

Los Angeles Times Book Review, August 1, 1982.

Nation, November 26, 2001, "Freedom Stumped Its Toe," review of *Jefferson's Pillow,* p. 40.

National Review, August 20, 1982, Joseph Sobran, review of *A Man's Life,* p. 1032.

Newsweek, August 2, 1982, Gene Lyons, review of *A Man's Life,* p. 58.

New York Review of Books, April 20, 1995, review of *A Man's Life,* p. 34.

New York Times, June 14, 1982.

New York Times Book Review, June 20, 1982.

Publishers Weekly, April 30, 1982, Genevieve Stuttaford, review of *A Man's Life,* p. 49; May 28, 2001, review of *Jefferson's Pillow: The Founding Fathers and the Dilemma of Black Patriotism,* p. 60.

Reason, April, 2002, Mark Goldblatt, "America's Black History: Reconciling Patriotism with Slavery's Legacy," review of *Jefferson's Pillow,* pp. 60-63.

Trial, September, 1983, Gary Tolchinsky, review of *A Man's Life,* p. 34.

Washington Post Book World, June 6, 1982.*

*   *   *

WILKINSON, (Arthur) Warren (Jr.) 1945-

PERSONAL: Born February 13, 1945, in Fitchburg, MA; son of Arthur Warren (a sales engineer) and Katherine Esther (a homemaker; maiden name, Keating) Wilkinson; married Barbara Boardman, December 23, 1967 (divorced, 1970); children: Arthur Warren III, Jan Elaine Garrett. *Education:* Attended University of Bridgeport and Keene State College. *Politics:* Republican. *Religion:* Episcopalian. *Hobbies and other interests:* Civil War enthusiast.

ADDRESSES: Agent—William Morris Co., 1350 Avenue of the Americas, New York, NY 10019.

CAREER: Honeywell Inc., Peterboro, NH, assistant engineer, 1967-70; self-employed general contractor, New Hampshire and Texas, 1970-80; U.S. Merchant Marines, Louisiana and Texas, mate, 1980-83; Connecticut Valley Arms Inc., Norcross, GA, operations manager, 1983-85; writer, 1985—. National Park Service volunteer, Andersonville National Historical Site; performer in Civil War reenactments.

MEMBER: North-South Skirmish Association, Fitchburg Historical Society.

AWARDS, HONORS: Mother, May You Never See the Sights I Have Seen: The Fifty-seventh Massachusetts Veteran Volunteers in the Army of the Potomac, 1864-1865 was selected as a History-Book-of-the-Month by *History Book Club Review.*

WRITINGS:

Mother, May You Never See the Sights I Have Seen: The Fifty-seventh Massachusetts Veteran Volunteers in the Army of the Potomac, 1864-1865, Harper (New York, NY), 1990.

(With Steven E. Woodworth) *A Scythe of Fire: The Civil War Story of the Eighth Georgia Infantry Regiment,* Morrow (New York, NY), 2002.

Contributor to periodicals, including *Civil War Times Illustrated.*

SIDELIGHTS: Warren Wilkinson is a writer who has won praise for his publications about the Civil War. In his first book, *Mother, May You Never See the Sights I Have Seen: The Fifty-seventh Massachusetts Veteran Volunteers in the Army of the Potomac, 1864-1865,* Wilkinson relates the activities of the Union regiment that included his great-great-grandfather. He researched the regiment by examining a range of sources, including diaries, military records, and written correspondence. Joseph T. Glatthaar, writing in the *Washington Post Book World,* declared that *Mother, May You Never See the Sights I Have Seen* "will delight and impress buffs and scholars alike."

Wilkinson followed *Mother, May You Never See the Sights I Have Seen* with *A Scythe of Fire: The Civil War Story of the Eighth Georgia Infantry Regiment,* wherein he chronicles the Confederate regiment that fought in some of the war's key battles, including conflicts at Gettysburg and Appomattox. In preparing the book, Wilkinson—in collaboration with Steven E. Woodworth—again turned to sources such as diaries and written correspondence. *Booklist* reviewer Jay Freeman hailed *A Scythe of Fire* as "a gritty and gripping account of men at war," and *Library Journal* critic Robert Flatley noted the book's "vivid battle descriptions." In *Kirkus Reviews,* meanwhile, a critic summarized *A Scythe of Fire* as "a superior example of unit history" and added that it "provides an almost inexhaustible treasure trove for history buffs." Another enthusiast, Dave Larson, wrote at the *8th Georgia Infantry Home Page* that *A Scythe of Fire* "is an excellent book" and a "unique and exciting account of one of the most well-known Confederate regiments."

BIOGRAPHICAL AND CRITICAL SOURCES:

PERIODICALS

Booklist, February 15, 2002, Jay Freeman, review of *A Scythe of Fire: The Civil War Story of the Eighth Georgia Infantry Regiment,* p. 989.

Kirkus Reviews, December 1, 2001, review of *A Scythe of Fire.*

Library Journal, January, 2002, Robert Flatley, review of *A Scythe of Fire,* p. 126.

Washington Post Book World, May 20, 1990, Joseph T. Glatthaar, review of *Mother, May You Never See the Sights I Have Seen: The Fifty-seventh Massachusetts Veteran Volunteers in the Army of the Potomac, 1864-1865.*

ONLINE

8th Georgia Infantry Web site, http://home.earthlink. net/ (July 17, 2002), Dave Larson, review of *A Scythe of Fire.**

WORTIS, Avi 1937-
(Avi)

PERSONAL: Given name is pronounced "*Ah*-vee"; born December 23, 1937, in New York, NY; son of Joseph (a psychiatrist) and Helen (a social worker; maiden name Zunser) Wortis; married Joan Gabriner (a weaver) November 1, 1963 (divorced); married Coppelia Kahn (an English professor; divorced); married Linda C. Wright (a businesswoman); children: Shaun Wortis, Kevin Wortis; Gabriel Kahn (stepson; all from second marriage); Hayden, Catherine, Robert, Jack Spina. *Education:* Attended Antioch University; University of Wisconsin-Madison, B.A., 1959, M.A., 1962; Columbia University, M.S.L.S., 1964.

ADDRESSES: Home—Denver, CO. *Agent*—Gail Hochman, Brandt & Brandt Literary Agents, Inc., 1501 Broadway, New York, NY 10036.

CAREER: Writer, 1960—. New York Public Library, New York, NY, librarian in Performing Arts Research Center, 1962-70; Lambeth Public Library, London, England, exchange program librarian, 1968; Trenton State College, Trenton, NJ, assistant professor and humanities librarian, 1970-86. Visiting writer in schools across the United States.

MEMBER: PEN, Authors Guild, Authors League of America.

AWARDS, HONORS: Newbery Honor Award and *Boston Globe-Horn Book* Award, 1991, for *The True Confessions of Charlotte Doyle,*1992, for *Nothing but the Truth,* and 1996, for *Poppy;* Mystery Writers of America Special Award; Scott O'Dell Award for historical fiction; Judy Lopez Memorial Award; Golden Kite Award; American Library Association (ALA) citations; Best Book of the Year (British Book Council), Best Books (*School Library Journal*), and International Reading Association citations.

WRITINGS:

AS AVI

Things That Sometimes Happen (picture book), illustrated by Jodi Robbin, Doubleday (Garden City, NY), 1970.

Avi Wortis

Snail Tale: The Adventures of a Rather Small Snail (picture book), illustrated by Tom Kindron, Pantheon (New York, NY), 1972.

No More Magic, Pantheon (New York, NY), 1975.

Captain Grey, Pantheon (New York, NY), 1977.

Night Journeys, Pantheon (New York, NY), 1979.

Encounter at Easton (sequel to *Night Journeys*), Pantheon (New York, NY), 1980.

The Man from the Sky, Morrow Junior Books (New York, NY), 1980.

History of Helpless Harry: To Which Is Added a Variety of Amusing and Entertaining Adventures, Pantheon (New York, NY), 1980.

A Place Called Ugly, Pantheon (New York, NY), 1981.

Who Stole the Wizard of Oz?, Knopf (New York, NY), 1981.

Sometimes I Think I Hear My Name, Pantheon (New York, NY), 1982.

Shadrach's Crossing, Pantheon (New York, NY), 1983.

The Fighting Ground, Lippincott (New York, NY), 1984.

S.O.R. Losers, Bradbury (Scarsdale, NY), 1984.

Devil's Race, Lippincott (New York, NY), 1984.

Bright Shadow, Bradbury (New York, NY), 1985.

Wolf Rider: A Tale of Terror, Bradbury (New York, NY), 1986.

Romeo and Juliet Together (and Alive!) at Last (sequel to *S. O. R. Losers*) Orchard Books (New York, NY), 1987.

Something Upstairs: A Tale of Ghosts, Orchard Books (New York, NY), 1988.

The Man Who Was Poe, Orchard Books (New York, NY), 1989.

The True Confessions of Charlotte Doyle, Orchard Books (New York, NY), 1990.

Windcatcher, Bradbury (New York, NY), 1991.

Nothing but the Truth, Orchard Books (New York, NY), 1991.

Who Was That Masked Man, Anyway?, Orchard Books (New York, NY), 1992.

Blue Heron, Bradbury (New York, NY), 1992.

Emily Upham's Revenge; A Massachusetts Adventure, Morrow Junior Books (New York, NY), 1992.

Punch with Judy, Bradbury, 1993.

City of Light, City of Dark: A Comic Book Novel, Orchard Books (New York, NY), 1993.

The Barn, Orchard Books (New York, NY), 1994.

The Bird, the Frog, and the Light: A Fable, Orchard Books (New York, NY), 1994.

Tom, Babette, & Simon: Three Tales of Transformation, Macmillan Books for Young Readers (New York, NY), 1995.

Poppy, Orchard Books (New York, NY), 1995.

Beyond the Western Sea: The Escape from Home, Orchard Books (New York, NY), 1996.

Beyond the Western Sea: Lord Kirkle's Money, Orchard Books (New York, NY), 1996.

What Do Fish Have to Do with Anything?: And Other Stories, Candlewick Press (Cambridge, MA), 1997.

Finding Providence: The Story of Roger Williams, HarperCollins (New York, NY), 1997.

Poppy and Rye, Avon (New York, NY), 1998.

Perloo the Bold, Scholastic (New York, NY), 1998.

Ragweed, Avon (New York, NY), 1999.

(Editor) *Second Sight: Stories for a New Millennium,* Philomel Books (New York, NY), 1999.

Abigail Takes the Wheel, HarperCollins (New York, NY), 1999.

Midnight Magic, Scholastic (New York, NY), 1999.

Ereth's Birthday, HarperCollins (New York, NY), 2000.

The Christmas Rat, Simon & Schuster (New York, NY), 2000.

Prairie School, HarperCollins (New York, NY), 2001.

The Secret School, Harcourt (San Diego, CA), 2001.

Don't You Know There's a War On?, HarperCollins (New York, NY), 2001.

The Good Dog, Atheneum (New York, NY), 2001.
Crispin: The Cross of Lead, Hyperion (New York, NY), 2002.
Silent Movie, Atheneum (New York, NY), 2002.

Also author of *The Shortest Day,* Orchard Books; author of numerous plays. Contributor to books, including *Performing Arts Resources, 1974,* edited by Ted Perry, Drama Book Publishers, 1975. Contributor to periodicals, including *New York Public Library Bulletin, Top of the News, Children's Literature in Education, Horn Book,* and *Writer.* Book reviewer for *Library Journal, School Library Journal,* and *Previews,* 1965-73.

Translations of Wortis's books have been published in Germany, Austria, Denmark, Norway, Spain, and Japan.

ADAPTATIONS: A recording of *The Fighting Ground* was produced by Listening Library, and many other books have been recorded on audio cassette. *Emily Upham's Revenge, Shadrach's Crossing, Something Upstairs, The Fighting Ground,* and *The True Confessions of Charlotte Doyle,* were produced on the radio programs *Read to Me,* Maine Public Radio, and *Books Aloud,* WWON-Rhode Island; *Something Upstairs* was adapted as a play performed by Louisville (KY) Children's Theater, 1997; *Nothing but the Truth* was adapted as a play by Ronn Smith. *Something Upstairs, The True Confessions of Charlotte Doyle, Night Journeys, Sometimes I Think I Hear My Name,* and *City of Light, City of Dark* have all been optioned for film.

SIDELIGHTS: Critics, teachers, parents, and young readers recognize Avi Wortis, known only by his first name, for a body of work highlighted by colorful characters and intricate plots. Encompassing a wide variety of genres, Avi's books typically offer complex, thought-provoking, and sometimes disturbingly realistic reflections on American history and culture. A longtime champion of literary issues involving young readers, the author said in *Twentieth-Century Children's Writers*: "I try to write about complex issues—young people in an adult world—full of irony and contradiction, in a narrative style that relies heavily on suspense with a texture rich in emotion and imagery. I take a great deal of satisfaction in using popular forms—the adventure, the mystery, the thriller—so as to hold my reader with the sheer pleasure of a good

story. . . . In short, I want my readers to feel, to think, sometimes to laugh. But most of all I want them to enjoy a good read."

Avi once noted that his first career step was reading. He learned more from reading— from comic books and science magazines to histories, plays, and novels—than he learned in school. Though his teachers were skeptical, Avi was determined to write for a career. Eventually, he enrolled in some playwriting classes at the University of Wisconsin.

"That's where I really started to write seriously," he once commented. "The first playwriting instructor that I had would say, 'this is the way you do it.' You didn't have much choice in it, you had to do it in a very specific way. He even had charts for you to fill out. And I think I learned how to organize a story according to this man's precepts. It didn't even matter what [his system] was except that I absorbed it."

After obtaining two master's degrees and working at a variety of jobs, Avi began a twenty-five year career as a librarian, working in the theater collection of the New York Public Library. Avi's determination to be a writer never flagged; in fact, the author had written nearly 800 pages of his "great American novel" before turning to children's literature. This change in focus came about largely because Avi found that he had such fun telling stories to his two sons. "My oldest would tell me what the story should be about—he would invent stuff, a story about a glass of water and so forth. It became a game, and here I had a writing background so I was telling some fairly sophisticated stories," Avi remarked.

Avi's first children's book, *Things That Sometimes Happen,* appeared in 1970. Since then, Avi has produced a number of works whose structure defies genre classification. He is perhaps best known for experimenting with the historical novel format. Several of his early books, including *Captain Grey, Night Journeys,* and *Encounter at Easton,* place fictional characters against the backdrop of actual historical events. Avi told *Booklist's* Ilene Cooper that the research required for historical fiction is rigorous, although he admitted to having an edge: "I was, however, a research librarian for 25 years, so I always have a leg up on finding out things." Avi's work has been recognized for the thoroughness of the historical recreation.

The Fighting Ground, the tale of a young boy caught up in the horror of the Revolutionary War, received the Scott O'Dell Award for children's historical fiction. His Newbery Award-winning *The True Confessions of Charlotte Doyle,* in which a young girl encounters a mutinous crew on a journey across the Atlantic, also draws on a carefully rendered nineteenth-century backdrop. In other books, such as *Something Upstairs* and *The Man Who Was Poe,* Avi combines elements from history, traditional ghost stories, mythology, and science fiction to effectively mix fantasy and reality.

The author is by no means tied to the historical novel. His contemporary tales about young people, such as *S.O.R. Losers, A Place Called Ugly,* and *Nothing but the Truth* (also a Newbery Honor book), have proven as popular with readers as his historically-based stories. Avi's fantasy fiction, such as his *Poppy* series featuring a mouse heroine, has also been successful.

Avi travels around the United States, talking in schools about his work. He has noticed that his readers are increasingly hungry for well-told stories to which they can relate. With this in mind, Avi strives to keep his books both timely and lively. "More than anything else," he said in a *Horn Book* interview. "children's literature is about the place and role of the child in society. . . . If we—in the world of children's literature—can help the young stand straight for a moment longer than they have done in the past, help them maintain their ideals and values, those with which you and I identify ourselves, help them demand—and win—justice, we've added something good to the world."

BIOGRAPHICAL AND CRITICAL SOURCES:

BOOKS

Behind the Covers: Interviews with Authors and Illustrators of Books for Children and Young Adults, Libraries Unlimited, 1985, pp. 33-41.

Bloom, Susan P., and Cathryn M. Mercier, *Presenting Avi,* Twayne (New York City), 1997.

Markham, Lois, *Avi,* Learning Works (Santa Barbara, CA), 1996.

Twentieth-Century Children's Writers, St. Martin's, 1989, pp. 45-46.

PERIODICALS

Booklist, April 15, 1994, Julie Corsaro, review of *The Bird, the Frog, and the Light,* p. 1538; March 15, 1995, Barbara Baskin, review of *The Fighting Ground,* p. 1343; February 1, 1997, Hazel Rochman, review of *Beyond the Western Sea: The Escape from Home,* p. 930, and review of *Finding Providence: The Story of Roger Williams,* p. 949; November 15, 1997, Michael Cart, review of *What Do Fish Have to Do with Anything?,* p. 557; October 1, 1998, review of *City of Light, City of Dark,* p. 317; January 1, 1999, Michael Cart, "Carte Blanche" (article and interview with Avi), p. 846; March 1, 1999, Sally Estes, review of *The Barn,* p. 1212; April 1, 1999, Hazel Rochman, review of *Abigail Takes the Wheel,* p. 1421; "Spotlight on Historical Fiction" (interview with Avi), p. 1609; June 1, 2001, Hazel Rochman, review of *Don't You Know There's a War On?,* p. 1876; October 15, 2001, Lolly Gepson, review of *Ragweed,* p. 428. May 15, 2002, Ilene Cooper, review of *Crispin: The Cross of Lead,* p. 1604.

Bulletin of the Center for Children's Books, June, 1984, p. 180; October, 1989, p. 27.

Girls' Life, Kim Childress, review of *Midnight Magic,* p. 40.

Horn Book, August, 1979, p. 410; April, 1980, pp. 169-70; October, 1980, pp. 517-18; April, 1981, p. 136; June, 1981, pp. 297-98; August, 1983, p. 439; June, 1984, p. 325; January-February, 1985, p. 49; September-October, 1987, pp. 569-576; January-February, 1992, p. 24-27; January-February, 1995, review of *Smugglers' Island,* p. 80; May-June, 1997, Maeve Visser Knoth, review of *Finding Providence: The Story of Roger Williams,* pp. 313-314; November-December, 1997, Marilyn Bousquin, review of *What Do Fish Have to Do with Anything?,* p. 676; July-August, 1998, Ann A. Flowers, review of *Poppy and Rye,* pp. 482-483; March, 1999, Marilyn Bousquin, review of *Abigail Takes the Wheel,* p. 206; May, 2000, Kitty Flynn, review of *Ereth's Birthday,* p. 306; November, 2000, Roger Sutton, review of *The Christmas Rat,* p. 751; November-December, 2001, Betty Carter, review of *The Secret School,* p. 741; January-February, 2002, Peter D. Sieruta, review of *The Good Dog,* p. 75.

Kirkus Reviews, October 1, 2001, review of *The Good Dog,* p. 1418.

New York Times Book Review, September 11, 1977; March 1, 1981, p. 24.

Publishers Weekly, January 30, 1981, p. 75; November 16, 1984, p. 65; December 26, 1986, p. 61; August 28, 1987, p. 81; September 14, 1990, p. 128; September 6, 1991, p. 105; January 17, 1994, review of *The Bird, the Frog, and the Light,* p. 432; June 15, 1998, review of *Poppy and Rye,* p. 60; October 4, 1999, review of *Perloo the Bold,* p. 78; May 8, 2000, review of *Ereth's Birthday,* p. 222; October 29, 2001, review of *Midnight Magic,* p. 67; November 5, 2001, review of *The Good Dog,* p. 68; June 3, 2002, review of *Crispin: The Cross of Lead,* p. 88.

School Library Journal, March, 1978, p. 124; May, 1980, p. 64; November, 1980, p. 68; September, 1984, p. 125; October, 1984, p. 164; December, 1986, pp. 111-12; January, 1987, p. 21; April, 2000, Louise L. Sherman, review of *Perloo the Bold,* p. 78; May, 2000, Eva Mittnick, review of *Ereth's Birthday,* p. 166; May, 2001, Carol Schene, review of *Prairie School,* p. 108; June, 2001, Marie Orlando, review of *Don't You Know There's a War On?,* p. 142; September, 2001, B. Allison Gray, review of *The Secret School,* p. 223.

Storyworks, September, 2002, Melody Zhang, review of *The True Confessions of Charlotte Doyle,* p. 6.

Voice of Youth Advocates, August, 1981, pp. 23-24; August, 1982, p. 27; December, 1984, pp. 261-62; February, 1985, p. 321; February, 1989, p. 293.

ONLINE

McDougal Littell Web site, http://www.mcdougallittell.com/ (March 3, 2003), biography of Avi Wortis.*

* * *

WRIGHT, Richard B(ruce) 1937-

PERSONAL: Born March 4, 1937, in Midland, Ontario, Canada; son of Laverne and Laura Willette (Thomas) Wright; married Phyllis M. Cotton (a library technician), September 2, 1966; children: Christopher, Andrew. *Education:* Ryerson Polytechnic Institute, graduate, 1959; Trent University, B.A., 1972. *Politics:* Conservative. *Religion:* Anglican. *Hobbies and other interests:* Walking, reading, music.

ADDRESSES: Home—52 St. Patrick Street, St. Catharines, Ontario, Canada L2R 1K3. *Agent*—The Cooke Agency, 278 Bloor Street East, Apt. 305, Toronto, Ontario H4W 3MI.

CAREER: CFOR-Radio, copywriter, 1959-60; Macmillan Publishing Co., Inc., Toronto, Ontario, Canada, editor and sales manager, 1960-68; Oxford University Press, sales representative, 1969-70; Ridley College, St. Catharines, Ontario, Canada, teacher of English, 1975-2001, head of department, 1976-79. Sales representative, Oxford University Press, 1969-70.

AWARDS, HONORS: Canada Council junior fellow, 1971-72, senior fellow, 1973-74; Book award from City of Toronto, 1974, and Faber Memorial Prize, 1975, both for *In the Middle of a Life;* Ontario Arts Council fellow, 1975-76; Governor General's Literary Award, government of Canada, and Giller Prize for Canadian Fiction, 2001, both for *Clara Callan,* 2001. Several honorary degrees.

WRITINGS:

Andrew Tolliver (juvenile), St. Martin's (New York, NY), 1965.

The Weekend Man, Farrar, Straus (New York, NY), 1971.

In the Middle of a Life, Farrar, Straus (New York, NY), 1973.

Farthing's Fortunes, Atheneum (New York, NY), 1971.

(Editor, with Robin Endres) *Eight Men Speak, and Other Plays from the Canadian Workers' Theatre,* New Hogtown Press (Toronto, Ontario, Canada), 1976.

Final Things, Dutton (New York, NY), 1980.

The Teacher's Daughter, Macmillan (Toronto, Ontario, Canada), 1982.

Tourists, Walker (New York, NY), 1984.

One John A. Too Many (juvenile), Schoolhouse Press (Independence, OH), 1986.

Sunset Manor, Seal Books (Toronto, Ontario, Canada), 1990.

The Age of Longing (novel), HarperCollins (Toronto, Ontario, Canada), 1995.

Clara Callan, HarperFlamingoCanada (Toronto, Ontario, Canada), 2001, HarperCollinsPublishers (New York, NY), 2002.

Editor, *The Malarkey Review.*

SIDELIGHTS: Richard B. Wright has been praised for his ability to make ordinary lives seem fascinating. In novels such as *The Weekend Man, In the Middle of a*

Life, and *Clara Callan,* he has featured protagonists whose lives are constrained or even failed. Wright is "a smooth and natural stylist," according to James Doyle, a contributor to *Dictionary of Literary Biography;* he "creates his characters and settings by means of a brilliantly figurative and ironic language." Doyle further praised Wright for "his attempts to capture in fiction the moral and aesthetic complexity of urban Canadian life," which constitute "a valuable contribution to the imaginative literature of his country."

Wright's first novel, *The Weekend Man,* relates a few days in the life of its narrator, Wes Wakeham. Wes is a textbook salesman, a job also held by Wright for a time. Profoundly dissatisfied with life, Wes goes through a temporary estrangement from his wife shortly before Christmas, which leads to a series of adventures that are not particularly remarkable. Yet Wright has a unique ability to present his characters authentically, according to Richard P. Brickner of the *New York Times Book Review,* and "he gets types, situations, conversations, down so sharply that we chuckle at recognizing what we may have never, in our own experience, seen." Brickner especially noted the author's talent for "making the boring glamorous—glamorous because so vivid, and, sometimes, funny." L. J. Davis, a contributor to the *Washington Post Book World,* concurred that *The Weekend Man* is "a brilliant first effort, a breath-taking stylistic tightrope act where a single, small misstep (never taken) could have sent the author plunging." Davis concluded that *The Weekend Man* is "a haunting book and very nearly a perfect one."

Davis regarded Wright's next book, *In the Middle of a Life,* with less enthusiasm. This novel told of another middle-aged man in crisis, and was described as very much like *The Weekend Man* by numerous critics. Davis found this follow-up "disappointing," but Walter Clemons in *Newsweek* praised Wright for again demonstrating his "gift of making ordinariness enthralling." A *Times Literary Supplement* reviewer allowed that there was no great moral revealed through *In the Middle of a Life;* the protagonist "is just there to be relished. All the clichés come to life again: irony, pathos, compassion."

The picaresque life story of a ninety-five-year-old man in a nursing home is the basis of *Farthing's Fortunes,* a work of historical fiction that takes in Victorian Toronto, the Klondike Gold Rush, World War I, and the

Great Depression. "As a work of historical fiction the novel is convincing," stated Doyle, adding, "As a fable of North American life the story takes on allegorical implications." Wright returned to contemporary times with *Final Things.* This novel's main character, Charlie Farris, bears some resemblance to those in *The Weekend Man* and *In the Middle of a Life;* like them, he is a quiet failure in urban Toronto, struggling with ordinary problems of alcoholism, marital failure, and a disappointing job. This life of quiet desperation is interrupted by the brutal murder of Charlie's son. The novel details how "the distraught parent is exposed to the ordeals of funeral, police investigation, and the reactions of friends and relatives, the irrational and self-centered response of human beings to crisis situations are relentlessly laid bare," commented Doyle.

Wright's novel *Clara Callan* earned two major Canadian awards for its author, the Governor General's Literary Award, and the Giller Prize. The title character is an unmarried schoolteacher living in Ontario during the 1930s. Her life appears sterile, but in fact she has a rich, passionate secret life, which includes an affair with a married man in Toronto. Wright delves into "Clara's hidden reserves of passion with a skill that makes her one of the most compelling heroines of recent Canadian fiction," commended John Bemrose in *Maclean's.* Doyle defined Wright as "a polished, sensitive, thoroughly professional writer," who "may well emerge in time as one of the more important Canadian novelists of his period."

BIOGRAPHICAL AND CRITICAL SOURCES:

BOOKS

Contemporary Literary Criticism, Volume 6, Gale (Detroit, MI), 1976.
Dictionary of Literary Biography, Volume 53: *Canadian Writers since 1960,* First Series, Gale (Detroit, MI), 1986.

PERIODICALS

Atlantic, December, 1973.
Best Sellers, May 15, 1971; March, 1977; December, 1980, review of *Final Things,* p. 318.

Booklist, November 1, 1984, review of *Tourists,* p. 345.

Books in Canada, December, 1978, "Life to Wright," pp. 10-12; November, 1980, review of *Final Things,* p. 12; December, 1980, review of *Final Things,* p. 34; January, 1982, review of *Final Things,* p. 27; September, 1982, review of *The Teacher's Daughter,* p. 59; October, 1982, review of *The Teacher's Daughter,* p. 17; January, 1985, review of *Tourists,* p. 13.

Book World, June 6, 1971.

Canadian Book Review Annual, 1996, review of *The Age of Longing,* p. 178.

Canadian Forum, December, 1976; December, 1982, Meredith Yearsley, review of *The Teacher's Daughter,* p. 40.

Canadian Literature, September, 1981.

Chatelaine, February, 2002, review of *Clara Callan,* p. 20.

Choice, December, 1973; April, 1977.

Essays on Canadian Writing, spring, 1987, review of *Tourists,* p. 133.

Kirkus Reviews, August 15, 1980, review of *Final Things,* p. 1114; September 1, 1984, review of *Tourists,* p. 826.

Library Journal, April 1, 1971; September 15, 1973; September 15, 1976; November 1, 1980, review of *Final Things,* p. 2348.

Maclean's, November 17, 1980, Douglas Hill, review of *Final Things,* p. 70; December 3, 2001, John Bemrose, "Hero of the Humdrum: Richard B. Wright Proves That the Tale of a Dull Life Can Be Extraordinary," p. 64.

New Republic, May 29, 1971.

Newsweek, October 1, 1973, Walter Clemons, review of *In the Middle of a Life,* p. 96.

New Yorker, June 12, 1971.

New York Times Book Review, September 23, 1973, Richard P. Brickner, review of *In the Middle of a Life;* January 2, 1977; December 14, 1980, Todd Walton, review of *Final Things,* p. 10.

Publishers Weekly, September 5, 1980, review of *Final Things,* Barbara A. Bannon, p. 64; March 5, 1982, review of *Final Things,* p. 68; November 2, 1984, review of *Tourists,* p. 68.

Quill & Quire, December, 1980, review of *Final Things,* p. 29; September, 1982, review of *The Teacher's Daughter,* p. 59; December, 1984, review of *Tourists,* p. 31; July, 1990, review of *Sunset Manor,* p. 57; April, 1995, review of *The Age of Longing,* p. 28.

Saturday Night, November, 1982, review of *The Teacher's Daughter,* p. 72.

Saturday Review, July 3, 1971.

Studies in Canadian Literature, summer, 1977, Sheila Campbell, "The Two Wes Wakehams: Point of View in *The Weekend Man,*" pp. 289-305.

Times Literary Supplement, April 2, 1971; February 15, 1974, review of *In the Middle of a Life,* p. 149; November 13, 1981, review of *Final Things,* p. 1330.

Washington Post Book World, September 23, 1973, L. J. Davis, review of *In the Middle of a Life.**

Y-Z

YACCARINO, Dan 1965-

PERSONAL: Born May 20, 1965, in Monclair, NJ. *Education:* Graduated from the Parsons School of Design, New York, NY, 1987.

ADDRESSES: Home—New York, NY. *Agent*—c/o Author Mail, HarperCollins/Joanna Cotler Books, 1350 6th Avenue, New York, NY 10019.

CAREER: Freelance artist, writer, and producer. Images created for advertising campaigns, including Cotton Inc., AT&T, Gardenburger, Sony, and Nikkei. *Exhibitions:* Has exhibited sculptures and large-scale paintings in galleries in New York, Tokyo, Los Angeles, and Rome.

AWARDS, HONORS: ADDE Award, *How Magazine*-Society of Illustrators of Los Angeles; AIGA Award, Association of Educational Publishers; Parents' Choice Award; ALA Notable and Parent Guide Award; has received awards from the Society of Illustrators, Communication Arts, and American Illustration; invited to read his books at 2002 Easter festivities at the White House.

WRITINGS:

SELF-ILLUSTRATED BOOKS FOR CHILDREN, EXCEPT AS NOTED

Big Brother Mike, Hyperion (New York, NY), 1993.
If I Had a Robot, Viking (New York, NY), 1996.
An Octopus Followed Me Home, Viking (New York, NY), 1997.

Good Night, Mr. Night, Harcourt (San Diego, CA), 1997.
Zoom! Zoom! Zoom! I'm Off to the Moon, Scholastic, Inc. (New York, NY), 1997.
Deep in the Jungle, Atheneum (New York, NY), 2000.
Oswald, Atheneum (New York, NY), 2001.
Unlovable, Holt (New York, NY), 2001.
So Big!, HarperFestival (New York, NY), 2001.
The Lima Bean Monster, illustrated by Adam McCauley, Walker & Company (New York, NY), 2001.
Where the Four Winds Blow, Joanna Cotler Books (New York, NY), 2003.

Also author, with Lisa Desimini, David Ricceri, and Sara Schwartz, of *All Year Round: A Book to Benefit Children in Need,* for Scholastic, and illustrator for *Discover 2000: The New York State 2000 Summer Reading Program,* by Lisa von Drasek.

"BLAST OFF BOY AND BLORP" SERIES; SELF-ILLUSTRATED

First Day on a Strange New Planet, Hyperion (New York, NY), 2000.
New Pet, Hyperion (New York, NY), 2001.
The Big Science Fair, Hyperion (New York, NY), 2002.

ILLUSTRATOR

Catherine Friend, *The Sawfin Stickleback: A Very Fishy Story,* Hyperion (New York, NY), 1994.
Eve Merriam, *Bam! Bam! Bam!,* Holt (New York, NY), 1995.

M. C. Helldorfer, *Carnival,* Viking (New York, NY), 1996.

W. Nikola-Lisa, *One Hole in the Road,* Holt (New York, NY), 1996.

Kevin Henkes, *Circle Dogs,* Greenwillow Press (New York, NY), 1998.

Five Little Pumpkins, HarperFestival (New York, NY), 1998.

Laura Godwin, *Little White Dog,* Hyperion (New York, NY), 1998.

Andrea Zimmerman and David Clemesha, *Trashy Town,* HarperCollins (New York, NY), 1999.

Rebecca Kai Dotlich, *Away We Go!,* HarperFestival (New York, NY), 2000.

Naomi Shihab Nye, *Come with Me: Poems for a Journey,* Greenwillow Books (New York, NY), 2000.

Laurie Myers, *Surviving Brick Johnson,* Clarion Books (New York), 2000.

Robert Burleigh, *I Love Going through This Book,* HarperCollins (New York, NY), 2001.

Abigail Tabby, *Baby Face,* HarperFestival (New York, NY), 2001.

Jack Prelutsky, *Halloween Countdown,* HarperFestival (New York, NY), 2002.

I Met a Bear, HarperFestival (New York, NY), 2002.

Margaret Wise Brown, *The Good Little Bad Little Pig,* Hyperion (New York, NY), 2002.

Dan Yaccarino's Mother Goose, Little Golden Books (New York, NY), 2003.

ILLUSTRATOR; PLAY-AND-LEARN KIT

Paul Kepple and Ann Keech, *Move It!,* Running Press (Philadelphia, PA), 1998.

Paul Kepple and Ann Keech, *Bugs,* Running Press (Philadelphia, PA), 1999.

Also animator for television commercials. Yaccarino's illustrations have been featured on maps, Jack in the Box, picture frames, growth charts, sewing cards, stationary, playing cards, travel games, bed linens, and other products. Yaccarino has contributed illustrations to magazines, including *Rolling Stone, Playboy, New York,* and *Fast Company.*

ADAPTATIONS: Yaccarino has adapted several of his books for animation; *Oswald* was adapted for an animated television series, Nickelodeon network, 2001. Several of Yaccarino's characters have been made into plush toys.

WORK IN PROGRESS: Writing and illustrating children's books; television and feature film projects.

SIDELIGHTS: Dan Yaccarino is a children's book writer and illustrator who first broke into print with his self-illustrated *Big Brother Mike,* a "visually offbeat take on sibling rivalry," according to a reviewer for *Publishers Weekly.* Since that time, Yaccarino has authored many more titles of his own as well as illustrated numerous books by other authors, including the works of Jack Prelutsky and Margaret Wise Brown. Best known for *Oswald,* which has become a popular and critically acclaimed series on the Nickelodeon network, Yaccarino has also penned a trio of books about Blast Off Boy and Blorp, a pair of "unlikely intergalactic exchange students," according to a contributor for *Kirkus Reviews.* Other books from the versatile and prolific author/artist include *Deep in the Jungle, Good Night, Mr. Night, The Lima Bean Monster,* and the juvenile fantasy novel from 2003, *Where the Four Winds Blow.* Writing in *Bulletin of the Center for Children's Books,* Deborah Stevenson applauded the "retro air" to much of Yaccarino's work. "There's no glamorized, adult-appealing nostalgia here," Stevenson further commented. "Rather there's a robustness reminiscent of the energetic illustrative work of the colorful 1950s and even at times . . . of Diego Rivera's glistening monumental figures." Employing bold, bright colors and sturdy figures, Yaccarino's illustrations have a "refreshening unfussiness," according to Stevenson.

Yaccarino has parlayed a career in editorial illustration and advertising with children's illustration. With his first solo title, *Big Brother Mike,* he tells a story of typical older brother and younger brother relationships, including the usual ups and downs. While older brother Mike can come to the aid of the younger narrator against bullies or to help him bury his pet hamster, he can also be irritating when battling for the television remote control. A reviewer for *Publishers Weekly* called this a "spunky first book." *Booklist*'s Lisa Napoli recognized Yaccarino's "ability to use color, form and composition to show feelings" in this debut title, and a critic for *Kirkus Reviews* also had praise for his "vibrantly expressive illustrations, with emotion-indicative colors."

In his second solo effort, *If I Had a Robot,* Yaccarino tells of young Phil, who dreams of having a robot so that the machine could finish up his vegetables for him or go to school and do his homework for him. Once again, reviewers focused on Yaccarino's "visually emphatic" illustrations, as John Peters characterized them in *School Library Journal. Booklist*'s Susan Dove Lempke also commented on the "retro-style artwork . . . [which] carries through the time-honored concept" of childish wish-fulfillment. A contributor for *Publishers Weekly* likewise felt that the book's "main appeal comes from the quirky sci-fi illustrations." Yaccarino returns to a similar premise in *The Lima Bean Monster,* in which Sammy unwittingly unleashes a monster when trying to get rid of unwanted food stuffs. In this case, lima beans need to be emptied from the plate, and Sammy does so by slipping them into his sock and then burying them in a vacant lot. When a Lima Bean Monster results from this and starts to eat all the adults in the neighborhood, Sammy and the other kids protect them by gathering around the monster and eating him up. Sally R. Dow, writing in *School Library Journal,* found this a "fast-paced story . . . [with] surefire appeal for youngsters who won't touch their vegetables."

Working on a bedtime premise, Yaccarino presents a bowler-hatted Mr. Night, who puts the world to bed and also helps children fall asleep in the picture book *Good Night, Mr. Night.* "Simple forms and Matisse-like colors match the innocence of the story, told in a series of simple lines," wrote a critic for *Kirkus Reviews.* Writing in *Bulletin of the Center for Children's Books,* Janice M. Del Negro commented on Yaccarino's "Rousseauian landscape," concluding that the book is a "storytime natural," and that young readers would "appreciate Yaccarino's controlled text and flamingly colorful illustrations." Similarly, a reviewer for *Publishers Weekly* called the book a "calming bedtime tale" and further remarked that the "quiet narration and undulating illustrations have an almost hypnotic quality." Lauren Peterson, writing in *Booklist,* felt *Good Night, Mr. Night* was a "gentle bedtime tale that stirs the imagination." Peterson also went on to praise Yaccarino's "rich, vibrant" double-page spreads, which "complement the text beautifully."

Moon exploration is the focus of *Zoom! Zoom! Zoom! I'm Off to the Moon,* about a boy astronaut who takes an adventurous trip to the moon done in rhyming narrative. The text itself climbs diagonally up the page, reducing in size as the boy's spaceship takes off and gains altitude. A contributor for *Publishers Weekly* called this an "effervescent" picture book that readers could use as a "launch pad for their own imaginations," and *Horn Book*'s Roger Sutton felt the book is "a perfect space story for the toddler realm" and a "lilting bedtime story." Sutton also commented on Yaccarino's signature "rounded retro shapes" in the illustrations, reminiscent of 1950s toys. Shelle Townsend-Hudson, reviewing the same title in *Booklist,* felt that Yaccarino's "fanciful illustrations pull children into this exuberant picture book and make the launch a special event." More rhyming text is presented in *An Octopus Followed Me Home,* in which a child whines to be allowed to keep the stray octopus that has followed her home. But her father reminds her of all the other animals that have followed her home, including the crocodile under the bed and the giraffe with its neck up the chimney. No more, says dad, but then the last page shows an even more monstrous critter following the girl home. *Booklist*'s Hazel Rochman felt that the verses and "bright illustrations give an uproarious spin" to the usual tale of a kid pleading to keep a stray. A reviewer for *Publishers Weekly* wrote that Yaccarino "specializes in simple text and whimsically distorted shapes," and *Newsweek*'s Malcolm Jones, Jr., dubbed the tale a "beguilingly simple can-I-keep-it story."

A reviewer for *Publishers Weekly* called Yaccarino's year 2000 title *Deep in the Jungle* "perhaps his best book yet," and a "tongue-in-cheek look at an arrogant king of beasts." Tricked one day into leaving the jungle for the confines of a zoo, the lion decides he does not really care for captivity, nor for a taste of the medicine he regularly dosed out to underlings in the jungle. So he eats his tamer, and returns home where he helps the other jungle animals against another trickster trying to get them into the zoo. The same reviewer concluded that Yaccarino "humorously twists the savage-versus-civilized formula." *Booklist*'s Connie Fletcher felt that Yaccarino's "bright and cartoony" illustrations help take the "bite out of the tale."

Yaccarino has also penned three titles in a series about an earthling student, Johnny Smith, and an alien boy from the planet Meep, Blorp Gorp, who trade places. Smith, dubbed Blast Off Boy, is chosen from millions of applicants to represent Earth on Meep; at the same time Blorp, all green except for his black eyes, tries to adjust to his new life at Blast Off Boy's former elementary school. *First Day on a Strange Planet* chronicles the outset of this strange arrangement. While Blast Off Boy becomes the center of attention on Meep, Blorp is put in detention. A reviewer for *Publishers Weekly* felt that Yaccarino "puts a fresh and funny spin on ordinary events like lunchtime and gym class" in this "auspicious debut" to the series. Stevenson, reviewing the same title in *Bulletin of the Center for Children's Books,* found the book "an enjoyable armchair excursion into space." Blorp is living with the Smiths and Blast Off Boy resides with Blorp's family on Meep in the second title of the series, *New Pet.* A critic for *Kirkus Reviews* thought that while this second book "won't send any young readers into orbit, it will appeal to those who adore aliens of any variety." John Peters, writing in *Booklist,* had higher praise for the book, commending Yaccarino's "daffy spin on familiar themes," and noting that the author/illustrator once again "deftly intertwin[es] his two story lines." The dual story line continues in *The Big Science Fair,* and both students are preparing for fairs on each planet: Blorp with real exuberance and Blast Off Boy with more of a sense of dread, faced with "all the brainy aliens [who] are planning their macaroni models of hydrogen molecules," as a contributor for *Kirkus Reviews* noted. The same critic concluded that the series is a "welcome addition to the library of those just blasting off out of easy readers." Marlene Gawron, writing in *School Library Journal,* thought that Yaccarino's name should be added to the list of those authors "who have nailed the schoolroom scene."

Another popular offering from Yaccarino is the 2001 *Oswald,* illustrated with computer-generated images. In this cumulative story, Oswald and his dog, Weenie, move to a new city and though the eight-armed wonder is worried that they will remain friendless, the canine is not so worried. Attempting to catch a runaway piano, they in fact begin to meet a cast of odd new locals, including trees that can walk and hat-wearing eggs. Gillian Engberg, writing in *Booklist,* felt that youngsters three to seven would enjoy the "zany, random comedy."

BIOGRAPHICAL AND CRITICAL SOURCES:

PERIODICALS

Booklist, March 15, 1993, Lisa Napoli, review of *Big Brother Mike,* p. 1363; July, 1996, Susan Dove Lempke, review of *If I Had a Robot,* p. 1831; August, 1997, Hazel Rochman, review of *An Octopus Followed Me Home,* p. 1908; November 1,

1997, Lauren Peterson, review of *Good Night, Mr. Night,* p. 485; November 15, 1997, Shelle Townsend-Hudson, review of *Zoom! Zoom! Zoom! I'm Off to the Moon,* p. 568; December 15, 1998, Carolyn Phelan, review of *Five Little Pumpkins,* p. 754; March 1, 2000, Connie Fletcher, review of *Deep in the Jungle,* p. 1253; July, 2001, Gillian Engberg, review of *Oswald,* p. 2022; September 1, 2001, John Peters, review of *The Lima Bean Monster,* p. 118; December 1, 2001, John Peters, review of *New Pet,* p. 645.

Bulletin of the Center for Children's Books, September, 1996, p. 38; September 1, 1998, Deborah Stevenson, "Rising Star: Dan Yaccarino"; January, 1998, Janice M. Del Negro, review of *Good Night, Mr. Night,* p. 182; December, 2000, Deborah Stevenson, review of *First Day on a Strange New Planet,* p. 167; June, 2001, Deborah Stevenson, review of *Oswald,* pp. 392-393.

Horn Book, July-August, 1995, pp. 452-453; May-June, 1996, p. 324; September-October 1997, Roger Sutton, review of *Zoom! Zoom! Zoom! I'm Off to the Moon,* p. 567; March-April, 2000, review of *Deep in the Jungle,* p. 191.

Horn Book Guide, fall, 1993, p. 280; spring, 1997, p. 54; spring, 1999, Marilyn Bousqin, review of *Five Little Pumpkins,* p. 20; spring, 2001, Anita L. Burkam, review of *First Day on a Strange New Planet,* p. 68.

Kirkus Reviews, March 1, 1993, review of *Big Brother Mike,* p. 308; July 15, 1997, p. 1119; August 15, 1997, review of *Good Night, Mr. Night,* p. 1315; December 15, 2000, review of *So Big!,* p. 1768; September 1, 2001, review of *New Pet,* p. 1304; November 1, 2001, review of *Unlovable,* p. 1556; October 1, 2002, review of *The Big Science Fair,* p. 1484.

Newsweek, December 1, 1997, Malcolm Jones, Jr., review of *An Octopus Followed Me Home,* p. 78.

New York Times Book Review, March 16, 1997, p. 26; May 11, 1997, p. 24; July 21, 1997, p. 200.

Publishers Weekly, March 15, 1993, review of *Big Brother Mike,* p. 85; October 3, 1994, p. 68; January 30, 1995, p. 99; December 18, 1995, p. 53; June 24, 1996, review of *If I Had a Robot,* p. 58; August 12, 1996, pp. 82-83; July 21, 1997, review of *Good Night, Mr. Night,* and *Zoom! Zoom! Zoom! I'm Off to the Moon,* p. 200; October 20, 1997, review of *An Octopus Followed Me Home,* pp. 74-75; January 3, 2000, review of *Deep in the Jungle,* p. 75; October 30, 2000, review of *First Day on a Strange New Planet,* p. 75; July 30,

2001, review of *The Lima Bean Monster,* p. 84; December 17, 2001, review of *Unlovable,* pp. 89-90.

School Library Journal, August, 1993, p. 155; December, 1994, p. 74; July, 1995, p. 73; September, 1996, John Peters, review of *If I Had a Robot,* p. 195; March, 1996, p. 189; September, 1996, p. 195; October, 1996, p. 103; October, 1997, p. 114; December, 1997, Susan M. Moore, review of *Zoom! Zoom! Zoom! I'm Off to the Moon,* p. 103; January, 1998, p. 95; February, 1999, Blair Christolon, review of *Five Little Pumpkins,* pp. 83-84; February, 2000, Joy Fleishhacker, review of *Deep in the Jungle,* p. 106; July, 2001, Linda M. Kenton, review of *Oswald,* p. 91; September, 2001, Sally R. Dow, review of *The Lima Bean Monster,* p. 209; December, 2001, Gay Lynn Van Vleck, review of *New Pet,* p. 116; January, 2002, Karen Land, review of *Unlovable,* p. 114; December, 2002, Marlene Gawron, review of *The Big Science Fair,* p. 114.

Time, December 9, 1996, pp. 78-79.

ONLINE

Dan Yaccarino Homepage, http://www.danyaccarino.com/ (March 9, 2003).

* * *

ZIMMER, Jill Schary
 See ROBINSON, Jill